T0393392

Springer International Handbooks of Education

The *Springer International Handbooks of Education* series aims to provide easily accessible, practical, yet scholarly, sources of information about a broad range of topics and issues in education. Each *Handbook* follows the same pattern of examining in depth a field of educational theory, practice and applied scholarship, its scale and scope for its substantive contribution to our understanding of education and, in so doing, indicating the direction of future developments. The volumes in this series form a coherent whole due to an insistence on the synthesis of theory and good practice. The accessible style and the consistent illumination of theory by practice make the series very valuable to a broad spectrum of users. The volume editors represent the world's leading educationalists. Their task has been to identify the key areas in their field that are internationally generalizable and, in times of rapid change, of permanent interest to the scholar and practitioner.

Joerg Zumbach • Douglas A. Bernstein •
Susanne Narciss • Giuseppina Marsico
Editors

International Handbook of Psychology Learning and Teaching

Volume 1

With 64 Figures and 92 Tables

 Springer

Editors
Joerg Zumbach
Department of Educational Research
University of Salzburg
Salzburg, Austria

Susanne Narciss
School of Science -
Faculty of Psychology, Psychology
of Learning and Instruction
Technische Universitaet Dresden
Dresden, Sachsen, Germany

Douglas A. Bernstein
Department of Psychology
University of South Florida
Tampa, FL, USA

Giuseppina Marsico
Department of Human, Philosophical and
Educational Sciences (DISUFF)
University of Salerno
Fisciano, Italy

ISSN 2197-1951 ISSN 2197-196X (electronic)
Springer International Handbooks of Education
ISBN 978-3-030-28744-3 ISBN 978-3-030-28745-0 (eBook)
https://doi.org/10.1007/978-3-030-28745-0

This Springer imprint is published by the registered company Springer Nature Switzerland AG.
The registered company address is: Gewerbestrasse 11, 6330 Cham, Switzerland

Preface

As reflected in its title, this *International Handbook of Psychology Learning and Teaching* was designed to be a comprehensive reference text devoted to presenting ideas for how to improve the learning and teaching of psychology worldwide. Its chapters are aimed at a broad audience, including psychology teacher trainees and new faculty members who are interested in the basics of how and what to teach, as well as more experienced professors who are interested in training psychology teachers or in evaluating and improving the effectiveness of their own teaching.

We were motivated to create the handbook partly because, although teaching and learning can be designed and evaluated from a general educational perspective, psychology, like all other academic disciplines, has its own traditions, course content, and approaches to teaching and learning, a phenomenon sometimes referred to as *pedagogical content knowledge* (cf. Koehler & Mishra, 2008). We wanted to showcase that knowledge by providing a comprehensive description of psychology's core goals, contents, and topics, as well as the methods, approaches, and resources available for teaching psychology in psychology programs and elsewhere.

We hope the handbook will also inspire psychology teachers to engage in research in the scholarship of teaching and learning (SoTL; e.g., Felten, 2013). SoTL has been defined as "the systematic study of teaching and learning, using established or validated criteria of scholarship, to understand how teaching (beliefs, behaviors, attitudes, and values) can maximize learning, and/or develop a more accurate understanding of learning, resulting in products that are publicly shared for critique and use by an appropriate community" (Potter & Kustra, 2011, p. 2).

In psychology, that community is growing dramatically as the role of pedagogical content knowledge in our discipline has received more and more attention in recent years from psychology teachers who conduct, share, and discuss research on psychology learning and teaching (Dunn et al., 2010). Their ideas and results are being published in such US journals as *Teaching of Psychology* and *The Scholarship of Teaching and Learning in Psychology*, as well as in *Psychology Learning and Teaching*, the journal of the European Society of Psychology Learning and Teaching (ESPLAT), and elsewhere. Their work is also being presented at numerous national and international teaching conferences (e.g., ESPLAT and the U.S.'s National Institute on the Teaching of Psychology) as well as in teaching strands at research-oriented international conferences such as those of the American Psychological Association, the

Association for Psychological Science, and the International Congress of Psychology. We hope that this handbook will contribute to, expand, and inspire further the discussion among members of this community.

The handbook's chapters were written by expert psychology teachers from all over the world and cover topics germane to the teaching of all core courses in psychology, whether taught in psychology programs or as part of curricula in other disciplines. Each chapter includes an introduction to its topic, provides some historical context, a review of relevant literature, a summary of theory- and evidence-based approaches to teaching course content, including in various educational and cultural contexts, and advice on best practices in those contexts. Some chapters also provide guidelines and checklists designed to support psychology teachers in their daily work.

The handbook includes three major sections, each of which contains several chapters. The first section, "Teaching Psychology as Main Discipline in Undergraduate and Graduate Programs," focuses on psychology teaching and learning as a main discipline in undergraduate and graduate psychology programs. The chapters in this section address each of the major psychological sub-disciplines and offers evidence-based advice on how best to teach the courses within those sub-disciplines. The second section, "Psychology Learning and Teaching for All Audiences," focuses on several target audiences within and outside tertiary education. The third section includes several chapters on "General Educational and Instructional Approaches to Psychology Learning and Teaching."

Because it covers all central fields of Psychology, all major target groups, and all major relevant educational and instructional approaches, we hope that this handbook will provide a solid base for psychology teachers worldwide, serving as a stimulus for SoTL research in psychology, as an introductory text for new teachers, and as a guide for those involved in the development of teacher training programs, course and curriculum design, syllabus writing, assessment of teacher and student performance, and the like.

December 2022   Joerg Zumbach
                                                              Douglas A. Bernstein
                                                                 Susanne Narciss
                                                              Giuseppina Marsico

References

Dunn, D. S., Beins, B. B., McCarthy, M.A., & Hill, G. W. (Eds.). (2010). *Best practices for teaching beginnings and endings in the psychology major: Research, cases, and recommendations.* Oxford: University Press.

Felten, P. (2013). Principles of good practice in SoTL. *Teaching and Learning Inquiry, 1*(1), 121–125.

Koehler, M., & Mishra, P. (2009). What is technological pedagogical content knowledge (TPACK)? *Contemporary Issues in Technology and Teacher Education, 9*(1), 60–70.

Potter, M. K., & Kustra, E. (2011). The relationship between scholarly teaching and SoTL: Models, distinctions, and clarifications. *International Journal for the Scholarship of Teaching and Learning, 5*(1). http://www.georgiasouthern.edu/ijsotl

Contents

Volume 2

About the Editors

Joerg Zumbach received his Diploma in Psychology in 1999 from Ruprecht-Karls-University Heidelberg, Germany. He got his Dr. phil. in Educational Psychology 2003 from Ruprecht-Karls-University Heidelberg, Germany. Since 2006 he is Full Professor for Science Teaching and Learning Research and e-Learning at the Paris-Lodron University Salzburg, Austria. He served there as head of department and co-director of the School of Education. He also was and is in different editorial boards (e.g., *Journal of Educational Multimedia and Hypermedia*, *International Journal of Learning Technologies*, *Journal of Interactive Learning Research*, *Computers in Human Behavior*, *Psychology Teaching and Learning*). He authored and co-authored various research articles and textbooks in the areas of Multimedia and Hypermedia Learning, Higher Education, Problem-Based Learning, and Violent Media and Aggression among others.

Doug A. Bernstein received his bachelor's degree in psychology at the University of Pittsburgh in 1964 and his master's and Ph.D. degrees in clinical psychology at Northwestern University in 1966 and 1968, respectively. From 1968 to 1998, he was on the psychology faculty at the University of Illinois at Urbana-Champaign where he served as Associate Department Head and Director of Introductory Psychology. He is currently Professor Emeritus at Illinois and Courtesy Professor of Psychology at the University of South Florida. In 2013, he stepped down after 30 years as chairman of the National Institute on the Teaching of Psychology, and in 2018 he founded the Biennial International Seminar on the Teaching of Psychological Science in Paris. He has written or co-authored a book on the teaching of psychology, as well as textbooks on introductory, clinical, and abnormal psychology and on criminal behavior and progressive relaxation training.

Susanne Narciss is full professor and head of the research team "Psychology of Learning and Instruction (PsyLI)" at the Technische Universitaet Dresden. Her current interests include research on (a) promoting self-regulated learning, (b) the role of motivation and meta-cognition in instructional contexts, (c) conditions and effects of interactive learning tasks, and (d) conditions and effects of informative tutoring feedback strategies. Her work on feedback strategies was considered cutting-edge by the American Association on Educational Communication and Technology (AECT) and was awarded the prestigious AECT Distinguished Development Award 2007. Susanne Narciss is not only a productive scholar but also dedicates her expertise, time, and effort to improve the teaching and learning of psychology. She has been member of the founding executive board of the European Society for Psychology Teaching and Learning (ESPLAT) and was elected ESPLAT's President in September 2021.

Giuseppina Marsico is Associate Professor of Development and Educational Psychology at the University of Salerno (Italy) and Visiting Professor at Ph.D. Programme in Psychology, Federal University of Bahia (Brazil). She is President Elect of the American Psychological Association – Division 52 International Psychology and President Elect of the European Society of Psychology Learning and Teaching (ESPLAT). She has 20 years of experience as a researcher, with a proven international research network. She is Editor-in-Chief of the Book Series Cultural Psychology of Education (Springer), Latin American Voices – Integrative Psychology and Humanities (Springer), co-editor of SpringerBriefs Psychology and Cultural Developmental Sciences (together with Jaan Valsiner), and Annals of Cultural Psychology: Exploring the Frontiers of Mind and Society (InfoAge Publishing, N.C., USA, together with Carlos Cornejo e Jaan Valsiner). She is also co-editor of *Human Arenas: An Interdisciplinary Journal of Psychology, Culture and Meaning* (Springer), and of *Trends in Psychology* (Springer); Associate Editor of *Cultural & Psychology Journal* (Sage) and *Social Psychology of Education* (Springer); and member of the editorial board of several international academic journals (i.e., IPBS – *Integrative Psychological & Behavioural Science*, Springer). Her academic tracks and list of publications include two complementary lines of investigations: (1) an educational-focused research activity where Giuseppina Marsico is the leading figure of the new field of Cultural Psychology of Education and (2) a cultural-oriented interdisciplinary perspective based on both theoretical and empirical investigation, focusing on the borders as a new ontogenetic perspective in psychology and other social sciences. Giuseppina Marsico has established a new research field called Developmental Mereotopology.

Contributors

Francesca Amenduni University of Rome 3, Rome, Italy

Ruggero Andrisano Ruggieri University of Salerno, Fisciano, Italy

Anna N. Bartel Department of Psychology, University of Wisconsin, Madison, WI, USA

Martin Baumann Department of Human Factors, Ulm University, Ulm, Germany

Melissa J. Beers The Ohio State University, Columbus, OH, USA

Pedro F. Bendassolli Universidade Federal do Rio Grande do Norte, Natal, Brazil

Douglas A. Bernstein Department of Psychology, University of South Florida, Tampa, FL, USA

Swarnima Bhargava School of Human Ecology, Tata Institute of Social Sciences, Mumbai, India

Lisa Durrance Blalock Department of Psychology, University of West Florida, Pensacola, FL, USA

Thomas Boll Department of Cognitive, and Behavioural Sciences, Institute for Lifespan Development, Family, and Culture, University of Luxembourg, Esch-sur-Alzette, Luxembourg

Annette Bolte Faculty of Psychology, Technische Universität Dresden, Dresden, Germany

Angela Uchoa Branco Department of Psychology, University of Brasilia, Brasilia DF, Brazil

Robert G. Bringle Indiana University Purdue University Indianapolis, Indianapolis, IN, USA

Brian L. Burke Psychology, Fort Lewis College, Durango, CO, USA

Joanne Butt School of Sport & Exercise Sciences, Liverpool John Moores University, Liverpool, UK

Stefano Cacciamani University of Valle D'Aosta, Aosta, Italy

Luna Carpinelli Department of Medicine, Surgery, and Dentistry 'Scuola Medica Salernitana', University of Salerno (Italy), Fisciano/Baronissi, Italy

Leighann R. Chaffee University of Washington, Tacoma, Tacoma, WA, USA

Nandita Chaudhary Department of Human Development and Childhood Studies, Lady Irwin College, University of Delhi, Delhi, India

Andrew Christopher Albion College, Albion, MI, USA

Lewis L. Chuang Institute for Informatics, Ludwig-Maximilians-Universität München, München, Germany

IfADo – Leibniz Research Centre for Working Environment and Human Factors, Dortmund, Germany

Kevin Click Department of Psychology, California State University, Chico, CA, USA

Fellipe Coelho-Lima Universidade Federal do Rio Grande do Norte, Natal, Brazil

Emanuela Confalonieri Catholic University of the Sacred Heart of Milan, Milan, Italy

Michael J. Cortese Department of Psychology, University of Nebraska at Omaha, Omaha, NE, USA

Jacquelyn Cranney Psychology, University of New South Wales, Sydney, NSW, Australia

Ruby A. Daniels Texas A&M University - San Antonio, San Antonio, TX, USA

Moritz M. Daum Department of Psychology, Developmental Psychology: Infancy and Childhood, University of Zurich, Zurich, Switzerland

Jacobs Center for Productive Youth Development, University of Zurich, Zurich, Switzerland

Maria Cláudia Santos Lopes de Oliveira Institute of Psychology, University of Brasília, Brasília, Brazil

Dana S. Dunn Moravian University, Bethlehem, PA, USA

Christopher J. Ferguson Stetson University, DeLand, FL, USA

Pablo Fossa Universidad del Desarrollo de Chile, Santiago, Chile

Jane A. Foster Department of Psychiatry and Behavioural Neurosciences, McMaster University, Hamilton, ON, Canada

Robert Gaschler Department of Psychology, FernUniversität in Hagen, Hagen, Germany

David Gibson Curtin University, Perth, Australia

Sonia Gondim Universidade Federal da Bahia, Salvador, Brazil

Ricardo Gorayeb School of Medicine, São Paulo University, Ribeirão Preto, Brazil

Thomas Goschke Faculty of Psychology, Technische Universität Dresden, Dresden, Germany

Samuel Greiff University of Luxembourg, Esch-sur-Alzette, Luxembourg

Martin Greisel Lehrstuhl für Psychologie m.b.B.d. Pädagogischen Psychologie, University of Augsburg, Augsburg, Germany

Regan A. R. Gurung Psychological Science, Oregon State University, Corvallis, OR, USA

Jane S. Halonen Department of Psychology, University of West Florida, Pensacola, FL, USA

Bridgette Martin Hard Duke University, Durham, NC, USA

Viviana Hojman Universidad del Desarrollo de Chile, Santiago, Chile

Julie A. Hulme School of Psychology, Keele University, Keele, Staffordshire, UK

Dirk Ifenthaler Curtin University, Perth, Australia
University of Mannheim, Mannheim, Germany

Stephanie A. Jesseau University of Nebraska-Omaha, Omaha, NE, USA

Gordana Jovanović Belgrade, Serbia

Mariam Katsarava Department of Psychology, FernUniversität in Hagen, Hagen, Germany

Maya M. Khanna Department of Psychological Science, Creighton University, Omaha, NE, USA

Mary E. Kite Ball State University, Muncie, IN, USA

Susanne Knappe Institute of Clinical Psychology and Psychotherapy, Technische Universität Dresden, Dresden, Germany
Evangelische Hochschule Dresden (ehs), University of Applied Sciences for Social Work, Education and Nursing, Dresden, Germany

Ingo Kollar Lehrstuhl für Psychologie m.b.B.d. Pädagogischen Psychologie, University of Augsburg, Augsburg, Germany

Veit Kubik Department of Psychology, Universität Bielefeld, Bielefeld, Germany

M. Beatrice Ligorio University of Bari, Bari, Italy

Marie Lippmann California State University, Chico, CA, USA

Mirella Manfredi Department of Psychology, Developmental Psychology: Infancy and Childhood, University of Zurich, Zurich, Switzerland

Tiziana Marinaci Department of Medicine, Surgery, and Dentistry 'Scuola Medica Salernitana', University of Salerno (Italy), Fisciano/Baronissi, Italy

Giuseppina Marsico Department of Human, Philosophical and Educational Sciences (DISUFF), University of Salerno, Fisciano, Italy

Rob McEntarffer Lincoln Public Schools, Lincoln, NE, USA

Jennifer M. J. McGee Department of Psychology, Oxford College of Emory University, Atlanta, GA, USA

Katherine McLay University of Queensland (AU), Brisbane, Australia

M. David Merrill Utah State University, St. George, UT, USA

Günter Mey University of Applied Sciences Magdeburg-Stendal, Stendal, Germany

Leslie A. Miller LanneM TM, LLC and Rollins College, Winter Park, FL, USA

M. Cristina Miyazaki School of Medicine, FAMERP, São José do Rio Preto, Brazil

Maria Elisa Molina Universidad del Desarrollo de Chile, Santiago, Chile

Monica Mollo University of Salerno, Fisciano, Italy

David G. Myers Hope College, Holland, MI, USA

Susanne Narciss School of Science - Faculty of Psychology, Psychology of Learning and Instruction, Technische Universitaet Dresden, Dresden, Sachsen, Germany

Luzelle Naudé University of the Free State, Bloemfontein, South Africa

Helmut Niegemann Saarland University, Educational Technology, Saarbrücken, Germany

Faith Ong Ngee Ann Polytechnic, Singapore, Singapore

Sebastian Pannasch Faculty of Psychology, Technische Universität Dresden, Dresden, Germany

Jennifer Parada Bellevue College, Bellevue, WA, USA

Scott Plous Wesleyan University, Middletown, CT, USA

Claudia Prescher Technische Universität Dresden, Dresden, Germany

Ayesha Raees Department of Human Development and Childhood Studies, Institute of Home Economics, University of Delhi, Delhi, India

Vanessa R. Rainey Department of Psychology, University of West Florida, Pensacola, FL, USA

Roger N. Reeb University of Dayton, Dayton, OH, USA

Paul Rhodes Clinical Psychology Unit, University of Sydney, Sydney, Australia

Lia da Rocha Lordelo Federal University of Recôncavo of Bahia, Santo Amaro da Purificação, Brazil

Ana I. Ruiz Alvernia University, Reading, PA, USA

U. Arathi Sarma Department of Psychology, University of Kerala, Thiruvananthapuram, Kerala, India

Juergen Sauer Department of Psychology, University of Fribourg, Fribourg, Switzerland

Giulia Savarese Department of Medicine, Surgery, and Dentistry 'Scuola Medica Salernitana', University of Salerno (Italy), Fisciano/Baronissi, Italy

Niclas Schaper Psychology, University of Paderborn, Paderborn, Germany

Manfred Schmitt Department of Psychology, University of Koblenz-Landau, Landau, Germany

Neil H. Schwartz Department of Psychology, California State University, Chico, CA, USA

Danilo Silva Guimarães Universidade de São Paulo, São Paulo, Brasil

Timothy A. Sisemore St. Louis Behavioral Medicine Institute, St. Louis, MO, USA

Sujata Sriram School of Human Ecology, Tata Institute of Social Sciences, Mumbai, India

Christoph Steinebach ZHAW Zurich University of Applied Sciences, School of Applied Psychology, Zürich, Switzerland

Arianna M. Stone Oregon State University, Corvallis, OR, USA

Luca Tateo University of Oslo, Oslo, Norway

Tissy Mariam Thomas Department of Psychology, University of Kerala, Thiruvananthapuram, Kerala, India

J. Lukas Thürmer Department of Psychology, University of Salzburg, Salzburg, Austria

Mila Tuli Department of Human Development and Childhood Studies, Institute of Home Economics, University of Delhi, Delhi, India

Maria Tulis Department of Psychology, University of Salzburg, Salzburg, Austria

Maria Carmen Usai Department of Educational Sciences, University of Genova, Genova, Italy

Jaan Valsiner Centre of Cultural Psychology, Department of Communication and Psychology, Aalborg University, Aalborg, Denmark

Sigmund Freud Privatuniversität, Vienna, Austria

Paola Viterbori Department of Educational Sciences, University of Genova, Genova, Italy

Robert Weinberg Department of Sport Leadership and Management, Miami University, Oxford, OH, USA

Kristin Whitlock Davis High School, Kaysville, UT, USA

Megan C. Wrona Fort Lewis College, Durango, CO, USA

Tatiana Yokoy School of Education, University of Brasília, Brasília, Brazil

Mirella Zanobini Department of Educational Sciences, University of Genova, Genova, Italy

Joerg Zumbach Department of Educational Research, University of Salzburg, Salzburg, Austria

Part I

Teaching Psychology as Main Discipline in Undergraduate and Graduate Programs

Teaching Introductory Psychology

Melissa J. Beers and Bridgette Martin Hard

Contents

Abstract

One of the most popular courses taken by undergraduates in North America is introductory psychology. Although the course serves as a gateway to the psychology discipline, most students taking introductory psychology in North America are not psychology majors, instead representing a diversity of career interests. Acquainting such diverse students with the expansive discipline of psychology is a daunting task, made more daunting by the diversity of the course's format and instructors. It is difficult to imagine a single course that attempts to accomplish something so significant, with such breadth of content, in a context with so many variables and degrees of freedom. Yet, the introductory course is an opportunity

---

M. J. Beers (✉)
The Ohio State University, Columbus, OH, USA
e-mail: beers.3@osu.edu

B. M. Hard
Duke University, Durham, NC, USA
e-mail: bridgette.hard@duke.edu

© Springer Nature Switzerland AG 2023
J. Zumbach et al. (eds.), *International Handbook of Psychology Learning and Teaching*,
Springer International Handbooks of Education,
https://doi.org/10.1007/978-3-030-28745-0_2

to provide students' first exposure to some of the most exciting and influential ideas in the field – a tour of psychology's "greatest hits." In this chapter, we encourage teachers to understand and apply principles of effective course design in planning and teaching the course to maximize the benefits for both teaching and learning. We also review a framework for balancing breadth and depth while emphasizing the integrated nature of modern psychology. Introductory psychology provides a singular opportunity for teachers to grow in our understanding and appreciation of our discipline as well as to build our skills as evidence-based, scholarly teachers. While there are few courses in the psychology curriculum that are as challenging as introductory psychology, there are few courses as extraordinary in their far-reaching potential for impact.

Keywords

Teaching introductory psychology · Backward course design · Evidence-based teaching

Teaching Introductory Psychology

Psychology is one of the most popular majors on most North American college campuses. According to the US Department of Education, National Center for Education Statistics (NCES), psychology is the fourth most popular individual major overall, with 118,000 bachelor's degrees in psychology awarded in 2014–2015 alone (NCES, 2018). Nearly all these students are introduced to the field of psychology through an introductory course. Virtually every psychology department in the United States offers an introductory or general psychology course as a starting point for further study in the field (Norcross et al., 2016). Introductory psychology is required for the major at 98% of colleges in North America and is a prerequisite for all other psychology courses at 82% of colleges (Stoloff et al., 2010). Harry Potter once reflected: "every great wizard in history has started out as what we are now, students" (Rowling, 2003). Similarly, every psychological scientist contributing to new knowledge in the field today likely started their career in "Intro Psych."

Acquainting new students with the expansive discipline of psychology is a daunting task. As of 2019, the American Psychological Association (APA, 2017) had no fewer than 54 different divisions representing areas of specialization in psychology from brain science and cognitive psychology to climate and environmental psychology to forensic psychology and rehabilitation science. Psychology is not only a broad field, but it also has broad impact. As a "hub science," psychology influences advancements in fields such as medicine, public health, engineering, and education that span both theoretical and applied areas of inquiry (Boyack, Klavans, & Borerner, 2005). Thus, a course in introductory psychology could cover a seemingly endless set of possible topics and applications.

Introducing students to psychology is made even more daunting by the diversity of the course's students, format, and instructors. Most students taking introductory psychology, at least in North America, are not psychology majors. An estimated 1.2–1.8 million students enroll in introductory psychology courses each year (Gurung et al., 2016); the majority to fulfill general curriculum requirements intended to equip students with a broad educational foundation for their future careers. Introductory psychology students are thus a diverse population representing all ages and walks of life and with every possible area of interest. Most students taking the course are unlikely to pursue additional formal study in psychology and thus are temporary visitors to the discipline, rather than future citizens. The characteristics of its students make introductory psychology an opportunity to engage, inform, and impact society on a remarkably large scale.

Because of this diversity in its students, introductory psychology is offered in virtually every course format imaginable. Depending on the institutional context, students may take the course in cavernous lecture halls seating hundreds or in small, interactive seminars. They may take the course partly or fully online, completing assignments in their kitchens or bedrooms early in the morning or late in the evening. In a few programs, the course can still be taken by mail as a "correspondence course." Course length within and across institutions can range from a multi-term series of two or three courses to an intensive 4- or 6-week concentrated course – even as a full year of study in secondary education (high school).

Teachers of introductory psychology are equally diverse, ranging from advanced postgraduate students to seasoned full professors. In most contexts, there is no specific degree or training requirement to teach introductory psychology. Some teachers of the course may have no formal training in psychology at all, as is the case for many teachers of psychology in high schools who are typically licensed to teach social studies or history.

In short, teaching introductory psychology may well be viewed by some new teachers as an impossible task. It is difficult to imagine a single course that attempts to accomplish something so significant, with such breadth of content, in a context with so many variables and degrees of freedom. As long-time teachers of this course (and trainers of those who teach the course), we are both well acquainted with its inherent challenges. We have also seen the transformational impact the course can have for students as well as instructors. For students, this course can dispel persistent and harmful myths about human behavior and develop skills and knowledge that can improve students' academic performance, resilience, and well-being long after they turn in their final assignments. Some of them may even decide to major in psychology after taking the course. Whatever the case, for teachers, the course is an opportunity to provide students' first exposure to some of the most exciting and influential ideas in the field – a tour of psychology's "greatest hits."

The goal of this chapter is to provide relevant history and guidance for instructors teaching this course. We will begin by briefly considering the history and evolution of the introductory psychology course in North America. Next, we will provide guidance for designing a contemporary course that strikes a sound balance between breadth and depth, using principles of backward design (e.g., Fink, 2003; Wiggins & McTighe, 2005). We will consider how to assess student learning as well as one's own teaching effectiveness, specifically, how to teach in an evidence-based way.

Whether you are teaching introductory psychology for the first, third, or thirtieth time, we hope this chapter will inspire you to approach teaching the course the same way that students ideally approach learning in your class: with intention, patience, persistence, and self-reflection. The experience of teaching introductory psychology can be both challenging and rewarding and can grow with you as you develop and as a teacher.

How Did We Get Here: The Evolution of Introductory Psychology

Introducing students to a field as broad as psychology requires designing a course with tremendous breadth. Instructors approaching the course in high schools, community colleges, and 4-year institutions across North America may regard all the possible topics to include in their courses and ask, "How can I cover all this?" The following quote conveys an all-too-common sentiment:

> "Many professors of psychology have been saying that the traditional design of Introductory Psychology is no longer appropriate for the typical, present-day student....now, most college students want some exposure to psychology not for career purposes but for intellectual and personal development...Yet academic psychology seems reluctant to reflect this change in values in the textbooks it uses. Writers of new textbooks seem determined to follow the traditional pattern of including a smattering of everything."

Would you believe these words were, in fact, written almost half a century ago, when psychology as a field was not even 100 years old? This quote from Lazarus (1974) captures a long-standing complaint that introductory courses seem to try to "do it all" and cover an unmanageable amount of information. How did we get where we are today, and where are we headed?

Little is known about the first psychology courses, but it seems that they were offered in the earliest days of the discipline. The first introductory psychology course taught at Ohio State University, for example, met in 1879 – the same year Wilhelm Wundt opened his laboratory in Leipzig – but no course syllabus or lesson plans remain. This particular course, like many others of the time, was taught by a philosophy professor and focused on the mind and brain – topics considered so complex and advanced that students had to be at least juniors to enroll.

Textbooks for introductory psychology, still a common feature in North American courses, began to appear in psychology's infancy at the turn of the twentieth century. Early courses might have used books authored by Wilhelm Wundt (in German, *naturlich*), John Dewey, George Ladd, or Edward Titchener. These texts were not entirely objective but were "treatises" that tended to advance the theoretical orientation of the authors (Weiten & Wight, 1992). For example, Titchener's, 1915 text *A Beginner's Psychology*, for example, was deeply rooted in the structuralist perspective, while John Watson's *Psychology from the Standpoint of a Behaviorist* (Watson, 1919) appealed to teachers who embraced the emerging behaviorist view of the field.

Perhaps the most highly regarded early text was William James' two-volume *Principles of Psychology* (James, 1890) or his abridged (500-page) *Briefer Course* (James, 1892). These volumes were considered the standard psychological texts in the United States and across Europe at the turn of the twentieth century, cementing James' reputation as the "father of American psychology." According to Hothersall (2004), "a whole generation of psychologists learned from these books, referring to them affectionately as 'the James' and 'the Jimmy' (p. 337)." James himself was considered an exceptional teacher of psychology and was notable for being one of the few professors of his day who allowed students to ask questions during his lectures at Harvard. To support teachers in applying lessons from psychology to education, James gave a series of lectures which he published as *Talks to Teachers* (James, 1899); chapters included *Psychology and the Teaching Art*, *Education and Behavior*, and *The Acquisition of Ideas*, *Interest*, *Attention*, and *Memory*. James' advice from 120 years ago is still sound today: "The art of remembering is the art of thinking. When we wish to fix a new thing in either our own mind or a pupil's, our conscious effort should not be so much to impress and retain it as to connect it with something else already there" (James, 1899, p. 148).

By the early 1970s, introductory psychology was an almost universal undergraduate course offering; an APA survey commissioned at that time found an introductory course was taught at 99% of all universities (Kulik, Brown, Vestewig, & Wright, 1973). Arguably the most significant factor in the growth and popularity of the introductory psychology course was the advancement in the United States of general education. The term refers to the requirement of a strong "common core" of foundational courses, independent of students' major program, that are intended to develop a broad, integrated base of knowledge and intellectual skills (O'Banion, 2016). As a cornerstone of most general education curricula, introductory psychology courses experienced soaring enrollments – for example, by the 1980s enrollment in general psychology at Ohio State University exceeded 8000 students a year at the main campus alone.

Course materials and resources increased to meet the growing demands of both instructors and students. But introductory "survey" courses taught at this time tended to review a broad array of research and consequently were content-heavy with little to no integration across topics. Students and instructors struggled with a lack of coherence, leading to recommendations to replace the single general survey course with an introductory curriculum of four or more courses, such as physiology, cognition, development, and social behavior (Senn, 1985). Others recommended revising the course to be a less content-intensive experience that incorporated skills and application of concepts to students' lives. For example, Walker and McKeachie (1967) recommended ten objectives for teachers of introductory psychology courses:

1. Communicate elementary concepts.
2. Communicate facts in support of the concepts.
3. Introduce the student to the full range of subject matter.
4. Integrate course material.
5. Communicate basic attitudes of the discipline.

6. Communicate the intrinsic interest of the subject matter.
7. Present the newest developments of the field.
8. Provide individual guidance and monitoring.
9. Develop selected intellectual skills.
10. Provide a suitable identification model for the student.

Notably, only half of these ten objectives focus on developing content knowledge (1–4, 7). Considering the prevailing approach to survey courses at the time, urging instructors of the course to communicate intrinsic interest, support skill development, and integrate ideas across the course constituted rather revolutionary guidance! These ten objectives for instructors were synthesized into three broad student-centered goals for introductory courses, putting more emphasis on personal development and application of skills (Senn, 1985):

1. Improved attitudes and skills, specifically an appreciation of the scientific method and its application to the study of human behavior.
2. Greater knowledge, meaning an understanding of core principles in the discipline as well as an ability to apply them to new situations.
3. Better personal adjustment, in the form of productivity, happiness, and social effectiveness.

It seems McKeachie's advice was ahead of its time, because in the mid-1980s, critics of the introductory course continued to bemoan its content-heavy nature, contending this structure ignored psychology's own fundamental principles of learning and memory (Lenthall & Andrews, 1985). For example, some of the most popular textbooks at the time had over 1500 references and covered an amount of content that reviewers described as "staggering" in an attempt to achieve "scholarly sophistication" (Weiten & Wight, 1992). Critics of these "encyclopedic" texts called for courses to be restructured thematically and integratively so that students would have a more holistic view of the field (Dimond & Senter, 1985; Lenthall & Andrews, 1985). Among the examples of texts that embraced this perspective were volumes by Gleitman (1981) and Myers (1986), which synthesized and clarified complex ideas and introduced pedagogical graphics and illustrations – innovative additions that aimed to help facilitate students' understanding of the concepts (Weiten & Wight, 1992).

The changing structure of textbooks across time also reveals patterns and trends in the evolution of the course. Weiten and Wight (1992) analyzed introductory textbook content from the 1890s to the 1980s and found most texts converged on a now-familiar set of topics organized by chapter: history, methods, biological bases of behavior, learning, memory, sensation/perception, language/thought, motivation/emotion, development, intelligence, consciousness, psychological disorders and treatments, personality, and social psychology. While the proportion of coverage each topic receives has changed over the years, these topics have consistently formed the core of the course – and preview the broader curriculum of the psychology major: a strong foundation of research methods and core content domains including the biological basis of behavior, development, sociocultural issues, and cognition (Dunn, 2018). This core organization continues in many modern textbooks today (Griggs & Jackson, 2013) and parallels the way many courses are structured (Griggs, 2014). Yet, despite similarities in core topics, there remains great variability in the specific content that is covered in both textbooks and introductory psychology courses. For example, while chapters in different texts may have similar names, studies examining the content within these chapters reveal considerable variation in terms and theories discussed within (Griggs, Bujak-Johnson, & Proctor, 2004; Gurung et al., 2016; Zechmeister & Zechmeister, 2000).

A look back at the history of the introductory course thus reveals that, as psychology has grown and developed as a field, its introductory course has matured to include a relatively standard set of core topics and a focus that goes beyond content toward essential skills and applications. Yet, there has always remained tremendous variability in the way that introductory psychology is taught. For example, 1 study reviewed 158 syllabi for introductory courses and found great variability in whether courses were designed to meet specific learning objectives and even what those objectives might be (Homa et al., 2013). Ultimately, the content and character of introductory psychology is at the discretion of the individual instructor (or instructional team) as courses are designed and delivered.

Given the many varied formats and contexts for introductory courses, it seems unlikely (and untenable) that there can ever be a "one size fits all" approach that standardizes introductory psychology. Such an approach would be unnecessarily restrictive and potentially detrimental, in that it may well prevent instructors from making course decisions that best fit their institutional contexts and student needs. Mindful of this reality, the American Psychological Association has avoided being overly prescriptive in advising instructors who teach the course (e.g., APA, 2014; Gurung et al., 2016). Instead, it seems far more valuable to encourage teachers to understand and adopt principles of effective course design in planning and teaching the course to maximize the benefits for both teaching and learning. In the sections that follow, we describe these principles and specific strategies for implementing them within introductory psychology.

Weaving It All Together: The Importance of Backward Design

Many seasoned instructors of introductory psychology recall their early experience with course design as going something like this: open the assigned textbook, look at the table of contents, and assemble a course calendar that more or less follows the order of chapters, adding in as much content as you have time to cover during the academic term and administering an examination every few weeks. In other words, for generations of teachers in higher education, course planning involved far more consideration of what content to cover than what learning objectives students should meet by the end of the course.

A more effective process for planning a course involves *backward design*, in which courses are developed by "deconstructing" the learning process. Backward design starts with the question, "what will students learn in my course, and how will I know they have learned it?" By prioritizing the desired end result of the teaching and learning process, we can ensure that our courses are organized to emphasize and support our goals for student learning (cf., Fink, 2013; Wiggins & McTighe, 2005). In courses planned primarily around content, instructors can only hope that students will latch on to important ideas in the flow of course material and demonstrate that knowledge later on. When courses are planned around student learning goals, assessment tools and teaching strategies align to meaningfully support learning. Starting with the end of the course in mind seems particularly challenging for an expansive course such as introductory psychology, yet that expansiveness is precisely why it is so important to work backward. An integrated, well-aligned course increases the likelihood that students will have a positive experience that results in learning.

Effective course design is a complex and iterative process, beginning with several key steps:

Consider your Context

Teaching any course involves making choices about what you will ask your students to do and why. External factors such as your institutional context (e.g., high school, community college, 4-year institution), student demographics, and the support structures available to you should influence the curricular choices you make. These situational factors present both challenges and opportunities for course design (Fink, 2013). For example, if you teach many students who are in their first year of college and/or are the first in their family to attend college ("first-generation college students"), you may need to provide more study skills resources to support their transition to higher education. While such situations can present challenges in planning, they simultaneously present opportunities to leverage course content (e. g., learning and memory) and develop learning activities that promote application of this content to students' personal experiences.

As another example, consider whether your course enrolls students who do not intend to be psychology majors or even to take another course in the field. Such students form the majority in introductory psychology classes at North American institutions, because they must take courses in many disciplines to fulfill a "general education" requirement. Their presence will challenge you to make the course content and assignments relevant to a broad range of interests but also gives you an opportunity to reach students who might not otherwise encounter psychology and to help them learn how psychology can benefit them personally and professionally. Other contextual factors to consider are the size of your course (15 or 500?), whether your course has a research or laboratory component, whether you will teach fully or partly online, and whether you will work with others in a coordinated course or with teaching assistants. In planning to teach the course, begin by considering the "big picture" surrounding your course and what resources and supports you will need to teach the course effectively and manageably.

Prioritize Learning Objectives

Your course learning objectives for introductory psychology may be defined by your institution or department, or you may have the freedom to determine some or all of these objectives for yourself. Once you have considered important contextual factors in your course, the next step in course planning is to identify the core learning objectives, or the most important "enduring understandings" you want students to remember, not just at the end of the course but 6 months or even 6 years later (Wiggins & McTighe, 2005). Enduring understandings are important, meaningful ideas that cut across specific topics and inform the structure of the course. While there is a vast amount of content that is helpful for students to know or is worth being familiar with, a well-designed course is organized around and prioritizes a small set of objectives. One enduring understanding common to many introductory courses is for students to recognize psychology as an empirical science, that is, that psychologists use scientific evidence to draw conclusions about behavior and mental processes. This is an idea that an instructor would want to make integral to the course design and revisit multiple times across multiple topics.

For example, Hardin (2016) describes a central organizing theme of "thinking like a psychologist" into her introductory course, meaning she prioritizes applying the process of scientific inquiry to create an impact on students' habits of mind. She structures her course so that as students encounter core topics, they are not merely memorizing facts but rather developing a sense of curiosity and critical thinking. She shapes their approach to acquiring new information by encouraging them to ask such questions as "what is the evidence for this claim," "is it possible to find evidence that would prove this claim to be false," and "what other explanations are there?"

The American Psychological Association's *Introductory Psychology Initiative* recently recommended a set of expected student learning outcomes to articulate what introductory psychology students should know and be able to do as a result of completing the course (Halonen et al., in press). Like enduring understandings, these objectives can help instructors identify and establish priorities for their introductory courses:

Psychology Content: Identify basic concepts and research findings:
  1.1. Define and explain basic psychological concepts.
  1.2. Interpret research findings related to psychological concepts.
  1.3 Apply psychological principles to personal growth and other aspects of everyday life.

Scientific Thinking: Solve problems using psychological methods:
  2.1. Describe the advantages and limitations of research strategies.
  2.2. Evaluate, design, or conduct psychological research.
  2.3. Draw logical and objective conclusions about behavior and mental processes from empirical evidence.

2.4. Examine how psychological science can be used to counter unsubstantiated statements, opinions, or beliefs.

Key Themes: Provide examples of psychology's integrative themes:
   A. Psychological science relies on empirical evidence and adapts as new data develop.
   B. Psychology explains general principles that govern behavior while recognizing individual differences.
   C. Psychological, biological, social, and cultural factors influence behavior and mental processes.
   D. Psychologists strive to promote respect for human diversity in its many forms.
   E. Our perceptions and biases filter our experiences of the world through an imperfect personal lens.
   F. Applying psychological principles can change our lives, organizations, and communities in positive ways.
   G. Ethical principles guide psychology research and practice.

Compared to Walker and McKeachie's (1967) recommended course objectives presented earlier, the contemporary objectives are more student-centered than teacher-centered, articulating what students should know and be able to do at the end of the course rather than what instructors should do in order to teach it. The contemporary objectives also focus more on integrated themes and enduring understandings and emphasize skills that promote scientific thinking and ethical reasoning in psychology. Goals for student learning should be one's foremost consideration in planning to teach any course, but especially a course as broad as introductory psychology – not only to focus and streamline one's teaching, but to communicate to students what they should expect to learn in the course.

Align Assessments with Learning Goals

Once you have prioritized goals for student learning, the next step is to determine how you will know whether students have achieved the desired results. What should students be able to do to demonstrate they have learned, and what kind of assignments or activities give students an opportunity to practice and demonstrate their learning? These are questions of assessment that determine how instructors will structure student work and measure learning outcomes in the course. These decisions should be based not merely on what we want students to do within the limits of the course but rather what we want the long-term impact of the course to be.

All forms of assessment that are aligned to learning objectives provide data on students' mastery of the course learning objectives and also on their progress. Analyzing measures of student learning already present in the classroom such as exams, assignments, or papers is known as *embedded assessment* (McCarthy, Niederjohn, & Bosack, 2011). Embedded assessments offer a rich set of data that instructors can use to understand student learning and inform teaching strategies. For example, if the results of tests or quizzes suggest that students are struggling with particular topics (e.g., heritability, schedules of reinforcement, or experimental research methods), instructors can consider the teaching strategies they use for these topics and adjust them to better support student learning.

Assessments not only measure learning, but they also *produce* learning by giving students opportunities to practice applying their knowledge and skills. For example, if a long-term goal for introductory psychology students is to be able to critically analyze claims about behavior they encounter in the media, an assessment could involve students reading news stories about research and evaluating whether the results are conveyed accurately given the nature of the evidence. An assignment might ask students to write a response to the article's author or propose a revision to the original article. Such an assessment would be considered "authentic" in the sense that it mimics a real-world task that involves meaningful application of knowledge beyond the classroom. "Authentic assessments" allow students to demonstrate their understanding of an objective and frequently involve complex tasks, problem-solving, and application of knowledge to meaningful problems. This kind of assessment gives students the opportunity to synthesize and apply what they are learning and can result in new meaning and knowledge (Mueller, 2018). In contrast to traditional forms of assessment such as exams, quizzes, and student response papers that only an instructor might see, authentic assessments give students opportunities to create work that can be shared outside the classroom. These can take many forms, such as blog posts, videos, tutorials, or teaching tools for other students (cf., Seraphin et al., 2018).

Of course, traditional forms of assessment like tests and quizzes can also produce learning. Indeed, a central goal in any foundational course is to build a strong knowledge base for future use and application. Research from cognitive science reveals a "testing effect": compared to just repeated studying, the retrieval practice provided by repeated testing enhances learning (Roediger & Karpicke, 2006; Roediger, Agarwal, McDaniel, & McDermott, 2011; Nguyen & McDaniel, 2015). Classroom tests and quizzes can thus boost long-term retention. Several studies show that when retested years after taking the course, students can remember a significant amount of information from introductory psychology (Hard, Lovett, & Brady, 2019; Landrum & Gurung, 2013). A challenge to harnessing the benefits of testing is that many psychology instructors are not trained in writing test items or constructing examinations, although many resources exist to learn to construct valid and reliable assessments of student learning (cf., Rodriguez & Albano, 2017; Xu, Kauer, & Tupy, 2016). Although most textbooks provide instructors with supplemental teaching resources and banks of test questions to use as a starting point, the structure of any exam still must be aligned with the overall course objectives.

Multiple forms of assessment are usually necessary in introductory psychology to capture progress toward the full range of course objectives and to maximally affect students' knowledge and skills. While authentic assignments give students the opportunity to demonstrate their learning and apply knowledge to new issues and topics, traditional exams and quizzes boost retention and give students feedback on their mastery of a topic. Particularly in a foundational survey course, some combination of tests and authentic assignments is valuable. Mueller (2018) draws an analogy to assessing whether people are ready to have a driver's license: In many countries, new drivers must pass a knowledge test to demonstrate they understand the rules and regulations for driving (a traditional form of assessment), as well as a driving test to demonstrate they have the necessary skills (an authentic assessment). Ensuring success in both tasks is likely to produce the best long-term outcomes.

Plan Learning Experiences

Once instructors have identified key learning outcomes and planned for how they will assess them, the next question to consider is "What is the best way to support student learning to achieve those outcomes?" The first instructional strategy that comes to mind for many instructors is the most common technique in higher education: lecturing. Lectures are most likely to support student learning when instructors draw on the material they are teaching and apply principles from psychology to teaching psychology. Based on a review of research in learning science, Cerbin (2018) recommends that instructors can maximize the impact of learning in lecture by activating students' prior knowledge, effectively managing cognitive load during lecture, and creating opportunities for students to engage in deep, elaborative processing and retrieval practice, such as by asking students to make a prediction about the results of a study the instructor is explaining or by asking students to periodically answer questions about recent material.

The content of introductory psychology affords many opportunities to harness stories to enhance the meaningfulness, coherence, and memorability of lectures (Landrum, Brakke, & McCarthy, 2019). Psychology is, after all, mainly about people and people are natural protagonists in stories. Stories can illustrate important concepts or convey the history of the discipline in a narrative format, featuring such key figures as Phineas Gage, H.M., or Jean Piaget. As part of lecture, stories are easy to remember, provide deeper meaning to information, convey the values of the field, and help students see the relevance of psychology in their everyday lives (for more on the value of stories in teaching, see Brakke & Houska, 2015).

Although lecture has potential benefits, the technique can become too teacher-centered and has thus been criticized in recent years for putting students in a passive role (Bernstein, 2018). Incorporating more active forms of learning has been shown to produce student learning outcomes that are superior to traditional lecture in STEM fields (Deslauriers, Schelew, & Wieman, 2011; Weiman, 2014). Active learning can take many forms, from asking students to make and discuss their predictions about a study with a nearby peer (also known as "peer instruction") to more involved forms of experiential learning such as conducting in-class experiments, debating or discussing controversial topics, or asking students to engage in writing exercises during class time. Indeed, the entire introductory courses can be planned and delivered via "flipped" or problem-based-learning approaches, in which students gain access to basic course content outside of class and spend their in-class time engaging with the instructor and other students as they apply that content to novel problems and situations (c.f., LoGiudice & Kim, 2016).

Bernstein (2018) cautions that there are not currently evidence-based guidelines for choosing and using active learning strategies. He advises that new teachers and teachers inexperienced with active learning techniques should take a measured approach, focusing on methods supported by the highest-quality evidence and that are most relevant and feasible for their teaching context. For example, a starting point for incorporating active learning into one's class may be to start with easy-to-incorporate strategies such as retrieval practice, asking students to make a prediction or write a minute paper reflection after watching a video. Gradually instructors can incorporate more complex or varied techniques, depending on the learning objective and intended assessment.

When applying backward design, decisions about what teaching and learning activities to use in introductory psychology should be driven primarily by the learning objective and planned assessment. For example, if student learning will be assessed with an application-focused exam, then teaching strategies should be selected to train students to apply concepts to the kinds of problems and questions that will ultimately appear on the exam. If, however, student learning will be assessed with a research project or proposal, then teaching and learning strategies should give students the opportunity to practice the skills they need to be successful on the assignment, such as developing original hypotheses and finding/using empirical research studies. In other words, decisions about how to teach should be based on helping students to gain the knowledge and skills that will be measured on the course assessments.

Core Contents and Topics: Striking the Right Balance

You may have noticed that the course design process described in this chapter has not yet considered what *content* to include. What to teach in an introductory course has been the subject of vigorous debate among teachers of this course. As we saw in reviewing the history of the course, decisions about what topics to include, how to present them, and how much to cover have traditionally dominated the course design process for introductory psychology. Backward course design emphasizes goals for student learning that are of a higher order than simply memorizing specific content. In backward design, decisions about content are made *after* learning objectives, assessment, and teaching strategies are planned. For some teachers of this course, this may be an uncomfortable process. You may be wondering, "how can I know what my assignments will be if I don't first know what content I will cover?" As mentioned earlier, the curriculum for introductory psychology in North America has more or less coalesced into 16 broad topics which parallel the main content domains of the psychology major and are (for the most part) consistent across texts in the discipline. For many instructors, the possibility of covering 16 broad topics is overwhelming, as is the wealth of potential information that could be taught more deeply within each topic. With learning objectives as a guide, instructors still must make many decisions about what to include in their courses, and these decisions will naturally vary by institutional context and instructor.

The challenge of selecting course content led the APA to establish a working group to make recommendations for a "common core" that would guide instructors in making content choices while promoting more consistency in student experience and learning outcomes. The working group's recommendations (APA, 2014; Gurung et al., 2016) did not *prescribe* specific content the course should cover, but rather recommended a framework for balancing breadth and depth while emphasizing the integrated nature of modern psychology.

In this framework, instructors are encouraged to consider content as organized around five clusters of topics, or *pillars*, drawn from the APA Guidelines for the Psychology Major (APA, 2013). To ensure breadth of coverage across these pillars, the framework encourages instructors to select *at least two topics* from each pillar:

- Biological (neuroscience, sensation, consciousness).
- Cognitive (cognition, memory, perception, intelligence).
- Development (learning, development, language).
- Social and personality (social, personality, emotion, multicultural, gender, motivation).
- Mental and physical health (abnormal, health, therapies).

By encountering multiple topics from each of these five pillars, students can gain a more holistic appreciation of the discipline. Having this broad view should better equip them to see how psychology can apply in their personal and professional lives. The subset of topics that teachers select from each pillar reflects the content that works best in their institutional context as well as in relation to their own expertise and knowledge. Further, students may benefit from exposure to fewer topics covered in greater depth rather than to a wider array of topics covered only briefly.

Beyond including content from each of these five pillars, the recommendations also encouraged instructors to *integrate* content across units and to incorporate recurring themes that cut across each topic area, including research methods, cultural and social diversity, individual differences/variations in human functioning, applications to everyday life, and ethics. By encountering each theme in the context of each topic, students can learn what ideas unify the diverse field of psychology and appreciate the multifaceted and multiply-determined nature of human behavior and mental processes. Students can also learn how psychologists approach a given topic using various approaches and questions. For example, in a unit on lifespan development, cross-cutting themes might involve longitudinal methods for studying development over time, ethical considerations in conducting research with children and other vulnerable populations, how social and cultural practices impact development, how environmental influences impact gene expression to create individual differences, and how to apply research from developmental psychology to education or health care for elderly adults.

The challenge instructors face in making choices about content can also be an opportunity to tailor some content choices to the interests and needs of their students. For example, many students choose to take introductory psychology to prepare for medical school or other allied health professions. Instructors can incorporate medical examples throughout the course to appeal to such students. Instructors might highlight the connection between classical conditioning and drug tolerance, the potential for cognitive bias in physicians' decision-making, and how stereotypes can contribute to disparities in health care. Similarly, instructors can draw upon examples relating course content to business and industry, communications or public relations, psychology and the law, and important contemporary issues such as climate change or social justice. Better yet, instructors can create assignments that allow students to explore for themselves the connections between psychology and their own interests and planned careers.

It can be difficult for first-time instructors or advanced graduate student instructors to see these opportunities. Even highly experienced instructors can be challenged when teaching this course. Given that psychologists are trained primarily in one specific area of specialty (e.g., developmental, cognitive, social, clinical, and so on), teaching a broad introductory psychology course means that most instructors have little (if any) training in many of the topics covered in the course. Know that all instructors teaching this course are in the same boat, as illustrated by the fact that the entire books have been written about *Teaching What You Don't Know* (Huston, 2009). Fortunately, there are strategies you can use to overcome this challenge. First, capitalize on your own areas of strength as you are designing the course. Leverage the pillar model to incorporate topics you have the most expertise in or are most confident to teach, at least the first time. Remember that teaching is an iterative process and that each academic term you can make adjustments based on your students' outcomes and your own priorities to improve and enhance the course. Approach teaching with the same learning mindset you want to encourage in your students, that is, with curiosity and a willingness to learn alongside your students about topics you don't know well.

Another strategy for success is to leverage the knowledge and experience of others in your institution or social network. Colleagues can help you build your knowledge and resources in areas that are not your strength. For example, we were trained as social (Beers) and cognitive psychologists (Hard). Neither of us has had a single day of graduate training in abnormal psychology. Fortunately, we both work alongside other teachers of psychology whose training was primarily in clinical psychology. By sharing resources with one another, observing each other's classes, and talking informally about teaching strategies, we have built our skills and confidence teaching students about psychological disorders and treatments. In exchange, we have helped others build their resources to teach social and cognitive psychology. Many institutions have teams of instructors teaching introductory courses. If you are fortunate to have a teaching community for support, take advantage of it. For support beyond our own departments, use social media to extend your social networks. The Society for the Teaching of Psychology (STP) has an openly accessible Facebook page and many free teaching resources on their website (http://TeachPsych.org). You might even reach out to your own former professors or mentors for resources and guidance. Teaching conferences can also serve as opportunities to connect with other teaching professionals, especially those who teach introductory psychology. In fact, the annual Psych One Conference (http://www.psychoneconference.org/) is dedicated specifically to the teaching of introductory psychology.

Ultimately, there are as many ways to teach introductory psychology as there are teachers of the course. Beyond traditional approaches covering content in separate units or chapters, a more advanced approach is to structure the course thematically, such as organizing the course around the development of workplace skills (Landrum, 2016), integrative concepts that cut across topics (Nordmeyer, Hard, & Gross, 2016), or by organizing the content around myths and illusions we experience in everyday life (Bernstein, 2017). In the latter model, instead of organizing an introductory course around topic areas, a course could be organized around common myths or misperceptions, like "subliminal messages can change your behavior" instead of a traditional lecture on persuasion or "eyewitness testimony is the best kind of evidence" instead of a traditional unit on memory. Instead of requiring students to memorize terms and concepts, such a model encourages students to research myths for themselves and evaluate the evidence for and against each hypothesis through discussion or group work.

In short, there is no one "right" way – or even one "best" way – to teach introductory psychology. This may be frustrating for many new instructors, but with experience, we've found it to be one of the things we love most about the course. Each of us has to consider our personal strengths, our students' needs, and our course and institutional learning objectives in making our teaching decisions. Additionally, it is important to leverage our skills as scientists to inform our teaching. We can be scholarly teachers by using evidence-based practices that empirical research has shown to have a positive impact on student learning (e.g., Dunn, Saville, Baker, & Marek, 2013). Evidence-based practices can be discovered by using scholarly articles that rigorously evaluate teaching practices and by examining evidence about our own students' learning by analyzing the embedded assessments in our own courses. We can also listen to our students and systematically collect feedback on their learning experiences at midterm and at the end of our courses. The recommendation to approach teaching in a scholarly way is not unique to introductory psychology, but is particularly relevant given that course's focus on applying the scientific method to understanding human behavior and mental processes. What better way to model a scientific mindset and approach for students than by applying it to our own teaching? For additional guidance on scholarly teaching, see McKeachie and Svinicki (2013) or Bernstein, Frantz, and Chew (2020).

Concluding Thoughts

For some students, an introductory psychology course sparks an interest that fires a career in psychology. For others, the course plants seeds of knowledge about wellness, interpersonal relationships, or development that bloom long after the course ends. We firmly believe that everyone who takes the course can benefit from the generalizable knowledge and skills it affords, in their college careers and far beyond. No matter what problems or issues students seek to address in their future careers, understanding psychology is valuable. The discipline offers both an understanding of human behavior and a set of critical, scientific thinking strategies that are indispensable for addressing the most significant challenges facing society today. John Cacioppo, an ardent advocate for introductory courses, wrote, "Introductory Psychology is one – and perhaps the only – course in which we have the opportunity to teach our future public about the importance and impact of our scientific discipline" (Cacioppo, 2013, p. 309).

Introductory psychology is just as valuable for its instructors. This course presents a singular opportunity to take a bird's-eye view of our field, to examine human behavior and mental processes through varied lenses, and to uncover new and emerging findings alongside our students. Psychologists are largely trained in a narrow area of specialty, which can unfortunately result in subfields adopting a "siloed" structure. Introductory courses demand that we broaden our view of the field and examine how subfields complement and enhance one another. And most importantly, as we assess and evaluate our students' learning and make evidence-informed adjustments in our teaching methods, we grow and develop as teachers.

While there are few courses in the psychology curriculum that are as challenging as introductory psychology, there are few courses as extraordinary in their far-reaching potential for impact. Introductory psychology courses strengthen and support a department's psychology major and fuel research programs through research participation of introductory psychology students (Hard & Gross, 2016). What students learn contributes to their well-being both as individuals and citizens of their community and the world.

Resources for Teaching Introductory Psychology

The American Psychological Association's Introductory Psychology Initiative: Learn more about the APA's most recent recommendations for the introductory psychology course:

https://www.apa.org/ed/precollege/undergrad/introductory-psychology-initiative/

Lesson plans for teaching introductory psychology from APA's Teachers of Psychology in Secondary Schools (TOPSS):

https://www.apa.org/ed/precollege/topss/lessons/

The Society for the Teaching of Psychology (APA Division 02): Explore free E-books and other resources for psychology instructors: http://teachpsych.org/

A free E-book for new teachers of introductory psychology, published by the Society for the Teaching of Psychology (STP):

Afful, S. E., Good, J. J., Keeley, J., Leder, S., & Stiegler-Balfour, J. J. (2013). *Introductory Psychology teaching primer: A guide for new teachers of Psych 101.*

Retrieved from the Society for the Teaching of Psychology website: http://teachpsych.org/ebooks/intro2013/index.php

A free STP e-book on storytelling in teaching, including examples and teaching resources:

Brakke, K., & Houska, J. A. (Eds.). (2015). *Telling stories: The art and science of storytelling as an instructional strategy.* Society for the Teaching of Psychology. Retrieved from the Society for the Teaching of Psychology web site: http://teachpsych.org/ebooks/tellingstories.html

A collection of essays from introductory psychology instructors describing a variety of thematic approaches to teaching the course:

Dunn, D. S. & Hard, B. M. (Eds.). (2016) *Thematic Approaches for Teaching Introductory Psychology.* Boston: Cengage Learning.

A collection of essays from introductory psychology instructors describing their philosophies, course designs, and techniques:

Sternberg, R.J. (Ed.) (1997). *Teaching introductory psychology: Survival tips from the experts.* Washington, DC: American Psychological Association.

A collection of science-focused lesson plans from the Association for Psychological Science (APS) to reorganize introductory psychology content around persistent myths and misconceptions:

https://www.psychologicalscience.org/members/teaching-psychology/reinventing-introductory-psychology

A collection of popular myths and misconceptions about psychology that can provide examples and resources for helping students think critically and evaluate evidence:

Lilienfeld, S. O., Lynn, S. J., Ruscio, J., & Beyerstein, B. L. (2011). 50 great myths of popular psychology: Shattering widespread misconceptions about human behavior. John Wiley & Sons.

A comprehensive guide for preparing and teaching any course in psychology:

Bernstein, D. A., Frantz, S., & Chew, S. (2020). *Teaching psychology: A step by step guide.* (third ed.) New York: Routledge.

A peer-reviewed collection of case studies for undergraduate and graduate STEM education including teaching notes and resources from the National Center for Case Study Teaching in Science:

http://sciencecases.lib.buffalo.edu/cs/

References

American Psychological Association. (2013). *APA guidelines for the undergraduate psychology major 2.0.* Washington, DC: Author. Retrieved from www.apa.org/ed/resources.html.

American Psychological Association. (2014). *Strengthening the common core of the introductory psychology course.* Washington, DC: American Psychological Association, Board of Educational Affairs. Retrieved from www.apa.org/ed/governance/bea/intro-psych-report.pdf.

American Psychological Association, Working Group on Introductory Psychology Assessment. (2017). *Assessment of outcomes of the introductory course in psychology.* Retrieved from http://www.apa.org/ed/precollege/undergrad/index.aspx.

Bernstein, D. (2018). Does active learning work? A good question, but not the right one. *Scholarship of Teaching and Learning in Psychology, 4,* 290–307.

Bernstein, D. A. (2017). Bye-bye intro: A proposal for transforming introductory psychology. *Scholarship of Teaching and Learning in Psychology, 3,* 191–197.

Bernstein, D. A., Frantz, S., & Chew, S. (2020). *Teaching psychology: A step by step guide* (3rd ed.). New York, NY: Routledge.

Boyack, K. W., Klavans, R., & Borerner, K. (2005). Mapping the backbone of science. *Scientometrics, 64*(3), 351–374.

Brakke, K., & Houska, J. A. (Eds.). (2015). *Telling stories: The art and science of storytelling as an instructional strategy.* Society for the Teaching of Psychology. Retrieved from the Society for the Teaching of Psychology web site: http://teachpsych.org/ebooks/tellingstories.html

Cerbin, W. (2018). Improving student learning from lectures. *Scholarship of Teaching and Learning in Psychology, 4,* 151–163.

Deslauriers, L., Schelew, E., & Wieman, C. (2011). Improved learning in a large-enrollment physics class. *Science, 332,* 862–864.

Dimond, R. E., & Senter, R. J. (1985). An organizational framework for the teaching of basic psychology. In L. Benjamin, R. Daniel, & C. Brewer (Eds.), *Handbook for teaching introductory psychology.* Hillsdale, NJ: Lawrence Erlbaum Associates.

Dunn, D. S. (2018). On the primacy of introductory psychology. In D. S. Dunn & B. Martin Hard (Eds.), *Thematic approaches for teaching introductory psychology* (pp. 1–9). Boston, MA: Cengage Learning.

Dunn, D. S., Saville, B. K., Baker, S. C., & Marek, P. (2013). Evidence-based teaching: Tools and techniques that promote learning in the psychology classroom. *Australian Journal of Psychology, 65,* 5–13.

Fink, L. D. (2003). *Creating significant learning experiences: An integrated approach to designing college courses.* San Francisco, CA: Jossey-Bass.

Gleitman, H. (1981). *Psychology.* New York, NY: Norton.

Griggs, R. A. (2014). Topical coverage in introductory textbooks from the 1980s through the 2000s. *Teaching of Psychology, 41,* 5–10.

Griggs, R. A., Bujak-Johnson, A., & Proctor, D. L. (2004). Using common core vocabulary in text selection and teaching the introductory course. *Teaching of Psychology, 31,* 265–269.

Griggs, R. A., & Jackson, S. L. (2013). Introductory psychology textbooks: An objective analysis update. *Teaching of Psychology, 40,* 163–168.

Gurung, R. A. R., Hackathorn, J., Enns, C., Frantz, S., Cacioppo, J. T., Loop, T., & Freeman, J. (2016). Strengthening introductory psychology: A new model for teaching intro psych. *American Psychologist, 471*(2), 112–124.

Halonen, J. S., Thompson, J. L. W., Whitlock, J., Landrum R. E., & Frantz, S. (in press). Measuring meaningful learning in introductory psychology: The IPI student learning outcomes. In R. A. R. Gurung & G. Neufeld (Eds.), *Transforming introductory psychology: Expert advice on teaching, training, and assessing the course.* American Psychological Association.

Hard, B. M., Lovett, J. T., & Brady, S. T. (2019). What do students remember about introductory psychology, years later? *Scholarship of Teaching and Learning in Psychology, 5,* 61–74.

Hardin, E. E. (2016). Seeing the world like a psychologist. In D. S. Dunn & B. Martin Hard (Eds.), *Thematic approaches for teaching introductory psychology* (pp. 187–203). Boston, MA: Cengage Learning.

Homa, N., Hackathorn, J., Brown, C., Garczynski, A., Solomon, E., Tennial, R., . . . Gurung, R. A. R. (2013). An analysis of learning objectives and content coverage in introductory psychology syllabi. Teaching of Psychology, 40, 169–174.

Hothersall, D. (2004). *History of psychology.* New York, NY: McGraw-Hill.

Huston, T. (2009). *Teaching what you don't know.* Harvard University Press.

James, W. (1890). *The principles of psychology* (Vol. 1–2). New York, NY: Holt.

James, W. (1892). *Psychology, briefer course*. New York, NY: Holt.

James, W. (1899). *Talks to teachers: Psychology, and to students on some of life's ideals*. London, England: Longmans, Green.

Kulik, J. A., Brown, D. R., Vestewig, R. E., & Wright, J. (1973). *Undergraduate education in psychology*. Washington, DC: American Psychological Association.

Landrum, R. E. (2016). A skills theme for the introductory psychology course. In D. S. Dunn & B. M. Hard (Eds.), *Thematic approaches for teaching introductory psychology*. Boston, MA: Cengage Learning.

Landrum, R. E., Brakke, K., & McCarthy, M. A. (2019). The pedagogical power of storytelling. *Scholarship of Teaching and Learning in Psychology, 5*, 247–253.

Landrum, R. E., & Gurung, R. A. (2013). The memorability of introductory psychology revisited. *Teaching of Psychology, 40*, 222–227.

Lazarus, R. A. (1974). A riddle review: An author speaks. *Teaching of Psychology, 1*, 41–42.

Lenthall, G., & Andrews, D. (1985). Psychological seduction: Effective organization of the introductory course. In L. Benjamin, R. Daniel, & C. Brewer (Eds.), *Handbook for teaching introductory psychology*. Hillsdale, New Jersey: Lawrence Erlbaum Associates.

LoGiudice, A. B., & Kim, J. A. (2016). A focus on problem-based learning. In D. S. Dunn & B. Martin Hard (Eds.), *Thematic approaches for teaching introductory psychology* (pp. 46–65). Boston, MA: Cengage Learning.

McKeachie, W., & Svinicki, M. (2013). *McKeachie's teaching tips*. Cengage Learning.

Mueller, J. (2018). *What is authentic assessment?* Retrieved from http://jfmueller.faculty.noctrl.edu/toolbox/index.htm

Myers, D. G. (1986). *Psychology*. New York, NY: Worth.

National Center for Education Statistics. (2018). *Fast facts: Most popular majors*. Retrieved from https://nces.ed.gov/fastfacts/display.asp?id=37.

Nguyen, K., & McDaniel, M. A. (2015). Using quizzing to assist student learning in the classroom: The good, the bad, and the ugly. *Teaching of Psychology, 42*, 87–92.

Norcross, J. C., Hailstorks, R., Aiken, L. S., Pfund, R. A., Stamm, K. E., & Christidis, P. (2016). Undergraduate study in psychology: Curriculum and assessment. *American Psychologist, 71*, 89–101.

Nordmeyer, A., Hard, B. M., & Gross, J. J. (2016). Using integrative concepts as a theme in introductory psychology. In D. S. Dunn & B. M. Hard (Eds.), *Thematic approaches for teaching introductory psychology*. Boston, MA: Cengage Learning.

O'Banion, T. (2016). A brief history of general education. *Community College Journal of Research and Practice, 40*, 327–334.

Rodriguez, M., & Albano, A. (2017). *The college instructor's guide to writing test items: Measuring student learning*. New York, NY: Routledge.

Roediger, H. L., & Karpicke, J. D. (2006). Test-enhanced learning: Taking memory tests improves long-term retention. *Psychological Science, 17*, 249–255.

Rowling, J. K. (2003). *Harry potter and the order of the phoenix*. New York, NY: Listening Library.

Senn, D. J. (1985). Introductory psychology: Should it be taught as a general survey class? In L. Benjamin, R. Daniel, & C. Brewer (Eds.), *Handbook for teaching introductory psychology*. Hillsdale, New Jersey: Lawrence Erlbaum Associates.

Seraphin, S. B., Grizzell, J. A., Kerr-German, A., Perkins, M. A., Grzanka, P. R., & Hardin, E. E. (2018). A conceptual framework for non-disposable assignments: Inspiring implementation, innovation, and research. *Psychology Learning and Teaching, 18*, 84–97.

Stoloff, M., McCarthy, M., Keller, L., Varfolomeeva, V., Lynch, J., Makara, K., Simmons, S., & Smiley, W. (2010). The undergraduate psychology major: An examination of structure and sequence. *Teaching of Psychology, 37*, 4–15.

Titchener, E. B. (1915). *A beginner's psychology*. New York, NY: Macmillan.

Walker, E. L., & McKeachie, W. J. (1967). *Some thoughts about teaching the beginning course in psychology*. Belmont, CA: Brooks/Cole.

Watson, J. B. (1919). *Psychology from the standpoint of a behaviorist*. Philadelphia, PA: Lippincott.

Weiman, C. (2014). Large-scale comparison of science teaching methods sends clear message. *PNAS, 111*, 8319–8320.

Weiten, W., & Wight, R. D. (1992). Portraits of a discipline: An examination of introductory psychology textbooks in America. In C. L. Brewer, A. Puente, & J. R. Matthews (Eds.), *Teaching of psychology in America: A history* (pp. 453–504). Washington DC: American Psychological Association.

Wiggins, G., & McTighe, J. (2005). *Understanding by Design* (2nd ed.). Alexandria, VA: ASCD.

Xu, X., Kauer, S., & Tupy, S. (2016). Multiple-choice questions: Tips for optimizing assessment in-seat and online. *Scholarship of Teaching and Learning in Psychology, 2*, 147–158.

Zechmeister, J. S., & Zechmeister, E. B. (2000). Introductory textbooks and psychology's core concepts. *Teaching of Psychology, 27*, 6–11.

Learning and Teaching in Clinical Psychology

2

Susanne Knappe

Contents

Abstract

Clinical Psychology (abnormal psychology) addresses, though is not limited to, behavioral and mental health issues faced by individuals across the life span including intellectual, emotional, psychological, social and behavioral maladjustment, disability and discomfort, as well as severe psychopathology. Core elements to its practice are psychological assessment, clinical evaluation, and psychotherapy. The field bridges to other disciplines within Psychology as well as to the neurosciences, psychiatry and medicine, public health, as well to

S. Knappe (✉)
Institute of Clinical Psychology and Psychotherapy, Technische Universität Dresden, Dresden, Germany

Evangelische Hochschule Dresden (ehs), University of Applied Sciences for Social Work, Education and Nursing, Dresden, Germany
e-mail: susanne.knappe@tu-dresden.de

© Springer Nature Switzerland AG 2023
J. Zumbach et al. (eds.), *International Handbook of Psychology Learning and Teaching*,
Springer International Handbooks of Education,
https://doi.org/10.1007/978-3-030-28745-0_3

biology, pedagogic, and educational psychology. The science-practitioner model aims at integrating scientific research and clinical practice for curricula spanning from basics of describing human behavior across the life span to the science of behavior change. To these aims, students in Clinical Psychology are trained in basic research and clinical skills, including knowledge of psychological theory and practice, sensitive listening and questioning skills, abilities and strategies to cope with emotionally demanding situations, as well as research skills and scientific methods, along with academic, teamworking and communication skills. Following a student-centered approach in teaching, learning of course material is supplemented by initiating reflections of attitudes, enhancing thinking skills, and helping students to mature into more ethical or compassionate individuals. In order to direct student's learning activities, teachers use lectures, invite special guests and topics, present standardized patients and enroll students in role plays, support in-class activities using experiential learning, as well as between-class assignments in course-linked labs and hands-on-learning (internships). Teaching Clinical Psychology comes along with a particular responsibility for the teacher, namely to be capable of the desire to increase self-referential thinking versus to protect the student's welfares, and to balance between entertainment and education. Hence, the chapter closes with four premises of an experienced teacher and author of one of the most famous textbooks in the field that may serve as guiding principles for teaching in Clinical Psychology and likely beyond.

Keywords

Psychopathology · Psychological assessment · Experiential learning · Abnormal psychology

Introduction

Clinical Psychology is an integration of the science, theory, and clinical knowledge on human behavior and behavior change for the purpose of understanding, preventing, and relieving psychologically based distress or dysfunction and to promote subjective well-being and personal development (APA, 1996; Plante, 2005; Wittchen, Knappe, & Hoyer, 2021). Clinical Psychology addresses, though is not limited to, behavioral and mental health issues faced by individuals across the life span including intellectual, emotional, psychological, social, and behavioral maladjustment, disability and discomfort, minor adjustment issues, as well as severe psychopathology. In the USA, the term abnormal psychology is usually preferred over Clinical Psychology, which dominates in the European community. Core elements to its practice are psychological assessment, clinical evaluation, and psychotherapy, although clinical psychologists also engage in research, teaching, consultation, forensic testimony, and program development and administration (Brain, 2002). The field bridges to other disciplines within Psychology as well as to the neurosciences, psychiatry, and medicine, public health as well to biology, pedagogic, and educational psychology.

Because of its central relevance for therapeutic services, the American Psychological Association refers to Clinical Psychology as "(...) the psychological specialty that provides continuing and comprehensive mental and behavioral health care for individuals and families; consultation to agencies and communities; training, education and supervision; and research-based practice. It is a specialty in breadth — one that is broadly inclusive of severe psychopathology — and marked by comprehensiveness and integration of knowledge and skill from a broad array of disciplines within and outside of psychology proper" (URL from 07.03.2021, https://www.apa.org/ed/graduate/specialize/clinical). In many countries, Clinical Psychology is a regulated mental health profession and administration of psychotherapy requires a specific license.

The field of Clinical psychology was substantially influenced by the experimental work of Wilhelm Wundt in Leipzig, Germany, in the late 1890s. Wundt founded the first formal laboratory for psychological research and thereby helped to establish psychology as a separate science from other disciplines. He collaborated with prominent psychologists, psychiatrists, and philosophers of his time. For example, Wundt and Emil Kraeplin studied psychopathology, and developed and formalized a wide range of psychological methods. Clinical psychology in the sense of a mental health profession is generally considered to have begun in 1896 with the opening of the first psychological clinic at the University of Pennsylvania by Lightner Witmer. In the first half of the twentieth century, Clinical Psychology was focused on psychological assessment, with little attention given to treatment of mental health problems. This changed after the 1940s when World War II resulted in the need for a large increase in the number of trained clinicians. At least in the US-American countries and from there, also in many European countries, three main educational models have been developed: the Clinical Science model which is primarily focused on research, the practitioner-scholar model focusing on clinical theory and practice, and the science-practitioner model which aims at integrating scientific research and practice (Norcross & Karpiak, 2012).

Purposes and Rationale of the Curriculum in Clinical Psychology

Clinical Psychology spans towards a multitude of specialties such as clinical health, clinical child, forensic, clinical gerontopsychology, community, clinical neuropsychology, family psychology, and pharmacotherapy (for those with prescription privileges). Clinical Psychology encompasses all ages, multiple diversities, and varied systems. This variety is also reflected in the number of occupational areas: Clinical psychologists are most commonly employed in independent practice (41%) and higher education (26%), medical schools (8%), Veteran's Affairs settings (5%), and various hospitals and clinics, each averaging about 4% (Norcross & Karpiak, 2012). Other locations include schools, residential treatment centers, and corporations.

To meet the breadth and depth of this variety, curricula in Clinical Psychology teach advanced theoretical and scientific knowledge on (APA, https://www.apa.org/ed/graduate/specialize/clinical):

- Understanding of psychopathology and diagnostic/intervention considerations
- Mental health issues across the life span based on a solid understanding of psychopathology
- Assessment: ability to integrate and synthesize personality test data with additional standardized assessment measures
- Consultation: ability to consult with other health and behavioral health care professionals and organizations regarding severe psychopathology, suicide, and violence
- Research base: engagement with specific research and critical review of science, knowledge, and methods pertaining to those areas identified as distinct to Clinical Psychology

Hence, the curriculum covers basics of describing human behavior across the life span as well as the science of behavior change (Nielsen et al., 2018), at best substantiated by research knowledge and skills.

Core Teaching and Learning Objectives

Clinical psychologists work to reduce psychological distress in people with mental or physical health problems by providing services to individuals, families, and groups with mental health problems or mental disorders. Based on psychological theories, clinical psychologists assess, diagnose, and treat people with acute concerns and chronic conditions. Clinical psychologists interview patients and sometimes family members or friends, administer diagnostic tests, and provide therapy to individuals and their families. Typical responsibilities of the job include:

- Assessing clients' behavior and needs via observation, interviews, and psychometric tests
- Developing, administering, and monitoring appropriate treatment therapies and strategies
- Undertaking research
- Writing reports
- Providing support and advice to caregivers
- Meeting, advising, and liaising with other health care providers and professionals
- Helping clients to make positive changes to their lives

Three quarters of clinical psychologists conduct psychotherapy, accounting for an average of 35% of professional time; 58% routinely perform diagnosis or assessment; and approximately 50% are involved in teaching, clinical supervision, consultation, research, and administration on a weekly basis (Norcross & Karpiak, 2012).

Lessons for all Clinical Psychology Students

Norcross and Karpiak (2012) formulated four lessons that all psychology students, from those enrolled in the introductory course to those completing an advanced elective in Clinical Psychology, can master. These lessons map directly on research directions in the field: (1) understanding the strong connection between clinical work and psychological science that (ideally) characterizes modern Clinical Psychology, (2) commitment to evidence-based practice, (3) commitment to adapting treatment to the person and its environment, and (4) becoming all that a clinical psychologist can be (in contrast to providing only psychotherapy). To these aims, students in Clinical Psychology are trained in basic research and clinical skills, including knowledge of psychological theory and practice, sensitive listening and questioning skills, abilities and strategies to cope with emotionally demanding situations, as well as research skills and scientific methods, along with academic, teamworking, and communication skills (Table 1).

There is, however, no absolute distinction between learning objectives for undergraduate versus majors or graduate, albeit functional competencies are usually more often taught and trained in major psychology courses or graduate studies. Most undergraduates who choose to be psychology majors are interested in psychotherapy, and a majority of these students are not especially interested in investigative scientific thinking. Some psychology majors with practice interests become literate in psychological science, they rarely come to view psychology as a scientific field or psychological science as of prominent value to clinical pursuits (e.g., Holmes & Beins, 2009). Practice as clinical psychologist, i.e., provision and administration of psychotherapy, usually requires additional (graduate or postgraduate) education and training.

Graduate Education in Clinical Psychology

The master's degree in psychology with focus on Clinical Psychology and Psychotherapy usually follows a modular structured curriculum over four semesters. Students acquire all the necessary knowledge and skills in diagnostics, conversation, disorder models, intervention procedures, as well as clinical research methods and evaluation, and get insights into subareas of Clinical Psychology or related disciplines, e.g., occupational fields.

In Europe, much of the education and training in Clinical Psychology is at the bachelor and master's level, with the latter usually being a necessary prerequisite for graduate or postgraduate psychotherapeutic training and studies. There are, however, noteworthy differences across the curricula across universities and across countries.

In Australia, psychology is a regulated health profession under the Australian Health Practitioner Regulation Agency via the Psychology Board of Australia. Accordingly, a clinical psychologist undertakes 8 years of education and training in the assessment, formulation, diagnosis, and psychological treatment of mental health problems to become endorsed by the Psychology Board of Australia (PsyBA) which regulates the registration as a psychologist under the National Registration

Table 1 Foundational and functional research and clinical skills in Clinical Psychology (URL https://www.marquette.edu/psychology/documents/competencies-rubric.pdf)

Foundational competencies	
Reflective practice/self-assessment	Practices within the boundaries of competencies; demonstrates commitment to lifelong learning; engages with scholarship; capable of critical thinking; demonstrates a commitment to the development of the profession
Scientific method	Demonstrates a respect for scientifically derived knowledge; understands research and research methodology; understands biological bases of behavior, cognitive-affective bases of behavior, and life span human development
Relationships	Demonstrates capacity to relate effectively and meaningfully with individuals, groups, and/or communities
Individual/cultural diversity	Awareness and sensitivity in working professionally with diverse individuals, groups, and communities who represent various cultural and personal background and characteristics
Ethical/legal standards	Application of ethical concepts and awareness of legal issues regarding professional activities individuals, groups, and organizations. Advocating for the profession
Interdisciplinary systems	Professional and competent cooperation with colleagues and peers in related disciplines
Functional competencies	
Psychological evaluation	Assessment, diagnosis, and conceptualization of problems and issues of individuals, groups, and/or organizations
Psychological interventions	Interventions designed to alleviate suffering and to promote health and well-being
Consultation	The ability to provide expert guidance or professional assistance in response to a client's needs or goals
Research and evaluation	The generation of research that contributes to the scientific knowledge base and/or evaluates the effectiveness of various professional activities
Supervision	Supervision and training of professionals
(optional) teaching	Demonstrates rudimentary understanding of teaching theories and has gained some relevant experience in teaching

and Accreditation Scheme (2010). A 3-year accredited undergraduate psychology sequence is followed by a 1-year accredited psychology studies for completing an accredited honors degree or postgraduate diploma in psychology, and an additional 1-year internship pathway or postgraduate study. The current standard is to complete the MPsych, MPsych/PhD or DPsych for that area of practice, followed by a registrar program. Entry into the registrar program can only be achieved once the candidate has completed an MPsych degree, or for MPsych/PhD and DPsych students, once they have completed all coursework and placement requirements, and made sufficient progress on their thesis. Participation in a registrar program is required for registered psychologists who wish to qualify for an area of practice endorsement in one of the nine PsyBA-approved areas of practice (clinical neuropsychology, clinical psychology, community psychology, counselling psychology, educational and developmental psychology, forensic psychology, health psychology, organizational psychology, and sport and exercise psychology). Detailed information about these requirements are set out in the area of practice endorsement registration standard; supporting information is provided in the guidelines for area of practice endorsement (https://www.psychologyboard.gov.au/endorsement.aspx).

In the UK, standards for proficiency for clinical psychologists are set out by the Health and Care Professions Council, and the British Psychological Society accreditation criteria for training in Clinical Psychology. These theoretical frameworks are deemed suitable for Clinical Psychology training as they target studies to describe and understand the complexities of human development. By paying attention to biological, psychological, environmental, social, and cultural factors, curricula aim to chart the diverse pathways that may contribute to the development of psychological difficulties, or conversely optimal functioning. An example for a strong focus on clinical science comes from the Clinical Psychology program of Harvard. The main emphasis of the program is research, especially on severe psychopathology. The program and course work is committed to training clinical psychologists whose research advances scientific knowledge of psychopathology and its treatment, and who are capable of applying evidence-based methods of assessment and clinical intervention. Requirements for admission and the curriculum are available online (https://psychology.fas.harvard.edu/clinical-psychology).

In Canada, Clinical Psychology study programs usually require a minimum of 300 hours of practicum training for the MA degree, and a minimum of 700 additional hours for the PhD degree (1000 hours at the MA and PhD levels combined). An additional 1000 h of practicum prior to the year-long predoctoral internship is recommended. Students are required to engage in research across their enrollment in Clinical Psychology study programs (www.cpa.ca).

To allow for comparison and in recognition of studies in Clinical Psychology across different countries and educational systems, the European Federation of Psychologists' Association (EFPA) has set a European standard of education and professional training in psychology. EuroPsy is not a license in a particular country, but a European qualification that complements national standards. For example, standards for education (at least 5 years) and supervised practice (at least 1 year) and who have signed a statement of ethical conduct can obtain EuroPsy. Any psychologist who meets this standard can obtain a certificate and be included in the Register of European Psychologists. The model is called "EuroPsyT – A framework for education and training of psychologists in Europe" and was established by EFPA in 2001. Note that the holder of the specialist EuroPsy Certificate in Psychotherapy qualifies for the European Certificate in Psychotherapy (which is issued by the European Association for Psychotherapy).

Doctoral and Higher Education in Clinical Psychology

Training for doctoral psychology fellows is often organized in summer schools, doctoral programs, or graduate academies. Most of them follow curricula that aim to teach in-depth knowledge, training of and special competences in clinical research and practice (Table 2).

For example, the University of London's Doctorate in Clinical Psychology is the largest professional training course for clinical psychologists in the *UK*. The course

Table 2 Competencies in clinical research and practice, illustrated by individual competencies

Communication and interpersonal skills
• Communicates effectively
• Forms positive relationships with others
• Manages complex interpersonal situations
• Demonstrates self-awareness as a professional
Individual and cultural diversity
• Demonstrates awareness of diversity and its influence
• Develops effective relationships with culturally diverse individuals, families, and groups
• Applies knowledge of individual and cultural diversity in practice
• Pursues professional development about individual and cultural diversity
Professional values, attitudes, and behavior
• Displays professional behavior
• Engages in self-assessment and self-reflection
• Demonstrates accountability
• Demonstrates professional identity
• Engages in self-care essential for functioning effectively as a psychologist
Ethical and legal standards
• Demonstrates awareness of ethical and legal standards applicable to health service psychology practice, training, and research
• Recognizes and manages ethical and legal issues in health service psychology practice, training, and research
• Adheres to the APA ethical principles and code of conduct
Assessment
• Conducts clinical interviews
• Appropriately selects and applies evidence-based assessment methods
• Collects and integrates data
• Summarizes and reports data
Intervention
• Formulates case conceptualizations and treatment plans
• Implements evidence-based interventions
• Monitors the impact of interventions
Consultation and interprofessional/interdisciplinary, and systems-based practice
• Provides consultation (e.g., case-based, group, organizational systems)
• Engages in interprofessional/interdisciplinary collaboration
• Engages in systems-based practice
Supervision
• Seeks and uses supervision effectively
• Use supervisory feedback to improve performance
• Facilitates peer supervision/consultation
• Provides individual supervision (if applicable)
Research and scholarship
• Displays critical scientific thinking
• Uses the scientific literature
• Implements scientific methods

provides a first-rate training in clinical psychology, leading to a doctoral qualification accredited by the UK's Health and Care Professions Council (HCPC) and the British Psychological Society (BPS). The Course's overarching aim is to "train independently minded, scientifically-oriented and compassionate clinicians who are committed to anti-discriminatory practice and capable of taking a leadership role in health services at home or abroad" (https://www.ucl.ac.uk/clinical-psychology-doctorate/teachingprogramme/teach_docs/teach_curriculum, URL from April 14, 2021).

Similarly, doctoral trainings in *Canada* are accredited by the Canadian Psychological Association (www.cpa.ca). To become a psychologist in Canada, after obtaining a bachelor's degree in psychology, one must attend graduate school and obtaining a master's degree and/or doctoral degree. At the PhD level, one can obtain a PhD in clinical or experimental psychology, or a PsyD. In a PhD program, students normally take courses, pass comprehensive examinations, conduct original research, and write and defend their dissertation. For those wishing to provide psychological services to clients (i.e., PhD in clinical psychology), they have to spend at least one additional year interning and receiving supervision. Thus, a PhD program in clinical psychology requires research and practitioner expertise.

Given the history of the field, psychological assessment and intervention are pivotal to the field. Already in the early 1950s, the Boulder Conference (Raimy, 1950) identified personality appraisal (assessment) as one of the core areas in Clinical Psychology, including "all the methods available to the clinical or non-clinical psychologist for evaluating the individual and groups of individuals (. . .) in addition to testing methods, (. . .) interviewing, observation techniques and alike" (Raimy, 1950, p. 69). That is, knowledge on the theories and methods of diagnostic assessment and evaluation is required. More recently, the American Psychological Association accreditation recommended Clinical Psychology doctoral programs to train students in psychological assessment (APA, 1995, Guidelines and Principles for Accreditation of Programs in Professional Psychology, Domain B, Section 3 C, p. 6) in order to acquire substantial understanding of and competencies in the definition and diagnoses of mental health issues and mental disorders.

Similarly, clinical psychologists are expert in providing psychotherapy, so higher education programs focus on training in at least one of the four primary theoretical orientations – psychodynamic, humanistic, cognitive-behavioral therapy, and systems or family therapy (Lambert, 2013), sometimes also with special focus on children and adolescents versus adults versus older adults. Examples are mapped in training guidelines for various forms of specialty training within Clinical Psychology (e.g., training for clinical scientists, training for cognitive-behavioral therapists, training for behavioral health practitioners). Each of these guideline rests on the assumption that doctoral students will receive foundational training in core areas (e.g., psychopathology, evidence-based assessment, evidence-based treatment) and will receive clinical supervision in the development of core clinical skills (e.g., case formulation, differential diagnosis, treatment/intervention conceptualization, ethics, sociocultural competence). Training in these core competencies is usually organized in structured programs consisting of multiple experiences and across a 2–3-year period. The progress of fellows in developing these competencies is assessed by supervisors and advisors informally throughout the year and sometimes also formally through written assessments.

Core Contents and Topics of Clinical Psychology

Following the four lessons listed by Norcross and Karpiak (2002) and in line with Kramer, Bernstein, and Phares (2019), and Wittchen et al. (2021), core contents in Clinical Psychology include:

- Basic features, methods, and strategies of clinical assessment
- The variety of clinical interventions such as psychodynamic and humanistic psychotherapies, behavioral and cognitive-behavioral psychotherapies, system or family therapies, including their theoretical principles, empirical evidence as well as variations across settings, translation into prevention and intervention strategies
- Knowledge on the clinical phenomenology, diagnostic features, epidemiological characteristics of mental disorders according to current diagnostic classificatory systems and across the life span
- Knowledge on research designs, methods, statistical analyses, and procedures to plan, conduct, and evaluate research in the field

The sheer amount of theories makes it impossible to provide a full list of theories and associated research paradigms. Clinical Psychology has strong associations with other fields in psychology to map the development of adaptive and maladaptive behavior across the life span, such as with developmental psychology and attachment theory, as well key cognitive, interpersonal, and social processes that shape development throughout life. Since understanding of the development, onset, and course of mental disorders plays a pivotal role in the field, the vulnerability-stress model (or diathesis-stress-model) provides an atheoretical heuristic approach to explain the onset, manifestation, or trajectory of a disorder, as the result of an interaction between predisposing risk or vulnerability factors (the diathesis), and stress caused by life experiences. The heuristic was introduced by Zubin and Spring in 1977 for Schizophrenia (Zubin & Spring, 1977), but still is compelling today due to its simplicity and applicability across developmental ages, disorder categories, and cultures. The heuristic does not explain why or how vulnerability and stress work together, but it allows to collect evidence so far and to delineate research questions and hypotheses on the development of mental disorders.

Traditionally, knowledge of and skills in basic features, methods, and strategies of clinical assessment are considered as fundamental for clinical psychologists. Cross-reading of recent guidelines and current curricula suggest three general themes in assessment courses (Childs & Eyde, 2002), namely (1) knowledge about psychological assessment techniques including an understanding of psychometric concepts such as reliability, validity, objectiveness as well as of other issues such as professional ethics (who to test, why, critical evaluation), legal issues, and assessment of diverse populations; (2) training in psychological assessment techniques including supervised practice in selecting assessment methods, administering and scoring, interpreting, and communicating assessment results; (3) training in psychological assessment techniques in course-linked labs as well as hands-on-learning. Assessment courses predominantly teach intelligence and personality assessment, and often to a much lesser degree, behavioral assessment in adults. Also, some courses also cover clinical assessment in children and adolescents.

Given the relevance of assessment courses, Childs and Eyde (2002) listed for components for assessment training programs:

- Coursework in psychometrics, such as validity, reliability, as well as in general measurement principles based on test/item bias, classical test theory, and item response theory.
- Coursework in types of assessment, the assessment of specific populations (i.e., by age or culture), and the use of specific instruments, test development, and norming.
- Course-linked labs where assessment techniques and the use of specific instruments are taught through closely supervised assessment exercises, with students usually assessing volunteers (often friends, family, or fellow students with the stipulation that assessment results remain undisclosed to the volunteer).
- Internships in a clinic or hospital, in which actual clients are assessed by the student, usually under the supervision of a licensed psychologist (psychotherapist).

Preferably, assessment trainings are combined with trainings in communication and interpersonal skills, diagnoses, and intervention for optimal integration of theory, research, and clinical practice. Still though, comprehensive assessment curricula would encompass clinical interviewing and behavioral observation as well as formal psychological testing and coursework in basic psychometric concepts, professional ethics, legal issues, and assessment of diverse populations (Childs & Eyde, 2002).

The second core content field relates to clinical interventions, which is marked by at least four leading models guiding clinical psychology practice (https://www.ucl. ac.uk; Hoyer, Knappe, & Wittchen, 2021). *Behavior therapy* is delineated from theories, evidence-based knowledge and skills for developing behavioral conceptualizations to psychological distress found across the life span. In its first substantial amendment of Cognitive Behavior Therapy, individual cognitions (i.e., beliefs, expectations, attitudes, schemes) are considered in addition to observable antecedents and consequences of human behavior. Based thereupon, *Cognitive Behavior Therapy* is grounded on (diverse) cognitive models to understand individuals' distress and its etiology. In fact, current evidence suggests that mental disorders can be best understood and treated from a cognitive behavioral perspective (such as anxiety, obsessive compulsive disorder, and post-traumatic stress disorder). More recent amendments to Cognitive Behavioral Therapy include Acceptance Commitment Therapy, Mindfulness-Based Stress Reduction, or Schema Therapy (Hoyer & Knappe, 2021). The development of adaptive and maladaptive behavior (mental disorders) can also be conceptualized from the perspective of *Psychoanalytic Psychotherapy.* According to the origins of Freud's psychoanalytic theory of personality development, personality is formed through conflicts among three fundamental structures of the human mind: the id (unconscious source of primitive sexual, dependency, and aggressive impulses), the superego (subconsciously interjects societal mores, setting standards to live by), and the ego (representing a sense of self, mediating between realities of the moment and psychic needs and conflicts) (Freud, 2020). Since then, numerous psychoanalytic schools evolved been developed, applying the core concepts also to the conceptualization, assessment, and treatment of mental disorders (Frosh, 2012; Lemma, 2015). More recently, *Systemic Therapy* has been delineated form the theoretical developments and clinical applications of systems theory over the past 30 years, shifting the individual-centered focus to a variety of contexts for individual work, family work, and systemic consultation.

During the twentieth century, psychology moved into the realm of the paradigmatic science (Scotti, Jacoby, Cohen, & Hicks Patrick, 2010). Developing a strong proficiency in research design and statistical analysis has become a critical aspect of the psychologist identity in the USA and in many other countries around the world. Psychologists thus need at the very minimum to be familiar with various research designs and statistical techniques, and some psychologists should also be able to effectively teach these techniques and contribute to the development of new statistical designs and techniques (Field, 2017; Scotti et al., 2010). In addition to traditional statistical techniques, such as analysis of variance (ANOVA), more recent graduate and doctoral programs also cover advanced statistical skills such as structural equation modelling, multilevel modelling, hierarchical linear modelling, and other (Aiken, West, & Millsap, 2008). Furthermore, the Committee on Accreditation of the American Psychological Association (APA, 2013) requires all accredited doctoral programs in professional psychology to include courses in research methodology and techniques of data analysis in their curricula. Ord, Ripley, Hook, and Espamer (2016) surveyed 153 APA-accredited doctoral programs in clinical and counselling psychology, and conducted a review of 320 statistics course syllabi. Results indicated relative consistency among courses and programs in the concepts that were covered and the materials that were utilized. Moreover, all programs required at least one course in basic research design and statistics that addressed at least simple statistics analyses such as descriptive statistics, ANOVA, and multiple regression. SPSS was the most commonly used statistical software program, and most courses had statistics labs to teach students the practical use of computer programs. In the past 5 years, statistical software programs that were predominantly used for research activities in Clinical Psychology have been included in the curricula as well, such as STATA, MATLAB, R, and others.

Teaching, Learning, and Assessment in Clinical Psychology

Clinical Psychology is likely a discipline within the field of Psychology and Health Sciences where students are especially motivated to learn the content and skills. Pearlman and McCann (1999) referred to Clinical Psychology as the most popular of the specialized content classes in the undergraduate psychology major, maybe because students expect the course to clarify personal questions about mental health of family and friends and because students desire to learn how to manage the impact of mental disorders in their own lives (Connor-Greene, 2001). At the same time, students taking Clinical Psychology may also believe to have or have had the symptoms of the particular syndrome about which they are learning (i.e., "first-year-medical-student syndrome"). Thus, teachers are especially responsible to (re-) frame the sheer facts and need to be prepared that the action of teaching produces reaction in students beyond learning about theories and skills (i.e., self-reference, see below).

Broadly, teaching Clinical Psychology (and most likely other related disciplines as well) can be based on three pedagogical approaches (Halonen, 2005), namely (1) lecture centered, (2) diagnosis-centered, and (3) outcome-centered. The lecture-centered approach (1) uses clinical stories to help students extract critical concepts from the stories to convey basic course contents. For example, the lecturer illustrates the case of a patient or experiences from treatment. There is a range of prominent patient histories documented, such as the case of Bertha Pappenheim (Anna O) that illustrates the impact of previous traumas and subconscious ideas on the conscious mind, and gave rise to the use of "talking therapy," along with hypnosis and regression, to identify the possible causes of mental disorders (Freud, 2020). The teacher will then outline that Breuer's work with Berta Pappenheim significantly formed the psychoanalytic theories on hysteria and treatment methods. Lecturing can be highly efficient as loads of information is presented in quite a short time. However, students remain passive and thus, also learning is likely to be passive. When it comes to more recent (i.e., current cases), the lecturer runs risk of violating confidentiality and the patient's right of privacy. Thus, cases are strictly required to be anonymized, such as Breuer and Freud did with the story of Bertha Pappenheim who was usually named as Anna O.

Alternatively, the diagnoses-centered approach (2) focuses on diagnostic criteria, as depicted in current diagnostic classificatory systems of the APA (2013) or WHO (1992). Students are being taught to delineate an accurate diagnosis in response to a clinical story. This is an analytic process that requires active learning, rather than absorbing information from a lecture. Some students develop sincere enthusiasm for the diagnostic process (Halonen, 2005), while others find dealing with diagnostic criteria, thresholds, and taxonomy tedious.

As an intermediate approach that includes both lectures and the delineation of diagnoses is reflected by the outcome-centered approach (3), which teaches Clinical Psychology "as a liberal art in a science context rather than as a clinical entertainment or predoctoral training" (Halonen, 2005, p. 44). That is, an outcome-centered approach defines desired student achievement as competencies in clinical research and practice as illustrated above. Hence, learning of course material or facts is one preferred outcome, especially when it comes to the need for exams. However, important learning outcomes may also include changing the student's attitudes, enhancing thinking skills, and helping students to mature into more ethical or compassionate individuals (Halpern & Desrochers, 2005). Thus, teachers are well advised to use didactic elements that help to create a stimulating learning atmosphere, for example, lectures and seminars, special guests and topics, standardized patients and role plays, in-class activities using experiential learning, between-class assignments and supervision of clinical practice training by experienced therapists, etc.

Lectures. Allow for questions, even in large lectures. Students are then required to keep a minimum of attention, may feel welcomed and respected for their status: as Zimbardo pointed out "there are no right answers to discover but their perceptions and insights to uncover "(Zimbardo, 2005, p. 16).

Seminars are usually formed of smaller groups of students and thus allow discussions of theory and research driven published work, facilitated by an academic member of staff. Seminars focus on competencies rather than fact-based knowledge, aiming to develop and promote the students' ability to critically examine the evidence by paying close attention to the results of published research and examine the validity and reliability of conclusions drawn. Students are sometimes asked to read one or two key articles or chapters that reflect an important area for debate within academic clinical psychology, with a particular emphasis on the interface between theory and practice. These sessions provide a unique environment for students to lead discussions and engage in academic debate in a discursive manner, with the guidance of members of the academic team. Seminars also provide an opportunity to practice formal academic or clinical presentations and to develop their capacity to communicate complex clinical material in a clear and concise manner (https://www.ucl.ac.uk/clinical-psychology-doctorate/teachingprogramme/teach_docs/teach_curriculum).

Invite special guests, so students meet the expert. This tool is especially helpful in case the teacher is less familiar with a special topic or to allow for discourses. In Clinical Psychology, inviting patients to the class can be informative for students (i.e., to experience a given mental health problem from the perspective of the patient), for teachers (i.e., communication and interpersonal skills of the students), as well as the therapist of the patient (i.e., using the situation in class as behavioral observation or even more, given informed consent of the patient, as therapy experience). Also, learning about the realities of professional work in clinical research and practice can be promoted by direct experiences in service learning, featuring guest-speakers, asking students to chronicle their course of their career.

Standardized patients support practice-oriented teaching in clinical psychology and psychotherapy. They help students to test and experience the administration and outcome of prototypical interventions, and students may also experience themselves as counsellor or therapist.

Multiple in-class activities and *between-class assignments* help to engage students with the material. The latter is often based on homework such as reading and discussing literature, presenting research papers or writing essays about a given topic.

Experiential learning. One core didactic element in Clinical Psychology is experiential learning which refers to the process of learning through experience, and which can be more specifically defined as "learning through reflection on doing." Students conduct exercises in order to reflect the patient's role, therapist's behavior, and to observe and learn from others. Notably, students are free to choose not to participate in exercises. Hence, the social context of the classroom, the ambience of the setting, or the place of a particular course in the overall schedule can make a difference. An example is described in Box 1.

Box 1 "What's It Like to Reveal Personal Information About Yourself in Psychotherapy. Why Do Clients Show "Resistance?" (Suler, http://truecenterpublishing.com/tcp/resist.html, URL from 09.03.2021)

The students are instructed to write down on a small piece of paper something important and personal about themselves that they have never told anyone else – a secret wish, fantasy, feeling, belief, or something from their past. If they can't think of anything, they are suggested to write down something they have told maybe only one or two people who are close to them. The teacher then promises sincerely that no one will see what they have written. When the students are finished, they are asked to fold the paper up several times, very tightly. The teacher then walks around the room and asks some students, one at a time, if they will hand the paper. A few do so with little worry, or a few refuse, but most of the students will comply but with some hesitation. For those who do agree, the teacher takes the paper and does one of the following, usually in a humorous way:

- Ask them if you can open it (but refrain from doing so).
- Hold it to your head and pretend you can mind-read it.
- "Carelessly" toss it into the air
- Ask if you can give it to someone else (but don't do so).
- Stick it into your pocket and pretend to forget it's there (always give it back).
- Take one person's paper in your right hand, another in your left, wave your arms back and forth over each other, and pretend that you have confused whose secret is whose

This exercise illustrates putative reactions of patients to diagnostic assessments (i.e., in clinical interviews), to the therapist's approach into the very private feelings, thoughts, or behaviors of the client. For example, students discuss how they would have felt if the paper was read by someone: anxiety, anger, embarrassment, shame, helplessness – the same feelings that clients struggle with in psychotherapy, and that may account for their "resistance." How would the therapist react to your revealing such information?

Of note, instructions like these have direct, likely also, self-referential importance to students (cf. Snyder, 2005). So teachers (instructors) should be aware of the repercussions of their instructions on how students react and think about themselves.

Supervision is particularly relevant for graduate or postgraduate students when they start clinical work with "real" patients. That is, learning to apply treatment techniques in practice is often challenging, and in order to consolidate theory-practice links, and to enhance practical skills learned on placement, students are required to regularly attend individual or group supervision. Trainees bring clinical material that is discussed in their group, moderated and guided by an experienced clinical psychology supervisor. His/her task is to ensure that all trainees are competent in the treatment techniques by the end of their training and to ensure patient safety. The overarching aim is to support trainees in developing their understanding of treatment theory and their capacity to apply this in clinical practice.

Challenges and Lessons Learned

Curriculum design and implementation is a challenging task and requires addressing several alignment issues, including the alignment of the goals and affordances of (1) the academic discipline with those of the diverse professional fields in which the graduates of this discipline will work, (2) the curriculum with the goals and resources of the local settings, and (3) the curriculum with the goals and capabilities of the target students. Furthermore, the current state of art in an academic domain such as Clinical Psychology is constantly progressing, professional domains are changing depending on societal affordances and/or technical developments, and students' goals and capabilities are diverse and also changing (cf. Narciss, 2019).

In the past 25 years, Clinical Psychology curricula from colleges, universities up to doctoral training programs put emphasis on evidence-based practice in Clinical Psychology (Beck et al., 2016; Maki & Syman, 1997) which may be regarded as a turn from the long-lasting claim for empirical-supported treatment. It may also be regarded as a future trend, emerging from lessons learned in empirical-supported treatment. Here again, the interplay between clinical research and practice serves as an invaluable source of professional vitality and growing fascination (Norcross & Karpiak, 2012). Also, the emerging emphasis on internationalizing curricula in Clinical Psychology by including international dimensions of abnormal behavior enfolds a growth opportunity for teaching future scholars (Halonen, 2005).

Course concepts have also almost consistently included examples of application-oriented courses in Clinical Psychology, providing practical exercises in which students gain initial experiences with psychotherapeutic techniques on personally relevant problems. In case seminars, students apply their acquired skills to treat an actual outpatient case, while translating basic psychological knowledge into an individualized treatment plan. For example, the Master-seminar "Different approaches to psychotherapy in practice" (Philipps-Universität Marburg, Germany) offers the opportunity to explore six different patients coming from a variety of treatment setting (Wilhelm, Rief, Haberkamp, von Blanckenburg, & Glombiewski, 2020). Nonetheless, new modules for teaching practical skills are needed in order to meet the extensive requirements for a license to practice psychotherapy, for example, as in Germany. The innovative method of acting or simulation patients (standardized patients) seems to be particularly well suited to train and reflect on skills in clinical psychological communication. Experienced therapists' views indicate that very realistic interactions with patients can be simulated with reasonable effort. The students' evaluations reflect high satisfaction with the new teaching method. In addition, the pre-post comparison of the participating students shows an increased therapeutic self-efficacy – especially for the topics which were actually practiced (Alpers, & Steiger-White, 2020).

Clinical Psychology has gone through substantial development in the past decades with enormous increase in knowledge on research methods, designs, and strategies, increase in the provision of empirical supported treatments and health care utilization that have informed standards of proficiency in the field. Clinical Psychology has become a health profession, comparable to other, i.e., medical, professions. The challenge is to assert next to other health caregivers, to identify common grounds on the one hand, and to preserve and promote the expertise specific to Clinical Psychology on the other.

At least, also the Covid-19 pandemic has stimulated teaching and learning in almost every academic field and across occupational areas worldwide. Hence, blended learning and online-based learning have gained massive attention. For the field of Clinical Psychology, a number of challenges arise from social distancing between teachers and students, as well as patients and therapists. Until 2020, Clinical Psychology and in particular learning the clinical practice of administering interventions was predominantly based on face-to-face observational learning and training under supervision. Here, legal regulations (i.e., need for face-to-face contacts to qualify for psychotherapy in some countries), data protection and security, or ethical concerns (i.e., availability of the therapist or therapy strategies in acute crises) have challenged teaching concepts in Clinical Psychology.

Teaching, Learning, and Assessment Resources

Teaching Clinical Psychology (as most likely any other filed) can be considered as a privilege since teachers are trusted to teach their knowledge, skills, and expertise to others. So teaching goes beyond providing knowledge or specific information from one (expert) to another (any student); it can also be seen as a linchpin that decides on whether the student's motivation is appreciated and promoted. At the same time, teaching is a reciprocal process that emphasized the role of the student as an active agent in the learning process (Halpern & Desrochers, 2005). The idea of student-centered learning also requires the teacher to direct the student's learning activities.

That is, teachers present the facts, but at the same time, these facts likely have self-reference for the individual student. As a consequence, students may develop (promote, affirm) new and more sophisticated views about other people and about themselves (Snyder, 2005). This process adds responsibility to those who teach Clinical Psychology, especially when it comes to students presenting with mental health issues. Course contents likely deal with information about how students view themselves and also information about mental health of their own or their friends and families. So teachers need to be capable of the desire to increase self-referential thinking and keeping the balance with regard to protect the student's welfares (Snyder, 2005).

In line with teaching as a reciprocal process, commitment of both the teacher and the students is helpful. Think back over the course of your own education and recall those teachers who really made a difference for you (Snyder, 2005). What do you remember of these teachers, and do you have an idea what has made this learning experience so memorable? From a teacher, we would expect knowledge and expertise of past and ongoing developments in the field, but also commitment to teaching, creativity, humor, and understanding of the student's need. Teachers can contribute to the student's commitment to learning by acknowledging that (some) learning will require cognitive effort, sustained attention, and hard work. At the same time, teachers put a lot of work into tasks such as grading papers, meeting with students, planning demonstrations, and other engaging classroom activities (Halpern & Desrochers, 2005).

Recommendations for Teaching

Teaching is so much more than didactic information exchange; teaching can also serve as an agent of change, not only in Clinical Psychology. So how to stimulate this process? It may be that teachers who never stop being curious, who continually work on their teaching skills to keep it fresh for both the students and themselves, are better able to elicit interest and enthusiasm for the course content than others. However, keeping the balance between entertainment and education is needed to promote learning of facts, competencies, and skills, and to meet the motivation of both students and yourself as the teacher.

When it comes to didactic skills, ask for help from more senior teachers and take advantage of further training in teaching skills, for example, on blended learning and use of digital media to reach students even aside the campus. Though it might be tempting to present as much information as possible, to bridge to other contents or courses – also keep in mind, that the amount of data and details that can be processed, is limited (at least in the very moment of presenting information). So keep it simple and focus on three to four key points (take home messages). Plan, test, and update demonstrations, as a successful demonstration often has a major impact on student's commitment and interest in the field. Also make clear from the beginning what is needed to do in order to succeed (to pass the exam in this course).

Following Zimbardo's Premises on Teaching

Philipp G. Zimbardo, author of a prominent textbook providing a comprehensive introduction into the field of psychology that almost every student comes across in the first courses of psychology, described four premises for teaching. They are based on his extensive teaching experiences in undergraduates and involve making it (1) memorable, (2) right, (3) relevant, and (4) better next time: The more interesting the subject, the greater the memory strength. So teachers, who are able to describe psychological theories and promote students to relate to some personally relevant aspects, will likely promote deeper encoding and the more the content of the course will qualify as memorable. Also, read the primary resources and acknowledge your limits in expertise, rather than present half-truths. Rethink, use students' evaluations and feedback on your course to rework the introduction or how to chunk the big ideas, to integrate better examples, to improve the pacing or overall tempo.

These premises may serve as guiding principles for teaching, though not only in Clinical Psychology.

Further Reading Suggestions for Clinical Psychology Teachers

- (Clinical) psychological associations in your country often accredit curricula for undergraduate, graduate, and postgraduate education aiming to promote the professional development in the field. For example, the Australian Clinical Psychological Association (www.acpa.org) supports the requirements of the Psychology Board of Australia (PsyBA) for Continuing Professional Development (CPD); the British Psychological Society (BPS) set out what is considered necessary for safe and effective clinical practice in the UK, describe what professionals must know, understand and be able to do at the time they apply to join the HCPC Register (April 2021; https://www.bps.org.uk/news-and-policy/hcpc-standards-proficiency). These resources can inform teachers about county-specific requirements and proficiency in Clinical Psychology.
- *www.eaclipt.org* The European Association of Clinical Psychology and Psychological Treatment (EACLIPT) was founded in 2017 with the aims to foster research, education, and dissemination of scientifically evaluated findings on diagnostics and classification of mental disorders, psychological and psychobiological mechanisms of health and disease, psychological treatments, psychotherapy, prevention and rehabilitation, health care issues in mental disorders, and dissemination and implementation of evidence-based psychological treatments. The Journal Clinical Psychology in Europe is the official Journal of the EACLIPT and is available as open access resource. In addition, there is an annual congress of the EABCT reporting latest developments in clinical research and practice.
- *Prominent textbooks* in Clinical Psychology on the national and international level have been edited by Kramer et al. (2019) and Barlow (2014). They likewise provide excellent introductions to the field and it may simply depend on the lecturer's preference which one to choose. For Kramer et al., they provide a

scholarly portrait of the history, content, professional functions, and the future of Clinical Psychology. The textbook of Comer and Comer (2018) is widely adopted on Clinical Psychology courses and collects, explains, and illustrates theoretical approaches, starting from assessment procedures and diagnostic classification, mental disorders across the life span, their biological underpinnings up to treatment planning and evaluation. With respect to Clinical Psychology in non-Western countries, the casebooks by Lange and Davidson (2015) and Rich, Jafaar, and Barron (2020) provide comprehensive case formulations on the diagnosis, classification, and treatment of mental disorders in Asia, with special focus on the critical sociocultural, clinical, and health issues and perspectives in psychology in South East Asia.

- *Courses on research designs and statistical analyses* are usually required as mandatory, though some students find it difficult to engage in probability estimates, variance, sample size calculations, etc. A standard reference in the field was provided by Pedhazur and Pedhazur Schmelkin (2013); for a lively and enthusiastic application, check out the bestselling textbook "Discovering Statistics using IBM SPSS Statistics: and sex and drugs and rock n' roll" by Andy Field which is accompanied by social media activities and webpages such as https://www.discoveringstatistics.com

- The sheer number of textbooks on representatives of the four primary theoretical orientations as well as the more recent developments in the field of psychotherapy makes it almost impossible to pick a selection. Read as much as you can. When it comes to *understanding underlying therapeutic agents, active ingredients, and mechanisms of behavior change*, you may wish to follow the classic by Strupp (1993) and his research at Vanderbilt University. Initially focused on the empirical study of therapeutic techniques by the beginning of the 1950s, the work soon drew attention to therapists' attitudes toward the patient and the manner in which these attitudes were intertwined with therapists' clinical judgments and their communications to the patient.

- John Suler provides a plenty of *ideas and resources for teaching courses* in Clinical Psychology, especially at the undergraduate level, with strong preference for *experiential and hands-on learning.* Many of his ideas are presented on the webpage http://truecenterpublishing.com/tcp/tcp.html, but for more detailed information, refer to his books, manuals, and essays. Of note, Suler just recently published the Instructor Manual for Cyberpsychology (Suler, 2016) on how people think, feel, and behave in online environments. The manual includes a sample syllabus, student exercises, and online resources, and may be inspiring for teachers with online-teaching requirements.

- The Society for the Teaching of Psychology (STP, www.teachpsych.org) provides peer-reviewed teaching and advising materials for Clinical Psychology and other fields in psychology, for use to all teachers of psychology from school teachers, to undergraduate and graduate teaching. The resources are available as open access documents and can pertain to any aspect of teaching, spanning from abnormal/clinical/counselling psychology to statistics and research methods.

- The European Society of Psychology Learning and Teaching (www.esplat.org) aims to advance the learning and teaching of scientific psychology at all educational levels on the basis of scientific evidence. The associated journal *Psychology Learning and Teaching (PLAT)* publishes research articles, reviews, target articles and corresponding comments, as well as reports on good and innovative learning, teaching, and assessment practices in Clinical Psychology and other fields of psychology.
- Similarly, though not limited to Clinical Psychology, *online platforms* provide open access learning resources for students and teachers, for example, www.coursera.org and www.psychologylecturer.com, with the latter particularly focusing on digital learning scenarios using video tutorials and demonstrations, podcasts, chat bots, etc.
- Zimbardo's plea for *"Optimizing the power and magic of teaching,"* i.e., reflecting his four premises on teaching, is summarized in a peer-review article, and though published in 2005, his arguments are timeless.

References

Aiken, L. S., West, S. G., & Millsap, R. E. (2008). Doctoral training in statistics, measurement, and methodology in psychology: Replication and extension of Aiken, West, Sechrest, and Reno's (1990) survey of PhD programs in North America. *American Psychologist, 63*, 32–50.

Alpers, G. W., & Steiger-White, F. (2020). Standardized patients in university-level psychology programs: Introduction of an innovative method to strengthen practice-oriented teaching in clinical psychology and psychotherapy. *Verhaltenstherapie, 30*(2), 104–116.

American Psychiatric Association (APA). (2013). *Diagnostic and statistical manual of mental disorders, fifth edition (DSM-5)*. Arlington: American Psychiatric Association.

American Psychological Association. (1995). *Guidelines and principles for accreditation of programs in professional psychology*. Washington, DC: Author.

American Psychological Association. (1996). *About clinical psychology. American Psychological Association, Division 12 Society of Clinical Psychology*, URL /http:/www.apa.org/divisions/div12/aboutcp.html

American Psychological Association. (2013). *Guidelines and principles for accreditation of programs in professional psychology*. Washington, DC: American Psychological Association.

Barlow, D. (2014). Oxford handbook of clinical psychology. OUP USA; Updated edition,

Beck, G., Castonguay, L. G., Chronis-Tuscano, A., Klonsky, E. D., McGinn, L. K. & Youngstrom, E. A. (2016). *Evidence based psychology: Models for the graduate curricula in clinical psychology*. Prepared by the Division 12 Task Force on teaching evidence based practice in Clinical Psychology. URL https://div12.org/teaching-evidence-based-practice-in-clinical-psychology-new-material/

Brain, C. (2002). *Advanced psychology: Applications, issues and perspectives*. Cheltenham: Nelson Thornes.

Childs, R. A., & Eyde, L. D. (2002). Assessment training in clinical psychology doctoral programs: What should we teach? What do we teach? *Journal of Personality Assessment, 78*(1), 130–144.

Comer, R. J., & Comer, J. S. (2018). *Abnormal psychology* (10th ed.). Worth.

Connor-Greene, P. A. (2001). Family, friends, and self: The real-life context of an abnormal psychology class. *Teaching of Psychology, 28*, 210–232.

Field, A. (2017). *Discovering statistics using SPSS* (5th ed.). Sage Publications.

Freud, S. (2020). *Studien ueber Hysterie: Fruehe Arbeiten zur Neurosenlehre (1892–1899)*. Inktank Publishing.

Frosh, S. (2012). *A brief introduction to psychoanalytic theory*. Red Globe Press.

Halonen, J. S. (2005). Abnormal psycholoy as liberating art and science. *Journal of Social and Clinical Psychology, 24*(1), 41–50.

Halpern, D. F., & Desrochers, S. (2005). Social psychology in the classroom. Applying what we teach as we teach it. *Journal of Social and Clinical Psychology, 24*(1), 51–61.

Holmes, J. D., & Beins, B. C. (2009). Psychology is a science: At least some students think so. *Teaching of Psychology, 36*, 5–11. https://doi.org/10.1080/00986280802529350.

Hoyer, J., & Knappe, S. (2021). Verhaltenstherapie [behavior therapy]. In J. Hoyer & S. Knappe (Eds.), *Klinische Psychologie und Psychotherapie* (3rd ed.). Heidelberg: Springer.

Hoyer, J., Knappe, S., & Wittchen, H.-U. (2021). Klinisch-Psychologische und Psychothera-peutische Verfahren: Ein Überblick. [clinical-psychological and psychtherapeutic schools: An overview]. In J. Hoyer & S. Knappe (Eds.), *Klinische Psychologie und Psychotherapie* (3rd ed.). Heidelberg: Springer.

Kramer, G. P., Bernstein, D. A., & Phares, V. (Eds.). (2019). *Introduction to clinical psychology* (8th ed.). Cambridge University Press.

Lambert, M. J. (Eds.). (2013). Bergin & Garfield (2013). *Bergin and Garfield's handbook of psychotherapy and behavior change* (6th ed.). Wiley.

Lange, G., & Davidson, J. (Eds.). (2015). *Clinical psychology in Singapore: An Asian casebook*. NUS Press.

Lemma, A. (2015). *Introduction to the practice of psychoanalytic psychotherapy* (2nd ed.) Wiley-Blackwell.

Maki, R. H., & Syman, E. M. (1997). Teaching of controversial and empirically validated treat-ments in APA-accredited clinical and counseling psychology programs. *Psychotherapy, 34*(1), 44–57.

Narciss, S. (2019). Curriculum design for (non-)psychology programs – A reflection on general and specific issues, and approaches on how to address them: Comment on Dutke et al., 2019. *Psychology Learning and Teaching, 18*(2), 144–147.

Nielsen, L., Riddle, M., King, J. W., & NIH Science of Behavior Change Implementation Team. (2018). The NIH science of behavior change program: Transforming the science through a focus on mechanisms of change. *Behavior Research and Therapy, 101*, 3–11.

Norcross, J. C., & Karpiak, C. P. (2012). Teaching clinical psychology: Four seminal lessons that all can master. *Teaching of Psychology, 39*(4), 301–307.

Ord, A. S., Ripley, J. S., Hook, J., & Espamer, T. (2016). Teaching statistics in apa-accredited doctoral programs in clinical and counseling psychology: A syllabi review. *Teaching of Psy-chology, 43*(2), 221–226.

Pearlman, B., & McCann, L. I. (1999). The most frequently listed courses in the undergraduate psychology curriculum. *Teaching of Psychology, 26*, 177–182.

Pedhazur, E. J., & Pedhazur Schmelkin, L. (2013). *Measurement, design, and analysis: An integrated approach*. Psychology Press.

Plante, T. (2005). *Contemporary clinical psychology*. New York: Wiley.

Raimy, V. C. (Ed.). (1950). *Training in clinical psychology*. Prentice Hall: Englewood Cliffs.

Rich, G. J., Jafaar, J. L., & Barron, D. (Eds.). (2020). *Psychology in Southeast Asia. Sociocultural, clinical, and health perspectives*. New York: Routledge.

Scotti, J. R., Jacoby, V. M., Cohen, S., & Hicks Patrick, J. (2010). Design and analysis. In J. C. Thomas & M. Hersen (Eds.), *Handbook of clinical psychology competencies* (pp. 367–396). New York: Springer.

Snyder, C. R. (2005). Dispelling the fable of those who can, do, and those who can't, teach. *Journal of Social and Clinical Psychology, 24*(1), 1–2.

Strupp, H. H. (1993). The Vanderbilt psychotherapy studies: Synopsis. *Journal of Consulting and Clinical Psychology, 61*(3), 431–433.

Suler, J. (2016). *Psychology of the digital age: Humans become electric*. New York: Cambridge University Press.

Wilhelm, M., Rief, W., Haberkamp, A., von Blanckenburg, P., & Glombiewski, J. A. (2020). Master's graduates as state-licensed psychotherapists – Both a challenge and an opportunity: Practical university teaching concepts in clinical psychology and psychotherapy. *Verhaltenstherapie, 30*(2), 117–227.

Wittchen, H.-U., Knappe, S., & Hoyer, J. (2021). Was Ist Klinische Psychologie? Definitionen, Konzepte und Modelle [What is clinical psychology? Definitions, concepts and models]. In J. Hoyer & S. Knappe (Eds.), *Klinische Psychologie und Psychotherapie* [Clinical psychology and psychotherapy] (3. Vollst. überarb. Aufl). Heidelberg: Springer.

World Health Organization (WHO). (1992). *The ICD-10 classification of mental and behavioural disorders: Clinical descriptions and diagnostic guidelines.* Geneva: World Health Organization.

Zimbardo, P. G. (2005). Optimizing the power and magic of teaching. *Journal of Social and Clinical Psychology, 24*(1), 11–21.

Zubin, J., & Spring, B. (1977). Vulnerability: A new view of schizrenia. *Journal of Abnormal Psychology, 86*(2), 103–126.

Mapping Normality: Teaching Abnormal Psychology

3

Brian L. Burke and Megan C. Wrona

Contents

Abstract

This chapter provides a framework for developing an undergraduate course in abnormal psychology. Authors make recommendations about how to structure the course and outline necessary competencies, including the M.A.P.S. framework for understanding the limits of diagnostic classification systems. By identifying challenges associated with defining abnormality, problems with a strict medical model for understanding mental illness, not understanding the etiology of symptoms, pigeonholing individuals, and only paying attention to superficial

B. L. Burke (✉)
Psychology, Fort Lewis College, Durango, CO, USA
e-mail: burke_b@fortlewis.edu

M. C. Wrona
Fort Lewis College, Durango, CO, USA
e-mail: mcwrona@fortlewis.edu

© Springer Nature Switzerland AG 2023
J. Zumbach et al. (eds.), *International Handbook of Psychology Learning and Teaching*,
Springer International Handbooks of Education,
https://doi.org/10.1007/978-3-030-28745-0_4

49

symptoms, the authors suggest ways to ensure that students view the classification of mental disorders through a critical lens and take a wider view of diagnosis. Concrete tools and sample activities are included to help instructors expand their teaching repertoire for abnormal psychology.

Keywords

DSM · ICD · Diagnosis · Abnormal · Mental illness · Symptoms · Active learning · Disorders · Etiology · Medicine · Learning objectives · Case studies

Introduction

Teaching a course in abnormal psychology is a rare opportunity and a delightful adventure. Of all the courses in psychology and beyond, students are typically most interested in learning about abnormal psychology. In fact, we have removed the prerequisite courses from our abnormal psychology class where we teach so that students from a wide variety of majors can access what we consider the core "export" of psychology – understanding psychological disorders and how to work with people who suffer from them. Accordingly, the content in an abnormal psychology course is often recommended for students in a range of healthcare professions, including physical therapy and medicine, due to its importance for dealing with people. Furthermore, an abnormal psychology class presents unique opportunities to reduce bias surrounding mental illness. Whereas contact with people diagnosed with disorders is the best stigma-reduction technique, education is also promising and can be accomplished as part of course content coverage (Strassle 2018). Finally, one of the privileges of teaching abnormal psychology is also its greatest risk or burden, which is that the content often prompts students in the class to share about their own or family members' battles with the very mental disorders you are discussing. If handled skillfully, this can be an opportunity for students to access resources on campus or in the community that could help them or their family members in their recovery.

Foundations of an Abnormal Psychology Course

In terms of content, the central material of a typical abnormal psychology course is centered around a list of diagnosable mental disorders. For those who use a textbook (e.g., Burke et al. 2016), it is almost always built around the *Diagnostic and Statistical Manual of Mental Disorders*, currently DSM-5 (APA 2013), or its counterpart, the *International Statistical Classification of Diseases and Related Health Problems* (ICD-11, World Health Organization 2019). Often, the stage is set with a couple of introductory lectures to provide historical context, research methods, and biopsychosocial models used to understand mental disorders. Then, the DSM or

ICD classification system is explained. The remainder of the course constitutes an investigation of each of 15–20 major categories of mental disorders ranging from depression and anxiety to schizophrenia, autism, and Alzheimer's disease. For each disorder, content chiefly coalesces around three aspects: (a) diagnosis, the symptoms that comprise the diagnostic criteria of DSM/ICD and the way these disorders are identified; (b) cause, what research has shown us thus far about biological, psychological, and social factors that create or maintain the disorder; and (c) treatment, which biological (medication) and psychosocial (therapy) approaches have been effective in reducing symptoms of the disorder and promoting recovery.

Despite its ubiquity, the DSM and ICD classification systems have been criticized for lack of cultural sensitivity and for taking a disease-oriented categorical (e.g., depressed vs. non-depressed) rather than continuous (i.e., how depressed is the person) approach to describing psychological disorders. Nevertheless, virtually every textbook of abnormal psychology is organized around the DSM/ICD, and all hospitals or mental health settings to our knowledge are oriented toward its usage (DSM throughout North America and DSM or ICD internationally depending on the setting). Thus, as we will elucidate further below, we recommend highlighting the limitations of the DSM/ICD system (Frances 2013) along with its benefits at the very onset of your course. As Joel Paris (2013) puts it, the goal is for students to learn the classification system but not to blindly believe it.

The Diagnostic and Statistical Manual of Mental Disorders, one of two books (along with the ICD) used worldwide for the classification of mental disorders. (Public domain image by F.RdeC. Available at https://commons.wikimedia.org/wiki/File:DSM-5_%26_DSM-IV-TR.jpg)

Setting the Scene

Even though students often want to jump right into a discussion of the specifics of mental disorders (the "sexy" parts of the course), we believe it is essential – and well worth the investment – to spend some time setting the stage before you drill down deeper. We recommend taking time to focus on three broad strands of topical material in the first few days of class: defining abnormality, understanding the language of the DSM/ICD, and introducing the theoretical models of etiology/cause.

Defining abnormality. First, it is valuable to discuss the definition of abnormal psychology. Many students (and instructors!) may be uncomfortable with the title of "abnormal psychology" as this title itself implies the true existence of normal and abnormal behavior. Societally, abnormal tends to conjure negative feelings and associations and reduces the nuance of behavior into categorical terms. Our understanding of abnormal behavior has changed over the years, as evidenced by the revisions to the DSM and ICD over time. One prominent example is the history of homosexuality as a diagnosis in early versions of the DSM. The diagnosis of homosexuality was removed in 1973, largely due to research indicating that homosexuality was not pathological as well as mounting cultural and societal pressure for the APA to reconsider its stance on homosexuality (Drescher 2015). Meanwhile, the World Health Organization (WHO) only removed homosexuality from its ICD classification with the publication of ICD-10 in 1992 (Burton 2015).

The question of what constitutes a mental disorder and the corollary issue of what is and is not "abnormal" are foundational elements of courses in abnormal psychology and provide rich opportunities for critical thinking. The vast majority of abnormal psychology textbooks address the definition of abnormality as defined through a psychological disorder within their first pages (see, e.g., Comer 2011; Burke et al. 2016). This definition often sparks rich classroom discussion regarding the difficulty of identifying and naming psychological dysfunction, including the usage of the term disorder itself (Rounsaville et al. 2002). What is abnormal for one person may not be for another, and these symptoms in the DSM/ICD are generally defined from one cultural context. Psychiatrist Thomas Szasz (1996) argued that our culture has pathologized behavior to the extreme and that "abnormal" behavior is not necessarily the problem of an individual but rather society's response to the individual. For example, Szasz believed that attention-deficit hyperactivity disorder is not a diagnosis per se but rather the result of age-inappropriate standards placed on children (e.g., sitting in a kindergarten classroom with worksheets and minimal play time).

In efforts to more clearly acknowledge that "abnormal" occurs across a spectrum, the DSM-5 introduced an updated definition of a mental disorder that builds on the modern notion of a harmful/distressing dysfunction. The new definition retains the ideas of distress/disability, cultural context, and individual dysfunction found in DSM-IV (APA 1994), but adds the concepts of emotion regulation and developmental processes:

A mental disorder is a syndrome characterized by clinically significant disturbance in an individual's cognition, emotion regulation, or behavior that reflects a dysfunction in the psychological, biological, or developmental processes underlying mental functioning. Mental disorders are usually associated with significant distress or disability in social, occupational, or other important activities. An expectable or culturally approved response to a common stressor or loss, such as the death of a loved one, is not a mental disorder. Socially deviant behavior (e.g., political, religious, or sexual) and conflicts that are primarily between the individual and society are not mental disorders unless the deviance or conflict results from a dysfunction in the individual, as described above. (APA 2013, p. 20)

Note that ICD-11 has a very similar definition:

Mental, behavioural and neurodevelopmental disorders are syndromes characterized by clinically significant disturbance in an individual's cognition, emotional regulation, or behaviour that reflects a dysfunction in the psychological, biological, or developmental processes that underlie mental and behavioural functioning. These disturbances are usually associated with distress or impairment in personal, family, social, educational, occupational, or other important areas of functioning. (https://icd.who.int/browse11/lm/en#/http%3a%2f%2fid.who.int%2ficd%2fentity%2f334423054)

By including "emotion regulation" in its revised definition, DSM-5 and ICD-11 affirm that mental health does not arise so much from reducing certain emotions but rather from adaptively managing the range of human "positive" and "negative" emotions. This reflects researchers' rapidly growing understanding of the deep primary roles played by human affective systems (Davidson et al. 2000; Sander 2013). Further, the inclusion of "developmental processes" as a potential area of dysfunction emphasizes the move toward a lifespan developmental approach to classification (Klott 2012).

Understanding the language of the DSM/ICD and disorders. The second major goal before delving into the specifics of diagnoses is to establish a baseline understanding of the language of the DSM/ICD and how we talk about disorders. The language of these classification manuals is sometimes complex and obtuse, so translating it into simpler language helps to make the information more palatable. For instance, one textbook (Burke et al. 2016) has a feature called *DSM-5 in Simple Language*, which describes the diagnostic criteria for depression as follows.

The person shows at least five of the following nine symptoms most days for two or more weeks:

1. Sad mood
2. Lack of interest or pleasure in activities

   Physical changes, like:

3. Low energy
4. Sleeping more or less than usual
5. Eating more or less than usual
6. Moving faster or slower than usual

Changes in thinking, like:

7. Thinking negative thoughts about himself or herself
8. Trouble making decisions
9. Thoughts of suicide

In this way, complicated terms like hypermotor agitation or retardation (used in both the DSM-5 and the ICD-11) are decoded so that the student can comprehend more clearly what each symptom means and how to spot it. Additionally, it is helpful to introduce terms that students may be unfamiliar with, such as "comorbidity" and "differential diagnosis."

Finally, in an effort to destigmatize mental disorders and increase compassion and empathy for those who experience them, expectations should be set at the beginning of the semester about appropriate language to use. For example, helping students understand that casually using psychological terms (e.g., "I can't stop cleaning my dorm room; I am so OCD") can minimize the very real distress of people who suffer from such disorders. Similarly, talking with students about the negative implications of labeling a person solely as disorder (e.g., "She's a Borderline") and providing them tools for alternative language (e.g., "she is a person with borderline personality disorder") serves to humanize people with mental illness. Opening this discussion to the class can help them set ground rules for students' comfort and set the expectation of mutual respect.

Introduction of theoretical models for etiology. The third and final introductory topic that we recommend for a successful course in abnormal psychology is to define and unpack current models and explanatory lenses by which to optimally understand psychological disorders. For us, we begin with the biopsychosocial perspective because this model considers contributing factors in the development of mental health disorders in terms of three vital categories (biological, psychological, and social). Students may enter the class with a bias toward one of these categories of causes, but the presentation of how these three contributors interact helps deepen student understanding of disorders and the need for varied intervention options. Biological components of mental disorders encompass the medical/disease model, genetics, and other physiological contributions to the disorder (e.g., brain injury) and often utilize psychotropic medication as a primary arm of treatment. Psychological aspects that contribute to the development of a disorder include motivations, cognitions, and a person's (potentially misguided) behavioral attempts to solve their problems, with important cross-links to stand-alone courses in personality psychology. Treatments center around psychotherapy, ranging from psychodynamic approaches to cognitive-behavioral therapy. Social factors acknowledge the important layers of media, culture, and family history and add group treatments and social advocacy as treatment interventions. One effective way to teach the biopsychosocial model is to take any recent human-caused event from the news or a character from a movie (e.g., Eeyore from Winnie the Pooh) and ask the class to generate possible causal explanations for the event or for the character's personality. The instructor can jot down those answers in three distinct categories of causes:

biological, psychological, and social/cultural. The point can then be emphasized that anything involving humans (or even Eeyores) – including a person's mental disorder – can be optimally explained by considering and exploring the interactions among these three categories.

Original Winnie-the-Pooh stuffed toys. Clockwise from bottom left: Tigger, Kanga, Edward Bear (a.k.a Winnie-the-Pooh), Eeyore, and Piglet. (Public domain image by Spictacular. Available at https://commons.wikimedia.org/wiki/File:The_original_Winnie_the_Pooh_toys.jpg)

General Competencies

By the end of any undergraduate course in abnormal psychology, the authors believe that several key competencies should be achieved by the students. This class affords an opportunity for students to learn basic information about mental illness that can be applied in their future lives. For example, it is not expected (or appropriate) for a student to leave this course with the ability to clinically diagnose depression. However, if students can recognize common signs of depression, they may be able to help a friend or family member seek professional help. Similarly, a student who enters a medical or healthcare-related profession will hopefully be able to recognize sudden changes in behavior in a patient that might suggest the need for an outside referral.

To that end, one of the core competencies for this course is to help students to understand the prevalence of mental illness and its basic signs and symptoms.

Students are often surprised when presented with prevalence data. By highlighting this and inviting students to talk openly about mental illness in the course, students will ideally leave with a reduced tendency to see a stigma related to mental health problems and an enhanced ability to challenge stereotypes they may encounter. For example, one of our students who was a business major identified that the most impactful part of the course for him was learning about suicidality and the associated pain a person is feeling. He described that he used to view suicide as a selfish act (a common misperception!) but he now understood the inaccuracy of that belief. He further explained that his approach to talking about suicide with others would be very different in the future.

Another core competency of an abnormal psychology class is to help students understand the development of mental health problems. As described previously, these problems exist in a social and cultural context, and this should not be neglected. By helping students understand the biopsychosocial model and Urie Bronfenbrenner's ecological perspective (1979), students are able to better grasp the interconnected factors that contribute to mental illness. For example, if an American Indian or other indigenous college student is seeking treatment for depression, Bronfenbrenner's ecological perspective reminds clinicians that the student's roommate (microsystem), family (mesosystem), recent loss of a parent's job (exosystem), and cultural upbringing (macrosystem) all interact with the student's presentation and treatment. Additionally, the final layer of Bronfenbrenner's model, the chronosystem, acknowledges the historical trauma of indigenous peoples in the United States and elsewhere (see Hartmann et al. 2019) and how this may also impact the individual's symptoms.

Competencies Related to the Limitations of the DSM/ICD: M.A.P.S. of the Territory

In addition to the overarching competencies described above, abnormal psychology courses should explore the limitations of diagnosis and the DSM/ICD manuals. Whereas we do not want to discredit these classification systems completely or minimize their real benefits, it is important for students to understand their limitations and the ever-evolving nature of these manuals. We believe that students should be able to grasp four foundational principles that highlight shortcomings of the DSM/ICD system. These principles are illustrated by the acronym M.A.P.S. – medical myths, attempted answers, prejudicial pigeonholing, and superficial syndromes.

M = *Medical myths*. Despite the urgings of powerful drug companies and the potential increases in diagnosis of mental disorders in DSM-5 (Frances 2012) and ICD-11 (Reed et al. 2019), the medical model alone cannot explain mental illness, and pills are not always (or even often) the optimal first-line treatment for most psychological disorders (Hofmann et al. 2012), with the exception of bipolar disorders (Smith et al. 2007) and schizophrenia (Miyamoto et al. 2012). Furthermore, the biological/medical model is only one lens through which we view disorders, and the biological/genetic underpinnings have not yet been firmly established for any of the mental disorders in DSM/ICD (Paris 2013). It is tempting to take the simplest route possible to explaining mental disorders, for instance, to view depression as resulting merely from low serotonin levels in the brain. But understanding mental disorders as diseases stemming from a single cause is over-simplified and sometimes just plain wrong (this is where an understanding of the biopsychosocial model and the ecological perspective are so critical!).

Relatedly, it has been widely acknowledged that the categorical nature of the DSM/ICD, which is grounded in a medical model of symptomology, is problematic (Kotov et al. 2017). Whereas criteria often must be written with a requisite number of symptoms (e.g., five of nine symptoms of depression, two symptoms of substance use disorders), these numbers are often arbitrarily assigned and may not reflect distress of an individual. For example, if clients only exhibit four symptoms of depression, they may not be diagnosed with depression even though they may be just as impacted as those who exhibit six symptoms of depression. Many experts suggest the need for a more dimensional approach to the DSM/ICD in order to describe the range of symptoms more accurately (Kotov et al. 2017). In accordance with this view, more dimensional approaches have been incorporated into the ICD-11 classification, particularly for personality disorders and primary psychotic disorders (Reed et al. 2019). Students in an abnormal psychology course would benefit from understanding this ongoing categorical/dimensional debate with regard to diagnostic classification systems.

A = *Attempted answers*. We view mental disorders not as diseases but as a collection of potentially interrelated symptoms – subjective observations (by people themselves or those around them) indicating that something might be wrong. However, these symptoms often arise as the person's attempted solution to a problem. For instance, delusions may create meaning for people who are depressed; compulsive behaviors (e.g., handwashing) may temporarily reduce the anxiety caused by obsessional thoughts (e.g., worries about getting sick); children with autism may seek sameness/rituals to manage their social discomfort; and children with ADHD may overstimulate themselves to "wake their brains up." It is vital to understand *why* specific symptoms might emerge in specific situations and what function they might serve for the person who may have generated them. By strictly looking at DSM/ICD criteria and symptoms, students may miss the underlying reason for the exhibited behaviors, which may be a key to successful treatment. Yet another good example of "attempted answers" can be seen with the rising rates of anxiety and depression amidst the 2020 global pandemic as people try to cope with the unthinkable and unexpected.

P = *Prejudicial pigeonholes*. "Pigeonholing" an individual by placing the person into a diagnostic category or attaching a DSM or ICD label can sometimes be problematic. Even in modern times, the labels included in each version of the DSM/ICD and first-line treatments are partly reflections of historical trends and sociocultural attitudes. For example, as noted previously, homosexuality was included in past versions of the DSM/ICD, and several scholars still argue that the remaining sexual disorders in DSM/ICD, now called paraphilic disorders, should be removed as well (Silverstein 2009). Pigeonholing someone, or unfairly judging the person as belonging to a particular group, can have dire consequences. For example, DSM diagnostic criteria codify "masculine-based assumptions about what behaviors are healthy and what behaviors are crazy" (Kaplan 1983), and this shows up especially in diagnosis of personality disorders.

In one study (Ford and Widiger 1989), psychologists read a case history that illustrated either antisocial personality disorder (APD; diagnosed more often in males) or histrionic personality disorder (HPD; diagnosed more often in females). Psychologists were either told that their case involved a female or male client. For the antisocial case, the psychologists failed significantly more often to diagnose APD for the female (15%) than for the male (42%). The reverse was true for the HPD case; the psychologists significantly underdiagnosed this disorder in males (44%) compared with females (76%). The diagnosis of personality disorders in DSM-5 may result in prejudicial gender-based pigeonholing using data that go beyond the relevant symptoms of each client. It is noteworthy, however, that ICD-11 completely overhauls the section on personality disorders, which is where it most clearly departs from the DSM-5 system (Reed et al. 2019). The clinician now first determines whether the individual's clinical presentation meets the ICD-11's general diagnostic requirements for personality disorder, which is then labeled as mild, moderate, or severe, and measured in terms of five trait domains with an optional qualifier termed "borderline pattern" (Reed et al. 2019). It is not yet clear whether this new classification scheme for personality disorders represents a clear step forward (Watts 2019).

Furthermore, the DSM and ICD were initially conceptualized and written from the perspective of a medical model in a Western culture. Whereas this approach offers a wealth of information, it may be limited in its ability to accurately understand conditions and/or symptoms over a range of cultures and social contexts. For example, an individual may present with symptoms that are consistent with psychosis but are actually more closely related to spiritual experiences within a culture where they might not be considered problematic. In another instance, a therapist working with an individual who recently experienced an event in which they were racially discriminated against may need to consider that the client's feelings of depression may be clearly warranted and not pathological per se. If the clinician only focuses the individual symptoms rather than the cultural and environmental situations, treatment is likely to be misguided and less effective. Accordingly, both classification systems are improving in this regard with each iteration. Culture-related information was systematically incorporated based on a review of the literature on cultural influences on psychopathology and its expression for each ICD-11 diagnostic grouping (Reed et al. 2019), and the DSM-5 has a section that outlines how to take culturally relevant information into account when conducting a diagnostic assessment.

S = *Superficial symptoms*. The last several versions of the DSM (III, IV, and 5) and the ICD (10, 11) have had high interrater reliability in diagnoses because the diagnostic criteria are chiefly based on superficial signs and symptoms. In other words, diagnosis is made using features that clinicians or clients can easily observe, such as depressed mood, overt restlessness, or hypervigilance, rather than by any deeper understanding of cause. Whereas we diagnose medical diseases like diabetes based on blood sugar data and biopsies, research does not currently enable us to accurately diagnose depression based on any causal elements – i.e., low serotonin or genes or brainwave activities may be related to depression but are not reliable markers for its diagnosis. In our view, we are therefore left merely with what we can see or what the person tells us without any medical tests. We have used humorous photos in which cactus plants are diagnosed with mental disorders to illustrate the key caveat that both DSM and ICD systems are based on observable syndromes rather than diseases per se (Paris 2013). In your abnormal psychology class, we urge you to explore abnormality behind the cactus (and people!) to get at what causes these disorders and how to treat them, and not just how to spot them based on surface characteristics.

The goal of any good abnormal psychology course should be to get beyond the superficial view of signs and symptoms, such as this photo of a cactus diagnosed with dissociative identity disorder due to its apparent splitting into two distinct "alters" or alternate identities. (Source: Brian L. Burke, Atacama Region, Chile)

To sum up, M.A.P.S. outlines four foundational principles essential to any serious study of abnormal psychology and suggests that the diagnosis of mental disorders is frequently based on oversimplified medical assumptions and surface characteristics of human beings, as well as influenced by sociopolitical climate and stereotypes, rather than on a profound and real understanding of mechanism and cause. As Paris puts it (2013, pp. 183–184):

Thirty-odd years after DSM-III, we are still in the dark about the nature of most disorders…Advances in neuroscience have not succeeded in explaining ANY mental disorder. Genetics has raised more questions than it can answer. Neurochemistry turns out to be much more complex than most people believed. And the beautiful pictures of neuroimaging will be seen by future generations as, at best, suggestive and, at worst, primitive. Clinical observation and consensus from experts, rather than hard facts, are still the guiding forces behind the manual.

Additional Learning Objectives

In addition to the competencies delineated above, an abnormal psychology course may also have the following superordinate learning objectives: First, that students will learn about different potential careers related to identifying and treated mental illness, ranging from counseling, social work, and psychology to nursing and psychiatry. Second, whereas cognitive-behavioral therapy (CBT) is not the only treatment that is effective for a wide variety of mental disorders, it has the strongest evidence base for its usage and is the most customizable (David et al. 2018; Hofmann et al. 2012). Because of this, students should practice how to design CBT that specifically fits what research has uncovered about a particular mental disorder. For instance, studies have revealed that many people with panic disorder fear their own internal bodily cues for anxiety; accordingly, optimal treatment involves interoceptive exposure to induce a panic attack in treatment and then learn to endure/desensitize to the physical cues of anxiety (Barlow 1989). Once students have read about the basic tenets of CBT, they can brainstorm in groups and try to generate aspects of this groundbreaking treatment from their own budding understanding of panic disorder. This, of course, has cross-links to other stand-alone psychology classes, notably those in counseling and psychotherapy.

Teaching Methods

We have provided an overview of *what* content should be included in an abnormal psychology course, and we turn now to a focus on the *how* – the process and pedagogical tools that you can employ to bring the content to life for your students. Like many courses, abnormal psychology is most effectively taught when a range of approaches is employed to appeal to varied student learning preferences. We provide some of our best ideas below; our hope is that some of these activities will be useful in your classrooms as well.

Instructor's manual. Those who use a textbook will find that most of them offer instructor's manuals with teaching tips arranged around specific pieces of content. These types of materials are especially useful for new instructors or those who may be teaching this course for the first time.

Dynamic lectures. Although research continues to show the value of incorporating active learning into college classrooms (Mello and Less 2013), segments of organized and engaging lectures remain important (Bligh 2000). Students typically have many questions about psychological disorders, and so time should be left for questions and answer sessions as well as class discussion about the material. Given the extensive content in an abnormal psychology course (i.e., diagnostic criteria, treatment, etc.), brief lectures often help with providing basic information that is then illuminated via other teaching methods below.

Videos. Utilizing videos can be an especially helpful way to demonstrate how symptoms might actually appear in a particular person. Often textbooks provide supplemental materials with video examples, and a number of clinical presentation videos can be found online. For instance, there are free online video labs available for use at https://www.academicmediasolutions.com/burke-abnormal-psychology-2e-ovl.

Contemporary and famous examples of mental illness can also be impactful in reducing stigma as students may relate more closely to examples that are already familiar to them. For example, Demi Lovato, a child Disney star and current pop artist, is recognizable to many current undergraduate students in the United States. Her 2017 *Simply Complicated* documentary details her struggle with bipolar disorder, substance abuse, and disordered eating. In the documentary, she discusses the tangible ways in which her symptoms influenced her life and career. Adele, Lena Dunham, J.K. Rowling, Dwayne Johnson, Ruby Rose, and Kristen Stewart are other international celebrities who have spoken candidly about their own challenges with mental illness.

J.K. Rowling, for example, confirmed that the dementors in her *Harry Potter* series were a symbol for depression (White 2016): "It was entirely conscious. And entirely from my own experience. Depression is the most unpleasant thing I have ever experienced. It is that absence of being able to envisage that you will ever be cheerful again. The absence of hope. That very deadened feeling, which is so very different from feeling sad. Sad hurts but it's a healthy feeling. It's a necessary thing to feel. Depression is very different." Showing clips of these dementors in class can help bring the feeling that Rowling describes to life for students who may not have experienced depression themselves.

Dementor puppet from "The Making of Harry Potter" at the Warner Brothers Studio Tour in London, UK. (Public domain image by Peyton Eyre from Lille, France. Available at https://commons.wikimedia.org/wiki/File:Dementor_(8514403186).jpg)

Other visual material. PowerPoint and other presentation programs were designed as visual media, so it is valuable to include powerful images and artwork wherever possible in your presentation of abnormal psychology material (Tyler and Likova 2012). In addition to photos of a dementor to illustrate depression or of Saguaro cacti in the apparent throes of various psychological disorders, you can use the work of famous artists who may themselves have suffered from mental illness, including Vincent van Gogh's self-portraits, which may provide a clue as to his experience with depression and possibly bipolar disorder. Further, Edvard Munch's iconic paintings (*The Scream*, *Anxiety*, and *Despair*) can effectively illustrate the similarities and differences between a panic attack, generalized anxiety, and depression, all of which he reports having experienced first-hand (Rothenberg 2015).

An 1889 self-portrait by Vincent van Gogh with a bandaged ear. (Public domain image from the web museum. Available at https://commons.wikimedia.org/wiki/File:VanGogh-self-portrait-with_bandaged_ear.jpg)

Research articles. As stated above, we want students to get beyond the superficial diagnostic criteria of DSM/ICD and into the etiological realm of the plethora of interacting known and theorized causes of these psychological disorders. One way of facilitating this process is to have students gain an appreciation for how the causal theories are tested and refined – i.e., scientific research in the field of abnormal psychology. A possible assignment is to have students – individually or in groups – find a study in the psychology literature using your library's topical database (e.g., PsycINFO) and summarize its key findings either in writing or as a short (10-min) oral presentation to the class. We have pairs of students sign up at the beginning of the term for a specific topic area on the course syllabus, and then they come up at some point during the class period on their chosen topic to present a current research study to the class. Alternatively, class periods could be devoted to "micro-research" projects wherein students conduct group research in class using electronic journal databases or other appropriate online resources and formulate a presentation of their ideas within one class session.

In vivo experiences. Another way to foster a deep understanding of mental disorders is to allow students to "experience" the symptoms. This can be a tricky task and should be presented thoughtfully in order to not trivialize the real experiences of those with mental illness. For example, Depression Quest (http://www.depressionquest.com/) is an online tool that allows students to walk through what depression feels like, including some of the associated cognitions and feelings, while considering choices that might improve or worsen symptoms. As students progress through the simulation, they are asked to make decisions that then impact the information they receive as they continue. There is no end to this simulation, which signifies the potential risk for relapse and highlights the need for ongoing management of our own self-care and mental health.

In-class simulations can also illustrate disorders more vividly. In one demonstration (developed by Dr. Lori Ernsperger) designed to simulate experiences of those with autism, students are asked to form groups of three and assigned a role/task. Two students are instructed to talk with one another about a common topic while ignoring the third student. The third student is asked to communicate details of the sensory system to their peers (information provided on their instruction sheet) and interject this information into the conversation whenever possible. Following this brief interaction, time should be devoted to processing the experiences of students in each role. This leads to a discussion about the potential isolation and frustration that individuals with autism may experience as well as ideas for how neurotypical individuals might be able to respond more openly to them. The materials and questions for this activity can be found on page 39 of the document at http://airpnetwork.org/sites/default/files/2017-02/autism_friendly_youth_organizations.pdf.

Another example of a class simulation is a short activity designed to quickly mirror the experience of auditory hallucinations. In this paired activity, one student completes basic math problems, while the other plays the role of auditory hallucinations and talks to the person with negative statements, such as "you can't do this," "you are worthless," "you won't succeed," etc. After the simulation, students who were working on the math problems are invited to describe their experience and speculate on how this might impact a person who experiences regular auditory hallucinations, which are frequently negative and self-deprecating.

If possible and depending on your class size and other practical constraints, you can inject even more high-impact educational experiences (HIPs; Kuh 2008) into your abnormal psychology classes, including internships in or visits to a hospital or mental health setting and/or guest speakers who come to your class to discuss their personal experiences with specific mental disorders. Students generally respond very well to these types of activities as the disorders become more real, not just lists of symptoms in a textbook or other readings.

Application to the self. One benefit of teaching abnormal psychology is that many of the concepts and symptoms are familiar to students even if they themselves do not have a specific diagnosis (though many will have at least one!). For instance, almost every college student is able to identify with the feeling of anxiety. To help demonstrate the relationship between anxious thoughts and feelings and behaviors (and how anxious thoughts may intensify and rise to the level of a diagnosis), simple polling software (such as www.polleverywhere.com) can be used to generate common anxious thoughts and associated negative cognitions. Anonymous polling may allow students to be more honest in their responses and receive real-time feedback. Figure 1 shows a word cloud generated from one abnormal psychology class when students were asked to describe something they worried about in the past week. The follow-up question, shown in Fig. 2, asks students to go deeper and identify a worry they have that they would not typically share with others. As evidenced by the responses shown here, the negative thoughts of "I'm a failure" or "I'm not good enough" can then be used to demonstrate the cognitive triangle in CBT (the relationship between thoughts, feelings, and behaviors). After mapping out associated feelings, students are asked to generate alternative thoughts and how those thoughts might lead to improved mood for an individual with anxiety. After completing this activity, students can be encouraged to challenge some of their own negative thinking patterns the next time they encounter a stressful event.

Fig. 1 Abnormal Psychology Class - "What You Worry About" Word Cloud

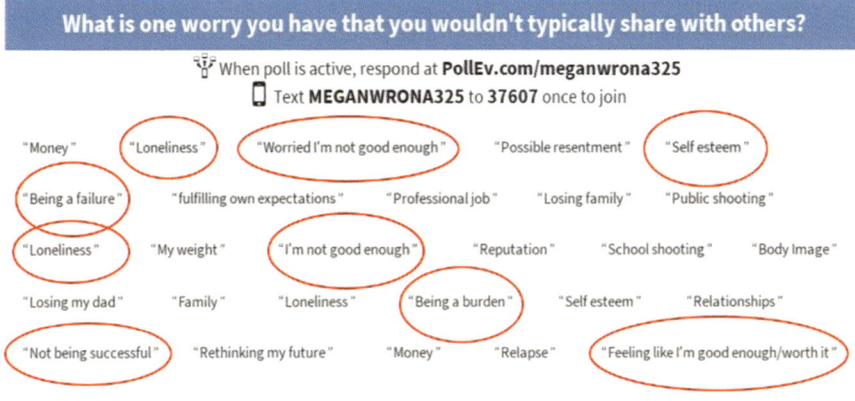

Fig. 2 Abnormal Psychology Class - "Secret Worry" Poll

Another assignment that relates back to the definition of a mental disorder discussed above is to have students explore one of the *Conditions for Further Study* found in DSM-5's Section III (e.g., Internet Gaming Disorder, Caffeine Use Disorder), which are also among the newest disorders included in ICD-11 (Reed et al. 2019). Students can write a case study illustrating how they or a "friend" might fit the definition of having a mental disorder based on use of video games or caffeine (both used very frequently by today's students). Students' case studies can (a) identify a dysfunction in psychological, biological, or developmental processes and (b) describe what a clinically significant disturbance in cognition, emotion regulation, or behavior would look like. Students can conclude the assignment by addressing whether or not they believe these new conditions are best conceptualized as mental disorders as per ICD-11 or left out of the official disorder list as per DSM-5.

Integrating structured trainings. Another method of teaching in abnormal psychology is to integrate opportunities for trainings related to the concepts in the course that can also give students certifications that might be valuable for their current or future jobs. Specifically, both of the authors of this chapter now incorporate brief (1-class) suicide intervention trainings into abnormal psychology content. Suicidality is a common symptom of several disorders and an increasing concern internationally. By providing an evidence-based training, such as Question, Persuade, and Refer (QPR; https://qprinstitute.com/), students learn about the signs and symptoms of suicidality and develop tangible skills to help people they may encounter in their own life. Another such program is Mental Health First Aid (https://www.mentalhealthfirstaid.org/).

Case studies and conceptualizations. Although students are not trained to professionally diagnose after the completion of an abnormal psychology course, activities that allow students to practice diagnosing are generally interesting and engaging for students. One assignment that lets students be creative and explore their own interests is to ask students to diagnose a character in a movie or a television show. In this assignment, students write a case conceptualization of the character including presenting problem, background information, diagnostic impressions, and treatment recommendations. Students generally describe this assignment as fun and like that they get to watch a movie or show as part of their school work! This written conceptualization can also be paired with a brief presentation of the character, with short video clips to illustrate the symptoms that were observed.

One of the most classic and effective techniques to engage all students in a classroom is to employ the jigsaw method (Aronson 1978), wherein each student is privy to specific information that they then need to share with a group in order to complete a collaborative task. Groups of 4–5 students can work on case in which each student is given a different part of the case material to read in class (e.g., one student gets the person's past medical history, another the presenting episode, another the previous treatment or family history, etc.). Each group therefore has an expert on each particular aspect of the case example, and so each student has to contribute and share individual perspectives and information with the group in order to answer questions collaboratively on diagnosis, cause, and treatment of the case.

Case studies can also be useful in demonstrating the complexity of comorbidity. For example, in the case described in the box on this page, Jen is clearly exhibiting symptoms of depression, but students may be less likely to pick up on symptoms associated with attention-deficit hyperactivity disorder (ADHD). Her ADHD symptoms may be interacting with her depression, however, and it would be helpful to address both in treatment planning for Jen.

Finally, in a comprehensive, experiential approach suggested by Jane Halonen of the University of West Florida (Neufeld and Landrum 2017), students can gain experience in diagnosing and clinical interviewing when you invite a former student or teaching assistant to come into your class to role play a client. In this activity, students are given no information about the client and must use their knowledge of symptoms, criteria, developmental background, and sociocultural beliefs to ask the appropriate questions in order to home in on a potential DSM/ICD diagnosis. This experience helps students learn more about the difficulty of identifying symptoms and the nuances of diagnosis that can be challenging to capture simply through memorizing a list of symptoms.

Summary

In sum, teaching abnormal psychology is one of our favorite jobs because it provides a rich opportunity for instructors to influence the way people understand and relate to mental illness. By laying a solid foundation for content and expectations at the beginning of the semester through exploring the meaning of abnormality, understanding the language of the DSM/ICD, and learning the models that explain the multitude of contributors to the development of mental disorders, instructors can delve into the details of these fascinating disorders with a range of evidence-based teaching techniques. Ideally, students should leave this course with increased compassion and empathy for people with mental illness, an understanding of the basic signs and symptoms of various disorders, and a critical and holistic view of diagnosis. Students are often engaged and hungry to learn more in this course, which tends to make the varied teaching techniques we describe here even more effective.

Final Teaching Tips

1. **Facilitate stigma reduction**. An abnormal psychology course provides an excellent opportunity to educate others about psychology and mental disorders, which in turn can serve to reduce the stigma often experienced by people with mental illness (Strassle 2018). As an instructor, you can make a real difference in how mental illness is perceived.
2. **Recognize that course content can be uncomfortable**. Given that at least one in five people struggle with mental illness (NIMH 2017), many students in your class have likely been affected in a significant way by these disorders. As such, we recommend that teachers be sensitive and considerate to students who have personal or family histories of mental disorders. Whether or not to use actual "trigger warnings" for the course content, however, is highly debatable (see Lilienfeld et al. 2018, for a thorough coverage of the debate taking place in North America).
3. **Make the material applicable**! Like most content, students learn best when they can apply concepts and ideas to their own lives. Whereas we do not want students to diagnose themselves or others, we do want them to be able to recognize symptoms that may indicate that professional help may be warranted.
4. **Encourage students to think critically about diagnosis**. Help students understand the complexity of diagnosis and some of the inherent flaws of the DSM/ICD classification systems. A diagnosis often carries a lot of weight and students should understand the implications.
5. ... **But, don't throw out the DSM/ICD systems completely**. Even though these are not perfect diagnostic tools, they are still the primary ones used to diagnose mental disorders worldwide and to foster critical communication within the field of psychology and beyond.
6. **Focus on the biopsychosocial and multicultural nature of diagnosis**. Given the challenges with the DSM/ICD and their emphasis on pathology, you can help students conceptualize symptoms and diagnosis from a more holistic approach. Even if you are a medical doctor, you are teaching what is, above all, a psychology class.
7. **Don't get bogged down by content**. Diagnosing is complicated and there is *no* way to cover all of the material in the DSM/ICD thoroughly in a single semester.

We thus suggest that you follow the interests of your students to ensure that the content that they are exposed to really sinks in and stays with them beyond exams. For example, a student may not remember the difference between positive and negative symptoms of schizophrenia in 5 years, but they will likely remember how it felt when they tried to complete math problems while experiencing simulated auditory hallucinations.

8. **Remember that students tend to love this class**! Students frequently identify abnormal psychology as one of their favorite undergraduate courses. Students are truly interested in the course precisely because they already see how the content overlaps with their own experiences and those of others close to them. This interest gives you, as the educator, an advantage that makes the class feel even more rewarding for your students and for yourself.

Further Reading

American Psychiatric Association. (2013). *Diagnostic and statistical manual of mental disorders (5th ed.)*. Arlington, VA: Author.

The *Diagnostic and Statistical Manual of Mental Disorders* (DSM), published by the American Psychiatric Association (APA), offers a common language and standard criteria for the classification of mental disorders. It is used by clinicians, researchers, psychiatric drug regulation agencies, health insurance companies, pharmaceutical companies, the legal system, and policy makers together with alternatives such as the ICD Classification of Mental and Behavioural Disorders (see below). The DSM is in its fifth edition, the DSM-5, published on May 18, 2013. The DSM evolved from systems for collecting census and psychiatric hospital statistics and from a US Army manual. Revisions since its first publication in 1952 have incrementally added to the total number of mental disorders and removed those no longer considered to be mental disorders due to expert consensus.

Barnhill, J. W. (Ed). (2014). *DSM-5: Clinical Cases*. Washington, DC: American Psychiatric Publishing.

This text, published shortly after the release of the DSM-5, includes case examples of most of the clinical diagnoses in the DSM. The text is organized by categories of disorders, and case studies are provided for each of the diagnoses within a category. Cases range in complexity and a discussion of the appropriate diagnosis is included. This is an excellent resource for realistic case study scenarios to use in the classroom.

Frances, A. (2012). *The Health Care Blog: Everything you always wanted to know about the Health Care system. But were afraid to ask* [blog]. https://thehealth careblog.com/blog/tag/allen-frances/

Dr. Alan Frances was Chair of the DSM-IV Task Force and has since been writing about his thoughts on healthcare in general and mental health more specifically. His blog began as a scathing but trenchant critique of DSM-5 and its perceived pandering to drug companies and has been expanded to encompass other related topics such as the political economy of DSM, what doctors do when they do not know what to do, the medicalization of modern life, and the perils of over-diagnosing mental illness.

Neufeld, G., & Landrum, E. (Producers). *Psych sessions: Convos about teaching and stuff* [Audio podcast]. Retrieved from https://psychsessionspodcast.libsyn.com/

Garth Neufeld and Eric Landrum host this podcast, which is a series of interviews with top educators in the field of psychology. Interviews include information about the individual educators and as well as rich discussion about teaching pedagogy, practices, and innovation. Podcast guests share their teaching ideas and perspectives. Although this podcast does not focus exclusively on abnormal psychology, many of the principles and ideas can be applied across a range of psychology courses.

Paris, J. (2013). *The intelligent clinician's guide to the DSM-5*. New York: Oxford University Press.

The Intelligent Clinician's Guide to the DSM-5 explores all revisions to the latest version of the Diagnostic and Statistical Manual and shows clinicians how they can best apply the strong points and shortcomings of psychiatry's most contentious resource. Written by a professor of psychiatry, this book uses evidence-based critiques and new research to point out where DSM-5 is right, where it is wrong, and where the jury's still out. Along the way, *The Intelligent Clinician's Guide to the DSM-5* sifts through the many public controversies and clinical debates surrounding the drafting of the manual and shows how they inform a modern understanding of mental disorders, diagnosis, and treatment.

Peterson, C. (2006). The Values in Action (VIA) Classification of Strengths: The un-DSM and the real DSM. In M. Csikszentmihalyi & I. Csikszentmihalyi (Eds.), *A life worth living: Contributions to positive psychology* (pp. 29–48). New York: Oxford University Press.

Positive Psychology's answer to the DSM and ICD is the VIA (Values in Action) Classification of Strengths. This is work undertaken by Chris Peterson and Martin Seligman that lists character strengths and virtues instead of abnormal/pathological symptoms or syndromes. The Values in Action (VIA) Classification of Strengths project means to complement the DSM and ICD by focusing on what is right about people and specifically about the strengths of character that make the good life possible. The VIA classification was the first major project deliberately developed from the perspective of positive psychology. Seligman and Peterson admit that many other thinkers have articulated what makes good character but what is different about their work is their attempt to define and measure these strengths. Their VIA Inventory of Strengths is a self-report questionnaire of 240 items which can be completed online for free at http://www.authentichappiness. sas.upenn.edu.

Society for the Teaching of Psychology, www.teachpsych.org

The Society for the Teaching of Psychology (STP), also known as Division 2 of the American Psychological Association, maintains a website rich in resources and information about teaching, including teaching abnormal psychology. Specifically, clicking on the resource link will lead instructors to e-books, websites, teaching competencies, and more. Of note, within the resource section, instructors can find a wealth of information through Project Syllabus, which is a repository of sample syllabi that have been submitted by instructors and peer-reviewed. These syllabi include ideas for texts, grading, assignments, and more.

Szasz, T.S. (1974). *The myth of mental illness: Foundations of a theory of personal conduct.* New York: Harper & Row.

Thomas Szasz was a staunch critic of the DSM/ICD classification systems and warned of the dangers of society over-pathologizing mental illness. His perspective is invaluable to instructors as they consider the strengths and weaknesses of the DSM/ICD and the implications of diagnoses on society.

World Health Organization (2019, July). *International classifications of diseases* (ICD). https://icd.who.int/en/

This is the only current legitimate competitor and alternative to the DSM-5, especially outside of North America, although in practice the two manuals are frequently employed in a complementary manner (e.g., DSM-5 and insurance companies use ICD codes for diagnosis and reimbursement). The *International Statistical Classification of Diseases and Related Health Problems* (ICD) is the bedrock for health statistics. It maps the human condition from birth to death: any injury or disease we encounter in life – and anything we might die of – is coded, including mental disorders. ICD is widely used and recognized internationally and is updated every 20–30 years with minor revisions even more frequently, much like the DSM (above).

Case Study
Jen is a 29-year-old woman who presents to your clinic in distress. She reports a significant decrease in her mood due to conflict with her husband and problems at work. She reports feeling depressed most of the time and has withdrawn from many of her typical activities. She starts crying almost

(continued)

immediately during the session and says she cries multiple times a day without knowing why. She says that she had lost about 10 pounds in recent months, without the intent to lose weight. She also reports that she cannot sleep through the night and consequently feels like she does not have energy to do anything or concentrate for long. When asked directly about suicidal thoughts, she reports that she sometimes thinks about how her family might respond if she died but denies any intent to harm herself.

In the interview, Jen fidgets and has a hard time sitting still. She tearfully tells you that she is in a major fight with her husband of 1 year because he is ready to have children but she fears that she is "too disorganized to be a good mother." As you break down some of the processes that have led to her current crises, you learn that she has difficulty with time management and does indeed tend to be disorganized. She chronically misplaces everyday objects like her keys and runs late to appointments. Although she wants her work to be perfect, she is prone to making careless mistakes. The struggle for perfection makes starting a new task feel very stressful, leading her to procrastinate. As a consequence, she has recently received a number of warnings from her boss related to missing deadlines for assignments and errors in her work, which has led to her acute fear of being fired. As her performance at work has plummeted and she has grown increasingly anxious and doubting of herself, she has grown even more pessimistic about starting a family.

Cross-References

► Basic Principles and Procedures for Effective Teaching in Psychology
► Problem-Based Learning and Case-Based Learning

References

American Psychiatric Association. (1994). *Diagnostic and statistical manual of mental disorders* (4th ed.). Arlington: Author.
American Psychiatric Association. (2013). *Diagnostic and statistical manual of mental disorders* (5th ed.). Arlington: Author.
Aronson, E. (1978). *The jigsaw classroom*. Oxford: Sage.
Barlow, D. (1989). Behavioral treatment of panic disorder. *Behavior Therapy, 20*(2), 261–282. https://doi.org/10.1016/s0005-7894(89)80073-5.
Bligh, D. A. (2000). *What's the use of lectures?* San Francisco: Jossey-Bass.
Bronfenbrenner, U. (1979). *The ecology of human development*. Cambridge, MA: Harvard University Press.

Burke, B. L., Trost, S., deRoon-Cassini, T., & Bernstein, D. (2016). *Abnormal psychology* (2nd ed.). Solon: Academic Media Solutions.

Burton, N. (2015, September 18). When homosexuality stopped being a mental disorder. *Psychology Today.* Retrieved from https://www.psychologytoday.com/us/blog/hide-and-seek/201509/when-homosexuality-stopped-being-mental-disorder

Comer, R. J. (2011). *Fundamentals of abnormal psychology* (6th ed.). New York: Worth.

David, D., Cristea, I., & Hofmann, S. G. (2018). Why cognitive behavioral therapy is the current gold standard of psychotherapy. *Frontiers in Psychiatry, 9,* 4. https://doi.org/10.3389/fpsyt.2018.00004.

Davidson, R. J., Jackson, D. C., & Kalin, N. H. (2000). Emotion, plasticity, context, and regulation: Perspectives from affective neuroscience. *Psychological Bulletin, 126,* 890–909. https://doi.org/10.1037//0033-2909.126.6.890.

Drescher, J. (2015). Queer diagnoses revisited: The past and future of homosexuality and gender diagnoses in DSM and ICD. *International Review of Psychiatry, 27*(5), 386–395. https://doi.org/10.3109/09540261.2015.1053847.

Ford, M. R., & Widiger, T. A. (1989). Sex bias in the diagnosis of histrionic and antisocial personality disorders. *Journal of Consulting and Clinical Psychology, 57*(2), 301–305. https://doi.org/10.1037/0022-006X.57.2.301.

Frances, A. (2012). DSM 5 is guide not bible – Ignore its ten worst changes [Web logpost]. In *DSM-5 in Distress.* Retrieved 20 May 2013 from http://www.psychologytoday.com/blog/dsm5-in-distress/201212/dsm-5-is-guidenot-bible-ignore-its-ten-worst-changes

Frances, A. (2013, January 7). *Last plea to DSM-5: Save grief from the drug companies* [Blog post]. Retrieved 29 Aug 2013 from http://www.huffingtonpost.com/allen-frances/saving-grief-from-dsm-5-a_b_2325108.html

Hartmann, W. E., Wendt, D. C., Burrage, R. L., Pomerville, A., & Gone, J. P. (2019). American Indian historical trauma: Anticolonial prescriptions for healing, resilience, and survivance. *American Psychologist, 74*(1), 6–19.

Hofmann, S. G., Asnaani, A., Vonk, I. J., Sawyer, A. T., & Fang, A. (2012). The efficacy of cognitive behavioral therapy: A review of meta-analyses. *Cognitive Therapy and Research, 36,* 427–440. https://doi.org/10.1007/s10608-012-9476-1.

Kaplan, M. (1983). A woman's view of DSM-III. *American Psychologist, 38*(7), 786–792. https://doi.org/10.1037/0003-066X.38.7.786.

Klott, J. (2012). *DSM-5: Revolutionizing diagnosis and treatment* [DVD]. Eau Claire, WI: CMI Education Institute.

Kotov, R., Kruegar, R. F., Watson, D., Achenbach, T. M., Althoff, R. R., ... Zimmerman, M. (2017). The hierarchical taxonomy of psychopathology (HiTOP): A dimensional alternative to traditional nosologies. *Journal of Abnormal Psychology, 126*(4), 454–477. https://doi.org/10.1037/abn0000258.

Kuh, G. D. (2008). High-impact educational practices: What they are, who has access to them, and why they matter. *American Association of Colleges and Universities.* https://www.aacu.org/leap/hips

Lilienfeld, S. O., Ceci, S. J., & Williams, W. M. (2018, October 18). The one-time-only trigger warning. *Inside Higher Ed.* Retrieved from https://www.insidehighered.com/views/2018/10/18/way-handle-trigger-warnings-develop-one-time-only-one-opinion

Mello, D., & Less, C. A. (2013). Effectiveness of active learning in the arts and sciences. *Humanities Department Faculty Publications & Research. Paper 45.* Retrieved from http://scholarsarchive.jwu.edu/cgi/viewcontent.cgi?article=1044&context=humanities_fac

Miyamoto, S., Miyake, N., Jarskog, L. F., Fleischhacker, W. W., & Lieberman, J. A. (2012). Pharmacological treatment of schizophrenia: A critical review of pharmacology and clinical effects of current and future therapeutic agents. *Molecular Psychiatry, 17,* 1206–1227. https://doi.org/10.1038/mp.2012.47.

National Institutes of Mental Health. (2017). *Mental Illness.* Retrieved from https://www.nimh.nih.gov/health/statistics/mental-illness.shtml

Neufeld, G., & Landrum, E. (2017, October). *E006: Jane Halonen: Mastery and Magic of Teaching* [Audio podcast]. Retrieved from https://www.iheart.com/podcast/263-psychsessions-conve-29214144/episode/e006-jane-halonen-mastery-and-magic-29220630/

Paris, J. (2013). *The intelligent clinician's guide to the DSM-5*. New York: Oxford University Press.

Reed, G. M., First, M. B., Kogan, C. S., Hyman, S. E., Gureje, O., Gaebel, W., et al. (2019). Innovations and changes in the ICD-11 classification of mental, behavioural and neurodevelopmental disorders. *World Psychiatry, 18*(1), 3–19. https://doi.org/10.1002/wps.20611.

Rothenberg, A. (2015, March 24). Creativity and mental illness II: The scream. *Psychology Today*. Retrieved from https://www.psychologytoday.com/us/blog/creative-explorations/201503/crea tivity-and-mental-illness-ii-the-scream

Rounsaville, B. J., Alarcón, R. D., Andrews, G., Jackson, J. S., Kendell, R. E., & Kendler, K. (2002). Basic nomenclature issues for DSM-V. In D. J. Kupfer, M. B. First, & D. A. Regier (Eds.), *A research agenda for DSM-V* (pp. 1–29). Washington, DC: American Psychiatric Association.

Sander, D. (2013). Models of emotion: The affective neuroscience approach. In J. Armony & P. Vuilleumier (Eds.), *The Cambridge handbook of human affective neuroscience* (pp. 5–53). New York: Cambridge University Press.

Silverstein, C. (2009). The implications of removing homosexuality from the DSM as a mental disorder. *Archives of Sexual Behavior, 38*, 161–163. https://doi.org/10.1007/s10508-008-9442-x.

Smith, L. A., Cornelius, V., Warnock, A., Tacchi, M., & Taylor, D. (2007). Pharmacological interventions for acute bipolar mania: A systematic review of randomized placebo-controlled trials. *Bipolar Disorders, 9*, 551–560. https://doi.org/10.1111/j.1399-5618.2007.00468.x.

Strassle, C. G. (2018). Reducing mental illness stigma in the classroom. *Teaching of Psychology, 45* (4), 351–357. https://doi.org/10.1177/0098628318796922.

Szasz, T. S. (1996). *The meaning of mind: Language, morality and neuroscience*. New York: Praeger.

Tyler, C. W., & Likova, L. T. (2012). The role of the visual arts in enhancing the learning process. *Frontiers of Human Neuroscience, 6*, 8.

Watts, J. (2019). Problems with the ICD-11 classification of personality disorder. *The Lancet Psychiatry, 6*(6), 461–463.

White, H. (2016). 22 J.K. Rowling Facts That Prove She Is ACTUALLY a Magical Human. *Popsugar*. Retrieved on 8 Aug 2019 from https://www.popsugartech.com/photo-gallery/41180052/image/41180427/Rowling-created-Dementors-metaphor-depression

World Health Organization (2019, July). *International classifications of diseases* (ICD-11). Retrieved 13 July 2019 from https://icd.who.int/en/

Sensation and Perception

4

Robert Gaschler, Mariam Katsarava, and Veit Kubik

Contents

Abstract

Often being covered in introductory psychology, the topic of sensation and perception offers ample opportunity to strengthen identification of students with psychology. On the one hand, this is due to the many recipes for classroom demonstrations of specific effects which should help to create durable memories of what it is to be in a psychology course. Reviewing these recipes, we draw attention to the challenges of linking classroom events to core content. On the

R. Gaschler (✉) · M. Katsarava
Department of Psychology, FernUniversität in Hagen, Hagen, Germany
e-mail: robert.gaschler@fernuni-hagen.de

V. Kubik
Department of Psychology, Universität Bielefeld, Bielefeld, Germany

© Springer Nature Switzerland AG 2023
J. Zumbach et al. (eds.), *International Handbook of Psychology Learning and Teaching*,
Springer International Handbooks of Education,
https://doi.org/10.1007/978-3-030-28745-0_6

other hand, the topic can be presented such that its central role for future work as a psychologist (e.g., in organizational or industrial psychology) becomes clear. It offers many opportunities for future psychologists to apply their methodological and content knowledge to tackle societal, economic, and ecological challenges. On the other hand, the topic can be used as a starting point to discuss core theoretical questions of psychology. Work in science studies suggests that sensation and perception are the domains where other science disciplines often need input from psychology.

Keywords

Grouping · Top-down influences · Psychology of science · Data graphs · Metaphors of attention · Change blindness · Human-machine interaction · Environmental psychology

Introduction

The literature on teaching psychology contains various recipes to convey the content of perceptual phenomena (see Table 5) to students. In these recipes, readers can easily grasp the scientific fascination that researchers have for specific phenomena and for psychology in general. Asking students what they remember from introductory psychology, students often mention classroom demonstrations – such as using prism goggles, in which the visual field can be shifted to the right or the left (VanderStoep, Fagerlin, & Feenstra, 2000), though only few events were recalled from class that were primarily relevant to the course material. This state of affairs is unfortunate but can be enhanced. Importantly, learning material on sensation and perception can be presented and learned in ways that make events better memorable and linked to core contents of the course material. Before we will provide recipes for teaching specific concepts (see Table 5, for a summary), we will illustrate the central role that the topic of *sensation* and *perception* can have in the curriculum of psychology.

From Telescope to Data Graph

Topics of sensation and perception strongly relate to the foundations of psychology as a science. Work in psychophysics was driven by the demands of early astronomers and particle physicists to better understand the limitations of the human perceptual system (cf. Brewer, 2012). Stars have, for instance, been ordered by brightness since the time of ancient Greek astronomers, calling for profound understanding of the human capabilities to perceive brightness and differentiate different levels of brightness, promoting the development of psychophysics (e.g., the Weber-Fechner law). In some cases, psychological research on perception revealed that alleged discoveries were not related to an external object at astronomic distance but instead could tell about the characteristics of an internal object nearby: the human brain. For instance, repeated observations of canals on Mars were early on attributed to the specific wiring of the perceptual system. Even when this fact was known, these canals were "perceived" as if they were existent (cf. Evans & Maunder, 1903). Early on, students can be introduced to the primacy of psychological knowledge: as humans rely on their sensations and perceptions, science disciplines build on psychological knowledge about the human perceptual system. Discussing the role of the human observer in other research disciplines might increase identification of the students with psychology and convey that exchange with other disciplines is strengthening the own discipline.

There are many examples from history of science that underline the role of psychological processes by direct observation, and they often involve the power of expectations in perceptual processes (Brewer, 2012). For instance, in discovering planets, it has proven highly important to know where to search. In 1846, Urbain Le Verrier reported to Johann Galle a deviation between the observed orbit of Uranus and predictions based on mechanics by Newton. Receiving this letter just days before a starry night, Johann Galle was able to discover Neptune within a few hours. Another more recent example of how perceptual limitations and expectations in astronomy can interact is the discovery of the Pluto moon Charon in 1990. In earlier photographs, the moon Charon was already detectable (i.e., elongation of Pluto due to atmospheric turbulences), but was not yet discovered. One reason was that observers did not have the expectations to find a moon at such a short distance from a planet.

Furthermore, there are various examples in the history of particle physics, in which scientists – guided by their expectations – discovered events or objects that in fact are not existent (cf. Brewer, 2012; Galison, 1997). For instance, Rutherford and Chadwick had observed light flashes under the microscope when targeting some (but not other) chemicals with specific radiation (i.e., alpha rays). They concluded that flashes occur only for elements that emit protons. However, the Vienna laboratory of Pettersson and Kirsch reported to have observed light flashes with virtually all probes. The experimental conditions (e.g., darkness before the test starts) were identical except for the expectations that differed between research groups: observers of the Vienna group continued to report light flashes even when (unbeknown to them) the source was replaced.

The interplay of perceptual limitations and expectations can also be demonstrated with data graphs. According to Brewer (2012), psychology of science should focus on this topic, as direct observation has become rare in science, while researchers view their object of study through data graphs instead. For example, Lewandowsky, Ballard, Oberauer, and Benestad (2016) showed that data graphs on climate change that raise opposing interpretations by climate skeptics and mainstream researchers are interpreted consensually in case the same data graphs are used with labels that are not relevant for climate change. Compared to numbers in tables, data graphs provide us with access to relational information at low effort (c.f. Schnotz & Bannert, 2003). For instance, we can perceive differences and variability in different measures at a glance. Yet, using the power of the perceptual system to grasp characteristics of data sets might come at the cost that in some cases perceptual biases lead to systematic errors. For instance, means are systematically underestimated in bar graphs (c.f. Godau, Vogelgesang, & Gaschler, 2016), suggesting that a different graph format (e.g., point graphs) should be chosen when an unbiased impression of the mean level is important. Students of psychology can learn these regularities and how the fit between communication purpose and data graph format can be empirically determined.

Data graphs are frequently used to convey research results to educational target groups (e.g., at schools), the public (e.g., the media), and the scientific community, specifically when conducting and communicating interdisciplinary research (cf. the Fifth Assessment Report of the United Nations Intergovernmental Panel on Climate Change; IPCC, 2014). Data graphs from public sources are central in debates on climate change. Students of psychology should learn how to select formats that can be easily and correctly comprehended by the specific target audience and should learn how to identify and quantify motivational biases in perception of data graphs of high societal relevance. For instance, the blind expert test conducted by Lewandowsky et al. (2016) might serve as a basis of student projects in research practice courses.

Purposes and Rationale of the Curriculum in Sensation and Perception

Qualification frameworks for future psychologists by the American Psychological Association (APA, 2013, 2018;) as well as on the European level (Lunt, Job, Lecuyer, Peiro, & Gorbena, 2014) emphasize that the curriculum should enable students to apply psychological knowledge in the field: "Professional psychologists apply psychology and psychological knowledge and understanding to real-life questions in order to enhance the well-being and effectiveness of individuals, groups and systems" (Lunt et al., 2014, p. 20). The APA guidelines for psychology undergraduate majors list five generic goals the curriculum should pursue which can be linked to examples from the domain of sensation and perception (Table 1).

Sensation and Perception within Areas of Applied Psychology

Lunt et al. stress that specialized theoretical and practical training usually takes place within an area of applied psychology. The most prominent areas of application are clinical and health psychology (working in the health system), followed by educational psychology (working in education), and work and organizational psychology (working in organizations and industry). While most of the teaching concerning sensation and perception takes place in the bachelor program before students have lectures and seminars in the area of applied psychology, applied questions should be integrated early to motivate students and to help in contextualizing their knowledge. With respect to clinical and health psychology, this might, for instance, involve

Table 1 Five goals for undergraduate psychology majors (APA, 2013) and examples from sensation and perception

Five goals for undergraduate psychology major	Issues in sensation and perception
Knowledge base in psychology	Profound knowledge about functions and structures involved in perception is needed to comprehend theoretical questions, understand and master appropriate methods, and deliver approaches to practical problems
Scientific inquiry and critical thinking	Theorizing, methodological, and empirical basis to question lay-concepts of vision and other senses
Ethical and social responsibility in a diverse world	Cultural diversity affects perceptual processes (c.f., Kitayama, Duffy, Tadashi, & Larsen, 2003; Luria, 1976)
Communication	By displaying data in graphs, we make use of the powerful computational system of visual perception. Yet, visual biases and neglect of information can result if purpose and format of information do not match. Appropriate design and usage of data graphs should be informed by empirical psychological research. The latter can help to uncover motivated cognition in graph interpretation (e.g., climate data, Lewandowsky et al., 2016)
Professional development	Using knowledge on sensation and perception can, for instance, be used to pursue career goals by applying self-regulation prompts, using flowcharts for project management or achieving high layout quality and usability in (electronic) presentations, portfolios, and CV

Fig. 1 Adaptation of the example provided by Wertheimer (1938). For many observers, the form determines what is being perceived, and the elements it consists of are not easily recognized despite the high number of prior encounters

covering work on the role of body image disturbance in the onset, maintenance, and relapse of anorexia nervosa (i.e., Glashouwer, Veer, Adipatria, Jong, & Vocks, 2019), the impact of visual feedback (cf. Wittkopf, Lloyd, & Johnson, 2018) and age on pain perception (Lautenbacher, Peters, Heesen, Scheel, & Kunz, 2017), or the possible interplay of depression and pain perception (Thompson, Correll, Gallop, Vancampfort, & Stubbs, 2016). Concerning educational psychology, this might involve a reflection on variations in data graph literacy in potential clients, interventions to raise these capabilities, and acquiring data graphing skills to communicate scientific results. According to Pittenger (1995), a first step might be to raise attention toward data graph usage in the teaching materials. Graphing techniques are an essential component of data analysis, as they can help to discover unexpected results, plan appropriate further analyses, and summarize results of research.

Communication between specialists and management is one domain where data graph design based on psychological research can be applied in organizations and industry. This might, for instance, involve work on comprehensible labeling of graphs (Huestegge & Philipp, 2011), usage of Gestalt principles to avoid errors in reading information from three-variable graphs (Ali & Peebles, 2013), or the impact of motivation involving economic or political factors on information sampling from graphs (i.e., Luo & Zhao, 2019). Furthermore, the organizational and industrial perspective involves safety issues related to expectation and perception. For instance, Lawton and Ward (2005) have documented that high-speed train drivers need to keep expectations active about when and where to decode which specific signal. Under adverse light conditions or in bends, an eyeblink alone would be sufficient to miss the status of an important signal. In an analysis of over 100 Australian railway accidents, Edkins and Pollock (1997) identified that expectation of a green signal was a common cause for drivers going through a red signal. From the perspective of the literature on errors in human-machine interaction, Dekker (2002) underlined the demand for studies that investigated how and why people use shortcut strategies that spare effort at the expense of overlooking critical displays or signals (cf. Gaschler, Marewski, & Frensch, 2015). Using examples from operating trains and aircrafts, Dekker (2002) stated that a warning light does not solve a human error problem but rather creates a new one as it might be safely ignored in some but not in other situations as operators might state "It lit up yesterday and meant nothing" and ask "Why care today?" Given that warning lights have to be tested occasionally to secure that they work when needed, it seems hardly possible to design security systems such that warning signs never operate when no real threat is likely. Probe-based vaccination preventing shortcuts (Gaschler & Frensch, 2009) and boosting surveillance performance by expectations (Gaschler, Schwager, Umbach, Frensch, & Schubert, 2014) can be applied. The question how expert knowledge drives perception can be discussed based on work on how expert radiologists visually inspect scans for anomalies (Bilalić, Grottenthaler, Nägele, & Lindig, 2016).

The control of room temperature is one literally "hot topic" where psychology teaching can have a strong economic and ecological impact in organizations and industry. Cooling and heating houses has a large share in energy consumption, and climate change might lead to further demands. So far comfortable room temperature in business and public buildings is often controlled based on psychological studies and rating scales that fail to take into account local and seasonal specifics (cf. Schweiker et al., 2017) and the potential to reduce cooling or heating by granting workers the opportunity to apply fans or other temperature regulation on their own demand when needed (cf. Luo et al., 2016). Schweiker, Huebner, Kingma, Kramer, and Pallubinsky (2018) suggest that understanding individual differences in human thermal perception is important, due to climate change and an ageing society. Training future psychologists to design and administer better scales for measuring and controlling thermal comfort can have a substantial economic and ecologic impact.

Lunt et al. (2014) state that psychological education should build up the competences that future psychologists need to address the needs of individuals, groups, and systems. Future psychologists should be trained with generic functions and tasks that can be mapped to contents from the domain of sensation and perception (Table 2).

Core Contents and Topics of Sensation and Perception

Serial Teaching of Nonserial Processing

It is difficult to provide basic knowledge about sensation and perception in an ordered manner while avoiding students to erroneously conclude that perception takes place in a step-like sequential way. Riener (2019) discusses these didactical difficulties and reports that most introductory psychology textbooks only poorly take them into account. Instead they simply describe the process of visual perception as a clear series of orderly and insulated steps carried out by a visual system composed of the eyes and the brain. For example, light reflects off surfaces and objects in the world. Structures in the eyes filter and focus the reflected light. The photoreceptors on the retina transform the light into neural firing rates. A series of brain areas process the pattern of neural activity emerging from the retina. After drawing this picture of sequential processing, Riener (2019) makes clear that it is wrong but potentially can serve as a useful first step in understanding how perception works. In line with work in computer vision (cf. Feng, Jiang, Yang, Duc, & Li, 2019), work in psychology and cognitive neuroscience shows that information processing does not wait for one potential stage being completed to start processing on the next potential stage. Riener (2019) furthermore lists examples of embodied perception studies suggesting that processing in the perceptual system is influenced by expectations, goals, and bodily states of the organism. For instance, objects appear closer when holding a tool that would enable the observer to reach it – but only when the observer intends to use that tool (Witt, Proffitt, & Epstein, 2005). In line with classic new look studies (Bruner & Goodman, 1947; Bruner & Postman, 1949), bodily states and resources have been found to influence conscious percepts. Hills appear steeper to people who are fatigued or carry a heavy backpack (cf. Proffitt, 2006; Proffitt, Bhalla, Gossweiler, & Midgett, 1995). Such experimentally induced biases are found in conscious perception, but not in the visual processing stream informing psychomotor adjustment. Perception informs decisions. We perceive the hill as too steep to take the risk trying to climb it, when we are not well prepared. Yet, when we would actually try, we would not stumble: our vision would grant our motor system with unbiased angle estimates. This illustrates the differentiation of vision for perception versus vision for action (Westwood & Goodale, 2011).

Riener (2019) highlights that the question "How can researchers measure what you see and not just what you *say* you see?" should be repeatedly posed in class to foster linking methodology in perception research to questions of high theoretical

Table 2 Generic tasks of psychologists (Lunt et al., 2014) and examples from sensation and perception

| Generic task (Lunt et al.) | Examples | | |
	Watch out for cyclists	*Consumer warnings*	*Optimize accuracy scanning of hand luggage*
Goal specification, goal setting for the intervention or service to be provided	Help avoid traffic accidents involving cyclists	Consumers should be aware that product is dangerous when taking (non)buying decision	Train staff to guard against pitfalls in visual search
Psychological assessment at the individual, group, and organizational level	Observational study with individual drivers and groups (i.e., truckers). Check information and hardware provided by organization (i.e., logistics firm) to individuals	Rate of involuntary fixations on different variants of warning signs. Evaluate which signs have high mean and low interindividual variability. Evaluate mixing procedure to avoid habituation	Measure to what extent low target rate or prior encounter of a different relevant item leads to search misses in the individual. Compare groups potentially differing in quality culture. Check training and information provided by organization
Development of services to be provided	Identify locations in town with high risk of blind-angle accidents	Eyetracking study to measure effectiveness of different warning signs to catch attention	Develop training program involving information on factors compromising search accuracy and strategies to acquire and maintain high levels of performance
Psychological intervention or service/product implementation	Raise level of expectations that cyclists are encountered: Posts, (social) media campaign, collaborate with local initiatives. Raise level of knowledge in cyclists about blind angle	Optimize drawing from set of effective warning signs across product items to avoid habituation	Training with staff and training multipliers
Evaluation to draw conclusion on the effectiveness of the interventions	Knowledge about blind angle and number of cyclists in town pre-post. Higher rate of precaution in observational study pre-post.	Panel study to track amount of processing of warning signs over the years	Pre-post comparison of knowledge about facts about visual search as well as about training strategies
Literature	Koustanaï, Boloix, Van Elslande, & Bastien, 2008	Chéron, 2015; Gaschler, Mata, Störmer, Kühnel, & Bilalic, 2010	Krüger & Suchan, 2016; Mitroff & Biggs, 2014

and practical relevance. For instance, Firestone and Scholl (2016) argued that proposed top-down influences on perception are effects not on perception itself but on responses or judgments, or on the input to perception, rather than on the early perceptual process. Such debates can be relevant for future practicing psychologists. They might, for instance, deal with the question whether reports of disturbing infrasound from wind energy farms are due to expectations or would occur irrespective of expectations (Crichton, Dodd, Schmid, Gamble, & Petrie, 2014). As automatization can leave boring checking tasks for humans, human-machine interaction studies deal with the problem of disentangling whether people have (a) gradually come to ignore an aspect of a to-be-checked display without knowing that they no longer check as instructed or (b) knowingly started to ignore the display as it for a long time did not show relevant information (cf. Gaschler et al., 2015).

The influence of prior information on the perceptual processes working on elements (i.e., top-down influence) is further illustrated by studies on scene perception. Humans can within very short time (and before identifying objects) process the gist of a scene (Brady, Shafer-Skelton, & Alvarez, 2017) based on basic textural information. A scene with lots of small edges might be a furnished living room. A scene with a long, horizontal edge and few small ones might be a beach. Early scene identification in turn determines whether (non)fitting objects are identified (cf. Biederman, 1972; Palmer, 1975).

Gestalt Psychology Fog Free and Objective

Gestalt psychology has provided many examples illustrating top-down influences in perception, demonstrating that the whole is something different than the sum of the elements and that the identification of the elements is determined by processing of the global level. Different from many other mechanisms that are covered in teaching psychology, perceptual grouping can be made directly apparent to students by example stimuli. For example, grouping by proximity predicts that when for the first time looking at the night sky of the other hemisphere, we are the more likely to perceive stars as belonging together in a constellation the closer they are to each other in perceived distance (Kubovy & van den Berg, 2006). Classic Gestalt papers (cf. Koffka, 1922; Wertheimer, 1938) involve pictures in which the overall form (rather than the elements) determines what we perceive. Examples we have repeatedly used to trigger discussions on the strength of form perception relative to the strength of the influence of learning in perception are Figs. 35 and 36 in Wertheimer (1938): when showing a "W" directly mounted on an "M," most observers in class report that they see an ornamental form. With a void between the "W" and the "M," it is obvious that letters are being shown. The demonstration suggests that billions of prior encounters with "W" and "M" cannot compete with grouping. We rather see a novel ornamental form than the letters we are highly experienced with.

In classic Gestalt papers and textbook examples, readers see the picture, engage in metacognition on what they consciously perceive, map it to the argument in the paper, and then often agree with it. Effects are often very large such that data collection, aggregation, and reporting do not seem to be necessary. Kubovy and van den Berg (2008) report that Gestalt phenomena are illustrated in psychology textbooks, because they are striking examples of psychological emergent properties – properties that a whole does not share with its parts. The Gestalt psychologists were the first to study these phenomena empirically. Kubovy and van den Berg (2008) suggest that their thinking has the reputation of being vague and wooly. Before they counter this evaluation, they cite Marr (1982) as a proponent of such a negative view of Gestalt psychology. Laying the ground for a computational analysis of the processes involved in vision, Marr (1982) distanced himself from the qualitative, post hoc, and highly subjective accounts of perceptual phenomena he attributed to Gestalt psychology. While his criticism might in part hold for the Gestalt psychologists of the early twentieth century, modern work has ruled it out by transferring older theorizing in a framework of mathematical modeling and clear-cut empirical operationalization (cf. Kubovy & van den Berg, 2008). The latter authors claim that it is possible to work "fog free and objective" (p. 131) when measuring Gestalt principles. They used lattices of dots as stimuli which grant high experimental control and allow for high numbers of measurements per observer. In particular, they operationalized grouping by proximity (the closer the dots are together, the more likely they are seen as connected) and grouping by similarity (the closer the luminance of the dots is on the scale, the more likely they are seen as connected) with this class of well-defined stimuli. Results showed that the probability of grouping scales very regularly with the amount of pixels dots is shifted together in space or in terms of luminance values. The highly regular relationship between similarity and probability of seeing dots as connected is apparent on the level of individual observers (and therefore also on the aggregate level). In our own teaching, we have used the dot lattice stimuli of Kubovy and van den Berg (2008) in a master course successfully. Students came to appreciate that the term "law" (Halvor Teigen, 2002) might be suitable with respect to Gestalt principles when discussing the minuscule deviation of their grouping data from the regression line. In fact, some students found it difficult to understand why a regression line should be computed, as in their view, the line was already there (in form of the arrangement of the highly ordered arrangement of the data points).

While the above paragraphs provide some possible lines of discussion and differentiation that can be helpful to order and link topics in teaching sensation and perception, Table 3 lists suggestions for a possible syllabus.

Teaching, Learning, and Assessment in Sensation and Perception: Approaches and Strategies

The Touch Metaphor for Vision

Material on vision dominates teaching of sensation and perception (cf. Prull & Banks, 2005). Yet, separating teaching on vision from the teaching concerning other senses might, as a side effect, help to sustain wrong lay-theories about

Table 3 Suggestions for a syllabus on sensation and perception

Unit	Content
Introduction	(1) Perception in science studies and ecologic and economic problems: other scientific disciplines and practical questions need input from psychology (2) Evolutionary development and functional value of sensation and perception (cf. Braitenberg, 1984) (3) Categorization problem: how and why do we categorize the chair in front of us as a chair? Resources for the introduction and other parts can be found in textbooks such as Goldstein (2013)
Physiological principles in receptors	(1) How are neural firing patterns generated in receptors in vision, hearing, touch, and smell? (2) Active sampling of information: Eye movements and eye tracking
Psychophysical methods	How does physical intensity map to psychological intensity? Implications for the intensity-range receptors can cover
Processing of sensory information in specialized brain areas	(1) Visual cortices: Organization in columns (including ontogenetic development), retinotopic coding, and binding problem (2) Perception of configurations (fusiform face area, prosopagnosia) (3) Streams of visual processing: Vision for object identification vs. vision for action, visuomotor coordination despite cortical blindness
Failures show strength of perceptual system	Visual and auditory illusions: Differences between lay-concepts of perception and characteristics demonstrated in illusions. Relevance for practical psychology (e.g., design of data graphs). Modularity of processing discussed based on illusions that are resistant to knowledge
Scene and element	(1) Gestalt principles of grouping by proximity and grouping by similarity (2) Features used in scene perception and influence of scene perception on identification of elements
Perception for action	(1) Observing and taking actions: Which information is used in sports (e.g., catching a ball), running, driving? (2) Influence of bodily and motivational states on perception
Art, grocery, and consumer electronics	(1) Which characteristics are relevant for esthetics (cf. Menninghaus et al., 2019)? (2) Which aspects of sensation and perception are relevant when designing and marketing consumer products?
Attention	(1) Visual search: pop-out search (one feature) vs. serial search (feature conjunction) (see, e.g., Thornton & Gilden, 2007). Discuss factors threatening success in real-life settings such as luggage scanning (cf. Mitroff & Biggs, 2014) (2) Spotlight metaphor vs. filter metaphor (cf. Fernandez-Duque & Johnson, 1999); "cause" theories, in which attention is presumed to modulate information processing

(continued)

Table 3 (continued)

Unit	Content
	(e.g., attention as a spotlight; attention as a limited resource); (b) "effect" theories, in which attention is considered to be a by-product of information processing (e.g., the competition metaphor) (see Fernandez-Duque and Johnson (2002)) (3) Predictive coding principle (e.g., Bubic, Cramon, & Schubotz, 2010; Clark, 2013): the brain as constantly operating prediction machinery. We process events in terms of how they deviate from our predictions
Expertise in perception	What are expert skills in perception, and how are they acquired? The unit should involve examples such as radiological expertise (cf. Bilalić et al., 2016) or the state of research on hand luggage scanning (cf. Krüger & Suchan, 2016)
Perception in human-machine interaction	Usability principles for user interfaces. Pitfalls of automatization. Testing and training attention and perceptual processing in the work place
Multimedia	How should multimedia material be designed to support knowledge acquisition by scaffolding perception and attention (cf. Mayer, 2014)? How do people integrate text and picture information? What do we know from psychological experiments about how data graphs should be designed and which graph format suits which communication purpose?
Diversity and perception	Cultural diversity (c.f., Kitayama, 2003; Luria, 1976), age effects (cf. Lautenbacher et al., 2017), and perception in clinical settings (Glashouwer et al., 2019; Thompson et al., 2016)
Speech perception	(1) Characteristics of human and computer-based speech perception (2) Training programs for developmental difficulties
Environmental psychology	Perception of built environments; recreational value of environments; psychophysics and evaluative components of noise (i.e., airport close to primary school, wind park noise); thermal comfort in working environments (for an overview of environmental psychology, see Steg & de Groot, 2019)

visual perception (cf. O'Regan, 2011). O'Regan in turn suggested to use a touch metaphor to correct misbeliefs about vision: w access details of visual scenes similar to exploring an invisible object (e.g., a harmonica) in a bag. Density of receptors on the retina differs and so does the density of receptors on the skin (e. g., fingertip vs. back of the hand). We actively sample from different locations from the visual scene (by fixating different parts) just as we explore an object by moving our hand on it. An object can be identified by using the fingertips or the palm or a pencil as point of contact. While the firing of the pressure-sensitive receptors differs strongly, there is commonality in the dynamics of changes in firing when moving across the object. Similarly, the physical characteristics of the light reflected from a "red" apple change dramatically under different lighting conditions and when projected on different parts of the retina. We perceive an object as red, because it features the changes characteristic for red when seen under different conditions.

Change Blindness

The touch metaphor for vision is useful to explain why we are wrong when assuming that vision grants us with a highly detailed representation of the world around us. Rather, we can access details of different parts of the visual environment similarly to exploring a part of an object in detail with our hands. O'Regan suggests that change blindness demonstrations are effective in conveying that we only sample detailed information from one part of the visual environment at a time: we do not realize if parts are changed at other locations. Change blindness demonstrations come in different variants. These variants have in common that observers witness that a change which seems large and obvious to people who know about it remains undetected for a long time for a large part of the audience not informed about what is changing. Take as an example the lab counter change blindness situation (there are many variants on YouTube) which we have also tried with our students with visitors of a public science event: a student waiting behind the counter welcomes the visitor approaching the entry of the lab and asks for a second to get a form sheet from beneath the counter. The student ducks. A different student (who had been waiting behind the counter) rises instead and hands over the form sheet. The visitor is led into the lab and can work on the sheet asking if anything unusual had been noticed. Only a minority reports anything related to the trick. Yet, when visitors are than granted the opportunity to witness the procedure from an angle that allows them to see the approaching visitors *and* the gymnastics taking place behind the counter, many find it very surprising that the change in person attending the visitor go unnoticed.

The flicker paradigm is the technically most simple variant to set up a change blindness demo. Students need a photograph (e.g., a scene from the campus). In a copied variant of the file, a part is being removed or exchanged. For instance, two houses in the background might flip positions between the original and the edited copy. Now the two variants of the picture are being displayed in alternation with a 100 ms blank screen between the original and edited copy. The blank screen is needed to avoid that attention is directed to the changed parts automatically. Students can show their variant to the class and have peers raise their hand as soon as they have found out what is constantly changing back and forth in the picture. Own teaching suggests that this activity is helpful in conveying the sampling character of vision. Students are astonished by that some peers are much faster than others to detect the change (because they by chance happened to fixate the part of the picture that was changing). Also, once detected, it is hard to believe that such a large change was so hard to detect for most of the audience. In one variant, the authors combined the flicker paradigm with eye tracking (see also Hollingworth, Schrock, & Henderson, 2001). One student was trying to find the changing part in the campus picture, while the audience could watch a projection containing the stimulus together with the location her eyes were fixating. This allowed the audience to track live that change detection was depending on (by chance) fixating the position of the change when it occurred.

Transfer Tasks

Didactic pairing of topics (such as touch and vision) and usage of student-run live demonstrations should be complemented by other tasks handed out to the students. Kreiner (2009) suggested to have students work on open tasks or problems to acquire knowledge about sensation and perception as well as skills to apply this knowledge. Psychophysics might be taught via a task to make recommendations on formulating and packaging a sports beverage. Knowledge about attention in the visual system as well as sensitivity to contrast, moving objects, and color information in different light conditions might be acquired in a task to make recommendations on lighting for nighttime road construction. Work on color perception might be triggered by a task to recommend colors for emergency vehicles to maximize detection. Development of recommendations on configuring emergency vehicle sirens might be used to motivate dealing with auditory perception. Students might practice to communicate knowledge in a supportive way by working on the task to develop a presentation for a senior center on the topic of presbyacusis. An introduction to neural pathways of visual processing might be given by asking for the development of a series of neuropsychological questions and tests to identify a person's visual perception problems. Awareness to the power of speech perception might be raised by a task to explain why artificial speech recognition systems might not be as good as human speech recognition. An overview of cutaneous senses can be reached by handing out the task to identify consequences for the loss of various cutaneous senses. Finally, knowledge about chemical senses can be acquired by having students compile a list of concepts that could be included in a lesson on taste perception for professional chefs.

Challenges and Lessons Learned

Teaching sensation and perception involves dealing with abundant resources and challenges (Prull & Banks, 2005). For example, sensation and perception chapters are among the most lengthy (Griggs, Jackson, Christopher, & Marek, 1999) and contain the highest number of psychological terms and concepts (Landrum, 1993). Nonetheless, chapters on sensation and perception in full-length introductory textbooks decreased from the 1980s (10%) to the 1990s (9%) and 2000s (7%) as other topics were increasingly covered (cf. Griggs, 2014). Yet in brief introductory textbooks, the percentage of text devoted to topics related to sensation and perception has not changed (9%, 8%, 8%, in the same decades).

Most of the published teaching recipes relevant to sensation and perception (see Table 5) come with only a very coarse evaluation (if any). When explaining to our students how psychology with evidence-based practice can help to meet societal challenges and pursue individual goals, we should take this as a reminder that evidence-based practice should also be a guiding principle for our teaching and efforts to obtain more thorough evaluations need to be intensified.

One aspect of aligning content and practice of teaching might be the use of data graphs. Peden and Hausmann (2000) suggest that there is a lack of work on how to teach students to make and interpret data graphs. They report that the journals on psychology didactics lack such work and that the variety, number, and quality of data graphs in textbooks can be improved. According to Butler (1993), the number of pages with data graphs in introductory psychology textbooks has not increased from the 1940s to the 1990s, while it increased in psychology research journals. Data graph literacy of future psychologists should be fostered more rigorously.

Current textbooks (e.g., Goldstein, 2013) and the material presented in this chapter suggest that there is a multitude of issues to be covered with a large array of demonstrations and tools at hand. Sensation and perception relate to profound theoretical questions in psychology and to many relevant fields of application. Given that course time is limited, the largest problem might be to select among the topics and materials. Yet, this problem might be eased somewhat as sensation and perception overlap with other domains such as consciousness, memory, cognition, cognitive neuroscience, and engineering psychology, which are treated in other chapters of this book. Sensation and perception can be taught in units that are explicitly dedicated to this topic as well as in units that are closely linked.

Teaching, Learning, and Assessment Resources

Online resources for teaching sensation and perception are developing at high rate. This short list of recommendations (Table 4) contains those of the sites we find inspiring and useful that have been maintained technically and with respect to content over the last years.

There are many recipes for teaching specific aspects of sensation and perception in the literature. In Table 5, we provide an overview of some published recipes sorted by sense and author.

Table 4 Online resources for teaching sensation and perception

Resource	Source
Collection of over 100 optical phenomena and visual illusions (including short discussions and suggestions for further reading)	https://michaelbach.de/ot/
Demonstrations (and texts) on psychophysics, receptive fields, perception of color, form, depth, and motion	http://elvers.us/perception/
Collection of demonstrations of auditory phenomenal grouping	http://faculty.virginia.edu/kubovylab/demo.php
Some of the classic gestalt texts showing examples and providing arguments for why and how emergence should be tackled	https://psychclassics.yorku.ca/topic.htm#gestalt
Collection of sound and image stimuli for creating own experiments	https://www.cmu.edu/dietrich/psychology/tarrlab/stimuli/index.html
Biological motion (e.g., walking person based on moving white dots)	https://www.biomotionlab.ca/demos/
Online and lab experiments and demos based on JavaScript	https://lab.js.org/
Library for web-based dynamic data graphs	https://d3js.org/
Collection of examples of interactive visualizations (and information on how to build them)	https://shiny.rstudio.com/gallery/
Free and open-source digital audio editor and recording application software for different platforms	https://www.audacityteam.org/
Free and open-source raster graphics editor for different platforms	https://www.gimp.org/
Free computer software package for speech analysis and synthesis in phonetics for different platforms	https://www.praat.org

Table 5 Recipes for presenting specific aspects of sensation and perception

Source	Keyword	Do/show what?	Convey what?
Auditory			
Barsz (1990)	Coding by position in basilar membrane	Have students observe where the travelling wave peaks that is generated by shaking a rope tied to a doorknob at low vs. high frequency	Lower frequencies lead to longer distance covered by travelling wave before peak coding of pitch by position in basilar membrane at which wave peaks
Grosofsky (1996)	Making use of audio software (e.g., audacity) to show wave patterns	Record the sentence "what are you wearing to that party?," and display the wave pattern. Students should try to parse the sentence based on the visual display	Speech stream is continuous, and pronunciation is variable among speakers

(continued)

Table 5 (continued)

Source	Keyword	Do/show what?	Convey what?
		Generate pure tones of different wavelength and amplitude	Show that wavelength maps to pitch and amplitude maps to loudness
		Have students try to record more vs. less pure tones by using their voice (or tools such as tuning fork), and have them order the records based on the display	Show mixing of wavelengths
		Record different sounds, and have them classify as noise or music based on the visual display	Discuss about variant and level of structuredness being evaluated positively
Larsen and Fritsch (1998)	Missing fundamental	We "hear" the fundamental (e.g., a 110 Hz tone) if a series of overtones (e.g., 220 Hz, 330 Hz; 440 Hz, 550 Hz, 660 Hz) is being played, even when the fundamental is not actually being played. With a whistle that can produce one or two sounds, one sound is heard when one is played, but three are heard when two are played (the third being the Hz difference of the two sounds played)	Pitch perception fills in the fundamental. Small loudspeakers that cannot play low frequencies can give the impression of a low tone by playing the overtones
Haptic			
O'Dell and Hoyert (2002)	Cookie cutter shapes at the fingertip	Try to infer which cookie cutter shape was actively touched (e.g., explored by moving palm and fingers) vs. encountered in passive touch (gently pressed into palm)	Differentiate active and passive touch: While active touch offers astonishing amounts of information, passive touch leaves us guessing. Learn about research methodology (blinding, multiple trials, chance baseline, confounds in earlier research papers on this topic)
Haptic + visual			
Horner and Robinson (1997)	Size-weight illusion	Lifting two objects of equal weight, the larger is perceived as lighter than the smaller. When large vs. small cans (filled with stones) are lifted with strings, haptic information	Driven by vision or haptics, a larger object automatically leads to different expectations and initial force than a smaller one

(continued)

Table 5 (continued)

Source	Keyword	Do/show what?	Convey what?
		is identical. When lifted directly, haptic information differs. Blindfolding and lifting with strings should quit the illusion	
Ideomotor			
Lawson and Crane (2014)	Dowsing rods	Have students move rods over covered cup with/ without water. Vary whether students have correct/incorrect beliefs with respect to the location of the cup filled with water	Discuss how the ideomotor principle leads people to believe that they unconsciously can sense water, etc.: The observer is involuntarily producing the movements
Olfactory			
Mason (1981)	Smell butyl and propyl acetate	Have students assign numerical values to strength of smell in sensitive, adapted, or cross-adapted state to later normalize these values	Introduce psychophysical method of magnitude estimation with an odorant as well as adaptation and cross-adaptation
Taste			
Fantino (1981)	Blind tasting	Have students taste different food such as apple, pear, potato, or onion when (1) blindfolded and deprived of smell or (2) artificially colored	Show cue integration in food tasting: Show low differentiation of food if smell is blocked. Show impact of visual cues (i.e., color)
Touch			
Nazzaro (1981)	Cutaneous two-point thresholds	Students touch different areas (i.e., palm, biceps) with caliper varying the distance of the two points of touch and report whether they feel one vs. two points of contact	Demonstrate that different parts of the skin have different densities of pressure receptors
Visual			
Beins (1983)	Color additivity	Arrange picture on monitor by mixing patches of red, green, and blue, shown to students at different viewing distances	Show white light as being combined of color light sources
Corey and Tatz (1990)	Müller-Lyer illusion	Have students estimate the length of a line ended by inward- vs. outward-pointing arrows. For an interactive slider arrangement, see https://	Shapes on arrows resemble depth cues found in many environments. The Müller-Lyer illusion leads to a surprisingly strong effect and does not change when one knows about the

(continued)

Table 5 (continued)

Source	Keyword	Do/show what?	Convey what?
		michaelbach.de/ot/sze-muelue/index.html	illusion. It can serve as a starting point to discuss modularity of information processing
Cushman (1981)	Distribution of blue-sensitive receptors	Small and dim flashing blue light will disappear when directly looking at it, but not when looking a few degrees to the side of the source	Color receptors are not uniformly distributed across the retina. Blue might not be a good choice to display small details. Blue-sensitive receptors have maximum density at the border of the fovea and decrease toward center
Duda (1981)	Blind spot	Print X (left) and Y (right) at 10 cm distance to make Y disappear and reappear when slowly approaching from arm-length distance while fixating the X with the right eye and keeping the left closed	There are no photoreceptors at the part of the retina, where nerve fibers from different parts of retina collect to form the optic nerve
Kunkel (1993)	Moon illusion: Introduce estimation procedure	Make students mentally select an object that would cover the moon when held at arm's length	Introduction to a simple but psychometrically sound estimation procedure. Size is overestimated and especially so when closed to the horizon. Different bases for illusion can be discussed. Factual knowledge can be acquired: Moon covers one degree of the night sky irrespective of altitude or time of year and can be occluded by a pea held at arm,s length
LaVoie (1987)	Emmert's law	Have students look at a unicolor shape of high luminance to then look at the plain wall. Depending on distance to the wall, the perceived size of the afterimage will vary	Computation of size combines size of object on the retina with context cues. Retinal images of the same size will appear of different size depending on distance to the wall
Neuhoff (2000)	Apparent motion and conjunction – Presentation software is sufficient	Apparent motion: (1) sequence of pictures showing object at successive positions is interpreted as if the object was moving (2) when a picture with	Phi phenomenon (Wertheimer, 1912): visual system automatically interprets movement. Binding problem: different features of visual objects are processed by different

(continued)

Table 5 (continued)

Source	Keyword	Do/show what?	Convey what?
		objects A and B is replaced by a picture with object A, viewers interpret that A occludes B (3) sequence of pictures with an object being shown left and right of a void is interpreted as movement illusory conjunctions: Briefly show three large letters in three different colors. Students will reliably be able to report the letters and the colors but fail to report which colors came with which letters	brain structures in the visual system; binding might work via coupling of neuronal firing frequencies (i.e., same frequency for those that belong together)
Prull and Banks (2005)	Classroom-sized pinhole camera	Show inverted projection of scene outside of the classroom clear and dim (small pupil) or blurry and bright (large pupil). Apply lens at optimal distance vs. simulating nearsightedness vs. farsightedness	Upside-down projection in mammalian eye. Tradeoff between image brightness and clarity of a large vs. small pupil shows role of the lens
Solomon (1980)	Magical illusions	(1) Basic vanishes: Movement of objects between hands suggests that object is being passed while it is not. Can be acquired by faculty or students within hours of training	We see what we expect to see. Starting point for discussing the role of experience in perception. Past experience with dynamics of objects determines perception. Predictive coding account (e.g., Clark, 2013)
		(2) After seeing a ball being thrown up in the air several times, the same movement will result in the illusion of a ball being thrown up to never return (if the ball is instead dropped)	See above
		(3) Auditory illusion of multiple coins vanish: The illusion that coins are (invisibly) still in the hand they apparently have been passed to is strengthened by shaking the coins in the hand. Observers don't notice that the sound comes from the other hand	Make transparent the acuity in localization of sound

(continued)

Table 5 (continued)

Source	Keyword	Do/show what?	Convey what?
		(4) Oversized playing cards with pips partially being occluded by hands, turning cards over creates impression of pips being added	Observers "see" the full pattern of pips; what is missing is being filled in automatically, when occluded by hands. Gestalt principle of good figure/figure completion
		(5) Use sleight of hand techniques to produce very unlikely events with cards (i.e., selecting four aces apparently at random from a deck of cards)	There is automatic processing of likeliness. Get students to discuss when they accept that something has occurred due to chance. Discuss type I and type II errors in null hypothesis testing

Cross-References

▶ Neuroscience in the Psychology Curriculum
▶ Teaching Engineering Psychology
▶ Teaching Introductory Psychology

References

Ali, N., & Peebles, D. (2013). The effect of gestalt laws of perceptual organization on the comprehension of three-variable bar and line graphs. *Human Factors: The Journal of the Human Factors and Ergonomics Society, 55*(1), 183–203. https://doi.org/10.1177/0018720812452592.

American Psychological Association. (2013). *APA guidelines for the undergraduate psychology major*: Version 2.0. Retrieved from http://www.apa.org/ed/precollege/undergrad/index.aspx

American Psychological Association, Task Force on Guidelines for Master's Programs in Psychology. (2018). *APA guidelines on core learning goals for master's degree graduates in psychology*. Retrieved from https://www.apa.org/ed/precollege/about/psymajor-guidelines.pdf

Barsz, K. (1990). Auditory sensory processes: The travelling wave on the basilar membrane. In V. Parker Makosky, C. C. Sileo, & L. G. Whittemore (Eds.), *Activities handbook for the teaching of psychology* (Vol. 3, pp. 70–71). Washington, DC: American Psychological Association.

Beins, B. C. (1983). The light box: A simple way of generating complex color demonstrations. *Teaching of Psychology, 10*, 113–114.

Biederman, I. (1972). Perceiving real-world scenes. *Science, 177*, 77–80. https://doi.org/10.1126/science.177.4043.77.

Bilalić, M., Grottenthaler, T., Nägele, T., & Lindig, T. (2016). The faces in radiological images: Fusiform face area supports radiological expertise. *Cerebral Cortex, 26*(3), 1004–1014. https://doi.org/10.1093/cercor/bhu272.

Brady, T. F., Shafer-Skelton, A., & Alvarez, G. A. (2017). Global ensemble texture representations are critical to rapid scene perception. *Journal of Experimental Psychology: Human Perception and Performance, 43*, 1160–1176. https://doi.org/10.1037/xhp0000399.

Braitenberg, V. (1984). *Vehicles: Experiments in synthetic psychology*. Cambridge, MA: MIT Press.

Brewer, F. W. (2012). The theory ladenness of the mental processes used in the scientific enterprise. In R. W. Proctor & J. E. Capaldi (Eds.), *Psychology of science: Implicit and explicit processes* (pp. 290–233). New York, NY: Oxford University Press.

Bruner, J. S. & Goodman, C. C. (1947). Value and need as organizing factors in perception. Journal of Abnormal and Social Psychology, 42, 33–44. https://doi.org/10.1037/h0058484. Online: https://psychclassics.yorku.ca/Bruner/Value/

Bruner, J. S. & Postman, L. (1949). On the perception of incongruity: A paradigm. Journal of Personality, 18, 206–223. https://doi.org/10.1111/j.1467-6494.1949.tb01241.x. Online: https://psychclassics.yorku.ca/Bruner/Cards/

Bubic, A., von Cramon, D. Y. & Schubotz, R. I. (2010) Prediction, cognition and the brain. Frontiers in Human Neuroscience, 4: e25. https://doi.org/10.3389/fnhum.2010.00025.

Butler, D. L. (1993). Graphics in psychology: Pictures, data, and especially concepts. *Behavior Research Methods, Instruments, & Computers, 25*, 81–92. https://doi.org/10.3758/BF03204481.

Chéron, E. (2015). Effect of graphic images in cigarette health warning: A call for stricter packaging regulation in Japan. *Journal of International Consumer Marketing, 27*(2), 137–151. https://doi.org/10.1080/08961530.2014.979306.

Clark, A. (2013). Whatever next? Predictive brains, situated agents, and the future of cognitive science. *Behavioral and Brain Sciences, 36*, 181–204. https://doi.org/10.1017/S0140525X12000477.

Corey, J. R., & Tatz, S. J. (1990). Classroom measurement of visual illusions. In V. Parker Makosky, C. C. Sileo, & L. G. Whittemore (Eds.), *Activities handbook for the teaching of psychology* (Vol. 3, pp. 63–65). Washington, DC: American Psychological Association.

Crichton, F., Dodd, G., Schmid, G., Gamble, G., & Petrie, K. J. (2014). Can expectations produce symptoms from infrasound associated with wind turbines? *Health Psychology, 33*(4), 360–364. https://doi.org/10.1037/a0031760.

Cushman, W. B. (1981). Blue-blindness in the central fovea. In L. T. Benjamin Jr. & K. D. Lowman (Eds.), *Activities handbook for the teaching of psychology, Volume 1* (pp. 36–37). Washington, DC: American Psychological Association.

Dekker, S. (2002). *The field guide to human error investigations*. Hampshire, UK: Ashgate.

Duda, J. J. (1981). Blind spot in vision. In L. T. Benjamin Jr. & K. D. Lowman (Eds.), *Activities handbook for the teaching of psychology, Volume 1* (pp. 43–44). Washington, DC: American Psychological Association.

Edkins, G. D., & Pollock, C. M. (1997). The influence of sustained attention on railway accidents. *Accident Analysis & Prevention, 29*, 533–539. https://doi.org/10.1016/s0001-4575(97)00033-x.

Evans, J. E., & Maunder, E. W. (1903). Experiments as to the actuality of the 'Canals' observed on Mars. *Monthly Notices of the Royal Astronomical Society, 63*, 488–499.

Fantino, B. (1981). Taste preferences: Influence of smell and sight. In L. T. Benjamin Jr. & K. D. Lowman (Eds.), *Activities handbook for the teaching of psychology, Volume 1* (pp. 29–30). Washington, DC: American Psychological Association.

Feng, X., Jiang, X., Yang, X., Duc, M., & Li, X. (2019). Computer vision algorithms and hardware implementations: A survey. *Integration, 69*, 309–320. https://doi.org/10.1016/j.vlsi.2019.07.005.

Fernandez-Duque, D., & Johnson, M. L. (1999). Attention metaphors: How metaphors guide the cognitive psychology of attention. *Cognitive Science, 23*(1), 83–116. https://doi.org/10.1016/S0364-0213(99)80053-6.

Fernandez-Duque, D., & Johnson, M. L. (2002). Cause and effect theories of attention: The role of conceptual metaphors. *Review of General Psychology, 6*(2), 153–165. https://doi.org/10.1037/1089-2680.6.2.153.

Firestone, C., & Scholl, B. J. (2016). Cognition does not affect perception: Evaluating the evidence for "top-down" effects. *Behavioral and Brain Sciences, 39*, 1–72. https://doi.org/10.1017/S0140525X15000965.

Galison, P. (1997). *Image and logic: A material culture of microphysics*. Chicago, IL: University of Chicago Press.

Gaschler, R., & Frensch, P. A. (2009). When vaccinating against information reduction works and when it does not work. *Psychological Studies, 54*, 43–53. https://doi.org/10.1007/s12646-009-0006-5.

Gaschler, R., Marewski, J. N., & Frensch, P. A. (2015). Once and for all – How people change strategy to ignore irrelevant information in visual tasks. *Quarterly Journal of Experimental Psychology, 68*, 543–567. https://doi.org/10.1080/17470218.2014.961933.

Gaschler, R., Mata, J., Störmer, V., Kühnel, A., & Bilalic, M. (2010). Change detection for new food labels. *Food Quality and Preference, 21*, 140–147. https://doi.org/10.1016/j.foodqual.2009.08.013.

Gaschler, R., Schwager, S., Umbach, V. J., Frensch, P. A., & Schubert, T. (2014). Expectation mismatch: Differences between self-generated and cue-induced expectations. *Neuroscience and Biobehavioral Reviews, 46*, 139–157. https://doi.org/10.1016/j.neubiorev.2014.06.009.

Glashouwer, K. A., van der Veer, R. M. L., Adipatria, F., & de Jong, P. J., & Vocks, S. (2019). The role of body image disturbance in the onset, maintenance, and relapse of anorexia nervosa: A systematic review. Clinical Psychology Review https://doi.org/10.1016/j.cpr.2019.101771.

Godau, C., Vogelgesang, T., & Gaschler, R. (2016). Perception of bar graphs – a biased impression? *Computers in Human Behavior, 59*, 67–73. https://doi.org/10.1016/j.chb.2016.01.036.

Goldstein, E. B. (2013). *Sensation and perception*. Wadsworth, OH, Cengage Learning.

Griggs, R. A. (2014). Topical coverage in introductory textbooks from the 1980s through the 2000s. *Teaching of Psychology, 41*(1), 5–10. https://doi.org/10.1177/0098628313514171.

Griggs, R. A., Jackson, S. L., Christopher, A. N., & Marek, P. (1999). Introductory psychology textbooks: An objective analysis and update. *Teaching of Psychology, 26*(3), 182–189. https://doi.org/10.1207/S15328023TOP260304.

Grosofsky, A. (1996). Audition laboratory activities for teaching sensation and perception. *Teaching of Psychology, 23*(1), 49–51. https://doi.org/10.1207/s15328023top2301_13.

Halvor Teigen, K. (2002). One hundred years of laws in psychology. *The American Journal of Psychology, 115*(1), 103–118. https://doi.org/10.2307/1423676.

Hollingworth, A., Schrock, G., & Henderson, J. M. (2001). Change detection in the flicker paradigm: The role of fixation position within the scene. *Memory & Cognition, 29*(2), 296–304. https://doi.org/10.3758/BF03194923.

Horner, D. T., & Robinson, K. D. (1997). Demonstrations of the size–weight illusion. *Teaching of Psychology, 24*(3), 195–197. https://doi.org/10.1207/s15328023top2403_12.

Huestegge, L., & Philipp, A. M. (2011). Effects of spatial compatibility on integration processes in graph comprehension. *Attention, Perception, & Psychophysics, 73*(6), 1903–1915. https://doi.org/10.3758/s13414-011-0155-1.

IPCC. (2014). Climate change 2014: Synthesis report. In Core Writing Team, R. K. Pachauri, & L. A. Meyer (Eds.), *Contribution of working groups I, II and III to the Fifth Assessment Report of the Intergovernmental Panel on Climate Change*. Geneva, Switzerland: IPCC. 151 pp.

Kitayama, K., Duffy, S., Tadashi, K., & Larsen, J. (2003). Perceiving an object and its context in different cultures: A cultural look at new look. *Psychological Science, 14*(3), 201–206. https://doi.org/10.1111/1467-9280.02432.

Koffka, K. (1922). Perception: An introduction to the Gestalt-theorie. *Psychological Bulletin, 19*, 531–585. https://doi.org/10.1037/h0072422. Online: https://psychclassics.yorku.ca/Koffka/Perception/perception.htm

Koustanaï, A., Boloix, E., Van Elslande, P., & Bastien, C. (2008). Statistical analysis of "looked-but-failed-to-see" accidents: Highlighting the involvement of two distinct mechanisms. *Accident Analysis and Prevention, 40*(2), 461–469. https://doi.org/10.1016/j.aap.2007.08.001.

Krüger, J. K., & Suchan, B. (2016). You should be the specialist! Weak mental rotation performance in aviation security screeners – Reduced performance level in aviation security with no gender effect. *Frontiers in Psychology, 7*, e333. https://doi.org/10.3389/fpsyg.2016.00333.

Kubovy, M., & van den Berg, M. (2006). Grouping in random-dot patterns. *Journal of Vision, 6*(6), 758–758. https://doi.org/10.1167/6.6.758.

Kubovy, M., & van den Berg, M. (2008). The whole is equal to the sum of its parts: A probabilistic model of grouping by proximity and similarity in regular patterns. *Psychological Review, 115* (1), 131–154. https://doi.org/10.1037/0033-295X.115.1.131.

Kunkel, M. A. (1993). A teaching demonstration involving perceived lunar size. *Teaching of Psychology, 20*(3), 178–180. https://doi.org/10.1207/s15328023top2003_14.

Larsen, J. D., & Fritsch, K. (1998). A valid demonstration of the missing fundamental illusion. *Teaching of Psychology, 25*(1), 29–31. https://doi.org/10.1207/s15328023top2501_8.

Lautenbacher, S., Peters, J. H., Heesen, M., Scheel, J., & Kunz, M. (2017). Age changes in pain perception: A systematic-review and meta-analysis of age effects on pain and tolerance thresholds. *Neuroscience and Biobehavioral Reviews, 75*, 104–113. https://doi.org/10.1016/j.neubiorev.2017.01.039.

LaVoie, A. L. (1987). Emmert's law. In V. Parker Makosky, L. G. Whittemore, & A. M. Rogers (Eds.), *Activities handbook for the teaching of psychology* (Vol. 2, pp. 46–48). Washington, DC: American Psychological Association.

Lawson, T. J., & Crane, L. L. (2014). Dowsing rods designed to sharpen critical thinking and understanding of ideomotor action. *Teaching of Psychology, 41*(1), 52–56. https://doi.org/10.1177/0098628313514178.

Lawton, R., & Ward, N. J. (2005). A systems analysis of the Ladbroke grove rail crash. *Accident Analysis & Prevention, 37*, 235–244. https://doi.org/10.1016/j.aap.2004.08.001.

Lewandowsky, S., Ballard, T., Oberauer, K., & Benestad, R. (2016). A blind expert test of contrarian claims about climate data. *Global Environmental Change, 39*, 91–97. https://doi.org/10.1016/j.gloenvcha.2016.04.013.

Lunt, I., Job, R., Lecuyer, R., Peiro, J. M., & Gorbena, S. (2014). *Tuning-EuroPsy: Reference points for the design and delivery of degree programmes in psychology.* Retrieved from http://www.efpa.eu/professional-development/tuning-europsy-_-tuning-educational-structures-in-europe

Luo, M., Cao, B., Ji, W., Ouyang, Q., Lin, B., & Zhu, Y. (2016). The underlying linkage between personal control and thermal comfort: Psychological or physical effects? *Energy and Buildings, 111*, 56–63. https://doi.org/10.1016/j.enbuild.2015.11.004.

Luo, Y., & Zhao, J. (2019). Motivated attention in climate change perception and action. *Frontiers in Psychology, 10*, e1541. https://doi.org/10.3389/fpsyg.2019.01541.

Luria, A. R. (1976). *The cognitive development: Its cultural and social foundations.* Harvard University Press.

Marr, D. (1982). *Vision: A computational investigation into the human representation and processing of visual information.* San Francisco, CA: Freeman.

Mason, J. R. (1981). A novel experiment for introductory psychology courses: Psychophysical assessment of olfactory adaptation. *Teaching of Psychology, 8*(2), 117–119. https://doi.org/10.1207/s15328023top0802_21.

Mayer, R. E. (2014). *The Cambridge handbook of multimedia learning.* Cambridge, UK: Cambridge University Press.

Menninghaus, W., Wagner, V., Wassiliwizky, E., Schindler, I., Hanich, J., Jacobsen, T., & Koelsch, S. (2019). What are aesthetic emotions? *Psychological Review, 126*(2), 171–195. https://doi.org/10.1037/rev0000135.

Mitroff, S. R., & Biggs, A. T. (2014). The ultra-rare-item effect: Visual search for exceedingly rare items is highly susceptible to error. *Psychological Science, 25*(1), 284–289. https://doi.org/10.1177/0956797613504221.

Nazzaro, J. R. (1981). Cutaneous two-point thresholds. In L. T. Benjamin Jr. & K. D. Lowman (Eds.), *Activities handbook for the teaching of psychology, volume 1* (pp. 31–32). Washington, DC: American Psychological Association.

Neuhoff, J. (2000). Classroom demonstrations in perception and cognition using presentation software. *Teaching of Psychology, 27*(2), 142–144. https://doi.org/10.1207/S15328023TOP2702_11.

O'Dell, C. D., & Hoyert, M. S. (2002). Active and passive touch: A research methodology project. *Teaching of Psychology, 29*(4), 292–294. https://doi.org/10.1207/S15328023TOP2904_07.

O'Regan, J. K. (2011). Why red doesn't sound like a bell: Understanding the feel of consciousness. Oxford University Press. Draft version as PDF: http://nivea.psycho.univ-paris5.fr/

Palmer, S. E. (1975). The effects of contextual scenes on the identification of objects. *Memory & Cognition, 3*, 519–526. https://doi.org/10.3758/BF03197524.

Peden, B. F., & Hausmann, S. E. (2000). Data graphs in introductory and upper level psychology textbooks: A content analysis. *Teaching of Psychology, 27*(2), 93–97. https://doi.org/10.1207/S15328023TOP2702_03.

Pittenger, D. J. (1995). Teaching students about graphs. *Teaching of Psychology, 22*(2), 125–128. https://doi.org/10.1207/s15328023top2202_9.

Proffitt, D. R. (2006). Embodied perception and the economy of action. *Perspectives on Psychological Science, 1*, 110–122. https://doi.org/10.1111/j.1745-6916.2006.00008.x.

Proffitt, D. R., Bhalla, M., Gossweiler, R., & Midgett, J. (1995). Perceiving geographical slant. *Psychonomic Bulletin & Review, 2*, 409–428. https://doi.org/10.3758/BF03210980.

Prull, M. W., & Banks, W. P. (2005). Seeing the light: A classroom-sized pinhole camera demonstration for teaching vision. *Teaching of Psychology, 32*(2), 103–106. https://doi.org/10.1207/s15328023top3202_5.

Riener, C. (2019). New approaches and debates on top-down perceptual processing. *Teaching of Psychology, 46*(3), 267–272. https://doi.org/10.1177/0098628319853943.

Schnotz, W., & Bannert, M. (2003). Construction and interference in learning from multiple representation. *Learning and Instruction, 13*(2), 141–156. https://doi.org/10.1016/S0959-4752 (02)00017-8.

Schweiker, M., Fuchs, X., Becker, S., Shukuya, M., Dovjak, M., Hawighorst, M., & Kolarik, J. (2017). Challenging the assumptions for thermal sensation scales. *Building Research and Information, 45*(5), 572–589. https://doi.org/10.1080/09613218.2016.1183185.

Schweiker, M., Huebner, G. M., Kingma, B. R. M., Kramer, R., & Pallubinsky, H. (2018). Drivers of diversity in human thermal perception – A review for holistic comfort models. *Temperature, 5*(4), 308–342. https://doi.org/10.1080/23328940.2018.1534490.

Solomon, P. R. (1980). Perception, illusion, and magic. *Teaching of Psychology, 7*(1), 3–8. https://doi.org/10.1207/s15328023top0701_1.

Steg, L., & de Groot, J. I. M. (2019). *Environmental psychology: An introduction*. Wiley-Blackwell.

Thompson, T., Correll, C. U., Gallop, K., Vancampfort, D., & Stubbs, B. (2016). Is pain perception altered in people with depression? A systematic review and meta-analysis of experimental pain research. *The Journal of Pain, 17*(12), 1257–1272. https://doi.org/10.1016/j.jpain.2016.08.007.

Thornton, T. L., & Gilden, D. L. (2007). Parallel and serial processes in visual search. *Psychological Review, 114*(1), 71–103. https://doi.org/10.1037/0033-295X.114.1.71.

VanderStoep, S. W., Fagerlin, A., & Feenstra, J. S. (2000). What do students remember from introductory psychology? *Teaching of Psychology, 27*(2), 89–92. https://doi.org/10.1207/S15328023TOP2702_02.

Wertheimer, M. (1912). Experimentelle Studien über das Sehen von Bewegung. *Zeitschrift für Psychologie, 61*, 161–265.

Wertheimer, M. (1938). Laws of organization in perceptual forms. In W. Ellis, W (Ed. & Trans.), *A source book of gestalt psychology* (pp. 71–88). London, England: Routledge & Kegan Paul. Online: https://psychclassics.yorku.ca/Wertheimer/Forms/forms.htm

Westwood, D. A., & Goodale, M. A. (2011). Converging evidence for diverging pathways: Neuropsychology and psychophysics tell the same story. *Vision Research, 51*(8), 804–811. https://doi.org/10.1016/j.visres.2010.10.014.

Witt, J. K., Proffitt, D. R., & Epstein, W. (2005). Tool use affects perceived distance, but only when you intend to use it. *Journal of Experimental Psychology: Human Perception and Performance, 31*, 880–888. https://doi.org/10.1037/0096-1523.31.5.880.

Wittkopf, P. G., Lloyd, D. M., & Johnson, M. I. (2018). The effect of visual feedback of body parts on pain perception: A systematic review of clinical and experimental studies. *European Journal of Pain, 22*(4), 647–662. https://doi.org/10.1002/ejp.1162.

Teaching the Psychology of Learning

5

Stephanie A. Jesseau

Contents

S. A. Jesseau (✉)
University of Nebraska-Omaha, Omaha, NE, USA
e-mail: sjesseau@unomaha.edu

© Springer Nature Switzerland AG 2023
J. Zumbach et al. (eds.), *International Handbook of Psychology Learning and Teaching*,
Springer International Handbooks of Education,
https://doi.org/10.1007/978-3-030-28745-0_7

Abstract

While teaching psychology is always demanding, teaching courses about the psychology of learning presents unique challenges for instructors. Learning courses have specialized language and procedures not found in other areas of psychology, students tend to enter courses with certain misconceptions, and published materials related to teaching learning can be lacking. This chapter discusses these and other challenges and potential ways to overcome them. Being aware of these pitfalls can help instructors to understand any confusion students might have or develop about the material and take actions to correct it. Also included is a brief history of learning as a field, and proposed core content and learning outcomes for learning courses. Evidence-based teaching and assessment strategies are discussed in general, along with specific examples pertaining to learning courses. A way of approaching the teaching of operant conditioning based on common student difficulties is also outlined. Lastly, some general teaching tips as well as teaching resources (some general, some specific to learning courses) are provided. Though this chapter is aimed at instructors of learning courses (or those looking for guidance in teaching the learning portion of an introductory psychology course), many of the strategies can be applied widely.

Keywords

Learning · Behaviorism · Operant conditioning · Pavlovian conditioning · Teaching strategies · Learning strategies

Introduction

The Study of Learning in Historical Context

Of all the subfields of psychology, the study of learning is certainly one of the oldest, with roots dating back to the ancient Greek philosophers. Aristotle observed that knowledge is acquired through experience, which was in opposition to his teacher Plato's view that knowledge is innate. In the seventeenth century, René Descartes incorporated both of these ideas by stating that humans are born with knowledge that becomes realized through experience. Despite the importance of these early philosophers, their ideas lacked empirical support.

More recently, other figures have significantly contributed to the field of learning including Charles Darwin, Ivan Pavlov, and B.F. Skinner. Darwin proved crucial to the study of learning and many other fields by proposing his theory of evolution by natural selection. As outlined in *The Descent of Man*, Darwin (unlike Descartes and many of his own contemporaries) felt that "there is no fundamental difference between man and the higher mammals in their mental faculties" (Darwin, 1871, p. 46). This paved the way for the use of animals in the study of memory and cognition, as well as the understanding that the ability to learn is itself an adaptation.

Pavlov observed that behavior can be elicited not only by certain stimuli directly (unconditioned stimuli), but also by other stimuli (conditioned stimuli) that have only been associated with an unconditioned stimulus. Modern psychologists continue to build on Pavlov's work, and the study of Pavlovian conditioning is certainly one of the enduring areas of psychology (Rescorla, 1988). Skinner's work focused on the prediction and control of behavior, specifically the role of reinforcers and punishers, and Skinner's behaviorism has been a dominant paradigm in psychology, particularly in the 1940s and 1950s. Skinner was not just a towering figure in the field of learning, but he was also one of the most important psychologists of the modern era. An analysis including qualitative (e.g., membership in the National Academy of Sciences and election as American Psychological Association President) and quantitative (e.g., overall citation numbers and citations in introductory textbooks) variables put Skinner at the very top of the list of the most influential psychologists of the twentieth century (Haggbloom et al., 2002), and Skinner's ideas continue to have a wide impact.

Learning Versus Cognition

The modern scientific study of learning was in some ways a reaction to the subjectivity of Sigmund Freud's psychoanalysis, Wilhelm Wundt's and Edward Titchener's introspection, and other nonempirical speculation that was taking place in psychology in the early twentieth century. To behaviorists such as Skinner and John B. Watson, what was important in the study of psychology was observable behavior (Skinner, 1974, 1977). The cognitive revolution that began in the 1950s was a reaction to the behaviorist view that the mind could not be studied empirically. As cognitive psychologists ushered in the application of scientific methods to the study of mental process such as thinking, memory, and attention, some claim that this spelled the end of behaviorism (Braat, Engelen, van Gemert, & Verhaegh, 2020; Robins, Gosling, & Craik, 1999; Watrin & Darwich, 2012), and that psychology as a whole needed to distance itself from behaviorism so that cognitive psychology could regain scientific respectability (Miller, 2003). Some even refer to the period of the dominance of behaviorism as a "behaviorist dark age," followed by a "cognitivist renaissance" (Roediger, 2004; Watrin & Darwich, 2012). Despite the rise of cognitive psychology, Skinner continued to argue that the focus of learning research should be on observable behavior, and he even called cognitive science "the creationism of psychology" in his last address to the APA in 1990 (Wasserman & Blumberg, 2006).

Textbook accounts often indicate that the cognitive perspective replaced behaviorism, and therefore students might be led to believe that the study of learning in the behaviorist tradition is outdated and unimportant in modern psychology (Abramson, 2013; Machado & Silva, 1998). Even among faculty, behaviorists are sometimes viewed as anachronistic and even "simple minded," while cognitive psychologists are seen as being on the cutting edge of science (Abramson, 2013). However, it is perhaps more accurate to consider cognitive psychology as building on the work of behaviorists rather than replacing it, and that the so-called cognitive revolution merely represented a shift rather than a revolution per se (Leahey, 1992). Citations of Skinner continued to increase throughout the period of the cognitive revolution (Thyer, 1991), as did the number of professional associations and publications related to behaviorism (Wyatt, Hawkins, & Davis, 1986). Though behaviorism is unlikely to return to the dominance it held prior to the cognitive revolution (Overskeid, 2008), research in the behaviorist tradition is very much alive today (Roediger, 2004). The tenets of behaviorism lie at the center of much of modern psychology, and any perceived decline in its dominance is simply because it is so pervasive that all psychologists doing empirical research are doing so in the behaviorist tradition (Brown & Gillard, 2015), even much of cognitive psychology (Morgan & Buskist, 1990). As one cognitive psychologist put it, "Behaviorism is alive and most of us are behaviorists" (Roediger, 2004).

Current Trends

Since the study of learning appears across many different domains of psychology, it is difficult to pinpoint a single direction in which the field is heading. Comparative cognition, functional neurology, and animal models of human behavior have been and continue to be important avenues of learning research (Domjan, 1987, 2010). One notable area where the study of learning is currently gaining prominence is in the applied disciplines of psychology such as cognitive behavior therapy and applied behavior analysis (ABA). While these approaches are perhaps best known as treatments for childhood disorders such as autism or attention deficit hyperactivity disorder (ADHD), they can be applied to a variety of targets including animal welfare, addiction, conduct disorders, workplace behavior, marriage and family problems, classroom management, eating disorders, sleep disorders, phobias, and post-traumatic stress disorder (PTSD), among others. Behaviorist concepts continue to be successfully applied to promoting animal and human welfare, which demonstrates the field's importance not just in academia but for society as well.

Purpose and Rationale for the Curriculum in Learning

According to the American Psychological Association Guidelines for the Psychology Major, there are four main content domains in psychology in the USA, including biological bases, learning and cognition, lifespan development, and sociocultural approaches (APA, 2013; see also Dunn et al., 2010). Learning is therefore considered a foundational course that gives students majoring in psychology a broad base of knowledge in the psychological sciences. In 1997, learning ranked fifth in the percentage of US institutions offering such a class (after introductory psychology, abnormal psychology, social psychology, and personality psychology among all institution types, [Perlman & McCann, 1999]). Another more recent study showed that in 2005, 80% of US institutions offered a class on learning, 24% of psychology majors completed such a class, and learning ranked eleventh on the list of most frequently offered courses (Stoloff et al., 2010). While this might indicate a slight decline over time in the popularity of the learning course, it might also simply indicate an increase in course specialization (Dunn et al., 2010). Regardless of specific enrollments, learning has been and continues to be a popular and foundational course in psychology in the USA.

Learning Objectives

Even though "learning is ideally suited to address a broad range of important issues in science in general and psychology in particular" (Machado & Silva, 1998, p. 216), students may view the study of learning as separate from other areas of psychology. As such, students should leave a learning course with an understanding of how important learning processes are to all aspects of human and animal life. In addition, there are certain learning outcomes or competencies that students should possess. By the end of the course, students should be able to:

- Understand what learning is (and is not) and articulate the differences and similarities between learning and instinct.
- Understand the evolutionary underpinnings of learning in animals, including humans.
- Understand the main types of learning (Pavlovian and operant conditioning), how they work, and their similarities and differences.
- Apply knowledge of learning processes including Pavlovian and operant conditioning to real-world scenarios.
- Understand and be able to apply research methods in the study of learning.
- Gather, compile, and interpret data related to learning processes.

Core Content and Topics of the Learning Course

As with many areas of psychology, it is impossible to cover everything that is known about learning in a single course. Learning as a concept has been studied in many disparate fields such as neuroscience, animal behavior, evolutionary biology, computer science, and educational psychology, among others. A cursory look at textbooks written for the learning course reveals titles that include many terms, such as learning, memory, cognition, evolution, adaptation, conditioning, the brain, behavior, and behavior analysis. Even the titles of learning courses themselves may cross over into other areas of psychology including learning and memory, learning and motivation, and learning and cognition (Barron et al., 2015; Stoloff et al., 2010). This diversity opens up a wide range of possibilities for the major themes presented in a psychology of learning course. Regardless of the precise content instructors might choose to include, I suggest below a way to organize content into four units, and discuss ways to present portions of the material.

- Unit 1: Introduction and Background
  - Introduction to and definitions of learning
  - Introduction to evolutionary theory, including its importance to learning

- – Research methods and experimental design, including operational definitions
- – Simple forms of learning (habituation and sensitization)
- Unit 2: Pavlovian Conditioning
  - – Introduction to Pavlovian conditioning (conditioned stimulus and response, unconditioned stimulus and response)
  - – Acquisition, extinction, and spontaneous recovery, including the Rescorla-Wagner model
  - – Variables affecting Pavlovian conditioning, including contingency and contiguity
  - – Pavlovian procedures and their effects, including latent inhibition, blocking, US pre-exposure, higher-order conditioning, sensory preconditioning, disinhibition, external inhibition, conditioned suppression, stimulus discrimination, and stimulus generalization.
  - – Contributions of John B. Watson and "Little Albert"
  - – Practical applications of Pavlovian conditioning, including counterconditioning, systematic desensitization, advertising, aversion therapy, and addiction treatment
- Unit 3: Operant Conditioning
  - – Introduction to operant conditioning (positive and negative reinforcement, positive and negative punishment)
  - – Comparisons of operant to Pavlovian conditioning
  - – Comparisons of operant conditioning to evolution by natural selection.
  - – Contributions of Thorndike and Skinner
  - – Intrinsic versus extrinsic reinforcement
  - – Contingency and contiguity in operant conditioning
  - – Reinforcer and species characteristics and their effects on reinforcement.
  - – Theories of reinforcement (drive reduction, relative value, response deprivation, and behavioral bliss point)
  - – Simple schedules of reinforcement (fixed and variable ratio, fixed and variable interval)
  - – Complex schedules of reinforcement and the matching law
  - – Noncontingent, partial, and intermittent reinforcement and their effects on behavior
  - – Shaping and chaining
  - – The problems with and variables affecting punishment
- Unit 4: Other Learning-Related Topics
  - – Operant conditioning in everyday life (e.g., in schools, hospitals, and zoos, or in interacting with other humans or animals)
  - – Using what we know about operant conditioning to improve self-control
  - – The role of learning in insight and creativity
  - – Social learning (humans and other animals)
  - – Animal cognition (deception, theory of mind)
  - – Language acquisition (humans and other animals)

Since learning is such a broad field, the last unit of the course in particular can encompass a wide variety of additional topics depending on instructor expertise, or instructor and/or student interests, including machine learning, the neurobiology of learning, behavioral economics, memory systems, applied behavior analysis, and information processing, among others (see Machado & Silva, 1998 for additional ideas on topics and approaches for learning courses). I suggest that, when possible, instructors allow students to choose among these potential topics so as to heighten student interest and to keep the course different and interesting for the instructor over time as well.

Suggestions for Introducing the Course

Definitions of Learning

The very first thing I do in my learning course is ask the students to submit online definitions of learning as they see it. I gather their answers from the campus learning management system prior to the first day of class so that we can spend part of that initial meeting discussing what learning means. Students are instructed to give their answers spontaneously and without any assistance from outside resources, and I generally get a variety of thoughtful and interesting answers with a few overlapping themes. Many students touch on the idea of change in one form or another. Some focus on the academic repercussions of learning (e.g., studying for exams or quizzes), while others mention acquiring skills (e.g., learning how to cook or ride a bike). A few, like Supreme Court Justice Potter Stewart in his definition of obscenity in 1964, claim "I know it when I see it" (as quoted in Gewirtzt, 1996). Students are often surprised at how difficult it is for them to define something as ubiquitous as learning, and many are equally surprised that even scientists who study learning utilize different definitions (Barron et al., 2015).

Indeed, many of the course textbooks used in the USA avoid defining learning entirely (Barron et al., 2015). Most of those that attempt to do so present definitions similar to the following: A relatively permanent change in behavior due to individual experience (Barron et al., 2015; Lachman, 1997). However, even a cursory examination of this definition by most people (my students included) seems lacking (see De Houwer, Barnes-Holmes, & Moors, 2013), and many students argue that learning can in fact happen in the absence of behavioral change. Having a discussion about what constitutes learning at the beginning of the course opens up a dialogue with students about the nature of science and knowing (e.g., can we know learning has happened in the absence of measurable change, and if so, how?), and demonstrates that even well-established fields still have many unanswered questions. Promoting this awareness is important because it helps students understand that the study of learning specifically and science more generally are not simply collections of facts to be memorized, but are dynamic and exciting enterprises.

Evolution by Natural Selection

After exploring definitions of learning, I next present the topic of evolution. This might not seem to be an intuitive choice, but there are several important reasons for it. First, having an understanding of evolution by natural selection helps students to see learning in a broader context (i.e., why do organisms have the capability to learn in the first place?). Second, it provides a framework in which to understand how learning takes place within the lifetime of an organism. Operant conditioning has much in common with the process of natural selection (Brown & Gillard, 2015; Donahoe, 2012). After all, "learning is the study of a major product of phylogenetic adaptation, and a major process of ontogenetic adaptation" (Machado & Silva, 1998, p. 225). Skinner has been described as the "Darwin of ontogeny" (Donahoe, 1984), and he himself made such comparisons between natural section and operant conditioning (Ghiselin, 2018). Through natural selection, individuals whose heritable traits are better suited to their environment are more likely to survive and reproduce, leading to a greater proportion of those traits in subsequent generations. The opposite is also true, with traits that are ill-suited to the environment becoming less common over time. Similarly, in operant conditioning, behaviors that are well suited to an individual due to their consequences are "selected for," and become more common in the future (reinforcement), and behaviors that are poorly suited to an individual due to their consequences become less common in the future (punishment). Having a basic understanding of evolution by natural selection early in the class helps students to view learning as part of a bigger picture while providing ways to think about selection that will be useful for understanding operant conditioning.

Research Methods

Research methods are important to all areas of psychology, and learning is no exception. Even if most students have already taken a methods course, it is useful to revisit the topic since some of the research methods that students encounter in a learning course differ from those that are emphasized in other areas of psychology (Machado & Silva, 1998; Pilgrim, 2003). Covering research methods also provides an opportunity to discuss the costs and benefits of the different research designs. For example, under what circumstances is a between-subjects design a better choice compared with a within-subjects design? When would a laboratory experiment be preferable to a more naturalistic design? Grappling with these sorts of problems will help students to understand why learning experiments are conducted the way they are, and connect the study of learning to the overall discipline of psychology.

Teaching, Learning, and Assessment in Learning Courses: Approaches and Strategies

B.F. Skinner himself noted that graduate schools train scholars rather than teachers, and that teaching at a university is one of the only professions where there is no professional training (Skinner, 1956). Though many graduate students receive pedagogical experience in the form of teaching assistantships, these are often structured to benefit faculty and the institution rather than the students themselves (Austin, 2002). Graduate schools tend to place a greater emphasis on research over teaching, and may even actively devalue teaching (Chew et al., 2018). This means that new faculty are often lacking in the basic pedagogical knowledge and experience to make them effective teachers. In addition, there is a dearth of published information regarding the instruction of learning courses in particular. Machado and Silva (1998) found that only 1.2% of articles in the journal *Teaching of Psychology* specifically addressed learning courses. Of the resources that exist, some of them are unnecessarily muddled and confusing (see Flora & Pavlik, 1990 for example, regarding operant conditioning). Despite these and other challenges inherent to teaching at the university level in general and teaching a learning course in particular, there are many data-supported pedagogical techniques for instructors to utilize.

Something that is important to keep in mind, especially early in a teaching career, is that there is not one single best way to teach (D. J. Bernstein et al., 2010; Holmes, 2016; Jakobsen & Daniel, 2019). Before constructing a class, however, instructors should think about what they want students to learn or be able to do, and adjust their techniques accordingly (i.e., backward design; Wiggins & McTighe, 2005). In addition, using teaching and learning techniques that include active engagement by students is the best way to encourage learning and deeper understanding of the material (Dolan & Collins, 2015; Halpern et al., 2010).

Indeed, as instructors we can use what we know about cognition to our advantage in the classroom. Many of the pedagogical techniques I use have their roots in cognitive psychology (see Parker, 1993). Some of my favorites for teaching a learning course in particular include using interactive lectures, having students predict outcomes, using retrieval practice, using classroom response systems and peer instruction, using spaced practice, and connecting material to existing knowledge. Regardless of the specific techniques chosen for a given course, a variety of teaching and learning techniques should be used in order to maximize impact (Halpern et al., 2010). Below I will outline strategies that I have found to be useful with learning courses, though the overall principles apply to pedagogy in general.

Interactive Lectures

Few teaching techniques have been as vilified as the lecture in recent years. Lecturing has been accused of being outdated and inefficient due to what some perceive to be short attention spans and passivity on the part of students (Matheson, 2008), and has even been called a waste of time (see Parker, 1993). These criticisms have always struck me as straw man arguments since the reasons for criticizing lectures do not tend to have a great deal of evidence, especially for all learners in all circumstances, and even the meaning of lecture is not adequately defined by many researchers (Bernstein, 2018; Holmes, 2016). Most people when criticizing lectures are not taking aim at lectures per se, but rather at bad lectures (Parker, 1993). It is easy to attack the image of a stereotypical professor who speaks in a monotone to a large lecture hall for an entire class period without so much as making eye contact with the students, let alone asking them if they have questions. Most college instructors still use lecture as a dominant teaching strategy (Barkley & Major, 2018), but most (myself included) also incorporate student-centered, active learning components in their lectures (Burkill, Dyer, & Stone, 2008).

I mention lectures here not because I think they are the best way of teaching in all circumstances, but because lecture is as good as other methods of delivering content (Bligh, 2000). Even in literature specifically devoted to denigrating them, lectures tend to be included in the overall pedagogical strategy in some form, such as short introductory lectures during class time, or recorded lectures for students to watch before coming to class. When students have little or no prior knowledge about a subject, lecture can be an efficient way to give students some of the basic, factual information they need. From there, instructors can employ a variety of active learning techniques (some of which I will outline below) to help students with the progression from the foundational, more fact-based levels of Bloom's taxonomy (e.g., remembering and understanding) to the higher levels where students are analyzing, evaluating, and applying information (Anderson et al., 2001). This type of interactive lecturing (Barkley & Major, 2018; Bernstein, Frantz, & Chew, 2020; White, 2011) is a great way to deliver content while maintaining student engagement and challenging students to go beyond simple memorization.

The field of learning contains a large number of terms and procedures that do not generally appear in other psychology courses (Machado & Silva, 1998), and the meanings of those terms are not always obvious and are sometimes even counterintuitive, which can lead to misunderstandings (see the "Challenges and Lessons Learned" section below for specific examples regarding operant conditioning). Despite the focus many instructors have on the higher levels of Bloom's taxonomy, the factual information in any course is still extremely important because it provides a foundation on which students can build further knowledge and understanding (see Christodoulou, 2014). Therefore, lectures can be useful to teachers of learning courses for introducing unfamiliar (and potentially confusing or counterintuitive) material, and pointing out common misconceptions before moving on to more complex ways of thinking about and processing the material.

Another advantage of interactive lectures is that components can be added over time. Even if an instructor currently exclusively utilizes lectures without any additional active learning components and does not have the time or desire to engage in a grand redesign of a course, incorporating elements of interactive lecture each time the course is taught can lead to incremental improvements in student learning with only a small investment of time each academic term (see Lang, 2016).

It should be noted, however, that simply adding active learning components to a class is not a guarantee of greater comprehension on the part of students (Clark & Mayer, 2008). There are many factors that influence whether a particular technique will be effective in the classroom such as student population, class size, instructor characteristics, and discipline, among others, so any given active learning technique will not be universally successful (Bernstein, 2018). Instructors should therefore utilize a "scientist-educator" model for teaching (D. J. Bernstein et al., 2010). With this model, instructors examine existing data on pedagogy to make educated decisions about how to teach. From there, instructors can use data from their own courses to improve successive offerings and contribute when possible to the body of knowledge encompassing teaching and learning. We generate an enormous amount of data each time we deliver a course in the form of formative and summative assessments, as well as student evaluations. These data should be examined and reflected upon in order to determine if interventions are working and to guide future pedagogy. Since no two courses are identical, teaching should be reflective and iterative in order to achieve maximum learning gains for students in each particular context (Bernstein, 2018; Halpern et al., 2010).

Making Predictions

Studies indicate that when people make a prediction about something, they are better able to recall information about it in the future, even if their initial prediction was wrong (Kornell, Hays, & Bjork, 2009). Asking students to predict an outcome encourages them to engage with the material in a way that simply providing them with information would not, and gives them an emotional investment in the outcome of their prediction. In other words, they become curious as to whether their prediction was correct or not (Lang, 2016). The implications of this research are important for education in general, and I have found that asking students to make predictions is particularly useful with helping them to learn the nuances of conditioning. For example, after going over the basic tenets of Pavlovian conditioning, I ask students to predict what would happen if the parameters of the situation change. I have students imagine one of Pavlov's dogs that has been conditioned over a large number of trials in which the dog got a bit of food immediately after hearing a tone. Students are well aware of the salivation that will happen when the dog hears the tone by itself after conditioning. But what will happen if the dog is now presented with the same tone, but also a simultaneous light shortly before receiving food for a number of trials? Will the dog now salivate when just hearing the tone? Just seeing the light? Only when both are presented? Not salivate at all regardless of what is presented? Having time to consider the situation and make a prediction about the outcome helps students to think about the relationship between variables, and better understand and remember the outcome when it is revealed. (In this case, the dog will continue to salivate when it hears the tone, but not when it sees the light by itself.) The scenario described above is a classic example of blocking, but asking students to predict outcomes can be used with any of the procedures involving Pavlovian conditioning including overshadowing, latent inhibition, and conditioned suppression, among others.

Asking for predictions can also be useful when teaching operant conditioning. For example, in order to help students understand schedules of reinforcement, I ask them to predict how they think they (or another person or animal) would respond under different schedules. Most students are able to accurately predict how organisms will respond to different schedules based on when reinforcement is available. Even if they get it wrong, the process of predicting and receiving feedback will help them to understand and remember the effects of different schedules. I ask students to imagine certain hypothetical behavior modification situations and tell me which schedule of reinforcement would be best for producing the desired outcome. For example, if students were hiring workers to perform some task such as mowing lawns or washing dishes, which schedule(s) would be best at getting high rates of responding (i.e., work), and which would be least effective? What are some other implications of schedules of reinforcement that a person doing the reinforcing would need to take into account, such as quality of work? What would be the most desirable schedule from the workers' perspective? Addressing such questions helps students to grasp how schedules affect work, and how they operate in the real world.

Having students make predictions can be especially useful when an outcome is somewhat surprising. For example, I ask students to predict how a pigeon will behave after conditioning when a light is presented on one side of a long (1 meter) Skinner box followed immediately by several seconds of food presentation on the opposite side. Most students guess that after conditioning, the pigeon will begin to wait by the food hopper shortly after the light comes on. At this point, I show a video of a pigeon in a long box after it has experienced the conditioning procedure described above. (See "Teaching, Learning, and Assessment Resources" section below for the link to this and several other excellent videos demonstrating basic conditioning concepts.) Students tend to be surprised (and amused) that instead of waiting where the food is distributed as they predicted, the pigeon not only orients toward the light on the far end of the Skinner box, but it also goes over to and pecks the light as well, even though pecking at the light is inconsequential to food delivery. As a result of this behavior, the pigeon misses out on several seconds of food access that would have occurred had the bird moved to the food hopper as soon as the light came on. Having students predict the outcome of this scenario is a great introduction to sign tracking (also known as autoshaping) because this nonintuitive and seemingly maladaptive behavior is surprising and therefore memorable. It also allows for further discussion about the nature of Pavlovian conditioning (e.g., under what circumstances, if any, are Pavlovian responses not reflexive? What is the role of awareness in Pavlovian conditioning? Is sign tracking adaptive?).

Retrieval Practice

Students should have ample opportunities to practice retrieving information from memory with low- or no-stakes formative assessments before requiring them to demonstrate their knowledge on a summative assessment such as a midterm or final exam, or before moving to more complicated or nuanced topics (Karpicke & Roediger, 2008). As one example, I distribute ungraded worksheets in class that students can work on together, and that we then go over as a group. This exercise gives students a chance to work with peers, and get immediate feedback from me as to the right or wrong answers. They can then take the worksheet home as a reference and study aid. This type of retrieval practice is particularly important for learning new terms and definitions. In classical conditioning, for example, there are many fundamental procedures that can easily be confused, such as conditioned inhibition, conditioned suppression, disinhibition, external inhibition, and latent inhibition. These in-class retrieval exercises help to ensure that students remember and understand these procedures, which prepares them to learn about more complex areas of the field later on.

Classroom Response Systems and Peer Instruction

In addition to retrieval practice, I also intersperse class time with more involved "understanding checks," particularly in the form of multiple-choice or short answer questions. Where student response system (i.e., "clickers") technology is available and does not create an undue financial burden for students, it can be useful for asking students many types of questions to which they can respond immediately and anonymously. (See Caldwell, 2007, for best practices regarding clickers, and Beatty, Gerace, Leonard, & Dufresne, 2006 for how to construct effective "clicker questions.") One important benefit of this form of questioning is that the responses can be immediately compiled, shared with the class, and used to provide instructors as well as students with a check on comprehension in real time. Without such checks, students often have the illusion that they grasp the material when in fact they do not. Another advantage is that students can respond to questions without fear of being embarrassed if they publicly answer the question incorrectly. Anonymity encourages all students to participate, including those who tend to be reticent to speak up in class.

When presenting clicker questions, if a large proportion of students answer a particular question correctly, the instructor can move on. When clicker checks show that a large percentage of students have difficulty with a particular question, it signals the perfect opportunity to utilize peer instruction (Mazur, 1997). In this procedure, after the students are shown how the group as a whole answered the question, they are organized into small groups to discuss the question and their individual answers, to explain their reasoning and to try to convince one another of the correct answer. They then vote again for what they believe to be the correct answer, the results are shown to the class and discussed, and the instructor can address any remaining difficulties or misunderstandings before moving on. Though there can be disadvantages to showing the class everyone else's answers (Perez et al., 2010), peer instruction, when implemented correctly, has the potential to greatly enhance student understanding (Vickrey, Rosploch, Rahmanian, Pilarz, & Stains, 2015).

Though electronic student response systems have many advantages, some of the same benefits of discussion of in-class questions are attainable through other means (Lasry 2008; Vickrey et al., 2015). Students can hold up colored cards to indicate their answers, write their answers on small chalk or dry-erase boards, or simply raise their hands to indicate their answer choice. The point is that answering in-class questions and having opportunities to practice and receive feedback on their answers is a simple and effective way to bolster students' learning.

Distributed Practice

Few things are as stereotypical to the college experience as students waiting until the night before an exam to study, and then staying up all night in an effort to cram all the information into their heads. Though many students choose to study in one long session (massed practice), we know from more than a century of research that distributed practice leads to greater retention under many circumstances (Cepeda, Pashler, Vul, Wixted, & Rohrer, 2006; but see Donovan & Radosevich, 1999). Distributed practice, also known as spaced practice, occurs when a learner leaves a temporal gap between study sessions. In one study examining 10 popular learning techniques, distributed practice (along with practice testing, see below under Assessments) was shown to have the highest utility to learners (Dunlosky, Rawson, Marsh, Nathan, & Willingham, 2013). Even if some students are not inclined to space out their study sessions on their own, we as instructors can make distributed practice part of the structure of our courses. Several days after being introduced to material and practicing it in class, I ask students to do homework on their own outside of class. This allows students to not only obtain additional practice, but it also spaces out their practice, which will lead to better and longer-lasting learning (also see the Assessments section below for information about using a cumulative final exam to further encourage distributed practice).

Students tend to be poor judges of the usefulness of particular pedagogical tools (Wesp & Miele, 2008). Indeed, students' feelings about how much they have learned using a particular method can be quite different from their actual learning (Deslauriers, McCarty, Miller, Callaghan, & Kestin, 2019). I tell students that I assign homework or other tasks not because I want them to do "busy work" or because I think it is fun to torture them, but because ultimately it will help them to learn the material better, and therefore perform better in the class. Telling students, and reminding them throughout the course, why I assign particular materials helps to increase buy-in about the assignments they are given. It also demonstrates to them that I am not their adversary, but rather their partner in learning who has their best interests in mind when constructing and assigning homework, projects, exams, and other work.

Connecting Information

Students tend to learn better when they can relate new information to existing knowledge (Lang, 2016). One way to connect information about learning processes to what students already know is to illustrate the prominence those processes have in their everyday lives. A poignant example of this involves conditioned taste aversion. Most people have had the experience of avoiding a particular food or beverage due to becoming ill after ingesting it, and many students are willing to share first- or second-hand accounts of conditioned taste aversion. I also explicitly ask students if they can willfully overcome their aversion, particularly in instances where they are aware that their illness was caused by something other than what they ingested, such as a flu virus or chemotherapy. Having students discuss conditioned taste aversion not only connects the concept to their own personal experience (which should help them better retain the information), but it also highlights the reflexive nature of Pavlovian conditioning (i.e., it happens automatically), which is something that students often find difficult to grasp.

Assessment of Student Learning

Instructors have many choices when it comes to formative and summative assessment of students' learning in the learning course. Regardless of the form this assessment takes, students should be provided frequent low-stakes quizzes or no-stakes practice exams prior to high-stakes summative exams (see the "Retrieval Practice" section above). This serves two purposes. First, simply engaging in some form of testing helps students learn (Roediger & Karpicke, 2006). Second, it allows students to monitor their learning. In general, students' judgment about how well they have learned particular material (i.e., their metacognition) is fairly poor (Dunlosky & Lipko, 2007). Practice exams or other low-stakes quizzes can help students better understand how well they know the material, and can allow them the opportunity to enhance their knowledge if needed before a summative assessment. In my learning class, I give students online practice exams that are similar in length and scope to the actual exams. Studies examining this "testing effect" show that taking practice exams is one of the most useful procedures for learning that students can utilize (Adesope, Trevisan, & Sundararajan, 2017; Dunlosky et al., 2013).

The types of questions I include on summative exams vary somewhat depending on practical considerations such as the number of students in the class, and whether I have grading assistance available. However, my exams always include multiple-choice questions. Many instructors assume that despite their popularity, multiple-choice questions can only measure superficial knowledge, and that higher-order thinking skills can only be measured with essay or other types of free-response questions (see Holmes, 2016). However, evidence suggests that multiple-choice and open-ended questions actually measure the same constructs (Bennett, Rock, & Wang, 1991; Lukhele, Thissen, & Wainer, 1994), and that scores from the two question types tend to be highly correlated (Bleske-Rechek, Zeug, & Webb, 2007; Rodriguez, 2003). It is absolutely possible to assess higher-order thinking using multiple-choice questions, though as with any exam, care must be taken in constructing the questions (Hancock, 1994). There are many excellent resources available for the construction of high-quality multiple-choice questions that measure higher-order thinking (see Haladyna, Downing, & Rodriguez, 2002; Scully, 2017; Xu, Kauer, & Tupy, 2016). It is important to include such questions because students who are given assessments that include higher-order thinking develop a better understanding of and memory for the material by the end of the course compared with students who are asked to answer only surface-level types of questions (Jensen, McDaniel, Woodard, & Kummer, 2014).

Some authors feel it is best to use the same types of questions in practice opportunities as students will encounter on summative assessments (Lang, 2016). However, even if the format of summative assessments is not multiple-choice, giving multiple-choice practice exams helps students perform better on those assessments (Roediger & Karpicke, 2006; Smith & Karpicke, 2014). One problem with multiple-choice practice exams, however, is that students can sometimes remember misinformation simply by being exposed to the incorrect answer choices (Marsh, Roediger, Bjork, & Bjork, 2007; Roediger & Marsh, 2005). Providing relatively immediate feedback (e.g., right after the exam is over) can help to mitigate this effect (Butler & Roediger, 2008). Therefore, I recommend practice exams with multiple-choice questions and immediate feedback, which will give students the best chance at accurately retaining the material.

I also feel it is important to include a cumulative final exam in my learning course. Though it is unreasonable to expect students to remember every detail of the material for the rest of their lives, having students retain information beyond the end of the term is likely important for most instructors. The ideal amount of time between study intervals increases as the time between when information is learned and when it needs to be recalled increases (Cepeda et al., 2006). A cumulative final exam naturally increases the time between study intervals, therefore increasing the odds of a longer retention period. Students might also approach how to study for a course differently if they are aware of a cumulative final (Royal, 2017; Szpunar, McDermott, & Roediger, 2007), making them more likely to remember the information for a longer period of time than they would otherwise. One study (Khanna, Brack, & Finken, 2013) found that students did better on a content exam after a course with a cumulative final compared to a course without one. Therefore, including a cumulative final exam will facilitate the long-lasting learning that most instructors desire for their students. I remind students in my learning course throughout the term of the existence of the cumulative final, and explain to them why it is something I have chosen to administer.

My final exam also has a unique format that provides additional opportunities for students. The exam is divided into four sections that are equivalent in content to the four units of the course. If students perform better on a unit of the final exam than they did on the original unit exam, I count the higher score as their grade for that exam. For example, if a student scores 80% on their unit 2 exam, but a 90% on the second unit of the final (which covers the same material), that student's grade for exam 2 will be corrected to 90%. The final exam itself is still worth a certain percentage of the overall grade (usually the same as a regular unit exam) to ensure that students who have consistently done well throughout the course are still motivated to take it. Having the ability to raise previous exam grades through improved performance on the final exam reduces some of the pressure students may feel about regular unit exams. It essentially means that there are two testing opportunities for each exam, which can be a relief for students who are overly anxious about taking exams. It can also provide a second chance for students who are falsely overconfident about how much they know when going into an exam, or who are dealing with situational stressors such as an illness or death in the family. In short, I do not necessarily care *when* students learn course information, just as long as they *have* done so by the end of the term. Having unit and final exams structured this way ensures that even if students are not necessarily prepared for any given unit exam, they still have the opportunity to learn the material and demonstrate their knowledge on the final exam.

Operant Project

The American Psychological Association recommends an applied experience as part of a quality undergraduate education in psychology (Halpern et al., 2010). Accordingly, as a capstone experience of the learning course, I have students complete a research project in which they apply what they know about operant conditioning in a real-world context (see Sperling, Reeves, Follmer, Towle, & Chung, 2016 for a description of a similar project for educational psychology students). For this project, students must come up with a plan to use operant conditioning in an attempt to change the behavior of someone they know (e.g., a parent, child, or roommate), a pet, or even themselves. Students first collect baseline and intervention data, and then write up their results in a report that includes a presentation of the data (e.g., graphs or tables), and why they think their intervention did or did not work based on operant principles. Students are specifically not graded on whether their intervention succeeded (many do not), but on the quality of the analysis of their results, and on what they say about how they would change things in order to get better results if they were to institute their plan again. This is the type of "messy" real-world problem (Dolan & Collins, 2015) that requires students to go beyond factual information and apply what they know to situations that are not clearly defined. It also allows for an examination of ethics in relation to operant conditioning, particularly those surrounding punishment. For example, when would it be acceptable (if ever) to utilize positive punishment, and why? Also, does the intention or awareness of the individual doing the conditioning matter? Planning and conducting this type of project helps students to gain a deeper understanding of the variables that affect whether conditioning is successful or not, and to see for themselves the effects of conditioning in the real world.

Challenges and Lessons Learned

There are a number of specific challenges that instructors and students of learning courses face. Below I outline some of these challenges with regard to operant conditioning and give suggestions for addressing them. For topics that tend to be confusing, I recommend starting slowly and gradually increasing the difficulty level for students while ensuring their mastery at each step. Though I give examples using operant conditioning below, the same general, recursive technique could apply to any topic that students often have difficulty with, particularly in advanced courses on learning.

In the USA, students are usually required to take a general or introductory psychology course prior to taking a learning course, so instructors might justifiably think that students in their learning courses already understand the fundamentals of conditioning (i.e., reinforcement and punishment). This assumption could lead instructors to do no more than briefly touch on the basics of conditioning before continuing on to more complicated and detailed information. In my experience, this is a mistake. Despite being deceptively simple, understanding the processes of operant conditioning can be especially challenging (Epting, 2011; Sperling et al., 2016), and students often arrive in learning classes holding certain misconceptions such as that punishment is a useful means of behavioral change (Sperling et al., 2016), or that negative reinforcement and punishment are the same thing (Shields & Gredler, 2003).

The difficulties students have in understanding operant conditioning likely begin even before they have any university instruction in psychology. On a pretest for an introductory psychology course, 73% of students said that negative reinforcement decreases behavior, and 76% said that individuals would not look forward to negative reinforcement (Tauber, 1988). Worse yet, taking an introductory course can result in even greater confusion. Sheldon (2002) found that 97% of introductory textbooks contained at least one confusing explanation, contradiction, or error regarding operant conditioning. For example, the importance of a change in future response rates, which is a central tenet of operant conditioning, is often not mentioned. So, a child talking back to a teacher and being made to stay after school might be described as a punishment and a child being made to stay in her room until she finishes her homework might be described as reinforcement. But since it is unclear if behavior changed in the future in either case, there is no way to know whether either of these consequences was reinforcement, punishment, or neither. Many textbooks also fail to point out that when an individual is attempting to use operant conditioning to reinforce or punish another, the intention of the individual doing the conditioning does not matter (Sheldon, 2002). For example, if a teacher tries to punish a student's disruptive behavior by giving a reprimand, but the student's disruptive behavior continues, this was not punishment – despite the intention of the teacher. Many textbooks also fail to highlight the fact that reinforcers and punishers might have different effects on different individuals and/or at different times (Sheldon, 2002). The opportunity to play outside might be considered a reward for some children but not for others, or it might be considered a reward for some children when the weather is nice, but not if it is raining.

The persistence of erroneous beliefs about learning was illustrated by the results of a true/false survey (DeBell & Harless, 1992) about B.F. Skinner taken by first-year and advanced undergraduates, first-year and advanced graduate students, and faculty. Some survey items contained factual statements (e.g., Skinner felt the focus of research should be observable behavior) whereas others conveyed myths (e.g., Skinner did not believe genetics play an important role in behavior). Participants in all groups more often responded correctly to factual than mythical items, but advanced undergraduates endorsed significantly more myths than the other groups. These studies indicate that instructors of learning courses need to be aware that students are likely to harbor misconceptions about the material upon entering their classrooms, and take steps to ensure those misconceptions do not persist.

Part of the difficulty in understanding operant conditioning lies in the use of the terms "positive" and "negative" to describe reinforcement and punishment. One reason many students find this confusing is because their previous experience with those words suggests that they mean "good" or "bad," rather than adding or subtracting something. This prior association renders the idea of positive punishment especially difficult to grasp (Shields & Gredler, 2003). Moreover, simply presenting correct definitions of operant conditioning terms is not generally sufficient to debunk misconceptions and allow students to grasp the meaning of these terms, let alone to help them think about how operant conditioning could be used in the real world to change behavior. A better strategy is to work slowly upward through Bloom's taxonomy (Anderson et al., 2001; Bloom, Engelhart, Furst, Hill, & Krathwohl, 1956) by giving students many opportunities to practice and get feedback on their understanding of basic terminology before advancing to higher levels of complexity.

So, when introducing operant conditioning, I first give definitions of the different kinds of reinforcement and punishment (positive and negative), along with a two-by-two matrix as described by Flora and Pavlik (1990). This matrix has "stimulus" (present or remove) on one axis, and "behavior probability or rate" (increases or decreases) on the other axis. The types of reinforcement and punishment fill the quadrants such that reinforcement always leads to an increase in behavior, and punishment a decrease, while positive indicates that a stimulus was added, and negative indicates that a stimulus was removed. (I make sure at this point and throughout the discussion of operant conditioning to remind students that "positive" and "negative" do not mean "good" or "bad.") Tauber (1988) presents a similar matrix, though the subjective terms "dreaded" and "desired" are used. This should be avoided in a discussion of operant conditioning since behavior is something that can be measured directly, but subjective desires cannot (Shields & Gredler, 2003). Giving students this simple matrix helps them to more easily see the categorical nature of reinforcement or punishment, and to accurately identify instances of both (but see Shields & Gredler, 2003 for possible disadvantages of using a matrix format).

Next, I provide many examples of operant conditioning that are already mapped out for students. That is, I give examples and explain whether they are reinforcement or punishment, and whether they are positive or negative. In general, I recommend using a multitude of everyday examples in the teaching of operant conditioning (Baldwin & Baldwin, 1999; Epting, 2011; but see Machado & Silva, 1998 for arguments against using such examples). Seeing how operant conditioning changes behavior in common scenarios helps students understand the relevance of conditioning to their own lives rather than seeing it as abstract and pertaining only to rats in mazes or pigeons in Skinner boxes (see the "Connecting Information" section above). If students understand how important and ubiquitous operant conditioning is to their own and others' lives (including animals), the information is more likely to be retained.

I then give students many more operant examples and ask them to decide for themselves what kind of reinforcement or punishment is represented. Students work alone at first, then in groups to discuss their answers (think-pair-share). Students will often come up with answers that differ from those of their classmates (especially with regard to negative reinforcement and punishment), which allows for discussion and a careful consideration of the examples by the entire class to get the correct answer. This process requires the students to map out the scenario, in particular identifying (1) the behavior of interest, (2) what the consequence of the behavior is, and (3) how the behavior changed.

Though working on problems in a group setting is a good way to help students understand material, online assessments that students complete on their own have several advantages as well. Therefore, after the students have practiced with identifying types of reinforcement and punishment in class, I ask them to complete an online homework assignment that requires them to do the same identification of reinforcement or punishment, but with different examples. For this and all of my online homework assignments, I use behaviorist principles to assist with learning, similar to the teaching machines described by B.F. Skinner (Skinner, 1968; see also Root & Rehfeldt, 2020). This includes allowing unlimited time so that individuals can learn at their own pace. Students who grasp the material quickly can move on, while those who are struggling can take extra time to consider their answers. Also, assignments can be configured so that students receive immediate feedback about whether they got a particular answer right or wrong (Skinner, 1968). These online assessments are low-stakes, allow students to revise their responses, to proceed at their own pace, and to receive immediate feedback, making them a great way to help students succeed with tricky material.

Once students have had a multitude of opportunities to practice identifying examples of operant conditioning, I then ask them to generate their own examples of each type of reinforcement and punishment. Students often begin this exercise with a modicum of confidence. However, even if students are at the point where straightforward instances of reinforcement and punishment are easily identified, they often have difficulty generating their own unique examples of operant conditioning, especially of negative reinforcement and punishment. Students' self-generated examples of negative reinforcement commonly include something like the following: "A parent takes away a child's phone in order to encourage studying."

Students may argue (incorrectly) that this is negative reinforcement because studying increased (reinforcement), and a treasured item was removed (negative), but those students failed to pay attention to what behavior led to the phone being taken away, and *when* the item is taken away. In other words, what was the consequence of the behavior? As this particular example is written, the child in question has not yet exhibited any behavior. The parent has simply removed a potential distractor in the hope that doing so will lead the child to study more. This example is therefore neither reinforcement nor punishment since the removal of an item was not contingent on any particular behavior. If, however, the item was removed *after* the child gets a bad grade, then the behavior that elicited the consequence was not studying, but getting the bad grade. Thus, removal of the phone could be considered negative punishment for getting a bad grade (assuming that the child gets fewer bad grades in the future). When students are given timely feedback of this sort, most recognize the flaws in their reasoning and are able to resubmit the assignment with a correct response (though some need several iterations before getting it right). This is why I encourage students to map out examples in the form of behavior leading to consequences leading to future behavior in order to better understand how conditioning works. Once students have tried this exercise on their own, received feedback, and had a chance to revise, I provide another in-class exercise that is more difficult than the previous ones.

After spending a significant amount of time grading student-generated examples of operant conditioning (such as the one mentioned above), I realized that analyzing and giving feedback to students about their incorrect examples gave me a sharper understanding of the process itself. Therefore, I ask students to analyze examples of operant conditioning that I have gathered from various places including online sources, popular television shows and movies, and anonymized student responses from prior academic terms, many of which are incorrect and/or confusing. One particularly useful ambiguous example comes from Gillespie and Simmons (1995) in a paper presented at the annual meeting of the American Psychological Association. They described a vignette that they used with their learning classes as a demonstration of operant conditioning. In their scenario, one member of a couple wants to go out for the evening, while the other wants to stay home in order to study. After some escalation, the spouse wanting to stay home agrees to go out after the other spouse pounds a fist on the table. The authors claim this is negative reinforcement since one spouse giving in to the demands of the other "relieved the anger" of the cajoling spouse.

There are several reasons why this example is so useful. First, it is not clear which person in the scenario the students are supposed to focus on. In general, students have more trouble correctly analyzing two-person scenarios compared with single-person scenarios (Shields & Gredler, 2003), and both people in the aforementioned situation are behaving and the behavior of each can be reinforced or punished by the other. Also, we are not given any information about how either party's behavior changed in the future. Without that information, it cannot be determined whether a consequence resulted in reinforcement, punishment, or neither. As the authors say, the scenario could be considered negative reinforcement if the spouse who agreed to go out continues to agree to go out in the future, and if doing so avoids arguments. But this information is not specified. However, it was removal of the behaviors associated with anger (yelling, fist pounding), not dissipation of anger, that is the focus of the conditioning involved (indeed, anger itself is difficult to measure). This is an opportunity to revisit the importance of operational definitions and observable behavior in the study of operant conditioning, as well as to allow students to grapple with ambiguous scenarios in order to get a better understanding of the process.

Teaching, Learning, and Assessment Resources

Teaching Tips

Below are several teaching tips that I try to consistently keep in mind:

- **Keep an eye on best practices for undergraduate education.** Chickering and Gamson (1989) outlined seven principles for undergraduate education including communicating high expectations, encouraging contact between faculty and students, and giving prompt feedback. I return to and reexamine these principles from time to time in order to zoom out and refocus on the big picture of teaching and learning.

- **Try to do the things that good teachers do, and avoid the things that bad teachers do.** The Teacher Behavior Checklist (Buskist, Sikorski, Buckley, & Saville, 2002; Keeley, Smith, & Buskist, 2006) provides a validated and reliable list of behaviors that constitute best practices for teaching, including being approachable, being respectful toward students, and being humble. A group of behaviors associated with poor teaching has also been identified (Busler, Kirk, Keeley, & Buskist, 2017), and includes being disrespectful, not giving feedback, and being overconfident.
- **Learn from previous iterations of the course.** Students are constantly giving us data we can work with to improve the next offering of a course (e.g., exam or in-class question scores, homework answers, etc.). Pay close attention to those data in order to see if any changes you make to the course have their intended effect, and make adjustments as needed.
- **Try to remember what it was like when you were a student.** Instructors in higher education no longer face the struggles of comprehending fundamental material in their field, even if they once found it difficult. Remembering what it was like to be a new student in an academic area can help instructors gain insight into the struggles that their beginning students are facing and inform decisions about how to present material in ways that are helpful to students.

Resources

Below is a collection of links and recommended further reading. Some are specific to courses on learning, while others are useful for teaching in general.

- https://www.youtube.com/user/daleswartzentruber/videos:A collection of YouTube videos created by Dale Swartzentruber of Ohio Wesleyan University, USA. It includes 10 useful demonstrations of learning phenomena in rats and pigeons, including habituation, dishabituation, spontaneous recovery, auto-shaping (in a regular and long box, and with different unconditioned stimuli), and conditioned suppression.
- https://bfskinner.org: The home page for the B.F. Skinner foundation. It includes many helpful resources about Skinner, including articles and quotes as well as videos that are useful for the learning classroom.
- Sniffy the Virtual Rat (sniffythevirtualrat.com) is a computer-simulated rat in a Skinner box. Students can manipulate the variables Sniffy experiences so as to see the effects of Pavlovian and operant conditioning. Sniffy is a good option for instructors who want to incorporate a laboratory component into a learning course but either cannot or do not want to work with live animals.
- Ware, M. E., & Johnson, D. E. (Eds.). (2000). *Handbook of demonstrations and activities in the teaching of psychology volume II: Physiological-comparative,*

perception, learning, cognitive, and developmental (2nd ed.). Mahwah, NJ: Lawrence Erlbaum Associates, Inc.

There are several handbooks of this sort, but this volume is the most relevant for learning courses. It includes instructions for demonstrations of conditioning in planarians, zoo animals, and humans, among others.

- Lang, J. M. (2016). *Small teaching: Everyday lessons from the science of learning*. Jossey-Bass.

Cited several times in this chapter, this book contains suggestions for a number of relatively easy changes teachers can make to improve their teaching and their students' learning. It is divided into three sections encompassing how to increase student knowledge, how to increase student understanding, and how to inspire students.

- Brown, P. C., Roediger, H. L., & McDaniel, M. A. (2014). *Make it stick: The science of successful learning*. Cambridge, MA: The Belknap Press of Harvard University Press.

This book contains information on how to learn more effectively, though instructors can use the principles for teaching as well. The recommendations include advice for avoiding illusions of knowing, embracing difficulties, and going beyond learning styles.

- Bernstein, D. A., Frantz, S., & Chew, S. (2020). *Teaching psychology: A step-by-step guide* (3rd ed.). New York, NY: Routledge.

This is an excellent and comprehensive resource for how to teach psychology courses. The authors include evidence-based pedagogical strategies for all stages of teaching from preparing the course and the first few days of class, through how to assess and improve future offerings of classes.

- Yancy McGuire, S. (2015). *Teach students how to learn: Strategies you can incorporate into any course to improve student metacognition, study skills, and motivation*. Sterling, VA: Stylus.

Many students simply have not figured out efficient ways of learning material, and this book offers concrete steps that instructors can recommend to students in order to improve their metacognition, and ultimately learn and perform better in classes.

- Angelo, T. A., & Cross, K. P. (1993). *Classroom assessment techniques: A handbook for college teachers.* (3rd ed.). San Francisco, CA: Jossey-Bass.

This is the quintessential handbook for all things related to assessment. The authors provide information about how to think about assessment, examples of successful projects, and ways to assess student attitudes, among other assessment-related resources.

- Bain, K. (2004). *What the best college teachers do* (1st ed.). Cambridge, MA: Harvard University Press.

Bain examined one hundred excellent teachers from varying disciplines and institutions. Despite very different personal styles, he discovered commonalities these teachers shared, including creating a critical learning environment, and an ability to simplify complex topics in ways that are understandable to students.

Cross-References

▶ Assessment of Learning in Psychology
▶ Basic Principles and Procedures for Effective Teaching in Psychology
▶ Formative Assessment and Feedback Strategies
▶ Problem-Based Learning and Case-Based Learning
▶ Small Group Learning
▶ Technology-Enhanced Psychology Learning and Teaching
▶ Topics, Methods, and Research-Based Strategies for Teaching Cognition

References

Abramson, C. (2013). Problems of teaching the behaviorist perspective in the cognitive revolution. *Behavioral Science, 3*(1), 55–71. https://doi.org/10.3390/bs3010055.

Adesope, O. O., Trevisan, D. A., & Sundararajan, N. (2017). Rethinking the use of tests: A meta-analysis of practice testing. *Review of Educational Research, 87*(3), 659–701. https://doi.org/10.3102/0034654316689306.

American Psychological Association. (2013). APA guidelines for the undergraduate psychology major: Version 2.0. Retrieved from http://www.apa.org/ed/precollege/undergrad/index.aspx

Anderson, L. W., Krathwohl, D. R., Airasian, P. W., Cruikshank, K. A., Mayer, R. E., Pintrich, P. R., . . . Wittrock, M. C. (Eds.). (2001). *A taxonomy for learning, teaching, and assessing: A revision of Bloom's taxonomy of educational objectives.* New York, NY: Longman.

Angelo, T. A., & Cross, K. P. (1993). *Classroom assessment techniques: A handbook for college teachers* (3rd ed.). San Francisco, CA: Jossey-Bass.

Austin, A. E. (2002). Preparing the next generation of faculty: Graduate school as socialization to the academic career. *The Journal of Higher Education, 73*(1), 94–122. https://doi.org/10.1080/00221546.2002.11777132.

Bain, K. (2004). *What the best college teachers do* (1st ed.). Cambridge, MA: Harvard University Press.

Baldwin, J. D., & Baldwin, J. I. (1999). The value of everyday examples in the teaching of learning: A comment prompted by Machado and Silva (1998). *Journal of the Experimental Analysis of Behavior, 72*(2), 269–272. https://doi.org/10.1901/jeab.1999.72-269.

Barkley, E. F., & Major, C. H. (2018). *Interactive lecturing: A handbook for college faculty*. San Francisco, CA: Jossey-Bass.

Barron, A. B., Hebets, E. A., Cleland, T. A., Fitzpatrick, C. L., Hauber, M. E., & Stevens, J. R. (2015). Embracing multiple definitions of learning. *Trends in Neurosciences, 38*(7), 405–407. https://doi.org/10.1016/j.tins.2015.04.008.

Beatty, I. D., Gerace, W. J., Leonard, W. J., & Dufresne, R. J. (2006). Designing effective questions for classroom response system teaching. *American Journal of Physics, 74*(1), 31–39. https://doi.org/10.1119/1.2121753.

Bennett, R. E., Rock, D. A., & Wang, M. (1991). Equivalence of free-response and multiple-choice items. *Journal of Educational Measurement, 28*(1), 77–92.

Bernstein, D. A. (2018). Does active learning work? A good question, but not the right one. *Scholarship of Teaching and Learning in Psychology, 4*(4), 290–307. https://doi.org/10.1037/stl0000124.

Bernstein, D. A., Frantz, S., & Chew, S. (2020). *Teaching psychology: A step-by-step guide* (3rd ed.). New York, NY: Routledge.

Bernstein, D. J., Addison, W., Altman, C., Hollister, D., Komarraju, M., Prieto, L., ... Shore, C. (2010). Toward a scientist-educator model of teaching psychology. In *Undergraduate education in psychology: A blueprint for the future of the discipline* (pp. 29–45). Washington, DC: American Psychological Association. https://doi.org/10.1037/12063-002.

Bleske-Rechek, A., Zeug, N., & Webb, R. M. (2007). Discrepant performance on multiple-choice and short answer assessments and the relation of performance to general scholastic aptitude. *Assessment & Evaluation in Higher Education, 32*(2), 89–105. https://doi.org/10.1080/02602930600800763.

Bligh, D. A. (2000). *What's the use of lectures?* (1st ed.). San Francisco, CA: Jossey-Bass.

Bloom, B. S., Engelhart, M. D., Furst, E. J., Hill, W. H., & Krathwohl, D. R. (Eds.). (1956). *Taxonomy of educational objectives: The classification of educational goals, handbook 1: Cognitive domain*. New York, NY: David McKay.

Braat, M., Engelen, J., van Gemert, T., & Verhaegh, S. (2020). The rise and fall of behaviorism: The narrative and the numbers. *History of Psychology, 23*(3), 252–280. https://doi.org/10.1037/hop0000146.

Brown, F. J., & Gillard, D. (2015). The "strange death" of radical behaviourism. *The Psychologist, 28*(1), 24–27.

Brown, P. C., Roediger, H. L., & McDaniel, M. A. (2014). *Make it stick: The science of successful learning*. Cambridge, MA: The Belknap Press of Harvard University Press.

Burkill, S., Dyer, S. R., & Stone, M. (2008). Lecturing in higher education in further education settings. *Journal of Further and Higher Education, 32*(4), 321–331. https://doi.org/10.1080/03098770802392915.

Buskist, W., Sikorski, J., Buckley, T., & Saville, B. K. (2002). Elements of master teaching. In S. F. Davis & W. Buskist (Eds.), *The teaching of psychology: Essays in honor of Wilbert J. McKeachie and Charles L. Brewer* (pp. 27–39). Mahwah, NJ: Lawrence Erlbaum Associates.

Busler, J., Kirk, C., Keeley, J., & Buskist, W. (2017). What constitutes poor teaching? A preliminary inquiry into the misbehaviors of not-so-good instructors. *Teaching of Psychology, 44*(4), 330–334. https://doi.org/10.1177/0098628317727907.

Butler, A. C., & Roediger, H. L. (2008). Feedback enhances the positive effects and reduces the negative effects of multiple-choice testing. *Memory & Cognition, 36*(3), 604–616. https://doi.org/10.3758/MC.36.3.604.

Caldwell, J. E. (2007). Clickers in the large classroom: Current research and best-practice tips. *CBE Life Sciences Education, 6*(1), 9–20. https://doi.org/10.1187/cbe.06-12-0205.

Cepeda, N. J., Pashler, H., Vul, E., Wixted, J. T., & Rohrer, D. (2006). Distributed practice in verbal recall tasks: A review and quantitative synthesis. *Psychological Bulletin, 132*(3), 354–380. https://doi.org/10.1037/0033-2909.132.3.354.

Chew, S. L., Halonen, J. S., McCarthy, M. A., Gurung, R. A. R., Beers, M. J., McEntarffer, R., & Landrum, R. E. (2018). Practice what we teach: Improving teaching and learning in psychology. *Teaching of Psychology, 45*(3), 239–245. https://doi.org/10.1177/0098628318779264.

Chickering, A. W., & Gamson, Z. F. (1989). Seven principles for good practice in undergraduate education. *Biochemical Education, 17*(3), 140–141. https://doi.org/10.1016/0307-4412(89) 90094-0.

Christodoulou, D. (2014). *Seven myths about education*. London: Routledge.

Clark, R. C., & Mayer, R. E. (2008). Learning by viewing versus learning by doing: Evidence-based guidelines for principled learning environments. *Performance Improvement, 47*(9), 5–13. https://doi.org/10.1002/pfi.20028.

Darwin, C. (1871). *The descent of man, and selection in relation to sex* (Vol. 1). London: John Murray.

De Houwer, J., Barnes-Holmes, D., & Moors, A. (2013). What is learning? On the nature and merits of a functional definition of learning. *Psychonomic Bulletin & Review, 20*(4), 631–642. https://doi.org/10.3758/s13423-013-0386-3.

DeBell, C. S., & Harless, D. K. (1992). B.F. Skinner: Myth and misperception. *Teaching of Psychology, 19*(2), 68–73. https://doi.org/10.1207/s15328023top1902_1.

Deslauriers, L., McCarty, L. S., Miller, K., Callaghan, K., & Kestin, G. (2019). Measuring actual learning versus feeling of learning in response to being actively engaged in the classroom. *Proceedings of the National Academy of Sciences, 116*(39), 19251–19257. https://doi.org/10.1073/pnas.1821936116.

Dolan, E. L., & Collins, J. P. (2015). We must teach more effectively: Here are four ways to get started. *Molecular Biology of the Cell, 26*(12), 2151–2155. https://doi.org/10.1091/mbc.E13-11-0675.

Domjan, M. (1987). Animal learning comes of age. *American Psychologist, 42*, 556–564. https://doi.org/10.1037/0003-066X.42.6.556.

Domjan, M. (2010). *The principles of learning and behavior* (6th ed.). Belmont, CA: Wadsworth, Cengage Learning.

Donahoe, J. W. (1984). Skinner – The Darwin of ontogeny? *The Behavioral and Brain Sciences, 7*, 487–488.

Donahoe, J. W. (2012). Reflections on behavior analysis and evolutionary biology: A selective review of evolution since Darwin – The first 150 years. Edited by M. A. Bell, D. J. Futuyama, W. F. Eanes, & J. S. Levinton. *Journal of the Experimental Analysis of Behavior, 97*(2), 249–260. https://doi.org/10.1901/jeab.2012.97-249.

Donovan, J. J., & Radosevich, D. J. (1999). A meta-analytic review of the distribution of practice effect: Now you see it, now you don't. *Journal of Applied Psychology, 84*(5), 795–805.

Dunlosky, J., & Lipko, A. R. (2007). Metacomprehension: A brief history and how to improve its accuracy. *Current Directions in Psychological Science, 16*(4), 228–232. https://doi.org/10.1111/j.1467-8721.2007.00509.x.

Dunlosky, J., Rawson, K. A., Marsh, E. J., Nathan, M. J., & Willingham, D. T. (2013). Improving students' learning with effective learning techniques: Promising directions from cognitive and educational psychology. *Psychological Science in the Public Interest, 14*(1), 4–58. https://doi.org/10.1177/1529100612453266.

Dunn, D. S., Brewer, C. L., Cautin, R. L., Gurung, R. A. R., Keith, K. D., McGregor, L. N., ... Voigt, M. J. (2010). The undergraduate psychology curriculum: Call for a core. In *Undergraduate education in psychology: A blueprint for the future of the discipline* (pp. 47–61). Washington, D.C.: American Psychological Association.

Epting, L. K. (2011). Connecting the fundamental science of behavior analysis to everyday experience: An assignment for students. *Journal of Behavioral and Neuroscience Research, 9* (2), 7.

Flora, S. R., & Pavlik, W. B. (1990). An objective and functional matrix for introducing concepts of reinforcement and punishment. *Teaching of Psychology, 17*(2), 121–122.

Gewirtzt, P. (1996). On "I know it when I see it". *The Yale Law Journal, 105*, 27.

Ghiselin, M. T. (2018). B.F. Skinner and the metaphysics of Darwinism. *Perspectives on Behavior Science, 41*(1), 269–281. https://doi.org/10.1007/s40614-018-0139-8.

Gillespie, D., & Simmons, S. (1995, August). *A classroom activity to demonstrate the principle of negative reinforcement.* Paper presented at the 103rd Annual Meeting of the American Psychological Association, New York, NY.

Haggbloom, S. J., Warnick, R., Warnick, J. E., Jones, V. K., Yarbrough, G. L., Russell, T. M., . . . Monte, E. (2002). The 100 most eminent psychologists of the 20th century. *Review of General Psychology, 6*(2), 139–152. https://doi.org/10.1037/1089-2680.6.2.139.

Haladyna, T. M., Downing, S. M., & Rodriguez, M. C. (2002). A review of multiple-choice item-writing guidelines for classroom assessment. *Applied Measurement in Education, 15*(3), 309–333. https://doi.org/10.1207/S15324818AME1503_5.

Halpern, D. F., Anton, B., Beins, B. C., Bernstein, D. J., Blair-Broeker, C. T., Brewer, C. L., . . . Rocheleau, C. A. (2010). APA principles for quality undergraduate education in psychology. In *Undergraduate education in psychology: A blueprint for the future of the discipline* (pp. 161–173). Washington, D.C: American Psychological Association.

Hancock, G. R. (1994). Cognitive complexity and the comparability of multiple-choice and constructed-response test formats. *The Journal of Experimental Education, 62*(2), 143–157.

Holmes, J. D. (2016). *Great myths of education and learning.* Hoboken: Wiley Blackwell.

Jakobsen, K. V., & Daniel, D. B. (2019). Evidence-inspired choices for teachers: Team-based learning and interactive lecture. *Teaching of Psychology, 46*(4), 284–289. https://doi.org/10.1177/0098628319872411.

Jensen, J. L., McDaniel, M. A., Woodard, S. M., & Kummer, T. A. (2014). Teaching to the test...Or testing to teach: Exams requiring higher order thinking skills encourage greater conceptual understanding. *Educational Psychology Review, 26*(2), 307–329.

Karpicke, J. D., & Roediger, H. L. (2008). The critical importance of retrieval for learning. *Science, 319*(5865), 966–968. https://doi.org/10.1126/science.1152408.

Keeley, J., Smith, D., & Buskist, W. (2006). The teacher behaviors checklist: Factor analysis of its utility for evaluating teaching. *Teaching of Psychology, 33*(2), 84–91. https://doi.org/10.1207/s15328023top3302_1.

Khanna, M. M., Brack, A. S. B., & Finken, L. L. (2013). Short- and long-term effects of cumulative finals on student learning. *Teaching of Psychology, 40*(3), 175–182. https://doi.org/10.1177/0098628313487458.

Kornell, N., Hays, M. J., & Bjork, R. A. (2009). Unsuccessful retrieval attempts enhance subsequent learning. *Journal of Experimental Psychology: Learning, Memory, and Cognition, 35*(4), 989–998. https://doi.org/10.1037/a0015729.

Lachman, S. J. (1997). Learning is a process: Toward an improved definition of learning. *The Journal of Psychology, 131*(5), 477–480. https://doi.org/10.1080/00223989709603535.

Lang, J. M. (2016). *Small teaching: Everyday lessons from the science of learning.* San Francisco, CA: Jossey-Bass.

Lasry, N. (2008). Clickers or flashcards: Is there really a difference? *The Physics Teacher, 46*(4), 242–244. https://doi.org/10.1119/1.2895678.

Leahey, T. H. (1992). Questions of psychology's evolution: The mythical revolutions of American psychology. *American Psychologist, 47*(2), 308–318.

Lukhele, R., Thissen, D., & Wainer, H. (1994). On the relative value of multiple-choice, constructed response, and examinee-selected items on two achievement tests. *Journal of Educational Measurement, 31*(3), 234–250.

Machado, A., & Silva, F. J. (1998). Greatness and misery in the teaching of the psychology of learning. *Journal of the Experimental Analysis of Behavior, 70*(2), 215–234. https://doi.org/10.1901/jeab.1998.70-215.

Marsh, E. J., Roediger, H. L., Bjork, R. A., & Bjork, E. L. (2007). The memorial consequences of multiple-choice testing. *Psychonomic Bulletin & Review, 14*(2), 194–199. https://doi.org/10.3758/BF03194051.

Matheson, C. (2008). The educational value and effectiveness of lectures. *The Clinical Teacher, 5*(4), 218–221. https://doi.org/10.1111/j.1743-498X.2008.00238.x.

Mazur, E. (1997). *Peer instruction: A user's manual*. Upper Saddle River, NJ: Prentice-Hall.

Miller, G. A. (2003). The cognitive revolution: A historical perspective. *Trends in Cognitive Sciences, 7*(3), 141–144. https://doi.org/10.1016/S1364-6613(03)00029-9.

Morgan, D. L., & Buskist, W. (1990). Conversations with the keepers of the internal order: A review of B.J. Baars' the cognitive revolution in psychology. *The Behavior Analyst, 13*(2), 199–200.

Overskeid, G. (2008). They should have thought about the consequences: The crisis of cognitivism and a second chance for behavior analysis. *The Psychological Record, 58*(1), 131–151. https://doi.org/10.1007/BF03395606.

Parker, J. K. (1993). Lecturing and loving it: Applying the information-processing model. *The Clearing House: A Journal of Educational Strategies, Issues and Ideas, 67*(1), 8–11. https://doi.org/10.1080/00098655.1993.9956006.

Perez, K. E., Strauss, E. A., Downey, N., Galbraith, A., Jeanne, R., & Cooper, S. (2010). Does displaying the class results affect student discussion during peer instruction? *CBE Life Sciences Education, 9*(2), 133–140. https://doi.org/10.1187/cbe.09-11-0080.

Perlman, B., & McCann, L. I. (1999). The most frequently listed courses in the undergraduate psychology curriculum. *Teaching of Psychology, 26*(3), 177–182. https://doi.org/10.1207/S15328023TOP260303.

Pilgrim, C. (2003). Science and human behavior at fifty. *Journal of the Experimental Analysis of Behavior, 80*(3), 329–340. https://doi.org/10.1901/jeab.2003.80-329.

Rescorla, R. A. (1988). Pavlovian conditioning: It's not what you think it is. *American Psychologist, 43*(3), 151–160.

Robins, R., Gosling, S., & Craik, K. (1999). An empirical analysis of trends in psychology. *The American Psychologist, 54*, 117–128. https://doi.org/10.1037/0003-066X.54.2.117.

Rodriguez, M. C. (2003). Construct equivalence of multiple-choice and constructed-response items: A random effects synthesis of correlations. *Journal of Educational Measurement, 40*(2), 163–184. https://doi.org/10.1111/j.1745-3984.2003.tb01102.x.

Roediger, H. L. (2004). What happened to behaviorism. *APS Observer, 17*, 40–42.

Roediger, H. L., & Karpicke, J. D. (2006). Test-enhanced learning: Taking memory tests improves long-term retention. *Psychological Science, 17*(3), 249–255. https://doi.org/10.1111/j.1467-9280.2006.01693.x.

Roediger, H. L., & Marsh, E. J. (2005). The positive and negative consequences of multiple-choice testing. *Journal of Experimental Psychology: Learning, Memory, and Cognition, 31*(5), 1155–1159. https://doi.org/10.1037/0278-7393.31.5.1155.

Root, W. B., & Rehfeldt, R. A. (2020). Towards a modern-day teaching machine: The synthesis of programmed instruction and online education. *The Psychological Record, 71*(1), 1–10. https://doi.org/10.1007/s40732-020-00415-0.

Royal, K. D. (2017). Why veterinary medical educators should embrace cumulative final exams. *Journal of Veterinary Medical Education, 44*(2), 346–350. https://doi.org/10.3138/jvme.0216-035R.

Scully, D. (2017). Constructing multiple-choice items to measure higher-order thinking. *Practical Assessment, Research and Evaluation, 22*(4). https://doi.org/10.7275/CA7Y-MM27.

Sheldon, J. P. (2002). Operant conditioning concepts in introductory psychology textbooks and their companion web sites. *Teaching of Psychology, 29*(4), 281–285. https://doi.org/10.1207/S15328023TOP2904_04.

Shields, C., & Gredler, M. (2003). A problem-solving approach to teaching operant conditioning. *Teaching of Psychology, 30*(2), 114–116. https://doi.org/10.1207/S15328023TOP3002_06.

Skinner, B. F. (1956). A case history in the scientific method. *The American Psychologist, 11*(5), 221–233.

Skinner, B. F. (1968). *The technology of teaching*. New York, NY: Appleton-Century-Crofts.

Skinner, B. F. (1974). *About behaviorism*. New York, NY: Knopf.

Skinner, B. F. (1977). Why I am not a cognitive psychologist. *Behavior, 5*(2), 1–10.

Smith, M. A., & Karpicke, J. D. (2014). Retrieval practice with short-answer, multiple-choice, and hybrid tests. *Memory, 22*(7), 784–802. https://doi.org/10.1080/09658211.2013.831454.

Sperling, R. A., Reeves, P. M., Follmer, D. J., Towle, A. L., & Chung, K. S. (2016). Teaching behaviorism to support self-regulation, integration, and transfer. In M. C. Smith & N. DeFrates-Densch (Eds.), *Challenges and innovations in educational psychology teaching and learning* (pp. 15–28). Charlotte, NC: Information Age Publishing.

Stoloff, M., McCarthy, M., Keller, L., Varfolomeeva, V., Lynch, J., Makara, K., … Smiley, W. (2010). The undergraduate psychology major: An examination of structure and sequence. *Teaching of Psychology, 37*(1), 4–15. https://doi.org/10.1080/00986280903426274.

Szpunar, K., McDermott, K., & Roediger, H. (2007). Expectation of a final cumulative test enhances long-term retention. *Memory & Cognition, 35*, 1007–1013. https://doi.org/10.3758/BF03193473.

Tauber, R. T. (1988). Overcoming misunderstanding about the concept of negative reinforcement. *Teaching of Psychology, 15*(3), 152. https://doi.org/10.1207/s15328023top1503_15.

Thyer, B. A. (1991). The enduring intellectual legacy of B. F. Skinner: A citation count from 1966-1989. *The Behavior Analyst, 14*(1), 73–75.

Vickrey, T., Rosploch, K., Rahmanian, R., Pilarz, M., & Stains, M. (2015). Research-based implementation of peer instruction: A literature review. *CBE Life Sciences Education, 14*(1), es3. https://doi.org/10.1187/cbe.14-11-0198.

Ware, M. E., & Johnson, D. E. (Eds.). (2000). *Handbook of demonstrations and activities in the teaching of psychology volume II: Physiological-comparative, perception, learning, cognitive, and developmental* (2nd ed.). Mahwah, NJ: Lawrence Erlbaum Associates.

Wasserman, E. A., & Blumberg, M. S. (2006). Designing minds. *APS Observer, 19*(10), 25–26.

Watrin, J. P., & Darwich, R. (2012). On behaviorism in the cognitive revolution: Myth and reactions. *Review of General Psychology, 16*(3), 269–282. https://doi.org/10.1037/a0026766.

Wesp, R., & Miele, J. (2008). Student opinions of the quality of teaching activities poorly predict pedagogical effectiveness. *Teaching of Psychology, 35*(4), 360–362. https://doi.org/10.1080/00986280802374617.

White, G. (2011). Interactive lecturing. *The Clinical Teacher, 8*(4), 230–235. https://doi.org/10.1111/j.1743-498X.2011.00457.x.

Wiggins, G. P., & McTighe, J. (2005). *Understanding by design* (2nd ed.). Alexandria, VA: Association for Supervision and Curriculum Development.

Wyatt, W. J., Hawkins, R. P., & Davis, P. (1986). Behaviorism: Are reports of its death exaggerated? *The Behavior Analyst, 9*(1), 101–105.

Xu, X., Kauer, S., & Tupy, S. (2016). Multiple-choice questions: Tips for optimizing assessment in-seat and online. *Scholarship of Teaching and Learning in Psychology, 2*(2), 147–158. https://doi.org/10.1037/stl0000062.

Yancy McGuire, S. (2015). *Teach students how to learn: Strategies you can incorporate into any course to improve student metacognition, study skills, and motivation.* Sterling, VA: Stylus.

Teaching of General Psychology: Problem Solving

David Gibson, Dirk Ifenthaler, and Samuel Greiff

Contents

Abstract

This chapter defines problem solving and its research history. In addition to this, it introduces data science approaches to research on problem solving for psychology students, educators, and researchers. The chapter describes four new core content and topical areas on the immediate horizon: data science, Internet of things, network analyses, and artificial intelligence. The chapter elucidates

D. Gibson
Curtin University, Perth, Australia

D. Ifenthaler
Curtin University, Perth, Australia

University of Mannheim, Mannheim, Germany

S. Greiff (✉)
University of Luxembourg, Esch-sur-Alzette, Luxembourg
e-mail: samuel.greiff@uni.lu

© Springer Nature Switzerland AG 2023
J. Zumbach et al. (eds.), *International Handbook of Psychology Learning and Teaching*,
Springer International Handbooks of Education,
https://doi.org/10.1007/978-3-030-28745-0_8

implications for data science education in general psychology, focusing on research in problem solving and on how problem solving can be taught in higher education.

Keywords

Problem solving · Data science methods · Learning science · Individual and group psychology

Introduction

The nature of human problem solving has been studied by psychologists for the past hundred years. Early conceptual work of German Gestalt psychologists (e.g., Duncker, 1935; Wertheimer, 1959) and experimental research on problem solving in the 1960s and 1970s typically operated with relatively simple, laboratory tasks (e.g., Duncker's famous "X-ray" problem; Ewert and Lambert's 1932 "disk" problem, later known as "Tower of Hanoi") that appeared novel to participants. Reasons for the choice of simple but novel tasks include the clearly defined optimal solutions, being solvable within a relatively short time frame, and researchers could trace participants' problem solving steps. The underlying assumption that simple tasks such as the Tower of Hanoi captured the main properties of "real world" problems and that the cognitive processes underlying participants' attempts to solve simple problems were representative of the processes they engaged in when solving "real world" problems has been the center of these empirical investigations. Thus, researchers used simple problems for reasons of convenience. The aim remained to generalize research findings in order to explain how people solve more complex problems (Greiff & Wüstenberg, 2014; Seel et al., 2009).

Psychologists generally agree on the point that problem solving should be considered as information processing that is relevant across a number of areas. However, different lines of research focusing on problem solving emerged, for example, in North America and in Europe. While researchers in North America focused successfully on the implementation of problem solving in computer systems, European researchers focused on the simulation of complex environments to empower human problem solving and decision making within complex domains (Berry & Broadbent, 1984, 1988; Newell & Simon, 1972). Interestingly, research on complex problem solving is closely related to research on cognitive structures and mental model research insofar as researchers such as Funke (1992) agree on the point that complex problem solving necessarily presupposes the process of mental model building (Ifenthaler & Seel, 2005, 2011, 2013). Further, Krems (1995) identified differences between novices and experts in complex problem situations in terms of domain-specific knowledge, strategies applied, and available cognitive flexibility. As such, the link between researching the construction and development of cognitive structures and mental models as well as complex problem solving provides a major challenge for research in the field of psychology (Jacobson, 2000).

Problem solving has been taught as a subfield of psychology beginning in the 1930s and received a boost from theorists who were aware of and involved with the then emerging field of computer science in the 1940s. By the early 1970s, the field had fully begun to embrace computational approaches, metaphorically if not fully operationalized, and proceeded alongside traditional psychological studies. More recently, with the advent of fully globally connected cloud computing services, massive access to the Internet, and advances in data science such as artificial intelligence, the subfield of problem solving is undergoing rapid change toward integrating and better understanding the psychological factors evidenced with the digital signatures of individual- and group-based problem solving.

So, while the topic of problem solving has traditionally been included in lectures either in cognitive or general psychology, practitioners and researchers need more than historical awareness of developments such as the "General Problem Solver" or the work of key historical figures. In this chapter, we expand from the historical perspective on problem solving in three ways: (1) as an educationally relevant competence for both practitioners and researchers; (2) as a variable of individual difference and potential factor in psychological processes; and (3) as a measurement challenge of the digital age that is amenable to new and emerging data science methods.

Purposes and Rationale of the Curriculum in Problem Solving

A curriculum focusing on problem solving skills should be based on current research findings in the field of problem solving and requires learners to solve meaningful problems. Hence, relevant problems for the curriculum have to be chosen judiciously (Lester, 1983; Silver, Ghousseini, Gosen, Charalambous, & Strawhun, 2005).

Mayer and Wittrock (1996) identified and recommended three general principles for problem solving instruction (p. 299):

1. Domain-specific principle: It is better to teach problem solving skills within specific disciplines rather than attempting to teach general problem solving heuristics.
2. Near-transfer principle: It is better to expect that problem-solving skills will be largely restricted with respect to their range of applicability rather than expecting problem-solving skills to be applicable to a wide range of problems.
3. Knowledge integration principle: It is better to integrate teaching of facts, concepts, and strategy knowledge within guided problem solving tasks rather than focusing mainly on teaching.

Core Contents and Topics of Problem Solving

This section is organized into two parts: the historical core contents and topics of problem solving and emerging data science core contents and topics.

Historical Core Content and Topics

The following list documents the core historical content and its focus. In particular the earlier works are, by and large, outdated and are rather of historical value, but they can be important to students when trying to get an overview of what early problem solving research proposed.

- Duncker, K. (1935). *The Psychology of Productive Thinking*. Springer. This book discusses functional fixedness and mental restructuring as relevant parts of problem solving. It was one of the first works that systematically looked at the topic.
- Pólya, G. (1945). *How to Solve It*. Princeton University Press. This book discusses heuristics for solving any kind of problem and includes the infamous "We need heuristic reasoning when we construct a strict proof as we need scaffolding when we erect a building."
- Newell, A., & Simon, H. A. (1972) *Human Problem Solving*. Prentice-Hall. This book introduces the idea of problem spaces and associated with it the Problem Space Hypothesis that postulates that all goal-oriented behavior can be represented as a search through a space of possible states while attempting to achieve a goal. The first consequence of the principle of bounded rationality is that the intended rationality of an actor requires one to construct a simplified model of the real situation in order to deal with it. The actor behaves rationally with respect to this model, and such behavior is not even approximately optimal with respect to the real world. To predict the actor's behavior, we must understand the actor's psychological properties as a perceiving, thinking, and learning animal.
- Kahneman, D. Slovic, P., Tversky, A. (1982) *Judgment Under Uncertainty: Heuristics and Biases*. Cambridge University Press. This work argues that people rely on a limited number of heuristic principles, which reduce the complex tasks of assessing probabilities and predicting values to simpler judgmental operations: representativeness, availability, adjustment, and anchoring

Coming from this historical perspective, problem solvers need to learn *effective strategies for all the cognitive processes* (Ifenthaler & Seel, 2013; Margulieux, 2019), which provide us with targets for considering data science and artificial intelligence in problem solving.

Whereas scientific inquiry into problem solving previously focused primarily on cognitive processes of individuals, in the era of data science, it has recently turned attention to *cognitive systems* composed of people, machines, and networked information. In the era of big data, artificial intelligence, and cloud computing, the traditional definitions of problem solving, strategies, and processes take on new meaning because instances of people, machines, and cyberspace can increasingly work together as a *problem solving system*.

People engaged in the system are the source of questions, the motivation for inquiry, and the ultimate arbiters of the value of any solution and knowledge produced. People also reason with far less data than machines, using complex human processes that have led to new strategies in machine learning – in particular, reinforcement learning and deep learning. Machines in the system handle enormous amounts of data at extremely high velocity and apply algorithms that automate reasoning and extend it creatively by learning on the fly and building and testing computational models. Cyberspace is the context of the new problem solving system, which integrates knowledge via open science to represent information and people. Thus, the purposes and rationale for the psychology curriculum has expanded to advance the use of data science knowledge, methods, tools, and approaches to further use and understand problem solving.

New Data Science Core Content and Topics

The emergence of data science (Stanton, 2012) has brought new possibilities and approaches to research on problem solving. New methods for dealing with dynamic systems, large data sets, streaming data flows from interactive applications, and smart applications support a new kind of science of educational research, such as research on unobtrusive observation, automated analysis, and personalized feedback to learners and instructors. Examples of data science in cognitive sciences indicate additional possibilities for re-imagining data analyses and visualization of network relationships in educational contexts. See, for example, Goldstone, Pestilli, and Börner (2015), Sporns (2011), and van den Heuvel and Sporns (2013) for application of data science to information processing from physical to mental states. This section is organized into four areas: Data science, Internet of things, network analyses, and artificial intelligence.

Data Science

The publication of A New Kind of Science (Wolfram, 2002) identified a groundswell in computation that had been building since 1890 when Poincare concluded that the challenging three-body problem (i.e., a dynamic system with earth, moon, and sun) could not be solved in terms of algebraic formulas and integrals. With the advent of computers in the mid-twentieth century and the rapid expansion of computational sciences (Blei & Smyth, 2017), Poincare's conclusion can now be modeled at very high scale and fine resolution, creating a new approach in scientific inquiry. The new kind of inquiry and representation (Wolfram, 2002) depends on massive scale computation and exhaustive modeling as proofs. For example, the four-color theorem was proven in 1976 with the aid of a computational method that required an exhaustive search of all possible combinations of abstraction from a mapping (Gonthier, 2008). A debate ensued within mathematics because the proof could not be "analytically checked" by humans as it would take an excessive amount of time to replicate the computer's process. Events such as these signaled the coming of age of computation-enhanced science, preparing the ground for the field now referred to as "data science." This field is closely connected to problem solving in the sense that the increased capabilities of computational science have promoted the growth of dynamic systems and nonlinear methods in educational research, including problem solving. Computational science includes globalized data from an increasingly interconnected web of sensor networks, multimodal data sources, application sharing on a massive scale, network analysis methods, and artificial intelligence.

Internet of Things

While the traditional Internet is focused on serving requests and responses, the Internet of things (IoT), which allows the connectedness of sensors and actuators to global cloud-based services, focuses instead on sensing and responding (Etzion, Fournier, & Arcushin, 2014; Evans, 2011). Within the IoT, consumer products and enterprise services are connected to each other and the rest of the Internet, leading to the phrase "Internet of Everything." This conception allows for connecting smart objects into bigger cognitive systems. For example, a smart refrigerator could maintain the supply of groceries by monitoring their supply and ordering them for you, keeping a stocked shelf of all ingredients you usually need for cooking. This, in fact, could be understood as some type of automatic problem solving with a clearly defined algorithm. The refrigerator communicates with the grocery store and delivery services and perhaps negotiates with more than one service and forms contracts for services. The refrigerator places and accepts or verifies the order, maintains its portion of your food expense financial system, and calls upon other objects, agents, and services in the supply chain as needed. The systems woven together into the Internet of Everything include things (e.g., milk container), people (e.g., clerks and delivery people or robots), places (e.g., the fridge, store, and transport locations), and systems (e.g., drone-based delivery, apartment security, and food network). Working with problems where an integration among data types, people, and machines has multiple nuanced meanings at several levels of complexity is not so much a "big data" problem as one of finding a solution with just enough information in a short period of time – more like a human learns to recognize a face or associate a smell with a place and an emotion – in short, more like cognition. In this development, humans and machines are linked to work better together than when apart, opening several avenues for problem solving research. The term "cognitive computing" evolved from knowledge discovery, cognitive science, and big data (Chen, Herrera, & Hwang, 2018) and designates the use of computerized models to simulate human thought processes. The Internet of things, cloud computing, and reinforcement and deep learning analytics and algorithms form the foundation of human-centered cognitive computing. Such technologies underpin the goal of machine-based reasoning analogous to the human brain working in partnership with and guided by problem solving humans. Critical to human-centered cognitive computing is having humans continuously in the loop with machines and cyberspace. As such, they serve as a bridge to the question of how networks of machines, information, and other people are changing the nature of research on problem solving. In such networks of people, machines, and information, it is clear that several sciences need to be integrated: learning sciences, including the psychology of individual and group learning as the epistemological focus and source of relevant questions; data science, including information and computer sciences as the lab bench and method of the new kind of science; and cyberspace as the ubiquitously distributed laboratory.

Since a key context of research and analysis of problem solving with the IoT concerns how these human, machine, and information systems can be integrated and interactively networked, we next turn attention to a variety of network analyses before briefly discussing artificial intelligence as a partner in problem solving research.

Network Analyses

Information networks are becoming increasingly popular to capture complex relationships across various disciplines, such as social networks, citation networks, and biological networks (Aktas, Akbas, & Fatmaoui, 2019). Thus, the tools and approaches of network mining are arising as an important frame for studying problem solving. In the following sections, we introduce three types of network analysis that can be applied to problem solving research – social, ecological, and epistemic network analyses – we briefly describe them and give illustrative examples of their use in problem solving research. A network by definition is an arrangement of intersecting horizontal and vertical lines representing, for example, a group or system of interconnected people or things (https://www.lexico.com/en/definition/network). As a system of people, things, and intersecting connections, networks are broadly applicable to many learning, teaching, and educational situations. For example, the "people" might be learners, teachers, parents, or administrators singly or in combinations and clusters; and the "things" might be communications, power relationships, educational data, curriculum materials, and artifacts created during learning processes. Networks can flexibly represent psychological processes, social relationships, and structural relationships as well as to understand flows of information, making network analysis an essential new data science toolkit for the learning sciences.

Network analysis relies on graph theory and methods. Graph-theoretic measures (Diestel, 2006) such as density and centrality are based on counts of the nodes (entities) and edges (relationships or links) of the graph; similarity measures, in particular, are based on differences between either node or edge measurements or correlations. Newer topological approaches such as persistent homology (Aktas et al., 2019) measure network features that persist across multiple scales, indicating the accurate patterns in the data. Such approaches examine distances between specific node structures (triangles, tetrahedrons, and higher-dimensional objects) through filtrations, which are mathematically rigorous subset formalisms of the topology. However, these existing methods have been mainly used on static networks and cannot be directly applied to large-scale evolving networks as needed in some educational contexts, particularly those that capture and represent data from multiple, diverse, and dynamic data sources.

We refer to dynamic complexes, similar to those arising out of the topological analysis of networks as motifs, using a concept from music that refers to a salient recurring figure, fragment, or succession of events. Graph theory defines a clique as a subgraph of any directly connected node to another node. A motif, which adds time and evolving complex structure to the concept of a clique, is composed of relatively persistent cliques changing over time while maintaining a substantial portion of the subgraph composition relevant to some unit of analysis. A motif is a complex code and is a flexible concept that can be applied at multiple levels of analysis from micro to meso to macro features, with homological features preserved over time and network scope (Aktas et al., 2019). For example, a motif of interest might be the experience of "being a doctor" in a simulation, as defined and bounded by the simulation leverage points of having a patient to talk to, noticing things from the patient interview, and making a reasoned decision about a therapy (Sharkasi, 2010).

In epistemic network analysis, which we will discuss below, the nodes of the network are complex codes (i.e., narrative assignment or identification by experts or machines) that might represent a combination of action, communication, cognition, and other relevant features of group interaction (Gašević, Joksimović, Eagan, & Shaffer, 2019). This characterizes part of the meaning of a motif – that it has a semantic import as well as a physical syntactic reality – but we want to extend the idea further to give it capability for persisting over time and evolving within its semantic position in the network. We will thus refer to network nodes as "motifs" if they play a significant structural role in the network (e.g., centrality, density, and using higher level concepts from ecological, social, and epistemic frameworks) and can be described in terms of persistent homology. In a network analysis, a motif can thus be considered a summarized complex node, a composition of complex elements, in the sense that each node has depth and breadth in both frequency and magnitude at many scale lengths. For example, in an ego analysis of an individual learner who is acquiring new knowledge in a guided group discussion, a single node (e.g., an individual) can be understood (e.g., microscopically further represented) as a complex and layered evolving motif and can be further combined with other motifs to create a layered global network. In a learning setting, a single instant of a learner's private experience (e.g., a motif representation) might be manifested as an observable behavioral change influenced by both individual and group elements; as a unit of analysis, the individual motif can be seen to evolve or maintain across time, depending on the context.

From these foundational ideas, we hold that when a learning design or curriculum or classroom environment is implemented by an instructor and is encountered by a learner or a group of learners, an ecological network ensues. When learners interact with other people, social networks are generated. When a learner has a personal experience of a learning situation, an epistemic network may be formed. In the following sections, we introduce these kinds of networks and link them to the psychological study of problem solving.

Ecological Networks

Ecological networks are a standard method for representing and analyzing a multitude of interactions between different species (Ings & Hawes, 2018) via interactions that are trophic (consumer-resource) or symbiotic (coaction resulting

Table 1 Interaction types in ecological networks

Symbiosis type	Species 1	Species 2
Mutualism	Benefit (+)	Benefit (+)
Commensalism	No effect (0)	Benefit (+)
Parasitism	Harm (−)	Benefit (+)
Neutralism	No effect (0)	No effect (0)
Amensalism	Harm (−)	No effect (0)
Competition	Harm (−)	Harm (−)

in one of six types of benefit-harm). Trophic interactions in biological networks concern the food chain (e.g., a trophic level of an organism is the position or number of steps it occupies in a food web). There may be a valid generalization of the consumer-resource relationship that applies to learning and problem solving. We can think of learners as both consuming and creating instructional resources for themselves and others while learning. Similarly, problem solving can be seen as both using (consuming) and deploying (creating) internal and external resources to solve the problem. The application of ecological perspectives and networks to learning and education requires a re-thinking of education as a system and applying consumer-resource relations in learning networks. For example, can teachers and students (or students and students; or students and interactive learning materials) be treated as two different "species" and thus amenable to various ecological indicators, with new possibilities for interpretation? Is the "food chain" metaphor translatable to a generic energy web where students "consume" some resources (e.g., learning content materials) to "create" different resources (e.g., brain structures to store new knowledge)? We discuss these possibilities further below.

Symbiotic relations, in contrast, require even less of a leap than the metaphor of trophic transformation of energy. With the lens of symbiosis, six types of interactions identify when one or both species benefit from each other, have no effect, or are harmed (Table 1). The possibilities for interpreting some of these as peer-to-peer and novice-to-expert have begun to be explored by data scientists interested in learning analytics.

Applying ecological networks to learning and educational systems is relatively new. Davis and colleagues have developed an ecological perspective on educational change theory (Davis, 2012) and the structure of educational systems (Davis, Eickelmann, & Zaka, 2013).

Social Networks

Social network analysis (SNA) is a strategy for investigating social structures (Otte & Rousseau, 2002) via two primary forms: ego analysis (one person) and global network analysis (relationships between people). In the psychological study of problem solving, the addition of "things" such as curriculum materials, goals of learning, and performance indicators adds new dimensions to the foundations, which we will refer to as SNA+, which we discuss further in the sections on ecological and epistemic networks.

Cohesion	How a network is interlinked
Centralization	Extent to which the network depends on a small number of actors
Structural equivalence	Whether there are actors that have similar roles in the network
Prominence	Popularity of an actor in the network
Range	Extent to which an actor is connected to others in the network
Brokerage	How an actor connects different parts of the network that are otherwise disconnected

Epistemic Networks

The term "epistemic frame" (Shaffer, 2006) refers to the ways of knowing, of deciding what is worth knowing, and of adding to a collective body of knowledge and understanding of a community of practice. The concept was initially proposed as a possible mechanism through which sufficiently rich experiences in computer-supported games could be based on real-world practices. The concept expanded to include a specific type of network analysis – epistemic network analysis (Shaffer et al., 2009) for examining interactions within a digital learning system (DLS). A DLS environment is composed of a theory of learning and its accompanying method of assessment, linked into an evidence-based, digital intervention, particularly salient for assessing performance in context and learning in progress.

The SENS model (Gašević et al., 2019) combines SNA and ENA to address the different "species" of people and learning resources – the social and content perspectives – specifically in collaborative learning environments. As we will soon encounter in the section below on artificial intelligence, the collaborating entity may be a machine or dynamic educational resource as well as a person, which suggests that the six types of symbiosis may be relevant as a general framework in all cases. In the initial research in 2019, indicators from both frameworks were combined for complementary roles in an analysis (e.g., the authors suggested that an external analysis method should be used such as regression analysis, mixed models, or statistical tests for comparisons of groups p. 5).

Integrated properties from both SNA and ENA have been shown to better predict team outcomes than ENA alone, SNA alone, and when the two are combined but not fully integrated. Researchers have named the integrated method iSENS, focusing on analyzing cognitive and social aspects of learning (Swiecki & Shaffer, 2020). Interestingly, this mixing of internal factors with externally exhibited factors suggests the mixing of different species in the ecological framework and lends support to the idea of integrated ego-social-ecological network methods having a role in setting a larger context for scientific inquiry into problem solving.

Artificial Intelligence

Zawacki-Richter and Latchem (2018) identified four broad uses of artificial intelligence in higher education: profiling and prediction, intelligent tutoring systems, assessment and evaluation, and adaptive learning systems. In addition, Chen, Xie,

Zou, and Hwang (2020) conducted a systematic analysis of 45 highly cited articles to identify the development, trends, and technologies adopted, as well as major research issues concerned by the artificial intelligence in education community. They listed typical techniques of three approaches: deep learning (DL) as a subset of machine learning (ML) as a subset of the broad perspective of general AI in education (AI).

DL	Artificial neural networks, deep belief networks, deep neural networks, recurrent neural networks, convolutional neural networks, long- and short-term memory, generative adversarial networks, variational autoencoders, adversarial learning
ML	Reinforcement learning, decision trees, support vector machines, regression analysis, Bayesian networks, genetic algorithms
AI	Fuzzy logic, rule-based systems, agent system, heuristic algorithms

Common approaches to solving problems with artificial intelligence include via searching, including searching in complex environments, adversarial search, and games, and by satisfying constraints (Russell & Norvig, 2009).

Teaching, Learning, and Assessment in Problem Solving: Approaches and Strategies

Looking at the previous sections of this chapter, it becomes clear that problem solving is an ongoing and active field of research that is not confined to psychological science but extends into fields such as computer science and education, in particular when considering the digital aspects of problem solving. However, the origins of problem solving are in psychology and over the last century researchers who would identify themselves as psychologists have studied problem solving from various angles with an initial focus on the cognitive aspects in the twentieth century. This focus has recently been extended to include also the motivational and socio-emotional aspects of problem solving. For instance, in the Programme for International Student Assessment (PISA), an assessment of individual problem solving was included in the 2012 edition. This assessment was extended to problem solving in groups (labelled collaborative problem solving) in the 2015 edition to additionally consider the social dimension of problem solving.

Problem solving as a content topic is relevant for studies in many fields but maybe most for psychology. Consequently, content on problem solving is found in many Bachelor and Master programs of psychology to familiarize students with the topic and to provide relevant theoretical and empirical background. Traditionally, problem solving is covered in Bachelor-level lectures of general psychology or cognitive psychology. Contents typically cover the historical beginnings of problem solving research starting with Duncker and cover milestones of the development of our understanding of problem solving such as the seminal work on the General Problem Solver (GPS) by Newell and Simon (1972). As problem solving research advances and gets increasingly connected to the digitalized world of the twenty-first century, content nowadays often includes some of the more recent and still developing topics outlined above such as problem solving in the context of data science, the IoT, network analyses, and artificial intelligence.

Problem solving is also a topic that is often considered as part of empirical seminars in Bachelor programs of psychology, in which students set up their own experiments to gather initial experience with the process of experimental work. The reason behind this is that the fundamental contents of problem solving research are easily accessible at the Bachelor level, and many experiments related to problem solving performance are straightforward. In addition, experimental setups might target differences among problem solvers or even more prominently, the manipulations of problem features that are expected to lead to subsequent differences in problem solving performance and the underlying processes. To this end, the field of problem solving has been a use-case of early experimental and practical work in the education of psychology students in addition to and beyond the theoretical contents mentioned above and is a cornerstone of contemporary higher education of psychologists.

While problem solving as a content-related field that psychology students should know about is fairly established in tertiary education in psychology, a second question concerns whether and in which way psychology programs should develop actual problem solving skills in students to prepare them for working as psychologists later on. This question is clearly different from teaching problem solving-related content. This also holds for the complexity of the underlying question: Whereas teaching factual knowledge on problem solving as research topic within lectures or within experimental courses is rather straightforward, it is a completely different context and challenge to facilitate actual problem solving skills in students throughout tertiary education (for some thoughts on the role of transversal skills such as problem solving in tertiary education, see Zlatkin-Troitschanskaia, Pant, & Greiff, 2019).

The question on how to make students good problem solvers is not new but has been mainly targeted in the context of secondary education. In fact, some have labelled the challenge of bringing students to the level of well-skilled and competent problem solvers as the biggest task that schools and educational systems face (Mayer & Wittrock, 2006). As indicated above, this is also evidenced by the fact that large international studies with student populations such as PISA (with 15-year-old students) that aim at comparing the performance of educational systems across the world have repeatedly included problem solving in their assessments to provide international comparisons. These studies have mostly been run with student populations but also studies that focus on adult populations such as the Programme for the International Assessment of Adult Competencies (PIAAC) have included problem solving as a core skill for success at work and life in more general.

To this end, teachers and instructors in tertiary education would easily agree that becoming good problem solvers while not explicit is yet an important goal of tertiary education, and this holds for the teaching and learning of psychology as well. At the same time, it is important to acknowledge that the type of problem solving that is required and the contextual embedding of problem solving varies greatly across different study programs (such as computer science, problem solving, medicine, and so forth) and, later on in life, occupations. But even within psychology, the problems that one needs to successfully master are by no means similar or coherent. For instance, the collaborative aspects of solving problems in a group might be in the focus for an I/O psychologist who is asked to mediate conflicts and improve team spirit in a small business; the adaptive and meta-cognitive components of problem solving might be the focus when working as an educational psychologist in the classroom to consider several students' learning needs and challenges simultaneously in an attempt to help them master curricular content; and hands-on practical problem solving dimensions as well as the emotional dimensions of problem solving are likely to be key to successful treatment of patients when working as a clinical psychologist.

With these different foci that problem solving might take, it comes as no surprise that it is a great challenge to combine all this in a study program. In addition to this, it can be assumed that there are few explicit resources and guidelines on how to teach problem solving – on the one hand because research does not have answers yet to the question on how to best teach problem solving and on the other hand because curricula in psychology are more organized along content than along skills.

One promising method to increase students' problem solving skills aligned with their specific area of occupation is problem-based learning (PBL). PBL represents a major development in educational practice that continues to have a large impact across subjects and disciplines worldwide. The claims made for PBL promise an important improvement in outcomes for education, including increased retention of knowledge and enhanced integration and application of basic science concepts (e.g., Schmidt et al., 2007). However, empirical evidence to support these claims is less straightforward (Capon & Kuhn, 2004; Şendag & Odabaşi, 2009), and it remains an open question whether PBL can help to sustainably lift occupationally relevant problem solving skills in psychology students.

In this chapter, three suggestions for teaching problem solving are offered concerning the history, professional competence, impacts on individuals, and the use of data science in psychology.

Suggestion 1: Balance lectures with real-world experiences that engage students through individual- and team-based problem solving.

Suggestion 2: Ensure that the psychology curriculum spends adequate time and resources for students to experience iterative reflection and receive timely, effective feedback on problem solving in four aspects:
  1. Knowing and applying the field's history in clinical practice and research
  2. Developing personal professional competence in problem solving as an individual and as a team member
  3. Acquiring and honing observational and clinical skills for assisting others in problem solving in individual- and team-based psychological practice
  4. Making extensive use of data science methods and knowledge in research and practice

Suggestion 3: Because data science is a new addition to the curriculum of general psychology, the psychology faculty team should review and improve its knowledge of data science research practices, methods, and findings in order to build and maintain a shared vision of its role in the field.

Challenges and Lessons Learned

Despite the relevance of problem solving skills for the psychologists of the future, it is not easy to implement problem solving as key feature of curricula in tertiary education of psychology. Please note that, in contrast, this is rather unproblematic for the research area of problem solving as this involves the mere teaching of relevant content knowledge. Thus, this section on challenges and lessons learned will be mainly about the question of what the core challenges are when trying to facilitate problem solving skills during tertiary education of psychology.

In fact, there are several reasons that might undermine a clear and evidence-based focus on psychology-relevant teaching of problem solving skills. The first is that problem solving and the dimensions (cognitive, motivational, and emotional) that are associated with it are a moving target. The research area continues to evolve and the nature of problem solving has likely changed to a substantial degree due to the level of digital tools that we use in our everyday life (Greiff et al., 2017) and that have not stopped at the doorstep of the profession of psychology. Secondly, many initiatives on assessment, learning, and instruction of problem solving have been focused on primary and secondary education, so knowledge and empirical evidence of facilitating problem solving skills in tertiary education is lacking. Thirdly, problem solving shares one concern with many other skills that are not primarily related to specific content knowledge: Students in tertiary programs, for instance, in psychology, are expected to acquire these skills but little explicit support is provided – neither to educators on how to teach the relevant set of skills nor to students on how to acquire the relevant set of skills. Mayer and Wittrock (2006) label this situation as "hidden curriculum" in the context of secondary education, but the same label adequately describes the situation in tertiary education.

These three challenges in combination lead to the conclusion that, at present, learning and instruction of problem solving as a skill happen largely on an implicit basis in psychology programs with huge individual differences, for instance, with regard to the focus a specific instructor might put on problem solving and appropriate instructional methods such as PBL. However, the picture that we paint here should not be too negative. Many courses, in particular in Master programs, that are meant as preparation for an occupation in a subfield of psychology such as I/O psychology or clinical psychology or (mandatory) internships are likely to include components that are relevant for problem solving. To this end, it is reasonable to assume that many students, once they leave tertiary education with a degree, have obtained a reasonable or for some even a high level of problem solving skills that will help them to successfully start their occupation as psychologist irrespective of the specific subdiscipline. In addition to this, often the most intensive period of learning and development is on the job, and there are many case reports on psychologists that go through an intensive period at the beginning of their occupational career when being faced with working on a job with specific demands and duties. In broad terms, this period could be described as being almost permanently faced with new problems and being confronted with the demand to solve them. This "learning by doing" will have beneficial effects on the majority of graduates and on their problem solving skills. To the extent possible, some of these crucial experiences should be integrated in a more protected environment, that is, into the period of formal tertiary education, for instance, through developing explicit and curricular anchored requirements on teaching problem solving skills.

Recommended Further Reading

Historical Approaches to Problem Solving

Empirical research on problem solving and problem posing: a look at the state of the art. (Liljedahl & Cai, 2021)

While the context of this special issue is mathematics, and not all problem solving is as well-defined or well-studied, there are a number of lessons that can be transferred to other fields. This collection introduces sixteen empirical papers that add nuance to what is known about problem solving and problem posing. The issue covers problem solving through the ages, the role of collaboration in problem solving, the role of professional development in problem solving, task variables, technology, and problem solving as a cognitive activity.

Professional Competence

Scaffolding students' problem-solving processes in an ill-structured task using question prompts and peer interactions. (Ge & Land, 2003)

This quasi-experimental study supported by case examples examines the effects of question prompts and peer interactions in scaffolding undergraduate students' problem solving processes in an ill-structured task in problem representation, developing solutions, making justifications, and monitoring and evaluating. The study investigated both the outcomes and the processes of student problem solving performance. The quantitative outcomes revealed that question prompts had significantly positive effects on student problem solving performance and the qualitative findings indicated positive effects of peer interactions in facilitating cognitive thinking and metacognitive skills.

The construction of shared knowledge in collaborative problem solving. (Roschelle & Teasley, 1995)

This study examines the interaction between participants analyzed with respect to a "joint problem space" created in collaboration, which comprises an emergent, socially negotiated set of knowledge elements, such as goals, problem state descriptions, and problem solving actions. The analysis shows how this shared conceptual space is constructed through the external mediational framework of shared language, situation, and activity. This approach has particular implications for understanding how the benefits of collaboration are realized and serves to clarify the possible roles of the computers in supporting collaborative learning.

Individual Differences

Measuring Problem Solving with Technology : A Demonstration Study for NAEP (Bennett, Persky, Weiss, Jenkins, & Russell, 2010)

In this study, two computer-delivered assessment scenarios were designed, one on solving science-related problems through electronic information search and the other on solving science-related problems by conducting simulated experiments. The assessment scenarios were administered to nationally representative samples of 8th-grade students in over 200 schools. Results are reported on the psychometric functioning of the scenarios and the performance of population groups.

Data science in educational assessment (Gibson & Webb, 2015)

This article introduces four psychometric challenges of data science or "big data" in educational assessments that are enabled by technology: (1) dealing with change over time via time-based data; (2) how a digital performance space's relationships interact with learner actions, communications, and products; (3) how layers of interpretation are formed from translations of atomistic data into meaningful larger units suitable for making inferences about what someone knows and can do; and (4) how to represent the dynamics of interactions between and among learners who are being assessed by their interactions with each other as well as with digital resources and agents in digital performance spaces. The article calls for the restructuring of training of the next generation of researchers and psychometricians to specialize in data science in technology enabled assessments.

Data Science in Psychology

Making use of data for assessments: Harnessing analytics and data science. (Ifenthaler, Greiff, & Gibson, 2018)

This chapter focuses on how data with a large number of records, of widely differing data types, and arriving rapidly from multiple sources can be harnessed for meaningful assessments and supporting learners in a wide variety of learning situations. Distinct features of analytics-driven assessments may include self-assessments, peer assessments, and semantic rich and personalized feedback as well as adaptive prompts for reflection. The chapter concludes with future directions in the broad area of analytics-driven assessments for teachers and educational researchers which is of interest to educational psychologists.

References

Aktas, M. E., Akbas, E., & Fatmaoui, A. E. (2019). Persistence homology of networks: methods and applications. *Applied Network Science, 4*(1). https://doi.org/10.1007/s41109-019-0179-3

Berry, D.C., & Broadbent, D.E. (1984). On the relationship between task performance and associated verbalizable knowledge. *Quarterly Journal of Experimental Psychology, 36A*, 209–231.

Berry, D.C., & Broadbent, D.E. (1988). Interactive tasks and the implicit–explicit distinction. *British Journal of Psychology, 79*, 251–272.

Blei, D., & Smyth, P. (2017). Science and data science. *Proceedings of the National Academy of Sciences, 114*(33), 8689–8692. https://doi.org/10.1073/pnas.1702076114

Chen, M., Herrera, F., & Hwang, K. (2018). Cognitive computing: Architecture, technologies and intelligent applications. *IEEE Access, 6*, 19774–19783. https://doi.org/10.1109/ACCESS.2018.2791469

Chen, X., Xie, H., Zou, D., & Hwang, G.-J. (2020). Application and theory gaps during the rise of Artificial Intelligence in Education. *Computers and Education: Artificial Intelligence, 1-*(August), 100002. https://doi.org/10.1016/j.caeai.2020.100002

Davis, N. (2012). *Leadership for online learning within and across secondary schools: An ecological perspective on change theories.* In International federation of information processing working group 3.3 (pp. 1–15).

Davis, N., Eickelmann, B., & Zaka, P. (2013). Restructuring of educational systems in the digital age from a co-evolutionary perspective. *Journal of Computer Assisted Learning, 29*, 438–450. https://doi.org/10.1111/jcal.12032

Diestel, R. (2006). *Graph theory.* https://doi.org/10.1103/PhysRevLett.107.085504

Duncker, K. (1935). *Zur Psychologie des produktiven Denkens.* Berlin: Springer.

Etzion, O., Fournier, F., & Arcushin, S. (2014). *Tutorial on the Internet of everything.* In Proceedings of the 8th ACM international conference on distributed event-based systems – DEBS '14 (pp. 236–237). https://doi.org/10.1145/2611286.2611308

Evans, D. (2011, April). *The Internet of Things – How the next evolution of the Internet is changing everything.* CISCO white paper, pp. 1–11. https://doi.org/10.1109/IEEESTD.2007.373646

Funke, J. (1992). *Wissen über dynamische Systeme: Erwerb, Repräsentation und Anwendung.* Berlin: Springer.

Ge, X., & Land, S. M. (2003). Scaffolding students' problem-solving processes in an illstructured task using question prompts and peer interactions. *Educational Technology Research and Development, 51*(1), 21–38.

Gibson, D. C., & Webb, M. (2015). Data science in educational assessment. *Education and Information Technologies, 20*(4), 697–713. https://doi.org/10.1007/s10639-015-9411-7

Ifenthaler, D., Greiff, S., & Gibson, D. C. (2018). Making use of data for assessments: harnessing analytics and data science. In J. Voogt, G. Knezek, R. Christensen, & K.-W. Lai (Eds.), *International handbook of IT in primary and secondary education* (2 ed., pp. 649–663). Springer. https://doi.org/10.1007/978-3-319-71054-9_41

Jacobson, M.J. (2000). Problem Solving About Complex Systems: Differences Between Experts and Novices. In B. Fishman & S. O'Connor-Divelbiss (Eds.), *Fourth international conference of the learning sciences*, pp. 14–21. Mahwah, NJ: Erlbaum.

Krems, J. (1995). Cognitive flexibility and complex problem solving. In P.A. Frensch & J. Funke (Eds.), *Complex problem solving. The European perspective*, pp. 201–218. Hillsdale, NJ: Lawrence Erlbaum.

Gašević, D., Joksimović, S., Eagan, B. R., & Shaffer, D. W. (2019). SENS: Network analytics to combine social and cognitive perspectives of collaborative learning. *Computers in Human Behavior, 92*(May), 562–577. https://doi.org/10.1016/j.chb.2018.07.003

Goldstone, R. L., Pestilli, F., & Börner, K. (2015). Self-portraits of the brain: Cognitive science, data visualization, and communicating brain structure and function. *Trends in Cognitive Sciences, 19*(8), 462–474. https://doi.org/10.1016/j.tics.2015.05.012

Gonthier, G. (2008). Formal proof–the four-color theorem. *Notices of the AMS, 55*(11), 1382–1393. Retrieved from https://www.ams.org/notices/200811/tx081101382p.pdf

Greiff, S., Scheiter, K., Scherer, R., Borgonovi, F., Britt, A., Graesser, A., Kitajima, M., & Rouet, J. F. (2017). *Adaptive problem solving. Moving towards a new assessment domain in the second cycle of PIAAC* (OECD education working papers, no. 156). Paris: OECD. https://doi.org/10.1787/90fde2f4-en

Greiff, S., & Wüstenberg, S. (2014). Assessment with microworlds: Factor structure, invariance, and latent mean comparison of the MicroDYN test. *European Journal of Psychological Assessment, 30*, 1–11. https://doi.org/10.1027/1015-5759/a000194

Ifenthaler, D., & Seel, N. M. (2005). The measurement of change: Learning-dependent progression of mental models. *Technology, Instruction, Cognition and Learning, 2*(4), 317–336.

Ifenthaler, D., & Seel, N. M. (2011). A longitudinal perspective on inductive reasoning tasks. Illuminating the probability of change. *Learning and Instruction, 21*(4), 538–549. https://doi.org/10.1016/j.learninstruc.2010.08.004

Ifenthaler, D., & Seel, N. M. (2013). Model-based reasoning. *Computers & Education, 64*, 131–142. https://doi.org/10.1016/j.compedu.2012.11.014

Ings, T. C., & Hawes, J. E. (2018). The history of ecological networks. In *Ecological networks in the tropics* (pp. 15–28). Springer. https://doi.org/10.1007/978-3-319-68228-0_2

Lester, F. K. (1983). Trends and issues in mathematical problem-solving research. In R. Lesh & M. Landau (Eds.), *Acquisition of mathematics concepts and processes* (pp. 229–261). Academic Press.

Margulieux, L. (2019). *Chapter summary: Mayer & Wittrock (2006) Problem solving | Lauren Margulieux*. Retrieved March 22, 2021, from https://laurenmarg.com/2019/04/21/chapter-summary-mayer-wittrock-2006-problem-solving/

Mayer, R., & Wittrock, M. (1996). Problem-solving transfer. In D. Berliner & R. Calfee (Eds.), *Handbook of educational psychology* (pp. 47–62). Simon & Schuster Macmillan.

Newell, A., & Simon, H. (1972). *Human problem solving*. Englewood Cliffs, NJ: Prentice-Hall.

Otte, E., & Rousseau, R. (2002). Social network analysis: A powerful strategy, also for the information sciences. *Journal of Information Science, 28*(6), 441–453. https://doi.org/10.1177/016555150202800601

Russell, S., & Norvig, P. (2009). *Artificial intelligence: A modern approach* (3rd ed.). Englewood Cliffs, NJ: Prentice Hall Press.

Seel, N. M., Ifenthaler, D., & Pirnay-Dummer, P. (2009). Mental models and problem solving: Technological solutions for measurement and assessment of the development of expertise. In P. Blumschein, W. Hung, D. H. Jonassen, & J. Strobel (Eds.), *Model-based approaches to learning: Using systems models and simulations to improve understanding and problem solving in complex domains* (pp. 17–40). Sense Publishers.

Shaffer, D. W. (2006). Epistemic frames for epistemic games. *Computers & Education, 46*(3), 223–234. https://doi.org/10.1016/j.compedu.2005.11.003

Shaffer, D., Hatfield, D., Svarovsky, G., Nash, P., Nulty, A., Bagley, E., … Mislevy, R. (2009). Epistemic network analysis: A prototype for 21st-century assessment of learning. *International Journal of Learning and Media, 1*(2), 33–53.

Sharkasi, N. (2010). The doctor will be you now: A case study on medical ethics and role. In K. Schrier & D. Gibson (Eds.), *Ethics and game design* (pp. 275–290). Hershey, PA: IGI Global.

Silver, E. A., Ghousseini, H., Gosen, D., Charalambous, C., & Strawhun, B. T. F. (2005). Moving from rhetoric to praxis: Issues faced by teachers in having students consider multiple solutions for problems in the mathematics classroom. *Journal for Mathematical Behavior, 24*, 287–301.

Sporns, O. (2011). *Networks of the brain*. Cambridge, MA: MIT Press.

Stanton, J. (2012). *An introduction to data science*. Syracuse University.

Swiecki, Z., & Shaffer, D. W. (2020). *ISENS: An integrated approach to combining epistemic and social network analyses*. In ACM International conference proceeding series, pp. 305–313. https://doi.org/10.1145/3375462.3375505

van den Heuvel, M. P., & Sporns, O. (2013). Network hubs in the human brain. *Trends in Cognitive Sciences*. https://doi.org/10.1016/j.tics.2013.09.012

Wertheimer, M. (1959). *Productive thinking* (Enlarged Ed.). New York: Harper & Row.

Wolfram, S. (2002). *A new kind of science*. Champaign, IL: Wolfram Media.

Zawacki-Richter, O., & Latchem, C. (2018). Exploring four decades of research in Computers & Education. *Computers & Education, 122*, 136–152. https://doi.org/10.1016/j.compedu.2018.04.001

Zlatkin-Troitschanskaia, O., Pant, H. A., & Greiff, S. (Eds.). (2019). Assessing generic and domain-specific academic competencies in higher education. *Zeitschrift für Pädagogische Psychologie*. https://doi.org/10.1024/1010-0652/a000236

General Psychology Motivation

7

Maria Tulis and J. Lukas Thürmer

Contents

Abstract

The willful pursuit of goals is one of the key capabilities that allow humans to thrive. Motivation Science is the interdisciplinary research field that investigates this fundamental capability. In the current chapter, we discuss the roots of this young field of psychology, outline an evidence-based curriculum of how to teach Motivation Science, and discuss some emerging research topics. We present a potential curriculum of an introductory course on Motivation Science, structured along the lines of the Rubicon model of action phases. We base our didactic approach on the principle of integrative teaching and learning, and spiral progression to structure our curriculum according to Motivation Science.

M. Tulis (✉) · J. L. Thürmer
Department of Psychology, University of Salzburg, Salzburg, Austria
e-mail: maria.tulis-oswald@plus.ac.at; lukas.thuermer@plus.ac.at

© Springer Nature Switzerland AG 2023   151
J. Zumbach et al. (eds.), *International Handbook of Psychology Learning and Teaching*,
Springer International Handbooks of Education,
https://doi.org/10.1007/978-3-030-28745-0_9

Keywords

Motivation Science · Spiral progression approach in teaching · Conceptual-change based learning · Integrative learning

Introduction

Motivation is a ubiquitous aspect of human behavior and a key concept in contemporary psychology. This is a blessing and a curse. A blessing because almost every student, teacher, and lay person expresses interest in this topic. It is therefore easy to engage people in teaching. The interest in motivation is a curse, however, because most people also have profound and deeply-rooted assumptions and lay-theories about motivation, supported by a vast popular literature of self-help books. Teaching motivation therefore at times may feel like an uphill battle against ill-founded knowledge and untestable theories.

To master these challenges, we suggest integrating the content of the course with pedagogic principles, motivating students through the application of Motivation Science. Furthermore, we propose the *Rubicon model of action phases* (Heckhausen & Gollwitzer, 1987) as a framework (also from a didactical point of view) in order to combine current goal concepts with traditional motivational psychology and illustrate the interrelationships. This chapter will proceed as follows: First, we will give a brief overview of the roots of Motivation Science. Second, we will introduce our contemporary perspective, which reflects the core topics we believe an undergraduate course on Motivation Science should cover. Thus, we will develop a curriculum for teaching Motivation Science organized along our contemporary perspective. Finally, we will highlight some approaches and strategies for teaching and learning in this domain.

Historical Roots of Motivation Science

Motivation can come about in different ways, as everyday experience shows: For some activities, motivation arises without intervention; for other activities, one must overcome considerable hindrances to instill motivation. Asking laypersons what they think it means "to be motivated" mostly converges to the idea of having and expending high energy in the pursuit of goals (i.e., investing effort). This answer reflects a conception of motivation that was considered in the early days of Motivation Science, from different but complementary perspectives but to answer one and the same question: What is the source of this "energy" that drives goal-directed behavior (i.e., *action*)?

In the history of Motivation Science, *drives* and *needs* were extensively analyzed in this regard, as well as intrapersonal dispositions (*motives*) and environmental affordances (*incentives*). From a psychodynamic view, Freud (1915) focused on (unconscious) drive impulses and drive satisfaction as a kind of "instinctual energy."

Freud believed that these unconscious processes are not accessible to quantitative-empirical investigation. Instead, Freud relied on qualitative descriptions of single cases to back his theory. Some scholars even argue that Freud's theories were designed to be untestable (Kempf, 2003). Current Motivation Science still assumes that many important processes run off with limited conscious awareness. But we have an arsenal of methods for measuring these processes (e.g., neuro-psychological measures: Murayama et al., 2015; Wieber, Thürmer & Gollwitzer, 2015) and are firmly rooted in a quantitative-empirical tradition.

In stark contrast to this psychodynamic approach, (neo-)behaviorists such as Hull (1943, 1952) only considered observable processes as "fair game" for science. Nevertheless, their motivation account also focuses on the drive concept. Hull's drive theory developed the concept of drive reduction as an "energizer" (i.e., as a central motivating principle). He and his colleagues emphasized the link between (biological) drives as an *un*specific source of energy that can be directed by learning processes and incentives. This conceptualization introduced a clear distinction between need and drive: Whereas needs were viewed as (observable) specific deficiencies or disturbances within the organism that elicit a nonspecific drive (which in turn initiates a specific behavior), drives constituted theoretical (hypothetical) constructs. In keeping with a behaviorist tradition, Hull accordingly operationalized drives in terms of deprivation. The longer a certain need was unfulfilled (e.g., time without food), the larger the organism's drive was assumed to be. Importantly, this drive was assumed to be unspecific. The assumption, therefore was that the deprivation of a specific need (e.g., withholding food) should not only energize related behavior (i.e., obtaining food) but also unrelated behavior (e.g., obtaining water, mates, etc.). Since Hull assumed that habit and drive were both necessary to energize behavior, he expressed his theoretical assumptions in a multiplicative association; behavior thus requires all components, because if either factor is zero, the entire term is zero – an important assumption in later theories on human motivation, too: $E_R^{nergy} = Drive \times {}_sh_R^{abit}$

Perhaps unsurprisingly, the strong assumption of unspecific drive received mixed empirical support. For instance, even rodents perform behaviors that match their specific needs (e.g., eat when they are hungry) instead of any learned behavior (e.g., drink when they are hungry; Perin, 1942). Such observations led to a gradual shift towards incorporating more elaborate inner states in motivation theory, which later led to the *cognitive revolution.* For instance, Hull later extended his theory with the assumption that environmental conditions (incentives) become motivators of behavior. Situational incentives (e.g., food) attract the individual, and thus, trigger a certain behavior. Current motivation theory does incorporate a host of inner states that were off-limits in a behaviorist tradition.

Nevertheless, Motivation Science focuses on empirical observation that reflects these processes. In this sense, we are "all behaviorists" (Smith, 2014).

Lewin's (1939, 1951) field theory focuses on human's subjective experience of the world and is based on a third theoretical tradition, *Gestalt-psychology.* As a key foundation for modern Motivation Science, Lewin proclaimed that behavior is the product of person and the environment. Lewin thus assumed that the fit of personal needs, goals, and intentions with his or her *subjective perceptions* of environmental hindrances and opportunities produce motivated behavior, much like different gravitational forces move an inanimate object. Lewin's untimely death prevented him from completing his work on field theory, such as the mathematical formulations of the field at a given time. Lewin, nevertheless, laid the foundation for modern motivation research with his focus on *intentions* as proximal predictors of action as well as the interplay between person and environment.

Although not integrated at the time, the work by Ach (1935) provides an important complementary view with respect to goals. Ach distinguished between *goal setting* and *goal realization*. This distinction opens up the possibility that one may set a goal but fail to realize it, a common occurrence in everyday experience. Ach analyzed the processes that play a role in the realization of set intentions. While processes of goal setting are determined by incentives (value) and feasibility (expectancy of success), processes of goal realization are subject to the influence of *volition*, such as persistence. Ach (1935) already investigated volitional processes that determine which motivational tendencies are implemented, at which opportunity, and in what manner. Ach's work was largely neglected by his contemporaries but the goal-setting/goal-striving distinction has been key to Motivation Science since the 1980s.

Lewin's work was also of far-reaching importance for the development of *expectancy-value theories* (in the field of educational psychology: Wigfield & Eccles, 2000; in the field of social psychology: Fishbein & Ajzen, 1975; in the field of work and organizational psychology: Vroom, 1964), which highlight *rational thought as determinant of motivation* – an idea that was first taken up and further specified by Atkinson (1957, 1964). In his model, behavior is conceptualized as a function of *motives*, incentives (*value*), and subjective *expectancies*. Heckhausen (1963) further differentiated the conceptualization of motives in terms of different *types of expectations*: (1) Situation-outcome expectancies express the assessment of how likely the desired outcome is to occur even without one's own action. (2) Action-outcome expectancies relate to the impact of one's own actions, and (3) outcome-consequence expectancies refer to the extent to which the outcome will also result in the desired consequences. On the other hand, in the field of education, Wigfield and Eccles (1992, 2000) further differentiated *types of task value* into (1) attainment value (i.e., personal importance of the task which affirms a valued aspect of an individual's identity), (2) intrinsic value (i.e., personal enjoyment from engaging in the task for its own sake), (3) utility value (i.e., perceived usefulness of the task for future short-term or long-term goals), and (4) cost (i.e., competition with other goals).

A highly important motivation framework that can contribute to understanding how individuals derive their expectancies is *attribution theory* (Heider, 1958; Kelley, 1973; Weiner, 1985). According to this perspective, humans evaluate events as "lay scientists" who seek to determine the causes for certain events (e.g., the situation or the person) to predict and alter future events. A host of research indicates that such attributions can have far-reaching consequences on the responses that people show to seemingly similar situations (review by Weiner, 2018). Attribution theory addresses multiple motivational domains, including achievement and affiliation, which is why it is considered to be a general theory of motivation (Graham, 2020). Concerned with the perceived causes of achievement success and failure, the distinction of three causal dimensions (Weiner, 1985) – locus, stability, and controllability – particularly found prominence in the field of educational psychology in particular as well as psychology and related fields more generally. Such evaluations of past events then likely impact individuals' expectations regarding future events.

Another strand of Motivation Science focuses on the *content of motivation*. Murray (1938) explained goal-directed behavior in terms of needs (as rather stable personal quantities) in correspondence with appropriate opportunities for action offered by incentives in the environment (so-called *press*). A person's individual needs modulate the specific situational prompting character, that is, how he/she perceives the environmental incentives. Murray differentiated a bundle of human physiological and psychological needs, including the motives of achievement, affiliation, and power (McClelland, Atkinson, Clark & Lowell, 1953; Murray, 1938; Atkinson, Heyns & Veroff, 1954), which are still the focus of current motivation research. The *affiliation motive* concerns establishing, maintaining, and restoring positive relationships with other people and describes a person's need to feel a sense of involvement and "belonging" within a social group. Thus, situational incentives are characterized by positive social interaction and cooperation. The personal *motive "need for achievement"* is characterized by an enduring and consistent concern with setting and meeting high standards of achievement. High need for achievement motivates an individual to succeed in competition, and to excel in activities important to them (cf. Murray, 1938; Atkinson, Heyns & Veroff, 1954). The overriding incentive is to experience competence or avoid incompetence.

Motives can be distinguished from needs in terms of their broader scope. For example, the affiliation motive is not solely directed to satisfying the need for affiliation, but related to the satisfaction of needs for protection, nurturance, and warmth (Scheffer & Heckhausen, 2018, p. 84). The *achievement motive* is related to the satisfaction of needs for competence and proves one's performance, for instance, whereas the underlying needs for the power motive might be to "feel strong" and having influence or control. Maslow (1954) took an alternative approach to classify motives in terms of needs. He proposed a hierarchical model of groups of needs, based on the principle of relative priorities in motive activation: Lower needs (e.g., physiological needs) must always be satisfied, before higher needs (e.g., self-respect, or self-actualization) will emerge and can determine behavior. On the other hand, a need activates and influences behavior only as long as it remains unsatisfied. Thus, motivated behavior is rather "*pulled*" by the external consequences of its satisfaction than "*pushed*" from within the organism. Unfortunately, Maslow's conceptualization of hierarchical groups of needs remained rather vague and has never been empirically verified. Nevertheless, it offers an alternative view on motives within the scope of *Positive psychology* and, above all, it points to their culture specificity. All these historical approaches, extensions, and differentiations have paved the way for modern Motivation Science.

Central Issues of Motivation Science

The willful regulation of behavior is key for human thriving, and Motivation Science accordingly spans a wide array of fields and uses a variety of concepts (Murphy & Alexander, 2000). For instance, educational psychology focuses on other (aspects of) motivation theories than those studied in social psychology, cognitive psychology, neuroscience, or organizational psychology. For instance, educational psychology often draws to the differentiation of *intrinsic motivation* (i.e., engagement in an activity for its own sake) versus *extrinsic motivation* (i.e., engagement in an activity from the desire for some external reward or to avoid punishment) and *self-determination theory* (Deci & Ryan, 1985, 2000) which proposes a developmental continuum of extrinsic to intrinsic motivation – both experienced as self-determined (more details in section "Core Contents and Topics of Motivation Science"). In neuroscience, there is emerging interest in the neuropsychological aspects of motivation (e.g., Ryan & Di Domenico, 2016), and motivation in the workplace for a long time has been understood in terms of extrinsic rewards, but nowadays seen as a multilevel phenomenon where individual, group, organizational, and cultural variables must be considered (Kanfer, Chen & Pritchard, 2008). In recent years, researchers have recognized the importance of integrating these cross-disciplinary approaches under the rubric of Motivation Science (Braver et al., 2014), which is now an emerging field (Kruglanski, Chernikova & Kopetz, 2015; Murayama, 2019).

Instead of a unified theory, the history of motivation research has yielded a wide range of theories and motivational concepts – each addresses motivation within a particular context and from a certain perspective. As outlined in the previous chapter, theories of human motivation stem from different conceptual frameworks: psychoanalytic, drive, field, achievement, social learning, attributional, and humanistic (for more comprehensive descriptions see Weiner, 2013). The abundance of significant contributions to understanding human motivation creates a desire to organize them and integrate them in a structuring framework (Anderman, 2020; Dweck, 2017; Forbes, 2011). A structured model of general human motivation, such as the 3×3 matrix provided by Forbes (2011) – based on three foci $\times$ three levels of aspiration – has value for contemporary Motivation Science in several ways: It can provide a common and more precise language for both academic and applied psychologists who work in the field of motivation, it structures and systematically organizes theories and insights of the past century as well as future work on motivation, and it may contribute to conceptual clarity. Indeed, over the past two decades, the question of conceptual overlap between theories and constructs remained unanswered (a continued conversation in terms of motivational theories prominent in the field of Educational Psychology provide Murphy & Alexander, 2000; Wigfield & Koenka, 2020). Contemporary Motivation Science thus engages in an interactive dialog on alternative perspectives and ongoing discussion of how constructs are similar to or distinct from constructs in other models.

Finally, current trends in motivation research emphasize the dynamic nature of motivational processes and the impact of the situation (Eccles & Wigfield, 2020; Nolen, 2020; Nolen & Ward, 2008). Therefore, new methods of both study and data analyses have developed to capture the situated nature of motivation. In addition, the importance of the social environment and the broader context for motivation is increasingly coming into focus (Wigfield & Koenka, 2020). In this regard, someone may also think of the cultural context and cross-cultural nuances (e.g., for the role of culture in goal pursuit see Oettingen, Sevincer & Gollwitzer, 2008; in achievement goal theory see Zusho & Clayton, 2011).

Purposes and Rationale of the Curriculum in Motivation Science

Teaching psychology in higher education aims to provide students with psychological knowledge and skills, such as scientific and critical thinking, and to demonstrate opportunities to apply psychological principles to real-world problems. Motivation Science lends itself to attaining these goals in teaching due to its rich theoretical background, its interdisciplinary nature, and its immediate applicability.

Therefore, our proposed selection of traditional (see previous section) and more recent motivation concepts and research (see section below) are based on the following questions:

- How relevant and representative is each theory/concept for the field of Motivation Science and for understanding human behavior?
- How does it contribute to, or is related to, the fundamental conceptions of traditional motivation research?
- How important is a theory/concept for the students' everyday experiences?

Motivational processes are based on the complex interaction between personal and environmental factors. For this reason, a curriculum for teaching motivation must present different motivation theories in relation to each other. As a case in point, we used one Motivation Science model, the *Rubicon model of action phases* (Gollwitzer, 1990, 2012; Heckhausen & Gollwitzer, 1987; Heckhausen, 1989; Keller, Gollwitzer & Sheeran, 2020), to structure the curriculum, and as a framework in order to combine different motivation theories (Fig. 1b). The Rubicon model, which subdivides the stream of action from the emergence of a desire to the achievement of a goal into four phases (pre-decisional, pre-actional, actional, and post-actional) will be explained in the next section (and illustrated in Fig. 1a). It is important to note that Motivation Science is a vast and interdisciplinary field and that our curriculum therefore necessarily represents a selection. Other approaches integrate a host of additional variables that go beyond the central question of how individuals attain goals. In this regard, PSI theory (*theory of personality-systems-interactions*: Kuhl, 2001) is a highly ambitious and comprehensive theory that refers to the ensemble of cognitive and motivational-affective processes, and how they interact differentially in individuals to determine behavior and experience (Kuhl, Quirin & Koole, 2020). Another such topic for further elaboration would be *Terror Management Theory* (e.g., see "The Oxford Handbook of Human Motivation" by Ryan, 2019) which addresses existential aspects of human motivation. Our goal is to

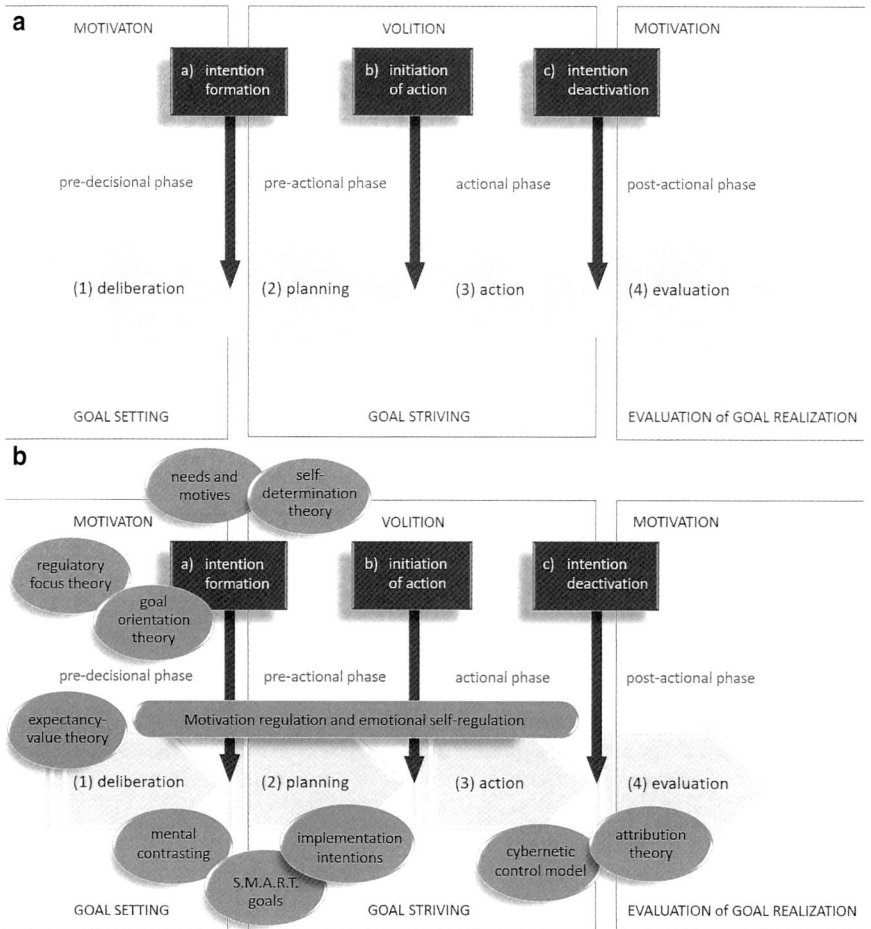

Fig. 1 (**a**) Rubicon model of action phases (own illustration). (**b**) Motivation theories and goal concepts along the four action phases (own illustration)

present a potential curriculum of an introductory course on Motivation Science on the general processes with regard to human motivation. Specific areas of psychology may therefore refer to Motivation Science literature in their sub-fields.

With reference to the competency areas identified in the APA guidelines for the undergraduate psychology program (2016), students ideally will acquire the following competencies in a course on Motivation Science:

1. *Content and Knowledge Base in Motivation Science: Core concepts and research*
   Students should demonstrate fundamental knowledge and comprehension of the major concepts of Motivation Science (historical and current), theoretical perspectives and trends, and empirical findings.

1.1 Define and explain psychological motivation theories and principles, their development, and interrelations.

1.2 Describe the complexity of the persistent questions in Motivation Science.

1.3 Distinguish between goal setting and goal striving.

1.4 Compare and relate Motivation Science to other psychology sub-disciplines.

1.5 Apply psychological principles and motivational concepts to everyday problems.

2. *Scientific Thinking and Critical Thinking Skills*

Within the field of Motivation Science, students should gain skills and conceptual knowledge in interpreting behavior, studying research, and applying research design principles to drawing conclusions about motivation-related phenomena.

2.1 Interpret motivation research findings from the backdrop of different theoretical perspectives.

2.2 Use motivation concepts to predict, explain, and change one's own behavior and the behavior of others (e.g., in counseling, therapy, or leadership).

2.3 In this regard, it is important to recognize the potential as well as the pitfalls of common intuitions about motivation. The intuitions provide an easy connecting point to Motivation Science; however, they may also lead to resistance when it comes to accepting counter-intuitive findings such as the intention-behavior gap or coasting.

2.4 Meet motivational challenges in an evidence-based manner.

2.5 Evaluate popular literature on motivation in the light of psychological knowledge, scientific reasoning, and empirical evidence. Describe the effectiveness and limitations of strategies proposed in self-help books.

3. *Ethical and Social Responsibility*

3.1 Consider the potential impact on global concerns of interventions on motivational issues (e.g., pro-environmental behavior, effective responses to the Coronavirus pandemic).

3.2 Devise motivational interventions in a way that empowers people to attain their goals; avoid conflicts of interests and the violation of ethical principles when using Motivation Science.

3.3 Ensure that Motivation Science speaks to people of diverse backgrounds.

3.4 Explain differences in individual needs and personal motives, and how social or cultural characteristics may influence motivation.

3.5 Devise interventions for motivational challenges of diverse groups of people with specific needs and conditions.

4. *Personal and Professional Development*

Students should apply motivation-specific content and skills for effective self-reflection, self-regulation, personal growth, and professional development.

4.1 Apply Motivation Science content knowledge and skills to personal growth and personal goal attainment.

4.2 Understand how and why we do (not) attain our goals.

4.3 Describe how Motivation Science applies to business, health care, education, and other workplace settings.

4.4 Apply Motivation Science to facilitate a more effective learning environment or workplace (e.g., project management, responses to setbacks and failure). Devise interventions for motivational challenges.

4.5 Demonstrate competence in writing and in oral and interpersonal communication skills in order to engage in discussion of motivational challenges and interventions with a specific audience (peer, lay, and professionals).

Across subdisciplines in Motivation Science, the *goal concept* has proven useful for analyzing motivated behavior (Gollwitzer, 2018). It is intuitively plausible that goals are a source of motivated behavior. However, the goal concept is also subject to misguided intuitions. For instance, one may assume that strong goal commitment will ensure successful goal attainment – in accordance with the maxim "where there is a will, there is a way." There is some truth to such intuitions as a complete lack of commitment most certainly will be detrimental to goal attainment. However, even strong commitment is no guarantee for goal attainment. Further complicating this situation, those who have a goal but fail to act on it are quick to provide excuses to the effect that their initial motivation must have been insufficient. In line with this reasoning, correlational research shows a medium-to-large correlation between self-reported goal strength and goal attainment. However, experimental studies show that a medium-to-large increase of commitment only translates into a small-to-medium change in respective behavior (Webb & Sheeran, 2006); an *intention-behavior gap* exists (Sheeran, 2002; Sheeran & Webb, 2016). This analysis suggests that humans waste tremendous potential between setting and attaining goals. In our experience, students identify with this observation and we therefore believe that teaching Motivation Science benefits from focusing on how to explain and improve intention-behavior relations.

Core Contents and Topics of Motivation Science

To fully comprehend intention-behavior relations, one needs to unpack a host of processes leading up to successful goal pursuit. A useful way to structure these processes is to look at the different action phases as specified in the *Rubicon model* (Gollwitzer, 1990, 2012; Heckhausen & Gollwitzer, 1987; Heckhausen, 1989; Keller, Gollwitzer & Sheeran, 2020). The Rubicon model differentiates four phases (pre-decisional, pre-actional, actional, and post-actional) which are concerned with completing four different tasks (deliberation, planning, action, and evaluation) and which are separated by three distinctive transitions (formation of a goal intention, action initiation, and goal attainment). The Rubicon model incorporates the distinction between goal setting and goal striving. The pre-decisional phase and the post-actional phase are concerned with deliberating different potential goals (motivation). In contrast, the pre-actional and actional phases are concerned with the implementation of a set goal (volition). Figure 1a depicts the main action phases (1–4) and transitions (a, b, and c) from intentions to action and its evaluation. *Intention formation* (in the pre-decisional phase) marks a shift from the motivational phase of deliberation on motivational tendencies to the volitional phases of planning and action. The *initiation of action* marks a shift from the volitional phase of planning (pre-actional phase) to that of acting (goal engagement in the post-decisional phase and action phase). Once an action has been completed or abandoned (post-actional phase), the *intention deactivation* marks another shift from a volitional to a motivational phase that involves evaluation processes of the achieved action outcomes, for example, attributions of success or failure (for a detailed overview see Achtziger & Gollwitzer, 2018, p. 485 ff.). We believe that this comprehensive and clear temporal structure not only helps motivation scientists to guide their research but also empowers students to develop a firm grasp on the topic.

Building on the basic findings of motivational psychology, psychology undergraduates need to learn about and be able to classify current research approaches and models of Motivation Science – based on the examination of how goals can be set, how goal realization occurs, and what self-regulatory processes are activated by goals. The focus of teaching Motivation Science is on combining the goal concept with the developments of traditional Motivation Science on the one hand, and on applying a meaningful selection of modern theoretical approaches to one's own actions in everyday life on the other. Personally relevant questions in this context can guide the discussion and inspire interest in the topic. Which kinds of goals do people set and what determines their goal commitment? How do people succeed in setting and committing to attractive and at the same time realistic goals? How can specific plans help the implementation and attainment of goals? What does the ideal goal pursuit and the necessary self-regulation look like in order to actually achieve one's goal? Figure 1b provides a conceptual overview of the covered curriculum. Traditional as well as more recent motivation research can be located in this framework, which is used in terms of both theory and didactics, illustrating ongoing progress and sequential development in Motivation Science.

The Pre-decisional Phase: Theories About Goal Setting

All goals are not created equal. Whereas some goals leave "wiggle room" for excuses, others already imply a path for action. A course on Motivation Science therefore necessarily contains sections on goal content and structure.

a) Goal content

Goals can be geared towards attaining positive outcomes or avoiding negative outcomes. The concepts of *approach* versus *avoidance goals* reflect this distinction: Approach goals refer to a specified positive state to be attained. Avoidance goals refer to a negative state to be avoided. With regard to the impact of more stable personal traits – in terms of the three motives (McClelland, 1985) explained in the previous section – "hope for success" (approach) versus "fear of failure" (avoidance) relate to the achievement motive; striving for control versus fear of loss of control constitute these two dimensions within the power motive; and desire for affiliation versus fear of rejection regarding the affiliation motive – all of them rather acquired through learning experiences in early childhood.

Similarly, the *regulatory focus theory* (Higgins, 1997) distinguishes goals in terms of their framing. Based on early learning processes and parental education, individuals with a dispositional *promotion focus* strive for how they would like to be and for personal gains (in all respects). Their goal pursuit is characterized by active, joyful engagement and is directed toward positive outcomes. In contrast, individuals with dispositional *prevention focus* strive for how they should be and for loss avoidance and security. The overarching goal of prevention-focused individuals is to avoid the occurrence of a negative undesirable outcome (loss). More recent research examines the *regulatory fit* of promotion vs. prevention-focused goals and the promotion vs. prevention-oriented means available to attain these goals (Higgins, 2000).

In contrast, the *self-determination theory* (Deci & Ryan, 1985, 2000) distinguishes three fundamental innate psychological needs: (experiences of) competence, autonomy, and social relatedness. This theory proposes a successive adoption (i.e., integration) of externally imposed behavioral standards, and a developmental continuum of extrinsic to intrinsic motivation – both experienced as self-determined. The goals people set for themselves are guided by these basic psychological needs and they determine their intrinsic motivation. Self-determination theory has gained some popularity, particularly among researchers in educational psychology (Niemiec & Ryan, 2009).

b) Goal structure

Beyond identifying which goals people set, Motivation Science has clarified how to set goals.

An enormous body of research on *goal-setting theory* by Locke and Latham (1990, 2013) shows that individuals perform better when they set specific and challenging goals (e.g., I will exercise five times a week) instead of easy goals ("I will exercise once a week!") or vague goals (e.g., "I will exercise as often as possible"). Although people are less likely to attain specific and challenging goals, these goals lead to higher performance because they motivate continued effort and make it easy to determine whether one has already attained the goal. Important prerequisites for goal setting effects to occur are a person's sufficient skills, his or her confidence in mastering the task (i.e., in goal realization), goal commitment, and feedback on goal progress (Latham & Locke, 2007). In an extension, more recent research proscribes to S.M.A.R.T goals – goals that are **S**pecific, **M**easurable, **A**ttractive, **R**ealistic, and **T**ime-Bound.

A personal determinant of the desirability (cf. value) and subjective feasibility of goals (cf. expectancy of success) has been addressed in the *goal orientation theory* (Dweck, 1986; Elliot & McGregor, 2001; Nicholls, 1984). Empirical findings by Dweck and Leggett (1988) laid the foundation for the distinction between mastery versus performance goals and the development of goal orientation theory, which also returns to the basic notion of approach and avoidance in the course of its theoretical differentiation. Mastery approach goal orientation refers to a focus on personal skill development and individual improvement. In contrast, performance-approach goal orientation refers to a focus on social comparison and performing better than others, whereas performance-avoidance goal orientation refers to a focus on avoiding the demonstration of lack of competence compared to others. The findings of Dweck and colleagues were highly relevant for practical (motivational) questions in various contexts and finally transformed into the so-called *mindset theory*. Mindset theory attributes people's motivation to learn and develop to their beliefs about the fixed or alternatively mutable nature of their basic qualities, like their intelligence. In these terms, a *growth mindset* primarily centers on the belief that everyone can increase their abilities given the appropriate effort and guidance. On the other hand, in a *fixed mindset*, people believe that their intellectual abilities are static givens that cannot be changed in any meaningful way. This has important implications for goal setting in achievement situations: People who are convinced that their intellectual abilities are fixed, their overriding goal can only be to demonstrate them (performance approach goal) or to hide respective deficits (performance avoidance goal). On the other hand, if they believe in the possibility of change, they will be eager to mastery goals and individual development despite obstacles and failure experiences (Tulis & Ainley, 2011), and they show more adaptive action-related responses to setbacks (Tulis, Steuer & Dresel, 2017).

Finally, setting "good" goals requires the assessment of how feasible or realistic a goal is. The process of systematically comparing and contrasting positive and negative aspects of an impending future (i.e., thinking about the positive consequences of achieving a specific goal alternating with thoughts about the obstacles that need to be overcome on the way to that goal) is known as *mental contrasting* (Oettingen, 2012; Oettingen & Reininger, 2016). The technique of mental contrasting promotes commitment to attractive and attainable goals. It allows people to drop goals that appear unrealistic and instead commit to realistic goals, which is the precondition for successful goal striving.

More recent research has started investigating motivation at the team level. This field of research is highly relevant because many important goals require acting together. However, the team level also adds considerable complexity. For instance, individual and team goals can be at odds. A mature literature on goal setting in teams (review by Nahrgang et al., 2013) speaks to these processes.

The Pre-actional and Actional Phases: Theories About Goal Striving

The Rubicon model assumes that people do not blindly embark on attaining their newly set goals; instead, they first prepare for action. In this regard, Gollwitzer (1993) proposed supplementing a set goal intention (goal) with an if-then plan or *implementation intention*. While goal intentions specify a desired end state, implementation intentions specify when, where, and how to act, ideally in an "If Situation S occurs, then I will perform goal-directed Response R!" format (reviews by Bieleke, Keller & Gollwitzer, 2020; Gollwitzer, 1999; Gollwitzer & Sheeran, 2006). A host of research in a range of areas demonstrates that implementation intentions promote goal attainment (meta-analysis by Gollwitzer & Sheeran, 2006; for a meta-analysis of meta-analyses see: Keller, Gollwitzer & Sheeran, 2020). A younger and growing literature analyses how teams can support their goals with "We-if-then" plans (see below) or *collective implementation intentions* (reviews by Thürmer, Wieber & Gollwitzer, 2020b, 2021).

Once people have set a plan and start to act, they need to control the direction of their actions as well as the velocity of their progress towards their goal. One goal-striving approach that can explain both processes is the *cybernetic control model* (Carver & Scheier, 1990, 2009, 2017; Powers, 1973). The model explains goal-directed action through the function of a set of feedback loops. One loop monitors the discrepancy between a current state (where I am) and a reference value (goal; where I want to be). Discrepancies between the reference and the current state elicit actions designed to minimize the discrepancy and move closer towards the goal (i.e., direction). Carver and Scheier (1990, 1998) further argued that another loop monitors the rate of discrepancy reduction towards the goal (i.e., velocity).

Rather than action, the output function of the second loop is assumed to be affective in nature: Negative affect occurs when progress is slower than the expected or needed reference value; positive affect occurs when progress is faster than expected, needed, or desired (for greater detail see Carver & Scheier, 1998). The authors assume that negative affect leads to increased effort (*pushing*); positive affect leads to reduced effort (*coasting*). The pushing hypothesis is quite intuitive and has received ample empirical support (e.g., Schmidt & DeShon, 2007). In contrast, coasting and shifting have only been demonstrated in a small number of studies and represent an emerging field of research (Fulford, Johnson, Llabre & Carver, 2010; Thürmer, Scheier & Carver, 2020a). Other applied research has observed that both negative-activating and positive-activating emotion states (for this distinction see Barrett, 2006) during challenging tasks were positively associated with persistent engagement in learning and achievement settings (Tulis & Fulmer, 2013). Emotions have finally been studied along with the belief of self-efficacy (as described in social cognitive theory, Bandura, 1986) which has consistently been shown to be positively related to motivation (e.g., Schunk & DiBenedetto, 2020).

The Post-actional Phase: Evaluation of Goal Realization

Finally, the achieved outcomes of the goal-directed behavior are evaluated by looking backward (i.e., people question the success of their goal-directed behavior) and forward (i.e., seeking what still needs to be done to achieve the desired outcomes implied by one's goal). Furthermore, post-actional evaluations affect future pre-decisional deliberations – for instance, the estimation of expected values should become more accurate – goal intention and planning. Intra- and interpersonal attributions after an event regulate cognitions and emotions, which determine motivation and predict future behavior (Weiner, 2018). Attribution theory research has expanded in scope over the past two decades (Graham, 2020). Research not only increased its emphasis on emotions (Pekrun & Linnenbrink-Garcia, 2012), functional as well as dysfunctional strategies to alter attributions (e.g., self-handicapping, review by Török, Szabó & Tóth, 2018), or on attributional retraining (review by Perry & Hamm, 2017) but there has also been an increase in research on attributional (feedback) processes in stigmatized groups and ethnic minorities (e.g., Graham, 2016; Harber, 1998).

Table 1 summarizes the concepts and theories that should be addressed in the teaching of Motivation Science.

Table 1 Overview of the proposed curriculum for teaching Motivation Science based on the Rubicon model of action phases

Theories about	Basics and fundamentals	Relevant current concepts	Deepening and addenda
... goal setting	• Drives and needs • Approach versus avoidance • Intrinsic versus extrinsic motivation • Expectancies and values • Intentions	• Achievement, affiliation, and power motives • Regulatory focus • Self-determination theory • Goal orientations, mindset theory • S.M.A.R.T. goals • Mental contrasting	• PSI-theory • Goal setting in teams
... goal striving	• Volition • Self-regulation • Intention-behavior gap • Self-efficacy	• Implementation intentions • Action regulation • Cybernetic control model	• PSI-theory • Activating and deactivating emotional states (e.g., Tulis & Fulmer, 2013) • Motivation regulation strategies (e.g., Wolters, 2003) • Co-regulation and socially shared monitoring (e.g., Hadwin, Järvelä & Miller, 2018) • Collective implementation intentions (e.g., Thürmer et al., 2020b, 2021)
... **evaluation of goal realization**	Attribution theory	Determinants and consequences of attributions on goal-directed behavior	• Emotions (e.g., Reeve, 2018) • Attributional feedback and retraining (e.g., "positive feedback bias" Harber, 1998)

Approaches and Strategies for Teaching, Learning, and Assessment in Motivation Science

Motivation Science covers the complex interaction between personal traits and states, and environmental factors. Human motivation can best be described, explained, predicted, or modified if it is viewed or treated from different perspectives. The Rubicon model may serve as a framework for the integration of various theoretical directions and approaches from a behaviorist, cognitivist, and systemic point of view. Based on such different paradigms of psychological research (for an introductory textbook following this approach see: Glassman & Hadad, 2009), developments in Motivation Science are thus vividly conveyed and compared in a didactically reduced way.

Generally, fostering student motivation is an important issue for teaching Motivation Science as for any other subject. Undergraduate psychology *students' motivation* to study the *subject of motivation* will affect the way they learn it. Derived from the key theories and relevant determinants for motivation that were described in this chapter, teaching Motivation Science itself should also utilize the various evidence-based strategies and practices to trigger, maintain, and enhance students' motivation. For example, according to *self-determination theory*, students feel competent within a course when they are able to track their progress in developing skills or an understanding of course material (Deci & Ryan, 2000). Therefore, higher education teachers should set and communicate high but achievable (and specific!) learning *goals* (Locke & Latham, 2013), signal confidence in students' abilities to meet these high expectations, include multiple low-stakes assessments with (peer) feedback, and provide a safe environment for students to fail and then learn from their mistakes (Steuer & Dresel, 2015). When students know what is expected of them, and have clearly defined goals, they are more likely to experience high *expectancy* (Pajares, 1996), likewise when difficulty of course material matches students' skill levels (for an overview see Eccles & Wigfield, 2002). Providing students with options to choose – within a structure – supports students' *autonomy*, and *social relatedness* is fostered when students feel a sense of belonging in the course. To facilitate a sense of community, students could be paired into stable or altering working groups to work on specific tasks together and experience co-regulation of learning motivation. Referring to the personal relevance and usefulness of the content mentioned at the beginning of this chapter, simple interventions – like as a short writing task, for example – help students to connect what they are learning to their personal lives and/or the real world, increasing the likelihood that they experience high *value* (Hulleman, Godes, Hendricks & Harackiewicz, 2010).

Academic motivation as a goal-directed process is closely related to self-regulation competencies (cf. Schunk, Meece & Pintrich, 2014). Further important for *goal striving* are both a high level of *goal commitment* (resulting effort, and the time and energy spent on goal attainment even in the face of difficulties) and feasible realization conditions. Course design should provide opportunities for students to set individual learning goals for each chapter/topic, and self-evaluation whether these goals are realistic, specific, and challenging. Students could be prompted to reflect and compare their study *habits* and personal *motives*, and they could be encouraged to try out specific interventions, such as *implementation intentions* (Gollwitzer, 1999) and *mental contrasting* (Oettingen, 2012) for studying and exam preparation, which is conveniently available in the free-to-use WOOP app.

In line with the idea of goal orientation theory (Dweck, 1986), teachers can establish mastery goal structures in terms of prevailing practices that make mastery (instead of performance) goals salient. An emphasis on individual improvement instead of being better than others and task-mastery by valuing effort and providing individualized learning environments with appropriate challenging tasks for each student makes a mastery goal structure salient (for an overview see Ames, 1992). In contrast, course characteristics and practices that emphasize competition, extrinsic motivation, and overtly social comparison of students' performance outcomes are likely to foster a performance goal structure (e.g., Kaplan, Middleton, Urdan & Midgley, 2002). According to the importance of person-environment fit, the congruence between personal goals and goal structures may particularly enhance motivation (Murayama & Elliot, 2009). Hence, again, providing different options for students to work and perform is important.

Challenges and Lessons Learned

Studying Motivation Science not only provides an opportunity to gain theoretical understanding but useful practical know-how. In fact, students can immediately experience the application and usefulness of the learned content during class. Students' initial interest in the topic is usually high, too. However, the high relevance to everyday life and students' various personal experiences and naive theories about human motivation may impede the acquisition, or rather the *re*construction, of (psychological) knowledge in Motivation Science classes. Students do not simply exchange their lay conceptions for scientific concepts but rather supplement, differentiate or refine their intuitions with (personally valued!) evidence-based knowledge. Therefore, it is relevant to systematically identify students' pre-conceptions in order to subsequently question them critically together and supplement them by a more differentiated, theory-based view that can be applied in everyday life (for a more comprehensive description of this conceptual change-based approach see: Tulis, 2021).

With this in mind, we suggest starting each topic with actual cases and real-word scenarios around motivational issues, where students can contribute their experience-based explanations and solution attempts, then providing the relevant theory, and finally placing it in the Rubicon model that is referred to throughout the course. In this way, integration of knowledge takes place in a spiral structure and successive expansion of the fundamentals, illustrated in the framework of action phases. Allowing students to contribute their intuitive ideas to explain motivational issues, finally followed by the application of theory on common situations also fosters increased mastery in evidence-based problem solving and feelings of competence.

Teaching, Learning, and Assessment Resources

We so far have discussed our view of a curriculum for teaching Motivation Science. But how can we translate this content into practice? We believe that one can derive the following concrete advice from our discussion for teaching Motivation Science:

1. People often use the term *motivation* and related termini (e.g., a person's *motive* to act) in various everyday situations when referring to ambition, enthusiasm, perseverance, or willingness to perform. Teachers and learners sometimes do not understand each other because they think in different contexts, "speak a different language." For teaching the subject of Motivation Science it is important to listen and investigate the ideas behind what learners say and think about motivation. Learners do not simply exchange their everyday experiences and naive concepts for scientific knowledge. Therefore, learning can (and from our point of view it should) only be done *with* them.

2. The significance of research findings and theories may be even more apparent to students when naive assumptions are obviously insufficient to predict or explain motivational issues. Therefore, ask students to make predictions on specific situations and behavior. Students will differ in their explanations and considerations. Being confronted with different perspectives as well as evidence that may contradict one's beliefs and expectations encourages seeking knowledge that accounts for the respective behavior.

3. When selecting and preparing learning material, focus on the practical use and applicability of knowledge, thinking, and action in everyday life and in solving individual, social, and societal problems. Consider where the chosen example and its underlying motivational mechanisms would be located in our proposed framework, the Rubicon model, to ensure the necessary theoretical reference.

4. Theory on human motivation is concerned with goal-directed behavior in terms of people's needs, motives, and orientations, and ranging from intention formation and goal setting to persistence, intensity of goal striving, and goal attainment. Motivation Science considers a complex interaction of affective, cognitive, and physiological processes as well as characteristics of the environment. Ensure your students' understanding of the fundamental principles of approach and avoidance and person-environment interaction before you gradually introduce specific motivation theories. Use the proposed framework to illustrate their relation to each other.

5. Our thinking first and foremost is for our doing. Even more than other courses, a course on Motivation Science should heed this advice. The field offers a host of good studies to discuss as well as applied fields that students can devise evidence-based interventions for.

Recommended further reading references and online resources about teaching, learning, and assessment of Motivation Science (for complete citation of books see list of references):

- Gendolla and Wright (2016) provide an excellent review of the development of the field in the Editorial of the Journal *Motivation Science.*
- Brandstätter, Schüler, Puca, and Lozo (2018) have published a nicely structured introductory book on motivation and emotion with an excellent discussion of the historical background (that focuses on the essentials) as well as goal setting and goal striving, in German.
- *Motivation and action* edited by Heinz Heckhausen and his daughter Jutta Heckhausen (2018) is another introductory book on motivation with a more detailed presentation of the historical roots and traditional motivation concepts (e.g., motives) as well as motivation theory development. This book also includes a chapter on PSI theory and another on the Rubicon model of action phases.
- The book *Understanding Motivation and Emotion* (Reeve, 2018) highlights the connection between motivation and emotions. In the introduction, it provides a comprehensible overview of the unifying themes of motivation and emotion, followed by four parts that address (a) needs and motives, (b) cognitions (goal setting and goal striving, mindsets, beliefs, and values), (c) emotions (very recommendable synopsis!), and (d) the application of motivation theory with a focus on growth mindsets/positive psychology, unconscious motivation (i.e., psychodynamic perspective) and interventions.
- Within the field of developmental and educational psychology, Eccles and Wigfield (2002) provide a paper in *Annual Review of Psychology* that allows for a deeper examination of expectancy-value theory (inclusive Heckhausen's differentiation), and related motivational constructs such as flow, interest, self-efficacy, attribution theory, and self-determination theory.
- We strongly recommend the recently published Special Issue in *Contemporary Educational Psychology* on "Prominent Motivation Theories: The Past, Present, and Future" edited by Allan Wigfield and Alison Koenka (2020). Particularly interesting is a comparison with the Special Issue on "A motivated exploration of motivation terminology" published two decades ago (Murphy & Alexander, 2000).
- For motivating students during the course in general: Hulleman and colleagues (2016) summarize various research-based sources that positively impact students' expectancy beliefs, perceptions of task value, and perceptions of cost.
- Another perspective takes the book "Emotion, Motivation, and Self-regulation: A Handbook for Teachers" edited by Hall and Goetz (2013). It links research findings from Motivation Science as well as emotion and self-regulated learning research for students *and teachers* alike.
- For a further examination of PSI theory we recommend a book (in German) written by Julius Kuhl himself (2001), or a well understandable recent summary in English by Kuhl, Quirin, and Koole (2020). PSI-theory is also addressed in the most recent volume of the series "Advances in Motivation Science" (Vol. 8, 2021,

edited by Andrew Elliot). Advances in Motivation Science provide an overview of key research programs conducted by highly respected scholars working in this area.

Online resources:

- The Society for the Science of Motivation (interdisciplinary academic society with most up-to-date information on the field), https://www.scienceofmotivation. org/
- WOOP (Practical online tool and mobile app for generating one's own plan, based on MCII), https://woopmylife.org/

References

Ach, N. (1935). Analyse des Willens. In E. Abderhalden, Handbuch der biologischen Arbeitsmethoden (6, Part E 460). Berlin: Urban & Schwarzenberg.

Achtziger, A., & Gollwitzer, P. M. (2018). Motivation and volition in the course of action. In J. Heckhausen & H. Heckhausen (Eds.), *Motivation and emotion* (pp. 485–527). Berlin: Springer.

American Psychological Association. (2016). Guidelines for the undergraduate psychology major: Version 2.0. *American Psychologist, 71*(2), 102–111. https://doi.org/10.1037/a0037562

Ames, C. (1992). Classrooms: Goals, structures, and student motivation. *Journal of Educational Psychology, 84*(3), 261–271.

Anderman, E. (2020). Achievement motivation theory: Balancing precision and utility. *Contemporary Educational Psychology, 61*, 101864. https://doi.org/10.1016/j.cedpsych.2020.101864

Atkinson, J. W. (1957). Motivational determinants of risktaking behavior. *Psychological Review, 64*, 359–372.

Atkinson, J. (1964). *An introduction to motivation*. Princeton: Van Nostrand.

Atkinson, J. W., Heyns, R. W., & Veroff, J. (1954). The effect of experimental arousal of the affiliation motive on thematic apperception. *Journal of Abnormal and Social Psychology, 49*, 405–410.

Bandura, A. (1986). *Social foundations of thought and action: A social cognitive theory*. Englewood Cliffs: Prentice Hall.

Barrett, L. F. (2006). Solving the emotion paradox: Categorization and the experience of emotion. *Personality and Social Psychology Review, 10*, 20–46.

Bieleke, M., Keller, L., & Gollwitzer, P. M. (2020). If-then planning. *European Review of Social Psychology, 32*, 1–35. https://doi.org/10.1080/10463283.2020.1808936

Brandstätter, V., Schüler, J., Puca, R. M., & Lozo, L. (2018). *Motivation und emotion. Allgemeine Psychologie für Bachelor [Motivation and emotion. General psychology for bachelor's degree progam]*. Berlin: Springer.

Braver, T. S., Krug, M. K., Chiew, K. S., Kool, W., Westbrook, J. A., Clement, N. J., . . . Somerville, L. H. (2014). Mechanisms of motivation-cognition interaction: Challenges and opportunities. *Cognitive, Affective, & Behavioral Neuroscience, 14*(2), 443–472. https://doi.org/10.3758/s13415-014-0300-0.

Carver, C. S., & Scheier, M. F. (1990). Origins and functions of positive and negative affect: A control-process view. *Psychological Review, 97*(1), 19–35. https://doi.org/10.1037/0033-295X.97.1.19

Carver, C. S., & Scheier, M. F. (1998). *On the self-regulation of behavior*. Cambridge, UK: Cambridge University Press.

Carver, C. S., & Scheier, M. F. (2009). Action, affect, and two-mode models of functioning. In E. Morsella, J. A. Bargh, & P. M. Gollwitzer (Eds.), *Oxford handbook of human action* (pp. 298–327). New York: Oxford University Press. http://www.redi-bw.de/db/ebsco.php/

search.ebscohost.com/login.aspx?direct=true&db=psyh&AN=2008-14699-015&site=ehost-live

Carver, C. S., & Scheier, M. F. (2017). Self-regulatory functions supporting motivated action. In A. J. Elliot (Ed.), *Advances in motivation science* (Vol. 4, pp. 1–37). New York: Academic Press. https://doi.org/10.1016/bs.adms.2017.02.002

Deci, E. L., & Ryan, R. M. (1985). *Intrinsic motivation and self-determination in human behaviour.* New York: Plenum Press.

Deci, E. L., & Ryan, R. M. (2000). The "what" and "why" of goal pursuits: Human needs and the self-determination of behavior. *Psychological Inquiry, 11,* 227–268.

Dweck, C. S. (1986). Motivational processes affecting learning. *American Psychologist, 41,* 1040–1048.

Dweck, C. S. (2017). From needs to goals and representations: Foundations for a unified theory of motivation, personality, and development. *Psychological Review, 124,* 689–719. https://doi.org/10.1037/rev0000082

Dweck, C. S., & Leggett, E. L. (1988). A social-cognitive approach to motivation and personality. *Psychological Review, 95*(2), 256–273. https://doi.org/10.1037/0033-295X.95.2.256

Eccles, J. S., & Wigfield, A. (2002). Motivational beliefs, values, and goals. *Annual Review of Psychology, 53*(1), 109–132.

Eccles, J. S., & Wigfield, A. (2020). From expectancy-value theory to situated expectancy-value theory: A developmental, social cognitive, and sociocultural perspective on motivation. *Contemporary Educational Psychology, 61,* 101859.

Elliot, A. J., & McGregor, H. A. (2001). A 2 x 2 achievement goal framework. *Journal of Personality and Social Psychology, 80*(3), 501–519.

Fishbein, M., & Ajzen, I. (1975). *Belief, attitude, intention, and behavior: An introduction to theory and research.* Addison-Wesley.

Forbes, D. L. (2011). Toward a unified model of human motivation. *Review of General Psychology, 15*(2), 85–98.

Freud, S. (1915/1952). *Triebe und Triebschicksale* (GW, Bd. X). Frankfurt: Fischer.

Fulford, D., Johnson, S. L., Llabre, M. M., & Carver, C. S. (2010). Pushing and coasting in dynamic goal pursuit: Coasting is attenuated in bipolar disorder. *Psychological Science, 21*(7), 1021–1027. https://doi.org/10.1177/0956797610373372

Gendolla, G. H. E., & Wright, R. A. (2016). Gathering the diaspora: Aims and visions for Motivation Science. *Motivation Science, 2*(3), 135–137. https://doi.org/10.1037/mot0000035

Glassman, W. E., & Hadad, M. (2009). *Approaches to psychology* (5th ed.). Maidenhead: McGraw-Hill.

Gollwitzer, P. M. (1990). Action phases and mind-sets. In E. T. Higgins & R. M. Sorrentino (Eds.), *Handbook of motivation and cognition: Foundations of social behavior* (Vol. 2, pp. 53–92). New York: Guilford Press.

Gollwitzer, P. M. (1993). Goal achievement: The role of intentions. *European Review of Social Psychology, 4,* 141–185.

Gollwitzer, P. M. (1999). Implementation intentions: Strong effects of simple plans. *American Psychologist, 54*(7), 493–503. https://doi.org/10.1037/0003-066X.54.7.493

Gollwitzer, P. M. (2012). Mindset theory of action phases. In P. A. M. Van Lange, A. W. Kruglanski, & E. T. Higgins (Eds.), *Handbook of theories of social psychology* (Vol. 1, pp. 526–545). Thousand Oaks: Sage Publications Ltd. https://doi.org/10.4135/9781446249215.n26

Gollwitzer, P. M. (2018). The goal concept: A helpful tool for theory development and testing in motivation science. *Motivation Science, 4*(3), 185–205. https://doi.org/10.1037/mot0000115

Gollwitzer, P. M., & Sheeran, P. (2006). Implementation intentions and goal achievement: A meta-analysis of effects and processes. In M. P. Zanna (Ed.), *Advances in experimental social psychology* (Vol. 38, pp. 69–119). San Diego: Elsevier Academic Press. https://doi.org/10.1016/S0065-2601(06)38002-1

Graham, S. (2016). An attributional perspective on motivation in ethnic minority youth. In J. DeCuir-Gunby & P. Schutz (Eds.), *Researching race and ethnicity in the study of teaching, learning, and motivation in educational contexts.* New York: Routledge.

Graham, S. (2020). An attributional theory of motivation. *Contemporary Educational Psychology, 61*, 101861.

Hadwin, A. F., Järvelä, S., & Miller, M. (2018). Self-regulation, co-regulation and shared regulation in collaborative learning environments. In D. Schunk & J. Greene (Eds.), *Handbook of self-regulation of learning and performance* (2nd ed.). New York: Routledge.

Hall, N. C., & Goetz, T. (2013). *Emotion, motivation, and self-regulation: A handbook for teachers.* Bingley: Emerald Group Publishing.

Harber, K. D. (1998). Feedback to minorities: Evidence of a positive bias. *Journal of Personality and Social Psychology, 74*(3), 622–628.

Heckhausen, H. (1963). *Hoffnung und Furcht in der Leistungsmotivation.* Meisenheim/Glan: Hain.

Heckhausen, H. (1989). Volition: Realisieren von Intentionen. In *Motivation und Handeln* (pp. 189–218). Berlin/Heidelberg: Springer.

Heckhausen, H., & Gollwitzer, P. M. (1987). Thought contents and cognitive functioning in motivational versus volitional states of mind. *Motivation and Emotion, 11*, 101–120. https://doi.org/10.1007/BF00992338

Heckhausen, J., & Heckhausen, H. (Eds.). (2018). *Motivation and emotion.* Berlin: Springer.

Heider, F. (1958). *The psychology of interpersonal relations.* New York: Wiley. https://doi.org/10.1037/10628-000

Higgins, E. T. (1997). Beyond pleasure and pain. *American Psychologist, 52*, 1280–1300.

Higgins, E. T. (2000). Making a good decision: Value from fit. *American Psychologist, 55*, 1217–1230.

Hull, C. L. (1943). *Principles of behavior: An introduction to behavior theory.* New York: Appleton Century Crofts.

Hull, C. L. (1952). *A behavior system: An introduction to behavior theory concerning the individual organism.* Westport: Greenwood Press.

Hulleman, C. S., Godes, O., Hendricks, B. L., & Harackiewicz, J. M. (2010). Enhancing interest and performance with a utility value intervention. *Journal of Educational Psychology, 102*(4), 880–895.

Hulleman, C. S., Barron, K. E., Kosovich, J. J., & Lazowski, R. A. (2016). Student motivation: Current theories, constructs, and interventions within an expectancy-value framework. In A. A. Lipnevich et al. (Eds.), *Psychosocial skills and school systems in the 21st century.* Berlin: Springer.

Kanfer, R., Chen, G., & Pritchard, R. D. (Eds.). (2008). *Work motivation: Past, present, and future* (The organizational frontiers series) (Vol. 27). New York: Routledge/Taylor & Francis Group.

Kaplan, A., Middleton, M. J., Urdan, T., & Midgley, C. (2002). Achievement goals and goal structures. In C. Midgley (Ed.), *Goals, goal structures, and patterns of adaptive learning* (pp. 21–53). Mahwah: Erlbaum.

Keller, L., Gollwitzer, P. M., & Sheeran, P. (2020). Changing behavior using the model of action phases. In M. S. Hagger, L. Cameron, K. Hamilton, N. Hankonen, & T. Lintunen (Eds.), *The handbook of behavior change* (pp. 77–88). New York: Cambridge University Press.

Kelley, H. H. (1973). The processes of causal attribution. *American Psychologist, 28*(2), 107–128. https://doi.org/10.1037/h0034225

Kempf, W. (2003). Forschungsmethoden der Psychologie. Zwischen naturwissenschaftlichem Experiment und sozialwissenschaftlicher Hermeneutik (Band 1: Theorie und Empirie) [Methods of Psychology. Between Scientific Experiment and Social Science Hermeneutics]. Regener.

Kruglanski, A. W., Chernikova, M., & Kopetz, C. (2015). Motivation science. In R. A. Scott & S. M. Kosslyn (Eds.), *Emerging trends in the social and behavioral sciences* (pp. 1–16). New York: Wiley. https://doi.org/10.1002/9781118900772.etrds0104

Kuhl, J. (2001). *Motivation und Persönlichkeit: Interaktionen psychischer Systeme.* Göttingen: Hogrefe.

Kuhl, J., Quirin, M., & Koole, S. (2020). The functional architecture of human motivation: Personality systems interactions theory. In A. J. Elliot (Ed.), *Advances in motivation science* (Vol. 7). Cambridge, UK: Elsevier.

Latham, G. P., & Locke, E. A. (2007). New developments in and directions for goal-setting research. *European Psychologist, 12*(4), 290–300. https://doi.org/10.1027/1016-9040.12.4.290

Lewin, K. (1939). Field theory and experiment in social psychology: Concepts and methods. *American Journal of Sociology, 44*(6), 868–896. https://doi.org/10.1086/218177

Lewin, K. (1951). Behavior and development as a function of the total situation. In D. Cartwright (Ed.), *Field theory in social science. Selected theoretical papers by Kurt Lewin* (pp. 238–303). New York: Harper.

Locke, E. A., & Latham, G. P. (1990). *A theory of goal setting and task performance.* Englewood Cliffs: Prentice Hall.

Locke, E. A., & Latham, G. P. (Eds.). (2013). *New developments in goal setting and task performance.* New York: Routledge.

Maslow, A. H. (1954). The instinctoid nature of basic needs. *Journal of Personality, 22*(3), 326–347. https://doi.org/10.1111/j.1467-6494.1954.tb01136.x

McClelland, D. C. (1985). *Human motivation.* Glenview: Scott, Foresman.

McClelland, D. C., Atkinson, J. W., Clark, R. W., & Lowell, E. L. (1953). *The achievement motive.* New York: Appleton Century Crofts.

Murayama, K. (2019). Neuroscientific and psychological approaches to incentives: Commonality and multi-faceted views. In A. Renninger & S. Hidi (Eds.), *Cambridge handbook on motivation and learning* (pp. 141–162). Cambridge, UK: Cambridge University Press.

Murayama, K., & Elliot, A. J. (2009). The joint influence of personal achievement goals and classroom goal structures on achievement-relevant outcomes. *Journal of Educational Psychology, 101*(2), 432–447. https://doi.org/10.1037/a0014221

Murayama, K., Matsumoto, M., Izuma, K., Sugiura, A., Ryan, R. M., Deci, E. L., & Matsumoto, K. (2015). How self-determined choice facilitates performance: A key role of the ventromedial prefrontal cortex. *Cerebral Cortex, 25*(5), 1241–1251.

Murphy, P. K., & Alexander, P. A. (2000). A motivated exploration of motivation terminology. *Contemporary Educational Psychology, 25*(1), 3–53.

Murray, H. A. (1938). *Explorations in personality.* New York: Oxford University Press.

Nahrgang, J. D., DeRue, D. S., Hollenbeck, J. R., Spitzmuller, M., Jundt, D. K., & Ilgen, D. R. (2013). Goal setting in teams: The impact of learning and performance goals on process and performance. *Organizational Behavior and Human Decision Processes, 122*(1), 12–21. https://doi.org/10.1016/j.obhdp.2013.03.008

Nicholls, J. G. (1984). Achievement motivation: Conceptions of ability, subjective experience, task choice, and performance. *Psychological Review, 91*(3), 328–346. https://doi.org/10.1037/0033-295X.91.3.328

Niemiec, C. P., & Ryan, R. M. (2009). Autonomy, competence, and relatedness in the classroom: Applying self-determination theory to educational practice. *Theory and Research in Education, 7*(2), 133–144. https://doi.org/10.1177/1477878509104318

Nolen, S. (2020). A situative turn in the conversation on motivation theories. *Contemporary Educational Psychology, 61*, 101866. https://doi.org/10.1016/j.cedpsych.2020.101866

Nolen, S., & Ward, C. J. (2008). Sociocultural and situative research on motivation. In M. Maehr, S. Karabenick, & T. Urdan (Eds.), *Social psychological perspective on motivation and achievement* (pp. 428–460). London: Emerald Group Publishing.

Oettingen, G. (2012). Future thought and behavior change. *European Review of Social Psychology, 23*, 1–63.

Oettingen, G., & Reininger, K. M. (2016). The power of prospection: Mental contrasting and behavior change. *Social and Personality Psychology Compass, 10*, 591–604.

Oettingen, G., Sevincer, A. T., & Gollwitzer, P. M. (2008). Goal pursuit in the context of culture. In R. Sorrentino & S. Yamaguchi (Eds.), *The handbook of motivation and cognition across cultures* (pp. 191–211). San Diego: Elsevier/Academic Press.

Pajares, F. (1996). Self-efficacy beliefs in academic settings. *Review of Educational Research, 66*(4), 543–578. https://doi.org/10.3102/00346543066004543

Pekrun, R., & Linnenbrink-Garcia, L. (2012). Academic emotions and student engagement. In S. L. Christenson, A. L. Reschly, & C. Wylie (Eds.), *The handbook of research on student engagement* (pp. 259–292). New York: Springer.

Perin, C. I. (1942). Behavioral potentiality as a joint function of the amount of training and the degree of hunger at the time of extinction. *Journal of Experimental Psychology, 30*, 93–113.

Perry, R., & Hamm, J. (2017). An attribution perspective on competence and motivation. In A. Elliot, C. Dweck, & D. Yeager (Eds.), *Handbook of competence and motivation* (2nd ed., pp. 61–84). New York: Guilford Press.

Powers, W. T. (1973). *Behavior: The control of perception*. Chicago: Aldine.

Reeve, J. (2018). *Understanding motivation and emotion* (7th ed.). Hoboken: Wiley.

Ryan, R. M. (Ed.). (2019). *The Oxford handbook of human motivation*. New York: Oxford University Press.

Ryan, R. M., & Di Domenico, S. I. (2016). Distinct motivations and their differentiated mechanisms: Reflections on the emerging neuroscience of human motivation. In S. Kim, J. Reeve, & M. Bong (Eds.), *Advances in motivation and achievement: Recent developments in neuroscience research on human motivation* (pp. 349–369). Bingley: Emerald Group Publishing.

Scheffer, D., & Heckhausen, H. (2018). Trait theories of motivation. In J. Heckhausen & H. Heckhausen (Eds.), *Motivation and action* (pp. 67–112). Berlin: Springer. https://doi.org/10.1007/978-3-319-65094-4_3

Schmidt, A. M., & DeShon, R. P. (2007). What to do? The effects of discrepancies, incentives, and time on dynamic goal prioritization. *Journal of Applied Psychology, 92*(4), 928–941. https://doi.org/10.1037/0021-9010.92.4.928

Schunk, D. H., & DiBenedetto, M. K. (2020). Motivation and social cognitive theory. *Contemporary Educational Psychology, 61*, 101832. https://doi.org/10.1016/j.cedpsych.2019.101832

Schunk, D., Meece, J., & Pintrich, P. (2014). *Motivation in education. Theory, research and application* (4th ed.). London: Pearson.

Sheeran, P. (2002). Intention-behavior relations: A conceptual and empirical review. *European Review of Social Psychology, 12*(1), 1–36. https://doi.org/10.1080/14792772143000003

Sheeran, P., & Webb, T. L. (2016). The intention–behavior gap. *Social and Personality Psychology Compass, 10*(9), 503–518. https://doi.org/10.1111/spc3.12265

Smith, L. D. (2014). Behavior, overview. In T. Teo (Ed.), *Encyclopedia of critical psychology*. New York: Springer. https://doi.org/10.1007/978-1-4614-5583-7_448

Steuer, G., & Dresel, M. (2015). A constructive error climate as an element of effective learning environments. *Psychological Test and Assessment Modeling, 57*(2), 262–275.

Thürmer, J. L., Scheier, M. F., & Carver, C. S. (2020a). On the mechanics of goal striving: Experimental evidence of coasting and shifting. *Motivation Science, 6*(3), 266–274. https://doi.org/10.1037/mot0000157

Thürmer, J. L., Wieber, F., & Gollwitzer, P. M. (2020b). Management in times of crisis: Can collective plans prepare teams to make and implement good decisions? *Management Decision, 58*(10), 2155–2176. https://doi.org/10.1108/MD-08-2020-1088

Thürmer, J. L., Wieber, F., & Gollwitzer, P. M. (2021). How can we master the 2020 Coronavirus pandemic? The role of planning across social levels. *European Review of Social Psychology, 32*(1), 1–46. https://doi.org/10.1080/10463283.2020.1852699

Török, L., Szabó, Z. P., & Tóth, L. (2018). A critical review of the literature on academic self-handicapping: Theory, manifestations, prevention and measurement. *Social Psychology of Education, 21*, 1175–1202.

Tulis, M. (2020). Konzeptverändernde Psychologiedidaktik. Eine Fortführung der Überlegungen von Seiffge-Krenke [Concept changing psychology didactics. A continuation of the considerations of Seiffge-Krenke]. In P. G. Geiß & M. Tulis (Eds.), *Psychologie unterrichten. Fachdidaktische Grundlagen für Deutschland, Österreich und die Schweiz [Teaching psychology. Didactic basics for Germany, Austria and Switzerland]* (pp. 158–186). Opladen: UTB-Barbara Budrich.

Tulis, M. (2021). *Achieving conceptual growth in the teaching of psychology* [Manuscript submitted for publication]. Department of Psychology, University of Salzburg.

Tulis, M., & Ainley, M. (2011). Interest, enjoyment and pride after failure experiences? Predictors of students' state–emotions after success and failure during learning mathematics. *Educational Psychology, 31*(7), 779–807. https://doi.org/10.1080/01443410.2011.608524

Tulis, M., & Fulmer, S. (2013). Students' motivational and emotional experiences and their relationship to persistence during academic challenge in mathematics and reading. *Learning and Individual Differences, 27*, 35–46.

Tulis, M., Steuer, G., & Dresel, M. (2017). Positive beliefs about errors as an important element of adaptive individual dealing with errors during academic learning. *Educational Psychology, 38*, 139–158. https://doi.org/10.1080/01443410.2017.1384536

Vroom, V. H. (1964). *Work and motivation*. Wiley.

Webb, T. L., & Sheeran, P. (2006). Does changing behavioral intentions engender behavior change? A meta-analysis of the experimental evidence. *Psychological Bulletin, 132*(2), 249–268. https://doi.org/10.1037/0033-2909.132.2.249

Weiner, B. (1985). An attributional theory of achievement motivation and emotion. *Psychological Review, 92*(4), 548–573. https://doi.org/10.1037/0033-295X.92.4.548

Weiner, B. (2013). *Human motivation*. New York: Psychology Press.

Weiner, B. (2018). The legacy of an attribution approach to motivation and emotion: A no-crisis zone. *Motivation Science, 4*(1), 4–14. https://doi.org/10.1037/mot0000082

Wieber, F., Thürmer, J. L., & Gollwitzer, P. M. (2015). Promoting the translation of intentions into action by implementation intentions: Behavioral effects and physiological correlates. *Frontiers in Human Neuroscience, 9*. https://doi.org/10.3389/fnhum.2015.00395

Wigfield, A., & Eccles, J. S. (1992). The development of achievement task values: A theoretical analysis. *Developmental Review, 12*(3), 265–310. https://doi.org/10.1016/0273-2297(92)90011-P

Wigfield, A., & Eccles, J. S. (2000). Expectancy–value theory of achievement motivation. *Contemporary Educational Psychology, 25*(1), 68–81. https://doi.org/10.1006/ceps.1999.1015

Wigfield, A., & Koenka, A. C. (2020). Where do we go from here in academic motivation theory and research? Some reflections and recommendations for future work. *Contemporary Educational Psychology, 61*, 101872. https://doi.org/10.1016/j.cedpsych.2020.101872

Wolters, C. A. (2003). Regulation of motivation: Evaluating an underemphasized aspect of self-regulated learning. *Educational Psychologist, 38*(4), 189–205. https://doi.org/10.1207/S15326985EP3804_1

Zusho, A., & Clayton, R. (2011). Culturalizing achievement goal theory and research. *Educational Psychologist, 46*, 239–260.

Topics, Methods, and Research-Based Strategies for Teaching Cognition

8

Maya M. Khanna and Michael J. Cortese

Contents

Abstract

In this chapter, we review the basic contents and structure of our courses in cognition and cognitive psychology as well as pedagogical approaches to teaching. Topics range from an historical overview of the areas of science that lead up to the formation of cognitive science to detailed discussions of published articles within each of the major subfields of cognition (e.g., perception, attention, short-term working memory, long-term memory, language, and decision-making).

M. M. Khanna (✉)
Department of Psychological Science, Creighton University, Omaha, NE, USA
e-mail: mayakhanna@creighton.edu

M. J. Cortese
Department of Psychology, University of Nebraska at Omaha, Omaha, NE, USA

© Springer Nature Switzerland AG 2023
J. Zumbach et al. (eds.), *International Handbook of Psychology Learning and Teaching*,
Springer International Handbooks of Education,
https://doi.org/10.1007/978-3-030-28745-0_11

Throughout our courses, we also focus extensively on the practical applications to cognitive theory. Furthermore, we emphasize the importance of research design and data analyses and discuss how we guide our students in the practice of using theory to arrive at specific numerical predictions. In addition, we discuss our major learning objectives that we hope our students achieve in completing our courses and highlight ways that we assess student work toward these objectives. We also share some of the best practices for teaching cognition that we have developed ourselves and ones that we acquired from others. In particular, we discuss our style of teaching the course as well as examples of in-class activities and demonstrations. Finally, we share a list of resources that interested readers can review to help in the design of their courses on cognition, or in any courses, in general. This overview can serve as both a good starting point for beginning instructors and a useful resource for more experienced instructors.

Keywords

Research methods · Mental processes · Learning objectives · Cognitive domains · Mental processing theories · Cognitive theory applications

Introduction

Major Themes

Cognitive psychology is the scientific study of cognitive processes associated with perception, memory, attention, language, problem-solving, decision-making, and more. Cognitive psychology is part of a broader framework known as cognitive science. Cognitive science is an interdisciplinary field that encompasses cognitive psychology, cognitive neuroscience, psycholinguistics, artificial intelligence, and the applications of each in real-world settings. We advocate a cognitive science approach to teaching cognitive psychology because we believe that one's overall understanding of the field benefits from a diversity of perspectives. More specifically, we believe that one's understanding of cognition is enlightened by knowledge of how the brain works (i.e., cognitive neuropsychology and cognitive neuroscience), through simulation models (i.e., connectionism, artificial intelligence), and by the knowledge of the structure of language and understanding how real-world context can influence mental processes.

Historical Influences

Being a subdiscipline of psychology, cognitive psychology has a common history with psychology in general but gained independent status during the "cognitive revolution" that occurred around 1960. One can trace the antecedents of cognitive psychology to the Greek philosophers Plato and Aristotle who wrote about the structure of knowledge and thought processes. In addition, cognitive psychology was influenced by work on human physiology and neurology. For example, Broca, Wernicke, and others' associated left hemisphere structures with language, and these discoveries have influenced how we study language in terms of both semantics (meaning) and syntax (grammar, etc.; Goodglass & Kaplan, 1972). In addition, von Helmholtz's first reaction time (RT) experiments introduced a method, whereby RT could be used to delineate a process (see, e.g., Donders, 1868-69/1969; Sternberg, 1969). Later, Sternberg's additive factor logic provided a framework to interpret patterns of RT data. In short, Sternberg proposed that if two factors influence the same processing stage, then the two factors will produce an interaction on RT. Otherwise, they will produce additive (i.e., independent) effects. Within this tradition, cognitive psychologists have developed a reputation for executing well-conceived experimental designs to examine cognition via behavior. Of course, other accuracy measures (e.g., number or proportion correct) have been used to infer the nature of cognitive processes as well.

In addition, cognitive theory has been strongly influenced by cognitive neuropsychology (i.e., examining cognition via brain damage). Cognitive neuropsychology can be thought of as a branch of cognitive neuroscience that examines the relationship between cognition and the brain. The advancement of neuroscientific methods (e.g., functional magnetic resonance imaging, fMRI) has helped fuel the increasing interest in cognitive neuroscience. While cognitive neuropsychology's influence on cognitive psychology is clear, the value of neuroimaging to elucidate cognitive processes has been more controversial (see Coltheart, 2013). In contrast, some neuroscientists believe that we will replace descriptions of cognitive processes with biological and neurological descriptions.

We espouse the middle ground; cognitive psychology and cognitive neuroscience are complementary approaches to studying cognition. Cognitive psychologists will need to continue evaluating the degree to which our understanding of cognition can be enhanced via the understanding of the brain. But, at the very least, knowledge of the relationship between the brain and cognition provides a more comprehensive understanding of the cognitive system. In addition, a cognitive science approach to cognitive psychology practically requires a detailed examination of cognitive neuroscience.

Current Trends

In addition to the influence of cognitive neuroscience on cognitive psychology, there are three additional current trends that are worthy of mention. First, connectionism, or the application of computer programs to simulate cognitive processes, has been very influential. In fact, the seminal book on parallel distributed processing (PDP, Rumelhart & McClelland, 1986) has been cited no less than 23,000 times according to Google Scholar. Simulating cognitive processes allows for a better understanding of a process because the theory, as simulated, forces the theoretician to be precise and unambiguous. In addition, one of the most important debates within cognitive psychology concerns whether symbolic or non/sub-symbolic models better capture and help explain the nature of cognition (see, e.g., McClelland et al., 2010). Specifically, traditional symbolic models (e.g., Pinker, 1999) operate using explicit rules and representations, whereas non-/subsymbolic approaches (e.g., Joanisse & Seidenberg, 1999) propose that these "rules" and "representations" emerge from fundamental processing systems that consist of simple processing units that learn associations between inputs and outputs based on an individual's experiences. Second, there has been increasing support for an embodied approach to cognition (e.g., Barsalou, 2008). Embodiment refers to the relationship between cognition (e.g., conceptual processing) and sensory/perceptual systems (e.g., motor processing, visual processing, etc.). For example, it is proposed that our understanding of a concept (e.g., *to write*) requires the recruitment of perceptual processes (e.g., sensory and motor networks utilized in writing) associated with that concept. The evidence to support this theory is abundant and inherently interesting. For example, one activates motor regions of the brain tied to the tongue when reading *lick* and foot areas when reading *kick* (Hauk, Johnsrude, & Pulvermu'ller, 2004). Third, there has been a wide interest in applying cognitive principles to practical situations (e.g., Dunlosky, Rawson, Marsh, Nathan, & Willingham, 2013). Cognitive scientists believe that the better we understand the nature of a cognitive process, the better we should be at developing strategies to solve problems that involve those processes. For example, if we truly understand how people recognize printed words, then we should be better equipped to teach reading. If we understand the processes of human memory (e.g., encoding, storage, and retrieval), then we should be able to present information in a way that facilitates memory and understanding in those who are trying to acquire information (i.e., all of our students). We would argue that students who complete a course in cognitive psychology are better prepared for future classes that require memory, language, attention, problem-solving, decision-making, and more because they have acquired some explicit knowledge into the nature of these processes. Ultimately, this better understanding can then lead to effective strategies that capitalize on personal strengths.

Purpose and Rationale of Our Curriculum in Cognition

Taking a course in cognitive psychology should involve much more than acquiring knowledge about mental concepts. In studying the mind, students will explore cognitive processes, and they will be able describe these processes. However, students should also (a) understand basic experimental design, (b) understand theories and the predictions that can be derived from them, (c) interpret data from figures and tables, (d) interpret data presented in text-based and statistical notation, (e) evaluate studies, and (f) draw conclusions. Many textbooks in cognitive psychology do not include a chapter on research methodology, but we think it is important to include this topic early in the course and emphasize it throughout. This, in part, is due to the fact that many students take cognitive psychology before completing the research methods and statistics courses within our department.

However, knowledge of research methods and analysis is vital to understanding the classic and contemporary experiments that we discuss in cognition. As an example of this, many theories in cognition apply additive factors and subtractive logic (both are explained in detail below). These research designs and the related analyses require a deep understanding of the principles of statistical main effects and interactions as well as factorial designs. Thus, when we discuss research methods and statistical procedures in cognitive psychology, we emphasize the theoretical implications of potential interactions and main effects of experimental factors.

Core Contents and Topics of Cognition

In our classes, we discuss a wide range of topics with our students. We typically organize the course to cover the following topics across four sections that correspond to four section exams.

Section 1
  A) Introduction and history
  B) Methodology
  C) General themes

Section 2
  D) Neuroscience methods
  E) Attention
  F) Sensation, perception, and pattern recognition

Section 3
  G) Short-term working memory
  H) Long-term memory
  I) Semantic memory

Section 4
  J) Language
  K) Decision-making
  L) Problem-solving

A number of other topics could also be included in a cognitive psychology course. Some of these topics are cognitive development, social cognition, application of cognitive psychology principles to real-world situations, and the like.

We strongly advocate requiring a cumulative final exam at the end of the course. The implementation of this aspect of our courses is based on complementary learning systems (CLS) theory (McClelland, McNaughton, & O'Reilly, 1995). This theory proposes that two complementary long-term memory systems are involved in the acquisition and storage of information. Initial acquisition of information is fairly rapid and relies on a hippocampal-based system that is subject to decay; repeated processing of the information leads to gradual and more permanent changes in the lateral cortex (e.g., the anterior temporal lobe). Because information decays relatively quickly from the hippocampal-based system, information about the course material likely will be lost without repeated practice. Incorporating a cumulative final exam means that students will process information repeatedly which encourages longer-term storage that is less subject to decay. One study, for example (Khanna, Badura Brack, & Finken, 2013), found that students who completed a course with a cumulative exam performed better on a test of the course material than those who did not even 18 months after the course had been completed.

Theories in Cognition

We emphasize the themes described above in our cognition course because we consider them to be general principles or patterns in the approach that cognitive scientists use to study mental processes. We typically also discuss specific mental processes that are uniquely examined by cognitive psychologists and often highlight particular studies and researchers who have been pioneers in the field. One example is the landmark publication alluded to earlier (McClelland et al., 1995) which thoroughly describes the dual representation of memory in hippocampal regions and in the neocortex CLS (see, e.g., O'Reilly, Bhattacharyya, Howard, & Ketz, 2014). These authors also describe the process through which memories are initially represented within the hippocampal regions but then transfer to the neocortex. Discussing this paper with students highlights many principles of cognition. For example, it highlights how synaptic connections serve as the bases of learning and representations of memories. It also substantiates the existence of separate but related long-term memory systems: the hippocampal system that is responsible for rapid short-term learning often of an arbitrary nature (e.g., associating names with faces) and the neocortical system in which learning reflects the gradual accumulation of knowledge. McClelland et al. (1995) propose that the gradual learning system is similar to that described by parallel distributed processing (PDP) models, whereas the learning associated with the hippocampus is not because it establishes associations much quicker. In addition, the decay of information occurs more quickly from the hippocampal-based system than the neocortical system. In other words, hippocampal-based memories are somewhat more fragile than those associated with the neocortical system. This example highlights how computational models can serve as a representation of human mental processing and how these models can be tested by examining human behavior. Another reason to discuss this type of article is that it makes more explicit the link between cognitive theory and neuroscience. That is, it helps students realize that cognitive psychologists are interested in explaining behavior by examining brain-based processes. Our view is that theories must hold up to the physiological reality of how thinking works within the brain.

Another major theory that we explore in cognitive psychology is the idea of relying upon what we know about brain-based incremental learning to explain some mental phenomena that seem hard to explain. One example is the seemingly innate ability of children to learn language. For decades, it was commonly assumed that much of language – especially grammatical understanding – was innate and initial representations were not dependent upon experience (Chomsky, 1965). According to this view, children were born with a deep representation of language, including the syntactically acceptable structure of sentences. More recent research has used techniques such as habituation/dishabituation, computational modeling, and the recording of electrophysiological responses to demonstrate that even before children are talking, they are learning – really they are extracting – the acceptable structure of speech and language from conversations they hear. One study (Saffran, Aslin, & Newport, 1996) demonstrated that 8-month-old infants can hear a novel string of sounds (e.g., from an unfamiliar language) for 2 min and, based on that brief exposure, become familiar with that language's typical speech patterns (also see Marcus, Vijayan, Bandi Rao, & Vishton, 1996). They can even identify word boundaries from a subsequent stream of speech, again, based on the initial 2 min of exposure. This suggests that pre-verbal infants are learning linguistic constraints from mere exposure and that this learning is so quick and impressive that it can appear innate.

The previous example highlights another recurring point covered in our courses in cognition. Many times, mental processes that underlie behavior are more compli- cated than initially expected. In the case of language learning just described, carefully designed experiments can reveal and explain subtle processes that allow fast – seemingly innate –language acquisition. Similarly, it seems sensible that children learn to read by learning typical phonics rules. However, experiments have shown that experienced readers use at least two routes to reading aloud. Exactly how one defines these routes depends on theoretical perspectives. More symbolic approaches (e.g., Coltheart, Rastle, Perry, Langdon, & Ziegler, 2001) posit a lexical (i.e., a known word-based) and a sublexical orthographic-to-phonological conver- sion route. In contrast, PDP models (Seidenberg & McClelland, 1989) propose a triangle framework consisting of distributed representations for orthography, pho- nology, and semantics. In this model, the reader may generate a phonological output directly from orthography, or a phonological code is generated indirectly via orthog- raphy-to-semantics-to-phonology. Evidence for these distinct processing pathways can be found in individuals with acquired dyslexia that specifically impacts one route but leaves the other intact. For example, surface dyslexia impacts the lexical/ semantic route – thus, readers will have trouble with words that do not follow typical phonics rules (e.g., words such as *pint*, or *were* in which the ending sounds, *int*, and *ere* are not pronounced according to the phonics rules that accurately predict the pronunciations of *mint* and *here*). On the other hand, phonological dyslexia impacts the sublexical or orthographic-to-phonological route that decodes unfamiliar words. Thus, a person with phonological dyslexia will be able to read words via the lexicon or via the orthographic-to-phonological-to-semantic route but will struggle with unfamiliar words. Evidence for the use of multiple routes for reading has also been supported by carefully designed experiments with typical readers (e.g., Zevin & Balota, 2000). The use of multiple methods or routes to complete a task is found in many areas of cognition beyond reading aloud, including decision-making, attention allocation, and memory representation.

Of course, one of the most widely explored and discussed topics in cognition is the processing and representation of material in memory. We spend one-third to one-half of our cognition course discussing theories and studies of memory. We discuss the multiple divisions of memory – sensory memory, short-term working memory, and long-term memory and the many subdivisions of each. We also discuss ways to test memory experimentally. In addition, we explore many theories of memory and highlight the ways that knowledge of these theories can help students enhance their learning and their performance on tests and other assessments. For example, we discuss levels of processing theory (LOP; Craik & Lockhart, 1972). In LOP theory, memory will be better when attention is focused on meaningful information (e.g., semantic information) during study than when attention is focused on superficial information (e.g., orthographic information). We help our students link this theory to the familiar phenomenon in which they study for an exam by repeatedly reading or recopying their notes. We ask them to compare their exam performance after using those relatively low levels of processing with how they perform when they think about course material in a more meaningful way. For example, we ask them to create visual representations of what we have discussed in class (e.g., create a tree representing the divisions and processes involved in memory). Or, we ask them to create their own quizzes based on the material that we have discussed. We also encourage students to quiz each other using their self-generated quizzes to enjoy the benefits of test-enhanced learning along with the deeper, semantic processing.

We encourage students to modify their study strategies based on transfer-appropriate processing theory (Morris, Bransford, & Franks, 1977). According to this theory, performance on a test will benefit to the extent that processes utilized during acquisition are the ones required during testing. For example, we invite students to consider the potential testing formats that they may encounter (e.g., multiple choice, essay, oral exam, etc.) and to modify their study approaches to mimic those testing formats. If they can mimic the testing situation during study, those experiential properties may transfer to their testing experience.

Related to this overlap of study and testing processes is the increasingly influential theory of embodied or grounded cognition (Barsalou, 2008). According to this theory, our cognition (e.g., semantic memory) is grounded in sensory and perceptual processes. For example, when processing concepts related to hand-action words (e.g., writing, throwing, etc.), motor areas related to these processes are hypothesized to become active. In addition, there is increasing evidence that our knowledge of semantic relations between concepts (e.g., *attic-basement*) includes spatial relationships that are associated with the right hemisphere (see, Zwaan & Yaxley, 2003), perceptions related to color (Connell & Lynott, 2009), and more. The hub-and-spoke model (e.g., Patterson & Lambon Ralph, 2015) provides a precise account of how modal and amodal systems may interact in semantic memory. We discuss these theories in our classes not only to review key and influential theories but also to highlight for our students how these theories can influence their study and practice. One take-home message about embodied cognition is that the semantic knowledge that we acquire is represented in multiple modes, and we can take advantage of all of those modes when studying to enhance our representation of that semantic knowledge. For example, in studying French, a student can focus on the meaning of new words, on their pronunciations, and on the way they would interact with the referents of the word. When thinking about *petit dejeuner*, one might think not only about its orthographic and phonological representation but also about the smell of a fresh baguette and butter or jam. Similarly, students can anticipate their testing context and format (e.g., an oral exam in French) and try to emphasize those aspects of the material during study (e.g., focus on the phonology and articulation rather than the orthography) to enhance the connection of that context to embodied representations of the knowledge they are acquiring.

Research Paradigms Used in Cognitive Research

Human Mental Chronometry

As already mentioned, we integrate the discussion of research methods within the coverage of the core contents and themes in our cognition courses because we believe that doing so encourages our students' analytical thinking. So when we discuss attention, memory, language processing, and other topics, we also discuss the ways in which researchers conduct experiments on them. We describe how experimental findings drive the development of theories in cognition. In particular, we emphasize how studies that rely on reaction time and accuracy measures can be used to reveal relationships among mental processes. In particular, we discuss the overarching principle of human mental chronometry and the subtraction and additive factor methods of Donders and Sternberg, respectively (described, above; see Donders, 1868-69/1969; Sternberg, 1969). We discuss how examining patterns of reaction times across various experimental conditions can reveal how mental processes relate to one another.

We also highlight some of the common experimental tasks that cognitive scientists use. For example, much cognitive research focuses on word processing. Thus, we discuss the reading aloud task, the lexical decision task (i.e., indicating if a given letter string is a word or a nonword), recognition memory, free recall, and more. Within our discussion of semantic memory and the lexicon, we discuss semantic priming in which one observes facilitated reading aloud reaction times for words (e.g., *nurse*) preceded by words related in meaning (e.g., *doctor*). We explain how finding facilitation for the target word is more than a simple result; it informs us about how the concepts of the prime and target may be represented in memory. For example, mediated priming – in which the prime (e.g., *lion*) and target (e.g., *stripes*) are related only via a mediator (e.g., *tiger*) – can be explained and understood in terms of a spreading activation model (e.g., Collins & Loftus, 1975). That is, activation spreads in a semantic network from the mental representation associated with the prime to the mediator and finally to the target.

The Influences of Neuropsychological Research

After presenting a broad overview of historical studies that laid the foundation for modern cognitive psychology, we jump into a discussion of how to examine individuals with brain damage to help elucidate cognitive theory. We do this because of the rich and long-lasting traditions that link cognitive psychology and cognitive neuropsychology. Along this vein, we emphasize the principles of association, dissociation, and double dissociation as ways to determine the relative independence of two or more cognitive processes. Furthermore, we highlight how the transcranial magnetic stimulation (TMS) technique, which is used to create temporary "virtual" lesions, represents an important breakthrough in cognitive neuropsychology. We believe TMS to be a powerful approach because it allows for the disruption of processes associated with precise brain areas at specific times during the course of completing a within-subjects design with relatively large sample sizes (see, e.g., Woollams, Madrid, & Lambon Ralph, 2017). We also discuss how the emphasis of relating structure to function has shifted to using methods in cognitive neuroscience that do not require examining people who have incurred brain damage but instead rely on typical functioning. In particular, we discuss the techniques used in cognitive neuroscience ranging from single-cell electrode recordings to event-related potentials (ERPs), magnetoencephalography (MEG), and functional magnetic resonance imaging (fMRI). We compare and contrast these methods and discuss how research questions and environmental constraints often dictate the most appropriate research methods.

Techniques in Memory Research

Within our section on memory, we discuss the variety of tests that have been developed to query explicit and implicit memory as well as short-term/working memory and long-term memory. These methods are sometimes surprisingly simple. For example, a common method for testing explicit memory is a simple list-learning free recall paradigm in which participants study a list of 12–20 unrelated words presented on a computer monitor, one at a time, and then recall as many of those words as possible in any order. Characteristics of the words can be predictive of recall. For example, even a very slight variation in how the words are presented (e.g., a change in font for some items) may result in different patterns of recall. We also discuss how memory for lists of words can be tested using basic free recall (as described above), serial recall (i.e., recalling the words in the order of presentation), and/or a recognition memory test where subjects study a list of words and are later tested with a list that contains the studied words and an equal number of unstudied words for which subjects make "old" (i.e., studied) and new (i.e., unstudied) decisions. Students find it particularly easy to understand the relative ease of *recognizing* something that they have seen before as compared to *recalling* the same thing because it links up to the difference between multiple-choice and essay test items. Of course, we relate all this material back to the neuropsychological and neuroscientific evidence showing that these two types of memory processes (recognition and recall) are dissociable based on behavioral and neuroimaging studies.

Using Cognitive Neuroscience to Inform Cognitive Theory

In fact, over the years, we have dedicated more and more time to discussing the links between cognitive psychology and cognitive neuroscience. Each of us also teaches a separate course on cognitive neuroscience, in which a thorough discussion of neuroscience techniques is more appropriate. However, we do present the basic principles of cognitive neuroscience in our cognitive psychology courses as a natural extension of our discussion of neuropsychology. This is because some aspects of cognitive psychology are influenced by neuroimaging techniques. For example, positron emission tomography (PET) and functional magnetic resonance imaging (fMRI) have long been used to test the neurological validity of many of the mental process models first introduced in cognitive psychology. A nice illustration comes from a study by Smith and Jonides (1999) in which they used PET to demonstrate the separate representations of verbal and spatial working memory and a task domain-independent area serving as central executive. They were able to provide support for a model of working memory that had been introduced 25 years earlier (Baddeley & Hitch, 1974).

In discussing the techniques of cognitive neuroscience, we also highlight the distinctions among various neuroimaging techniques, especially those pertaining to each technique's spatial and temporal resolution. In addition, we discuss how the scientific question at hand can determine which technique is most appropriate. For example, many psycholinguistic researchers favor techniques with high levels of temporal resolution for studies of speech perception and processing. Thus, event-related potentials (ERPs) and magnetoencephalography (MEG) are better choices than PET and fMRI. When studying speech perception and comprehension processes that are ongoing and changing at a millisecond pace as a person interprets the speech they hear, it may be better to use PET and fMRI techniques because they allow millisecond-level resolution.

Using Big Databases to Explore Empirical and Theoretical Questions

To best serve our students, it is important to keep up to date with the current trends and paradigm shifts in cognitive science, including the collection and use of "big data." Of course, this "new" approach is not entirely new. For example, the child data language exchange system (CHILDES) that now serves as a repository for massive amounts of language data across 26 different languages was established in the early 1980s (e.g., MacWhinney & Snow, 1985). CHILDES allows researchers to access large samples of language interactions.

A more recent version of big data comes from the megastudy paradigm (see Keuleers & Balota, 2015). Megastudies involve the collection of performance measures for a large number of stimuli. For example, the English Lexicon Project (ELP) involved the collection of reaction time and accuracy measures for over 40,000 English words in reading aloud and lexical decision across 6 different universities. These data have served as the primary evidence in many different studies (e.g., Yap & Balota, 2009) and have motivated similar lexicon projects in many other languages. The megastudy paradigm has been extended to semantic priming (Hutchison et al., 2013), recognition memory (Cortese, Khanna, & Hacker, 2010), and more. Conducting megastudies offers many advantages over the traditional factorial design (see Balota, Yap, Hutchison, & Cortese, 2012, for a thorough description of these issues). For one thing, due to the sheer number of stimuli, the megastudy offers a statistically powerful way to examine relationships among variables. Also, the data obtained from megastudies are usually easily accessible to researchers who wish to test novel hypotheses. In one study (Adelman & Estes, 2013), researchers were interested in how valence (i.e., positivity or negativity of a stimulus referent) and arousal (i.e., how boring or exciting a stimulus is) are related to recognition memory. They accessed previously published recognition memory data from Cortese et al., (2010) and then, using multiple regression, they entered valence and arousal values in the final step of the analyses, after controlling for the variables analyzed by Cortese et al. (2010). Interestingly, they found that as valence got increasingly positive or negative, recognition memory improved, whereas arousal was unrelated to memory. Later, we discuss how students can use megastudy data to test certain hypotheses in undergraduate cognitive psychology courses and laboratory classes.

Another major emphasis of our courses is a discussion of how a researcher can combine a series of methods and techniques to help explore scientific questions. By discussing the many methods that we use in cognition and relating them to cognitive neuropsychology and cognitive neuroscience, we hope that it becomes very obvious to students that continued technological development and interdisciplinary work will only further and deepen our understanding of cognition. Perhaps the most important application of this principle is seen in the design of experiments in cognitive neuroscience. The best-designed studies using neuroimaging are ones that use the well-planned and controlled designs of experiments in cognitive psychology.

Teaching, Learning, and Assessment in Cognition: Approaches and Strategies

One of the nicest things about teaching a course in cognition is that students can apply much of what we are discussing to their own learning. After all, the focus of the course is on mental processes such as attention and memory. It is easy for students to become interested in these processes because part of their academic success depends on maximizing their attention and memory capabilities. To enhance the students' level of interest, we both use what we think of as dynamic lectures and active lectures. That is, in addition to presenting material via traditional lectures illustrated by PowerPoint slides, we include many opportunities for active discussions and ask students to think of how topics in cognition are related to their own lives. For example, relatively early in the course, we discuss perception and the fact that it is a subjective experience. We ask students to think of examples from their own lives in which they have had a perception that was different from that of another person. Students typically come up with examples ranging from things that they have heard and interpreted differently than their friends (e.g., the sounds of an AC unit may be calming to one and menacing to another) to examples of visual stimuli that they have interpreted differently (e.g., seeing a color as blue vs. green).

Throughout the course, we ask students to apply our discussions to their lives and to share these examples with their classmates. Sometimes we ask students to do this individually, and sometimes we ask them to use the "think-pair-share" technique in which they generate examples of their own, pair up with a classmate to compare their examples, and then share their combined examples with the rest of the class. As teachers, we find it pleasant and satisfying to hear students engaging in lively discussions of examples from real-life-related to course topics. Students are often surprised when they realize how much of their everyday lives relate to principles in cognition.

Another example of the practical value of cognition research for students' lives comes when we discuss retrieval practice and test-enhanced learning (e.g., Agarwal, Bain, & Chamberlain, 2012; McDaniel, Agarwal, Huelser, McDermott, & Roediger, 2011). There has been a recent surge in research in the practical applications of retrieval practice (i.e., repeatedly recalling previously learned information) to increase the likelihood of remembering the information on a future assessment. One form of retrieval practice is simply taking a test or quiz on a set of material. Doing so can enhance the durability of memory for that material, leading to better performance on subsequent assessments – including graded exams. Thus, in our classes, we discuss how students can use retrieval practice and self-testing to improve their memory for material in preparation for exams (and hopefully even after exams). This also helps us to justify our use of various forms of retrieval practice in our courses (e.g., quizzes, practice problems, research projects, etc.). For our graded learning assessments, we each use four to five exams throughout the academic term, each of which covers three to four major topics or chapters of material.

To further illustrate applications of cognitive science research to student, we discuss common mnemonic devices and related study strategies. This discussion can range from how to use acronyms and acrostics (e.g., phrases such as "please excuse my dear aunt Sally" to help remember the order of mathematical operations) to how to reorganize notes to encourage retention. Students really seem to perk up when we are discussing these strategies and the best ways to use them. We discuss not only how these strategies can help them study for our class and others but also how using these memory strategies can help them with everyday problem-solving (e.g., how to remember items on a grocery list).

We also highlight the practical nature of cognitive science by using many in-class demonstrations of experimental designs used in cognition research. One example is the Stroop task and the Stroop effect (Stroop, 1935). In this task, participants are shown a series of words printed in various colors. Participants are asked to ignore the word meaning and say aloud the color of ink in which the word is printed. The classic Stroop design includes words that spell color names (e.g., *blue*) as well as words unrelated to color (e.g., *book*). Some of the color words are presented in the color of ink that is congruent with the word meaning (e.g., *blue* printed in blue), whereas other words are presented in an incongruent color (e.g., *blue* printed in red). Participants are slower to respond correctly on incongruent trials compared to congruent trials; response times on neutral trials (e.g., *keep* printed in black) fall somewhere in between. We ask students to complete the Stroop task in class, either by having one student perform the task in front of the other students or in pairs in which one student is the participant and the other is the tester who presents a sheet of Stroop stimuli. When performing this task, students can experience the need to override their prepotent reading response (i.e., to focus on word meaning) in order to complete the color-naming task in the incongruent condition, but not in the congruent condition. This experience serves as the basis for our discussion of how this task can be used as a measure of attention allocation and inhibition. Moreover, we discuss how simple reaction time and accuracy measures can help us understand the nature of the mental processes that are involved in performing the task.

We use many other demonstrations of research topics and common research paradigms. These include everything from simple free recall tasks (e.g., orally presenting a list of 12–15 words and asking students to remember them in any order), to demonstrations about word processing (e.g., using reading aloud and lexical decision tasks), to more complicated demonstrations about dichotic listening and multitasking. A list of research method demonstrations is presented in the Resources section at the end of the chapter.

Throughout our courses in cognition, we relate research findings from studies of memory, learning, attention, decision-making, and other realms to the strategies that teachers and students use to improve learning. Even in early lectures when we are discussing basic cognitive processes (e.g., auditory working memory), we discuss how we can use theoretical principles to improve study habits and learning. For example, we discuss early research in phonological working memory (e.g., Conrad, 1960) that highlights the fact that people often recode written information into an auditory representation. Our presentation about this phenomenon can help students see the advantage of studying information in both written and phonological format. In other words, students realize that talking out loud while problem-solving or even rehearsing information can help them retain it. These are just a few examples of how we link discussion of basic research findings to tips that can help students study more effectively.

Student Learning and Assessment

In teaching cognition, we are guided by several fundamental learning objectives. They are student-focused and transparent. They appear on the first page of each of our syllabi (i.e., a document that outlines the course content and objectives for students). Each learning objective takes the form of a statement about what we hope students will gain from the course, and each begins with the same words: "Students will be able to..." (SWBAT). These learning objectives fall into three main categories. The first is focused on students acquiring a basic understanding of cognition (e.g., SWBAT identify models of working memory). The second category is focused on the importance of relating data to theory (e.g., SWBAT use data collected from experiments to inform cognitive theories and to make specific predictions regarding these theories). The third set focuses on using cognitive theory for practical applications (e.g., SWBAT use research from studies in retrieval practice to identify successful study strategies). There are several learning objectives within each of these categories, and we discuss them all with students on the first day of class. Students are sometimes at first surprised by our focus on data and our requirement for them to be comfortable working with data, but we quickly dispel their misconception that data are the exclusive domain of courses on statistics and research methods.

We are careful to make sure that we have created learning objectives that are measurable. Thus, we map our assessments back to learning objectives before the beginning of each semester. We ask ourselves, "What is it that I want my students to learn from this course?" Our next question is "How am I going to measure that?" For example, with regard to the learning objective, "Students will be able to use data collected from experiments to inform cognitive theories and to make specific predictions regarding these theories," there are several assessment options. One of these could be an essay exam question which asks students to first describe an experiment and sample data collected from it and then to explain how the data inform a theory (e.g., LOP theory). Finally, they would have to say how their new understanding of LOP can lead them to make predictions about a proposed experiment. Such essay questions are very detailed but also very doable.

Another way to assess the same learning objective is through a research proposal assignment. The students are asked to read material from an area of cognitive science (e.g., attention training, working memory, decision-making, etc.) and propose an original experiment whose results would extend our understanding of cognition within that area. Doing this requires students to develop a relatively deep understanding of the cognitive research related to their proposal. In addition to submitting the written proposal, the students prepare and deliver a 10–12-min presentation about it. This assignment requires students to engage in deep processing and retrieval practice, both while writing the proposal and while making their research presentations. Because they do not actually have to conduct the experiment, there are no limits to what they can propose. The study can focus on children, older adults, or left-handed synesthetes (one student actually proposed that population!). Our only requirement is that students provide a theory-based justification for including specific participant types. We also encourage students to propose research designs that are practical and doable. Furthermore, we ask students to make predictions about the results of their proposed experiment and explain how that pattern of results will expand our understanding of cognitive theory.

The research proposal assignment has many practical benefits. Every semester at least a handful of students remark on how completing this assignment helped them to understand assignment-related course material. In fact, several students have used their proposals as the basis for later independent studies or honors projects, some of which have been published. One student even used her proposed project when she entered graduate school. It is also satisfying for us to see how knowledgeably our students are able to respond to their classmates' questions about their proposals and how they are able to "think on their feet" about the theories related to their proposed research.

We use a variety of additional assessments to help us gauge student learning, as well as to provide students with the opportunity to engage in retrieval practice and relatively deeper processing with the material. For example, we often use ungraded, unannounced ("pop") quizzes. These usually include 10–15 multiple-choice, fill-in-the-blank, or short-answer questions. We encourage our students to treat them as they would a graded quiz by setting them up in a closed-note, closed-book, and individually completed format. Although the quizzes are not graded, we do review the questions and appropriate answers in class. No-stakes quizzes such as these have been shown to provide beneficial retrieval practice without causing anxiety students typically experience in relation to graded pop quizzes (Khanna, 2015). Most of all, students can gauge their performance and use that information to direct their study strategies.

In short, when we map our assessments back to learning objectives, we are mindful that students vary in their feelings about various forms of assessment. Many students dread exams and prefer in-class, long-term group projects. Others have the opposite preferences. We try to please and annoy both types of students to about the same degree. Thus, we use exams, research proposals, database research projects, in-class quizzes (usually ungraded), in-class assignments (e.g., think-pair-share work or demonstrations), and long-term group projects. Each of our assessments is centered on at least one learning objective but often more.

Teaching Strategies Informed by Theory and Research

We try our best to structure our class sessions in ways that both convey important course information and – as illustrated by the research proposal assignment – allow students to actively engage with the material. We do this in several different ways.

Active Lecturing The most frequent of these is to structure our classes in an active lecture format (e.g., Bernstein, Frantz, & Chew, 2020). That is, we do follow the "sage on the stage" trope, but we also make sure that the students are active participants in our lectures. As already mentioned, one of the most common ways that we do this in cognitive courses is by providing demonstrations of classic research paradigms and asking students to participate or "play along." In the free recall demonstration alluded to above, for example, after students have written down in any order as many as possible of the 12–15 words they heard, we ask them to score their performance and then lead a discussion about what they did and did not remember. This discussion allows us to highlight numerous patterns, including the serial position curve, in which participants typically remember items from the beginning and end of the list better than the items in the middle. We can also discuss the lexical factors that can influence memory. For example, words that are highly imageable (i.e., easy to think of as an image) tend to be more memorable than those that are not. By using such demonstrations of research paradigms, we can convey raw information about research methods and cognitive processes while encouraging students to think more deeply about these processes as they experienced them for themselves.

Socratic Methods We also integrate Socratic teaching methods into our lectures. One way that we do this is by asking questions throughout our lectures and waiting (sometimes for a very long time) for students to answer them before moving on to another topic. Often these questions ask students to think of ways that specific cognitive theories are applicable to their own lives. For instance, when we discuss limits on attention capacity, we ask students to provide their own examples. We typically get examples involving texting and driving or integrating words that they are saying in a conversation into a paper they are writing for a class at the same time. Using active lecture formats and Socratic questioning is another way to encourage our students to engage in retrieval practice and relatively deep processing (ala LOP theory) that can facilitate learning and retention of course information. In addition, during the "think-pair-share" activities described earlier, we often ask students to relate course concepts to their personal experiences. This enables them to connect current course topics with memories and experiences from their lives, therein requiring relatively deep processing. These techniques alongside the retrieval practice provided by the in-class ungraded pop quizzes (discussed, above) give our students many opportunities for deep processing course material in several different ways.

Big Data Assignments Our "big data" processing assignment brings together all of the above techniques to encourage active learning, retrieval practice, deep thinking, and the like. For this assignment, students must access the English Lexicon Project (ELP; Balota et al., 2007) to help them answer questions about cognition. As already mentioned, the ELP is a megastudy in which thousands of participants across several universities were each asked to read aloud and/or make lexical (i.e., word/nonword judgments) on thousands of items (i.e., words and nonwords). The reaction time and accuracy of pronunciation and lexical decisions were recorded for each person for each item. These reaction time and accuracy measures are now archived and publicly available to anyone interested on the ELP database website (www.elexicon.wustl. edu). In addition, the database includes detailed information about each of the items, including each word's frequency of usage (according to three published measures), number of syllables, number of letters, it's part of speech, a measure of how similar its spelling pattern is to other words pronounced similarly, and many other "word nerd" characteristics. Using this information allows a person to access a specified list of words that have specific features (e.g., they are high or low frequency) and see how that characteristic influences participants' reaction time and accuracy for that word.

For the big data assignment, we ask students to hypothesize how these word characteristics should influence pronunciation or lexical decision responses. We then ask them to make specific predictions (e.g., high-frequency words should have shorter reaction times than low-frequency words). Next, the students are to access the ELP database and see if their predictions were correct. Then, we ask them to provide support for what they found in the ELP database but also in previously published articles (based on smaller-scale studies) that have examined these lexical factors. This assignment allows us not only to get students really thinking about how lexical representation and lexical characteristics influence behavior but also to raise the question of whether big data sets offer a legitimate and efficient way to investigate mental processing. To conclude the assignment, we ask students to apply their findings to an everyday problem. For example, one group of students used the ELP to investigate the reading aloud performance of words according to their part of speech and imageability (they also accessed the Cortese & Fugett, 2004 imageability ratings). They found that nouns and highly imageable words were associated with faster reaction times and higher levels of accuracy. They translated these findings into a recommendation for preparing reading instruction materials for children that included a high concentration of very imageable nouns. This was not an earth-shaking recommendation, but it showed that the students learned how big data and research results can be used to support the development of curricular materials and even education policy.

In short, this assignment prompts deep processing of course information, provides retrieval practice, and requires relating the purpose of the study back to a real-world problem. We think the assignment is an excellent tool that students can use to help them answer future research questions in a scientific way. To assess the degree to which this is true, our final exams include questions in which students must outline a plan of action for using the ELP (or another publicly available big database) to answer a question about cognition.

Challenges and Lessons Learned

We have developed our methods for instruction in cognition courses over many semesters, and yet we still change some things each semester. Although we try to integrate what cognitive science tells us about learning, some things we do are not necessarily exciting or innovative. One of those things is to give PowerPoint-based lectures. We have found that in most classes, students need to have a basic vocabulary and need to hear and see the facts at least once before they can be expected to extrapolate or apply those facts. Similarly, though we give multiple-choice exams that include applied and detailed questions, we also ask some straightforward fact-based questions.

We also realize that although lecturing about basic course information is necessary, students learn best by doing. Thus, our lectures are presented in an active, engaging format with lots of in-class demonstrations and student activities. For example, we often ask students to participate in mock experiments that are similar to ones we are discussing. We ask them to note how they performed, and many times we will compare the "data" collected from the class to the published results. As an example, we ask students to engage in a variation of the classic Deese-Roediger-McDermott (DRM) false memory paradigm. In the classic DRM paradigm, participants receive lists of words related in meaning (e.g., *bed*, *rest*, *awake*, *pillow*, *peace*, etc.) to a central theme item (i.e., critical lure; e.g., *sleep*) that is not on the list. Participants are just as likely to recall this critical lure as they are to recall many of the items that actually appear on the list (e.g., Roediger & McDermott, 1995). We ask our students not only to engage in this classic version of the task but to also engage in a version that highlights how lexical representations include semantic (i.e., meaning-based) features but also phonological (i.e., sound-based) features. We do this by first asking students to pair up in class. We then give one person within each pair three lists that we ask them to read aloud (one list at a time) to their partner – we randomize the order of the lists across students before class. They are to read each list at a pace of 2 s per word and then record all of the words recalled by their partner for each list, one list at a time. One of the lists contains a classic DRM list such as the *sleep* list provided above. Another list will contain a series of words that are all phonological neighbors (e.g., *fog, log, dot, bog, doll*, etc.) to a critical lure (e.g., *dog*). Another list will be a hybrid list in which there will be semantically related as well as phonologically related words to a critical lure (a list such as *sugar, sweat, heart, meet, bitter, beet,* etc. for the critical lure, *sweet*). We ask students to test their in-class partner on each of these lists. Students will see that although there are high rates of false recall for the critical lure for the semantic and phonological lists, there is a higher rate of false recall for the hybrid list (e.g., Watson, Balota, & Roediger, 2003). From this demonstration, we can discuss how lexical representations contain not only meaning-based but also sound-based codes. Furthermore, this 5-min demonstration allows us to discuss a major theory in cognition, generate data, and examine patterns of results and relate these data back to the original theory.

A final important lesson from our experiences teaching cognition is that not all results of laboratory research in cognitive psychology apply equally well in real classrooms. For example, cognitive science researchers have encouraged instructors to use frequent pop quizzes to provide students with retrieval practice that should lead to better performance on unit exams as well as cumulative final exams (e.g., Roediger, Agarwal, McDaniel, & McDermott, 2011). However, we have found that giving frequent, graded pop quizzes actually causes students to feel so anxious about the material and the class, in general, that it impairs rather than enhances learning. This doesn't negate the theory, though. When we have reduced the anxiety factor by giving *ungraded* (no stakes) pop quizzes, we see the expected higher performance on cumulative final exams. Moreover, students like ungraded pop quizzes because the ungraded feedback helps them to know where to concentrate their study efforts before the next test (Khanna, 2015). Our experience with pop quizzing illustrates a more general point, namely, that even the best theories and most impressive research results about pedagogical practice must be evaluated in real classrooms before they can be recommended for broad adoption. We are trying to do some of that evaluation ourselves by investigating how students' characteristics might help teachers select the pedagogical techniques best suited to their students. Consider, for example, that our results from graded vs. ungraded pop quizzes were collected at a university enrolling mainly high-achieving, goal-oriented, and anxious students. Would the same trepidation and distracting anxiety about graded pop quizzes occur in a different sample of students? This is a research question.

In short, we have found that the science of teaching is similar to the science of learning – you teach/learn best by doing. So we encourage you to try new things in your cognitive psychology courses, make incremental changes at first, and then see how well those new things suit you and your students.

Teaching, Learning, and Assessment Resources

We have found countless resources about teaching and articles about applying cognitive science to teaching practice. Here are just a few of our favorites. The articles are also listed in the References:

Craik, F. I. M., & Lockhart, R. S. (1972). Levels of processing: A framework for memory research. *Journal of Verbal Learning and Verbal behavior, 11*, 671–684.

Dunlosky, J., Rawson, K. A., Marsh, E. J., Nathan, M. J., & Willingham, D. T. (2013). Improving students' learning with effective learning techniques: Promising directions from cognitive and educational psychology. *Psychological Science in the Public Interest, 14*, 4–58.

Khanna, M. M., Badura Brack, A. S., & Finken, L, L. (2013). Short- and long-term effects of cumulative finals on student learning. *Teaching of Psychology, 40*(3), 175–182.

Khanna, M. M. (2015). Ungraded Pop-Quizzes: Test-enhanced learning without all the anxiety. *Teaching of Psychology, 42*(2), 174–178.

Khanna, M. M., & Cortese, M. J. (2016). The benefits of quizzing in content-focused versus skills-focused courses. *Scholarship of Teaching and Learning in Psychology, 2*(1), 87–97.

https://www.retrievalpractice.org/ – a student and teacher oriented website highlighting why retrieval practice can help students retain information.

http://gocognitive.net/ – a great resource for online demonstrations in cognitive psychology

http://www.simonslab.com/index.html – a great researcher website with links to videos demonstrating attentional limitations.

Cognitive Psychology In-Class Demonstrations

Here is a list of many of the demonstrations that we conduct with our students in class. We will include details for the first few and a brief list for several others. Please email us if you would like more details or more specific examples: mayakhanna@creighton.edu; mcortese@unomaha.edu.

Free Recall List Short-term memory – Create a list of 12–15 words. Depending upon what you want to demonstrate, these can vary in length, imageability, frequency, etc. You can present these to your students verbally or visually or both. Present words one word per 2 s. At the end of the list, indicate to "Recall Now." This can be shown on the screen or give them a signal (we simply look up from the list) to start recall. After students have recorded all of the words that they recall, ask them to indicate how many words they recalled (hold up fingers corresponding to recall number). This is related to the 7+/− 2 short-term memory constraint. You can read through the list and ask students to raise their hands when a word they recorded is read aloud. This can help them visualize the list position effect. You can also discuss proportion of items recalled that correspond to any of the lexical characteristics (e.g., frequency, length, etc.) that you may have embedded within your list.

Serial Recall Short-term memory – Similar to free recall, except specify that items must be recalled in order. When students are indicating the items that they recalled (i.e., raising their hands for the words they recorded), highlight how serial and free recall performance are different. Also, the primacy and recency effects are apparent (recalling relatively more items from the beginning and the end of the lists, respectively).

Stroop Attention – You can simulate a few trials of the classic paradigm within a PowerPoint slideshow. Create slides with the color words (e.g., *blue*, *green*, *red*, etc.), and vary the color of ink in which the words are presented. Ask a student volunteer to focus and report out the color of ink of each item while ignoring the actual word written. Use at least nine trials (three congruent, three incongruent, and three neutral items). Discuss the relative ease of color identification in the congruent versus the incongruent trials.

Levels of Processing Theory Memory – Create a list of words to be presented and remembered in a free recall test. These words should be presented visually (this is easy with PowerPoint). For each item, also include a question. One-third of the words should have a question based on the meaning of the words, another third should have questions related to the sound of the word, and the final third should have questions related to the spelling pattern of the words. For example, for a meaning-based question, if the word is *fox* this can be paired with the question, "Does this have a fuzzy tail?" For a sound-based question, the word *light* could be paired with the question, "Does this word rhyme with fight?" For a spelling-based question, the word could be *rural*, and the question could be, "How many *r*s are in the word?" At the end of the recall list, ask the students to recall all of the items that they can. After that, follow the reporting procedure for the free and serial recall lists (above). Invite students to reflect on which words had the highest recall rates across the class. Discuss this as it relates to LOP from Craik and Lockhart (1972).

Brief List of Other Possible Demonstrations
Visual Perceptual Distortions
Dichotic Listening with Shadowing: Attention
Dual-Task Performance – show how increased difficulty in primary task leads to increased RT in the secondary task
Release from Proactive Interference: Wickens (1975)
Analogical Problem-Solving
Deese-Roediger-McDermott Lists and False Memory – We especially like using lists that interleave semantic and phonological associates (see Watson et al., 2003)

Cross-References

► Neuroscience in the Psychology Curriculum
► Sensation and Perception
► Teaching the Foundations of Psychological Science

References

Adelman, J. S., & Estes, Z. (2013). Emotion and memory: A recognition advantage for positive and negative words independent of arousal. *Cognition, 129*, 530–535. https://doi.org/10.1016/j.cognition.2013.08.014.

Agarwal, P. K., Bain, P. M., & Chamberlain, R. W. (2012). The value of applied research: Retrieval practice improves classroom learning and recommendations from a teacher, a principal, and a scientist. *Educational Psychology Review, 24*, 437–448.

Baddeley, A. D., & Hitch, G. (1974). Working memory. In G. H. Bower (Ed.), *The psychology of learning and motivation: Advances in research and theory* (Vol. 8, pp. 47–89). New York, NY: Academic.

Balota, D. A., Yap, M. J., Cortese, M. J., Hutchison, K. A., Kessler, B., Loftus, B., Neely, J. H., Nelson, D. L., Simpson, G. B., & Treiman, R. (2007). The English lexicon project: A users guide. *Behavior Research Methods, 39*, 445–459. https://doi.org/10.3758/BF03193014.

Balota, D. A., Yap, M. J., Hutchison, K. A., & Cortese, M. J. (2012). Megastudies: Large scale analyses of lexical processes. In J. S. Adelman (Ed.), *Visual word recognition Vol. 1: Models and methods, orthography and phonology* (pp. 90–115). New York, NY: Psychology Press.

Barsalou, L. W. (2008). Grounded cognition. *Annual Review of Psychology, 59*, 617–645. https://doi.org/10.1146/annurev.psych.59.103006.093639.

Bernstein, D. A., Frantz, S., & Chew, S. L. (2020). *Teaching psychology: A step by step guide* (3rd ed.). New York, NY: Routledge.

Chomsky, N. (1965). *Aspects of the theory of syntax*. Cambridge, MA: MIT Press. ISBN:9780262260503.

Collins, A. M., & Loftus, E. F. (1975). A spreading-activation theory of semantic processing. *Psychological Review, 82*(6), 407–428.

Coltheart, M. (2013). How can functional neuroimaging inform cognitive theories? *Perspectives on Cognitive Science, 8*(1), 98–103. https://doi.org/10.1177/1745691612469208.

Coltheart, M., Rastle, K., Perry, C., Langdon, R., & Ziegler, J. (2001). DRC: A dual route cascaded model of visual word recognition and reading aloud. *Psychological Review, 108*, 204–256. https://doi.org/10.1037//0033-295X.108.1.204.

Connell, L., & Lynott, D. (2009). Is a bear white in the woods? Parallel representation of implied object color during language comprehension. *Psychonomic Bulletin & Review, 16*(3), 573–577. https://doi.org/10.3758/PBR.16.3.573.

Conrad, R. (1960). Serial order intrusions in immediate memory. *British Journal of Psychology, 51*(1), 45–48.

Cortese, M. J., & Fugett, A. (2004). Imageability ratings for 3,000 monosyllabic words. *Behavior Research Methods, Instruments, & Computers, 36*(3), 384–387.

Cortese, M. J., Khanna, M. M., & Hacker, S. (2010). Recognition memory for 2,578 monosyllabic words. *Memory, 18*, 595–609. https://doi.org/10.1080/09658211.2010.493892.

Craik, F. I. M., & Lockhart, R. S. (1972). Levels of processing: A framework for memory research. *Journal of Verbal Learning and Verbal Behavior, 11*, 671–684.

Donders, F. (1868-69/1969). On the speed of mental processes. In W.G. Koster (ed.) *Acta psychologica 30: Attention and performance II* (pp. 412-431). Amsterdam, The Netherlands: North-Holland Press Company.

Dunlosky, J., Rawson, K. A., Marsh, E. J., Nathan, M. J., & Willingham, D. T. (2013). Improving students' learning with effective learning techniques: Promising directions from cognitive and educational psychology. *Psychological Science in the Public Interest, 14*, 4–58.

Goodglass, H., & Kaplan, E. (1972). *The assessment of aphasia and related disorders*. Philadelphia, PA: Lea & Febiger.

Hauk, O., Johnsrude, I., & Pulvermüller, F. (2004). Somatotopic represen-tation of action words in human motor and premotor cortex. *Neuron, 41*, 301–307.

Hutchison, K. A., Balota, D. A., Neely, J. H., Cortese, M. J., Cohen-Shikora, E., Tse, C., Yap, M. J., Bengson, J. J., Niemeyer, D., & Buchanon, E. (2013). The semantic priming project. *Behavior Research Methods, 45*, 1099–1114. https://doi.org/10.3758/s13428-012-0304-z.

Joanisse, M. F., & Seidenberg, M. S. (1999). Impairments in verb morphology after brain injury: A connectionist model. *Proceedings of the National Academy of Sciences, 96*, 7592–7597. https://doi.org/10.1073/pnas.96.13.7592.

Keuleers, E., & Balota, D. A. (2015). Megastudies, crowdsourcing, and large datasets in psycholinguistics: An overview of recent developments. *The Quarterly Journal of Experimental Psychology, 688*, 1457–1468. https://doi.org/10.1080/17470218.2014.945096.

Khanna, M. M. (2015). Ungraded pop-quizzes: Test-enhanced learning without all the anxiety. *Teaching of Psychology, 42*(2), 174–178.

Khanna, M. M., Badura Brack, A. S., & Finken, L. L. (2013). Short- and long-term effects of cumulative finals on student learning. *Teaching of Psychology, 40*(3), 175–182.

MacWhinney, B., & Snow, C. (1985). The Child Language Data Exchange System. *Journal of Child Language, 12*, 271–295.

Marcus, G. F., Vijayan, S., Bandi Rao, S., & Vishton, P. M. (1996). Rule learning by seven-month old infants. *Science, 283*(1), 77–80. https://doi.org/10.1126/science.283.5398.77.

McClelland, J. L., McNaughton, B. L., & O'Reilly, R. C. (1995). Why there are complementary learning systems in the hippocampus and neocortex: Insights from the successes and failures of connectionist models of learning and memory. *Psychological Review, 102*(3), 419–457.

McClelland, J. L., et al. (2010). Letting structure emerge: Connectionism and dynamical systems approaches to cognition. *Trends in Cognitive Science, 14*(8), 348–356.

McDaniel, M. A., Agarwal, P. K., Huelser, B. J., McDermott, K. B., & Roediger, H. L. (2011). Test-enhanced learning in a middle school science classroom: The effects of quiz frequency and placement. *Journal of Educational Psychology, 103*, 399–414.

Morris, C. D., Bransford, J. D., & Franks, J. J. (1977). Levels of processing versus transfer appropriate processing. *Journal of Verbal Learning and Verbal Behavior, 16*(5), *519–533*. https://doi.org/10.1016/s0022-5371(77)80016-9.

O'Reilly, R. C., Bhattacharyya, R., Howard, M. D., & Ketz, N. (2014). Complimentary learning systems. *Cognitive Science, 38*(6), 1229–1248. https://doi.org/10.1111/j.1551-6709.2011.01214.x.

Patterson, K., & Lambon Ralph, M. (2015). The hub-and-spoke hypothesis of semantic memory. In G. Hickok & S. L. Small (Eds.), *Neurobiology of language* (pp. 765–773). London, UK: Academic. https://doi.org/10.1016/B978-0-12-407794-2.00061-4.

Pinker, S. (1999). *Words and rules: The ingredients of language* (1st ed.). New York, NY: Basic Books.

Roediger, H. L., & McDermott, K. B. (1995). Creating false memories: Remembering words not presented in lists. *Journal of Experimental Psychology: Learning, Memory, and Cognition, 21* (4), 803–814.

Roediger, H. L., Agarwal, P. K., McDaniel, M. A., & McDermott, K. B. (2011). Test-enhanced learning in the classroom: Long-term improvements from quizzing. *Journal of Experimental Psychology: Applied, 17*, 382–395.

Rumelhart, D. E., & McClelland, J. L. (Eds.). (1986). *Parallel distributed processing: Explorations in the microstructure of cognition (V1 and V2)*. Cambridge, MA: MIT press.

Saffran, J. R., Aslin, R. N., & Newport, E. L. (1996). Statistical learning by 8-month-old infants. *Science, New Series, 274*(5294), 1926–1928.

Seidenberg, M. S., & McClelland, J. L. (1989). A distributed, developmental model of word recognition and naming. *Psychological Review, 96*(4), 523–568. https://doi.org/10.1037/0033-295X.96.4.523.

Smith, E., & Jonides, J. (1999). Storage and executive processes in the frontal lobes. *Science, 283*, 1657–1661.

Sternberg, S. (1969). The discovery of processing stages: Extensions of Donders' method. *Acta Psychologica, Amsterdam, 30*, 276–315.

Stroop, J. R. (1935). Studies of interference in serial verbal reactions. *Journal of Experimental Psychology, 18*(6), 643–662.

Watson, J. M., Balota, D. A., & Roediger, H. L. I. I. I. (2003). Creating false memories with hybrid lists of semantic and phonological associates: Over-additive false memories produced by converging associative networks. *Journal of Memory and Language, 49*(9), 95–118.

Wickens, D. (1975). A test of four proposed new dimensions of semantic space. *Bulletin of the Psychonomic Society, 6*(4), 381–382.

Woollams, A. M., Madrid, G., & Lambon Ralph, M. A. (2017). Using neurostimulation to understand the impact of pre-morbid individual differences on post-lesion outcomes. *Proceedings of the National Academy of Sciences, 114*(46), 12279–12284. www.pnas.org/cgi/doi/10.1073/pnas.1707162114.

Yap, M. J., & Balota, D. A. (2009). Visual word recognition of multisyllabic words. *Journal of Memory and Language, 60*, 502–529. https://doi.org/10.1016/j.jml.2009.02.001.

Zevin, J. D., & Balota, D. A. (2000). Priming and attentional control of lexical and sublexical pathways during naming. *Journal of Experimental Psychology: Learning, Memory, & Cognition, 26*, 121–135. https://doi.org/10.1037//0278-7393.26.U21.

Zwaan, R. A., & Yaxley, R. H. (2003). Hemispheric differences in semantic relatedness judgments. *Cognition, 87*, B79–B86. https://doi.org/10.1016/S0010-0277(02)00235-4.

How to Design and Teach Courses on Volition and Cognitive Control

9

Thomas Goschke and Annette Bolte

Contents

T. Goschke (✉) · A. Bolte
Faculty of Psychology, Technische Universität Dresden, Dresden, Germany
e-mail: thomas.goschke@tu-dresden.de; annette.bolte@tu-dresden.de

© Springer Nature Switzerland AG 2023   201
J. Zumbach et al. (eds.), *International Handbook of Psychology Learning and Teaching*,
Springer International Handbooks of Education,
https://doi.org/10.1007/978-3-030-28745-0_12

Abstract

While volition has long been a topic of philosophical debates, in the past decades the mechanisms underlying voluntary action have become a central research topic in experimental psychology and cognitive neuroscience. Volitional control is conceived of as the result of cognitive control mechanisms, which enable humans to flexibly adapt behavior to changing goals and task demands and to override habitual or impulsive responses in favor of long-term goals or social norms. Understanding these mechanisms is not only a key challenge for basic research but highly relevant in wide range of applied (educational, work, and clinical) contexts. Courses on volition and cognitive control are thus an essential part of the training of psychologists both at undergraduate and graduate levels. Designing and teaching such courses pose specific challenges for lecturers, given that research on these themes cuts across various disciplines (cognitive, motivational, social, and clinical psychology as well as cognitive neuroscience) and levels of analyses (behavioral, computational, neural). Given that especially undergraduates often experience cognitive control as an abstract and difficult topic, it is important to not only convey why the theme is important for a scientific understanding of human behavior but also to provide examples of its relevance for practical applications. We present a systematic overview of key contents a course on volition and cognitive control should cover and provide recommendations: (i) how to tailor course contents to the learning objectives of different study programs (B.Sc. psychology programs versus M.Sc. programs in clinical psychology or cognitive neuroscience), (ii) how to provide students with knowledge of psychological and neural mechanisms underlying cognitive control and its impairments in mental or neurological disorders, (iii) how to enable them to apply this knowledge in practical contexts, and (iv) how to critically reflect on implications of this research for ethical and philosophical questions related to concepts of free will and personal responsibility. Moreover, we give tips how to instigate students' motivation and interest in the topic and how to promote deep and elaborative encoding of the course contents.

Keywords

Volition · Cognitive control · Executive functions · Goal-directed action · Self-control · Willpower · Intention · Prefrontal cortex

Introduction

Human volitional action exhibits a remarkable flexibility and future directedness, which shows up in our ability to adapt behavior to changing goals and task demands and to override impulsive or habitual responses in order to render behavior consistent with long-term goals or social norms. In experimental psychology, volitional actions are not attributed to an undetermined "free will," which is independent from any causal antecedents. Rather, what sets volitional action apart from reflexes is that they are not completely determined by fixed stimulus-response associations, but depend on intentions, goals, and anticipations of future consequences (Goschke, 2013; Haggard, 2019). The term cognitive control denotes a set of mechanisms, which are required when routine behaviors do not suffice to achieve a goal or accomplish a task, but response dispositions must be configured in novel ways, new action sequences must be planned, or competing desires or habits must be overridden to attain long-term goals (Cohen, 2017). The concept of cognitive control overlaps with the construct "executive functions," which is used as umbrella term for "higher-order" cognitive processes that coordinate perceptual, emotional, and motor activity during the execution of new and complex tasks (Diamond, 2013). Cognitive control also overlaps with the concept "self-control," which denotes the ability to resist momentary temptations and to override short-term desires in the service of long-term goals or social norms (Kotabe & Hofmann, 2015). Finally, apart from its use as a summary term for mechanisms underlying goal-directed action, the term volition is sometimes used to refer to the subjective experience of agency associated with intentional actions (Haggard, 2019; Roskies, 2010).

In the past decades, research on volition and cognitive control has advanced to one of the most active fields in experimental psychology and cognitive neuroscience (the number of peer-review articles listed in the Web of Science, which contain one of the terms "volition," "cognitive control," "self-control," or "executive functions" in their title, increased from a handful in 1980 to currently more than 1000 per year). Substantial progress has been made in elucidating the cognitive, computational, and neural mechanisms underlying volition and cognitive control, due to the integration of behavioral tasks from experimental psychology, advanced neuroimaging techniques, and computational modeling approaches (for a recent selection of authoritative reviews, see the handbook by Egner, 2017).

Importantly, insights into the mechanisms of volition and cognitive control are not only of interest from a scientific perspective but are relevant in a wide range of applied domains of high societal relevance. For instance, individual differences in cognitive control account for the degree of persistence or the tendency to procrastinate in academic or work contexts (Johnson, Lin, & Lee, 2018). Moreover, cognitive control plays an important role in self-regulated learning, explanations of insufficient academic effort, or deficient impulse control in educational contexts (Duckworth, Taxer, Eskreis-Winkler, Galla, & Gross, 2019; Job, Friese, & Bernecker, 2015; Panadero, 2017). More generally, deficient self-control is a key characteristic of a wide range of maladaptive and harmful behaviors, such as unhealthy eating habits, lack of physical exercise, shortsighted and impulsive choices, as well as substance abuse and behavioral addictions (Goschke, 2014; Volkow & Baler, 2015). Finally, cognitive control impairments are a key characteristic of the decline of cognitive abilities in old age and neurodegenerative diseases (Reuter-Lorenz, Festini, & Jantz, 2016; Stuss & Craik, 2019). Given the adverse personal consequences and immense societal costs that are directly or indirectly caused by deficient cognitive control abilities, elucidating their causal antecedents and underlying mechanisms is of central importance for mechanism-based prevention, intervention, and training.

Purposes and Rationale of a Curriculum in Volition and Cognitive Control

Given the wide range of theoretical frameworks, empirical findings, and methodological approaches in research on volition and cognitive control, it is important to specify the knowledge, skills, and competencies students should acquire in a respective course. Course contents and learning objectives should be tailored to the course level (undergraduate, graduate, postgraduate) (cf. the APA competency-based approach to psychology program curriculum development (Association, 2020a, 2020b).

For an introductory-level first or second year course in a general B.Sc. psychology program, a course should provide a broad overview of theories and empirical results on volition and cognitive control (see also the list of learning outcomes and skill-based goals in APA's (2020) guidelines for the psychology undergraduate major). For more specialized B.Sc. or advanced M.Sc. courses, additional learning aims will be defined, which will depend on whether it is a research-focused or applied track. For instance, in a specialized study program in organizational psychology, the focus will be on applied themes like cognitive effort investment and self-control in work contexts. In contrast, in a master's program in cognitive neuroscience, the emphasis will be on neural systems and computational mechanisms underlying cognitive control, while in a clinical psychology or neuropsychology program, the focus will be on impairments of cognitive control in mental or neurological disorders, neuropsychological tests assessing executive functions, and interventions to improve cognitive control competencies. Table 1 shows key learning objective for different types and levels (B.Sc., M.Sc.) of study programs.

Core Contents and Topics of a Curriculum on Volition and Cognitive Control

In the following sections, we outline key topics that should be addressed in a one- or two-semester course on volition and cognitive control. Our selection of topics must necessarily be incomplete, and we focus on topics we consider particularly

Table 1 Key learning objectives of a course on volition and cognitive control in different types of study programs

Study program	Learning objectives
B.Sc. Program in psychology: Introductory-level 1st or 2nd year course	–Sound understanding of key theoretical constructs, major theories and models, exemplary tasks and experimental paradigms, and key empirical findings in the field of volition and cognitive control –Basic ability to relate this knowledge to other research fields (e.g., the role of impaired cognitive control as a possible vulnerability factor for certain mental disorders) –Basic ability to transfer knowledge about cognitive control to applied problems (e.g., the use of tests to assess executive functions; the role of self-control strategies for impulse control, procrastination, and cognitive effort in school contexts)
M.Sc. program in Psychology or Cognitive Neuroscience: Research-focused track	–Deeper understanding of neural systems and circuits underlying volition and cognitive control (e.g., role of prefrontal cortical regions in different control functions, response inhibition, and goal-directed action; neural correlates of self-control; neural representation of intentions and task sets) –Ability to derive novel predictions from theories of cognitive control, to develop experimental paradigms, and to design own experiments to test these predictions –Ability to conduct basic analysis of functional magnetic resonance imaging (fMRI) and EEG data from simple cognitive control tasks using standard software packages (e.g., SPM, EEGLab) –Deeper understanding of computational models of cognitive control (e.g., neural network models). Depending on the course level, basic experience in computer simulations of simple cognitive control models with Matlab or neural network simulation software
M.Sc. program in Psychology: Applied or clinical track	–Ability to apply knowledge about cognitive control in the context of clinical psychology and psychotherapy (e.g., cognitive-behavioral interventions to promote self-control; interventions to enhance the monitoring of one's own behavior and the use of precommitment strategies) –Ability to apply knowledge about cognitive control in the context of neuropsychological assessment (e.g., competence to apply, analyze, and interpret tests and task batteries assessing executive functions) –Ability to transfer knowledge about cognitive control in further applied contexts (e.g., promotion of self-regulated learning and cognitive effort mobilization in school and work contexts)

relevant for an introductory undergraduate course, but also point to more specialized themes that could be addressed in an advanced course in a master program in psychology or cognitive neuroscience (see Table 2 for a condensed overview).

Table 2 Overview on key learning objectives, topics, and concepts for a course on volition and cognitive control

Course unit	Learning objective	Key concepts and themes
1. Introduction	General course overview and introduction to key concepts (goal-directed action, volition, cognitive control) using real-life examples	−Voluntary actions are not determined by the current stimulus situation but depend on goals, intentions, and anticipated outcomes −Goals as mental representations of distal action effects −Examples of the relevance of cognitive control in applied contexts and everyday life behavior −Optional: Brief historical overview of classical research on volition (e.g., James, Ach, Lewin)

2. Key concepts and research questions	Knowledge of the definitions of the core constructs of volition, intention, cognitive control, executive functions, self-control, and understanding the adaptive functions of cognitive control	−Open discussion of possible adaptive functions of cognitive control from an evolutionary perspective
		 −Key functional features of human volitional action
		   −Extended future time perspective and ability to anticipate and evaluate long-term consequences of actions
		   −Ability to anticipate own future needs and motivational states as the basis for precommitment strategies
		   −Ability to generate hierarchical action plans and to represent intentions and instructions in a verbal format as the basis for the flexible and rapid reconfiguration of behavioral dispositions
		 −Overview of central research questions

3. Cognitive mechanisms of intentional action	Understanding the distinction between automatic and controlled processes and knowledge of experimental tasks assessing the two types of processes and their interaction	Introduction to the distinction between automatic versus control processing
		   −Everyday life examples of automatic and controlled behavior
		   −Classical definition of automatic vs. controlled processes (e.g., Posner & Snyder, 1975)
		   −Standard tasks used to investigate the interplay of automatic and controlled processes (e.g., Stroop color naming task)
		 Preconditions for automatic processing and conditions requiring controlled processes
		   −Does the current stimulus information specify the correct response and all execution parameters, or is planning or problem solving required to determine the correct response?
		   −Has the agent acquired all necessary skills to perform a task?
		   −Are there conflicts between an intended action and competing responses or motivational tendencies?
		 Critical reflection on the distinction

		–Critique of dual processes models assuming a dichotomy of automatic and controlled processes –Alternative models of "conditional automaticity" and of intentional control as the modulation of automatic processes –Understanding that most tasks are not "process-pure" but involve an interplay of automatic and controlled processes Optional expansions and advanced themes –Role of conscious intentions and unconscious processes in the causation of intentional actions –Classical experiment by Libet et al. (1983) –Overview of the debate whether voluntary actions are caused by unconscious brain processes and the subjective feeling of conscious will is an illusion (e.g., Wegner's theory of apparent mental causation) –Neuroimaging studies showing that free choices can be decoded from neural activity patterns in prefrontal cortex several seconds before individuals become conscious of their choices
4. Functional decomposition and assessment of cognitive control abilities	Understanding that cognitive control can be decomposed into a set of specific mechanisms and knowledge of tasks assessing cognitive control	–Functional decomposition of cognitive control and executive functions into sub-mechanisms (goal maintenance and shielding, set shifting, response inhibition, emotion regulation, episodic future thinking, action planning) –Standard tests and tasks assessing cognitive control and executive functions (e.g., task-switching, n-back, go/nogo, stop signal tasks, Stroop and flanker interference tasks, emotion regulation) –Individual difference studies and latent variable analyses of task batteries assessing executive functions, which suggest that set shifting, working memory updating, and inhibition are three core executive functions –Recent critique and revisions of the three factor model of executive functions
5. Self-control and volitional strategies	Understanding the concepts of intertemporal choice and self-control and being familiar with key theories of self-control,	Intertemporal choice conflicts –Intertemporal choice conflicts in everyday life and laboratory tasks to investigate intertemporal choices –Temporal discounting (optional: mathematical discounting models in behavioral economics)

(continued)

Table 2 (continued)

Course unit	Learning objective	Key concepts and themes
	relevant empirical evidence, and theoretical critiques	– Preference reversals and explanation why they violate rationality axioms of standard expected utility theory – Different explanations of preference reversals and shortsighted choices **The concept of self-control** – Definition of self-control as a summary term for strategies that serve to override temporary temptations or competing habits in order to render behavior consistent with long-term goals – Commonalities and differences between self-control and the constructs cognitive control, executive functions, and volitional strategies – Different forms of self-control (preventive self-control and precommitment; interventive self-control and response inhibition; formation of beneficial habits) **Major theories of self-control** – Baumeister's strength model and ego depletion effect; theoretical critique of resource theories of self-control; failures to replicate the ego depletion effect and alternative interpretation of the effect in terms of a motivational shift – Dual systems/dual process models of self-control and theoretical critique of the assumption two competing "impulsive" and "reflective" systems; behavioral and neuroimaging evidence for dual systems – Alternative models of self-control as the top-down modulation of a common value signal and relevant evidence from neuroimaging studies – Theories of volitional strategies in motivational psychology; distinction between motivation (goal selection) and volition (goal realization) **Optional expansions** – Meta-analyses reporting little-to-no relationships between trait self-control and performance on response inhibition tasks; discussion of alternative explanations for this dissociation (e.g., low retest-reliability of laboratory tasks; trait self-control and behavioral tasks reflecting distinct mechanisms underlying self-control) – Individual differences: action vs. state-orientation as a moderator of the mobilization of self-control strategies

| 6. Neural mechanisms underlying volition and cognitive control | Knowledge of exemplary neuropsychological and neuroimaging studies of cognitive control and of brain systems and networks mediating cognitive control functions | Optional propaedeutic tutorials (depending on student's prior knowledge and on selected studies)
–Functional neuroanatomy (subregions and connectivity of the prefrontal cortex, PFC)
–Basic principles of functional magnetic resonance imaging (fMRI) and fMRI data analyses
–Basic principles of EEG and ERPs, noninvasive brain stimulation (TMS), single cell recordings
–Advantages and limitations of different methods (e.g., spatial and temporal resolution in hemodynamic and electrocortical measures)
–Importance of theoretically derived experimental tasks and control conditions for neuroimaging studies
Neuropsychological studies of cognitive control
–Impaired executive functions after brain lesions in the PFC and other relevant regions ("dysexecutive syndrome")
–Concept and interpretation of single and double functional dissociations
–Understanding that there is not a one-to-one mapping of cognitive functions to brain regions
–Neuroimaging studies of cognitive control
–fMRI studies of cognitive control functions to demonstrate that cognitive control is not located in single brain region
–Concept of the "control network" ("central executive network")
–Functional fractionation of the control network into sub-regions and exemplary studies of their functions
–"Brain-as-predictor" studies combining fMRI with experience sampling of real-life behaviors and self-control failures
Advanced themes
–Hierarchical (rostral-to-caudal) organization of the lateral prefrontal cortex
–Conflict-monitoring theory
–Expected value of control theory
–Control dilemmas and meta-control
–Modulation of cognitive control by emotions, reward, stress, and associated neuromodulatory systems |

(continued)

Table 2 (continued)

Course unit	Learning objective	Key concepts and themes
7. Computational models of cognitive control	Basic knowledge of computational models of cognitive control and their relevance for psychological research	General introduction to computational models in psychology –Relevance of mechanistic explanations and computational models; advantages compared to verbal theories –Explanation how testable predictions can be derived and how they can be fit to empirical data –Limitations of computational models Discussion of an exemplary "toy" model –Connectionist model of the Stroop task –Distinction between activation-based and connection-based processing; automatic responses as the result of the incremental strengthening of direct stimulus-response connections via learning –Demonstration how goals and task rules can be represented as neural activation patterns, how cognitive control emerges from the capacity for (a) rapid updating and active maintenance of activation patterns and (b) top-down biasing of perceptual processes by currently active goal or task representations –Demonstration how "lesions" of a network can impair goal maintenance and lead to interference and stimulus-driven behavior Advanced themes –Additional modeling approaches (e.g., Bayesian inference, reinforcement learning) –More complex neural network models of cognitive control –Practical training in implementing models using Matlab or specialized simulation software (e.g., the "Leabra" framework –practical exercises with neural network simulations of cognitive control tasks
8. Cognitive control in applied contexts	Understanding why cognitive control is relevant in applied or clinical contexts and ability to transfer knowledge of cognitive control mechanisms to practical problems	Exemplary applications of cognitive control research in practical or clinical contexts –Role of cognitive control dysfunctions as transdiagnostic mechanism or vulnerability factor for mental disorders (e.g., substance use, behavioral addictions, impulsivity-compulsivity spectrum disorders, ADHD) –Training of executive functions in children with ADHD or in elderly people with age-related cognitive decline –Meta-analyses suggesting that effects of executive function trainings are usually

		limited to near transfer tasks –Cognitive control training as a tool in psychotherapy (e.g., attentional bias training in anxiety and/or substance use disorder) –Cognitive control in work and engineering psychology (e.g., in the context of man-machine interactions, software engineering, high-tech multitasking environments)
9. Philosophical issues and implications	Basic understanding of philosophical foundations of research on volition and cognitive control and its implications for concepts of free will, agency, and personal responsibility	Guiding questions for an open discussion –Do insights into neurocognitive mechanisms of self-control and volitional action show that lay concepts of free will are illusory? –Does psychology and neuroscience undermine our view of humans as autonomous agents? –Should knowledge about cognitive and neural mechanisms underlying self-control influence our moral evaluation of actions? –Should neurobiological markers of impaired self-control play a role in the assessment of an offender's criminal responsibility and culpability? Key concepts and themes –Main positions and arguments in the philosophy of free will (e.g., incompatibilistic/libertarian versus compatibilistic theories; concepts of causality and determinism) –Implications of incompatibilistic and compatibilistic theories of free will for concepts of personal responsibility, agency, and authorship –Relevance of empirical research on self-control for philosophical theories of weakness of will, akrasia, and intentionality –Critical reflection about what psychology and neuroscience can and cannot contribute to philosophical debates (distinction between empirical, conceptual, and normative questions)

Section 1: Introducing the Topic and Learning Objectives and Instigating Students' Interest

In an introductory section, students should be given a broad overview of the topic and acquire an intuitive understanding of the concepts volition and cognitive control. Students should understand that the defining feature of voluntary actions is that they are not fully determined by the immediate stimulus situation, but depend on intentions, mental representations of goals, and anticipated consequences. This includes understanding that voluntary action rests on subjective knowledge about the probability and value of short- and long-term outcomes of actions, which enables humans to select actions of which they have learned that they will produce desired effects (Hommel & Wiers, 2017). Students should understand that goals can be conceived as mental representations of distal effects of actions and that they have a hierarchical structure and differ widely in their abstractness and temporal distance.

The introductory section should instigate students' interest and ensure that they understand the relevance of the topic both for the scientific quest for the mechanisms underlying human action and for understanding voluntary behavior in applied contexts. One way to achieve this is to introduce key concepts with reference to real-life examples that illustrate why cognitive control is an important and personally relevant topic. Moreover, students' motivation can be stimulated by an exchange about their prescientific understanding of folk-psychological concepts like willpower, weakness of will, and self-control and a discussion of situations in daily life involving choice conflicts or examples of persistence versus procrastination in the pursuit of goals. Moreover, the societal relevance of the theme can be documented by pointing to the fact that deficient self-control increases the risk of a wide range of maladaptive behavioral patterns such as shortsighted choices, unhealthy eating habits, substance use, and behavioral addictions (Goschke, 2014; Volkow & Baler, 2015), which have adverse personal consequences and incur immense societal costs due to reduced health, educational deficits, and even premature death. Finally, interest in the topic can often be instigated by initiating a nontechnical discussion about whether knowledge about psychological and neural mechanisms underlying human action challenges concepts of free will, autonomy, and personal responsibility.

Optionally, one may include a brief historical exposition of classical research in early psychology of "the will" as represented by late nineteenth- and early twentieth-century scholars like William James, Narciss Ach, and Kurt Lewin.

Section 2: Basic Concepts, Theoretical Constructs, and Key Research Questions

Section 2 should provide more precise working definitions of core constructs (volition, cognitive control, executive functions, self-control) and their differences and commonalities. This should not simply consist in presenting a list of definitions, but be combined with a discussion of the *adaptive functions* of cognitive control from an evolutionary perspective. Guiding questions for such a discussion could be:

- Why have humans (and to lesser degrees nonhuman animals) evolved cognitive control capacities?
- What are universal adaptive problems that goal-directed agents must cope with in changing and uncertain environments?
- What are adaptive advantages of the ability to pursue long-term goals and shield temptations from short-term temptations?
- Have simpler levels of behavioral control (e.g., reflexes, instincts, Pavlovian and instrumental conditioning) been extinguished in the course of the evolution of "higher" forms of volitional control, or do they still determine human behavior?

The discussion should then focus on functional properties that set volitional actions apart from other forms of behavior, while making clear that differences between different forms of behavioral control are often gradual and reflect a continuum of increasing cognitive complexity and flexibility. Key functional features of volitional action that students should understand are:

- An extended future time perspective, which shows up in the ability to anticipate and evaluate long-term consequences of actions.
- The ability to anticipate own future needs and motivational states as the basis for precommitment strategies, which serve to restrict the space of one's future behavioral choices and to prevent or avoid temptations and self-control conflicts.
- The ability to generate hierarchically structured action plans and to represent intentions and instructions in a verbal format, which enables flexible and rapid reconfiguration of behavioral dispositions.

Based on this discussion, an overview of key research questions should be presented:

- Which cognitive mechanisms underlie the ability to persist in pursuing long-term goals in the face of transient temptations or competing habits?
- How and when are cognitive control processes recruited, and why do some people succeed in mobilizing control better than others do?
- Why do people sometimes act against their long-term goals and make short-sighted choices?
- Does cognitive control reflect a unitary capacity, or can it be decomposed into specific sub-mechanisms (e.g., response inhibition, goal maintenance, task switching), which can be functionally dissociated?
- Which brain systems mediate volition, cognitive control, and flexible goal-directed action?
- How are cognitive control processes modulated by emotions, reward, and stress?
- How do cognitive control abilities develop across the lifespan?

- Are impairments of cognitive control vulnerability factors and/or transdiagnostic mechanisms increasing the risk of mental disorders such as substance use, behavioral addictions, attention deficit/hyperactivity disorder, major depression, and impulsivity-compulsivity spectrum disorders?

Section 3: Cognitive Mechanisms of Intentional Action

Section 3 focuses on the influential distinction between automatic and controlled processes. This distinction can be introduced by reference to everyday life examples. Every student will have had the experience that highly practiced actions can often be executed with minimal conscious control, whereas novel actions or complex problems require effortful cognitive control and put high demands on working memory. For instance, an experienced driver may steer a car through rush hour traffic without having to consciously control each individual action (braking, changing gears, etc.). By contrast, a novice driver maneuvering in an unfamiliar big city must allocate full attention to the task and will consciously control each individual action. Based on such examples, students can be invited to reflect about the preconditions under which actions can run off automatically. They should come to understand that actions require minimal conscious control when (i) the current stimulus information in conjunction with a currently active goal is sufficient to specify which action should be executed and how it should be executed, (ii) the person has the skills required to execute the action, (iii) no additional planning or problem-solving is required to determine the correct response, and (iv) there are no conflicts between the intended action and competing responses.

Based on this discussion, students should be familiarized with the classical definition of Posner and Snyder (1975), according to which automatic processes are triggered in an obligatory manner by stimuli, are unconscious, and require little processing capacity, whereas controlled processes depend on intentions, are conscious, and put high demands on limited processing capacity.

Importantly, students should learn that subsequent research called into question that automatic and controlled processes constitute a strict dichotomy, because the different criteria for automaticity and control can dissociate (Hommel, 2019). This point can again be illustrated by everyday life examples (e.g., the case of an experienced driver who shifts gears to pass another car "automatically" in response to the sight of a slow car in front of her, but whose action nevertheless depends on (and is "controlled" by) the intention to arrive at an important meeting in time). In addition, one may discuss experimental evidence showing that responses, which are automatic in the sense that they are triggered by stimuli without conscious control, can nevertheless depend on prior intentions or instructions. These findings led to alternative models, which conceive of intentional control as the modulation of automatic processes by goals and task instructions, by which certain response disposition is set into a state of readiness, while individual responses may be triggered directly by stimulus conditions specified by the intention (Bargh, 1989; Goschke, 2003; Hommel, 2019).

In this section, students should also be introduced to standard tasks used to investigate the interplay of automatic and controlled processes (e.g., the Stroop color naming task), and they should understand that there are no "process-pure" tasks measuring exclusively automatic or controlled processes, but that most tasks involve a dynamic interplay of both types of processes.

In an optional expansion of this section, one might discuss the role of conscious intentions and unconscious processes in the causation of intentional actions. A good starting point is the classical experiment by Libet et al. (1983), which showed that the readiness potential (a negative potential shift in the electroencephalogram (EEG) that precedes a self-initiated movement) started several 100 milliseconds before participants became aware of their intention to move. This and related findings (see review by Haggard, 2008) provoked a heated debate as to whether willed actions are caused by unconscious neuronal processes rather than by conscious intentions (Sinnot-Armstrong & Nadel, 2011) and whether conscious will is an "illusion" (Wegner, 2003). The discussion may also include neuroimaging studies showing that individuals' free choices between two simple actions can be decoded from neural activity in the prefrontal cortex already several seconds before participants reported that they consciously made their choice (Soon, He, Bode, & Haynes, 2013).

Section 4: Functional Decomposition and Assessment of Cognitive Control Abilities

Building on the discussion of automatic and controlled processes, Section 4 provides a more differentiated perspective on the concept of cognitive control. In particular, students should understand that cognitive control does not denote a unitary function, but can be decomposed into a set of specific mechanisms (see Table 3).

A second learning objective is that students acquire knowledge about standard tests and tasks used to measure cognitive control abilities, as well as experimental paradigms used to investigate underlying mechanisms and their temporal dynamics. Examples are task-switching paradigms assessing cognitive set shifting, n-back tasks assessing working memory updating, go/no-go and stop signal tasks assessing response inhibition, Stroop and flanker tasks assessing interference control, and cognitive reappraisal tasks assessing emotion regulation. Students should acquire an understanding that such tasks are no process-pure measures of a single control function, but involve several cognitive processes to varying degrees. A good example is the Wisconsin Card Sorting task that is often considered a neuropsychological test of cognitive flexibility, but does not only require participants to switch between response rules but also to update working memory, to inhibit no-longer-relevant rules, to process feedback, and to adjust behavior accordingly.

This section should also include a discussion of individual difference studies of task batteries assessing executive functions, which revealed that confirmatory factor models with a small number of latent variables yielded a moderate to good fit to the observed pattern of inter-task correlations (Miyake et al., 2000; Wolff et al., 2016).

These variables have been interpreted as *set shifting* (the ability to switch quickly between tasks or response rules), *updating* (the ability to maintain and update information in working memory), and *inhibition* (the ability to suppress prepotent but unwanted responses). These latent variables are moderately correlated with each other, which offers an opportunity to discuss with students possible interpretations of the shared variance between tasks measuring executive functions (e.g., whether all such tasks rest on the ability to maintain task-relevant information in working memory and whether response inhibition may be just a by-product of the goal-directed focusing of attention on task-relevant information in conjunction with lateral inhibition) (cf. Karr et al., 2018). Instead of a separate section, tasks and experimental paradigms to measure cognitive control and executive functions may alternatively be addressed at various points throughout a course when specific control functions (e.g., response inhibition, task switching) are discussed.

Section 5: Self-Control and Volitional Strategies

In contrast to simple response conflicts in laboratory tasks (e.g., the Stroop task), in everyday life conflicts often arise when long-term goals stand in conflict with transient temptations and current desires (Hofmann, Baumeister, Förster, & Vohs, 2012). A typical example is a person who intends to maintain a healthy diet, but experiences a strong craving for a tasty but high-caloric dessert. Section 5 focuses on self-control, which can be defined as the ability to override impulsive or habitual responses in order to render behavior congruent with long-term goals or social norms (Duckworth et al., 2019; Kotabe & Hofmann, 2015).

One may start this section with an open discussion about possible alternative explanations for why people make shortsighted ("impulsive") choices and do not act in accordance with their long-term goals. The learning objective of such a discussion is the insight that there are multiple explanations for self-control failures, including a lack of future-directed thinking, overly steep discounting of the value of future outcomes, deficient inhibitory control, or deficient conflict monitoring resulting in an insufficient mobilization of cognitive control. Such an introductory discussion can also serve to underline the practical relevance of the topic, given that deficient self-control is associated with a wide range of maladaptive behaviors such as unhealthy eating habits, lack of exercise, insufficient academic effort, substance use, and impulsive aggression.

Next, one should introduce more formally the concept of intertemporal choice conflicts, i.e., situations in which individuals must choose between a smaller sooner reward and a larger later reward (e.g., between 5$ now and 8$ in 6 months). Students should understand the concepts of temporal discounting and of preference reversals (i.e., the finding that individuals often prefer a later larger reward over a smaller sooner reward when both options are delivered in the future, but choose the smaller reward when it is immediately available). They should understand why preference reversals violate rationality axioms of standard expected utility theory and are often

Table 3 Sub-functions and mechanisms of cognitive control

Sub-process	Short description
Goal shielding	Ability to maintain goals, task instructions, and intentions in working memory and shield them from distracting stimuli
Set shifting	Ability to flexibly update goal representations and to reconfigure behavioral dispositions in order to adapt to changing contexts or task demands
Top-down modulation	The biasing of processes in perceptual, emotional, and response systems by currently active goals, intentions, and task sets
Response inhibition	Ability to suppress strong but unwanted habitual, automatic, or impulsive responses
Emotion regulation	Ability to voluntarily self-regulate emotions (e.g., via cognitive reappraisal strategies)
Anticipation and episodic prospection	Ability to anticipate future consequences of actions and engage in future-directed thinking
Planning	Ability to generate and mentally simulate novel action sequences before their execution

interpreted as an indicator of impulsivity (Kable, 2014). In a more advanced course, one should discuss mathematical models of temporal discounting and explain why exponential discounting conforms to normative rationality rules, whereas hyperbolic discounting models account for violating of these rules such as preference reversals.

Building on the concept of intertemporal choice conflicts, one can then discuss cognitive strategies supporting self-controlled choices. The learning objective is that students understand that self-control comprises a variety of cognitive strategies, which can be classified into preventive, interventive, and habitual strategies (Hofmann & Kotabe, 2012):

- *Preventive self-control* refers to precommitment strategies that serve to avoid self-control conflicts before they arise or to restrict one's future behavioral options in order to reduce the likelihood of giving into an anticipated temptation (Studer, Koch, Knecht, & Kalenscher, 2019).
- *Interventive self-control* denotes strategies that serve to render behavior congruent with long-term goals when self-control conflicts and temptations cannot be avoided, but one finds oneself in a situation, in which goal pursuit is challenged by competing desires or habits. These strategies include episodic future thinking (Peters & Büchel, 2011) and modulation of value representations by anticipated future outcomes (Hare, Malmaud, & Rangel, 2011; Krönke et al., 2020), control of selective attention (Harris, Hare, & Rangel, 2013; Mischel, Ebbesen, & Raskoff Zeiss, 1972), downregulation of craving (Hofmann, Friese, & Roefs, 2009; Kober, Kross, Mischel, Hart, & Ochsner, 2010; Kruschwitz et al., 2018), and response inhibition (Berkman, Falk, & Lieberman, 2011; Krönke et al., 2018).
- *Habitual self-control* has recently attracted increasing attention due to studies showing that self-controlled behavior often relies on the formation of beneficial

habits, which support the goal pursuit without requiring effortful interventional self-control (e.g., Galla & Duckworth, 2015).

At this point one may include a discussion of recent meta-analyses, which found little-to-no relationships between trait self-control and performance on tasks measuring response inhibition (Saunders, Milyavskaya, Etz, Randles, & Inzlicht, 2018). Students should discuss possible reasons for this dissociation (e.g., whether it may reflect the low retest reliability of many laboratory tasks of cognitive control or whether self-report scales and behavioral tasks may assess separate components or mechanisms mediating of self-control).

Building on the introductory discussion of different possible explanations for self-control failures, one should introduce important theories of self-control. This should include a discussion of the influential yet controversial *strength model*, which conceives of self-control as a limited and exhaustible "willpower" resource (Baumeister, Tice, & Vohs, 2018). A section on the strength model should include a discussion of recent failed attempts to replicate the so-called ego depletion effect (e.g., Friese, Loschelder, Gieseler, Frankenbach, & Inzlicht, 2019) as well as a discussion of alternative accounts and theoretical critiques of the strength model (Inzlicht, Schmeichel, & Macrae, 2014; Job, Dweck, & Walton, 2010; Lurquin & Miyake, 2017).

A second influential class of self-control theories that should be discussed is *dual systems* or *dual process models*, which conceive of self-control as the suppression of an impulsive (hot) by a deliberative ("cool") control system (Hofmann, Friese, & Strack, 2009; McClure, Laibson, Loewenstein, & Cohen, 2004). In addition to behavioral evidence, one may refer to early neuroimaging studies, which yielded evidence for separate neural valuation systems (McClure et al., 2004). Dual systems theories should be contrasted with more recent evidence for the alternative view that behavioral choices are determined by a *common neural value signal* that integrates short- and long-term outcomes (Hare, Camerer, & Rangel, 2009; Krönke et al., 2020). According to this view, self-control does not reflect the suppression of an impulsive by a reflective system, but rests on the modulation of this common value signal by anticipated future outcomes (Hare et al., 2009; Krönke et al., 2020).

Finally, a discussion of self-control theories should also include theories of volitional strategies that emerged from motivational psychology, in particular Kuhl's action control theory (Kuhl, 2018; Kuhl & Goschke, 1994) and Heckhausen and Gollwitzer's model of action phases (Achtziger & Gollwitzer, 2018). These theories distinguish between *motivational* processes, which mediate the selection of goals and *volitional* processes, which comprise cognitive strategies (e.g., the focusing of attention on goal-relevant information or the formation of so-called implementation intentions) that serve to support the realization of goals in face of competing motivational tendencies. In this context, one should also discuss the personality disposition action-state orientation (Kuhl, 2018) as an important moderator of the mobilization of volitional strategies (Wolff et al., 2016). Section 5 may be concluded by discussing recent attempts to integrate different self-control mechanisms within general process models (Inzlicht, Werner, Briskin, & Roberts, 2020; Kotabe & Hofmann, 2015).

Section 6: Neural Mechanisms Underlying Volition and Cognitive Control

In the past decades, knowledge about neural systems and circuits underlying volition and cognitive control has dramatically increased, and a vast body of evidence has accumulated from studies of patients with focal brain lesions and experiments using neuroimaging methods such as functional magnetic resonance imaging (fMRI) and electrophysiological measures (EEG and event-related potentials). The neural basis of cognitive control could thus easily be the sole topic for a one- or two-semester course. In a general introductory course on volition and cognitive control, where cognitive neuroscience studies are just one of many themes, one must therefore decide which topics to include. Once again, this will obviously depend on the course level and overall learning objectives of the study program. In the following paragraphs, we suggest selected key topics that should be addressed in an undergraduate course on volition and cognitive control program, and we make some suggestions how these topics could be expanded in more advanced courses in a master program in cognitive neuroscience or clinical psychology/neuropsychology.

Given that not all psychology students are intrinsically interested in functional neuroanatomy, it is a particular challenge for lecturers to instigate interest in the study of brain systems underlying cognitive control and to convey why knowledge about neural correlates is also relevant for understanding *psychological* processes. One should make clear that the aim of cognitive neuroscience is not merely a mapping of psychological functions to brain structures, but that knowledge about neural mechanisms can provide important constraints for psychological theories of human behavior. Moreover, one should make clear that neuroimaging methods do not call into question the relevance of behavioral experiments, but that, to the contrary, well-designed behavioral tasks are an essential precondition to ensure that neuroimaging findings can be interpreted in meaningful ways.

Optional Propaedeutic Tutorial on Neuroanatomical and Neuroscience Methods

To ensure that students profit optimally from this section, depending on their prior knowledge, a propaedeutic tutorial on functional neuroanatomy and neuroscience methods is recommended.

Functional neuroanatomy. Students should have basic knowledge of brain anatomy and subregions of the prefrontal cortex (PFC) in particular (including dorsolateral, orbitofrontal, ventromedial, frontopolar regions and the anterior cingulate cortex). A tutorial should also convey a basic understanding of the connectivity between the PFC and other relevant cortical (e.g., posterior parietal) and subcortical regions (e.g., basal ganglia). For an introductory course on cognitive control, knowledge at the level of standard cognitive neuroscience textbooks (e.g., Gazzaniga, Ivry, & Mangun, 2018; Purves et al., 2013) should suffice.

Cognitive neuroscience methods. To understand and be able to critically reflect on cognitive neuroscience studies, students need basic knowledge of the most important methods. If students have not yet acquired the respective knowledge in other courses (e.g., biopsychology), a propaedeutic tutorial should convey basic knowledge about the following aspects:

- Basic principles underlying the blood oxygen level-dependent (BOLD) response in fMRI; the preprocessing of fMRI data (motion correction, normalization, coregistration); experimental designs of fMRI studies (i.e., block, event-related, and parametric designs); basic principles of statistical analyses of fMRI data (generalized linear model, statistical parametric mapping, regions of interest analyses, subtraction logic and its limitations, multiple testing problem); basic principles of functional connectivity, network analyses, and multi-voxel pattern analyses.
- Basic knowledge of how event-related potentials are generated in the brain and how they are derived from the EEG. Depending on the selection of studies to be discussed, basic knowledge of noninvasive brain stimulation methods (transcranial magnetic stimulation) and single-cell recordings may also be required.
- Advantages and limitations of different methods (e.g., tradeoffs between spatial and temporal resolution in hemodynamic and electrocortical measures).
- Importance of theoretically derived and carefully designed experimental tasks and control conditions for neuroimaging studies and important methodological caveats in fMRI studies (reverse inference, circular analyses).

For an introductory course on cognitive control, knowledge at the level of the abovementioned cognitive neuroscience textbooks should suffice; for advanced courses with a focus on neuroimaging studies, several excellent introductory textbooks on neuroimaging are available (e.g., Huettel, Song, & McCarthy, 2014).

Suggestions for Key Themes from the Cognitive Neuroscience of Volition and Cognitive Control

Given that the cognitive neuroscience of cognitive control is an extremely broad field, lecturers must decide which themes to include, depending on the overall learning objectives of a course. For an introductory course in a B.Sc. psychology program, we recommend including the following topics.

Neuropsychological studies. A good starting point that usually instigates students' interest is neuropsychological studies of cognitive control impairments in patients with lesions in the prefrontal cortex. Students should obtain knowledge about the profile of intact and impaired functions associated with prefrontal lesions (sometimes termed the dysexecutive syndrome) (Stuss & Knight, 2013). They should also learn that the prefrontal cortex is not a unitary "central executive," but that different prefrontal regions mediate dissociable control functions. Students should be made familiar with the concept of functional dissociations and understand why double dissociations (where a lesion in a region X affects performance in task A but leaves task B intact, while a lesion in another region Y has the reverse effect) are critical for mapping psychological functions to brain structures. Moreover, students should acquire the competence to reflect critically on methodological limitations of brain lesion studies and understand why an impaired cognitive function following injury to a particular brain structure does not necessarily imply that this structure is exclusively responsible for the function in the healthy brain (e.g., because impaired functions may reflect disrupted connectivity between brain regions). More generally, they should understand that there is usually not a one-to-one mapping of cognitive functions to brain regions, but that brain regions are often involved in multiple functions and cognitive functions are often mediated by multiple brain systems.

Neuroimaging studies of cognitive control. Given the vast number of neuroimaging studies of cognitive control, the selection of studies will depend heavily on the focus and aims of a course. We can thus give only some general recommendations for exemplary topics and learning objectives as regards neural correlates of cognitive control. A starting point can be a discussion of the so-called control network (also termed "central executive network" or "multi-demand network") (Duncan, 2010), which comprises the lateral PFC, parts of the parietal cortex, and the dorsal anterior cingulate cortex (dACC) as core nodes. Students should learn that this control network can be functionally fractionated into subregions, which can be conveyed by discussing selected fMRI studies on neural correlates of central control functions (e.g., on the role of the dorsolateral PFC in active maintenance of task-relevant information and top-down modulation of attention; of the right inferior-frontal gyrus in response inhibition; of the ventrolateral PFC and inferior-frontal junction area in the retrieval and implementation of response rules; of the frontopolar cortex in planning, prospective memory, multitasking, and metacognitive strategies; of the ventromedial PFC in emotion regulation and value-based decision-making; and of the dACC in conflict monitoring) (cf. Egner, 2017; Gazzaniga et al., 2018; Purves et al., 2013). An overarching learning objective is that students understand that cognitive control is not located in single brain region, but emerges from dynamic interactions between the prefrontal cortex and other cortical and subcortical brain systems.

Hierarchical organization of the prefrontal cortex. In addition to specific control functions, one should discuss general principles of the functional organization of the prefrontal cortex. In particular, one should discuss evidence for a hierarchical organization of the lateral PFC that unfolds along an axis from caudal (posterior) to rostral (anterior) regions (Badre & Nee, 2018). Students should learn that more rostral regions play a role in action planning and control by higher-level or longer-term goals, whereas more posterior regions mediate lower-level sensory-motor rules and response selection based on the current context.

Neural correlates of self-control. Building on the discussion of self-control in Section 5, a particularly interesting expansion may be recent studies using a "brain-as-predictor" approach, which combine neuroimaging in laboratory tasks with the smartphone-based ecological momentary assessments of real-life behavior. These studies showed that activity in brain regions involved in cognitive control and decision-making reliably predicts individual differences in the proneness to commit daily self-control failures, i.e., to execute behaviors that satisfy short-term desires even if they stand in conflict with personal long-term goals (Berkman et al., 2011; Krönke et al., 2018).

Conflict monitoring and cognitive control. A fundamental question that should be addressed in a section on neural mechanisms of cognitive control is how to explain the context-dependent recruitment and allocation of control without postulating a homunculus-like "executive controller" in the brain. One influential attempt to answer this question is the conflict-monitoring model (Botvinick, Cohen, & Carter, 2004; Mansouri, Egner, & Buckley, 2017), according to which the dACC monitors response conflicts and in case of a conflict signals the demand for enhanced control to brain systems such as the dorsolateral PFC, which mediates goal maintenance and the top-down biasing of perceptual processing and response selection. More recently, this idea has been integrated into a broader framework, the expected value of control theory (Shenhav, Botvinick, & Cohen, 2013), which assumes that the dACC integrates rewards and costs of effortful control and computes the expected value of control, which determines how much control is recruited and to which task it is allocated.

In the following we suggest a number of optional themes for more advanced courses with a focus on neural mechanisms of cognitive control.

Control dilemmas and meta-control. A central unresolved challenge and emerging field of research concerns the problem of meta-control, i.e., the question how the brain regulates the balance between complementary modes of control serving antagonistic functions. An example is the stability-flexibility dilemma: While the pursuit of goals often requires shielding a goal from distracting information or competing responses, in a constantly changing and uncertain environment, agents must also be prepared to switch rapidly between goals and adapt behavior to unexpected changes. While goal shielding promotes persistence and cognitive stability, it may also lead to dysfunctional perseveration and rigidity. Conversely, while weak goal shielding facilitates flexible goal switching, it may increase distractibility and susceptibility to interference. Another example is the exploitation-exploration dilemma. It is usually adaptive to select actions that were rewarded in the past (*exploitation*). However, in order to discover such actions (or even better options), agents must select novel but potentially risky actions (*exploration*). Such control dilemmas require that agents regulate the balance between complementary control modes in an adaptive and context-sensitive manner (Goschke, 2003, 2013; Goschke & Bolte, 2014). It is currently a mostly unresolved question, which computational mechanisms and neural systems underlie this regulation. As the basis for a discussion of this emerging field of research in an advanced course, we recommend a recent special issue on psychological, computational, and neural perspectives on meta-control (Eppinger, Goschke, & Musslick, 2021).

Modulators of cognitive control. A related optional theme concerns modulators of cognitive control. The learning objective is that students understand that the prefrontal cortex not only plays a key role in cognitive control, but is strongly modulated by brain systems involved in emotion, reward, stress, and associated brainstem neuromodulatory systems. Specific topics may include effects of positive affect and reward (e.g., Braver, 2016; Goschke & Bolte, 2014) as well of psychosocial stress on cognitive control (Tsai, Eccles, & Jaeggi, 2019). Moreover, one may include a discussion of the influence of neuromodulators like dopamine and serotonin on prefrontal control processes (Cools, 2019; Ott & Nieder, 2019). Given that the latter theme is a complex research field, given that effects of neuromodulators depend on a multitude of variables (e.g., target brain regions, receptor types, tonic versus phasic activity), it may be more apt to cover it in an advanced course with a focus on the neurobiology of cognitive control.

Section 7: Computational Models of Cognitive Control

Complementing the section on neural correlates of cognitive control, we consider it important to also discuss computational mechanisms underlying cognitive control (for an overview see Verguts, 2017). A special challenge for lecturers is that psychology students often find it difficult to understand why computational models are needed in psychology. We thus recommend introducing this topic by discussing the relevance of mechanistic explanations in psychology in general and the specific advantages of computational models in comparison to verbal ("arrows-and-boxes") theories. For instance, one should point to the fact that computational models (especially when implemented as computer simulations) contain no "magic" or "homunculus," that they support a particularly stringent derivation of testable hypotheses and can demonstrate unexpected behaviors of nonlinear dynamic systems that are not easily predicted by verbal theories.

While current computational models of cognitive control are often highly complex, basic principles can be conveyed even with relatively simple "toy models," which put modest demands on students' mathematical skills. An example is simple connectionist models of cognitive control such as the "guided activation model" by Cohen and colleagues, which has been used to account for cognitive control processes in the Stroop color-word interference task (Botvinick & Cohen, 2014; Cohen, Dunbar, & McClelland, 1990). In this model, goals and task rules are represented as activation patterns over simple interconnected processing units, which bias perceptual processing such that task-relevant information gains a stronger impact on response activation, while irrelevant information is suppressed. For didactic purposes, this model has several advantages: it is relatively easy to understand; it illustrates general principles of connectionist networks and shows how goals and task sets can be represented and maintained as self-sustaining activation patterns over simple processing units; it shows how automatic responses emerge from the gradual strengthening of stimulus-response connections; it shows how active goal representations can bias "top-down" perceptual processes such that automatic responses can be overridden; it explains how impaired goal maintenance leads to interference and stimulus-driven behavior; and it can be used to demonstrate how testable predictions can be derived from a computational model and fit to empirical data.

In more advanced and specialized courses in a master program with a focus on cognitive or computational neuroscience, one may discuss a wider variety of modeling approaches to cognitive control (e.g., Bayesian inference, reinforcement learning) and more complex neural network models of cognitive control (e.g., Herd et al., 2014). Moreover, an advanced course may include practical training in the implementation of models using general software packages such as MATLAB or dedicated software packages for the simulation of neural network such as the "Leabra" framework by O'Reilly and colleagues (O'Reilly et al., 2020), which includes practical exercises with neural network models of a range of cognitive control tasks.

Section 8: Cognitive Control in Applied Contexts

Insights into mechanisms of cognitive control are relevant in a wide range of applied contexts, and students' interest can often be increased by examples of where cognitive control becomes practically relevant. While we address this theme in a separate section of this chapter, from a didactic perspective, we recommend integrating applied themes directly into discussions of specific research themes at various points throughout a course. Here, we just mention mental disorders and cognitive training as two examples of applied contexts in which cognitive control is relevant.

Dysfunctions of cognitive control in mental and neuropsychiatric disorders. Impairments and dysfunctions of cognitive control have been conceived as (possibly transdiagnostic) mechanisms and vulnerability factors increasing the risk of various mental disorders, including substance use disorders, behavioral addictions, impulsivity-compulsivity spectrum disorders, attention deficit and hyperactivity disorder, and major depression (Goschke, 2014; Santens, Claes, Dierckx, & Dom, 2020).

Training of cognitive control. A question of high practical relevance is whether and how executive functions and cognitive control abilities can be improved via training, as, for instance, in children with attention deficit/hyperactivity disorders or in elderly people with age-related cognitive decline. Meta-analyses suggest that training of executive functions and working memory significantly improves performance in older adults (Karbach & Verhaeghen, 2014) as well as in children and adolescents (Strobach, Salminen, Karbach, & Schubert, 2014). However, one should also critically discuss that training effects are usually short-lived or confined to tasks that are similar to the training tasks (Kassai, Futo, Demetrovics, & Takacs, 2019; Melby-Lervag & Hulme, 2013), although recent evidence suggests that cognitive training seems to promote far transfer in developmentally at-risk children (Scionti, Cavallero, Zogmaister, & Marzocchi, 2020).

Cognitive control and attentional bias training in psychotherapy. A related applied theme concerns the use of cognitive control trainings as a part of psychotherapeutic interventions. Examples include trainings to reduce attentional biases and enhance attention control in anxiety disorders (Linetzky, Pergamin-Hight, Pine, & Bar-Haim, 2015; MacLeod & Clarke, 2015) and substance use disorders (Heitmann, Bennik, van Hemel-Ruiter, & de Jong, 2018).

Section 9: Philosophical Issues and Implications

Although research on volition and cognitive control is primarily the domain of experimental psychology and cognitive neuroscience, we consider it important that students acquire a basic understanding of philosophical foundations as well as implications of this research for concepts of free will, agency, and personal responsibility. Questions that have proven useful to instigate an open discussion on these themes include the following:

- Do insights into neurocognitive mechanisms of self-control and volitional action show that lay concepts of free will are illusory?
- Does psychology and neuroscience undermine our view of humans as autonomous agents (Roskies, 2010)?
- Should knowledge about cognitive and neural mechanisms underlying self-control influence our moral evaluation of actions (Roskies, 2012)?
- Should psychological or neurobiological markers of impaired cognitive control play a role in the assessment of an offender's criminal responsibility and culpability (Glannon, 2015; Meixner, 2015)?

Some of these questions may appear purely hypothetical given our limited current knowledge of cognitive control and the modest reliability of measures of control abilities, which hardly justify it to apply them to individual cases. Nevertheless, we believe that the next generation of clinical, educational, or forensic scientists and practitioners should be able to critically reflect on the rapid development of the cognitive neuroscience of volition and cognitive control in order to competently participate in the societal discourse on implications of this research for moral, philosophical, and legal questions. We thus recommend addressing at least some of the following specific themes in a psychology or cognitive neuroscience course on volition and cognitive control:

- Key positions and arguments in the philosophy of free will (e.g., incompatibilistic (libertarian) versus compatibilistic theories; concepts of causality and determinism).
- Implications of incompatibilistic and compatibilistic theories of free will for concepts of personal responsibility, agency, and authorship.
- Relevance of empirical research on self-control for philosophical theories of "weakness of will," akrasia, and intentionality.
- Reflection about what psychology and neuroscience can and cannot contribute to philosophical debates (i.e., students should understand the difference between empirical questions concerning causal mechanisms, conceptual questions as how to define free will, and normative questions related to moral responsibility).

As a basis for discussing these questions, there are excellent short and nontechnical introductions to the philosophy of free will (e.g., Kane, 2005) as well as edited volumes on psychological perspectives on free will (e.g., Baer, 2008).

Teaching and Learning in Courses on Volition and Cognitive Control: Approaches and Strategies

In this section, we will not recapitulate general teaching and learning strategies that can be applied across different topics and that have been excellently summarized in other chapters of this volume (e.g., Chap. 20, "▶ Psychological Assessment and Testing," by Miller and Daniels in this handbook). We rather describe two alternative organizing frameworks for a course on volition and cognitive control.

A fundamental decision when planning such a course is whether to structure course contents along *research fields and (sub)disciplines* or along *research topics and questions*, which cut across disciplinary boundaries. Both organizing principles have complementary advantages and challenges. When using a disciplinary scheme, a course would be structured along the main (sub)disciplines in which research on volition and cognitive control is conducted:

– In *cognitive psychology*, research on cognitive control emerged in the 1970s with the distinction between automatic and controlled processing (Posner & Snyder, 1975) and focuses on laboratory experiments with the aim to elucidate mechanisms underlying the configuration of perceptual and motor processes according to intentions and task instructions, as well as the processing of task-relevant information in the face of interfering stimuli or competing responses (Cohen, 2017).
– In *motivational psychology*, research on volitional control originated in the 1980s, when researchers distinguished between motivational processes mediating goal selection and volitional processes mediating goal pursuit (for overviews see Achtziger & Gollwitzer, 2018; Kuhl, 2018). The focus is on volitional control strategies, which support the realization of intentions when goal pursuit is challenged by competing motivational tendencies or habitual responses.
– In *social psychology*, research focuses on self-control strategies that underlie the ability to resist temptations and to override transient desires or impulsive responses in order to render behavior consistent with long-term goals or social norms (Kotabe & Hofmann, 2015).
– In *cognitive and clinical neuropsychology*, the focus is on impairments of executive functions in patients with prefrontal brain lesions, which show up in deficient action planning and cognitive flexibility, increased susceptibility to interference, and a predominance of stimulus-driven over goal-directed behavior (Stuss & Knight, 2013).
– In *cognitive neuroscience*, tasks and paradigms from cognitive psychology are combined with functional neuroimaging or noninvasive brain stimulation methods to elucidate the neural systems and networks underlying cognitive control (Cohen, 2017; Gazzaniga et al., 2018; Purves et al., 2013).
– In *educational and lifespan developmental psychology*, cognitive control is an important topic in research on self-regulated learning and impulse control in childhood and adolescence (Duckworth et al., 2019; Job et al., 2015; Panadero, 2017), as well as in research on cognitive decline in old age and neurodegenerative diseases (Reuter-Lorenz et al., 2016; Stuss & Craik, 2019).

– In *clinical psychology*, dysfunctions of cognitive control play an important role as putative vulnerability factors and mechanism of mental disorders including substance abuse, behavioral addictions, obsessive-compulsive spectrum disorders, and major depression (Goschke, 2014; Volkow & Baler, 2015; Zelazo, 2020).

Such a disciplinary organization has the advantage that one can introduce key concepts using the coherent terminology within a particular research field, convey the inherent logic of consecutive studies, and delineate the evolution of theories within a given subdiscipline. However, a major disadvantage is that such an approach renders cross-disciplinary overlap between key concepts less obvious. Despite different methodologies and theoretical frameworks, the lines of research listed above all share a largely overlapping subject matter. There will thus be considerable redundancy when explaining the overlapping concepts of cognitive control, executive functions, and self-control repeatedly from different disciplinary angles. More importantly, a disciplinary course organization may create the impression of an artificial segregation of actually closely related topics, which may make it more difficult to convey important interrelations between behavioral studies of self-control, neuropsychological studies of executive functions, and neuroimaging studies of cognitive control.

Thus, although it is still a common practice in psychology curricula and textbooks to address cognitive control, volition, and self-control as separate subjects, teaching them as a coherent theme in a systematic and integrative manner has several advantages. First, a systematic course organization along key research questions that cut across disciplines makes the overlap between key concepts transparent. More importantly, central topics (e.g., response inhibition, cognitive flexibility, intentional action) can be discussed across different (behavioral, computational, neural) levels of analyses, which promotes deeper encoding and more elaborative knowledge representations in students. While such an approach may initially put higher demands on students' ability to relate theoretical concepts from different research traditions with often idiosyncratic terminologies and methodologies, the cost of this increased intellectual effort is outweighed by the benefits of a more comprehensive understanding of the field, the ability to take different perspectives on volition and cognitive control and to integrate levels of analyses. In fact, in the long run, such an integrative cross-disciplinary approach is often experienced as intellectually more rewarding by students, because it helps to counteract the impression (prominent in novice students) that psychology consists of a bewildering array of segregated research paradigms.

Challenges and Lessons Learned

Volition and cognitive control are complex themes, which pose various challenges to students. First, as this chapter shows, the topic cuts across several (sub)disciplines and demands an understanding of theoretical concepts and models from profoundly different research traditions, as well as knowledge of a wide range of methods (cognitive tasks, neuropsychological assessments, functional neuroimaging, computational modeling). Moreover, especially first-year students often experience theoretical constructs in this field as abstract and difficult to grasp. This impression is further fueled by the fact that cognitive control research mostly employs experimental paradigms that may appear remote from real-life behavior. Thus, instigating students' interest and maintaining their motivation pose challenges that go beyond the general aim to convey contents in a systematic and clearly structured manner. Instructors should therefore pay attention not only to the contents of a curriculum and ways to ensure that students understand core concepts, but they should also make students personally care about what they learn; see why topics are relevant, both for the scientific aim to elucidate mechanisms underlying human action and for applied problems; and motivate them to actively and critically reflect about what they have learned. In the following we give some recommendations from our own teaching experience for how to increase students' interest and engagement in a course on volition and cognitive control.

Tip 1: Include Real-Life Examples and Instigate Transfer to Daily Behavior

Examples demonstrating the relevance of cognitive control for real-life behavior or clinical conditions usually instigate students' interest and increase the motivation even of those who are not primarily interested in basic science but in practical applications of psychological knowledge. Applied themes should ideally not be discussed in a separate section at the end of a course, but be integrated in thematic sections through-out a course. Moreover, students should learn to transfer their knowledge to real-life contexts and be invited to provide examples of where findings from experiments on cognitive control are relevant for daily behaviors. For example, when introducing the distinction between goal-directed and automatic or habitual behavior, students may be asked to generate everyday life examples of both types of behaviors, to discuss their costs and benefits, and to critically reflect upon whether real-life behaviors can be neatly classified as being either automatic or controlled. Likewise, when discussing experimental tasks to investigate cognitive flexibility, students may be asked to provide examples of task switching or dual tasking in daily life and to discuss their phenomenology and behavioral consequences. Analogously, in a section on self-control, students may be asked to provide examples of real-life self-control failures and discuss possible causes and strategies for how to avoid them. In a similar vein, when discussing neural mechanisms of cognitive control, one may include recent studies using a "brain-as-predictor" approach (see Section 6), which combines neuro-imaging with ecological momentary assessments to examine whether brain activation measured in laboratory tasks predicts self-control in real-life contexts.

Tip 2: Use Socratic Dialogues

Students' interest and involvement can be significantly increased by Socratic dia-logues to encourage active reflection and critical thinking. This holds in particular, but by no means exclusively, for theoretical topics (e.g., competing models of self-control) and philosophical themes (e.g., theories of free will). Some examples for questions that have proven helpful for instigating Socratic dialogues in a course on volition and cognitive control include the following:

- Why is cognitive control important for understanding human behavior?
- What are the benefits and costs of automatic or habitual behavior?
- In which daily contexts is cognitive control practically relevant?
- Which conceptual problems does the view of self-control as a limited willpower resource face?
- What are strengths and weaknesses of dual systems theories of self-control?
- Is self-control always adaptive, or can it also have adverse consequences for mental health or well-being (e.g., in cases of chronic "overcontrol")?
- Is addiction a brain disease that reflects impaired cognitive control abilities?
- Does neuroscience show that free will is merely an illusion, and if so, what does this imply for our concept of personal responsibility and agency?
- If intentions can be decoded from brain activity before persons become conscious of their intention, does this imply that conscious intentions play no role in the causation of behavior?
- How might the ecological validity of experimental paradigms used to investigate cognitive control be increased without sacrificing experimental control?
- What might be interventions to improve self-control competencies?

Although Socratic dialogue is more easily instigated in face-to-face seminars with small groups of students, it is worthwhile to integrate them also in lectures. We recommend to regularly insert discussion periods into lectures, where students can be engaged in Socratic questioning to increase their interest, curiosity, and critical reflection. Moreover, often it is possible to not simply present a chunk of knowledge to students, but rather motivate them to *actively generate* the to-be-learned knowledge. As a concrete example, instead of describing the go/no-go task or the task-switching paradigm, students may be asked to come up with ideas how one might measure response inhibition and cognitive flexibility.

Tip 3: Motivate Students to Read and Critically Reflect on Original Research Papers

It is strongly recommend that a course on volition and cognitive control be not exclusively based on textbooks or review articles, but that one motivates students to read, critically reflect on, and discuss selected original journal articles. This is indispensable if students are to acquire the competence to search, understand, and evaluate research results in a rapidly progressing research field. Moreover, reading original research articles usually leads to more engaging and profound classroom discussions. It should be stressed that this will not only be relevant for those students aiming for a research career, but is also important for practitioners (e.g., psychotherapists, neuropsychologists, educational psychologists) who should acquire the competence to keep up with relevant developments in research fields of relevance for their professional activity.

Tip 4: Use Multimedia and Classroom Demonstrations of Experimental Tasks

It is a truism that courses can be made more interesting and stimulating by employing various media and demonstration tools. This may include video documentaries of neuropsychological case studies, video tutorials of brain anatomy, and principles underlying functional neuroimaging. Moreover, it is recommended to include classroom demonstrations of experimental tasks and paradigms. In fact, many tasks used to assess cognitive control (e.g., go/no-go, Stroop, or set-switching tasks) can easily be demonstrated in the classroom. Having students actively execute these tasks not only improves their understanding, but usually stimulates a much more lively discussion about the cognitive processes required in a task and possible limitations of experimental paradigms. Building on this, one may initiate small-group discussions on how to overcome such limitations and improve tasks to investigate cognitive control functions.

Tip 5: Promote Deep and Elaborative Encoding

It is well established by research on memory and learning that memorization and understanding of new material is enhanced by deep (semantic) encoding, elaborative processing, critical reflection, and active generation rather than passive reception of to-be-learned materials. Some of these principles form the basis for the PQ4R method (Thomas & Robinson, 1972), which specifies six stages of active learning from textbooks, but which can be transferred to learning in a classroom context (see Table 4).

Table 4 Six stages of active learning according to the PQ4R method

Stage	Learning/teaching objective
Preview	Provide a broad overview of relevant themes and identify the key topics to be covered
Questions	Encourage students to formulate questions for each theme
Read	Encourage students to read the relevant literature prior to each thematic session and to follow the classroom discussion while trying to answer the aforementioned questions
Reflect	Encourage students to find examples and counterexamples, critically review arguments given, and develop additional arguments, and relate these to their previous knowledge of the subject
Recite	Encourage students to try to actively recall the content, preferentially in small learning groups
Review	After a topic has been completed, students should review the most important points of the new knowledge they acquired

Tip 6: Provide Examples from Your Own Research and Show Your Passion for the Topic

As we noted, theories and experiments in the field of volition and cognitive control are often experienced as abstract, difficult, and remote from real life. It thus matters the more that instructors succeed in motivating students and in instigating their interest by presenting knowledge in an engaging and passionate manner. While the way this is achieved will obviously depend in large part on the personality and teaching style of lecturers, it has proven useful to refer to one's own research and explain why one chose volition and cognitive control as a topic for teaching or as a research focus in one's academic career and which unresolved questions one finds particularly fascinating. Including such a personal perspective is contagious and often enhances students' interest over and above a didactically skillful, but impersonal, exposition of theories and empirical findings.

Teaching and Learning Resources

Recommended Nonfiction Book on Cognitive Control

Badre, D. (2020). *On Task: How Our Brain Gets Things Done.* Princeton, NJ: Princeton University Press.

An excellent nontechnical, up-to-date, and well-written overview of cognitive control research with many examples of its relevance for daily tasks and behaviors and consequences of impaired cognitive control.

Selected Handbooks and Review Articles on Cognitive Control

Egner, T. (2017). *The Wiley handbook of cognitive control.* Wiley Blackwell.

Comprehensive handbook that may serve as the basis for a one- or two-semester course on volition and cognitive control. Contains authoritative reviews on a wide range of topics, including theoretical concepts, neural mechanisms, and computational models of cognitive control, the interaction of cognitive control with other domains of cognitive and emotional functioning, as well as applied themes (e.g., cognitive control in aging, training of cognitive control, cognitive control in brain-injured patients and mental disorders).

Gazzaniga, M., Ivry, R. & Mangun, R. (2018). *Cognitive neuroscience. The biology of the mind (5th. Ed.).* Norton. (Chapter 12: Cognitive Control).

A textbook chapter providing an introductory overview of the cognitive neuroscience of cognitive control.

Diamond, A. (2013). Executive functions. *Annual Review of Psychology, 64,* 135–168.

Review article on executive functions with a focus on the development of cognitive control.

Eppinger, B., Goschke, T., & Musslick, S. (2021). Meta-control: From psychology to computational neuroscience. *Cognitive, Affective, & Behavioral Neuroscience, 21*(3), 447–452.

Introduction to a special issue dedicated to the emerging field of meta-control.

Selected Chapters and Review Articles on Volition and Intentional Action

Haggard, P. (2019). The neurocognitive bases of human volition. *Annual Review of Psychology, 70,* 9–28.

A review of cognitive neuroscience research on volitional action with a focus on the role of conscious intentions in the control of willed action and the feeling of agency.

Goschke, T. (2013). Volition in action: Intentions, control dilemmas and the dynamic regulation of cognitive control In W. Prinz, A. Beisert, & A. Herwig (Eds.), *Action science: Foundations of an emerging discipline* (pp. 409–434). Cambridge, MA: MIT Press.

A theoretical chapter on the role of cognitive control in goal-directed action including a discussion of the concept of control dilemmas.

Handbook and Selected Review Chapters on Volition and Self-Control

Vohs, K. D., & Baumeister, R. F. (Eds.). (2017). *Handbook of Self-Regulation. Research, Theory, and Applications* (3rd ed.). New York, NJ: Guilford Press.

Handbook with authoritative reviews on a wide range of topics related to self-control.

Inzlicht, M., Werner, K. M., Briskin, J. L., & Roberts, B. W. (2021). Integrating Models of Self-Regulation. *Annual Review of Psychology, 72(1),* 319–345.

An integrative review summarizing research and theories of self-control.

Achtziger, A., & Gollwitzer, P. (2018). Motivation and volition in the course of action. In J. Heckhausen & H. Heckhausen (Eds.), *Motivation and action* (3rd ed., pp. 485–527). Berlin: Springer.

Textbook chapter summarizing research on Gollwitzer and Heckhausen's model of action phases and on implementation intentions as a self-regulatory strategy.

Kuhl, J. (2018). Individual differences in self-regulation. In J. Heckhausen & H. Heckhausen (Eds.), *Motivation and action* (3rd ed., pp. 529–577). Berlin: Springer.

Textbook chapter summarizing research on Kuhl's theory of volition and action control with a focus on individual differences between action- and state-oriented individuals.

Position Paper on the Role of Cognitive Control in Mental Disorders

Goschke, T. (2014). Dysfunctions of decision-making and cognitive control as transdiagnostic mechanisms of mental disorders: advances, gaps, and needs in current research. International Journal of Methods in *Psychiatric Research, 23(S1)*, 41–57.

Position paper on the role of cognitive control as a transdiagnostic mechanism and vulnerability factors for a range of mental disorders.

Selected Books on the Philosophy and Psychology of Free Will

Kane, R. (2005). *A contemporary introduction to free will*. Oxford: Oxford University Press.

A short and nontechnical introduction to main positions and arguments in the philosophy of free will.

Cross-References

▶ Psychological Assessment and Testing

Acknowledgments Work on this chapter and the authors' research on volition and cognitive control has been supported by the German Research Foundation within the Collaborative Research Centre "Volition and Cognitive Control" (SFB 940/1, SFB 940/2, SFB 940/3).

References

Achtziger, A., & Gollwitzer, P. M. (2018). Motivation and volition in the course of action. In J. Heckhausen & H. Heckhausen (Eds.), *Motivation and action* (3rd ed., pp. 485–527). Springer.

Association, A. P. (2020a). APA guidelines for the psychological undergraduate major. Retrieved from https://www.apa.org/ed/precollege/about/undergraduate-major.

Association, A. P. (2020b). Promoting excellence in professional psychology education and training through best practices in defining and measuring competence. Retrieved from https://www.apa.org/ed/graduate/competency.

Badre, D., & Nee, D. E. (2018). Frontal cortex and the hierarchical control of behavior. *Trends in Cognitive Sciences, 22*(2), 170–188. https://doi.org/10.1016/j.tics.2017.11.005

Bargh, J. (1989). Conditional automaticity: Varieties of automatic influences in social perception and cognition. In J. S. Uleman & J. A. Bargh (Eds.), *Unintended thought* (pp. 3–51). The Guilford Press.

Baumeister, R. F., Tice, D. M., & Vohs, K. D. (2018). The strength model of self-regulation: Conclusions from the second decade of willpower research. *Perspectives on Psychological Science, 13*(2), 141–145. https://doi.org/10.1177/1745691617716946

Berkman, E. T., Falk, E. B., & Lieberman, M. D. (2011). In the trenches of real-world self-control: Neural correlates of breaking the link between craving and smoking. *Psychological Science, 22*(4), 498–506. https://doi.org/10.1177/0956797611400918

Botvinick, M. M., & Cohen, J. D. (2014). The computational and neural basis of cognitive control: Charted territory and new frontiers. *Cognitive Science, 38*(6), 1249–1285. https://doi.org/10.1111/cogs.12126

Botvinick, M. M., Cohen, J. D., & Carter, C. S. (2004). Conflict monitoring and anterior cingulate cortex: An update. *Trends in Cognitive Sciences, 8*(12), 539–546. https://doi.org/10.1016/j.tics.2004.10.003

Braver, T. (Ed.). (2016). *Motivation and cognitive control*. Taylor & Francis.

Cohen, J. D. (2017). Cognitive control Core constructs and current considerations. In T. Egner (Ed.), *Wiley handbook of cognitive control*. Wiley.

Cohen, J. D., Dunbar, K., & McClelland, J. L. (1990). On the control of automatic processes: A parallel distributed processing account of the Stroop effect. *Psychological Review, 97*(3), 332–361. https://doi.org/10.1037/0033-295x.97.3.332

Cools, R. (2019). Chemistry of the adaptive mind: Lessons from dopamine. *Neuron, 104*(1), 113–131. https://doi.org/10.1016/j.neuron.2019.09.035

Diamond, A. (2013). Executive functions. *Annual Review of Psychology, 64*, 135–168. https://doi.org/10.1146/annurev-psych-113011-143750

Duckworth, A. L., Taxer, J. L., Eskreis-Winkler, L., Galla, B. M., & Gross, J. J. (2019). Self-control and academic achievement. In S. T. Fiske (Ed.), *Annual review of psychology* (Vol. 70, pp. 373–399). https://doi.org/10.1146/annurev-psych-010418-103230

Duncan, J. (2010). The multiple-demand (MD) system of the primate brain: Mental programs for intelligent behaviour. *Trends in Cognitive Science, 14*(4), 172–179. https://doi.org/10.1016/j.tics.2010.01.004

Egner, T. (Ed.). (2017). *The Wiley handbook of cognitive control*. Wiley-Blackwell.

Eppinger, B., Goschke, T., & Musslick, S. (2021). Meta-control: From psychology to computational neuroscience. *Cognitive, Affective, & Behavioral Neuroscience, 21*(3), 447–452. https://doi.org/10.3758/s13415-021-00919-4

Friese, M., Loschelder, D. D., Gieseler, K., Frankenbach, J., & Inzlicht, M. (2019). Is ego depletion real? An analysis of arguments. *Personality and Social Psychology Review, 23*(2), 107–131. https://doi.org/10.1177/1088868318762183

Galla, B. M., & Duckworth, A. L. (2015). More than resisting temptation: Beneficial habits mediate the relationship between self-control and positive life outcomes. *Journal of Personality and Social Psychology, 109*(3), 508–525. https://doi.org/10.1037/pspp0000026

Gazzaniga, M. S., Ivry, R. B., & Mangun, G. R. (2018). *Cognitive neuroscience: The biology of the mind* (5th ed.). W. W. Norton.

Glannon, W. (Ed.). (2015). *Free will and the brain: Neuroscientific, philosophical, and legal perspectives*. Cambridge University Press.

Goschke, T. (2003). Voluntary action and cognitive control from a cognitive neuroscience perspective. In S. Maasen, W. Prinz, & G. Roth (Eds.), *Voluntary action: Brains, minds, and sociality* (pp. 49–85). Oxford University Press.

Goschke, T. (2013). Volition in action: Intentions, control dilemmas, and the dynamic regulation of cognitive control. In W. Prinz, M. Beisert, & A. Herwig (Eds.), *Action science: Foundations of an emerging discipline* (pp. 409–434). MIT Press.

Goschke, T. (2014). Dysfunctions of decision-making and cognitive control as transdiagnostic mechanisms of mental disorders: Advances, gaps, and needs in current research. *International Journal of Methods in Psychiatric Research, 23*(S1), 41–57. https://doi.org/10.1002/mpr.1410

Goschke, T., & Bolte, A. (2014). Emotional modulation of control dilemmas: The role of positive affect, reward, and dopamine in cognitive stability and flexibility. *Neuropsychologia, 62*, 403–423. https://doi.org/10.1016/j.neuropsychologia.2014.07.015

Haggard, P. (2008). Human volition: Towards a neuroscience of will. *Nature Reviews: Neuroscience, 9*(12), 934–946. https://doi.org/10.1038/nrn2497

Haggard, P. (2019). The neurocognitive bases of human volition. *Annual Review of Psychology, 70*, 9–28. https://doi.org/10.1146/annurev-psych-010418-103348

Hare, T. A., Camerer, C. F., & Rangel, A. (2009). Self-control in decision-making involves modulation of the vmPFC valuation system. *Science, 324*(5927), 646–648. https://doi.org/10.1126/science.1168450

Hare, T. A., Malmaud, J., & Rangel, A. (2011). Focusing attention on the health aspects of foods changes value signals in vmPFC and improves dietary choice [Research Support, U.S. Gov't, non-P.H.S.]. *Journal of Neuroscience, 31*(30), 11077–11087. https://doi.org/10.1523/JNEUROSCI.6383-10.2011

Harris, A., Hare, T., & Rangel, A. (2013). Temporally dissociable mechanisms of self-control: Early attentional filtering versus late value modulation. *Journal of Neuroscience, 33*(48), 18917–18931. https://doi.org/10.1523/JNEUROSCI.5816-12.2013

Heitmann, J., Bennik, E. C., van Hemel-Ruiter, M. E., & de Jong, P. J. (2018). The effectiveness of attentional bias modification for substance use disorder symptoms in adults: A systematic review. *Systematic Reviews, 7*(1), 160–160. https://doi.org/10.1186/s13643-018-0822-6

Herd, S. A., O'Reilly, R. C., Hazy, T. E., Chatham, C. H., Brant, A. M., & Friedman, N. P. (2014). A neural network model of individual differences in task switching abilities. *Neuropsychologia, 62*, 375–389. https://doi.org/10.1016/j.neuropsychologia.2014.04.014

Hofmann, W., Baumeister, R. F., Förster, G., & Vohs, K. D. (2012). Everyday temptations: An experience sampling study of desire, conflict, and self-control. *Journal of Personality and Social Psychology, 6*, 1318–1335. https://doi.org/10.1037/a0026545

Hofmann, W., Friese, M., & Roefs, A. (2009). Three ways to resist temptation: The independent contributions of executive attention, inhibitory control, and affect regulation to the impulse control of eating behavior. *Journal of Experimental Social Psychology, 45*(2), 431–435. https://doi.org/10.1016/j.jesp.2008.09.013

Hofmann, W., Friese, M., & Strack, F. (2009). Impulse and self-control from a dual-systems perspective. *Perspectives on Psychological Science, 4*(2), 162–176.

Hofmann, W., & Kotabe, H. (2012). A general model of preventive and interventive self-control. *Social and Personality Psychology Compass, 6*(10), 707–722. https://doi.org/10.1111/j.1751-9004.2012.00461.x

Hommel, B. (2019). Binary theorizing does not account for action control. *Frontiers in Psychology, 10*, 2542. https://doi.org/10.3389/fpsyg.2019.02542

Hommel, B., & Wiers, R. W. (2017). Towards a unitary approach to human action control. *Trends in Cognitive Sciences, 21*(12), 940–949. https://doi.org/10.1016/j.tics.2017.09.009

Huettel, S. A., Song, A. W., & McCarthy, G. (2014). *Functional magnetic resonance imaging* (2nd ed.). Sinauer.

Inzlicht, M., Schmeichel, B. J., & Macrae, C. N. (2014). Why self-control seems (but may not be) limited. *Trends in Cognitive Sciences, 18*(3), 127–133. https://doi.org/10.1016/j.tics.2013.12.009

Inzlicht, M., Werner, K. M., Briskin, J. L., & Roberts, B. W. (2020). Integrating models of self-regulation. *Annual Review of Psychology, 72*(1), 319–345.

Job, V., Dweck, C. S., & Walton, G. M. (2010). Ego depletion – Is it all in your head? Implicit theories about willpower affect self-regulation. *Psychological Science, 21*(11), 1686–1693. https://doi.org/10.1177/0956797610384745

Job, V., Friese, M., & Bernecker, K. (2015). Effects of practicing self-control on academic performance. *Motivation Science, 1*(4), 219–232. https://doi.org/10.1037/mot0000024

Johnson, R. E., Lin, S.-H., & Lee, H. W. (2018). Self-control as the fuel for effective self-regulation at work: Antecedents, consequences, and boundary conditions of employee self-control. In A. J. Elliot (Ed.), *Advances in motivation science* (Vol. 5, pp. 87–128). https://doi.org/10.1016/bs.adms.2018.01.004

Kable, J. W. (2014). Valuation, intertemporal choice, and self-control. In P. W. Glimcher & E. Fehr (Eds.), *Neuroeconomics. Decision making and the brain* (2nd ed., pp. 173–192). Academic Press. https://doi.org/10.1016/b978-0-12-416008-8.00010-3

Karbach, J., & Verhaeghen, P. (2014). Making working memory work: A meta-analysis of executive-control and working memory training in older adults. *Psychological Science, 25*(11), 2027–2037. https://doi.org/10.1177/0956797614548725

Karr, J. E., Areshenkoff, C. N., Rast, P., Hofer, S. M., Iverson, G. L., & Garcia-Barrera, M. A. (2018). The unity and diversity of executive functions: A systematic review and re-analysis of latent variable studies. *Psychological Bulletin, 144*(11), 1147–1185. https://doi.org/10.1037/bul0000160

Kassai, R., Futo, J., Demetrovics, Z., & Takacs, Z. K. (2019). A meta-analysis of the experimental evidence on the near- and far-transfer effects among children's executive function skills. *Psychological Bulletin, 145*(2), 165–188. https://doi.org/10.1037/bul0000180

Kober, H., Kross, E. F., Mischel, W., Hart, C. L., & Ochsner, K. N. (2010). Regulation of craving by cognitive strategies in cigarette smokers [Research Support, N.I.H., extramural]. *Drug and Alcohol Dependence, 106*(1), 52–55. https://doi.org/10.1016/j.drugalcdep.2009.07.017

Kotabe, H. P., & Hofmann, W. (2015). On integrating the components of self-control. *Perspectives on Psychological Science, 10*(5), 618–638. https://doi.org/10.1177/1745691615593382

Krönke, K. M., Wolff, M., Mohr, H., Kraplin, A., Smolka, M. N., Buhringer, G., & Goschke, T. (2018). Monitor yourself! Deficient error-related brain activity predicts real-life self-control failures. *Cognitive, Affective, & Behavioral Neuroscience, 18*(4), 622–637. https://doi.org/10.3758/s13415-018-0593-5

Krönke, K. M., Wolff, M., Mohr, H., Kraplin, A., Smolka, M. N., Buhringer, G., & Goschke, T. (2020). Predicting real-life self-control from brain activity encoding the value of anticipated future outcomes. *Psychological Science, 31*(3), 268–279. https://doi.org/10.1177/0956797619896357. Article 0956797619896357.

Kruschwitz, J. D., Ludwig, V. U., Waller, L., List, D., Wisniewski, D., Wolfensteller, U., . . . Walter, H. (2018). Regulating craving by anticipating positive and negative outcomes: A multivariate pattern analysis and network connectivity approach. *Frontiers in Behavioral Neuroscience, 12*, 297. https://doi.org/10.3389/fnbeh.2018.00297, Article 297.

Kuhl, J. (2018). Individual differences in self-regulation. In J. Heckhausen & H. Heckhausen (Eds.), *Motivation and action* (3rd ed., pp. 529–577). Springer.

Kuhl, J., & Goschke, T. (1994). A theory of action control: Mental subsystems, modes of control, and volitional conflict-resolution strategies. In J. Kuhl & J. Beckmann (Eds.), *Volition and personality: Action versus state orientation* (pp. 93–124). Hogrefe.

Libet, B., Gleason, C. A., Wright, E. W., & Pearl, D. K. (1983). Time of conscious intention to act in relation to onset of cerebral activity (readiness-potential). The unconscious initiation of a freely voluntary act. *Brain, 106*(Pt 3), 623–642. https://doi.org/10.1093/brain/106.3.623

Linetzky, M., Pergamin-Hight, L., Pine, D. S., & Bar-Haim, Y. (2015). Quantitative evaluation of the clinical efficacy of attention bias modification treatment for anxiety disorders. *Depression and Anxiety, 32*(6), 383–391. https://doi.org/10.1002/da.22344

Lurquin, J. H., & Miyake, A. (2017). Challenges to ego-depletion research go beyond the replication crisis: A need for tackling the conceptual crisis. *Frontiers in Psychology, 8*, 568. https://www.ncbi.nlm.nih.gov/pubmed/28458647

MacLeod, C., & Clarke, P. J. F. (2015). The attentional bias modification approach to anxiety intervention. *Clinical Psychological Science, 3*(1), 58–78. https://doi.org/10.1177/2167702614560749

Mansouri, F. A., Egner, T., & Buckley, M. J. (2017). Monitoring demands for executive control: Shared functions between human and nonhuman primates. *Trends in Neurosciences, 40*(1), 15–27. https://doi.org/10.1016/j.tins.2016.11.001

McClure, S. M., Laibson, D. I., Loewenstein, G., & Cohen, J. D. (2004). Separate neural systems value immediate and delayed monetary rewards. *Science, 306*(5695), 503–507. https://doi.org/10.1126/science.1100907

Meixner, J. B., Jr. (2015). Applications of neuroscience in criminal law: Legal and methodological issues. *Current Neurology and Neuroscience Reports, 15*(2), 513. https://doi.org/10.1007/s11910-014-0513-1

Melby-Lervag, M., & Hulme, C. (2013). Is working memory training effective? A meta-analytic review. *Developmental Psychology, 49*(2), 270–291. https://doi.org/10.1037/a0028228

Mischel, W., Ebbesen, E. B., & Raskoff Zeiss, A. (1972). Cognitive and attentional mechanisms in delay of gratification. *Journal of Personality and Social Psychology, 21*(2), 204–218. https://doi.org/10.1037/h0032198

Miyake, A., Friedman, N. P., Emerson, M. J., Witzki, A. H., Howerter, A., & Wager, T. D. (2000). The unity and diversity of executive functions and their contributions to complex 'frontal lobe' tasks: A latent variable analysis [empirical study]. *Cognitive Psychology, 41*(1), 49–100. https://doi.org/10.1006/cogp.1999.0734

O'Reilly, R. C., Munakata, Y., Frank, M. J., Hazy, T. E., & Contributors. (2020). *Computational cognitive neuroscience*. Wiki Book (4th ed.). https://github.com/CompCogNeuro/ed4.

Ott, T., & Nieder, A. (2019). Dopamine and cognitive control in prefrontal cortex. *Trends in Cognitive Sciences, 23*(3), 213–234. https://doi.org/10.1016/j.tics.2018.12.006

Panadero, E. (2017). A review of self-regulated learning: Six models and four directions for research [review]. *Frontiers in Psychology, 8*(422). https://doi.org/10.3389/fpsyg.2017.00422

Peters, J., & Büchel, C. (2011). The neural mechanisms of inter-temporal decision-making: Understanding variability. *Trends in Cognitive Sciences, 15*(5), 227–239. https://doi.org/10.1016/j.tics.2011.03.002

Posner, M. I., & Snyder, C. R. (1975). Attention and cognitive control. In R. L. Solso (Ed.), *Information processing and cognition* (pp. 55–85). Lawrence Erlbaum.

Purves, D., LaBar, K. S., Platt, M. L., Wolfdorff, M., Caebzoa, R., & Huettel, S. A. (2013). Principles of cognitive neuroscience. In S. Ass (ed.), (2nd ed.).

Reuter-Lorenz, P. A., Festini, S. B., & Jantz, T. K. (2016). Executive functions and neurocognitive aging. In K. W. Schaie & S. L. Willis (Eds.), *Handbook of the psychology of aging* (pp. 245–262). Academic Press. https://www.sciencedirect.com/science/article/pii/B9780124114692000133

Roskies, A. L. (2010). How does neuroscience affect our conception of volition? *Annual Review of Neuroscience, 33*(1), 109–130. https://doi.org/10.1146/annurev-neuro-060909-153151

Roskies, A. L. (2012). How does the neuroscience of decision making bear on our understanding of moral responsibility and free will? *Current Opinion in Neurobiology, 22*(6), 1022–1026. https://doi.org/10.1016/j.conb.2012.05.009

Santens, E., Claes, L., Dierckx, E., & Dom, G. (2020). Effortful control – A transdiagnostic dimension underlying internalizing and externalizing psychopathology. *Neuropsychobiology, 79*(4–5), 255–269. https://doi.org/10.1159/000506134

Saunders, B., Milyavskaya, M., Etz, A., Randles, D., & Inzlicht, M. (2018). Reported self-control is not meaningfully associated with inhibition-related executive function: A Bayesian analysis. *Collabra: Psychology, 4*(1), Article 39. https://doi.org/10.1525/collabra.134

Scionti, N., Cavallero, M., Zogmaister, C., & Marzocchi, G. M. (2020). Is cognitive training effective for improving executive functions in preschoolers? A systematic review and meta-analysis [systematic review]. *Frontiers in Psychology, 10*(2812). https://doi.org/10.3389/fpsyg.2019.02812

Shenhav, A., Botvinick, M. M., & Cohen, J. D. (2013). The expected value of control: An integrative theory of anterior cingulate cortex function. *Neuron, 79*(2), 217–240. https://doi.org/10.1016/j.neuron.2013.07.007

Sinnot-Armstrong, W., & Nadel, L. (Eds.). (2011). *Conscious will and responsibility*. Oxford University Press.

Soon, C. S., He, A. H., Bode, S., & Haynes, J. D. (2013). Predicting free choices for abstract intentions. *Proceedings of the National Academy of Sciences of the United States of America, 110*(15), 6217–6222. https://doi.org/10.1073/pnas.1212218110

Strobach, T., Salminen, T., Karbach, J., & Schubert, T. (2014). Practice-related optimization and transfer of executive functions: A general review and a specific realization of their mechanisms in dual tasks. *Psychological Research, 78*(6), 836–851. https://doi.org/10.1007/s00426-014-0563-7

Studer, B., Koch, C., Knecht, S., & Kalenscher, T. (2019). Conquering the inner couch potato: Precommitment is an effective strategy to enhance motivation for effortful actions. *Philosophical Transactions of the Royal Society of London. Series B: Biological Sciences, 374*(1766), 20180131. https://doi.org/10.1098/rstb.2018.0131

Stuss, D. T., & Craik, F. I. M. (2019). Alterations in executive functions with aging. In K. M. Heilman & S. E. Nadeau (Eds.), *Cognitive changes and the aging brain* (pp. 168–187). Cambridge University Press. https://doi.org/10.1017/9781108554350.012

Stuss, D. T., & Knight, R. T. (2013). *Handbook of frontal lobe function* (2nd ed.). Oxford University Press.

Thomas, E. L., & Robinson, H. A. (1972). *Improving reading in every class: A sourcebook for teachers*. Houghton Mifflin.

Tsai, N., Eccles, J. S., & Jaeggi, S. M. (2019). Stress and executive control: Mechanisms, moderators, and malleability. *Brain and Cognition, 133*, 54–59. https://doi.org/10.1016/j.bandc.2018.10.004

Verguts, T. (2017). Computational models of cognitive control. In T. Egner (Ed.), *Wiley handbook of cognitive control*. Wiley.

Volkow, N. D., & Baler, R. D. (2015). NOW vs LATER brain circuits: Implications for obesity and addiction. *Trends in Neurosciences, 38*(6), 345–352. https://doi.org/10.1016/j.tins.2015.04.002

Wegner, D. M. (2003). The mind's best trick: How we experience conscious will. *Trends in Cognitive Sciences, 7*(2), 65–69. https://doi.org/10.1016/s1364-6613(03)00002-0

Wolff, M., Krönke, K. M., Venz, J., Kraplin, A., Buhringer, G., Smolka, M. N., & Goschke, T. (2016). Action versus state orientation moderates the impact of executive functioning on real-life self-control. *Journal of Experimental Psychology: General, 145*(12), 1635–1653. https://doi.org/10.1037/xge0000229

Zelazo, P. D. (2020). Executive function and psychopathology: A neurodevelopmental perspective. *Annual Review of Clinical Psychology, 16*, 431–454. https://doi.org/10.1146/annurev-clinpsy-072319-024242

Developmental Psychology

10

Moritz M. Daum and Mirella Manfredi

Contents

M. M. Daum (✉)
Department of Psychology, Developmental Psychology: Infancy and Childhood, University of Zurich, Zurich, Switzerland

Jacobs Center for Productive Youth Development, University of Zurich, Zurich, Switzerland
e-mail: moritz.daum@uzh.ch

M. Manfredi
Department of Psychology, Developmental Psychology: Infancy and Childhood, University of Zurich, Zurich, Switzerland

© Springer Nature Switzerland AG 2023
J. Zumbach et al. (eds.), *International Handbook of Psychology Learning and Teaching*,
Springer International Handbooks of Education,
https://doi.org/10.1007/978-3-030-28745-0_13

Abstract

Developmental Psychology is the scientific study of mind and behavior from the perspective of change across the entire lifespan. In the present chapter, we provide a comprehensive and modern view on current topics particularly relevant when teaching Developmental Psychology. We start with the attempt to derive a contemporary definition of development and Developmental Psychology. Over historical time, perspectives on development changed. These different perspectives were regularly challenged, and we discuss some of the questions of scientific dispute such as the influence of nature and nurture on the development of an individual from a contemporary perspective. The perspectives often resulted in larger theoretical constructs. We will not describe individual theories comprehensively but rather focus on general issues of theoretical approaches and highlight one recent approach, the dynamic systems theories. Theories need to be supported by empirical evidence. Accordingly, we will briefly describe the major research designs used to measure developmental change. We will conclude the chapter with a focus on one topic particularly relevant when teaching Developmental Psychology, the development of communication, and discuss further topics that can potentially be included in a Developmental Psychology curriculum and describe some ideas on how to teach them. In all, we intend to provide a contemporary overview of the scientific study of developmental change.

Keywords

Developmental psychology · Change · Methods · Nature · Nurture · Theories · Questions

Introduction

Developmental Psychology is one of the most diverse fields in Psychology; it covers all aspects of Psychology and adds the aspect of change over the lifespan. This makes the task of giving a concise overview of the topics to teach in Developmental Psychology in one single book chapter not an easy endeavor. Available textbooks usually prioritize a selection of topics or age ranges and never claim to include all possible aspects of development.

The present chapter is not intended to provide an overview of specific topics and aspects of development such as the development of emotions, cognitive skills, or language. Rather, we aim to promote critical thinking and problem-solving among teacher educators, teachers, and/or prospective teachers about current topics in the field. We aim to do so by providing a contemporary view of the science of development more generally. To teach development and Developmental Psychology, it is essential to have profound knowledge about the science of development, about different concepts and models of development, and what the current status of theory-building and methodological approaches is. We will begin with an attempt to define development and Developmental Psychology and discuss matters of scientific dispute regarding development such as the influence of nature and nurture on the development of an individual. We then briefly focus on theoretical perspectives. We will not comprehensively describe individual theories but rather focus on general issues of development and highlight one contemporary theoretical approach, the dynamic systems theories. In the remainder, we will cover the aspect of how change can be measured and describe currently available research paradigms. The chapter includes one concrete example of development within none particular domain: the development of communication. We conclude the chapter with suggestions on how to teach Developmental Psychology.

Purposes and Rationale of the Curriculum in Developmental Psychology

The present chapter has the following main learning objectives: First, readers should be able to demonstrate appropriate and accurate professional content for teaching Developmental Psychology. Second, readers should think about and revise already existing courses to incorporate current research and/or best practices. Overall, readers should acquire knowledge about scientific disputes and recent trends in Development Psychology. In particular, based on the standards of qualification frameworks (e.g., Standards of Teacher Education), teachers should stimulate students to think critically about the content of Developmental Psychology. In addition, teachers might engage students in active research in the field of Developmental Psychology and suggest they establish connections between newly acquired knowledge and previously acquired contexts and perspectives. Finally, teachers should encourage the students to reflect on their own learning and apply personal life experiences to the knowledge learned in the field of Developmental Psychology.

Core Contents and Topics of the Curriculum in Developmental Psychology

Developmental Psychology: A Definition

Psychology (from Greek *psyche* = breath, spirit, soul and *logos* = science, study, research) is a relatively young scientific discipline. Among the first to define Psychology was James (1890) who defined it as "the science of mental life, both of its phenomena and their conditions." Today, Psychology is usually defined as the science of mind and behavior including their description, explanation, prediction, and intervention of behavior and mental processes (Schacter, Gilbert, Wegner, & Hood, 2011). The subdiscipline *Developmental Psychology* covers all these aspects from the perspective of change across the entire lifespan (e.g., Daum, Greve, Pauen, Schuhrke, & Schwarzer, 2020; Schwarzer & Walper, 2016). The range of topics in Developmental Psychology covers all parts of Psychology in general; it includes physical growth; cognitive, emotional, and motivational processes; and their neuro-psychological foundations. It further includes social processes of normative and non-normative behavior and experience and the effects of education and other forms of intervention on developmental events.

When asking non-experts about when and how individuals develop, the variability of the answers will be large. Development is often described as a series of distinct, qualitative, and irreversible changes (as compared to merely quantitative growth). These changes are described as being directed toward a final state, and each subsequent step is of a higher value than the previous one, and the previous one is a necessary prerequisite for the subsequent one. Developmental changes are closely related to the advancing age, and they are universal, natural, and mostly culture-independent. The question about when development takes place is traditionally seen as predominantly comprising childhood and adolescence.

While all these aspects seem to be intuitively compelling, the question arises of whether they are valid. For example, the search for a universally valid sequence of stages or states is no longer the central motif of today's theoretical and empirical considerations. In contrast, the dominant view of contemporary research is the notion of differential developmental trajectories, which are understood as sustainable, multi-directional changes with age. As a result, modern definitions are less presupposition-rich (and thus at the same time broader and humbler): Developmental Psychology is concerned with *intra-individual changes* in human behavior and experience over the entire lifespan as well as with *inter-individual differences* between these intra-individual changes (e.g., Baltes, 1987). From this perspective, the focus of Developmental Psychology has been expanded from childhood and adolescence to the entire lifespan (although not everybody agrees with this notion; see Bischof, 2020, who defines development "as the structural unfolding of an organic shape"). According to Baltes (1987), development needs to be considered from a broader perspective: It is a process covering the entire lifespan; it consists of a dynamic process that includes gains and losses with gains being more prominent in younger individuals and older individuals having to deal with more losses. Development takes place within a certain context, which can be defined by spatial location (e.g., culture), the available financial and social resources (e.g., the socioeconomic status), and the historical time (for different historical perspectives on development, see the previous contributions by Reinert (1976), Trautner (2003), or Daum and Manfredi (2021)). This modern view comes with several challenges. To shed more light on this question, we will look at past and current matters of controversy about the nature of development and how they have been and are discussed.

Questions of Scientific Dispute and Concepts About Development

Questions about how humans develop have occupied philosophy and science for millennia: What is innate? What is acquired? What is the effect of age on development? Should development be understood as following universal laws or describing individual trajectories? Are development principles domain-general or domain-specific or cross-cultural or culture-specific? As a result of the abovementioned broader definition of Developmental Psychology, the attempts to answer these questions have slowly moved away from an either-or pattern. Today, it is assumed that development is determined multi-directionally and multi-causally (e.g., Baltes, 1987). To describe and explain developmental processes, it is important not to restrict the perspective to the time that starts with birth, not even to the time that starts with the fertilization of the ovum; some factors influence the development of an individual that often lie before these points in time. Evolutionary processes thus play just as much a role as biological maturation and environmental experiences. At the same time, development may be regarded to not necessarily end with a person's death; an individual can substantially influence further generations through the actions during his or her lifetime. In the following, we focus on three major questions, the influence of age, the influence of biology vs. environment, and the question of whether, when describing development, one should focus on group means or individual data. Other questions are important to discuss as well, to which extent a child is an active shaper of their environment or passively exposed to maturational processes, whether development can be generalized across domains or cultures or not. However, discussing all aspects goes beyond the scope of this chapter, and the reader is referred to other sources.

The Effect of Age and Time on Development

Developmental change is often related to age. Around their first birthday, children start to speak their first words and to make their first independent steps. This age is one of the major milestones and results in the terminological shift of a child from being called "infant" (from Latin *infans* = unable to speak) to "toddler" (that describes the particular type of toddling locomotion, observed at this age). However, this uni-dimensional focus on age has limitations. Age is only one possible factor related to developmental change. It furthermore comes in different units. Usually, developmental change is described as taking place in weeks, months, or years. However, changes occur in the course of days, hours, minutes, or even seconds. One prominent example of short-term but extensive changes is the child's physical adjustment processes from at birth when regular breathing and ventilation of the lungs have their onset, as well as the switch from parallel fetal to postnatal serial cardiac circulation. Next to maturational processes, changes are triggered by significant life events that are not necessarily or not at all related to age. These events can be positive, as the beginning of the first romantic relationship or the birth of a child. The events can also be negative, like the death of a loved one or being confronted with a serious illness or job loss. Finally, development includes the aspect of stabilization, that is, the deliberate control of non-change by maintaining cognitive and motor functions in old age, whereby stabilization at a certain level usually implies changes at other levels at the same time.

Nature vs. Nurture

One of the questions developmental psychologists (and researchers from many other fields) discuss is how much the genes (i.e., *nature*) and the environment (i.e., *nurture*) contribute to an individual's development, in particular to the plasticity in brain structure and function (Meaney, 2010). The difficulty to answer these questions becomes obvious in the fact that nature and nurture are often regarded as being "in contrast to" each other. Furthermore, it is often expected to know which factor influences an individual's development more strongly, be it in an "either-or" answer or at least in a precise quantification (e.g., in percentages) of the respective influence. The impression that the contribution of nature and nurture can be quantified is often inferred from twin and adoption studies, for example, on intelligence. The results of these studies are usually reported as a quantified correlation between the intelligence of siblings that is stronger for monozygotic (MZ) than dizygotic twins or regular siblings being raised together (e.g., Plomin, DeFries, Craig, & McGuffin, 2003; Plomin & Spinath, 2004). This information is important to understand the interplay between genes and the environment. However, one might be inclined to misinterpret a correlation of $r = 0.86$ (e.g., for MZ twins, Plomin & Spinath, 2004) as a value about the percentage of genetic influence that holds for each individual, which it is not.

This does not mean that there aren't cases that can be quantified, quite the opposite: Eye color and natural hair color are primarily defined by our genes with little to no potential for changes caused by the environment. In contrast, while the ability of humans to speak and process language is an innate feature of the human brain in combination with the human vocal tract, the specific language a person speaks is exclusively defined by the linguistic environment in which this person is born and grows up.

The specific paths from biology to behavior continue to remain an issue for further investigation (Meaney, 2010). Before starting, we need to define two important terms: the *genotype* is the complete heritable genetic identity of an individual, and the *phenotype* is the description of an individual's characteristics, including appearance, behavior, and general disposition. There are several possible ways how genes and environment interact in the development and result in the particular genotype and phenotype of an individual. The interaction can be *passive*, for example, parents provide an environment that correlates with their own predispositions (parents inherit genes and environment); evocative, the child's predispositions evoke certain reactions in others; and *active*, individuals seek out niches that correspond to their predispositions:

1. *Genotype → Genotype:* The most obvious path is that the genotype of parents is combined and transferred to the genotype of their children when the egg is fertilized and genes and chromosomes are inherited by the offspring.
2. *Environment → Phenotype:* It is not only the genotype but also an individual's environment that influences an individual's phenotype. The genotype provides the potential of a phenotype to be expressed, but this potential is influenced by the particular environment a child grows up in.
3. *Phenotype → Environment:* Vice versa, a child's phenotype can likewise influence their environment. Imagine parents having a colicky, that is, a baby who suffers from colics and, as a result, cries a lot. These parents' responses to their

child probably differ from the same parents' responses to non-colicky. They are likely to be more exhausted and will, as a result, be less responsive to the colicky, which might have an impact on his/her attachment pattern and, thus, his/her phenotype.

4. *Genotype → Environment:* The individual genotype influences the individually chosen environment. A child that has a genetic preference for listening to and playing music will prefer a different kind of environment (e.g., taking music lessons, meeting friends with similar interests) than a child with a genetically determined preference for visual arts or doing sports. Accordingly, children seek their niche based on their (genetically determined) interests.

5. *Environment → Phenotype:* Siblings typically grow up in the same family, that is, in a similar environment, and the *shared environmental influences* are sources of behavioral similarity. But siblings are often found to be dissimilar (e.g., Plomin & Spinath, 2004). These differences can – to some extent – be traced back to the *nonshared environmental influences*, the sources of behavioral dissimilarity. For example, parenting practices might differ based on whether a child is the first or the last born; the home environment may change due to the move of a family to a new place at the point in time the second child is born (e.g., Tarantino et al., 2014), resulting in differences between siblings.

6. *Environment → (Epi)genotype:* Finally, environmental influences, such as nutrition, education, and substance use, can influence the function of an individual's genes. Importantly, it is not the genome (i.e., the genetic material of an organism) that is changed, but the epigenome (i.e., a multitude of chemical compounds that "tell the genome what to do"; for further information, see Meaney, 2010).

The Difficulty of Differentiating Between the Influence of Nature and Nurture, an Example

A second aspect of the difficulty to answer the abovementioned question about the individual impact of nature and nurture lies in the scope for interpretation of the data. To explain this, we refer to the story of the three little pigs (adapted from Lindenberger, 2013). In this story (following roughly the rhymes of the US Band Green Jellÿ), the mother of three little pigs had not enough to keep them and sent them out to seek their fortune. The first little pig went off, found a grainfield, and built a house from straw. The second little pig found a forest and built a house from wood. The third pig found a stone quarry and built a house from stones. Then, the big, bad, and hungry wolf appeared at each of the three houses and yelled "Little pig, little pig, let me in!". The little pigs refused, and the wolf started to blow their houses in. He was successful with the houses of straw and wood, but not with the one of stones.

This story can be seen as scientific observation, and the data can be interpreted as evidence for both the influence of nature and nurture on the (un)successful development of the individual pigs. In support of an influence of nature, it provides evidence for genetically based differences in "house-building" intelligence. Only the third little pig has inherited enough intelligence to build a house solid enough to serve as a secure home. In contrast, the same data are evidence in support of an effect of the environment: Each little pig found – more or less by accident – material that can be used to build a house. And it was only good or bad luck which little pig found which material. If the first little pig would have taken another road, he would have found stones and built a house from them instead of straw and, as a consequence, survived. Accordingly, depending on the perspective, the very same data can serve as evidence for both perspectives.

The question about the influence of nature and nurture is today discussed in a very differentiated way. The adherence to extreme positions is no longer tenable today, nicely framed by Spencer, Thomas, and McClelland (2009): "The nativist-empiricist debate [...] continue[s] to distract attention from the reality of developmental systems" (p. 79). These authors suggest using a developmental systems approach and argue that it embraces the concept of epigenesis, that is, the view that development emerges via cascades of interactions across multiple levels of causation, from genes to environments. According to this view, development always takes place as a dynamic interaction of both genes and environment (e.g., Meaney, 2001). We will discuss this in more detail later (section "A Potential Candidate for an Integrative Theory: The Dynamic Systems Theories").

Continuous vs. Non-continuous Development

A second controversially discussed question is whether idea development proceeds as a discontinuous series of distinct and stepwise levels or as smooth and more or less continuous progress. The idea of a discontinuous development has several roots: First are several prominent theoretical approaches such as the genetic epistemology by Piaget (e.g., Piaget, 1954), the theory of psychosocial development by Erikson and Erikson (e.g., Erikson & Erikson, 1998), the theory of stages of moral development by Kohlberg (e.g., Kohlberg, 1973), attachment theory by John Bowlby (e.g., Bowlby, 1999), the theory of human development and education by Havighurst (e.g., Havighurst, 1972), or Sigmund Freud's theory of psychosexual development (e.g., Freud, 1930). Second is the idea of sensitive phases, that is, phases in development of increased plasticity (e.g., Werker & Hensch, 2015) suggest that development seems to proceed in a discontinuous way with phases of developmental accelerations. Third, the way how empirical findings are reported suggests a stage-like development, for example, when children at the age of 12 months do use index finger pointing but not yet at the age of 10 months. Finally, nature provides numerous examples for (seemingly) discontinuous development, be it a caterpillar that pupates and then becomes a butterfly or in the form of *Dicrocoelium dendriticum* (D.D.), a small parasite fluke that lives in ruminant mammals such as cows and sheep and that has a fascinating life cycle including the digestive tract of snails to the submandibular ganglion of ants, to the final host, cows and sheep (who eat the ants), where D.D. then lives out their adult lives inside the animal and the cycle of reproduction starts over again. These examples emphasize relatively long states of (relative) stability rather than the (seemingly) short phases of transition from one state into another and might be interpreted that the development of an individual is as a series of distinct stages where the individual on one stage has little similarities with the same individual on a different stage.

However, the transition from one stadium to the next is by no means an abrupt step, and there are vast examples from nature and cognitive development that suggest that development may likewise follow a continuous trajectory. Like trees grow, vocabulary size, the number of solved mathematical problems, processing speed, and working memory continuously increase across childhood. These are facts that brought different theorists to assume that development seems to follow a rather continuous trajectory (e.g., Munakata, Snyder, & Chatham, 2012).

How can these two opposing viewpoints be brought together? To explain this, we refer to the idea of two different perspectives on development (e.g., Thelen & Smith, 1996), a view-from-above (*macro-view*) and a view-from-below (*micro-view*) on development. In the macro-view, ontogeny is described as a continuous, linear process, displaying regularity, with a clear direction and being irreversible. In contrast, from a micro-view, development appears to be "messy" and depends on the context and situational constraints. This idea has been further developed by Adolph et al. (2008; see, e.g., Fig. 2, p. 530). They measured the development of independent standing on a day-to-day basis which resulted in different developmental patterns: Some infants exhibited an abrupt, irreversible, and stagelike development from independent standing being absent on 1 day to being present the next day. Other infants had more variable developmental trajectories, where independent standing being present or absent oscillated over the course of several days to weeks.

To sum up, continuities and discontinuities seem to exist alongside one another, and their relative salience depends very much on the perspective and each individual's development. Continuous development might be missed or overlooked because phases of relative stability are more salient than the phases of transition. And it is to date not clear whether discontinuities are real or just accelerations in underlying continuous processes (van Geert, 1998).

Nomothetic vs. Idiographic Research Approaches

The third example refers to the question of whether developmental science should search for universal valid laws (i.e., *nomothetic* research; from the Greek "nomos," which means "law," and "thesis" meaning "to build") or focus on individual development (i.e., *idiographic* research; from the Greek "idios" meaning "own" or "private" and "graphos" meaning "drawn" or "written"). Nomothetic theories abstract from phenomena. They represent a widely applied way of thinking in the natural sciences. Usually, the average values of a whole group of participants or population are analyzed to formulate predictions about how people perceive, act, or feel. The strength of nomothetic research lies in the possibility to make at least an estimate for a prediction of behavior, the investigation of larger groups, and the application of objective methods that allow for replication and generalization. Limitations lie in the fact that the predictions only provide a rough estimate and that the group averages may not necessarily apply to the individuals constituting the group. Idiographic research, in contrast, investigates the individual. The idea is that predicting what a particular person will do in a particular situation cannot be based on group averages but needs to take into account the individual more strongly.

To illustrate the importance of disentangling the two, we refer to a (hypothetical) example by Hamaker (2012). It describes the relationship between the speed of typing on a keyboard (number of words per minute) and the percentage of typos made. The intuitive expectation is that faster typing is correlated with an increase in typos. This is true when looking at the intra-individual (idiographic) level. In contrast, when looking at the inter-individual (nomothetic) level, the results counterintuitively suggest that faster typing is related to fewer typos. The reason for this counterintuitive finding is that on a group level, more experienced typers both type faster and make fewer typos. Hamaker (2012) concludes that "qualifying large sample research as nomothetic, and thus – indirectly – as more scientific than other approaches because it is concerned with finding general laws, is erroneous" (p. 44). For this reason, the nomothetic approach has been accused of losing sight of the individual person. But yet, a substantial amount of Developmental Psychology research still applies a nomothetic research approach.

Application in Teaching

Vignette 1: Nature vs. Nurture

Paul comes from a family where his parents, grandparents, siblings, cousins, uncles, and aunts have great talent as musicians. All the members of the larger family play at least one instrument, some of the older family members are professional musicians, and some of the younger members think about doing so. Paul's friend Peter has a rather different family situation than Paul. None of the members of his immediate or extended family has any affiliation with music.

It does not require a great deal of expertise to assume that Paul is significantly more likely to become a professional musician than Peter. The question is whether this means that chances are 100% that Paul will be a musician and love to play an instrument and 0% that Peter will do so? Of course not. However, there are reasons that Paul has a higher genetic predisposition for musical talent as well as an environment that supports and facilitates such talent. Yet, both, one, or neither of them might become a musician.

Vignette 2: Continuous vs. Non-continuous Development

Sarah and Lynn are enthusiastic mountaineers who are standing at the base of the Matterhorn. They plan to go all the way up to the peak of that mountain and are discussing potential strategies on how to manage their forces. Sarah views the climb as a steady path and suggests making a pause every hour. But Lynn focuses more on distinct sections of the climb such as steeper and less steep parts, a plateau, and a small mountain shelter and suggests adjusting the timing of the climb to these stages.

These two views reflect the views of continuous and discontinuous development. The continuity view says that development is a gradual and cumulative process, just like a steady ascent that leads to the top of the mountain. In contrast, the discontinuity view says that development consists of a series of stages that are qualitatively different from each other, just like walking a series of stages, or steps, to get to the top of that mountain. But in the end, both views describe the same climb to the summit of the Matterhorn.

Theories of Development

From these different questions of scientific dispute and historical contexts, different theoretical views have emerged, given the respective *Zeitgeist* and the available research techniques. These different views have been described at numerous places, and we will only describe them briefly in Table 1 but do not describe them in greater detail at this place.

We will, however, spend some time on the description of an (actually not so) recent theoretical approach that originates from mathematics and the natural sciences and that combines some parts of these previous ones: the *dynamic systems theories* (DSTs, e.g., Thelen & Smith, 2007). DSTs do not adopt an either-or perspective. DSTs try to answer what can be considered the *core question* of all developmental sciences: How can the emergence of order (structure) from a diffuse initial state be explained? Or, as Smith and Thelen (2003) Running Head: Developmental Psychology 17 wrote "How does the human mind, with all its power and imagination, emerge from the human infant, a creature so unformed and helpless?" (p. 343). DSTs have been developed to explain developmental change through processes of self-organization and emergence. DSTs, therefore, aim to include many of the variables influencing development; short- and long-term experiences; changes in cognition, motor behavior, and motivation, as well as in physiology; and context.

A Potential Candidate for an Integrative Theory: The Dynamic Systems Theories

Definitions
We start by defining the basic elements of DSTs. A *system* is a set of distinct elements connected by recursive relationships. A *systems theory* helps to explain what processes cause pattern formation and change in a system of elements and how it is possible for qualitatively new properties to emerge in the process. Central concepts of DSTs are *self-organization* and *emergence*, that is, systems can generate novelty through their own activity. *Self-organization* means that the parts of a system are coordinated without an organizational (executive) entity that provides explicit instructions and that the pattern and the order of occurrence *emerge* from the dynamic interactions of the components of the (complex) system (Thelen & Smith, 2007). Emergence can be observed when an entity has properties not inherent in its single parts but only emerge when these parts interact. Numerous fascinating examples in nature are based on emergence. The flocking of birds can be described by three very simple processes (Reynolds, 1987):

1) Collision avoidance: Individuals should maintain a minimum distance between nearby animals to avoid collisions.

Table 1 Brief descriptions including exemplary theories and main authors of different theoretical perspectives

Theoretical perspective	Main assumptions	Exemplary theories and main authors
Biology	The development in all domains (motor, emotions, cognition, etc.) is rooted in the biologically determined maturation of the body and the brain. Often behavior (e.g., the inborn reflexes) is considered as being adaptive and having a survival value. The grasping reflex is seen as being adaptive because it allows the newborn child to cling to its mother's fur	Maturational theory (Arnold Gesell); ethological theory (Konrad Lorenz)
Learning	Based on the ideas of Aristotle and Locke (among others), development is seen as learning from experiences an individual makes. The learning can occur as a basis of reinforcement, which increases the likelihood of a behavior to be learned or punishment, which reduces this likelihood. The observation that children learn without reinforcement and punishment has led Bandura to the conclusion that children try actively to understand what other people are doing and whether or not to learn from them	Behaviorism (John Watson); classical (Pavlov) and operant (Skinner) conditioning; social cognitive theory (Albert Bandura)
Psychodynamic	Development is mainly determined by conflicts individuals are confronted with during different phases of the lifespan and, in particular, how well individuals solve these conflicts. The nature of these conflicts differs in the theories, Freud emphasizes psychosexual aspects, Erikson and Erikson focus on psychosocial aspects, and Havighurst focuses on developmental tasks in different stages of the lifespan	Psychosexual development (Sigmund Freud); psychosocial development (Erik H and Joan Erikson); developmental tasks (Robert Havighurst)

(continued)

Table 1 (continued)

Theoretical perspective	Main assumptions	Exemplary theories and main authors
Cognitive development	(Cognitive) Development is mainly determined by changes in children's thinking as they grow older. The most prominent candidate is Piaget's theory of genetic epistemology in which he emphasizes changes in children's thinking by a process of adaptation in which new information results in either the adaption of the child's own thinking (accommodation) or the reinterpretation of the information based on existing schemas (assimilation). He describes four distinct phases of development (sensorimotor, preoperational, concrete operational, and formal operational)	Genetic epistemology or constructivism (Jean Piaget)
Moral development	Piaget and after him Kohlberg formulated a stage theory for moral development in which children progress in their moral thinking as a result of their advances in cognitive development	Theories of moral development (Jean Piaget, Lawrence Kohlberg)
Context	Similar to learning theories, contextual theories oppose to some extent the idea of purely maturational processes taking place during development. These theories emphasize socio-cultural context as determining development. This context can refer to culture, to the specific language that is spoken that transfers knowledge in a language-specific way, that differs between different languages	Social constructivism (Lew Vygotsky, Luria), the bioecological model (Urie Bronfenbrenner), shared intentionality (Michael Tomasello), personality influenced by context (Walter Mischel)
Dynamic systems (see section "A Potential Candidate for an Integrative Theory: The Dynamic Systems Theories")	Development is determined by the dynamic interaction between changes in the individual in the particular	See different forms of application of the DST in Developmental Psychology

(continued)

Table 1 (continued)

Theoretical perspective	Main assumptions	Exemplary theories and main authors
	environment. Dynamic system means that a system (e.g., a child growing up in an environment) consists of elements that change over time. Development is a continuous interaction of all the levels of the developing system, from molecules to culture	by Esther Thelen, Linda B. Smith, or Paul van Geert
Information processing	The human cognitive system is compared to a computer with hardware (structure) that includes memory (short-term and long-term), processing units (processing speed), and input and output units and software including strategies and content. Development is determined by changes in information processing by the human cognitive system: the increase in processing speed, working memory capacity, and automated information processing, the use of more efficient strategies, an increase in knowledge content	

2) Velocity matching: Individuals should attempt to match velocity with nearby flockmates.

3) Flock centering: Individuals should attempt to stay close to nearby flockmates. Accordingly, the seemingly complex flocking behavior emerges from the particular (and simple) way individuals interact with each other. There is no innate, pre-specified movement pattern in these individuals, and there is no alpha individual telling the others how to move.

Application of DSTs to Development

The ideas of self-organization and emergence in combination with multi-causality have a long tradition in the natural sciences. Dynamic systems have been formulated as an area of mathematics and physics and in the areas of electrical networks, biological processes, and national economies. And while the idea of DSTs as guiding principles of development seems to be a relatively recent development, first approaches to this line of thinking have already been formulated by researchers such as Waddington, Lewin, or Gesell. These authors have formulated hypotheses according to which development occurs as a result of the interplay of a multitude of external and internal factors. Only recently, the ideas of the development of mind and behavior based on emergence and self-organization have been taken up more systematically by developmental psychologists who started to interpret salient developmental changes such as the development of walking or the A-not-B-Error from a DST perspective (for overviews, see Thelen & Smith, 2007; van Geert, 2017). Smith and Thelen (2003) conclude that "Developmental change evolves from the real-time activities of the infant" (p. 347). Complex systems self-organize to produce cohesive patterns, and due to the multi-causal nature and different timescales, development becomes highly non-linear and sometimes highly sensitive to initial conditions during particular developmental phases. Smith and Thelen conclude "that small changes in one or more components of the dynamic system can lead to reorganisation and large differences in behaviour" (p. 347).

Application of DSTs to Existing Developmental Theories

The idea of development as a self-organizing process in which novel patterns emerge has not only been applied to individual phenomena but also been related to explain and extend previously formulated broader theoretical considerations. Here, we highlight one prominent example by Thelen and Smith (1996) and van Geert (1994, 2017) who applied DSTs to explain the process of adaptation in Piaget's theory of genetic epistemology (from the Greek *genetikos* = related to the formation; *episteme* = science, knowledge; and *logos* = reason). Piaget considered development to proceed in relatively short periods of transition intermitted by relatively long periods of stability. Van Geert (2017) describes the cognitive structures in these periods of stability as a system of "related, interacting, or interdependent components that, as a consequence of those relationships, form a unified whole" (p. 21). In the course of development, these structures are subject to change. Van Geert defines two distinct forms, *structure-preserving change* and *structure-altering change*. Structure-preserving change is observed when components of the system and their relations are changed but the higher-order structure remains unchanged. Piaget described this process as *assimilation*. Structure-altering change, in contrast, occurs when the current structure (or schema) cannot be applied any longer to a current problem. As a consequence, the schema has to be adjusted, which Piaget referred to as *accommodation*.

Van Geert (1998, 2017) brings together the basic principles of Piaget's theory with DSTs. Both approaches overlap with the notion of a self-organizing system with dynamic transformations, self-maintaining attractor states, resistance to perturbation (assimilation), return to stability after perturbation, and the existence of self-maintaining states over longer periods of time. However, DSTs add one particular explanation for which Piaget struggled, the development of novel (cognitive) structures. DSTs use the concept of emergence in the sense that structure or its components and their relationships "may, under certain conditions, spontaneously result in the arising [i.e., emergence] of novel properties" (van Geert, 2017, p. 22). In contrast to Piaget who describes the developing child as being actively involved in the construction of her/his cognition and behavior, the genesis of cognitive structure and behavioral patterns is the consequence "of activity patterns governed by deep properties of organisation of the brain-body-world system" (van Geert, 2017, p. 23), with the components interacting on several different timescales (Fischer & van Geert, 2014; van Geert, 1998). To sum up, according to DSTs, the emergence of cognitive structure is not based on some form of pre-existing internal or external construction plan; rather, emergent patterns result spontaneously from simple activity principles in the interacting individuals.

To conclude, DSTs have the potential to explain and integrate several different previously formulated theoretical approaches beyond constructivist approaches such as those formulated by Piaget or Vygotsky. They share with nativist theories the idea of core processing mechanisms; however, they differ in that DSTs do not assume any form of core knowledge or modules. They share with learning theories that information and acquired experience result in a change of existing "schemas." DSTs thus have the potential to bridge the gap between opposing views and allow to move beyond either-or thinking by integrating ideas from different perspectives under the core assumptions of emergence and self-organization.

Application in Teaching

Vignette 3: Different Theories on the Development of Drawing

Max is a 4-year-old boy who is developing his drawing skills. Over the past few weeks, Max's drawing skills have improved significantly. Why? What has brought about this change? Let's try to describe the emergence of Max's drawing skills through the lens of some of the most important theoretical perspectives on development. According to biological theories, the ability to draw is determined by the maturation of certain brain structures responsible for fine motor skills. Differently, learning and contextual theories ascribe the improvement of Max's drawing skills to his experience and practice in this activity and to the reinforcement he received from both his parents and teachers. Finally, according to dynamic systems theories (DSTs), the development of Max's drawing skills reflects the interaction between his developmental changes (i.e., cognition, motor, motivation) in the particular environment he grows up in. Although the first two approaches make important contributions in explaining the emergence of a specific skill, they only focus on only one single aspect of development. In contrast, DSTs provide an integrated view of development, by trying to combine different perspectives.

Vignette 4: Dynamic Systems Theories vs. Piaget's Theory of Genetic Epistemology

Jeff and Kate are two passionate young chefs who just opened their own restaurants in Manhattan. Both are very creative and meticulous in the preparation of their dishes, but they follow different paths and procedures to create new culinary specialties. Jeff likes to creatively combine products and ingredients that are already available in his kitchen, while Kate, in addition to combining the ingredients she already owns, sometimes generates a new product (i.e., spices, cheeses) that she will use for her dishes.

These two culinary techniques reflect the DSTs and Piaget's theory on development. Piaget's theory describes development as the consequence of activity patterns characterized by deep properties of organization of the brain and body system, like a well-equipped kitchen that already has all its ingredients and products to create unique delicacies. In contrast, according to DSTs, a cognitive structure and patterns may result in the emergence of novel properties, just as a dish created from new ingredients.

Research Methods

In the previous sections, human development was discussed from a theoretical and historical perspective. However, to validate or refute theoretical considerations, empirical data is essential. In the following, we will discuss different approaches to how developmental change can be assessed. We start with the differentiation between two main categories, quantitative and qualitative methods, and then move to different designs to assess developmental change.

Qualitative and Quantitative Research Methods

In general, two main research directions are applied, described as qualitative and quantitative research methods (Przyborski & Wohlrab-Sahr, 2013). *Qualitative research* approaches aim to reconstruct phenomena, to generate hypotheses and theories. The methods are often not standardized, exploratory with open questions such as "What kind of practices and values are predominant in different cultures? Are there common practices between cultures and what do they mean?". Typical data collection methods are naturalistic observations, group discussions, or narrative interviews.

The major goal of *quantitative research* approaches is to make phenomena measurable, to test hypotheses and theories empirically using rigorous statistical analyses. Typical testing situations are highly standardized to reduce the amount of noise in the data and the potential for confounding factors as much as possible. Typical questions include "Are certain cultural values present in a group of people?" or "Do persons who have a strong expression of the cultural value x also have a strong expression of y?". Typical methods of data collection include standardized questionnaires, experiments, and systematic interventions. The two approaches are not as clear-cut as often assumed. For this reason, it has been suggested to distinguish between standardized and reconstructive methods or between hypothesis-testing and theory-building studies.

Research Designs

The discovery that infants have visual preferences for certain patterns (e.g., faces) over others (e.g., monochrome areas; Fantz, 1963) has provided looking time as a powerful measure to assess infants' perception and cognition. More recent technical advances in the application of eye tracking, encephalography (EEG), functional near-infrared spectroscopy (fNIRS), functional magnetic resonance imaging (fMRI), magnetoencephalography (MEG), and other neurophysiological techniques to developmental populations have provided a large variety of measurement techniques that can be applied to assess the development of mind and behavior even in very young children.

Whichever technique is used, developmental researchers additionally need to consider how perception, cognition, and behavior change over time. Basically, there are two approaches to this question. Either, change is inferred (not measured!) from differences between the assessment of the behavior of different age groups (*cross-sectional assessment*). Or, change is measured by following the same groups across a certain amount of time (*longitudinal assessment*). Depending on the exact application of longitudinal research designs, for example, concerning the density of the measurement points, longitudinal designs can further be differentiated in sequential or microgenetic designs (Shaffer & Kipp, 2010).

Cross-Sectional Research Designs

In cross-sectional designs, different people from different age groups are studied at the same point in time. This approach allows us to identify age-related differences (but not changes). The possibility to collect data from different age groups in a short period of time is an advantage of the cross-sectional design. However, it also comes with limitations. Most importantly, participants in each age group are from different cohorts. This can cause so-called cohort effects: any difference between the age groups might be due to the different age or may reflect individual differences that characterize the members of different cohorts. Another limitation is that because each person is tested only at one point in time, it does not provide information about individual development and the respective (in)stability of individual development.

Longitudinal Research Designs

Already Vygotsky (1978) raised the concern that a cross-sectional approach primarily focuses on age-dependent and stable endpoints in development. Similarly, Adolph et al. (2008) stated that this kind of research has resulted in "a gallery of before and after snapshots, studio portraits of newborns, and fossilised milestones" (p. 527). With these static developmental pictures, little can be learned about developmental processes. This shortcoming is compensated for by longitudinal research paradigms. In a longitudinal design, the same cohort of participants is studied repeatedly over a certain period of time. Longitudinal designs allow the investigation of the change and stability of one specific aspect across time.

The advantages of longitudinal designs lie in the possibility to compare the developmental trajectories of different children and that actual development is measured and not only age differences. Disadvantages are that due to the repeated measurement and potentially resulting training effects, the study material is limited and longitudinal research takes time and requires (often substantially) more resources than cross-sectional research. The sample underlies selection effects in the sense that participants drop out for several reasons (relocation, limited desire to continue participating).

Sequential Research Designs

Sequential research designs (e.g., Schaie, 2015) combine the features of the two previously discussed designs, implying that participants from different age groups are studied repeatedly over a period of months/years. This allows to make both longitudinal and cross-sectional comparisons within and between cohorts and to control for cohort effects. In general, sequential designs are more efficient than standard longitudinal designs; however, they are even more expensive and time-consuming.

Microgenetic Research Designs

One major shortcoming of most longitudinal studies is that it often remains unknown what happens between the measurement points. According to Adolph et al. (2008), "sampling rates typically used by developmental researchers may be inadequate to accurately depict patterns of variability and the shape of developmental change" (p. 527). That is, when the sampling rate is chosen too low, it is not possible to say anything about the shape of a developmental trajectory, for example, whether it reflects a continuous or discontinuous transformation.

Microgenetic research paradigms are a potential tool to overcome this shortcoming. This method assesses developmental change in short-term intervals such as weeks or even days. Microgenetic assessments are defined by several key features (e.g., Siegler, 2016), for example, the observation needs to span the complete period in which a developmental change of a particular skill is expected to occur. Further, the frequency of the measurements during this period is high, optimally day-to-day observations either in the lab or at home. Microgenetic research paradigms have shed light on children's motor development (Adolph et al., 2008), strategies for solving problems (Siegler & Svetina, 2002), arithmetic skills (Siegler & Jenkins, 2014), memory (Coyle & Bjorklund, 1997), and language skills (Gershkoff-Stowe & Smith, 1997). A microgenetic research design is a powerful tool to document development and to infer the processes that give rise to change. At the same time, it requires a great effort from both scientific staff and participating parents; it is costly and time-consuming. The high measurement frequency often results in the measurement period being limited in time, reduced to days or a few weeks. In addition, in a microgenetic study, children's behavior change is stimulated to occur and, therefore, may not reflect what children would normally encounter in a real situation.

Summary

The big challenge in developmental research is to measure change and not only age differences. The description of the most commonly used paradigms suggests that there is no silver bullet that can be applied and researchers have to choose from the available options the technique and the design that is most suitable to address the formulated research question, given the available resources.

Application in Teaching

Vignette 5: Qualitative and Quantitative Research Methods

Lisa and Anne are two developmental psychologists who are planning to test altruistic behavior in children of primary school. They apply two different research strategies. Anne starts to schedule interviews with parents and teachers and to conduct structured observations of children's behavior at school. Lisa prepares standardized questionnaires and one computer experiment for her study in which she presents invented situations of different children who show different levels of helping behavior. While the children observe these situations, Anne measures their looking behavior and skin conductance as two dependent variables.

This example describes the two research approaches discussed at the beginning of this section: Anne applies a qualitative research approach, while Lisa applies a quantitative approach. The results of Anna and Lisa's studies will highlight different aspects of the same complex phenomenon. The combination of these methodological approaches provides important and complementary insights into the development of altruistic behavior.

Vignette 6: Longitudinal and Cross-sectional Research Designs

Alexander and Edward are two school psychologists who want to analyze the development of language in a group of elementary school children. Alexander chooses to analyze the development of the same group of children over time, while Edward prefers to test the language abilities of children of different ages and grades. Therefore, Alexander will test the development of language by employing a longitudinal design, whereas Edward will investigate the same phenomenon adopting a cross-sectional design. Over the years, Alexander, although he has undoubtedly gone through several dropouts, has gained important insights into the actual language development of individual children in an elementary school. On the other hand, Edward, albeit comparing children from different cohorts, was able to compare language development in children of different ages in a short period of time.

Exemplary Domain: Communication Development

Human infants are born with a predisposition to interact with other people. Infants notice contingencies between their own actions and the environment from the first weeks of life. Around the age of 3 months, infants interpret intentional actions as goal-directed.

The Saliency of Faces

One of the first visual stimuli a child is likely to see after birth is the face of the mother, the father, a midwife, or a pediatrician. Human faces and the look of the eyes are important sources of information in connection with an interaction with a social partner. From facial features, information can be extracted about the direction of attention (e.g., where someone is looking) and about their emotional state (e.g., whether someone is sad or happy). This information allows conclusions to be drawn about what someone is about to do (Baron-Cohen, 1995). Children have no prenatal experience of perceiving faces, but they show a preference for faces from birth (e.g., Valenza, Simion, Cassia, & Umilta, 1996). Even more, newborns prefer faces that look directly at them to faces that avert their gaze (Farroni, Massaccesi, Pividori, & Johnson, 2004), and they prefer faces with eyes open to faces with eyes closed

(Batki, Baron-Cohen, Wheelwright, Connellan, & Ahluwalia, 2000). This face preference suggests that children distinguish from birth between a social agent and a non-social physical object and respond to whether the face-bearing social agent wants to interact with them and whether to expect something interesting to learn from this person.

Infants are not only sensitive to the configuration of a face at birth; they rapidly develop a preference for certain faces thereafter. After only a few hours, infants prefer to look at the face of their mother to that of another woman (Bushneil, Sai, & Mullin, 1989). This preference increases in the first days of life with the length of time infants have seen their mother's face (Walton, Bower, & Bower, 1992).

Early Forms of Communication

Gaze Following

To communicate with and learn from others, other aspects than just the perception of faces are required. The direction of a person's gaze, for example, says something about what or where they are currently focusing their attention and who or what they might interact with next. The place a person looks marks the focus of their interest and their possible next action step. A shift of attention as a consequence of an observed gaze shift is shown by children as early as 3 to 6 months of age (Hood, Willen, & Driver, 1998). When children of this age see a face that suddenly directs their gaze to the left or right, they look more quickly at a subsequently appearing object if it appears in a position that is congruent with the direction of gaze than if it appears in an incongruent position. Even newborns show this shift of attention; however, they also need information on the movement of the eyes. They show the congruency effect only when the shift of gaze is observable (Farroni et al., 2004), while older children also shift their attention when observing a static image of a face with gaze directed to the side (Hood et al., 1998). Gaze following also depends on the context; toddlers between 12 and 18 months were more likely to follow a gaze shift when the observed agent had her eyes open compared to closed (Brooks & Meltzoff, 2002).

Joint Attention

Gaze following and pointing are crucial elements in understanding social behavior and are an early form of *joint attention*. Joint attention is characterized by the coordination of attention with another person regarding objects and events (Mundy & Newell, 2007). The development of joint attention is fundamental to the development of social and cognitive competencies and linguistic abilities. The frequency with which infants engage in joint attention is positively correlated with the development of their linguistic skills (Mundy et al., 2007), and joint attention influences information processing in 9-month-old infants (Striano, Chen, Cleveland, & Bradshaw, 2006).

Two types of joint attention are evident in infancy (Mundy & Newell, 2007): responding joint attention (RJA) and initiating joint attention (IJA). RJA refers to the infants' following of others' gaze and gestures; IJA involves infants' use of gestures and eye contact to direct others' attention to an object, event, or themselves. It is considered an involuntary and early system that develops in the first months of life. IJA "involves infants' use of gestures and eye contact to direct others' attention to objects, to events, and to themselves" (Mundy & Newell, 2007, p. 269). The function of IJA is to show or spontaneously seek to share interests or pleasurable experiences with others.

Development of Communication

Human communication is multimodal and involves verbal and nonverbal forms of information transmission. Infants start to communicate long before they speak their first words. By the end of the first year, children develop a gestural communication system that allows them to successfully interact with their caregivers (Bruner, 1983). Yet, along the course of the development, gestures and speech become closely connected for realizing effective and mature communication (McNeill, 1992).

In the next section, we will describe significant acquisitions that typically characterize the development of communication in early childhood. According to the interactionist theory, communication develops in the context of social interactions during which children try to interact with their social partners (Bohannon & Bonvillian, 1997; Callanan & Sabbagh, 2004). In this context, communication skills are considered as the result of a complex interaction between biological maturation, cognitive development, and dynamic linguistic environment.

In the past years, psycholinguists noticed that communication strategies can promote and improve language learning. For example, it has been observed that before the acquisition of productive language skills, infants recognize regularities of language and conversational turn-taking by playing reversible roles with their social partners (Bruner, 1983). Specifically, by 9 months of age, infants understand the alternation rules of social games, and if this regular alternation is interrupted, they might try to re-establish the alternation of turn-taking (Ross & Lollis, 1987).

Moreover, different research showed that caregivers often communicate with children using infant-directed speech (IDS, Kuhl, 2004), a speech mode that is typically characterized by exaggerated pitch (Cooper & Aslin, 1990), expanded intonation (Fernald & Simon, 1984), higher variable speech rate and rhythm (Lee et al., 2014; Leong et al., 2017), and lexical and syntactic modifications (Soderstrom, 2007). In particular, the intonation is modulated to communicate different messages to the infants (Katz, Cohn, & Moore, 1996). For example, to recapture the infant's attention, parents use it to increase the intonation, while to reassure or comfort the infant, they usually adopt a falling intonation. Previous evidence revealed that 2- to 6-month-old infants react with vocalizations characterized by an intonation similar to that produced by their parents (Masataka, 1992).

As the child's language improves, parents' infant-directed speech becomes longer and more complex. They start to respond to the child's incorrect speech by providing a correct and extended version of the child's statement (i.e., expansion). During the prelinguistic phase of development (from birth to 10–13 months of life), infants show clear sensitivity and responsivity to language. For example, while hearing speech, newborns usually open their eyes, look at the speaker, and by 2 months of age begin to use vocalization to communicate their needs (Rheingold & Adams, 1980; Rosenthal, 1982). By 4 to 6 months of age, infants start to babble by combining consonant and vowel sounds, and toward the end of the first year, children start to adjust their babbling to the tonal features of the language surrounding them (Blake & Boysson-Bardies, 1992; Davis & MacNeilage, 2000).

Toward the end of the first year of life, preverbal infants begin to use nonverbal communication such as gestures to interact with their social partners (Acredolo & Goodwyn, 1990). In particular, around 12 months of age, children usually show two types of preverbal gestures: "protoimperative" pointing and "protodeclarative" pointing. Protoimperative pointing is used to obtain an object (Baron-Cohen, 1989) and does not require a comprehension of others' mental states. On the other hand, protodeclarative pointing is used to direct the attention of another person toward something of interest to the infant. The use of protodeclarative pointing implies that the infant is aware of another person's mental state and, thus, could be considered an early indicator of the "theory of mind" (Baron-Cohen, 1989).

Even when children acquire advanced linguistic skills, they continue to use gestures to accompany speech or substitute missing words (Goldin-Meadow, 2000). Around 2 years, children acquire several pragmatic abilities that make them sensitive to other social features. The achievement of these pragmatic skills has a significant impact on efficient communication. For example, around 2 years of age, children learn to appropriately use vocal turn-taking and begin to show awareness about their partners' knowledge when they choose to discuss a specific topic. Moreover, children start to use some social communication norms, such as polite words when making requests (Baroni & Axia, 1989; Garton & Pratt, 1990). During the preschool period, children develop several conversational skills that help them to communicate more successfully. For example, at around 3 years of age, they begin to understand that the real meaning of an utterance may not always correspond to the literal meaning of the words (i.e., illocutionary intent). By age 6 to 7, children's communication and sociolinguistic skills enable them to adapt their speech to the needs of their listeners.

In conclusion, communicative development can be used as an example for the dynamics of development as proposed by dynamic systems theories because it is the result of a complex interaction between biological maturation and a highly dynamic social environment, which is constantly influenced by the child's interactions with their social partners (McKee & McDaniel, 2004; Tomasello, 1995).

Application in Teaching

Vignette 7: The Emergence of Joint Attention

Emily, a 5-month-old infant, has an older brother, Jack, who is 2 years old. Emily's dad loves to spend time on the mat with his little girl. However, during their interactions, he is often distracted by Jack, who loves to climb all over the place looking for new adventures. Emily's dad, therefore, while interacting with her, often turns his gaze toward Jack, and Emily will begin to observe her brother, following her father's gaze. When Emily turns 11 months, Jack's activities become of common interest for Emily and her dad. Indeed, Emily is now the one to call her father's attention (using pointing and eye contact) toward her brother's activities and to respond in turn with smiles and vocalizations when her father calls her attention to Jack.

This example well describes the emergence of social behavior. Emily learned to shift her attention as a consequence of her dad's gaze shift. Moreover, over the months, she showed an early form of *joint attention* behavior by both following her dad's gaze and directing his attention to her brother.

Vignette 8: The Development of Communication and Social Interaction

Peter is a very talkative and communicative 7-year-old who loves to tell jokes and chat with his parents and friends. How has he developed his social and communication skills? Peter's parents are very social people, who establish new friendships very easily. In addition, Peter's parents communicated with their child during all stages of his development, naturally adapting the form of communication to Peter's current communicative skills. For example, when Peter was a newborn, his mother communicated with him by using the so-called infant-directed speech to which Peter responded with vocalizations and body movements. With the passing of the months, the communication between Peter and his parents became progressively richer. Peter appreciated the first illustrated animal books that his parents used to name each animal by reproducing the verse (i.e., onomatopoeic words). At about 18 months, he began to name the animals in his books, by saying the onomatopoeic words corresponding to each animal. As the months went by, Peter's social and communication skills became more and more refined, thanks also to the continuous feedback and reinforcement he received from his parents. For example, around the age of 3 to 4, Peter began to learn to wait his turn to speak and that it was important to use polite words when making requests.

From this description, it is possible to infer that the development of social and communication skills derives from interaction with the environment, constantly influenced and stimulated by social interactions whose nature and type change over time.

Teaching, Learning, and Assessment in Developmental Psychology: Approaches and Strategies

We close this chapter with a brief and exemplary overview of how Developmental Psychology can be taught in class, what the important topics are that we think can be covered in a curriculum, how age groups are categorized across the entire lifespan, and what forms of teaching can be applied. Section (1) includes *relevant topics* which a Developmental Psychology syllabus can choose from, (2) describes how *age groups* are categorized across the lifespan, and (3) describes how the *topics can be taught in a class*, for example, by providing applied classroom demonstrations.

Relevant Topics

The potential content of the curriculum is rich because Developmental Psychology covers all aspects of Psychology with a particular emphasis on change over (particular phases of) the lifespan. When we start teaching Developmental Psychology in a new class, one of the first aspects to cover is to discuss the "big questions" of Developmental Psychology. Ultimately, all studies and theories are directed toward answering these big questions, although very specific aspects of development are examined during the course. In Table 2, we describe a selection of potential topics including some major keywords for each topic. The selection is by far not complete and rather represents a guiding proposal than a complete overview. To teach individual topics, the reader is referred to textbooks such as mentioned in the section Selected References.

Age Groups

As said before, Developmental Psychology covers all the aspects mentioned in Table 2 from the perspective of change across the entire lifespan (e.g., Daum et al., 2020; Schwarzer & Walper, 2016). Because body, mind, and behavior are subject to substantial changes over the lifespan, it is not always appropriate or even possible to compare the competencies across different age groups. Here, in line with previous thoughts, we suggest using the following broad categorization to differentiate between different phases of the lifespan: prenatal (before birth), neonatal or newborn period (up to 3 months after birth), infancy (Although often used in the literature, we suggest to refrain from the use of the term "preverbal infants." The word "infant" comes from Latin "infans" meaning "unable to speak." Accordingly, "preverbal infants" is a pleonasm.) (up to 1 year), early childhood (comprising toddlerhood (The term toddler comes from the "toddeling" gait of young children, the typical staggering and wobbling and yet unstable way of independent walking that is first observed around the child's first birthday.), 1–3 years, and preschoolers, 3–5 years), later childhood/school-aged children (6–10 years), adolescence, (early, 11–14 years; late, 15–17 years), young adulthood (18–29 years; this also includes the potential phase of emerging adulthood (e.g., Arnett, 2007)), middle adulthood (30–64 years), early older adulthood (65–84 years), and late older adulthood (85 years and older). Please note that these phases are not set in stone and that depending on competencies and inter-individual variability, the boundaries of these phases can be dynamic.

Suggestions on How to Teach Topics of Developmental Psychology

It is not our goal to provide a comprehensive list and description of specific teaching formats for particular topics of Developmental Psychology. This is covered by collections and textbooks that present different formats and empirical findings on

Table 2 Suggestions for topics to teach in Developmental Psychology and most important keywords

Topic	Major keywords
Basic foundations	
What is (child) development	Historical foundations: Questions of dispute; practical implications; societal relevance
Theories of development	Nature vs. nurture; active vs. passive child; nativism; behaviorism; core knowledge; constructivism; information processing; socio-cultural theories; dynamic systems; domain-specific vs. domain-general theories
Research designs to measure development	Cross-sectional; longitudinal; sequential cohort design; microgenetic
Basic functions	
Brain development	Brain maturation; brain plasticity; specialization of different brain areas and functions; critical/sensitive periods; development of neurons; neurotransmitters
Biology and behavior	Genes and environment and their interaction; differentiation of cells and structures; behavioral genetics; heritability; epigenetics; twin studies
Body growth	Anatomical development before and after birth; growth spurts; timing of growth
Motor development	Prenatal movements; reflexes and their function and plasticity; reaching and grasping; coordination of changing bodies; perception and action; locomotion; navigating in the environment
Perception	Sensation vs. perception vs. cognition; higher senses (vision, hearing); lower senses (taste, smell, touch, pain); object perception; face perception; depth perception; categorical perception; intermodal perception; multisensory integration
Cognition	Working memory; short-term memory; long-term memory; attention; information processing; executive functions (planning, shifting, and inhibition); cognitive flexibility
Knowledge about concepts	Artifacts; living entities; causality; objects, space, time, and numbers; play (pretend, sociodramatic)
Language	Preverbal and verbal communication; nonverbal communication; language acquisition; language spurt; multilingualism; gestures; use and understanding of symbols; infant-directed speech; sign language
Intelligence	Concepts of intelligence; measuring intelligence; IQ scores; predictive validity; heredity; genes X environment
School-related competencies	Reading; writing; mathematics; individual and collaborative learning; influence of teachers, parents, SES; use of gestures in teaching
Emotions	Primary emotions (anger, disgust, fear, happiness, sadness, and surprise); secondary emotions; self-related emotions; emotion expression; emotion understanding; emotion regulation; temperament; stress
Social cognition	Intersubjectivity; joint attention (joint action, following attention, directing attention); imitation; understanding intentions; theory of mind

(continued)

Table 2 (continued)

Topic	Major keywords
Self	Self-concept; mirror self-recognition; contingency detection; identity; self-esteem
Sex/gender differences	Biological, social, motivational, cognitive, and cultural influences; body image; gender identity; gender stability and flexibility
Moral development	Theories of moral development; prosocial behavior; antisocial behavior; moral judgment; aggression; altruism
Influences of context	
Attachment	Attachment theory; strange situation test; secure and insecure attachment; attachment network; cultural variations
Family relations	Parenting; parenting styles; parent-child interactions; family structures; family dynamics; socioeconomic context
Peer relations	Friendships; peer interactions; status in peer groups; bullying

how the design effective teaching (e.g., Buskist & Benassi, 2011; Chalmers & Fuller, 2012, Schneider & Mustafić, 2015). Our goal is to provide some applied examples about how the findings can be implemented in everyday teaching and how critical thinking can be fostered among students (and teachers; see Dunn, Halonen, & Smith, 2008, for a more in-depth discussion on teaching critical thinking).

Similar to other areas in Psychology, applied examples of the different topics can be found everywhere (see Vignette 2: Continuous vs. Non-continuous Development). The Ph.D. supervisor of one of the authors often suggested that research ideas are virtually lying on the street (Wilkening; 2002, personal communication). The vignettes attached to the individual sections are some (out of an infinite number of) examples of how a particular topic can be introduced in class. Some of them are particularly suitable for the format of a debate where two groups prepare the pros and cons of a respective point of view which are then discussed in a plenary discussion. Others are more suitable for thinking about different aspects of development. Contemporary textbooks provide many more examples for vignettes (see section Textbooks in the section "Teaching, Learning, and Assessment Resources") for some examples of suitable textbooks.

Examples for Applied Teaching Techniques

One of the most important issues when teaching Developmental Psychology is the aspect of how development can be measured (see section "Research Methods"). This aspect can easily be addressed in an applied way in class. Change not only occurs in periods of months and years, but more short-term changes and fluctuations such as heart rate or respiratory frequency can be made visible with the students. A short exemplary intervention study would include the measurement of a physical aspect such as heart rate and a cognitive aspect such as mathematical abilities in two groups of children at two measurement points. The members of an intervention and a control group are tested before and after running around the building for 10 min. Their performance will be compared to a control group of students who read a short story for the same duration of 10 min. With such a procedure, the effects of an intervention (physical activity) on both physical and cognitive (or emotional, etc.) performance can be made visible, and the effects of moderating factors such as sex, age, fitness, and math grades can be discussed and included in the analyses.

More systematically, students might be guided to work on a small research project in which they need to identify a theoretically grounded research question, formulate hypotheses, operationalize the research question, run a short experiment, analyze the data, and relate the results to the previously formed hypotheses. For the derivation of a *theoretical basis*, one promising approach is "theory mapping" (e.g., Gray, 2017). Theory mapping involves drawing out links between constructs using different elements such as associations, moderations, and fundamental elements. It can be used to develop a simple theoretical background from which a well-justified research question can be derived. *Assessing* development requires the application of sophisticated research technologies and differentiated material. It often requires extensive offline coding from previously recorded looks toward a monitor or the measurement of gaze behavior using eye-tracking technology. However, there are several easy-to-apply paper-pencil tests such as the Stroop Colour and Word Test (e.g., Stroop, 1935), the Grass/Snow Task (Carlson & Moses, 2001), or a Backward Digit Span Task (Davis & Pratt, 1995). Further, children's behavior can be assessed via structured observations on playgrounds or in childcare institutions. In this setting, research topics can include the use of pretend play (as an indicator for the social-cognitive development), the number of conflicts with peers (as an indicator for their pro- and antisocial behavior), and the number of utterances made in a period of, for example, 5 min (as an indicator of their language status). The data is then compared between the same child across different situations (to assess the intra-individual variability), between different children of the same age (to assess inter-individual variability), and between children of different age groups (to assess the effect of age and the accompanying age-related differences). These different types of approaches provide a set of tools with which Developmental Psychology can be experienced by students first-hand by systematically looking at how similar and how different children of different age groups are.

The final example highlights how students can experience directly how a particular competence such as language is acquired (http://www.devpsy.org ©). This can be achieved by employing a game in which students learn to acquire language solely through the ability to produce phonemes: the instructor will provide the students with shapes in different colors and sizes and a list of phonemes that they will have to associate to a specific characteristic (e.g., color, shape). The students will work in small groups. In each group, one student will produce a picture with the shapes, and he/she will use only phonemes to describe the picture to the other students who have the task of creating the same picture, but without seeing it. This game gives students an active role in their learning of how skills develop.

Challenges and Lessons Learned

To conclude, we aimed to provide a comprehensive and contemporary view on current topics particularly relevant when teaching Developmental Psychology. The chapter by no means intended to cover all aspects of Developmental Psychology. Even Developmental Psychology textbooks do not manage to do so. But we highlight some of the major questions and challenges discussed in the field. This includes statements such as (1) development is not just the maturation of the body and the brain; (2) development does not occur in a stepwise fashion; rather, (3) development occurs as an interaction between biological and environmental processes; (4) group means are not necessarily reflecting the development of an individuum; and (5) a growing child is constantly and dynamically changing and so is the content of the topic Developmental Psychology. With this, we hope to enrich the portfolio of Developmental Psychology teachers with information about the origins and future directions of Developmental Psychology with the ultimate goal to foster critical thinking about the development of individuals across the entire lifespan.

Teaching, Learning, and Assessment Resources

For recommendations and advice, please see the section above entitled "Suggestions on How to Teach Topics of Developmental Psychology."

Textbooks

Siegler, R. S., Saffran, J. R., Eisenberg, N., Gershoff, E. T., & Leaper, C. (2019). *How children develop* (6th ed.). Worth Pub.
Keil, F. (2013). *Developmental psychology: The growth of mind and behavior: international student edition*. W. W. Norton & Company.
Kail, R. V. (2015). *Children and their development* (Global ed.). Pearson Education Limited.
Tomasello, M. (2019). *Becoming human: A theory of ontogeny*. Harvard University Press.
German: Schneider, W., & Lindenberger, U. (2018). *Entwicklungspsychologie: Mit Online-Material* (Originalausgabe, 8., vollständig überarbeitete). Beltz.

Theories

van Geert, P. L. C. (1994). *Dynamic systems of development: Change between complexity and chaos* (pp. xii, 300). Harvester Wheatsheaf.

Specific Topics

Meaney, M. J. (2010). Epigenetics and the biological definition of gene × environment interactions. *Child Development, 81*(1), 41–79. https://doi.org/10.1111/j.1467-8624.2009.01381.x

Cross-References

▸ Basic Principles and Procedures for Effective Teaching in Psychology
▸ Developmental Psychology: Moving Beyond the East–West Divide
▸ Psychology in Social Science and Education
▸ Teaching the Foundations of Psychological Science

References

Acredolo, L. P., & Goodwyn, S. W. (1990). Sign language among hearing infants: The spontaneous development of symbolic gestures. *Springer Series in Language and Communication*, 68–78. https://doi.org/10.1007/978-3-642-74859-2_7

Adolph, K. E., Young, J. W., Robinson, S. R., & Gill-Alvarez, F. (2008). What is the shape of developmental change? *Psychological Review, 115*(3), 527–543. https://doi.org/10.1037/0033-295x.115.3.527

Arnett, J. J. (2007). Emerging adulthood: What is it, and what is it good for? *Child Development Perspectives, 1*(2), 68–73. https://doi.org/10.1111/j.1750-8606.2007.00016.x

Baltes, P. B. (1987). Theoretical propositions of life-span developmental psychology: On the dynamics between growth and decline. *Developmental Psychology, 23*(5), 611–626. https://doi.org/10.1037/0012-1649.23.5.611

Baron-Cohen, S. (1989). Perceptual role taking and protodeclarative pointing in autism. *British Journal of Developmental Psychology, 7*(2), 113–127. https://doi.org/10.1111/j.2044-835x.1989.tb00793.x

Baron-Cohen, S. (1995). *Mindblindness: An essay on autism and theory of mind*. Cambridge, MH: MIT Press.

Baroni, M. R., & Axia, G. (1989). Children's meta-pragmatic abilities and the identification of polite and impolite requests. *First Language, 9*(27), 285–297. https://doi.org/10.1177/014272378900902703

Batki, A., Baron-Cohen, S., Wheelwright, S., Connellan, J., & Ahluwalia, J. (2000). Is there an innate gaze module? Evidence from human neonates. *Infant Behavior & Development, 23*(2), 223–229.

Bischof, N. (2020). Life Span an der Lahn. *Psychologische Rundschau, 71*(1), 36–38.

Blake, J., & Boysson-Bardies, B. D. (1992). Patterns in babbling: A cross-linguistic study. *Journal of Child Language, 19*(1), 51–74. https://doi.org/10.1017/s0305000900013623

Bohannon, J. H., & Bonvillian, J. D. (1997). Theoretical approaches to language acquisition. *The Development of Language, 4*, 259–316.

Bowlby, J. (1999). *Attachment and loss: Vol. 1. Attachment* (2nd ed.). Basic Books.

Brooks, R., & Meltzoff, A. N. (2002). The importance of eyes: How infants interpret adult looking behavior. *Developmental Psychology, 38*(6), 958–966. https://doi.org/10.1037/0012-1649.38.6.958

Bruner, J. S. (1983). Play, thought, and language. *Peabody Journal of Education, 60*(3), 60–69. https://doi.org/10.1080/01619568309538407

Bushnell, I. W. R., Sai, F., & Mullin, J. T. (1989). Neonatal recognition of the mother's face. *British Journal of Developmental Psychology, 7*(1), 3–15. https://doi.org/10.1111/j.2044-835X.1989. tb00784.x

Buskist, W. F., & Benassi, V. A. (Eds.). (2011). *Effective college and university teaching: Strategies and tactics for the new professoriate* (1st ed.). SAGE.

Callanan, M. A., & Sabbagh, M. A. (2004). Multiple labels for objects in conversations with young children: Parents' language and children's developing expectations about word meanings. *Developmental Psychology, 40*(5), 746–763. https://doi.org/10.1037/0012-1649.40.5.746

Carlson, S. M., & Moses, L. J. (2001). Individual differences in inhibitory control and children's theory of mind. *Child Development, 72*(4), 1032–1053. https://doi.org/10.1111/1467-8624. 00333

Chalmers, D., & Fuller, R. (2012). *Teaching for learning at university.* Routledge.

Cooper, R. P., & Aslin, R. N. (1990). Preference for infant-directed speech in the first month after birth. *Child Development, 61*(5), 1584–1595. https://doi.org/10.1111/j.1467-8624.1990. tb02885.x

Coyle, T. R., & Bjorklund, D. F. (1997). Age differences in, and consequences of, multiple and variable-strategy use on a multitrial sort-recall task. *Developmental Psychology, 33*(2), 372–380. https://doi.org/10.1037/0012-1649.33.2.372

Daum, M. M., Greve, W., Pauen, S., Schuhrke, B., & Schwarzer, G. (2020). Positionspapier der Fachgruppe Entwicklungspsychologie: Versuch einer Standortbestimmung. *Psychologische Rundschau, 71*(1), 15–23. https://doi.org/10.1026/0033-3042/a000465

Daum, M. M., & Manfredi, M. (2021). The history of developmental psychology. *PsyArXiv.* https://doi.org/10.31234/osf.io/s2ckp

Davis, B. L., & MacNeilage, P. F. (2000). An embodiment perspective on the acquisition of speech perception. *Phonetica, 57*(2–4), 229–241. https://doi.org/10.1159/000028476

Davis, H. L., & Pratt, C. (1995). The development of children's theory of mind: The working memory explanation. *Australian Journal of Psychology, 47*(1), 25–31. https://doi.org/10.1080/ 00049539508258765

Dunn, D., Halonen, J. S., & Smith, R. A. (2008). *Teaching critical thinking in psychology a handbook of best practices.* Wiley-Blackwell.

Erikson, E. H., & Erikson, J. M. (1998). *The life cycle completed.* W. W. Norton & Company.

Fantz, R. L. (1963). Pattern vision in newborn infants. *Science, 140*(3564), 296–297. https://doi.org/10.1126/science.140.3564.296

Farroni, T., Massaccesi, S., Pividori, D., & Johnson, M. H. (2004). Gaze following in newborns. *Infancy, 5,* 39–60.

Fernald, A., & Simon, T. (1984). Expanded intonation contours in mothers' speech to newborns. *Developmental Psychology, 20*(1), 104–113. https://doi.org/10.1037/0012-1649.20.1.104

Fischer, K. W., & van Geert, P. L. C. (2014). Dynamic development of brain and behavior. In *Handbook of developmental systems theory and methodology* (pp. 287–315). The Guilford Press.

Freud, S. (1930). *Three contributions to the theory of sex: Authorized transl. By AA Brill. With introduction by James J. Putnam, and AA Brill.* Nervous and Mental Disease Publishing Company.

Garton, A. F., & Pratt, C. (1990). Children's pragmatic judgements of direct and indirect requests. *First Language, 10*(28), 51–59. https://doi.org/10.1177/014272379001002804

Gershkoff-Stowe, L., & Smith, L. B. (1997). A curvilinear trend in naming errors as a function of early vocabulary growth. *Cognitive Psychology, 34*(1), 37–71. https://doi.org/10.1006/cogp. 1997.0664

Goldin-Meadow, S. (2000). Beyond words: The importance of gesture to researchers and learners. *Child Development, 71*(1), 231–239. https://doi.org/10.1111/1467-8624.00138

Gray, K. (2017). How to map theory: Reliable methods are fruitless without rigorous theory. *Perspectives on Psychological Science.* https://doi.org/10.1177/1745691617691949

Hamaker, E. L. (2012). Why researchers should think "within-person": A paradigmatic rationale. In M. R. Mehl & T. S. Connor (Eds.), *Handbook of research methods for studying daily life* (pp. 43–61). Guilford.

Havighurst, R. J. (1972). *Developmental tasks and education* (3rd ed.). New York: David McKay Company.

Hood, B. M., Willen, J. D., & Driver, J. (1998). Adult's eyes trigger shifts of visual attention in human infants. *Psychological Science, 9*(2), 131–134. https://doi.org/10.1111/1467-9280.00024

James, W. (1890). *The principles of psychology.* Holt.

Katz, G. S., Cohn, J. F., & Moore, C. A. (1996). A combination of vocal f0 dynamic and summary features discriminates between three pragmatic categories of infant-directed speech. *Child Development, 67*(1), 205. https://doi.org/10.2307/1131696

Kohlberg, L. (1973). *Moral development.* McGraw-Hill Films.

Kuhl, P. K. (2004). Early language acquisition: Cracking the speech code. *Nature Reviews Neuroscience, 5*(11), 831–843. https://doi.org/10.1038/nrn1533

Lee, C. S., Kitamura, C., Burnham, D., & McAngus Todd, N. P. (2014). On the rhythm of infant-versus adultdirected speech in Australian English. *The Journal of the Acoustical Society of America, 136*(1), 357–365.

Leong, V., Kalashnikova, M., Burnham, D., & Goswami, U. (2017). The temporal modulation structure of infantdirected speech. *Open Mind, 1*(2), 78–90.

Lindenberger, U. (2013, September 10). Lifespan psychology: Challenges for the future. *21. Tagung Fachgruppe Entwicklungspsychologie.* Tagung der Fachgruppe Entwicklungspsychologie der DGPs, Saarbrücken.

Masataka, N. (1992). Pitch characteristics of Japanese maternal speech to infants. *Journal of Child Language, 19*(2), 213–223. https://doi.org/10.1017/s0305000900011399

McKee, C., & McDaniel, D. (2004). Multiple influences on children's language performance. *Journal of Child Language, 31*(2), 489–492. https://doi.org/10.1017/s0305000904006130

McNeill, D. (1992). *Hand and mind: What gestures reveal about thought.* University of Chicago Press.

Meaney, M. J. (2001). Nature, nurture, and the disunity of knowledge. *Annals of the New York Academy of Sciences, 935*(1), 50–61. https://doi.org/10.1111/j.1749-6632.2001.tb03470.x

Meaney, M. J. (2010). Epigenetics and the biological definition of gene × environment interactions. *Child Development, 81*(1), 41–79. https://doi.org/10.1111/j.1467-8624.2009.01381.x

Munakata, Y., Snyder, H. R., & Chatham, C. H. (2012). Developing cognitive control: Three key transitions. *Current Directions in Psychological Science, 21*(2), 71–77. https://doi.org/10.1177/0963721412436807

Mundy, P., Block, J., Delgado, C., Pomares, Y., Van Hecke, A. V., & Parlade, M. V. (2007). Individual differences and the development of joint attention in infancy. *Child Development, 78*(3), 938–954. https://doi.org/10.1111/j.1467-8624.2007.01042.x

Mundy, P., & Newell, L. (2007). Attention, joint attention, and social cognition. *Current Directions in Psychological Science, 16*(5), 269–274. https://doi.org/10.1111/j.1467-8721.2007.00518.x

Piaget, J. (1954). *The construction of reality in the child.* Basic Books.

Plomin, R., DeFries, J. C., Craig, I. W., & McGuffin, P. (2003). Behavioral genetics. In R. Plomin, J. C. DeFries, I. W. Craig, & P. McGuffin (Eds.), *Behavioral genetics in the postgenomic era* (pp. 3–16). American Psychological Association.

Plomin, R., & Spinath, F. M. (2004). Intelligence: Genetics, genes, and genomics. *Journal of Personality and Social Psychology, 86*(1), 112–129. https://doi.org/10.1037/0022-3514.86.1.112

Przyborski, A., & Wohlrab-Sahr, M. (2013). *Qualitative Sozialforschung: Ein Arbeitsbuch.* Walter de Gruyter.

Reinert, G. (1976). *Grundzüge einer Geschichte der Human-Entwicklungspsychologie.* Univ., Fachbereich I, Psychologie.

Reynolds, C. W. (1987). Flocks, herds and schools: A distributed behavioral model. *ACM SIGGRAPH Computer Graphics, 21*(4), 25–34. https://doi.org/10.1145/37402.37406

Rheingold, H. L., & Adams, J. L. (1980). The significance of speech to newborns. *Developmental Psychology, 16*(5), 397–403. https://doi.org/10.1037/0012-1649.16.5.397

Rosenthal, M. (1982). Vocal dialogues in the neonatal period. *Developmental Psychology, 18*(1), 17–21. https://doi.org/10.1037/0012-1649.18.1.17

Ross, H. S., & Lollis, S. P. (1987). Communication within infant social games. *Developmental Psychology, 23*(2), 241–248. https://doi.org/10.1037/0012-1649.23.2.241

Schacter, D., Gilbert, D., Wegner, D., & Hood, B. M. (2011). *Psychology: European edition.* Macmillan International Higher Education.

Schaie, K. W. (2015). Cohort sequential designs (convergence analysis). In R. L. Cautin & S. O. Lilienfeld (Eds.), *The encyclopedia of clinical psychology* (pp. 1–6). American Cancer Society. https://doi.org/10.1002/9781118625392.wbecp098

Schneider, M., & Mustafić, M. (2015). *Gute Hochschullehre: Eine evidenzbasierte Orientierungshilfe: Wie man Vorlesungen, Seminare und Projekte effektiv gestaltet.* Springer-Verlag.

Schwarzer, G., & Walper, S. (2016). Entwicklungspsychologie. In *Dorsch Lexikon der Psychologie.* Verlag Hans Huber. https://m.portal.hogrefe.com/dorsch/gebiet/entwicklungsp sychologie/.

Shaffer, D. R., & Kipp, K. (2010). *Developmental psychology: Childhood and adolescence* (8th ed.). Wadsworth/Cengage Learning. http://thuvienso.vanlanguni.edu.vn/handle/Vanlang_TV/11689

Siegler, R. S. (2016). Continuity and change in the field of cognitive development and in the perspectives of one cognitive developmentalist. *Child Development Perspectives, 10*(2), 128–133. https://srcd.onlinelibrary.wiley.com/doi/abs/10.1111/cdep.12173. https://doi.org/10.1111/cdep.12173

Siegler, R. S., & Jenkins, E. A. (2014). *How children discover new strategies.* Psychology Press.

Siegler, R. S., & Svetina, M. (2002). A microgenetic/cross-sectional study of matrix completion: Comparing short-term and long-term change. *Child Development, 73*(3), 793–809. https://doi.org/10.1111/1467-8624.00439

Smith, L. B., & Thelen, E. (2003). Development as a dynamic system. *Trends in Cognitive Sciences, 7*(8), 343–348. https://doi.org/10.1016/S1364-6613(03)00156-6

Soderstrom, M. (2007). Beyond babytalk: Re-evaluating the nature and content of speech input to preverbal infants. *Developmental Review, 27*(4), 501–532. https://doi.org/10.1016/j.dr.2007.06.002

Spencer, J. P., Thomas, S. C., & McClelland, J. L. (2009). *Toward a unified theory of development: Connectionism and dynamic systems theory re-considered.* Oxford University Press.

Striano, T., Chen, X., Cleveland, A., & Bradshaw, S. (2006). Joint attention social cues influence infant learning. *European Journal of Developmental Psychology, 3*(3), 289–299. https://doi.org/10.1080/17405620600879779

Stroop, J. R. (1935). Studies of interference in serial verbal reactions. *Journal of Experimental Psychology, 18*, 643–662.

Tarantino, N., Tully, E. C., Garcia, S. E., South, S., Iacono, W. G., & McGue, M. (2014). Genetic and environmental influences on affiliation with deviant peers during adolescence and early adulthood. *Developmental Psychology, 50*(3), 663–673. https://doi.org/10.1037/a0034345

Thelen, E., & Smith, L. B. (1996). *A dynamic systems approach to the development of cognition and action.* MIT Press.

Thelen, E., & Smith, L. B. (2007). Dynamic systems theories. In *Handbook of child psychology.* American Cancer Society. https://doi.org/10.1002/9780470147658.chpsy0106

Tomasello, M. (1995). Joint attention as social cognition. In C. Moore & P. J. Dunham (Eds.), *Joint attention: Its origins and role in development* (pp. 103–130). Lawrence Erlbaum Associates.

Trautner, H. M. (2003). *Allgemeine Entwicklungspsychologie.* Kohlhammer Verlag.

Valenza, E., Simion, F., Cassia, V. M., & Umilta, C. (1996). Face preference at birth. *Journal of Experimental Psychology-Human Perception and Performance, 22*(4), 892–903.

van Geert, P. L. C. (1994). *Dynamic systems of development: Change between complexity and chaos* (p. xii, 300). Harvester Wheatsheaf.

van Geert, P. L. C. (1998). A dynamic systems model of basic developmental mechanisms: Piaget, Vygotsky, and beyond. *Psychological Review, 105*(4), 634–677. https://doi.org/10.1037/0033-295X.105.4.634-677

van Geert, P. L. C. (2017). Constructivist theories. In B. Hopkins, E. Geangu, & S. Linkenauger (Eds.), *The Cambridge encyclopedia of child development* (2nd ed., pp. 19–34). Cambridge University Press. https://doi.org/10.1017/9781316216491.005

Vygotsky, L. S. (1978). *Mind and society: The development of higher mental processes*. Harvard University Press.

Walton, G. E., Bower, N. J. A., & Bower, T. G. R. (1992). Recognition of familiar faces by newborns. *Infant Behavior & Development, 15*(2), 269–265. https://doi.org/10.1016/0163-6383(92)80027-R

Werker, J. F., & Hensch, T. K. (2015). Critical periods in speech perception: New directions. *Annual Review of Psychology, 66*(1), 173–196. https://doi.org/10.1146/annurev-psych-010814-015104

Developmental Psychology: Moving Beyond the East–West Divide

11

Nandita Chaudhary, Mila Tuli, and Ayesha Raees

Contents

N. Chaudhary (✉)
Department of Human Development and Childhood Studies, Lady Irwin College, University of Delhi, Delhi, India

M. Tuli · A. Raees
Department of Human Development and Childhood Studies, Institute of Home Economics, University of Delhi, Delhi, India

© Springer Nature Switzerland AG 2023
J. Zumbach et al. (eds.), *International Handbook of Psychology Learning and Teaching*,
Springer International Handbooks of Education,
https://doi.org/10.1007/978-3-030-28745-0_14

Abstract

Developmental Psychology is the science of human growth and development across
the life span. Drawing from its parent discipline, Psychology's developmental subdiscipline has continued with a focus on Western, industrialized, and educated
populations while describing behavior. By eliminating cultural contexts from its
discourse, the discipline of Psychology has largely ignored the majority world in
constructing the notion of childhood and later development. Standards and norms are
mostly based on these assumptions. This chapter outlines some shortcomings of
mainstream Psychology and the impact this has had in creating a unidimensional,
narrow, and skewed understanding of human development and behavior. These
criticisms are not new. Yet the refusal to recognize the obvious continues to plague
the discipline. By choosing to align with the "scientific" methods of experimentation
and lab-based study developed by the physical sciences, by emphasizing standards
and norms of human behavior, by insisting on Western/European/American interpretations of behavior, Psychology has created a hegemonic discipline that still continues
to use the "one (costly) glove fits all" premise. Using research examples from Asia
(specifically India) and Africa, the chapter systematically demonstrates how well-
established tools, techniques, systems, and theoretical binaries are inadequate to
explain the diversity of human existence. Some instances of traditional, context-
specific ideas and wisdom have been shared to emphasize the need to recognize and
hear multiple voices. Using the cultural understanding of childhood as the focus, the
association between science and culture has also been examined. Furthermore, the
chapter introduces the student of Psychology to the idea of globally valid and
sustainable ideas to respond to the changing needs and situation of a new world order.

Keywords

Developmental psychology · Culture · Context · Methods · Childhood ·
Learning · Language

Introduction

Developmental psychology is the scientific study of growth, continuity, and changes
in a developing organism. It includes the exploration of different dimensions of
human behavior and psyche including physical, cognitive, language, social, and
emotional aspects across the life span. These domains relate to the specific tradition
of mainstream Psychology, the configuration of which can be remarkably different in
different traditions, although guided by similar preoccupations of understanding

human behavior and thought. Historically, the "objects of interest" for psychologists are constructed and can be vastly different based on problems, assumptions, and categories that cannot be reduced to specifics. Psychological categories are not "exempt from the flux of history" (Danziger, 1997, p. 12).

Some important developmental concerns relate to the contributions of nature and nurture and biological predispositions and the environment; descriptions of changes and continuity and the nature of transformations, and their stage-like quality. The primary objectives of the science are to be able to describe, understand, explain, and predict human behavior and to consolidate findings from research to expand and refine our theoretical understanding of life, from childhood to maturity and old age. In fulfilling these tasks, Developmental Psychology has accomplished a great deal. We now know a lot more about children's developing minds and activities, what they think about the world around them, their social relationships, and their fears. Yet, these descriptions have been collected from the study of a relatively small number of people and there has been a failure to adequately represent diversity, both by minimizing the study of contexts (Kagan, 2012), conceptual and practical debates (Burman, 1994/2017), and samples used for research (Henrich, Heine, & Norenzayan, 2010). A thorough examination of research studies over the years demonstrates a WEIRD bias in sampling (Western, Educated, Industrialized, Rich and Democratic societies) mostly easily accessible groups like University students. Despite intense criticisms and extensive debates there remains a persistent sampling bias in developmental research based on methodological (also see ▶ Chap, 18, "The Methodology Cycle as the Basis for Knowledge," by Valsiner and Branco, this volume) and theoretical preferences (Nielsen, Haun, Kärtner, & Legere, 2017).

The subject of Psychology can be reverse constructed through several channels, by looking at University curricula, research topics, contents of books, but we can also look another way, at public imagination. What do lay people understand as Psychology? Psychology in this space is understood as a body of work based largely on theories and experimentation related to self-knowledge, intimate relations, well-being, and therapy. A quick look at public libraries or bookstores will provide an easy access to this understanding. Yet, even in academic circles, higher education, and research laboratories, these domains are popular. In this sense, Psychology has failed to address worldwide concerns, and remains driven by a relatively narrow range of assumptions about human behavior that persist as epistemological errors caused by historical amnesia (▶ Chap. 46, "Epistemology of Psychology," by Jovanović, this volume).

In this chapter, we will reflect on several of these issues drawing from scholarly writing and social debates about content and processes and provide some alternative perspectives about the future of Psychology with social justice, sustainability, and inclusion.

Theoretical Perspectives and a Brief History

For the social sciences, context is constitutive. After all, it is our own selves and our connections to circumstances that we attempt to study. The person and environment are in constant dialogue and any attempt to separate these processes is artificial and incomplete. In the case of Psychology, phenomena are subjective, ephemeral, and even elusive, making access a constant challenge. Sensitivity to context, time, and person adds to the complexity of investigating phenomena that makes the template of the natural sciences, physics in particular, an inappropriate model for Psychology. This emphasis on observations, measurement, and objectivity resulted in significant gaps in the pursuit of our understanding of psychological phenomena. Despite the long-standing history of work on qualitative methodologies, the valuable contributions made to the field of psychology have not had the kind of impact on the discipline as in other social sciences (▶ Chap. 19, "Qualitative Methodology," by Mey, this volume). The acceptance of qualitative research in psychology has had limited expression, in the use of interviews and qualitative content analysis, and the mixed-methods paradigm (Demuth & Mey, 2015).

In an attempt to explain psychological phenomena, theories developed in limited contexts were adopted as universal principles, guidelines, and norms for behavior and development. Not unlike the blind men and their individual ideas of an elephant's form in a well-known tale (see notes below), the study of Psychology has been fragmented and incomplete, but sometimes also erroneous (▶ Chap. 46, "Epistemology of Psychology," by Jovanović, this volume). Psychology has remained rather uncomfortable with "culture" and a common strategy has been to ignore context and treat real-life circumstances as "noise" or distraction. In this tradition, the laboratory is promoted as a "pure setting," but for us context-dependent humans, this (the lab) is also an environment, with its own peculiar properties that impinge upon our responses. Despite this awkwardness, Psychology requires to be committed to the study of phenomena in context, but it need not be bound by context either. In practical applications, there is no denying that Psychology has failed to find relevance in several parts of the world, but because of that disconnect, we will argue that mainstream Psychology has, in fact, seriously failed even the "West."

It is believed that history is written by the victors, and this may also be true of mainstream Psychology, although there are significant challenges to the dominant position promoted in journal articles (Kagan, 2012). The uneven political landscape of the nineteenth century clearly defined what would be taught as Psychology. This period experienced the surge of modernism, the industrial revolution, and the clear separation of State and Religion. Also, many ideological facets lingered, the pursuit of science and philosophy became subjects of academic study. It was not inconsequential that Physics (rather than Biology) was the chosen ideal for a science to develop further. The prevailing pragmatism in the USA resulted in a preference for the study of laboratory-based, measurable phenomena. As experimentation in Behaviorism flourished, the project of explaining differences between groups and individuals became assumed to be a consequence of different experiences, with little regard to the context in which things were happening. Or to the inherent limitations of the tools that were used to measure these differences. Across the Atlantic, European scholars were more concerned with the mind than with behavior, guided by the writings of theorists like Freud and Piaget. The failure to explain the expanse of human behavioral phenomena then led to the cognitive revolution in the 1980s, eagerly exploiting machines to measure biological processes and brain activity to explain hard-to-understand phenomena, giving the impression of purifying scientific procedures. Brain circuits became seen as underlying reasons for behavior in all domains of activity. The main problem with these studies was the assumption that experimental conditions would seamlessly transfer to real-life settings, when a person was alone or in a strange place, or at a festive occasion. This was and continues to be a serious problem with outcomes of the neurosciences.

It is important to table that these criticisms of psychology are not new. As early as 1965, scholars were aware of the problems related to isolating individuals in a lab and conducting experiments. Yet the distance achieved by the discipline have been so dramatic that this trend has continued unabated, and little has changed in the last five decades (Kagan, 2012).

A History of "Western Psychology"

In ancient Greek and Roman culture, nativists like Plato (427–347 BCE) proposed several key ideas that helped lay the foundation of Western philosophy and scholarship. The idea that knowledge is inborn and that children are endowed with knowledge required for functioning can be traced back to Plato, whereas empiricists like Aristotle believed that knowledge is acquired through sensory experiences. During the Medieval period, around the fifteenth century in European society, records display that children were seen as miniature adults and even dressed like them, but were also considered to be fragile and in need of protection. The notion of the original sin prevailed and children were believed to be in need of correction by society. It was during the Renaissance period (1300–1600 A.D.) that society became responsible for caring and protecting children. Play activities were considered to be essential for growth and development of children. Following that, the Reformation period (1500 A.D.) was a time when the emphasis was placed on imparting education to children and that is when child rearing was taken seriously. Descartes (1596–1650 A.D.) presented a dualistic model, which focused on our shared biological development with other species. The only thing that differed was the mind, which consisted of ideas about self, time, motion, etc., which could not be derived from experience. Around the same period, Locke compared children's mind to a blank slate (Tabula Rasa) and believed that all the knowledge emerged from experience. During the eighteenth-century AD, Rousseau considered innate biological processes to be motivating factors behind development. Further, it was believed that human development unfolds naturally along the pathways set by nature with the support of society. This was followed by the work of several scholars whose work contributed to the study of human development, notable among them being Darwin in the nineteenth Century, who believed that organisms evolve by the process of natural selection and the competition for survival helps them in evolving into more mature and efficient forms. The role of nature or nurture in development of children has been a critical topic for scientists and philosophers regarding the development of children and the influence of social factors.

Following these early developments, the first Psychology experiments were set up by Wundt in Leipzig in Germany where the academic discipline was founded and expanded, gradually moving to different parts of the world. From these early ideas, theories of behaviorism, humanism, social learning theory, psychoanalysis, psychosocial development, cognitive development, and scores of others emerged, creating a robust range of writing and scholarship around the changes and continuities in children's growth from conception to maturity and into adulthood (see Baldwin, 1967; Maier, 1988; for overview).

Some Examples of Alternative Perspectives

Owing to the wide range of scholarship in Europe and America, the discipline of Developmental Psychology advanced into a thriving field of study and the practical applications of theory and research in everyday life began to gain importance through applications in child care and development, education, therapy, and other related fields. Psychological assessments became a popular field related to measurement and assessments of developmental norms and standards with practical relevance in clinical and classroom practice. Despite these advancements, an important domain that remained relatively unexplored was the significance and meaning of cultural context and social diversity in the intersection between a child and its environment. Furthermore, child development also became distant from other related fields of study like anthropology, medicine, sociology, social work, economics, history, literature, and others. We will not dwell on intersectionality in this chapter because that requires separate attention, but we will take up the issue of culture and diversity.

In a review of global perspectives on childhood and human development, Pence (2011) questions the dependence of terms like standards and norms in development as narrowly sourced and defined. For instance, "there is a virtual absence of African-led contributions to research on early childhood care and development" in international interventions (p. 112). This holds true for South-East Asia, the Far East, and the Southern America. In fact, wherever ideology and practice in the care of children departs from Eurocentric notions of childhood, standards and norms are imposed in the attempt to correct local views about children. "Why is mainstream psychology hegemonic?" Bhatia (2018) asks, arguing that because it attempts to speak for everyone, subordinates others, and is used for the purpose of marginalizing other explanation systems through power structures that obscure and silence other voices. An alternative psychology is needed that which "goes beyond the mechanistic, universalizing, essentializing, and ethnocentric dimensions that make the hegemony of Euro-American psychological science" (Bhatia, 2018, p. 13).

In an effort to conceptualize the emerging field of Indian Psychology, it is possible to view this as a significant scholarship that has potential contribution to the main field a school of thought primarily rooted in the diverse Indian philosophical systems with universal appeal. Particular emphasis is available regarding the vast expanse of the human consciousness from transcendental, dynamic experiential perspectives. The increasing popularity of the practice of yoga and mindfulness have gained widespread appeal across the world, and we believe there is a lot to be gained from including these in academic study (Rao, & Paranjpe, 2008; Paranjpe, 2021). The inclusive, first-person positions of everyday human phenomena and their practical applications are significant for Psychological theory and practice to notice and learn from (Bhawuk, Srinivas, Dalal, & Misra, 2010). Several important sources about Indian views on issues like justice, intergroup relations, intelligence, gender, activism, and spirituality are available in volumes like New Directions in Indian Psychology by Dalal and Misra (2002).

Examples from India

Let us take some examples from Indian traditions about development and person-hood that stands in contradiction to mainstream notions in Psychology.

Childhood and the Care of Children

In Indian thought, for example, birth and childhood are believed to represent a paradoxical, insoluble reality of life and the child is assumed to be a link between generations, which guaranteed continuity. Children are viewed as close to divinity, with male and female offspring holding different spiritual significance in family life. The male child has different responsibilities for family continuity, especially among agricultural communities, whereas the female child will have the potential for its expansion as she grows older. For this reason, some ritual practices among upper caste Hindus (for instance) are defined for male children and their learning like the *Yagnopavita* (sacred thread ceremony) from where the phase of learning and forma-tion is initiated. Principles of *dharma*, *karma*, and reincarnation are underlying beliefs of the Hindu population, but social practices in children's care are more often shared between families of a region than not. Multiple caregiving in large households in the company of several children, siblings and cousins, is the predom-inant style of child care. The separation of children from family occupations is not common, and incidental learning through observation and apprenticeship is frequent, especially in traditional occupations. Regional differences are often far more signif-icant than religious ones, since child care is seen as adaptive to ecological contexts. Furthermore, changes occurring due to education, mobility, urbanization, techno-logical advancement, and global influences are undeniable. Childhood in the major cities of India has begun to look very different from its rural and tribal versions.

Notwithstanding ethnic, religious, and cultural diversity, children have a special status in family life and their arrival is celebrated as a symbol of renewal and continuity of the life cycle of the family (Saraswathi, 2017). With some exceptions of matriarchal groups, families in the region are predominantly patriarchal, with agriculture and related careers as a major occupation in rural areas, although changes in technological development and industrial advancement has resulted in many significant changes in the economic and social profile of people, including within country migration, as mentioned before.

Generally, children are not separated from the family, growing up in close connection with siblings, cousins, uncles, aunts, and grandparents. There are some important differences between rural and urban family life on account of occupational and other demands; but the joint household and close associations within the kin network sustain. Furthermore, it remains popular to address outside the family relationships (neighbors, friends, colleagues) with kin terminology (fictive kinship) demonstrating the sustained importance of the family in defining social relationships and interpersonal dynamics (Chaudhary, 2004). Cultural context is the center of activities related to bringing up a child. Children are guided toward keen attention to person, place, and time in their actions and the demands for social appropriateness are guided by context-sensitivity rather than uniform standards. Thus, from a very early age, children growing up in Indian homes learn to regulate their conduct, in speech, stance, and self-presentation (Saraswathi, 2017).

The Ashrama Theory

Roles and relationships within the family are largely gender-specific but fungible within that paradigm. In keeping with this ideology, children are socialized to perform their respective roles in the society and not particularly for their individual development. "Otherness" is a key component of people's self-construction as is evident in conversations and narratives about the self. Childhood and adult life are characterized by continuity and it is neither common nor advisable to separate children from their kin network. Children are traditionally believed to "grow" by themselves as well as by inputs from the family and the culture in which they lived, the emphasis being on socially appropriate conduct in socialization. Some important features of family and community life shared in the majority world that have been marginalized and even pathologized by the standard notion of childhood include the ideology of a stage-like sequence of developmental tasks through life, multiple generation households and the daily presence of the elderly, the prevalence of multiple carers and siblings. The belief in reincarnation in Hinduism, Buddhism, and Jainism is a fundamental departure from the Western notion of the life cycle, since a single life is seen as transitory in the journey of a person's Aatman, sometimes translated as soul. Similarly the principles of dharma (righteousness) and Karma (actions and their consequences) are also fundamental principles of life's journey. It is very hard to capture these constructs without going into details, but these are mentioned here so as not to silence their local significance in ideology and action.

The Ashrama theory (Table 1) is a belief in a sequence of developmental tasks for each stage of life. Sometimes compared with Erikson's theory of psychosocial development on account of similarities of stage and life span, the Ashrama theory proposes that an individual has certain age- and stage-related responsibilities that contribute toward the social significance of his or her life. Speaking of similarities

Table 1 Stages in Ashrama dharma. (Source: https://iskconeducationalservices.org/HoH/practice/dharma/the-four-ashrams/)

Age	Stage	Tasks
Under 2 years of age		No moral codes defined
Childhood to 24 years	Bhrahmacharya	Student life
25 – 48 years	Grihastha	Householder, occupied with work and family life
49 – 72 years	Vanaprastha	Retirement
Beyond 73 years	Sanyasa	Renunciation

between these two approaches (Erikson's theory and Ashrama theory), Kakar (1996) writes that despite some similarities, it is important to table the fact that the first three stages of Erikson's theory are not addressed in the conceptualization of the Ashramas that deal more with the social aspects of a person's engagement with the world and himself. Yet, the visualization of the life span as a sequence of progressive stages with a spectrum of experiences that will make an impact on forthcoming experiences within a range of possibilities is a similar approach between the two positions, Erikson's theory and Ashrama dharma. As a former student of Erikson, Kakar has written widely about similar issues in the study of spirituality and selfhood.

The Indian Sense of Self

Hindu philosophy has an ancient tradition of spiritual discourse about self-knowledge within the religious tradition. The Vedas, of which the Upanishads are a part, have extensive debates about the nature of the self and self-knowledge and core aspects of Hindu philosophy. Although there has been a recent inclusion of some aspects of these traditions in the syllabus of Indian Psychology, mostly these texts have been avoided because of the conflicts between science and religious thinking, whether from Hinduism, Buddhism, Islam, or Jainism, or any other of the pluralistic traditions that flourish in India. Gaining wisdom about the nature of the self and its relationship with the outside world is the primary objective of these texts and including their study is an important way of understanding the background of cultural practices in the region. The pursuit of Yoga, for instance (not to be confused with Yoga as physical exercise), is a practice in self-knowledge and mind-body union through concentration and control.

Although ancient texts are not universally known or followed, there are several ripples of this ancient tradition on prevailing notions of self and social relations: socially oriented notions of self and the importance of "otherness," encouragement of cooperation and interdependence as a virtue, discouragement of preoccupations with the self, connectedness with ancestors and large kinship networks, higher fertility rates and the primacy of the family and community over the individual. Roland (1988) refers to this predilection as "familism" to contrast it with the ideology of "individualism," remarking that it was not just anyone, but others in the family toward whom a person is expected to have close representations in one's sense of self (Chaudhary, 2012). Furthermore, and the continuity of household activities and spaces including co-sleeping of adults and children reinforces connectedness with others. Several important scholarly articles have argued against the limited interpretations of the individualism-collectivism paradigm to understand the Indian Psyche (Chaudhary, 2004; Sinha, & Tripathi, 1994). Several publications have also looked into the matter of India's spiritual traditions to examine the influence of that in self-configuration (Paranjpe, 2002; Rao, Paranjpe, & Dalal, 2008).

Learning Differently

The construct of intelligence in academic Psychology has been guided primarily by measurability and standardized testing. In a detailed analysis of people's lay understanding of intelligence, Dalal and Misra (2002) found that elements of social wisdom and relational acuity are especially valuable for the shared sense of who an intelligent person is. These elements do not get adequate attention in conventional views that have tended to remain loyal to the standard purpose and outcomes of intelligence testing (Sternberg, 2019). In the domain of learning some noteworthy features are: distributed and shared learning in informal settings, apprenticeship and incidental learning, rote memorization, and an oral orientation to literature.

Knowledge or truth (according to Hinduism, Buddhism, and Jainism) has three dimensions (*Tirupati*):

- The knower (pramAtr),
- The knowable (prameya) and
- The process by which we learn (pramAna), of which there are six types:
  - Pratyaksh – Sensation
  - Anuman – Presumption
  - Upaman – Analogy
  - Anuplabdhi – Awareness of absence
  - Arthapatti – Contradiction (with what is already known)
  - Shabd – Words

In this scheme of learning and knowledge, some noteworthy aspects are the importance given to wisdom as well as orality (Jha, 2008). Another interesting aspect is learning the significance of something or someone from appreciating its absence. This is only one of the many traditions of learning described in the Nyaya tradition of Hindu thought (Rao, Paranjpe & Dalal, 2008).

Emotional Landscapes

Another important point of departure from Developmental Psychology's global version is the ways in which emotions, emotional expression, and management is constructed. One important feature is the importance given to context in the significance and assessment of the positive or negative function of emotional expression. Furthermore, there is a separate discussion about the underlying emotion and its outward expression apart from the larger variety of emotions conceptualized. The study of emotions as per the Natyashastra is the Rasa theory (Pandit, 2011). The realization of Rasa is the result of the union of *Sthaibhavas* (underlying emotions, 49 in number, 9 stable ones), *Vibhavas* (situations), *Anubhavas* (experiences), and *Vyabhikaribhavas* (mental states). There is a distinction between real-life experience and artistic or theatrical expressions in dance and song. Here is an overview of the vocabulary of emotions:

- Emotions: Nine stable (49 in all) – *Sthaibhavas*: Love, Humor, Sorrow, Anger, Enthusiasm, Fear, Disgust, Wonder, and Passiveness
- Situations (*Vhibhavas*) facilitate emergence of sthaibhavas
- Experience (*Anubhava*): Experience of or effect of the emotion on a person
- Mental States (*Vyabhikaribhavas*) like anxiety, depression, despair, determination

As can be understood, this formulation of emotions departs from the visualization of six basic emotions and their development.

The Social Construction of Gender

As a predominantly agricultural society, India's communities are also patriarchal, although several pockets of matriarchal networks have also thrived: the Khasi and Garo tribes in the North-Eastern State of Meghalaya, the Nairs and Ezhavas from Kerala in the South, and the Bant and Billavas in Karnataka State. By and large the large contingent of tribal groups in different parts of India, despite the increasing impact of incursion from urban culture, retains cultural practices unique to their group. There are over 500 tribal groups in India and their community organization, beliefs, and cultural practices are distinct from the mainstream ethnic groups.

Although social dynamics among majority communities are guided by age and gender the ways in which gender is understood is somewhat distinct from global culture (Pandey, 2002).

Contemporary Perspectives

Despite long-standing and favorable traditions of a nurturing context in the company of multiple caregivers, children in India are the most vulnerable under conditions of poverty and disadvantage, natural and man-made disasters. This reality has several historical and ecological antecedents, but the crisis of poverty is undeniable, as we scan reports and witness children on our streets. In this regard, any discussion of childhood in India cannot escape the attention from governmental services, nongovernmental organizations, multinational companies, and international donor agencies. The contemporary understanding of childhood still bears the traces of the colonial past that the region has shared, and children continue to be seriously affected. Issues of child health, education, children at work, street children, and child trafficking are some crucial concerns that need to be addressed.

The importance of understanding childhood in its context has taken a backseat due to the extra attention that was put on quantifying the results of studies done on poverty and related problems, in order to come to a definite conclusion and the ease of generalizability, and there is need for finding local solutions to these issues, for as long as even one child goes hungry, or fails to receive medical attention when needed, is a failure of a nation to fulfill its responsibilities toward children. The intense importance of a family in a child's life is sometimes seen as a reason for the State's negligence in providing services, as is seen in the case of disability studies (Sharma, 2011).

The significance of looking at alternate perspectives of childhood for social, political, environmental, economic, and cultural expansion is undeniable. But the consistent and deliberate biases in the issues addressed by Psychology in general and Developmental Psychology in particular, which have tended to remain wedded to small populations and limited ideologies, has had several consequences for theoretical advances and practical outcomes in Psychology.

Global Consequences of Local Psychology

Let us examine some of the substantive consequences that the above bias in sampling of the populations on which Psychology and its Developmental domain is based for which there is sufficient evidence for debate.

"Humpty Dumpty Had a Great Fall": The Fragmented Individual

The embryonic field of Psychology has been characterized as "pretentious and blinkered," Hampden-Turner claims (1982, p. 11), and there is an urgent need for it to be put back together like the shattered Humpty Dumpty. The psyche is broken up into domains of affect, cognition, learning, sensation, perception, and the like, which have become scattered across numerous books and journals, and a consolidated view of a person is hard to construct. Furthermore, hyphenated expressions like psycho-somatic, psycho-biological have added to this disconnect (Laing, 1965). Especially in therapy, these fractures result in obscuring the access to and addressing of the difficulties faced by individuals. The tripartite division of physical, cognitive, and emotional is another instance of fractures created by the separation of domains and specialization. Added to the separation of mind and body, between the psychological and physical, a separation that prevented advanced understanding of both the body and the mind (Van Kolk, 2000), domains became fields in themselves and dedicated journals rarely address common problems. As the domains and distributions became smaller and more distant, the conceptualization of the whole individual and the connection with the context was obscured.

These domains that we have been treating as essential features of the human condition are conventions, emerging from a specific tradition of psychological study, and far from universal (Danziger, 1997). In fact, the reification of these constructs has created an illusion of their existence as identifiable features. As Cole (1996) remarks about the invisibility of one's own culture as a way of life, perhaps psychologists too were blind to their own cultural roots!

Methodological "Purity" and an Indifference to Context

Driven by the inspiration to emulate the physical sciences (physics in particular) and a parallel discomfort with context, psychological investigations have tended to favor laboratory experiments, structured observations, and measurement. Research in the quantitative tradition is placed at a higher status, and although it may have been initially proposed as "the Second Psychology" by the founders of the subject (Wundt in particular), other methods became subordinated. Wundt's recommendations for systematic experimentation were adopted, but the importance of self-examination and introspection as legitimate techniques also became ignored along the journey of Psychology from Europe to America, as was his extensive work on *Volkerpsychologie*, or Folk Psychology, regarding human beings' participation in culture (see Valsiner, 2004).

Although the qualitative tradition from other fields and mixed methods has gained in significance, the superiority of quantification and "objectivity" remains undefeated. This has had many consequences on the content of psychological research and its "weirdness" (Chaudhary & Sriram, 2020). The conditions demanded of standardized techniques are often far too expensive and inconvenient to be replicated in other countries, even if the tasks may be fully applicable, which is not often the case. Thus, the bulk of research retains its "purity" by undermining other forms of enquiry, thereby perpetuating the myth of measurability of psychological phenomena and their independence of context (Kagan, 2012). Valsiner (2014) has argued extensively about the need to bring data and phenomena closer together in order to better grasp psychological reality.

The Embryonic Fallacy, Intersubjectivity and Interobjectivity

The myth of the independent individual is a strong feature of Psychology, resulting in a preference for intramental phenomena. The greater attention to issues of individual, inside-the-head phenomena has had several consequences. This is also related to the assumption that whatever transpires in a human life is an outcome of a single lifetime, and has little to do with social circumstances and cultural setting. Moghaddam writes that this is a major blind-spot in psychological theorizing, identifying the embryonic fallacy as the (false) assumption that everything that happens to us as individuals is the consequence of a single individual's lifetime. This approach tends to mute intersubjectivity, the relationships between people and its co-dependence upon interobjectivity, or the ways in which social relationships are structured by collective culture. Another significant and related issue is the phenomenon of treating all human conduct as emerging from thought.

Psychologization and Biologization

Psychologism literally means "to make something psychological," and psychologization implies the deliberate or otherwise transformation of social, political, or moral issues into psychological factors like well-being or self-processes. The unprecedented growth of Psychology in the twentieth century is an important reason for this phenomenon (Madsen, & Brinkmann, 2010) that has captured our imagination and sustained specific forms of psychological theory and practice, especially psychoanalysis, within which powerful myths about the human condition are proposed. We remain seduced by our own sense of self-importance and must heed the warning to seriously consider alternative versions.

Burman, (1994/2017) argues that psychologization is a persistent problem despite the many changes in the world order in recent decades. Although global relations, immigration, and environmental crises have heightened, and neoliberalism has impacted how we understand childhood in the contemporary, technologically connected world, we persist in attributing performance and participation of individuals and groups primarily to psychological factors, and everyone lands up becoming a psychologist (de Vos, 2008).

Another important phenomenon is the biologization of conduct, and the renewed importance of the neurosciences in explaining behavioral outcomes. Madsen and Brinkmann (2010) argue that attributions to neural activity has in fact thrived on the foundation laid by psychologization, that origins of our world lay in the understanding of the mind as separated from and superior to the rest of the body as well as social reality. Bruer (2001) argues that "the purported new breakthroughs were in fact 'old' neuroscience. These results have been carefully selected, oversimplified, and overgeneralized and then woven into an argument to support U.S. legislation to fund programmes. Neuroscience and the brain have a strong hold on the popular imagination. Once claims that the first three years of life were critical for brain development appeared on the covers of Newsweek and Time magazines, upper middle-class parents world-wide became students of the new brain science and consumers of brain-based products like Baby Einstein, My Baby Can Read, and Mozart CDs" (Bruer, 2001, p. 21). Most importantly, the myth has its origin in policy and advocacy circles, not in the scientific community. Neuroscience was chosen as the scientific vehicle for public relations campaign to promote early childhood programs more for rhetorical, than scientific reasons. When questioned, "Based on neuroscience what can you tell parents about choosing a preschool for their children?" he answered, "Based on neuroscience, absolutely nothing" (Bruer, 2001, p,1). Regardless, the trend has persisted. In fact, the use of the neurosciences argument can be explained as a sort of hyper-generalization in the theater of research (Valsiner, 2019), a sort of exaggerated posturing to impress consumers, influence policy, and silence dissent. The strategy has been widely successful. The notion of neuroliberalism is invoked here as the rise of the use of research in the behavioral sciences in governance and assumptions of economic progress under neoliberalism. Children's minds become positioned as baby brains and our worlds are captured by ideas of personal progress as a consequence. With the entry of behavioral economics there has been a further escalation of the use of research in the drafting of public policy worldwide (see de Vos, 2016).

Pathologizing of "Others"

Another negative outcome of a unitary view of childhood development is pathologizing of the "other." Consequences can be seen in various fields of application, from assessments, therapy, intervention, and education, with adverse positioning of people belonging to other cultures. In the case of child care, for instance, recent immigrants to a State where Child Protection policies are firmly in place in fact stand at a serious risk of losing custody of their children for practicing their own cultural ways of bringing up their offspring. There is a serious need for a global debate on this issue where a clear mandate for the separation of unfamiliar practices must be considered from the position of cultural norms of place of origin. Unless such a review is completed, Child Protection Services can in fact land up perpetuating the very damage to children and families that they are working so hard to prevent.

Cultural practices in children's care, may not be "universal" for the majority world, but they are significant in their prevalence. Yet, Developmental Psychology has systematically treated these conditions as outside of the norm while conducting assessments of development (individual testing), laboratory studies (absence of individualized spaces), measurement (unfamiliarity with quantification, dyadic discourse (as opposed to multilogues, see Chaudhary, 2012), mind-body continuity, and the differential view of the psyche, to name a few. Consequences for schooling have been dealt in a later section, but the judgments placed on child-care practices of immigrants that come under the scanner of Child Protection Services and intervention programs developed in wealthy nations as applicable to other cultures especially the poor are all direct outcomes of the dominance of this singular view of development. Yet again, for the purpose of social justice and global understanding, this limited stance needs to change, and we have to adopt a more expansive view of the world of childhood by reexamining the key messages of Developmental Psychology in the name of social justice and representation of the world's people. Another important reason for this call for change is sustainability and ecological wisdom. The ways in which children are brought up in the West is unsustainable for the world on account of the disproportionately high investment. Keeping these as golden standards for care is uneconomical apart from being unethical and unscientific.

The Family Unit and the Life Cycle of the Family

The question of who looks after children is a critical one, as we raised earlier. Since the "family" is defined as a unit that has children, and not just couples living together (Van Ever, 1992, from Burman, 1994/2017), makes the caregiving role a key to the definition of a family. Yet, this view of a couple with children as a family with its own dateline of the "family life cycle" is again a singular one, and it excludes all other forms of family, extended and joint. This has serious consequences for policy and practice, since key members are left outside the unit within which the mother and, now more recently as a token, fathers have also been included. Ignoring the importance of other family members has had important consequences. In fact, what is most alarming is the outcomes of the breakup of the family, where single parenthood has become a frequent outcome for children growing up in the West. In contrast, when we look elsewhere, divorced, separated, or widowed individuals in other cultures can almost always depend upon the kin network for support with children and household responsibilities. It is rare to see a single parent on their own, caring for young children, even if the assistance maybe periodic.

In fact, if we search for a more appropriate metaphor for the family life cycle as imagined in Developmental Psychology, one could better represent it as a Family merry-go-round, in which infancy, old-age, ill-health, dependence, youthfulness, and household responsibility are ongoing themes. The advantage of this system is in fact its circularity and the opportunities it provides for experiences one would miss otherwise. For instance, it is rare for a young person to grow up into adulthood without experiencing the birth and development of someone else's infant. The first child you hold and care for, even sporadically, is not your own. This is true for both men and women. Furthermore, one encounters the condition of growing older well before your own parents reach their end, thereby providing important practice for tasks of nurturing older people as you grow. It must be noted that this is not an attempt to romanticize large kin networks and family settings, since these are also scenes for conflict and disagreement, but merely to state facts about the different view of family life, one that is completely outside of the paradigm of Developmental Psychology, despite the fact that more people live in multiple member households than otherwise. This is another consequence of Psychology's WEIRDness. Yet, we continue to visualize the family timetable as a cycle, which must complete one phase before the other one can be manifested! This weirdness also has several consequences that are not favorable. For instance, because large families are usually associated in wealthy nations with migration and poverty, results of research are uncritically applied to families in other parts of the world where such family systems may be the norm and not the exception! The shrinking model of the family has been idealized with several important negative outcomes for the study of childhood and the fragility of relationships where legal support and State services for single and out-of-wedlock parents may be more an issue of economics rather than social practice. In fact, if we look carefully, where State support for children is strong, couples do not even feel the need to be married perhaps because they don't believe they need any social support outside of the State. In such circumstance, domestic violence and child abuse can be an isolated and thus, more exaggerated experience for the child.

Burman writes:

> While the 'environment' for children's development has often been treated as synonymous with the mother... the family as the context for child rearing is central to social policy and welfare provision and is also the site for heated debate about social relations and social change. The significance of these national and international social policy debates – in particular at the level of specific national policies – and the ways they enter into developmental research is the topic of this chapter. State and family interact in complex ways. And when the idealized notion of the family is minimized, several consequences occur as we have discussed. It isolates significant others, and piles on complete responsibility with parents. And if the parents find they are unable to get along, it is usually one parent, or two conflicted individuals who care for children (Burman, 1994/2017, p. xxi).

Constricted Collectivism and Other Dualisms

Creating polar oppositions in human phenomena has resulted in limiting our vocabulary for a more favorable and valid discourse. Instances of constructions like interdependent-independent, collectivist-individualist, foreclose the possibility of unity and mutuality, which is in fact the ways in which phenomena play out. The myth of collectivism, for instance, once applied to a people predisposes similarity between very different ideologies that may be clubbed under the same label. Collectivism as a socialist ideology is dramatically different from the familism and interconnectedness of Indians in several domains and not in others. Dualisms created this false sense of simplistic imagination about people and suppresses both within group differences and between group similarities. It is a discourse in which the autonomous dimensions of the Indian Psyche and the family orientation of the American are not only minimized, they are ignored! One consequence of this has been the easy assumptions of Indians being a friendly, welcoming people for all others, whereas the reality is very far removed from this.

The Lonely Mother and Her Precariously "Attached" Infant

The nuclear family model and the central role of the mother has resulted in a persistent burden of holding mothers responsible for the primary care as well as outcomes of childhood. This feminization of development has been intensely criticized in the work of Burman (1994/2017). She argues that despite the shift in the inclusion of fathers, the ways in which fatherhood is constructed still perpetuates the myth of a primary caregiver within the same old paradigm of the nuclear family. There is little or no space for the inclusion of grandparents as primary carers despite that fact that a significant number of the world's children grow up in the care of extended kin along with mothers. The consideration of fathers, grandparents, and siblings is constrained by the format of the nuclear family, where the attachment to and love for a single carer is key to a child's development, and others can sometimes step in. These positions have significant consequences for policy and it remains to be seen how the view of the family is going to respond to the increasing difficulties with single parent families in some parts of the world. In fact, single parent families are far greater consequences of the transformations in selfhood and neoliberalism than we realize. And in fact, research has repeatedly pointed to the fact that far more danger of outcome is placed on the child if he or she is growing in a single parent household than in large families.

Language Shrinkage: Idealizing Monolingualism and Word Count

Research on language is one of the most vibrant and dynamic areas in Developmental Psychology. Yet the norms and standards of language usage have been based primarily on the premise of single language users. For many of the world's children, linguistic diversity and multilingualism are the norm, and quantitative measures of vocabulary keep in sharp focus the noun (versus verbs) and expression (versus comprehension), single language competence (versus multiple languages), literacy (versus language use) as important assumptions. Mostly, imagine pre-literate persons is outside the frame of this model, which considers parents or children who have not had or do not have access to schooling or literacy as disadvantaged in the same way as school drop-outs are. There is no denying the consequences of the lack of literacy in the contemporary world, but such an approach tends to assume that people are also lagging intellectually. In fact, this is a gross injustice, a serious one since the first failure to reach schooling to the people is a failure of the State and not the person, and to that we pile on another injustice, that of treating people as if they have been incapable of learning.

Further, apart from language differences, there are certain patterns in discourse that characterize a people. For instance, the immense complexity of kin terminology in all Indian language that mark every nuance of age, gender, and distance in the kin network is something children develop and gain expertise in at very early ages. They are experts in person deixis and, in fact, the play with kin terminology is a fascinating area of study (Chaudhary, 2012). Furthermore, there is the predominance of oral modes of learning rather than written, and narrating stories usually by older family members (rather than a parent reading to the child at night-time) is a common practice. Treating reading (from books at night) as the gold standard for literacy training tends to ignore family dynamics, multiple roles, and responsibilities and cultural traditions. The collective narration of folk tales and mythological stories is a strong tradition that is tending to be replaced by the "literate" inputs that parents feel compelled to perform. Besides, there is a much greater focus on "following instructions" and comprehension, rather than on articulation which many children will hesitate to do before a stranger, a teacher, or a researcher. School curricula tend to mimic these patterns of language use that silence local linguistic practices and local languages, one important reason for children's poor performances.

Psychology of language needs review and revision to include other paradigms of language-reality representation. This form of language use tends to separate the child from the context and assume that the child's language use is an isolated intramental act. This could not be farther from the truth as anthropological linguists have informed us. As Rogoff (1993) reminds us, participation rather than transmission is a much more favorable way of understanding learning, whether it is between individuals or groups. The notion of "subtractive education" refers to curriculum policies, processes, or practices that remove students' culture or language from classroom contexts as a resource for learning or as a source of personal affirmation. Subtractive education assumes that students' academic successes depend on the degree to which they give up their own cultures or linguistic practices or traditions to assimilate into mainstream culture, a process often referred to as "Americanization" in the USA (Valenzuela, 1999). These are just a few examples of how local ideas became global and are then imposed onto the local in psychology.

Let's take a look at the "word-gap" phenomenon that has come under heavy criticism by linguistic anthropologists because it promotes a very specific version of language use, where the motivation to market a software developed for use is not an insignificant player in the promotion of the links of word count with development. But the point that this research fails to acknowledge is precisely the existing differences between the cultures "express and understand language use." The indicators of command over language varies across language communities. Whereas some societies focus more on advancement of vocabulary, others treat comprehension as an indicator of maturity. Such differences place children who grow up among different language practices at an automatic disadvantage.

The association between mothers who don't talk to their children as being distant or uncaring or inadequate mothers is another fallout of this principle of word gap that depends exclusively on dyadic and expressive language use and book reading cultures.

Learning As Schooling

The wider issue of how children learn has become conflated with schooling, with the reduced importance of forms of learning outside of the classroom. The fact that the classroom as the setting is understood almost universally draws from the European idea of a group of children of similar ages being seated together in a confined space, being taught by teachers. The dominance of school in contemporary society has resulted in this being among the two most important institutions in children's lives. Yet there are consequences of this. For those children who do not have access to school, of which there are large numbers in the global south, who do not attend school not because they are unwilling to attend school but because they don't have access to schools, are unfortunately clubbed with children who voluntarily drop out of school. This is a problem because it carries assumptions that have long-term consequences for the ways in which these children and families are categorized. Another consequence is the underestimation of the importance of incidental informal learning outside the classroom, which has a very important role in life lessons, cooperated or distributed learning that happens among children in mixed groups where teaching younger ones, learning to care for them, and complementarily respecting older children and learning from them builds strong social bonds. School as an institution underestimates these forms of family and community learning and social relationships, sometimes even treating them as barriers to classroom learning. The 'single adult many children' model of the classroom is a primary and often exclusive template for schools, at the cost of a wide range of informal opportunities from which children learn that could effortlessly and with little cost be incorporated into schooling or treated as complementary to school learning. Within the deficit paradigm of school–community relationships, it is quite commonplace to treat the child either as a blank slate, or as someone who has to be cleaned up in preparation for school. This is a position that, at the outset, creates an antagonism not only between home and school, but also between the child and school. Young children find it very hard to understand this antagonism, and the outcomes can push a child to school refusal or if she/he is successful at schooling, a rejection of home. Between these two extreme possibilities, children live through this difficulty in comprehending why such an opposition is present in the first place (Chaudhary, & Pillai, 2014).

The East–West Divide and the Failure to Understand Mutuality

Valsiner (2020) writes that:

> It has been customary to present the Eastern and Western views on the human beings as two discrete and mutually competitive perspectives. I think this starting point is unproductive from the outset. Instead, we are better off starting from an axiomatic stance where the basic assumption is that of universal unity of the human psyche, with versions in different societies that on their external specifications seem mutually irreconcilable. (p.7)

While endorsing the "unproductive" nature of this divide, we will argue further that this opposition has failed to recognize the great deal of scholarship even from the West, in Psychology and other human sciences, which favorably addresses cultural context as well as the blind followership of borrowed ideas in other cultures, especially in the advancement of neuroliberalism, the practical application of borrowed ideas in policy and interventions. We propose that it is timely now to dissolve these categories and address issues of disembodiment, entrenchment, and disconnectedness (both intrapsychic and interpersonal) as the key elements of mainstream Psychology that need to be addressed and abandoned. Vision 2020 (taking from the symbol of perfect eyesight, 20/20) for the discipline needs to have a more global approach that is inclusive, plural, and draws from mutuality rather than singularity. This is the only way forward for a sustainable, socially just future, free of the problems of Psychology's ghosts (Kagan, 2012).

Suppressing Dialogues Between Global-Local and Science-Culture

Assuming that global is scientific and local as cultural has created other fractures in the system, ignoring both "global culture" and local science' (see Table 2). The association of reason with (global) science and (local) culture with its opposite has been unfortunate for fully grasping people's relationship with social, psychological, environmental, and other phenomena. It is also a principle on which colonialism was falsely justified for centuries. Let us make an attempt to examine these associations. For the sake of discussion, if we separate local and global as well as science and culture, we can visualize the matrix thus:

In common discussions, we sometimes fail to recognize two of the above dimensions, mostly assuming automatically that culture is local and science is global. Local Science and Global Culture have received relatively little attention in comparison. Although it may be seen as a perpetuation of the artificial separation between culture and science, acknowledging local science may in fact be an important interim step to the advancement of knowledge with a dialogical perspective.

There is a subtle but significant shift in recent times between the cultural notions of childhood as understood by communities and the task of national development. Whereas the latter is linked primarily to social history and ethnic membership, national development aims toward understanding children as future citizens. The dialogue between these two positions is important to reflect on.

Table 2 Dialogue between culture and science

	SCIENCE	CULTURE
LOCAL	LOCAL SCIENCE	LOCAL CULTURE
GLOBAL	GLOBAL SCIENCE	GLOBAL CULTURE

Culture and Communities: Childhood As a Project

The project of building a universalized notion of childhood that is a recommended experience for all nations, and within nations all people, relates to the task of developing intervention programs for the welfare of children everywhere.

"Development in the human form is an epigenetic process of the emergence of more complex structures in which each new level of organization is associated with a new relevant context and a new form of mediation between the individual and at least one other human being" (Cole, 2002, p. 316).

The variations in culture are not sudden changes that happen in and around us, these are adaptive processes that take place gradually and are passed down from one generation to other. The capacity of the human mind to create different forms of culture is what makes human mind distinct (Chaudhary, 2017). The erosion of traditional cultures and ways of life has become a growing concern in the face of modernity and a number of social and economic challenges facing our societies. In areas characterized by strong oral traditions and unique characteristics largely shaped by their cultural behaviors, such as storytelling, music, and mechanisms of social integration, this is particularly disturbing. Aspects of traditional culture deserve more attention in the current environment of change and cultural loss in understanding the change in contemporary community and positive development.

The different strategies that have been prescribed in these scriptures have been lost in the modernization of education. After the British arrived, the conventional education system in India suffered damage. The schooling system became crippled with the advent of Western missionaries who scattered throughout the country and Western schooling became a way of educating the supposedly uncivilized children of the country. This change had a long-standing effect on the way of imparting education as well as the values being reinforced, which had an impact on the relationship between school and the community. Indigenous systems of education were a norm before the entry of the British. Temples and mosques were places where education was imparted to the elementary school children, but primarily to young boys. Elementary education was practical in nature whereas higher education was literary. With the introduction of missionaries, Western education became a norm. Other groups also started following the same pathway where children from other minority communities (ethnic and religious) received education. The complexity caused by extremely diverse ecological, social, and financial backgrounds makes the schooling system to be complex, which makes it even more difficult to make any generalizations about the Indian system of education. The lack of connection between the local environment of children and the lessons taught in the classroom could be summed up in this statement "In creating a sanitary idea of citizenship, modern education has amputated our primordial affinity with the world around us" (Viswanathan, 2016, p.10).

Skutnabb-Kangas (2009) highlighted that the linguistic genocide evident in the tribal education in India may lead to psychological hurdles and learning difficulties. Panda (2004) who conducted her study among Saora tribals concluded that any learning cannot be studied after separating it from its cultural context. Kumar (2014) did a study on the Musahar (pig rearing) community, which according to the legend used to be rat-eaters. The children from these communities were considered to be impure and hence faced discrimination against them, which indirectly affected their learning and development. Similar to this, children with special needs also face discrimination at the hands of peers and sometimes school authorities when they are provided with facilities needed by them which have an impact on their psyche and well-being.

Children when admitted to schools have ascribed to a developing cultural identity, which may be different for different children coming to the same school. The schooling system uses a uniform code to be followed by all children, which may or may not be in consonance with the existing cultural identity of children.

Research Limitations

We now provide selected examples of research studies that present support for our claims. Research studies done on Japanese children reported a 1 year delay in acquisition of theory of mind as compared to children from the West, which could be attributed to the fact that in Asian cultures, an action is evaluated with reference to context. The concept of eCOM (entering the Community of Minds) was proposed by Nelson et al. (2003) over the concept of ToM (theory-of-mind). Personal narratives and stories are important features of CoM, which represents the social-cultural world in which the child lives. In another study by Correa-Chavez and Rogoff (2005), children of indigenous mothers with low schooling were attentive to activities but asked fewer questions as compared to children of highly educated Euro-American mothers who focused their attention on one activity at a time. The "cognitive disadvantage" hypothesis fails in case of children engaged in informal trading. These children may fail at math problems in school but they could easily be seen solving the same math problems in their day-to-day lives. The difference is doing it in the head and doing it on paper.

The difference in chronological age and educational age misguides the study of cognitive outcomes in children. It is believed that more than the chronological age, the educational age can provide the extent of learning more accurately. Most Western studies have catered to the connection between the chronological age and schooling, which may not present a clear idea of the learning outcomes. Children face a lot of informal cognitive problems in their day-to-day lives, which are put forward to them in school much later, so to relate schooling with higher cognitive functioning is an unhealthy comparison. A large part of children in developing countries like India are from rural areas with access to basic primary education or sometimes not even that. The development of these children and those coming from the urban areas may be at the same level but the ways to measure them and the research methods applied to study them need to be context-specific in order to present a clearer picture. Generalizations in such diverse locales would be unfair and hence there is a need to learn, absorb, and reflect on childhoods in different contexts to be able to compare it with the West and observe the qualitative changes that exist in different domains, communities, and cultures. To understand the same, this quote illustrates the above mentioned: "drawing on analyses of the 1989 United Nations Convention on the Rights of the Child, conceptual limitations of a shift from generalization to naturalization are identified. These culminate in a globalization of childhood that is particularly evident in models of psychological development. The article outlines how the assumptions about the separation of individual and society, and development from culture, play a key role in this process. At the level of practice, therefore, the article argues for the need to maintain a critical vigilance on the adequacy of the conceptual resources that inform policy and programmes for children" (Burman, 1996, p.45).

As cited in Chaudhary (2017), the changes to a newborn's care in today's world were explained in the statement ahead.

"But the care of the newborn baby should not be limited to preserving it from death, to isolating it from infection, as is done today in the more modern clinics where the nurses who approach it cover their faces with bandages so that the microbes from their breath should not reach it. There are the problems of the psychic care of the child-from the very moment of birth-and those of measures to facilitate his adjustment to the world. To this end, experiments have still to be made in clinics, and propaganda is required in families in order that the attitude towards the newly born should be changed." (Montessori, 1966/2013, p.19)

Montessori (1966) expressed concerns over protection and overprotection of children. Scientific approaches to care need to be balanced and the natural exploration of natural phenomena should be the path to be followed in order to let children explore maximum potential. Global patterns are increasingly defining how children should be cared for and how they should develop. There is a huge difference between Western and Asian parenting and care practices for example, co-sleeping (primary caretaker and children) in Asian cultures is believed to foster attachment between the mother and the child whereas in Western countries, it may be seen as abuse. Another example could be feeding with the hands, which may be interpreted as force-feeding in the West whereas in Asian cultures it is a sign of feeding with love and affection. Such contrasting caring beliefs are bound to create confusion and term one culture to be better at caring than the other, which should not be the case. There is no right way to care for children. Cultural practices adapted to the specific ecological, social, and geographical context may reveal developmental pathways, which are culturally appropriate and help in unfolding development along the natural lines. Eagleton (2000) stated that access to reality of an area could be gained through the culture of that particular area. Planning for childhood should be revisited in order to check the reality and relevance of the practices, at the same time retaining the practices that stand the test of time (Chaudhary, 2017).

A review of three studies done by Chaudhary and Pillai (2014) on Indian children in rural and urban settings regarding their methodological choices provides evidence of the importance of context and shared understanding gained by participating in cultural events. Differences in moral reasoning can be expected based on those different values that have greater acceptance. According to them, an individual is a person with a separate set of intramental activity, which results in an internal reality.

Children could be studied where they are not separated from their dynamic social networks or where they are separated from the social settings. In a longitudinal, ethnographic study on mealtimes by Ishiguro (2016), conducted on a Japanese child from 9 to 78 months of age, portrayed how children perceive about their culture and communities. The findings of this study showed that children learn about their communities' beliefs in a complex interplay when physical conditions are constrained by environmental arrangements and when the child is cared for by the partner on whom he/she is dependent for care, at the same time understanding himself as a separate entity.

Cultural specificity needs to be a fundamental concern in conducting research with children from diverse backgrounds. In other words, a range of standards have to be put in place rather than just one to assess development in different cultural groups. The tests should be such which facilitate thinking and problem solving. Test questions should help in understanding the context and the concept. In order to facilitate the process of investigation, one might carefully choose the way in which the questions are asked. Baer (1970) states that by proper sequencing of events, the process of development can be revealed. Sequence plays an important role in eliciting appropriate responses. Quantitative methods have usually been seen as the reserve of those interested in the "positivist identification" of facts. Whereas qualitative techniques focus on the "interpretive paradigm" and the social construction of meaning (Tulloch, 2000). This does not mean that they are mutually exclusive, or that they cannot be used in conjunction. Tulloch (2000) suggests that social research constructed by combining techniques can provide a basis on which to challenge generalizable adult assumptions. Qualitative or quantitative data is a representation of the findings; the findings are not inherently qualitative or quantitative in nature. Essentially the basic difference between representation being data presented in numeric and data presented in texts, observations, or narratives. The mixed methods approach is useful to understand child development in a particular context where quantitative approach can be applied to study prevalence while qualitative approach can be applied to study meaning (Weisner, 2002). Conventional psychological research considers the individual as a separate entity to be studied irrespective of the context, which proves to be a superficial way of looking at things. For research to be inclusive, individual agency is to be explored by situating the self in research encounters that mobilize subjective but also intersubjective processes (Chaudhary & Pillai, 2014). Cultural psychology is not a single subdiscipline, but a family of approaches (▶ Chap. 24, "Cultural Psychology," by Tateo, Marsico, and Valsiner, this volume) that provide an effective and productive approach for the future of psychology on account of the fundamental commitment to cultural context and multidisciplinarity.

Summing Up

In this chapter, we made an attempt to expand the perspective to include the understanding of development from other traditions, hoping that this will help in reexamining some of the basic assumptions of Developmental Psychology and the understanding of the human life span. In this regard, the place of cultural psychology, with the emphasis on meaning-making, human agency, cultural context, and systemic approach to human, cultural phenomena (see ▶ Chap. 24, "Cultural Psychology," by Tateo, Marsico, & Valsiner, this volume) is of critical importance. As the world becomes more connected than ever before, as populations are on the move more than ever before, and as our world's resources are becoming depleted by the expansion of globalization, neocolonial and neoliberal policies, and privatization, it is no longer possible to ignore sustainability and ecological validity of our ideas. As academics also, we will do well to look around to different ways of living, as people engage with their physical and social environments in different, often more sustainable ways and means. Our world is calling for a new world-order, and academic Psychology is being called out to respond.

References

Erikson, E. H., & Erikson, J. M. (1998). *The life cycle completed*. New York, NY: Norton.

Baer, D. (1970). An age-irrelevant concept of development. *Merrill-Palmer Quarterly, 16*, 238–245.

Baldwin, A. L. (1967). *Theories of child development*. New York, NY: Wiley.

Bhatia, S. (2018). *Decolonizing psychology: Globalization, social justice and youth identities*. New York, NY: Oxford University Press.

Bhawuk, D. P. S., Srinivas, E. S., Dalal, A. K., & Misra, G. (2010). The core and context of Indian Psychology. *Psychology and Developing Societies, 22*(1), 121–155.

Bruer, J. T. (2001). *The myth of the first three years: A new understanding of early brain development and lifelong learning*. New York, NY: The Free Press.

Burman, E. (1994/2017). *Deconstructing developmental psychology* (3rd ed.). New York, NY: Routledge.

Burman, E. (1996). Local, Global or Globalized? Child Development and International Child Rights Legislation. *Childhood, 3*(1), 45–66.

Chaudhary, N., & Sriram, S. (2020). Psychology in the "Backyards of the world": Experiences from India. *Journal of Cross-Cultural Psychology.* https://doi.org/10.1177/0022022119896652

Chaudhary, N. (2004). *Listening to culture. New Delhi: Constructing reality from everyday talk*. New Delhi, Delhi: Sage.

Chaudhary, N. (2012). Negotiating with autonomy and relatedness: Dialogical processes in everyday lives of Indians. In H. J. M. Hermans & T. Gieser (Eds.), *Handbook of dialogical self theory* (pp. 169–184). Cambridge, UK: Cambridge University Press.

Chaudhary, N. (2017). Childhood, culture and social science: What we have gained and may be in the process of losing. In T. S. Saraswathi, A. Madan, & S. Menon (Eds.), *Childhoods in India: Traditions, trends and transformations*. New Delhi, Delhi: Routledge.

Chaudhary, N., & Pillai, P. (2014). Research and the Young Child in India: Shifting from Alienation to Adaptability Using an Expanded Framework. *European Journal of Psychology of Education., 31*(1), 29–42.

Cole, M. (1996). *Cultural psychology: A once and future discipline*. Cambridge, MA: Harvard University Press.

Cole, M. (2002). Culture and development. In H. Keller, Y. H. Poortinga & A. Schölmerich, *Between culture and biology: Perspectives on ontogenetic development.* (pp. 303–319). Cambridge: Cambridge University Press.

Correa-Chavez, M., & Rogoff, B. (2005). Cultural research has transformed our ideas of cognitive development. *International Journal of Behavioral Development, 29*(3), 7–10.

Dalal, A. K., & Misra, G. (2002). Social Psychology in India: Evolution and emerging trends. In A. K. Dalal & G. Misra (Eds.), *New directions in Indian Psychology, Vol. 1* (pp. 19–52). New Delhi, Delhi: Sage.

Danziger, K. (1997). *Naming the mind: How Psychology found its language*. New Delhi, Delhi: Sage Publications. Retrieved from http://kurtdanziger.com/Naming%20the%20Mind.pdf

Demuth, C., & Mey, G. (2015). Qualitative methodology in developmental psychology. In J. D. Wright (Ed.), *International encyclopedia of social and behavioral sciences* (Vol. 19, 2nd ed., pp. 668–675). Oxford, UK: Elsevier.

De Vos, J. (2008). From Panopticon to Pan-psychologisation. *International Journal of Zizek Studies, 2*(1), 1–20. https://journals.sagepub.com/doi/10.1177/097133360902200105

De Vos, J. (2016). The metamorphoses of the brain and its discontents.

Eagleton, T. (2000). *The idea of culture*. Oxford, UK: Blackwell.

Hampden-Turner, C. (1982). *Maps of the Mind*. New York, NY: Macmillian.

Henrich, J., Heine, S. J., & Norenzayan, A. (2010). The weirdest people in the world. *Behavioural and Brain Sciences, 33*(2-3), 61-83. https://doi.org/https://doi.org/10.1017/S0140525X0999152X

Ishiguro, H. (2016). How a young child learns how to take part in mealtimes in a Japanese day-care center: A longitudinal case study. *European Journal of Psychology of Education., 31*(1), 13–27.

Jha, V. N. (2008). (Chapter 13): The Nyāya-Vaiśeṣika theory of perceiving the world of our experience. In I. R. Rao, A. C. Paranjpe, & A. K. Dalal (Eds.), *Handbook of Indian Psychology*. New Delhi, Delhi: Cambridge University Press.

Kagan, J. (2012). *Psychology's ghosts: The crisis in the profession and the way back*. New Haven, CT: Yale University Press.

Kakar, S. (1996). *The Indian psyche*. New Delhi, Delhi: Viking.

Kumar, S. (2014). Inclusive classroom and social diversity in India: Myths and challenges. *Journal of Indian Research, 2*(1), 126–140.

Laing, R. D. (1965). *The divided self: An existential study in sanity and madness*. London, UK: Penguin.

Madsen, O. J., & Brinkmann, S. (2010). The disappearance of Psychologisation. *Annual Review of Critical Psychology, 8*, 179–199.

Maier, H. W. (1988). *Three theories of development* (3rd ed.). New York, NY: University Press of America.

Montessori, M. (1966). *The secret of childhood* (M. Joseph Costelloe, Trans.). New York: Ballantine Books. (Original work published in 1936).

Nelson, K., Skwerer, P. D., Goldman, S., Henseler, S., Presler, N., & Walkenfeld, F. (2003). Entering a Community of Minds: An Experiential Approach to 'Theory of Mind'. *Human Development, 46*, 24–46. https://doi.org/10.1159/000067779

Nielsen, M., Haun, D., Kärtner, J., & Legere, C. H. (2017). The persistent sampling bias in developmental psychology: A call to action. *Journal of Experimental Child Psychology, 162*, 31–38. https://doi.org/10.1016/j.jecp.2017.04.017

Panda, M. (2004). Culture and mathematics: Case study of Saora in Orissa. In K. Chanana (Ed.), *Transformative links between higher education and basic education: Mapping the field*. New Delhi, Delhi: Sage.

Pandey, J. (2002). *Psychology in India revisited, Vol. 2*. New Delhi, Delhi: Sage.

Pandit, S. A. (2011). The concept of "Rasa" in Indian Psychology. *Journal of Psychological Research, 6*(1), 139–157.

Paranjpe, A. C. (2021). Situating systems of psychology within the traditional Indian and modern Western knowledge systems. In G. Misra, N. Sanyal, & S. De (Eds.), *Psychology in modern India: Historical, methodological and future perspectives* (pp. 487–502). Singapore, Singapore: Springer.

Paranjpe, A. C. (2002). *Self and identity in modern Psychology and Indian thought*. Boston, MA: Springer.

Pence, A. (2011). Early childhood care and development research in Africa: Historical, conceptual, and structural challenges. *Child Development Perspectives, 5*(2), 112–118.

Rao, R., & Paranjpe, A. C. (2008). (Chapter 11): Yoga Psychology. In R. Rao, A. C. Paranjpe, & A. K. Dalal (Eds.), *Handbook of Indian Psychology*. New Delhi, Delhi: Cambridge University Press.

Rao, R., Paranjpe, A. C., & Dalal, A. K. (2008). *Handbook of Indian Psychology*. New Delhi, Delhi: Cambridge University Press.

Roland, A. (1988). *In search for self in India and Japan: Towards a cross-Cultural psychology*. Princeton: Princeton University Press.

Rogoff, B. (1993). Children's guided participation and participatory appropriation in sociocultural activity. In R. Woxniak & K. Fischer (Eds.), *Development in context: Acting and thinking in specific environments* (pp. 121–153). Hillsdale, NJ: Erlbaum.

Saraswathi, T. S. (2017). Preface. In T. S. Saraswathi, A. Madan, & S. Menon (Eds.), *Childhoods in India: Traditions, trends and transformations* (pp. xviii–xxii). New Delhi, Delhi: Routledge.

Sharma, N. (2011). *Understanding adolescence*. New Delhi, Delhi: National Book Trust.

Sinha, D., & Tripathi, R. C. (1994). Individualism in a collectivist culture: A case of coexistence of opposites. In U. Kim, H. C. Triandis, C. Kagitcibasi, S. C. Choi, & G. Yoon (Eds.), *Individualism and collectivism: Theory, method, and applications* (pp. 123–136). Thousand Oaks, CA: SAGE.

Skutnab-Kangas, T. (2009). The role of mother tongues in the Indigenous, tribal, minority and minoritized children- what can be done to avoid crimes against humanity? In P. W. Orelus (Ed.), *Affirming language diversity in schools and society. Beyond linguistic apartheid*. New York/London: Routledge.

Sternberg, R. (2019). *Time Bomb: How the Western Conception of Intelligence is Taking Down Humanity*. SRCD Keynote, Baltimore, 22nd March, 2019, SRCD.

Tulloch, M. (2000). The meaning of age difference in fear of crime: Combining qualitative and quantitative approaches. *British Journal of Criminology, 40*, 451–467.

Valenzuela, A. (1999). *Subtractive schooling: U.S.-Mexican youth and the politics of caring*. Albany, NY: State University of New York.

Valsiner, J. (2020). Where Occidental Science Went Wrong: Failing to See Systemic Unity in Diversity. *Psychology and Developing Societies, 32*(1), 7–14. https://doi.org/10.1177/0971333620903880

Valsiner, J. (2019). Hypergeneralisation by the human mind: The role of sign hierarchies. In *First presented at 4th Hans Kilian Preis Lecture Bochum, April 28, 2017*. Giessen: Psychosozial Verlag.

Valsiner, J. (2014). The need for cultural psychology: Methodology in a new key. *Culture and Psychology, 20*(1), 3–20. https://doi.org/10.1177/1354067X13515941

Valsiner, J. (2004). *Culture in minds and societies; Foundations for Cultural Psychology*. New Delhi, Delhi: Sage.

Van der Kolk, B. (2000). Post-traumatic stress disorder and the nature of trauma. *Dialogues in Clinical Neuroscience, 2*(1), 7–22.

Viswanathan, S. (2016). *Confessions of a bird-man*. The Hindu, December 1, 2016. https://www.thehindu.com/opinion/op-ed/Confessions-of-a-bird-man/article16731708.ece

Weisner, T. S. (2002). Ecocultural understanding of children's developmental pathways. *Human Development, 45*(4), 275–281.

Teaching Physiological Psychology

12

Using News and Social Media to Engage Students in Active Learning

Jane A. Foster

Contents

Abstract

Physiological psychology in North America is an undergraduate course that introduces students to the neurobiology that controls behavior. It complements other psychology courses and includes key concepts and content related to the structure and function of the nervous system. To engage students, instructors can utilize interactive teaching strategies and styles and can consider integrating technology into their course design and organization. This chapter provides an overview of undergraduate *physiological psychology* and provides teaching strat-

J. A. Foster (✉)
Department of Psychiatry and Behavioural Neurosciences, McMaster University, Hamilton, ON, Canada
e-mail: jfoster@mcmaster.ca

© Springer Nature Switzerland AG 2023
J. Zumbach et al. (eds.), *International Handbook of Psychology Learning and Teaching*,
Springer International Handbooks of Education,
https://doi.org/10.1007/978-3-030-28745-0_15

egies and assessment tools based on the integration of news media and use of the social media platform, Twitter, in the classroom. Several resources are provided.

Keywords

Brain and behavior · Twitter · Social media · Science in the news

Introduction

Physiological psychology courses in North America provide an opportunity for students to gain an understanding of the biological basis of brain function and behavior. In general, undergraduate courses in *physiological psychology* are offered in second or third year of university study and require prior completion of an introductory psychology course. Additional upper-level courses that consider sub-topics of physiological psychology are often offered as electives in many undergraduate programs. Course titles vary across programs and may include *biological psychology, behavioral neuroscience, and foundations of brain and behavior,* among others. Their common foundation lies in providing an opportunity for students to advance their knowledge of the dynamic interaction between physiology and psychology.

From a historical perspective, the First International Congress of Physiological Psychology was held in Paris, France, in 1889, with the aim of separating psychology from philosophy (Sabourin & Cooper, 2014). Development of the topic of physiological psychology in the late nineteenth and early twentieth century occurred at a time when scientists were advancing theories to understand the relationship between the brain and behavior (Milner & White, 1987). Advances in neurology and anatomy provided a road map to how sensory and motor systems were organized in the brain and provided the neurobiological framework that contributed to the development of the field (Milner & White, 1987). In addition, biomedical research activities aimed at generating physiological explanations for diseases of the nervous system also provided evidence that behavior was associated with particular brain regions. From there, the concept that these associations were applicable to normal behavior developed more and more throughout the twentieth century (Milner & White, 1987).

Over time, research studies related to physiological psychology advanced our knowledge through the simultaneous consideration of both the brain and behavior and, as such, courses on this topic include an in-depth analysis of neurobiological systems and how these systems influence behavior. A recent trend in university teaching in North America has been to integrate technology into course design for the purpose of enhancing student engagement and improving teaching and learning. Accordingly, this chapter will not only provide an overview of physiological psychology, but will also suggest some innovative and engaging ways to integrate technology such as news media and social media into course content and consider its potential use as a learning assessment tool.

Purposes and Rationale of the Curriculum in Physiological Psychology

The curriculum in *physiological psychology* is a core feature of undergraduate psychology course work in North America. It links psychology and neuroscience while providing a comprehensive introduction to the neurobiological systems that influence behavior. The American Psychological Association guidelines for undergraduate psychology provide the framework for core teaching and learning objectives in psychology courses in general (American Psychiatric Association, 2013). Based on these guidelines, students completing an undergraduate course in physiological psychology should:

1. Demonstrate fundamental knowledge and understanding of the content and concepts of physiological psychology and be able to describe how neurobiological systems contribute to normal behavior and to diseases of the nervous system.
2. Develop skills related to critical thinking and scientific inquiry including an ability to read scientific literature in an evaluative manner.
3. Become familiar with ethical and socially responsible standards in psychological studies and to develop professional skills by participating and contributing to a positive learning experience for themselves and their peers.
4. Develop skills related to communicating about science and scientific findings.
5. Develop an understanding for the use of technology in learning and actively use these tools to engage in learning physiological psychology content from a variety of information sources.

Core Contents and Topics of Physiological Psychology

Physiological psychology provides an overview of the neurobiological basis of behavior. It is recommended that instructors provide a general overview of what is physiological psychology and provide several examples of current research findings in the area, and why the study of physiological psychology is important to understanding animal and human behavior. A foundational topic that should be covered prior to other system-level topics is the structure and function of the nervous system. This topic would include the cellular and anatomical organization of the nervous system, concepts related to neuronal signaling, and would highlight brain regions and circuits that are important to behavior. Additional topics include neuroanatomy, sensory and motor systems, learning, memory, and cognition, sleep, stress systems, emotion, and psychological disorders. An emphasis on linking the course content to current areas of research and to recent publications in the literature will increase student engagement and promote class discussion. It is likely that a degree of overlap in course content will exist between a course in physiological psychology and other courses such as psychopharmacology, perception, and abnormal psychology, among others. The basic principles of nervous system function provide key information that students can apply to other courses.

Approaches and Strategies for Teaching and Assessment in Physiological Psychology

Despite the many advances in teaching strategies in the past decade, including flipped classrooms, problem-based learning, peer mentoring, and the like, the predominant method of teaching in undergraduate psychology is a combination of textbook readings and traditional lectures. Traditional lectures are effective in providing foundational information on a topic, and this is true for *physiological psychology*. In addition, there are well-written and well-organized textbooks on the topics that provide a comprehensive overview of the course content described above. It is recommended that instructors include a textbook as a key resource for *physiological psychology* as this is a comprehensive and convenient resource for students. Similarly, the use of traditional lectures to deliver key course content is valuable. However, it is recommended that instructors consider a variety of teaching styles and levels of engagement to improve the learning experience for the student (▶ Chaps. 54, "Assessment of Learning in Psychology," ▶ 58, "Learning and Instruction in Higher Education Classrooms," ▶ 31, "Teaching Psychopharmacology for Undergraduates," and ▶ 8, "Topics, Methods, and Research-Based Strategies for Teaching Cognition"). Different levels of engagement including interactive engagement, constructive engagement, active engagement, and passive engagement can be considered in course organization and in the delivery of course material (for more information see ▶ Chap. 58, "Learning and Instruction in Higher Education Classrooms," by Schwartz and Bartel, in this handbook). Further, teaching styles that demonstrate the instructor's enthusiasm and knowledge of the topic contribute to an outstanding lecture. That enthusiasm and knowledge can be communicated by using personal examples, focusing on one key research group that contributed to a research area, telling the story of how a recent research topic or a specific research finding developed over time, describing the challenges that occurred in certain areas of the field, and how new approaches may have helped overcome those challenges. If there is a key discovery or key person who provided foundational work in an area, it can be interesting to examine former trainees of that lab, their contributions, and where they have gone and what they have done to continue to work in that field or in other areas. The use of short YouTube videos or references to podcasts by researchers in the field can have a great impact on student interest and enthusiasm, which may lead to better learning in the long run. If your institution provides opportunities for undergraduate research projects, arranging for students to collaborate with local research teams to provide these opportunities in parallel with course work can also benefit student learning (Lloyd, Shanks, & Lopatto, 2019).

Integrating Technology into the Physiological Psychology Course

As numerous online resources including those found in news media, social media, podcasts, YouTube videos, university and government websites, scientific organizations, and many more are accessible to all, integration of these resources inside and outside the classroom has the potential to enhance students' learning opportunities. As described below, arranging for students to explore these online resources can be a useful endeavor, but some resources may be more useful than others.

For example, a recent analysis of the use of web-based resources for delivery of educational materials to medical students in the clinical phase of their studies suggests that podcasts, case studies, and subject-specific apps are suitable but social media such as Twitter and Facebook were less so (Vogelsang, Rockenbauch, Wrigge, Heinke, & Hempel, 2018). Interestingly, the perception and use of social media differs to some extent between educators and their students (El Bialy & Jalali, 2015). This discrepancy highlights the need for educators to engage with students and listen to their perspectives and their feedback. Certainly, the reliability of the resource is a key consideration for instructors. In addition, exploring these resources and integrating them from an instructional perspective can be time consuming and this may limit uptake for undergraduate psychology courses. Multimedia classrooms provide an alternative to using online resources for integrating technology into the course's content delivery system. Such classrooms offer the possibility of including interactive questions using student response systems ("clickers") as well as the use of animations to deliver content (Stoloff, 1995). The availability of interactive classrooms varies at different institutions, of course, but instructors who do not have access to them can consider some of the suggestions provided in this chapter and tailor them to their own teaching situation.

Using Science in the News to Engage Students in the Classroom

There are several reasons to highlight science-based news in classroom lectures and discussions in a physiological psychology course. First, the general public and media outlets are interested in science. Indeed, news outlets typically serve as the first line of communication between the public and the results of scientists' research. Understanding how science is communicated to the public, the various forums involved, the quality of the communication, and the topics that warrant attention is an important component of an undergraduate science education. Second, focusing on science news can help students understand the public importance of key topics in the course, to excite them about recent research findings that are directly related to the course content, and to engage in active learning as they explore news media reports on the topic. Third, well-written news articles can help students to decipher complicated research papers and to identify its key points. Fourth, encouraging students to evaluate the quality, accuracy, and source of science news provides a framework to discuss and consider the key features and aspects of research findings that come from scientific work. Fifth, applying active learning methods to science in the news can open useful classroom dialogues support homework assignments that prompt students to think more deeply about science communication. Sixth, drawing students' attention to science writers' use of terminology that provides laypersons with an understandable overview can provide useful examples for undergraduate students to follow in learning how to communicate with others about topics in physiological psychology. Finally, as described below, combining the use of science in the news with the introduction of social media apps such as Twitter can provide an alternative tool for assessing students' class participation.

One particularly useful way to integrate science news into your course design is to assign students to find recent news articles that are related to physiological psychology. They can do so as in-class activity, a discussion board activity, or as part of some other kind of writing or research assignment. The best approach for your particular course will depend on the scheduled length of class time and the number of students enrolled. With small classes, it is easy to assign students to make short classroom presentations, whereas in larger classes, peer-driven discussion boards may be a scalable way to include students' findings about science in the news. Providing students with the proper framework for finding and considering the available news articles is an important instructional step to ensure that students are prepared and will get the most value out of this exercise. Table 1 outlines the information you can provide to students in order for them to get them started with a science in the news exercise.

As an in-class activity, completing a science in the news exercise can contribute to class participation credit or could be graded as a stand alone presentation. Depending on the number of students and the time available, students can work individually or in small groups to prepare 5- to 10-min classroom presentations. The content of the presentations ought to highlight the key findings that were included in a news story related to physiological psychology. The topics selected can be matched to course content or can be broader in nature, in which case, students have the opportunity to explore topics in which they are particularly interested, but that may not be directly covered in lecture or in other aspects of the course. A possible format for these classroom presentations would include a maximum number of slides (3–5 recommended) and focus on: (1) What is the primary scientific finding in the news article? (2) How does it relate to physiological psychology? (3) Why did it warrant attention in the news? and (4) How accurate was the information provided?

Using Twitter in Support of a Course in Physiological Psychology

As you probably know, Twitter is a social media platform used extensively for communication among scientists, educators, and media, not to mention the general public. Users can share links to news articles, research papers, photos, websites, videos, and include a message or "tweet" of up to 280 characters. There are many good reasons to consider using Twitter as a social media platform in support of teaching physiological psychology, and in general. First, it is an open platform such that all tweets are accessible by all users. Second, academic researchers are active on twitter, so by following other researchers in physiological psychology, it is easy to share recent findings and to keep up to date on literature in the area. Further, as an active user, you can build your network and connect with individuals with similar interests outside your local environment. In addition to scientists, many journals, science organizations, and media are active on Twitter, meaning that both teachers

Table 1 Strategies for finding science in the news

Finding news items
Google News
www.google.com
Science news for students
www.sciencenewsforstuents.org
Social media
Twitter, Facebook, Instagram – Twitter is an excellent source for scientific news
Linked In
News posts by academic and business individuals highlight important news and the attention it is getting

Determining the news story relevance
Consider the source: The more reliable the source, the better the information
- Major news outlets: Radio, newspapers, magazines.
- Scientific journal websites: Often feature research published in their journals.
- University websites: Often feature media articles by the university's public relations office coming from their researchers.
Take a look to see if multiple sources cover the same research or news; often a story put out by a university or journal website is picked up and shared by other media outlets
Evaluate the content
- General information or specific details related to the topic.
- Is there a link to a recent publication?
- Are experts on the topic quoted in the article?
- What is the quality and accuracy of the information provided?
- Is it clear why this finding warrants media attention?.

Who is the target audience?
- General public.
- Scientists and researchers.
- Health care practitioners.
- Other stakeholders.

Identify the primary literature related to the news
PubMed
- PubMed is an online database search engine which comprises more than 28 million citations for biomedical literature from MEDLINE, life science journals, and online books. It is a major literature tool used in the research world.
- Online access to PubMed is available through the following website: https://www.ncbi.nlm.nih.gov/pubmed/
Google scholar
- *Google scholar* provides a simple way to broadly search for *scholarly* literature. From one place, you can search across many disciplines and sources: Articles, theses, books, abstracts, and court opinions from academic publishers, professional societies, online repositories, universities, and other web sites.
- Online access to Google scholar is available through the following website: https://scholar.google.ca/

and students can have access to engaging and interesting course-related information. Third, there is no cost to create a Twitter account and there are no fees associated with its use. Each user is identified by a unique handle, for example, mine is @jfosterlab, and my undergraduate physiological psychology course is @htsci4BB3. Fourth, topics of interest can be highlighted by users in their tweets through the use of hashtags, for example, #phsyiologicalpsychology. Hastags are useful to gather topic-related tweets on relevant topics or ongoing events. Often, organizers of conferences provide attendees with a hashtag for the event so that attendees tweet activities in real time as an event is taking place. Accessing related content by hashtag is easy; when you click on the hashtag in a Twitter post and it takes you to the other posts with the same hashtag.

If you are not yet on twitter, it is easy to get started. The online Twitter guide (https://help.twitter.com/en/twitter-guide) provides step by step instructions to set up your account and profile, as well as tips for getting the most out of using the app. You can stay up to date with topics you are interested in, learn about what other people are talking about, and join in the conversation with people from all areas of the world.

Twitter as a Tool for Sharing Course Content

The fact that Twitter users can share links to other Internet sites or resources provides opportunities to use it not only to provide educational content to a group of students, but also to the public and other interested parties. In a recently published example, Twitter was used to disseminate surgical videos. Links to YouTube videos were embedded in the tweets, allowing users from 28 countries and six continents to have access to this educational material (Cassidy et al., 2020). Further, the producers of the videos were able to monitor the activity of all the users who were connected to their tweets by taking advantage of Twitter analytics. Using this analytical tool provided by Twitter, it is possible to monitor the level of engagement with a tweet, a hashtag, or with a particular account in general (see analytics.twitter.com). Twitter analytics measure the number of times a post is viewed (referred to as "impressions"), the number of times a user interacted with the tweet by clicking a link (referred to as "engagements"), the number of times a post was "liked," or the number of times the tweet was shared (referred to as a "retweet"). In addition, users can select to follow others who share their interests. Based on who you follow and what tweets you like, when you open the app, Twitter algorithms tailor the content that appears on your twitter feed to match your prior activity.

Twitter in the Classroom

The use of twitter in the classroom has expanded in the past decade. Early adopters of twitter in the classroom used live tweets by faculty or teaching assistants during lectures to increase engagement with the course across enrolled students and the larger university community. A concern related to live tweeting is the quality of the information disseminated. Thus educational researchers have suggested strategies to increase content quality through presenter-initiated approaches, such as having the speakers or instructors provide students or teaching assistants with the key take-home points so as to improve the accuracy of the tweets (Tomlinson et al., 2017). To date there has been very little research in this area, and so far, much of it is related to medical education (Feito & Brown, 2018).

Research demonstrating the benefits of using Twitter and other social media to enhance student engagement is emerging (Chawinga, 2017), and there are many blogs, websites, and educational resources available that provide ideas and options for Twitter-based classroom activities (e.g., https://wabisabilearning.com/blogs/technology-integration/18-twitter-based-classroom-activities). Not all of these ideas and options are appropriate for an undergraduate course in physiological psychology, however, the suggestions may provide ideas that can be tailored for that course and other psychology courses.

Using Twitter as an Alternative to Traditional Class Participation

For several years, I have integrated Twitter participation as one of the methods by which students can get class participation credit. In the courses with a biological framework, it is possible to combine the above-noted science in the news activities with Twitter participation. To start, create a Twitter account and profile for your physiological psychology course and generate a couple key hashtags to share with students. Each student would also need to create a Twitter account and profile. The goal of the exercise is for you, your teaching assistant (if you have one), and your students to (1) "tweet" key news articles linked to physiological psychology and (2) "tweet" the research evidence that supports the news article (see Fig. 1).

Here are some instructions and examples of news articles and related scientific papers, as well as formatting of tweets as part of a class participation exercise.

Each tweet ought to tag the course twitter account (e.g., @hthsci4BB3), and refer to the hashtags that you have created. Inclusion of these two identifiers makes it easier for you to track the Twitter activity in the course. Assessing participation through Twitter can be accomplished by following the Twitter activity of student users directly in Twitter, or as described above, using Twitter analytics. Users can also have access to their own Twitter activity and the Twitter activity of a hashtag, and can generate a report of this activity. You can thus ask your students to submit a Twitter analytical report for their activity related to the physiological psychology course. The standard formatting and accessible nature of Twitter analytics makes participation easy to track and easy to grade.

Challenges Faced and Lessons Learned

For more than 15 years, I have integrated science in the news into course design including lecture material, student presentations, and written assignments. Feedback from students has been positive and many have expressed appreciation for the

Science in the News

- Find a News Article and Tweet it out

Tweeting the original news items

- Tweet always begins with 'NEWS:' followed by:
    - first few words of the headline in quotations, to indicate the article's headline
    - link to the news story and any appropriate hashtags

Tweeting the evidence

- Find the research article that related to the news item
- Tweet always begins with 'EVIDENCE:' followed by:
    - the key findings of the paper or main take home

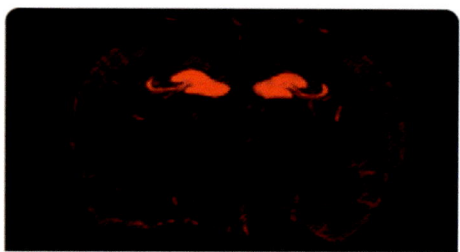

@hthsci4bb3 NEWS:"This Receptor Mediates the Effects of Chronic Stress in the Brain"-Psychological stress contributes to anxiety & depression as a result of neuroinflammation-Actions on hippocampal neurons influence cognitive & mood alterations with stress

This Receptor Mediates the Effects of Chronic Stress in the Brain
The neuronal receptor for IL-1 has been linked to chronic stress in a rodent model.
🖉 technologynetworks.com

@hthsci4bb3 EVIDENCE: "Interleukin-1 receptor on hippocampal neurons drives social withdrawal and cognitive deficits after chronic social stress"-Showed the neuronal receptor for IL-1 straddles the interaction between social stress, inflammation, & anxiety
...-nature-com.libaccess.lib.mcmaster.ca/articles/s4138...

Fig. 1 Twitter participation on topics related to physiological psychology

opportunity to explore topics not directly covered in the course content but related to course topics. Over the past 3 years, I have found using Twitter in the classroom to be successful in providing an active learning option for students. Participating in Twitter activities is one option available to students to earn participation credit and more than 90% of them choose it. I like that option, too, because measuring participation via Twitter is easy to translate into a grade using a simple rubric of 1 grade or 1.5 points per tweet.

One of the challenges associated with using Twitter or other social media activity as part of determining course credit is that a small subset of students do not use these media, but this can be managed by providing other avenues for class participation. Generally, students find participating in twitter as an easy and enjoyable way to earn participation credit, and it is more popular than the option of making short presentations. Still, in one second-year class with over 100 students, the science in the news article assignment was very successful and all students participated, either individually or in groups to present key findings in the news and on related topics. Several times over the years, I have changed the format for integrating news media and social media in my classrooms, but always in response to helpful feedback and suggestions from the students.

Teaching, Learning, and Assessment Resources for Physiological Psychology

My teaching philosophy is simple – be creative, enthusiastic, energetic, present the most up-to-date science, and keep the students involved. To increase the overall effectiveness of my teaching, I try to provide a positive learning environment and use a variety of pedagogical skills and techniques. In addition, I believe that teachers of any course in psychology should engage in professional development activities including teaching attending teaching conferences, workshops, and courses (online or in person) that can expand their knowledge of teaching styles and new teaching techniques. The information and ideas gained can help any teacher to improve teaching effectiveness and move beyond the traditional lecture approach to undergraduate teaching.

Recommended Resources:

1. **Effective Teaching Strategies** (https://www2.le.ac.uk/offices/lli/developing-learning-and-teaching/enhance/strategies). Several universities have teaching resources for professional development and to assist educators. It is often difficult to find a good overview of the current and best teaching strategies. This website at the University of Leicester Learning Institute provides an updated list and description and is a great place to find new ideas.
2. **Linked In Learning** (www.linkedin.com): This online resource requires membership but offers extensive resources for professional development. Some universities provide access for their faculty.
3. **Brainfacts.org** (https://www.sfn.org/outreach/brainfactsorg):
   Often students in physiological psychology do not have a strong biological or neuroscience background. Providing online resources that can help them understand some of the concepts and content related to basic neuroscience and behavior. The Society for Neuroscience provides outreach to the public, including the brainfacts.org website, which offers simple explanations of key concepts about brain function. It provides summaries of research discoveries and information on many diseases and disorders that effect the brain.
4. **Ted Talks** (https://www.psychreg.org/ted-talks-psychology/):
   Ted talks are a fabulous way of gaining insight into a topic and hearing it from an expert on the topic. This site provides links to great TED talks on psychology. These may be of interest to educators and may also be useful to integrate into lectures.
5. **University of Waterloo Centre for Teaching Excellence** (https://uwaterloo.ca/centre-for-teaching-excellence/teaching-resources/teaching-tips/alternatives-lecturing/active-learning/varying-your-teaching-activities).
   This center offers numerous resources for teachers, including teaching tips and links to many resources that can help in course organization, teaching strategies, and professional development.

References

American Psychiatric Association. (2013). APA guidelines for the undergraduate psychology major: Version 2.0., Retrieved from http://www.apa.org/ed/precollege/undergrad/index.aspx.

Cassidy, D. J., Mullen, J. T., Gee, D. W., Joshi, A. R. T., Klingensmith, M. E., Petrusa, E., & Phitayakorn, R. (2020). #SurgEdVidz: Using social media to create a supplemental video-based surgery didactic curriculum. *The Journal of Surgical Research, 256*, 680–686. https://doi.org/10.1016/j.jss.2020.04.004.

Chawinga, W. D. (2017). Taking social media to a university classrom: Teaching and learning using twitter and blogs. *International Journal of Educational Technology in Higher Education, 14*, 3. https://doi.org/10.1186/s41239-017-0041-6.

El Bialy, S., & Jalali, A. (2015). Go where the students are: A comparison of the use of social networking sites between medical students and medical educators. *JMIR Med Educ, 1*(2), e7. https://doi.org/10.2196/mededu.4908.

Feito, Y., & Brown, C. (2018). A practical approach to incorporating twitter in a college course. *Advances in Physiology Education, 42*(1), 152–158. https://doi.org/10.1152/advan.00166.2017.

Lloyd, S. A., Shanks, R. A., & Lopatto, D. (2019). Perceived student benefits of an undergraduate phsyiological psychology laboratory course. *Teaching of Pscyhology, 46*, 215–222.

Milner, P. M., & White, N. M. (1987). What is physiological psychology? *Psychobiology, 15*, 2–6.

Sabourin, M., & Cooper, S. (2014). The first international congress of physiological psychology (Paris, august 1889): The birth of the International Union of Psychological Science. *International Journal of Psychology, 49*(3), 222–232. https://doi.org/10.1002/ijop.12071.

Stoloff, M. (1995). Teaching physiological psychology in a multimedia classroom. *Teaching of Pscyhology, 22*, 138–141.

Tomlinson, S., Haas, M., Skaugset, L. M., Cico, S. J., Wolff, M., Santen, S., . . . Huang, R. (2017). Using twitter to increase content dissemination and control educational content with presenter initiated and generated live educational tweets (PIGLETs). *Medical Teacher, 39*(7), 768–772. https://doi.org/10.1080/0142159X.2017.1317727.

Vogelsang, M., Rockenbauch, K., Wrigge, H., Heinke, W., & Hempel, G. (2018). Medical education for "generation Z": Everything online?! - an analysis of internet-based media use by teachers in medicine. *GMS Journal for Medical Education, 35*(2), Doc21. https://doi.org/10.3205/zma001168.

Teaching Social Psychology Effectively

A Practical Guide

13

Scott Plous, David G. Myers, Mary E. Kite, and Dana S. Dunn

Contents

S. Plous (✉)
Wesleyan University, Middletown, CT, USA
e-mail: splous@wesleyan.edu

D. G. Myers
Hope College, Holland, MI, USA

M. E. Kite
Ball State University, Muncie, IN, USA

D. S. Dunn
Moravian University, Bethlehem, PA, USA

© Springer Nature Switzerland AG 2023
J. Zumbach et al. (eds.), *International Handbook of Psychology Learning and Teaching*,
Springer International Handbooks of Education,
https://doi.org/10.1007/978-3-030-28745-0_16

313

Abstract

Social psychology is the scientific study of how people think about, influence, and relate to one another – a subfield of psychology that began more than a century ago with experiments on social facilitation and social loafing. In the aftermath of World War II, social psychology subsequently broadened to tackle pressing social issues such as prejudice, genocide, obedience to authority, and school desegregation. In this chapter, we provide a practical guide on how to teach social psychology to undergraduate students, including "action teaching" – a relatively new educational approach in which students take action on social issues as part of the learning process. After discussing the curricular goals of social psychology, the chapter outlines six core ideas that emerge from research and theories in social psychology. Next, it describes several teaching, learning, and assessment strategies, beginning with "backward course design" (a design method in which instructors first identify learning objectives and then work backward to create course content, learning activities, and student assessments to achieve the objectives). The chapter also offers advice on how to address some of the most common challenges and questions that social psychology teachers face: *(1) What if class members vary widely in psychology training? (2) Do the results of social psychology research generalize? (3) Are social psychology findings replicable? (4) How should research ethics be discussed? (5) What's the best way to teach about difficult or controversial topics? (6) How can social psychology be taught effectively online?* Finally, the chapter ends with an annotated list of published and online resources related to teaching, learning, and assessment, all of which should be useful to both new and veteran social psychology instructors.

Keywords

Social psychology · Teaching · Action teaching · Online · MOOC · Undergraduate · Assessment

Introduction

We humans are social animals. Our ancestors hunted, gathered, and found protection in groups. As their descendants, our lives are connected by a web of invisible threads. Social psychology explores these connections as it illuminates our beliefs and our attitudes, our conformity and our individuality, and our capacity to help and love one another and to dislike or harm others.

Social Psychology's Focus

Reduced to its essence, social psychology is *the scientific study of how we think about, influence, and relate to one another:*

- *Social thinking* – Social psychologists observe and experiment with how we view ourselves and others, both consciously and unconsciously (implicitly). How do we explain people's behavior? How do we assess and explain our own behavior?
- *Social influence* – Social psychologists study both the subtle social forces that induce conformity, persuasion, and group behavior and the counterforces that lead us to assert our uniqueness, resist indoctrination, and sway our groups. They also explore the cultural roots of social behavior.
- *Social relations* – Social psychologists plumb the depths of our helping or hurting others. Why do we like or love some people and dislike or distrust others? What explains our individual prejudices and systemic racism? What kindles social conflict, and how can we transform closed fists into open arms?

Moreover, social psychologists shine the light of these concepts on everyday life. Thus, we have a social psychology of health and well-being, of courtroom justice, and of behaviors that enable a sustainable future.

Social Psychology's History

Although humans have been social throughout recorded history, sociality is on the rise, as the Google Ngram in Fig. 1 suggests. In today's world of unprecedented population density and ever-increasing connectedness, our species has devised social media, social security, social services, social work, and, yes, social psychology.

The earliest experiments in social psychology explored *social facilitation* – as in Norman Triplett's (1898) finding that people exert more energy when performing tasks such as bike riding in the presence of others – and of *social loafing*, as in Maximilien Ringelmann's (1913) studies of people's expending less effort in a tug of war when their own contributions were not identifiable.

But as Thomas Pettigrew (in press) notes, it was World War II and its aftermath that led to social psychology's emergence as a robust discipline. European social psychologists Kurt Koffka, Wolfgang Köhler, Max Wertheimer, and – most notably – Kurt Lewin immigrated to the United States and leavened the academic loaf. Social psychologists at Yale University and elsewhere studied soldier morale and mass persuasion. Interdisciplinary institutes were founded to conduct social research and national surveys. Gordon Allport's (1954) classic volume, *The Nature of Prejudice*, became, in its 1958 abridged version, a best-selling contribution to public under-standing. In 1954, reports Pettigrew, social psychologists Kenneth Clark, Isidor Chein, and Stuart Cook "supplied the major scientific support" for the US Supreme Court's landmark school desegregation decision.

During the latter half of the twentieth century, the "cognitive revolution" prior-itized studies of social thinking, including automatic processing that fuels our stereotypes and drives our behavior. Simultaneously, European social psychology made the discipline's focus less individualistic by emphasizing the importance of

Relative Frequency of the Word "Social" in English Language Books

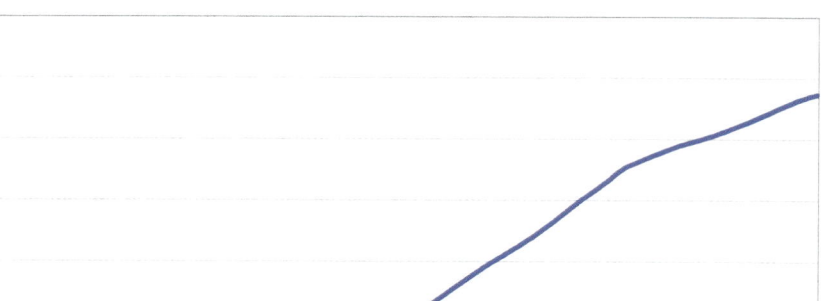

Fig. 1 An increasingly social world
Source: http://books.google.com/ngrams

social identity. Social psychology has also grown worldwide, including in Central and South America, Australia, South Africa, and Asia.

Action Teaching

As this brief history suggests, social psychology began with studies on social facilitation and social loafing, but after the upheaval of World War II, researchers increasingly began to tackle pressing social issues such as prejudice, violence, and obedience to authority. Kurt Lewin, who left Nazi Germany for the United States in 1933, was deeply troubled by anti-Semitism and anti-Black prejudice, and in the 1940s, he proposed "action research" as a way to address societal problems while also advancing scientific knowledge (Lewin 1946, 1948). "No action without research," wrote Lewin, and "no research without action" (Marrow, 1969, p. 193). This two-track approach to social research had an enduring effect on social psychology that is still visible today in the form of behavioral science-based efforts to address racial injustice (Eberhardt, 2019), climate change (Fielding et al., 2014), the COVID-19 pandemic (Van Bavel et al., 2020), and other social problems (Fig. 2).

Building on Lewin's approach, "action teaching" is the educational counterpart to action research (Plous, 2000). What distinguishes action teaching from traditional pedagogy is that it contributes directly to the betterment of society, while it teaches students about the topic being studied. That is, students don't merely listen to lectures, complete reading assignments, or write term papers – they take actions that promote peace, social justice, sustainable living, and the well-being of others.

Fig. 2 Kurt Lewin, who
advocated action research and
helped found contemporary
social psychology
Source: http://vlp.mpiwg-
berlin.mpg.de/people/data?
id=per638

By incorporating prosocial action into the learning process, action teaching tends to
increase student motivation, improve learning outcomes, and provide students with a
foundation for future civic action (Velez & Power, 2020).

Although action teaching has been used in a variety of courses and disciplines, it
is especially well suited to courses in psychology because the field covers social,
cultural, and political topics such as intergroup conflict, stereotyping, climate
change, human rights, criminal justice, and the development of empathy. Here are
a few examples featured on ActionTeaching.org, a web-based repository of action
teaching ideas and resources:

- Psychology students at Buffalo State College learned about culture and the daily
  life of refugees by teaching a local refugee family how to set up and balance a
  checking account, handle telephone solicitations, and avoid credit card debt,
  thereby helping family members while learning from them (Norvilitis, 2010).
- An organizational psychologist at the University of Pennsylvania taught students
  about the principles of persuasion, negotiation, leadership, and teamwork by
  challenging students to create fundraising campaigns for the Make-a-Wish Foundation, which serves children with life-threatening medical conditions. Students

in classes that included this assignment learned so much and were so engaged that they ended up raising more than \$100,000 in donations to the foundation (Grant, 2013).

- Grand Valley State University psychology students learned about research methods and statistics by comparing the effectiveness of different social influence techniques that they employed to solicit volunteers for a local anti-hunger organization. Over a 4-year period, students not only learned first-hand how to collect and analyze psychological data, but the volunteers they signed up decorated more than 13,000 meal bags for children in need of food and emotional support (Jones, 2020).

Depending on the learning objectives and associated curricular goals and constraints, action teaching activities can be used in social psychology classroom demonstrations, student assignments, field experiences, or web-based exercises, and they can take a number of different forms, such as required course assignments, extra-credit assignments, honors work, half-credit courses, lab components, tutorial projects, or independent study opportunities. Action teaching has also been used in online education, where it has the potential to reach thousands of students (for an example, see the sidebar "Action Teaching Assignment: The Day of Compassion"). Regardless of the form that action teaching takes, the central idea is that students contribute to the welfare of others as they learn about course topics, often in highly memorable ways that lead to meaningful and lasting educational outcomes.

Action Teaching Assignment: The Day of Compassion

The "Day of Compassion" is an action teaching assignment that has been used in both online and campus-based social psychology courses since the 1990s (Day of Compassion, 2021). The goal of the assignment is to teach students about compassion and empathy by challenging them to live as compassionately as possible for 24 hours. Specifically, students are asked to spend the day trying their best "to reduce suffering, help other people in need, be considerate and respectful, and avoid causing harm to any living being." After the day is over, students then submit a paper answering questions such as:

- If your behavior was different than normal, which person did you like more: the "Day of Compassion you" or the "normal you"?
- If you preferred the "Day of Compassion you," what are the psychological factors that prevent this "you" from coming out?
- If you wanted to encourage others to behave as you did during the Day of Compassion, what techniques would you use?

Most students find the Day of Compassion assignment to be enlightening, and some describe it as life-changing (Plous, 2009). For example, many students report that they like their "Day of Compassion self" more than their "normal self" and that they intend to continue behaving more compassionately in the future. Others come to realize that compassion is easier and more fun to practice than they had expected. Still others report that their acts of kindness and compassion were reciprocated by those they helped, creating a positive feedback loop in which compassion begat compassion. In the context of a social psychology course, the assignment can be used to teach about prosocial behavior, bystander intervention, conflict resolution, social identity, intergroup bias, and participant-observation research methods, among other topics.

In keeping with the twin goals of action teaching – to promote learning and contribute to the welfare of others – the Day of Compassion tends to generate a wide assortment of prosocial outcomes. For instance, students often report resolving conflicts with estranged friends or family members, helping homeless strangers, rescuing animals, donating money to nonprofit groups, and volunteering time at community organizations. In fact, when the Day of Compassion was assigned in a massive open online course on social psychology (mentioned later in this chapter), thousands of students in dozens of countries spent so much time helping and caring for their friends, colleagues, family members, and community that a BBC News article dubbed the event "the world's most compassionate 24 hours" (Stephens, 2014).

Purposes and Rationale of the Curriculum in Social Psychology

Social psychology courses address two key competencies that the US National Association of Colleges and Employers (2019) has identified as essential for under-graduates' career readiness: critical thinking/problem-solving and global/intercultural fluency. In addition, the teaching of social psychology contributes to liberal education with its three broad aims:

1. *Understanding oneself and others*: Empowering students to accurately under-stand and interpret behavior with less gut feeling and more evidence-based thinking
2. *Enlarging hearts*: Replacing judgmentalism with empathy and compassion – to respect our social diversity while appreciating our human kinship
3. *Enabling social flourishing*: Educating global citizens to contribute to a thriving, sustainable, peaceful future

As teachers, we strive toward these aims by training students how to think critically when it comes to human behavior – to repeatedly ask *What do you mean?* and *How do you know?* And we seek to equip them with powerful concepts that have wide applicability to everyday life.

To help social psychology instructors move from these broad aims to crafting specific course learning objectives, we recommend consulting the American

Psychological Association's (2013) *Guidelines for the Undergraduate Psychology Major: Version 2.0* (the current guidelines are scheduled for renewal and revision on or before 2023). APA's guidelines represent a set of expectations for learning and performance by undergraduate students who are majoring in psychology or enrolled in a psychology course, such as social psychology. Five learning goals appear in the *Guidelines 2.0:* knowledge base in psychology, scientific inquiry and critical thinking, ethical and social responsibility in a diverse world, communication, and professional development. These learning goals can be incorporated into a social psychology course that either follows introductory psychology or is taught as an entry-level course without prerequisite coursework (Dunn et al., 2020).

For instance, instructors teaching an introductory social psychology class might state early in the syllabus that students who successfully complete the course will be able to:

- Demonstrate knowledge of the major concepts, theoretical perspectives, empirical findings, and historical trends in social psychology
- Identify and critique research methods in social psychology
- Use critical thinking, skeptical inquiry, and, when possible, the scientific method to identify and solve problems related to social behavior and social thinking
- Apply social psychological theories and principles to understand people's everyday behavior and relationships, including one's own
- Recognize, understand, and respect the complexity of human diversity

These learning objectives are typical in an introductory social psychology class, but there is no single codified set of objectives applicable to all social psychology courses. What is most important is that learning objectives be explicit, clearly written, and closely linked to the required readings, assignments, and classroom activities.

Core Content and Topics of Social Psychology

What are social psychology's core ideas? Our short list includes this half dozen.

Attitudes and Actions Feed Each Other

As but one determinant of our behavior, our internal attitudes are imperfect predictors. Yet an attitude can matter, particularly when it's directly relevant to a behavior, such as exercising, and when we're reminded of it. Persuasion – whether viewed as "education" (by those who believe it) or "propaganda" (by those who don't) – can therefore change our attitudes and sway our behavior.

But our attitudes not only influence our behavior; they are also shaped by it. When we act and accept responsibility for our actions, our attitudes tend to fall in line. The resulting self-persuasion may lead us to believe more strongly in those things for which we have suffered or given public witness.

We Construct Our Social Reality

We humans have an urge to explain behavior – to attribute it to some cause. As intuitive lay scientists, we typically attribute behavior efficiently and with enough accuracy to serve our needs. For example, when people's behavior is distinctive and consistent, we attribute it to their personal traits and attitudes.

But in ways that may go undetected, our attributions and judgments often predictably err. Especially in individualist cultures, we may attribute people's behavior to their dispositions without noticing situational factors that constrain and influence behavior – as when thinking that a shy teacher's classroom talkativeness reflects an extraverted personality. Likewise, we are sometimes biased by our pre-conceptions; we see what we expect.

We may also misperceive illusory associations and causes. Thus, we may treat others in ways that lead them to fulfill our expectations. And we may be influenced more by vivid, memorable – and, therefore, cognitively available – anecdotes than by statistical reality. Finally, failing to recognize our vulnerability to bias, we may be overconfident and self-serving in our social judgments.

Social Influences Powerfully Guide Our Behavior

Faced with powerful social forces such as norms, expectations, and orders, our actions may diverge from our attitudes and values. Depending on the situation, the very same person may act kindly or viciously, submissively or independently, and foolishly or wisely. As a result, even good people sometimes do bad things. Evil situations may overwhelm the best of intentions, leading people to accept falsehoods or capitulate to cruelty. And race-based unfair treatment may result not only from bad-apple individuals with explicit prejudice but from systemic injustice and implicit bias.

Cultures matter, too. If you tell social psychologists where in the world you live, how old you are, how educated you are, and what media you read and view, they will predict your likely attitudes toward same-sex relationships, whether you prefer a slim or voluptuous body, and whether you focus relatively more on yourself or on your community.

Persons and Situations Interact

Although powerful situations may override our individual inclinations, we are not passive tumbleweeds blown hither and yon by the social winds. Facing the same situation, some (depending on their dispositions, their cultural experience, and their convictions) may acquiesce, while others may assert themselves. Therefore, people may react to restore their sense of freedom, and a numeric minority may change a group's direction. We are not only the creatures of our social world but also its creators.

As Social Animals, We Have a Deep Need to Belong

We long to connect, to be esteemed, and to bond with others. Separated from significant others, as when physically distancing under COVID-19, we find new ways to socially connect. Ostracism from one's family or friends creates genuine pain. Short of torture, solitary confinement can be the severest punishment. Because of this need to belong, we are driven to bond with friends, fall in love, or check social media (in the United States, on a daily basis; Kunst, 2020). Given supportive, close, enduring relationships – such as a healthy marriage or intimate friendships – we express greater happiness and are at less risk of depression. And, for better and worse, we develop strong ingroup loyalties: We prefer and favor "us" over "them."

Our Social Behavior Has Biological Roots

Many of our social behaviors reflect biological wisdom. As evolutionary psychologists remind us, we share a human kinship – a human nature that inclines us to behave in ways and to exhibit likes and dislikes that helped our ancestors survive and reproduce. Whether dating and mating, caring and sharing, or hating and hurting, our biological nature has prepared us with dispositions that will help send our genes into the future.

Our brain, behavior, and relationships form an interconnected system. Because of this, social neuroscientists can explore brain networks that underlie our experiences of love, rejection, excitement, aggression, and other social and emotional states. We are the products of both "under-the-skin" biological influences and social influences.

Teaching, Learning, and Assessment in Social Psychology: Approaches and Strategies

The assessment of learning outcomes is an essential element of teaching social psychology effectively. For our purposes, assessment can be defined as the measurement and evaluation of how well students are learning key information and skills from the course they are taking (Maki, 2004; Mentkowski et al., 2000). The goal is for social psychology teachers to be able to show various stakeholders (e.g., administrators, colleagues, the students themselves, and their families) that class members are benefitting from their studies. In short, the question is simply this: *How well have students mastered the field's subject matter?*

To assess student mastery, we advise instructors to begin by outlining their course's learning objectives and then employ "backward course design" (Wiggins & McTigue, 2005) to build a framework for the course content and assessments. Identifying the learning goals in advance affords instructors the opportunity to tie course activities and evaluative elements to them, increasing the likelihood that the assessments demonstrate desired results. After identifying the desired learning outcomes, there remain two steps in backward course design (Hard et al., in press):

1. Designing the instructional activities, readings, and other course elements that will best achieve the learning objectives (e.g., lectures, classroom demonstrations, small-group discussions, assigned readings, projects)
2. Finding or creating assessment instruments that accurately measure the degree to which students have met the course's learning objectives (e.g., exams, quizzes, graded papers, oral presentations)

Backward course design, then, encourages instructors to be intentional and goal-oriented in their teaching plan from the start.

Assessing Outcomes Tied to Teaching and Student Learning

Traditional outcome measures, such as exam scores and course grades, have their place, but ideally, social psychology courses should include assessments tied to assignments and activities occurring throughout the course. As many assessment enthusiasts have long advocated, it is generally better to employ *formative assessments* – in-process, low-stakes evaluations of students' understanding and progress during the course – than to focus on high-stakes *summative assessments* that occur at the end of a course unit or the course itself (Dunn et al., 2004, 2012).

One central piece of advice for social psychology educators as they develop assessments for their courses is this: Students will benefit if their instructor helps them to perform well on assessments (Pusateri et al., 2009). Evaluating student learning and performance should never be mysterious; rather, the exercise should be transparent. Here are recommendations on how to achieve transparency where assessment is concerned:

Help Students Understand What Matters
Go beyond providing mere definitions of social phenomena by explaining why an assignment or activity is important when it comes to learning a core concept or phenomenon in social psychology (e.g., the role of confirmation bias in science, politics, and medicine; Nickerson, 1998). To solidify students' grasp of why a concept matters, instructors might also invite students to generate and share examples from their own observations or experiences.

Provide Detailed Instructions
Tell the students exactly what to do and how to do it, and explain concretely how their work will be evaluated. When feasible, it's often helpful to provide a scoring rubric for a given assignment (Greenberg, 2015) and teach students how to critique their own work.

Share Samples or Models from Prior Social Psychology Classes
Share a few examples of successful student work in the past, such as a self-reflection paper (e.g., "When do you conform?"; Asch, 1956) or an application of a social psychological theory to an everyday situation ("How does the just world hypothesis influence the way we react to other people's health problems?"; e.g., Lerner, 1980). Exemplars can illustrate what good work looks like and help students satisfy the goals of an assignment.

Provide Timely Feedback on Student Performance
In the spirit of formative rather than summative assessment, offer clear, detailed, and constructive feedback on the work so that students learn to improve in the future.

Introduce Students to Effective Learning Strategies

Research on learning and cognition reveals a variety of techniques that can promote student learning (for a summary, see Dunlosky et al., 2013). Some of these strategies include:

- *Elaborative processing* – Encourage students to reflect on the meaning of what they are learning. When students actively link new terms, theories, and research results with previously known information, learning tends to deepen and endure (e.g., "How is Asch's conformity paradigm related to yet different from Milgram's research on obedience to authority?"; Asch, 1956; Milgram, 1963).
- *Retrieval practice or the "testing effect"* – Provide repeated opportunities for low-stakes testing in which new course material is recalled from memory. Quizzes can be given during class or online to encourage study, strengthen recall, and prepare students for higher-stakes exams.
- *Distributed practice* – Let students know that they're more likely to retain information when they break their study time into a series of short sessions over a lengthy period of time than when they "cram" all studying into one long study session right before an exam.
- *Metacognition* – Ask students to think about how they are processing course material and applying it to their own life, which should be easy given that social psychology relates directly to daily life and relationships. When students become aware of their own thoughts and reactions to course material, the information is more likely to be remembered down the road.

These basic steps can help students master, integrate, and retain new material as the course unfolds.

Consider High-Impact Practices as Opportunities for Assessment

Kuh (2008) identified several educational practices that have been tied to successful student performance, known as "high-impact practices," or "HIPs." Besides engaging students in active learning opportunities, HIPs also present assessment opportunities for social psychology instructors. In other words, while using HIPs to involve students in deep learning about social psychology, they can also be leveraged as formative assessments. Here are three broad HIP categories:

Writing Intensive Activities Aimed at Different Audiences Students benefit from learning to do different types of writing aimed at distinct audiences. In academic settings, the default option is for students to write descriptive papers for the instructor (e.g., describing the hypothesis, methodology, results, and conclusions of a social psychology experiment). However, various types of reflective writing can be done as well. For example, students might write a personal account of how a psychological phenomenon affects them in daily life (e.g., overconfidence; West & Stanovich, 1997), or they might apply social psychology research findings to a societal issue by writing a mock newspaper letter to the editor (e.g., the effect of affective forecasting biases on materialism; Wilson & Gilbert, 2005).

Collaborative Assignments and Projects Collaborative efforts allow students to learn from and instruct their peers, just as they afford students the opportunity to experience this important aspect of professional work life. To do so, instructors can form teams of 3–5 students to prepare in-class demonstrations of readily replicable social psychological effects (e.g., social loafing; Karau & Williams, 1993). Alternatively, teams of students can conduct conceptual replications of simple social psychology experiments, adding new variables in order to expand understanding of a given effect (e.g., positive affect and problem-solving; Isen, 2004).

Undergraduate Research Depending on class size, collaboration can be taken even further by having an entire class develop hypotheses, research procedures, and stimulus materials and then collect, analyze, and present or write up results. These sorts of undergraduate research activities require considerable organizational effort, yet they provide substantial benefits in terms of professional training as well as reinforcing the idea that cooperation among investigators is a hallmark of contemporary psychological science. Alternatively, if a department or program has a research participation requirement that includes social psychology, students can learn about the subfield by taking part in relevant studies.

Challenges and Lessons Learned

Teaching social psychology is a richly rewarding experience, in large measure because it helps students understand themselves and their social world based on the results of theory-driven empirical research. Nonetheless, social psychology instructors face a number of challenges worth considering. Here are a few of the most common challenges and questions that instructors encounter when teaching introductory social psychology courses, along with suggestions on how to effectively address them.

What If Class Members Vary Widely in Psychology Training?

Because introductory social psychology classes often include students with widely different levels of prior training in psychology, competency in research methods cannot be assumed. Thus, early in the term, instructors should provide an overview of basic research methodology. Key issues are how social psychologists form and test hypotheses, the distinction between correlational and experimental research (and the conclusions that can be drawn from each), the purposes of random sampling and random assignment, and the generalizability of research findings. Students should understand that social psychologists blend the logical positivist tradition with a social constructionist approach that recognizes how researchers' values and expectations can influence the scientific process. These values affect who chooses to become a social psychologist, the research topics those individuals decide to pursue, and how the findings from those inquiries are interpreted (e.g., Else-Quest & Hyde, 2016). Students should be encouraged to critically examine the strengths and weaknesses of various research methods, including a consideration of how researchers' values might constrain or buttress social psychologists' understanding of the social world.

Do the Results of Social Psychology Research Generalize?

There are two reasons why the generalizability of social psychology research findings is especially important to cover. First, social psychology research is based heavily on convenience samples that overrepresent college students and people from Western Europe, Canada, and the United States. For example, Henry (2008) examined prejudice research in three top social psychology journals and found that more than 90% of all articles used student samples. Social science research findings are also disproportionately based on WEIRD (Western, Educated, Industrialized, Rich, and Democratic) samples (Henrich et al., 2010), and social psychology is no exception. Moreover, Arnett's (2008) analysis of six top psychology journals found that more than two thirds of empirical research articles relied on samples from the United States, whereas the people of Africa, Asia, the Middle East, and South America were only rarely represented. Although the trend toward obtaining participant samples through crowdsourcing is encouraging, these samples also fail to fully represent humankind. For instance, even though participants from Amazon's Mechanical Turk are generally older than most college students, they still tend to overrepresent college graduates, employed people, and White people (Buhrmester et al., 2011; Chandler et al., 2014). Thus, we suggest instructors acknowledge these limitations and make students aware of high-quality research from a variety of countries, as well as cross-cultural research spanning collectivist and individualist (or tight and loose) cultures (see Matsumoto & Juang, 2017).

A second reason instructors should attend to generalizability is that it serves as a starting point for discussions of diversity regarding not only race, age, and culture but social class, (dis)ability, sexual orientation, gender identity, ethnicity, and other attributes. Considering who is included and excluded from research can lead to conversations about how such decisions affect our understanding of the world (Kite & Littleford, 2015). More generally, when instructors include the experiences of people from diverse backgrounds, they help students gain scientifically valid knowledge about human behavior (Trimble et al., 2003). Moreover, discussions of sociocultural diversity invite students to sharpen their critical thinking and problem-solving skills (Bowman, 2010; Dunn et al., 2013). Finally, addressing diversity can increase students' civic engagement and help equalize the educational environment for members of marginalized groups because students achieve more when they see themselves and their social groups represented (Bowman, 2011; Elicker et al., 2010).

Are Social Psychology Findings Replicable?

Several years ago, the Open Science Collaboration (2015) published a landmark report calling into question the replicability of social psychology research. Specifically, an international coalition of 270 researchers attempted exact replications of 100 experimental and correlational psychology studies, and the coalition found that 64% of the studies failed to replicate. Indeed, the successful replication rate was especially low for social psychology studies (23% for articles from the *Journal of Personality and Social Psychology* and 29% for social psychology articles in *Psychological Science*). These results suggest that instructors should help students exercise caution with respect to social psychology findings that have yet to be replicated, and they provide an opportunity to discuss how scientific progress works, beginning with information about how to distinguish between exact replications that recreate a study and conceptual replications that test the same hypothesis with a different set of operational definitions (Kite & Whitley, 2018). Instructors might also explain why it is difficult to know whether findings from an original study or its replication are "true" (Open Science Collaboration, 2015).

Instructors can also use the topic of replication to discuss recent changes being made to strengthen confidence in research results. One such change is greater attention to whether a study's sample size has adequate statistical power for testing the proposed hypotheses. Another is the increased use of preregistration, whereby a study's rationale, methodology, and proposed statistical analyses are peer reviewed prior to data collection (Nosek et al., 2018). At the same time, we recommend assuring students that social psychology textbook authors serve as gatekeepers who endeavor to present research findings that are reliable and well validated. Although errors occasionally creep in, the social psychological theories and findings covered in an introductory course overwhelmingly represent results that can be counted on.

How Should Research Ethics Be Discussed?

The ethical behavior of social psychologists is, of course, germane to the discussion of research practices, and all the more so because social psychology is the home of two prominent psychologists associated with ethically controversial studies: Philip Zimbardo and Stanley Milgram. In Zimbardo's Stanford prison study, several research participants experienced significant distress for hours or days, but the study continued for nearly a week before being shut down (Haney et al., 1973). Likewise, in Milgram's (1974) research on obedience to authority, a number of participants experienced acute distress yet were urged by the experimenter to continue despite their protestations, thus violating the now-established right to withdraw without penalty. Although ethical standards have advanced considerably since the time of these classic studies, both cases offer instructors an excellent chance to discuss the importance of informed consent, US Institutional Review Boards and other ethics committees that regulate research on human participants, post-experimental debriefing procedures, data security, codes of ethical conduct, and other measures designed to protect the health and welfare of research participants.

One unresolved issue in social psychology concerns the use of deception, which is often used to disguise the true purpose of a study and reduce the likelihood that participants will respond artificially to an experimental situation. This deception can range from the creation of fictitious materials distributed in a laboratory experiment (e.g., a news article summarizing made-up research findings) to outright lying (e.g., giving participants false feedback about their personality or abilities). The level of harm caused by such procedures is hard to assess, but most social psychologists would surely agree with Sieber's (1992) conclusion that it is indefensible to use deception to trick people into doing something they would avoid if they fully understood what was happening. As with the other issues we have discussed, a thoughtful consideration of research ethics can situate social psychological research findings in the broader context of risk-benefit analysis. Where the line should be drawn is ultimately a matter of opinion and conscience, but students need an understanding of the ethical issues at stake in order to reach their own conclusion.

What's the Best Way to Teach About Difficult or Controversial Topics?

The issues discussed so far focus on controversies concerning the scientific method, but social psychology topics themselves can arouse strong emotions – hot button topics that run the gamut from racism to sexual orientation to partner violence and beyond. For example, studies on prejudice and stereotyping suggest that most people exhibit ingroup favoritism and harbor implicit biases toward others with respect to race, gender, age, or other attributes. When students learn that they may hold unconscious biases toward certain groups, many are understandably troubled. Yet when students learn that biases arise in part from a reliance on common cognitive heuristics, and when they are challenged to confront their biases, the result can be greater openness, understanding, and multicultural competency. In fact, providing students with individualized feedback about their biases and how they operate can lead students to accept that they have unconscious racial biases (Casad et al., 2013) and to feel more positively about the learning process in general (Morris & Ashburn-Nardo, 2010). Interestingly, learning about personal biases may be especially helpful for people high in prejudice. For instance, when Adams et al. (2014) asked students to complete the Implicit Association Test followed by teaching modules on conscious and unconscious bias, it turned out that the students who initially displayed the highest levels of bias reported the greatest motivation to control their prejudice.

Students do not always have experience discussing emotional issues in a classroom setting, and some students find the prospect of doing so unsettling or even frightening (Vespia & Filz, 2013). To help them manage difficult conversations, students need to be assured that they are in a safe classroom environment with clearly established ground rules for discussion (ideally, rules that the students have had a voice in creating; Goldstein, 2021). Students and instructors must both be mindful of how privilege affects classroom dynamics – who is in the room, who has social power, and how instructors can make sure that students from underrepresented groups have a voice (Warner et al., 2021). Instructors also need to consider their own level of multicultural competence and take steps to ensure they're prepared to teach about complex emotional topics (Kite & Littleford, 2015).

How Can Social Psychology Be Taught Effectively Online?

Because classroom instruction tends to feel more personal than online instruction, it may seem daunting to teach social psychology online, particularly when it comes to the controversial and emotional topics mentioned earlier. There is no reason, however, that social psychology can't be taught in a supportive, educational, and engaging way online. Indeed, Coursera's massive open online course (MOOC) in social psychology has enrolled more than a million students since it was first offered in 2013, and Coursera's MOOC on the science of well-being (based heavily on social psychology) has enrolled more than three million. During the COVID-19 pandemic, thousands of social psychology courses were taught either partially or wholly online, and even before the pandemic, an estimated 43% of US undergraduates reported taking at least one class online (Snyder et al., 2019). The primary question, then, is not whether social psychology can or will be taught online, but how to do it most effectively. Although research on this question is limited, here are some preliminary recommendations:

Choose a Course Format that Fits Student Needs and Learning Objectives One of the most important decisions an online instructor faces is whether to teach synchronously (i.e., in live sessions), asynchronously (with materials that students can watch, read, or listen to on their own), or some blend of the two (e.g., alternating live and recorded lectures or recording live lectures for students who prefer to watch them later). In general, synchronous courses are more interactive and responsive to student questions and input – a format well suited to seminars and other small classes – whereas asynchronous and blended formats have the advantage of allowing students greater flexibility in choosing when to watch the class sessions (see Martingano, 2020, for further distinctions).

Harness the Advantages of Online Teaching Rather than focusing on the limitations of online instruction, concentrate on the pedagogical advantages. For instance:

- Teaching online makes it relatively easy and affordable for instructors to host guest speakers for part or all of a class session, regardless of where guests are located. To take just one example, instructors can discuss a social psychology experiment and then surprise the class with a guest appearance of the experimenter to talk with students about the study.
- Teaching synchronously with a videoconferencing app such as Zoom allows the instructor to conduct anonymous polls to solicit student opinions, assess

mid-lecture comprehension, carry out in-class demonstrations, and see if students can predict research findings before learning of experimental outcomes.

- If a synchronous lecture class has teaching assistants and a videoconferencing app with a chat window, instructors can ask TAs to answer any questions that students post during the lecture in real time, thereby clearing up confusion without interrupting the lecture. Teaching assistants can also open each class session a few minutes early with background music that welcomes students or relates to the topic being discussed (e.g., the Dar Williams song *Buzzer* about Stanley Milgram's obedience research).

- In contrast with campus-based courses, asynchronous and blended online courses have the advantage of allowing students to pause videotaped lectures to take notes, replay the videos if something isn't clear, and rewatch lectures to help prepare for upcoming exams.

- One great advantage of MOOCs and other open-access courses is that they enroll students from around the world, thus facilitating cross-cultural dialogue. For example, in the social psychology MOOC mentioned earlier, class members from nearly 200 countries were able to interact with each other, and the class discussion forum included a Coronavirus Pandemic subforum with nearly 500 threads addressing questions such as *How can social psychology be used to reduce the pandemic?* and *What is daily life like in your country, culture, and community?* Similarly, a Black Lives Matter subforum fostered cross-cultural exchange with questions such as:
  - *How much racism is there in your country?*
  - *How can social psychology be used to reduce racism and promote respect for all people?*
  - *If there were any one video, website, book, or article on anti-racism that you wish people around the world would see or read, what would it be, and why?*

As these examples suggest, each mode of online teaching offers unique advantages, some of which would be hard to duplicate in traditional classroom settings.

Master the Technology To make the most of online teaching, it's essential that instructors take time to master the necessary technology. Depending on the course and instructional needs, this mastery might include learning how to administer online exams; edit digital videos; crop and resize images; share online documents; use Moodle, Blackboard, or other learning management systems; and smoothly operate videoconferencing apps such as Zoom, which offer an array of customizable settings and options (Levy, 2021). Although it takes time to learn new technologies, in the long run, many of them save time and have the potential to improve the quality of teaching.

Adapt to the Medium Just as a movie is more than a filmed play, an effective online course is more than a set of videotaped classroom lectures (Moore, 2016). To hold student attention online, instructors generally need to energize the delivery with faster pacing and more interactivity, theatricality, questions, stories, and audiovisuals than a campus-based class would commonly have. For example, rather than simply quoting from a book, online instructors might occasionally hold up the book like a prop and read from it. Rather than talking about an experiment that randomly assigned participants based on a coin toss, online instructors might toss a coin on camera or share their screen and show students how to conduct random assignment using Randomizer.org. Rather than discussing social traps such as "the dollar auction game" (Teger, 1980), online instructors might auction off a dollar or other unit of currency to members of the class. Finally, a word about pacing: In his book *What the Best College Teachers Do*, Bain (2004) reported that effective teachers tended to vary the rhythm and content of their delivery every 10–12 minutes; in the world of MOOCs and other online courses, however, instructors would be well advised to change gears even more frequently and break up course content so that each videotaped lecture runs only 6–12 minutes (Bhattacharya, 2020; Hickey et al., 2020). In other words, student learning and engagement tend to be better with 5–10 brief videos covering an hour of content than with a single video showing the same hour of content.

Teaching, Learning, and Assessment Resources

Although there are thousands of excellent teaching, learning, and assessment resources available, here are a few we find especially useful for instructors teaching social psychology to undergraduates.

Recommended Reading

American Psychological Association. (2013). *APA guidelines for the undergraduate psychology major: Version 2.0.* http://www.apa.org/ed/precollege/about/psymajor-guidelines.pdf

These guidelines are designed to help psychology educators teach and assess student learning related to content-oriented and skills-based goals. Although the guidelines do not focus exclusively on social psychology, they contain a wealth of valuable recommendations for anyone teaching courses in this area.

Pusateri, T., Halonen, J. S., Hill, B., & McCarthy, M. (2009). *The assessment cyberguide for learning goals and outcomes* (2nd ed.). American Psychological Association. http://www.apa.org/ed/governance/bea/assessment-cyberguide-v2.pdf

This online guide offers advice on how to implement a range of assessment activities in psychology courses, including courses in social psychology. The text has four sections that help instructors (1) understand assessment in departmental, institutional, educational, and societal perspectives; (2) design viable assessment plans; (3) maintain a culture of assessment; and (4) apply assessment strategies in psychology.

Myers, D. G. (2005, March 1). Teaching tips from experienced teachers. *APS Observer, 18*(3), pp. 39–40, 48–50. http://www.psychologicalscience.org/observer/teaching-tips-from-experienced-teachers

This article includes ten valuable teaching tips from master teachers in psychology. Even though the tips are intended mainly for new psychology instructors, they're useful at any level of experience, and the article includes additional advice from award-winning teachers (gathered by William Buskist) as well as six other suggestions based on David Myers' experience teaching dozens of sections of introductory and social psychology.

Recommended Websites

- *Social Psychology Network*

http://www.socialpsychology.org/
Founded in 1996, Social Psychology Network has received more than 375 million page views and is one of the oldest, largest, and most active Internet gateways in the behavioral and social sciences. The central hub of the Network, SocialPsychology.org, features searchable databases of more than 20,000 classified resources, 16,000 psychology-related news stories, 10,000 members, 2,000 social psychology experts, and 650 career mentors for students from underrepresented groups. All resources in the Network – including thousands of teaching-related links, interactive activities, and student learning aids – are available free of charge.

- *Resources for the Teaching of Social Psychology*

http://jfmueller.faculty.noctrl.edu/crow/
This website offers an annotated collection of more than 6,000 links to activities, exercises, class assignments, online videos, examples, and other resources for teaching social psychology and related courses. The site is organized by topic and curated by social psychologist Jon Mueller.

- *Action Teaching*

http://www.actionteaching.org/
ActionTeaching.org is the world's largest repository of action teaching materials, including a searchable archive of more than 40 award-winning classroom activities, field experiences, student assignments, and web resources that instructors are welcome to freely use or adapt.

- *SPSSI Action Teaching Program*

  http://www.spssi.org/action-teaching

  The Society for the Psychological Study of Social Issues maintains an Action Teaching Program designed to (1) recognize excellence in action teaching with an annual award honoring innovative teaching that addresses social issues such as climate change, immigration, human rights, or intergroup conflict; and (2) facilitate the development of new action teaching resources by providing grants to develop, enhance, or measure the impact of an action teaching activity, assignment, field experience, or web-based resource.

- *Teaching Current Directions in Psychological Science*

  http://www.psychologicalscience.org/tag/teaching-current-directions

  This compendium offers educators a trove of creative ideas and practical tips for teaching about research topics covered in *Current Directions in Psychological Science* – a peer-reviewed journal published by the Association for Psychological Science. The compendium includes dozens of teaching ideas related to social psychology and other subfields of scientific psychology.

- *The Stanford Prison Experiment*

  http://www.prisonexp.org/

  This website features detailed information on one of the most famous and controversial social psychology studies ever conducted: the Stanford Prison Experiment, a simulation study of prison life in which college-aged participants were randomly assigned to play the role of prisoner or guard over a period of 6 days. The site contains material in seven languages and includes archival documents, photos, videos, related links, critiques of the study, and rebuttals from the principal investigator and others associated with the study.

- *UnderstandingPrejudice.org*

  http://www.understandingprejudice.org/

  UnderstandingPrejudice.org, whose pages have been visited more than 40 million times, offers a "Teacher's Corner" with more than 35 college-level classroom activities and student assignments, a "Reading Room" that includes a prejudice research literature review available in 10 languages, and interactive demonstrations that permit visitors to learn about different forms of prejudice, explore the dynamics of segregation, test their knowledge about US slavery and Native American issues, and compare their score on the Ambivalent Sexism Inventory with the average scores of people from 25 different countries.

- *Project Implicit*

  http://www.projectimplicit.net/

Project Implicit allows visitors to learn about implicit biases and stereotypes that operate outside conscious awareness and to take a variety of online Implicit Association Tests to see whether they themselves hold biases related to race, gender, age, sexual orientation, gender identity, weight, disability, and other social, demographic, and physical characteristics. Project Implicit was founded in 1998 by social psychologists Tony Greenwald, Mahzarin Banaji, and Brian Nosek and has thus far administered more than 25 million tests.

- *Research Randomizer: Random Sampling and Random Assignment Made Easy*

http://www.randomizer.org/
Research Randomizer is a free online resource that provides researchers and students with an easy way to generate random numbers and assign participants to experimental conditions. In addition, the site offers an interactive tutorial that teaches students how random sampling and random assignment work. Thus far, the Research Randomizer tutorial has been completed by more than 100,000 students, and the site has been used to generate more than 30 billion sets of random numbers.

- *Teaching Resources from the Society for Personality and Social Psychology*

http://www.spsp.org/resources/teaching
The Society for Personality and Social Psychology maintains a teaching resource page with a curated list of sample syllabi, teaching aids, textbooks, videos, and links to other websites offering useful ideas and materials for teaching personality and social psychology.

References

Adams, V. H., Devos, T., Rivera, L. M., Smith, H., & Vega, L. A. (2014). Teaching about implicit prejudices and stereotypes: A pedagogical demonstration. *Teaching of Psychology, 41*(3), 204–212. https://doi.org/10.1177/0098628314537969.

Allport, G. W. (1954). *The nature of prejudice*. Reading, MA: Addison-Wesley.

American Psychological Association. (2013). *APA guidelines for the undergraduate psychology major: Version 2.0.* http://www.apa.org/ed/precollege/about/psymajor-guidelines.pdf

Arnett, J. (2008). The neglected 95%: Why American psychology needs to become less American. *American Psychologist, 67*(7), 602–614. https://doi.org/10.1037/0003-066X.63.7.602.

Asch, S. E. (1956). Studies of independence and conformity: I. A minority of one against a unanimous majority. *Psychological Monographs: General and Applied, 70*(9), 1–70. https://doi.org/10.1037/h0093718.

Bain, K. (2004). *What the best college teachers do*. London: Harvard University Press.

Bhattacharya, P. (2020, November 23). *Why your ideal online course video must be 6-12 minutes long.* HubSkills.com. http://hubskills.com/online-course-video-to-be-6-12-minutes/

Bowman, N. A. (2010). College diversity experiences and cognitive development: A meta-analysis. *Review of Educational Research, 80*(1), 4–33. https://doi.org/10.3102/0034654309352495.

Bowman, N. A. (2011). Promoting participation in a diverse democracy: A meta-analysis of college diversity experiences and civic engagement. *Review of Educational Research, 81*(1), 29–68. https://doi.org/10.3102/0034654310383047.

Buhrmester, M., Kwang, T., & Gosling, S. D. (2011). Amazon's Mechanical Turk: A new source of inexpensive, yet high-quality, data? *Perspectives on Psychological Science, 6*(1), 3–5. https://doi.org/10.1177/1745691610393980.

Casad, B. J., Flores, A. J., & Didway, J. D. (2013). Using the implicit association test as an unconsciousness raising tool in psychology. *Teaching of Psychology, 40*(2), 118–123. https://doi.org/10.1177/0098628312475031.

Chandler, J., Mueller, P., & Paolacci, G. (2014). Nonnaïveté among Amazon Mechanical Turk workers: Consequences and solutions for behavioral researchers. *Behavioral Research, 46*(1), 112–130. https://doi.org/10.3758/s13428-013-0365-7.

Day of Compassion. (2021, June 16). In *Wikipedia.* https://www.wikipedia.org/wiki/Day_of_Compassion

Dunlosky, J., Rawson, K. A., Marsh, E. J., Nathan, M. J., & Willingham, D. T. (2013). Improving students' learning with effective learning techniques: Promising directions from cognitive and educational psychology. *Psychological Science in the Public Interest, 14*(1), 4–58. https://doi.org/10.1177/1529100612453266.

Dunn, D. S., Baker, S. C., Mehrotra, C. M., McCarthy, M., & Landrum, R. E. (Eds.). (2012). *Assessing teaching and learning in psychology: Current and future perspectives.* Cengage.

Dunn, D. S., Coffman, C., Bhalla, M., Boysen, G. A., Diaz-Granados, J. L., McGregor, L. N., Morgan, B., & Smith, P. (2020). Doing assessment well: Advances for undergraduate psychology programs and psychology educators. *Teaching of Psychology, 47*(4), 251–261. https://doi.org/10.1177/0098628320945097.

Dunn, D. S., Gurung, R. A. R., Naufel, K. Z., & Wilson, J. H. (2013). Teaching about controversial issues: An introduction. In D. S. Dunn, R. A. R. Gurung, K. Z. Naufel, & J. H. Wilson (Eds.), *Controversy in the psychology classroom: Using hot topics to foster critical thinking (pp. 3–10).* American Psychological Association. https://doi.org/10.1037/14038-000.

Dunn, D. S., Mehrotra, C., & Halonen, J. S. (Eds.). (2004). *Measuring up: Educational assessment challenges and practices for psychology. American Psychological Association.* https://doi.org/10.1037/10807-000.

Eberhardt, J. L. (2019). *Biased: Uncovering the hidden prejudice that shapes what we see, think, and do.* Viking.

Elicker, J. D., Snell, A. F., & O'Malley, A. L. (2010). Do student perceptions of diversity emphasis relate to perceived learning of psychology? *Teaching of Psychology, 37*(1), 36–40. https://doi.org/10.1080/00986280903425706.

Else-Quest, N. M., & Hyde, J. (2016). Intersectionality in quantitative psychological research: 1. Theoretical and epistemological issues. *Psychology of Women Quarterly, 40*(3), 155–170. https://doi.org/10.1177/0361684316629797.

Fielding, K. S., Hornsey, M. J., & Swim, J. K. (2014). Developing a social psychology of climate change. *European Journal of Social Psychology (Special Issue: The Social Psychology of Climate Change), 44*(5), 413–420. https://doi.org/10.1002/ejsp.2058.

Goldstein, S. (2021). Ground rules for discussing diversity: Complex considerations. In M. E. Kite, K. A. Case, & W. R. Williams (Eds.), *Navigating difficult moments in teaching diversity and social justice* (pp. 17–29). American Psychological Association.

Grant, A. M. (2013). Bringing organizational psychology to life through fundraising. http://www.actionteaching.org/award/organizational-fundraising

Greenberg, K. P. (2015). Rubric use in formative assessment: A detailed behavioral rubric helps students improve their scientific writing skills. *Teaching of Psychology, 42*(3), 211–217. https://doi.org/10.1177/0098628315587618.

Haney, C., Banks, W. C., & Zimbardo, P. G. (1973). A study of prisoners and guards in a simulated prison. *Naval Research Review, 30*, 4–17.

Hard, B. M., Dunn, D. S., Hudson, D., Musselman, R., & Richmond, A. (in press). Designing the introductory psychology course: An evidence-informed framework. In R. A. R. Gurung & G. Neufeld (Eds.), *The introductory psychology initiative*. American Psychological Association.

Henrich, J., Heine, S. J., & Norenzayan, A. (2010). The weirdest people in the world? *Behavioral and Brain Sciences, 33*(2–3), 61–135. https://doi.org/10.1017/S0140525X0999152X.

Henry, P. J. (2008). College sophomores in the laboratory redux: Influences of a narrow data base on social psychology's view of the nature of prejudice. *Psychological Inquiry, 19*(2), 49–71. https://doi.org/10.1080/10478400802049936.

Hickey, A., Urban, A., & Karsten, E. (2020). *Drivers of quality in online learning: How to increase engagement, satisfaction, skill development, and career impact worldwide*. Coursera. http://about.coursera.org/press/wp-content/uploads/2020/10/Coursera_DriversOfQuality_Book_MCR-1126-V4-lr.pdf

Isen, A. M. (2004). Some perspectives on positive feelings and emotions: Positive affect facilitates thinking and problem solving. In A. S. R. Manstead, N. Frijda, & A. Fischer (Eds.), *Feelings and emotions: The Amsterdam symposium* (pp. 263–281). Cambridge University Press. https://doi.org/10.1017/CBO9780511806582.016.

Jones, E. (2020). *Teaching research methods with an anti-hunger project*. http://www.actionteaching.org/award/anti-hunger

Karau, S. J., & Williams, K. D. (1993). Social loafing: A meta-analytic review and theoretical integration. *Journal of Personality and Social Psychology, 65*(4), 681–706. https://doi.org/10.1037/0022-3514.65.4.681.

Kite, M. E., & Littleford, L. N. (2015). Teaching about diversity across the undergraduate psychology curriculum. In D. S. Dunn (Ed.), *The Oxford handbook of undergraduate psychology education* (pp. 129–141). Oxford University Press. https://doi.org/10.1093/oxfordhb/9780199933815.013.012.

Kite, M. E., & Whitley, B. E., Jr. (2018). *Principles of research in behavioral science* (4th ed.). Routledge. https://doi.org/10.4324/9781315450087.

Kuh, G. D. (2008). *High-impact educational practices: What they are, who has access to them, and why they matter*. Association of American Colleges & Universities.

Kunst, A. (2020, November 19). Social network usage by frequency in the U.S. 2020. *Statistica*. http://www.statista.com/forecasts/997198/social-network-usage-by-frequency-in-the-us

Lerner. (1980). *The belief in a just world: A fundamental delusion*. Plenum.

Levy, D. (2021). *Teaching effectively with Zoom: A practical guide to engage your students and help them learn* (2nd ed.). Author.

Lewin, K. (1946). Action research and minority problems. *Journal of Social Issues, 2*(4), 34–46. https://doi.org/10.1111/j.1540-4560.1946.tb02295.x.

Lewin, K. (1948). *Resolving social conflicts: Selected papers on group dynamics*. Harper.

Maki, P. L. (2004). *Assessing for learning: Building a sustainable commitment across the institution*. Stylus.

Marrow, A. J. (1969). *The practical theorist; the life and work of Kurt Lewin*. Basic Books.

Martingano, A. J. (2020, August 20). *The best of both worlds: The benefits of online and offline teaching*. http://www.spsp.org/news-center/announcements/benefits-online-offline-teaching

Matsumoto, D., & Juang, L. (2017). *Culture and psychology* (6th ed.). Cengage.

Mentkowski, M., Rogers, G., Doherty, A., Loacker, G., Hart, J. R., Richards, W., O'Brien, K., Riordan, T., Sharkey, S., Cromwell, L., Diez, M., Bartels, J., & Roth, J. (2000). *Learning that lasts: Integrating learning, development, and performance in college and beyond*. Jossey-Bass.

Milgram, S. (1963). Behavioral study of obedience. *Journal of Abnormal and Social Psychology, 67*(4), 371–378. https://doi.org/10.1037/h0040525.

Milgram, S. (1974). *Obedience to authority*. Harper and Row.

Moore, S. (2016, February 22). *A filmed play is not a movie: Improving online learning*. Extension Engine. http://blog.extensionengine.com/innovative-online-learning/

Morris, K. A., & Ashburn-Nardo, L. (2010). The Implicit Association Test as a class assignment: Student affective and attitudinal reactions. *Teaching of Psychology, 37*(1), 63–68. https://doi.org/10.1080/00986280903426019.

National Association of Colleges and Employers. (2019, January). *Career readiness for the new college graduate: A definition and competencies.* http://www.naceweb.org/uploadedfiles/pages/knowledge/articles/career-readiness-fact-sheet-jan-2019.pdf

Nickerson, R. S. (1998). Confirmation bias: A ubiquitous phenomenon in many guises. *Review of General Psychology, 2*(2), 175–220. https://doi.org/10.1037/1089-2680.2.2.175.

Norvilitis, J. M. (2010). *Bringing culture alive by offering financial education to refugees.* http://www.actionteaching.org/award/refugees

Nosek, B. A., Ebersole, C. R., DeHaven, A. C., & Mellor, D. T. (2018, March). The preregistration revolution. *Proceedings of the National Academy of Sciences of the United States of America., 115*(11). https://doi.org/10.1073/pnas.1708274114.

Open Science Collaboration. (2015). Estimating the reproducibility of psychological science. *Science, 349*, 943. https://doi.org/10.1126/science.aac4716.

Pettigrew, T. F. (in press). Social psychology in mid-20th century United States. In P. Hegarty (Ed.), *Oxford encyclopedia of the history of psychology.* Oxford: Oxford University Press.

Plous, S. (2000). Responding to overt displays of prejudice: A role-playing exercise. *Teaching of Psychology, 27*(3), 198–200. http://www.understandingprejudice.org/pdf/roleplay.pdf.

Plous, S. (2009, Winter). Are you an action teacher? Win $1,000 while making the world a better place. *Psychology Teacher Network, 18*(4), 1, 4, 8, 10, 11. http://www.socialpsychology.org/pdf/psychteacher2009.pdf

Pusateri, T., Halonen, J. S., Hill, B., & McCarthy, M. (2009). *The assessment cyberguide for learning goals and outcomes* (2nd ed.). American Psychological Association. http://www.apa.org/ed/governance/bea/assessment-cyberguide-v2.pdf

Ringelmann, M. (1913). Recherches sur les moteuers animés: Traveil de l'homme [Research on animate sources of power: The work of man]. *Annales de l'Instiut National Agronomique,* 2nd série – tome XII, 1–40. https://gallica.bnf.fr/ark:/12148/bpt6k54409695.image.f14.langEN

Sieber, J. (1992). *Planning ethically responsible research.* Sage https://doi.org/10.4135/9781412985406

Snyder, T. D., de Brey, C., & Dillow, S. A. (2019). *Digest of Education Statistics 2018* (NCES 2020-009). National Center for Education Statistics, Institute of Education Sciences, U.S. Department of Education. https://nces.ed.gov/pubs2020/2020009.pdf

Stephens, P. (2014, October 8). The world's most compassionate 24 hours. *BBC News.* http://www.bbc.com/news/business-28882749

Teger, A. I. (1980). *Too much invested to quit.* Pergamon Press.

Trimble, J. E., Stevenson, M. R., & Worrell, J. P. (2003, September 15). *Toward an inclusive psychology: Infusing the introductory psychology textbook with diversity content* (APA Commission on Ethnic Minority Recruitment, Retention, and Training, Textbook Initiative Work Group). American Psychological Association. https://www.apa.org/pi/oema/programs/recruitment/inclusive-textbooks.pdf

Triplett, N. (1898). The dynamogenic factors in pacemaking and competition. *American Journal of Psychology, 9*(4), 507–533. https://doi.org/10.2307/1412188.

Van Bavel, J. J., Baicker, K., Boggio, P. S., Capraro, V., Cichocka, A., Cikara, M., et al. (2020). Using social and behavioural science to support COVID-19 pandemic response. *Nature Human Behavior, 4*, 460–471. https://doi.org/10.1038/s41562-020-0884-z.

Velez, G., & Power, S.A. (2020). Teaching students how to think, not what to think: Pedagogy and political psychology. *Journal of Social and Political Psychology, 8*(1), 388–403. https://doi.org/10.5964/jspp.v8i1.1284

Vespia, K. M., & Filz, T. E. (2013). Preventing and handling classroom disruptions. In D. S. Dunn, R. A. R. Gurung, K. Z. Naufel, & J. H. Wilson (Eds.), *Controversy in the psychology classroom: Using hot topics to foster critical thinking* (pp. 23–32). American Psychological Association. https://doi.org/10.1037/14038-002.

Warner, L. R., Wagner, L. S., & Grzanka, P. (2021). White privilege in the classroom. In M. E. Kite, K. A. Case, & W. R. Williams (Eds.), *Navigating difficult moments in teaching diversity and social justice* (pp. 151–163). American Psychological Association.

West, R. F., & Stanovich, K. E. (1997). The domain specificity and generality of overconfidence: Individual differences in performance estimation bias. *Psychonomic Bulletin & Review, 4*(3), 387–392. https://doi.org/10.3758/BF03210798.

Wiggins, G. P., & McTighe, J. (2005). *Understanding by design* (2nd ed.). Association for Supervision and Curriculum Development.

Wilson, T. D., & Gilbert, D. T. (2005). Affective forecasting: Knowing what to want. *Current Directions in Psychological Science, 14*(3), 131–134. https://doi.org/10.1111/j.0963-7214. 2005.00355.x.

Teaching Health Psychology Here, There, and Everywhere

14

Arianna M. Stone and Regan A. R. Gurung

Contents

Abstract

Health psychology is a student favorite given its easy applicability to life. In this chapter, we overview the origins and growth of the health psychology course and review current information regarding how the course is taught. We review three major studies of content outlines for the course highlighting course learning outcomes, major assessments used, and the main topics covered and thought to be important by instructors. Together with providing a comprehensive overview of current teaching resources in the field, we map the evolution of one textbook over nine editions to demonstrate changes in the health psychology course over

A. M. Stone
Oregon State University, Corvallis, OR, USA

R. A. R. Gurung (✉)
Psychological Science, Oregon State University, Corvallis, OR, USA
e-mail: Regan.Gurung@OregonState.edu

© Springer Nature Switzerland AG 2023
J. Zumbach et al. (eds.), *International Handbook of Psychology Learning and Teaching*,
Springer International Handbooks of Education,
https://doi.org/10.1007/978-3-030-28745-0_17

time. We then discuss how the course is taught around the world with a focus on the United States, the United Kingdom, and Australia, highlighting areas where more information is needed. Finally, we address major challenges to teaching the course and future directions of the field.

Keywords

Health psychology · Biopsychosocial model

Health psychology is now a thriving subarea of psychology, especially in North America. Several peer-reviewed journals are disseminating research on the topic, multiple professional organizations around the world are devoted to it, and many health psychologists are playing major roles in psychology in general (Revenson & Gurung, 2019). From its origins in the 1970s, the field has now grown dramatically. In the 1990s, only 26% of US psychology departments offered a health psychology course (Perlman & McCann, 1999), but that figure reached 48% in 2005 (Stoloff et al., 2010) and nearly 70% in 2016 (Norcross et al., 2016). Health psychology is featured in many introductory psychology textbooks (e.g., Griggs, 2014) and rated by students as one of the most important and interesting topics covered in introductory psychology (McCann et al. 2016). After briefly reviewing the origins of the health psychology course and summarizing how the course is taught in the United States, we take a detailed look at how the course is taught around the world. We conclude with a description of new directions in health psychology that teachers of the course will want to follow.

Introduction

Health psychology is commonly conceptualized as studying the ways in which health and illness are affected by interactions between biological (e.g., genetics, nervous system) and psychological factors (e.g., personality, attitudes) on health. The field focuses on promoting and maintaining physical health, preventing and treating illness, and identifying the origins and process of illness (Taylor, 1990). The topics most commonly covered include stress and coping, health-risk behaviors, factors surrounding illness (e.g., access, adherence), and chronic and terminal diseases. Health psychology is largely based on the *biopsychosocial model* (Engel, 1977), which highlights the need to include physiological, psychological, and social factors in understanding health and illness.

Current estimates for the emergence of health psychology as a distinct field of study in North America are in the 1960s, which saw the formal adoption of the field in North America and other parts of the world (Lubek & Murray, 2018). In the United States, health psychology is overseen by the American Psychological Association (APA), which creates the guidelines for its practice and standards for its teaching and accreditation.

The first health psychology course was developed in the 1980s (DiMatteo & Friedman, 1982), as were the first of the many health psychology textbooks available today (see Appendix A). Those textbooks vary in their focus, their pedagogical features, and how they have evolved across editions in parallel with changes in the field. The textbook described in Table 1, for example, takes on a less medicalized/clinical perspective across editions, in favor of a more humanized view of individuals and their health and a greater emphasis on practical applications. So although

Table 1 Evolution of Health psychology: an introduction to behavior and health 1st-9th editions

First edition: 1988 | Length: 14 chapters, 434 pages	Second edition: 1992 Length: 16 chapters, 544 pages
1. Introducing Health Psychology	1. Introducing Health Psychology
2. Psychological Principles in Behavioral Medicine	**2. Conducting Research in Psychology and Epidemiology**
3. Physiological Foundations of Health Psychology	**3. Defining and Measuring Stress**
4. The Psychology of Being Sick	4. *Understanding Stress and Illness*
5. Stress and Stress Management	**5. Understanding Pain**
6. Pain and Pain Management	**6. Coping with Stress and Pain**
7. Behavioral Factors in Cardiovascular Disease	7. *Identifying* Behavioral Factors in Cardiovascular Disease
8. Behavioral Factors in Cancer	8. *Identifying* Behavioral Factors in Cancer
9. Personal Control and Health	**9. Receiving Health Care**
10. Smoking Tobacco	10. *Adhering to Medical Advice*
11. Drinking Alcohol	**11. Living with Chronic Illness**
12. Eating to Control Weight	12. Smoking Tobacco
13. Exercising	13. *Using Alcohol and Other Drugs*
14. The Challenge to Health Psychology	14. Eating to Control Weight
	15. Exercising
	16. *Health Psychology: Premise and Promise*

Note: Additions to the second edition are shown in **Bold** with significant revisions to chapter titles shown in *italics.* Summaries of changes to additional editions are shown below.

Third Edition: 1997 \| **Length:**17 chapters, 567 pages
- *The chapter on research is now concisely referred to as "Conducting Health Research" without reference to epidemiology.*
- *Rather than being oriented toward "Receiving" health care, as in the previous edition, this edition frames it as "Seeking Health Care."*
- *Adds an additional chapter on "Staying Healthy."*

Fourth Edition: 2000 \| **Length:**16 chapters, 608 pages
- *It isn't clear exactly when the new section about stress appeared (since the previous two editions' contents were pulled from study guides); however, at least in this edition, there is an entire section devoted to Stress, Pain, and Coping.*
- *Compared with the first edition's section on Behavior and Illness, this edition refers to Behavior and Chronic Disease for Part III, which is reflected in Chapter 6, where "Understanding Stress and Illness" has been changed to "Understanding Stress and Disease."*
- *The chapter on "Staying Healthy" has been changed to "Preventing Injuries."*
- *The final chapter has been edited to "Future Challenges" and will remain so in all future editions.*

Table 1 (continued)

Fifth Edition: 2004 | **Length:** 17 chapters, 593 pages

The only major change in this edition is that the "behavioral factors" language was removed from the Cardiovascular Disease section and altered in the Cancer section, but only for this edition. It was returned in the next edition.

Sixth Edition: 2007 | **Length:** 17 chapters, 599 pages

- *An interesting change is the difference between "coping with" stress and pain, as in the previous edition, and "managing" stress and pain in this edition.*

- *The reference to behavioral factors in cardiovascular disease returns in this edition.*

- *Likely the most notable change is the language around eating – in previous editions, the chapter referring to diet talked about "eating to control weight," while now it only vaguely refers to "eating and weight."*

Seventh Edition: 2010 | **Length:** 16 chapters, 571 pages

Instead of two separate chapters, this edition merges "understanding" and "managing" pain.

The entire chapter on "Preventing Injuries" is removed without a clear replacement.

Eighth Edition: 2014 | **Length:** 16 chapters, 521 pages

- **Contents:** *"Receiving" returns to the chapter about Seeking health care, making it "Seeking and Receiving Health Care."*

- *Chapter 4 has been altered to indicate how to adhere to "Healthy Behavior," rather than "Medical Advice," as in the previous editions.*

- *Chapter 6 adds information regarding immunity to "Understanding Stress and Disease."*

Ninth Edition: 2018 | **Length:** 16 chapters, 531 pages

While the main chapter titles and organization have not changed since the previous edition, the following updates are contained in this edition:

- *Up-to-date coverage*

- *Revised to maintain student interest (containing more relevant examples/case studies, e.g.)*

- *Online multimedia lists*

- *Real-world profile*

some content has remained consistent (e.g., drugs/alcohol/exercise), the addition of sections on stress, chronic illness, accessibility of healthcare, and alternative approaches to managing various health problems reflect a broader, more humanistic, and less purely academic approach to teaching health psychology. The focus on applying health psychology to students' everyday lives mirrors the inclusion of "personal development" in the American Psychological Association's Guidelines for the Undergraduate major (APA, 2013).

Today, there are clear pathways to advanced degrees in health psychology in North America with 22 institutions offering a health psychology-focused Ph.D. program, several of which also offer a master's-level degree (Panjwani et al., 2017). Many of these programs utilize the "embedded" rather than "exclusive" formula, where the health psychology content is combined into a related field within psychology rather than offered stand-alone (Martin et al., 2014). The field of health psychology has evolved significantly over 30 years, but most programs have a clinical focus (Murray, 2014), and undergraduate psychology programs are overall fairly consistent in the types of topics they cover (i.e., in textbooks), although they may not be entirely uniform in their teaching (Panjwani et al., 2017).

Purposes, Rationale, and Content of the Health Psychology Curriculum

The Society for Health Psychology (Division 38 of the American Psychological Association) lists ten major course objectives for the health psychology course (Society for Health Psychology, n.d.). They are:

1. Develop an understanding and appreciation of the complex interplay between one's physical well-being and a variety of biological, psychological, and social factors.
2. Learn how psychological research methods, theories, and principles can be applied to enhance biomedical approaches for promoting health and treating illness.
3. Learn the nature of the stress response and its impact in the etiology and course of many health problems.
4. Discover how behavioral and cognitive methods can help individuals cope with stress.
5. Develop skills for designing programs to improve one's own and others' personal health habits and lifestyles.
6. Acquire an understanding of the difficulty patients experience in deciding whether or when to seek treatment for disturbing symptoms.
7. Become aware of the experiences of patients in the hospital setting, factors that affect adherence to medical regimens, and sources of problems in patient/practitioner relationships.
8. Determine how psychological and medical methods for relieving pain differ and are often combined to enhance treatment effectiveness.
9. Become aware of the impact that disabling or life-threatening illnesses have on patients and their families.
10. Discover how psychological methods and principles can be applied to help patients manage and cope with chronic illness.

A small number of studies have examined the extent to which these learning objectives are reflected in health psychology courses as they are taught in the United States. The first study to shine a light on the health psychology course, and the one best positioned to unpack the purposes and rationale of the course, reviewed 300 course catalogs from a random sample of institutions of higher education (Brack et al., 2010). The reviewers first read course descriptions to identify the titles used for the course (e.g., health psychology, behavioral medicine) and then conducted a survey of course instructors. The catalog review showed that at 93% of the institutions, the course was considered to be an elective and at 63% of them, it was offered only in alternative academic terms. The study also provided a good look at the topics frequently taught in the course. The most common topics (shown here as percent of respondents) included the biopsychosocial model (93%), chronic illnesses (90%), adherence (87%), alcohol/drugs (83%), and behavior modification (80%). Most instructors in this study reported using lecture to teach (97%) and videos to provide supplemental information (77%). The most common assessments included writing assignments and examinations (both 97%). Half the sample reported using personal health change assignments (53%).

A second study (Gurung & Rittenhouse, 2015) examined 50 health psychology course outlines collected in response to a national call and found 13 major themes:

1. General learning (e.g., build active learners and develop careful reading and oral communication skills)
2. Critical thinking
3. Health-related professionals (e.g., understand the challenge involved in health behavior change)
4. Terms and concepts (e.g., acquire an understanding of the components of the field of health psychology)
5. History (e.g., the history of healing in different cultures)
6. Scientific methods (e.g., understand the scientific method)
7. Interpreting research (e.g., basic conceptual skills for interpreting research)
8. Role of psychology (e.g., the role of psychology in health risks and outcomes)
9. Roles of other psychological constructs (e.g., personality and social support)
10. The biopsychosocial model
11. Patterns of health behavior problems (e.g., disease risk)
12. Personal health
13. Importance of culture and diversity (e.g., the role of culture in disease)

In general, course outlines contained specific learning outcomes relating to a wide range of topics. Whereas many learning objectives (e.g., critical thinking, general learning, terms and concepts, interpreting research, and the scientific method) were applicable to any psychology course, a number were specific to health psychology (e.g., health-related professions, roles of psychosocial constructs, biopsychosocial model, patterns of health behavior, and personal health).

The most recent study found that the ten course topics considered most important by instructors were stress, health behavior change, coping, chronic illness, health behavior theories, social support, health disparities, pain, interventions, and cardiovascular disease (Panjwani et al., 2017, Table 2).

Teaching, Learning, and Assessment in Health Psychology

Over the years, several resources have appeared to aid in the teaching of the health psychology course, especially at the graduate level. These include articles in the Society for Health Psychology's flagship journal *Health Psychologist*, and in peer-reviewed journals such as *Annals of Behavioral Medicine*, as well as a wide array of handbooks and specialized volumes (e.g., Benyamini et al., 2017; Gurung, 2014; Revenson & Gurung, 2019; see Appendix B).

A more detailed picture of exactly how the health psychology course is taught in the United States comes from a survey of 126 instructors who described their course format, teaching tools, views about the importance of covering specific topics, and resources needed (Panjwani et al., 2017). A principal component analysis of the topic importance ratings described above revealed five domains: chronic illness, stress and adjustment processes, health psychology in practice, health behavior change, and basics and background. A review of the course outlines provided by 30 of these instructors showed that the most common teaching formats were lecture (97%), discussion (87%), and video presentations (77%). Not surprisingly, exams were the most common form of learning outcome assessment, but 20–25% of instructors also assigned graded papers, projects, discussion boards, quizzes, and presentations[1]. Survey responses also showed that there is some inconsistency in how the course is taught and that there is a clear need for additional teaching resources, including integrated digital media and suggestions for class activities.

New guidelines in teaching health psychology in the United States are trending toward a more diverse and inclusive model that represents greater training in cultural aspects, with a particular focus on social justice and critical psychology, which springs from critical theory and focuses on social critique of structures of power and their contributions to social ills like prejudice and discrimination, especially more "hands-on" training in these perspectives (Ertl et al., 2020). There is also a larger focus in global health education, which has resulted in more opportunities for cross-cultural collaboration in health psychology (Berić-Stojšić et al., 2020), and LGBTQ+ issues (Nic Giolla Easpaig et al., 2014), as well as a community health-centered psychology practice designed to better focus on the needs of a given community from within rather than from the perspective of outsiders (Campbell & Murray, 2004).

A Global View of Health Psychology

Most of the material presented in the preceding sections is well-known in the United States, but because little attention has been paid to how health psychology is taught around the world, we allocate the bulk of this chapter to rectifying that information

---

[1]Survey respondents noted that health psychology textbooks provided inadequate coverage of topics related to diversity and to health disparities across demographic groups. A need for integrating digital media and class activities as teaching tools was apparent.

gap. The following review covers some major themes in the teaching of health psychology globally, but it is incomplete because of the difficulty we encountered in finding relevant information from some parts of the world, because what we in the United States call "health psychology" may be given other names in other countries (in Australia and New Zealand, e.g., the field is often referred to as "behavioral health"; Hamilton & Hagger, 2014), and because many countries have yet to establish health psychology courses. Additionally, in many countries, there is significant overlap between health psychology and community psychology such that it would be inaccurate to divide the two areas fully.

Canada

In Canada, the professional organization that is responsible for generating standards for psychological research and teaching is the Canadian Psychological Association (CPA). This organization has a specific sub-group that represents health psychology, the Health Psychology and Behavioral Medicine Section (*Health Psychology and Behavioural Medicine Section*, n.d.). As in the United States, health psychology is ubiquitous in Canada and is often taught within undergraduate introductory psychology courses as well as in stand-alone health psychology courses, under the guidance of the Canadian Psychological Association (Canada Health Psychology University Programs, Health Psychology and Behavioural Medicine Section). At least five Canadian institutions offer Ph.D.- and/or master's-level degrees specifically in health psychology, and at least one undergraduate institution offers a program at the bachelor's level (Programs in Health Psychology, n.d.). Most programs in Canada have a significantly different emphasis as compared to their US counterparts, mainly because they tend to be framed as community health psychology (Reich, 2007), and particularly because of their focus on a critical approach to the field (Stam et al., 2018), characterized by their critique of the mainstream perspective of psychology (Campbell & Cornish, 2014; MaClachlan, 2006).

Central and South America

Central and South America are very large and complex regions with unique and varied experiences in the development and implementation of health psychology; however, there are some commonalities that can be observed across their trajectories. Overarching themes indicate that health psychology as a discipline is under-practiced in Central and South America (with a few notable exceptions) in favor of a more distinctly community-focused, social change approach (Reich, 2007). The large number of countries involved makes it difficult to render sweeping generalizations, but a critical approach to health psychology that openly opposes problematic, colonized systems of power and emphasizes collective, community response to health concerns in their areas is vastly favored in this region over accommodationist perspectives that seek compromise and conciliation with such systems (Campbell & Murray, 2004; Reich, 2007). In both regions, Freire's *Popular Education*, an educational movement focusing on social class and rejecting the traditional roles of student and teacher in favor of a more equitable, community-centered model, has been utilized (Montero, 1996).

Programs in South America tend to be in community psychology with a focus area in health and extend in many cases to the master's and Ph.D. level. In Brazil, as is common across South America, health psychology is often divided into two main practice areas: hospitals and public health initiatives (Lubek & Murray, 2018). A critical perspective with a focus on social change is the cornerstone common to both of these programs and will generally diverge from similar social psychology or clinical psychology courses by paying specific attention in the curriculum to researching interventions while simultaneously practicing them in the community (Reich, 2007). Community psychology in Chile was founded upon the mental health framework, and its engagement in health is rooted in those origins, as well as the subsequent critical pushback against traditional psychiatric care (Hanitio & Perkins, 2017). Like other countries in Central and South America, Chile's community-based education has courses in many private and public universities focusing on such issues as economic development, social work, and health (Hanitio & Perkins, 2017). This community health perspective in academic programming has been prevalent in other South American countries (e.g., Colombia, Peru, and Venezuela) since the 1960s (Montero, 1996).

In Central America, a similar view is favored. While countries such as Guatemala and Honduras have no specific programs or are only developing programs in community psychology, others (e.g., El Salvador, Costa Rica) have created programs with a strong emphasis in critical psychology and a robust connection to a social as opposed to a clinical psychological perspective (Montero, 1996). While this region has seen simultaneous growth in academic programming for community psychology alongside countries in South America, the process hasn't been identical; there has been a dual model in which one area is focused primarily on traditional approaches to health in the community, whereas the other has utilized a more critical, grassroots perspective that is typical across South America (Montero, 2008).

Several professional organizations that support the training and development of community psychologists in Central and South America, such as the Interamerican Society of Psychology (Sociedad Interamericana de Psicología; SIP), help to establish guidelines for the field (Reich, 2007) as it continues to grow. While community psychology focuses on several different dimensions of public life, a renewed emphasis on community health and health promotion, preventative care, and the impact of social support on health in community settings has been marked in the broad Latin American literature (Montero, 2008). More academic programming is likely to become available as this unique perspective on health psychology continues to grow in these regions.

The United Kingdom

Health psychology in the United Kingdom is overseen by the British Psychological Society (BPS; Quinn et al., 2020). As is the case in North America, there are a long history of health psychology in the United Kingdom, a curriculum reflecting health psychology as a priority in undergraduate psychology education, and journals, textbooks, and training programs (Quinn et al., 2020). And as in the United States, Australia, and Europe, "Health Psychologist" is a protected title in the United Kingdom that requires practitioners to have at least master's-level training for certification. Training programs are offered by 32 institutions, 9 of which are at the Ph.D. level (Martin et al., 2014). There are fewer health psychology textbooks in the United Kingdom than in the United States, but they present a more balanced view of the field, including both the quantitative "hard science" approach that is popular in the United States and a more classical positivist perspective that prioritizes the experiential, qualitative method in community-based, critical work that is popular in Central and South America (Murray, 2014).

The main focus of the UK curriculum is on promoting research in health psychology, and, as in Central and South America, there is a burgeoning critical psychology paradigm, as well as a trend toward separating health psychology from clinical psychology (Martin et al., 2014). Community psychology is a distinct but related focus in health psychology in the United Kingdom, where there is a call to evolve from scientist-practitioners into "scholar-activists" and to transform the curriculum to reflect a broader mission to promote social justice (Campbell & Murray, 2004).

Europe

EuroPsy, also referred to as the European Qualification in Psychology, is a European standard of education, professional training, and competence in psychology set by the European Federation of Psychologists' Associations (EFPA) that complements national standards that already exist in individual European nations. Since 2009, EFPA has been responsible for oversight of standards and practices for health psychology in Europe. This organization makes no distinction between clinical psychology and health psychology overall, so its requirements are such that training programs at most European institutions would not meet the standards for doctoral-level specialists in health psychology in the United States. Further, in many European countries, there are no particular requirements for licensure or certification in health psychology (Martin et al., 2014). Still, there are now undergraduate and postgraduate degree programs in health psychology in at least nine European countries (Martin et al., 2014).

The competencies in health psychology that are required for the European Certificate in Psychology focus primarily on assessment, development, intervention, and other skills that are particularly relevant to clinical practice (Bartram &

Roe, 2005). The European Health Psychology Society (EHPS), too, has worked in recent years to establish a consensus on the content of the health psychology curriculum in the countries it represents. That content reflects a view of health psychology as an offshoot of medicine, rather than behavioral science, albeit with a strong biopsychosocial orientation (Plass & Ingmar, n.d.). Many programs are also considering adding more virtual opportunities for learning, as in community psychology programs in Italy that are beginning to offer entire programs at full distance (Francescato, 2013).

Australia

In Australia, where health psychology is overseen by the Australian Psychological Society (APS), and particularly the College of Health Psychologists, the training curriculum is more research-oriented than in it tends to be in Europe, and it has also become increasingly focused on developing intercultural competence in health psychologists (Mak, 2012). As in the United Kingdom, graduate-level certification in health psychology is typically embedded in clinical psychology (Fisher et al., 2008; Hamilton & Hagger, 2014; Martin et al., 2014). Though health psychology appeared more recently in Australia than in other parts of the world, it has generated intense interest among students. Unfortunately, the growth of the field has been curtailed by an inadequate number of training programs (Hamilton & Hagger, 2014). Though efforts are now being made to include health psychology courses as part of the undergraduate core curriculum (Lubek & Murray, 2018), psychology departments are not required to do so. This situation, combined with too few training programs at the graduate level, means that there are not enough new health psychologists entering the field (Hamilton & Hagger, 2014).

Organizations such as the Australasian Society for Behavioral Health and Medicine, alongside the APS, have attempted to address this problem in a country where the demand for training in health psychology has far outpaced the supply (Hamilton & Hagger, 2014). Undergraduate courses in psychology in Australia tend to use standard North American textbooks with little specific information to Australia, while the concepts of social justice, particularly as it relates to indigenous issues and the notion of Aboriginal land rights, are paramount in the Australian psychological discourse (Fisher et al., 2008; Reich, 2007). Thus, a push has been made to reorient the discourse to a critical community perspective and promote health psychology as a core curriculum (Lubek & Murray, 2018).

Other Regions

In South Africa, health psychology is remarkable for the claim that "there is no health psychology in South Africa" (Yen, 2016). Instead, as in parts of Central and South America, one sees a focus on health as part of the broader field of community psychology (Yen, 2016). This focus reflects what has been described as a rejection of the narrow, North American view of health that was imposed upon African society by colonialism and is echoed in other parts of the continent. In Ghana, for example, community psychology examines health and illness from a perspective that seeks to link them to the impact of colonialism (Lubek & Murray, 2018). While there are some clinical psychology graduate programs and some health psychology under-graduate courses throughout Africa (Yen, 2016), health psychology per se remains an underdeveloped field in the region.

In Hong Kong, there are no professional organizations or licensing bodies related to health psychology, but the field has nevertheless appeared as a channel through which to provide community-based clinical services (Reich, 2007). Community psychology grew in Hong Kong out of a need for more applied research and community-based delivery of mental health services, more as an extension of clinical psychology than as a stand-alone area of behavioral medi-cine (Lam & Ho, 1989). Recently, an orientation toward social justice and community issues has taken the forefront of this discipline and will likely guide its growth (Reich, 2007).

In Egypt and Lebanon, as with many other regions, a focus on community-based health psychology is influenced by the Western model and is supported by a Master of Arts program in community psychology offered through the American University in Cairo; however, this program has not been successful in reaching Egyptian and Lebanese psychologists due to its use of the English language and primarily American programming, which are less accessible to this population (Amer et al., 2015). Palestinian universities, such as Birzeit University, have been prominent in rejecting the Westernized educational forces that persist in the Arab world and focus instead on anti-colonial, critical community psychology frame-works that draw inspiration from Central and South America as well as post-Apartheid South Africa (Makkawi, 2017). As more programs become available throughout this region, a primary focus on social justice in health, education, and scholarship is likely to be the primary perspective through which health psychol-ogists are educated.

Challenges and Future Directions

Teaching the health psychology course creates some unique challenges. First, some students find it difficult to deal with course topics such as death, euthanasia, health-risky sex, and other dangerous behaviors (Gurung & Bruns, 2013). They may want to deny or ignore these uncomfortable topics and thus show little motivation to talk about them in class. Even in the face of clear evidence for racial differences in the probability of contracting and dying from COVID, many students do not believe health disparities exist among different demographic groups.

Another challenge for health psychology teachers lies in the effort required to keep up with the rapid growth of health psychology research and applications. Building on successes in the twentieth and early twenty-first century in terms of spanning different levels of analysis, contemporary health psychology research may focus on social, environmental, biological, behavioral, and even a cellular analysis, all in one project. For example, the movement in health psychology toward studying biological processes surrounding health at a molecular and cellular level (c) brings with it a greater need for health psychology teachers to discuss basic biology, neuroscience, and neurochemistry. Health psychologists are also highlighting the ways in which biopsychological processes influence socioeconomic forces and interact with culture (Ruiz et al., 2019). As a result, some of them are advocating a new *biopsychosociocultural* model for health psychology (Revenson & Gurung, 2019).

Health psychology is a continually growing area of psychology with new advances in medicine, closer collaboration between different disciplines, and an increase in interdisciplinary research. Especially after remote teaching in response to the COVID pandemic (2020–2021), there has been a greater focus on pedagogy and instructional methods, which promises new ways to teach this intrinsically interesting course.

Annotated List of Teaching Resources

Teaching Resources for Health Psychology (https://societyforhealthpsychology. org/training/training-resources/teaching-resources-for-health-psychology/). This website is the online home of the Society for Health Psychology and together with sample syllabi also provides sample course descriptions and typical course content.

Teaching Health Psychology (Gurung & Rittenhouse, 2015). This chapter in Oxford Handbook of Undergraduate Psychology Education (Dunn, 2015) provides a detailed discussion of the evolution of the health psychology course, together with information on the course gleaned from a national study of 50 syllabi in areas such as learning outcomes, textbooks, varieties of content delivery, and assessment.

Appendixes

Appendix A
Appendix B

Appendix A Health Psychology textbook resources with most recent edition prior to 2015

Author	Title	Originally published	Edition (date)	Pages	Chapters	Focus	Cost paper/ eBook	Publisher
Forshaw M. & Sheffield D.	Health Psychology in Action	2012	1 (2012)	256	20	Clinical	$65/52	Wiley
French, D., Vedhara, K., Kaptein, A. A., & Weinman, J.	Health Psychology	2010	2 (2012)	432	31	Biopsychosocial	$71	Wiley
Friedman, H. S.	Health Psychology	2001	2 (2002)	528	15	Clinical/social	$259	Prentice Hall
Hadjistavropoulos, T., & Hadjistavropoulos, H. D.	Fundamentals of Health Psychology	2012	2 (2015)	399	15	Clinical	$NA/ 112	Oxford University Press
Harrington, R.	Stress, Health, and Well-Being: Thriving in the 21st Century	2013	1 (2013)	538	15	Social	$107/ 25	Cengage Learning
Jones, K. & Creedy, D.	Health and Human Behavior	2003	3 (2012)	352	16	Clinical	$92/80	Oxford University Press
Karren, K. J., Smith, N. L., & Gordon, K. J.	Mind/Body Health: The Effects of Attitudes, Emotions, and Relationships	1996	5 (2014)	616	21	Clinical/social	$117/ 34	Pearson
Murray, M.	Critical Health Psychology	2004	2 (2015)	368	16	Socio-cultural	$NA/ 50	Red Globe Press
Stroebe, W.	Social Psychology and Health	1995	3 (2011)	376	8	Social	$99	Open University Press

Appendix B Other written resources for teaching Health Psychology

Author	Title	Originally published	Edition (date)	Pages	Chapters	Focus	Cost paper/ eBook	Publisher
Andrasik, F., Goodie, J. L., & Peterson, A. L.	Biopsychosocial Assessment in Clinical Health Psychology	2015	1 (2015)	512	15	Clinical	$NA/ 82	The Guildford Press
Benyamini, Y., Johnston, M., & Karademas E. C.	Assessment in Health Psychology	2016	1 (2016)	345	18	Clinical	$NA/ 49	Hogrefe Publishing
Caltabiano, M. L., & Ricciardelli L.	Applied Topics in Health Psychology	2012	1 (2012)	560	36	Clinical	$66/53	Wiley
Kazarian, S. S. & Evans D. R.	Handbook of Cultural Health Psychology	2001	1 (2001)	488	16	Social	$129/ 126	Elsevier
Marks, D. F., Murray, M., & Estacio E. V.	Health Psychology: Theory, Research, and Practice	1999	5 (2018)	832	25	Critical/public policy	$126	SAGE
Pickren, W. E.	Psychology and Health: Culture, Place, and History	2020	1 (2020)	116	6	Socio-cultural	$60/19	Routledge
Revenson, A. T. & Gurung, R. A. R.	Handbook of Health Psychology	2019	1 (2019)	540	40	Multidisciplinary	$130/ 117	Routledge
Revenson, A. T., Saab, P. G., Zoccola, P. M., & Traeger, L. N.	Becoming a Health Psychologist	2020	1 (2020)	210	9	Mentorship/ guidance	$29/26	Routledge
Rohleder, P.	Critical Issues in Clinical and Health Psychology	2012	1 (2012)	226	8	Clinical	$NA/ 25	SAGE
Suls, J. M., Davidson, K. W., & Kaplan R. M.	Handbook of Health Psychology and Behavioral Medicine	2010	1 (2010)	608	36	Clinical	$115	The Guildford Press

References

American Psychological Association. (2013). *APA guidelines for the undergraduate psychology major: Version 2.0*. Retrieved from http://www.apa.org/ed/precollege/undergrad/index.aspx

Amer, M. M., El-Sayeh, S., Fayad, Y., & Khoury, B. (2015). Community psychology and civil society: Opportunities for growth in Egypt and Lebanon. *Journal of Community Psychology, 43*(1), 49–62. https://doi.org/10.1002/jcop.21688.

Bartram, D., & Roe, R. A. (2005). Definition and assessment of competences in the context of the European diploma in psychology. *European Psychologist, 10*(2), 93–102. https://doi.org/10.1027/1016-9040.10.2.93.

Benyamini, Y., Johnston, M., & Karademas, E. C. (2017). *Assessment in Health Psychology (E. C. Karademas, Ed.)*. Hogrefe Publishing.

Berić-Stojšić, B., Doobay-Persaud, A., & Neubauer, L. (2020). How do we teach for global health reviewing and renewing to advance pedagogy for global health and health promotion. *Pedagogy in Health Promotion*. https://doi.org/10.1177/2373379919900647.

Brack, A. B., Kesitilwe, K., & Ware, M. E. (2010). Taking the pulse of undergraduate health psychology: A nationwide survey. *Teaching of Psychology, 37*(4), 271–275. https://doi.org/10.1080/00986283.2010.510962

Campbell, C., & Cornish, F. (2014). Reimagining community health psychology: Maps, journeys and new terrains. *Journal of Health Psychology, 19*(1), 3–15. https://doi.org/10.1177/1359105313500263.

Campbell, C., & Murray, M. (2004). Community health psychology: Promoting analysis and action for social change. *Journal of Health Psychology, 9*(2), 187–195. https://doi.org/10.1177/1359105304040886.

DiMatteo, M. R., & Friedman, H. S. (1982). A model course in social psychology and health. *Health Psychology, 1*(2), 181–193. https://doi.org/10.1037/0278-6133.1.2.181.

Engel, G. L. (1977). The need for a new medical model: A challenge for biomedicine. *Science, 196*(4286), 129–136. https://doi.org/10.1126/science.847460

Ertl, M. M., Agiliga, A. U., Martin, C. M., Taylor, E. J., Kirkinis, K., Friedlander, M. L., Kimber, J. M., McNamara, M. L., Pazienza, R. L., Cabrera Tineo, Y. A., & Eklund, A. C. (2020). "Hands-on" learning in a health service psychology doctoral program through social justice consultation. *Training and Education in Professional Psychology*. https://doi.org/10.1037/tep0000311.

Fisher, A. T., Gridley, H., Thomas, D. R., & Bishop, B. (2008). Community psychology in Australia and Aotearoa/New Zealand. *Journal of Community Psychology, 36*(5), 649–660. https://doi.org/10.1002/jcop.20242.

Francescato, D. (2013). Community psychology practice competencies in undergraduate and graduate programs in Italy. *Global Journal of Community Psychology Practice, 4*(4). https://doi.org/10.7728/0404201303.

Griggs, R. A. (2014). *Psychology: A Concise Introduction (Fourth edition)*. Worth Publishers.

Gurung, R. A. R. (2014). *Multicultural Approaches to Health and Wellness in America* (1st Edition, Vol. 1–2). ABC-CLIO.

Gurung, R. A. R., & Bruns, D. (2013). Health psychology and policy: When politics infiltrate science. *Controversy in the Psychology Classroom: Using Hot Topics to Foster Critical Thinking*, 225–241. https://doi.org/10.1037/14038-014.

Gurung, R. A. R., & Rittenhouse, E. M. (2015). Teaching health psychology. In *The Oxford Handbook of Undergraduate Psychology Education*. Oxford University Press. https://doi.org/10.1093/oxfordhb/9780199933815.013.039.

Hamilton, K., & Hagger, M. S. (2014). The 'health' of health psychology in australia: behavioural approaches and interventions: Guest editorial. *Australian Psychologist, 49*(2), 63–65. https://doi.org/10.1111/ap.12051.

Hanitio, F., & Perkins, D. D. (2017). Predicting the emergence of community psychology and community development in 91 countries with brief case studies of Chile and Ghana. *American Journal of Community Psychology, 59*(1–2), 200–218. https://doi.org/10.1002/ajcp.12127.

Health Psychology and Behavioural Medicine Section – Canadian Psychological Association. (n.d.). Retrieved October 7, 2020, from https://cpa.ca/sections/healthpsychology/

Lam, D. J., & Ho, D. Y. F. (1989). Community psychology in Hong Kong: Past, present, and future. *American Journal of Community Psychology, 17*(1), 83–97.

Lubek, I., & Murray, M. (2018). Doing Histor{y/ies} of Health Psycholog{y/ies}. *Journal of Health Psychology, 23*(3), 361–371. https://doi.org/10.1177/1359105317753627.

MaClachlan, M. (2006). Towards a global health contribution for critical health psychology: Some comments on Hepworth. *Journal of Health Psychology, 11*(3), 361–365. https://doi.org/10.1177/1359105306063304.

Mak, A. S. (2012). Embedding intercultural competence development in the psychology curriculum. *Psychology Learning & Teaching, 11*(3), 365–369. https://doi.org/10.2304/plat.2012.11.3.365.

Makkawi, I. (2017). The rise and fall of academic community psychology in Palestine and the way forward. *South African Journal of Psychology, 47*(4), 482–492. https://doi.org/10.1177/0081246317737945.

Martin, P. R., Cairns, R., Lindner, H., Milgrom, J., Morrissey, S., & Ricciardelli, L. A. (2014). The training crisis in health psychology in Australia: Training crisis in health psychology. *Australian Psychologist, 49*(2), 86–95. https://doi.org/10.1111/ap.12042.

McCann, L., Immel, K., Kadah, L., & Adelson, S. (2016). The importance and interest of introductory psychology textbook topics: Student opinions at technical college, 2-, and 4-year institutions. *Teaching of Psychology, 43*. https://doi.org/10.1177/0098628316649477.

Montero, M. (1996). Parallel lives: Community psychology in Latin America and the United States. *American Journal of Community Psychology, 24*(5), 589–605. https://doi.org/10.1007/BF02509715.

Montero, M. (2008). An insider's look at the development and current state of community psychology in Latin America. *Journal of Community Psychology, 36*(5), 661–674. https://doi.org/10.1002/jcop.20241.

Murray, M. (2014). Social history of health psychology: Context and textbooks. *Health Psychology Review, 8*(2), 215–237. https://doi.org/10.1080/17437199.2012.701058.

Nic Giolla Easpaig, B. R., Fryer, D. M., Linn, S. E., & Humphrey, R. H. (2014). A queer-theoretical approach to community health psychology. *Journal of Health Psychology, 19*(1), 117–125. https://doi.org/10.1177/1359105313500259.

Norcross, J. C., Hailstorks, R., Aiken, L. S., Pfund, R. A., Stamm, K. E., & Christidis, P. (2016). Undergraduate study in psychology: Curriculum and assessment. *The American Psychologist, 71*(2), 89–101. https://doi.org/10.1037/a0040095.

Panjwani, A. A., Gurung, R. A. R., & Revenson, T. A. (2017). The teaching of undergraduate health psychology: A national survey. *Teaching of Psychology, 44*(3), 268–273. https://doi.org/10.1177/0098628317712786.

Perlman, B., & McCann, L. I. (1999). The Structure of the psychology undergraduate curriculum. *Teaching of Psychology, 26*(3), 171–176. https://doi.org/10.1207/S15328023TOP260302.

Plass, A. M., & Ingmar, S. (n.d.). Health psychology practice in Europe and other countries represented in the EHPS: A first step to moving forward together. *19*(6), 8.

Programs in Health Psychology. (n.d.). *Society for Health Psychology.* Retrieved October 7, 2020, from https://societyforhealthpsychology.org/training/programs/programs-in-health-psychology-non-clinical/.

Quinn, F., Chater, A., & Morrison, V. (2020). An oral history of health psychology in the UK. *British Journal of Health Psychology, 25*(3), 502–518. https://doi.org/10.1111/bjhp.12418.

Reich, S. M. (Ed.). (2007). *International community psychology: History and theories.* New York: Springer.

Revenson, T. A., & Gurung, R. A. R. (Eds.). (2019). *Handbook of Health Psychology* (1st edition). Routledge.

Ruiz, L. D., Zuelch, M. L., Dimitratos, S. M., & Scherr, R. E. (2019). Adolescent obesity: Diet quality, psychosocial health, and cardiometabolic risk factors. *Nutrients, 12*(1), E43. https://doi.org/10.3390/nu12010043.

Society for Health Psychology. (n.d.). https://www.apa.org. Retrieved October 7, 2020, from https://www.apa.org/about/division/div38

Stam, H. J., Murray, M., & Lubek, I. (2018). Health psychology in autobiography: Three Canadian critical narratives. *Journal of Health Psychology, 23*(3), 506–523. https://doi.org/10.1177/1359105318755409.

Stoloff, M., McCarthy, M., Keller, L., Varfolomeeva, V., Lynch, J., Makara, K., Simmons, S., & Smiley, W. (2010). The undergraduate psychology major: An examination of structure and sequence. *Teaching of Psychology, 37*(1), 4–15. https://doi.org/10.1080/00986280903426274.

Taylor, S. E. (1990). Health psychology: The science and the field. *American Psychologist, 45*(1), 40–50. https://doi.org/10.1037/0003-066X.45.1.40.

Yen, J. (2016). Psychology and health after apartheid: Or, Why there is no health psychology in South Africa. *History of Psychology, 19*(2), 77–92. https://doi.org/10.1037/hop0000025.

Educational Psychology: Learning and Instruction

Neil H. Schwartz, Kevin Click, and Anna N. Bartel

Contents

Abstract

Educational psychology is a field that straddles two large domains: education and psychology. Reaching far back into antiquity, the field was borne from philosophies and theories that weaved back and forth between each domain all with the intent of understanding the way learners learn, teachers teach, and educational settings should be effectively designed. This chapter tells the story of educational psychology – its evolution, its characteristics, and the insights it provides for

N. H. Schwartz (✉) · K. Click
Department of Psychology, California State University, Chico, CA, USA
e-mail: kclick1@csuchico.edu

A. N. Bartel
Department of Psychology, University of Wisconsin, Madison, WI, USA
e-mail: anbartel@wisc.edu

J. Zumbach et al. (eds.), *International Handbook of Psychology Learning and Teaching*,
Springer International Handbooks of Education,
https://doi.org/10.1007/978-3-030-28745-0_67

357

understanding it as a field of study, teaching it at the tertiary level of education, and leveraging its findings in the classroom. The chapter begins with a rationale for a curriculum of educational psychology, tracing its core teaching and learning objectives. It describes the topics that are core to the field, as well as the theory-based and evidence-based strategies and approaches for teaching it effectively. It discusses the basic principles of effective teaching, including problem-based learning, inquiry-based learning, and small-group and service-based learning, among others. Finally, it addresses technology in learning, open-university teaching and learning, and closes with a discussion of the best approaches – both theory-based and evidence-based – for assessing the core competencies of the field.

Keywords

Educational psychology · Teaching · Learning · Post-secondary teaching · Teacher training · Educational curriculum · Teaching core competencies · Assessing core competencies · Theory-based teaching strategies · Evidence-based teaching strategies

Introduction

Educational psychology, as a field of study, is devoted to the application of a wide variety of theories to understand the way humans learn so that the most effective practices of instruction can be implemented. Yet, while educational psychology seems rather simple to describe, its application to education is complex. After all, when we examine the two words individually, "education" exists in a myriad of contexts, both formal and informal, over the course of one's life, and "psychology" is an ocean of concepts, principles, and processes across layers of dynamic human-environmental transactions. We are not alone in noticing the complexities, as some contemporary and popular textbooks of educational psychology (Ormrod, Anderman, & Anderman, 2020; Santrock, 2021; Slavin, 2021; Snowman & McCown, 2015; Woolfolk Hoy, 2019) comprise a wide collection of vectors pointing to the target of the field; and while the field is divided into two main sections within the current volume, the collection is no less daunting for the present chapter. That is, the subsection of learning and instruction within educational psychology traditionally includes multiple theoretical and conceptual domains (e.g., human development, complex cognitive processes, behavioral and social-cognitive views of learning, social-constructivist views of learning, self-regulation and classroom management, classroom assessment strategies, and motivation) – domains that are intersectional within culture, language, technology, and levels of schooling.

What is common to the field of educational psychology, as represented in the textbooks above, are five common domains: 1. Developmental Theories; 2. Learning and Motivation; 3. Student Heterogeneity; 4. Classroom Instruction; and 5. Assessment and Evaluation. The first domain, developmental theories, addresses the development of cognition and language, as well as social, emotional, and moral development. The second domain, learning and motivation, encompasses behavioral and social learning theory, motivation, and cognitive views of learning. Given that learners are very different across a wide swath of the student landscape, the third domain, student heterogeneity, is addressed with a focus on culture and diversity as well as students' special needs. Fourth, classroom instruction focuses on (a) how instruction may be organized, (b) models for managing the learning environment, (c) use of technology for teaching, and (d) how to think about instructional strategies given what we know about how students actively construct knowledge. Finally, the fifth domain, assessment and evaluation, underscores the importance of evidence-based practices and making educational decisions empirically. Thus, the field of educational psychology has, over the decades, embraced – and continues to embrace – the need for the measurement of student performance both formatively and summatively.

However, a look through the history of educational psychology reveals that making empirically based educational decisions was not always common practice. Indeed, tracing its beginning to the early twentieth century some six generations of thinkers ago, most would agree that the field's evolution was often adversarial if not conceptually competitive (Berliner, 1993). After all, the field grew from a collection of convergent and divergent ideas centuries before that – for example, Democritus in the fifth century B.C. (see Watson, 1961); Plato and Aristotle a century later (see Adler, 1952); Quintilian around 35–100 A.D. (Quintilian, translated by Butler, 1953; Quintilian translated by Smail, 1966); and Vives during the early years of the sixteenth century (see Vives, 1913; Charles, 1987). Thus, from those beginnings in antiquity, Berliner (1993) traced the agreed-upon ideas at the time that can be considered precursory thinking of the field today. Those ideas were:

1. Getting to know and leveraging the unique characteristics of students
2. Developing criteria for selecting teachers
3. Making teaching engaging within an interesting curriculum to circumvent behavior problems of students
4. Using visual material to enhance learning
5. Focusing on understanding rather than rote learning
6. Ordering instruction and deploying it from higher-order ideas to specific details
7. Making certain all material to be taught is vetted in experience
8. Recognizing that students teaching other students is the best way to learn
9. Involving parents in the education of their children

In 1899, James published educational psychology's first definitive book: *Talks to Teachers on Psychology* (James, 1899, 1983) following his publication of one of the first books on psychology – *Principles of Psychology* (James, 1890). In his psychology text, James espoused that the science of the mind's laws, while not elemental as the Europeans viewed it, was important to study experimentally as a stream – an indivisible continuous flow of consciousness – that required careful observation for the purpose it served rather than the cause by which it arose. This was a teleological point of view that gave rise to a decidedly American perspective called *pragmatism*

– a philosophical theme that became the cornerstone of educational psychology as a field. From this perspective, James, in his lectures to teachers on psychology, came to believe that the new science of psychology could not provide "definite programmes and schemes and methods of instruction for immediate school-room use" (James, 1899; 1983, p. 15). That is, he was loath to transform teachers into psychologists. Instead, he believed that psychology could only offer heuristics that teachers could explore within the parameters of their own knowledge and experience – to offer guidelines and directions within which teachers could apply their own wisdom when teaching their students. James said it best when he wrote, "Psychology is a science, and teaching is an art; and sciences never generate arts directly out of themselves" (James, 1899; 1983, p. 15). Thus, James' (1899) contribution to the field of educational psychology was to see psychology as offering: (a) deeper logical thinking to underlying common instructional beliefs, (b) guardrails to ensure teachers avoided errors of instruction, and (c) well-thought-out support for the pedagogical choices he believed teachers should be making on their own (Berliner, 1993). This was in stark contrast to his former doctoral student, E. L. Thorndike.

While Thorndike was remarkably influenced by James' thinking about psychology's application to education – even as an undergraduate student – Thorndike preserved a steadfast commitment to the experimental science of psychology and statistics. In fact, dominating the field of educational psychology for over 40 years with scores of books and hundreds of articles, Thorndike believed that only a strict experimental and disciplined study of psychology should provide prescriptions to education – just as in any other discipline with an applied arm (Thorndike, 1910). Furthermore, and rather unbelievably, Thorndike admonished educational psychologists from spending any time in schools or classrooms. Instead, he was quite strong in his opinions that *only* methods of exact science should be applied to educational problems and that opinions and perspectives of those people teaching and learning in the schools were essentially irrelevant.

Fast forward to the present, educational psychology has found a common ground between these two extremes; and that ground is due in no small part to the trajectory of thought from the field's other early forebears – principally, G. Stanley Hall and John Dewey. Indeed, Berliner (1993) wrote:

> In Hall and Dewey, our granduncles, we have former classroom teachers who respected teachers and the complexity of teaching more than did James. Hall's science had a common sense to it; he trusted teachers to be good observers and data collectors, and he defended passion, sentiment, and love as elements in the making of a good science of child and educational study. Although generally poorly carried out, his was a science more naturalistic than laboratory based, more clinical than experimental, and more qualitative than quantitative. Dewey held to a holistic psychology, understood the teacher as a social being, and thought that if psychology presented its findings as truths to be applied it would necessarily put teachers in a position of servitude. He saw laboratory psychology as limited and all psychological findings as tentative, as working hypotheses for teachers to test. (pp. 14–15)

Thus, today, educational psychologists show great respect for the complexities and vagaries of teaching and the individuals who do it, recognizing that listening to teachers and students and observing them both in real time are essential. Educational psychologists recognize that there must be a tight reciprocal and recursive relationship between the lab and the classroom that allows generating theories and testing hypotheses borne from each source. This contemporary way of conceptualizing and conducting the field has paid dividends in understanding the teaching-learning process.

Rationale of the Curriculum in Educational Psychology

Presently, the American Psychological Association (APA) is the largest scientific organization for the field of psychology. Psychologists around the world follow APA guidelines related to ethics, writing, and research. While the APA is home to many different fields of psychology, the focus of this chapter is targeted to educational psychology. According to the APA, the primary goal of educational psychologists is to study how people learn. Educational psychologists use their knowledge to improve learning among students, aiming to ensure that all students are successful learners. In order for educational psychologists to meet this goal, they need to take into account many facets of learning. These facets of learning include not only cognitive processes but also social and emotional processes.

Furthermore, educational psychology is inherently interdisciplinary. It is a broad domain that covers many different subgroups: human development, learning sciences, quantitative methods, school psychology, learning analytics, and educational technology – and all of these different subgroups have specific curricula. However, when speaking of curricula broadly in educational psychology, the goals of each subgroup align. The primary purpose of the overarching curriculum is to provide psychology students with opportunities to critically evaluate learning theories, conduct progressive research, and acquire skills to become successful communicators of information. All of these goals aim to improve educational outcomes both for psychologists and for students across educational contexts.

These curricula may not be explicitly defined in any one educational psychology program but will typically follow an apprenticeship model of student training and mentoring. This type of apprenticeship model is called a cognitive apprenticeship. Cognitive apprenticeship is an instructional model that focuses on cognitive skills and the knowledge that learning is situated in authentic contexts. Cognitive apprenticeships assume that people learn from each other in authentic contexts, and the model advocates for using teaching methods that include modeling, scaffolding, reflection, and exploration (Collins, 1991; Collins, Brown, & Holum, 1991). For example, students trained in educational psychology are frequently matched with faculty mentors based on corresponding research interests. The faculty serve as mentors, working closely with students at a graduate or undergraduate level, to improve each student's research and teaching skills. Throughout their training, students will likely work with different faculty members given the interdisciplinary nature of educational psychology as a field of study.

Core Teaching and Learning Objectives

Like most training programs, student learning is assessed by providing learning objectives. Often, these learning objectives are based on qualification frameworks. One specific type of qualification framework is called a competency model. Competency models provide a standard of competence that should be met by trainees. Specifically, in the field of psychology, there have been efforts and difficulties in defining acceptable standards of competence (Nash & Larkin, 2012). In fact, the only mention of competencies from the APA is through their Code of Ethical Principles and Standards of Conduct, which indeed highlights the importance of standards of competence in the field (American Psychological Association [APA], 2016). Further, APA designates that psychologists may only teach and conduct research within the bounds of their competence. These bounds of competence are "based on education, training, supervised experience, consultation, study, or professional experience" (p. 5).

On the other hand, while the APA does not designate a specific competency model, they do provide a general Benchmark Evaluation System (APA, 2012). This Benchmark Evaluation System was designed to help graduate programs in professional psychology, not specifically educational psychology, evaluate their success in meeting the above defined standard competence in the field. The Benchmark Evaluation System is organized into six general benchmark clusters, all of which have corresponding core competencies. The six clusters and their core competencies can be seen in Table 1.

The Benchmark Evaluation Systems goes into further detail by describing the core competencies at three different developmental levels. However, these developmental levels are specific to professional psychology and not easily applied to

Table 1 Benchmark Evaluation System as designated by the APA (2012)

Benchmark Evaluation System	
Benchmark cluster	Core competency
Professionalism	Professional Values and Attitudes
	Individual and Cultural Diversity
	Ethical, Legal Standards and Policy
	Reflective Practice/Self-Assessment/Self-Care
Relational	Relationships
Science	Scientific Knowledge and Methods
	Research/Evaluation
Application	Evidence-Based Practice
	Assessment
	Intervention
	Consultation
Education	Teaching
	Supervision
Systems	Interdisciplinary Systems
	Management/Administration
	Advocacy

different types of psychology courses (see Benchmark Evaluation System, APA, 2012; Peterson, Peterson, Abrams, & Stricker, 2010; Rodolfa, Bent, Eisman, Nelson, Rehm, & Ritchie, 2005). As such, while the Benchmark Evaluation System provides generally useful information, the specific competencies beyond professional psychologists remain undefined (Kelly, 2016; Nash & Larkin, 2012).

Despite the importance of assessing competence for educational psychologists, many of the existing competency models are specific to professional psychology careers, such as clinical psychology (see Benchmark Evaluation System, APA, 2016; Peterson, Peterson, Abrams, & Stricker, 2010; Rodolfa, Bent, Eisman, Nelson, Rehm, & Ritchie, 2005). Consequently, many programs that train educational psychologists who are interested in teaching and conducting research do not have such formalized and specific competency models (Kelly, 2016; Nash & Larkin, 2012).

Competencies Students Should Acquire

There is currently no specific role of qualification frameworks in educational psychology, and there has been no clear understanding of how qualification frameworks might be defined (Kelly, 2016). As it pertains to training contexts in educational psychology, it is possible that qualification frameworks could be based on theoretical and practical perspectives. A unique skill of educational psychologists is that they are required to learn theoretical frameworks, practice frameworks, and understand the relationship between the two (Kelly, 2016).

For educational psychologists, having an understanding of theoretical frameworks is a core competency because the frameworks describe different learning theories and how these theories might be applied. Through understanding many different theoretical perspectives of learning, educational psychologists may conduct innovative research that brings together seemingly disparate theories of learning. In this case, combining multiple theoretical perspectives may lead to a wider range of practical applications. Practical applications may only be fully understood by gaining knowledge of practice frameworks, which are defined as a series of actions that support the application of theoretical frameworks in authentic contexts (Kelly, 2016). It is key for educational psychologists to have an understanding of practice frameworks as they serve to bridge the gap between theoretical frameworks in research and help to effectively apply those theories in practice.

As previously stated, the goal of educational psychologists is to better understand and improve student learning. In order to achieve this goal, educational psychologists need training that produces an understanding of the complex relationship between learning theories and educational practice. What follows is an understanding of the role of evidence in educational psychology. Understanding what constitutes evidence is a large undertaking, one that warrants its own task force (see APA Presidential Task Force on Evidence-Based Practice, 2006). To briefly describe the main points, evidence has an important role for educational psychologists because understanding what constitutes good evidence for demonstrating successful learning can, and probably should, lead to a substantive change in instructional practice (Boyle & Kelly, 2016). In an effort to gain understanding of what exactly constitutes good evidence, educational psychologists should have a solid foundation in the hierarchy (Pilcher & Bedford, 2011) and typology (Petticrew & Roberts, 2003) of evidence, as well as sufficient training in research methods to apply that foundational knowledge to measuring and refining elements of their own teaching practice.

Superordinate Learning Objectives

In all, the superordinate learning objective for students of educational psychology is to reduce the gap between research and practice in learning. Through their years of training, educational psychologists gain expertise in the multiple theoretical perspectives of learning. Further, educational psychologists master the creation and implementation of rigorous psychological research designed to build understanding and address educational issues relevant to learning in different, authentic, contexts.

Core Topics of Educational Psychology

Educational psychologists are the liaisons between psychology and education. As such, they have the responsibility of identifying those areas of psychology pertinent to the field of education; they also have the responsibility to curate the scholarly, empirical, and in-practice evidence relevant to educational application. Perhaps the best source of curation is those sources tasked with informing future practitioners and scholars in the field: textbooks of educational psychology and the seminal works written over the decades that form the bedrock of the field.

As described at the top of this chapter, there are five educational psychology domains that form the core topics of the field. Of the five textbooks examined, each shares consistent treatment of the topics within those domains.

As for the seminal works, Kirschner and Hendrick (2020) assembled an interpretive collection of the most influential researchers in the fields of educational psychology and cognitive psychology, explaining how their findings illuminate how learners learn and what learners need to have, in order to be able to learn efficiently, effectively, and successfully. Not only does their collection inform the core topics of educational psychology, but the collection informs the delivery of the field's combined knowledge to teachers and learners. For example, with regard to the development of cognition, Kirschner and Hendrick (2020) explain the work of Chi, Feltovich, and Glaser (1981), a seminal paper on experts and novices in physics problem-solving. Not only do novices have less knowledge than experts, the experts think differently than the novices. That is, experts cognitively represent physics problems differently by categorizing problem features based on their specific knowledge of physics principles; novices, on the other hand, use superficial features of the problems, generally leading the novices to generate erroneous or misleading solution strategies and pathways.

Applying the question of core topics exclusively to cognition, Kirschner and Hendrick (2020) also contend that the field of educational psychology has brought to educational classrooms the sine qua non gems of cognitive load theory, the importance of prior knowledge – subsumption theory – and depth of processing during learning, elaboration theory. Cognitive Load Theory (Sweller, 1988, 2020) is the idea that humans have only so much room in working memory to process information, and the nature of that information creates different types of strain (load) during processing; some of that load is germane to problem-solving, some is irrelevant or extraneous, and some is immutable because it is intrinsic to the structure and complexity of a problem. After closely examining findings on the way experts bring to mind the configurations of a problem they already know, Sweller (1988) realized that when cognitive load was being spent by experts to deploy their memory of problem state configurations, the load was not only utilitarian but also was germane to the problem's solution. This led Sweller (1988) to conclude that educators must find ways to guide their learners to manipulate information not only to reach solution of particular types of problem sets but also to remember those effective cognitive machinations.

Subsumption theory was borne from Ausubel (1960, 1968) who hypothesized that knowledge held in memory is organized hierarchically into higher-order concepts that subsume sub-concepts and specific data of information within those sub-concepts. Ausubel (1960, 1968) demonstrated that when educators provide organizers in advance of instruction that tap these higher-order memory stores, subsequent learning of new related information is easier, more effective, enduring, and more utilitarian. Multiple examples of the application of Ausubel's theory to education have been published since the early 1960s, with nearly 18,000 citations of his 1968 publication. Ausubel's work was also one of the essential precursors to schema theory (c.f. Alba & Hasher, 1983) – another integral core topic of psychology's application to education.

As for the other seminal topics of cognition, depth of processing theory (Craik & Lockhart, 1972) added to the field the idea that enduring memory of information is the result of more and more deliberate processing – going beyond sensory analysis and pattern recognition of stimuli (essentially shallow processing) to deeper processing characterized by a learner's quest to actively process semantic associations to what the learner already knows. One of the ways to build these associations into an effective structure of new knowledge can be seen in the Elaboration Theory of Instruction (Reigeluth & Stein, 1983) – a theory that is a good example of the topic domain of organizing instruction. According to elaboration theory, classroom lessons should be presented as simple as possible at first and then increased in complexity relative to the learners' knowledge base. This synergy between what a learner already knows and what needs to be learned emphasizes the importance of appropriate content structure, context that is meaningful to the learner, and systematic integration and review at the end of each lesson. Endemic to elaboration theory is a recursive process where teachers guide learners to zoom in and out of new concepts at each level of complexity.

Other examples of seminal works illuminating core topics of the field can be seen in the domains of social cognitive theory and motivation. With regard to social cognition, Zimmerman (1989) suggested that effective learners are self-regulated – that is, they have agency, purpose, and regulation over the actions they take to learn. However, this agency of actions is not exclusively internal to the learner. Rather, it is comprised of personal, behavioral, and environmental aspects that work harmoniously with each other to form what Zimmerman calls "triadic reciprocality." The notion of triadic reciprocality refers to the recursive transaction between (a) what a learner brings to learning – the learner's knowledge and beliefs about their level of efficacy to learn; (b) what the environment affords for that learning, teacher modeling, verbal persuasion, direct assistance from a teacher, and the way the learning context is structured; and (c) the learners behavior, that is, their regulatory use of specific learning strategies and self-monitoring of performance manifest in the planning, decision-making, and activities they engage in before, during, and in reflection of their learning.

What is interesting about self-efficacy (Bandura, 1977) and beliefs is that they are both also core topics under the domain of motivation. Both are also braided with concepts like "goal orientation" (Pintrich, 2000) and Attribution theory (Weiner, 1985). In essence, teachers can motivate their students by helping them believe that whatever intellectual capacity they have is not immutable; that is, they can get "smarter" and work harder or in more effective ways to achieve at levels higher than they currently believe. For example, Dweck and Leggett (1988) explained that learners show two patterns of behavior – mastery and helpless – with regard to the learning beliefs they have about themselves and the way they approach goals based on those beliefs. The mastery disposition leads a learner to seek challenging tasks where they maintain a level of striving even under conditions of failure. The helpless disposition, on the other hand, is characterized by a learner's tendency to pull the throttle back on their effort to perform and avoid challenges when they encounter obstacles. These dispositions lead learners to create very different approaches to learning – the mastery students, when encountering obstacles, work to *improve* their ability, whereas helpless students pursue the goal of *proving* their ability. These are strikingly different ways of approaching challenging learning situations that can be altered by teachers with respect to what learners believe about themselves (see Kirschner and Hendrick, 2020, for a discussion of these alterations).

The final example of core topics to be illustrated comes under the category of technology. Within that category, the Cognitive Theory of Multimedia Learning (Mayer, 2005) serves as an excellent example.

Technology has become ubiquitous across educational contexts. PowerPoint and Prezi are software that have become staples in blending words, pictures, animations, videos, and sound effects in the delivery of instruction; indeed, Canva, Renderforest, Google Slides, and Visme, for example, are other multimedia presentation software available for instructional use. The question for educational psychology is how to use them effectively during instruction. Mayer (2005) worked out and tested 12 design principles for multimedia-based instruction that led to prescriptions of the design, development, and implementation of multimedia learning material.

These principles have at their base the core theories of information processing, cognitive load theory, and a theory of the way knowledge is stored in memory – for Mayer, dual-coding theory (Clark & Paivio, 1991). In essence, Mayer (2005) contends that learners process multimedia presentations by first selecting relevant words from the text or narration in the presentation; at the same time, they select relevant images from the visual graphical illustrations presented along with the words; then, within two separate but parallel cognitive channels, they organize the words into a coherent verbal representation and organize the relevant images into a coherent pictorial representation; finally, they integrate together the pictorial and verbal representations into a cognitive framework blended with the knowledge they already have. In short, the value of Mayer's (2005) multimedia theory is the degree to which its 12 design principles lead to the assembly of visual and verbal presentation material that can efficiently and effectively prime these processes.

Approaches and Strategies in Educational Psychology

Any approach to instructing university students in the best practices of learning and instruction is founded upon the problems and goals of curricular design. Curricular design must do a large part of the work that is necessary to demonstrate the relevance of educational psychology to non-psychologists – especially in relation to the training of students, such as pre-service teachers, who will not become psychologists (Berliner, 1993). Over the last three decades, many modern reformers (e.g., Anderson et al., 1995; Greenwood & Fillmer, 1999; Ormrod, 2006; Ormrod & McGuire, 2007; Sudzina, 1997; Woolfolk Hoy, 1996, 2008) have advocated for prioritizing educational psychology principles in curriculum design.

A critical mission, then, for educational psychology is designing curriculum that promotes an understanding by key stakeholders of how basic principles derived from psychological science are applied to teaching in the classroom (Patrick, Anderman, Bruening, & Duffin, 2011). These key stakeholders may include teachers-in-training; university students studying psychology or other disciplines who may become higher education faculty; or existing university faculty in psychology and other disciplines. In other words, the role of educational psychologists in training their students is threefold: (1) help non-psychologists relate key concepts from psychological theory to problems and goals within their own field of practice; (2) help non-psychologists build knowledge of how to apply that theory to their own field of practice; and (3) train developing psychologists to promote these types of learning in their own classrooms. Thus, educational psychologists must learn how to build bridges between the knowledge base of psychology and other professional fields.

The public image of psychology as a whole discipline – not just within the field of educational psychology – depends upon the attitudes that non-psychology majors develop about the usefulness of psychological principles (Dutke et al., 2019), lending a broader sense of urgency to the endeavor. While specific data describing nonmajors' experience with psychology courses is sparse, Dutke et al. (2019) argued that students who take courses in psychology departments are much more likely to be nonmajors than to be psychology majors, citing reports from Germany (Statistisches Bundesamt, 2017) and the Czech Republic (The Czech Ministry of Education, Youth and Sports, 2018, as cited in Dutke et al., 2019; Slovak Centre of Scientific and Technical Information, 2018).

Although data is also sparse in the United States, similar reports suggest that the number of undergraduate students who take an Introduction to Psychology course is an order of magnitude higher than the number of undergraduate students who earn a bachelor's degree in psychology (Gurung et al., 2016; National Center for Education Statistics, 2019). Because many students who earn a bachelor's degree in psychology undertake careers outside of psychological science or applied psychological practice, those graduates act as ambassadors to other professional communities regarding the benefit and application of psychological knowledge (Cranney, 2013). Such convergence of interest between psychologists and non-psychologists calls for collaboration between psychologists and experts in other fields, particularly regarding psychological curriculum development (Berliner, 1993, 2006; Dutke et al., 2019; Patrick et al., 2011).

Theory-Based and Evidence-Based Approaches to Teaching Core Competencies

The quality of collaboration in fields of professional practice between psychologists and non-psychologists is increased when non-psychologists better understand the methods involved in deriving and implementing psychological principles (Dutke et al., 2019). Moreover, collaboration with experts in other fields helps educational psychologists create and maintain the relevance of both their curriculum and their research to a broad array of students in psychology classrooms. Cross-disciplinary cooperation serves to familiarize psychologists with the real problems faced by professionals in other fields – leading to better, and more relevant, curriculum design (Berlin, 1993, 2000; Dutke et al., 2019). Collaboration with field-specific experts (e.g., educational faculty, supervisors of teacher induction programs, and pre-service teachers) serves to generate a framework of "desirable competencies" (Dutke et al., 2019, p. 8) on which constructing relevant curricula can be focused (e.g., see ▶ Chap. 33, "Psychology in Teacher Education," by Narciss and Zumbach in this volume for an extensive discussion of psychology curricula for pre-service teacher training). Maintaining relevance of psychological research and curriculum to psychology students who will work in other professions, as well as for students not who are nonmajors, is squarely within the role of educational psychologists because it facilitates the relation of psychological concepts to the problems and goals of a broad range of fields.

Making the case for relevance of psychological knowledge to students majoring in psychological study is more straightforward than making the same case to students of other disciplines. Thus, Dutke et al. (2019) propose five criteria for the selection of content in courses that are aimed to develop psychological knowledge among students who will not become psychologists. First, the content should be specific to the field of study (e.g., education, law, medicine, or management), rather than assuming that all psychological principles are equally useful to constituent groups. Second, content should be need oriented, selection being driven by specific practical problems or epistemological considerations of the constituent groups. Third, content should be process oriented – in other words, derived from theoretical perspectives and research methodologies that are consistent with those used by – and, thus, well understood by, the constituent group. Fourth, content should be limited to information that is relevant to the professional or academic field of the constituent group. Students of other disciplines, such as teachers, do not need to become psychologists and consequently do not require breadth of coverage. For instance, psychology curricula aimed at pre-service teachers should include only those elements of theory and application that can make them better teachers. Fifth, with the goal of fostering deep understanding of this relevant psychological material, the content should remain internally consistent while systematically offering depth of coverage.

The aim of these criteria is to meet what Narciss (2019) describes as a challenging task for instructional faculty "to align the goals and affordances of the academic discipline with those of the diverse professional fields in which the graduates of this discipline will work" (p. 2). It is also challenging to achieve alignment with the constraints and the goals of local settings. In short, educational psychologists should provide professionally relevant curricula for non-psychological professions and enable appropriate application of that knowledge.

Unfortunately, although the five criteria provided by Dutke et al. (2019) are a useful framework for discussion, the framework does not necessarily provide concrete recommendations for curriculum design. Thus, Narciss (2019) suggests a strategy in addition to interdisciplinary collaboration: use existing resources – including competency frameworks and domain-specific guidelines – such as the European Qualifications Framework for Higher Education, to structure curriculum in a way that meets the same goals and results in the delivery of psychology knowledge that students will value when working in applied settings.

Within the field of traditional education, the content of teacher education curriculum already includes key educational psychology content areas (Patrick et al., 2011). Widespread integration of psychological principles into expectations for teacher competencies is evidenced by numerous reports and teacher education standards (e.g., Educational Testing Service [ETS], 2004, 2009; Klieme and Maag Merki, 2008; Interstate New Teacher Assessment and Support Consortium, 1992; Darling-Hammond, and Baratz-Snowden, 2007; National Council for the Accreditation of Teacher Education, 2008; Queensland College of Teachers, Professional Standards Unit, 2011; Training and Development Agency for Schools, 2007). Educational psychology theorists have also identified key content areas. For instance, Woolfolk Hoy (2000) identified five psychological knowledge domains central to pre-service teachers, namely:

1. Developmental changes in student thinking and metacognition
2. Socially supported learning as a function of dialogue, interaction, and collaboration

3. Matching classroom instruction to students' learning abilities
4. Utilizing effective communication to foster successful inquiry and learning
5. Assessment strategies that are effective for refining student learning

As discussed earlier in this chapter, there are five general psychological knowledge domains represented in the most commonly used educational psychology textbooks. Four of these (1. Developmental Theories; 2. Learning and Motivation; 3. Classroom Instruction; and 4. Assessment and Evaluation) align with Woolfolk Hoy's (2000) domains of knowledge. While teachers are only a subset of the professional fields of study to which Dutke et al. (2019) refer, they are no less important; and it is safe to conclude that the process of teaching and learning makes up an integral component necessary for all fields of study, both in the university classroom and in their field of practice. Thus, the domains identified by Woolfolk Hoy (2000) are informative to psychology instructors when teaching the full range of students in their classrooms.

And yet, like Narciss (2019), Lohse-Bossenz, Kunina-Habenicht, & Kunter (2013) suggested that such broad category domains provide insufficient guidance to instructors who seek to develop a curriculum that meets the needs of applied professionals, like teachers in the classroom. The category domains are also not particularly useful as standards for pre-service teacher instruction, per se. Thus, Lohse-Bossenz et al. (2013) sought to quantitatively assess which specific topics within the common domains were seen as important, relevant, and of practical utility to the three important groups of education-specific constituents: education faculty; supervisors of teacher induction programs; and pre-service teachers. Using a list of topics drawn from textbooks, literature, interviews, and educational governing standards, Lohse-Bossenz et al. (2013) tested 43 topic areas across the categories of learning, development, and assessment. Consensus among the three constituent groups pointed to the following as important:

1. In the area of learning: problem-solving and creativity; social learning; learning motivation; achievement motivation; knowledge acquisition; knowledge transfer; and metacognition and self-regulated learning
2. In the area of development: cognitive development; development of conceptual knowledge; development of motivational, emotional, and behavioral regulation; and development of social cognition
3. In the area of assessment: data collection methods and procedures; test theories and test construction; test score interpretation; theory, hypothesis, scientific observation, falsification, and internal/external validity; and qualitative research methods

In addition to meeting the real-world needs of professional teachers, these topics also map onto a broad array of professional applications and are thus relevant to a wide range of psychology students. Moreover, these topics, as well as the broad content areas discussed by others (e.g., Woolfolk Hoy, 2000) and those covered by popular textbook authors mentioned earlier in this chapter, are among the psychological principles addressed in depth by other chapters in this volume. We will briefly discuss of a few of them here.

Basic Principles of Effective Teaching (see also Bernstein, ▶ Chap. 48, "Basic Principles and Procedures for Effective Teaching in Psychology"). One central goal of teaching psychology is to cultivate psychological literacy (Cranney, 2013). Development of psychological literacy promotes an appreciation for, and valuation of, evidence-based teaching practices among education faculty and administrators at universities and among their students. Dutke, Bakker, Papageorgi, & Taylor (2017) wrote that psychology has generated well-supported ideas about teaching and learning that generally apply across subject matters (e.g., collaborative learning, spaced learning, multimodal learning). As experts in the field then, psychologists should apply these principles in their own classrooms. As instructors, psychologists should *adapt* these principles to the "demands and constraints of the specific learning situation and content" (Dutke et al., 2017, p. 174). For example, pre-service teachers benefit from a combination of training in general best practices, as well as in subject-specific teaching practices. Thus, training psychological literacy in pre-service teachers results in a better application by *classroom* teachers of the psychological principles of good teaching to the demands of subject-specific teaching (Buskist, 2013).

Psychologists have also developed numerous principles of good teaching that are supported by substantial bodies of evidence and can be implemented with relative ease in classrooms (Dunn, Saville, Baker, & Marek, 2013). These practices include (a) testing to enhance memory (e.g., Butler and Roediger, 2007; Karpicke, Butler, & Roediger, 2009) and transfer (e.g., Carpenter, 2012), (b) distributed practice or spaced learning (e.g., Cepeda, Pashler, Vul, Wixted, & Rohrer, 2006; Wahlheim, Dunlosky, & Jacoby, 2011), (c) metacognitive skills such as reflective note-taking (e.g., Dunn, 2011), (d) writing to learn (e.g., Berninger, 2012; Dunn 1994, 2011), and (e) interteaching (e.g., Boyce & Hineline, 2002; Saville, Lambert, & Robertson, 2011; Saville & Zinn, 2009). Students profit from guidance and reminders from their instructors on the benefits of these strategies, as well as on the effects of other habits and behaviors known to impact academic success (Dunn et al., 2013). Thus, the application and development of evidence-based teaching practices such as these is vital to improving student learning outcomes.

There are also other models that are noteworthy for their promise of enhancing psychological literacy and leveraging the principles above. For example, the Scholarship of Teaching and Learning (SoTL) model proposes that faculty adopt a scholarly approach to the continual development of good teaching practices (Wilson-Doenges & Gurung, 2013). The SoTL model suggests that faculty deliberately combine best practices in teaching with science-driven experimentation, curiosity, creativity, and self-reflection toward their own practice of teaching. Thus, teachers can and should become, according to SoTL, teacher-scholars who contribute to the field of educational psychology, as well as to the practice of instruction, by deliberately and scientifically examining teaching and learning across disciplines in settings of applied teaching practice. While the model underscores the need to disseminate the results of scientifically evaluating their teaching practices to others within the education community, there are caveats to such an implementation. That is, challenges to accomplishing the goals of the SoTL model include the difficulties associated with producing true experiments in the classroom, gathering data of adequate quantitative depth and accuracy, obtaining diverse and representative samples in the classroom, and constructing experimental conditions that do not violate ethical applications of educational standards.

And yet, even if a teacher-scholar perspective is not necessarily adopted by teachers per se, there are still principles that are borne from it, as well as from the promotion of psychological literacy and other principles of instruction discussed above. Consider the first principles of instruction espoused by Merrill (2002).

First Principles of Instruction (see also ▶ Chap. 49, "First Principles of Instruction Revisited," by Merrill). Merrill (2002, pp. 44–45) argued that there are five first principles about learning – basic, key truths – that underpin all successful teaching practices:

1. *Learning is promoted when learners are engaged in solving real-world problems.*
2. *Learning is promoted when existing knowledge is activated as a foundation for new knowledge.*
3. *Learning is promoted when new knowledge is demonstrated to the learner.*
4. *Learning is promoted when new knowledge is applied by the learner.*
5. *Learning is promoted when new knowledge is integrated into the learner's world.*

What Merrill's (2002) first principles add is another set of "truisms" collected across multiple theoretical accounts that help facilitate a better understanding and deployment of instructional practices, as well as helping to organize programs of instruction that are composed of these practices. In short, any program or practice has the potential to successfully promote learning, provided that it applies the first principles accurately and effectively. What follows is a brief description of Merrill's first principles and an example of teaching practices that exemplify the application of those principles.

Learning is more successful when it centers on relatable, real-world problems, beginning with a demonstration of the process by the instructor, followed by conceptual instruction, scaffolding the learner toward mastery of more complex versions of the problems, and a more comprehensive understanding of abstract concepts inherent in the problems. Comprehensive understanding is more likely when relevant prior knowledge is activated to provide a framework for the construction of mental models for new information, and connections between prior knowledge and new knowledge are made explicit through an instructor's expert guidance, as with the cognitive apprenticeship model (Collins, 1991; Collins et al., 1991), for instance.

An instructor's expertise can be used to demonstrate the application of new skills or knowledge in multiple ways, consistent with the learning goals, along with explicit mapping of these differing demonstrations to the same problem structure, for the learner to compare and contrast under the instructor's guidance. Regular and repeated applied practice opportunities, combined with feedback, error correction, and redirection, form a supporting framework from which the instructor can gradually withdraw, as the learner's performance accuracy increases. As the learners' performances improve, they should be encouraged to integrate – or transfer – their new skill or knowledge to other situations. Public demonstrations of new knowledge and skills are intrinsically motivating to learners, particularly when they are encouraged to reflect on or to defend their new knowledge, finding application to their everyday life.

As an example in practice, these principles might take the form of walking through the critical analysis of a few short, formal arguments from a recent or well-known political debate: The instructor would begin by identifying, describing, and demonstrating the various steps and showing whether the argument is sound, prior to providing a detailed theoretical description of each step taken in the analysis. The process of demonstration would serve as a conceptual anchor for the learning process, and the relatable aspects of the political argument would serve to activate prior experience and knowledge, which would allow the learner to more successfully create a mental model of the key analysis concepts. Asking the learner to participate in comparing and contrasting multiple example arguments on the same topic would allow the learner to circumscribe their understanding of concepts involved in the analysis while providing opportunities for performance with corrective feedback from the instructor. Assigning the learner to present their own longer form argument on a self-chosen public policy topic takes the learned concepts out of abstraction and into application in everyday life.

Another approach to reifying instruction through the application of instructional principles and psychological literacy (cf., Cranney, 2013; Cranney & Dunn, 2011) is problem-based learning.

Problem-Based Learning (see also Zumbach, Prescher, Niegemann, Blalock et al., ▶ Chap. 50, "Problem-Based Learning and Case-Based Learning"). Problem-based learning (PBL) is a pedagogical style that is student-centered, where learners often work in groups, solving open-ended problems, with the aim of developing self-directed learning skills (Wiggins, Chiriac, Abbad, Pauli, & Worrell, 2016). In PBL, a "problem" represents an issue for investigation, analysis, or discussion, with no pre-determined correct solution. Students each take responsibility for independently researching and presenting relevant content to the group. The group then collaborates to produce a solution to the problem. PBL does not represent a single pedagogical model but rather serves as a foundation for several models, each with a slightly different set of parameters and each deployed differently depending on disciplinary or course-specific learning objectives.

In psychology programs, direct benefits of PBL on learning outcomes include better long-term knowledge retention, conceptual synthesis, and transfer to novel applications (e.g., Hmelo, 1998; Hung, Jonassen, & Liu, 2008). On the other hand, for psychology majors who do not go into a psychological profession, it can be difficult to focus PBL in a psychology course on desirable or useful outcomes (e.g., Cranney & Voudouris, 2012; Trapp et al., 2011). For implementation of PBL to be successful at achieving its goals, support is needed from administrators, and buy-in is needed from students (Wiggins et al., 2016). As Wiggins et al. (2016) describe, this can take the form of whole programs of study – such as with Linköping University where there is broad departmental and institutional support for the pedagogy. Psychology students at Linköping University form groups at the beginning of their 5-year combined bachelor and master's degree program, remaining with their group throughout their years in the program; PBL is integrated across all the academic courses within the program, where PBL takes the form of deployment in short course modules or entire semester-long courses.

Like PBL, inquiry-based learning leverages the features of student self-direction and open-ended problems.

Inquiry-Based Learning (see also Lipmann, ▶ Chap. 51, "Inquiry-Based Learning in Psychology"). Inquiry-based learning (IBL) is a way of approaching the learning process that aims to mimic the process of discovery outlined by the scientific method (Keselman, 2003). IBL pedagogy has developed through constructivist and discovery-based learning theories – indeed, it is sometimes described synonymously with discovery-based learning (e.g., Pedaste et al., 2015). IBL began to achieve a prominent place in primary and secondary education programs within the last few decades (Abd-El-Khalick et al., 2004; Alfieri, Brooks, Aldrich, & Tenenbaum, 2011), in part, because of the inclusion of key tenets of the practice in a prominent National Research Council report by Bransford, Brown, and Cocklin (2000). The purpose of IBL, then, is to involve students in self-directed construction of knowledge that results both in the conceptual understanding of information within the investigated domain and promoting problem-solving skills and scientific thinking (Abd-El-Khalick et al., 2004; Pedaste et al., 2015).

In IBL, as it is also in PBL, the learning process is predicated on self-direction. Self-directed knowledge construction allows learners to situate new knowledge within their own experiences, rather than simply as an abstract concept. It is also effective. Meta-analyses continue to find positive effects on student achievement when implementing inquiry-based learning (e.g., Furtak, Seidel, Iverson, & Briggs, 2012; Lazonder & Harmsen, 2016; Zheng, Li, Tian, & Cui, 2018), although the inquiry-based feature of self-direction still requires expert guidance to be truly successful. That is, learners face challenges to achievement within an inquiry-based framework due to both domain-specific knowledge gaps and deficits in meta-cognitive skillsets required for productive scientific inquiry (Keselman, 2003). Thus, the positive effects of inquiry-based learning still rely on guidance, scaffolding, and support in order to be more effective than traditional instructional delivery (e.g., Alfieri et al., 2011; Furtak et al., 2012), and effectiveness may depend on the type of guidance received (e.g., Lazonder & Harmsen, 2016).

One example of inquiry-based learning incorporating modern instructional technology can be seen in the European Union's Global Online Science Labs for Inquiry Learning in Schools (Go-Lab). The Go-Lab is described by the project team as an online collection of virtual and remote laboratories, as well as archival datasets designed specifically for educational use at scale (de Jong, Sotiriou, & Gillet 2014). The Go-Lab federation collects dozens of inquiry-based learning projects across these three main laboratory types, including a remote experiment involving synthesis of methyl orange (cf. van Rens, Van Dijk, Mulder, &

Nieuwland, 2013). This experiment requires equipment and supplies that many chemistry laboratories may not possess. Instructors can use the Go-Lab web portal to customize the phases of the inquiry cycle, the progression, and the available guidance – such as process constraints, hints, and heuristics, as well as other supports – while students learn concepts related to pH and chemical reactions (de Jong et al., 2014). The value of the Go-Lab portal as an example is that it reveals how a rich environment can be established for students to dive into the learning process by using available resources to learn about the subject matter while also learning how to learn.

Another way of importing psychological literacy and principles of instruction into learning environments is through evidence-based small-group learning. Small-group learning scales down the learning environment to a level more manageable for students to learn.

Small-Group Learning (see also Dollar and Grease, ▶ Chap. 52, "Small Group Learning"). Evidence-based small-group learning strategies have three main aims: (1) to leverage the characteristics of more intimate, small-group interactions in comparison to large, lecture-based teaching; (2) to involve students in aspects of teaching-to-learn; and (3) to involve students in contributing to projects or activities based on their own competencies. Small-group learning strategies include reciprocal teaching (e.g., Palincsar & Brown, 1984; Hattie, 2009), interteaching (Boyce & Hineline, 2002; Saville et al., 2011; Saville & Zinn, 2009), and team-based learning (TBL). TBL is a form of small-group learning originally developed in the late 1970s. Its purpose was to address perceived problems with large courses (Sibley & Ostafichuk, 2015) by helping students develop skills needed for the professional workforce, including tackling real-world problems (Parmelee, Michaelsen, Cook, & Hudes, 2012). TBL incorporates evidence-based teaching and learning practices such as frequent assessment and interleaved practice, as well as elaborating, explaining, and defending positions (Dunlosky, Rawson, Marsh, Nathan, & Willingham, 2013; Hattie, 2012). Liu and Beaujean (2017) conducted a meta-analysis of TBL studies, showing that there is a reliable benefit to using TBL as a pedagogical technique, with some variance in effectiveness according to the type of program.

When using TBL in a course, teams are formed deliberately and transparently, aiming to balance each group's strengths and weakness, thus maximizing team effectiveness (e.g., Michaelsen & Sweet, 2008). The learning sequence is prescribed, and teams remain together throughout the duration of the course. Sequentially, learners begin with individual preparation where they study preparatory material; then, the students assure their readiness to learn by being formatively tested on lower-order knowledge at the individual and group level; finally, the group applies their course content by collaboration and discussion where they exercise and assess their newly acquired higher-order knowledge of challenging, complex concepts (Liu & Beaujean, 2017). At first, TBL was developed and deployed primarily in post-graduate medical programs but has since been adopted across a variety of disciplines and levels of tertiary education (e.g., Burgess, McGregor, & Mellis, 2014; Haidet, Kubitz, & McCormack, 2014).

Service-Based Learning (see also Bring et al., ▶ Chap. 53, "Service Learning"). Another learning method that leverages psychological knowledge and effective teaching practice is service-based learning. Service-based learning (SL) "integrates community service with academic study to enrich learning, teach civic responsibility, and strengthen communities" (Fiske, 2002, p. 6). As a pedagogical strategy, SL aims to facilitate student application of abstract academic concepts to resolving real-world social problems while developing long-term commitments to civic involvement after graduation. The strategy results in learning that is identity transformative (Macías Gomez-Estern, Arias-Sánchez, Marco Macarro, Cabillas Romero, and Martínez Lozano, 2019). SL research has a history of demonstrating achievement in the concomitant goals of improving students' academic learning while also developing a sense of greater social responsibility (e.g., Boland, 2014; Katz, DuBois, & Wigderson, 2014; Meyer et al., 2016; Rockquemore & Schaffer, 2000; Shek, Ma, & Yang, 2019).

One empirical example of the efficacy of SL was conducted by Macías Gomez-Estern et al. (2019). They experimented with university students enrolled in two sections of the same psychology courses. Students in one course were assigned to an SL-based curriculum that included teaching children at a primary school, primarily populated by an under-served ethnic minority. Their involvement in teaching the children included leading collaborative learning groups, giving guidance to the children, and providing classroom support. Students in the other course were assigned to the same program of study but had no involvement with the children. In support of the efficacy of SL model, students in the SL course section reported higher valuation of the course, more personal growth, and better knowledge of the course content.

Technology-Enhanced Psychology Learning (see also Niegemann, ▶ Chap. 56, "Technology-Enhanced Psychology Learning and Teaching"). Technologies that are successful at improving learning outcomes tend to incorporate features that leverage well-established principles of cognitive architecture (Sweller, 2020). The process of acquiring knowledge that is pertinent to culture – rather than knowledge that simply meets the demands of survival – is effortful, demands attention, requires guidance, and benefits from effective supports. Alongside other effective teaching strategies, well-designed technology-assisted learning strategies can provide support, particularly in circumstances where it would be otherwise difficult to reduce cognitive load for learners. Ensuring that learning technologies are well-designed requires the incorporation of sound psychological principles of teaching and learning into the design and deployment of those technologies (Crompton, Bernacki, & Greene, 2020).

Crompton et al. (2020) reviewed six modern learning technologies – identified by experts (Brown et al., 2020), and in use by modern higher education institutions – with a focus on the underlying psychological principles that inform their potential and their success: adaptive learning technologies; learning analytics; artificial intelligence; improved instructional design tools; X-reality systems; and Open Educational Resources. Adaptive learning technologies modify the learning experience based on real-time analysis of student responses, adjusting the presentation of content, and the level of learner support, to optimize learning efficiency (Aleven, McLaughlin, Glenn, & Koedinger, 2016). Adaptive learning technologies are learning systems designed to employ a framework of support, based on cognitive task analysis and other psychological principles, like metacognitive self-analysis by learners engaged in solving complex problems (Aleven et al., 2016). When the design of these systems incorporates such well-established psychological principles, adaptive learning systems can be as effective as human tutors in promoting learner success (VanLehn, 2011).

Using evidence-based psychological principles to provide optimal support for learning requires the capacity to understand the processes of learners and the contributions of their environments. Learning analytics seeks to provide data and analysis that can be used for this purpose (Fischer et al., 2020). Such data and analyses can detect the use – or lack of use – of important and well-researched components of learning, including retrieval practice, self-explanation, metacognitive self-regulation, performance feedback, and strategy adaptation (Crompton et al., 2020). Successful application of detailed data and analyses can be supported by complex software systems, such as with the use of artificial intelligence (AI) in educational contexts.

Artificial intelligence (AI) describes computing systems performing human-like cognitive and metacognitive processes (Popenici & Kerr, 2017). In higher education, AI use learning analytics to predict low performance among students and then use adaptive learning supports to improve student strategies and meta-cognitions (Bernacki, Crompton, & Greene 2020). These adaptive supports allow for personalization of the learning experience, customizing, scaffolding, and fading support, and improved outcomes (van de Pol, Volman, & Beishuizen, 2010) with massive scalability. Expanded adoption and development of instructional design tools and learning platforms have led to a focus on the deliberate incorporation of central psychological principles of learning, such as multimedia learning theory and cognitive load, into frameworks informing user interface design (Bernacki et al., 2020). Modern applications of those design principles can be seen in the development of complex content delivery interfaces, such as X-reality systems.

X-reality systems are capable of overlaying, mixing, or subsuming real environments with artificially supplied information (augmented, mixed, and virtual realities, respectively). Research shows that involving X-reality in teaching and learning can facilitate improved learning outcomes (e.g., Al Janabi et al., 2020), provided that design and implementation are informed by well-established psychological principles of learning (Crompton et al., 2020). Such systems can enhance the realism of training environments, enhancing the efficiency for learners establishing their emerging ability to put abstract concepts into practice.

Online and Open-University Teaching and Learning (see also Jesseau, ▶ Chap. 5, "Teaching the Psychology of Learning"). Finally, online and distance-based education has risen in public consciousness and discourse since the COVID-19 pandemic forced educational systems to find ways to combine continued curriculum delivery with precautions to protect public health and safety (e.g., Aguilera-

Hermida, 2020; Ali, 2020). While online education is a relatively new educational format, its adoption in higher education has become increasingly commonplace (e.g., Gikandi, Morrow, & Davis, 2011; Nguyen, 2015) – including models that blend in-person instruction with some online course delivery.

Despite the relative novelty of online education, researchers and educational theorists have been grappling with the structure, benefits, and challenges of online learning for decades (e.g., Gikandi et al., 2011; Kebritchi, Lipschuetz, & Santiague, 2017; Lou, Bernard, & Abrami, 2006; Means, Toyama, Murphy, Bakia, & Jones, 2009; Nguyen, 2015; Nichols, 2003; Oliver, 1999). Nichols (2003) argued that online learning should be thought of as a new expression of education, and a pedagogy-independent collection of tools for delivering education, rather than as a separate system. Kebritchi et al. (2017) described online education as being "post-secondary and credit bearing coursework completely delivered through online courses via a learning management system" (p. 6).

The broad term "open education" has historically described educational practices aimed at providing inclusion and access to educational opportunities across wider populations (Weller, Jordan, DeVries, & Rolfe, 2018). Cronin (2017) notes that the concept of openness is multidimensional, referring at times to admission standards, cost, resources, or practices. Modern conceptualizations of open education have grown from the expansion of the Open Educational Resources movement and further magnified by the very modern development of open educational practices and massive open online courses (Weller, et al., 2018).

McCutcheon, Lohan, Traynor, & Martin (2015) contend that students can have equivalent, or better, learning outcomes (e.g., Means et al., 2009; Nguyen, 2015) in online courses then they might in face-to-face courses. However, the student outcomes supporting such a position are variable; success frequently depends on factors such as (a) learner characteristics (e.g., readiness for distance learning, self-direction), (b) the structure and delivery of the course, (c) the availability and quality of interaction opportunities between learners and their peers or instructor, and (d) time spent by the learners on learning tasks (e.g., Gikandi et al., 2011; Lou et al., 2006; Means et al., 2009; Nguyen, 2015). Successful online education continues to face numerous challenges: 1) expectations, readiness, and participation of the learner; 2) preparation, time management, and teaching style of the instructor; 3) development, delivery, and instructional strategies for the content; as well as 4) student preparation, instructor development, and logistical support from the institution (Kebritchi et al., 2017).

Assessing Core Competencies: Theory-Based and Evidence-Based Approaches

Summative Assessment (see also Blalock et al., ▶ Chap. 54, "Assessment of Learning in Psychology"). Summative assessment is a process of evaluation defined by Taras (2005) as "a judgement which encapsulates all the evidence up to a given point" (p. 468). Typically, assessment that is summative in nature represents the final evaluation of the state of a learner's mastery of a topic or skill, often tied to a high-stakes decision or certification (e.g., Harrison et al., 2013; Harrison, Könings,

Schuwirth, Wass, & van der Vleuten, 2015; van der Vleuten et al., 2012; Yorke, 2003). In other words, a summative assessment measures the degree to which a learner has met the standard represented by a learning goal, and that measurement facilitates making judgments that are a necessity in the course of education and in everyday life (Taras, 2005).

Many authors agree that summative assessment affects learning, despite its focus on measuring learning outcomes. This is particularly the case given the power of the well-understood "testing effect" (Roediger & Karpicke, 2006), whereby the act of taking tests during learning improves later retrieval. Schwieren, Barenberg, & Dutke (2017), for example, conducted a recent meta-analysis of the contributions of testing to learning in psychology classrooms, finding a moderate benefit from intermediate testing between the initial acquisition of knowledge and a final test of that knowledge, even without the intermediate provision of feedback.

And yet, summative assessments are not without their disadvantages. Boud (2000) suggests that a summative assessment provides a framework for focusing student attention on specific elements of the curriculum, but that such a framework suffers from ambiguity. Others, such as Harrison et al. (2015), have argued that summative assessment focuses learners on a fear of failure, often to the detriment of learning progress.

Still, best practices in summative assessment do help to attenuate some of these risks when close attention is paid to reliability and validity of the assessments, clarity about the standards for achievement, and close connection of the assessment to clearly articulated learning goals (e.g., Kibble, 2017).

Formative Assessment and Feedback Strategies (see also Narciss and Zumbach, ► Chap. 55, "Formative Assessment and Feedback Strategies"). Black and Wiliam (1998, 2009) wrote that assessment serves a formative function when it provides information that instructors, learners, and peers can use to modify, support, plan, or facilitate decisions about regulating the process of future learning, in a way that will likely result in better learning outcomes. In other words, assessment is formative insofar as it provides actionable information used in metacognitive processing that is involved in monitoring and directing efforts made toward achieving a learning goal.

This definition of formative assessment provides differentiation from summative assessment by virtue of how the information provided by the assessment is exchanged, interpreted, and applied – rather than by virtue of the form the assessment takes as an information-gathering tool. For instance, Taras (2005) suggests that formative assessment "focuses on the process of assessing and using feedback, whereas summative assessment tends to focus on product" (p. 472). Consequently, assessments can be formative in utility when information is gathered using formalized instruments such as tests and exams or when information is gathered using less formal methods (e.g., Yorke, 2003) such as online discussion boards or verbal exchanges in a classroom setting.

All of these types of assessment have the potential to provide feedback to the instructor, learner, or the learner's peers, in the form of evidence about a learner's current progress or state of mastery. What is critical to applying such assessments formatively is to ensure that this evidence is "used in a way that fits formative purposes" (Gikandi et al. 2011, p. 2337). In other words, the feedback must be available to, and understood by, the learner, who must also have a chance to apply the feedback to their learning process (Boud, 2000).

Feedback, Black and Wiliam (2009) conclude, is most useful when instructors possess valid models of student learning that allow them to predict in advance which types of feedback will result not only in use by the learner but also in beneficial effects upon learning processes. Like Sadler (1989, 1998), Nicol and Macfarlane-Dick (2006) argued that those benefits should include the development of self-regulated learning – a metacognitive process. In addition, sustained development of self-regulated learning requires the feedback to be in the form of dialectic exchanges between learners, their peers, and their instructors (Nicol & Macfarlane-Dick, 2006). Such exchanges help ensure that feedback is appropriate for, is understood by, and is more likely to be applied successfully by the learner (Black & Wiliam, 2009; Boud, 2000; Nicol, 2010; Nicol & Macfarlane-Dick, 2006; Sadler, 1989, 1998; Yorke, 2003). Boud (2000) calls the practice of this type of assessment "sustainable" because it represents assessment that both "meets the needs of the present and prepares students to meet their own future learning needs" (p. 151).

Still, formative assessments and summative assessments are, by some accounts, not clearly differentiated (Gikandi et al., 2011), and their use is "inextricably woven together" in higher education (Boud, 2000, p. 154), with summative assessment central to – and a necessary condition of – formative assessment (Taras, 2005). Yet others suggest adopting assessment regimes that strategically and purposefully integrate the use of both methods – sometimes called programmatic assessment (e.g., van der Vleuten et al., 2012). Additionally, formative assessments can often overlap in utility with summative assessments, as assessments designed to be formative may also serve summative purposes – providing information about the state of a learner's progress at the time of the assessment (Yorke, 2003).

Finally, it is important to note that the most prototypically summative of in-class assessment tools can also serve a formative purpose if feedback is both provided to, and utilized by, learners to inform their future learning efforts (Gikandi et al. 2011; Taras, 2005). While not all learners make equal use of feedback after summative assessments (e.g., Harrison et al., 2013, 2015; Heeneman, Schut, Donkers, van der Vleuten, & Muijtjens, 2017), Harrison et al. (2013) found that learners who valued feedback more, and those who performed better on summative assessments, were more engaged with available feedback. In sum, it may be difficult to argue that any assessment is not formative in some way, unless the results of the assessment are unavailable to provide feedback for the learner, their peers, or the instructor – or unless all of the parties ignore the information when it is available.

Teaching, Learning, and Assessment Resources

In this chapter, we have woven issues, concepts, theories, and practices with evidence – both historically and contemporarily – into as clear a picture as possible of the field of educational psychology. Thus, we recommend the following practices for those psychology teachers teaching in higher education with a focus on learning and instruction in the context of educational psychology:

1. Be cognizant of the fact that teaching and learning consists of dynamic human-environment interactions. Thus, when teaching, try and take into account multiple perspectives (e.g., human development, complex cognitive processes, behavioral and social-cognitive views of learning, social-constructivist views of learning, self-regulation and classroom management, classroom assessment strategies, and motivation). However, be sensitive to and embrace the intersectionality of these perspectives within the culture and language of both teachers and learners.

2. Begin the instructional process at the point where students have knowledge as close as possible to the new knowledge they are being asked to build. Students do not think like experts when attempting to learn; instead, their strategic naivete leads them to deploy simple and typically erroneous approaches toward problem-solving. Thus, it is important to guide student learning by scaffolding information and strategies of acquisition from simple to complex, modeling effective knowledge building approaches, and providing feedback and cues during the knowledge construction process.

3. There is a reciprocal and recursive relationship between the lab and the classroom. Keep this relationship in mind because it reflects one of the superordinate learning objectives of educational psychology: to reduce the gap between research and practice in learning.

4. In the year 2020, online learning and teaching rose to the forefront of the public discussion around education – and the practice of education – at all levels, due to a global health pandemic. However, online learning will likely continue to grow in use and in importance, even though a return to traditional classrooms occurred for the majority of teachers and learners worldwide. Online teaching and learning offer the possibility of (a) reducing some of the traditional constraints limiting delivery of education, (b) reducing or eliminating barriers of educational access due to educational inequities, and (c) improving opportunities to learn across age groups, socioeconomic groups, and learning goals. Thus, constructing efficient, accessible, and effective online learning environments has never been more important. Understand and communicate how effective learning and teaching practices can be built and leveraged online.

5. Students can be cognitively and emotionally inspired to change their beliefs about themselves as learners – to become their own champions in taking on the challenges of learning situations they experience as difficult. This can be done by helping students migrate their goals from *performance* goals to *learning* goals while gradually scaling up the difficulty of lessons. Guiding and supporting students away from a focus on performance goals toward learning goals shift their disposition to one of mastery, rather than helplessness. Mastery dispositions empower to students to believe that they can take on more and more challenging tasks and succeed based on their effort rather than their ability.

6. Psychologists have developed principles of effective teaching that can be implemented with relative ease in classrooms. These practices include testing to enhance memory and transfer, distributed practice or spaced learning, meta-cognitive skills such as reflective note-taking, and interteaching. The application and development of evidence-based teaching practices, such as these, is vital to improving student learning outcomes.

7. Formative assessment should be used as extensively as is practical, bearing in mind the necessity of providing high-quality feedback following assessment performance. The practical considerations include the size of the class, the complexity of the assessment for which feedback will be provided, and the time constraints of the instructor. One way to minimize the time required to provide in-depth feedback to a larger class is to assign low-stakes assessments (such as reading quizzes or quick-writes) during a class meeting. Other options include classroom response technology such as iClickers or PollEverywhere, where it is possible to check knowledge and provide immediate, high-quality, corrective feedback to the entire class at once.

Recommended Readings and Resources

Berliner, D. C. (2006). Educational psychology: Searching for essence through-out a century of influence. In P.A. Alexander and P. H. Winne (Eds.), *Handbook of educational psychology* (pp. 3–28). Routledge. Berliner has produced a (now-classic) comprehensive analysis that traces the history and development of ideas about what educational psychology should be as a discipline, across the course of the twentieth century. In this (2006) update to his earlier (1999) version, he reflects on how those ideas have developed and changed while discussing the intertwined influences of theory, research, and practice on the current (2006) state of the field. By producing a clear and comprehensible description of the educational psychology, Berliner (2006) both highlights the ideas and debates that are structural to the discipline, and he challenges current and future educational psychologists to continue pushing toward a fulfillment of the discipline's promise and potential.

Cranney, J. (2013). Towards psychological literacy: A snapshot of evidence-based learning and teaching. *Australian Journal of Psychology*, 65, 1–4. In a brief introduction to a special issue of the *Australian Journal of Psychology*, Cranney (2013) succinctly calls for a move toward the scholar-teacher model. This call underscores two important points about psychology in education. First, dissemination of psychological knowledge and facilitating an understanding of how such knowledge is produced – especially to people who will not become psychologists themselves – are part of the responsibility of psychologists as educators. She calls this responsibility the production of psychological literacy. Second, effective dissemination of this goal requires psychologists to apply what they know about human learning to the aim of producing psychological literacy. Thus, a teacher-scholar uses existing knowledge to implement evidence-based teaching techniques and then observes the resulting effect on learning. Observations are reported to the psychological community. The teacher-scholar makes adjustments to their teaching practice, and the cycle of refinement and testing begins again. Despite acknowledged challenges to implementing such a model, Cranney suggests that aspiring to this "gold standard" is both possible and necessary.

Kirschner, P.A., and Hendrick, C. (2020). How learning happens: Seminal works in educational psychology and what they mean in practice. Routledge. This book is a compendium of seminal works designed to inventory and explain the most important papers published in the field of learning and teaching. As such, the book not only is a historical record of the major thinkers in the field but also provides the most important research findings that have formed the bedrock for educational psychology's best practices. As Schwartz (2020) wrote, "the authors give voice, reason, and seasoned erudition to the findings, perspectives, and applications of these classics—in short, a level of percipience that is well-nigh beyond what most authors are typically able to do"(p.120).

Taras, M. (2005). Assessment – summative and formative – some theoretical reflections. *British Journal of Educational Studies*, *53*(4), **466–478.** We have suggested here that testing and assessment form a core piece of effective teaching. We have cited many theorists and researchers (e.g., Black & Wiliam, 2009; Gikandi et al., 2011) who have reflected in some depth on assessment, particularly formative assessment. Numerous authors discuss both formative and summative assessment – at least briefly. Taras (2005) differs from others we have cited by virtue of her in-depth consideration of the application, appropriateness, and interrelationship of *both* summative assessment and formative assessment within the same discussion. She argues that using both forms of assessment is critical to developing, refining, and producing an effective educational environment. In addition, she makes a strong effort in this discussion to more clearly define each assessment type, along with describing the role of each in the classroom – an issue that psychologists continue to struggle with.

Other valuable digital resources include:

1. https://www.learningscientists.org/downloadable-materials. These free resources were put together by cognitive psychologists interested in education and are based on research from cognitive psychology. The site suggests that these materials be used to provide flexible guiding principles to help guide learning.
2. https://www.retrievalpractice.org/library. These are additional free resources, also put together by a team of cognitive psychologists. This site condenses cognitive and educational research related to teaching strategies, why they enhance learning, and how to implement them in the classroom.
3. https://theeffortfuleducator.com/downloadables/. This website was designed by a high school psychology teacher who wanted to highlight the connections between research being done on learning, memory, and cognition and the classroom. The website contains many resources directly relevant to teaching (e.g., how to enhance multiple-choice questions).

Cross-References

▶ Assessment of Learning in Psychology
▶ Basic Principles and Procedures for Effective Teaching in Psychology
▶ First Principles of Instruction Revisited
▶ Formative Assessment and Feedback Strategies
▶ Inquiry-Based Learning in Psychology
▶ Problem-Based Learning and Case-Based Learning
▶ Psychology in Teacher Education
▶ Service Learning
▶ Small Group Learning
▶ Teaching the Psychology of Learning
▶ Technology-Enhanced Psychology Learning and Teaching

References

Abd-El-Khalick, F., Boujaoude, S., Duschl, R., Lederman, N. G., Mamlok-Naaman, R., Hofstein, A., . . . Tuan, H. L. (2004). Inquiry in science education: International perspectives. *Science Education, 88*(3), 397–419.

Adler, M. (Ed.). (1952). *The great ideas: A syntopicon of the great books of the Western world.* Encyclopedia Britannica.

Aguilera-Hermida, A. P. (2020). College students' use and acceptance of emergency online learning due to Covid-19. *International Journal of Educational Research Open, 1*(2020), 100011.

Alba, J. W., & Hasher, L. (1983). Is memory schematic? *Psychological Bulletin, 93*(2), 203.

Al Janabi, H. F., Aydin, A., Palaneer, S., Macchione, N., Al-Jabir, A., Khan, M. S., . . . Ahmed, K. (2020). Effectiveness of the HoloLens mixed-reality headset in minimally invasive surgery: A simulation-based feasibility study. *Surgical Endoscopy, 34*(3), 1143–1149.

Aleven, V., McLaughlin, E. A., Glenn, R. A., & Koedinger, K. R. (2016). Instruction based on adaptive learning technologies. In R. E. Mayer & P. Alexander (Eds.), *Handbook of research on learning and instruction* (pp. 522–560). Taylor & Francis.

Alfieri, L., Brooks, P. J., Aldrich, N. J., & Tenenbaum, H. R. (2011). Does discovery-based instruction enhance learning? *Journal of Educational Psychology, 103*(1), 1–18.

Ali, W. (2020). Online and remote learning in higher education institutes: A necessity in light of COVID-19 pandemic. *Higher Education, 10*(3), 16–25.

American Psychological Association. (2012). *A practical guidebook for the competency benchmarks.* American Psychological Association.

American Psychological Association. (2016). Revision of Ethical Standard 3.04 of the "Ethical Principles of Psychologists and Code of Conduct" (2002, as amended 2010). *The American Psychologist, 71*(9), 900.

Anderson, L. M., Blumenfeld, P., Pintrich, P. R., Clark, C. M., Marx, R. W., & Peterson, P. (1995). Educational psychology for teachers: Reforming our courses, rethinking our roles. *Educational Psychologist, 30*(3), 143–157.

APA Presidential Task Force on Evidence-Based Practice. (2006). Evidence-based practice in psychology. *The American Psychologist, 61*(4), 271.

Ausubel, D. P. (1960). The use of advance organizers in the learning and retention of meaningful verbal material. *Journal of Educational Psychology, 51*(5), 267.

Ausubel, D. P. (1968). *Educational Psychology: A cognitive view.* Holt Rinehart and Winston.

Bandura, A. (1977). Self-efficacy: Toward a unifying theory of behavioral change. *Psychological Review, 84*(2), 191.

Berliner, D. C. (1993). The 100-year journey of educational psychology: From interest, to disdain, to respect for practice. In T. K. Fagan & G. R. VandenBos (Eds.), *Master lectures in psychology. Exploring applied psychology: Origins and critical analyses* (pp. 37–78). American Psychological Association. https://doi-org.mantis.csuchico.edu/10.1037/11104-002

Berliner, D. C. (2006). Educational psychology: Searching for essence throughout a century of influence. In I. P. A. Alexander & P. H. Winne (Eds.), *Handbook of educational psychology* (pp. 3–28). Routledge.

Bernacki, M. L., Crompton, H., & Greene, J. A. (2020). Towards convergence of mobile and psychological theories of learning. *Contemporary Educational Psychology, 60*(2020), 101828.

Berninger, V. W. (Ed.). (2012). *Past, present, and future contribution of cognitive writing research to cognitive psychology*. Psychology Press.

Black, P., & Wiliam, D. (1998). Assessment and classroom learning. *Assessment in Education: Principles, Policy & Practice, 5*(1), 7–74.

Black, P., & Wiliam, D. (2009). Developing the theory of formative assessment. *Educational Assessment, Evaluation and Accountability, 21*(1), 5–31.

Boland, J. A. (2014). Orientations to civic engagement: Insights into the sustainability of a challenging pedagogy. *Studies in Higher Education, 39*(1), 180–195.

Boud, D. (2000). Sustainable assessment: Rethinking assessment for the learning society. *Studies in Continuing Education, 22*(2), 151–167.

Boyce, T. E., & Hineline, P. N. (2002). Interteaching: A strategy for enhancing the user-friendliness of behavioral arrangements in the college classroom. *The Behavior Analyst, 25*(2), 215–226.

Boyle, J., & Kelly, B. (2016). The role of evidence in educational psychology. In B. Kelly, L. M. Woolfson, & J. Boyle (Eds.), *Frameworks for practice in educational psychology: A textbook for trainees and practitioners* (2nd ed.). Jessica Kingsley Publishers.

Bransford, J. D., Brown, A. L., & Cocklin, R. R. (2000). How people learn: Brain, mind, experience, and school: Expanded edition. In National Research Council (Ed.), *Early childhood development and learning: New knowledge for policy* (pp. 57–86). National Academy Press.

Brown, M., McCormack, M., Reeves, J., Brooks, D. C., Grajek, S., Alexander, B., . . . Weber, N. (2020). *2020 Educause horizon report: Teaching and learning edition*. EDUCAUSE.

Burgess, A. W., McGregor, D. M., & Mellis, C. M. (2014). Applying established guidelines to team-based learning programs in medical schools: A systematic review. *Academic Medicine, 89*(4), 678–688.

Buskist, W. (2013). Preparing the new psychology professoriate to teach: Past, present, and future. *Teaching of Psychology, 40*(4), 333–339.

Butler, A. C., & Roediger, H. L., III. (2007). Testing improves long-term retention in a simulated classroom setting. *European Journal of Cognitive Psychology, 19*(4–5), 514–527.

Carpenter, S. K. (2012). Testing enhances the transfer of learning. *Current Directions in Psychological Science, 21*(5), 279–283.

Cepeda, N. J., Pashler, H., Vul, E., Wixted, J. T., & Rohrer, D. (2006). Distributed practice in verbal recall tasks: A review and quantitative synthesis. *Psychological Bulletin, 132*(3), 354–380.

Charles, D. C. (1987). The emergence of educational psychology. In J. A. Glover & R. R. Ronning (Eds.), *Historical foundations of educational psychology*. Plenum Press.

Chi, M. T., Feltovich, P. J., & Glaser, R. (1981). Categorization and representation of physics problems by experts and novices. *Cognitive Science, 5*(2), 121–152.

Clark, J. M., & Paivio, A. (1991). Dual coding theory and education. *Educational Psychology Review, 3*(3), 149–210.

Collins, A. (1991). Cognitive apprenticeship and instructional technology. *Educational values and cognitive instruction: Implications for reform, 1991*, 121–138.

Collins, A., Brown, J. S., & Holum, A. (1991). Cognitive apprenticeship: Making thinking visible. *American Educator, 15*(3), 6–11.

Craik, F. I., & Lockhart, R. S. (1972). Levels of processing: A framework for memory research. *Journal of Verbal Learning and Verbal Behavior, 11*(6), 671–684.

Cranney, J., & Dunn, D. S. (Eds.). (2011). *The psychologically literate citizen: Foundations and global perspectives*. Oxford University Press.

Cranney, J., & Voudouris, N. J. (2012). Psychology education and training in Australia: Shaping the future. In S. McCarthy, K. L. Dickson, J. Cranney, V. Karandashev, & A. Trapp (Eds.), *Teaching psychology around the world* (Vol. 3, pp. 2–14). Cambridge Scholars Press.

Cranney, J. (2013). Towards psychological literacy: A snapshot of evidence-based learning and teaching. *Australian Journal of Psychology, 65*, 1–4.

Crompton, H., Bernacki, M., & Greene, J. A. (2020). Psychological foundations of emerging technologies for teaching and learning in higher education. *Current Opinion in Psychology, 36*, 101–105.

Cronin, C. (2017). Openness and praxis: Exploring the use of open educational practices in higher education. *The International Review of Research in Open and Distance Learning, 18*(5), 15–34.

Darling-Hammond, L., & Baratz-Snowden, J. (2007). A good teacher in every classroom: Preparing the highly qualified teachers our children deserve. *Educational Horizons, 85*(2), 111–132.

de Jong, T., Sotiriou, S., & Gillet, D. (2014). Innovations in STEM education: The Go-Lab federation of online labs. *Smart Learning Environments, 1*(3), 1–16.

Dunlosky, J., Rawson, K. A., Marsh, E. J., Nathan, M. J., & Willingham, D. T. (2013). Improving students' learning with effective learning techniques: Promising directions from cognitive and educational psychology. *Psychological Science in the Public Interest, 14*(1), 4–58.

Dunn, D. S., Saville, B. K., Baker, S. C., & Marek, P. (2013). Evidence-based teaching: Tools and techniques that promote learning in the psychology classroom. *Australian Journal of Psychology, 65*(1), 5–13.

Dunn, D. S. (1994). Lessons learned from an interdisciplinary-writing course: Implications for student writing in psychology. *Teaching of Psychology, 21*(4), 223–227.

Dunn, D. (2011). *A short guide to writing about psychology* (3rd ed.). Longman.

Dutke, S., Bakker, H. E., Papageorgi, I., & Taylor, J. (2017). PLAT 16 (2) 2017: Introduction to the special issue on evidence-based teaching (EBT): Examples from learning and teaching psychology. *Psychology of Learning & Teaching, 16*(2), 175–178.

Dutke, S., Bakker, H., Sokolová, L., Stuchlikova, I., Salvatore, S., & Papageorgi, I. (2019). Psychology curricula for non-psychologists? A framework recommended by the European Federation of Psychologists' Associations' Board of Educational Affairs. *Psychology Learning & Teaching, 18*(2), 111–120.

Dweck, C. S., & Leggett, E. L. (1988). A social-cognitive approach to motivation and personality. *Psychological Review, 95*(2), 256.

Educational Testing Service. (2004). *Study guide: Principles of learning and teaching* (2nd ed.). Educational Testing Service.

Educational Testing Service. (2009). *About the praxis series™ tests*. Educational Testing Service.

Fischer, C., Pardos, Z. A., Baker, R. S., Williams, J. J., Smyth, P., Yu, R., … Warschauer, M. (2020). Mining big data in education: Affordances and challenges. *Review of Research in Education, 44*(1), 130–160.

Fiske, E. B. (2002). *Learning in deed: The power of service-learning for American schools*. National Commission on Service-Learning.

Furtak, E. M., Seidel, T., Iverson, H., & Briggs, D. C. (2012). Experimental and quasi-experimental studies of inquiry-based science teaching: A meta-analysis. *Review of Educational Research, 82*(3), 300–329.

Gikandi, J. W., Morrow, D., & Davis, N. E. (2011). Online formative assessment in higher education: A review of the literature. *Computers & Education, 57*(4), 2333–2351.

Greenwood, G. E., & Fillmer, H. T. (1999). *Educational psychology cases for teacher decision-making*. Merrill.

Gurung, R. A., Hackathorn, J., Enns, C., Frantz, S., Cacioppo, J. T., Loop, T., & Freeman, J. E. (2016). Strengthening introductory psychology: A new model for teaching the introductory course. *American Psychologist, 71*(2), 112–124.

Haidet, P., Kubitz, K., & McCormack, W. T. (2014). Analysis of the team-based learning literature: TBL comes of age. *Journal on Excellence in College Teaching, 25*(3–4), 303–333.

Harrison, C. J., Könings, K. D., Molyneux, A., Schuwirth, L. W., Wass, V., & van der Vleuten, C. P. (2013). Web-based feedback after summative assessment: How do students engage? *Medical Education, 47*(7), 734–744.

Harrison, C. J., Königs, K. D., Schuwirth, L., Wass, V., & van der Vleuten, C. (2015). Barriers to the uptake and use of feedback in the context of summative assessment. *Advances in Health Sciences Education, 20*(1), 229–245.

Hattie, J. (2009). *Visible learning. A synthesis of over 800 meta-analyses relating to achievement.* Routledge.

Hattie, J. (2012). *Visible learning for teachers: Maximizing impact on learning.* Routledge.

Heeneman, S., Schut, S., Donkers, J., van der Vleuten, C., & Muijtjens, A. (2017). Embedding of the progress test in an assessment program designed according to the principles of programmatic assessment. *Medical Teacher, 39*(1), 44–52.

Hmelo, C. E. (1998). Problem-based learning: Effects on the early acquisition of cognitive skill in medicine. *Journal of Learning Science, 7*(2), 173–208.

Hoy, A. W. (2019). *Educational psychology.* Pearson.

Hung, W., Jonassen, D. H., & Liu, R. (2008). Problem-based learning. In: *Handbook of Research on Educational Communications and Technology, 3*(1), 485–506.

Interstate New Teacher Assessment and Support Consortium. (1992). Model standards for beginning teacher licensing, assessment and development: A resource for state dialogue. Interstate New Teacher Assessment and Support Consortium.

James, W. (1890). *Principles of psychology.* New York: Henry Holt. Reprinted: Harvard.

James, W. (1983). *Talks to teachers on psychology and to students on some of life's ideals.* Harvard University Press. (Original work published 1899).

Karpicke, J. D., Butler, A. C., & Roediger, H. L., III. (2009). Metacognitive strategies in student learning: Do students practise retrieval when they study on their own? *Memory, 17*(4), 471–479.

Katz, J., DuBois, M., & Wigderson, S. (2014). Learning by helping? Undergraduate communication outcomes associated with training or service-learning experiences. *Teaching of Psychology, 41*(3), 251–255.

Kebritchi, M., Lipschuetz, A., & Santiague, L. (2017). Issues and challenges for teaching successful online courses in higher education: A literature review. *Journal of Educational Technology Systems, 46*(1), 4–29.

Kelly, B. (2016). Frameworks for practice in educational psychology. In B. Kelly, L. M. Woolfson, & J. Boyle (Eds.), *Frameworks for practice in educational psychology: A textbook for trainees and practitioners* (2nd ed.). Jessica Kingsley Publishers.

Keselman, A. (2003). Supporting inquiry learning by promoting normative understanding of multivariable causality. *Journal of Research in Science Teaching, 40*(9), 898–921.

Kibble, J. D. (2017). Best practices in summative assessment. *Advances in Physiology Education, 41*, 110–119.

Kirschner, P. A., & Hendrick, C. (2020). *How learning happens: Seminal works in educational psychology and what they mean in practice.* Routledge.

Klieme, E., & Maag Merki, K. (2008). Introduction of educational standards in German-speaking countries. In J. Hartig, E. Klieme, & D. Leutner (Eds.), *Assessment of competencies in educational contexts* (pp. 215–224). Hogrefe.

Lazonder, A. W., & Harmsen, R. (2016). Meta-analysis of inquiry-based learning: Effects of guidance. *Review of Educational Research, 86*(3), 681–718.

Liu, S. N. C., & Beaujean, A. A. (2017). The effectiveness of team-based learning on academic outcomes: A meta-analysis. *Scholarship of Teaching and Learning in Psychology, 3*(1), 1–14.

Lohse-Bossenz, H., Kunina-Habenicht, O., & Kunter, M. (2013). The role of educational psychology in teacher education: Expert opinions on what teachers should know about learning, development, and assessment. *European Journal of Psychology of Education, 28*(4), 1543–1565.

Lou, Y., Bernard, R. M., & Abrami, P. C. (2006). Media and pedagogy in undergraduate distance education: A theory-based meta-analysis of empirical literature. *Educational Technology Research and Development, 54*(2), 141–176.

Macías Gomez-Estern, B., Arias-Sánchez, S., Marco Macarro, M. J., Cabillas Romero, M. R., & Martínez Lozano, V. (2019). Does service learning make a difference? Comparing students' valuations in service learning and non-service learning teaching of psychology. *Studies in Higher Education*, 1–11.

McCutcheon, K., Lohan, M., Traynor, M., & Martin, D. (2015). A systematic review evaluating the impact of online or blended learning vs. face-to-face learning of clinical skills in undergraduate nurse education. *Journal of Advanced Nursing, 71*(2), 255–270.

Means, B., Toyama, Y., Murphy, R., Bakia, M., & Jones, K. (2009). Evaluation of evidence-based practices in online learning: A meta-analysis and review of online learning studies. US Department of Education.

Merrill, M. D. (2002). First principles of instruction. *Educational Technology Research and Development, 50*(3), 43–59.

Mayer, R. E. (2005). Cognitive theory of multimedia learning. *The Cambridge handbook of multimedia learning, 41*, 31–48.

Meyer, C. L., Harned, M., Schaad, A., Sunder, K., Palmer, J., & Tinch, C. (2016). Inmate education as a service learning opportunity for students: Preparation, benefits, and lessons learned. *Teaching of Psychology, 43*(2), 120–125.

Michaelsen, L. K., & Sweet, M. (2008). The essential elements of team-based learning. *New Directions for Teaching and Learning, 2008*(116), 7–27.

Narciss, S. (2019). Curriculum design for (non-) psychology programs–a reflection on general and specific issues, and approaches on how to address them: Comment on Dutke et al., 2019. *Psychology Learning & Teaching, 18*(2), 144–147.

Nash, J. M., & Larkin, K. T. (2012). Geometric models of competency development in specialty areas of professional psychology. *Training and Education in Professional Psychology, 6*(1), 37.

National Center for Education Statistics. (2019). Integrated postsecondary education data system (IPEDS) fall 2000 through fall 2018, completions component. US Department of Education.

National Council for the Accreditation of Teacher Education. (2008). Professional standards for the accreditation of teacher preparation institutions. National Council for the Accreditation of Teacher Education.

Nguyen, T. (2015). The effectiveness of online learning: Beyond no significant difference and future horizons. *MERLOT Journal of Online Learning and Teaching, 11*(2), 309–319.

Nicol, D. J., & Macfarlane-Dick, D. (2006). Formative assessment and self-regulated learning: A model and seven principles of good feedback practice. *Studies in Higher Education, 31*(2), 199–218.

Nicol, D. (2010). From monologue to dialogue: Improving written feedback processes in mass higher education. *Assessment & Evaluation in Higher Education, 35*(5), 501–517.

Nichols, M. (2003). A theory for eLearning. *Journal of Educational Technology & Society, 6*(2), 1–10.

Oliver, R. (1999). Exploring strategies for online teaching and learning. *Distance Education, 20*(2), 240–254.

Ormrod, J. E. (2006). Commentary: Similarities and differences among educational psychology textbooks: An author's perspective. *Teaching Educational Psychology, 1*(3), 1–4.

Ormrod, J. E., Anderman, E. M., & Anderman, L. H. (2020). *Educational psychology: Developing learners*. Pearson.

Ormrod, J. E., & McGuire, D. J. (Eds.). (2007). *Case studies: Applying educational psychology* (2nd ed.). Merrill.

Parmelee, D., Michaelsen, L. K., Cook, S., & Hudes, P. D. (2012). Team-based learning: A practical guide: AMEE guide no. 65. *Medical Teacher, 34*(5), e275–e287.

Patrick, H., Anderman, L. H., Bruening, P. S., & Duffin, L. C. (2011). The role of educational psychology in teacher education: Three challenges for educational psychologists. *Educational Psychologist, 46*(2), 71–83.

Palincsar, A. S., & Brown, A. L. (1984). Reciprocal teaching of comprehension-fostering and comprehension-monitoring activities. *Cognition and Instruction, 1*(2), 117–175.

Pedaste, M., Mäeots, M., Siiman, L. A., De Jong, T., Van Riesen, S. A., Kamp, E. T., ... Tsourlidaki, E. (2015). Phases of inquiry-based learning: Definitions and the inquiry cycle. *Educational Research Review, 14*(2015), 47–61.

Peterson, R. L., Peterson, D. R., Abrams, J. C., Stricker, G., & Ducheny, K. (2010). The National Council of schools and programs of professional psychology: Educational model 2009. In M. B. Kenkel & R. L. Peterson (Eds.), *Competency-based education for professional psychology* (pp. 13–42). American Psychological Association.

Petticrew, M., & Roberts, H. (2003). Evidence, hierarchies, and typologies: Horses for courses. *Journal of Epidemiology & Community Health, 57*(7), 527–529.

Pilcher, J., & Bedford, L. A. (2011). Hierarchies of evidence in education. *The Journal of Continuing Education in Nursing, 42*(8), 371–377.

Pintrich, P. R. (2000). Multiple goals, multiple pathways: The role of goal orientation in learning and achievement. *Journal of Educational Psychology, 92*(3), 544.

Popenici, S. A., & Kerr, S. (2017). Exploring the impact of artificial intelligence on teaching and learning in higher education. *Research and Practice in Technology Enhanced Learning, 12*(1), 1–13.

Queensland College of Teachers, Professional Standards Unit. (2011). *Australian professional standards for teachers*. Queensland College of Teachers.

Quintilian, F. B. (1953). *Institutio oratoria* (4 Vols.; H. E. Butler, Trans.). Harvard University Press.

Quintilian, F. B. (1966). *Quintilian on education* (W. M. Smail, Trans.). Teachers College Press.

Reigeluth, C. M., & Stein, F. (1983). The elaboration theory of instruction. In C. M. Reigeluth (Ed.), *Instructional design theories and models* (pp. 335–381). Erlbaum.

Rockquemore, K. A., & Harwell Schaffer, R. (2000). Toward a theory of engagement: A cognitive mapping of service-learning experiences. *Michigan Journal of Community Service Learning, 7*(1), 14–25.

Rodolfa, E., Bent, R., Eisman, E., Nelson, P., Rehm, L., & Ritchie, P. (2005). A cube model for competency development: Implications for psychology educators and regulators. *Professional Psychology: Research and Practice, 36*(4), 347.

Roediger, H. L., III, & Karpicke, J. D. (2006). Test-enhanced learning: Taking memory tests improves long-term retention. *Psychological Science, 17*(3), 249–255.

Sadler, D. R. (1989). Formative assessment and the design of instructional systems. *Instructional Science, 18*(2), 119–144.

Sadler, D. R. (1998). Formative assessment: Revisiting the territory. *Assessment in Education: Principles, Policy & Practice, 5*(1), 77–84.

Santrock, J. W. (2021). *Educational psychology*. McGraw-Hill.

Saville, B. K., & Zinn, T. E. (2009). Interteaching: The effects of quality points on exam scores. *Journal of Applied Behavior Analysis, 42*(2), 369–374.

Saville, B. K., Lambert, T., & Robertson, S. (2011). Interteaching: Bringing behavioral education into the 21st century. *The Psychological Record, 61*(1), 153–165.

Schwieren, J., Barenberg, J., & Dutke, S. (2017). The testing effect in the psychology classroom: A meta-analytic perspective. *Psychology Learning & Teaching, 16*(2), 179–196.

Shek, D. T. L., Ma, C. M. S., & Yang, Z. (2019). Transformation and development of university students through service-learning: A corporate-community-university partnership initiative in Hong Kong (Project WeCan). *Applied Research in Quality of Life, 15*(2020), 1375–1393.

Sibley, J., & Ostafichuk, P. (2015). *Getting started with team-based learning*. Stylus Publishing, LLC.

Slavin, R. E. (2021). *Educational psychology: Theory and practice*. Pearson.

Slovak Centre of Scientific and Technical Information. (2018). *Štatistická ročenka - vysoké školy [Statistic yearbook – higher education]*. Ministerstvo školstva, vedy, výskumu a športu Slovenskej Republiky [Ministry of Education, Science, Research and Sports of the Slovak Republic].

Snowman, J., & McCown, R. R. (2015). *Educational psychology*. Wadsworth/Cengage Learning.

Statistisches Bundesamt. (2017). *Bildung und Kultur. Prüfungen an Hochschulen 2016 [Education and culture. Examinations at universities 2016]*. Statistisches Bundesamt.

Sudzina, M. R. (1997). Case study as a constructivist pedagogy for teaching educational psychology. *Educational Psychology Review, 9*(2), 199–218.

Sweller, J. (1988). Cognitive load during problem solving: Effects on learning. *Cognitive Science, 12*(2), 257–285.

Sweller, J. (2020). Cognitive load theory and educational technology. *Educational Technology Research and Development, 68*(1), 1–16.

Taras, M. (2005). Assessment–summative and formative–some theoretical reflections. *British Journal of Educational Studies, 53*(4), 466–478.

Thorndike, E. L. (1910). The contribution of psychology to education. *Journal of Educational Psychology, 1*, 5–12.

Training and Development Agency for Schools. (2007). Professional standards for teachers. Training and Development Agency.

Trapp, A., Banister, P., Ellis, J., Latto, R., Miell, D., & Upton, D. (2011). The future of undergraduate psychology in the United Kingdom. Higher Education Academy Psychology Network, University of York.

Van de Pol, J., Volman, M., & Beishuizen, J. (2010). Scaffolding in teacher–student interaction: A decade of research. *Educational Psychology Review, 22*(3), 271–296.

van der Vleuten, C. P., Schuwirth, L. W. T., Driessen, E. W., Dijkstra, J., Tigelaar, D., Baartman, L. K. J., & van Tartwijk, J. (2012). A model for programmatic assessment fit for purpose. *Medical Teacher, 34*(3), 205–214.

van Rens, L., Van Dijk, H., Mulder, J., & Nieuwland, P. (2013). Using a web application to conduct and investigate syntheses of methyl orange remotely. *Journal of Chemical Education, 90*(5), 574–577.

VanLehn, K. (2011). The relative effectiveness of human tutoring, intelligent tutoring systems, and other tutoring systems. *Educational Psychologist, 46*(4), 197–221.

Vives, J. L. (1913). De tradendis disciplinis. In *Vives on education* (F. Watson, Trans.). Cambridge University Press. (Original work published 1531).

Wahlheim, C. N., Dunlosky, J., & Jacoby, L. L. (2011). Spacing enhances the learning of natural concepts: An investigation of mechanisms, metacognition, and aging. *Memory & Cognition, 39*(5), 750–763.

Watson, R. I. (1961). A brief history of educational psychology. *Psychological Record, 11*, 209–242.

Weiner, B. (1985). An attributional theory of achievement motivation and emotion. *Psychological Review, 92*(4), 548.

Weller, M., Jordan, K., DeVries, I., & Rolfe, V. (2018). Mapping the open education landscape: Citation network analysis of historical open and distance education research. *Open Praxis, 10*(2), 109–126.

Wiggins, S., Chiriac, E. H., Abbad, G. L., Pauli, R., & Worrell, M. (2016). Ask not only 'what can problem-based learning do for psychology?' but 'what can psychology do for problem-based learning?' A review of the relevance of problem-based learning for psychology teaching and research. *Psychology Learning & Teaching, 15*(2), 136–154.

Wilson-Doenges, G., & Gurung, R. A. R. (2013). Benchmarks for scholarly investigations of teaching and learning. *Australian Journal of Psychology, 65*(1), 63–70.

Woolfolk Hoy, A. (1996). Teaching educational psychology: Texts in context. *Educational Psychologist, 31*(1), 41–49.

Woolfolk Hoy, A. (2000). Educational psychology in teacher education. *Educational Psychologist, 35*(4), 257–270.

Woolfolk Hoy, A. (2008). *Educational psychology in teacher education*. Teachers College Record.

Yorke, M. (2003). Formative assessment in higher education: Moves towards theory and the enhancement of pedagogic practice. *Higher Education, 45*(4), 477–501.

Zheng, L., Li, X., Tian, L., & Cui, P. (2018). The effectiveness of integrating mobile devices with inquiry-based learning on students' learning achievements: A meta-analysis. *International Journal of Mobile Learning and Organisation, 12*(1), 77–95.

Zimmerman, B. J. (1989). A social cognitive view of self-regulated academic learning. *Journal of Educational Psychology, 81*(3), 329.

Neuroscience in the Psychology Curriculum

16

Jennifer Parada and Leighann R. Chaffee

Contents

J. Parada (✉)
Bellevue College, Bellevue, WA, USA
e-mail: jennifer.parada@bellevuecollege.edu

L. R. Chaffee
University of Washington, Tacoma, Tacoma, WA, USA
e-mail: LChaffee@uw.edu

© Springer Nature Switzerland AG 2023
J. Zumbach et al. (eds.), *International Handbook of Psychology Learning and Teaching*,
Springer International Handbooks of Education,
https://doi.org/10.1007/978-3-030-28745-0_19

Abstract

Neuroscience, as an academic concentration and area of research, has grown significantly in past decades and has influenced the content and methods of closely related fields. Psychology programs have expanded biopsychology course offerings, increased the hiring of faculty with neuroscience academic concentrations, and provide considerable emphasis on the biology of behavior in introductory psychology courses. The goals of this chapter are to provide instructors with an understanding of neuroscience content in psychology programs, outline the competencies that students gain from taking biopsychology courses, and offer teaching resources. The chapter begins with a review of the history of neuroscience, including its current role in psychology programs and in shaping undergraduate curriculum. We then outline biopsychology competencies and organize content into three core concepts: foundational knowledge of the nervous system, application of the foundational knowledge, and understanding the clinical/social impact. Each core concept is connected to prompts for addressing influential themes in biopsychology (scientific literacy, evolution, and neuroplasticity and adaptability). Example learning activities and teaching resources that align with core concepts and themes are provided. The final sections of the chapter discuss the opportunities, challenges, and lessons learned in teaching biopsychology with evidence-based pedagogical approaches, including self-regulated learning, active learning through the use of high-impact practices, centering professional development skills through course work, and tips for successful instruction.

Keywords

Teaching neuroscience · Teaching biopsychology · Evidence-based teaching · Self-regulated learning · High-impact practices

Introduction

Neuroscience is an interdisciplinary field, drawing from disciplines like psychology, biology, mathematics, and chemistry to investigate nervous system functions (Stead, Wiseman, & Hellemans, 2019). Applying a neuroscientific level of analysis to psychological phenomena, for instance, pinpointing the biological correlates of cognition, emotion, and mental illnesses, has grown significantly in recent decades (Schwartz, Lilienfeld, Meca, & Sauvigné, 2016). This *neuroscience movement* within psychology has not only influenced areas of research and experimental methods but has also impacted the training and requisite knowledge of psychology students (Homa et al., 2013; Norcross et al., 2016). This chapter aims to provide instructors a foundation for teaching biopsychology courses (also titled "physiological psychology," "biological psychology," or "behavioral neuroscience") by summarizing the role of neuroscience in psychology programs, discussing core content areas in biopsychology, including learning activities and resources, outlining assessment options, and overcoming teaching challenges.

The History of Neuroscience in Psychology

The field of neuroscience was initially concerned with understanding the electrical and chemical properties of neurons, localized functions of brain regions, development and organization of neural tissue, and functions of neurotransmitters (Palermo & Morese, 2019; Stead et al., 2019). The foundational basis of neuroscience has expanded rapidly in the past century, resulting in many disciplines adopting neuroscientific approaches and methodologies, with psychology being no exception. Psychology has become a top area of research in neuroscience (Yeung, Goto, & Leung, 2017), and neuroscience-driven subfields of psychology, including behavioral and cognitive neuroscience, social neuroscience, evolutionary psychology, and comparative neuroscience, have expanded. Technological advances, particularly in imaging and microscopy, have made it more feasible to incorporate neuroscience variables into behavioral science research (Schwartz et al., 2016; Yeung et al., 2017). This growth is also attributed to increases in funding, the growing number of individuals with advanced neuroscience degrees, and the general public's growing interest in the brain (Akil et al., 2016).

Neuroscientific findings greatly inform our understanding of behavior and cognition; yet, the early allure of neuroscience information perpetuated several unsupported claims about the brain and behavior. For instance, the emergence of "brain-based learning" led many educators to trust myths like brain hemisphere dominance and learning styles (Bowers, 2016; Goswami, 2006; Lindell & Kidd, 2011), which could have negatively impacted instruction quality and led to misuse of instructional resources. Fortunately, the belief in neuroscience myths has decreased among educators and experts alike. The general public and students continue to perceive psychological explanations that contain neuroscience information as more compelling, even when the neuroscience information is irrelevant or inaccurate (see Weisberg, Keil, Goodstein, Rawson, & Gray, 2008). This suggests that the way we use neuroscience information to interpret psychological phenomena matters, particularly for those that do not have a thorough understanding of neuroscience and the philosophy of science.

Science communication and outreach have not always been prioritized or regarded as essential for neuroscience students (Kerchner, Hardwick, & Thornton, 2012). Fortunately, undergraduate and graduate training programs have made significant efforts to center science communication across disciplines and accurate representation of findings to combat the misapplication of neuroscientific information (Akil et al., 2016; Brownell, Price, & Steinman, 2013). Similarly, psychology programs are recommended to provide students with a broad knowledge base of psychology, incorporating multiple levels of analysis (e.g., biological, social, developmental, cultural) while fostering critical thinking skills (Schwartz et al., 2016). This chapter highlights influential themes and learning activities across core content areas in biopsychology as ways to promote critical thinking. The themes of scientific literacy and research, genetics and evolutionary influences, and neuroplasticity and adaptability align with content- and skill-based competencies outlined in this chapter and by other neuroscience education groups (e.g., Faculty for Undergraduate Neuroscience; Kerchner et al., 2012). These themes, outlined in subsequent sections, provide students with opportunities to critically evaluate the course content and their learning.

Given the rapid growth and application of neuroscience in psychology, it is no surprise that undergraduate psychology programs have also shifted toward highlighting the biological correlates of behavior, from introductory psychology courses through advanced course work.

Neuroscience in Undergraduate Psychology Programs

Neuroscience content is heavily incorporated into the undergraduate psychology curriculum. Homa et al. (2013) found that introductory psychology instructors spend significantly more time covering biopsychology content compared to other areas like social, clinical, or developmental psychology. This focus on biopsychology content in introductory psychology could reflect the role neuroscience plays in our understanding of behavior, an increase in the number of instructors with a specialty in neuroscience (Akil et al., 2016), and the fact that foundational neuroscience content can be applied to several psychological domains (e.g., brain development across the lifespan, the neurological correlates of psychological disorders). In fact, Gurung et al.'s (2016) model for introductory psychology content coverage highlights biology as a major pillar/domain of knowledge. Despite the reasoning, from the beginning of their undergraduate education, psychology students' understanding of behavior is shaped considerably by a biopsychological perspective.

Introductory biopsychology courses are commonly offered (Norcross et al., 2016). The number of psychology programs in the United States that offer such a course has increased from 89% in 2005 to 93% in 2013. Despite the rise in biopsychology course offerings, there remains substantial variability in the number of programs that require students to take biopsychology to fulfill degree requirements (Norcross et al., 2016; Stoloff et al., 2009). Estimates suggest that only between 25 and 49% of programs require biopsychology, while the rest of programs give students the option to pick biopsychology out of a group of other required courses or count the course as an elective. It is rare for universities to offer a dedicated major in biopsychology (Stoloff et al., 2009), and only about 1% of students in the biological and life sciences major in cognitive science and biopsychology (Carnevale, Strohl, & Melton, 2013).

The variability in biopsychology requirements is particularly interesting as it is a popular course and has been shown to benefit psychology students in several ways. Betancur, Rottman, Votruba-Drzal, and Schunn (2019) found that high performance in biopsychology (and research methods) was uniquely predictive of high performance in subsequent psychology courses. Content covered in biopsychology and research methods can be inherently difficult for students; thus, gaining a thorough understanding of such content areas could benefit students in future courses by allowing them to apply this knowledge more critically to other areas of psychology. Using biopsychology as an opportunity to foster critical thinking could be a way to combat persistent misinformation based on irrelevant neuroscience explanations (see Weisberg et al., 2008).

Biopsychology is one of the few courses in psychology programs that is occasionally accompanied by a lab. Approximately 28% of psychology programs in the United States offer a biopsychology lab course (Norcross et al., 2016). This low number could represent the unique challenges faced by lab faculty and students. A prominent challenge to offering and maintaining lab courses is a lack of resources (Peterson & Sesma Jr, 2017). Labs require additional space and facilities, funding to obtain equipment and supplies (e.g., dissection tools, personal protective equipment, lab manuals), and coordination of faculty to run the lab. Access to the resources necessary for lab courses varies significantly across 2- and 4-year institutions, particularly when it comes to the teaching load of instructors and funding (Hailstorks, Stamm, Norcross, Pfund, & Christidis, 2019). For students, labs can pose both financial and time-related burdens as they may require more course fees and an additional 2–3 hours of on-campus presence per week. Despite these challenges, the benefits of lab courses are well documented such as increasing students' content knowledge and interest (Thieman, Clary, Olson, Dauner, & Ring, 2009) and their interest in pursuing graduate school (Lloyd, Shanks, & Lopatto, 2019) or research careers (Adedokun, Bessenbacher, Parker, Kirkham, & Burgess, 2013). See Parada and Birkett (2020) for an overview of psychology lab benefits and teaching resources.

Though biopsychology primarily serves students majoring in psychology, it is often taken by pre-medical and nursing students. The revised Medical College Admissions Test (MCAT) emphasizes biological, psychological, and social aspects of behavior, making courses like biopsychology important for pre-medical students (Hong, 2012). Psychology and neuroscience are interdisciplinary fields, which lends to their relevance and application to several professions, especially those that are service-oriented, like medicine.

Purposes and Rationale of the Curriculum in Neuroscience

Considering the importance of neuroscience in psychology and related programs, it is essential to understand the core learning objectives of the course. As with the course requirements, there is vast variability in the learning objectives across biopsychology courses. Generally, though, the course learning objectives can be organized under content- and skill-focused competencies as displayed in Table 1. These competencies are consistent with those proposed by the Faculty for Undergraduate Neuroscience (FUN; Kerchner et al., 2012) and align with two standards in higher education, the American Psychological Association (APA) Guidelines for the undergraduate psychology major (Version 2.0; APA, 2018) and the European Higher Education Area (EHEA) framework of qualifications (EHEA, 2005).

The following sections provide an overview of the core content areas in biopsychology: *foundational knowledge of the nervous system*, *application of foundational knowledge*, and an *understanding of social/clinical impact*. Core concepts are

Table 1 Content- and skill-focused competencies for biopsychology courses

Content-focused core competencies	Skill-focused core competencies
Foundational Nervous System Knowledge • Examples: Structure and function of neurons and neural communication; brain structures and associated functions; influence of endocrine and immune systems.	*Research Methods* • Basic understanding of neuroscience methods. • Comprehension of the strengths and weaknesses of common biopsychology methods. • Ethical standards for animal and human research.
APA goal 1: Knowledge base in psychology	**APA goal 2**: Scientific inquiry and critical thinking
EHEA: Demonstrated knowledge and understanding in a field of study that builds on previous education	**EHEA**: Gather and interpret relevant data to inform judgments
Application of Foundational Knowledge • Examples: Survival/motivation-based behaviors such as eating, sleeping, reproduction; responding to stressors; sensation and perception; movement.	*Scientific Literacy* • Finding credible sources of information, reading research articles, critically evaluating evidence. • Applying biopsychology knowledge to own life (e.g., sleep patterns, taste perception, stress management, reflexes).
APA goal 1: Knowledge base in psychology	**APA goal 2**: Scientific inquiry and critical thinking
EHEA: Apply knowledge and understanding and problem-solving abilities within broader contexts	**EHEA**: Critical analysis, evaluation, and synthesis of new and complex ideas
Understanding Clinical/Social Impact • Examples: Biological basis of substance use and reward; psychological disorders; neurological disorders such as dementia and head trauma.	*Communication* • Written communication, including scientific writing. • Communicating with peers and instructor.
APA goal 3: Ethical + social responsibility in a diverse world	**APA goal 4**: Communication **APA goal 5**: Professional development
EHEA: Integrate knowledge and handle complexity, formulate judgments, and reflect on social or ethical responsibilities	**EHEA**: Communicate conclusions plus knowledge and rationale to specialists and non-specialists clearly and unambiguously

demonstrated across three influential themes related to students' understanding of biopsychology: *scientific literacy and research*, *genetics and evolutionary influences*, and *neuroplasticity and adaptability*. The goal of incorporating themes into biopsychology courses is twofold. First, it encourages students to apply their knowledge of core content areas, and second, it provides an opportunity for students to think critically about the real-world application of these areas; see Table 2.

Core Contents and Topics of Neuroscience

Core Concept 1: Foundational Knowledge of the Nervous System

Consider the following subcategories for Core Concept 1: cells of the nervous system, neural communication, neuroanatomy, and spinal cord and peripheral nervous system functions. Core Concept 1 content is consistent with topics of introductory and advanced neuroscience courses (see Kerchner et al., 2012; Stevenson, Shah, & Bish, 2016), which reflect popular areas of neuroscience research including cellular, molecular, and anatomical (Yeung et al., 2017). Core Concept 1 provides students with foundational knowledge of nervous system functions applied in Core Concepts 2 and 3. It is recommended that instructors spend as much time as they think is necessary on the recommended topics for Core Concept 1 (see Table 3). The topics covered and time allotted will depend on their specific course learning outcomes.

Core Concept 2: Applications of Foundational Knowledge

Application of foundational knowledge allows for more complex understanding of psychological processes. These areas are relevant to students, as they can observe concepts from class in their daily life and apply the principles from earlier chapters to their academic interests. Coverage of sensation and perception, plus movement and motor systems, transition from anatomical pathways to applied topics such as top-down and bottom-up processing. The study of motivated behaviors and the reward system transitions to a selection of the remaining topics, including eating, sleeping and biological rhythms, and sexual development and reproduction. Additional applications include language and development or emotions and stress anchored in a broader discussion of health. It is recommended that instructors select a couple of the recommended topics from Core Concept 2 (see Table 4) that best align with their course learning outcomes.

Core Concept 3: Clinical Applications

Core Concept 3 merges foundational knowledge and the understanding of basic behavioral processes to challenge students to consider the impact of atypical

Table 2 Core concepts and themes for biopsychology courses

	Core Concept 1: Foundational knowledge of the nervous system	Core Concept 2: Applications of foundational knowledge	Core Concept 3: Clinical/social impact
Scientific literacy and research	How do neuroscientists study the nervous system? Note methods (anatomical and neurobiological techniques, neuroimaging, psychophysiology) including strengths and limitations. Clarify ethics of research with animal subjects and human participants, including the practical limitations of these models.	How do we locate credible sources of information about the brain? Distinguish types of information, identify peer-reviewed sources, and critically evaluate evidence behind common neuroscientific claims. Note the role of human and animal research in the generation of knowledge related to each topic.	What are the limitations in our knowledge and areas for future research? Identify pseudoscience and pop-neuroscience claims around health and disease, and debunk common myths about the brain and behavior.
Genetics and evolutionary influences	How do brain sizes and shapes differ across primates? What explains the similarities and differences? What factors could have contributed to the large number of neurons that make up the human brain? Discuss how comparative neuroanatomy can be used to elucidate basic principles in natural selection and evolution of the human brain.	How might these behaviors have contributed to the survival of our hunter-gatherer ancestors? Do these behaviors continue to serve the same evolutionary benefit today? Provide examples of simple genetic inheritance, such as single nucleotide polymorphisms, and more complex patterns of inheritance, including epigenetics, on these functions.	How do genes and experience interact to influence the presentation of neurological diseases and psychological disorders? Describe the potential for experiences such as stress to impact our phenotype through epigenetic mechanisms.
Neuroplasticity and adaptability	How does the brain change, grow, and adapt across the lifespan? Describe neurogenesis, synaptogenesis, and dendritic branching and under what circumstances each of these processes occur. What are the functional impacts of changes to brain architecture?	How does learning, memory, and our environment play a role in these behaviors? Processes of associative and social learning can be modeled for behaviors in each chapter. More complex memory functions can then be incorporated in the persistence of these behaviors.	How do rehabilitative treatment options for neurological disorders work? Describe pharmacological and psychological treatment options for psychological disorders. Identify environmental and social influences that impact the development of substance use disorder and psychological disorders.

Table 3 Recommended biopsychology content for Core Concept 1

	Description	Recommended content
Cells of the nervous system	What is our brain made of? How do these fundamental elements work together? Note the number of neurons the human brain has and highlight the underlying biological principles that govern the workings of the structures that allow neurons to function. *Key theme: Genetics and evolutionary influences*	Functions of internal neuron structures: • Nucleus • Organelles: Smooth and rough endoplasmic reticulum, mitochondria, lysosomes • Cytoplasm Functions of external neuron structures: • Cell membrane • Cell body or soma • Dendrites • Axon, myelin sheath including nodes of Ranvier • Terminal buttons and vesicles Glial cell functions: Astrocytes, oligodendrocytes, Schwann cells, microglia
Neural communication	How do neurons communicate with each other? How do different neurotransmitters influence the brain and behavior? Note the electrical and chemical properties of neural communication, including action potentials and the influence of neurotransmitter systems. *Key theme: Scientific literacy and research*	Resting membrane potential principles: • Uneven ion distribution: The role of diffusion and electrostatic pressure • Voltage-gated ion channels when neurons are at rest • Sodium-potassium pumps Action potentials: • Threshold of excitation • Postsynaptic potentials (excitatory and inhibitory) • Saltatory conduction Neurotransmitter release: • Steps of exocytosis • Synaptic gap • Postsynaptic receptor binding (ionotropic and metabotropic receptors) • Neurotransmitter deactivation via reuptake or enzymatic degradation Neurotransmitter systems including release, deactivation, and behavioral correlates: • Amino acids (GABA, glutamate) • Monoamines (dopamine, serotonin, norepinephrine, epinephrine) • Acetylcholine • Neuropeptides

(continued)

Table 3 (continued)

	Description	Recommended content
Brain structures and functions	Do our brain regions have specific functions? How do these regions communication with each other? Note basic elements of the nervous system, including early development, and highlight the various functions associated with specific brain regions. *Key themes: Scientific literacy and research; genetics and evolutionary influences*	Protective elements of the nervous system: • Meninges (dura mater, arachnoid membrane, pia mater) • Ventricular system and production of cerebrospinal fluid • Blood-brain-barrier Fundamental brain elements and terminology: • Difference between gray and white matter • Gyri, sulci, and fissures • Directional terms: Anterior (rostral), posterior (caudal), medial, lateral • Planes: Coronal, horizontal, sagittal. Early brain development and the formal divisions of the brain (e.g., hindbrain, midbrain, forebrain) Functions associated with specific brain regions: • Hindbrain regions: Medulla, pons, reticular formation, cerebellum • Midbrain regions: Inferior and superior colliculi, substantia nigra, ventral tegmental area. • Forebrain regions: Limbic system structures (e.g., amygdala, hippocampus, fornix), basal ganglia structures (globus pallidus, striatum, nucleus accumbens), thalamus, hypothalamus, cerebral cortices (frontal, parietal, occipital, temporal)
Spinal cord and peripheral nervous system	How does our nervous system control our reflexes? How do environmental factors influence our voluntary and involuntary behavior and bodily functions? This section provides an overview of the functions associated with spinal cord regions and branches of the peripheral nervous system. *Key theme: Genetics and evolutionary influences*	Spinal cord divisions: • Cervical • Thoracic • Lumbar • Sacral. Peripheral nervous system divisions and functions: • Somatic division; highlight efferent and afferent nerves • Autonomic division; note sympathetic and parasympathetic functions

Table 4 Recommended biopsychology content for Core Concept 2

	Description	Recommended content
Sensation and perception	How does our brain receive and represent stimuli from our sensory organs? How does the process of perception guide our interpretation of sensory stimuli? Note principles of sensory system organization: Hierarchy, functional segregation, and parallel processing. *Key theme: Scientific literacy*	For each of the five senses below, discuss the similarities and differences in the pathway from the sensory receptor to the cortex, and note additional processes for each: • Vision: Edge detection, color vision, cortical mechanisms, prosopagnosia • Audition: Auditory-visual interactions, damage to the auditory system • Somatosensation: Role of association cortex, agnosias, and pain perception • Gustation: Taste perception and taste sensitivity • Olfaction: Odor-evoked memories, taste-smell interactions Describe the role this system plays in our ability for selective attention
Movement	How does the brain guide the movement of our body? Note the role of reflexes and subconscious control of movement. Principles of sensorimotor function: Hierarchy, guiding by sensory input, learning changes locus of control. *Key theme: Neuroplasticity*	Top-down organization of pathway: • Sensorimotor association cortex • Secondary motor cortex • Primary motor cortex • Basal ganglia and cerebellum • Descending motor pathways Spinal circuits and reflexes; sensorimotor programs and learning
Motivated behaviors	How do motivated, or goal-directed, behaviors influence not only our survival but also our individual daily activities? Note the potential for neuroscience research to question common assumptions and conventional wisdom about these processes. *Key theme: Genetics and evolution*	Positive-incentive perspective (also Core Concept 3): • Contrast with homeostatic perspectives • Describe dopaminergic reward pathway • Berridge's incentive sensitization Ingestive behavior/eating: • Digestion, homeostasis, and metabolism • Contrast the set-point assumption from the positive incentive perspective • Integration: Gut-brain neuropeptides, hypothalamus, higher brain regions • Obesity and eating disorders Sleep and biological rhythms: • Stages of sleep and circadian rhythms • Sleep disorders • Impact of drugs on sleep Sexual development and reproductive behavior: • Neuroendocrine system • Hormones and development of the brain and body • Sexual behavior: Brain and hormonal mechanisms • Sexual orientation and gender identity

(continued)

Table 4 (continued)

	Description	Recommended content
Emotion and stress	How do emotions and the stress response cycle complement motivational processes? Note the potential to apply information in this section for understanding the self and improving well-being. *Key theme: Neuroplasticity*	Emotional responses and communication: • Autonomic nervous system • Brain mechanisms • Facial expression • Fear, defense, and aggression Contrast theories and historical perspectives with the modern biopsychological view of constructed emotions Stress responses: • Sympathetic-adrenal-medullary (SAM) system and hypothalamic-pituitary-adrenal (HPA) axis • Chronic stress, inequality, the hippocampus • Psychoneuroimmunology
Language	How does human communication rely on other processes in this concept area? Distinguish between human and animal communication and the evidence for lateralization of function. *Key theme: Scientific literacy*	Cerebral lateralization of function and the split brain Cortical localization of language: • Evolutionary perspectives on lateralization • Evidence for and against the Wernicke-Geschwind model of language Cognitive neuroscience of language and functional imaging Disorders of reading and writing: Dyslexia

nervous system function. These applications include real-world phenomena that psychologists address in research and practice, including substance abuse, neurological disorders (e.g., dementia, head trauma, brain tumors, stroke), and psychological disorders like depression, anxiety, and schizophrenia. It is recommended that instructors select a couple of the recommended topics from Core Concept 3 (see Table 5) that best align with their course learning outcomes.

Teaching, Learning, and Assessment in Neuroscience and Psychology Courses: Approaches and Strategies

Similar to other science courses, traditional didactic approaches are commonly used to teach biopsychology content. Several scholars critique the effectiveness of these approaches and instead focus on accessibility of course content through active learning strategies (see Smith, Howard, & D'Alessandro, 2020; Willard & Brasier, 2014). The next section discusses the benefits of integrating active and self-regulated learning strategies. Here, example lessons that align with one of the three core concepts and themes plus additional resources and tools adaptable to face-to-face, hybrid, or online instruction are described.

Table 5 Recommended biopsychology content for Core Concept 3

	Description	Recommended content
Substance abuse and reward	How do psychoactive drugs impact our brain and behavior? Distinguish mechanisms of action and associated risks of commonly used drugs. Note the evidence for various theories of addiction in explaining drug abuse, relapse, and recovery. *Key theme: Scientific literacy*	Basic principles of drug action: • Pharmacokinetics • Pharmacodynamics • Behavioral/learning processes Commonly used drugs and their effects: • Distinguish legal and illicit substances • Note mechanism of action and associated risks Theories of addiction: • Physical dependence theories • Positive-incentive perspective (also Core Concept 2) • Reward pathways • How does each theory account for addiction, relapse, and recovery? How do they inform treatment?
Neurological disorders	What are the range of events that cause brain damage and disease? Distinguish acute causes of brain damage and their lasting effects, plus types of neurological disease. Are these preventable and/or treatable? Describe the potential and limitations of brain repair and reorganization. *Key theme: Neuroplasticity*	Causes of brain damage: • Head injury: Concussion, contusion, and chronic traumatic encephalopathy (CTE) • Brain tumors • Cerebrovascular disease • Infections and neurotoxins Neurological disease: • Epilepsy • Neurodegenerative diseases • Types of dementia and etiology • Types of amnesia and etiology Response to brain damage: • Degeneration, reorganization, recovery • Neurotrophic factors and neuroplasticity
Psychological disorders	How do we currently describe psychological disorders, and what perspectives are used for the categorization of these disorders? What does neuroscience research tell us about the etiology and genetic basis of these disorders? Describe the process of clinical trials research and the associated controversies. *Key theme: Genetics and evolution*	Contrast approaches: • Historical perspectives through the *Diagnostic and Statistical Manual of Mental Disorders* (DSM–5) • Biopsychological explanations Describe categories of psychological disorders, including the symptoms, etiology of the disorder (known genetic contributions), treatment, and prognosis • Schizophrenia • Mood disorders • Anxiety disorders Clinical trials • How are new drugs developed? Note the stages in clinical trials research • Discuss controversies in clinical trials, e.g., representing subgroups, financial conflicts of interest, targets for pharmacotherapy

Lesson: Neuroanatomy Exploration through the Whole Brain Atlas

Aligns with:

- Core Concept 1: Foundational Knowledge of the Nervous System
- Theme: Scientific Literacy

The Whole Brain Atlas is a free repository of neuroimages of individuals with and without underlying conditions, including cerebrovascular diseases, tumors, and neurodegenerative diseases. This lesson, which typically follows lectures on neuroanatomy and neuroimaging techniques, asks students to use magnetic resonance images (MRIs) to explore several brain regions in a healthy individual as well as brain changes in an individual with Alzheimer's disease. Learning outcomes include reviewing anatomical planes (e.g., horizontal, coronal, sagittal), identifying brain regions across the different planes, exploring brain differences in someone with Alzheimer's disease, and contrasting noticeable brain changes between individuals with and without Alzheimer's disease.

1. Have students access the Whole Brain Atlas homepage (http://www.med.harvard.edu/AANLIB/home.html) and select the second link, *NEW: Normal Anatomy in 3-D with MRI/PET (JavaScript)*.
2. Allow students to familiarize themselves with the interface (e.g., functions of the top panel, up and down arrows, "2x" option).
   a. Instructors may provide a walkthrough of these functions or implement screenshots into written instructions.
3. Once students are familiar with the interface, have them select common brain structures across all anatomical planes (e.g., transaxial, sagittal, coronal). Common brain regions include the thalamus, hypothalamus, structures of the limbic system, and structures of the basal ganglia.
   a. First and second dropdown menus should be set to "Brain-hemispheric" and "MR-T1," respectively.
4. Students may switch the first dropdown menu to "Brain-axial" to explore other brain regions, such as the hypothalamus, thalamus, pons, mammillary bodies, and inferior colliculus, or to "CSF/Vascular" to explore the ventricular system.
5. Finally, students can explore the case study titled *Alzheimer's Disease with a tour* to compare and contrast brain changes as a result of a neurological condition.

Additional Lesson Planning Resources for Core Concept 1

The following resources can be modified and adapted for face-to-face and online instruction, as well as lecture and lab-based courses.

- *Models of the Nervous System.* A common challenge for biopsychology students is being unable to visualize the microscopic elements of the nervous system, particularly neurons. Similarly, learning neuroanatomy without access to an actual brain can be challenging. Typically, introductory biopsychology instructors do not have access to microscopy equipment or dissection supplies to help students grasp these elements. Luckily, neurons can be modeled with simple and inexpensive supplies (e.g., Play-Doh, pipe cleaners, beads) and with creative 3D brain model alternatives. See modeling resources below:
  - The University of Washington's Neuroscience for Kids website (https://faculty.washington.edu/chudler/chmodel.html) provides several neuron model examples made from Play-Doh or clay, beads, and pipe cleaners. **Tip**: Advanced neuron modeling activities can ask students to build a network of neurons, instead of one neuron, and to describe how this network communicates, which can incorporate elements of chemical communication and post-synaptic cell activation.
  - The brain hemisphere hats by Ellen McHenry (http://ellenjmchenry.com/brain-hemisphere-hat/) can be used to understand cortical anatomy and associated functions. Students can also keep their brain hemisphere model and reference it for future content.
  - Latimer, Bergin, Guntu, Schulz, and Nair (2018) describe open-source software for teaching neuroscience courses.
  - Schettino (2014) outlines the use of NeuroLab graphical simulations.
- *Action Potential Simulations*. The conduction of action potentials is by far one of the most challenging topics in biopsychology. For many students, this is their first exposure to molecular biology principles. Understanding action potentials is also difficult without additional, hands-on exploration. Fortunately, there are several easy-to-use action potential simulations.
  - The University of Colorado Boulder's PhET website (https://phet.colorado.edu/en/simulation/neuron) provides an easy-to-use, guided inquiry action potential simulation. Students can visualize the resting potential, the membrane permeability, and the refractory period.
  - A more advanced virtual stimulation using MetaNeuron (http://www.metaneuron.org) has students explore various aspects of action potentials such as resting potentials, refractory periods, and all-or-none responses. See Newman and Newman (2013) for additional information.
  - BrainU provides a narrated action potential animation (http://brainu.org/movies; select "Action Potential") that highlights ion concentration changes and the roles of voltage-gated ion channels and the sodium-potassium pumps.
- *Understanding Neurotransmitters*. Cammack (2018) provides an interactive, "Mystery Neurotransmitter" activity where students determine the deactivation mechanisms for two mystery neurotransmitters and how drugs influence the chemical properties of neural communication.
- *Comparative Neuroanatomy*. Providing students with comparative neuroanatomy tools can allow for a more thorough understanding of evolutionary brain

principles, an ability to observe structural brain differences and similarities across species, linking brain size and regional sophistication with abilities, and an understanding of experimental neuroanatomy methods. Grisham et al. (2018) use a comparative neuroanatomy approach to teach students quantitative skills. Resources can be found on the University of California Los Angeles Comparative Neuroanatomy webpage (https://mdcune.psych.ucla.edu/modules/cna).

Students can contrast mouse, primate, and human brain slices with the following atlases:

- Mouse brain atlas (http://developingmouse.brain-map.org/).
- Primate brain atlas (https://www.blueprintnhpatlas.org/).
- Human brain atlas (http://human.brain-map.org/).

Lesson: Are You a Supertaster?

Aligns with:

- Core Concept 2: Applications of Foundational Knowledge.
- Themes: Scientific Literacy, Genetics, and Evolutionary Influences.

Learning outcomes for this activity include review of sensory pathways for gustation and olfaction, hypothesis generation around taste preferences, and description of individual variability of gustatory experiences. In advance of the lesson, order taste test/n-propylthiouracil (PROP) strips from online retailer.

1. Have students reflect on their "palate" and taste preferences, including the foods they like, dislike but tolerate, and simply cannot eat. Have them compare with a classmate or a family member or roommate in the case of online/remote learning.
2. Allow students to explore what we know about taster status. To address the theme of scientific literacy, contrast coverage and style of writing in a popular source vs. a scientific article.
   a. Popular source options:
      i. Fadiman, A. (2017, September 30). How science saved me from pretending to love wine. The New Yorker. https://www.newyorker.com/tech/annals-of-technology/how-science-saved-me-from-pretending-to-love-wine
      ii. Rupp, R. (2014, September 30). Are you a supertaster? National Geographic. https://www.nationalgeographic.com/culture/article/are-you-a-supertaster
   b. Scholarly source options:
      i. Bartoshuk et al. (1994). PTC/PROP tasting: Anatomy, psychophysics, and sex effects. *Physiology & Behavior, 56*(6), 1165–1171.
      ii. Hayes et al. (2008). Supertasting and PROP bitterness depends on more than the TAS2R38 gene. *Chemical Senses, 33*(3), 255–265.

3. Provide a student collaboration opportunity by forming predictions and testing taster status.
   a. In groups or pairs, have students compose a set of questions to make a prediction of taster status for each student, and then administer those questions.
   b. Have students complete PROP test for taste status in class. The PROP substance is very safe, but is not advised for students who may be pregnant.
   c. Visualize distribution of class responses to both the survey administered and the PROP taste tests. Discuss reasons for any discrepancy (e.g., cultural determinants of food preferences, social desirability).

Lesson: College Success and Sleep

Aligns with:

- Core Concept 2: Applications of Foundational Knowledge.
- Themes: Genetics and Evolutionary Influences, Neuroplasticity, and Adaptability.

This activity is best completed in phases as the course moves through sleep content. Learning outcomes include understanding the impact of sleep deprivation on memory, behavior, and academic performance, applying content knowledge to own sleep hygiene, and exploring measures of sleep quality. Access a sleep quality questionnaire, such as the Pittsburgh Sleep Quality Index (PSQI; Buysse, Reynolds III, Monk, Berman, & Kupfer, 1989), in advance of the activity.

1. During the first lesson on sleep, have students self-report hours slept each night for the past week and then complete a sleep quality questionnaire.
2. After a brief overview of biological rhythms and sleep, have students read literature on the impact of sleep deprivation on learning and memory. Example: Curicio et al. (2006). Sleep loss, learning capacity and academic performance. *Sleep Medicine Reviews, 10*(5), 323–337.
   a. Students may also explore the impact of sleep deprivation on prejudice and stereotyping as demonstrated by Ghumman and Barnes (2013).
3. Provide students with Scullin's (2019) Sleep Tips. Once students have reviewed the tips, have them to address the following prompts:
   a. What sleep tips do you currently do or have done in the past? Were these tips helpful?
   b. Next, consider tips that you can try that you haven't already and try to implement these tips during the next week. (Stick to one or two, as implementing all of these tips can be hard!)
4. Reassess self-reported sleep, PSQI, and inventory of tips in 3 weeks or at the end of the term. This can be done as an informal or formal (i.e., graded) assessment and as an individual reflection or class discussion.

Additional Lesson Planning Resources for Core Concept 2

- *Evaluating Neuroscience Claims.* Provide students with examples of valid *and* false claims about the brain (e.g., lateralization, targeted enrichment, the Mozart effect, gender differences). Use lesson to explain the allure of simple explanations for complex phenomena. Resource: Weisberg et al. (2008).
- *Collaborative Journal Article Review.* This activity follows the jigsaw method – each student in a small group (4–6) is assigned a different scholarly article on a topic central to the course (e.g., language, sleep, biological rhythms). Outside of class, students read their assigned article, write a summary, and prepare a brief (5–10-minute) presentation to describe their article to peers. On the due date, students join their group and hear the short presentation on the 4–6 different articles.
  - Resource: Chaffee, L. (2015). Collaborative journal article review. In M. Birkett (Ed.). *Teaching Neuroscience: Practical activities for an engaged classroom.* http://teachpsych.org/ebooks/teachingneuroscience
- *Health and Stress.* Students explore the impact of social factors on the development and reactivity of the stress response systems. Discussion topics include epigenetics, brain development, emotional responses, psychoneuroimmunology, and psychological disorders.
  - Resources on the impact of adverse childhood experiences (ACEs):
    - Burke Harris, N. (2014, September). *How childhood trauma affects health across a lifespan* [Video]. TED Conferences. https://www.ted.com/talks/nadine_burke_harris_how_childhood_trauma_affects_health_across_a_lifetime?language=en
    - Starecheski, L. (2015, March 2). Take the ACE quiz – and learn what it does and doesn't mean. NPR. https://www.npr.org/sections/health-shots/2015/03/02/387007941/take-the-ace-quiz-and-learn-what-it-does-and-doesnt-mean
  - Sources on the impact of discrimination on physiological stress responses:
    - Busse et al. (2017). Social context matters: Ethnicity, discrimination and stress reactivity. *Psychoneuroendocrinology, 83*, 187–193.
    - Busse et al. (2017). Discrimination and the HPA axis: current evidence and future directions. *Journal of Behavioral Medicine, 40*(4), 539–552.
    - Kaholokula, et al. (2012). Association between perceived racism and physiological stress indices in Native Hawaiians. *Journal of Behavioral Medicine, 35*(1), 27–37.

Lesson: Understanding Epigenetics and Schizophrenia

Aligns with:

- Core Concept 3: Clinical/Social Impact.
- Theme: Genetics and Evolutionary Influences.

This lesson uses the case study titled *Identical Twins, Identical Fates?* from the National Center for Case Study Teaching in Science (https://sciencecases.lib.buffalo. edu/). The case study illustrates the influence of epigenetics on schizophrenia development in identical twins. The case can be modified to better fit the outcomes associated with the lesson. For instance, students in an introductory biopsychology course might only be assigned Parts 1–4, while students in an upper division biopsychology course could more easily navigate through Part 5. Students should work in small groups to address the discussion questions for each part; consider only providing one part at a time.

Additional Lesson Planning Resources for Core Concept 3

- *Case Studies.* Case studies are effective teaching tools, lending themselves to in-depth understanding of content. Meil (2007) provides three distinct recommendations of how students can use case studies in neuroscience courses and a list of case studies for a variety of disorders. The following are additional case study resources:
- National Center for Case Study Teaching in Science (https://sciencecases.lib. buffalo.edu/) is a repository of cases and lesson plans for multiple psychological and neurological conditions. Example case studies:
  - *Skinny Genes? An Interdisciplinary Look at a Complex Behavioral Disorder.*
  - *Are you Blue? What can you do? A Case Study on Treatment Options for Depression.*
  - *Anxiety doesn't Work: Treatment options for SAD.*
- The Journal of Undergraduate Neuroscience Education (JUNE) often contains a case study section in published issues. The case studies provide descriptions, learning outcomes, assessment techniques, and student data. Example: https:// www.funjournal.org/2019-volume-18-issue-2/
- Virtual case studies on the Whole Brain Atlas (https://www.med.harvard.edu/ AANLIB/home.html). The case studies include various neurodegenerative disorders like Alzheimer's disease and multiple sclerosis, including corresponding brain images and changes across disease progression.
- *Research History and Harm.* Have students explore historical examples of biomedical and behavioral research harm, perpetuation of unsupported "research" claims, and connections to current research and clinical practices in neuroscience, psychology, and medicine, as well as conversations around the public's trustworthiness in medicine and science.
  - Eugenics Crusade Documentary: https://www.pbs.org/wgbh/americanex perience/films/eugenics-crusade/#part01
  - Garrison, N. A. (2013). Genomic justice for Native Americans: Impact of the Havasupai case on genetic research. *Science, Technology, & Human Values, 38* (2), 201–223.
  - Skibba, R. (2019, May 20). The disturbing resilience of scientific racism. Smithsonian Magazine. https://www.smithsonianmag.com/science-nature/ disturbing-resilience-scientific-racism-180972243/

- Roberts, D. (2015, November). *The problem with race-based medicine* [Video]. TED Conferences. https://www.ted.com/talks/dorothy_roberts_the_problem_with_race_based_medicine/up-next?language=en
- *Exploring Chronic Traumatic Encephalopathy (CTE)*. Many students are familiar with chronic traumatic encephalopathy (CTE) from its disproportionate impact on contact sport players (e.g., boxers and football players). Students can further explore CTE neuropathology, its application to contract sport policy, and overall social implications.
  - Overview of CTE-related brain changes from the Franklin Institute: https://www.fi.edu/your-brain/video/head-games
  - Video summary of Mez et al. (2017) findings: https://edhub.ama-assn.org/jn-learning/video-player/14591368
  - Barlow, R. (2017, November 9). Aaron Hernandez' CTE worst seen by BU experts in a young person. The Brink. http://www.bu.edu/articles/2017/aaron-hernandez-cte-worst-seen-in-young-person/

Opportunities, Challenges, and Lessons Learned

A significant reward in teaching neuroscience content within psychology courses is celebrating student's growing confidence throughout the quarter. This reward provides insight into the challenge of students' anxiety around the difficulty of course content and their initial intimidation of neuroscience.

In addition to anecdotal experiences of student anxiety around learning neuroscience, the phenomenon of "neurophobia" was first used to describe medical students' anxiety in Jozefowicz's, 1994 letter, attributing neurophobia to a lack of integration between coursework in basic sciences and clinical experiences. Subsequent research confirms that medical students and residents suffer a disconnect between basic neuroscience education and clinical expertise, undermining confidence in treating patients with neurological disease (Zinchuk, Flanagan, Tubridy, Miller, & McCullough, 2010). In the context of undergraduate biopsychology courses, neuroscience anxiety is a distinct form of apprehension experienced by students (Birkett & Shelton, 2011), which can prevent students from enrolling in biopsychology or neuroscience courses and hinder degree progress. Biopsychology course performance is predicted by a *positive attitude about science* and *science efficacy* (Moore & Foy, 1997 as cited by Sgoutas-Emch, Nagel, & Flynn, 2007).

How do instructors overcome the challenges of student anxiety, boost students' attitudes and self-efficacy for course material, and help students succeed in neuroscience coursework? Evidence-based teaching strategies, such as active learning and self-regulated learning, are recommended.

Active Learning An instructional approach to engage students in material through classroom involvement such as discussion, problem-solving exercises, collaboration with peers, and invited reflection to learn from mistakes. Best practices require advanced preparation by the instructor, authentic tasks for the student, and timely feedback (Wieman, 2014). The evidence for active learning is robust; a meta-analysis showed that active learning improved performance and decreased student failure rates over traditional lecture courses (Freeman et al., 2014). Active learning reduces the achievement gap between traditional college students and students from systemically non-dominant groups (Haak, HilleRisLambers, Pitre, & Freeman, 2011). The benefits of active learning span the STEM disciplines, large and small courses, and introductory to advanced courses (Wieman, 2014). Active learning practices increase self-efficacy and classroom belongingness, particularly for students from systemically non-dominant groups (Ballen et al., 2017).

Self-Regulated Learning One type of active learning, where students monitor and adjust their progress through opportunities for practice and timely feedback. The ability to control our learning processes and environment includes cognitive and motivational processes. The cognitive skills required to encode and recall information are controlled and monitored through metacognition. Self-regulatory capacity includes the motivation to use and develop cognitive and metacognitive abilities (Schraw, Crippen, & Hartley, 2006). Metacognitive activity is related to student motivation and self-efficacy, so efforts to boost self-regulated learning may improve motivation (Bell & Kozlowski, 2008). Self-regulated learning is tied to beliefs about the value of the task (Pintrich, 1999); thus, we recommend instructors communicate the value of the process and material to students. One way to accomplish this is to incorporate the Transparency in Learning and Teaching (TILT) framework (Winkelmes et al., 2016) to explicitly outline the purpose of assignments, knowledge gained, skills practiced, and criteria for success (https://tilthighered.com/tiltexamplesandresources).

The Association of American Colleges and Universities (AAC&U; Kuh, 2008) recognizes a variety of **high-impact practices**, including learning communities, collaborative assignments, undergraduate research, diversity/global learning, and community-based learning, described below.

In addition to the concept-specific resources below, these references detail high-impact practices aimed at enhancing accessibility and student learning in biopsychology courses.

- Levit Binnun and Tarrasch (2014) provide evidence for the utility of contemplative exercises within biopsychology.
- McFarlane and Richeimer (2015) describe avenues for using perspectives from humanities for teaching neuroscience to nonmajors.
- Ramirez (2020) describes current challenges of neuroscience education, emphasizing lived experiences of college students and the influence of the COVID-19 pandemic on student success.
- Stevenson et al. (2016) provide practical tools for learning outcome assessment.

Online Learning While biopsychology courses are typically offered face-to-face, technologies for online teaching and learning can support remote instruction of courses in this area. Online learning is helpful for college students for whom scheduling conflicts or other obligations make it difficult to attend a scheduled, on-campus course. We have seen an increase of online course offerings in psychology and the majority of other disciplines, likely in response to the changing needs of students (Hailstorks et al., 2019). At present, the transition to remote instruction is advantageous during public health efforts to combat a global pandemic. While some remain critical of the efficacy and equivalency of online classes, a robust meta-analysis sponsored by the US Department of Education (Means, Toyama, Murphy, Baki, & Jones, 2009) found *better* learning outcomes for online learning as compared to purely face-to-face instruction. Evidence-based techniques for high-quality instruction are essential in all learning environments, and the literature emphasizes interaction (student-faculty and student-peer), incorporating self-regulated learning practices to enhance motivation, and collaborative learning in the online classroom (Abrami, Bernard, Bures, Borokhovski, & Tamim, 2011). In fact, student motivation is predictive of success in online psychology courses (Waschull, 2005). Some courses, such as those with a hands-on or lab component, certainly pose challenges to online teaching. Virtual labs are available through a variety of textbook publishers, research institutes such as the Howard Hughes Medical Institute (HHMI), and Faculty for Undergraduate Neuroscience (FUN). The resources and lesson plans shared in this chapter are intentionally low-cost and accessible for instructors, whether in a brick-and-mortar or virtual classroom.

In sum, the challenge of neuroscience courses can sometimes undermine student confidence and thus success in the course. Evidence-based strategies for active learning and self-regulated learning improve student confidence, motivation, and self-efficacy and thus improve student performance in the course. Active and self-regulated learning are essential for bridging achievement gaps between students in neuroscience courses.

Teaching, Learning, and Assessment Resources

Tip 1: Be Clear, Concise, and Transparent

Given the potential challenges in teaching biopsychology courses outlined in this chapter, transparency and clarity are essential for the success of these courses, for students and faculty alike. Students may be hesitant or even fearful of these classes, given the perceived difficulty and technicality as compared to other psychology courses. A key recommendation is clear and transparent articulation of expectations, learning objectives, and purpose for course assessments. Note that for many biopsychology students, this course is the first time they are being exposed to natural science content. Instructors are encouraged to integrate scaffolding practices that gradually fade immediate support and increase student ownership/responsibility to assist students in this transition (see Van de Pol, Volman, & Beishuizen, 2010).

Integration of the neuroscientific approach complements and extends psychology curricula. The themes align with standard programmatic and departmental learning objectives within psychology. The inherent interdisciplinary nature of neuroscience in psychology provides an opportunity for collaboration within and between academic disciplines, providing students a well-rounded perspective on the state of contemporary neuroscience.

Tip 2: Center Evidence-Based Strategies to Promote Student Success

Active learning is essential and can take various forms, from a dissection lab to computer simulation, case studies, and debates. The resources shared and referenced are accessible online and are useful in various teaching modalities. Active learning approaches can also help students see the "bigger picture." Neuroscience, as much as it is molecular, is more of a framework that can be applied to better understand complex behavioral phenomena and assess other influential factors, like the environmental or social settings.

Courses that integrate neuroscience in the psychology curriculum have a reputation for being challenging. However, active learning strategies and self-regulated learning boost student learning. Reflection and metacognitive monitoring are two techniques that are relatively easy to integrate and have a significant potential to boost student motivation and performance.

Tip 3: Use High-Impact Practices

The American Association of Colleges and Universities promotes a wide variety of educational practices, many of which are opportunities that extend beyond the classroom. Given the considerable commitment of resources and time, these opportunities are ideally integrated at a programmatic level to properly support faculty. The following are examples of two high-impact practices that could be implemented in biopsychology courses. See the Franklin Institute Neuroscience and Society website: https://www.fi.edu/your-brain/neuroscience-and-society-curriculum.

Course-based undergraduate research experiences (CUREs) provide students research opportunities in the classroom (see Sathy, Mahfuz, Strauss, & Hutson, 2020), centering use of the scientific method, student discovery, collaboration and agency, and science communication and impact. Traditional undergraduate research opportunities require students to seek limited faculty-led projects, commit to additional time on campus, or credit hours for independent study. These barriers can limit who participates in undergraduate research opportunities. Since CUREs occur in the classroom, their reach is broader and can provide similar benefits of undergraduate research participation. CUREs are especially beneficial for students of underrepresented groups, which could, in the long run, result in greater representation and diversity in STEM fields (Bangera & Brownell, 2014). See Sathy et al. (2020) for more on CUREs in psychology courses.

Project-based learning (PBL) is an inquiry-based instructional approach where students work toward an end product (e.g., a presentation, poster, portfolio, informational pamphlet), focusing on the knowledge and skills applied throughout the process (Aditomo, Goodyear, Bliuc, & Ellis, 2013). PBL requires faculty to explicitly assess and align the project deliverables with content- and skill-focused outcomes.

CUREs and PBL are student-centered, active learning approaches that provide opportunities to engage in self-regulated learning by setting clear goals, being reflective at every step of the way, and maintaining motivation to meet the student-set goals (English & Kitsantas, 2013). These high-impact practices help students gain and foster marketable knowledge, skills, and characteristics needed to succeed in the workforce (Appleby, 2018; Bell, 2010).

Tip 4: Incorporate Professional Development Opportunities

The majority of baccalaureate psychology and biopsychology students do not attend graduate school. Thus, it is imperative to provide opportunities to gain marketable skills to benefit them post-graduation. The knowledge, skills, and characteristics expected by employers in the top occupations include critical thinking, time management, attention to detail, cooperation with coworkers, and communication (Appleby, 2018). Faculty can use alternative assessment techniques that center science communication, such as class presentations, college- or community-based presentations through research symposium participation, building publicly available websites, and poster presentations for classroom "conferences" (Flanagan-Cato, 2019; Schwartz, Obeid, & Powers, 2018; Schwartz, Obeid, Shane-Simpson, Powers, & Thompson, 2020). The majority of students in biopsychology courses will not pursue this field of study as a career; thus, teaching transferable, marketable skills can ensure that students excel in other areas of their academic or professional endeavors.

Annotated List of Recommended Further Readings

Readings for Additional Classroom Activities and Curriculum Development

- Franklin Institute. (n.d.). *Neuroscience & society curriculum*. https://www.fi.edu/your-brain/neuroscience-and-society-curriculum
- Simon-Dack, S. L. (2011). *Interactive Teaching Activities for Introductory Biopsychology*. Society for the Teaching of Psychology. http://teachpsych.org/resources/Documents/otrp/resources/simon-dack12.pdf
- Oswald. B. B. (2019). *Authentic assessments for biopsychology: Encouraging learning and retention by applying biopsychological knowledge in real-world contexts*. Society for the Teaching of Psychology. http://teachpsych.org/resources/Documents/otrp/resources/oswald19.pdf
- Birkett, M. (2015). *Teaching Neuroscience: Practical activities for an engaged classroom*. Society for the Teaching of Psychology: http://teachpsych.org/ebooks/teachingneuroscience

Pedagogy-Related Readings

- Schwartz, S. J., Lilienfeld, S. O., Meca, A., & Sauvigné, K. C. (2016). The role of neuroscience within psychology: A call for inclusiveness over exclusiveness. *American Psychologist*, *71*(1), 52–70.

  This article offers an analysis of the growing prominence of neuroscience in psychology programs.
- McKeachie, W. & Svinicki, M. (2013). *McKeachie's Teaching Tips*. Cengage Learning.

  This book provides practical tools plus evidence-based strategies for college and university teaching.
- Sensoy, O. & DiAngelo, R. (2017). *Is everyone really equal? An introduction to key concepts in social justice education*. Teachers College Press.

  This book provides an introduction to critical social justice literacy, including key concepts on critical thinking, group identity and dynamics, prejudice and discrimination, plus examples and vignettes to illustrate these terms.

Content-Focused Readings

The following recommendations focus on a variety of core concepts outlined in this chapter. These readings can be used as supplemental to textbook readings.

- Sapolsky, R. M. (2017). *Behave: The biology of humans at our best and worst*. Penguin.
- Grisel, J. (2020). *Never enough: The neuroscience and experience of addiction*. Anchor Books.
- Kandel, E. R. (2018). *The disordered mind: What unusual brains tell us about ourselves*. Farrar, Straus and Giroux.
- Barrett, L. F. (2017). *How emotions are made: The secret life of the brain*. Houghton Mifflin.
- Roach, M. (2013). *Gulp: adventures on the alimentary canal*. W.W. Norton & Company.
- Roach, M. (2009). *Bonk: The curious coupling of science and sex*. W.W. Norton & Company.
- Kuhn, C., Swartzwelder, S., & Wilson, W. (2019). *Buzzed: The straight facts about the most used and abused drugs from alcohol to ecstasy*. W.W. Norton & Company.

Cross-References

▶ Inquiry-Based Learning in Psychology
▶ Problem-Based Learning and Case-Based Learning
▶ Sensation and Perception

► Teaching Introductory Psychology
► Teaching Physiological Psychology
► Teaching Psychopharmacology for Undergraduates

References

Abrami, P. C., Bernard, R. M., Bures, E. M., Borokhovski, E., & Tamim, R. M. (2011). Interaction in distance education and online learning: Using evidence and theory to improve practice. *Journal of Computing in Higher Education, 23*, 82–103.

Adedokun, O. A., Bessenbacher, A. B., Parker, L. C., Kirkham, L. L., & Burgess, W. D. (2013). Research skills and STEM undergraduate research students' aspirations for research careers: Mediating effects of research self-efficacy. *Journal of Research in Science Teaching, 50*(8), 940–951.

Aditomo, A., Goodyear, P., Bliuc, A. M., & Ellis, R. A. (2013). Inquiry-based learning in higher education: Principal forms, educational objectives, and disciplinary variations. *Studies in Higher Education, 38*(9), 1239–1258.

Akil, H., Balice-Gordon, R., Cardozo, D. L., Koroshetz, W., Norris, S. M. P., Sherer, T., . . . Thiels, E. (2016). Neuroscience training for the 21st century. *Neuron, 90*(5), 917–926.

American Psychological Association. (2018). Guidelines for the undergraduate psychology major, 2.0. https://www.apa.org/ed/precollege/about/undergraduate-major

Appleby, D. C. (2018). Preparing psychology majors to enter the workforce: Then, now, with whom, and how. *Teaching of Psychology, 45*(1), 14–23.

Ballen, C. J., et al. (2017). Enhancing diversity in undergraduate science: Self-efficacy drives performance gains with active learning. *CBE-Life Sciences Education, 16*(56), 1–6.

Bangera, G., & Brownell, S. E. (2014). Course-based undergraduate research experiences can make scientific research more inclusive. *CBE—Life Sciences Education, 13*(4), 602–606.

Bell, B. S., & Kozlowski, S. W. (2008). Active learning: Effects of core training design elements on self-regulatory processes, learning, and adaptability. *Journal of Applied Psychology, 93*(2), 296–316.

Bell, S. (2010). Project-based learning for the 21st century: Skills for the future. *The Clearing House, 83*(2), 39–43.

Betancur, L., Rottman, B. M., Votruba-Drzal, E., & Schunn, C. (2019). Analytical assessment of course sequencing: The case of methodological courses in psychology. *Journal of Educational Psychology, 111*(1), 91–103.

Birkett, M., & Shelton, K. (2011). Decreasing neuroscience anxiety in an introductory neuroscience course: An analysis using data from a modified science anxiety scale. *Journal of Undergraduate Neuroscience Education, 10*(1), A37–A43.

Bowers, J. S. (2016). The practical and principled problems with educational neuroscience. *Psychological Review, 123*(5), 600–612.

Brownell, S. E., Price, J. V., & Steinman, L. (2013). Science communication to the general public: Why we need to teach undergraduate and graduate students this skill as part of their formal scientific training. *Journal of Undergraduate Neuroscience Education, 12*(1), E6–E10.

Buysse, D. J., Reynolds, C. F., III, Monk, T. H., Berman, S. R., & Kupfer, D. J. (1989). The Pittsburgh sleep quality index: A new instrument for psychiatric practice and research. *Psychiatry Research, 28*(2), 193–213.

Cammack, K. M. (2018). Mystery neurotransmitters! An active learning activity on synaptic function for undergraduate students. *Journal of Undergraduate Neuroscience Education, 17*(1), A26–A33.

Carnevale, A. P., Strohl, J., & Melton, M. (2013). What's it worth?: The economic value of college majors. *Georgetown University Center on Education and the Workforce*. https://1gyhoq479ufd3yna29x7ubjn-wpengine.netdna-ssl.com/wp-content/uploads/2014/11/whatsitworth-complete.pdf

English, M. C., & Kitsantas, A. (2013). Supporting student self-regulated learning in problem-and project-based learning. *Interdisciplinary Journal of Problem-Based Learning, 7*(2), 128–150.

European Higher Education Area. (2005). The framework qualifications. http://www.ehea.info/page-qualification-frameworks

Flanagan-Cato, L. M. (2019). Everyday neuroscience: A community engagement course. *The Journal of Undergraduate Neuroscience Education, 18*(1), A44–A50.

Freeman, S., Eddy, S. L., McDonough, M., Smith, M. K., Okoroafor, N., Jordt, H., & Wenderoth, M. P. (2014). Active learning increases student performance in science, engineering, and mathematics. *PNAS, 111*(23), 8410–8415.

Ghumman, S., & Barnes, C. M. (2013). Sleep and prejudice: A resource recovery approach. *Journal of Applied Social Psychology, 43*, E166–E178.

Goswami, U. (2006). Neuroscience and education: From research to practice? *Nature Reviews Neuroscience, 7*(5), 406–413.

Grisham, W., Greta, S., Burre, A., Tomita, W., Rostamian, D., Schottler, N., & Krull, J. L. (2018). Using online images to teach quantitative skills via comparative neuroanatomy: Applying the directives of vision and change. *Journal of Undergraduate Neuroscience Education, 16*(3), A236–A243.

Gurung, R. A., Hackathorn, J., Enns, C., Frantz, S., Cacioppo, J. T., Loop, T., & Freeman, J. E. (2016). Strengthening introductory psychology: A new model for teaching the introductory course. *American Psychologist, 71*(2), 112–124.

Haak, D. C., HilleRisLambers, J., Pitre, E., & Freeman, S. (2011). Increased structure and active learning reduce the achievement gap in introductory biology. *Science, 332*, 1213–1216.

Hailstorks, R., Stamm, K. E., Norcross, J. C., Pfund, R. A., & Christidis, P. (2019). 2016 undergraduate study in psychology: Faculty characteristics and online teaching. *Scholarship of Teaching and Learning in Psychology, 5*(1), 52–60.

Homa, N., Hackathorn, J., Brown, C. M., Garczynski, A., Solomon, E. D., Tennial, R., ... Gurung, R. A. (2013). An analysis of learning objectives and content coverage in introductory psychology syllabi. *Teaching of Psychology, 40*(3), 169–174.

Hong, B. (2012, August). *The teaching of psychology and the new MCAT.* American Psychological Association. https://www.apa.org/ed/precollege/ptn/2012/08/mcat

Jozefowicz, R. F. (1994). Neurophobia: The fear of neurology in medical students. *Archives of Neurology, 51*(4), 328–329. https://doi.org/10.1001/archneur.1994.00540160018003.

Kerchner, M., Hardwick, J. C., & Thornton, J. E. (2012). Identifying and using 'core competencies' to help design and assess undergraduate neuroscience curricula. *Journal of Undergraduate Neuroscience Education, 11*(1), A27–A37.

Kuh, G. D. (2008). High-impact educational practices: What they are, who has access to them, and why they matter. *AAC&U Report*, Washington D. C. https://www.aacu.org/node/4084

Latimer, B., Bergin, D., Guntu, V., Schulz, D., & Nair, S. (2018). Open source software tools for teaching neuroscience. *Journal of Undergraduate Neuroscience Education, 16*(3), A197–A202.

Levit Binnun, N., & Tarrasch, R. (2014). Relation between contemplative exercises and an enriched psychology students' experience in a neuroscience course. *Frontiers in Psychology*, 5. https://doi.org/10.3389/fpsyg.2014.01296.

Lindell, A. K., & Kidd, E. (2011). Why right-brain teaching is half-witted: A critique of the misapplication of neuroscience to education. *Mind, Brain, and Education, 5*(3), 121–127.

Lloyd, S. A., Shanks, R. A., & Lopatto, D. (2019). Perceived student benefits of an undergraduate physiological psychology laboratory course. *Teaching of Psychology, 46*(3), 215–222.

McFarlane, H. G., & Richeimer, J. (2015). Using the humanities to teach neuroscience to non-majors. *Journal of Undergraduate Neuroscience Education, 13*(3), A225–A223.

Means, B., Toyama, Y., Murphy, R., Baki, M., & Jones, K. (2009). Evaluation of evidence-based practices in online learning: A meta-analysis and review of online learning studies. *U. S. Department of Education.* www.ed.gov/about/offices/list/opepd/ppss/reports.html.

Meil, W. M. (2007). The use of case studies in teaching undergraduate neuroscience. *Journal of Undergraduate Neuroscience Education, 5*(2), A53–A62.

Mez, J., Daneshvar, D. H., Kiernan, P. T., Abdolmohammadi, B., Alvarez, V. E., Huber, B. R., . . . Cormier, K. A. (2017). Clinicopathological evaluation of chronic traumatic encephalopathy in players of American football. *JAMA, 318*(4), 360–370. https://doi.org/10.1001/jama.2017.8334.

Moore, R. W., & Foy, R. L. H. (1997). The scientific attitude inventory: A revision (SAI II). *Journal of Research in Science Teaching, 34*(4), 327–336.

Newman, M. H., & Newman, E. A. (2013). MetaNeuron: A free neuron simulation program for teaching cellular neurophysiology. *Journal of Undergraduate Neuroscience Education, 12*(1), A11–A17.

Norcross, J. C., Hailstorks, R., Aiken, L. S., Pfund, R. A., Stamm, K. E., & Christidis, P. (2016). Undergraduate study in psychology: Curriculum and assessment. *American Psychologist, 71*(2), 89–101.

Palermo, S., & Morese, R. (2019). Introductory chapter: Neuroscience wants behavior. In S. Palermo (Ed.), *Behavioral Neuroscience*. https://www.intechopen.com/books/behavioral-neuroscience

Parada, J. C., & Birkett, M. A. (2020). In defense of labs: Maximizing academic, cognitive, and interpersonal skills through the teaching of psychology labs. In T. Ober, E. Che, J. Brodsky, C. Raffaele, & P. J. Brooks (Eds.), *How we teach now (Vol 2): The GSTA guide to transformative teaching*. http://teachpsych.org/ebooks/howweteachnow-transformative.

Peterson, J. J., & Sesma, A., Jr. (2017). Introductory psychology: What's lab got to do with it? *Teaching of Psychology, 44*(4), 313–323.

Pintrich, P. R. (1999). The role of motivation in promoting and sustaining self-regulated learning. *International Journal of Educational Research, 31*, 459–470.

Ramirez, J. J. (2020). Undergraduate neuroscience education: Meeting the challenges of the 21st century. *Neuroscience Letters, 739*. https://doi.org/10.1016/j.neulet.2020.135418.

Sathy, V., Mahfuz, N., Strauss, C., & Hutson, B. (2020). The CURE for broadening participation in undergraduate research. In T. Ober, E. Che, J. Brodsky, C. Raffaele, & P. J. Brooks (Eds.), *How we teach now (Vol 2): The GSTA guide to transformative teaching*. http://teachpsych.org/ebooks/howweteachnow-transformative.

Schettino, L. F. (2014). NeuroLab: A set of graphical computer simulations to support neuroscience instruction at the high school and undergraduate level. *Journal of Undergraduate Neuroscience Education, 12*(2), A123–A129.

Schraw, G., Crippen, K. J., & Hartley, K. (2006). Promoting self-regulation in science education: Metacognition as part of a broader perspective on learning. *Research in Science Education, 36*, 111–139.

Schwartz, A., Obeid, R., & Powers, K. (2018, May 15). *Teaching APA format in experimental psychology through poster design* [Blog post]. GSTA blog. https://teachpsych.org/page-1784686/6205676

Schwartz, A., Obeid, R., Shane-Simpson, C., Powers, K. L., & Thompson, L. (2020). Turning the undergraduate classroom into a research conference: Using poster presentations to target the APA guidelines 2.0. In T. Ober, E. Che, J. Brodsky, C. Raffaele, & P. J. Brooks (Eds.), *How we teach now (Vol 2): The GSTA guide to transformative teaching*. http://teachpsych.org/ebooks/howweteachnow-transformative.

Schwartz, S. J., Lilienfeld, S. O., Meca, A., & Sauvigné, K. C. (2016). The role of neuroscience within psychology: A call for inclusiveness over exclusiveness. *American Psychologist, 71*(1), 52–70.

Scullin, M. K. (2019). The eight-hour sleep challenge during finals exam week. *Teaching of Psychology, 46*(1), 55–63.

Sgoutas-Emch, S. A., Nagel, E., & Flynn, S. (2007). Correlates of performance in biological psychology: How can we help? *Journal of Instructional Psychology, 34*(1), 46–53.

Smith, P. L., Howard, J. R., & D'Alessandro, M. (2020). The use of magazine spreads as a tool in neuroscience pedagogy. *Psychology and Education, 57*(3), 191–197.

Stead, J., Wiseman, A., & Hellemans, K. (2019). Neuroscience and careers. In M. Norris (Ed.), *The Canadian handbook for careers in psychological science*. https://ecampusontario.pressbooks. pub/psychologycareers/.

Stevenson, J. L., Shah, S., & Bish, J. P. (2016). Use of structural assessment of knowledge for outcomes assessment in the neuroscience classroom. *Journal of Undergraduate Neuroscience Education, 15*(1), A38–A43.

Stoloff, M., McCarthy, M., Keller, L., Varfolomeeva, V., Lynch, J., Makara, K., ... Smiley, W. (2009). The undergraduate psychology major: An examination of structure and sequence. *Teaching of Psychology, 37*(1), 4–15.

Thieman, T. J., Clary, E. G., Olson, A. M., Dauner, R. C., & Ring, E. E. (2009). Introducing students to psychological research: General psychology as a laboratory course. *Teaching of Psychology, 36*(3), 160–168.

Van de Pol, J., Volman, M., & Beishuizen, J. (2010). Scaffolding in teacher–student interaction: A decade of research. *Educational Psychology Review, 22*(3), 271–296.

Waschull, S. B. (2005). Predicting success in online psychology courses: Self-discipline and motivation. *Teaching of Psychology, 32*(3), 190–192.

Weisberg, D. S., Keil, F. C., Goodstein, J., Rawson, E., & Gray, J. R. (2008). The seductive allure of neuroscience explanations. *Journal of Cognitive Neuroscience, 20*(3), 470–477.

Wieman, C. E. (2014). Large-scale comparison of science teaching methods sends clear message. *PNAS, 111*(23), 8319–8320.

Willard, A. M., & Brasier, D. J. (2014). Controversies in neuroscience: A literature-based course for first year undergraduates that improves scientific confidence while teaching concepts. *Journal of Undergraduate Neuroscience Education, 12*(2), A159–A166.

Winkelmes, M. A., Bernacki, M., Butler, J., Zochowski, M., Golanics, J., & Weavil, K. H. (2016). A teaching intervention that increases underserved college students' success. *Peer Review, 18*(1/2), 31–36.

Yeung, A. W. K., Goto, T. K., & Leung, W. K. (2017). The changing landscape of neuroscience research, 2006–2015: A bibliometric study. *Frontiers in Neuroscience, 11*. https://doi.org/10. 3389/fnins.2017.00120.

Zinchuk, A. V., Flanagan, E. P., Tubridy, N. J., Miller, W. A., & McCullough, L. D. (2010). Attitudes of US medical trainees toward neurology education: "Neurophobia" – a global issue. *BMC Medical Education, 10*, 49–56.

Teaching the Foundations of Psychological Science

17

Basic Research Methods and Statistics

Regan A. R. Gurung and Andrew Christopher

Contents

Abstract

In this chapter, we detail a number of considerations for teachers of research methods and statistics courses at the undergraduate level, particularly introductory courses on these topics. In particular, we provide a rationale for why students need to learn the information in these courses, address challenges we as teachers face in teaching this information, and provide suggestions for overcoming these challenges and turning them into opportunities for students to understand the importance of this material. We also provide ideas for organizing the material in each of these two courses, discuss the benefits and pitfalls of teaching this material in an integrated course sequence, and highlight resources to help teachers teach this difficult material.

R. A. R. Gurung (✉)
Psychological Science, Oregon State University, Corvallis, OR, USA
e-mail: Regan.Gurung@OregonState.edu

A. Christopher
Albion College, Albion, MI, USA
e-mail: achristopher@albion.edu

© Springer Nature Switzerland AG 2023
J. Zumbach et al. (eds.), *International Handbook of Psychology Learning and Teaching*,
Springer International Handbooks of Education,
https://doi.org/10.1007/978-3-030-28745-0_20

421

Keywords

Research methods · Statistics · Undergraduate teaching · Student professional development

Introduction

There has been a marked increase in global conversations about teaching psychology (Cranney & Dunn, 2011; Hanna, 2013). Finding optimal ways to teach students research methods and statistics in particular is a large part of the global conversation in higher education (Allen & Baughman, 2016; Roberts, 2016; Roberts & Allen, 2012; Sümer, 2016). In the United States, the American Psychological Association's (APA) Guidelines for the Undergraduate major (*Guidelines 2.0,* APA, 2013) and the National Standards for High School Psychology (APA, 2012) both stress the importance of research design and statistical knowledge and ability and provide useful language for shaping a focus on these two areas. The *Guidelines 2.0* lists "scientific inquiry and critical thinking," as one of the learning goals for an undergraduate psychology degree. Similarly, scientific inquiry is one of seven domains of the *Standards* for secondary education (APA, 2012). To accomplish this goal of fostering scientific inquiry and critical thinking ability requires, "the development of scientific reasoning and problem solving, including effective research methods," "applying research design principles to drawing conclusions about psychological phenomena," and "designing and executing research plans" (APA, 2013, p. 15).

Knowledge of basic research methods and statistical concepts are also foundational elements of the introductory psychology course (Gurung et al. 2016) and are featured explicitly in new student learning outcomes for the course developed for global implementation (APA, 2019). Consequently, research methods and statistics courses are the bedrock of education in psychological science (Dunn et al. 2010). Both courses hold a prominent position in the undergraduate psychology curriculum in the United States. Nearly every undergraduate psychology program offers introductory-level research methods and statistics courses (Norcross et al., 2016; Stoloff et al., 2010). Research Methods and Statistics, besides Introductory Psychology, are the most universally required courses of a psychology major in the United States (Friedrich, Childress, & Cheng, 2018) and are an important part of courses worldwide (Roberts, 2016).

In this chapter, we outline the rationale for teaching these courses, explore challenges teachers face when teaching this information to most undergraduates, and provide suggestions for turning pedagogical challenges into learning opportunities with undergraduate students. Furthermore, we provide resources for teaching these courses, suggestions on organizing course material, and a discussion of the trend to teach courses in an integrated sequence. Throughout, we offer key recommendations for teaching and learning the content and skills in both of these interrelated areas, ones that most undergraduate students are anxious about and dreading.

Rationale for Learning Research Methods and Statistics

One of the most common complaints we hear from our undergraduate psychology majors amounts to "Why do we have to take these boring research methods and statistics classes when there are so many more interesting psychology classes we could be taking?" Of course, as teachers of these subject matters, we often roll our eyes (at least figuratively) when we hear such reactions. Having gone on for advanced study in psychology, we fully understand the importance of these courses. In addition to being foundational for the science of psychology, stronger research training correlates with self-reported research self-efficacy, a greater willingness to engage in additional research, and better critical thinking and analytical skills (Burke & Prieto, 2019), attributes that graduate schools seek in new students. However, many of our students may not have the same professional aspirations or be financially able to attend graduate school. Thus, although the rationale for these courses may be clear to us as teachers, we need to convey that importance to our students on their terms. For many students, the rationale for taking any course may boil down to one question: how can taking a course help them get a job? Although we as teachers may cringe at hearing this question, the reality is that our students, particularly traditional-age undergraduates, are dealing with the "How can that help you get a job" question from others (e.g., parents). We need to help them answer it, remembering that we as their teachers already have jobs that we love.

What do faculty members see as the main reasons why students should take Research Methods and Statistics? Faculty in one survey saw the most important reason for the course as developing scientific thinking skills (79%), followed by increasing engagement in the research process (28%), and preparing for higher-level courses (22%) (Ciarocco, Strohmetz, & Lewandowski, 2017). Indeed, as mentioned previously, students themselves tend to see these courses as geared toward preparing them for graduate school, regardless of whether they intend to pursue advanced study. Although these courses are certainly relevant to our graduate-school-bound students, we argue that these courses offer wonderful opportunities to help all students develop skills and have experiences that employers (and graduate schools) value (see Gardner, 2007; Hart Research Associates, 2015). For instance, Hart Research Associates (2015) found that the six most important outcomes of an undergraduate education are: (1) the ability to effectively communicate orally; (2) the ability to work effectively with others in teams; (3) the ability to effectively communicate in writing; (4) ethical judgment and decision-making; (5) critical thinking and analytical reasoning skills; and (6) the ability to apply knowledge and skills to real-world settings. As Christopher and Batsell (2019) detailed, the research methods and statistics courses offer ample opportunities to design assignments that allow students to develop some of these desired outcomes. For example, the fairly traditional project of having students do some combination of designing a study, submitting a research ethics proposal, collecting data, analyzing those data with software, and presenting the data (in a paper and/or poster or platform format) inherently requires students to use many of these skills. Making that fact explicit to students will help them understand the importance of such a project, even if they are not aiming for a research-oriented graduate school program. Even more specific to making skill develop explicit to students, we ask our students to keep a journal that details how they developed these employer-desired skills so that they can draw on them in later endeavors, such as in constructing a resume, answering questions on an interview, or preparing a personal statement for a graduate school application. Every student, regardless of ability or motivational level, is interested in making or finding a job. Tying these courses (and all others) to this ultimate outcome can only serve to heighten students' interest in the material.

In addition to the skills that we can help students develop in these courses, we love teaching research methods and statistics because of the information in these classes. Of course, most of our students are not, at least initially, interested in research. Many of our best research students who go on to research-focused graduate programs found that passion only after enrolling in a research methods and statistics course. We try to start with something that students are actually interested in or at least can relate to before diving into anything technical, especially with statistics (Lawson, Schwiers, Doellmann, Grady, & Keinhofer, 2003). Indeed, likely one reason we as teachers find this information so appealing is because of how widely applicable it is. We need to convey that applicability to all of our students. For instance, one might introduce the topic of one-way analysis of variance (ANOVA) by asking students which wireless service they use. From there, you can ask which service is "the best," leading into a discussion of constructs and operational definitions. Once the class decides on a construct and its operational definition, discussion can lead into how to compare the three (or more) wireless services on that dimension. Typically, in our classes, students choose "customer satisfaction" as the construct of interest, leading into the one-way between-subjects ANOVA. From there, we do a conceptual example of what this analytic technique allows us to learn and the conditions necessary to use it. We then dive into conceptual discussions of the components of this analytic technique, such as between-group variability and within-group variability.

Key Challenges in Teaching Research Methods and Statistics

Every course has unique challenges that teachers must help students overcome. For instance, in abnormal psychology courses, teachers must help students overcome potential "medical student syndrome," in which students perceive that they see every psychological illness they read about appearing in themselves or someone they know. But what about the challenges teachers face in in the scholarship of teaching and learning suggests that faculty believe that the most common challenge in teaching these courses involves course design issues. Specific challenges included struggling with the balance between the different types of material, the available time to teach "everything," and making the material engaging. Other challenges involved teaching students how to conduct research, teaching data analysis, and teaching writing (Ciarocco et al., 2017). Perhaps one of the most salient challenges to teaching research methods and statistics is the students' perceptions of the course.

Boring/Irrelevant Content. One of our students once told us, "Psychology would be a perfect major if we didn't have to take these two classes" (or something close to that effect). Indeed, some – and perhaps most – psychology students may see research methods and statistics requirements as some sort of conspiracy that prevents them from taking other classes they would rather take. Indeed, these anecdotes are well-supported in empirical work. Research shows most students (75%) are not enthusiastic about taking research methods (Rajecki, Appleby, Williams, Johnson, & Jeschke, 2005), prefer to passively read or hear about research over actively conducting research individually or with a team (Rottinghaus, Gaffey, Borgen, & Ralston, 2006; Vittengl et al., 2004), hold negative attitudes towards research methods (Addison et al., 2015; Murtonen, 2005; Sizemore & Lewandowski, 2009), and fail to see the future relevance or utility of methods and statistics courses (Ciarocco, Lewandowski, & Van Volkom, 2013; Earley, 2014; Murtonen, 2015).

Research methods and statistics are the "core" tools of scientific psychology that allow researchers to draw conclusions about their work. As teachers, we appreciate this state of affairs. Our students, however, do not have this level of appreciation, and in many cases, have no desire to acquire it. Instead, they see these courses as barriers to what is otherwise a wonderful major! Thus, it is incumbent on us to demonstrate the importance of these courses to our students. For those aiming for graduate school, and particularly research-oriented programs, that is relatively easy to do. It is much more difficult to elucidate the importance of statistical knowledge to students who are taking the class because it is required in what is an otherwise interesting major.

Teacher-Student Enthusiasm Gap. A related challenge in teaching research methods and statistics courses is that students and instructors may not perceive the information in the same way. Strohmetz, Ciarocco, and Lewandowski (2018) reported students see learning to think scientifically and learning to do research as equally important, whereas their instructors place a higher value on learning to think scientifically. Students also saw these courses as preparation for graduate school more than as opportunities to cultivate employable skills. Whereas students worried about writing problems and learning how to design/conduct their own study, instructors were more likely to list student problems (e.g., lack of motivation and inability to engage in higher order thinking), as the most challenging aspects of the course. Students saw learning how to engage in research as a less important goal than their instructors did.

Given this enthusiasm gap, it is not entirely surprising that exposure to research methods and statistics courses can solidify attitudes that were already negative. After taking these courses, some students report seeing statistics and research knowledge as less useful (Sizemore & Lewandowski, 2009) and having less interest in scientific activities (Manning, Zachar, Ray, & LoBello, 2006).

Inherently Difficult and Abstract Content. Of course, in any given psychology course, there are some topics that students find particularly difficult, but in research methods and stats courses, the list of difficult topics seems much, much longer. Indeed, many of these topics serve as "potholes" or impediments to learning (Stoa,

Chu, & Gurung, in press). In a recent attempt to uncover potholes and repave the street in the United States, Stoa and colleagues asked undergraduate students to identify their challenges in research methods and statistics. The students could list up to five concepts that they found challenging, and then were asked to rate the difficulty of 63 research methods concepts (e.g., confound, effect size) derived from past research (Gurung & Landrum, 2013). The topics most often mentioned as challenging included types of validity (21%), quasi-experiments (5.8%), general knowledge of statistics (4.8%), and operational definition (4%).

A principle components analysis of difficulty ratings of the 63 concepts revealed five underlying factors: (a) Factor 1: items related to *Samples and Variables* (e.g., random assignment and confounds), (b) Factor 2: items related to *Ethics and Theory Data Cycle* (e.g., debriefing and informed consent), (c) Factor 3: items related to *Threats to Internal Validity* (e.g., attrition and demand characteristics), (d) Factor 4: items related to *Design Confounds* (e.g., systematic variability and third-variable problem), and (e) Factor 5: items related to *Scale Measurements* (e.g., Cronbach's alpha, and correlation coefficient). Do students in different educational systems across the globe find the same factors difficult? Research to answer this question is currently underway.

Overcoming Challenges to Teaching Research Methods and Statistics

Instructors have tried differing ways to address the challenges we have listed here, ranging from changing course design, to directly addressing how research methods and statistics classes are viewed by students.

Make the Course Applicable to Life. One of the biggest barriers is changing how students view the course. The good news is research methods and statistics are perhaps the classes in which we teach the most practical information in the major. The content is not only vital to our students' academic and professional development as discussed previously, but it is inherently interesting as well! We need to do a better job of highlighting the pragmatic value of the courses, and we can use the interesting content. Teachers can and should incorporate into these courses many "everyday" experiences that utilize core information about psychological science.

When teaching research methods, we suggest aiming to provide students with skills they can use in daily life and in the workforce, even if your course is aimed mainly at those bound for graduate school. Whereas most courses on the surface seem to be designed as preparation for graduate school (Lewandowski, Ciarocco, & Strohmetz, 2017), only a small portion of students will go on to graduate school. Consequently, start the course with many illustrations of how research design and analysis can be used in daily life can build student motivation for the course. For instance, to refer to a previous "real life" example from the one-way between-subjects ANOVA of phone service customer satisfaction, a research methods teacher could illustrate a variety of methodological designs. For instance, one could use survey research to gather customer ratings of different restaurants and compare value and meal quality. In fact, although we have not done so ourselves, teachers could have students construct such a survey themselves, using principles of good survey construction (Berk, 2009). Doing so not only teaches them basic methodological information, but it provides a great chance to do a "real world" project.

One significant way to change how the course is perceived is to include many opportunities for students to interact with the material in an active way with the guidance of the instructor. One study tested the efficacy of a multifaceted approach that included both active learning and a form of scaffolding in which the instructor provided a temporary structure to guide the student towards learning (Ciarocco et al., 2013). Students do better in the presence of the knowledge expert (the instructor) than if they were learning independently. As the student learns the new skills, the instructor slowly removes the guidance and structures. For example, students first read a published psychological study and wrote an in-class summary. The instructor provided scaffolding by discussing the article with the class and asking specific questions about the procedure and analyses, and giving feedback on the students' critiques. The instructor then did an in-class demonstration of the same research design as featured in the paper the students read, and where the students served as participants. Students then discussed the study results and design in small groups, finally writing up their results. US students exposed to this approach showed improved ability to write in accordance with APA style, higher perceived utility of research and statistics, more positive attitudes toward statistics, and higher perceived skills/abilities in statistics.

Other possible solutions to alleviate students' negative attitudes about these courses include arranging for students to collect their own data rather than have data handed to them. Students who actively design and conduct research as part of their methods course report more interest in doing research, feel more prepared to conduct their own research, and have more favorable impressions of the course overall (Roberts & Allen, 2012, 2013). One note of warning, there is evidence that even when students collect their own data, if they do so in an online course they score significantly lower on measures of quantitative mastery of statistical concepts than students who collect data in a face-to-face class (Goode et al., 2018).

Pay Attention to Course Design. A major consideration in teaching research methods in particular is whether the course will stress experimental methodology or balance that material with coverage of correlational and descriptive designs. Given the extent to which most workplaces utilize survey data collection, it may be prudent to train students in descriptive data collection methodologies, as this skill can be built on in the discussion of correlational and experimental designs. If the course is designed to prepare students for a wide array of careers, you may want to build in a discussion of qualitative methods and quasi-experimental methods, a common need identified by instructors (Gurung & Stoa, 2020). Again, doing so increases the perceived value of the course by demonstrating its real-life utility.

A related consideration in course planning is the order in which to present information. If you will be using a textbook, you will likely find that most books start with nonexperimental methods and progress through experimental designs. Therefore, it makes sense to organize the course in this order. However, we have found that students often have trouble understanding the limitations of various nonexperimental work without understanding the insights that experimental designs allow. Therefore, it might be a good idea to first introduce students to the basic two-group experiment, with a manipulated independent variable and random assignment to conditions, then address nonexperimental designs, including their strengths and weaknesses in relation to experiments. We know of no research that suggests incremental benefits of this topic organization, but we have found it useful.

Course organization is particularly important for statistics classes as well. Most statistics courses start with descriptive statistics, then present material on probability, hypothesis testing, and specific inferential techniques. Indeed, it would seem difficult for students to understand the latter areas without a foundation in the former. Within the realm of inferential statistics, however, there are a number of organizational options, depending on your teaching goals. You might want to link particular inferential statistics to the research designs with which they are typically associated. For instance, you could cover statistics such as correlations, univariate and perhaps multivariate regression, and nonparametric techniques such as chi-square in relation to analyzing data from nonexperimental research, and covers statistics such as one-way analysis of variance in relation to analyzing data from experimental research. One significant advantage of organizing the discussion of inferential techniques in this manner is that it allows students to see the connection between research methods and the statistical techniques needed to analyze the results of those methods. This organizational structure is especially easy to implement if you are teaching in a department in which research methods and statistics courses are combined or presented in a fixed sequence (see Christopher, Walter, Horton, & Marek, 2007, and our discussion to follow).

Another organizational decision involves whether and how to address "between-subjects" analyses vs. "repeated-measures" analyses. For example, one could cover the independent samples t test followed immediately by the paired samples t tests. This organization makes intuitive sense, as both analyses deal with comparing two means. However, it is equally sensible to follow the independent samples t test with the one-way between-subjects analysis of variance, as both analyses involve between-subject designs. We do not know of any empirical work that has assessed the relative effectiveness of these two approaches.

There are still other ways of organizing your presentation of inferential statistics tools. One of these is to start with the simplest ones. For most students, these would be the independent samples t test or possibly the Pearson correlation coefficient. You could start with the Pearson correlation, then extend that discussion into univariate (and perhaps multivariate) regression. You could next present the independent samples t test, followed by other mean-comparison tools as noted previously. Here again, we know of no empirical evidence that evaluates the effects of this plan on student learning.

Resources for Teaching Research Methods and Statistics

No matter how you chose to organize your course in research methods or statistics, we urge you to take advantage of the vast array of resources available to help you teach it well. Included in this array is a dense network of supportive colleagues who are eager to share their experiences and pedagogical ideas through listservs, blogs, and other social media such as twitter and Facebook. Here, we highlight only a few of the many books, websites, and other resources available to you.

An excellent starting source of ideas for both research methods and statistics is *Activities for Teaching Statistics and Research Methods* (Stowell & Addison, 2017). This compendium of 26 activities comes from a variety of teachers and includes, for example, having students repeatedly toss a pair of dice to create a frequency distribution table and bar graph (McEntarffer & Vita, 2017). We have found that this activity helps students to understand and appreciate the importance of large sample sizes by comparing the bar graph that results from 15 rolls of the dice compared with 75 rolls. The book includes another remarkably simple demonstration in which students draw slips of paper out of a container. It serves as the foundation for a useful discussion of sampling distributions and central limit theorem, two topics that, because of their hypothetical nature, tend to be among the most difficult for students to understand. These and other activities in this compendium can be used and/or adapted easily for classroom presentations or laboratory experiences.

Still other resources are to be found in the form of journals devoted to the scholarship of teaching and learning in psychology, especially *Teaching of Psychology* (http://teachpsych.org/top/index.php), the *Scholarship of Teaching and Learning in Psychology*, (https://www.apa.org/pubs/journals/stl/), *Psychology Teaching and Learning* (PLAT) (https://uk.sagepub.com/en-gb/eur/journal/psychology-learning-teaching). Each of these journals tends to publish a relatively large number of articles about teaching research methods and statistics material. For instance, in just one recent issue of *PLAT,* there were articles about managing statistics anxiety among undergraduates and student attitudes toward research. Indeed, it is the rare issue of these outlets that does not include information useful to teachers of these two classes.

Consider also the journal *Teaching Statistics* (https://onlinelibrary.wiley.com/journal/14679639) which, though not aimed specifically at teachers in psychology, provides a wide variety of ideas and activities for statistics teachers in any discipline. For instance, one recent issue contained a wonderful activity, using data about lead levels in the water supply in Flint, Michigan, USA, to illustrate descriptive statistics and the potentially life-altering effects they can reveal. The scholarly society associated with this journal, the Teaching Statistics Trust, also provides free resources to statistics teachers (http://teachingstatisticstrust.org.uk/).

In addition to scholarly journals, there are also conferences devote specifically to the teaching of psychology, and typically, there are numerous presentations on the teaching of research methods and statistics at these meetings. There are three such conferences in particular that we enjoy. First, there is the National Institute on the

Teaching of Psychology (NIToP: https://nitop.org/), which is held during the first week of January each year in St. Petersburg Beach, Florida USA. This conference provides 3.5 days of opportunities to learn about teaching in all areas of psychology, including platform presentations, poster sessions, idea exchanges, and numerous planned opportunities for informal interactions with other conference attendees who share similar teaching interests and responsibilities. Second, there is the Annual Conference on Teaching of Psychology (ACT: https://teachpsych.org/conferences/act.php), which is held each October in a different location in the United States. Typically, two full days, this meeting offers many opportunities similar to those offered at NIToP. Finally, the Association for Psychological Science holds a Teaching Institute as part of its annual convention, which is typically held in the USA or Canada during the last weekend each May (https://www.psychologicalscience.org/conventions/annual/teachinginstitute).

If you want to incorporate standard academic research into your methods and statistics classes, we suggest using primary sources on topics that tend to be of strong interest to students. A list of examples from clinical psychology is especially appropriate for use in research methods and statistics courses (Sizemore & Lewandowski, 2011). If you are interested in incorporating interdisciplinary issues into your courses, Christopher, Marek, and Benigno (2003) provided numerous examples, albeit somewhat dated now, of methodological and statistical exemplars from economic psychology.

We have found in both courses that the more we design assignments that are applicable to students' lives, the more likely it is that students will be motivated to learn the material. For example, on the first day of a research methods course, consider asking students answer a simple question such as: Is happiness relate to sleep? Ask each student to list how happy they are on a 10-point scale and to write down how much sleep they got the previous night. Open a statistical program such as SPSS or, for free easy-to-use software, JAMOVI, and enter all the data. Then calculate a correlation to answer the question. In one fell swoop, you have modeled the research process, namely, asking a question, collecting data, and analyzing it. This simple exercise can make the research process real while simultaneously demystifying statistics, software, and research design. It also provides the jumping off point for discussing shortcomings (e.g., why correlation does not establish causation) and proposing fixes (i.e., through designing an experiment). In short, take advantage of any and all activities and assignments that help demonstrate the importance of using statistics in ways that are relevant to the students' lives and to understanding psychological research.

Finally, using the previously discussed research on potholes and challenges, instructors should plan on covering the "hard" stuff together in class, in a low-stakes fashion. What are the concepts that your students find most problematic? Developing extra examples and applications for the most difficult concepts and allocating time in class for students to work together on assessing their comfort and knowledge of such concepts is critical. Explicitly signaling concepts proven to be difficult in advance may make students more likely and comfortable to ask for help when they have problems with the material.

Assessment of Learning in Research Methods and Statistics

Evaluation of the outcomes of research methods and statistics courses typically involves assessment of either student attitudes towards the material or their knowledge of that material. One measure of the former consists of a 30-item scale whose six subscales assess students' attitudes toward research, attitudes toward statistics, perceived utility of research, perceived utility of statistics, perceived ability in research, and perceived ability in statistics (Sizemore & Lewandowski, 2009). The scale includes items such as, "Reading articles about research in psychology is something that I enjoy" and "The concepts learned in a research class will be helpful to me in the future." Another scale (Allen & Baughman, 2016) measures students' confidence in seven different research methods skills, including, for example, their ability to "correctly identify the independent and dependent variables in an experiment," or to "run and interpret an independent samples t-test using SPSS."

Students' knowledge of research methods content can be measured in a number of ways, including total scores on the *Psychological Research Methods Survey* (Amsel, Allen, & Bauer 2014), a 10-item multiple-choice test about psychological research methods. One item, for example, reads as follows: "The part of an experiment that the experimenter deliberately manipulates is the: (a) hypothesis; (b) control group; (c) dependent variable; (d) independent variable." There is also a 20-item *Psychological Research Inventory of Concepts* (Veilleux & Chapman, 2017). It was developed using Item Response Theory, such that the multiple-choice items were derived from longer vignettes and validated on a diverse sample of students and Amazon Mechanical Turk workers.

Additional Considerations in Teaching Research Methods and Statistics

We once heard a colleague say that she had not really changed her research methods and statistics classes much during the past 20 years. On the surface, it may be true that a lot of the material that was important in these courses decades ago is still important today. However, the students enter higher education for a wide variety of reasons. Might these diverse goals affect what and how these courses will be taught in the future? We think so.

What Is Taught? There are five main factors that instructors in the USA believe are most important when teaching research methods and statistics: Basic Knowledge, Design, Skills, Statistics, and Other topics (Gurung & Stoa, 2020). In statistics classes, topics related to null hypothesis testing to be among the most essential (e.g., Giesbrecht, Sell, Scialfa, Sandals, & Ehlers, 1997). In fact, instructors of undergraduate statistics courses rated "statistical significance," "significance level," and "hypothesis testing" as among the seven most important terms (out of 374 examined) students needed to understand (Landrum, 2005). There was no mention of what are now called the "new statistics," such as effect sizes, confidence intervals, or meta-analytic techniques. Although these two particular studies are now relatively dated, they do point to the need for statistics teachers to rethink precisely what information undergraduates need to know about this subject matter, particularly at an introductory level.

As noted previously, discussions of hypothesis testing are still the norm in undergraduate statistics classes (Friedrich et al., 2018), despite calls to abandon hypothesis testing results in favor of reporting other statistics, such as effect sizes and confidence intervals (e.g., Cummings, 2014). Though effect sizes are now commonly reported in the results sections of psychology journal articles, the reporting of "new statistics" feels to us to be inconsistent not only across journals but sometimes even within the same journal. Indeed, hypothesis testing remains a staple, so teachers of research methods and statistics are more or less obligated to continue emphasizing both, lest students not understand what they are reading in those journals.

How Is it Taught? A recent survey of undergraduate psychology programs in the United States (Friedrich et al., 2018) found that large majorities of departments require statistics courses (80% of general schools, and 79% of top-ranked schools) and/or research methods courses (85% of general schools, and 65% of top-ranked schools). In the subset of 83/385 departments requiring both research methods and statistics, most (71%) required that statistics be taken first; 11% required that research methods be taken first. A little less than a third of the departments required an integrated research methods and statistics course (28% of general schools, and 24% of top-ranked schools).

Because there are many reasons to integrate research methods and statistics, we think combined courses are likely to become more common than they are now. Integrated courses provide a context for students to learn statistics, enhance the transfer of learning from one course to the other, and illustrate how science actually works (Christopher et al., 2007). In the life of most academics, research methods and statistics go hand-in-hand, and it is actually quite difficult to separate them. Furthermore, whereas many of the textbooks available to the instructor are dedicated exclusively to research methods or statistics, there is a growing number of books that integrate both topics.

Knowledge of research methods and statistics form the core foundation of the discipline of psychology. Having a basic understanding of both these areas can make for a psychological literate global citizen. Both classes have their challenges as outlined previously; however, the effort to teach them well can pay off with a better functioning citizenry. Our solutions do not cover all bases, and there is work to be done. We trust the resources and opportunities suggested will also stimulate significant reflection and potentially a range of systematic, intentional modifications to teaching research methods and statistics.

Cross-References

▶ Qualitative Methodology
▶ Teaching the Foundations of Psychological Science

References

Addison, W. E., Stowell, J. R., Reab, M. D. (2015). Attributes of introductory psychology and statistics teachers: Findings from comments on RateMyProfessors.com. *Scholarship of Teaching and Learning in Psychology, 1*, 229–234. https://doi.org/10.1037/stl0000034.

Allen, P. J., & Baughman, F. D. (2016). Active learning in research methods classes is associated with higher knowledge and confidence, though not evaluations or satisfaction. *Frontiers in Psychology, 7*, Article 279. https://doi.org/10.3389/fpsyg.2016.00279.

American Psychological Association (APA). (2012). Guidelines for preparing high school psychology teachers: Course-based and standards-based approaches. Retrieved from https://www.apa.org/education/k12/teaching-guidelines.pdf

American Psychological Association (APA). (2013). APA guidelines for the undergraduate psychology major: Version 2.0. Retrieved from http://www.apa.org/ed/precollege/undergrad/index.aspx

American Psychological Association (APA). (2019). The APA introductory psychology initiative: Envisioning the future: Charting new directions for introductory psychology. Retrieved from https://www.apa.org/ed/precollege/undergrad/introductory-psychology-initiative

Amsel, E., Allen, L., & Bauer, R. (2014, August). *Psychological literacy: Its nature, acquisition, and application*. Presented at the 6th international conference on psychology education, Flagstaff.

Berk, R. A. (2009). Using the 360-degree multisource feedback model to evaluate teaching and professionalism. *Medical Teacher, 31*, 1073–1080.

Burke, K. S., & Prieto, L. R. (2019). High-quality research training environments and undergraduate psychology students. *Scholarship of Teaching and Learning in Psychology, 5*(3), 223–235. https://doi.org/10.1037/stl0000156.

Christopher, A. N., & Batsell, W. R., Jr. (2019). Mentoring students in professional development. In R. Harnish (Ed.), *What I wish my mentor had told me* (pp. 87–102). Retrieved from: https://teachpsych.org/resources/Documents/ebooks/mentortoldme.pdf. Society for the Teaching of Psychology.

Christopher, A. N., Marek, P., & Benigno, J. (2003). Economic psychology: Its connections with research-oriented courses. *Teaching of Psychology, 30*(3), 209–215. https://doi.org/10.1207/S15328023TOP3003_02.

Christopher, A. N., Walter, M. I., Horton, R. S., & Marek, P. (2007). Benefits and detriments of teaching an integrated research methods and statistics course. In D. S. Dunn, R. A. Smith, & B. Beins (Eds.), *Best practices in the teaching of statistics and research methods in the behavioral sciences* (pp. 215–232). Mahwah, NJ: Lawrence Erlbaum.

Ciarocco, N. J., Lewandowski, G. W., & Van Volkom, M. (2013). The impact of a multifaceted approach to teaching research methods on students attitudes. *Teaching of Psychology, 40*(1), 20–23. https://doi.org/10.1177/0098628312465859.

Ciarocco, N. J., Strohmetz, D. B., & Lewandowski, G. W., Jr. (2017). What's the point? Faculty perceptions of research methods courses. *Scholarship of Teaching and Learning in Psychology, 3*(2), 116–131. https://doi.org/10.1037/stl0000085.

Cranney, J., & Dunn, D. S. (Eds.). (2011). *Educating the psychologically literate citizen: Global perspectives*. New York, NY: Oxford University Press. https://doi.org/10.1093/acprof:oso/9780199794942.001.0001.

Cummings, G. (2014). The new statistics: Why and how. *Psychological Science, 25*, 7–29. https://doi.org/10.1177/0956797613504966.

Dunn, D. S., Brewer, C. L., Cautin, R. L., Gurung, R. A. R., Keith, K. D., McGregor, L. N., ... Voigt, M. J. (2010). The undergraduate psychology curriculum: Call for a core. In D. F. Halpern (Ed.), *Undergraduate education in psychology: A blueprint for the future of the discipline; undergraduate education in psychology: A blueprint for the future of the discipline* (pp. 47–61, Chap xvi, 227 p) Washington, DC: American Psychological Association. https://doi.org/10.1037/12063-003.

Earley, M. A. (2014). A synthesis of the literature on research methods education. *Teaching in Higher Education, 19*, 242–253. https://doi.org/10.1080/13562517.2013.860105.

Friedrich, J., Childress, J., & Cheng, D. (2018). Replicating a national survey on statistical training in undergraduate psychology programs: Are there 'new statistics' in the new millennium? *Teaching of Psychology, 45*, 312–323.

Gardner, P. (2007). *Moving up or moving out of the company? Factors that influence the promoting or firing of new college hires* (CERI research brief 1-2007). East Lansing, MI: Michigan State University, Collegiate Employment Research Institute. Retrieved from http://ceri.msu.edu/pub lications/pdf/brief1-07.pdf.

Giesbrecht, N., Sell, Y., Scialfa, C., Sandals, L., & Ehlers, P. (1997). Essential topics in introductory statistics and methodology courses. *Teaching of Psychology, 24*(4), 242–246. https://doi.org/10.1207/s15328023top2404_2.

Goode, C. T., Lamoreaux, M., Atchison, K. J., Jeffress, E. C., Lynch, H. L., & Sheehan, E. (2018). Quantitative skills, critical thinking, and writing mechanics in blended versus face-to-face versions of a research methods and statistics course. *Teaching of Psychology, 45*, 124–131. https://doi.org/10.1177/0098628318762873.

Gurung, R. A. R., Hackathorn, J., Enns, C., Frantz, S., Cacioppo, J. T., Loop, T., & Freeman, J. E. (2016). Strengthening introductory psychology: A new model for teaching the introductory course. *American Psychologist, 71*(2), 112–124. https://doi.org/10.1037/a0040012.

Gurung, R. A. R., & Landrum, R. E. (2013). Bottleneck concepts in psychology: Exploratory first steps. *Psychology Learning & Teaching, 12*(3), 236–245. https://doi.org/10.2304/plat.2013.12.3.236.

Gurung, R. A. R., & Stoa, R. (2020). A national survey of teaching and learning research methods: Important concepts and faculty and student perspectives. *Teaching of Psychology, 47*(2), 111–120. https://doi.org/10.1177/0098628320901374.

Hanna, B. (2013). Toward psychological literacy: A snapshot of evidence-based teaching and learning. *Australian Journal of Psychology, 65*(1), 1–4.

Hart Research Associates. (2015). *Falling short? College learning and career success*. Association of American Colleges and Universities. Retrieved from https://www.aacu.org/sites/default/files/files/LEAP/2015employerstudentsurvey.pdf

Landrum, R. E. (2005). Core terms in undergraduate statistics. *Teaching of Psychology, 32*, 249–251.

Lawson, T. J., Schwiers, M., Doellmann, M., Grady, G., & Keinhofer, R. (2003). Enhancing students' ability to use statistical reasoning with everyday problems. *Teaching of Psychology, 30*(2), 107–110. https://doi.org/10.1207/S15328023TOP3002_04.

Lewandowski, G. W., Jr., Ciarocco, N. J., & Strohmetz, D. B. (2017). Research methods 2.0: A new approach for today's students. In R. Obeid, A. Schwartz, C. Shane-Simpson, & P. J. Brooks (Eds.), *How we teach now: The GSTA guide to student-centered teaching* (pp. 329–339). Society for the Teaching of Psychology.

Manning, K., Zachar, P., Ray, G., & LoBello, S. (2006). Research methods courses and the scientist and practitioner interests of psychology majors. *Teaching of Psychology, 33*, 194–196.

McEntarffer, R., & Vita, M. (2017). Getting dicey: Thinking about normal distributions and descriptive statistics. In J. R. Stowell and W. E. Addison (Eds.), *Activities for teaching statistics and research methods: A guide for psychology instructors* (pp. 28–32). Washington, DC: American Psychological Association.

Murtonen, M. (2005). University students' research orientations: Do negative attitudes exist toward quantitative methods? *Scandinavian Journal of Educational Research, 49*, 263–280. https://doi.org/10.1080/00313830500109568.

Murtonen, M. (2015). University students' understanding of the concepts empirical, theoretical, qualitative and quantitative research. *Teaching in Higher Education, 20*, 684–698. https://doi.org/10.1080/13562517.2015.1072152.

Norcross, J. C., Hailstorks, R., Aiken, L. S., Pfund, R. A., Stamm, K. E., & Christidis, P. (2016). Undergraduate study in psychology: Curriculum and assessment. *American Psychologist, 71*(2), 89–101.

Rajecki, D. W., Appleby, D., Williams, C. C., Johnson, K., & Jeschke, M. P. (2005). Statistics can wait: Career plans activity and course preferences of American psychology undergraduates. *Psychology Learning & Teaching, 4*, 83–89. https://doi.org/10.2304/plat.2004.4.2.83.

Roberts, L. D. (2016). Editorial: Research methods pedagogy: Engaging psychology students in research methods and statistics. *Frontiers in Psychology, 7*, 3.

Roberts, L. D., & Allen, P. J. (2012). Student perspectives on the value of research participation. In S. McCarthy, K. L. Dickson, J. Cranney, A. Trapp, & V. Karandashev (Eds.), *Teaching psychology around the world* (Vol. 3, pp. 198–211). Newcastle, UK: Cambridge Scholars.

Roberts, L. D., & Allen, P. J. (2013). A brief measure of student perceptions of the educational value of research participation. *Australian Journal of Psychology, 65*, 22–29. https://doi.org/10.1111/ajpy.12007.

Rottinghaus, P. J., Gaffey, A. R., Borgen, F. H., & Ralston, C. A. (2006). Diverse pathways of psychology majors: Vocational interests, self-efficacy, and intentions. *The Career Development Quarterly, 55*, 85–93. https://doi.org/10.1002/j.2161-0045.2006.tb00007.x.

Sizemore, O. J., & Lewandowski, G. W. (2009). Learning might not equal liking: Research methods course changes knowledge but not attitudes. *Teaching of Psychology, 36*, 90–95. https://doi.org/10.1080/00986280902739727.

Sizemore, O. J., & Lewandowski, G. W. (2011). Lessons learned: Using clinical examples for teaching research methods. *Psychology Learning & Teaching, 10*(1), 25–31. https://doi.org/10.2304/plat.2011.10.1.25.

Stoa, R., Chu, A., & Gurung, R. A. R. (in press). *Potential potholes: Predicting challenges and learning outcomes in research methods in psychology courses.* Teaching of Psychology.

Stoloff, M., McCarthy, M., Keller, L., Varfolomeeva, V., Lynch, J., Makara, K., … Smiley, W. (2010). The undergraduate psychology major: An examination of structure and sequence. *Teaching of Psychology, 37*(1), 4–15. https://doi.org/10.1080/00986280903426274.

Stowell, J. R., & Addison, W. E. (2017). *Activities for teaching statistics and research methods: A guide for psychology instructors.* Washington, DC: American Psychological Association.

Strohmetz, D. B., Ciarocco, N. J., & Lewandowski, G. W., Jr. (2018). *Getting on the same page: Aligning student and instructor perception to facilitate learning in methods classes.* Presentation at the society for the teaching of psychology's annual conference on teaching, Phoenix.

Sümer, N. (2016). Rapid growth of psychology programs in Turkey: Undergraduate curriculum and structural challenges. *Teaching of Psychology, 43*(1), 63–69. https://doi.org/10.1177/0098628315620886.

Veilleux, J. C., & Chapman, K. M. (2017). Development of a research methods and statistics concept inventory. *Teaching of Psychology, 44*(3), 203–211. https://doi.org/10.1177/0098628317711287.

Vittengl, J. R., Bosley, C. Y., Brescia, S. A., Eckardt, E. A., Neidig, J. M., Shelver, K. S., & Sapenoff, L. A. (2004). Why are some undergraduates more (and others less) interested in psychological research? *Teaching of Psychology, 31*, 91–97. https://doi.org/10.1207/s15328023top3102_3.

The Methodology Cycle as the Basis for Knowledge

Teaching Basic Epistemological Thinking

Jaan Valsiner and Angela Uchoa Branco

Contents

Abstract

Teaching *methodology* in various social sciences is a complex problem that starts from the ambiguity about what is meant by the notion of methodology. In contemporary practices, the meaning of the terms has usually been associated with the notion of *methods* that are viewed as discrete tools applicable in research in their own terms. This is inadequate on epistemological grounds. We have introduced the system of methodology – the Methodology Cycle back in 1997. In this chapter, we examine the implications of different ways of using the cycle for research purposes and show how it is the necessary basis for teaching methodology at all levels of education.

Keywords

Epistemology · Methodology · Knowledge · Educated intuition

J. Valsiner (✉)
Centre of Cultural Psychology, Department of Communication and Psychology, Aalborg University, Aalborg, Denmark

Sigmund Freud Privatuniversität, Vienna, Austria
e-mail: jvalsiner@gmail.com

A. U. Branco
Department of Psychology, University of Brasilia, Brasilia DF, Brazil

Introduction

More than two decades ago, in despair about the proliferating practices of unreflective application of various specific methods in psychology and educational research Worldwide, we introduced a message of caution to the never-ending quest for "more data!". The message was simple:

> It is not the issue of "application" of different methods (as separate tools—chosen from the "toolbox" because of their convenience, current social fashion, or researchers' ideological inclinations) to the phenomena we study. Instead, the combination of methods of data acquisition has to represent the theoretical assumptions of the researcher. (Branco & Valsiner, 1997, p. 38)

The result of our critique of the equation of "methodology" with "methods" – and the consumerist attitude to the latter – was the introduction of the Methodology Cycle (Fig. 1).

The crucial feature of the Cycle is the dynamic unity of all four components that are involved in any research effort: PHENOMENA, BASIC ASSUMPTIONS (axioms, META-CODE), THEORY, and – last in the line – METHODS, the work of all of which is made productive by the researcher. Within the exposition of the Methodology Cycle, the researcher is similar to an artist who unifies the four components and builds one's knowledge constructive efforts. This is both based on – and leads further into – EDUCATED INTUITION about how the process of research through the Cycle needs to proceed.

The whole move through the Cycle is an act of positioning by the researcher – looking for an access route to the phenomena of interest by constructing appropriate methods. The frequently asked question of priorities – *what kind of methods to use* (quantitative, qualitative or "mixed")? – is replaced by another question – *what kinds of methods need to be created* given the specific parameters selected through the Methodology Cycle.

The DATA have a special role as an outcome of the intellectual work through the Cycle. The date are not "facts" about the phenomena but *derived signs* that represent the phenomena in some – META-CODE and THEORY based – capacity. Their *derivation from* the phenomena was equated to sign-making in semiotic sense (Valsiner, 1995, 2000, 2018). As such, *data are always partial representations of the phenomena and therefore not "objective" by themselves*. Instead, objectivity in research is a result of coordination of the whole of the Cycle in a counter-clockwise process that needs to begin from the researcher's intuitive feeling-in (*Einfühlung*) into the PHENOMENA that is socially positioned by the BASIC ASSUMPTIONS on which the researcher sets up one's epistemological efforts.

Why Is the Methodology Cycle Necessary? Countering Pseudo-empiricism

We felt the need to provide an epistemological framework for methodology in the middle of the 1990s as we saw the proliferation of empirical research of pseudo-empirical kind (Smedslund, 1991, 1995) going on in child and developmental

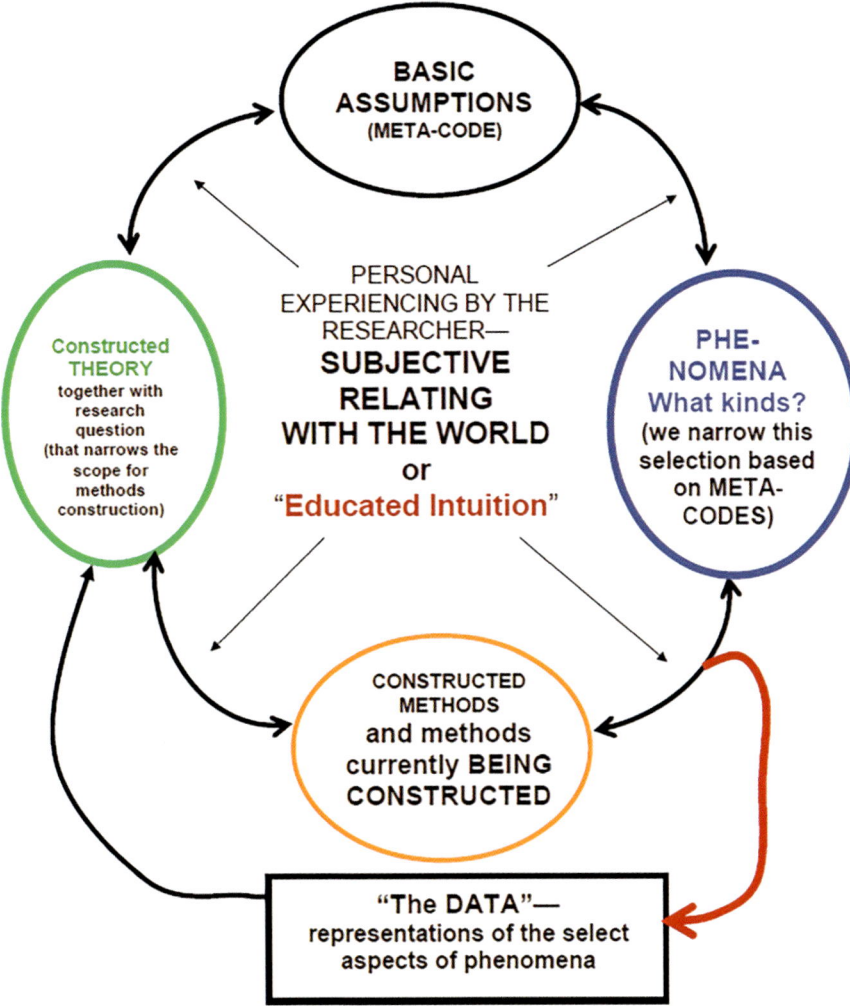

Fig. 1 The methodology cycle

psychology (Branco & Valsiner, 1997). The prevailing reality of the social practices in educational and psychological research was then – in the end of the 1990s – and continues to be now, deeply empiricist. DATA are still viewed as "objective" as they are "collected" – with the assumption that they are objectively given. Our current fascination with computer-collected "big data" has only fortified that illusion. The belief that data are granted objectivity if "collected" by consensually legitimized METHODS that are loosely linked with THEORIES prevails. Theories at worst are used as "conceptual umbrellas" for the inductive generalizations from the DATA or at best might prove or disprove some set hypothesis about the local knowledge

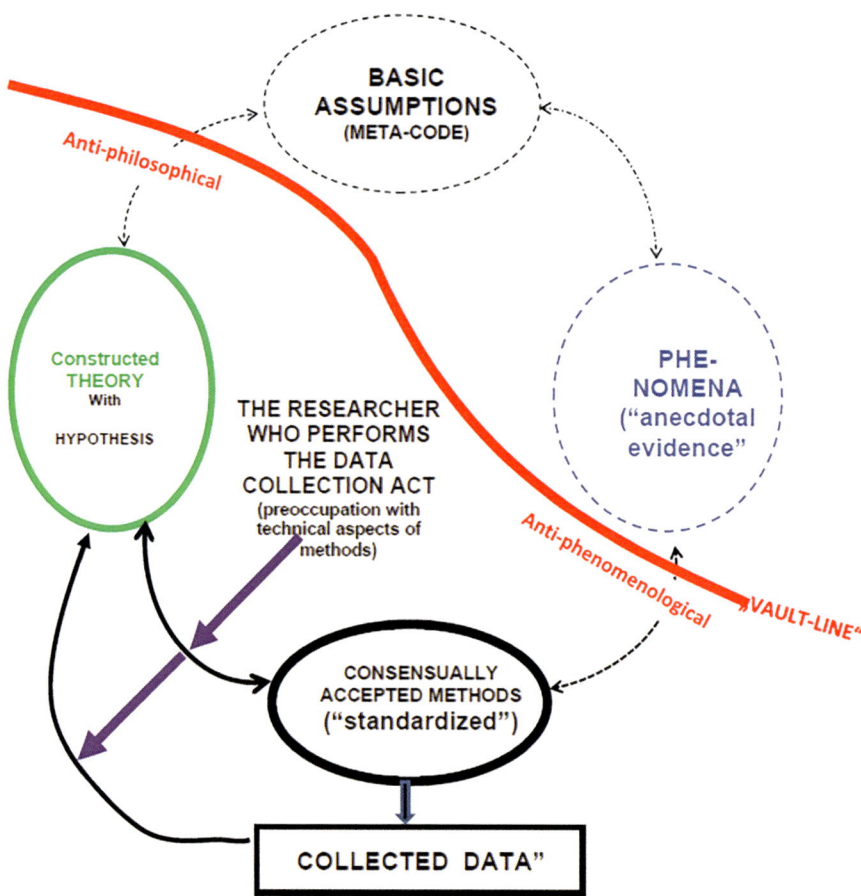

Fig. 2 The regular empirical practice of eliminating the cycle

presentable in the DATA. This reduction of the Methodology Cycle is depicted in Fig. 2.

The introduction of the exclusive barrier ("anti-philosophical and anti-phenomenological epistemic vault" – in Fig. 2) defines the *science* of psychology as if it is limited to never-ending data accumulation with episodically changing general frameworks ("theories"). Nothing can be further from reality of science (as *Wissenschaft*) – purely "empirical science" is a contradiction in terms, and empirical work that is philosophy-blind and phenomenology-aversive provides no new scientific knowledge.

The implications of such linearizing act for science are formidable. First, it creates the basis for pseudo-empiricism (Smedslund, 1991, 1992, 2012) – the collection of data that "prove" empirically that what we know already (as encoded in our common language) is "true." This is possible because of the exclusion of the META-CODE from consideration as shown in Fig. 2. The result of such exclusion is that one's hidden assumptions are not considered as part of the empirical research efforts. As a result, some empirical research projects may continue as social practices for a century or less—simply by the inertia that "this is the way we do things" in our field. In the early 2020s, it is about hundred years since the researchers of intelligence consensually agreed that this concept is what the IQ tests measure. The practice of continuous use of the intelligence notion is based on that test and its extensions to adjacent fields ("emotional intelligence," etc.). This leads to a paradoxical situation, that is, the accumulation of increasing sizes of data bases – now enabled by the computer technologies – need not enhance scientific progress but would camouflage its absence by way of changes of meta-theoretical fashions. There is no breakthrough in our understanding, for example, when the prevailing fashion leads to change from cognitive to positive psychology – with the focus on the data remaining the same.

Need to Restore the Role of the Experiencing Researcher: Educated Intuition
In the practices depicted in Fig. 2, the role of the researcher in this empirical data collection game has been reduced to that of the administrator of the selected METHODS. There is a general social tendency in social science research of the last half-century behind this reduction – that of administrative institutional control effort over the social and educational sciences. This is exemplified by increasing reliance of technical acts of research based on institutionally approved manuals. While the latter is not surprising in the *application* of scientific knowledge, it cannot be productive in the *production* of new knowledge.

The tendency toward manualization – using guidelines to act in one's profession – has been transposed from "evidence-based" medicine to psychology practices and research. It is believed that the data in and by themselves (and by some magical features –"standardization") would create our "objective knowledge" if enough data are collected. This clockwise move in the Cycle – starting from METHODS moving through DATA and ending in some discourse about THEORIES – is a deeply impoverished version of the Cycle that fits the inductive ideology that prevails in psychology and in the educational and social sciences. The general philosophical background of the social sciences (Valsiner, 2020) becomes reduced to the inductive imperative of "empirical science." Then the Cycle becomes eliminated by linearizing it, and the result of such impoverished approach can be summarized as follows:

RESEARCHER ➔ formulates a specific Hypothesis➔ selects a couple of tools (METHOD)➔ to reach out for a slice of PHENOMENA that manifests as DATA (considered as ultimate evidence) ➔ which reifies or not the initial Hypothesis, all leading to an accumulation of scientific "evidence"

Note that the epistemological framework (BASIC ASSUMPTIONS) that allows for the elaboration of a specific THEORY is left out of the picture. In addition, the THEORY itself is almost irrelevant from a perspective that considers the "objectivity" of DATA, assumed from a positivistic framework that is taken for granted. Neither the quality of the basic assumptions (epistemology) and their role in theory construction nor the quality of the "data" produced by the utilization of specific methods (which operate, in fact, as selective lens to "reveal" the PHENOMENA) is taken into account with the adoption of this linear process.

The second major deficiency that the linearization of the Cycle brings with it is the alienation of research from the phenomena. As the PHENOMENA in Fig. 2 are considered objective and not linked with the METHOD selection and "use" in the DATA obtaining act, it is the representational nature of the data [that] becomes eliminated. Such data alienation has devastating effects on bringing the accumulated data to the practical fields of clinical (Smedslund & Ross, 2014) or sports psychology (Lykkeskov, Askildsen, & Eckerdal, 2019). Professional institutional decisions, rather than the fit of the empirical research results with phenomena, replace the focus on the phenomena and limit the applicability of our knowledge to the needs of practices. Most of the data in the educational and social sciences represent the outcomes of inherent process of thinking, feeling or acting, while for practical intervention (i.e., therapies) it is the knowledge of the processes that lead to such outcomes that are needed. Outcome data do not inform about the needs of process change, or about the characteristics of the processes' dynamics.

Thirdly, the role of the researcher becomes reduced from an active constructor of knowledge – a creative person similar to an artist – into a kind of "research executive" whose role is to carry out the data collection act in accordance with existing rules and regulations, rather than think together with the unfolding encounters with the research participants. This pseudo-neutral, standardized role given to the researcher, as well as the "slave role" given to graduate and undergraduate research assistants, do not encourage them to become creative researchers. Everybody ends up in academic jobs but tends to be mere followers of the prevailing fashions in their disciplines.

History of developmental psychology provides a good example of how to de-standardize a method, young Jean Piaget's turning away from the META-CODE of "intelligence testing" to replace that with another one, the cognitive adaptation to the problem-solving tasks. Young Piaget was given as his first task the standardization of a British "intelligence test" to French school children in a Parisian suburb. In giving the tests, he became fascinated by the phenomena of how young children were *trying* – independently of whether they succeeded or failed – to solve the problems that the test items posed to them. Each test "item" (which, as such, would lead to becoming summarized into a "score") could be seen as a cognitive problem to solve. Piaget abandoned his given task and began his lifelong inquiry into development of cognitive processes. The "intelligence test" was left behind as a useless carcass of a method that no longer was productive – while its items creatively served as basis for Piaget's following work. His employers were obviously not amused by Piaget's youthful rebellion.

The idea that certain questions demand the use of specific tools – such as correlational, experimental or quasi-experimental designs, interviews, or naturalistic observations – is naively simplistic, unrealistic, and, ultimately, non-productive. The problem faced by such fast lane to carry out research projects is derived from a basic requirement that is *not* adequately fulfilled: all components of the Methodology Cycle, presented in Fig. 1, need to be well articulated with each other to maintain a strong coherence when adopted to respond to the research questions to be investigated. If such coherence is not achieved, the informative power of the data constructed is poor, and the theoretical relevance of the produced results either become substantively questioned, or simply does not exist. Pseudo-empiricism in psychology (Smedslund, 1991, 1995, 2016) is an inevitable result from the "cutting" of the Cycle as depicted in Fig. 2.

It is important to point out that our introduction of the Methodology Cycle in 1997 (Branco & Valsiner, 1997) was no news – at least when seen through the prism of the history of science. It merely represents – in a cyclical form – the basic science methodology that has been in place over the past three centuries, only forgotten in the twentieth-century psychology for historically particular extra-scientific reasons (Toomela & Valsiner, 2010; Valsiner, 2014). The META-CODE of the "Law of Large Numbers" – belief that the particular phenomena remain represented in populational aggregates – may have fitted the democratic representation models of politics in the Occidental societies, but it fails to provide evidence about the reconstructive uniqueness of ever new emerging persons in a society.

Examples of Use of the Cycle

Let us illustrate how the Methodology Cycle operates as a heuristic orientation to produce scientific knowledge concerning psychological phenomena. First, we make explicit the nature of our epistemological (BASIC ASSUMPTIONS) and theoretical (THEORY) approaches, and then, we describe the guiding questions of the research project and how such questions orient the selection and creation of specific innovative procedures (METHODS) to reach out for those aspects of the PHENOMENA under study, according to the theory.

Our major topic of investigative interest consists in making sense of human development as a whole. Here we depart from the axiomatic assumption that all human phenomena are developmental, systemic, complex, and dynamic. From this *epistemological* perspective, characterized by a qualitative, sociogenetic, and dialogical paradigm, active individuals continuously coconstruct each other as they interact within culturally structured contexts. To investigate the developmental nature of those complex processes involved in human phenomena, we have carried out many empirical research projects from a cultural psychology *theoretical* perspective, which stresses the mutual constitution of person and context along the irreversible time. For cultural psychology, the focus of any investigation concerning human psyche must concentrate on those *meaning-construction processes* (semiosis) occurring at both inter- and intra-individual levels as people relate to each other. Furthermore, any investigation should take into account practices and processes involving interactions among people occurring at micro, meso, and macro levels.

Cultural psychology highlights the fundamental role played in hypergeneralized affective-semiotic fields – situated at intra-individual level – that lie at the basis of internalization/externalization processes along individuals' life trajectories (Branco, 2016; Valsiner, 2014). Affective semiotic fields, coconstructed throughout life experiences with others, operate together with cultural canalizations and guide each person's perceptions, feelings, thoughts, and actions toward goals in the imagined future. According to this theoretical perspective, past experiences are continuously constructed and reconstructed under the influence of the imagined future, and those affective semiotic fields of particular relevance for the developing individual acquire a significant guiding function of her psyche. As they become hypergeneralized, we designate them as the person's *values*. Values, henceforth, orient individual psychological functioning and everyday interactions with self, others, and the world.

Cultural values and personal values are dynamic and constitute each other as much as the active subject and cultural contexts engage in mutual constitution along time. Therefore, to make sense of psychological processes and experiences, we need to identify and analyze aspects of the structured quality of sociocultural contexts as well as characteristics of individual's self-configurations, which, in the following example, were aspects of self-development as expressed by changes in the participants' self-positionings and values.

Example # 1

The brief description of our epistemological and theoretical grounds above was necessary to explain the two research projects we present next, in our effort to articulate all components of the Methodology Cycle (MC). The first empirical project (Roncancio-Moreno, 2015; Roncancio-Moreno & Branco, 2017) was carried out from two compatible frameworks: cultural psychology and dialogical self theory (Hermans, 2001; Hermans & Hermans-Konopka, 2010). Here we focus on its basic methodological characteristics due to the specific purpose of this chapter. The study's goal was to investigate possible dialogical self-developments in 5- to 6-year-old children during their transition from a public preschool to elementary schools located in the city of Brasilia, Brazil. As we conducted the research, we developed specific procedures (see Table 1) to obtain relevant information concerning the study's objectives. By bringing together all information, we were able to construct significant DATA, as we identified and analyzed indicators of each investigated child's self-development, revealed by changes observed in their self-positionings along the longitudinal study. However, how specific methods were constructed and used, in order to provide meaningful information for data construction and analysis?

The study took place during a period of 1 year (phase 1 in preschool and phase 2 in elementary school). After accepted in the school context, the researcher initiated an ethnographic approach, which allowed her to become familiar and accepted by children and adults within the educational context. During this time, she observed

Table 1 Procedures included in the study

1. Naturalistic observations
2. Field Notes
3. Video recording of daily routines
4. Video recording of structured activities: doll school
5. Video recording of structured activities: cube of emotions
6. Video recording of structured activities: frog story (by Max Velthuijs)
7. Individual interviews with children
8. Individual interviews with parents
9. Individual interviews with teachers
10. Drawing journal (a copybook or journal, where they should draw whatever they wanted)

children and educators within their classrooms and in the playground, registering relevant events and ideas in a field diary. Casual conversations with teachers and other adults occurred naturally and played a role in her social acceptance within the preschool context. The next step then was to select those subjects who would participate of the longitudinal research. After selecting one specific classroom in the preschool, and before any other procedure, the researcher attended to preschool's activities with children for 8 weeks. Thus, she was able to develop a good rapport with children, which later was fundamental for implementing the research procedures. After the immersion period, the researcher selected seven children to participate in the study, and their parents were contacted to obtain their consent. During the 1-year period, the researcher spent at least 3 days within the preschool and the elementary school's contexts in order to perform the procedures described in Table 1.

After bringing together the knowledge deriving from all procedures, we started data construction according to five levels of analysis:

1. Initial transcription of all relevant material in order to select a smaller number of subjects to be investigated in detail, as in case studies. Three subjects, two girls and one boy, were selected due to quality of their information, which would allow us to construct significant data for our purposes.
2. Analysis of children and adults' narratives.
3. Analysis of children's and adult-child's interactions.
4. Microgenetic analysis aiming at the construction and integration of data concerning meaning-making processes for each child. Data triangulation was performed in search for powerful indicators of each child's affective semiotic fields and self positionings along the year.
5. Elaboration of substantiated inferences about children's self-development and the proposal of theoretical explanations of those possible processes involved in children's self-development.

To investigate each children's trajectories (the three case studies), we used an analytical framework (Branco & Valsiner, 1997) that took into account specific sources of information. They were (a) children, narratives about themselves and their experiences at school and family; child-child and teacher-child interactions; (b) teachers, narratives about the child's development, peer interactions, academic performance, and teacher's relationship with the child's family; and (c) families, mother's narrative about the child and child's development in general. As the researchers analyzed the three case studies, the relevance of communication and metacommunication, cultural canalization, and anticipation processes (Branco, 2016; Valsiner, 2014; Zittoun, 2016) were discovered.

Three basic guidelines oriented the research construction of each child trajectory: (1) The expectations and meanings concerning social and affective relationships, recurrent in preschool and in the first grade; (2) the role of significant others; and (3) relevant changes in self-related meanings from preschool to elementary school.

A summary of each child's trajectory follows:

1. Helena: at preschool, she provided multiple indicators of social isolation, sadness, and a self-positioning of "I-as-rejected," particularly due to her father's abandonment after parents' divorce and to difficulties in engaging in relations with peers. At the first grade, with new extra-class activities provided by mother's support (meaningful at both phases), she moved on to much more positive self-positionings, toward an optimistic self-development trajectory due to the support and appreciation of her skills by teacher and peers in the first grade.

2. Giselle: from preschool to the elementary school, she experienced a somewhat ambivalent self-development trajectory. She is very much appreciated by teacher and peers at preschool, the new environment did not support her major affective-semiotic fields and self-positionings, related to being beautiful and popular. The new environment praised intellectual skills, and as she presented learning difficulties, this resulted in strong tensions, which made her sad but also hopeful, since her abilities to draw were then appreciated.

3. Anderson: the boy went through a very problematic self-development trajectory, mainly because in the first grade, his teacher and his mother contributed to the deconstruction of those previous positive self-meanings he had developed during preschool.

The idiographic and longitudinal approach to Giselle's, Helena's, and Anderson's trajectories, in conclusion, allowed for the investigation of self- developmental processes, as each child's affective-semiotic fields and self-positionings (Branco, 2016; Branco, Freire, & Roncancio-Moreno, in press; Roncancio-Moreno, 2015) were identified and analyzed in terms of emergence, disappearance, and transformation, within their developing dialogical self-systems. Had we not employed all procedures developed to produce several indicators of each child's dialogical self-positioning, we would not be able to make sense of such positionings as well as the whole set of social others and subjective resources used by the participants that resulted in their self-development.

The use of several procedures allowed the researchers to access to different aspects of children's lives, providing valuable information about the dynamics of the dialogical self-system of each child during that transition period. Social interactions, observed in videos, field notes, semi-structured tasks, together with narratives produced by participants, were the core of the investigation of children's meaning-making processes about themselves. As Zittoun (2016) argues, transitions entail identity redefinitions, learning, and sense making.

The study's major results pointed to the fundamental role of the internalization of significant others' voices in active dialogue with each child's own voices, creating tensions in their dialogical self-system that tended to promote development in specific directions. Possibilities for a creation of a third position to negotiate between opposite self-positionings were observed, and we argue that this emergence may have occurred because the dialogical self-system operates to release tension and achieve a reasonable level of integration and stability. Such emergence, therefore, can result from the dynamics of dialogical self-system resources in interaction with several catalytic conditions – as significant social others and activities – that enable new developments. Other significant results were obtained, with consequences to further theoretical elaborations on the dynamics of individuals' dialogical self-development along the irreversible time, but to discuss them would be out of the scope of this chapter. For further details concerning this study, we suggest the reader to consult (Roncancio-Moreno & Branco, 2017).

Example # 2

The second example here presented refers to an experiment we conducted in Brasília (Branco & Valsiner, 1992). Our goal was to analyze the role of social interactions' dynamic and structured contexts on cultural canalization processes related to specific patterns of children's interactions. We carried out an experiment with two triads composed by three 3-year-old children (two boys and one girl) that were instructed to play under the supervision of an adult. They were observed within two differently structured contexts: a cooperative context and a competitive context. Along six 25-minute consecutive sessions, each triad was invited to play with different materials but under a same social participation rule. Triads were then referred to as "cooperative" or "competitive."

Children in the "cooperative" triad were asked to interact with each other in order to build a unique structure from small pieces of a same material; or they were asked to play together within a fantasy-play context. In the "competitive context," children were asked to play alone and their performance were then compared. For instance, the adult took photographs of their constructions so people could later choose which was the best one; or their individual scores during competitive games were exposed. The materials used during the sessions were varied to keep children's motivation to participate is high and were selected to afford multiple coordination possibilities (wooden blocks, family doll sets, puzzles, bowling game, etc.). We also organized a test situation (the 7th session) when children of both triads (cooperative and competitive) were asked to perform a same cooperative task. Children were instructed to carry around a big doll pretended to be "ill," to undress her, pretend to bathe her, dry her, dress her again, carry her to the "hospital" for examination and medication, and, finally, bring the doll back "home."

All sessions were fully videotaped, and adult's and children's actions and interactions were fully transcribed. After that, we carried out a microgenetic analysis of the material, in order to be able to identify specific cues and strategies used by children along the experiment. The experiment's goals, then, did not only consisted of demonstrating the effect of cultural canalization on the emergence of specific patterns of social interactions. The study aimed, in addition, at identifying and analyzing all sorts of triggers, events, and strategies – at a microgenetic level – used by participants during play activities.

Results revealed the effects of cultural canalization processes, with a sharp contrast in the time spent in cooperative interactions between the triads. We verified an increasing number and duration of cooperative episodes among children belonging to the cooperative triad, in comparison to the triad submitted to competitively structured activities. Likewise, results from the test session (7th session) showed that the cooperative triad displayed cooperative interactions during 81% of the session time, while children who experienced competitive contexts spent only 8% of session time in cooperative interactions. Such results are, therefore, aligned with the work of cultural canalization processes, demonstrating that adult's verbal orientations, as well as the typical affordances and constraints of each situation, directed children's actions and interactions during the experiment.

When we analyzed the material from a microgenetic level of analysis, we observed a very interesting interplay between cooperative-oriented and competitively oriented interactions. We were able to closely analyze the events that triggered divergences as well as negotiation movements and strategies employed by the participants, and this led us to conclude for the intertwined nature of social interactive processes. This is next illustrated by an interesting episode taken from the first cooperative session. In the episode, divergent interactions occurring between two boys over the possession of an object finally resulted in a negotiation process, which gave rise to the emergence of a new cooperative coordination of their actions.

The experimental procedure we designed allowed for capturing relevant information concerning the dynamics of social interactions within culturally structured contexts. For instance, the adult, a female undergraduate student, was instructed to continuously negotiate with the three children to canalize their actions, either into cooperation or individual/competitive orientation, during the six sessions. Next, we present an extract of an episode with the "cooperative" triad that clarifies the dynamic interplay between different categories of social interaction. Gustavo (G), who plays the most active role in interacting with the adult (strongly resisting her efforts to promote cooperation) and with peers, initiates conflictual interactions with Pablo (PF) over the possession of an object. He picks a wooden block he pretends to be a "clock" from Pablo, Pablo struggles to take it back, Gustavo threats Pablo's construction and indeed destroys it. Then the adult takes to pieces Gustavo's construction, and the interactional flow goes on with Gustavo involved in conflictual interactions with both Pablo and the adult. The three children grab a part of the blocks for themselves, and the following interaction takes place:

[A = adult, in italic; G = Gustavo;   PF = Pablo;   P = Paola]

- *A: Folks, she smiles, what have you done?*
- G: I won't let him take these from me!
- PF: Neither will I!
- *A asks G: But why? Isn't he your friend?*
- G complains: No! I'm not his friend because he's taking... he doesn't let me take his clock...
- *A: But you also have a clock!*
- G: Where is the clock?
- *A picks up PF's clock: What if we have a clock here and we make a church?*
- PF takes his block back: No!! (emphasis)
- G: Where is my clock?
- *A: It's not yours, it belongs to everyone, Gustavo!*
- G: Where is my clock that was here?
- *A: I don't know... and then: Pablo could help you. He could lend you the clock and then you'd make something very big here!*
- **G to PF: So you lend it to me...**
- **PF moves towards P's construction: Look what we have here!! (he picks up a block-"clock" in P's construction and gives it to G)**
- **G to P: Give it to me! That's what I was looking for, this clock..**
- *A: But this belongs to everybody! (she firmly asserts this point, and picks up PF's clock) We can use two clocks if we do just one thing!*
- PF takes his block back immediately: OK, but this is mine!
- *A: Hum...*
- G: This belongs to him! Nobody should take it, isn't that right, Pablo? (G firmly holds the block PF gave to him from P's construction) This is mine... to build something like this, and nobody will get inside my building. I have to put all here, or they will get lost...
- *A: Isn't Gustavo going to help Paola? She's started to do it, it's turning into a very nice job!*
- **G moves towards P: Do you want me to help you? (G picks up a different block, which is lying in front of P and puts it in her construction)**
- *A: OK! That's it!*
- **G to A: *Like this. That's a good idea, isn't it?***
- *A: Good idea!*

The first thing that becomes evident in our analysis is how intensively and appropriately the adult tried to engage children in cooperation, consistently negotiating with them, insisting to trigger negotiations leading to mutual collaboration. In this episode, she finally succeeds, but a setback occurred when Pablo used a strategy to help Gustavo – metacommunicating to him he was indeed his friend – that could potentially upset Paola. The complex dynamics observed in such a short piece of the interactional flux among the four participants well demonstrates the adequacy of the experiment's design and the microgenetic analysis of the participants interactions.

Both allowed us to elaborate some relevant theoretical possibilities. It is noteworthy, for instance, that before the emergence of the conflict between Gustavo and Pablo, children were not interacting with each other, they were oriented to their individual activities. Therefore, we can speculate about the functional role of conflict interactions for the very emergence of cooperation among peers, since negotiations may include strategies – as the one used by Pablo – that can be considered as a key element to twist the quality of individuals' interchange. In the episode, Pablo's prosocial strategy toward Gustavo (his friend but immediate opponent in the flux of interactions) contrasted with a possible disrespect regarding Paola, whose block was taken away.

To sum up our point, we can, thus, conclude that the mere recording and evaluation of the occurrence of mutually excluding behavioral categories, such as cooperation and competition, would not allow for a deep understanding of social interactions dynamics. It would not, for example, provide relevant information – necessary for data construction – on how individuals constantly use all sorts of strategies to negotiate and change the quality of the flux of their interactions, ultimately affecting their relationships in different and multiple ways.

General Conclusion: What Does "Teaching Methodology" Mean?

Our story of the Methodology Cycle has immediate and profound importance for teaching methodology in psychological and educational sciences. We can summarize these as follows:

1. Teaching methodology *is not* equal to giving students an overview of existing methods and expecting them to evaluate and then select the already-available method in direct comparison with other methods at the researcher's disposal. Thus, questions about "what methods are better than others?" have no place in the teaching of methodology from the perspectives of our Methodology Cycle. Instead the productive questions about methods that need to be taught in the domain of methodology is how a particular designed method allows us to extract knowledge out of the raw phenomena through the help of the given theory that allows us to search for new knowledge.

   Any initial phase of teaching methodology starts from the work of the student's intuition when confronted with the selected phenomena. Implicit assumptions that the student carries into the first encounter need to be made explicit and analyzed by teacher and students in class. Some of such explicated assumptions can be personally upsetting for the students, and they need to get used to that. The flexibility of the scientific – as opposed to ideological – look at the phenomena entails multiple perspectives some of which may be personally rejectable by the student. Yet these disliked assumptions can have an equal status, among others. The student needs to bring all assumptions out to his or her personal philosophical consideration and then explain why some of these he/she prefers not to accept. For example, a researcher who ideologically claims to be of some particular persuasion (feminist, masculinist, Zoroastrian, vegetarian, nativist, nudist or any other) needs to learn not to dismiss the assumptions used by his or her declared "opponents" on ideological grounds but explicitly analyze these assumptions and then explain why one rejects these in favor of one's preferred ones.

2. The notion that each research project requires the construction of its own adequate methods needs to be developed through the use of the Cycle. The *coordination* of all parts of the Cycle needs to be emphasized. The methods must be well coordinated between THEORY and PHENOMENA to render adequate data.

3. Theories are not "umbrellas" for empirical efforts where "anything goes," as long as the conventional norms of inter-coder agreements, validity, and reliability are fulfilled. Instead, theories are, first of all, tools for thinking about how to adequately construct research methods that fit the phenomena.

4. META-CODES are axioms that are on the foundation of the whole research process. They differ from orthodoxies by being changeable if they are found to misfit the phenomena. In contrast, axioms that have become orthodox beliefs are not changeable. Orthodox beliefs have no place in science, while axioms are central in the research enterprise.

We also insist on the necessary active participation of the students in defining and discussing multiple research questions and all aspects and steps concerning a project coconstruction. Such approach can definitely be very productive. Hence, students' motivated engagement on such practices and activities can prove to be the best venue to put in motion successful teaching-learning processes that we, as teachers, look forward to develop with them.

It becomes obvious that the teaching of methodology is a clearly structured educational task that emphasizes creativity, subjectivity, and most of all – fresh ways of thinking – in the very first research efforts of young students. Such teaching is crucial for the future of the science – since exactly at this early stage the difference between axioms and orthodoxies becomes clarified. The eagerness of young students to innovate their worlds needs to be supported – rather than crushed – by the teaching of methodology.

References

Branco, A. U. (2016). Values and their ways of guiding the psyche. In J. Valsiner, G. Marsico, N. Chaudhary, T. Sato, & V. Dazzani (Eds.), *Psychology as the science of human being: The Yokohama Manifesto* (pp. 225–244). Cham: Springer.

Branco, A. U., Freire, S. F., & Roncancio-Moreno, M. (in press). Dialogical self system development: The permanent co-construction of Dynamic Self Positionings along life trajectory from a cultural psychology perspective. In M. C. Lopes-de-Oliveira, A. U. Branco, & S. F. Freire (Eds.), *Psychology as a dialogical science*. São Paulo: Springer.

Branco, A. U. & Valsiner, J. (1992, July 19–25). *Development of convergence and divergence in joint actions of preschool children: The emergence of cooperation and competition within structured contexts.* Paper presented at the 25th International Congress of Psychology, Brussels, Belgium.

Branco, A. U., & Valsiner, J. (1997). Changing methodologies: A co-constructivist study of goal orientations in social interactions. *Psychology and Developing Societies, 9*(1), 35–64.

Hermans, H. (2001). The dialogical self: Toward a theory of personal and cultural positioning. *Culture & Psychology, 7*, 243–281.

Hermans, H., & Hermans-Konopka, A. (2010). *Dialogical self theory: Positioning and counter-positioning in a globalizing society.* New York: Cambridge University Press.

Lykkeskov, M., Askildsen, M. A., & Eckerdal, A. (2019). Integrative synthesis of psychological support systems for enhancing athletic performance. *Human Arenas.* https://doi.org/10.1007/s42087-019-00065x

Roncancio-Moreno, M. (2015). *Dinâmica das significações de si em crianças na perspectiva dialógico-cultural* [Self-meanings dynamics in children from a dialogical cultural perspective]. Doctoral dissertation, University of Brasília, Brazil.

Roncancio-Moreno, M., & Branco, A. U. (2017). Developmental trajectories of the Self in children during the transition from preschool to elementary school. *Learning, Culture and Social Interactions, 14*, 38–50.

Smedslund, J. (1991). The pseudoempirical in psychology and the case for Psychologic. *Psychological Inquiry, 2*(4), 325–330.

Smedslund, J. (1992). Are Frijda's "laws of emotion" empirical? *Cognition & Emotion, 6*(6), 435–456.

Smedslund, J. (1995). Psychologic: Common sense and the pseudoempirical. In J. A. Smith, R. Harre, & L. van Langenhoeve (Eds.), *Rethinking psychology* (pp. 196–206). London: Sage.

Smedslund, J. (2012). The bricoleur model of psychological practice. *Theory & Psychology, 22*(5), 643–657.

Smedslund, J. (2016). Why psychology cannot be an empirical science. *IPBS: Integrative Psychological & Behavioral Science, 50*, 185–195.

Smedslund, J., & Ross, L. (2014). Research-based knowledge in psychology: What, if anything, is its incremental value for the practitioner. *IPBS: Integrative Psychological & Behavioral Science, 48*, 365–383.

Toomela, A., & Valsiner, J. (Eds.). (2010). *Methodological thinking in psychology: 60 years gone astray?* Charlotte, N.C.: Information Age Publishers.

Valsiner, J. (1995). Meanings of "the data" in contemporary developmental psychology: Constructions and implications. Gastvorträg am *12. Tagung der Fachgruppe Entwicklungspsychologie der Deutschen Gesellschaft für Psychologie*, Leipzig, 27. September (published version-Valsiner, 2018).

Valsiner, J. (2000). Data as representations: Contextualizing qualitative and quantitative research strategies. *Social Science Information, 39*(1), 99–113.

Valsiner, J. (2014). *An invitation to cultural psychology.* London: Sage.

Valsiner, J. (2018). Meanings of "the data" in contemporary developmental psychology: Constructions and implications. In G. Marsico & J. Valsiner (Eds.), *Beyond the mind* (pp. 421–452). Charlotte, NC: Information Age Publishers.

Valsiner, J. (Ed.). (2020). *Social philosophy of science for the social sciences.* New York: Springer. ISBN 978-3-030-33098-9.

Zittoun, T. (2016). Studying higher psychological functions: The example of imagination. In J. Valsiner, G. Marsico, N. Chaudhary, T. Sato, & V. Dazzani (Eds.), *Psychology as the science of human being: The Yokohama manifesto* (pp. 129–147). Cham: Springer.

Qualitative Methodology

19

Günter Mey

Contents

With the assistance of Paul Sebastian Ruppel

G. Mey (✉)
University of Applied Sciences Magdeburg-Stendal, Stendal, Germany
e-mail: guenter.mey@h2.de

© Springer Nature Switzerland AG 2023   453
J. Zumbach et al. (eds.), *International Handbook of Psychology Learning and Teaching*,
Springer International Handbooks of Education,
https://doi.org/10.1007/978-3-030-28745-0_22

Abstract

In this chapter, methods for qualitative data production and analysis relevant for psychological research are presented with respect to their importance for teaching and learning qualitative methodology in psychology. Beginning with a brief overview of epistemological and methodological foundations, the special features of qualitative research with regard to the question of design and case selection are highlighted. Since qualitative research follows different logical assumptions compared to quantitative research and works with smaller numbers of cases, it requires an appropriate overall framing of the respective research project. The use of software programs to support qualitative data analysis and the potential of working in research groups is discussed in this chapter. Lastly, questions are addressed about the presentation of qualitative research results as well as the consideration of quality criteria and research ethics.

Keywords

Qualitative research · Subjectivity · Interview · Arts-based research · Grounded theory

Introduction

Consider this rephrasing of a well-known sentence: Qualitative research in psychology has a long history, but no tradition. There exist two narratives: one emphasizes, because of "paradigm wars" and heated controversies, that qualitative approaches were marginalized in psychology for a long time, although qualitative methods had shaped the beginning of research in several sub-disciplines at one time. The other narrative points out that there are a growing interest in qualitative methodology in psychology and – stressed by Smith, Harré, and Van Langenhove (1995a, 1995b) – a need for "rethinking psychology" and "rethinking of methods in psychology" which includes its own history and seeks an exchange with other disciplines that have a lively practice in qualitative research, especially social sciences and anthropology (Schjødt Terkildsen & Demuth, 2015).

Many general handbooks in qualitative research have existed over time. One of the most prominent is edited by Norman Denzin and Yvonna Lincoln, first published in 1994, now in its fifth edition (Denzin & Lincoln, 2018). There are also handbooks on special approaches (e.g., grounded theory; Bryant & Charmaz, 2019) and methods (e.g., interviewing; Gubrium, Holstein, Marvasti, & McKinney, 2012). Many journals are published, dedicated explicitly to qualitative research. A prominent one is, e.g., the multi-lingual (English, Spanish, German) open-access journal *FQS* (Forum Qualitative Sozialforschung / Forum: Qualitative Social Research, www.qualitative-research.net) with more than 2000 peer-reviewed articles. In the last two decades, the number of special handbooks on qualitative research in the field of psychology has been growing in different countries: written in Danish, German, Italian, or Spanish and in English as the international scientific language (e.g., the revised version of Willig & Stainton-Rogers, 2017). The same development can be found with regard to disciplinary journals like *Qualitative Research in Psychology* (founded in 2004) or *Qualitative Psychology* (2019) and, lastly, the founding of specific divisions in psychological organizations, e.g., the APA division subgroup "Society for Qualitative Inquiry in Psychology" or the "Association of European Qualitative Researchers in Psychology" (EQuiP) (https://www.equipsy.org/).

In sum, today – compared to the situation two decades ago – a wide range of possible applications is conceivable doing psychological research with the aim of data-based theorizing on relevant questions in all fields of psychology. The status quo expresses the progress of qualitative research in psychology and emphasizes the need to place the diversity of qualitative research and the particular logic of qualitative methodology as an integral part of the teaching programs in psychological education.

Without any doubt, qualitative research is not limited to but necessarily indicated when it is not possible to answer a research question on the basis of existing theories by means of hypothesis generation and testing. But even in proven fields, new phenomena emerge all the time, especially through processes of social change for which no or only inadequate explanations are yet available. When existing theories can no longer claim validity, further or new developments become necessary. Furthermore, a qualitative approach is always suitable if the planned analysis presupposes the preservation of the complexity of the research objects to be investigated or if reference to individual cases is in the foreground. Lastly, some practical concerns could be mentioned: qualitative research is indicated if access via standardized research is not possible or if research situations are to be set up as non-artificially as possible in order to maintain the reference to everyday life.

In the following presentation, attention is paid to general topics of qualitative research in order to understand the very special logic of the approach (section "Theoretical-Methodological Foundations of Qualitative Research"). Then follows an overview of different designs (section "Planning and Design of Qualitative Studies"), data production (section "Data Production"), and data analysis (section "Qualitative Analysis"). Included are also remarks regarding organizing the research process (sections "Fixing the Data" and "Organization of the Work Process"), added by an outline to questions of quality criteria (section "Quality Criteria of Qualitative Research") and ethics (section "Research Ethics") and, lastly, some suggestions with regard to learning and teaching qualitative research methods (section "Teaching and Learning Qualitative Research").

Theoretical-Methodological Foundations of Qualitative Research

Theoretical Reference Points

It is a truism that qualitative research is an umbrella term for a wide variety of methods and approaches dedicated to a meaningful approach to everyday contexts. Important theoretical points of reference include hermeneutics, phenomenology, and American pragmatism – paradigms that were made theoretically and methodologically fruitful especially in symbolic interactionism and in ethnomethodology. Of particular importance for psychology are psychoanalysis as well as social constructionism, the theory of social representations, critical psychology, and especially research in cultural psychology.

These theoretical references point out that psychological, social, and cultural realities are the result of social processes of construction and negotiation. In this respect, qualitative research in psychology is dedicated to the subjective views and patterns of interpretation of the actors as well as their communication and interaction in their everyday world contexts. But latent structures of meaning can also be taken into account.

Paradigmatic Commonalities in Qualitative Research

The diversity of theoretical frameworks and the plurality in methods suggest that there are some characteristics ("essentials of qualitative research") which are generally significant insofar as they open up a special sensitivity for the communicative, interactive, and social moment for doing psychological research. These essentials are openness, contextuality (principle of communication), and reflexivity (cf. Flick, Kardorff, & Steinke, 2004, pp. 7–8; Mey, 2010).

The principle of openness refers to a basic attitude toward the researched and at the same time refers to the design of the entire research process. In particular, it demands that contextual assumptions or hypotheses are not specified or formed in advance, but ideally only in the course of the research process. This is to ensure that the structuring of the investigated subject field that was done by the researchers can flow into the theory development. In the meantime, however, researchers are granted a more theory-guided approach, whereby openness as "disclosure" of prior knowledge is to be consistently implemented.

Principle of communication/contextuality: Since research is understood as an interaction between all participants (researchers and researched), the data generated in the research situation are considered to be co-produced. This co-construction can be used to explore social processes and interactions and involve the researcher in the analysis. In addition, during data analysis, there is sometimes an intense communicative exchange between researchers that generates further data. Attention to these – often unconsidered – communicative group phenomena holds further potential for psychological approaches to shed light on the production process of qualitative research.

Reflectivity: In view of the principles mentioned above, researchers are encouraged to reflect on their working methods. After all, they structure the research situations with their interests and their approach (e.g., research question, choice of data collection and evaluation strategies, spatio-temporal arrangements). The researchers – as perceptible subjects/actors – themselves are the ones who interact and provoke reactions in the field. The ethnopsychoanalyst Georges Devereux (1967) speaks here of the "stimulus value" that persons have for other persons; of course, this stimulus value is not a fixed influencing variable, but varies depending on the person and the situation. Against this background, the overall demand for a reflected subjectivity is to be understood. However, the fact that contextual factors, differences in perception, and the subjectivity of the researcher are not regarded as confounding variables, but are essential and should be used for analysis, is pointedly advocated within the framework of qualitative programmatic research. An enormous amount in qualitative research practice is needed to take into account the joint construction process and the researcher's own involvement (his/her subjectivity) in the research (see Mruck & Mey, 2019).

Planning and Design of Qualitative Studies

The planning of qualitative studies is of great importance, since they often work with a small number of cases compared to quantitative studies. Even if single case studies are a rarity, studies with a case number of a few dozen participants occur frequently. In view of the relatively high effort involved, case numbers are often in the single digits in the context of students' qualification theses (BA/MA theses). In order to be able to generalize, however, special attention must be paid to sampling, so the procedure of purposive sampling has become widely established in the discipline.

Sampling

Theoretical sampling, which originates from grounded theory methodology (Glaser & Strauss, 1967), is a prominent strategy to sampling and a special case of purposive sampling. This is a so-called iterative procedure, in which data collection and analysis constantly alternate. The selection of the next data in each case does not take place as a theory-driven and pre-defined top-down strategy, but as a data-driven bottom-up process in which the specific criteria for the ongoing case selection are successively specified with regard to the theory to be developed on the basis of the analysis of the data material collected up to the respective point in time. Based on a selection of minimum and maximum comparisons, the best possible condensation or variation for the subject area of interest is to be sounded out step by step. It is important here, first, to make explicit the criteria for selecting the next case and not to form the next sample beforehand and, second, to counter the danger of seeking only confirming cases by deliberately including (potentially) divergent cases. Completion of this iteration of data collection and analysis occurs when further data are no longer expected to yield significant insight. In the language of grounded theory methodology, this is referred to as theoretical saturation.

Triangulation and Mixed Methods

Study design also includes the question of the extent to which it is based on one or more methodological approaches and how these can be justifiably related to each other. This combination of methodological approaches is called triangulation. Introduced by Denzin (1989) as a way of mutually examining different results, triangulation is now considered a way of obtaining findings from multiple perspectives, relating them to one another, and differentiating them. A distinction is made here between data triangulation, researcher triangulation, theory triangulation, and method triangulation (Flick, 2018).

Data triangulation describes the use of data from different times, places, persons, or sources to create a basis for comparison. Researcher triangulation refers to the fact that the collection and analysis is carried out by more than one person. In the case of theory triangulation, the analysis is carried out using different theories or approaches. For method or methodological triangulation, different procedural elements are used, whereby a distinction is made here between within-method (combination of similar methods) and between-method (use of divergent methods). In the latter case, qualitative and quantitative methods are often used together.

For the combination of qualitative and quantitative methods, the term "mixed methods" has become generally accepted, and one already speaks of the third research paradigm beside the quantitative and the qualitative. Depending on the research question, the appropriate combination models are selected (Todd, Nerlich, McKeown, & Clarke, 2004).

Secondary Analysis

Secondary analysis is relatively new on the research agenda of qualitative methodology. Here, existing data (so-called primary data) are subjected to repeated analysis. Secondary analysis, however, requires that data be made available for further use, especially through data archives. In addition to the data set, so-called metadata (information on the research context and collection situation) are also required for the analysis (Corti, Witzel, & Bishop, 2005).

Following Heaton (2004), a distinction is made between different forms of analysis: Data analysis takes place under a new research perspective (supra analysis), along questions that have only become relevant in the follow-up (supplementary analysis), and re-analysis with the same research question, which has the primary goal of developing alternative perspectives on the material (re-analysis). Secondary analyses can be performed on a single data set or on data sets from different studies (amplified analysis). In addition, they can be combined with the collection of new data (assorted analysis).

Participatory Approaches

Participation – the extent to which respondents can become an active part of the study as co-researchers – is also a planning issue (Bergold & Thomas, 2012). Although qualitative research is characterized by a "subject" understanding that sees the researched as self-reflective and interested in their everyday world and actions, it is often "traditionally" conceived in its design, that is, with a strict separation between researchers and researched. Participatory research, on the other hand, which is based on Kurt Lewin's action research (Lewin, 1946), questions this separation and tries to dissolve it, so that participation comes into play to different degrees: for example, the research question can be negotiated between the researcher and the researched. Participation can also be extended to the cooperative design of the entire research process, the course and (interim) results of which are jointly structured and presented by all participants.

Data Production

In the practice of psychological research, interviews as well as group discussions and observation methods were often used. Because there exists a variety of qualitative methods which developed in the interdisciplinary field of social research, there is also a plethora of other methods that have become established for addressing diverse research questions, and those will now be presented.

In general, the choice of the methods should not be made hastily and detached from the consideration of the research project as a whole, for which it is inevitably momentous. In this respect, the theoretical background and the specific understanding of the subject matter must be made clear. In addition, the relationship between the data to be generated and the analysis methods must be coordinated. In this context, the existing range of methods should not be misunderstood as a toolbox that can always be used with precision. The primacy of the phenomena under inquiry (and appropriateness of the method to the object) applies, and thus also the credo that the application of methods can or must also always be the development of methods. Qualitative researchers are therefore required to carry out methodological modifications and innovations in the examination of the research object, if necessary, and to present these in a comprehensible way.

Interviews

Variants of Qualitative Interviews

In interdisciplinary qualitative research as a whole, interviews are the most common method of data collection in psychology. This is hardly surprising if one takes a look at psychological topics such as opinions, attitudes, interpretations of self and others, and everyday theories. Interviews make it possible to record narratives, descriptions, explanations, argumentations, justifications, convictions, and statements of facts or hypothetical assumptions.

The abundance of available interviews can be distinguished according to:

- What extent they are structured – from open to semi-structured to structured – and thus determine the interviewers' scope for design and frame the interviewees' response options
- Which form of presentation they aim at in particular: for example, narratives, statements of facts/reports, and opinions
- Whether they are more dialogical-discursive or receptive (i.e., either they are closer to an everyday conversation and the interviewers intervene in a formative way or they act in a very restrained way)

The focused interview (Merton & Kendall, 1946) is considered the "original version" of all qualitative interviews, since it was here that the questioning technique was first systematized. As an introduction, it was suggested to present stimulus material (mostly films or newspaper commentaries, but also other texts, images, and/or sound materials) in order to then explore the subject area in detail. The interview questions should consider the following levels:

- Specificity, to go beyond the level of generalized statements
- Coverage of relevant aspects/themes "given" by the interviewers and "brought in" by the interviewees
- Affective, cognitive, and evaluative deepening in order to go beyond "abbreviated" naming
- Exploration of the biographical background as a prerequisite for appropriate interpretation

As an example of many existing interview forms (cf. Kvale & Brinkman, 2008) for the design of conversations, the problem-centered interview (Witzel & Reiter, 2012) will be presented here from the abundance of suggested procedures. Distinguished are:

- An open-ended introductory question, which does not necessarily have to be narrative in nature: a relevant social problem identified by the researcher forms the starting point. This problem-centeredness gives the method its name.
- Material-generating inquiries, for example, "How was that exactly?".
- Comprehension-generating follow-up questions. These include (with reference to Rogerian person-centered psychotherapy) reflection back for communicative validation, comprehension questions to clarify possible contradictions, and confrontation to further promote detail.
- In addition, ad hoc questions are provided, which can be taken from a flexibly applicable interview schedule.
- In addition, a short questionnaire can be used to outsource the collection of supplementary or socio-demographic data from the interview.

Each interview procedure is based on basic theoretical positions, e.g., psychoanalytically inspired (Kvale, 2003) or aligned to narrative theories (Wengraf, 2001), furthermore adapted for specific groups (e.g., children) or to address specific professions, like elite interviewing (Dexter, 2006).

Interview Schedules

In many interviews, and partly also in group discussions, schedules are used. They have to be developed anew in each case with regard to the research question, since it is usually not possible to fall back on existing schedules for similar research contexts – differently, for example, from the case of "the adult attachment interview" (George, Kaplan, & Main, 1996) in the context of research on attachment theory.

The quality of an interview depends primarily on how it is conducted and not on the design of the underlying guide. However, the interview schedule is a crucial link between research question, data collection, and analysis, because its construction presupposes the mental anticipation of the interview and offers the possibility to plan in advance desired framings, thematic emphases, or even forms of answers. Such framing, however, can easily be at the expense of the subjective relevance and orientation of the interviewees. This quickly violates the principle of openness, which should be avoided, if possible.

In general, an interview schedule should be clearly sorted and subdivided into topic blocks. Interview schedules should not be misunderstood as a corset-like set of questions that simply have to be "worked through." Rather, schedules serve as an orientation for conducting the interview. They also offer help in the run-up to the interview in order to organize one's own knowledge as well as to disclose pre-assumptions and discuss them in the research group (cf. Witzel & Reiter, 2012).

Lastly, it should be noted that completed guide development work does not have to mean that no modifications will be made from this point forward. If necessary, the guide can be adapted for further interviews, depending, for example, on the person to be interviewed, anticipated circumstances of the implementation, or the stage of the research process. Further adjustments can also be made on an ad hoc basis as needed during implementation.

Group Discussion

In psychology, group discussions – often titled "focus groups" (Krueger & Casey, 2000) – are an important method for recording group processes. Group discussions aim at the exchange about or the discussion of a given topic. The discussions are usually opened with a "basic stimulus" or "narrative stimulus." This can be a given topic, an open question, a provocative statement, or a given material, such as a film or a newspaper report. Ideally, the discussion then becomes "self-propelling," i.e., a discussion among the participants that does not need to be initiated again by the leaders. The groups can be heterogeneous or homogeneous in terms of age, status, gender, social orientations/practices, or horizons of experience. They can also exist in reality or be "artificially" arranged with regard to the research question (e.g., teachers from different schools). Accordingly, they are characterized by a different degree of cohesion, which, for example, may be more pronounced in families or long-standing "cliques" than in ad hoc groups. One of the special features of group discussions is that the addressee is always the group. In practice, the method of group discussion is often seen as equivalent to group interviews as a quick way to get much information from different people.

Observation and Ethnography

The method of observation is also frequently used in psychological research. Along with interviews, it is one of the methods employed and elaborated upon as a matter of course. In psychology, there are many classic studies that used observation to capture "live" social behavior.

Observation can be used in a wide variety of ways: in natural or artificial settings, participatory or non-participatory, overt or covert, unmediated or mediated, unstructured or structured, and as third-party or even self-observation. Within qualitative research, participant observation is a particularly fruitful approach. Somewhat more broadly, it is also referred to as ethnographic research. An example of this is the study "Street Corner Society" (Whyte, 1943), which is pioneering in terms of social psychology and qualitative methodology due to its focus on group processes and in-group-out-group phenomena. This research on the "Social Structure of an Italian Slum" examined how immigrant youths organize themselves and establish their social identity in a culture that is new to them.

Ethnography or participant observation aims at a comprehensive data collection that combines "pure" observation data with insights from conversations, being there and one's own experience. Likewise, documents found in the field enter into the analysis (see section "Documents and Artifacts").

Insights are also opened up by attempting to record how the field responds to the researchers, i.e., how it gives them access, excludes them, or interacts with them. This recording is referred to as ethnographic protocols. The principles of communication and strangeness come into particular play here and require a high degree of reflection on the research action, the researcher him−/herself, and the roles he/she has assumed or ascribed in the field. In the course of participant observation, the question of proximity-distance is problematized. A prominent term here is "going native" which refers to a phenomenon that sometimes occurs during longer field stays. The researchers then increasingly lose the outside perspective, adopt the ways of seeing and acting of the people in the field, and become group members. Similarly, there is debate about the extent to which observation protocols reveal more about the researchers' construction efforts than about the actions of those observed in the field.

The data generated during observation or ethnographic work can be recorded in different structured ways. Besides various forms of writing observation protocols, sheets, and schemes during or shortly after a field or observation phase, a research diary is recommended especially in the context of ethnographic studies. It can be used to reflect on one's own role, document the research process, and shed light on challenges such as the field's reactivity. Quite a few field researchers have pointed out that the duration of the protocol preparation exceeds the observation time many times over. Moreover, observational or ethnographic studies, especially when conducted covertly or partially covertly, face particular ethical issues for which situational and general answers must be found.

Documents and Artifacts

Qualitative research increasingly uses "found" documents and materials to address its research questions. This approach is sometimes referred to as a separate approach when talking about documents, artifacts, or visuals. Sometimes these are then classified as forms of data collection and elsewhere as analysis procedures.

The more general term "document analysis" is used when existing documents are used that were not specifically created with the research question in mind (Bowen, 2009). These can be, for example, expert reports; files; annual, case, or other reports with which institutional processes are reconstructed; or personal notes, diaries, and correspondence with which forms of sociality and biographical aspects can be worked out. Finally, newspaper articles or political speeches are also used to address socio-psychological questions, for example, to study discourses on social movements.

Artifact analysis (Froschauer & Lueger, 2020) is used when dealing with "objects" of material culture: objects (e.g., packaging), photographs (e.g., family pictures), written documents (e.g., fanzines), or traces in public spaces (e.g., graffiti).

In document analysis as well as artifact analysis, it is important not to interpret the objects of investigation exclusively as references to something "behind" them, but to consider the constructional character and thus the (e.g., usual, anticipated, intended) context of production as well as reception. Accordingly, the questions pertain to how the document/artifact is constituted, what functions it has in the original or newly placed context, and what meanings it has.

Videography and Visual Data

Video-based recording is increasingly used both in the course of field work and in observational studies. This is referred to more broadly as videography or video ethnography (Pink, 2021). These films, produced by researchers, differ from video analyses which focus on videos that are not produced by researchers, but sometimes by the researched, such as films of festivals or events or such videos that are uploaded to internet platforms. Because of the easy accessibility to video technology, everyday situations are now recorded with great ease. The advantages of video recordings lie primarily in repeatability; sequences can also be played back separately, for example, for single-frame analysis of interactions. However, the limitations associated with the use of video should not be underestimated. These are, in particular, the limited angle of view, which can lead to the misrecognition of situation logics as "tunnel vision," as well as the lack of bodily experienced perception. Videos, therefore, do not per se guarantee more comprehensive or detailed data than, for example, ethnographic protocols, and the choice of the use of videography can thus only be determined along the lines of the research interest.

Netnography and Online Research

When researching media worlds, it becomes particularly clear how social science objects and methodological-technical approaches are mutually dependent. With the growth of net communication and virtual communities, new research questions can be applied to psychological issues. The term netnography (Kozinets, 2015) was specifically coined for methodologically innovative approaches and for forms of "being on the net" by researchers.

The expansion of new media also makes them interesting for the implementation of research (Mann & Stewart, 2000). On the one hand, the new media are the "object" of investigation; on the other hand, they also provide the equipment: while interviews by telephone have long been taken for granted, synchronously – through the Covid-19 pandemic – designed e-interviews and group discussions in virtual spaces are now becoming established. For qualitative research, which has to reflect the contexts of data production in particular, this poses completely different challenges due to the very different modes of communication.

Qualitative Experiments

The experiment as a central method for psychological questions has also a special relevance for psychology. The classics – the Milgram experiment and the Stanford Prison experiment – have attracted attention beyond the boundaries of the discipline. In this context, the work on leadership styles that goes back to Lewin or Sherif's field experiments on group conflict is also significant, as are experiments in the case of ideographic research related to "Ganzheitspsychologie" (holistic psychology) (Diriwächter, 2009).

In contrast to the quantitative experiment, the qualitative experiment focuses neither on hypothesis testing nor on the establishment of rigid experimental conditions. Rather, it is characterized by a search movement that influences during the execution, that is modifiable and discovering, and that seeks great proximity to everyday life. In the context of qualitative experiments, the "interventions" can be physical-material modifications, as well as be carried out in the form of thought experiments.

Introspection, Autoethnography, and Arts-Based Research

Approaches in which researchers make themselves the subject of inquiry sharpen a salient moment of qualitative research: the involvement of researchers. Their perspective connects with introspection which was part of the common methodo-logical repertoire in the early stages of psychology's history (Valsiner, 2017). The scientific approach to introspection is to recollect experiences and events. The process of doing introspection varies. It could, for example, take place in a research group: at first, members write down their memories individually and in as much detail as possible, present their notes to each other, and finally expand and clarify again in writing what they have presented.

A second approach that works with self-reports is autoethnography (Ellis, 2004), which contains moments of autobiography and ethnography. As in a written self-interview, researchers detail their own experiences and ways of processing the field of study. However, description alone is not the goal of autoethnography. Rather, it is about broadening the perspective beyond the purely personal level to generalizable sociocultural processes.

Introspection and autoethnography could be combined (Mey, 2018), and from autoethnography, it is a short step to approaches labeled as arts-based research which uses artistic methods – coming from theatre, the arts like painting or documentary film, etc. – to explore the phenomena under research (Leavy, 2015).

Fixing the Data

In order for qualitative data to be used for later analysis, it must be fixed. This can be done through texts as results from introspection/autoethnography or through protocols from observations/ethnography. Because of the prominence of verbal accounts, transcripts are usually prepared based on the audio- or video-recorded interviews, group discussions, field conversations, etc.

Transcription is not to be misunderstood as a simple transformation from spoken language to written text. It is a sophisticated process of "transcription as theory" (Ochs, 1979). Beside theoretical discussions (Davidson, 2009), quite a few suggestions for transcription are available (cf. Kowal & O'Connell, 2004). They range from "standard orthography" (transcription according to the norms of written language) to "literary transcription" to "phonetic transcription," according to a catalog of specifications.

The decision about the adequate transcription should be made on the basis of the research question and the planned evaluation steps: a "simple" transcription oriented to the written language is recommended if the level of analysis focuses in particular on what was said (manifest content). If, in addition, or primarily, it is of interest how something was said (e.g., communicative-interactional aspects) or why it was said (latent meaning), more complex transcriptions are appropriate.

In the course of transcription, further decisions have to be made, for example, whether to transcribe completely or in excerpts and how detailed to make the transcripts, i.e., whether to include not only what was said but also para-linguistic features such as laughter or prosodic ones such as pauses, stresses, or stretches. The duration of a transcription depends on the recording quality and the chosen transcript format. It varies from about 1:4 to 1:10, i.e., for 1 hour of audio-taped interview, 4 to 10 hours of transcription time should be estimated. For video-taped data, the time required – depending on the demands of the transformation of image and voice information – can often be incomparably longer. For the fixation, it is recommended to use software (see section "Category-Oriented Methods").

In addition to transcripts and other fixations, it has become standard practice to create a postscript after an interview or group discussion (Witzel & Reiter, 2012). Here, the framework data of the situation (place, time, duration), conspicuous features (e.g., disturbances), impressions of the course (e.g., atmosphere, interactions), and unrecorded moments (e.g., greeting, warming up, and follow-up discussion) are fixed.

Qualitative Analysis

In qualitative social research, there are several methods for data analysis. They are in a process of being continuously developed, also because non-textual data are increasingly used in qualitative research. Which analysis method is suitable depends on the objective of the study. In addition, it is crucial which data are available in which form, because they must fit the method and meet its requirements. Finally, it should be noted that some analysis methods are designed as stand-alone procedures, while others can be combined with others. The choice and use of analysis methods are of great importance in qualitative social research, since the analysis work is usually the most time-consuming step, in which interpretation methods and results are determined.

Category-Oriented Methods

With qualitative content analysis (QCA) and grounded theory methodology (GTM), two methods are mentioned here that have in common how the results are presented in the form of categories. However, they do this in different ways: while QCA applies categories to the data material on the basis of theoretical assumptions and the research question or develops the categories further in discussion with the data material, the analysis work within the framework of GTM begins without categories that have been deduced in advance, because these are only developed and related to each other during the data analysis in order to arrive at complex statements about the topic of investigation.

Qualitative Content Analysis

Qualitative content analysis is characterized by the fact that categories are developed in an interplay between theory, the research question, and the concrete material. Many different kinds of QCA have existed (Schreier, 2012; Schreier, Stamann, Janssen, Dahl, & Whittal, 2019), but as a common understanding, this is the distinction between inductive and deductive categorization. Inductive category development means the elaboration of categories from the data. A predefined process model includes the steps of paraphrasing, generalizing, and reducing. In this way, the data are condensed so that complex statements about the content of the data material become possible. The deductive category application is different, using a coding guide in which clear category descriptions, descriptive anchor examples, and concrete coding rules are listed. This procedure is intended to ensure that the data are processed systematically and as unambiguously as possible. This serves the formal, the content-related, the typifying, and the scaling structuring of the data. In scaling, for example, the data material is estimated on an ordinal scale level (such as "much – medium – little"). In this respect, the quantification of qualitative data is also often seen as an advantage of QCA, which can thus be classified in the border area between qualitative and quantitative research.

Grounded Theory Methodology

Grounded theory methodology is an approach that provides sophisticated methodological implementation suggestions for data collection and analysis. Originally developed by Glaser and Strauss (1967), the authors each later developed it independently. In addition, further variants have been proposed by Kathy Charmaz and Adele Clarke, among others, and increasingly linkages with other approaches are being implemented (e.g., with narrative analysis or with regard to approaches to the analysis of visual data; see for an overview Ruppel & Mey, 2017).

The goal in applying this methodology is to develop a grounded theory, i.e., a theory grounded in the data. Through intensive engagement with the data, categories are formed and organized into a relational structure until a theory framework emerges. The particular strengths of GTM are its transparently comprehensible methodological path of theory generation, its handling of sampling questions, and its iterative procedure that systematically combines data collection and analysis.

Following Strauss and Corbin (1990), to date one of the most prominent GTM books, the analysis process can be divided into three phases – open, axial, and selective coding. In the first phase, open coding, the data are examined in a small-scale manner. For this purpose, the texts are broken down into segments and interpreted in terms of their conceptual meaning, and codes are assigned. The second phase is axial coding. Here the so-called coding paradigm can be used to expand the categories and to highlight their relations. A distinction is made between context, causal conditions, intervening conditions, strategies, and consequences, which are ordered with regard to the phenomenon of the study. This procedure should help to structure the data and to establish category-oriented connections, since even a strongly inductive approach cannot hope to elaborate theoretical structures purely on the basis of data. In the last phase – selective coding – the relational connections that have remained vague are specified. Furthermore, the categories are further condensed, integrated into a category network by establishing a core category, and finally formulated as grounded theory.

Sequence Analytical Procedures

In addition to analysis procedures that present the data material in categories, there are a variety of methods that focus on the sequential structuring and temporal dimensions of social phenomena. Sequential analytical methods differ, for example, in how small-scale they make the analysis and which data they prefer. The objects of sequential analyses are often micro-aspects of social interaction. An example of this is the change of speakers in conversational sequences, which are studied conversationally or narratively. However, meso- or macro-level phenomena can also be subject to sequential analysis, such as socially, historically, or institutionally shaped ways of speaking about gender, nation, or culture, where discourse analysis is then applied.

Narrative Analysis

Narrative psychology is interested in how people give meaning and significance to events and experiences by presenting and transmitting them in the form of narratives (Sarbin, 1986). For narrative analysis (e.g., Andrews, Squire, & Tamboukou, 2013), it is crucial whether the data are considered in terms of their narrative aspects, that is, whether narrative dimensions are considered significant reference points of the data in the analysis. Thematic analysis sheds light on the "what" of the narrative or what is narrated, whereas structural analysis sheds light on the "how."

Narrative analysis procedures are particularly suitable for the reconstruction of self- and other-positioning, with which the narrators indicate how they want to be seen and which positions they assign to others. On the basis of biographical interviews, for example, narrative analyses also enable the reconstruction of (life) events with their interactional, social, cultural, and historical reference points. Going beyond the individual biography, they represent a fruitful field of social psychological research, for example, with questions about dialogic and group dynamics and structures. In order to fully exploit the analytical potential of the narrative-analytical approach, distinct language-related knowledge is required. Then complex narrative reconstructions of social phenomena can be developed with the help of this method (e.g., in the field of identity research, see Bamberg, Demuth, & Watzlawick, 2021).

Conversation and Discourse Analysis

Conversation analysis (CA) was developed by Harvey Sacks, among others, in the 1960s. With it, a methodology is available that enables the analysis of social interactions, so that the organization of interactive action sequences can be examined and practical design rules of communication can be worked out. Accordingly, the analyses can be localized on the micro level. In addition, there is a close empirical reference that decisively shapes the conduct of the analyses: CA prefers natural, i.e., audio/video data of everyday and institutional origin, e.g., private conversations, telephone calls, or doctor-patient interactions, which were not created for the purpose of research. In CA data analysis, the focus is on sequentiality such as looking closely at speaker changes or sequence of contributions, and analysis is conducted on a case-by-case basis as well as comparatively and across cases.

In psychology, conversation analysis is sometimes labeled discourse analysis (Potter & Wetherell, 1987). In sociology, especially in European research, however, the term discourse analysis is associated with approaches that take a power-critical approach to discursive phenomena, for example, that of Michel Foucault

(Bührmann et al., 2007). Those are not identical with CA. In this respect, it must always be taken into account not only that the concept of discourse is understood quite differently but also that different varieties of "discourse analyses" coexist. Particularly with regard to Foucault, one tends to speak of "analytical glasses" rather than of small-scale methodological steps of analysis that have to be "worked through." Analytical orientations in the context of discourse analyses often aim at questions about the production of power relations, about inclusion and exclusion phenomena, moments of production and representation of reality, and truth and subjectivity. In addition, contextual, historical, social, and institutional points of reference are considered relevant. In this context, the "texts," and meant here are any forms of data in which traits of the discourse phenomenon of interest can be shown (e.g., newspaper articles and political speeches), are examined for discursive structures and practices.

Further Procedures and Basic Considerations

Without presenting further methods individually here in detail, at least some of them should be pointed out. They illustrate the special challenges of qualitative analyses which also guide the methods mentioned so far.

In objective hermeneutics (Reichertz, 2004), the central principles are contextuality, literalness, sequentiality, extensivity, and parsimony. The principle of contextuality prohibits interpreting the text hastily on the basis of contextual knowledge. The principle of literalness refers to the requirement to interpret the text in its existing form and to consistently elaborate the latent structures of meaning beyond the manifest meaning or textual intention. The principle of sequentiality demands that the interpretation be based without exception on the sequences and structures given by the data. Thus, it is forbidden to pick out passages arbitrarily or to skip them during the interpretation. The principle of extensivity states that the interpretations must be logically exhaustive. Therefore, all textual statements must be considered in depth, and all conceivable readings must be formed that are necessary for understanding and reconstructing the latent meaning. Finally, the principle of parsimony states that in the elaboration of possible readings, no additional assumptions are used, but only those "forced" by the text. Thus, interpretation proceeds in a methodologically controlled ("objective") manner, since only readings that can be verified against the text are taken into account.

Depth hermeneutics or, more generally, psychoanalytically oriented social research (Salling Olesen, 2012) applies a detailed interpretation of what is said (and meant, the latent meaning), first on a case-by-case basis and later across cases, including the conversational dynamics in the interviews and group discussions. Within the framework of the interpretation – based on the two fundamental operations of psychoanalysis: transfer and countertransfer – various meaning development questions are asked in order to enable a logical (factual content), psychological (relational content), scenic (manner of representations), and in-depth hermeneutic (latent intentions and meanings) understanding. Here, the associations, emotions, identifications, and dynamics triggered in the evaluators are consciously used for interpretation.

Lastly, there exist many other approaches like metaphor analysis based on the linguist theory by Lakoff and Johnsen (2003), variants of interpretative phenomenological analysis approaches rooted in phenomenology or phenomenological psychology, and more and more specific approaches like video analysis (Knoblauch, Baer, Laurier, Petschke, & Schnettler, 2008).

Organization of the Work Process

Software for Computer-Assisted Analysis of Qualitative Data

Qualitative (or more generally: non-numerical) data in the form of text, images, or video are nowadays largely analyzed using specially developed software. This is called computer-assisted/computer-aided qualitative data analysis (CAQDAS). Numerous tools are available (e.g., ATLAS.ti, MAXQDA, and NVivo), which are mainly used for category-forming procedures, but also for sequence-analytical procedures. For various film or video analyses, for example, special software has been developed. In addition to paid tools, there is also freeware such as freeQDA. Researchers sometimes also realize their analysis with the help of Word or Excel. In the end, the complexity of the data analysis decides which programs should be used (a helpful orientation is given by Lewins & Silver, 2007).

CAQDAS is not an independent analysis technique but merely supports the evaluation. The programs are aids in the application of one of the many evaluation methods possible in qualitative research. Just as in the past paper-pencil analysis was used to mark passages of text and assign codes or categories to them, for example, these steps are now mostly done using digital input on a computer screen. The most important functions of the programs are data management (for compiling text passages for special coding, so-called retrievals), category management (for compiling categories and subcategories and attaching notes to categories), and memoing (for recording ideas about text passages, categories, and entire cases). Many programs are characterized by further features, for example, for searching text segments or for visualizations by graphical representations (qualitative modeling).

An advantage of CAQDAS is the possibility to process large amounts of data, to structure them clearly, and to include different types of data and their multimedia links. In addition, this can facilitate documentation and thus increase transparency. The fact that the software supports teamwork when processing data sets is also a major advantage.

Working in Research Teams

Today, data analysis via CAQDAS is often taken for granted. The situation is completely different when it comes to working in groups which is realized much less frequently. Yet collaboration in teams or working groups – in doing research, but also in the context of studying and learning qualitative methodology – can help to make research decisions more explicit and provide input, for example, on case selection and through alternative "readings" in data analysis (Strauss, 1987). Teams are also helpful in checking the plausibility of, for example, the presentation of results. Working in groups also fulfills crucial demands of the quality criteria of qualitative research, especially that of intersubjectivity (Mruck & Mey, 2019).

It seems particularly important that research groups work together in a binding and regular manner. They are more productive if they are heterogeneously composed with respect to the topic or the state of the work, i.e., if they deal with different questions and the respective work is at different stages of development. Meanwhile, such research groups can also work virtually – for example, by using chats, discussion forums, or online conference tools. However, the specifics of network communication should be reflected and the necessary adaptations implemented.

Presentations of Qualitative Research and Performative Approaches

The modes of presentation of qualitative and quantitative studies differ to some extent. The articles resulting from quantitative studies are relatively standardized in structure, always including, for example, the state of the research, the hypotheses, the research design, information on the survey, the analysis, presentation of results, and finally the discussion. Qualitative research, on the other hand, cannot always – although all the study elements exist – follow such a scheme, if only because of its iterative procedure and its goal of theory development in, for example, the context of GTM studies. There is always a big gap between research work and its publication.

All studies, regardless of which methods they use, have in common that they must present the research process transparently. Especially for qualitative research, it means to give a deep insight into the individual decisions and steps, so that readers can understand the research process. To this end, it is not enough to merely mention the methods used by name.

Against the background of postmodern considerations on the staging of reality and truth, as well as the increased attention paid to the reception of scientific presentations of results, it has recently been discussed within qualitative research to fundamentally redesign the presentations and to enable new forms of appropriation. Under the general term performative social science (Jones et al. 2008; Mey, 2023), work has begun to develop new forms of presentation. As arts-informed research, artistic elements such as painting, theater, film, or multimedia installations and exhibitions are used to make social science results and findings accessible in new ways and for new audiences.

Quality Criteria of Qualitative Research

The comments on the presentation of qualitative studies already address the question of validity. Special weight is given to the "method-appropriate quality criteria" of qualitative research which means that the quality criteria of standardized research – objectivity, reliability, and validity – are largely rejected as a standard of evaluation.

Occasionally, however, the transfer of classical criteria can be found with, for example, reliability estimates in QCA to determine intercoder reliability. Rarer are positions that fundamentally reject the application of criteria for determining quality to qualitative research. The debate essentially boils down to different proposals and attempts to further develop criteria that genuinely relate to challenges of producing and demonstrating quality in qualitative research. In view of the diversity of methods for data production and analysis, specific criteria catalogs are discussed, and each criterion is weighted differently with respect to the areas of application (e.g., basic, application, and evaluation research). Against this background, the overarching criteria of transparency, intersubjectivity, and scope seem particularly important (see also the section "Debate: Quality of Qualitative Research" in *FQS* (https://www.qualitative-research.net/index.php/fqs/sections/deb/quality)).

Transparency: Since qualitative research involves a multitude of research decisions and the application of methods always means method development, the entire research process must be adequately documented – from the research question to the justification of choice of method, its adaptation within the framework of the study, and the concrete implementation of the research work with information on the sample. It must also be possible to clearly understand how the data were analyzed and interpreted. This presentation is part of the paper and should therefore not be separated into appendices.

Intersubjectivity: The evaluation should be plausibly explicated and juxtaposed with alternative interpretations. Against this background, the relevance of working in research groups is emphasized which helps to establish consensual validation or intersubjectivity. This includes reflecting on one's own role and disclosing the possible reflection of one's own thinking. Member checking, a presentation and discussion of the results with the participants, is recommended for studies in which an ability to agree in principle on the part of the respondents/co-researchers can be assumed.

Scope: Due to the comparatively small number of cases, it should be stated which generalization is intended and possible. Instead of statistical representativeness criteria, the "theoretical relevance" or "theoretical representativeness" should be estimated, and the scope should be defined. Against this background, any comments on the practical relevance of the research work can also be appropriately classified.

Research Ethics

It goes without saying that research must meet ethical criteria. This has been discussed in detail within psychology, most recently on the occasion of the Milgram experiment. Qualitative research is not ethically permissible per se, but it also must take into account the legitimate interests of those being researched – precisely because of its closeness to everyday life. In principle, the requirement of informed consent applies, i.e., all research participants must be informed about the aims, purposes, and possible effects of the study. As a rule, an information sheet is prepared for this purpose, in which information about the study is provided. The protection of the individual, the safeguarding of his or her integrity, and the protection of his or her rights must be ensured at all stages of the research process. On the other hand, it should be avoided to trigger crises among the research participants, for example, by designing the research situation, by insensitive formulations of interview questions. Finally, all personal data must be treated confidentially, and publications must be designed in such a way that no conclusions can be drawn about the participants. This commitment on the part of the researchers goes far beyond anonymization. Changing or omitting personal details such as names, places, or institutions is sometimes not enough, because certain narrative sequences or specific modes of presentation could also make a person identifiable. Therefore, written agreements regulating the details must be drawn up with all research participants. In particular, these are voluntary participation, information about the aims of the study, storage of data, and information about the use and status of the research.

Regulations on research ethics and data protection are provided by the respective professional societies. At the same time, it is also true that qualitative research, due to its special logic, must formulate and adapt the recommendations with regard to its concerns and demands. Here, reference should be made, by way of example, to process ethics, which understands ethical decisions as process-related and questions the extent to which all concrete ethical challenges in terms of content can be anticipated (see also the section "Debate: Qualitative Research and Ethics" in *FQS* (https://www.qualitative-research.net/index.php/fqs/sections/deb/ethics)).

Teaching and Learning Qualitative Research

General Considerations

Against the background of the explanations on qualitative research, it becomes clear that three perspectives must be always virulent in teaching/training programs on qualitative research (see also the section "Debate: Teaching and Learning Qualitative Methods" in *FQS* (https://www.qualitative-research.net/index.php/fqs/sections/deb/teaching)):

– First, it is to give (for the teacher) and to learn (for the students) broad knowledge of research approaches/theories and thus knowledge also about their differences.
– Second, an understanding of research as a "social arrangement" and thus as a process of communication and interaction must be conveyed (learned): this includes a willingness and ability to be open to the researched persons, their stories, and their attitudes/(self-)interpretations/ways of constructing (according to the "principle of openness") and includes the ability for (self-)reflection and recognition of subjectivity (committed to the "principle of communication").
– Third, abilities to act appropriately in the research process are to be taught; corresponding qualifications are to be acquired by the students. But again, this includes the ability to put aside one's own prior knowledge, as well as to endure contradictions and ambiguities.

Learning/teaching of – and that means socialization into – qualitative research takes place (at best) over several semesters, in which, from the teachers' perspective, knowledge transfer, demonstration of technical procedures, and coaching of student research constantly merge.

The principle of teaching includes a rotation of the work phases of individual and small group work and discussion in the plenum. The alternation of mediation and accompaniment is paralleled by the practice of interpretation skills as well as the implementation of studies on pre-selected or freely selectable topics.

Regarding application orientation of qualitative research, the process of learning is linked from the very beginning through close interlocking with later (professional) practice – for example, through the discussion of suitable studies as well as research into the field.

Integrated Method Education

With this goal of teaching/learning in mind, the task is to develop curricula to give a complete understanding of qualitative methodology in regard to research planning (research question, sampling, design including mixed methods, access to the field, tip sheets, agreements) as well as methods of data production (interview, group discussion, observation, etc.), data preparation (transcription, protocols, postscript), and analysis procedures. Some of these issues could be given as a lecture, but selected aspects (development of interview schedules, mock interviews with video feedback, moderation techniques in group discussions, reading transcripts) are studied in depth as exercises in small groups.

After providing this general understanding of qualitative research, especially in order to make theoretical and methodological claims of qualitative research recognizable as equal access to social, psychological, and cultural realities, the following courses should be much more practice-oriented by involving the students in conducting their own empirical study which systematically addresses the aspects of the research process covered before. All steps are then worked out together in the research team. In practical terms, the individual work packages could be implemented in small groups to promote teamwork, but all results have to be discussed in plenary sessions. Although the project phases are circular, the first part of the module should focus on preparation (formulation of research questions and development of schedules, agreements, etc.), implementation of the study (field access/acquisition), and starting data production (interviews, observations, etc.). In the second part, supervision of the interviews, group discussion, and ethnography take place – for example, in regard to interviewing, question formulation, and specifically communicative/interactive skills.

Based on these skills – gaining first experiences through conducting a small study – the students are well prepared to start writing a qualitative-empirical bachelor or master thesis. Because of the specificity of qualitative research, it is advisable to organize for the students a moderated peer-to-peer setting, in which projects are presented and supervised on an ongoing basis. All research concerns are discussed, and in particular, data are interpreted collaboratively to emphasize diversity of perspective.

Additionally, a course or a unit called "Presentation of scientific results using the example of qualitative research" could be implemented. Beside traditional dissemination strategies (articles, posters), alternative forms, such as performative social science (film, theater, exhibition), should be discussed. This prepares for interdisciplinary work and sensitizes students to the particularities of presentation in general and in particular for addressing results to different recipients.

Conclusion

Qualitative research has a firm foothold in many disciplines, as is evidenced by numerous handbooks and textbooks. Although the first comprehensive accounts for psychology are also available, qualitative research is still less established here, which can be attributed to the quantitatively dominated psychological teaching and learning content at universities.

The acceptance of qualitative research within psychology is expressed primarily in the use of interviews and qualitative content analysis, as well as in research that follows the mixed-methods paradigm (cf. Demuth & Mey, 2015). Genuinely qualitative work still has a hard time within the discipline. The same is true for the implementation of newer developments such as autoethnographic and performative approaches.

In view of the manifold and elaborate offers of qualitative research methods and the connectivity to formative research traditions of the discipline, their careless non-use is tantamount to self-restriction which wastes the potentials of qualitative research especially for psychological investigations. For future work, it is to be hoped that the discipline will more decisively exploit the breadth of qualitative research at the same time as it also participates in further development of these valuable tools.

Acknowledgments Thank you for inviting me to contribute to this handbook and for the expertise of Giuseppina Marsico as editor. Special thanks go to Monika Reuter for her careful copy editing.

References

Andrews, M., Squire, C., & Tamboukou, M. (Eds.). (2013). *Doing narrative research*. Los Angeles, CA: Sage.

Bamberg, M., Demuth, M., & Watzlawick, M. (Eds.). (2021). *The Cambridge handbook of identity*. Cambridge University Press.

Bergold, J., & Thomas, S. (Eds.). (2012). Participatory qualitative research. *Forum Qualitative Sozialforschung/Forum: Qualitative Social Research, 13*(1). Retrieved August 4, 2021 http://www.qualitative-research.net/index.php/fqs/issue/view/39

Bowen, G. A. (2009). Document analysis as a qualitative research method. *Qualitative Research Journal, 9*(2), 27–40. https://doi.org/10.3316/QRJ0902027

Bryant, A., & Charmaz, K. (Eds.). (2019). *The Sage handbook of current developments in grounded theory*. London, UK: Sage.

Bührmann, A. D., Diaz-Bone, R., Gutiérrez Rodríguez, E., Schneider, W., Kendall, G., & Tirado, F. (2007). Editorial FQS 8(2): From Michel Foucault's theory of discourse to empirical discourse research. *Forum Qualitative Sozialforschung/Forum: Qualitative Social Research, 8*(2). https://doi.org/10.17169/fqs-8.2.233

Camic, P. M., Rhodes, J. E., & Yardley, L. (Eds.). (2003). *Qualitative research in psychology: Expanding perspectives in methodology and design*. Washington, DC: American Psychological Association.

Corti, L., Witzel, A., & Bishop. L. (Eds.). (2005). Secondary analysis of qualitative data. *Forum Qualitative Sozialforschung/Forum: Qualitative Social Research, 6*(1). Retrieved August 4, 2021, from https://www.qualitative-research.net/index.php/fqs/issue/view/13

Davidson, C. R. (2009). Transcription: Imperatives for qualitative research. *International Journal of Qualitative Methods, 8*(2), 1–52. Retrieved August 4, 2021, from https://journals.library.ualberta.ca/ijqm/index.php/IJQM/article/view/4205

Demuth, C., & Mey, G. (2015). Qualitative methodology in developmental psychology. In J. D. Wright (Editor-in-chief), *International encyclopedia of social and behavioral sciences* (2nd ed., Vol. 19, pp. 668–675). Oxford, UK: Elsevier.

Denzin, N. K. (1989). *The research act* (3rd ed.). Englewood Cliffs, NJ: Prentice Hall.

Denzin, N. K., & Lincoln, Y. S. (Eds.). (2018). *The Sage handbook of qualitative research* (5th ed.). Thousand Oaks, CA: Sage.

Devereux, G. (1967). *From anxiety to method in the behavioral sciences*. The Hague, Netherlands: Mouton & Co.

Dexter, L. A. (1970/2006). *Elite and specialized interviewing*. Essex, UK: ECPR Press.

Diriwächter, R. (2009). Idiographic microgenesis: Re-visiting the experimental tradition of Aktualgenese. In J. Valsiner, P. C. M. Molenaar, M. C. D. P. Lyra, & N. Chaudhary (Eds.), *Dynamic process methodology in the social and developmental sciences* (pp. 319–352). New York, NY: Springer.

Ellis, C. (2004). *The ethnographic I: A methodological novel about autoethnography*. Walnut Creek, CA: AltaMira Press.

Flick, U. (2018). *Doing triangulation and mixed methods*. London, UK: Sage.

Flick, U., Kardorff, E., & Steinke, I. (2004). What is qualitative research? An introduction in the field. In U. Flick, E. Kardorff, & I. Steinke (Eds.), *A companion to qualitative research* (pp. 3–11). London, UK: Sage.

Froschauer, U., & Lueger, M. (2020). Artefaktanalyse. In G. Mey & K. Mruck (Eds.), *Handbuch Qualitative Forschung in der Psychologie. Vol. 2.: Designs und Verfahren* (2nd ed., pp. 773–794). Wiesbaden, Germany: Springer.

George, C., Kaplan, N., & Main, M. (1996). *Adult attachment interview protocol* (3rd ed.). Berkeley, CA: University of California. Unpublished manuscript.

Glaser, B. G., & Strauss, A. L. (1967). *The discovery of grounded theory: Strategies for qualitative research*. New York, NY: Aldine de Gruyter.

Gubrium, J. F., Holstein, J. A., Marvasti, A. B., & McKinney, K. D. (Eds.). (2012). *Sage handbook of interview research. The complexity of the craft* (2nd ed.). London, UK: Sage.

Heaton, J. (2004). *Reworking qualitative data*. London, UK: Sage.

Jones, K., Gergen, M., Yallop, J. J. G., Lopez de Vallejo, I., Roberts, B., & Wright, P. (Eds.). (2008). Performative social science. *Forum Qualitative Sozialforschung/Forum: Qualitative Social Research, 9*(2). Retrieved June 18, 2022. http://www.qualitative-research.net/index.php/fqs/issue/view/10.

Kleining, G., & Witt, H. (2000). The qualitative heuristic approach: A methodology for discovery in psychology and the social sciences. Rediscovering the method of introspection as an example. *Forum Qualitative Sozialforschung/Forum: Qualitative Social Research, 1*(1), Art. 13. https://doi.org/10.17169/fqs-1.1.1123

Knoblauch, H., Baer, A., Laurier, E., Petschke, S., & Schnettler, B. (2008). Visual analysis. New developments in the interpretative analysis of video and photography. *Forum Qualitative Sozialforschung/Forum: Qualitative Social Research, 9*(3), Art. 14. https://doi.org/10.17169/fqs-9.3.1170

Kowal, S., & O'Connell, D. C. (2004). The transcription of conversations. In U. Flick, E. Kardorff, & I. Steinke (Eds.), *A companion to qualitative research* (pp. 248–252). London, UK: Sage.

Kozinets, R. V. (2015). *Netnography. Redefined* (2nd ed.). London, UK: Sage.

Krueger, R. A., & Casey, M. A. (2000). *Focus groups: A practical guide for applied research.* Thousand Oaks, CA: Sage.

Kvale, S. (2003). The psychoanalytical interview as inspiration for qualitative research. In P. Camic, J. Rhodes, & L. Yardley (Eds.), *Qualitative research in psychology: Expanding perspectives in methodology and design* (pp. 275–297). Washington, DC: American Psychological Association Press.

Kvale, S., & Brinkman, S. (2008). *InterViews: Learning the craft of qualitative research interviewing* (2nd ed.). Thousand Oaks, CA: Sage.

Lakoff, G., & Johnsen, M. (2003). *Metaphors we live by.* London, UK: The University of Chicago Press.

Leavy, P. (2015). *Method meets art* (2nd ed.). New York, NY: The Guilford Press.

Lewin, K. (1946). Action research and minority problems. *Journal of Social Issues, 2,* 34–46. https://doi.org/10.1111/j.1540-4560.1946.tb02295.x

Lewins, A., & Silver, C. (2007). *Using software in qualitative research: A step-by-step guide* (2nd ed.). London, UK: Sage.

Mann, C., & Stewart, F. (2000). *Internet communication and qualitative research: A handbook for researching online.* London, UK: Sage.

Merton, R. K., & Kendall, P. L. (1946). The focused interview. *American Journal of Sociology, 51,* 541–557.

Mey, G. (2010). Qualitative developmental psychology. In A. Toomela & J. Valsiner (Eds.), *Methodological thinking in psychology: 60 years gone astray?* (pp. 209–230). Charlotte, NC: Information Age Publishers.

Mey, G. (2018). Outer silence-inner dialogue. An essay on the performative dining experience "The Silence Meal" at Zagreus-Projekt, Berlin. *Human Arenas, 1*(2), 143–150. https://doi.org/10.1007/s42087-018-0017-7

Mey, G. (2023/in press). Performative social science. In E. Tseliou, C. Demuth, E. Georgaca, & B. Gough (Eds.), *Routledge international handbook of innovative qualitative psychological research.* London: Routledge.

Mruck, K., & Mey, G. (2019). Grounded theory and reflexivity in the process of qualitative research. In A. Bryant & K. Charmaz (Eds.), *The Sage handbook of current developments in grounded theory* (pp. 470–496). London, UK: Sage.

Ochs, E. (1979). Transcriptions as theory. In E. Ochs & B. Schieffelin (Eds.), *Developmental pragmatics* (pp. 43–72). New York, NY: Academic Press.

Pink, S. (2021). *Doing video ethnography* (4th ed.). London, UK: Sage.

Potter, J., & Wetherell, M. (1987). *Discourse and social psychology. Beyond attitudes and behaviour.* London, UK: Sage.

Reichertz, J. (2004). Objective hermeneutics and hermeneutic sociology of knowledge. In U. Flick, E. Kardorff, & I. Steinke (Eds.), *A companion to qualitative research* (pp. 296–302). London, UK: Sage.

Ruppel, P. S., & Mey, G. (2017). Grounded theory methodology. In R. Parrott (Ed.), *Encyclopedia of health and risk message design and processing* (Oxford research encyclopedia of communication, pp. 1–20). New York, NY: Oxford University Press. https://doi.org/10.1093/acrefore/9780190228613.013.522.

Salling Olesen, H. (Ed.) (2012). Cultural analysis and in-depth hermeneutics – Psycho-societal analysis of everyday life culture, interaction, and learning. *Forum Qualitative Sozialforschung/*

Forum: Qualitative Social Research, 13(3). Retrieved August 4, 2021, from http://www.qualitative-research.net/index.php/fqs/issue/view/41

Sarbin, T. R. (Ed.). (1986). *Narrative psychology: The storied nature of human conduct.* London, UK: Praeger Press.

Schjødt Terkildsen, T., & Demuth, C. (2015). The future of qualitative research in psychology. A discussion with Svend Brinkmann, Günter Mey, Luca Tateo and Anete Strand, moderated by Carolin Demuth. *Integrative Psychological & Behavioral Science, 49*(2), 131–161.

Schreier, M., Stamann, C., Janssen, M., Dahl, T., & Whittal, A. (2019). Qualitative content analysis: Conceptualizations and challenges in research practice – Introduction to the FQS special issue "Qualitative content analysis I". *Forum Qualitative Sozialforschung/Forum: Qualitative Social Research, 20*(3), Art. 38, https://doi.org/10.17169/fqs-20.3.3393.

Schreier, M. (2012). *Qualitative content analysis in practice.* London, UK: Sage.

Smith, J. A., Harré, R., & Van Langenhove, L. (Eds.). (1995a). *Rethinking psychology.* London, UK: Sage.

Smith, J. A., Harré, R., & Van Langenhove, L. (Eds.). (1995b). *Rethinking methods in psychology.* London, UK: Sage.

Strauss, A. L. (1987). *Qualitative analysis for social scientists.* Cambridge, UK: Cambridge University Press.

Strauss, A. L., & Corbin, J. M. (1990). *Basics of qualitative research: Grounded theory procedures and techniques.* Newbury Park, CA: Sage.

Todd, Z., Nerlich, B., McKeown, S., & Clarke, D. D. (Eds.). (2004). *Mixing methods in psychology: The integration of qualitative and quantitative methods in theory and practice.* Hove, UK: Psychology Press.

Valsiner, J. (2017). *From methodology to methods in human psychology.* New York, NY: Springer.

Wengraf, T. (2001). *Qualitative research interviewing: Biographic narrative and semi-structured method.* London, UK: Sage.

Whyte, W. F. (1943). *Street corner society. The social structure of an Italian slum.* Chicago, IL: University of Chicago Press.

Willig, C., & Stainton-Rogers, W. (Eds.). (2017). *The Sage handbook of qualitative research in psychology* (2nd ed.). London, UK: Sage.

Witzel, A., & Reiter, H. (2012). *The problem-centred interview.* London, UK: Sage.

Further Readings

FQS – Forum Qualitative Sozialforschung/Forum Qualitative Social Research. www.qualitative-research.net

Willig, C., & Stainton-Rogers, W. (Eds.). (2017). The sage handbook of qualitative research in psychology (2nd ed.). London, UK: Sage.

Psychological Assessment and Testing

20

Leslie A. Miller and Ruby A. Daniels

Contents

Abstract

The field of psychological assessment is a multibillion-dollar business and probably touches more people than any other field of psychology. Various professionals, across different settings, administer psychological assessments and use the results to make important decisions about others. From childhood through adulthood, millions of individuals take and use psychological assessments to

L. A. Miller (✉)
LanneM TM, LLC and Rollins College, Winter Park, FL, USA
e-mail: DrLeslieAMiller@outlook.com

R. A. Daniels
Texas A&M University - San Antonio, San Antonio, TX, USA
e-mail: RDaniels@tamusa.edu

© Springer Nature Switzerland AG 2023
J. Zumbach et al. (eds.), *International Handbook of Psychology Learning and Teaching*,
Springer International Handbooks of Education,
https://doi.org/10.1007/978-3-030-28745-0_23

479

make important decisions about themselves and others. Given the wide-reaching use and effects of psychological assessments, effectively designing and teaching of psychological assessment courses is essential. For significant and valuable learning to occur, courses must be designed using a systematic and integrated competency-based approach, with purposeful and aligned course goals, outcomes, and learning objectives. Courses must be designed in a way that has personal meaning to students and extends beyond the classroom experience into the workforce. In this chapter, we present a systematic and integrated competency-based approach (based on Fink's taxonomy of significant learning) for teaching courses related to psychological assessment. The approach helps those who design and teach psychological assessment sources achieve two major goals. The first goal is to provide students with learning opportunities to acquire the knowledge base needed to be informed consumers of psychological assessment. The second goal is to offer individuals who take workforce roles that involve identifying, administering, and/or interpreting psychological assessments with opportunities to acquire the knowledge base and professional skills needed to properly use psychological assessments to make good decisions.

Keywords

Psychological assessment · Psychological testing · Tests and measurements · Teaching · Instruction

Introduction

Psychological assessment, also commonly referred to as psychological testing, is a multibillion-dollar business and probably touches more people than any other field of psychology. Each year hundreds of test publishing companies proactively market their assessments, with media reports indicating sales growing from approximately $7 million in 1955 to as high as $700 million in more recent years (WGBH Educational Foundation, 2015). Annually, states spend approximately $1.8 billion a year on standardized tests in US schools (Statistic Brain Research Institute, 2017), with parents investing about $1.1 billion on test preparation and tutoring (IBISWorld, 2019) and students taking approximately 112 tests between pre-K and Grade 12 (Hart et al., 2015). Workplace assessment alone is a $500 million a year industry, with 82% of US organizations administering pre-employment assessments (Zielinski, 2018). Over 2 million students took the SAT alone in 2019 (College Board, 2019), with over 10,000 companies using the Myers-Briggs Type Indicator personality assessment and 35 million people taking the assessment each year (Bajic, 2015).

Professionals, across disciplines, financially and personally invest in psychological assessments because they rely on the results to make objective, high-stakes decisions. For example, in clinical and counseling settings, psychologists use assessment results to make diagnoses, develop treatment plans, and assess treatment outcomes – even determine a person's competency to stand trial for a crime. In organizational settings, human resource professionals use psychological assessment results to make hiring/promotion decisions, measure employee performance, evaluate training effectiveness, and assemble effective teams. In educational settings, school administrators and educators use psychological assessment results to evaluate the success of curriculum, measure teacher performance, make college admission decisions, guide curriculum planning, and assign student grades. Similarly, government agencies and professional organizations use psychological assessment results for certification and licensure. Even individuals, such as yourself, who take psychological assessments use the results to make personal decisions, such as where to apply to college or graduate school and what degree to seek.

Given the heavy reliance on psychological testing to make decisions, it is critical that those who both take psychological assessments and those who administer them are well-informed about foundational concepts related to psychological assessment. For example, they must know how to distinguish well-designed (or psychometrically sound) assessments from others and how such assessments should and should not be used. Without understanding such foundational concepts, psychological assessments can be misunderstood and improperly used. For example, individuals may incorrectly conclude that psychological assessments are useless or even harmful. Or they may conclude that psychological assessments are extremely precise measurement instruments – when, in fact, they are not.

Because these foundational concepts are not intuitive, effective teaching about psychological assessment is essential. When students are interested in pursuing professions that use and rely on psychological assessments to make critical decisions, they must be prepared to identify and administer such assessments appropriately and ethically. Even if they do not pursue such careers, students are still likely to be consumers of psychological assessments. While in school and after graduating, they will continue to take standardized and/or teacher-made assessments throughout their professional and personal lives. Many are likely to be recipients of assessments administered to them in the workplace (e.g., as part of a job selection process). As a result, having a foundational understanding of testing concepts helps students become informed consumers of psychological assessment.

Carefully designing psychological assessment courses is also vital. Simply identifying the foundational concepts that must be taught and then providing students with resources to learn about these topics is not enough. For high-quality learning to occur, courses must be purposely and carefully designed to reflect emerging, competency-based teaching and learning best practices (American Psychological Association [APA], 2020a) and to influence students' perceptions of the material (Black, Daughtrey, & Lewis, 2014). Research indicates student engagement and learning improve dramatically when a systematic and integrated, competency-based approach to course design is used (Fink, 2007).

To build a strong foundation for learning, effective psychological assessment courses are ones that are purposefully designed to integrate the learning objectives, activities, and assessments needed for students to develop the competencies expected in high-quality undergraduate and graduate programs. Students who can demonstrate desired competences are more likely to be successful upon graduation.

The course design process begins with a clear understanding of critical competencies and clearly identified learning objectives so students understand the purpose – or "why" – of a course. In turn, instructors should then develop engaging learning activities that inspire students to achieve the intended objectives. To maximize learning, the pedagogical process should be both clear and engaging. Students should be active participants in their learning so they are slowly guided to deeper and higher-order thinking with interesting activities that appeal to different learning styles. When designed appropriately, assessments not only determine whether students understand foundational concepts but also evaluate if students can apply the concepts in a meaningful way (Fink, 2007). While instructors may be tempted to design courses "on the fly," failure to integrate learning objectives, activities, and assessments into a holistic, integrated course design – focused on developing critical competencies – increases the likelihood that students will feel disengaged and/or confused in a psychological assessment course.

In this chapter, our goal is to provide evidence-based advice about how to design and teach courses related to psychological assessment that strive for two major goals: first, providing students with learning opportunities to acquire the knowledge base needed to be informed consumers of psychological assessment and, second, offering individuals who take workforce roles that involve identifying, administering, and/or interpreting psychological assessments with opportunities to acquire the knowledge base and professional skills needed to properly use psychological assessments to make good decisions.

Nature of the Field

So, what exactly is psychological assessment? It is a process professionals use to systematically gather information about individuals, using a combination of methods and instruments. The information gathered is then used to make important decisions across a variety of settings, including clinical/counseling, educational, and organizational settings (Miller & Lovler, 2020). Within different settings, the types of professionals who use psychological assessments are varied, with some of the most common being clinical psychologists, counselors, administrators, school psychologists, educators, industrial-organizational psychologists, and human resource professionals.

Professionals use a variety of methods and instruments during the psychological assessment process. For example, in clinical and counseling settings, clinical psychologists and mental health counselors often use clinical interviews/observations, standardized tests (e.g., personality assessments and neuropsychological tests), as well as behavioral checklists. These instruments help professionals understand the nature and impact of a client's problem, diagnose mental illness/disease, determine a client's readiness for treatment, evaluate whether an individual will benefit from treatment, and develop the most effective interventions. In organizational settings, industrial-organizational psychologists, human resource professionals, and managers often use structured interviews, personality inventories, as well as tests of cognitive ability, aptitude, knowledge, and integrity. They use these assessment results to not only make human resource decisions, such as who to hire and promote, but to guide decisions related to development planning, employee performance, and training effectiveness. Within educational settings, school administrators, college admission personnel, school psychologists, and teachers use norm-referenced, criterion-referenced, and self-made tests to make admission and placement decisions, assess program and student learning outcomes, compare student performance to other groups, and evaluate whether students have developed critical competencies (collections of knowledge, skills, and abilities).

Professional and Scientific Issues/Objectives

As is true in most disciplines, those working in the field of psychological assessment must understand the relevant professional and scientific issues. Some of today's most prominent issues in psychological assessments are (a) using assessments appropriately and ethically, (b) using psychological assessments with good psychometric properties, and (c) not making critical decisions based on the results of a single psychological assessment. These issues stem from continued misunderstanding and improper use of psychological testing resulting in two extreme misconceptions: (a) psychological assessments provide little value (and can even be harmful), and (b) psychological assessments are perfectly precise measurement instruments.

Using Assessments Appropriately and Ethically Using assessments appropriately and ethically is critical to avoiding assessment misuse. To alleviate the potential for assessment misuse, all individuals who use psychological assessments should ensure they understand and abide by the guidelines, principles, and standards that exist for psychological assessment (Miller & Lovler, 2020; Society for Personality Assessment, 2006). Misuse can have significant consequences, including the assessment user making poor or improper decisions based on the information obtained from an assessment. Further, misuse can reflect poorly on test users and professional organizations that develop, market, and provide services related to psychological assessment.

Misuse of a psychological assessment is often not intentional. Rather, misuse is often the result of inadequate technical knowledge and misguided information about proper testing procedures. To help those who use psychological assessments act appropriately and ethically, a variety of professional associations and societies publish technical/professional guidelines, principles, and standards for constructing, evaluating, administrating, scoring, and interpreting psychological assessments. Intended to guide the work of members and nonmembers who practice in the field of psychological assessment, some of the most referred to guidelines, principles, and standards are:

- American Psychological Association's (APA) Ethical Principles of Psychologists and Code of Conduct (APA, 2010)
- Code of Fair Testing Practices in Education (Joint Committee on Testing Practices, 2004)
- Standards for Educational and Psychological Testing (American Educational Research Association [AERA], APA, and National Council on Measurement in Education [NCME], 2014)
- Code of Ethical and Professional Standards in Human Resource Management (Society for Human Resource Management [SHRM], 2019)
- Uniform Guidelines on Employee Selection Procedures (1978)

A more comprehensive listing of professional guidelines, principles, and standards can be found at the Buros Center for Testing (2019).

Assessment misuse may also be the result of purchasing and using psychological assessments without meeting the minimum training, education, and experience qualifications (Miller & Lovler, 2020). While publishers are responsible for ensuring those who purchase their assessments are qualified to use them, individuals purchasing assessments also have a responsibility to ensure they meet the required test user qualifications (background, training, and/or certifications). Most test publishers market their psychological assessments as A-, B-, and C-level tests (e.g., see Pearson, 2019). While A-level assessments typically do not require any special qualifications, B- and C-level assessments have increasingly stringent training, education, and experience requirements.

Using Psychological Assessments with Good Psychometric Properties Individuals who use psychological assessments should also ensure they only use assessments with good psychometric properties (Ayearst & Bagby, 2010; Miller & Lovler, 2020). The psychometric properties of a psychological assessment are determined by gathering evidence of reliability and validity for intended use. Because important decisions are made using the results of psychological assessments, it is critical that assessments produce dependable or consistent information and that the inferences and decisions made from this information are well justified.

To determine whether psychological assessments produce dependable or consistent information, we gather evidence of reliability. No one psychological assessment can be 100% dependable or consistent due to the measurement error associated with evaluating psychological constructs. However, the objective is to use psychological assessments where error is minimized. The less error, the more dependable and consistent the information is resulting from a psychological assessment.

Just using a psychological assessment that produces dependable and consistent information is not enough. Individuals who use psychological assessments should also ensure the psychological assessments they use have evidence of validity for intended use. Historically, those involved in psychological assessment have viewed validity as a property of an assessment instrument itself. For example, if evidence was gathered that an instrument measured what it claimed to measure or predicted what it claimed to predict, the instrument was considered valid. However, today assessment experts argue that the concept of validity is best understood by accumulating evidence to justify the inferences and decisions made based on the results of a particular psychological assessment (AERA, APA, & NCME, 2014).

Not Making Critical Decisions Based on the Results of a Single Psychological Assessment Last, individuals who use psychological assessments should also ensure they do not make critical decisions based on the results of a single assessment (Miller & Lovler, 2020). As shared above, psychological assessments are not perfectly accurate measurement instruments. Their results contain error that may be caused by factors related to the assessment itself (systematic error) or factors stemming from how the assessment was administered or taken (unsystematic or random error). Using the results of multiple assessments provides not only a more comprehensive understanding of what is being measured but also enhances the accuracy of information being used to make important decisions. If multiple assessments reveal similar, converging information, then we can feel more confident in the information obtained to make more informed decisions.

Historical Context and Current Trends

The use of psychological assessments is thought to have begun over 4000 years ago during the Xia Dynasty in Ancient China. At this time, there is some, though not confirmed, evidence that the Chinese emperor implemented royal examinations to determine whether officials should remain in office. While a thorough discussion of the history of psychological assessment is beyond this chapter, Fig. 1 includes a timeline summarizing many of the significant events in history described by Miller and Lovler (2020), leading to today's worldwide use of psychological assessments.

During the late 1800s, the use of psychological assessments gained in popularity, primarily due to the realization that just as important as studying individual similarities was studying individual differences, which is what psychological assessments do. Then, in the 1900s, the use of psychological assessments began to flourish with the publication of multiple intelligence tests: the Binet-Simon Scale (Binet & Simon, 1905), the Stanford-Binet Intelligence Scale (Terman, 1916), and the Wechsler-Bellevue Intelligence Scale for Adults/the Wechsler Adult Intelligence Scale (Wechsler, 1939). Various personality tests, such as the US Army's Personal Data Sheet (Papurt, 1930), the Rorschach inkblot test (Exner, 1993), and the thematic apperception test (Murray, 1943), were also published. Efforts then began, in the mid-1940s, to design vocational tests such as the General Aptitude Test Battery (U.S. Department of Labor, 1970).

In the early 1950s, given the increasing numbers of psychological assessments being used and the significance of the decisions being made based on testing results, psychologists began focusing efforts on protecting test taker rights. In 1953 the APA established the Committee on Ethical Standards for Psychology. This committee then led a larger group of psychologists to publish the Ethical Standards of Psychologists, of which an updated version is still in use today.

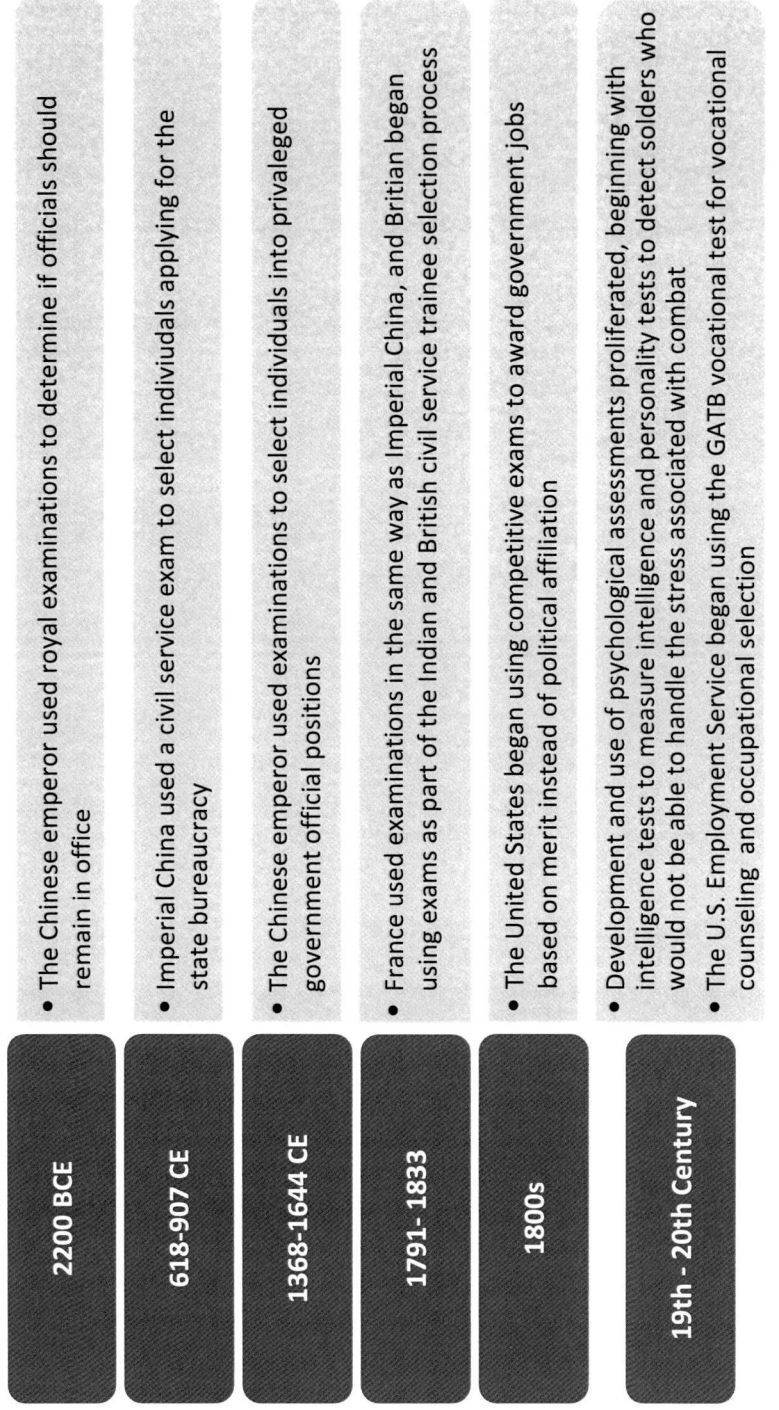

2200 BCE
- The Chinese emperor used royal examinations to determine if officials should remain in office

618-907 CE
- Imperial China used a civil service exam to select indiviudals applying for the state bureaucracy

1368-1644 CE
- The Chinese emperor used examinations to select individuals into privaleged government official positions

1791-1833
- France used examinations in the same way as Imperial China, and Britian began using exams as part of the Indian and British civil service trainee selection process

1800s
- The United States began using competitive exams to award government jobs based on merit instead of political affiliation

19th - 20th Century
- Development and use of psychological assessments proliferated, beginning with intelligence tests to measure intelligence and personality tests to detect solders who would not be able to handle the stress associated with combat
- The U.S. Employment Service began using the GATB vocational test for vocational counseling and occupational selection

Fig. 1 Timeline of historical events related to the use of psychological assessment

Purposes and Rationale of the Curriculum in Psychological Assessment

Various undergraduate and graduate programs offer core and/or elective courses to educate students about psychological assessment. The content included in these courses varies significantly depending on the level of the degree (associate, bachelor's, master's, or doctorate), the course level (introductory or advanced), and the degree program (e.g., BS in Psychology or Organizational Behavior, MA in Counseling, PhD in Clinical Psychology). Lower-level associate and bachelor's degree courses typically focus on enhancing student understanding of foundational concepts related to psychological assessments. These courses usually provide students with the information needed to be well-informed consumers, versus users, of psychological assessments. For example, an introductory-level course may focus on enhancing student understanding of what psychological assessments are, who uses them and for what reason, how to tell if an assessment is a quality one, and the ethical issues associated with psychological assessment.

In contrast, more advanced or graduate-level courses may focus on enhancing student understanding of specific types of psychological assessments and how to appropriately use them within the profession of a specific graduate program. For instance, psychological assessment courses in graduate clinical psychology programs are likely to focus on improving student understanding of how to administer and interpret the results of specific assessments clinical psychologists use to aid in diagnosing client problems, monitoring treatment progress, and assessing treatment outcomes. Examples include clinical interviews, behavior rating scales, and clinically oriented self-report tests, such as the Minnesota Multiphasic Personality Inventory (MMPI) or the Personality Assessment Inventory (PAI) (Miller & Lovler, 2020). Similarly, a psychological assessment course in a graduate industrial-organizational program is likely to focus on improving student understanding of the specific assessments used for employee selection and development. Examples include cognitive ability tests, job knowledge tests, personality tests, integrity tests, situational judgment tests, assessment centers, and behaviorally based structured interviews (SHRM Foundation, 2016).

All courses on psychological assessment, regardless of degree, course level, or program, should be carefully designed to follow today's best practices in curriculum development. Aligned with Covey's (2013) Habit 2 of the seven habits of highly effective people and the APA's competency-based approach to psychology program curriculum development (e.g., see APA, 2020a, b), instructors should *begin with the end in mind* when designing courses on psychological assessment. Beginning with the end in mind requires understanding the competencies (collections of knowledge, skills, and abilities) or outcomes students should be able to demonstrate at the end of the program of study and identifying the goals of the specific course being designed.

The competencies or outcomes students should be able to demonstrate at the end of a program of study vary depending on the program. For example, as shown in Fig. 2, APA's (2013) *Guidelines for the Undergraduate Psychology Major* indicate psychology departments should expect undergraduate students majoring in psychology to

Goal 1: Knowledge Base

- Describe key concepts, principles, and overarching themes in psychology
- Develop a working knowledge of psychology's content domains
- Describe applications of psychology

Goal 2: Scientific Inquiry & Critical Thinking

- Use scientific reasoning to interpret psychological phenomena
- Demonstrate psychology information literacy
- Engage in innovative and integrative thinking and problem solving
- Interpret, design, and conduct basic psychological research
- Incorporate sociocultural factors in scientific inquiry

Goal 3: Ethical & Social Responsibility in a Diverse World

- Apply ethical standards to evaluate psychological science and practice
- Build and enhance interpersonal relationships
- Adopt values that build community at local, national, and global levels

Goal 4: Communication

- Demonstrate effective writing for different purposes
- Exhibit effective presentation skills for different purposes
- Interact effectively with others

Goal 5: Professional Development

- Apply psychological content and skills to career goals
- Exhibit self-efficacy and self-regulation
- Refine project-management skills
- Enhance teamwork capacity
- Develop meaningful professional direction for life after graduation

Fig. 2 APA (2013) framework of guidelines for undergraduate majors

demonstrate 19 specific learning outcomes that are grouped into 5 skill-based goals (pp. 15–16).

The goals of a specific psychological assessment course will also vary. The goals will vary depending on whether the course is an introductory-level course or a graduate-level course. For introductory-level courses, we recommend two simple course goals:

1. To develop student understanding of the foundational knowledge and principles of psychological assessment
2. To develop student understanding of what types of professionals use psychological assessments, in what settings, and for what reasons

When developing a graduate-level psychological assessment course where students will be using profession-specific assessments after graduation, we recommend one additional course goal:

3. To develop student competency applying foundational psychological assessment principles when selecting and using assessment instruments in clinical, educational, organizational settings

Beginning with the end in mind, or a clear understanding of program-level competencies and course-level goals, leads to development of high-quality courses in psychological assessment, where students can experience more robust learning and assessment activities (APA, 2020a, b). Such an approach helps curriculum designers and teachers achieve the objectives of a college education, such as helping students develop work-related skills, grow personally and intellectually (Pew Research Center, 2011), and become globally competitive (Department of Education, 2020).

Taking time to carefully identify what course outcomes (as well as corresponding learning objectives) are needed to achieve program-level competencies and course-level goals establishes a foundation for a well-aligned course that not only engages students but also maximizes learning. Once course outcomes and learning objectives are identified, teachers can design learning activities or tasks (such as reading book chapters/articles, watching videos, or completing exercises) to help students achieve the desired learning objectives. Similarly, all assessments of student learning (such as quizzes, tests, etc.) should be designed to determine the extent to which the desired learning objectives are achieved.

Learning Objectives for Psychological Assessment Courses

As we previously discussed, the content of psychological assessment courses varies significantly by degree level, course level, and degree program. As a result, no standard set of learning objectives (what students should know and be able to do) is recommended for a course on psychological assessment. However, we believe that Fink's (2013) taxonomy of significant learning can serve as an extremely valuable framework to help instructors create course learning objectives – regardless of level or program. Fink's taxonomy builds upon Bloom's (1956) taxonomy, a powerful and commonly used framework for developing learning objectives (e.g., see Adams, 2015). While Bloom's (1956) taxonomy includes six hierarchical levels of learning based on how the brain processes information and how students learn, Fink's (2013) taxonomy includes six interactive categories of learning deemed important for *significant* learning to occur.

According to Fink (2013), for significant learning to occur, students must experience lasting learning, which only occurs when the concepts are important to a person's life. Therefore, course learning objectives should extend well beyond the typical objectives of understanding and application of core concepts and topics – which aligns extremely well with most competency-based program-level guidelines. To make the process important to a learner's life, Fink (2003) believes courses should include more challenging and exciting learning objectives that (a) lead to significant changes in students that continue after a course and graduation and (b) enhance students' lives by preparing them for experiences beyond the classroom, including the world of work. According to Fink (2003, 2013), significant learning occurs when courses are designed with learning objectives in each of six major categories (see Fig. 3).

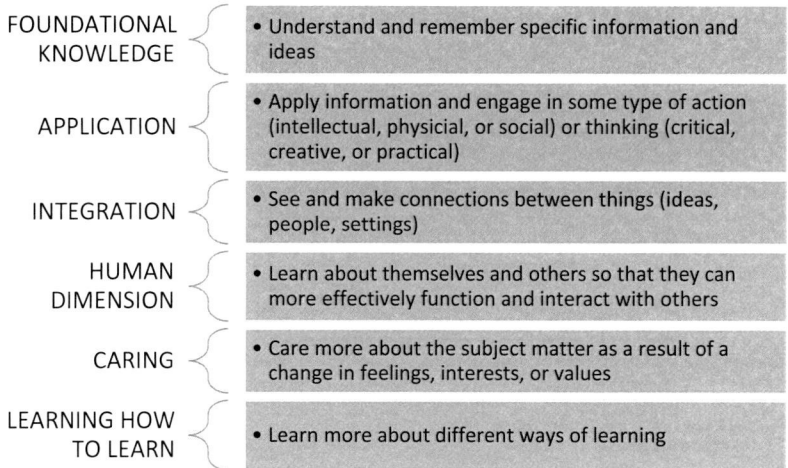

Fig. 3 Summary of Fink's (2013) taxonomy of significant learning

When designing courses, it is essential for instructors to align each course goal with corresponding course outcomes and learning objectives. Table 1 illustrates how the course goal of "developing student understanding of the foundational knowledge and principles of psychological assessment" aligns with six specific course outcomes. In turn, each course outcome has more specific learning objectives. For instance, the first course outcome in Table 1 indicates that students should be able to "explain key terms related to psychological assessment." To meet this outcome, students have the learning objectives to "define what a psychological assessment is," "identify common measures of central tendency," "define reliability and validity," etc.

When writing learning objectives, teachers should also consider Fink's taxonomy of significant learning. By using Fink's taxonomy to create learning objectives, courses on psychological assessment have the potential to add value that extends well beyond the classroom, the college experience, and graduation. Following Fink's (2003, 2013) taxonomy, Fig. 4 includes some general questions to help instructors reflect about the desired learning objectives for a psychological assessment course. For the most lasting learning to occur, Fink (2003, 2013) encourages teachers to identify learning objectives that promote all six kinds of learning. For more information on how to write objectives that promote all six kinds, of learning with examples, see Teacher and Educational Development, University of New Mexico School of Medicine (2005).

Core Contents and Topics of Psychological Assessment

To illustrate how to align specific topics with the course goals identified in the previous section, Table 2 lists the foundational concepts and principles instructors should include to meet the course goals of an introductory class about psychological

Table 1 Alignment of a course goal, course outcomes, and learning objectives by Fink's taxonomy of significant learning

Course goal
Develop student understanding of the foundational knowledge and principles of psychological assessment

Course outcomes	Learning objectives	Fink's taxonomy of significant learning				
		Foundational knowledge	Application	Integration	Human dimension	Caring
Explain key terms related to psychological assessment	Define what a psychological assessment is	•				
	Identify common measures of central tendency	•				
	Define reliability and validity	•				
	Define nominal, ordinal, interval, and ratio levels of measurement	•				
	Define test-retest, alternative forms, internal consistency, and scorer reliability	•				
	Define content, construct, and criterion-related validity	•				
Discuss how and why psychological assessments are used to make decisions	Identify reasons why different professionals, across various settings, use psychological assessments				•	•
	Discuss the types of decisions made based on the results of psychological assessments					
	Identify common examples of psychological assessments used by individuals and organizations				•	•
Describe ethical issues related to psychological assessment	Explain the ethical responsibilities of assessment publishers				•	•
	Describe the rights and responsibilities of assessment-takers				•	•
	Discuss ethical issues that may occur when assessing individuals with physical and mental challenges				•	•

(continued)

Table 1 (continued)

Course goal
Develop student understanding of the foundational knowledge and principles of psychological assessment

Course outcomes	Learning objectives	Fink's taxonomy of significant learning				
		Foundational knowledge	Application	Integration	Human dimension	Caring
Interpret the results of psychological assessments	Explain when the mean, median, and mode should be used to measure central tendency		•	•		
	Interpret the results of norm-referenced and criterion-referenced assessments		•	•		
	Interpret standard and normed scores		•	•		
Demonstrate best practices when developing a psychological assessment	Describe how to minimize response bias when developing a psychological assessment			•	•	•
	Explain how to use replication and cross-validation to measure the validity of a psychological test		•	•		
	Explain how to use common quantitative and qualitative techniques to analyze items in a pilot test		•	•		
	Describe best practices for validating a psychological assessment		•	•		
Analyze the psychometric properties of a psychological assessment	Determine whether a psychological assessment has evidence of reliability		•	•		
	Analyze whether a psychological test has evidence of validity for intended use		•	•		

Foundational Knowledge

- What can students do to demonstrate they understand critical psychological assessment facts, concepts, theories, etc.?

Application

- What can you have students do to show they have developed new actions and kinds of thinking as a result foundational knowledge acquired?

Integration

- What can you have students do to demonstrate they have made connections among psychological assessment concepts both within and beyond the learning experience?

Human Dimension

- What can you have students do to demonstrate they have learned about themselves and how to effectively interact with others based on psychological assessment learnings?

Caring

- What can students do to demonstrate a change in feelings, interests, or values as a result of psychological assessment learnings?

Learning How to Learn

- What can students do to demonstrate they have developed new ways of learning?

Fig. 4 General questions to consider when developing learning objectives for psychological assessment courses

assessment. The table clusters topics into four groups: overview, use/rationale, critical evaluation, and ethics. These categories indicate that by the end of the course, students should know what psychological assessments are (overview), who uses them and for what reason (use and rationale), how to tell if an assessment is a quality one (critical evaluation), and ethical issues associated with psychological assessment.

Based on these core concepts and topics, instructors should develop four to six general course outcomes to identify what students should be able to do by the end of an introductory psychological assessment course. For instance:

- Explain key terms related to psychological assessment.
- Discuss how and why psychological assessments are used to make decisions.
- Interpret the results of psychological assessments.
- Demonstrate best practices when developing a psychological assessment.
- Analyze the psychometric properties of a psychological assessment.
- Describe ethical issues related to psychological assessment.

Organizing Frameworks for Psychological Assessment Courses

There are various ways course developers organize instructional content to achieve learning objectives. For example, content might be organized categorically, chronologically/sequentially, by order of importance, from simple to complex,

Table 2 Foundational concepts and principles critical to an introductory psychological assessment course

	Concepts and principles	Description
Overview	Definition of psychological assessment	What constitutes a psychological assessment, including the similarities and differences between a psychological assessment, a psychological test, and a survey
	Common characteristics	The characteristics common to all well-designed psychological assessments
	Ways of classifying psychological assessments	The common ways professionals classify and refer to psychological assessments (maximal performance, behavior observation, self-report; standardized vs. nonstandardized; objective or projective; dimension/construct measured)
	Assumptions	The assumptions we must make when using psychological tests and steps we can take during test development to increase our confidence
	Locating information about psychological assessments	Where to locate appropriate psychological assessments (print and online), including information about their intended use, merits, and limitations
Use and rationale	Professionals who use psychological assessments	The types of professionals in different settings (e.g., clinical/counseling, educational, and organizational) who use psychological assessment results to make important decisions
	Types of psychological assessments used	The types of psychological assessments professionals in different settings use to make important decisions
	Types of decisions made	The types of important decisions individuals and institutions make, in different settings, using the results of psychological assessments, including the comparative or absolute method used by institutions
Critical evaluation	Critical concepts and procedures for interpreting results	Levels of measurement, normal distribution, histograms, measures of central tendency, measures of variability, standard scores, norms
	Methods for establishing reliability/precision	Test-retest, alternate forms, internal consistency, and scorer reliability
	Methods for gathering evidence of validity	The five sources of validity evidence described in the *Standards for Educational and Psychological Testing*: Evidence based on test content (content validity), evidence based on response

(continued)

Table 2 (continued)

	Concepts and principles	Description
		process, evidence based on internal structure (construct validity), evidence based on relations with other variables (criterion-related validity), evidence based on the consequences of testing
	General principles/methods for developing psychological assessments	The assessment development process, including common item types (objective and projective) and practices for minimizing response bias (e.g., social desirability, acquiescence, random responding/faking)
	General principles/process for conducting a pilot test to assess the psychometric quality of an assessment	Common quantitative (e.g., item difficulty, discrimination index, item-total correlations, interitem correlations, item bias) and qualitative (e.g., questionnaires, expert panels) techniques for evaluating the performance of test items, including the assessment revision process
	General principles/process for validating a psychological assessment	The process of replication and cross-validation; assessing measurement bias and differential validity; determining test fairness; developing norms and identifying cut scores
Ethical issues	Common professional practice standards	The professional practice standards of associations and societies most relevant to psychological assessment/testing, including the general ethical responsibilities of assessment/test publishers, test users, and test takers
	Ethical issues	Issues associated with testing special populations (e.g., individuals with physical and mental challenges)

hierarchically, or by focusing on the whole and then the parts. Regardless of how the content of a psychological assessment course is organized, the course should be structured in a way that is logical and meaningful to students.

Most psychological assessment courses have a core textbook upon which most content is drawn. Textbook content is organized into some logical, meaningful structure. One possible way to organize a psychological assessment course is to find a core textbook that you believe is meaningfully organized. Then, either map your learning objectives to the textbook content or use the learning objectives provided by the textbook author, supplementing them to ensure learning objectives are included from all six categories of Fink's (2013) taxonomy of significant learning.

Figure 5 includes a combination of *simple to complex* and *hierarchical* organizing framework, with the course divided into four sections, each with sub-units. The framework is *simple to complex* in that students are slowly introduced to the topic of

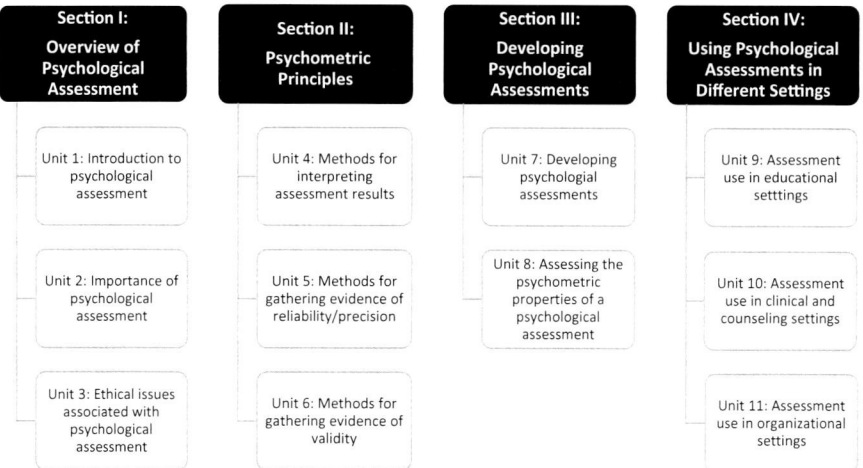

Fig. 5 Organizing framework for a psychological assessment course

psychological assessment (in section "Introduction") prior to focusing on more complex concepts related to psychometric principles and assessment design. The framework is also hierarchical because foundational knowledge, which is required for more higher-level knowledge/skills, is presented first. This organizing framework follows the structure of Miller and Lovler's (2020) *Foundations of Psychological Testing: A Practical Approach* textbook. Instructors who use this *simple to more complex* and *hierarchical* framework gradually introduce students to the field of psychological assessment by building their knowledge base and confidence prior to covering more complex concepts and practices.

Teaching, Learning, and Assessments: Approaches and Strategies

The complexity of psychological assessment demands a myriad of teaching and assessment strategies. Instructors should not only consider *what* to teach and *how* to assess whether students understand the core concepts but also *why* students should care about the information and *how* to keep students engaged during class. After discussing general strategies related to student engagement and type of instructional delivery (face-to-face, online, or hybrid), this section presents specific learning activities and assessments instructors should consider for their psychological assessment classes.

Teaching Strategies

Engagement Strategies Keeping students engaged in the learning process is particularly important when teaching a challenging subject like psychological assessment. Students often perceive theory-based, lecture-only approaches as boring, irrelevant, and confusing. Research indicates student attention starts to lapse after about 10 to 18 minutes of a lecture (Williamson & Schell, n.d.). To maximize student engagement, teachers of psychological assessment courses should leverage the technology, application, and dialogue strategies suggested in Table 3.

Activities that require students to apply the course concepts to specific problems or situations tend to increase student engagement (Fink, 2007). For instance, rather than merely providing general information about the widespread use of psychological assessments, instructors should have students work in small groups to identify and discuss psychological assessments they have personally taken in the past. Integration of real-world case studies, simulations, and problem-based learning also increase student engagement.

Using technology to reinforce psychological assessment concepts also helps capture student interest and attention. Several interactive quiz platforms, such as Kahoot, Quizizz, Quizlet Live, and/or Gimkit, allow students to use their laptops or smart phones to measure understanding of course concepts or provide the instructor with feedback. Instructors can also incorporate activities that teach students how to design psychological assessments and collect data with online survey-hosting platforms, such as Google Forms, SurveyMonkey, and SurveyPlanet (see Stickler, 2019).

Classroom dialogue, whether in-person or online, also significantly increases student engagement. Rather than merely providing information, instructors should use Socratic questioning to encourage participation and reflection about psychological assessment concepts. McQuain (2014) provides a list of various Socratic inquiries, including questions to probe about assumptions, information, reasons, evidence, causes, viewpoints, implications, consequences, and interpretations. For instance, psychological assessment teachers can ask students questions such as:

- Why should you care about psychological assessment?
- Who can benefit from the use of psychological assessments?
- What is the difference between reliability and validity?
- How do we know if a psychological assessment has evidence of validity?
- What evidence supports your interpretation of a psychological assessment's results?
- What is the difference between interval and ratio levels of measurement?
- When should you use norm-referenced assessments? Criterion-referenced assessments?

Regular use of Socratic questioning teaches students to think critically about psychological assessment concepts, rather than merely memorizing and repeating information.

Delivery Strategies Because traditional face-to-face (F2F) courses incorporate live interaction, instructors should reflect carefully about the way psychological assessment concepts are presented. F2F classes provide instructors with several options to

Table 3 Strategies to maximize student engagement in psychological assessment courses

Engagement strategies	Description	Examples	Description
Application	Integrate scenarios that require critical thinking about psychological assessment concepts	Simulations	Teachers provide students with hypothetical scenarios that require them to apply and interpret various psychological assessment concepts
		Real-world case studies	Instructors develop case studies issues related to popular psychological tests
		Problem-based learning	Teachers provide students with psychological assessment-related problems and require them to make recommendations, individually or in groups
		Real-life examples	Instructors design activities based on current events. For instance, the class could discuss how inappropriate sampling resulted in inaccurate conclusions about pilot readiness to fly Boeing 737 MAX aircraft (Pasztor, 2019)
Technology	Incorporate interactive hardware and software in the classroom to maintain student interest	Clickers	Instructors provide students with handheld devices that collect and analyze student responses to close-ended questions in real time (Bruff, 2019)
		Online assessments	Instructors demonstrate online testing platforms
		Interactive quiz platforms	Instructors use a free online quiz platform, such as Kahoot (2019), so students can anonymously self-assess their understanding of foundational concepts
		Survey software	Instructors incorporate activities that teach students how to design psychological assessments and collect data with online survey-hosting platforms (see Stickler, 2019)
		Excel activities	Instructors use Excel to demonstrate various statistical methods to calculate and interpret test scores

(continued)

Table 3 (continued)

Engagement strategies	Description	Examples	Description
Dialogue	Use interactive conversation between the instructor and students psychological testing	Socratic questioning	Instructors pose probing questions (rather than merely providing information) to encourage student self-discovery
		Peer interaction	Students work in pairs to discuss their thoughts about various psychological assessment concepts
		Group discussion	Students work in groups of 3 to 5 to discuss concepts and/or case scenarios
		In-class debate	Students debate the pros and cons of standardized testing in schools

engage students personally and use formative assessments to measure student understanding. A F2F environment also provides students with the opportunity to ask questions in real time, minimizing the chance of confusion about a particular concept.

However, traditional lectures can be problematic in psychological assessment courses. When lengthy, lectures may come across as tedious and/or complicated. As a result, teachers should consider "chunking" longer lectures into a series of shorter presentations so the information can be combined with activities to maximize student attention, interest, and curiosity. Figure 6 illustrates how a traditional 60-minute lecture can be modified into a more engaging "chunked" approach (Williamson & Schell, n.d.).

Learning Activities Before designing learning activities, teachers of psychological assessment should reflect about whether the activities align with at least one of the course's learning objectives. Purposefully selecting specific readings and videos for students to review is particularly important because these resources provide students with a preliminary understanding of psychological testing concepts. When the assigned readings and videos align with course learning objectives, students are in a stronger position to accomplish the course outcomes. In contrast, when readings and videos are disconnected with the learning objectives, accomplishing course goals/outcomes is significantly harder. Similarly, other learning activities should also align with one or more of the learning objectives. Table 4 identifies a variety of engaging learning activities that can be integrated into a psychological assessment course. For practical and critical thinking learning activities following the course structure in Fig. 6, see Rhoads, Pemble, Miller, and Lovler (2020).

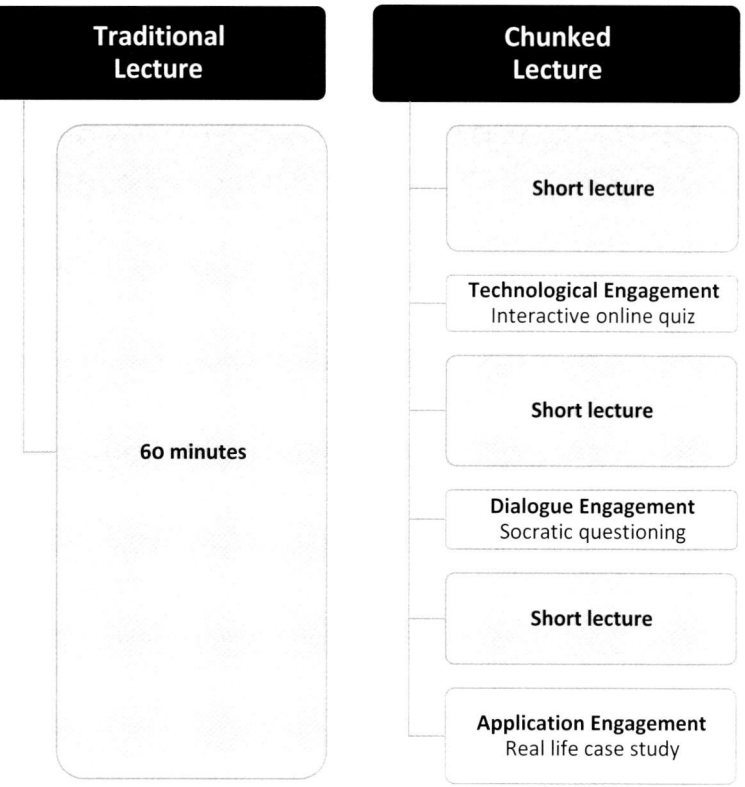

Fig. 6 Comparison of a traditional lecture with a chunked approach

Unlike F2F classes, online courses are asynchronous, with students participating at different times and from various locations. Because students are not in the same place as the instructor, online learning depends heavily on written (rather than oral) communication and may result in less instructor and peer-to-peer interaction. Because of these structural differences, online and hybrid psychological assessment instructors should proactively use technology to build relationships with students and provide opportunities for live dialogue. For instance, online instructors can record video lectures rather than relying exclusively on text-only information. They also can offer live office hours with telephone or video conferencing platforms to provide students with opportunities to discuss concepts in real time (see Watts, 2019).

Course-spanning learning activities, which include a series of activities spread throughout the course, are also an effective means for achieving desired learning objectives. The purpose of such activities is for students to apply psychological assessment concepts as they proceed through the course, culminating in a final deliverable submitted at the end of the class. For example, instructors can integrate an assessment critique activity where students identify a commercially available

Table 4 Alignment of potential learning activities with engagement strategies

Learning activity	Description	Engagement strategies		
		Application	Technology	Dialogue
Pair and share	Students work in pairs to share their thoughts on a discussion topic			●
Muddiest point	Students anonymously write down topics that are not clear at the end of a class. In the next class, the instructor discusses topics that are still "muddy"			●
Fishbowl	Students insert questions about a psychological assessment topic into a fishbowl (or other containers). The instructor then randomly selects questions for class discussion			●
Real-world case study	Students receive and analyze a case study based on actual events	●		
Daily journal	Students regularly write journal entries about the psychological assessment concepts and cases presented in class	●		●
Discussion	Students analyze questions that are presented in a F2F or online class	●	●	●
Build a survey	Students use an online survey-hosting platform to create a psychological assessment; they can also analyze data collected from their assessment	●	●	
Interactive quiz	Students respond to true/false and multiple-choice questions based on readings and videos about psychological assessment		●	●
Concept mapping	Students use online software to create concept maps about various psychological assessment topics	●	●	●

Note: Additional information about these activities can be found at Paulson and Faust (2019)

psychological assessment, conduct sequential research on the assessment, and complete an assessment critique worksheet (see Fig. 7). At the end of the course, students present their critique to classmates (either face-to-face or perhaps through an online video), demonstrating increasing levels of knowledge and skill. Instructors may also consider providing students with an opportunity to take a psychological assessment and receive coaching about their results (see Center for Application of Psychological Type, 2019; Morrison, 2019a, b, c). Students can then prepare a development plan based on the assessment's results or write an analysis of their key learnings.

Assessment Strategies

Measuring whether students are learning is particularly important in psychological assessment courses. Instructors are expected to "walk the talk" of assessment

Test/assessment Critique Worksheet

Part I: General descriptive information	
• What is the title of the test/assessment?	
• Who is the author of the test/assessment?	
• Who publishes the test/assessment, and when was it published? (Include dates of manuals, norms, and supplementary materials.)	
• How long does it take to administer the test/assessment?	
• How much does it cost to purchase the test/assessment?	
Part II: Purpose and nature of the test/assessment	
• What does the test/assessment measure and/or predict?	
• What behavior does the test/assessment require the test/assessment taker to perform?	
• What population was the test/assessment designed for (for example, age, type of person)?	
• What is the nature of the test/assessment (for example, maximal performance, behavior observation, self-report, standardized or nonstandardized, objective or subjective)?	
• What is the format of the test/assessment (for example, paper-and-pencil or computer, multiple choice or true/false)?	
• Is the test/assessment manual comprehensive? (Why or why not?)	
• Is the test/assessment easy or difficult to administer?	
• How clear are the administration directions?	
• How clear are the scoring procedures?	
• What qualifications and training does a test/assessment administrator need to have?	
• Does the test/assessment have face validity?	

Fig. 7 (continued)

Test/assessment Critique Worksheet

Part III: Technical evaluation	
• Is there a norm group, who comprises the norm group, and what types of norms are there (for example, percentiles, standard scores)?	
• What evidence exists that the test/assessment has evidence of reliability/precision?	
• What evidence exists that test/assessment has evidence of validity for intended use?	
Part IV: Test/assessment reviews	
• What do reviewers say are the strengths and weaknesses of the test/assessment?	
• How did the test/assessment perform when researchers or test/assessment users, other than the test/assessment developer or publisher, used it?	
Part V: Summary	
• Overall, what do you see as being the strengths and weaknesses of the test/assessment?	

Fig. 7 Sample psychological assessment critique worksheet

by demonstrating they can accurately identify when students have obtained the knowledge, skills, and abilities specified in the course outcomes. To maximize student learning, psychological assessment instructors should be familiar with both summative and formative assessment as well as key performance indicators.

Summative Assessment Psychological assessment courses frequently use summative assessments, which measure student learning at the end of an instructional unit. Tests, problem sets, discussion questions, individual or team papers, presentations, and/or projects are common summative assessments. Designed to evaluate understanding of key concepts, students take tests, write papers, participate in online discussion boards, complete computational problem sets, etc. While these assignments provide a global measure of understanding at the end of an instructional unit (e.g., after a chapter or a midterm exam), summative assessments only measure a student's understanding at a specific point in time. Because these tend to be high-stakes assignments (worth a significant percentage of the student's grade), summative assessments can be stressful and do not effectively provide feedback about student learning between each assignment.

Formative Assessment In contrast, formative assessments provide students with ongoing, low-stakes feedback to improve their learning throughout the course. Several of the learning activities in Table 4 are also formative assessments that can be used in psychological assessment courses. For instance, instructors can use an interactive quiz activity to anonymously assess students' understanding of key terminology about psychological assessment. As shown in Fig. 8, a series of true/ false or multiple-choice questions can be displayed for the class. Students then use their laptop or smart phone to select a response. After everyone indicates an answer, the correct response is displayed and can be discussed by the instructor. This type of formative assessment allows students an anonymous and engaging way to self-assess their understanding of psychological assessment concepts.

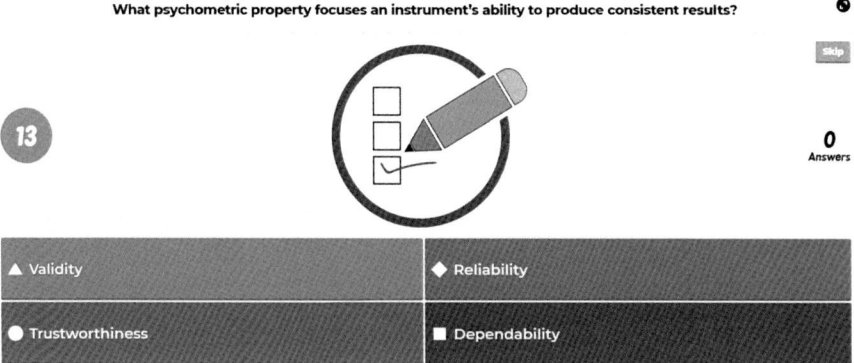

Fig. 8 Example of a formative assessment hosted on Kahoot's (2019) interactive quiz platform

It also provides students with insight about the content the instructor believes is important. The muddiest point, fishbowl, and concept mapping activities also provide instructors with an informal way to measure students' understanding of the course concepts.

Course Key Performance Indicators In addition to using specific assignments to measure learning, instructors should track overall course effectiveness with key performance indicators (KPIs). When crafting such indicators, Winkelmes (2014) suggests instructors should reflect about what essential knowledge students should be able to retain 5 years after taking a course. Table 5 provides sample KPIs for an introductory psychological assessment course. By clearly and transparently stating KPIs *before* a class starts, instructors make the course more intentional, while also empowering students with the ability to self-assess their understanding of important concepts during (as well as after) the class.

Table 5 Learning outcome key performance indicators (KPIs) for effective teaching of psychological assessment

Learning outcome KPIs	Description	Poor	Average	Excellent
Awareness of the importance of psychological testing	To what extent can the student describe how psychological assessments are used by individuals and organizations?	Describes less than two examples	Describes three to four examples	Describes five or more examples
Unprompted recognition of common psychological assessments	How many psychological tests can the student identify and describe without being prompted?	Identifies less than five assessments	Identifies six to nine assessments	Identifies ten or more assessments
Correct recollection of psychological assessment concepts	How accurately can the student remember key psychological testing concepts? Reliability Validity Instrumentation Sampling Data collection Data analysis/ interpretation	Accurately recalls a few (two or less) key concepts	Accurately recalls some (three to five) key concepts	Accurately recalls all six key concepts
Proper application of psychological assessment concepts	To what extent can the student appropriately apply psychological testing concepts in his/her personal and professional life?	Able to apply few (two or less) of the key concepts	Able to apply some (three to five) key concepts	Able to apply all six key concepts

Challenges and Lessons Learned

Designing and teaching a psychological assessment course that has maximal impact on students is not easy. Based on the material in this chapter, such courses should be designed and taught to achieve four pedagogical objectives:

- Keep students engaged in their learning.
- Enhance student understanding of core concepts and topics.
- Lead to significant changes in students that continue after a course and graduation.
- Enhance students' lives by preparing them for experiences beyond the classroom, including the world of work.

Achieving these four teaching objectives requires that individuals designing a psychological assessment course carefully identify aligned course goals, outcomes, learning objectives, activities, and assessments. The learning objectives must be carefully written, and action-oriented, to align with program-level competencies and to promote significant learning, including learning objectives across all six of Fink's (2013) categories of significant learning: foundational knowledge, application, integration, human dimension, caring, and learning how to learn. Instructors must then focus on keeping students engaged by incorporating purposeful learning activities that align with identified learning objectives, leveraging technology, application, and dialogue strategies. Further, instructors must incorporate formative and summative assessment strategies that can accurately identify whether students have the knowledge, skills, and abilities specified in the course outcomes. When such information is integrated effectively into a course, students are more likely to demonstrate the long-term KPIs of a psychological assessment course: awareness of the importance of psychological testing, unprompted recognition of common psychological assessments, as well as accurate recollection and appropriate application of psychological assessment concepts.

Achieving the four pedagogical objectives above becomes more challenging, requiring strategies above and beyond those discussed in this chapter, given the following:

- **Students often fear courses with statistics**, which are foundational to understanding methods for interpreting assessment/test results and establishing evidence of reliability/precision and validity. Therefore, it is critical that teachers employ strategies to get students to relax and feel comfortable learning about statistical concepts.
- **The demographics and learning environment of classrooms change over time**. Therefore, teachers must constantly update their approaches to teaching to meet the needs of both traditional and adult learners who have unique needs and learn in various ways (F2F classroom, online, and blended learning environments).

- **While many of the foundational concepts of psychological testing are old ones, the field of psychological assessment/testing constantly evolves.** Therefore, teachers must be lifelong learners themselves, remaining aware of current trends (e.g., changes in the way we conceptualize validity, focus on evidence-based assessment in clinical settings, use of simulations and gamification instead of paper-based assessments in educational and organizational settings, and electronic availability of tests compromising test security).
- **Students are savvy and will take every opportunity they can to question the assessments administered to them** – particularly in a psychological assessment course where they are learning about best practices in assessment development. Therefore, teachers must ensure their assessments are developed following best practices in assessment development, with good psychometric properties themselves.
- **Students demand relevance.** Therefore, students need to know *why* the concepts being taught are important before they can focus on *how* to apply/use the information.
- **Employers are less interested in content knowledge and more focused on graduates who write and think critically.** Therefore, instructions must integrate more critical thinking and writing learning activities into their courses.
- **Passion is contagious!** Some of the concepts in psychological assessment are dry and/or difficult to understand. Instructors must understand that delivery matters. Even in a well-designed course, teachers must excite and engage students by presenting information in an engaging, dynamic, and compelling manner to spark students' desire to learn.

Teaching, Learning, and Assessment Resources

The role of an instructor who teaches courses in psychological assessment is to demonstrate teaching excellence using evidence-based practices that maximize student engagement and learning of the field. Below are some final recommendations and advice for those who teach psychological assessment courses, followed by a brief list of annotated sources about teaching, learning, and assessment in the field of psychological assessment:

- **Tip 1**: Create alignments: Begin with the end in mind! Take time to align course goals, outcomes, and action-oriented learning objectives focused on what students should be expected to do. Similarly, align each learning objective with Fink's (2013) categories of significant learning using the course concepts and principles in Table 1 as a foundation.
- **Tip 2:** Keep students engaged by incorporating purposeful and aligned learning activities leveraging technology, application, and dialogue strategies.
- **Tip 3:** Incorporate formative and summative assessment strategies that accurately identify whether students have the knowledge, skills, and abilities specified in the course outcomes.

- **Tip 4:** Employ additional strategies to help students relax and feel comfortable, addressing the need of both traditional and adult learners who learn in classroom, online, and blended learning course.
- **Tip 5:** Stay current on current trends in psychological testing so you can explain *why* concepts are important before focusing on *how* to apply them.
- **Tip 6:** Design psychometrically sound formative and summative assessments based on best practices in assessment development.
- **Tip 7:** Integrate critical thinking and writing activities.
- **Tip 8:** Demonstrate passion in the classroom.

For more information about teaching, learning, and assessment in the field of psychological assessment, see the list of resources below.

American Educational Research Association, American Psychological Association, & National Council on Measurement in Education. (2014). *Standards for educational and psychological testing.* Washington, DC: American Educational Research Association.

The *Standards* is the gold standard guide on testing not only in the United States, but globally. Approved in 2013 as APA policy, the *Standards* is a 230-page book, providing those who develop and use standardized psychological assessments/tests with criteria for evaluating testing practices and tests. Some of the criteria included are related to validity, reliability/precision, measurement error, fairness in testing, test design and development, rights and responsibilities of test takers and test users, and applications in clinical, workplace, and educational settings.

Buros Center for Testing (https://buros.org)

The Buros Center for Testing is a nonprofit research and assessment resource center located within the Department of Educational Psychology at the University of Nebraska-Lincoln. The Center's mission is to improve both the science and practice of assessment and testing. The Center houses the largest and most comprehensive test review resources, such as the Mental Measurements Yearbook and Tests in Print. The Center also has many valuable print and video resources related to appropriate use of psychological assessments.

Course Design and Teaching

Fink, D. L. (2013). *Creating significant learning experiences: An integrated approach to designing college courses.* San Francisco, CA: Jossey Bass.

This book includes informative ideas that higher education instructors can use to improve teaching and how these improvements will benefit both them and students. A new taxonomy of significant learning extends beyond just remembering and application, with terms instructors can use to create learning goals. An integrated course design is presented in a new and novel manner with easy to understand and apply things course designers and students can do to engage student in active learning and achieve significant learning.

Rhoads, A., Pemble, S., Miller, L. A., & Lovler, R, L. (2020). *Student workbook to accompany Miller and Lovler's foundations of psychological testing: A practical approach* (6th ed.). Thousand Oaks, CA: SAGE Publications.

While written to accompany Miller and Lovler's 6th edition *Foundations of Psychological Testing: A Practical Approach* textbook, the workbook contains a variety of learning activities directly linked to critical psychological assessment learning objectives. Included are practical and critical thinking exercises that allow students to actively demonstrate one or more learning objectives by completing very applied activities. Also included are practice multiple-choice and short-answer questions.

Teacher & Educational Development, University of New Mexico School of Medicine. (2005). *Effective use of performance objectives for learning and assessment.* Retrieved from https://www.mtsac.edu/fclt/docs/EffectiveUseofLearningOb jectives.pdf

This PDF file provides detailed information about what learning objectives are and why have them. The authors discuss the key components of well-designed learning objectives, as well as how to create useful SMART learning objectives. Also included are example action verbs, example learning objectives, and suggested learning strategies using both Fink's dimensions of learning and Bloom's levels of thinking/learning.

Cross-References

▶ Assessment of Learning in Psychology
▶ Basic Principles and Procedures for Effective Teaching in Psychology
▶ Educational Psychology: Learning and Instruction
▶ First Principles of Instruction Revisited
▶ Formative Assessment and Feedback Strategies
▶ Inquiry-Based Learning in Psychology
▶ Problem-Based Learning and Case-Based Learning
▶ Psychological Literacy and Learning for Life
▶ Psychology in Professional Education and Training
▶ Psychology in Social Science and Education
▶ Psychology in Teacher Education
▶ Small Group Learning
▶ Teaching of Work and Organizational Psychology in Higher Education
▶ Teaching Psychology in Secondary Education
▶ Teaching the Foundations of Psychological Science
▶ Teaching the Psychology of Learning
▶ Technology-Enhanced Psychology Learning and Teaching
▶ Topics, Methods, and Research-Based Strategies for Teaching Cognition

References

Adams, N. E. (2015). Bloom's taxonomy of cognitive learning objectives. *Journal of the Medical Library Association, 103*(3), 152–153. https://doi.org/10.3163/1536-5050.103.3.010.

American Educational Research Association, American Psychological Association, & National Council on Measurement in Education. (2014). *Standards for educational and psychological testing*. Washington, DC: American Educational Research Association.

American Psychological Association. (1953). *Ethical standards of psychologists*. Washington, DC: Author.

American Psychological Association. (2010). *Ethical principles of psychologists and code of conduct: Including 2010 amendments*. Washington, DC: Author. Retrieved from http://www.apa.org/ethics/code/index.aspx

American Psychological Association. (2020a). *APA guidelines for the psychological undergraduate major*. Retrieved from https://www.apa.org/ed/precollege/about/undergraduate-major

American Psychological Association. (2020b). *Promoting excellence in professional psychology education and training through best practices in defining and measuring competence*. Retrieved from https://www.apa.org/ed/graduate/competency

Ayearst, L. E., & Bagby, R. M. (2010). Evaluating the psychometric properties of psychological measures. In M. M. Antony & D. H. Barlow (Eds.), *Handbook of assessment and treatment planning for psychological disorders* (pp. 23–61). New York, NY: The Guilford Press.

Bajic, E. (2015, September). *How the MBTI can help you build a stronger company*. Retrieved from https://www.forbes.com/sites/elenabajic/2015/09/28/how-the-mbti-can-help-you-build-a-stronger-company/#240084a7d93c

Binet, A., & Simon, T. (1905). New methods for the diagnosis of the intellectual level of subnormals. In H. H. Goddard (Ed.), *Development of intelligence in children (the Binet-Simon Scale)*. Baltimore, MD: Williams & Wilkins.

Black, G. S., Daughtrey, C. L., & Lewis, J. S. (2014, December 7). The importance of course design on classroom performance of marketing students. *Marketing Education Review, 24*(3), 213–226. https://doi.org/10.2753/MER1052-8008240303

Bloom, B. S. (1956). *Taxonomy of educational objectives: The classification of educational goals*. Retrieved from https://www.uky.edu/~rsand1/china2018/texts/Bloom%20et%20al%20-Taxonomy%20of%20Educational%20Objectives.pdf

Bruff, D. (2019). *Clickers and classroom dynamics*. Retrieved from http://www.nea.org/home/34690.htm

Buros Center for Testing. (2019). *Standards, codes, & guidelines*. Retrieved from https://buros.org/standards-codes-guidelines

Center for Applications of Psychological Type. (2019). *Take the MBTI assessment with personal feedback*. Retrieved from https://www.capt.org/take-mbti-assessment/mbti.htm?utm_source=MBF&utm_medium=link&utm_campaign=personal&bhcp=1

College Board. (2019). *SAT results: Class of 2019*. Retrieved from https://reports.collegeboard.org/sat-suite-program-results/class-2019-results

Covey, S. R. (2013). *7 habits of highly effective people*. New York, NY: Simon & Schuster.

Exner, J. E. (1993). *The Rorschach: A comprehensive system* (3rd ed.). New York, NY: Wiley.

Fink, L. D. (2003). *Creating significant learning experiences: An integrated approach to designing college courses*. San Francisco, CA: Jossey-Bass.

Fink, L. D. (2007, Winter). The power of course design to increase student engagement and learning. *Peer Review, 9*(1). Retrieved from https://www.aacu.org/publications-research/periodicals/power-course-design-increase-student-engagement-and-learning

Fink, L. D. (2013). *Creating significant learning experiences: An integrated approach to designing college courses*. San Francisco, CA: Jossey Bass.

Hart, R., Casserly, M., Uzzell, R., Palacious, M., Corcoran, A., & Spurgeon, L. (2015, October). *Student testing in America's great city schools: An inventory and preliminary analysis.*

Retrieved from https://www.cgcs.org/cms/lib/DC00001581/Centricity/Domain/87/Testing%20Report.pdf

IBISWorld. (2019, March). *Tutoring & test preparation franchises in the US market size 2005–2025.* Retrieved from https://www.ibisworld.com/industry-statistics/market-size/tutoring-test-preparation-franchises-united-states

Joint Committee on Testing Practices. (2004). *Code of fair testing practices in education.* Washington, DC: Author. Retrieved from http://www.apa.org/science/programs/testing/fair-testing.pdf

Kahoot. (2019). *Make learning awesome.* Retrieved from https://kahoot.com/

McQuain, W. (2014). *Questions for a Socratic dialogue.* Retrieved from http://courses.cs.vt.edu/cs2104/Spring14McQuain/Notes/SocraticQ.pdf

Miller, L. A., & Lovler, R. (2020). *Foundations of psychological testing: A practical approach* (6th ed.). Thousand Oaks, CA: SAGE Publications.

Morrison, I. (2019a). *CPI 260 coaching report for leaders.* Retrieved from http://www.discoveryourpersonality.com/cpi-260-lead.html

Morrison, I. (2019b). *FIRO-B test online.* Retrieved from http://www.discoveryourpersonality.com/firo-b.html

Morrison, I. (2019c). *Myers-Briggs Step II online (Form Q).* Retrieved from http://www.discoveryourpersonality.com/myers-briggs-step-2-online-form-q.html

Murray, H. A. (1943). *Thematic Apperception Test manual.* Cambridge, MA: Harvard University Press.

Papurt, M. (1930). A study of the Woodworth Psychoneurotic Inventory with suggested revision. *Journal of Abnormal and Social Psychology, 25*(3), 335–352.

Pasztor, A. (2019, September 26). Plane tests must use average pilots, NTSB says after 737 MAX crashes. *Wall Street Journal.* Retrieved from https://www.wsj.com/articles/plane-tests-must-use-average-pilots-ntsb-says-after-737-max-crashes-11569506401

Paulson, D. R., & Faust, J. L. (2019). *Active learning for the college classroom.* Retrieved from http://www.calstatela.edu/dept/chem/chem2/Active/main.htm

Pearson. (2019). *Qualifications policy.* Retrieved from https://www.pearsonassessments.com/professional-assessments/ordering/how-to-order/qualifications/qualifications-policy.html

Pew Research Center. (2011, June 2). *Purpose of a college education.* Retrieved from https://www.pewsocialtrends.org/2011/05/15/is-college-worth-it/

Rhoads, A., Pemble, S., Miller, L. A., & Lovler, R. L. (2020). *Student workbook to accompany Miller and Lovler's foundations of psychological testing: A practical approach* (6th ed.). Thousand Oaks, CA: SAGE Publications.

SHRM. (2019). *SHRM code of ethical and professional standards in human resource management.* Retrieved from https://www.shrm.org/about-shrm/pages/bylaws%2D%2Dcode-of-ethics.aspx#sthash.gcyad0s5.dpu

SHRM Foundation. (2016). *Choosing effective talent management to strengthen your organization.* Retrieved from https://www.shrm.org/hr-today/trends-and-forecasting/special-reports-and-expert-views/documents/effective-talent-assessments.pdf

Society for Personality Assessment. (2006). Standards for education and training in psychological assessment: Position of the Society for Personality Assessment. *Journal of Personality Assessment, 87*(3), 355–357.

Statistic Brain Research Institute. (2017). *Standardized testing statistics.* Retrieved from https://www.statisticbrain.com/contact/

Stickler, R. (2019). *11 free online survey tools compared.* Retrieved from https://www.webfx.com/blog/internet/11-free-online-survey-tools-compared/

Teacher & Educational Development, University of New Mexico School of Medicine. (2005). *Effective use of performance objectives for learning and assessment.* Retrieved from https://www.mtsac.edu/fclt/docs/EffectiveUseofLearningObjectives.pdf

Terman, L. M. (1916). *The measurement of intelligence.* Boston, MA: Houghton Mifflin.

U.S. Department of Education. (2020). *About ED*. Retrieved from https://www2.ed.gov/about/landing.jhtml

U.S. Department of Labor. (1970). *Manual for the USES General Aptitude Test Battery.* Washington, DC: U.S. Government Printing Office.

Uniform guidelines on employee selection procedures, 41 C.F.R. § 603 (1978).

Watts, R. (2019, April 29). *6 best free conference call services 2019.* Retrieved from https://fitsmallbusiness.com/best-free-conference-call-service/

Wechsler, D. (1939). *The measurement of adult intelligence.* Baltimore, MD: Williams & Wilkins.

WGBH Educational Foundation. (2015). *The testing industry's big four.* Retrieved from https://www.pbs.org/wgbh/pages/frontline/shows/schools/testing/companies.html

Williamson, Z., & Schell, J. (n.d.). *Chunking instruction.* Retrieved from https://craftx.org/sites/all/themes/craft_blue/pdf/Chunking-Instruction.pdf

Winkelmes, M. A. (2014). *Using transparent assignments to increase students' success equitably.* Retrieved from https://tilthighered.com/assets/pdffiles/Faculty%20Workshop%20Slides.pdf

Zielinski, D. (2018, January 22). *Predictor assessments give companies insight into candidates' potential.* Retrieved from https://www.shrm.org/resourcesandtools/hr-topics/talent-acquisition/pages/predictive-assessments-insight-candidates-potential.aspx

Individual Differences and Personality

21

Manfred Schmitt

Contents

Abstract

This chapter first introduces the aims, scope, history, achievements, and current state of personality and individual differences (PID) as a subdiscipline of psychology. Section "Purposes and Rationale of Curricula" describes guidelines for the composition of PID curricula provided by academic associations. The third section presents knowledge, comprehension, and competencies as components of

M. Schmitt (✉)
Department of Psychology, University of Koblenz-Landau, Landau, Germany
e-mail: schmittm@uni-landau.de

© Springer Nature Switzerland AG 2023   513
J. Zumbach et al. (eds.), *International Handbook of Psychology Learning and Teaching*,
Springer International Handbooks of Education,
https://doi.org/10.1007/978-3-030-28745-0_24

the content to be taught. Knowledge includes concepts, theories, research methods, controversies, and important research findings. Comprehension pertains to the location of PID in psychology, the hierarchical structure of personality, the bandwidth-fidelity dilemma, the difference between absolute and relative consistency and stability, the data box, and the meaning of heritability estimates. Competencies and skills consist of tracing literature and appropriate instruments, administering tests correctly, reading texts, designing and executing studies, and analyzing data. Section "Teaching, Learning, and Assessment: Approaches and Strategies" introduces teaching, learning, and assessment resources. Section "Challenges and Lessons Learned" describes challenges in teaching PID, resulting from confusion about the existence of multiple theories and research designs and from insufficient knowledge about research methods. Section "Teaching, Learning, and Assessment Resources" recommends books, journals, and online materials as teaching and learning resources.

Keywords

Temperament · Character · Ability · Skill · Attitude · Motive · Belief · Inerest · Emotion · Self-concept · Self-esteem · Disposition · Trait · State · Consistency · Stability

Introduction

Personality psychology or personality science is a subdiscipline of psychology. In this chapter, the more inclusive denomination personality and individual differences (PID) will be used. PID is interested in individual differences in thinking, feeling, and behaving. It seeks to describe and understand the pattern of psychic attributes that make individuals unique and constitute their personality. Individual differences are ubiquitous. People differ in their abilities, skills, knowledge, motives, attitudes, values, beliefs, interests, emotions, self-concept, and self-esteem. Some individual differences are quite consistent across contexts and are called broad or generalized dispositions. Others are more context-dependent and are called narrow or domain-specific dispositions. Some individual differences are rather stable over time and are called traits, whereas others fluctuate and are called states. These classifications are simplifications because consistency and stability are continuous. Behavior is neither fully consistent nor fully inconsistent and neither entirely stable nor entirely unstable. It is more or less consistent and more or less stable.

Describing individuals with a large number of typical thoughts, feelings, and behaviors would be inefficient and would go against the principle of scientific parsimony. Therefore, specific individual differences are combined into broader classes on the basis of their similarity. Intelligence, for example, is used as an abstract construct that includes a large number of correlated problem-solving abilities. Loss of accuracy is the price that is paid for the parsimony of abstract constructs. This trade-off is called the bandwidth-fidelity dilemma.

In addition to describing individual differences, PID explores the extent to which important life outcomes (e.g., educational achievement, job success, and health) can be predicted from personality. Next, PID wants to explain how individual differences emerge. Explanation means identifying the causal factors that shape personality. Causal knowledge is necessary for another task of PID: the modification of personality. Excessive feelings (anxiety), thoughts (suspiciousness), and behavior (gambling) can be maladaptive to a point where professional help is advisable. This example shows that PID can make important contributions to applied psychology.

PID has witnessed constancy, change, crises, and important advancements over its history of about 100 years. Some enduring goals have been to describe and explain individual differences, to assess personality traits, and to use them to predict important life outcomes. Considerable change has occurred in the theoretical paradigms guiding the discipline's epistemic agenda. Psychodynamic theories, humanistic theories, cognitive theories, social-learning theories, interactionist theories, psychobiological theories, trait theories, and process theories have each dominated personality research for a while before being superseded by other theories. Some theories, especially trait theories, have persisted for a long time, whereas others have reappeared in modified versions.

Whereas it is difficult to evaluate whether shifts in the theoretical mainstream are advances or mere alternations, this evaluation is easy for the research methods PID employs. These have become more elaborate due to progress in test theory, multivariate statistics, elaborate assessment methods such as virtual reality, ambulatory assessment, electronic sensing, online data collection, and big data mining. Most of this progress is due to the availability of increasingly powerful electronic hardware and software.

PID has had its crises. Its most devastating was sparked by Mischel's (1968) critique of the trait model. His review concluded that, except for intelligence, traits hardly ever predict behavior with a correlation over 0.30, suggesting that traits have little value for one of psychology's most important tasks: predicting behavior. As a consequence of this putative limitation, PID lost attraction, funding, its place in curricula, as well as research and teaching staff. Fortunately, not all scholars turned away from PID. Some engaged vividly in its defense, challenging Mischel's critique as exaggerated, simplified, and biased. Important lessons were learned from this debate (Funder, 2009) and eventually strengthened PID. Meanwhile, doubts about whether individual differences matter in predicting life outcomes have vanished (Roberts, Kuncel, Shiner, Caspi, & Goldberg, 2007).

A second critique argued that PID lacks scientific rigor because (a) its correlational research approach is unfit for revealing causes of behavior and (b) explaining behavior with traits is circular because traits are defined as behavioral dispositions. Both objections have some validity and need to be taken seriously. Yet, they are one-sided and draw only an incomplete picture. Sophisticated longitudinal designs combined with latent growth and true change models can detect cross-lagged effects reflecting the causal impact of personality differences over time on outcomes of interest. Experimental designs can be used to manipulate personality states and reveal state effects. Assuming the functional equivalence of states and traits

(Fleeson, 2001; Steyer, Schmitt, & Eid, 1999), state effects are suggestive regarding the causal impact of their trait counterparts.

A third critique is that causal mechanisms of behavior cannot be revealed with structural models of personality. Process-oriented research is needed for this task. The argument is reasonable but ignores the fact that PID has always been interested in both personality structure and process (Rauthmann, Funder, & Sherman, 2017) and attempts to integrate them (Baumert, Schmitt, et al., 2017; Jayawickreme, Zachry, & Fleeson, 2019).

A fourth objection against PID involves its alleged ignorance of the impact of situations on behavior. Though it is true that the trait approach cares more about persons than situations, other approaches have included situations systematically and have considered person x situation interactions for the explanation of behavior (Blum, Rauthmann, Göllner, Lischetzke, & Schmitt, 2018; Endler & Magnusson, 1976).

Finally, the trait model was accused of disregarding the modifiability of personality. As a consequence of the alleged immutability assumption, teacher education programs have taken little notice of personality as a source of teacher behavior in the classroom. The argument is that if personality cannot be changed during teacher education or later, knowing the impact of personality on teaching behavior is pointless. This attitude, which can also be found in other fields of applied psychology, is unfortunate. Despite the substantial stability of individual differences across the lifespan, personality does change, for instance, due to life transitions and events (Denissen, Luhmann, Chung, & Bleidorn, 2019), and can be changed through targeted interventions (Roberts et al., 2017).

These challenges have shaken PID but have also contributed to its progress and reputation. The latter is due to the high methodological standards of PID as well as to research findings of high relevance and replicability. To further increase the trustworthiness of its findings, PID is committed to open science guidelines (Asendorpf, Conner, et al., 2013).

Purposes and Rationale of Curricula

Curricula in PID vary across countries, universities, and levels (undergraduate, graduate, PhD). In the USA, many undergraduate curricula follow APA guidelines for the undergraduate psychology major (APA, 2013). These guidelines stipulate five learning goals: (a) knowledge base in psychology, (b) scientific inquiry and critical thinking, (c) ethical and social responsibility in a diverse world, (d) communication, and (e) professional development. Because these goals are defined for psychology majors in general, they need to be specified in curricula. APA does not provide similar guidelines for master and PhD programs. In Europe, the European Federation of Psychologists' Associations (EFPA) has established boards, standing committees, and project groups that are in charge of reviewing, informing, and advising the community of psychologists about research, teaching, and professional activities in Europe. Board 2 is responsible for educational affairs.

It monitors and assesses developments in the teaching of psychology, develops standards, and gives advice on issues of concern to students and teachers. The reports of this board show that despite the Bologna framework adopted by all members of the European Union, psychology curricula vary greatly across European countries. Because of this variability, the board's guidelines are phrased, like the APA guidelines, in general terms. Consequently, no report contains a blueprint for a curriculum in PID.

Higher degrees of standardization have been attained within countries. Most guidelines issued by national psychological societies recommend the subject areas that are to be taught and the number of CPs that should be devoted to these subjects. They do not contain recommendations about the content to be taught. This decision is left to the departments. When departments apply for program accreditation, they submit curricula, including module books. Module books describe content and learning goals. Although the module books of different departments overlap, each department is free to define its own profile.

Two remarkable observations can be made when inspecting typical PID modules. First, the content to be taught is defined in short and general terms. No specific theories, methods, and research findings are recommended. Thus, PID teachers are free but also obliged to choose the content they consider relevant. Second, learning goals can be sorted into three categories: knowledge, comprehension, and competencies/skills.

Core Contents and Topics

Adaptive Composition of Content

The content to be taught in a PID module depends on several factors:

1. The weight given to PID in a specific program as mirrored in the number of classes and workload devoted to PID.
2. Whether a PID module is part of a psychology major or minor or another major (education, teacher education, counseling, public health). If PID is taught as a minor or as part of another major, the selection of content should be aligned with the major.
3. The term it is taught in and the other modules that have been taught before. Some personality theories (e.g., need theories) explain individual differences but also general principles of behavior. Accordingly, they are taught in modules from other subjects such as motivation. A second case includes research methods. Ideally, PID is taught after students have acquired basic knowledge in statistics, test theory, and psychological assessment. Otherwise, the PID module has to transmit this knowledge, which is indispensable for understanding how PID research works and what the findings mean.
4. The level of the program. Bachelor PID modules provide basic knowledge, understanding, and competencies. Master PID modules build on the content of

bachelor modules and systematically advance it with an emphasis on methodological expertise and research skills.

To help PID teachers select content adaptively according to these conditions, the
following presentation of content, comprehension, and competencies seeks to be
exhaustive. It can hardly be covered in full in any PID module. Rather, it is meant to
serve as an offer from which PID teachers can choose.

Content Knowledge

Concepts

Like every science, PID uses specific concepts to communicate its theories, methods,
and findings. Despite their frequent use, these concepts are not always clearly
defined. Their ambiguous meaning results from their origin in ordinary language.
Because psychology explores phenomena (e.g., feelings) that ordinary people know,
reflect on, and talk about, the scientific description of these phenomena is intrinsically interwoven with natural language. According to the lexical approach, words are
created in natural language for all objects, phenomena, and attributes of relevance for
social interaction. Personality attributes are part of this vocabulary, which was
created over thousands of generations of human observers and was used as the
starting point for the scientific inquiry of personality traits (Allport & Odbert, 1936;
Cattell, 1950).

In light of the conflation of natural and scientific language and the potential
misconceptions resulting from it, some authors have provided definitions of crucial
concepts in their texts. For example, a target article by Baumert et al. (2017) contains
an Appendix with definitions of many of the concepts listed below. PID teachers are
well-advised to make students aware of the ambiguity issue and misconceptions
resulting from the conflation of scientific and natural language. Awareness can be
raised, for instance, by presenting dissenting definitions taken from different textbooks and dictionaries.

Core concepts of PID to know are personality, character, temperament, virtue,
ability, aptitude, achievement, performance, behavior, cognition, motivation, need,
drive, attitude, value, interest, emotion, variable (independent, dependent, mediator,
moderator, manifest, latent), disposition, trait, state, construct, factor, indicator,
correlation, consistency (absolute, relative), stability (absolute, relative), personality
structure, personality process, personality development, measurement, assessment,
and prediction. Depending on the program level and knowledge already acquired
before entering the PID module, additional concepts will have to be introduced, such
as:

1. Statistical concepts. Basic concepts of descriptive statistics: nominal scale, ordinal scale, interval scale, ratio scale, frequency distribution, mean, median, variance, standard deviation, covariance, correlation, regression. Advanced concepts
   of multivariate statistics: general linear model, multiple regression, factor

analysis, structural equation modeling. Basic concepts of inferential statistics: probability distributions z, t, F, chi-square and associated tests. Advanced concepts: fit criteria of structural equation models.

2. Research design concepts: experimental design, quasi-experimental design, between-subjects design, within-subjects design, mixed design, fully crossed design, nested design, round-robin design, internal validity, randomization, confound, control techniques, covariate, omitted variable, cross-sectional design, longitudinal design.

3. Psychological assessment concepts: performance test, questionnaire, behavior observation, biography, physiological measure, projective test, response time measure, self-description, peer rating, objectivity, reliability, validity, random measurement error, systematic measurement error, regression to the mean, attenuation due to restricted reliability and variance.

4. Concepts used in specific theories with Freud's psychoanalytic theory serving as an example: eros and libido, thanatos and aggression; id, ego, superego; conflict, identification; consciousness, preconsciousness, subconsciousness; oral stage, anal stage, oedipal stage, Oedipus complex, Electra complex, latent stage, genital stage, fixation; defense mechanism, repression, denial, projection, displacement, regression, sublimation.

Scope of the Personality Concept and Domains of Individual Differences

Some scholars use the personality concept in a narrow sense and restrict it to classical trait models such as the model proposed by Eysenck's (1953; psychoticism, extraversion, neuroticism), the five-factor model (Digman, 1990; neuroticism, extraversion, openness, agreeableness, conscientiousness), and the model proposed by Ashton and Lee (2007; honesty-humility, emotionality, extraversion, agreeableness, conscientiousness, openness). Such a narrow concept of personality covers *what* people typically do.

Other scholars prefer a broader personality concept that includes, besides the traits listed in the previous paragraph, temperament traits as proposed by Buss and Plomin (1975; activity, emotionality, sociability, impulsivity) or Strelau (1998; briskness, perseveration, sensory sensitivity, endurance, emotional reactivity, activity). This personality concept covers *what* people typically do (content characteristics of behavior) and *how* they typically do what they do (formal characteristics of behavior).

Next, some scholars prefer an even broader personality concept that includes, in addition to content (*what*) and style (*how*), motives, drives, and needs as reasons for *why* people do what they do. In his psychodynamic theory, Freud assumed two drives, eros and thanatos, that provide the psychic energy necessary for behavior. In addition to these drives and motives assumed in subsequent theories (Deci & Ryan, 1985; Maslow, 1954; McClelland, 1987; Murray, 1938; Rogers, 1954), values (Schwartz, 1992) and interests (Holland, 1973) entail motivational accounts of behavior.

Finally, the broadest personality concept possible includes all behavioral dispositions in which individuals differ consistently across situations and stably over time:

personality traits in the narrow sense, temperament, virtues, character strengths, motives, values, beliefs, attitudes, interests, emotions, self-concept, self-esteem, talents, abilities, knowledge, and skills.

Knowing that personality cannot be equated per decree with one of these definitions that vary in scope is important to avoid confusion among students. It helps to understand that consistent and stable individual differences in behavioral dispositions are the common denominator of all personality concepts, be they narrowly or broadly defined, and that denominating the field as PID is a wise compromise that can help scholars avoid fruitless debates about the "correct" or most appropriate definition of personality.

Theories and Models

The constructs mentioned in the last section are elements of theories and models. Theories consist of sets of assumptions that together explain consistent and stable individual differences in behavioral dispositions, how these develop and change over the lifespan, how they shape important life outcomes, and how they can be modified via targeted interventions. Models describe systematic patterns of variability in thoughts, feelings, and actions that constitute personality. Models are parts of theories, but they are not necessarily grounded in a specific theory. The personality trait model, for example, can be explained by biological theories or learning theories. Theories and models can be grouped into families on the basis of their most important assumptions and research paradigms. Basic PID modules should introduce at least one specific theory or model from each family. Advanced PID modules should address communalities among and differences between members of a family of theories or teach a specific theory in detail, including the research programs it initiated and important findings.

The boundaries between families of theories are fuzzy because their assumptions overlap. Therefore, specific theories can be assigned to more than one family; see below. Understanding this matter is important because personality textbooks and handbooks differ in their classification of theories, and these differences can be a source of confusion to students.

Psychodynamic theories assume that the management of conflicts between drives and social norms determine personality development. Freud's theory, which includes dynamic (drives: eros and thanatos), structural (id, ego, superego), topographical (conscious, preconscious, unconscious), and developmental (oral, anal, phallic, latent, genital) models, and psychoanalysis as a therapeutic method is the most influential representative of this family. Psychology students should know about its sustainable influence on subsequent theories. Other representatives that can be taught in advanced courses are the theories proposed by Alfred Adler, Carl-Gustav Jung, and Anna Freud.

Motive theories assume that individual differences in behavior are the product of differences in motive strength. Theories by Murray (1938), Maslow (1954), Rogers (1954), Deci and Ryan (1985), and McClelland (1987) are representatives of this family. Schwartz's (1992) theory of values and Holland's (1973) theory of interests can also be assigned to it.

Humanistic theories: The motive theories proposed by Maslow (1954) and Rogers (1954) are sometimes also termed humanistic theories because Maslow and Rogers were distinguished advocates of humanistic psychology, a movement powered by the idea that individuals are basically healthy and resilient, capable of self-healing, agents of their own personality development, and striving for self-actualization.

Learning theories assume that personality and its change can be explained by individuals' learning histories. Important learning principles are operant conditioning (Skinner, 1969), classical conditioning (Pavlov, 1927), and social learning via the observation of others and the consequences of their behaviors (Bandura, 1977).

Cognitive theories argue that individual differences in behavior result from informed (rational) choices people make on the basis of their values and beliefs. Theories by Kelly (1955), Rotter (1954, 1966), and Bandura (1977) represent this family.

Trait theories map individuals onto a limited set of dimensions that are considered necessary and sufficient for a comprehensive and parsimonious description of PID. Trait theories have had a persistent influence on PID research. Important representatives are the abovementioned PEN, the 16 PF, the five-factor, and the HEXACO models. The trait approach is not restricted to personality in a narrow sense. It is the most general model of PID. Importantly, ability constructs such as intelligence rely on the trait model. Influential representatives are Spearman's (1904) two-factor theory, Thurstone's (1938) theory of primary mental abilities, Vernon's (1950) common factors theory, Cattell's (1971) theory of fluid and crystallized intelligence, and the comprehensive Cattell-Horn-Carroll model of intelligence (Carroll, 1993). Most trait models are hierarchical and assign many narrow traits to the lowest level of the hierarchy and a few broad traits to the highest.

Biological theories assume that individual differences are caused by the architecture of the brain and physiological processes. Seminal biological trait theories were proposed by Eysenck (1953) and Gray (1972). Biological PID research also employs behavior genetics to estimate the heritability of individual differences and molecular genetics to reveal the genetic codes responsible for these differences (Lee, Wedow, et al., 2018; Plomin, DeFries, Knopik, & Neiderhiser, 2016).

Person x situation interaction theories emerged in response to Mischel's (1968) critique of the trait model. They argue that individual differences in behavior result from the interplay of individual propensities and situational affordances. Supporting this assumption, studies have found that the interaction between the two types of factors explained more behavioral variance than the main effects did (Endler & Hunt, 1966). Revealing patterns of person x situation interactions (Endler, 1975) and the mechanisms that account for these patterns (Blum & Schmitt, 2017) are important research goals.

Personality process theories seek to explain behavioral dispositions with perceptual, cognitive, motivational, and emotional processes operating in specific situations (Rauthmann et al., 2017). Process accounts of individual differences have primarily been employed to understand emotional disorders such as excessive and dysfunctional anxiety, aggression, and depression. Selective attention to threatening, provoking, and depressing stimuli and biased interpretations of ambiguous stimuli as dangerous, annoying, or oppressive are among the candidates for processes that have been confirmed in empirical studies (Mathews & MacLeod, 1994; Williams, Watts, MacLeod, & Mathews, 1991).

Dual-process theories distinguish between two systems of information processing and behavior control. One system is called reflective and the other impulsive (Strack & Deutsch, 2004). These theories assume that dispositions such as attitudes or self-esteem exist in explicit and implicit forms. People are aware of their explicit dispositions but have no introspective access to their implicit dispositions. Explicit dispositions can be measured directly via self-report. Implicit dispositions must be measured indirectly via procedures such as the Implicit Association Test (Greenwald, McGhee, & Schwartz, 1998). Explicit dispositions feed into reasoned action via the anticipation of behavioral outcomes. Implicit dispositions affect behavior automatically via the activation of schemata or scripts.

Systems theories integrate elements from the previously mentioned theories to achieve a comprehensive explanation of PID. Whole trait theory combines the trait model with mechanisms assumed in process theories to explain why personality states, defined as situation- and time-specific behavior, deviate from traits, defined as intraindividual averages of states (Jayawickreme et al., 2019). Personality systems interaction theory (Kuhl, Kazen, & Quirin, 2014; Kuhl, Quirin, & Koole, 2015) combines neurobiological and psychological principles and specifies seven functional personality levels, four cognitive macro-systems, and two affective modulators. The complex interactions among these elements shape behavior.

Ability theories describe and explain individual differences in performance. Abilities are stable and largely heritable. Competencies emerge from interactions between abilities (aptitudes) and learning (treatment). Skills are more narrowly defined than competencies and depend on practice. Intelligence is the most important ability because of its far-reaching impact on virtually all components of life success (Gottfredson, 2018). Different intelligence trait models were mentioned earlier. Besides academic intelligence, other kinds of intelligence have been proposed (Gardner, 2006), with emotional intelligence (Goleman, 1996) and social intelligence (Thorndike, 1920) as the most important examples. The number of competencies and skills that have been defined, measured, and used in diverse fields of applied psychology is virtually endless and not covered by a single theory.

Research Methods

Basic methodological knowledge is essential for understanding PID research findings and drawing reasonable conclusions from them. Students of advanced PID modules who are required or choose to conduct empirical studies need to acquire the methodological expertise that is necessary to investigate the research question at issue.

Ideally, research methods, test theory, and psychological assessment are taught in special modules. However, not all departments offer such modules or offer them after PID has been taught. Basic research methods are usually taught at the beginning of a bachelor program, whereas advanced courses covering multivariate statistics, test theory, and psychological assessment are usually taught, if at all, after or simultaneously with the PID module. This situation can generate challenges that will be addressed in section "Challenges and Lessons Learned."

Assessment methods: Students should know about the large repertoire of assessment methods used in PID research. These include tests, questionnaires, behavioral observation, physiological measures, interviews, content analyses, biographical data, projective tests, indirect procedures such as the IAT, apparatus tests, simulators, economic games, virtual reality, ambulatory assessment, electronic sensing, log file analyses, and big data mining. Beginning students should be introduced to the most frequently used methods, which are tests, questionnaires, behavioral observation, and physiological measures. Each method should be illustrated with a prominent example. Advanced students should be familiar with all kinds of assessment methods and should get acquainted with at least one example from each method.

Test theory: Students of basic PID modules should be introduced to classical test theory (CTT) because most assessment methods are based on it. Advanced PID modules should cover the five measurement models of CTT (congeneric, essentially equivalent, essentially parallel, equivalent, and parallel) and how these models can be tested via confirmatory factor analysis (CFA). Advanced PID modules should also teach item response theory (IRT), at least the Rasch model. Beginning students should know the meaning and relevance of measurement precision (objectivity, reliability, validity). Advanced students should know how to estimate these coefficients.

Correlational designs: These have been the most important and frequently used research designs in PID for a long time. Beginning students should learn how to design and run a simple correlational study. Advanced students need to acquire knowledge about more complex designs and designs needed for special purposes, for instance, multitrait-multimethod designs for estimating convergent and discriminant validity.

Experimental and mixed designs: These are primarily used in general psychology to determine the impact of stimuli and situations on behavior (Shadish, Cook, & Campbell, 2002). PID research employs experimental designs for similar purposes. The calibration of the stimuli and situations to be used in mixed designs requires systematic experimental manipulation. Personality process research exposes participants to situations that vary systematically in their affordance level to explore how it interacts with personality factors. Beginning students need basic knowledge about the logic and nature of experimental designs. Advanced students should know about more complex designs such as nested and multilevel designs.

Longitudinal and cross-sectional designs: Beginning students should know the difference between these designs and their specific benefits and costs. Associations between stable traits can be estimated in cross-sectional studies. Exploring personality change requires longitudinal designs, which are also necessary for revealing causal relations among variables. Advanced students should know designs that combine cross-sectional and longitudinal elements such as the cohort sequential design for disentangling age, time, and cohort effects that contribute to ability and personality change (Schaie, 1965).

Data box: Virtually all designs can be considered special cases of a multivariate data box (Cattell, 1966). Its simplest version includes three facets: persons, situations, and time points with cells containing scores on some measure. The box can be modified and extended at will depending on research interests. For instance, the situation facet can be replaced by personality constructs, or a facet of methods can be added. The basic idea behind this powerful framework should be taught on the basic level. Its full potential should be conveyed to advanced students.

Representative designs: Advanced students should learn about representative designs as proposed by Brunswik (1952). He argued that drawing random samples should not be restricted to the person facet of the data box but should include all facets such as situations, methods, and time points. Random samples on all facets are essential for unbiased generalizability estimates of facet main and interaction effects (Shavelson & Webb, 1991).

Special designs: Depending on the research focus of a PID module, research interests, or research assignments, master and PhD students need to know special designs such as the round-robin design for disentangling perceiver effects, target effects, and perceiver x target interactions (Kenny, 1994).

Debates and Important Findings

Over its history, PID has undergone several crises. Some were mentioned in section "Introduction." Although most controversies have been resolved, some recur from time to time. Students should know about them. Beginning students should know the most important arguments, whereas advanced students should dig deeper into the issues.

Person versus situation debate: This came up first time when Harthshorne and May (1928) discovered that individual differences in honest behavior generalized only weakly across situations with an average correlation of $r = 0.23$. Similar findings and Mischel's (1968) review led critics of the trait model to argue that the situation influences behavior more strongly than personality does. Today we know that this conclusion was premature. Richard, Bond, and Stokes-Zoota (2003) meta-analyzed over 16,000 studies and found similar average effects of the situation ($r = 0.22$) and personality ($r = 0.19$) on behavior. Both effects are small, implying that person x situation interactions account for most behavioral variance. Revealing the nature of interactions requires knowledge about the psychological characteristics of situations. Psychology has made many attempts to solve this issue. Meanwhile, there are taxonomies and assessment instruments for situations that match the quality of personality taxonomies and measures (Rauthmann, Gallardo-Pujol, et al., 2014). Basic PID modules should teach the idea of combining personality and situation measures, and advanced students should be familiar with situation taxonomies and measures.

Predictability of behavior and life outcomes: Hartshorne and May's (1928) study of honesty, Mischel's (1968) review, and the meta-analysis by Richard, Bond, and Stokes-Zoota (2003) converged on the conclusion that single instances of behavior in specific situations cannot be predicted very well from personality traits. However, predictability can be vastly improved via the appropriate aggregation of behavior

(Epstein & O'Brien, 1985; Steyer & Schmitt, 1990). Accordingly, important life outcomes can be predicted reliably and surprisingly well from personality and ability traits (Gottfredson, 2018; Roberts et al., 2007).

Nature versus nurture: The question of the extent to which personality and cognitive ability are the products of a person's genetic dowry (nature) or the person's environment (nurture) has engendered a most ideologically laden controversy in PID. If personality and ability are matters of genetic fate, efforts to change undesirable personality expressions or to boost intelligence seem fruitless. Hundreds of studies have been devoted to this issue. The facts are clear. All personality characteristics and abilities depend to some extent on the person's genetic outfit. On average and roughly speaking, about half of the phenotypic personality and ability variance is genetically determined (Plomin et al., 2016). At the same time, heritability varies across individual difference domains. Whereas fluid intelligence (reasoning) has a strong genetic component and cannot be elevated much by instruction, crystallized intelligence (knowledge), competencies, and skills can be promoted more easily via learning and practice.

Stability and change: Despite substantial heritability, personality changes in response to life transitions, critical life events (Denissen et al., 2019), and targeted interventions (Roberts et al., 2017). Students need to know this and the difference between absolute (mean-level) change (Roberts, Walton, & Viechtbauer, 2006) and relative (rank-order) change (Roberts & DelVecchio, 2000). Both types of change can result from biological factors (e.g., physiological decline) and from environmental factors (e.g., training, intervention, nutrition, or injury). The degree of change varies across personality domains with the rank order of intelligence remaining particularly stable from childhood to old age (Deary, 2014).

Traits and states: In addition to the degree of personality change, its pace is relevant for PID. Intelligence changes very little across the lifespan, and it also changes very slowly. Emotions, by contrast, can change from one moment to next.

Comprehension

The knowledge of facts is worth little if their relevance cannot be appreciated for a lack of comprehension. Students must learn to understand why concepts are needed, what purposes theories and models serve, what specific methods can achieve, and how basic research findings inform applied psychology.

Location of Personality and Individual Differences in Psychology

PID cannot be defined by the kinds of thoughts, feelings, and behaviors its theories and research address. Rather, it can be characterized by its specific perspective and methodological approach. PID is interested in individual differences in dispositions and how they are interrelated. These interests differ from those of general psychology and developmental psychology. General psychology is not interested in differences between individuals. Rather, it is interested in the psychological principles that explain the thoughts, feelings, and behaviors of all individuals. Developmental psychology is interested in changes in thoughts, feelings, and behaviors over the lifespan. These three perspectives correspond to the dimensions of a data box consisting of a person facet (PID); a stimulus, situation, or task facet (general psychology); and a time facet (developmental psychology). The three perspectives complement each other and together enable a comprehensive understanding of how people function the way they do. Students must understand these relations. Teachers can help students understand them by demonstrating how the same kind of behavior (e.g., aggression) can be studied meaningfully from general, differential, and developmental perspectives and that the results complement each other.

Hierarchical Personality Structure and the Bandwidth-Fidelity Dilemma

Describing individuals using a large number of thoughts, feelings, and behaviors would be precise but inefficient. A parsimonious description can be achieved by summarizing similar indicators. Students need to understand that factor analysis serves this purpose and does so in several steps that define the levels of the personality hierarchy. In Eysenck's model, similar (correlated) specific behaviors, located on the first level, are combined into habits on the second level. Similar habits are combined into first-order factors on the third level. First-order factors are combined into second-order factors on the fourth level. Students should understand that precision and parsimony are inversely related. If precision goes up, parsimony goes down. There is no best level of personality description. Which level is most appropriate depends on the research question or the task to be solved in applied psychology. As a general rule, the prediction of relevant outcomes from personality and ability factors succeeds best when predictors and criteria are located on the same level (symmetry principle; Ajzen & Fishbein, 1977; Brunswik, 1952).

Traits and States as Endpoints of Continua

Understanding that traits and states are not mutually exclusive alternatives but are rather endpoints of a change continuum is important. The relative stability of dispositions is neither ever perfect nor ever absent. All personality and ability constructs that have been submitted to latent state-trait analyses (Steyer et al., 1999) were found to be less than perfectly stable and to have some stability. Beginning students should have a basic understanding of this principle, and advanced students should understand whole trait theory (Jayawickreme et al., 2019) and latent state-trait theory (Steyer, Mayer, Geiser, & Cole, 2015).

Absolute and Relative Consistency and Stability

Absolute and relative consistency and stability are independent phenomena. Absolute consistency and stability mean that the intensity of personality expressions (thoughts, feelings, behaviors) does not change over situations and time, respectively. Because situational characteristics affect thoughts, feelings, and behaviors as much as personality does, absolute consistency and stability cannot be expected.

However, this is no challenge to the trait model. This model is valid and useful to the extent that thoughts, feelings, and behaviors are relatively consistent across situations and relatively stable over time, which means that individual differences remain equal in different situations and at different time points. Students at all levels should understand this.

Data Box

The data box described earlier is a powerful tool for designing PID research. It is also useful for explaining important concepts such as absolute and relative consistency and stability as addressed in the last section. It helps teachers illustrate the meaning of personality structure, personality process, personality development, how these perspectives on PID differ, how they complement each other, and how they can be integrated (Baumert et al., 2017). Comprehending the logic behind the data box is therefore a highly valuable resource that students at all levels should possess.

Meaning of Heritability Estimates

Few results from PID research have caused misunderstandings and fruitless disputes as often and vividly as heritability estimates have. It is important for students at all levels to understand what heritability means and what it doesn't mean. Heritability is defined as the proportion of phenotypic variance that can be attributed to genetic variation. It can vary from 0 to 1. The remaining proportion of phenotypic variance is accounted for by factors other than genetic factors. The concept of environment is used to summarize these other factors. The human gene pool and its variability have remained virtually invariant for the last 150,000 years or more. The environment we live in has changed dramatically due to technological progress, cultural change, and advances in formal education. If it were possible to compare the intelligence test performance of people who lived thousands of years ago with that of people living today, heritability estimates would be much lower than the ones estimated at a specific period in history such as today. In a similar vein, a study using a sample of participants from a country with either high or low educational standards will result in higher heritability estimates compared with a study including countries with far different educational standards. Heritability estimates cannot be considered anthropological constants but need to be interpreted in view of the genetic and environmental heterogeneity of a specific heritability study.

Relevance of Personality and Individual Differences for Applied Psychology

Students on all levels have to comprehend that PID is not an art for art's sake. PID theories, methods, and research findings are relevant for the solution of tasks in educational, industrial, personnel, and clinical psychology. Individuals do well and feel good when the environments they live, study, and work in fit their personality (in a broad sense). Job performance, for example, depends on the fit between job demands and employees' competencies, interests, and values.

Understanding the general principle of person x environment fit is motivating, especially for students who are more interested in applied psychology than basic research.

Competencies and Skills

In addition to knowledge and comprehension, students need to acquire competencies and skills.

Literature search: Students of basic PID modules will be provided with literature by their teacher in most but not all courses. Independent studies, for instance, require a literature search. Advanced students and those who choose a PID research question for their bachelor or master thesis will have to trace the relevant literature. Finding relevant research literature, reviews, meta-analyses, and handbook chapters by searching electronic databases (e.g., APA's PsycInfo) is therefore an important competency.

Reading skills: Students must develop the skill of reading articles, chapters, and books efficiently and effectively by extracting important information without distorting it. For research articles, this skill includes identifying research questions and hypotheses, grasping methods and procedures, and interpreting graphs and tables correctly. Reading skills can be practiced in seminars by having students report a paper and its essence and giving them detailed feedback from the teacher and fellow students.

Tracing and evaluating assessment instruments: PID research and application relies heavily on assessment. Students should be capable of finding instruments that fit the research task best and have the highest precision among alternatives. This can be a challenging task. Due to commercial interests of test authors and publishers, thousands of measurement instruments exist, and many of them are poor in quality. Students need to develop the skill of separating the wheat from the chaff by applying the criteria of objectivity, reliability, validity, fairness, standardization, and economy. Students also need to know and follow copyright rules. Instruments published in research articles are often free after obtaining permission from the authors. Students should know how to ask for it. Instruments from commercial publishers are not free, and copyright violations in these cases can result in painful fines. Knowing how to navigate data banks such as PsycInfo or Google Scholar, publishers' websites, and psychological assessment handbooks is also part of this skill.

Application of assessment instruments: Students have to know how to apply assessment instruments properly. This skill cannot be acquired alone by reading instructions. Test-taking must be practiced and supervised by the teacher and fellow students who give feedback.

Designing and implementing empirical studies: Students who are required or choose to conduct empirical studies must identify the most appropriate design, assessment instruments, and data collection procedure. They must know how to define a population, draw a sample from it, recruit participants, give clear instructions, offer incentives to avoid dropout, debrief participants, and submit their proposal to an ethics committee.

Analyzing data: Students who run empirical studies must analyze the data to test hypotheses and answer research questions. This task requires statistical expertise, the competency of using software packages such as SPSS, R, or Mplus, interpreting outputs correctly, translating them into tables and graphs, and drawing the right conclusions regarding the research questions and hypotheses.

Teaching, Learning, and Assessment: Approaches and Strategies

Teaching

Selecting from the content presented in the last section and composing it into a coherent curriculum requires competencies on the part of the teacher. In line with teacher education theory, these can be divided into content knowledge (CK), general pedagogical knowledge (GPK), and pedagogical content knowledge (PCK) (Shulman, 1986). Regarding CK, teachers need to be familiar with the content described in the last section. They need to update their knowledge by reading original research articles published in journals, reviews, meta-analyses, and handbooks. Regarding GPK, teachers should know how to motivate students, get them engaged in reading texts, design targeted take-home assignments, give feedback, and answer questions. Pedagogical models in higher education offer solutions for these tasks (Cook-Sather, 2009). PID teachers should be familiar with these models and invite experienced colleagues to attend their classes and supervise their teaching. Regarding PCK, PID teachers have to apply their GPK to the content they teach.

As a best practice example of PCK, consider how PID teachers can arouse interest in PID and convince students that it is a fascinating science. Begin the first session of your personality lecture or seminar with a mutual introduction. Tell students that working together will be more fun if students and teachers know each other. Ask students to introduce themselves in a way that is most informative and relevant for working together. Most students will begin with biographic information and then move on to talking about their interests and who they are as a person. In doing so, most will use habits (listening to certain music, reading certain books, watching certain movies, spending time with friends) and traits (curious, smart, generous, thoughtful) as descriptors. At the end of the mutual introduction, tell students that PID is interested in exactly what they just did: describing individuals on the basis of what they typically do. Next, ask your students how their best friend would describe them as a person and how that description would differ from the self-description they provided. This task is useful for illustrating that PID uses different assessment methods. Subsequently, ask students to compare their self-description with other students' self-descriptions. This exercise helps to point out another important task of PID: describing individual differences. Further, ask students to reflect on possible explanations for the differences the last exercise revealed. Most likely, they will come up with explanations that can be roughly split into nature and nurture. Again, you can use students' answers to introduce another important mission of PID:

understanding the causal origins of individual differences. Finally, ask your students whether they believe that personality changes easily or remains stable over a person's lifespan. Some students will contribute examples of people they have known for a long time who have not changed a bit. Others will counter the stability claim with examples of people who changed so much that they no longer seem recognizable as the same person. This exercise makes students curious about which viewpoint comes closer to capturing the truth.

Learning

Pedagogical models of higher education address principles of effective teaching and learning. One of these principles pertains to the class type x content fit. Typical class types are lectures, seminars, and practicums. Lectures are suited for teaching knowledge content as described in section "Content Knowledge." To learn content effectively and efficiently, students must prepare lectures with appropriate texts, take notes, and iterate the content after the lecture. Learning success from follow-up work can be enhanced when teachers share their presentation with students.

Seminars are useful for conveying comprehension as described in section "Comprehension." All content described in section "Content Knowledge" can be taught in a seminar. In lectures, students mostly listen. In seminars, they should present content and discuss it with their fellow students and the teacher. A typical seminar begins with a presentation, delivered by a student or a group of students, about a theory, method, empirical study, review, meta-analysis, or task from applied psychology requiring PID expertise. After the presentations, fellow students and the teacher provide feedback and highlight the strengths and limitations of the presentation regarding content, style, and pedagogical skill. Next, fellow students should be given the opportunity to ask questions to complement the presentation and prevent misunderstandings. The seminar can be concluded with a discussion of issues. Was the reported study well-done? Was the reported review informative? Is the presented theory coherent and convincing? How can the reported findings be used to address issues in applied psychology? Experience tells us that students engage in the discussion of such questions. For a teacher to competently moderate such a discussion, the teacher must summarize and integrate the views that have been exchanged and link them to the content presented in the lecture or a textbook.

Competencies and skills as described in section "Competencies and Skills" can be best acquired in practicums. Typical practicums are devoted to the design and implementation of empirical studies, to data analysis with proper software, to the application of assessment instruments, or to combinations of these skills. Students can practice them either alone or in groups. Groups have the advantage that students can learn from each other. Individual work offers the advantage that students must practice all components of a skill. Learning success depends greatly on supervision and feedback from the teacher.

Assessment

Appropriate feedback and adaptive teaching require the assessment of knowledge, comprehension, and competencies. Knowledge can best be assessed with written exams composed of multiple-choice and open questions. Comprehension can be assessed well via essays written in class and presentations. Students' contributions to discussions in seminars can also reveal how well they understand the presented content, its theoretical meaning, and practical significance. Competencies and skills can be evaluated via on-task observation, for instance, when a student is taking a test and via the evaluation of products (e.g., results obtained from a multivariate analysis performed with statistical software packages such as SPSS, R, or Mplus).

Challenges and Lessons Learned

Frequent challenges that PID teachers face result from (a) students' confusion about the multiplicity of personality theories and controversies, (b) difficulty understanding research methods and denial of their necessity, and (c) confusion about the various research designs used in PID.

Confusion About the Multiplicity of Personality Theories and Controversies

When students are introduced to various theories and models of PID, they sometimes want to know which one is correct, which are wrong, or which are better and which are worse. A clear-cut answer to this question is impossible because theories cannot be pitted directly against each other empirically. Teachers can reduce the confusion by explaining to students that theories are often created by single scholars who have their specific way of thinking and preconceptions about human nature. Moreover, theories are born in a historical context that codetermines research interests and research paradigms. In contrast to abstractly formulated theories, models can be compared more easily. For example, CFA can be employed to test different factor models of cognitive abilities.

When introduced to the controversies PID has experienced, such as the person versus situation debate, students sometimes wonder why the same data can be interpreted differently or even contrarily. Teachers can resolve this confusion by explaining to students that no absolute standard exists for evaluating results such as effect sizes. Explaining 20% of job performance variability with personality and ability factors can be considered a little or a lot depending on expectations and the power of alternative explanations. In the same vein, a heritability of 0.5 can be considered a little or a lot. Those interested in correcting dysfunctional personality or boosting cognitive abilities will evaluate a certain level of heritability differently than those interested in the selection of students and employees.

Trouble Understanding Research Methods and the Denial of their Necessity

PID research relies on powerful research methods, including test theory and multivariate statistics. Depending on students' knowledge, explaining these methods can be quite challenging. Teachers should respond to these challenges with adaptive teaching.

Students without basic knowledge in statistics definitely need a basic introduction to descriptive statistics. They have to understand the meaning of scales, frequency distributions, coefficients of central tendency such as the mean, coefficients of dispersion such as the variance, and coefficients of association such as the Pearson correlation. Moreover, students without knowledge of multivariate statistics should acquire a basic understanding of the general linear model and its application in factor analysis and multiple regression. It helps to explain these models verbally, mathematically as structural equations, and graphically as path diagrams.

Insight into the logic of the general linear model also helps us understand classical test theory (CTT), the decomposition of observed scores into true scores and error scores, and the decomposition of observed score variance into true score variance and error variance. Students who find it difficult to understand the logistic model equations of item response theory (IRT) often find it easier to grasp the graphical representation of IRT models as arrays of item characteristic and person characteristic curves.

Examples from applied psychology can help convince students that methodological expertise is not only indispensable for conducting PID research but also for interpreting the results of personality research correctly. Methodological expertise is necessary for translating research findings into employee selection, student selection, adaptive teaching, targeted interventions, and the evaluation of intervention success. Experience tells us that examples from clinical psychology are most convincing due to psychology students' fascination with disorders and their desire to become psychotherapists. If students understand that comparing the effectiveness of alternative therapies requires appropriate designs, assessment methods, and data analyses, they will accept that the acquisition of methodological expertise is unavoidable.

Confusion About the Multiplicity of Research Designs

Introducing the research designs described in section "Research Methods" can be challenging because there are so many. Confusion about this can be reduced if teachers patiently explain the suitability, costs, and benefits of different designs. Students understand, for example, that investigating the variability of states across time requires repeated measures. They also understand that a longitudinal study spanning decades is costly and risky because of dropout and institutional discontinuity. Advanced students will understand that separating actor, observer, and actor x observer interaction effects requires round-robin designs. Illustrating designs with the data box is advisable because this framework is most flexible. Systematically building up and modifying the data box depending on the research interest contributes to understanding the similarities and differences between designs.

Teaching, Learning, and Assessment Resources

Types of Resources

Resources to be used in teaching PID include books, journals, online resources, assessment resources, and services provided by associations of personality and individual differences.

1. Books: Textbooks are the most frequently used teaching and learning resource for basic modules. Most textbooks are easy to understand and support learning with examples and graphical material. Moreover, modern textbooks are linked to online support for both teachers and students. Depending on how closely a teacher wants to follow the structure of a textbook, one may suffice. However, the use of more than one textbook is recommended because students differ in their preferences for writing and illustration style. Because so many textbooks are available in English and other languages, recommending a specific textbook seems difficult and unfair to authors whose textbooks are not recommended.

   Handbooks and encyclopedias are valuable teaching and learning resources for seminars and advanced lectures. Their chapters were written by experts on the treated topic. Their level of elaboration and richness of detail exceeds that of textbooks. Because the numbers of handbooks and encyclopedias are much smaller than the number of textbooks, the recommendations made in the list of cross-references below seem fair.

   A special category of books are readers containing classic articles with a lasting impact on PID or chapters that revisit such classics. For a recent example, see the list of cross-references below.
2. Journals: Students should read original research articles as early as possible. Journal articles are an indispensable resource for seminars and advanced courses. Secondary literature such as textbooks always contain a certain number of misconceptions and errors. Tertiary texts (e.g., excerpts from textbooks, class notes, and summaries prepared by students) contain even more misrepresentations and errors. Moreover, students sometimes share their notes with students who missed a class. Each of these "recycling" steps increases the risk of errors and moves the product further away from the original. Teachers are advised to counteract this erosion of quality. Assigning students the reading of original papers is the best means to this end. The most important outlets of PID are listed in the cross-references section below.
3. Online resources: The Internet is crowded with material about PID of all kinds and quality: presentations of teachers and students, theses, conference presentations, preprints, articles on authors' websites, Wikipedia pages, digital versions of books, figures, tables, and an ever increasing number of videos of presentations, interviews with scholars, and lectukres. In addition, most textbook publishers

provide online material to complement the book. Some of these diverse materials are excellent; others are misleading or just plain wrong. Beginning students will be overwhelmed by separating the wheat from the chaff and will therefore need guidance from the teacher.

4. Assessment resources: Some textbooks contain questions at the ends of chapters to help students self-assess their state of knowledge and comprehension. Online material provided by textbook publishers also sometimes includes such questions. For reasons of test fairness, these questions cannot be used for exams. But they can serve as exemplars for exam questions to be developed by teachers.

5. Associations of personality and individual differences: Teachers and students can seek advice in their search for resources from PID associations. Navigating their websites and those of their executive committees and members can be of great help in finding all kinds of helpful material and guidelines. The most important PID associations are listed in the next section.

Cross-References to Resources

Handbooks and Encyclopedias

- John, O. P., Robins, R. W., & Pervin, L. A. (Eds.) (2008). *Handbook of Personality: Theory and Research*. New York: Guilford Press.
- McAdams, D. P., Shiner, R. L. & Tackett J. L. (Eds.) (2019). *Handbook of personality development*. New York: Guilford Press.
- Rauthmann, J. F. (Ed.) (2020). *The Handbook of Personality Dynamics and Processes*. New York: Elsevier.
- Zeigler-Hill, V. & Shackelford, T.K. (Eds.) (2020). *Encyclopedia of Personality and Individual Differences*. New York: Springer.

Readers

- Corr, P. (Ed.) (2019). *Personality and individual differences: Revisiting the classic studies*. London: Sage.

Journals

European Journal of Personality
Individual Differences Research
Journal of Individual Differences
Journal of Personality
Journal of Personality and Social Psychology
Journal of Personality Assessment
Journal of Personality Disorders
Journal of Research in Personality
Personality and Individual Differences
Personality and Social Psychology Bulletin
Personality and Social Psychology Review

Personality Science
Social Behavior and Personality

Associations of Personality and Individual Differences
Association for Research in Personality
European Association of Personality Psychology
International Society for the Study of Individual Differences
Society for Personality and Social Psychology
World Association for Personality Psychology

Conclusions and Outlook

Individual differences in feeling, thinking, and behaving are pervasive and have substantial impact on peoples' lives and life outcomes (e.g., educational achievement, job success, health, marital satisfaction). PID is a fascinating research field that has revealed intriguing insights into personality structure, process, and development. These findings are not only fascinating in themselves. They also inform other basic research fields (e.g., developmental psychology, social psychology, and psychological assessment), and they deliver indispensable knowledge to all domains of applied psychology (e.g., clinical psychology, counselling, educational psychology, legal psychology, sport psychology, industrial and organizational psychology). For these reasons, PID should be taught in every basic psychology program (bachelor) and be included as an optional field of research in advanced psychology programs (master, PhD).

Like every scientific discipline, PID has undergone substantial changes over its history. These were due to the changing Zeitgeist, to the steady accumulation of knowledge, to the diversification of psychology, to controversies, and to the dramatic advances in digital technologies. The growth of computational power and digital interaction via the Internet has opened new avenues for the online collection of data and eased collaboration among research groups independent of their geographic location. Digital technologies have shifted PID research from classic paper-and-pencil methodology and behavioral observation in the lab to data collection via electronic devices in natural environments, virtual realities, as well as online interaction and communication settings. Moreover, linking digital data from multiple sources makes it possible to explore types of individual differences that were inaccessible before. Obviously, advancement in digital technologies does not only create new research opportunities but also poses ethical challenges that the scientific community must address.

Advances in digital technology have also changed and will continue to change the ways we teach. This chapter was written in during the COVID-19 pandemic that boosted the development of tools for online teaching and remote learning. Not all but many of these tools will continue to exist and will be improved, diversified, and used in the future. Although it is difficult to predict in exactly which direction teaching in higher education will move, it seems safe to forecast that the times of exclusive in-class teaching are definitely over. Investigating empirically which blend of in-class and remote teaching contributes best to learning progress will be a task for education and psychology. PID should be a partner in this research because individuals differ in how they teach and learn best. From the perspective of PID, one size fits all approaches will be less successful as compared to adaptive teaching formats that take into account individual differences in abilities, skills, motives, interests, and personality traits such as the ones included in the prominent five-factor model.

References

Ajzen, I., & Fishbein, M. (1977). Attitude-behavior relations: A theoretical analysis and review of empirical research. *Psychological Bulletin, 84,* 888–918.

Allport, G. W., & Odbert, H. S. (1936). Trait-names: A psycho-lexical study. *Psychological Monographs, 47,* 1–171.

APA (American Psychological Association) (2013). *APA Guidelines for the Undergraduate Psychology Major.* New York: APA.

Asendorpf, J. B., Conner, M., et al. (2013). Recommendations for increasing replicability in psychology. *European Journal of Personality, 27,* 108–119.

Ashton, M. C., & Lee, K. (2007). Empirical, theoretical, and practical advantages of the HEXACO model of personality structure. *Personality and Social Psychology Review, 11,* 150–166.

Bandura, A. (1977). *Social learning theory.* New York, NY: General Learning Press.

Baumert, A., Schmitt, M., et al. (2017). Integrating personality structure, personality process, and personality development. *European Journal of Personality, 31,* 503–528.

Blum, G., Rauthmann, J. F., Göllner, R., Lischetzke, T., & Schmitt, M. (2018). The nonlinear interaction of person and situation (NIPS) model: Theory and empirical evidence. *European Journal of Personality, 32,* 286–305.

Blum, G., & Schmitt, M. (2017). The nonlinear interaction of person and situation (NIPS) model and its values for a psychology of situations. In J. F. Rauthmann, D. C. Funder, & R. Sherman (Eds.), *The Oxford handbook of psychological situations* (pp. 1–17). Oxford, UK: Oxford University Press.

Brunswik, E (1952). *The conceptual framework of psychology.* Chicago: University of Chicago Press.

Buss, A. H., & Plomin, R. (1975). *A temperament theory of personality development.* New York, NY: Wiley.

Carroll, J. B. (1993). *Human cognitive abilities. A survey of factor-analytic studies.* New York, NY: Cambridge University Press.

Cattell, R. B. (1950). *Personality: A systematical theoretical and factual study.* New York, NY: McGraw-Hill.

Cattell, R. B. (1966). The data box: Its ordering of total resources in terms of possible relational systems. In R. B. Cattell (Ed.), *Handbook of multivariate experimental psychology* (pp. 67–128). Chicago, IL: Rand McNally.

Cattell, R. B. (1971). *Abilities. Their structure, growth, and action.* Boston, MA: Houghton Mifflin.

Cook-Sather, A. (2009). *Learning from the student's perspective: A sourcebook for effective teaching.* Boulder, CO: Paradigm Publishers.

Deary, I. J. (2014). The stability of intelligence from childhood to old age. *Current Directions in Psychological Science, 23,* 239–245.

Deci, E. L., & Ryan, R. M. (1985). *Intrinsic motivation and self-determination in human behaviour.* New York, NY: Plenum.

Denissen, J. A., Luhmann, M., Chung, J. M., & Bleidorn, W. (2019). Transactions between life events and personality traits across the adult lifespan. *Journal of Personality and Social Psychology, 116,* 612–633.

Digman, J. M. (1990). Personality structure: Emergence of the five-factor model. *Annual Review of Psychology, 41*, 417–440.

Endler, N. S. (1975). A person - situation interaction model for anxiety. In C. D. Spielberger & I. G. Sarason (Eds.), *Stress and anxiety* (Vol. 1, pp. 145–164). Washington, DC: Hemisphere Publishing Corporation.

Endler, N. S., & Hunt, J. M. (1966). Sources of behavioral variance as measured by the S-R inventory of anxiousness. *Psychological Bulletin, 65*, 336–346.

Endler, N. S., & Magnusson, D. (1976). Toward an interactional psychology of personality. *Psychological Bulletin, 83*, 956–974.

Epstein, S., & O'Brien, E. (1985). The person-situation debate in historical and current perspective. *Psychological Bulletin, 98*, 513–537.

Eysenck, H. J. (1953). *The structure of human personality*. London, UK: Methuen.

Fleeson, W. (2001). Towards a structure- and process-integrated view of personality: Traits as density distributions of states. *Journal of Personality and Social Psychology, 80*, 1011–1027.

Funder, D. C. (2009). Persons, behaviors and situations: An agenda for personality psychology in the postwar era. *Journal of Research in Personality, 43*, 120–126.

Gardner, H. (2006). *Multiple intelligences: New horizons in theory and practice*. New York, NY: Basic Books.

Goleman, D. (1996). *Emotional intelligence: Why it can matter more than IQ*. New York, NY: Bantam Books.

Gottfredson, L. S. (2018). g theory: How recurring variation in human intelligence and the complexity of everyday tasks create social structure and the democratic dilemma. In R. J. Sternberg (Ed.), *The nature of human intelligence* (pp. 130–151). New York, NY: Cambridge University Press.

Gray, J. A. (1972). The psychophysiological nature of introversion-extraversion: A modification of Eysenck's theory. In D. Nebylitsyn & J. A. Gray (Eds.), *The biological bases of individual behaviour* (pp. 182–205). New York, NY: Academic Press.

Greenwald, A. G., McGhee, D. E., & Schwartz, J. L. K. (1998). Measuring individual differences in implicit cognition: The implicit association test. *Journal of Personality and Social Psychology, 74*, 1464–1480.

Hartshorne, H., & May, M. A. (1928). *Studies in the nature of character: I studies in deceit*. New York, NY: Macmillan.

Holland, J. L. (1973). *Making vocational choices*. Englewood Cliffs, NJ: Prentice-Hall.

Jayawickreme, E., Zachry, C. E., & Fleeson, W. (2019). Whole trait theory: An integrative approach to examining personality structure and process. *Personality and Individual Differences, 136*, 2–11.

Kelly, G. A. (1955). *The psychology of personal constructs*. New York, NY: Norton.

Kenny, D. A. (1994). *Interpersonal perception: A social relations analysis*. New York, NY: Guilford Press.

Kuhl, J., Kazen, M., & Quirin, M. (2014). The theory of personality systems interactions (PSI). *Revista Mexicana de psichologia, 31*, 90–99.

Kuhl, J., Quirin, M., & Koole, S. L. (2015). Being someone: The integrated self as a neuropsychological system. *Social and Personality Psychology Compass, 9*, 115–132.

Lee, J. J., Wedow, R., et al. (2018). Gene discovery and polygenic prediction from a genome-wide association study of educational attainment in 1.1 million individuals. *Nature Genetics, 50*, 1112–1121.

Maslow, A. H. (1954). *Motivation and personality*. New York, NY: Harper and Row.

Mathews, A., & MacLeod, C. (1994). Cognitive approaches to emotion and emotional disorders. *Annual Review of Psychology, 45*, 25–50.

McClelland, D. C. (1987). *Human motivation*. Cambridge, MA: Cambridge University Press.

Mischel, W. (1968). *Personality and assessment*. New York: Wiley.

Murray, H. A. (1938). *Explorations in personality*. Oxford, UK: New York, NY.

Pavlov, I. P. (1927). Conditioned reflexes: An investigation of the physiological activity of the cerebral cortex. *Nature, 121*(3052), 662–664.

Plomin, R., DeFries, J. C., Knopik, V. S., & Neidérhiser, J. M. (2016). Top 10 replicated findings from behavioral genetics. *Perspective of Psychological Science, 11*, 3–23.

Rauthmann, J. F., Funder, D. C., & Sherman, R. (Eds.). (2017). *The Oxford handbook of psychological situations*. Oxford, UK: Oxford University Press.

Rauthmann, J. F., Gallardo-Pujol, D., et al. (2014). The situational eight DIAMONDS: A taxonomy of major dimensions of situation characteristics. *Journal of Personality and Social Psychology, 107*, 677–718.

Richard, F. D., Bond, C. F., & Stokes-Zoota, J. J. (2003). One hundred years of social psychology quantitatively described. *Review of General Psychology, 7*, 331–363.

Roberts, B. W., & DelVecchio, W. F. (2000). The rank-order consistency of personality traits from childhood to old age: A quantitative review of longitudinal studies. *Psychological Bulletin, 126*, 3–25.

Roberts, B. W., Kuncel, N. R., Shiner, R., Caspi, A., & Goldberg, L. R. (2007). The power of personality: The comparative validity of personality traits, socioeconomic status, and cognitive ability for predicting important life outcomes. *Perspectives on Psychological Science, 2*, 313–345.

Roberts, B. W., Luo, J., Briley, D. A., Chow, P. I., Su, R., & Hill, P. L. (2017). A systematic review of personality trait change through intervention. *Psychological Bulletin, 143*, 117–141.

Roberts, B. W., Walton, K. E., & Viechtbauer, W. (2006). Patterns of mean-level change in personality traits across the life course: A meta-analysis of longitudinal studies. *Psychological Bulletin, 132*, 1–25.

Rogers, C. R. (1954). *On becoming a person*. Boston, MA: Houghton Mifflin Company.

Rotter, J. B. (1954). *Social learning and clinical psychology*. New York: Prentice-Hall.

Rotter, J. B. (1966). Generalized expectancies for internal versus external control of reinforcement. *Psychological Monographs, 80* (1, No. 609).

Schaie, K. W. (1965). A general model for the study of developmental problems. *Psychological Bulletin, 64*, 92–107.

Schwartz, S. (1992). Universals in the content and structure of values: Theoretical advances and empirical tests in 20 countries. In M. Zanna (Ed.), *Advances in experimental social psychology* (Vol. 25, pp. 1–65). Orlando, FL: Academic Press.

Shadish, W. R., Cook, T. D., & Campbell, D. T. (2002). *Experimental and quasi-experimental designs for generalized causal inference*. Boston, MA: Houghton Mifflin.

Shavelson, R. J., & Webb, N. M. (1991). *Generalizability theory: A primer*. Thousand Oaks, CA: Sage.

Shulman, L. S. (1986). Those who understand: Knowledge growth in teaching. *Educational Researcher, 15*, 4–14.

Skinner, B. F. (1969). *Contingencies of reinforcement: A theoretical analysis*. New York, NY: Meredith.

Spearman, C. (1904). General intelligence, objectively determined and measured. *American Journal of Psychology, 15*, 201–293.

Steyer, R., Mayer, A., Geiser, C., & Cole, D. A. (2015). A theory of states and traits-revised. *Annual Review of Clinical Psychology, 11*, 71–98.

Steyer, R., & Schmitt, M. (1990). The effects of aggregation across and within occasions on consistency, specificity. *and reliability. Methodika, 4*, 58–94.

Steyer, R., Schmitt, M., & Eid, M. (1999). Latent state-trait theory and research in personality and individual differences. *European Journal of Personality, 13*, 389–408.

Strack, F., & Deutsch, R. (2004). Reflective and impulsive determinants of social behavior. *Personality and Social Psychology Review, 8*, 220–247.

Strelau, J. (1998). *Temperament. A psychological perspective*. New York, NY: Plenum Press.

Thorndike, E. L. (1920). Intelligence and its use. *Harper's Magazine, 140*, 227–235.

Thurstone, L. L. (1938). *Primary mental abilities*. Chicago, IL: University of Chicago Press.

Vernon, P. E. (1950). *The structure of human abilities*. London, UK: Methuen.

Williams, J. M. G., Watts, F. N., MacLeod, C., & Mathews, A. (1991). *Cognitive psychology and emotional disorder*. Chichester, UK: John Wiley.

Teaching of Work and Organizational Psychology in Higher Education

22

Niclas Schaper

Contents

Abstract

Work and organizational (W/O-)psychologists are basically concerned with the experience and behavior of people in organizations and at work. The topics that W/O-Psychology deals with, both scientifically and practically, are enormously diverse and range from work analysis and work design as well as occupational health and safety to leadership, group work, and human factor issues to telework and corporate culture. This means that training in this discipline should also cover this breadth, at least in terms of the core areas, or it is offered a profile for specialization in one or more areas. W/O-psychologists usually work together with experts from other fields and are also required to familiarize themselves with new subject areas frequently. Therefore, they should be prepared for interdisciplinary cooperation and have special communication skills. Additionally, they

N. Schaper (✉)
Psychology, University of Paderborn, Paderborn, Germany
e-mail: niclas.schaper@upb.de

© Springer Nature Switzerland AG 2023
J. Zumbach et al. (eds.), *International Handbook of Psychology Learning and Teaching*,
Springer International Handbooks of Education,
https://doi.org/10.1007/978-3-030-28745-0_25

539

should be trained to familiarize themselves quickly and effectively with new areas of application and obtain thorough methodological training to make well-founded decisions in practice and choose methodological procedures that are scientifically sound and tested. The scientist-practitioner model is the central concept W/O-Psychology programs are based on. According to this model, psychologists are to be trained in a way that integrates science and practice such that activities in one domain would inform activities in the other domain. This dual emphasis on theory and practice is needed regardless of a student's intended career path. W/O-Psychology sees itself first and foremost as an applied discipline. Therefore, instructional design in the discipline is primarily based on a high degree of application orientation; i.e., students should not only learn relevant psychological theories and methods in their study programs. They should also be confronted with practical requirements of the future professional areas, and they should be given opportunities to test their expertise and gain experience in dealing with practice-related challenges. Furthermore, it is important that the links between science and practice are already established and improved in lectures, seminars, and training courses. Therefore, it is recommended to try out and implement a variety of approaches like case-based training courses or research-based project seminars. Instructional improvement in W/O-Psychology can also be obtained by using a pedagogical double decker, which puts concepts into practice in the course that are parallely taught theoretically. Finally, a competence-oriented instructional design is recommended – including the use of the constructive alignment concept – to develop the professional competences of future W/O-psychologists effectively.

Keywords

Work and organizational psychology · Applied psychology · Scientist-practitioner model · Case-based learning · Research-based learning · Pedagogical double decker · Development of professional competences

Introduction

Work and organizational (W/O-)psychologists are basically concerned with the experience and behavior of people in organizations and at work. This has to be observed, described, and explained as well as predicted and changed (Schaper, 2019; Conte & Landy, 2019). The two major fields of application are therefore work and organization, although in many cases, a third field of application is added: personnel management and how it can be effectively operated from a psychological perspective (cf. Campbell, 2002). In Anglo-American contexts, this area is also often classified and taught under the heading of Organizational Behavior (e.g., Griffin, Phillips, & Gully, 2019).

With regard to the field of work, W/O-psychologists are primarily interested in the functions and significance of work in people's lives. The central object of study in work psychology is thus the experience and behavior of people at work as a function of working conditions, work tasks, and the performance requirements necessary for this (Sonntag, Frieling, & Stegmaier, 2012). Other central topics of work psychology are theoretical concepts for the description, explanation, and prediction of work activities as well as for the motivation of work activities, strain and stress at work, job satisfaction, occupational safety, design of group work, training, and further education of employees.

W/O-psychologists are also interested in how the behavior and experience of organizational members are influenced by organizational characteristics and what effects result from this. The object of study in organizational psychology is thus the experience and behavior of people in organizations in general, but also as a function of various characteristics of organizational variables (structural, process, and goal characteristics of organizations) (Robbins & Judge, 2019). Central topics and issues in organizational psychology are theoretical concepts for describing and understanding organizational characteristics and structures, communication, interaction, and socialization processes and their role in organizations, leadership concepts, and diagnosing and changing organizations.

Finally, the third area of Work and Organizational (W/O-) Psychology deals with questions of personnel management in organizations. The main focus here is on analyzing how personnel management measures (selection, assessment, development) work and how they can be designed effectively (Campbell, 2002). Personnel psychology deals with aspects of behavioral control (e.g., through incentives or feedback) and how the aforementioned personnel functions can be effectively supported. These include, above all, issues relating to career choice and development, the analysis of occupational and task-related requirements, the recruitment of employees for organizations (personnel marketing), personnel selection, performance and potential assessment, and personnel development.

So, the topics that W/O-Psychology deal with, both scientifically and practically, are enormously diverse. They range from work analysis and work design as well as occupational health and safety to leadership, group work, and human factors issues to telework and corporate culture (cf. Conte & Landy, 2019; Schuler & Sonntag, 2008; Zedeck, 2011). Though, in the practice of W/O-Psychology, the focus is predominantly on personnel-related fields, e.g., training, recruitment and selection, and performance appraisal. Tasks concerning organizational and management development also fall into this context. Here, W/O-psychologists are active not only in conceptual and operational but also in managerial functions. W/O-psychologists perform these tasks as employees of industrial and service companies, public authorities, associations, and universities, as well as consultants and trainers in employed and self-employed forms. An employment survey of SIOP from 2011 reveals that 39.4% of W/O-psychologists in the United States work at universities (academia), 31.2% in consulting firms, 14.3% in private companies, 9.3% in governmental organizations, and 5.8% in other organizations (Spector, 2019). Concerning the question in what kind of organizations W/O-psychologists are active, it can be seen that this refers primarily to large industrial companies and service companies (SIOP, 2019). Much less often, W/O-psychologists are employed in medium-sized companies as well as public administrations, hospitals, and recreational organizations.

The increase in the number of W/O-psychologists employed in business and consulting organizations, particularly in the 1990s, shows that they now form a recognized professional group that is seen as making significant independent contributions and is trusted to master key challenges in business and organizational contexts (Schaper, 2019; Conte & Landy, 2019). In particular, the increasingly significant role of psychologists in business illustrates that challenges and problems can not only be solved via business and technological solutions, but also require the human-centered design of work and organizational processes and/or the empowerment of employees to achieve high levels of technical, economic, and social performance. For the practical fields of application of W/O-psychologists, it is also true that their tasks rarely present themselves as purely "psychological." Rather, the practical work of W/O-psychologists usually requires cooperation with specialists from other disciplines (e.g., business economists, engineers, computer scientists, lawyers) (Conte & Landy, 2019). Knowledge and skills of the corresponding neighboring disciplines (e.g., in labor law, production management and technology, marketing, or software engineering) are therefore usually just as important. Finally, the professional self-image of a W/O-psychologist also includes reflection on their ethical responsibility, which arises from their research or practical activities. In particular, they should be aware of the responsibility that their work or the concepts they develop can significantly influence people's living conditions. Therefore, it is always important to raise the voice against claims and procedures in which people are regarded solely as a resource or production factor.

The history of an independent psychology, which has human work as its object of knowledge, is still comparatively short (cf., e.g., Aamondt, 2015). A major developmental path to the emergence of W/O-Psychology as an independent discipline can be seen in the establishment of applied psychology at the beginning of the twentieth century and the rationalization of industrial work and its study from the end of the nineteenth century. With the publication of "Psychology and Economic Life" in 1912, Hugo Münsterberg (1912) attempted to programmatically and systematically place applied experimental psychology at the service of economic life. He thus founded the economic branch of the "Psychotechnik" approach, which focused on questions of optimizing human performance (Sonntag et al., 2012). Under the influence of the "human relations" movement, work psychology, which had been individualistically oriented until then, subsequently focused on a more social-psychologically oriented view of human work behavior and thus also became an organizational psychology. The "Hawthorne experiments" of Mayo (1945) and Roethlisberger and Dickson (1939) at the Hawthorne Works of the Western Electric Company were particularly groundbreaking in this phase. They were the first to clearly identify the importance of attitudes and work motivation as well as social relationships in workgroups for operational performance. The work of the Tavistock Institute for Human Relations at the beginning of the 1950s in the English coal industry on the introduction of a new partially mechanized mining method and the associated problems (poor working atmosphere, rising accident rates, etc.) and the development of the "socio-technical system" approach, which aimed at the joint optimization of the technical and the social system, was also very influential. Initiated by cognition and cybernetics research and the models of information processing, the cognitive structure of human work activities finally also increasingly became the subject of analysis and theory formation. Against this background, action regulation theory was developed to provide a comprehensive theory of the cognitive regulation of human work activities. Hacker (2015) and Volpert (1974) thus provide a theory on the basis of which it is possible to describe and explain in relatively concrete terms how humans deal with their environment in a goal-directed, thinking manner, change their environmental conditions, and also develop their personality at the same time. With the broad use of computer technologies in production, administration, and service and with the emergence of new forms of work (e.g., telework), the need for application-oriented work and organizational psychological knowledge has grown considerably in the current phase. Concepts of W/O-Psychology are thus a vital antagonist to counteract the adverse effects on people caused by the strongly technology-centered approaches within the framework of a human design of technology and work organization.

Central trends in disciplinary development can be identified above all for the following topics (Schaper, 2019):

- *Digitization of the world of work:* The ubiquitous introduction and use of computer technologies has triggered significant changes in the world of work. One key example of this is telecooperation or teleworking. This enables organizations and employees to perform or design work services and processes more flexibly. However, telecooperative forms of work also pose a number of potential risks (e.g., the risk of social isolation from colleagues or the lack of separation between work and private sphere), which have so far only been rudimentarily investigated.
- *Growth of service activities.* Service activities are also becoming increasingly important in our working world. This is due to their increasing prevalence. Service activities are primarily characterized by the fact that they are carried out in direct contact with the customer and place special demands on interaction skills and commitment. Which communication aspects, personal prerequisites, and organizational conditions contribute to the success or failure of such service relationships is still incompletely studied empirically. The stresses and strains arising from such demands, called "emotional work," also require intensive further research efforts.
- *Internationalization, globalization, and diversity.* The internationalization and globalization of the economy as well as the increasing cultural, demographic, and religious heterogeneity of workforces – called diversity – have resulted in changed requirements for human resource management (see, e.g., Hebl & Avery, 2013 or Kalargyrou & Costen, 2017). Specialists and managers who are sent abroad must be prepared in the process for their assignments abroad. In addition, new requirements for human resource management arise from increasingly

multicultural and heterogeneous compositions of workforces and workgroups (e.g., in multinational teams or mixed-age workgroups).

- *Increasing flexibilization and new forms of work.* The increasing flexibilization of the world of work, especially with regard to working hours and contractual ties, leads to increased employment risks for employees (e.g., through fixed-term employment contracts). Therefore, the latter should learn to assume personal responsibility to maintain their own employability and acquire skills for vocational self-management (cf., e.g., Gasteiger, 2007). Furthermore, new forms of work in the "platform economy" (e.g., Crowd or Gig-working) place new demands (e.g., be always ready for delivery on demand) and risks (e.g., to ensure their living in phases of no work) on the ‚employees of such platforms.

What conclusions can be drawn from this description of the disciplinary orientation? First of all, the description should have made clear that the topics of W/O-Psychology are enormously broad and diverse. This means that training in this discipline should also cover this breadth, at least in terms of the core areas. Alternatively, a profile for specialization in one or more areas can be developed and offered (e.g., for Personnel Psychology and HRM). It also became clear that in practice, W/O-psychologists usually work together with experts from other fields and are also required to familiarize themselves with new subject areas frequently. W/O-psychologists should therefore be prepared for interdisciplinary cooperation in their training. They should also have special communication skills and be trained to familiarize themselves with new areas of application quickly and effectively. Additionally, thorough methodological training is required so that W/O-psychologists are also able to make well-founded decisions in practice and choose methodological procedures that are scientifically sound and tested. Last but not least, it becomes clear that W/O-Psychology is a highly application-oriented science that derives its research and design topics primarily from problems and issues in practice. This should also be reflected in a high application orientation in the training of W/O-psychologists.

Objectives and Structure of Curricula in W/O-Psychology

The content of training in W/O-Psychology – which is mostly named, industrial and organizational psychology "in Anglo-American countries in contrast to the European countries where the title, work and organizational psychology" is relatively common – is taught at both the undergraduate and graduate level. At the undergraduate level, individual modules or courses are usually offered in generalist psychology programs or thematically related programs (e.g., management-oriented business study programs). On the other hand, there are also more extensive programs at the undergraduate level that focus on W/O-Psychology. In Germany, for example, a variety of Bachelor's degree programs in business psychology that cover a broad range of work and organizational contents are offered within Universities of Applied Science. More common, however, are extensive and in-depth training curricula in

W/O-Psychology in the context of graduate programs. At this level, a distinction is made in Anglo-American countries between master's and doctoral programs in W/O-Psychology. Graduate training in W/O-Psychology in the form of master's programs is usually limited to two to four semesters, and the focus is more on application and practice-oriented training. In the doctoral programs, which are often offered together with the master's programs, the focus is more on the training of scientific skills, and the programs are also more long-termed (about 4 years). All of the above educational offerings at both the undergraduate and graduate levels are subject to national accreditation requirements. Particularly for the more extensive master's programs, the respective national professional societies of W/O-Psychology have also developed educational guidelines to ensure content and professional standards of training (see, for example, the "Guidelines for Education and Training in industrial-organizational psychology" of the Society for Industrial and Organizational Psychology in the United States; SIOP, 2016/2017).

The scientist-practitioner model is the central concept W/O-Psychology programs are based on. Though it has its origins in clinical psychology, it is also mentioned as a central orientation for W/O-Psychology programs (Baker & Benjamin, 2000; Hays-Thomas, 2002). According to this model, psychologists are to be trained in a way that integrates science and practice such that activities in one domain would inform activities in the other domain. The application of the scientist–practitioner model in W/O-Psychology graduate training has been analyzed by Bartels, Macan, Gutting, Lemming, and McCrea (2005) in the US context. The authors found that 60% of master's and 63% of doctoral programs described their orientation as scientist-practitioner. Master's programs were more likely to describe themselves as "mainly applied" (30%), but doctoral programs were more commonly described as "mainly research" (26%). Among the scientist-practitioner programs, the most common technique for training in practice skills was reported to be supervised experience (88%). A similar analysis was conducted with W/O-Psychology academic training programs in Australia and New Zealand (Carless & Taylor, 2006), which came up with similar results. Even in the European context, the W/O-Psychology study programs refer to the scientist-practitioner model. This is mirrored in the ENOP-guidelines (1998), which present a reference model and minimal standards for study programs in W/O-Psychology in European countries.

This dual emphasis on theory and practice is needed regardless of a student's intended career path (Rupp & Beal, 2007). Those interested in academic careers need to understand both theory and practice to develop sound research. W/O-Psychology practitioners in industry, government, and consulting are required on the other hand to use their knowledge and skills to deliver services and intervention measures. Thus, students not only need to know each topic in a theoretical sense; they also need to know "how to" develop and implement associated services or intervention measures. Learning about a topic in a theoretical sense is not equivalent to the experience of applying that information. Doing it and having first-hand familiarity with the pitfalls, limits, and constraints of a technique (e.g., job analysis) is different from, and as critical as, theoretical knowledge.

Table 1 Two exemplary descriptions of the SIOP competences (SIOP, 2016/2017)

4. Professional skills (communication, business/research proposal development, consulting, and project-management skills)
In all employment sectors, success as a W/O-psychologist requires the development of a variety of professional skills. Communication, business development, and project management represent broad categories capturing some of the most essential professional skills
Effective communication is critical and required to interact with and influence others regardless of the context. Communication skills encompass using technology, writing, and presenting. They also involve interpersonal, negotiation, and conflict-management skills in order to build and maintain relationships and an ability to navigate relationships in a politically savvy way. Communication skills are particularly important in team contexts. An understanding of how individual efforts facilitate group performance and the ability to contribute as a member of a group are essential. W/O-psychologists must be able to translate scientific research to professional and layperson audiences effectively
(…)
10. Groups and teams
Much of human activity in organizations takes place in the presence of other people. This is particularly true of work behavior. The pervasiveness of interpersonal and task interdependence in organizations demands that I-O psychologists have a good understanding of the behavior of people in workgroups. It is also critical to have a familiarity with the growing teamwork literature. This requires an understanding that extends beyond familiarity with research and theory related to interpersonal behavior in small groups. The body of theory and research concerning groups and teams draws from social psychology, organizational psychology, sociology, and organizational behavior. A good background in group theory and team processes includes, but is not limited to, an understanding of leadership, motivation, interpersonal influence, group effectiveness, conformity, conflict, role behavior, and group decision making. Contemporary issues include but are not limited to multi-team systems, virtual teams, and cross-cultural teams

A SIOP report indicates that the primary goal of graduate training in W/O-Psychology is developing competences (Zelin et al., 2015). Taking a competence-based approach, these guidelines focus on the skills, behaviors, and capabilities necessary to function as a new member of the profession. Table 1 presents two exemplary descriptions of the SIOP competences (2016/2017), which show that both science and practice are inherent in each competence description.

In addition, there are, of course, a large number of other national guidelines that have been developed by the respective professional societies of W/O-Psychology. As an example, the guidelines of the German professional society may be mentioned here (Ellwart, Hertel, Lang, Trimpop, & Ohly, 2015), which are based on defined fields of work and the competences required there. Concerning the first aspect, four general fields of work in W/O-Psychology are mentioned: (1) Personnel and profession, (2) Work, health, and prevention, (3) organizational consulting and organizational development, (4) marketing and market research. Also, a framework of job-related competences is provided, resulting in a competence model with four successive stages (Table 2). Each level contains both scientifically based competences and a reference to application aspects. So, in addition to an empirical-theoretical foundation in W/O-Psychology training, the labor market with its practical occupation-related expectations is also taken into account. Therefore, the competence model serves to communicate to prospective students and the

Table 2 Competence level of the German education guidelines for Master's programs in W/O-Psychology (Ellwart et al., 2015)

Competence level 1: Orientation and structuring. At this level, the focus is on the systematic nature of the subject areas. Students know central concepts and theories of A/W-psychology and are able to present them systematically and relate them to each other

Competence level 2: Selecting and evaluating. At this level, students are able to evaluate diagnostic procedures or intervention measures in a well-founded and critical manner along with quality criteria, as well as to make recommendations for the selection of certain methods

Competence level 3: Apply and reflect. At this competence level, students can conduct, evaluate, and document instruments and procedures themselves. The focus goes beyond the application of classical quality criteria, as context and target group in the field of application have to be considered more strongly (e.g., social acceptance or practical usefulness). Students also develop their own skills (e.g., social and emotional competences) on the basis of experience and reflect on limits and development potential

Competence level 4: Designing and evaluating. At this level of competence, students are able to develop new procedures or interventions for specific areas of the application themselves and evaluate their effectiveness scientifically. They are able to develop and work on new problem areas in both practical issues and research-related contexts

labor market which competence acquisition is intended or which competences can be expected by the employer.

In summary, it becomes clear that study programs in W/O-Psychology exist at different levels of training and are relatively diverse overall. Despite this heterogeneity, attempts are made to ensure sufficient content-related and scientific quality of the study programs by means of educational guidelines of the national professional societies or an orientation toward higher-level standards (e.g., national accreditation guidelines).

Core Contents and Topics of W/O-Psychology

The contents and topics of W/O-Psychology are broadly diversified due to the diverse application possibilities of psychological concepts and methods in the world of work and organization. They refer to the application areas of work, organization, and personnel already presented in the introductory chapter. Further overviews of the relevant topics and contents of W/O-Psychology are provided by textbooks (e.g., Spector, 2019; Sonntag et al., 2012; Conte & Landy, 2019; Nerdinger, Blickle, & Schaper, 2019) as well as standards of various national professional societies of the discipline. As an example, we refer to the overview of SIOP (2016/2017), which presents the recommended areas of competence or knowledge to be developed in W/O-Psychology study programs (see Table 3).

In order to gain a structured insight into the different topics and professional areas of W/O-Psychology, the following text deals with different approaches to structuring these fields (Schaper, 2019). In connection with the classification of topics and core contents relevant for W/O-Psychology, different levels of observation and perspectives are often distinguished (e.g., Schuler, 2006):

Table 3 Areas of competence and knowledge to be developed in W/O-Psychology study programs (SIOP, 2016)

General knowledge and skills
1. Ethical, legal, diversity, and international issues
2. Fields of psychology
3. History and systems of psychology
4. Professional skills (communication, business/research development, consulting, and project-management skills)
5. Research methods
6. Statistical methods/data analysis

Core content
7. Attitude theory, measurement, and change
8. Career development
9. Criterion theory and development
10. Groups and teams
11. Human performance
12. Individual assessment
13. Individual differences
14. Job evaluation and compensation
15. Job/task/work analysis, competence modeling, and classification
16. Judgment and decision making
17. Leadership and management
18. Occupational health and safety
19. Organization development
20. Organization theory
21. Performance appraisal/management
22. Personnel recruitment, selection, and placement
23. Training: theory, delivery, program design, and evaluation
24. Work motivation

Related areas of competence
25. Consumer behavior
26. Human factors

- *Level of the individual:* The focus here is primarily on the behavioral and performance conditions of individuals in organizations as well as their diagnosis and development.
- *Level of groups or interaction relationships:* This level is primarily concerned with the forms, conditions, and processes of workgroups and leadership relationships.
- *Level of the organization as a whole:* At this level, the focus is on forms (e.g., functional organizations) and characteristics of the organization (e.g., organizational climate or culture) as well as the relationships of an organization to its environment.

With respect to a more process-oriented perspective, which puts a focus on the way objects of research and practice in W/O-Psychology are dealt with, the following distinctions are made:

- *Fundamental concepts:* Under this perspective, fundamental theoretical concepts (e.g., on the regulation of work actions) and issues (e.g., on the meaning of work) are primarily researched and developed.

- *Diagnosis:* This perspective focuses on the development of diagnostic methods in relation to the various objects of investigation in W/O-Psychology (e.g., methods for work analysis, aptitude diagnostics, and organizational and team diagnostics).
- *Intervention:* This involves the development of concepts and measures for changing and optimizing work, interaction, group, and organizational processes (e.g., through personnel development measures).
- *Evaluation:* This perspective focuses on reviewing the effectiveness of intervention measures at the various levels (e.g., individual training or team respective organizational development) and on the quality assurance of diagnostic instruments.

The mentioned classifications allow a further differentiation and structuring of objects and contents of W/O-Psychology, although the categories are not selective. However, they are quite useful as heuristic principles for differentiating different perspectives on the various objects of research and practice in W/O-Psychology.

W/O-Psychology sees itself first and foremost as an applied discipline because it finds its problems – similar to, e.g., clinical and educational psychology – predominantly in the practical world of human life. Since it also makes use of general theoretical concepts and findings as well as sophisticated scientific research methods, it is not a research discipline that is focused only on application. Its epistemological interest and research approaches are quite differently determined (cf. Sonntag et al., 2012):

- *Basic psychological research:* On the one hand, the cognitive interest of W/O-Psychology is shaped by the objectives and methodology of basic psychological research; i.e., W/O-psychologists are also interested in formulating generally valid statements (or theories). Therefore, they are testing their more fundamental hypotheses and models using systematically designed laboratory and field studies. In this context, the research topics arise in particular from questions and problems inherent in the theory and represent fundamental questions of W/O-Psychology (e.g., what role do goals play in motivating and controlling work actions).
- *Applied psychological research:* On the other hand, the interest in knowledge is characterized by procedures of applied psychology, which develops models and methods for problem solving with reference to one or more theories and disciplines. This approach generates concepts and instruments whose effectiveness for analyzing, predicting, and changing work- and organization-related problems is to be tested in a context-specific manner. By including situational variables, the explanatory models are generally more complex than in a more basics-oriented view. For example, to explain the effectiveness of training measures, not only learning concepts (e.g., on the effect of cooperative forms of learning), but also motivational concepts (e.g., on the expected benefits of learning outcomes) and socio-psychological variables (e.g., attitudes of supervisors toward the continuous development of their employees) are included in respective research approaches.

- *Practice-oriented analysis and development:* Furthermore, the epistemic interest can be characterized as practice-oriented since W/O-Psychology is also interested in the direct analysis and intervention in concrete individual cases. The object of development and investigation here is the optimal implementation and specific application of knowledge and methods of W/O-Psychology in order to meet the design needs of practitioners in organizations. Though, from a scientific perspective, this epistemic perspective is still a rather underdeveloped field, but also of particular importance in the training of practical skills in W/O-Psychology.

With regard to research methodological approaches, W/O-Psychology makes use of very different approaches (Blickle, 2019). In addition to predominantly quantitative research designs, qualitative designs are also used, either independently or in addition to quantitative designs. Furthermore, though the use of cross-sectional survey designs in W/O-Psychology is still predominant, longitudinal studies are very much increasing, and model-based analyses are also nowadays widespread in this discipline, with a large number of studies also based on multilevel models. Also, the application and use of different diagnostic methods concerning selection and appraisal methods, job and requirements analysis, or approaches of organizational diagnosis are essential tools of a W/O-psychologist. So, this research and diagnostic methodological knowledge and corresponding competences need to be addressed not only in research but also in practice-oriented study programs.

W/O-Psychology builds on various basic disciplines of psychology. So, it is also referred to as a cross-sectional discipline. General psychology, social psychology, and differential psychology play a special role here. For example, basic models of general psychology are usually used to clarify psychological issues of perception, thinking and learning, and motivation in work activities. Social psychology's theories and findings play a central role in the analysis and design of communication, cooperation, and conflict relationships between organizational actors and within workgroups or teams. Furthermore, the diagnosis of interindividual differences in employees' behavior, performance, and aptitude characteristics is inconceivable without reference to concepts and procedures of differential psychology. In addition, W/O-Psychology is also characterized by close links to other application areas of psychology. For example, in the context of psychological questions of personnel development as well as training and further education, there are relatively close thematic relationships to educational psychology.

Furthermore, the complexity and multifactorial nature of psychological problems in the world of work and organizations also requires W/O-Psychology to make use of the findings of other scientific disciplines and to cooperate with them in order to develop appropriate explanatory approaches and solutions. Significant neighboring disciplines are in particular economic and business science, medicine, computer science and engineering, sociology, law, and vocational or media education. For example, in order to determine and prove the economic benefit and efficiency of personnel development measures or personnel selection processes, reference to business cost-benefit models is required (Süßmaier & Rowold, 2007).

The overview of central contents and topics of W/O-Psychology illustrate how the teaching contents of the discipline can be structured from different perspectives. Not only do different aspects of content structuring come into play, but also the various application as well as research perspectives of W/O-Psychology. The design of the teaching should therefore also refer to this diversity of perspectives and the diversity of scientific approaches.

Teaching, Learning, and Assessment W/O-Psychology

In the following chapter, the main approaches to teaching W/O-Psychology with reference to its instructional design are presented. This covers the implementation of the scientist-practitioner model in W/O-Psychology teaching, case-based learning approaches, and principles of research-based learning in W/O-Psychology, as well as a pedagogical double decker approach.

Implementation of the Scientist-Practioner Model in W/O-Psychology Teaching

Instructional design in W/O-Psychology is primarily based on a high degree of application orientation; i.e., students should not only learn the relevant psychological theories and methods in their study programs. They should also be confronted with practical requirements of the future professional areas, and they should be given opportunities to test their expertise and gain experience in dealing with practice-related challenges. Therefore, the scientist-practitioner model was used as a guiding principle for the design of study programs in W/O-Psychology (see section "Objectives and Structure of Curricula in W/O Psychology"). However, the core idea of the scientist-practitioner approach has been only vaguely formulated and concretized with regard to its application (cf., e.g., Hays-Thomas, 2006; Rupp & Beal, 2007). However, one concrete aspect of the implementation of this model is that it is essentially pointed out that students should be guided and accompanied in internships by lecturers and practice supervisors who have experience or expertise in both areas – research and practice. Therefore, Shoenfelt et al. (2012) emphasize that internships play an important role in the education of master's and undergraduate-level W/O-Psychology students, as they provide applied learning experiences in organizational settings under qualified supervision. However, they also point to different problems concerning the implementation of adequate supervision and guidance for the interns (e.g., the frequency and quality of contact with the hosts). Furthermore, the interlocking of theory and practice in the course of studies should not only refer to the accompaniment of internships but should also be oriented toward an application-oriented design of teaching. However, few concrete suggestions are made in this regard in the educational guidelines of, for example, SIOP (2016/2017).

Design of Application and Case-Oriented Learning in W/O-Psychology

Although the scientist-practitioner model is certainly purposeful as a central principle for the curricular design, it is in great need of development concerning the instructional design of courses. In particular, more concrete recommendations are needed on how the links between science and practice can be established and improved already in lectures, seminars, and training courses of W/O-Psychology. For this purpose, a variety of approaches can certainly be used (Brame, 2016; Prince, 2004).

For example, in lectures with bigger audiences, the multimedia elements (e.g., videos of business cases) can be used to illustrate practical cases or to illustrate the application of a particular intervention methodology in practice (Han, Eomb, & Sug Shin, 2013). Furthermore, the inclusion of case-based elements, e.g., in the form of mini cases or case studies, has proven to be particularly useful for application-oriented didactics (Carloye, 2017). These instructional elements can also be integrated into seminars or training resp. exercise courses that accompany lectures. Additionally, role plays or role-play simulations can be used to gain experiences in taking on a specific professional task/role or applying and trying out certain techniques in professional communication or cooperation situations (DeNeve & Heppner, 1997). The authors implemented a role-play simulation in their work psychology course to transform students in leadership roles of a company and ask them to cooperatively solve different workplace or human resource-related problems (e.g., job dissatisfaction due to lack of challenge). This fostered student interest helped students apply the material to real-world situations, and improved the remembrance of learning contents well after the course ends. Furthermore, inviting practitioners into university courses to report on their experiences in implementing W/O-Psychology concepts or to talk to students about professional topics is also an effective element of application-oriented teaching that promotes motivation and learning.

However, in addition to integrating such application-oriented instructional elements, the entire course can be aligned with an application-oriented instructional strategy. For this purpose, e.g., complex case scenarios are suitable, which are to be solved by project groups (Farashahi & Tajeddin, 2018). Such case scenarios follow didactics of case-based learning (CBL), which means that the learners have to identify suitable solution concepts and the relevant state of research as well as to apply these concepts to the case and develop a context-adapted intervention approach. CBL is an instructional approach used across disciplines where students apply their knowledge and skills to real-world scenarios, promoting the application of complex concepts of a discipline and developing skills to transfer the knowledge by considering the context relevant conditions (He, 2015; Farashahi & Tajeddin, 2018). In CBL task assignments, students typically work in groups on case studies or stories involving one or more characters and/or scenarios. The cases present a disciplinary problem for which students develop solutions under the guidance of an instructor. This method involves guided inquiry and is grounded in constructivism, whereby students learn to apply their knowledge by interacting with the case, their co-learners, and the instructor (Lee, 2012). Other instructional approaches that are helpful to design an application and action-oriented instructional arrangement are the 4C/ID model (van Merriënboer & Kirschner, 2013) or problem-based learning (e.g., Zumbach & Spraul, 2007), though they still have not been used to design W/O-Psychology courses.

Schaper, Soyka, and Depenbusch (2023) presented an example of such a case-based learning approach for a W/O-Psychology training course. In addition to a lecture teaching fundamentals of W/O-Psychology at the undergraduate level, a training course is organized, which deepens the topics (e.g., work and requirement analysis, work motivation, and satisfaction) in an application-oriented way by conducting case studies. A complex problem scenario is developed in the case studies, which describes a prototypical application case for a specific topic (e.g., improving one's leadership behavior) as the starting point (Schaper et al., 2023). In this description of the initial situation of the case, essential characteristics of the involved company are depicted (e.g., type of products or services offered, the economic condition of the company, etc.) in order to present the current problems of the company as vividly and concretely as possible (see Table 4 for an example). On this basis, an assignment is formulated or derived for a project group (approximately three to four students), which puts the group into the role of a team of experts (e.g., a consulting team) and confronts them with a realistic assignment to analyze the problem and to develop a context adapted solution approach. The overall assignment is subdivided into approximately four to five sub-assignments, which the case study group has to work on by using the theoretical and methodical concepts of the relevant topic presented in the lecture.

Initial evaluations with competence-oriented survey items show that this type of training course significantly improves participants' skills in analyzing complex cases, transferring theoretical concepts to practical problems, and designing psychological interventions taking into account their application constraints (Schaper et al., 2023). In addition, there are clear motivational effects with regard to a more intensive occupation with topics and issues of W/O-Psychology in practice and the joy of solving challenging problems of this domain. Vodanovich and Piotrowski (1999) also demonstrated that CBL can be implemented in an online course arrangement of an Internet-based graduate course concerning legal issues in W/O-Psychology.

Orientation Toward Principles of Research-Based Learning in W/O-Psychology

Since the focus of the training in W/O-Psychology is also to be placed on abilities for the scientific analysis of practice-related problems, approaches of research-based learning or research-oriented teaching are also appropriate instructional measures. Research-based learning in the sense of learning through one's own research (from the "real" question to the presentation of results) represents only one type. Huber

Table 4 Example of a case study assignment in W/O-Psychology

Case study "work motivation"
Initial situation:
ProWare is a growing software company with around 4000 employees worldwide that develops and sells company-specific software solutions for customers in the financial services industry. The demand for such individually tailored programs has risen sharply in recent years, and an end to this trend is not in sight for the near future (...)
ProWare works in large project teams, which are also structured relatively hierarchically and in which the areas of responsibility are divided up very meticulously at the start of the project and are primarily carried out by the respective (sub-)project managers. The team members have to adhere primarily to the instructions of this team leader and therefore gain little insight into the context of the overall project. Coordinating team meetings very often take place only in the circle of the project managers. The software developers at the lower level are hardly included in the conceptual meetings. They are primarily responsible for the implementation of the concepts developed in the leader circle together with the customers. This leads to a lot of dissatisfaction at the lower level of project staff because they do not feel sufficiently involved in the project. The project team members are paid well for their tasks, but unfortunately, there are also few opportunities to develop further in the teams, as there are hardly any changes of tasks or positions within and between the teams (...)
Case study assignment:
As the head of HR at ProWare, you are asked by the management to analyze the lack of morale and turnover problems in the project teams and to take countermeasures
Consider the following questions to solve the case study:
1. Using the Job Characteristics Model, analyze which motivation problems exist among the software developers at ProWare
2. Make a corresponding analysis also on the basis of Vroom's VIE theory. What other theoretical concepts, if any, would you use to explain and analyze the motivation problems at ProWare?
3. Consider which measures would be useful to improve motivation in the software teams and, in particular, to increase the willingness to perform of the lower team members
4. Further elaborate on at least two of the measures. How would you design them and what should be considered? Which theoretical concepts of motivation theory can be used for this?
5. Finally, how can you evaluate or record whether employee motivation in your company has increased significantly after the implementation of the designed measures?

(2014), for example, divides research-based teaching into three types: In *research-based teaching*, learning is based on research, with students being introduced to the current state of research as well as the fundamental problems and initial questions of this research. *Research-oriented teaching* prepares students for independent research. Students should learn how to design the research process, with particular emphasis on the choice and implementation of research methods. Finally, *research-based learning* means that students conduct active and independent research, going through the complete research process. Therefore, "small formats" of research-based and -oriented teaching aim to practice the research-oriented view on certain questions and convey certain elements of research-oriented work. This could, for example, include smaller research tasks on subject-specific questions, the preparation of a review on the state of research on a certain topic, or the conception of a research design on a certain question. As a "large format" of research-based learning in W/O-Psychology, on the other hand, it is advisable to design and conduct research-oriented project seminars.

For this purpose, a project seminar for teaching W/O-Psychology was developed and evaluated (Schaper & Decius, 2023), which aimed at the research-based examination of practice-related topics or questions in W/O-Psychology. Based on project assignments given to project groups (approximately four to five students), the assignments usually refer to current topics or research questions (see Table 5 for an exemplary assignment), which has to be worked out by the project group both in terms of the current state of research and in terms of an own empirically based exploration (e.g., by interviews or surveys). First, the current state of research, including the underlying theoretical concepts or models and the state of development in practice, is researched and systematically evaluated. On this basis, the project groups derive their own research questions and research design. In the second project phase, the research designs are further elaborated and discussed with the instructor. In the next step, interviews and surveys are conducted with subjects relevant to the topics. Finally, the collected data have to be evaluated with the help of quantitative or qualitative methods (e.g., content analysis) and interpreted against the background of the state of research. Furthermore, practical implications and limitations of the own research approach as well as further research needs had to be worked out. In order to exchange and discuss these results with the other seminar participants, all project groups will present their results of the empirical phase.

The results of surveys of the participants at the end of the course (Schaper & Decius, 2023) showed that the students very much appreciate the instructional format of research-based learning because they have the opportunity to try out

Table 5 Exemplary project assignment for the project seminar on research-based learning in W/O-Psychology

Assignment sheet: *Relationship between work and family under conditions of the pandemic*
Project assignment: The Corona pandemic also led to the problem that many working parents have been confronted with considerable additional demands, i.e., work demands on the one hand and educational and care demands in relation to their children on the other. This is not only a matter of effective time management but also of dealing with transfer effects from one domain to the other (the so-called spillover effects) as well as boundary management in order to be able to live the two domains of life satisfactorily and to distinguish them appropriately from each other. This raises the question of how working parents have dealt with these particular demands, especially in different phases of lockdown, and how they have managed the conflicts that have arisen in this context
Learning objectives and project steps: • Review and systematically prepare literature on the topic of "work and family conflicts" with a focus on disruptive changes in the working world • (Internet) research of cases and examples in dealing with work-family challenges during the pandemic crisis • Prepare a presentation to present and discuss the state-of-the-art research on balancing work and family concerns and illustrative practical examples; also, derive research question for your own study • Plan and conduct structured interviews with working parents to identify, analyze, and discuss successful and problematic examples of balancing work and family concerns • Develop a concept or recommendations for balancing work and family concerns under pandemic conditions

scientific work and research with an authentic research topic and thus gain their own experience. The intensive supervision of the research work with corresponding support material was also judged positively because these are perceived as helpful for structuring and orienting the learning and research process.

Besides the described approach, "inquiry-based learning" or "experiential learning" are further approaches to reinforce scientific and critical analytic thinking that are needed to develop the scientific competences of future W/O-psychologists. Inquiry-based learning (IBL) is an educational approach that facilitates learning by engaging students in complex, authentic questions or problems (▶ Chap. 51, "Inquiry-Based Learning in Psychology"). In IBL, students typically apply methods and practices comparable to those of scientists, including the formulation of research questions and hypotheses and the testing of hypotheses through observation or empirical tests and experimenting. This process guides learners toward actively constructing new knowledge by discovering new insights in a domain. However, the results of meta-analyses (Furtak, Seidel, Iverson, & Briggs, 2012; Lazonder & Harmsen, 2016) show that it is essential to employ some level of guidance within IBL settings to help learners accomplish subtasks and overarching goals and to learn from the IBL activities effectively. Additionally, Gilardi and Lozza (2009) could show that an inquiry-based learning course in organizational psychology can successfully support professional identity development through reflective practice. Furthermore, "experiential learning" is another approach in higher education in which students gain knowledge through the application of theory (Clark, Threeton, & Ewing, 2010). Typically, students gain this experience in nonacademic settings, such as workplaces or a company, and the learning experience may be combined with research and the task of assisting a company. These approaches commonly make reference to Kolb's experiential learning theory, which is defined as "the process whereby knowledge is created through the transformation of experience" (Kolb, 1984). Luthanen, Sibert, Morris, Ohmer, and Lowden (2012) applied this approach as a field study that was conducted as an experiential learning research project. The goal of the project was to create an effective employee selection process (e.g., development of a situational judgment test) for this company. The authors resume that the project was a valuable experiential-learning opportunity for students and company members, which illustrates the importance of integrating the learning and research cycles in a manner that supports students and assists the company partner in meeting their needs.

Approach of the Pedagogical Double Decker in W/O-Psychology

Furthermore, Lisa Kath and colleagues (2021) have developed an interesting approach to instructional innovation and improvement of teaching in W/O-Psychology, which caused a lot of resonance and commentaries of other scholars (cf., e.g., Rogelberg, Summerville, & Ruggs, 2020). Their recommendations are to be understood in the sense of a "pedagogical double decker." That means that a course instructor not only teaches certain concepts but also uses the concept to design the learning process (e.g., moderation techniques that are not only presented and demonstrated by the instructor but also used to moderate the discussion in the course); in other words, the instructor puts into practice in the course what he parallelly teaches theoretically or what he is "preaching." Kath and colleagues start from the assumption that W/O-Psychology has developed findings and methods that can be used effectively to improve teaching in one's own discipline. In this context, they develop recommendations for changing one's own teaching, which require different degrees of change or adaptation of existing teaching concepts. In doing so, they distinguish between recommendations that lead to small, medium, or large changes in the teaching concept. Their recommendations are based on evidence-based concepts from research in W/O-Psychology on the topics of "training and development," "diversity and inclusion," "groups and teams," and "leadership." Table 6 shows excerpts of the authors' recommendations for two areas.

In the approach of Kath et al. (2021), the idea of the "pedagogical double decker," which is otherwise primarily practiced in educational science courses, seems to be particularly worth emphasizing. By applying concepts of W/O-Psychology when parallelly teaching them, students receive a living example of how an exemplary application of, e.g., team or leadership development concepts can look. By experiencing and being involved in the implementation of these concepts, students

Table 6 Exemplary needs-assessment questions and recommended changes for the areas of "training and development" and "leadership"

Needs assessment questions	Small changes	Medium changes	Large changes
Training/ development: Will your students retain what they learned well beyond the end of your course? Have you considered your teaching through the lens of any model of training design?	Encourage students to set goals focused on their own learning and behavior (rather than on their performance relative to other students)	Explain how course content might be useful to students in the near future	Ensure that students have repeated opportunities to practice in some fashion, receive feedback, and demonstrate that they paid attention to the feedback and improved
Transformational lead-ership: Are you modeling the type of leader you hope they will become? Are you able to create dynamic relationships that allow students to exceed typical expecta-tions, thereby trans-forming themselves?	Establish a shared vision for a course by explaining the "why" behind everything that goes into the course	Give more individual-ized feedback to stu-dents on their assign-ments, which can be done efficiently using well-designed rubrics	Assign team projects that allow the students to build efficacy and learn from each other

will gain and experience a more profound understanding, which can be used for reflection and professional development.

Lucas and Goodman (2015) reported a case study of project-based learning within an organizational psychology course that was designed to advance college students' knowledge on the intersection of leadership and well-being with reference to concepts of positive psychology. This was realized in the sense of a pedagogical double decker as the mentioned concept of leadership and well-being were not only used as central learning contents but also as significant concepts to provide guidance and support for the students. A major emphasis on this course was transforming the classroom into a laboratory where students applied relevant course concepts and interventions with client organizations. Evaluations of the course showed that the students were able to raise their self-assessment, stress management, and problem-solution abilities, as well as their resilience, self-efficacy, and social support.

Challenges and Lessons Learned

It has already been pointed out several times above that the training of W/O-psychologists requires a competence-oriented approach. This requirement is reflected both in a large number of framework recommendations of national professional societies and in the qualification framework models of higher education, especially in European countries. Study regulations and module descriptions of psychological study programs have concretized and implemented this recommendation in the form of corresponding learning outcomes. However, systematic implementation of competence-oriented didactics in teaching and the corresponding examination formats often does not yet take place in the elaborate and consistent manner that would be desirable. The lectures in W/O-Psychology are often still very theory based, the application tasks are not sufficiently related to the intended learning outcomes, and the examination formats and tasks also do not have a sufficient and systematic relationship to the learning outcomes, though there exist already effective concepts and tools to realize the desired level of competence orientation in W/O-Psychology (see section "Teaching, Learning, and Assessment Resources").

Another challenge is the appropriate and didactically meaningful use of digital media in higher education teaching. As already described above, on the one hand, they can be used very helpfully to present application examples and contexts in a more vivid, concrete, and lively way, which is of considerable benefit for application-oriented teaching. However, digital media should also be increasingly used in teaching W/O-Psychology to promote an active engagement with content and develop profession-oriented skills of analysis, evaluation, conceptual planning, and problem solving. All too often, teachers of W/O-Psychology still have to make their own efforts to create appropriate application scenarios for case- and problem-oriented learning instead of being able to use already proven and didactically sound collections of case studies or application scenarios.

Further challenges in the training of professionally oriented graduates in W/O-Psychology arise from the dynamic change in the world of work and the associated development trends. This refers not only to the rapidly advancing digitization of work and business processes. Also, the increasing spread of work contracts in the platform economy and the associated working conditions, the expansion of in-house socio-technical systems to organizational ecosystems which are also networked with external partners and actors (e.g., in healthcare systems), and the changing role of human actors in such systems, the change in organizational processes and structures toward agile systems and the associated demands on those involved, as well as the design of learning and development-oriented work environments in the context of "new work" approaches are just some of the trends that are leading to significant changes in working conditions and requirements. These trends are also challenging future workers as co-designers of work processes and structures as well as human resource management and development. On the one hand, these trends and the resulting changes in the world of work must be taken up in the training of W/O-psychologists and considered in the form of appropriate theoretical and analytical concepts. On the other hand, it is also important to prepare students for dealing with this changing world of work in terms of adapted professional competences (e.g., in terms of skills for dealing with digital media or skills for developing virtual teams).

Last but not least, further developments in theoretical and empirical-methodological approaches in W/O-psychological research must also be continuously integrated and taken into account in training so that not only future researchers but also practitioners benefit from these approaches for their professional actions. This involves, for example, more complex causal-analytic research approaches such as multilevel analyses or the increasingly extended survey and evaluation approaches for longitudinal analyses (e.g., in the form of event sampling methods in data collection or growth curve models in statistical evaluation). Thus, the integration of such approaches into research-oriented education requires didactic approaches to how these complex empirical research approaches can be taught in the context of application-oriented instruction.

Teaching, Learning, and Assessment Resources

The central basis and starting point for planning courses in W/O-Psychology should be well-formulated learning objectives or learning outcomes (Schaper, 2012). After an initial determination of the learning and knowledge content to be covered in a course, therefore, the next step is to determine which learning objectives are to be achieved and which competences are to be developed. In this context, the formulation of learning outcomes helps to determine and document the intended development goals as precisely as possible. For the derivation and formulation of learning goals or learning outcomes, it is advisable to use proven learning goal taxonomies (e.g., the taxonomy of Anderson et al., 2001, which provides categories for systematizing and deriving cognitive learning goals resp. outcomes). Learning goal taxonomies are important tools not only for the formulation of learning objectives but also for the analysis of requirements in learning and examination tasks and its comparison with the requirements formulated in the learning objectives (with reference to the constructive alignment principle). In view of the fact that the courses should contribute to the acquisition of competences by W/O-psychologists that are as professionally oriented as possible, learning outcomes for application-oriented learning as well as for the development of a research-oriented attitude in dealing with questions and problems of the organizational reality (in the sense of the scientist-practitioner model) must be taken into account.

The planning of courses in W/O-Psychology should, of course, also take into account the range of content required to prepare future W/O-psychologists (see the content catalogs of the professional societies in sections "Objectives and Structure of Curricula in W/O-Psychology" and "Core Contents and Topics of W/O-Psychology"). However, the learning content should be integrated into the curriculum in the context of a competence-oriented teaching strategy so that it can also be taught in a profession-oriented manner. Since a selection of learning content is necessary due to the large number of areas of application in W/O-Psychology, the professional societies recommend that reference should be made to the central fields of application of W/O-psychologists when selecting learning content.

Even when teaching the basics, teaching in W/O-Psychology should be oriented toward application *and* research. This can be achieved, for example, by integrating the so-called "small formats" of case-oriented learning, as already described above. In advanced study phases, the "large formats" of application- and research-oriented teaching should also be integrated into the curriculum. This is necessary with reference to the goals of a profession-oriented education in W/O-Psychology and to ensure that not only employment-relevant knowledge but also the respective skill elements are taught.

However, these more instructional approaches should be complemented by the integration of internship phases into the curriculum (cf. Shoenfelt, Kottke, & Stone, 2012). In the conception and implementation of such internship phases, it is crucial on the one hand that suitable internship offerings meet certain criteria (e.g., concerning the type and quality of support by the host organization). On the other hand, the internships should also be intensively supervised by the university. This includes support before the start of the internship (e.g., concerning the choice of an adequate internship or concerning the goals of the internship), but also during (e.g., concerning the support for practice projects) and after the internship (e.g., concerning the reflection of the internship experiences and the competence development). Appropriate supervision ensures that the experiences gained during the internship are also evaluated and used for professional competence development as well as the theory-practice interlocking. Other formats in which the inclusion of practice in teaching is in the foreground (e.g., inviting practitioners, projects with practice partners) should also be continuously included in the teaching of W/O-Psychology. This not only promotes the theory-practice linkage but also motivates students to develop their profession-oriented competences and attitudes.

Finally, when designing and implementing examination formats, care must be taken to ensure that the examination requirements are designed in accordance with the "constructive alignment" approach. At its core, constructive alignment is about matching (1) learning goals/learning outcomes with (2) instructional content and methods, as well as (3) examination forms and requirements when planning a course

(Biggs & Tang, 2011). This not only ensures the fit of the three central didactic resp. instructional elements of a course, but also ensures transparency about learning and examination requirements. Especially the examination tasks should appropriately reflect the learning outcomes and requirements of the learning tasks and activities in the courses. Constructive alignment thus prevents superficial learning and skill acquisition and calls for in-depth learning and targeted skill acquisition. Even in basic courses, exams should not only consist of knowledge questions but also require comprehension and application tasks as well as analysis and evaluation skills. Finally, to test learning performance in large formats of problem- or research-based learning, assessment forms other than written and oral exams should be considered to test the acquisition of competences adequately. If necessary, one should seek advice on this from instructional experts.

Following Kath, Salter, Bachiochi, Brown, and Hebl (2021), it can also be recommended not to always start with major changes in instructional redesign. Especially if one is inexperienced with instructional design and delivery, it is more appropriate to start with small changes in order to gain experience with implementing such changes. By this, novice or inexperienced teachers can learn how to prepare the changes, determine what should be considered during the implementation, and how to adequately evaluate the experiences made, etc. It can also be advisable to choose a subject area in which you feel confident and which you can use for instructional design in the sense of the pedagogical double decker.

Last but not least, it should be pointed out that it is highly recommended not to implement the instructional changes alone, but to coordinate the own projects with other lecturers, exchange experiences, and tackle joint projects of changing and innovating teaching. In this way, one better integrates one's strategy into the entire curricula of a study program. In addition, one protects oneself from mistakes and dead ends and benefits from the knowledge and experiences of others.

Further Reading

SIOP Web Site: The web pages of the US Society for W/O-Psychology (SIOP) offer a wealth of information about the research and practice fields of this psychological discipline. Furthermore, there is also a wide range of information about the pathways to undergraduate and graduate study and the professional establishment as a W/O-psychologist. As a professional society, SIOP also deals with the description and adoption of guidelines for the training of W/O-psychologists. In particular, the SIOP web pages include the Guidelines of Education and Training, described already in sections "Objectives and Structure of Curricula in W/O-Psychology" and "Core Contents and Topics of W/O-Psychology."

Textbooks of W/O-Psychology: In order to get an idea of the contents and subject areas of W/O-Psychology and get suggestions for the teaching of W/O-Psychology, reference can be made to various textbooks of the discipline. Paul Spector, as well as Jeffrey Conte and Frank Landy, have each written very well-founded and constantly updated textbooks that provide a good overview of the state of research and the body of knowledge in W/O-Psychology. The textbooks by Michael Aamondt (2015) and Donald Riggio (2017), as well as the textbook on Organizational Behavior by Stephen Robbins and Timothy Judge (2019), are also recommended. They are not only written in a very catchy and comprehensible way but also contain a number of additional instructional elements (e.g., case studies, experiential exercises, ethical dilemma, controversial topics (point and counterpoint), review questions) that lead to an active engagement with the topics and provide creative ideas for teaching the content.

Hays-Thomas, R. (2006): *Challenging the Scientist-Practitioner Model: Questions About I-O Education and Training.* The author has done extensive research on the scientist-practitioner model and its transferability, as well as the status of its implementation in W/O-Psychology. In the mentioned article, she describes the limitations of this approach and contrasts the scientist-practitioner model with two other approaches (scholar-practitioner and local clinical scientist approach), which, in her view, more appropriately reflect and address the training requirements for scientist-practitioner training in W/O-Psychology. Against this background, she discusses various questions for the further development of training in W/O-Psychology in the sense of more effectively linking research and practice (e.g., with regard to the supervision of students in practice fields).

Shoenfelt, E. L. (2012): *Master's and undergraduate I/O internships: Databased recommendations for successful experiences.* This paper discusses the role of internships for training in W/O-Psychology and describes the design aspects that need to be met in order to achieve the training goals associated with internships. The paper is not only characterized by clear recommendations for action regarding the design of the framework conditions for internships in W/O-Psychology at the graduate level. In addition, empirical data from surveys of internship providers and interns are also presented regarding the extent to which the recommended design aspects are actually implemented in practice.

Rynes-Weller, S. L. (2012): *The Research-Practice Gap in I/O Psychology and Related Fields: Challenges and Potential Solutions.* The author examines the different types and causes of the research-practice gap systematically. She distinguishes the following gaps: awareness gaps (unawareness of research or practice findings), belief gaps (attitudes/convictions regarding research or practice concepts), and implementation gaps (lack of implementation of already well-established research or practice concepts). On this basis, she also develops conclusive suggestions for overcoming the gaps. The gaps are not only relevant for the professional practice of W/O-psychologists, but they also should be addressed as a significant topic in W/O-Psychology training. Among other things, this can significantly shape the professional self-image as a scientist-practitioner.

Cross-References

▶ Formative Assessment and Feedback Strategies
▶ Inquiry-Based Learning in Psychology
▶ Problem-Based Learning and Case-Based Learning

▶ Service Learning
▶ Teaching Engineering Psychology
▶ Technology-Enhanced Psychology Learning and Teaching

References

Aamondt, M. G. (2015). *Industrial/organizational psychology: An applied approach*, 8th ed. New York: McGraw Hill Education.

Anderson, L. W., Krathwohl, D. R., et al. (Eds.). (2001). *A taxonomy for learning, teaching, and assessing: A revision of Bloom's taxonomy of educational objectives.* Boston: Allyn & Bacon, Pearson Education Group.

Baker, D. B., & Benjamin, L. T., Jr. (2000). The affirmation of the scientist-practitioner: A look back at Boulder. *American Psychologist, 55*(2), 241–247. https://doi.org/10.1037/0003-066X.55.2.241

Bartels, L. K., Macan, T., Gutting, B., Lemming, M. R., & McCrea, R. M. (2005). Teaching the practitioner side of the scientist-practitioner model. *Industrial-Organizational Psychologist.* https://doi.org/10.1037/e579182011-007

Biggs, J., & Tang, C. (2011). *Teaching for quality learning at university: What the student does* (4th ed.). Maidenhead: Open University Press.

Blickle, G. (2019). Methoden. In F. Nerdinger, G. Blickle, & N. Schaper (Eds.), *Arbeits- und Organisationspsychologie* (Lehrbuch) (pp. 29–44). Berlin: Springer.

Brame, C. (2016). *Active learning.* Vanderbilt University Center for Teaching. Retrieved [today's date] from https://cft.vanderbilt.edu/active-learning/

Campbell, W. J. (2002). Consideration of Consulting Psychology/Organizational Educational principles as they relate to the practice of Industrial–Organizational Psychology and the Society for Industrial and Organizational Psychology's education and training guidelines. *Consulting Psychology Journal: Practice and Research, 54*(4), 261–274.

Carless, S., & Taylor, P. (2006). Industrial and organisational psychology training in Australia and New Zealand. *Australian Psychologist, 41*(2), 120–129.

Carloye, L. (2017). Case study: Mini-case studies: Small infusions of active learning for large-lecture courses. *Journal of College Science Teaching, 46*(6), 63–67.

Clark, R. W., Threeton, M. D., & Ewing, J. C. (2010). The potential of experiential learning models and practices in career and technical education and career and technical teacher education. *Journal of Career and Technical Education, 25*(2), 46–62.

Conte, J. M., & Landy, F. J. (2019). *Work in the 21st century* (6th ed.). Hoboken: Wiley.

DeNeve, K. M., & Heppner, M. J. (1997). Role play simulations: The assessment of an active learning technique and comparisons with traditional lectures. *Innovative Higher Education, 21*(3), 231–246.

Ellwart, T., Hertel, G., Lang, J., Trimpop, R., & Ohly, S. (2015). Perspektiven für die AOW-Psychologie in Bachelor- und Masterstudiengängen. Verfügbar unter: http://www.fv-pasig.de/fileadmin/user_upload/Download_Texte/Perspektiven_AOW-Psychologie.pdf

ENOP-EAWOP. (1998). European curriculum reference model with minimum standards for W&O-Psychology: Basic and advanced. Verfügbar unter: http://www.eawop.org/uploads/datas/8/original/Enop%20-%20Eawop%20Reference%20model%202007.pdf

Farashahi, M., & Tajeddin, M. (2018). Effectiveness of teaching methods in business education: A comparison study on the learning outcomes of lectures, case studies and simulations. *International Journal of Management Education, 16*(1), 131–142. https://doi.org/10.1016/j.ijme.2018.01.003

Furtak, E. M., Seidel, T., Iverson, H., & Briggs, D. C. (2012). Experimental and quasi-experimental studies of inquiry-based science teaching: A meta-analysis. *Review of Educational Research, 82*(3), 300–329. https://doi.org/10.3102/0034654312457206

Gasteiger, R. (2007). *Selbstverantwortliches Laufbahnmanagement. Das proteische Erfolgskonzept.* Göttingen: Hogrefe.

Gilardi, S., & Lozza, E. (2009). Inquiry-based learning and undergraduates' professional identity development: Assessment of a field research-based course. *Innovative Higher Education, 34*(4), 245–256. https://doi.org/10.1007/s10755-009-9109-0

Griffin, R. W., Phillips, J. M., & Gully, S. M. (2019). *Organizational behavior: Managing people and organizations* (13th ed.). New York: McGraw Hill Education.

Hacker, W. (2015). *Psychische Regulation von Arbeitstätigkeiten.* Kröning: Asanger.

Han, I., Eomb, M. S., & Sug Shin, W. (2013). Multimedia case-based learning to enhance pre-service teachers' knowledge integration for teaching with technologies. *Teaching and Teacher Education, 34*, 122–129.

Hays-Thomas, R. (2002). Perspectives on the teaching of applied psychology. In D. C. Solly & R. Hays-Thomas (Eds.), *Mastering the future: Proceedings of the third national conference on master's psychology.* Pensacola/Richmond: CAMPP.

Hays-Thomas, R. (2006). Challenging the scientist – Practitioner model: Questions about I-O education and training. *Industrial-Organizational Psychologist, 44*(1), 47–53.

He, W. (2015). Developing problem-solving skills with case study in a conceptual management course. *Journal of Business Case Studies, 11*(2), 57–70.

Hebl, M. R., & Avery, D. R. (2013). Diversity in organizations. In N. W. Schmitt, S. Highhouse, & I. B. Weiner (Eds.), *Handbook of psychology: Industrial and organizational psychology* (pp. 677–697). Hoboken: Wiley.

Huber, L. (2014). Forschungsbasiertes, Forschungsorientiertes, Forschendes Lernen: Alles dasselbe? Ein Plädoyer für eine Verständigung über Begriffe und Unterscheidungen im Feld forschungsnahen Lehrens und Lernens. *Das Hochschulwesen, 62*(1–2), 32–39.

Kalargyrou, V., & Costen, W. (2017). Diversity management research in hospitality and tourism: Past, present and future. *International Journal of Contemporary Hospitality Management, 29*(1), 68–114. https://doi.org/10.1108/IJCHM-09-2015-0470

Kath, L., Salter, N., Bachiochi, P., Brown, K., & Hebl, M. (2021). Teaching I-O psychology to undergraduate students: Do we practice what we preach? *Industrial and Organizational Psychology, 13*(4), 443–460. https://doi.org/10.1017/iop.2020.47

Kolb, D. A. (1984). *Experiential learning: Experience as the source of learning and development.* Upper Saddle River: Prentice-Hall.

Lazonder, A. W., & Harmsen, R. (2016). Meta-analysis of inquiry-based learning: Effects of guidance. *Review of Educational Research, 86*(3), 681–718. https://doi.org/10.3102/0034654315627366

Lee, V. (2012). What is inquiry-guided learning? *New Directions for Teaching and Learning, 12*, 5–14.

Lucas, N., & Goodman, F. R. (2015). Well-being, leadership, and positive organizational scholarship: A case study of project-based learning in higher education. *Journal of Leadership Education*, 138–152. https://doi.org/10.12806/V14/I4/T2

Luthanen, A., Sibert, H., Morris, H., Ohmer, W., & Lowden, R. (2012). Experiential learning in industrial/organizational psychology: A case study. *Journal of the Indiana Academy of the Social Sciences, 15*(1), 95–110.

Mayo, E. (1945). *The social problems of an industrial civilization.* Cambridge, MA: Harvard University Press.

Münsterberg, H. (1912). *Psychologie und das Wirtschaftsleben. Ein Beitrag zur angewandten Experimental-Psychologie.* Leipzig: Barth.

Nerdinger, F., Blickle, G., & Schaper, N. (2019). *Arbeits- und Organisationspsychologie* (Lehrbuch). Berlin: Springer.

Prince, M. (2004). Does active learning work? A review of the research. *Journal of Engineering Education, 93*, 223–231.

Riggio, R. (2017). *Introduction to industrial and organizational psychology* (7th ed.). New York: Taylor & Francis.

Robbins, S. P., & Judge, T. A. (2019). *Organizational behavior*, 18th ed. London: Pearson.

Roethlisberger, F. J., & Dickson, W. J. (1939). *Management and the worker*. Cambridge, MA: Harvard University Press.

Rogelberg, S. L., Summerville, K., & Ruggs, E. N. (2020). I-O psychology for everyone: Use of culturally responsive teaching to increase diversity and inclusion in undergraduate classrooms. *Industrial and Organizational Psychology, 2020*(13), 509–514. https://doi.org/10.1017/iop.2020.78

Rupp, D. E., & Beal, D. (2007). Checking in with the scientist–practitioner model: How are we doing? *Industrial-Organizational Psychologist, 54*(1), 35–40.

Rynes-Weller, S. L. (2012). The research-practice gap in I/O psychology and related fields: Challenges and potential solutions. In S. Kozlowski (Ed.), *The Oxford handbook of organizational psychology: Psychology, organizational psychology, psychological methods and measurement* (Vol. 1). Oxford, UK: Oxford University Press.

Schaper, N. (2012). *Fachgutachten zur Kompetenzorientierung in Studium und Lehre*. Bonn: Hochschulrektorenkonferenz, Projekt "nexus". Verfügbar unter: https://www.hrk-nexus.de/fileadmin/redaktion/hrk-nexus/07-Downloads/07-02-Publikationen/fachgutachten_kompetenzorientierung.pdf

Schaper, N. (2019). Selbstverständnis, Gegenstände und Aufgaben der Arbeits- und Organisationspsychologie. In F. Nerdinger, G. Blickle, & N. Schaper (Eds.), *Arbeits-und Organisationspsychologie* (4th ed., pp. 3–18). Heidelberg: Springer.

Schaper, N., & Decius, J. (2023). Ein Ansatz zum forschenden Lernen zur Förderung von Forschungskompetenzen in der Arbeits- und Organisationspsychologie. In. B. Behrendt, A. Fleischmann, N. Schaper, B. Sczcyrba & M. Wiemer (Hrsg.), *Neues Handbuch Hochschullehre*, Band 112. Berlin: DUZ.

Schaper, N., Soyka, C., & Depenbusch, S. (2023). Fallbasiertes Lernen zur Vermittlung des Anwendungsbezugs arbeits- und organisationspsychologischer Konzepte. In. B. Behrendt, A. Fleischmann, N. Schaper, B. Sczcyrba & M. Wiemer (Hrsg.), *Neues Handbuch Hochschullehre*, Band 111. Berlin: DUZ.

Schuler, H. (2006). Gegenstandsbereich und Aufgaben der Personalpsychologie. In H. Schuler (Ed.), *Lehrbuch der Personalpsychologie* (pp. 4–13). Göttingen: Hogrefe.

Schuler, H., & Sonntag, K. (2008). *Handbuch Arbeits- und Organisationspsychologie*. Göttingen: Hogrefe.

Shoenfelt, E. L., Kottke, J. L., & Stone, N. J. (2012). Master's and undergraduate I/O internships: Database recommendations for successful experiences. *Teaching of Psychology, 39*(2), 100–106. https://doi.org/10.1177/0098628312437724

SIOP, Society for Industrial and Organizational Psychology. (2016/2017). Guidelines for education and training in industrial-organizational psychology. Verfügbar unter: https://www.apa.org/about/policy/industrial-organizational-guidelines.pdf

SIOP, Society for Industrial and Organizational Psychology. (2019). 2019 Income-and-Employment_Report. Verfügbar unter: https://www.siop.org/Research-Publications/Items-of-Interest/ArtMID/19366/ArticleID/4592

Sonntag, K., Frieling, E., & Stegmaier, R. (2012). *Lehrbuch Arbeitspsychologie*. Bern: Huber.

Spector, P. E. (2019). *Industrial and organizational psychology: Research and practice* (6th ed.). London: Macmillan.

Süßmaier, A., & Rowold, J. (Eds.). (2007). *Kosten-Nutzen-Analysen und human resources (HR)*. Weinheim: Beltz.

van Merriënboer, J. J. G., & Kirschner, P. A. (2013). *Ten steps to complex learning: A systematic approach to four-component instructional design* (2nd ed.). New York/London: Routledge.

Vodanovich, S. J., & Piotrowski, C. (1999). An Internet-based approach to legal issues in industrial-organizational psychology. *Journal of Educational Technology Systems, 28*(1), 67–73. https://doi.org/10.2190/a2ug-jb0j-6h98-lw31

Volpert, W. (1974). *Handlungsstrukturanalyse als Beitrag zur Qualifikationsforschung.* Köln: Pahl-Rugenstein.

Zedeck, S. (Ed.). (2011). *APA handbook of industrial and organizational psychology, vol. 2. Selecting and developing members for the organization.* Washington, DC: American Psychological Association. https://doi.org/10.1037/12170-000

Zelin, A. I., et al. (2015). Identifying the competencies, critical experiences, and career paths of I-O psychologists: Consulting. *Industrial-Organizational Psychologist, 52*(4), 122–130.

Zumbach, J., & Spraul, P. (2007). The role of expert and novie tutors in computer-mediated and face-to-face problem based learning. *Research and Practice in Technology Enhanced Learning, 2*(2), 161–187.

Teaching Engineering Psychology

Sebastian Pannasch, Martin Baumann, Lewis L. Chuang, and
Juergen Sauer

Contents

S. Pannasch (✉)
Faculty of Psychology, Technische Universität Dresden, Dresden, Germany
e-mail: sebastian.pannasch@tu-dresden.de

M. Baumann
Department of Human Factors, Ulm University, Ulm, Germany

L. L. Chuang
Institute for Informatics, Ludwig-Maximilians-Universität München, München, Germany

IfADo – Leibniz Research Centre for Working Environment and Human Factors, Dortmund,
Germany

J. Sauer
Department of Psychology, University of Fribourg, Fribourg, Switzerland

© Springer Nature Switzerland AG 2023   567
J. Zumbach et al. (eds.), *International Handbook of Psychology Learning and Teaching*,
Springer International Handbooks of Education,
https://doi.org/10.1007/978-3-030-28745-0_26

Abstract

Engineering psychology addresses our interactions with systems – from personal wearable devices to urban environments – that are designed to serve specific purposes. Research and teaching in engineering psychology is highly interdisciplinary. It is increasingly relevant given the growing complexity of technical systems and their prevalence in safety-critical domains. This chapter outlines the specific characteristics of engineering psychology and provides an overview of the relevant teaching issues. We propose a curriculum of key topics and discuss several factors that influence the nature of teaching, such as learning goals, format of teaching (e.g., lecture, seminar), and target audience (e.g., students of psychology, engineering, or computer science). Three examples illustrate how topics of engineering psychology could be taught in different formats. We also propose how to deal with several challenges in this field (e.g., teaching students with diverse academic backgrounds and career goals). Finally, several textbooks are recommended for teaching engineering psychology.

Keywords

Engineering psychology · Interface design · Human-machine interaction · Human factors · Cognitive ergonomics

Introduction: The Realm of Engineering Psychology

Professional aspects of engineering psychology relate to the application of psychological knowledge to designing tasks, human-operated equipment, and human-machine systems, typically in collaboration with engineers (Fitts, 1958). Thus, the scientific aspects of engineering psychology address the mental representations that humans hold of designed systems. These representations govern how we use systems and are defined by contributions from the biological and social sciences. In the real world, problems can arise when our representations do not correspond with how systems truly work. This can cause bad user experience or, worse, fatal accidents. There are many contemporary examples whereby engineering psychology could (or should) have contributed to system design. The following three examples demonstrate such contributions at different levels: major accidents at the macro-level, automation in everyday life at the meso-level, and design principles at the micro-level.

Macro-Level: Chernobyl

April 26, 1986, witnessed one of the worst accidents in commercial nuclear power generation. Two explosions at the Chernobyl-4 reactor blew off the 1000-tonne concrete cap sealing, releasing molten core fragments into the immediate vicinity and fission products into the atmosphere. Analyses of such accidents and failures are especially relevant to engineering psychology because they identify problems often obscured in complex systems, yet explainable by psychology. The Chernobyl disaster represents a case study where failures can be found across different levels in a hierarchy (Reason, 1990). First, there was a fallible management structure that was monolithic, remote, and slow to respond; for whom, safety ranked low in priority. Engineering psychology strives to understand such complex systems, which comprise interacting technical and human components, to identify potential problems and to involve the relevant stakeholders for implementing improvements. Second, the Chernobyl reactor was hazardous, complex, tightly coupled, opaque, and operated outside normal conditions. Third, there were operators with only a highly circumscribed and narrow understanding of the part of the system under their control. Engineering psychology should be involved in the design of such systems but also contribute to the definition of requirements with respect to the operators and their training.

   Being involved in the design of such systems represents one of the main responsibilities of engineering psychologists in order to facilitate the control of complex but also simple systems.

Meso-Level: Automation in Everyday Life

Our everyday environment contains numerous automated systems. For instance, incoming phone calls usually provide, unprompted, the name and even a picture of the person calling. This simple automation helps us identify the caller readily without need to decipher the incoming phone number and to associate it with the caller's identity. In a different example, houses are typically equipped with thermostats or air conditioning that automatically controls the room temperature. Once the desired temperature is set, no further human monitoring or adjustment of the room temperature is required. The washing machine represents another example for everyday automation. The procedural labor required for various types of laundering is subsumed into the selection of the appropriate program and a press of the button. All of these automated systems facilitate processes in everyday life and allow humans increased capacity to divert toward other activities. However, problems (and even fatalities) can occur when humans misjudge the responsibilities of automation, for instance, when users of semi-automated vehicles stop looking at the road even when they are required to do so. This can result in the misuse, disuse, or abuse of automation (Parasuraman & Riley, 1997). Thus, engineering psychology plays an important role in designing automated systems according to our concepts and mental representations of how these processes might work. This challenging task requires particular efforts to design processes and interfaces in the way that users can operate and control such systems without difficulties. The importance should be obvious for everyone who struggled with particular mobile phone apps, who has been faced with confusing remote controls, or who has tried to find the appropriate option in a poorly designed technical system. To summarize, the real challenge for engineering psychology lies in understanding technical systems and ensuring their compatibility to human cognition, conceptions, and expectations.

Micro-Level: Fitts' Law

Engineering approaches can serve to formalize psychological concepts. This allows for the parameterization of psychological concepts, which facilitates the systematic investigation of the fundamental properties of complex behavior, providing a common basis for designing systems that are sensitive to human capabilities. Describing the information capacity of human movement, Fitts' law is one of the most prominent examples of parameterizing a psychological concept (Fitts, 1966). By utilizing information theory, Paul Fitts was able to define human movements in terms of information requirements for changing one's motor actions. Difficult tasks that place high information requirements are those that involve highly precise movements, while simple ones are those that are less precise (i.e., it is easier to press a large button accurately than a small one because the former requires less precision). Besides size, limb movements are also more precise when they travel shorter distances compared to longer distances. With this in mind, the design parameters of size and distance can be readily employed to define the accessibility of elements in a human-machine interface. A familiar example is the placement of the minimize/maximize button of windows in most computer operating systems. Since the cursor cannot go any further than the corner of the screen, these buttons are infinitely large and easy to select, in spite of their small size and their large distance to the screen center.

Background and Interdisciplinary Character of Engineering Psychology

Three objectives characterize engineering psychology. First, it seeks to investigate how humans perceive, reason about, and interact with engineered systems – given their innate and acquired abilities to interact with the natural world in the first place. Unfortunately, engineered systems are not always compatible with our psychological concepts and expectations; non-psychological factors (e.g., production costs) can also influence how a system is designed. Second, engineering psychology aims to apply basic psychological methods and established theories of psychology to the design and optimization of systems. The goals are to promote user-centered systems that consider the user's psychological satisfaction as well as the implementation of effective support for the user-system interaction. While the former goal applies mainly to systems of everyday use, the latter addresses rather complex systems and workplace design. Third, engineering psychology research can identify how existing limitations of psychological processes and mechanisms (e.g., within-team communication, attention, memory, and reasoning) could benefit from an engineered solution (e.g., adaptive notifications, communication protocols).

Therefore, work in engineering psychology often aims to find answers to the following questions: (i) What are the problems that arise when humans interact with engineered systems? (ii) How can the cause of these problems be identified based on psychological theories, systematic investigations, and empirical research findings? (iii) How do behavioral phenomena observed in interaction with engineered systems contribute to confirming or extending psychological theories?

Given the interdisciplinary nature of engineering psychology, it is difficult to provide a precise definition of the field in relation to other disciplines – in fact, the authors of this chapter hold different views on these definitions, too. Following the distinction by Wickens, Hollands, Banbury, and Parasuraman (2016), engineering psychology can be understood as a subdiscipline of human factors. Together with other subdisciplines, such as physical ergonomics, engineering psychology endeavors to apply psychological and physiological principles to the design and engineering of products, processes, and systems. Thus, engineering psychology strives to provide a functional description of psychological concepts in a way that can inform the design of engineered (i.e., artificial) systems. It is distinct from human factors and work-related disciplines in that it does not necessarily seek to satisfy work domain requirements. In return, engineering psychology contributes to psychology by broadening the scope of existing theories, for instance, inspiring research on multiple attentional resources (Wickens, 1984). Work and organizational psychology is a close cousin to engineering psychology, given its interest in the relevance of psychological mechanisms to artificial systems (i.e., workspace design, management). Finally, engineering psychology is influenced by numerous disciplines outside of psychology that include, but are not limited to, economics, computer science, engineering science, and physiology.

Purposes and Rationale of the Curriculum in Engineering Psychology

For every individual teaching session, the instructor should decide on the weighted emphases across the following approaches: (i) definitions, theories, and models, (ii) empirical findings and practical applications, and (iii) methods relevant to this particular topic. When planning and preparing a teaching session, it can prove difficult to find the optimal balance between (i), (ii), and (iii). This decision is closely linked to the learning goals. Due to the characteristics of engineering psychology (see above), the field allows to focus on various learning goals in relation to the audience.

(i) *Definition, theories, and models*: This approach should focus on the understanding of abstract concepts. This means understanding the general concepts, research questions, and theoretical contributions related to the given topic. For instance, a session on usability would involve defining the term itself and discussing the different theoretical concepts that relate to it, across different use cases. Focusing on this learning goal would be most appropriate for students at level 6 (e.g., bachelor's degrees) of the European Qualifications Framework (EQF, Bologna Working Group, 2005). Relying on theory means that students learn to appreciate how abstract (and more generalizable) knowledge can be applied to novel domains, ranging from the design of virtual websites to physical kitchen devices. On the one hand, this could also mean that students acquire less concrete and applicable knowledge (e.g., how to examine the usability of a specific kitchen device). On the other hand, this means that students are better prepared to solve problems in novel domains that are yet to be addressed by textbooks.

(ii) *Empirical findings and practical applications*: This approach should provide empirical findings and support for work practices. For instance, the instructor could explain how results in color perception research inform color palettes in website designs or traffic signs. It should demonstrate how evidence informs theory formation, which in turn allows for general application to practical questions. As a rule, teaching is clearer and enhances student motivation when concrete examples are provided that demonstrate how basic theoretical knowledge can be applied to answer issues in the design of everyday objects. Nonetheless, it might be difficult to select representative examples. For instance, discussing the details about the position of car backlights and the estimates of observer-car distance (Buchner, Brandt, Bell, & Weise, 2006) can be helpful to explain the mechanisms of perception in the context of everyday application. However, a detailed discussion of this topic might only touch briefly upon 3D perception and distance while neglecting other relevant topics such as 2D perception. As such, this approach could be particularly useful for students who already possess a background in psychology at level 6 as well as at level 7 of the EQF as it demonstrates the practical application of psychological knowledge.

(iii) *Methods*: This approach should provide insights into the planning and execution of empirical investigations to gather relevant data. In particular, students should understand the difficulties of generalizing from well-controlled studies in the laboratory to address applied research questions. It shall be noted that a survey among human factors/ergonomics professionals showed that basic design methods were ranked as highly relevant for their job (Rantanen & Moroney, 2011). Many tools are available, and this approach should provide information about these tools and how to use them. For instance, different measurement techniques for the same operational concept (see, e.g., for the concept of situational awareness, Endsley, Selcon, Hardiman, & Croft, 1998) should be explained. Understanding the relationship between the design and use of these tools requires a certain knowledge about the underlying concepts as well as some background information about previous work with these tools. We think that intensive teaching of methods would be particularly beneficial for advanced students in the field of engineering psychology, i.e., for teaching at level 7 (e.g., master's degrees) of the EQF. Furthermore, when thinking about the learning goals in relation to methods, one should consider that learning about methods should always imply the possibility of applying these methods.

Core Contents and Topics of Engineering Psychology

The following topics present what the authors consider as suitable and fundamental for teaching engineering psychology. Therefore, this list may not be exhaustive and, instead, represents a starting point. The topics suggested would be suitable for a single-semester course. An overview of the topics is presented in Table 1. These topics may be considered to be part of the core curriculum of engineering psychology. Other topics could be added to respond to the particularities of local teaching institution (e.g., focus on ergonomics of maritime systems).

For each of the topics proposed, we recommend a similar structure for teaching each session. With the exception of history and methods, they should consistently provide definitions, theories and models, empirical findings, and practical applications. This will help students establish links between the different topics and, hence,

Table 1 Suggestions for topics that may constitute a lecture on engineering psychology

Topics	Short description
History and definition of engineering psychology	Historic development of field, historic milestones, boundaries of the field, interdisciplinary nature
Fundamentals of human performance	Attention, perception, selection of action, decision-making, cognitive processing, strengths and limitations of human performance
Central theories and concepts of engineering psychology	Fitts' law, Hick-Hyman law, mental workload, situation awareness, multi-tasking, etc.
Displays and controls	Designing the elements of human-machine interaction, design of mobile devices, compatibility of displays and controls
Automation	Design options (e.g., static, adaptive, and adaptable automation), automation levels, complacency, trust, mental model
Human error and safety	Case studies of major disasters (e.g., Chernobyl), alarms, warnings, risk assessment, theoretical approaches
Overview of methods	Lab-based experiments, simulation (e.g., computer-based, virtual reality), objective performance measures, psychophysiology, eye tracking, signal detection theory
Design methods	Ergonomics design principles, regulations, guidelines, human-centered design methods; design of hardware, software, tasks, and jobs
Social aspects of human-machine interaction	Teamwork, social support, distributed systems
Personnel selection and training	Cognitive styles, competencies, work and system analysis
Stress	Designing for emergencies, work stress (e.g., task-related, physical, social)
Usability, user experience, and accessibility	Design and testing of interactive consumer products and websites; universal design
Application domains of engineering psychology	Aviation, air traffic control, surface transportation, industrial process control, etc.

develop a perspective that is uniquely shaped by the application domain that most interests them (e.g., aviation).

We would like to point out that across this range of possible topics, "methods" is especially important. This is because engineering psychology has the option of providing students with numerous methodological tools for field investigations (e.g., mental workload questionnaires, usability testing, task analyses). Engineering psychologists can use these methods to evaluate human-machine systems (e.g., whether humans with certain functional limitations can use a certain smartphone, whether the design of a ship's bridge is suitable for operations with a reduced team size). The results of these evaluations will provide input for computer programmers, engineers, and designers to redesign the systems. The methodological tools typically encompass the measurement of primary and secondary task performance, psychophysiological data, eye tracking, and subjective state data (usually by means of rating scales) such as fatigue and mental effort. The methodological competence of students in engineering psychology represents an asset for them in their future professional career (Table 2).

Teaching, Learning, and Assessment in Engineering Psychology: Approaches and Strategies

There are different formats of teaching in engineering psychology, as they are in most subdisciplines of psychology. We may distinguish between traditional lecturing, more interactive formats (e.g., seminars), and classes that are organized like a project (e.g., small group practicals or laboratory classes). Each of these formats has its strengths and weaknesses and should be selected in accordance with the primary learning goals to be achieved in the course. Of course, there is considerable literature that is designed to support teaching at the university, describing a great deal of general techniques and approaches relevant for good teaching in general (see, for instance, ▶ Chaps. 48, "Basic Principles and Procedures for Effective Teaching in Psychology," ▶ 49, "First Principles of Instruction Revisited," and ▶ 50, "Problem-Based Learning and Case-Based Learning," in this book as well as Fry, Ketteridge, & Marshall, 2008; Sambell, Brown, & Graham, 2017). Since the focus of this chapter is teaching engineering psychology, we will concentrate on aspects of teaching formats that are especially important for engineering psychology. Nevertheless, we strongly recommend that these general approaches and strategies are considered to create a teaching experience that engages students in their learning.

The format of lectures is mainly appropriate to provide a broad introduction to the field and pertinent topics of engineering psychology, as presented in Table 1. This format provides the students with the opportunity to become familiar with the most relevant concepts, theories, and methodological approaches of engineering psychology. The instructors' challenge is to create a coherent structure of the diverse field of engineering psychology for the students. In Table 3, we provide an overview of textbooks that might be of help for structuring the lectures. The lectures need to bridge the gap between the generality of theories and frameworks and singularities of

Table 2 Example of structure of a seminar on automation

Session	Short description
Introduction to automation (I)	The lecturer gives an overview of the field of automation
Lab-based practical	Presentation of a computer-simulated automatic system to students in laboratory, including active participation of students in system management
Introduction to automation (II)	The lecturer builds on the previous lecturer by making multiple references the practical experience gained in the preceding session
Discussion of scientific articles	Discussion of 1–2 key scientific articles from the field of automation
Scientific presentation of students (I)	Students in small groups will give short presentations on different topics (e.g., deskilling, trust and system reliability, adaptive and adaptable automation)
Small group project: Preparation	In class, an interview schedule is prepared for collecting information in organization using automatic systems
Small group project: Working out and presenting methodological approach	Presenting interview guideline and other data collection method to fellow students in class, discussing and improving proposed methodological approach practical project
Small group project: Conducting work in organization	Small groups of students collect interview and observational data in an organization of their choice
Scientific presentation of students (II)	Students in small groups will give short presentations on different topics (e.g., automation in aviation, industrial process control, car driving)
Small group project: Presenting findings	After data analysis, the findings are presented to fellow students, using the style of presentation of a business consultancy being hired by the organization
Summary of seminar content	The lecturer summarizes the content of the seminar and revisits the main learning goals, followed by a seminar evaluation by students
Assignment	This could be in form of a written exam using mainly open questions (e.g., "Describe the concept of automation complacency!") or an essay (e.g., "How will increasing automation level affect operator workload? Please discuss!")

different application domains. This is because engineering psychology focuses on the mechanisms of human information processing in different contexts of human-technology interaction, whereas the different contexts are of more importance for engineers and system designers.

The instructor's task is to demonstrate, explain, and emphasize the common theories and mechanisms that underlie problems across different application domains (e.g., issues related to selective attention in driving a car and piloting an airplane). Understanding the common features of problems within a domain allows the students to recognize and understand the general nature of theories and models in

Table 3 Recommended textbooks for teaching engineering psychology

Book reference	Comments
(i) *Engineering Psychology and Human Performance* by Wickens et al. (2016)	This introduction to engineering psychology provides a broad coverage of the field in 12 chapters, emphasizing theoretical and empirical research on human information processing and performance applied to the human-machine interaction. Looking at the problems in system design from the perspective of human information processing, it somewhat lacks chapters on design and evaluation methods. It is mainly intended for psychology and engineering students and practitioners in the field of engineering psychology
(ii) *Designing for People: An Introduction to Human Factors Engineering* by Lee, Wickens, Liu, and Boyle (2017)	This recent textbook provides a broad introduction to human factors engineering. It emphasizes design principles and methodologies, but nevertheless shows how these principles are derived from "humans' psychological, biological, and physical characteristics" (Lee et al., 2017, p. iv). Primary audiences are engineering or computer science students with no prior experience in psychology. But, according to the authors, it can be also used in applied psychology courses
(iii) *Human Factors in Simple and Complex Systems* by Proctor and Van Zandt (2018)	This textbook has a major focus on human factors and ergonomics in general. Therefore, the part I provides a good introduction in the field of human factors. In the parts II–IV, the perceptual, cognitive, and action factors are introduced and discussed with regard to applications. For students with a background in psychology, this part might largely repeat already known issues, but since this is all set in the context of application, it can provide a good foundation. Part V focuses on environmental factors and is therefore dedicated to aspects that traditionally are related to human factors
(iv) *Designing the user interface: Strategies for effective human-computer interaction* by Shneiderman et al. (2018)	This classical textbook focuses on the evolution of user interfaces. It covers theoretical foundations and addresses all relevant steps in the design process. The book is written for a broad audience with diverse backgrounds such as psychology, computer science, business, sociology, and education
(v) *Human Factors Engineering and Ergonomics: A Systems Approach* by Guastello (2014)	This is another classical textbook for the field of engineering psychology (also here labelled as human factors engineering). The goal of the book "is for the engineers to think more like psychologists, and the psychologists to think

(continued)

Table 3 (continued)

Book reference	Comments
	more like engineers" (Guastello, 2014, p. xvii). Therefore, the book is structured in chapters which follow relevant topics of engineering psychology, such as visual displays; stress, fatigue, and human performance; and human-computer interaction. Each chapter provides the necessary information for psychologists and engineers
(vi) *An Introduction to Human Factors Engineering* by Wickens, Lee, Liu, and Gordon-Becker et al. (2014)	The structure of this textbook is also in accordance with the topics in engineering psychology. The book offers a more psychological perspective by describing the capabilities and limitations of the human operator and how these should be used to guide the design of systems with which people interact
(vii) *Human Factors Methods: A Practical Guide for Engineering and Design* by Stanton et al. (2013)	This is not a classical textbook but presents a comprehensive and well-arranged overview about most of the commonly used methods in the field of human factors. This book therefore can be understood as a valuable supplement to the aforementioned textbooks. For the preparation of a lecture, relevant details about particular methods can be found. Also for seminars, this can be used for the discussion of certain methods

engineering psychology. This would enable them to broadly apply fundamental knowledge to different problems and to innovate methodological approaches derived from theories and models for novel situations. As engineering psychology focuses on supporting the design of human-machine systems in the real world, it is important for students to learn how to apply the theoretical concepts and the different methodological approaches to practical problems. Consequently, the ultimate goal of lectures should be to present the students with an overview of the field so that they are – to a certain extent – able to apply appropriate theories and frameworks and methodological approaches to new problems by being able to classify these new problems according to their underlying causes.

If possible, lectures should be accompanied by exercises where specific content of the lecture can be practiced, relevant research papers can be discussed in detail, or questions of the students can be discussed more thoroughly than in the lecture itself. Exercises provide the opportunity to involve the students more actively in the lecture content and thereby to deepen their understanding.

More interactive teaching formats, such as seminars, may focus on a sub-sample of the topics presented in the lecture (e.g., seminar on *automation* or seminar on *human error and safety*), but may also combine several topics into a coherent seminar topic for a given teaching period, such as semester or trimester (e.g., seminar on *errors in automation*). We suggest applying a basic structure within a seminar that includes relevant general theoretical concepts, methodological approaches, practical exercises, and possibly domain-specific applications. Seminars provide the opportunity to explore relevant topics in greater depth. They should also address different viewpoints that are critically evaluated. In this format, the students are much more actively involved in the teaching and learning process than in traditional lectures, in particular if supported by hands-on activities (Moroney, 1995). Therefore, active learning approaches should be applied to ensure that the focus is shifted from the instructor delivering the course content to the students being actively engaged in the topics of the course. Examples of how to include hands-on activities in engineering psychology courses can be found elsewhere (e.g., Benne & Fisk, 2000; Jones, 1999). Possible teaching approaches include short presentations given by students on specific sub-topics, which are followed up by discussions in the class, or small group exercises where students apply the content of the previous short student presentation on real-world problems sketching out a possible solution. These possible solutions should then be discussed in the class again. This integration of general theoretical concepts and methodological approaches with their practical application to small real-world problems makes this teaching format an important element for teaching engineering psychology. It ensures that relevant topics can be taught in depth and, at the same time, that they are integrated into a broader context. Furthermore, seminars help to bridge the gap between theoretical knowledge and its practical application in the context of real-world problems. Last, but not least, the active involvement of students supports the development of a wide range of soft skills that are essential for any professional in the area of engineering psychology.

In laboratory classes, the focus is largely on the practical application of knowledge acquired in lectures and seminars in the form of student projects. In such formats, small groups of students or individual students work on a specific problem under the supervision of an instructor. Usually, the results are presented in a written report. However, we would encourage instructors to organize a final presentation session during which all projects are presented by students. The assigned projects can range from running an experiment to carrying out a usability test. Ideally, the projects are related to the research topics of the instructors or the institution responsible for the teaching unit. This will increase the probability that the students become familiar with very recent research topics, research findings, concepts, and methodological approaches, learning to apply them in practice. Including basic research questions from engineering psychology (e.g., addressed by a lab experiment) or rather applied projects (e.g., together with partners from the community in a service-learning project; see Furco, 2002) is in any case helpful to provide the students with hands-on experience, which they will later need as engineering psychology professionals in their daily work. This project-oriented format, especially when organized in small teams, supports the further development of project management skills.

The Importance of Case Studies

Case studies are indispensable when communicating the importance of considering the human operator as an integral component of engineered systems. There are numerous examples of poor human-machine system designs that communicate the consequences of how simple oversights can result in catastrophes. Examples range from prominent accidents (e.g., Chernobyl, Herald of Free Enterprise) to constantly pressing the wrong button on the TV remote control. There is some literature that provide good accounts of such case studies, which can be used in teaching (e.g., Casey, 1988; Reason, 1990; Wogalter, 2019).

Target Audience

Engineering psychology is most likely to be taught to students who major in psychology, although students from other disciplines (e.g., engineering, computer science) may also participate. This topic may also be taught at a graduate level to mature students with work experience. Teaching a potentially diverse audience raises challenges in achieving a balanced focus. Nonetheless, it also presents a unique opportunity for students across psychology, engineering, and computer science to work collaboratively, as it would be mirrored in the real world. Cognitively diverse teams share a larger knowledge base and will allow students with different backgrounds to learn from each other.

To some extent, the format of teaching will determine whether this diversity can be leveraged. For example, seminars will benefit more from a highly diverse audience than a lecture. This is because in a seminar students will benefit from the input of other students with a different scientific background (e.g., in a discipline other than psychology) or a different level of expertise (e.g., work experience), whereas such student input is less prominent in lectures. Furthermore, lectures are less able to cater for differences in the competence levels in students. Therefore, it is advisable to adapt the format of teaching to the expected degree of student heterogeneity.

Involvement of Practitioners

To what extent should engineering psychology teach relevant skills for practice (e.g., interview techniques for root cause analyses)? Engineering psychology provides a unique opportunity to help students understand how theories from other subdisciplines relate to the design of real-world systems (e.g., how displays for low-light environments can be designed based on our understanding of visual perception). Given that students often lack the personal experience to appreciate the challenges of work domains, we believe that they can benefit from the involvement of practitioners. We will now suggest different ways in which practitioners can be involved, including an estimate of the resources required (i.e., in terms of time and budget) for each suggestions.

(i) *Co-teaching approach.* An academic member of staff and a practitioner could run the class jointly (high resource requirements).

(ii) *Customer-based approach.* The practitioner is a "customer" to whom input is provided by students to solve the practitioners' problem, such as improving the interface of a technical system (moderate to high resource requirements).

(iii) *External speaker.* A practitioner is invited as an external speaker to talk about an academic topic from a practitioner's point of view (e.g., "How is mental workload in aircraft cockpits measured by aircraft manufacturing companies?"). This involves low resource requirements.

(iv) *Site visits.* A similar approach represents visiting an external organization to talk to practitioners in their work environments (low to moderate resource requirements).

(v) *Internship (work placement).* Related to this issue is the completion of an internship, which is mandatory in many university courses. It provides a very good possibility to get to know real-world problems and in best case to transfer academic knowledge to them (low to moderate resource requirements).

Examples for Teaching

In this section, we will outline three specific cases that exemplify how different forms of teaching can be implemented. They may serve as a model for a range of classes to be taught in engineering psychology. In case 1, we will provide several suggestions for seminars that can be implemented in addition to a series of lectures, which might be planned according to the topics listed in section "Purposes and rationale of the curriculum in engineering psychology". Case 2 is an example for a series of seminars dedicated to specific topics (e.g., automation, aviation, ship navigation, etc.). Finally, case 3 provides suggestions for sessions with a practical orientation.

Case 1: Small Group Teaching

Topics in engineering psychology have the advantage of being directly relevant to our everyday experiences. This can motivate course participants, providing a unique opportunity to bridge theory to practice. There are various forms of small group teaching, such as tutorials, seminars, and problem-solving classes. Small group teaching accompanying a lecture is based on the idea that students are already familiar with the relevant theories and can now focus on real-world applications. A teaching session could therefore begin with a short presentation (5–10 min) given by a student participant. For example, such a presentation could address how attention in applied settings relates to operational concepts, such as "situational awareness." This could be followed by a practical part, wherein course participants will identify potential risks across different operational domains. For example, they could determine how limitations of selective visual attention might result in failures when using a particular in-vehicle display. They could also propose solutions to alleviate identified risks, such as the appropriate placement of in-vehicle displays. Alternatively, students could work on explaining how technology they use in their everyday life can be improved by using psychological theories.

An alternative activity would be to discuss research articles and accident reports. Course participants will read pre-selected papers before each teaching session, which is guided by questions provided by the instructor beforehand. Following a discussion, students would be requested to transfer their acquired knowledge to other problems or a different operational domain. This transfer can also be discussed in class or in the form of a short essay that is either evaluated by the instructor or by fellow students. The latter procedure provides the advantage that students will have to perform their own transfer as well as read and evaluate the approach of fellow students, hence benefiting from the diversity of applied research solutions and possibly different academic backgrounds.

Finally, linking small group teaching less strongly to the lecture allows focusing on only a few selected topics by studying specific problems in greater detail. As an example, one can think of the analysis of a website, a widely used piece of software, or a ticket vending machine. Following this approach would allow employing particular methods for the development of one or multiple alternative solutions. During the teaching sessions, methods can be discussed and even applied to evaluate the obtained solutions. Furthermore, such a procedure would provide the opportunity that students can work in different teams. Working in competitive teams might have the advantage to demonstrate that often several distinct approaches can be found and implemented to address a particular question. This can serve as a unique experience of the work in the field of engineering psychology.

Case 2: Seminar on Automation

It is a challenge to teach domain-related topics (automation, aviation, healthcare, etc.) to students who lack corresponding work experience. For example, students may not understand the system operations of a safety-critical domain (e.g., aviation) that prevent them from appreciating the benefits or added complexities of automation, for example, in terms of how automation is applied in landing an aircraft or controlling a chemical plant. As such, they may not empathize with the challenges experienced by human operators (e.g., boredom-induced fatigue during supervisory control) and might consider accidents as avoidable "human errors."

Two complementary approaches may overcome this familiarity problem. First, the seminar could focus primarily on examples from the students' personal experience, which bear similarity to the challenges in real work domains. For example, car park assistance systems or in-car navigation systems represent devices to which many students can relate. Second, using computer-based dynamic simulations of complex systems in the classroom may help students understand more easily the principal underlying features of automatic systems. Despite the reduced complexity of these lab-based simulation (compared to systems in the real world), they still allow students to experience the underlying features of the real-world system (e.g., in the case of industrial process control, this may be opaqueness and sluggishness of the system). Such computer-based simulations may also be used to model the different automation levels proposed by theoretical frameworks from the automation domain, such as the taxonomy of automation levels by (Sheridan & Verplank, 1978).

The seminar should offer a mixture of different activities. Table 2 provides an example of how a seminar on automation may be structured. The core elements of the seminar are the theoretical input provided by the lecturer and the hands-on experience of students at two levels, that is, in the form of a lab-based practical and a small group project to be carried out in an organization. Furthermore, it involves short scientific presentations on a particular aspect of automation and the discussion of journal articles, and, finally, the seminar ends with the completion of an assignment by the students.

There are multiple learning outcomes of this seminar. Students will be able to explain options of automation design by using automation models and examples. They will be able to design an interview guideline for analyzing the positive and negative consequences of automation in organizational settings. Finally, they will have gained a good understanding of the different options in automation design, including the advantages and disadvantages associated with each of them.

Case 3: Small Group Practicals Based on Real-World Examples of Engineered Systems

For students of engineering psychology who might go on to be human factors/ ergonomics professionals, it is highly important to gain practical experience in methods as well as in applying theoretical concepts to addressing specific problems and research questions. Small group practicals are especially important for acquiring such experience. Practitioners are typically expected to define and evaluate systems, prior to implementing a proposed improvement that is subsequently validated (i.e., systems development life cycle; e.g., V-Model, Forsberg & Mooz, 1992), to perform root cause analyses of system inefficiencies, or to prepare accident reports. In addition, they are expected to be familiar with standardized norms by professional bodies (e.g., National Institute for Occupational Safety and Health). One goal of a practical class would be to familiarize students with these expectations, even if the professional training for a given domain is beyond the scope of a tertiary education.

In one example, students can be familiarized with basic techniques used by practitioners to improve systems and processes. One example, drawn from the Six Sigma process, is the SIPOC model, which is often performed to identify the *suppliers, inputs, process, outputs,* and *clients* of a given system (Stamatis, 2004). To relate this to an everyday experience, students could be provided with the scenario of doing the laundry. They would first identify the suppliers of critical inputs (e.g., water, electricity, dirty laundry, etc.) before detailing the process that utilizes these inputs to produce certain outputs, which are subsequently directed to clients. With this complete description of a system, they would then be tasked with identifying how the process could be optimized, perhaps by introducing an automated feature in the washing machine for ordering washing detergent. This activity could be extended by teaching students to formalize processes and the interactions between different system components with Unified Modeling Language (UML), whereby activity diagrams provide an overview of the workflow of activities of the user at different steps of a task and sequence diagrams describe the interactions between the user(s) and different components of the system (e.g., display readout, buttons, etc.).

In a different example, students can be trained on investigative techniques to determine the root cause of undesirable incidents (e.g., accidents). Simple techniques, such as *Five Whys* and *Fishbone Diagram*, are used in practice to guide interviewers in systematically identifying potential reasons for system errors and accidents (Moaveni & Chou, 2017). Given that students often lack domain expertise, it is necessary to select problems from their daily lives. For example, they could be asked to identify the root causes of why their parents make "avoidable" mistakes with consumer electronics, or suboptimal administrative processes at the university, or a messy communal living environment. After acquiring some experience with these interviewing techniques, students could role-play the investigator of a well-known accident (e.g., Hudson River Plane Crash; popularized by the film "Sully") with other students who could, themselves, role-play as other actors in the accident (pilot, passengers, passers-by, etc.).

The basic procedure applicable to most small group practicals consists of a first phase where all students meet regularly. In this phase, the presented problem should first be defined, the relevant theoretical concepts and methods should be introduced, and some basic concepts of project management should be presented. After this phase, the students should form teams of two to four students that work together on the problem. If possible, the teams should be interdisciplinary in order to train students in coordinating different skillsets and transdisciplinary communication. At the beginning of this working phase, each team should define a project plan with tasks and milestones. During this working phase, we recommend regular meetings of the teams with the instructor to discuss individual questions and the current state of the project. We also recommend at least one meeting of all teams, where the teams present their current state to all other teams in the mid of the working phase. This will train the students' communication skills. It will support the exchange of ideas and experience with the application of concepts and methods and the mutual support of the teams. Such a small group practical should be concluded by a presentation of the results of all teams in a kind of mini-workshop. If possible, we recommend that a broader audience is to be invited to this final workshop. Additionally, either each individual student or the team as a whole should document their results in a written report. Again, this will train a different important set of communication skills.

Challenges and Lessons Learned

Given the rapid technological advancements, we expect the need for experts in engineering psychology to rise in the future. Therefore, universities and other institutions of higher education need to offer attractive curricula that will encourage students to take a degree in engineering psychology. However, apart from the issues discussed in this chapter, there are three further challenges that are relevant to the field of engineering psychology, which we will briefly discuss.

First, the design and optimization of human-machine interaction from a user-centered design perspective is the main focus of engineering psychology. When comparing the two parties involved, humans and technology, it becomes obvious that both evolve at a different pace. While there are anthropological speed limits on the human side, an enormous speed has been observed over the last decades in the development of technology. These differences are less problematic when only considered from a user-centered design perspective: It requires adjusting technology according to the respective state of the art in order to support the human user in an optimal way. However, it may impede the potential of innovation, since technological improvements are bound to the human perspective (see, for instance, Shneiderman, 2020). Beyond the constantly changing requirements for the research in engineering psychology, this also represents challenges for teaching in this field. For example, designing an optimal interface is a central topic in engineering psychology. With the evolution from physical to more virtual interfaces that become less visible and partly disappear in modern technical systems, this central topic requires fundamental revision as well as new methods and approaches. While the topics regarding the human aspects (e.g., human information processing, capacity limits, etc.) evolve at a rather slow pace, the fast developments regarding machines, interfaces, and technology require a permanent updating in order to teach an up-to-date curriculum.

The second point is related to the first issue and refers to the compatibility of academic teaching and the requirements of diverse professional fields. Teaching abstract theories and methods creates abstract knowledge that needs to be elaborated further in the concrete professional field, accompanied by on-the-job training. However, the rapid development of technology means that gaps can appear between the systems that are taught and the technology that graduates may work with. This situation might come across as a paradox. On the one hand, academic research is often at the forefront of technological development. On the other hand, an understanding of how such technology is deployed and implemented in the field might require many years of systematic research. Furthermore, implementation of a single technology might vary immensely across different domains. Thus, teaching should cover established aspects in human-machine interaction rather than seek to follow fads. This will equip the students with broad general knowledge on highly relevant concepts and methodological approaches for the solution of paradigmatic problems. It will give the students the capability to apply this knowledge to specific cases and develop their appropriate expertise in their respective domain in the interaction with real-world problems.

Finally, it is challenging to adjust the teaching content to the goals and capabilities of the target audience. Students from technical disciplines most often lack basic knowledge from psychology, while students of psychology rarely have technological knowledge. Teaching both groups in the same course requires a good balance to make it as beneficial as possible for both groups. Furthermore, the field of engineering psychology often provides to psychology students their first opportunity to see how psychological knowledge can be applied in everyday life settings. Therefore, they are interested and motivated to apply their knowledge gathered so far. The opposite is often the case for students from technical disciplines. For them, it is more interesting and fascinating to learn about the theoretical foundations of human information processing. Given the constraints that have been discussed throughout this chapter, finding an appropriate balance for the target audience can be challenging.

This chapter provides some ideas and material that teaching staff in the field of engineering psychology may find helpful. The process of writing this chapter revealed – especially throughout the discussions among the authors – how complex and challenging teaching in such an interdisciplinary discipline can be. We hope that this chapter will stimulate discussions about what the best way of teaching this interesting subject would be.

Teaching, Learning, and Assessment Resources

There are several established textbooks, in the domain of engineering psychology, which may be used for teaching (see Table 3). These are listed under (i)–(vii) and provide a systematic and coherent overview of the most important topics in engineering psychology. We recommend these because their chapters typically build on each other, with cross-references that highlight these connections. These textbooks are mainly written for students and observe high pedagogical standards. This includes chapter summaries, further reading, and/or study questions at the end of the chapters. Furthermore, the length of each chapter, and depth of detail, is compatible with a course plan that addresses one topic per course session. Therefore, we believe that such textbooks are preferable to handbooks. In contrast, handbooks tend to be more diverse, with the different chapters (usually written by different authors) not being connected and not building on each other. The target audiences of handbooks are professionals that would like to be informed about a specific topic in a brief and concise way.

We acknowledge that these textbooks may not be universally compatible to every course program. One reason for this is the diverse application domains that engineering psychology pertains to. Our individual backgrounds might also bias our preferences to particular domains, such as aviation or surface transport. The fields of usability and UX or design methods are covered to the same extent in general textbooks on engineering psychology as other more traditional topics, such as attention, design of displays and controls, and workload. Therefore, they might be supplemented with chapters from handbooks and research papers. The selection of textbooks in Table 3 is highly selective and does not claim to be exhaustive. The selection is mainly based on the authors' experience with textbooks in their own courses on engineering psychology. Table 3 also contains a book that provides a comprehensive overview of the methods in the field of engineering psychology (vii).

In addition to these suggestions, there are available online resources that can be used for different teaching formats. We provide just a few examples here, such as the website of the Human Factors and Ergonomics Society (https://www.hfes.org/Resources/Education-Resources).

Additionally, educational material can be found at the website of the APA organization (https://www.apa.org/action/science/human-factors) or at MITOPEN-COURSEWARE (https://ocw.mit.edu).

Furthermore, it is highly recommended to explore the content of journals where research findings and theoretical contributions from the field of engineering psychology are published. We suggest the following journals, which is a non-exhaustive list: *Human Factors*, *Ergonomics*, *Applied Ergonomics*, *Reviews of Human Factors and Ergonomics*, *Theoretical Issues in Ergonomics Science*, *Proceedings of the Annual Meeting of the Human Factors and Ergonomics Society*, *Journal of Applied Psychology*, and *Journal of Experimental Psychology: Applied*.

Cross-References

▶ Basic Principles and Procedures for Effective Teaching in Psychology
▶ Educational Psychology: Learning and Instruction
▶ Problem-Based Learning and Case-Based Learning

References

Benne, M. R., & Fisk, A. D. (2000). Teaching applied experimental psychology using a living laboratory. *Proceedings of the Human Factors and Ergonomics Society Annual Meeting, 44*(9), 75–78. https://doi.org/10.1177/154193120004400902.

Bologna Working Group. (2005). *A framework for qualifications of the European Higher Education Area*. Bologna Working Group Report on Qualifications Frameworks (Copenhagen, Danish Ministry of Science, Technology and Innovation).

Buchner, A., Brandt, M., Bell, R., & Weise, J. (2006). Car backlight position and fog density bias observer-car distance estimates and time-to-collision judgments. *Human Factors, 48*(2), 300–317.

Casey, S. M. (1988). *Set phasers on stun: And other true tales of design, technology, and human error*. Santa Barbara, CA: Aegean Press.

Endsley, M. R., Selcon, S. J., Hardiman, T. D., & Croft, D. G. (1998). A comparative analysis of SAGAT and SART for evaluations of situation awareness. *Proceedings of the Human Factors and Ergonomics Society Annual Meeting, 42*(1), 82–86.

Fitts, P. M. (1958). Engineering psychology. *Annual Review of Psychology, 9*(1), 267–294.

Fitts, P. M. (1966). Cognitive aspects of information processing III: Set for speed versus accuracy. *Journal of Experimental Psychology, 71*, 849–857.

Forsberg, K., & Mooz, H. (1992). The relationship of systems engineering to the project cycle. *Engineering Management Journal, 4*(3), 36–43.

Fry, H., Ketteridge, S., & Marshall, S. (2008). *A handbook for teaching and learning in higher education: Enhancing academic practice* (3rd ed.). New York, NY: Routledge.

Furco, A. (2002). Is service-learning really better than community service? In A. Furco & S. H. Billig (Eds.), *Service-learning: The essence of pedagogy*. Greenwich, CT: Information Age Publishing.

Guastello, S. J. (2014). *Human factors engineering and ergonomics: A systems approach* (2nd ed.). Boca Raton, FL: CRC Press.

Jones, D. R. (1999). Hands-on human factors and ergonomics education. *Proceedings of the Human Factors and Ergonomics Society Annual Meeting, 43*(7), 535–538. https://doi.org/10.1177/154193129904300702.

Lee, J. D., Wickens, C. D., Liu, Y., & Boyle, L. N. (2017). *Designing for people: An introduction to human factors engineering* (3rd ed.). Charleston, SC: CreateSpace.

Moaveni, S., & Chou, K. (2017). Using the five whys methods in the classroom: How to turn students into problem solvers. *Journal of STEM Education, 17*(4).

Moroney, W. F. (1995). Strategies for teaching undergraduate human factors. In *Proceedings of the Human Factors and Ergonomics Society 39th annual meeting* (p. 405). Santa Monica, CA: Human Factors and Ergonomics Society.

Parasuraman, R., & Riley, V. (1997). Humans and automation: Use, misuse, disuse, abuse. *Human Factors, 39*, 230–253.

Proctor, R. W., & Van Zandt, T. (2018). *Human factors in simple and complex systems* (3rd ed.). Boca Raton, FL: CRC Press.

Rantanen, E. M., & Moroney, W. F. (2011). Educational and skill needs of new human factors/ ergonomics professionals. *Proceedings of the Human Factors and Ergonomics Society, 55*, 530–534. https://doi.org/10.1177/1071181311551108.

Reason, J. (1990). *Human error.* Cambridge, UK: Cambridge University Press.

Sambell, K., Brown, S., & Graham, L. (2017). *Professionalism in practice: Key directions in higher education learning, teaching and assessment.* London, UK: Palgrave McMillan.

Sheridan, T. B., & Verplank, W. L. (1978). *Human and computer control of undersea teleoperators.* Cambridge, MA: MIT Press. (Technical Report, Man-Machine Systems Laboratory, Department of Mechanical Engineering).

Shneiderman, B. (2020). Human-centered artificial intelligence: Three fresh ideas. *AIS Transactions on Human-Computer Interaction, 12*(3), 109–124. https://doi.org/10.17705/1thci.00131.

Shneiderman, B., Plaisant, C., Cohen, M., Jacobs, S., Elmqvist, N., & Diakopoulos, N. (2018). *Designing the user interface: Strategies for effective human-computer interaction* (6th ed.). Boston, MA: Pearson.

Stamatis, D. H. (2004). *Six sigma fundamentals: A complete introduction to the system, methods, and tools.* New York, NY: Productivity Press.

Stanton, N. A., Salmon, P. M., Rafferty, L. A., Walker, G. H., Baber, C., & Jenkins, D. P. (2013). *Human factors methods: A practical guide for engineering and design* (2nd ed.). Boca Raton, FL: CRC Press.

Wickens, C. D. (1984). Processing resources in attention. In R. Parasuraman & R. Davies (Eds.), *Varieties of attention* (pp. 63–101). New York, NY: Academic.

Wickens, C. D., Hollands, J. G., Banbury, S., & Parasuraman, R. (2016). *Engineering psychology and human performance* (4th ed.). London, UK: Routledge.

Wickens, C. D., Lee, J. D., Liu, Y., & Gordon-Becker, S. (2014). *An introduction to human factors engineering* (2nd ed.). Harlow, UK: Pearson.

Wogalter, M. S. (2019). *Forensic human factors and ergonomics: Case studies and analyses.* Boca Raton, FL: CRC Press.

Cultural Psychology

24

Luca Tateo, Giuseppina Marsico, and Jaan Valsiner

Contents

L. Tateo (✉)
University of Oslo, Oslo, Norway
e-mail: luca.tateo@isp.uio.no

G. Marsico
Department of Human, Philosophical and Educational Sciences (DISUFF), University of Salerno, Fisciano, Italy
e-mail: gmarsico@unisa.it

J. Valsiner
Centre of Cultural Psychology, Department of Communication and Psychology, Aalborg University, Aalborg, Denmark

Sigmund Freud Privatuniversität, Vienna, Austria

© Springer Nature Switzerland AG 2023
J. Zumbach et al. (eds.), *International Handbook of Psychology Learning and Teaching*,
Springer International Handbooks of Education,
https://doi.org/10.1007/978-3-030-28745-0_28

Abstract

The chapter presents an overview and the historical background of what can be considered the family of "cultural psychologies," that is, those approaches that, since the 1990s, have brought back the cultural context and the meaning-making at the center of psychological theories. First, the core principles of cultural psychology are defined. The historical roots and main authors are briefly presented, reconstructing the historical trajectory of an apparently new perspective with solid historical bases. Then, the current scholarly global landscape is sketched. The ideal curriculum of cultural psychology program is presented in terms of learning goals and descriptors. Afterward, selected instructional approaches are illuminated with examples of pedagogical scenarios that an instructor can implement and easily adapt to the different learning contexts. As a matter of conclusion, the challenges that cultural psychology is launching to the current curricula in psychology are presented. We emphasize the potentialities of cultural psychology to fertilize the different sub-areas of psychological sciences by introducing a perspective of integral humanism, that is, to re-appreciate the rich educational background that characterized psychology since its beginnings.

Keywords

Cultural psychology · Meaning-making · Qualitative experiment · History of ideas

I was. . . an intellectual first and a scientist in support. . . .I used psychology to pursue matters that existed for me in their own right. Psychology was (and remains) only one way to use mind in behalf of these pursuits. (Bruner, 1983, p. 77)

Introduction

Cultural psychology is a label that covers a range of theoretical and empirical approaches to the study of the relationship between meaning, mind, and human activities in the context of different cultural-historical systems. Cultural psychology's approaches – although coming from a long tradition, which dates back as earlier as the sixteenth century (Klempe, 2021; Tateo, 2015) – have been emerging since the 1980s as a productive and heterogeneous field. In this context, the approaches of psychology, gravitating around the use of the term "culture," dialogue with different disciplines, also interested in the developmental processes of the organism in its historicity and context, such as anthropology, ethnography, history, philosophy, epigenetics, ecology, human geography, theology, cultural studies, etc. (Valsiner, 2012). Cultural psychology embraces a truly transdisciplinary perspective.

The core question addressed by the manifold versions of cultural psychology (Boesch, 1991; Bruner, 1990; Cohen & Kitayama, 2019; Cole, 1996; Shweder,

1991; Wertsch, del Río, & Alvarez, 1995; Valsiner, 2014) is why do we need the concept of culture to understand the mind? The epistemological tenets of cultural psychology's approaches are:

- The centrality of the meaning-making processes
- The role of culture in the development of psychological functions
- The human agency, understood as both product and producer of culture
- The whole of systemic organism-environment relationships as unit of analysis
- The genetic-historical and temporal dimension of psychological processes

Following a general interest for the role of culture in the social sciences, contemporary "cultural psychologies" – understood as a way to look at psychic processes, rather than a specific academic discipline – formulated an explicit organization of the different perspectives that use the notion of culture in the beginning of the 1990s. A more detailed overview of what has happened since 1995 is overviewed in detail in various editorial summaries over the past 25 years of one of the main dedicated journals: *Culture & Psychology* (Valsiner, 1995, 1996, 2001, 2004, 2019).

Cultural psychology is decidedly theoretical in focus. It critically acknowledges the progressive detachment of psychology with basic human cultural phenomena, such as the complex intentional forms of feeling, thinking, and acting that characterize our everyday lives. Starting from the rewriting of its formal history, psychology has pursued the "scientific status" of the discipline by telling a story of empirical accumulation of "hard" data on rewarding or punishing humans with tokens of consumables – food, money, etc. – leading thus the way to its versions of explaining complexity by way of simple elementary "effects" of some variables. The scientific program of cultural psychology is to bring back under the spotlight the active persons – embodied soul-searchers filled with curiosity – who create, perform, and feel about theater, poetry, and music and who read novels, organize revolutions and political debates, and worry about cholesterol levels, diets, prices, and marriages.

Indeed, none of these precarious activities of unabashedly subjective human beings are explainable by way of lower psychological functions. Neither can they be captured in the form of simple variables or be unpacked in separated behavioral, physiological, or cognitive dimensions. In order to study complex psychological phenomena of the human beings, psychology needs to rethink the methodologies of the discipline in such ways so as to be able to address them (Valsiner, Marsico, Chaudhary, Sato, & Dazzani, 2016).

Historical Context

The focus on cultural phenomena – mostly music and language – antedates the birth of psychology as a separate discipline. A pioneer was the Italian philosopher Giambattista Vico (Tateo, 2015) in the early eighteenth century, who advocated the birth of a "new science" of the relationship between mind and culture through the mediation of language. A century later, the first systematic treatment of culture appears in the language philosophy of Wilhelm von Humboldt (von Humboldt, 1836). Even the institutionalization of the interest in culture antedates the experimental turn by 19 years. Indeed, the first professorship in psychology proper was not that of Wilhelm Wundt in Leipzig (1879), but that of *Völkerpsychologie* for Moritz Lazarus in Bern (1859) (Jahoda, 1993). The dominant historical narrative of psychology as a laboratory-experimental discipline shadowed the interest in cultural processes. Similarly, the biographies of the official forefather of modern psychology – Wilhelm Wundt – have traditionally undervalued the presence of *both* experimental and *Völkerpsychologie* traditions in his work.

Cultural psychology once again takes on the general orientation of their predecessors' holistic, dynamic, and developmental emphases. In particular, four continental European traditions flourished at the beginning of the twentieth century: *Völkerpsychologie*, *Ganzheitspsychologie*, the introspection-based traditions of the *Würzburg School* of Oswald Külpe and colleagues, and the various branches of the Austrian traditions of Franz Brentano, particularly the *Graz School* of Alexius Meinong (Diriwächter, 2004).

The other relevant source of cultural psychology is the cultural-historical soviet psychology initiated by Lev Vygotsky and his circle, including scholars such as Lurja, Galperin, Leontev, and Bernstein (Valsiner, 2012). The interest for the work of Vygotsky arose in the West with the first, uncertain, English translations of his work in the 1960s. Since then, a progressive work of critical rediscovery and the improvement of the works available in English (Van der Veer & Valsiner, 1991) have made the cultural-historical perspective one of the most fruitful theoretical sources. In particular, cultural psychology has adopted from the cultural-historical approach the focus on:

- The sociogenesis of the higher psychological functions
- The genetic epistemology
- The mediation of symbolic forms in all higher psychological functions
- The whole of organism-environment relationship as unit of analysis in psychology
- The notion of system of activity (Brown, Heath, & Pea, 1999)

There are further relevant theoretical influences shared by many versions of cultural psychology. In the USA, the so-called "culture and personality" tradition (Kluckhohn, Murray, & Schneider, 1948), during the 1950s, established a dialogue between anthropology and psychology about the role of culture in shaping personality traits. Another relevant turn was the introduction of the ideas of the Russian philosopher and literary critic Mikhail Bakhtin into psychology, leading to the so-called dialogical perspective (Clegg & Salgado, 2011).

Another attempt of (re)introducing the notion of culture into psychology in a deep intellectual project was Jerome S. Bruner's contribution (1983, 1990) to place the meaning-making process at the core of the psychological functioning and to restore the dignity of the human mind as a relevant object of investigation. Since the origins of the "cognitive revolution" in the 1960s, Bruner (1990) promoted a view of cognition embedded in culturally shared meanings. As Bruner (2012) pointed out:

> I am deeply convinced that psychology cannot go it alone. The life of mind is not isolated from or independent of the life of the cultural community in which it develops and lives. Nor is it independent of the history that has shaped that cultural community. Our fate as human beings is shaped not only by our individual qualities but by the cultural circumstances in which we live our lives. (2012, p. 12)

Finally, another interlocutor of cultural psychology is the theory of social representations by Serge Moscovici (Duveen, 1998; Sammut, Andreouli, Gaskell, & Valsiner, 2015), which shares the interest for common sense knowledge and the role of everyday communication in the psychological functioning.

Since the 1990s, we can observe several efforts to bring back culture into the core of psychological science. These efforts opened new avenues for psychologists' legitimate research practices – a turn toward the use of qualitative methods is on its way; theoretical schemes used often transcend the limits of psychology (e.g., borrowing concepts from sociology, like *habitus*, or from literary scholarship and music – such as *polyphony*).

Current Trends

The open, interdisciplinary, and critical nature of cultural psychology has fortunately avoided their crystallization into another disciplinary fence. Indeed, its openness allowed the constant dialogue with other psychological perspectives such as socio-constructivism, phenomenology, and dynamic humanist psychology. Thus, cultural psychology cannot be properly defined a disciplinary or academic field, rather a particular gaze on the way human psyche develops in relation to value-laden, collectively coordinated, and symbolically mediated everyday activities. In other words, cultural psychology is a special way of looking at human beings (Valsiner et al., 2016).

There are few established academic programs in cultural psychology, although related courses are often integrated in other psychology programs. A brief – although probably not exhaustive – list of sites would include the Centre for Cultural Psychology at Aalborg University in Denmark, the Laboratory for Comparative Human Cognition at University of California San Diego in the USA, the Hans Kilian and Lotte Köhler Center for Cultural Psychology and Historical Anthropology at the Ruhr-University Bochum in Germany, and Research Group on Social Interactions at the University of Salerno in Italy. Informal but very productive groups are active in Latin America especially in Brazil – at the Federal University of Bahia, Federal University of Pernambuco, University of Sao Paulo, and University of Brasilia – and in Chile at the Pontificia Universidad Catolica in Santiago. Other groups are active in Europe – Wien, Berlin, Neuchatel, and Luxembourg – and in Asia, Tokyo, Shanghai, and Yogyakarta.

It must be noted that – especially in the Anglo-Saxon cultural area – the term "cultural psychology" is sometimes used as synonym with "cross-cultural psychology" (see, for instance, Heine, 2020; Heiphetz & Oishi, 2021). This creates some confusion also to students, as the family of theories that we discuss in this chapter is in dialectic opposition to cross-cultural approaches, in epistemological, theoretical, and methodological terms. The idea of universal psychological constructs varying in magnitude depending on the influence of culture understood as independent variable is completely alien to cultural psychology (Anandalakshmi, 1974). Similarly, the idea of culture-free or context-independent methods and instruments to assess individual differences and aggregate them has been fully rejected by cultural psychology (Cole, 1996).

Purposes and Rationale of the Curriculum in Cultural Psychology

The curriculum in cultural psychology is inspired by the concept of *integral humanism* (Tateo & Marsico, 2021; Valsiner et al., 2016), that is, the recovery of the extensive educational background that characterized psychologists, especially in the European tradition, until the first half of the twentieth century. In the perspective of cultural psychology, the curriculum shall include the interest in the different branches of human activity and must be inherently interdisciplinary, not limited to the mere technical aspects of psychology. At BA and MA levels, the general learning goals of the curriculum include solid bases in the history, epistemology, and philosophy of psychology and a strong focus on qualitative methodologies and mixed methods and should explore its relations with humanities and liberal arts, linguistics and semiotics, social sciences, and developmental sciences (i.e., epigenetics, system theory, ecology, etc.).

After having completed a BA and MA program (level 7 of ETF) in cultural psychology, the student should have acquired the following knowledge, skills, and competences:

Knowledge
- Deep knowledge of history, epistemology, and methodologies of cultural psychology and its main theories
- Fundamental principles of linguistic and semiotics
- Fundamentals of history of ideas
- Fundamentals of cultural studies
- Deep knowledge of developmental, systemic, and ecosystemic approaches in human and social sciences
- Academic writing and research design in ecological settings
- Critical awareness of the main theoretical, epistemological, political, and methodological issues in psychological sciences

Skills
- Capability to work in multicultural environment and to effectively deal with ethno-epistemologies
- Skills in developing innovative and original methods and research designs adapted to local contexts
- Insights in the application of cultural psychological perspective to educational, professional, and therapeutic contexts

Competences, Responsibility, and Autonomy
- Competence in international scientific publishing
- Capability to establish and maintain international research and professional networks
- Competence in multimodal qualitative analysis
- Competence in innovative interventions in community empowerment and participatory research
- Competence to critically interpret, manage, and transform interdisciplinary and multicultural work contexts
- Competence to apply cultural psychology to pedagogy
- Open mindedness and critical capability to address ethical issues, social injustice issues, and inclusion issues

After having completed a doctoral program (level 8 of ETF) in cultural psychology, the candidate should have acquired the following knowledge, skills, and competences:

Knowledge
- Advanced knowledge of the cultural psychology theory, epistemology, and methodology
- Large interdisciplinary knowledge of the developmental sciences
- Large interdisciplinary knowledge of the study of human activity

Skills
- Advanced academic writing skills
- Capability to design innovative research methods
- Capability to identify critical issues in the current scientific or professional knowledge and to produce radical theoretical advancements

Competence, Responsibility, and Autonomy
- The doctoral candidate will become able to work in a borderless, international, and diverse environment, to adapt and travel across contexts with reflexive awareness.
- Demonstrate substantial intellectual autonomy and authority, professional integrity, and sustained commitment to the development of new ideas.

A completed education in cultural psychology is relevant for working in a multicultural environment and to address societal issues from a nonconventional perspective. Thus, it can be functional to work in social sciences research, education and social work, community development, and international cooperation.

Core Contents and Topics of Cultural Psychology

There are at least three major themes that compose the core contents of cultural psychology:

1) The recognition of the object of study as a whole
2) The definition of what is a psychological fact
3) The epistemological attitude of dealing with historically dynamic concepts, such as continuity and discontinuity, evolution and adaptation, tension, and ambivalence in the irreversible time

Wholeness as the Object of Study

Cultural psychology assumes the study not of the single person or the single psychological phenomenon occurring in a vacuum or in a neutral context (Valsiner, 2014). Persons, psychological processes, and contexts are part of a whole that we can call the phenomenon, in the sense of being in a systemic relationship. Hence, the first central focus in cultural psychology is the relationship between the parts of a whole. It is assumed that "a reductionistic approach to science involves an abstraction from wholeness and a focus on smaller and smaller parts, until encountering a part that appears manageable" (Piechocinska, 2005, p. 2). Psychology has generally pursued this way since the nineteenth century. For instance, memory, perception, language, and emotions have been treated as separate processes, albeit just for analytical purpose, and have been hardly reconnected again. According to Piechocinska (2005), quoting Heisenberg: "There is a fundamental error in separating the parts from the whole, the mistake of atomizing what should not be atomized. Unity and complementarity constitute reality" (Piechocinska, 2005, p. 3). Such a way to look at the history of the discipline helped the cultural endeavor of "rehabilitating" those approaches that focused on the realm of meaning, context, and wholeness of psyche, for a long time neglected.

Defining Psychological Facts

In general, psychology lacks a clear understanding of *what a fact is* – how it is created and how solidly it stands within the ocean of alternative interpretations.

Psychology as science is necessarily cultural in its core – as long as its object of investigation is the species of *Homo sapiens*. Members of that species do not merely respond to stimuli or enact behaviors. Humans act, construct new meanings, think, develop strategies of coalition making in social units, and feel in ways that are not explainable by the mere fight or flight reactions from an event suddenly encountered in a forest. Humans articulate motives in value-laden and subjectively organized systems of motivation (Gonzalez Rey, 2015). Therefore, they construct firearms to go hunting for the bears and build complex systems of meaning and rituals to control and predict both the bear's behavior and the contextual factors that may affect the hunting, but also the mutual conducts of their fellow hunters, finding moral justification for killing the catch. In the same vein, they believe in the powers of weapons of mass destruction, which they condemn, eat with curious attachments to the body (such as chopsticks, forks, knives), turn the freshest – raw – food into cooked, believe in deities and stock markets, and the like. Ever since the first representative of the human species started to behave in such erratic manner, it has been through the construction of life-relevant instrumental artifacts that has allowed the species to survive.

Thus culture as a set of socially created action, feeling, and thinking tools is an evolutionary emergent and constitutes part of any psychological fact.

In cultural psychology (especially in the so-called semiotic turn), fact is not a given ("true") entity, but knowledge that has been created at the intersection of the object of study and the subject who studies the object. As such, what is constructed out of the object of investigation as a fact is a sign – some meaning that stands for some aspect of reality. "Facts," in contrast to other signs, are presented as if they were "the truth." Yet, in psychology there is no "truth" outside of context dependency that the sociocultural paradigms emphasize and that was prominent already in Gordon Allport's personality theory in the 1930s (Allport, 1937).

Ontogenesis and Time

The third theme concerns ontogenesis and time. Psychology deals with unique phenomena in irreversible time (Valsiner, 2014). This implies that every psychological event is unique, but it is treated and described as repeating in a similar way. The personal and cultural meaning of a number of life incidents emerges by the axiomatic uniqueness and the constructed similarity of events. The first word of a toddler, the first school day, the first kiss, the first day on the job, etc. are prepared, interpreted, and celebrated through culture-specific rituals that contribute to the construction of personal meanings. This calls for the appreciation of developmental axiomatic systems for psychology as science, which implies the rethinking of methodology in a developmental and processual form, as already clearly stated by Vygotsky (Van der Veer & Valsiner, 1991). This insistence is based on the basic assumption that in the case of irreversible time – which governs all living organisms – it is only an explicitly developmental framework that can acquire the basis for the science of psychology as a whole. Why that basic axiom? Why refusal to accept the (seemingly) simpler axiom of ontological being ("X exists") rather than insist upon the complexity of "X exists *in the becoming of X*"? The key here is in viewing stability –

a steady state of a system – as a temporary stabilization point in the life-course development of the system. Superficially, (a) and (b) look the same in their current view:

(a) Ontological axiom: X is X.
(b) Developmental axiom: X is *in becoming* X.

The focus on becoming is the crucial feature: "X" emerges from whatever was before and becomes something different later. In the human case, "something later" involves sign-mediated construction of lifeworlds (Valsiner et al., 2016).

The focus on the whole, the nature of psychological facts, and dynamic, historical, and developmental perspective form the fundamentals of cultural psychology that help to reformulate the traditional syllabi of general psychology. Therefore, the common disciplinary organizations of psychology (i.e., social, developmental, educational, clinical, etc.) are overcome by the focus on processes, such as teaching-learning (Bruner, 2020), *affectivating* (Cornejo, Marsico, & Valsiner, 2018), imagining (Tateo, 2020a), becoming and healing (Ho, 2019), etc.

Teaching, Learning, and Assessment in Cultural Psychology: Approaches and Strategies

Cultural psychology is heavily theory-driven, as they criticize the concept of "evidence" itself as a self-evident, self-standing result of an extraction process of inductive "data" from the reality. Data mining is a human collectively organized and value-led activity that takes place in specific historical conditions and materially organized settings. Besides, the emphasis is put on the becoming, rather than the actual condition, of the learner according to Vygotsky's strong developmental perspective.

The teaching-learning process of cultural psychology also cultivates researcher's critical educated intuition. The researcher herself becomes the first instrument of inquiry. Her reflexivity, as in the ethnographic approaches, is what triggers the development of theory, rather than the mere accumulation of empirical "facts" or "evidences."

The third pedagogical principle in cultural psychology is the systematic deconstruction of cultural taken-for-granted. The learners should constantly question and observe human activity as an "anthropologist on Mars" (Sacks, 1995), implying that cultures are neither internally homogeneous nor temporally stable. They are rather a process of constant construction, maintenance, and demolition of meanings in which people are both producers and products.

From the abovementioned principles, it follows that the teaching-learning process in cultural psychology is a continuous movement, back and forth, from the theory to the concrete observation of everyday life collectively coordinated human activities. In order to illustrate how the epistemological approach of cultural psychology can be translated into concrete educational strategies and learning goals, we will provide some examples in the form of pedagogical scenarios.

Training Observation Skills

The first step of any training program in cultural psychology is the improvement of the capability to observe mundane human activities with a fresh gaze. As teaching strategy, we recommend that the instructors always introduce new concepts beginning with first-person experiences by the students (Table 1). For instance, the instructor can lead her class to a public space and give an observation task involving different aspects of individual conduct in collective context.

An alternative is to build some small-scale "social experiments" (Milgram, Sabini, & Silver, 1992), in which a familiar situation is potentially jeopardized by introducing minimal elements of perturbation. The temporary disruption of taken-for-granted, social suggestions and expectations (Table 2) will make visible the way

Table 1 Scenario making borders visible

Learning objective: improve observational skills by identifying visible and invisible borders in a public space
Description of the activity and task: Students walk in small groups around the site (e.g., the university building) and try to identify both *visible* and *invisible* kinds of borders. Then, they stop few minutes on the borders, take pictures, and draw a map of the place they have selected. They mark on the map all the borders they can discover Afterward, the group analyzes the experience with the instructor focusing on: • What is the *given structure* ("border as it seems to be") • What is the *given function* ("border as it seems to work") • *How can you describe the possibilities of direct modification of the present border?* (maximum of the movability of this border as it currently is) • *What kind of sign-mediated actions are possible to accomplish* on the border

Table 2 Scenario questioning interpersonal borders

Learning objective: improve observational skills and researcher's self-awareness by questioning interpersonal borders in a public space
Description of the activity: Students walk around the site in small groups of 2–3 (e.g., the campus or cafeteria). They stop an unknown person and ask if they can touch her hair. Students can of course explain that the action is for an academic task. One of the students is performing the task, while the other(s) act as observers and interviewers. The student preforming the touching can take time and touch the hair as she feels. Afterward, the interviewer asks the person who has been touched how did it feel. Answers can be recorded on paper or audio. Finally, also the student performing the touch shall be interviewed about her feelings Finally, the group analyzes the experience and the answers with the instructor focusing in particular on: • What kind of border has been experienced? • When the feeling of a border emerges? • There is any explicit marker of the border? • Any resistance? • What are the changes after crossing the border?

people make meaning of everyday situations, allowing the learner to reflect from a direct experience. Here, we provide a concrete example of two different scenarios, in which the instructor can introduce endless variations.

Scenarios 1 and 2 are examples of how to foster the systematic deconstruction of cultural taken-for-granted through the exercise of the students' direct observation and critical reflection among the ordinary action and things of everyday life. The following might be considered a showcase to how cultural psychology might be taught to better understand the cultural component of our psychological processes and individual and collective level.

Training Cultural *Defamiliarization*

In the diametrically opposite direction of cross-cultural psychology, cultural psychology understands "culture" as local set of solutions that human collectives produce to answer general existential problems (e.g., how to give birth and reproduce, how to coordinate and manage conflicts, how to deal with death, what is healthy, what is a happy life, etc.). The local solutions, built through different sets of messages, practices, organization of places, and artifacts, constitute local ecosystems (Tateo, 2020b). The cross-cultural is based on a common theoretical construct, supposedly universal, by which local systems are compared, collecting inductive evidences about personal variations of the construct between cultural (meaning national) groups and eventually finding just some similarities and some differences (Fig. 1).

Both variability and similarity would be grouped in a limited number of binary dimensions (e.g., dependence/independence, collectivistic/individualistic, attachment styles, etc.) and explained by the belonging to a given, and internally homogenous, culture. The universality of the theoretical construct is assumed in virtue of an ethnocentric epistemology, whose validity is cross-cultural by default. Recently, Bhatia (2018) has proved such an assumption to be false. Cultures are instead unique instances of local complex configurations of interacting elements that nevertheless follow generalizable laws. Constructs are thus the product of indigenous, historically situated scientific traditions. Some specific traditions, namely, the Western positivistic social science, have been particularly functional to the colonialist process,

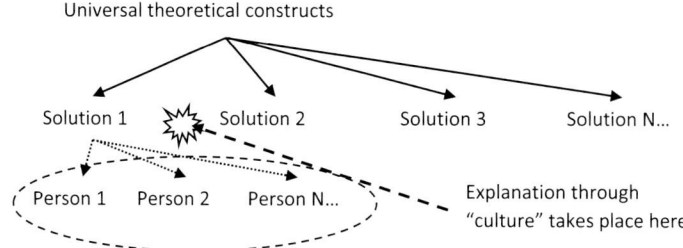

Fig. 1 Cross-cultural approach

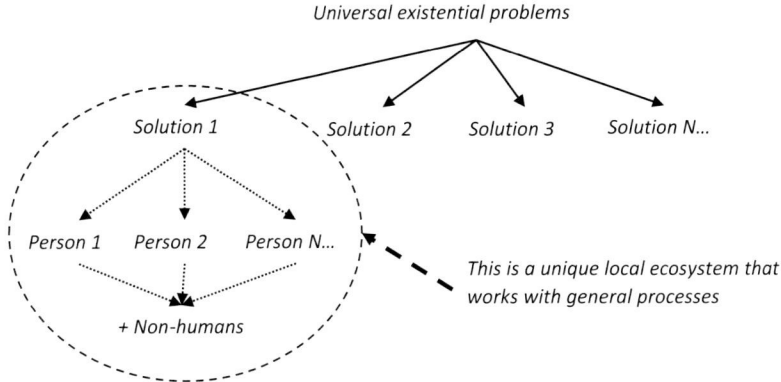

Fig. 2 Ecosystemic approach to cultural differences

which has legitimated this perspective as the only scientifically valid in return (Bhatia, 2018).

By deconstructing this set of assumption, the pedagogical goal of cultural psychology is to educate the learner to exert a new look at the local ecosystems of cultures. Human meaningful conduct cannot be generalized by observing and comparing its outcomes. Students must learn to discern and understand the processes beneath those variable outcomes. One can generalize the existential problems that human beings face both individually and collectively, not compare the local solutions developed in a specific space-time (Fig. 2) (Tateo, 2020b).

Through the systematic deconstruction of "familiar" cultural practices, the learner will be able to "defamiliarize" and recognize the sub-parts (both human and non-human elements) of a unique local configuration, without losing the whole, that is, the peculiar solution to existential problems that one can call "culture," such as "how do we organize family relationships" or "how do I differentiate myself from the other, but at the same time I do not appear an alien."

Yet, this learning process cannot be implemented by the learner alone, and it can emerge only in the context of social relationships of research as collective effort. Thus, we propose an innovative and culturally sensitive model of international learning mobility called "research tandem" (Xu & Marsico, 2020) as example (Table 3).

Training Dialogical Skills

The collective nature of scientific enterprise requires the learner to grasp the role of dialectic confrontation and collaborative construction of knowledge in psychology. For this sake, we propose a model of socialization to collaborative scientific work called "kitchen seminar." Invented as weekly face-to-face and videoconference meeting since 1997 by Jaan Valsiner at Clark University, the "kitchen seminar" is an informal group discussion of new or unfinished projects (e.g., research designs,

Table 3 Scenario the research tandem

Learning objective: improve collaborative research skills and cultural sensitivity through *defamiliarization*
Description of the activity: The innovative research/learning device, which can be implemented in students' international mobility, is called "research tandem." The idea of the device is to form a pair of one insider (host country student) with and an outsider (incoming student) based on common, previously explored research interests. In this process, both sides will be exposed to the experience of "defamiliarization": incoming students will be faced with totally a very different cultural and educational context, while host students will need to respond to their experienced doubts about their own cultural and educational context and curiosity for the other students' perspective. In the process, both sides need to re-examine their cultural beliefs and premises, which they have been taken for granted in their daily practice. The encounter between the students provides an opportunity for the "epoché" of phenomenology, opening to deeper analysis of the issues of inclusion (Xu & Marsico, 2020)

drafts of publications, new ideas for research, etc.). It operates on the basic principles of full equality of expression of constructive ideas independent of seniority or discipline. Its key restriction is the explicit avoidance of political discussions (of science, as well as of society). While these are important issues for sure, they also can divert scientists from concentration on research problems that need to be solved. Scenario 4 provides some hints on the discussion format that can become a powerful context for the socialization of students to cultural psychology (Table 4).

Challenges and Lessons Learned

From the abovementioned teaching-learning strategies, it adamantly appears that cultural psychology requires not only a complex, methodologically eclectic, inter-disciplinary, and historically deep syllabus but also a highly stimulating, diverse, and unconventional learning environment.

It is of fundamental importance the student's early direct and indirect contact with different cultural backgrounds. This is particularly challenging considering a general academic trend to limit the quality and quantity of higher education curricula to short, rigid, strongly practice-focused, and temporally constrained programs. The challenge is to provide a teaching-learning experience including the following affordances:

- Providing international and diversified literature of the topic to be discussed, which should not be limited to a single cultural area of origin. A good example would be, for instance, the study of the Self in a Western university from an Eastern perspective.
- Offering pedagogical support to questions rather than to acknowledge the accredited set of theories and authors.
- Promoting the theoretical elaboration (aside from the descriptive level of the phenomena under investigation).

Table 4 Scenario kitchen seminars

Learning objective: improve international scientific collaboration skills and ethic of research through collective development of ideas
The general rule of the format is that everybody can come and go whenever one desires, so the focus that keeps people together is joint interest in the topic discussed. The setting is informal and usually fueled by an abundant provision of coffee on the table

Every week, a person provides her own draft together with background readings to be discussed and sends the materials to a mailing list by the previous weekend. The list distributes these on directly to all the kitchen seminars list members. The author of the materials under discussion gives a short (10 min or so) introduction that further specifies in which direction she wishes the discussion could go and what are the open questions she needs to address. It is assumed that the participants will have read the materials – in reality it may sometimes be quick reading, requiring reminders of the relevant details. The discussion then starts for a couple of hours (giving time to the thought development is crucial), with some specific features:

• No formality (no introductions, beyond name if the person is new). Powerpoints are to be avoided (since these indicate ready-made presentational style) and are used only if there are materials that feed into discussion

• The tradition is not to think of time (even if, for technical reasons, the time is specified by the 2-h slot). This has been marked by the rule that "we start when the coffee is ready"

• When coffee is ready, it is directly being served (often starting from the most junior or new members in the group). This is important (in contrast to "coffee is out there, take it if you want" mentality) since it is a social gesture of offering. The offer for coffee is being made all through the 2-h period (until coffee resources last), so the offering by the server is constantly in the background of the discussion. There are often foods on the table – cookies or cakes – that are passed around by the participants from one another

• The group creates consensual local social norms that involve breaking (in small ways) the regular social norms of society. Through that, a specific unity of the group is being created and maintained for the event.

• The usual rule of conversations to honor one another's "keeping the floor" while speaking is blatantly violated in the discussions. People – when enthusiastic about an idea – "jump in" with elaboration of the idea at any moment, and that is the local social norm, accepted for the time of the event by all participants (but would be considered very rude in regular interactions). It allows for lively – yet at times highly diverse – collective growth of ideas, without boundaries. The mentality is we are here trying to solve the problem; if I have an insight, it should "burst out." of course, it is not always simple to accept that local convention of spontaneity. However, the spontaneity is not required – a participant can remain silent while observing others "burst out" ideas. This changed social norm is the centrally important feature of the event as it grants its freshness and creativity

• Combining different perspectives on the same topic (see the research-tandem strategy mentioned above).

Science Is One, and It Is Universal

Despite taking different forms – some European, some North-American – cultural psychologies are unified as being a part of science. In its ideal form, science has no national boundaries. There are no separate "American psychology," "Australian psychology," "Russian psychology," "indigenous psychology," etc. – but one general science that benefits from the work of scientists in every country. Yet, such ideal is far from being a reality in psychology, where the sociopolitical power structures either explicitly (by direct imposition of some classificatory scheme from one country to another) (e.g., APA telling clinical psychology programs in Canada to emphasize "cultural minorities" and evaluate these programs based on their inclusion of such "minorities") or implicitly monopolize the given discipline. In its history, psychology has moved from European to North-American dominance, with the latter resisting internationalization of the discipline's investigative practices at equal terms. Yet, it is precisely that restoration of international nature of the knowledge creation's enterprise that brings psychology back from having become a social tool, of any country's dominance over another on the epistemic markets of sciences, to universal domain of knowing (*Wissenschaft*).

Cultural psychology – a (re)new(ed) direction at the intersection of social and developmental psychology on the one hand and cultural anthropology on the other hand – is one of our contemporary efforts to break out of the closed circle of national dominance fights in psychology (Tateo & Marsico, 2019). Its emergence was prepared by the transposition of traditional empirical research on group comparisons to include materials from different societies. At the present time, cultural psychology has moved in a direction that is open to new theoretical models and to integration of approaches with cultural anthropology, social and developmental psychology, history, and sociology.

Teaching and Learning Resources

A list of fundamental readings to teach cultural psychology shall include the following books:

Boesch, E. E. (1991). *Symbolic action theory and cultural psychology*. Berlin: Springer-Verlag Publishing.

Bruner, J. (1990). *Acts of meaning*. Cambridge, MA: Harvard University Press. Cohen, D. & Kitayama, S. (Eds.) (2019), *Handbook of cultural psychology*. New York: The Guilford Press.

Cole, M. (1996). *Cultural psychology: A once and future discipline*. Cambridge, MA: Harvard University Press.

Shweder, R. A. (1991). *Thinking through cultures: Expeditions in cultural psychology*. Cambridge MA: Harvard University Press.

Valsiner, J. (2014). *An invitation to cultural psychology*. Sage.

Valsiner, J. (2021). *General human psychology*. Springer Nature.

Valsiner, J., Marsico, G., Chaudhary, N., Sato, T., & Dazzani, V. (2016). *Psychology as the science of human being*. The Yokohama Manifesto. Springer Nature.

Wertsch, J. V., del Río, P., & Alvarez, A. (Eds.). (1995). *Sociocultural studies of mind*. Cambridge UK: Cambridge University Press.

Some of the source journals, representing the range of approaches in cultural psychology, are (in alphabetical order):

- *Culture and Psychology.* Sage
- *Human Arenas.* An Interdisciplinary Journal of Psychology, Culture, and Meaning. Springer
- *Integrative Psychological and Behavioral Science.* Springer
- *Mind, Culture, and Activity.* Taylor & Francis

Online resources are available at:

- Institute of Cultural Psychology and Qualitative Social Research (https://ikus.cc/english-information/)
- Laboratory of Comparative Human Cognition (LCHC) (http://lchc.ucsd.edu/home)
- Centre for Cultural Psychology, Aalborg University (https://www.ccp.aau.dk/)
- Hans Kilian and Lotte Köhler Center for Cultural Psychology and Historical Anthropology (KKC) (http://www.kilian-koehler-centrum.de/)
- Research Group on Social Interactions - Laboratory of Psychology "Giovanni Abignente" University of Salerno (https://sites.google.com/unisa.it/gris)

Cross-References

▶ Developmental Psychology: Moving Beyond the East–West Divide
▶ Epistemology of Psychology
▶ Qualitative Methodology
▶ The Methodology Cycle as the Basis for Knowledge

References

Allport, G. W. (1937). *Personality: A psychological interpretation.* New York, NY: Holt.
Anandalakshmi, S. (1974). How independent is the independent variable? Problems and perspectives form New Delhi. In J. L. M. Dawson & W. J. Lonner (Eds.), *Readings in cross-cultural psychology* (pp. 79–89). Hong Kong, China: Hong Kong University Press.
Bhatia, S. (2018). *Decolonizing psychology.* New York, NY: Oxford University Press.
Boesch, E. E. (1991). *Symbolic action theory and cultural psychology.* Berlin, Germany: Springer-Verlag Publishing. https://doi.org/10.1007/978-3-642-84497-3
Brown, J. S., Heath, C., & Pea, R. (1999). *Perspectives on activity theory.* New York, NY: Cambridge University Press.
Bruner, J. (1990). *Acts of meaning.* Cambridge, MA: Harvard University Press.
Bruner, J. (2012). What psychology should study. *International Journal of Educational Psychology, 1*(1), 5–13.
Bruner, J. (2020). *The culture of education.* Cambridge, MA: Harvard University Press.
Bruner, J. S. (1983). *In search of mind: Essays in autobiography.* New York, NY: Harper and Row.

Clegg, J. W., & Salgado, J. (2011). From Bakhtinian theory to a dialogical psychology. *Culture & Psychology, 17*(4), 520–533.

Cohen, D., & Kitayama, S. (Eds.). (2019). *Handbook of cultural psychology*. New York, NY: The Guilford Press.

Cole, M. (1996). *Cultural psychology: A once and future discipline*. Cambridge, MA: Harvard University Press.

Cornejo, C., Marsico, G., & Valsiner, J. (Eds.). (2018). *I activate you to affect me*. Charlotte, NC: Information Age Publishers.

Diriwächter, R. (2004). Völkerpsychologie: The synthesis that never was. *Culture & Psychology, 10*(1), 85–109. https://doi.org/10.1177/1354067X04040930

Duveen, G. (1998). The psychosocial production of ideas: Social representations and psychologic. *Culture & Psychology, 4*(4), 455–472.

Gonzalez Rey, F. L. (2015). Human motivation in question: Discussing emotions, motives, and subjectivity from a cultural-historical standpoint. *Journal for the Theory of Social Behaviour, 45*(4), 419–439.

Heine, S. J. (2020). *Cultural psychology: Fourth international student edition*. New York, NY: WW Norton & Company.

Heiphetz, L., & Oishi, S. (2021). Viewing development through the lens of culture: Integrating developmental and cultural psychology to better understand cognition and behavior. *Perspectives on Psychological Science*. Online first, July 2021. https://doi.org/10.1177/1745691620980725

Ho, D. Y. (2019). *Rewriting cultural psychology: Transcend your ethnic roots and redefine your identity*. Irvine, CA/Boca Raton, FL: BrownWalker Press.

Jahoda, G. (1993). *Crossroads between culture and mind: Continuities and change in theories of human nature*. Cambridge, MA: Harvard University Press.

Klempe, S. H. (2021). *Sound and reason*. New York: Palgrave.

Kluckhohn, C., Murray, H. A., & Schneider, D. M. (Eds.). (1948). *Personality in nature, society, and culture* (2nd ed. Rev.). New York: Knopf.

Milgram, S., Sabini, J. E., & Silver, M. E. (1992). *The individual in a social world: Essays and experiments*. New York, NY: McGraw-Hill Book Company.

Piechocinska, B. (2005). *Physics from wholeness: Dynamical totality as a conceptual foundation for physical theories* (PhD dissertation, Acta Universitatis Upsaliensis). Retrieved from http://urn.kb.se/resolve?urn=urn:nbn:se:uu:diva-5915

Sacks, O. (1995). *An anthropologist from Mars: Seven paradoxical tales*. London, UK: Picador.

Sammut, G. E., Andreouli, E. E., Gaskell, G. E., & Valsiner, J. E. (2015). *The Cambridge handbook of social representations*. Cambridge, MA: Cambridge University Press.

Shweder, R. A. (1991). *Thinking through cultures: Expeditions in cultural psychology*. Cambridge MA: Harvard University Press.

Tateo, L. (2015). Giambattista Vico and the principles of cultural psychology: A programmatic retrospective. *History of the Human Sciences, 28*(1), 44–65.

Tateo, L. (2020a). *A theory of imagining, knowing, and understanding*. Cham, CH: Springer Nature.

Tateo, L. (2020b). The school as semiotic intercultural arena. In *Social ecology of a Chinese Kindergarten* (pp. 117–128). Cham, CH: Springer.

Tateo, L., & Marsico, G. (2019). Introduction: Framing a theory of ordinary and extraordinary in cultural psychology. In Marsico G. & Tateo, L. (Eds) (2019). *Ordinary things and their extraordinary meanings* (pp. xi–xxix). Charlotte, NC: InfoAgePublications.

Tateo, L., & Marsico, G. (2021). The creative synthesis and the global psychology. *Human Arenas, 4*(1), 1–4. https://doi.org/10.1007/s42087-021-00201-6

Valsiner, J. (1995). Editorial: Culture & psychology. *Culture & Psychology, 1*(1), 5–10. https://doi.org/10.1177/1354067X9511001

Valsiner, J. (1996). Editorial: After the first year. *Culture & Psychology, 2*(1), 5–8. https://doi.org/10.1177/1354067X9621001

Valsiner, J. (2001). The first six years: Culture's adventures in psychology. *Culture & Psychology, 7*(1), 5–48. https://doi.org/10.1177/1354067X0171002

Valsiner, J. (2004). Three years later: Culture in psychology – between social positioning and producing new knowledge. *Culture & Psychology, 10*(1), 5–27. https://doi.org/10.1177/1354067X04040925

Valsiner, J. (2014). *An invitation to cultural psychology.* London, UK: Sage.

Valsiner, J. (2019). *Culture & Psychology:* 25 constructive years. *Culture and Psychology, 25*(4), 429–469.

Valsiner, J., Marsico, G., Chaudhary, N., Sato, T., & Dazzani, V. (2016). *Psychology as the science of human being. The Yokohama manifesto.* New York, NY: Springer.

Valsiner, J. E. (Ed.). (2012). *The Oxford handbook of culture and psychology.* New York, NY: Oxford University Press.

Van der Veer, R., & Valsiner, J. (1991). *Understanding Vygotsky: A quest for synthesis.* Oxford, UK: Blackwell Publishing.

von Humboldt, W. (1988 [1836]). *Über die Verschiedenheit des menschlichen Sprachbaues und ihren Einfluss auf die geistige Entwickelung des Menschengeschlechts. – Wilhelm von Humboldt's gesammelte Werke. Kuudes nide.* Berlin, Germany: Walter de Gruyter.

Wertsch, J. V., del Río, P., & Alvarez, A. (Eds.). (1995). *Sociocultural studies of mind.* Cambridge, UK: Cambridge University Press. https://doi.org/10.1017/CBO9781139174299

Xu, S., & Marsico, G. (Eds.). (2020). *Social ecology of a Chinese Kindergarten: Where culture grows.* Cham, CH: Springer Nature.

Teaching Media Psychology

Or How Do I Distinguish the Data from the Dumpster Fire?

Christopher J. Ferguson

25

Contents

Abstract

The effects of cultural media can be one of the most difficult and controversial topics for psychology instructors to teach. It does not help that many textbooks get the subject matter wrong, claiming that effects are much stronger and better supported by evidence than they actually are. In fact, new evidence, particularly

C. J. Ferguson (✉)
Stetson University, DeLand, FL, USA
e-mail: cjfergus@stetson.edu

© Springer Nature Switzerland AG 2023
J. Zumbach et al. (eds.), *International Handbook of Psychology Learning and Teaching*,
Springer International Handbooks of Education,
https://doi.org/10.1007/978-3-030-28745-0_29

from preregistered studies, suggests that in most realms of media effects, whether media violence, body image, suicide-themed media, or pornography, effects on viewers' attitudes and behaviors are far less than was once imagined. Media effects research provides an excellent opportunity, however, to teach students how to weigh conflicting evidence and apply critical thinking to complicated, nuanced, and morally valenced debates.

Keywords

Media violence · Body image · Video games · Pornography · Sexualization · Suicide · Mass media · Aggression

Introduction

I will start with the premise that, as teachers of psychology, we often unwittingly lie to our students. Looking back on over 20 years of teaching, I cringe when I think now of the various origin myths and morality tales I passed along from introductory psychology texts to fascinated students as if I were a storyteller, passing along fables to youth around a campfire. The amazing story of the murder of Kitty Genovese and the 38 witnesses who did not help her (not true it turns out; Manning, Levine, & Collins, 2007). I described Zimbardo's Stanford Prison Experiment revealing how easily power corrupts us (now descending into chaos and accusations of experimenters pressuring participants to behave as the experimenters wished; Blum, 2018). We could probably think of countless other bits of nonsense we wish we could retract, writing furious e-mails to former students. "Remember when I told you that great story about X, Y, Z? Well, turns out it's not true. Sorry about that!" It is one of the greatest challenges of teaching psychology: separating the good data from the nonsense, particularly when teaching in areas that are not our specialty.

It is even more difficult when so many topics of human behavior, society, and welfare touch upon emotionally and morally valenced topics. Take, for example, the issue of whether males have more variance in IQ (thus resulting in both more cognitively impaired males than females, but also more geniuses). From an empirical view, it is a perfectly valid and testable hypothesis, but also one about which certain results could be upsetting to some people. Do textbooks, then, come under pressure to promote beliefs that advance certain moral agendas at the expense of clear data? Or, for that matter, are they biased in the direction of promoting psychology as a wonderland of clear results and fascinating stories when the reality is much murkier and sometimes embarrassing, such as for psychology's current replication crisis? One thing we know is that introductory textbooks are full of errors (Ferguson, Brown, & Torres, 2018; O'Donohue & Willis, 2018), and I have little confidence in upper division textbooks as well. So, what are teachers and professors to do?

The effects of media on behavior can be one of those difficult topics to teach for several reasons. First, the involved research fields have historically been very messy because of numerous problems with poor methodologies (Savage, 2004; Want, 2014;

Whyte, Newman, & Voss, 2016). Second, and related, there is overreliance on the Bandura bo-bo doll studies which, as I will discuss below, may be less informative than students are often told. The Bandura studies, small and flawed as they actually are, have become a kind of *origin myth* of psychology not unlike the now discredited Stanford Prison Experiment (Blum, 2018). Third, the widespread adoption of social learning theory (SLT) by psychology has undoubtedly created a bias in favor of evidence supporting media influences and against evidence questioning those influences. This creates an institutional bias in scholarly and professional organizations around the world, including the American Psychological Association (APA) and the World Health Organization (WHO), and results in the release of multiple seriously misleading policy statements on media effects (Elson et al., 2019). Fourth, issues of media effects are highly wrapped up with moral beliefs and moral advocacy related to a "saving lives" mentality. Fifth, many individuals including textbook authors and individual instructors have very strong opinions on the topic that may blind them to evidence conflicting with their personal views. And last, it has been well documented that there is a high rate of error in introductory psychology textbooks related to the issue of media effects, typically in the direction of vastly overstating the evidence for effects (Ferguson et al., 2018).

Taken together, these factors create a high degree of potential for instructors to *misinform* rather than inform students on this particular set of issues. Given that we have documentation that many introductory psychology textbooks (and certainly social psychology and other textbooks as well) have serious errors and biases about media effects and that even the APA's public statements have been discredited (also see Ferguson, Copenhaver, & Markey, 2020), covering this field in class creates significant challenges for psychology instructors. (I cannot say these challenges are unique, as textbooks are rife with biases on other morally and ideologically valenced topics.) Indeed, it is safe to say that many declarative statements made by textbook authors and instructors on the issue of media effects are false, particularly as illustrated by recent preregistered research. I will begin this chapter on teaching media psychology by taking a look at the violence in media debate before more briefly discussing several other related media effects realms, then offering some thoughts on how to refocus these debates into opportunities to engage students with critical thinking and appropriate scientific skepticism rather than to indoctrinate them in ideological or moral beliefs.

Media Effects in the Classroom

In most cases, media effects will be taught in classes outside of a course or module devoted specifically to the topic. Introductory psychology and social psychology textbooks typically, though briefly and often poorly, consider the topic of media violence. The potential impact of a "thin ideal" media on body image may be considered in courses on the psychology of women, or sexual behavior. Pornography effects may likewise be presented in courses on sexuality or gender. In most cases, though, textbooks struggle to present the research accurately, often falling back on misleading and morally valenced claims of public-health level effects that cannot, in fact, be supported by the evidence base in these areas. Indeed, psychology instructors' primary risk when talking about these matters is that they may hold and teach inaccurate information.

Relatively few universities offer "niche" courses that focus specifically on media effects, even though they are popular with students. At my university, I teach two of them; one is a seminar on media effects in general for third-year students, and the other is a first-year seminar for graduate students that focuses specifically on the effects of video games. Such media classes are typically taught at the undergraduate level; graduate-level examples are particularly rare other than at the few programs dedicated specifically to media psychology. Thus, in most cases, students' limited exposure to data on media effects may be in classes that are not devoted to the topic and are taught by instructors who are not particularly familiar with the issues at hand, relying on textbooks that are not particularly accurate in conveying the complexities of data and debate in these areas.

The Cautionary Tale of Media Violence

Interest in the idea that media might have deleterious effects on youth is nothing new and can be traced back to at least the ancient Athenians, some of whom worried about the effects of Greek plays on youth delinquency (Kutner & Olson, 2008). History is replete with societal concerns over new media and technology including, though not limited to, religious texts such as the Bible, phones, comic books, various styles of music (from waltzes through jazz, rock, and rap), Dungeons and Dragons, and, more recently, television and video games. In all such cases, the concern is generational, with older adults concerned about the new media creating a moral panic of alarm (Cohen, 1972). For instance, with video games, this same pattern has been demonstrated among the general public (Przybylski, 2014), clinicians (Ferguson, 2015a), and even scholars who study video games (Ferguson & Colwell, 2017). In each case, age (itself conflated with experience with games) as well as dislike of youth themselves was associated with greater belief in the harmfulness of video games. These surveys also show the inevitable death of moral panics as well…typically as the audience of older adults who believe the panic dies, the panic itself dies. This is why few people today worry about the deleterious effects of, say, the radio despite that academic journals in the 1940s published articles warning about its harming youth (e.g., Preston, 1941). In the surveys of clinicians and scholars noted above (see also Quandt et al., 2015), the belief that aggressive video games contribute to societal aggression is a minority view, typically espoused by 10–15% of scholars, with clinicians a bit higher at 39.5%, though once again mostly overrepresented among older clinicians.

Bandura's Origin Myth of Aggression

Most of psychology's unfortunate obsession with violent media can be traced back to the original Bobo doll studies with children. (I do not refer to them as studies of children's aggression as they are not, for reasons that will become clear in a moment.) These were not the first studies related to media violence by any means, but they helped (falsely) cement in the minds of many psychologists that children learned to become aggressive by watching adult models. The gist of these studies is probably known to most psychologists, so I will not repeat them in detail here. However, many flaws and limitations of these studies are typically glossed over when teaching them to students, such that these studies have become part of psychology's origin myths.

By origin myths, I mean that some studies and anecdotes are highlighted to students in order to represent psychology's power, although the stories themselves are flawed or simply untrue. As noted already, the parable of Kitty Genovese and the 38 witnesses and the debunked Stanford Prison Experiment are two such examples, but there are others, including exaggerations of the power of Watson's Little Albert experiment (Griggs, 2014), revelations that Milgram's obedience studies may be the product of demand characteristics and hypothesis guessing rather than real effects (Perry, Wanner, & Stam, in press), and the sensationalization of Phineas Gage's injuries and lack of coverage of his recovery (Griggs, 2015). Still other origin myths come from textbooks' failure to correct popular but low-quality studies in the context of psychology's replication crisis. Some phenomena that were once considered firmly established, such as social priming (Pashler, Coburn, & Harris, 2012) and stereotype threat (Stoet & Geary, 2012), now appear to be in serious trouble empirically, yet may be repeated to students by teachers and textbooks without mentioning replication failures. The issue of media violence effects, too, appears to be in this category.

To return to Bandura, his studies are often taught to students as if they tell us something about aggression, but, in fact, they are not aggression studies at all. Part of the problem relates to the severe limitations of a Bobo doll as an instrument through which to measure aggression, and part relates to flaws in the experimental design. It has long been understood that the Bobo doll paradigm is, in fact, a weak one for understanding aggression (Tedeschi & Quigley, 1996). After all, the Bobo doll is a toy whose *sole purpose* is to be hit! Generalizing from this play-like roughhousing to real-life aggression was always ill-advised. As Tedeschi and Quigley (1996) put it, "The Bobo modeling paradigm may not examine aggression at all, rather, imitative behavior of 'rough and tumble play' in which there is no intent to harm." Consider this thought experiment in which young children are exposed to videos of an adult hitting kittens with a hammer and are then brought into a room filled with kittens and hammers. Would most of the children imitate the behaviors they saw in the video? I doubt it. In fact, they likely would be traumatized by what they saw.

Indeed, one can see Bandura's Bobo studies as experiments on compliance, not aggression. He and others have made the arguably incorrect assumption that the children in the the study *felt* aggressive and wished to harm the doll. Yet, no evidence is offered to support that assumption. The children were shown the video, after which they entered the room where the Bobo doll awaited, but *given no other instructions.* Absent from further instructions from the experimenter, the children may well have assumed that the video had presented instructions as to what they were expected to do next. In effect, the results of Bandura's studies may have been strongly affected by *demand characteristics,* specifically, that when research participants figure out what experimenters want them to do, they tend to do it, even if it is not their natural inclination (Orne, 1962).

If this analysis is correct, the Bandura studies tell us nothing about aggression, as it is unlikely the children were feeling aggressive, and therefore tell us nothing about the impact of media violence. With these points in mind, I suggest that teachers of psychology should not encourage students to accept the descriptions found in many textbooks that link Bandura's results to conclusions about the dangers of media violence. Doing so would deprive students of a significant opportunity for critical thinking. Indeed, fully exploring the Bandura studies and their flaws can become an important learning experience. We can ask students what they do and do not consider convincing about the Bobo doll studies. Are there better ways to quantify aggression in the laboratory? Given ethical limitations, is it even possible to study aggression in the laboratory in a way that means anything for the real world? To what extent do we know that participants are responding in a study in a manner that reflects how they actually feel as opposed to what they think the experimenter wants them to do? Is human psychology really as straightforward as those of Bandura, Milgram, and Zimbardo suggest?

Some argue that the Stanford Prison Experiments should be dropped entirely from psychology courses (see Gray, 2013), and in the context of psychology's replication crisis, it may be time for us to let go of many other of these older cohort studies that have attained the status of origin myths. At the very least, these studies should be used as opportunities to dissect psychology's limitations, not as exemplars by which we indoctrinate students into believing nonsense.

The Pitfalls of Media Violence Research

Armed with Bandura's Bobo doll studies, psychology set upon a quixotic multi-decade effort to link media violence to everything from schoolyard bullying to mass shooting events. This effort has now crashed and burned. It is difficult to think of another field that went so rapidly from public prominence and the embrace of presidential-level politics to become a figurative dumpster fire and exemplar of how science should not be done.

I invoke the term "dumpster fire" to mean that the field has descended into both chaos and acrimony, and I do not do so lightly, but unfortunately the term is apt. This is because, in my view, some researchers in psychology (and some American psychological organizations such as the APA) have engaged in and supported pseudoscience or even antiscience in relation to the impact of media violence. Caught out finally during the replication crisis, the result has been the toppling of a house of cards, with considerable negative fallout for scientific credibility, professional relationships, and individual careers.

By the early 1970s, media researchers along with policy makers were adamant that television and movie violence (and, later, video game violence) were major causes not only of aggression but also criminal violence. Scholars claimed that perhaps half of all homicides (Centerwall, 1992) or 30% of all violent crime (Strasburger, 2007) could be attributed directly to media violence, and other scholars compared the effects to smoking and lung cancer (Bushman & Anderson, 2001). Ironically, some scholars aggressively bullied any who would question this belief, using ad hominem attacks, falsely claiming industry conflicts of interest where none existed, or comparing more skeptical scholars to Holocaust deniers (for specific examples, see Ferguson, 2015b). Statements by scholars believing in media violence effects became increasingly extreme, with frequent references to mass shootings and even the 9/11 attacks and comparison to important medical effects (for examples, see Markey, Males, French, & Markey, 2015).

Early on, however, some scholars (e.g., Freedman, 1984; Savage, 2004) were already warning that the evidence for these assertions was not strong and that inconsistent findings with weak effect sizes were being presented as more significant and certain than they actually were. These critics also pointed out other problems in the media field, including lack of standardized measures, and a tendency to ignore research results that were inconsistent with the emerging gospel. These warnings were either shouted down in print rebuttals or simply ignored. Not only did organizations like the APA fail to step in to provide scientific correction, but they also largely parroted researchers' most extreme claims in policy statements that ultimately proved to be erroneous and misleading (Elson et al., 2019). The American Academy of Pediatrics (2000) cited a pop psychology book in repeating the apocryphal claim that of 3500 studies of media violence only 18 failed to find harmful effects. In fact, at the time, there were only about 200 such studies, and the results were far more mixed (Freedman, 2002). In short, the history of media violence research is a case study of a remarkable lack of restraint or oversight of this research field, but in fairness it must be noted that acceptance of flawed research was influenced by the correlation between increased television viewing and an increase in the US crime rate that stretched from the 1970s through the mid-1990s. Similar correlations appeared in Canada and South Africa (Centerwall, 1989), though not in other countries (Zimring & Hawkins, 1997). Still, the idea of a link between media violence and violent behavior stuck.

The heyday of the media violence hypothesis lasted with only sporadic opposition until the early 2000s, at which point two things had become apparent. First, the crime wave in the United States that peaked in 1993 had evaporated; crime rates are now about where they were in the 1960s (though, it should be said, early data suggest a significant increase in 2020, likely due to a combination of unique events in that year). This is remarkable because the reduction in crime began just as violent video games were being introduced in the United States (Ferguson, 2015c), thus removing one pillar of the argument for the negative public health level effects of media violence. Ironically, many scholars who once pointed to increasing crime rates as evidence for those effects began to argue that decreasing crime rates were unimportant. But one cannot have it both ways. Certainly, violence is multiply determined. Yet, such a large negative correlation between recent media violence consumption and societal violence, coupled with the *sheer amount* of media violence consumed by society, provides a persuasive correlational argument against the notion that, at the very least, one-third to one-half of violent crimes are caused by media violence, or the effects are similar to smoking and lung cancer.

The second major recent development in the media violence research field is that the quality of some media violence studies improved and, by the mid-2010s, in the United States, at least, many of them began to be preregistered. This means that the researcher publishes his or her hypotheses, methods, and data analysis plans before collecting any data. Preregistration is important because, previously, most aggression measures used in media violence studies were unstandardized, allowing researchers to pick and choose data that best fit their hypotheses. Indeed, with some of the common measures used, it was possible with the *same sample* to show that violent media either increased, decreased, or had no effect on aggression by extracting data creatively from a single aggression measure (Elson, Mohseni, Breuer, Scharkow, & Quandt, 2014). During this time, it became clear that psychological research on media violence (and on many other topics) was unreliable and that many apparently well-established beliefs and theories were proving to be false under more rigorous testing. The problem was due in part to scholars injecting personal beliefs into their research by *p-hacking* or rerunning their analyses in creative ways until they got the results they expected or wanted. P-hacking is more difficult, though not impossible, following preregistration. Most preregistered studies of media violence have focused on violent video games, and almost none of them supports negative effects (Ferguson, 2020). In other words, the best preregistered research that uses standardized measures finds that media violence does not reliably affect violence, bullying, or milder aggression. Although most preregistered studies now focus on the effects of violent video games; to my knowledge, only one looked at the impact of movies (Mubarak & Ferguson, 2020).

What Is a Teacher to Do?

In a perfect teaching world, psychology teachers would have a set of definitively determined facts which we impart to students. Unfortunately, we often do not have clear facts about media psychology, or about other aspects of psychology. Add to this the fact that some textbooks contain significant biases, misinformation, or outright myths, and the psychology teacher's job becomes particularly challenging.

In the preceding section, I offered a synopsis of media violence research that may differ significantly from what you are likely to find in some textbooks. I believe it is the correct synopsis, but media psychology in general, and research on media violence in particular, is a field characterized by much continued debate, some of which is quite acrimonious. But all this debate and disagreement means that media psychology courses lend themselves particularly well to creating lively teaching and learning experiences focused on critical thinking. With this in mind, I offer a few suggestions.

Embrace the Debate

Teaching students that a field is in conflict is not necessarily a bad thing. Certainly, imparting definitive facts can be satisfying and exciting, but the truth is that psychology (and real life) is often messier than what appears in textbooks. So it can be even more satisfying and exciting to give students disparate pieces of evidence, ask them to weigh opposing arguments, and come to their own conclusions. Class exercises can be built around this. You can assign students to read review articles from both sides of the academic debate on the effects of media violence (or other course topics) and report on their conclusions. You can also organize in-class debates between students, perhaps asking them to represent the side of the issue that they personally oppose. Exercises like these help to give students a fuller view of science which, rather than discovering facts in a linear fashion, often proceeds in fits and starts, lumbering and lurching toward self-correction.

Highlight the Politics of Science

Ideally, science should be value neutral, with pieces of data carrying no moral or political value. But in psychology and other behavioral and social sciences, this is often not the case. This point is exemplified by media violence research, which though undoubtedly undertaken in good faith has taken on both political and moral valence. In the United States, its results played a role when the Supreme Court was considering the constitutionality of increased restrictions on free speech by artists (in this case, the authors of video games) in the name of *protecting children*. The court was not persuaded by the argument that violent games cause youth aggression and clarified that both game creators and players enjoy substantial free speech protections (Brown v EMA, 2011). The decision came as a disappointment to the many scholars, politicians, activists, and leaders of professional guilds such as the APA who had misrepresented research results (or disseminated misrepresentations) so as to make the research say what they *wanted* it to say, not what it actually said.

Introducing students to the politics of media violence research provides a relatively safe way to get them thinking about the more general problem of politics in psychological science. It is a problem that applies to many other fields in which data collected and analyzed in an utterly neutral way could have explosive emotional, political, and moral repercussions. Research related to race, gender, sexuality, and the like are obvious examples of topics which can be political minefields. We should be explaining this to our students, especially in media psychology courses, because the truth about human behavior may not always align with our cherished beliefs about the world, and misalignments may not sit well with those in the media who would preserve those beliefs at all costs. Students need to understand that scientists are influenced, consciously or not, by the impact their research can have on society, and that this influence may lead them to choose designs, analyses, and conclusions that are neither unbiased nor value free. To reinforce this point, we should ask students to consider what would happen to scientists who find data that supports certain aspects of racial stereotypes. What if they find evidence that there really are biological and genetic components to gender or ethnic differences? What if their data suggests that intelligence is a real, single construct that plays a major role in determining life success? What if college entrance exam scores are actually good predictors of college grades for all students, and what if students' evaluations are accurate measures of their teachers' performance? Asking such questions can help students begin to understand that, for scientists studying value-laden topics, there is an inherent tension between doing good science and the political agendas of the right or the left.

Arguments to Authority

One of the issues to emerge from the media violence debate is that a lot of very smart people can be extremely wrong. This goes back to Bandura, who undoubtedly was very smart, acted in good faith, and revolutionized our approach to psychology, but who I would argue did more to damage our understanding of how aggression works than any other single individual. I do not mean this assertion as a personal criticism. Sometimes, academics just get things wrong, and science must self-correct. That is the process, but we should be sensitizing our students to the danger of deifying individual psychologists as if their word on a matter is treated as evidence. This is the classic logical fallacy of *argument to authority*.

The same goes for professional guilds such as the APA. Students should be allowed to consider the argument that these organizations are not science organizations, rather that they exist to promote professions. Consequently, they tend to release public policy statements that benefit the profession or just the APA, even if the statements are not necessarily accurate. This general argument has been presented for some time (e.g., O'Donohue & Dyslin, 1996) and has been more recently focused on the APA's flawed policy statements on media violence (Elson et al., 2019). Presenting this information can help stimulate students to critically evaluate the worth of statements made by professional bodies.

The Limits of Meta-Analyses

Especially in advanced courses on media psychology, discussion of research on media violence provides an opportunity to highlight the limits and misuse of certain methodological approaches, especially meta-analyses. These analyses combine the results of individual studies into a pooled mass of data in order to examine mean effect sizes. They have mushroomed in popularity over the past several decades, but they can have serious flaws that threaten the validity of the conclusions drawn from them.

In most research fields, the pooled mean effect size between studies is not very meaningful, as that effect size may be driven by systematic methodological flaws rather than actual effects that exist in the real world. Also, given that meta-analyses are statistically powerful, and few mean effect sizes are exactly zero, poorly used meta-analyses tend to give undue advantage to the alternative hypothesis. In many, perhaps most, cases, effect sizes are tiny but are nonetheless interpreted as supporting hypotheses with little concern for methodological issues that can cause false positive results. As a result, meta-analyses are often misused as tools for dismissing the significance of between-study inconsistencies and allowing researchers to declare results in a field to be more consistent than they actually are.

As an example, for their 2015 Task force on media violence (mainly focused on video games), the APA conducted a meta-analysis on 18 studies (far fewer than 3500!) and declared them to provide consistent evidence for the effects of violence on aggression, though not on violent crime (APA, 2015). However, a more recent reanalysis found that the APA task force missed dozens of studies, included five studies that actually did not compare violent games to nonviolent controls, and that the evidence presented did not, in fact, support the hypothesis that violent games contributed to aggression (Ferguson, Copenhaver, & Markey, 2020). Other recent meta-analyses have found that publication bias (the tendency to publish positive findings but not negative ones) has been widespread in this field, which also limits the utility of meta-analysis (Hilgard, Engelhardt, & Rouder, 2017). Understanding the limits of meta-analysis can help students put their contribution into proper perspective.

Other Media Effects Fields

The observed discrepancy between public rhetoric and available data is not limited to the field of media violence. It appears to be endemic to most media effects theories, particularly those that warn of the dangers of morally naughty fictional media. Such fields tend to undergo a standard pattern, albeit over varying lengths of time: First, a hypothesis is formed, typically with a moral component to it. Second, data are collected, often heavily reliant on college student participants and usually employing laboratory analogues of stress or aggression that are not directly representative of aggression or gun violence or whatever topic that society is worried about. Third, a narrative process begins in which claims are made and for which data are *superfluous*. Indeed, data that do not confirm the claims are typically ignored; proponents of the asserted theory pretend those data do not exist. Inconsistent results are dressed up as consistent, and meta-analyses are employed to launder away between-study inconsistencies. Typically, the narrative pushes a moral narrative that scientists and society must *do something* to protect children or other groups from mental illness or even death. Fourth, professional guilds such as the APA, perhaps sensing a way to use this field to market the profession, release policy statements that, as already noted, rarely reflect the realities of the science, but typically further the moral and ideological agenda of the organization.

One of the best-known examples of this pattern can be found in the literature on the alleged causal link between thin-ideal media messages (i.e., that idolize slender models and actresses) and the occurrence of eating disorders in women, particularly anorexia nervosa. It might surprise your students to learn that there are exactly zero empirical studies that support the existence of such a causal link. You can explain that anorexia nervosa is exceedingly rare (occurring in 1% or less of women) making it difficult to obtain relevant research samples. Thus, most studies rely on either self-report surveys of eating disorder *symptoms* (some of which, like dieting to lose weight, are quite common and mild on their own), or a nonclinical condition called *body dissatisfaction.* Most studies are conducted with college students and use research designs that make it easy for participants to guess what the researchers' hypothesis is, thus causing some participants to respond or behave in accordance with what they think the experimenters want to see. Also, many studies do not use appropriate control groups. In an experiment on the impact of "thin ideals," the stimuli for the experimental group should be thin and attractive models, whereas control participants should see stimuli that are larger, but equally attractive. This arrangement separates the impact of thinness from that of, say, general attractiveness. However, many studies compare the impact of thin models to that of household appliances like refrigerators, not average-sized humans. This kind of control condition does not allow researchers to isolate the specific impact of thinness, or even humanness.

In short, serious methodological flaws run rampant in this field (Want, 2014), and as a result, the evidence is quite inconsistent. One of the best examples of flawed data being dressed up as more convincing than they are occurred in the "Fiji study," which examined the prevalence of eating disorders before and after the introduction of television on the island in the mid-1990s (Becker, Burwell, Herzog, Hamburg, & Gilman, 2002). On the basis of self-report surveys, the researchers concluded that eating disorders among Fijian girls increased after the introduction of television. However, a close examination of their main results indicates numerous inconsistencies with that conclusion (Ferguson, 2018). Although self-reported vomiting to reduce weight increased, as did overall eating symptoms, binging symptomatic of bulimia nervosa did not, nor did BMI decline as one might expect when girls embrace a thin ideal. A multivariate analysis of TV ownership and self-reported eating disorder symptoms became nonsignificant when only controlling for sample year (samples were collected in 1995 and 1998), and it is likely that effect sizes would have been further attenuated had other theoretically important variables been controlled. Thus, although the Fiji study reported increases in some, but not all, *self-reported* symptoms after television became available, there was no evidence that television resulted in actual weight-reducing behaviors among adolescent girls. Further, given the small sample size (63–65 girls), and the fact that the study design did not make it possible to isolate media effects from those of other social changes occurring in Fiji at the time, the Fiji study – though often interpreted as clear evidence for a media effect – does not provide strong support for that effect.

Indeed, for men and most women, there is no convincing evidence that thin-ideal media messages cause body dissatisfaction, let alone clinically diagnosed eating disorders, yet the studies that fail to find the claimed link tend to be ignored

(Ferguson, 2013). Ironically, those studies tend to be the ones with the best experimental designs (e.g., Bruns & Carter, 2015; Roberts & Good, 2010; Veldhuis, Konijn, & Seidell, 2014; Whyte et al., 2016).

After summarizing this body of evidence, it might be instructive to ask your students to consider other ways in which media messages might be related to eating disorders. One possibility is that, for women who *already* experience body dissatisfaction (caused by genetics, family influences, or peer competition), seeing thin models in the media may remind them of that dissatisfaction and amplify it.

Research on the impact of pornography is another which has long been heavily influenced by morality, but often divorced from good data. Even today, some scholars argue that pornography is a cause of sexual violence (e.g., Guggisberg, 2020), despite a dire lack of evidence to support that causal connection (e.g., Ferguson & Hartley, in press; Seto, Maric, & Barbaree, 2001). In fact, at the societal level, there is strong evidence for an inverse relationship between the availability of pornography and sexual violence.

Other false narratives about media influences abound. For example, it was briefly claimed that a US TV series called *13 Reasons Why*, which included the graphic suicide of a teenage girl, might be causing teen suicides until a closer examination of suicide data found no relationship to the release of the show (Romer, 2020). In the mid-2010s, both the US Centers for Disease Control and Prevention (CDC, 2017) and the United States Surgeon General (US Department of Health and Human Services (2014) had begun claiming that tens of thousands of Americans were dying each year as a result of having taken up smoking after watching movie or TV characters do so. The data supporting this claim appear to have been largely invented or extrapolated from very weak studies that actually, in the aggregate, found that movie smoking has little effect on teen smoking (Ferguson, Nielsen, & Markey, 2020).

Two more examples of debunked claims about media effects include that the movie *Jaws* was responsible for shark depopulation (that depopulation began before the movie was released and is related entirely to the impact of commercial overfishing), and that a radio broadcast of H.G. Wells' *War of the Worlds* in 1938 sent thousands of Americans fleeing for their lives because they thought the Earth was being invaded by Martians.

However, research on advertising provides strong evidence for causal effects of media messages, particularly on children (e.g., Emond et al., 2019). Making this point should stimulate your students to ask questions about what makes the effects of advertising more influential compared to those of video games, TV shows, or other fictional media. One possible answer is that the behaviors being influenced are relatively trivial (e.g., switching from Coke to Pepsi, eating French fries instead of apple slices) compared to those alleged to be caused by fictional media (increasing aggression, violent crime, or eating disorders). Another possibility is that advertisements are presented as repeated statements of fact (e.g., that X is the best shampoo or that Y is the best mobile phone) that are designed to tell (or more subtly persuade) consumers to change their behavior in some way. This format, like other forms of strong social influence, is likely to have a stronger causal impact than, say, seeing someone on TV shoot someone else. Couching advertisements as truth, accompanied by requests to make relatively minor behavior changes, may serve to circumvent cognitive and biological processes that normally help us to distinguish truth from fiction, processes that begin as early as age 3 (Petty, Cacioppo, & Kasmer, 2015; Woolley & Van Reet, 2006). A discussion of differences between advertisements and fictional media can be illuminating for students, and also helpful for pointing out that every hypothesis discussed in media psychology courses must be tested independently. It cannot be assumed that because one class of media has effects (advertisements) all of them do.

Tips for Teachers

As should by now be clear, media effects research is very controversial and people, whether scholars, politicians, or students, have passionate opinions about it. The suggestions below pertain mainly to helping teachers make good use of the debate, less as a way to inform students about *facts* (as these are often in dispute), but rather as an opportunity to teach critical thinking and how to debate controversial topics in a civil manner. For teachers who are so inclined, classroom analysis of the media effects controversy also creates an opportunity to discuss matters pertaining to free speech.

Check the Textbook

If you are teaching psychology in a country where it is traditional to assign a textbook for your courses, it is obviously important to choose your books with care. Having studied the content of introductory psychology textbooks (Ferguson et al., 2018), one thing that struck me is that the level of student engagement created by a book is a poor indicator of its accuracy. Put simply, some reader-friendly textbooks contain quite inaccurate information about media matters and other topics, whereas some less-engaging texts are far more accurate. Although few, if any, textbooks are entirely without sin, it would appear that serious errors in content tend to cluster in particular chapters, so if you find biased or erroneous coverage in a few key areas, there may be accuracy problems elsewhere, too. I suggest that you start your evaluation with the section on media or video game violence, which is usually in the chapter on learning. Does that section cover the debate in a fair and balanced manner? Does it take one side, while dismissing (or failing even to report) evidence to the contrary? Check a few other well-known problem areas for textbooks such as the Kitty Genovese fable or the Stanford Prison Experiment. If there is consistent misreporting across multiple areas, it may be wise to consider a different book. Correcting the text in a few areas is fine, but having to do so continuously during the academic term is likely to confuse students and make them wonder why you chose the book they are reading.

Highlight the Replication Crisis

Psychology is currently going through a massive realignment of knowledge based on an awareness of poor research practices in the past. Yet, we also want to get students excited about psychology, so how can we do that while also acknowledging psychology's serious failures? Discussion of research on media effects can help. The decline of the narrative about media-driven violence from "definitely true" into what has been called a dumpster fire provides an excellent perspective from which to discuss psychology's larger replication crisis. That discussion can lead to the realization that the news is not all bad. The process of self-correction in science is hardly ever peaceful and pleasant, and by reading articles in this field, students can study scientific self-correction in action. The classroom discussion might be intense, but handled correctly it can help students see that criticism of scientists by fellow scientists is what separates science from other ways of inquiring about the world (including, it may be worth noting, in nonscience disciplines). Far from depressing students about psychology, teachers have an opportunity to get them excited about possibly becoming part of the process of scientific self-correction.

Focus on Research Methods

Part of the problem with many studies on media effects is that the vast majority of them are simply of poor quality, including Bandura's Bobo doll studies. It should be easy for students, even in lower-level or introductory psychology classes, to identify the flaws in these studies, and as mentioned already, doing so provides excellent opportunities for critical thinking. So instead of presenting the Bobo doll studies as holy writ (as is often the case in psychology classes), you can encourage students to examine the design and methodology and ask themselves if the results really can be used to make sweeping claims about the nature of human aggression and on factors that influence it.

This kind of analysis also provides the opportunity to reinforce the "correlation doesn't equal causation" mantra, but, more than that, to point out that many scholars (and politicians) eschew this basic tenet when it suits their purposes. Both the Centerwall studies of television violence and violent crime and the Fiji study of thin-ideal media essentially drew causal conclusions from correlational data. Ask students to consider why scholars do this when they obviously should know better?

Promote Civil Debate

Media effects research presents an opportunity for students to learn how to disagree on a topic, but to do so civilly. As I write this, civil debate has all but broken down in North America, Europe, and elsewhere. As teachers, we have a role to play in helping students to focus on facts and methods and scientific reasoning rather than to allow themselves to be governed by political outrage and moral self-righteousness neither of which is healthy or scientific.

I suggest that you encourage your students to examine the pros and cons of media effects research while helping them to build skills in debate that takes a data-based approach rather than one that relies on emotion, personal attack, or anecdotal evidence. These skills take practice, yet teachers of psychology too seldom give students an opportunity to engage in that practice. Many classroom "debate" presentations are actually rather dry, and there is little in the way of exchange of ideas. Instead of having preplanned oral presentations, students could stage a formal debate, with opposing teams, clear rules – including an emphasis on civility – and a vote for winners (that should not affect course grades). Debates can also occur in the context of less formal group discussions.

Legitimize Uncertainty

Many scholars and professional guilds, and certainly many teachers, feel societal or student pressure to have *the* answer when it comes to issues like media effects. This pressure to find or present *the* answer has been the devil's lure, leading some scholars, teachers, and the APA to offer public statements or lectures that are faulty, and in some cases, deliberately misrepresentative of the research landscape. The APA, for example, has been told that its statements are wrong, in one case by a group of 230 scholars (Consortium of Scholars, 2013), yet failed to correct them. It is difficult to explain that failure without referring to the organization's need to create a sense of certainty about its science.

I suggest that you discuss with your students the possibility that the efforts of scholars and organizations to establish certainty where there is none can be attributed in part to concerns that it is difficult to market psychology as a science while admitting that it does not have definitive answers to many key questions. Ask them to consider the long-range consequences, such as that the certainty mindset may have actually damaged rather than burnished psychology's credibility because it results in causal claims that go out on scientifically fragile limbs. What is the alternative? Help students to see that one option is to recognize uncertainty can be acceptable, even exciting, because it drives psychological scientists toward new hypotheses and better data. Teaching students to be alright with uncertainty can be a valuable lesson.

Emphasize the Value of Free Speech

Media effects literature is rife with moral crusading and calls to restrict speech. As already documented above, scholars have been quick to generalize weak findings to create massive public health concerns, including claims that thousands of people are dying every year as a result of certain kinds of media depictions. That such ludicrous claims are readily repeated by otherwise smart people demonstrates how easily emotion and moral self-righteousness can overwhelm critical thinking. If we begin to restrict every kind of speech that someone somewhere passionately believes to be dangerous, what will remain? Who gets to decide what speech is protected and what is not? Are we content with the limits of the First Amendment, even though private multinational corporations may ultimately censor our online dialogues? On the other hand, when people are engaged in free but pernicious and ugly speech, how can we as individuals fight against that while maintaining free speech values?

The topic of freedom of speech as a civic value may not seem central to a course in media psychology, but it is. It is essential to the science of psychology, a science whose research results often challenge society's assumptions about the human condition. Our students, like the rest of us, tend to think of themselves as free speech advocates until they come across speech they do not like, and at that point may seek to restrict it in some way. A media psychology course in general, and an analysis of media effects in particular, can provide an arena in which to sensitize students to this issue.

Concluding Thoughts

Has psychological science royally screwed up the study of media effects? Absolutely. But the next chapter of that story tells how newer, better science is reevaluating old questions with better data. Teaching about media effects effectively in an introductory psychology course (or elsewhere) requires asking students to shift their thinking away from a search for "final answers" to embracing the controversy and debate generated by conflicting results. Helping students to do this will take them beyond rote memorization of course material and stimulate their skill at critical thinking, scientific evaluation, and civil debate. So although research on media effects may be a messy area for instructors to wade into, it is also full of potential for helping students to tolerate uncertainty and to thrive.

Cross-References

▶ Developmental Psychology: Moving Beyond the East–West Divide
▶ General Psychology Motivation
▶ Learning and Teaching in Clinical Psychology
▶ Teaching Social Psychology Effectively

References

American Academy of Pediatrics. (2000). Media violence policy statement. *Pediatrics, 108*(5), 1222–1226.
American Psychological Association. (2015). *APA review confirms link between playing violent video games and aggression*. Retrieved from: https://www.apa.org/news/press/releases/2015/08/violent-video-games.aspx
Becker, A. E., Burwell, R. A., Herzog, D. B., Hamburg, P., & Gilman, S. E. (2002). Eating behaviours and attitudes following prolonged exposure to television among ethnic Fijian

adolescent girls. *British Journal of Psychiatry, 180*(6), 509–514. https://doi.org/10.1192/bjp. 180.6.509.

Blum, B. (2018). The lifespan of a lie: The most famous psychology study of all time was a sham. Why can't we escape the Stanford prison experiment? *Medium.* Retrieved from: https://gen. medium.com/the-lifespan-of-a-lie-d869212b1f62

Brown v. Entertainment Merchants Association, 131 S. Ct. 2729. (2011). Retrieved from: http:// www.supremecourt.gov/opinions/10pdf/08-1448.pdf

Bruns, G. L., & Carter, M. M. (2015). Ethnic differences in the effects of media on body image: The effects of priming with ethnically different or similar models. *Eating Behaviors, 17*, 33–36. https://doi.org/10.1016/j.eatbeh.2014.12.006.

Bushman, B., & Anderson, C. (2001). Media violence and the American public. *American Psychologist, 56*, 477–489.

Centers for Disease Control (2017). *Smoking in the movies..* Retrieved from: https://www.cdc.gov/ tobacco/data_statistics/fact_sheets/youth_data/movies/index.htm

Centerwall, B. (1989). Exposure to television as a risk factor for violence. *American Journal of Epidemiology, 129*, 643–652.

Centerwall, B. S. (1992). Television and violence: The scale of the problem and where to go from here. *Journal of the American Medical Association, 267*, 3059–3063.

Cohen, S. (1972). *Folk devils and moral panics.* London, UK: MacGibbon and Kee.

Consortium of Scholars. (2013). *Scholar's open statement to the APA task force on violent media.* Retrieved from: http://www.scribd.com/doc/223284732/Scholar-s-Open-Letter-to-the-APA-Task-Force-On-Violent-Media-Opposing-APA-Policy-Statements-on-Violent-Media

Elson, M., Ferguson, C. J., Gregerson, M., Hogg, J. L., Ivory, J., Klisanin, D., . . . Wilson, J. (2019). Do policy statements on media effects faithfully represent the science? *Advances in Methods and Practices in Psychological Science, 2*(1), 12–25.

Elson, M., Mohseni, M. R., Breuer, J., Scharkow, M., & Quandt, T. (2014). Press CRTT to measure aggressive behavior: The unstandardized use of the competitive reaction time task in aggression research. *Psychological Assessment, 26*, 419–432. https://doi.org/10.1037/a0035569.

Emond, J. A., Longacre, M. R., Drake, K. M., Titus, L. J., Hendricks, K., MacKenzie, T., . . . Dalton, M. A. (2019). Influence of child-targeted fast food TV advertising exposure on fast food intake: A longitudinal study of preschool-age children. *Appetite, 140*, 134–141. https://doi-org. stetson.idm.oclc.org/10.1016/j.appet.2019.05.012

Ferguson, C. J. (2013). In the eye of the beholder: Thin-ideal media affects some but not most viewers in a meta-analytic review of body dissatisfaction in women and men. *Psychology of Popular Media Culture, 2*(1), 20–37.

Ferguson, C. J. (2015a). Clinicians' attitudes toward video games vary as a function of age, gender and negative beliefs about youth: A sociology of media research approach. *Computers in Human Behavior, 52*, 379–386.

Ferguson, C. J. (2015b). Pay no attention to that data behind the curtain: On angry birds, happy children, scholarly squabbles, publication bias and why betas rule metas. *Perspectives on Psychological Science, 10*, 683–691.

Ferguson, C. J. (2015c). Does movie or videogame violence predict societal violence? It depends on what you look at and when. *Journal of Communication, 65*, 193–212.

Ferguson, C. J. (2018). The devil wears Stata: Thin-ideal media's minimal contribution to our understanding of body dissatisfaction and eating disorders. *Archives of Scientific Psychology, 6*, 70–79.

Ferguson, C. J. (2020). Aggressive video games research emerges from its replication crisis (sort of). *Current Opinion in Psychology, 36*, 1–6.

Ferguson, C. J., Brown, J. M., & Torres, A. V. (2018). Education or indoctrination? The accuracy of introductory psychology textbooks in covering controversial topics and urban legends about psychology. *Current Psychology, 37*(3), 574–582.

Ferguson, C. J., & Colwell, J. (2017). Understanding why scholars hold different views on the influences of video games on public health. *Journal of Communication, 67*(3), 305–327.

Ferguson, C.J., Copenhaver, A. & Markey, P. (2020). Re-examining the findings of the APA's 2015 task force on violent media: A meta-analysis. *Perspectives on Psychological Science 15*(6), 1423–1443.

Ferguson, C. J., & Hartley, R. D. (in press). Pornography and sexual aggression: Can meta-analysis find a link? *Trauma, Violence & Abuse.*

Ferguson, C. J., Nielsen, R. K., & Markey, P. (2020) Movie smoking and teen smoking behavior: A critical methodological and meta-analytic review. *Psychology of Popular Media Culture, 9*(2), 247–254.

Freedman, J. L. (1984). Effect of television violence on aggressiveness. *Psychological Bulletin, 96* (2), 227–246. https://doi.org/10.1037/0033-2909.96.2.227.

Freedman, J. L. (2002). *Media violence and its effect on aggression.* Toronto, ON: University of Toronto Press.

Gray, P. (2013). Why Zimbardo's prison experiment isn't in my textbook. *Psychology Today.* Retrieved from: https://www.psychologytoday.com/us/blog/freedom-learn/201310/why-zimbardo-s-prison-experiment-isn-t-in-my-textbook

Griggs, R. A. (2014). The continuing saga of Little Albert in introductory psychology textbooks. *Teaching of Psychology, 41*(4), 309–317. https://doi-org.stetson.idm.oclc.org/10.1177/0098628314549702

Griggs, R. A. (2015). Coverage of the Phineas Gage story in introductory psychology textbooks: Was Gage no longer Gage? *Teaching of Psychology, 42*(3), 195–202. https://doi-org.stetson.idm.oclc.org/10.1177/0098628315587614

Guggisberg, M. (2020). Sexually explicit video games and online pornography – The promotion of sexual violence: A critical commentary. *Aggression and Violent Behavior, 53,* 101432. https://doi.org/10.1016/j.avb.2020.101432.

Hilgard, J., Engelhardt, C. R., & Rouder, J. N. (2017). Overstated evidence for short-term effects of violent games on affect and behavior: A reanalysis of Anderson et al. (2010). *Psychological Bulletin, 143*(7), 757–774. https://doi.org/10.1037/bul0000074.

Kutner, L., & Olson, C. (2008). *Grand theft childhood: The surprising truth about violent video games and what parents can do.* New York, NY: Simon & Schuster.

Manning, R., Levine, M., & Collins, A. (2007). The Kitty Genovese murder and the social psychology of helping: The parable of the 38 witnesses. *American Psychologist, 62*(6), 555–562. https://doi.org/10.1037/0003-066X.62.6.555.

Markey, P. M., Males, M. A., French, J. E., & Markey, C. N. (2015). Lessons from Markey et al. (2015) and Bushman et al. (2015): Sensationalism and integrity in media research. *Human Communication Research, 41*(2), 184–203. https://doi-org.stetson.idm.oclc.org/10.1111/hcre.12057

Mubarak, N., & Ferguson, C. J. (2020). Pride and prejudice and zombies. . .and statistics: Effects of powerful female role-models in media on attitudes towards women, and female viewer anxiety. *Current Psychology: A Journal for Diverse Perspectives on Diverse Psychological Issues.* https://doi-org.stetson.idm.oclc.org/10.1007/s12144-020-00605-7

O'Donohue, W., & Dyslin, C. (1996). Abortion, boxing and Zionism: Politics and the APA. *New Ideas in Psychology, 14*(1), 1–10. https://doi.org/10.1016/0732-118X(95)00025-C.

O'Donohue, W., & Willis, B. (2018). Problematic images of science in undergraduate psychology textbooks: How well is science understood and depicted? *Archives of Scientific Psychology, 6* (1), 51–62. https://doi-org.stetson.idm.oclc.org/10.1037/arc0000040.supp

Orne, M. T. (1962). On the social psychology of the psychological experiment: With particular reference to demand characteristics and their implications. *American Psychologist, 17*(11), 776–783. https://doi.org/10.1037/h0043424.

Pashler, H., Coburn, N., & Harris, C. R. (2012). Priming of social distance? Failure to replicate effects on social and food judgments. *PLoS One, 7*(8). https://doi-org.stetson.idm.oclc.org/10.1371/journal.pone.0042510

Perry, G., Wanner, A., & Stam, H. (in press). Credibility and incredulity in Milgram's obedience experiments: A reanalysis of an unpublished test. *Social Psychology Quarterly.*

Petty, R. E., Cacioppo, J. T., & Kasmer, J. A. (2015). The role of affect in the elaboration likelihood model of persuasion. In L. Donohew, H. Sypher, & E. Higgins (Eds.), *Communication, social cognition, and affect (PLE: Emotion)* (pp. 117–147). New York, NY: Psychology Press.

Preston, M. I. (1941). Children's reactions to movie horrors and radio crime. *The Journal of Pediatrics, 19*, 147–168. https://doi-org.stetson.idm.oclc.org/10.1016/S0022-3476(41)80059-6

Przybylski, A. K. (2014). Who believes electronic games cause real world aggression? *Cyberpsychology, Behavior and Social Networking, 17*(4), 228–234. https://doi-org.stetson.idm.oclc.org/10.1089/cyber.2013.0245

Quandt, T., Van Looy, J., Vogelgesang, J., Elson, M., Ivory, J. D., Consalvo, M., . . . Mäyrä, F. (2015). Digital games research: A survey study on an emerging field and its prevalent debates. *Journal of Communication, 65*(6), 975–996.

Roberts, A., & Good, E. (2010). Media images and female body dissatisfaction: The moderating effects of the five-factor traits. *Eating Behaviors, 11*(4), 211–216. https://doi.org/10.1016/j.eatbeh.2010.04.002.

Romer, D. (2020). Reanalysis of the Bridge et al. study of suicide following release of 13 Reasons Why. *PLoS One*. Retrieved from: https://journals.plos.org/plosone/article?id=10.1371/journal.pone.0227545

Savage, J. (2004). Does viewing violent media really cause criminal violence? A methodological review. *Aggression and Violent Behavior, 10*, 99–128.

Seto, M. C., Maric, A., & Barbaree, H. E. (2001). The role of pornography in the etiology of sexual aggression. *Aggression and Violent Behavior, 6*, 35–53.

Stoet, G., & Geary, D. C. (2012). Can stereotype threat explain the gender gap in mathematics performance and achievement? *Review of General Psychology, 16*(1), 93–102. https://doi-org.stetson.idm.oclc.org/10.1037/a0026617

Strasburger, V. (2007). Go ahead punk, make my day: It's time for pediatricians to take action against media violence. *Pediatrics, 119*, e1398–e1399.

Tedeschi, J., & Quigley, B. (1996). Limitations of laboratory paradigms for studying aggression. *Aggression and Violent Behavior, 2*, 163–177.

US Department of Health and Human Services. (2014). *The health consequences of smoking – 50 years of progress*. Retrieved from: https://www.surgeongeneral.gov/library/reports/50-years-of-progress/index.html

Veldhuis, J., Konijn, E. A., & Seidell, J. C. (2014). Negotiated media effects. Peer feedback modifies effects of media's thin-body ideal on adolescent girls. *Appetite, 73*, 172–182. https://doi.org/10.1016/j.appet.2013.10.023.

Want, S. C. (2014). Three questions regarding the ecological validity of experimental research on the impact of viewing thin-ideal media images. *Basic and Applied Social Psychology, 36*(1), 27–34. https://doi.org/10.1080/01973533.2013.856783.

Whyte, C., Newman, L. S., & Voss, D. (2016). A confound-free test of the effects of thin-ideal media images on body satisfaction. *Journal of Social and Clinical Psychology, 35*(10), 822–839. https://doi.org/10.1521/jscp.2016.35.10.822.

Woolley, J. D., & Van Reet, J. (2006). Effects of context on judgments concerning the reality status of novel entities. *Child Development, 77*(6), 1778–1793. https://doi.org/10.1111/j.1467-8624.2006.00973.x.

Zimring, F., & Hawkins, G. (1997). *Crime is not the problem: Lethal violence in America*. New York, NY: Oxford University Press.

Unfurling the Potential of the Counselor

A Perspective on Training

Sujata Sriram and Swarnima Bhargava

Contents

Abstract

Counseling and psychotherapy training in countries around the world have been imbued with theories and models developed in the Euro-American perspective. This chapter looks at the role of the therapist, therapist competence, and development as integral to therapy process and outcomes, from the perspective of developing countries in Asia. Training and education for counselors and therapists with reference to models of training, entry points, content of training programs, supervision, personal therapy, and deliberate practice have been examined. The lack of regulation and licensing and their impact on the professionalization of the field have been commented on. Encouraging open communication and dialogue across countries can help facilitate a culturally grounded approach to the training and supervision of therapists. Creating national bodies with the mandate of examining pedagogy and curriculum development in counseling training institutes across Asia may further help to establish common goals as well as enable sharing unique sociocultural specific practices and insights. Recommendations have been laid out for meeting the challenges to

S. Sriram (⊠) · S. Bhargava
School of Human Ecology, Tata Institute of Social Sciences, Mumbai, India
e-mail: sujatas@tiss.edu

© Springer Nature Switzerland AG 2023
J. Zumbach et al. (eds.), *International Handbook of Psychology Learning and Teaching*,
Springer International Handbooks of Education,
https://doi.org/10.1007/978-3-030-28745-0_30

global mental health resulting from the sociopolitical changes of the twenty-first century. The need to develop multicultural sensitivity and locally relevant codes of ethical standards is paramount.

Keywords

Counseling · Psychotherapy · Training · Supervision · Curriculum · Ethics · Multicultural sensitivity

Counseling and psychotherapy as professions have spread across the world, as means of alleviating distress for people with mental illness and difficulty. However, while the professions have benefitted multiple individuals, the methods used are often based on models and theories that have evolved in the Euro-American frameworks. While there is recognition that culture influences mental illness and wellness, counseling and psychotherapy practice and training have been slow to accept and include culture in the curricula used to train counselors. This chapter offers a perspective for training in counseling and psychotherapy from Asia.

From the Beginning: The Emergence of Counseling and Psychotherapy

People have turned to priests, gurus, philosophers, and doctors for guidance and advice in times of distress and confusion. The cure of mental suffering, earlier called "madness," has a long history from ideas of mental illness caused by evil spirits, to the present. Those who displayed any form of mental affliction were treated harshly and cruelly; they were whipped, beaten, starved, and isolated. In the United States, conditions for the mentally ill improved when the Quakers under the empathic guidance of Benjamin Franklin opened the first hospital in Pennsylvania "to care for the sick-poor and insane who were wandering the streets of Philadelphia." This gave rise to the Asylum Act of 1845, from which the profession of psychiatry evolved, for the care of the "insane," now referred to as "mentally ill."

From medicine and psychiatry evolved psychotherapy. The earliest physicians to call themselves psychotherapists were Van Renterghem and Van Eeden, who opened a clinic of Suggestive Psychotherapy in Amsterdam in 1887 (Ellenberger, 1970). By the late nineteenth century, psychotherapy was forged through the path-breaking work of pioneers like Freud.

In the twentieth century, Western counseling and psychotherapy have developed on three theoretical "schools" of thought: the psychodynamic, the behavioral, and the humanistic. Each had their views of human behavior; the psychodynamic school was based on unconscious urges and childhood antecedents; the behavioral school-based personality on learning and conditioning; and finally the humanistic school which introduced person-centered counseling and promoted the view of self-development. In the twenty-first century, myriad theoretical approaches have developed using these three perspectives as a base. Besides these three perspectives, other theoretical orientations have arisen, subsumed under the "fourth force" of psychology, such as transpersonal counseling, family systems approaches, feminist psychology, multicultural psychology, and ecopsychology. The social justice perspective in therapy has emerged in the context of the twenty-first century, as a fifth force, rooted in the human rights and social justice movements (Fleuridas & Krafcik, 2019).

Counseling vs. Psychotherapy The terms "counseling" and "psychotherapy" have dominated psychology literature since the inception of the field. Counseling encompasses a broad domain of helping professionals including specialist professional workers, but also encompasses paraprofessionals, volunteers, and those whose practice is embedded within other occupational roles. Psychotherapy involves deeper work, usually over a longer period of time with more disturbed clients. Essentially both groups do the same type of work, which is providing the client a confidential space to explore conflicted emotions. However, counseling has been portrayed in a "little sister" role in relation to psychotherapy. Counseling is still placed in a lesser position, while psychotherapy jobs are of a higher status and better paid than counseling posts, even when they involve doing equivalent work.

For the purpose of this paper, the term "psychotherapy" and "counseling" will be used synonymously to denote the talking cures used to alleviate distress.

Counseling and psychotherapy have their roots in the fields of medicine and psychiatry, and the term "psychological therapies" is used to denote the work of psychotherapists. A few countries make it mandatory to have a degree in psychology to gain training in psychotherapy. Apart from psychology, psychotherapy has been influenced by other fields such as philosophy, theology and religion, literature, and the arts. In recent times, psychotherapy has been influenced by Zen Buddhism. Mindfulness-based practices originating from the teachings of Buddhism have found their way into psychotherapy practice and have been used successfully along with cognitive therapies (Segal, Williams, & Teasdale, 2001. The field of arts, in particular, expressive arts such as music, dance, art, play, and drama, along with sculpture, and other visual media have evolved as modes of psychotherapy. In recent years, psychodrama and art therapy have developed their own distinctive theoretical models, training courses, and professional journals. Specific literature-based techniques have also been employed in counseling, such as autobiography, journal writing, poetry writing, and bibliotherapy.

Religion has played an important role in the evolution of psychotherapy. Since the 1800s, the Christian church believed that faith could heal people, and religious counseling, for example, the use of the confessional, was an important source of comfort, advice, and direction for distressed people. The work of theorists such as Wundt, Freud, and later Jung resulted in replacement of the moralistic flavor of counseling propagated by the church with a more spiritual and secular approach. As psychotherapy grew in prominence, it "took over" from religion by offering explanations for events that are difficult to understand, offering answers to the existential question "what am I here for?," defining social values, and supplying ritual ways of dealing with grief and other forms of distress. At present, the question that concerns therapists is not whether to include religion and spirituality while working with believers, but the manner and the timing of the inclusion. Literature has indicated that the adaptation of therapy to include religious and spiritual elements has been found to be demonstrably effective for clients who were oriented towards religion and spirituality (Gonsiorek, Richards, Pargament, & McMinn, 2009; Hook et al., 2019; Post & Wade, 2009).

Counseling and Psychotherapy in Asia

Literature on counseling and psychotherapy from Asian countries such as Korea, Japan, Taiwan, China, and India is limited. The need for counseling in many Asian countries has been recognized; however, mental health and illness have never received the attention that physical illness has received (Kumaraswamy, 2007). There is stigma associated with mental illness and a lack of awareness about ways of dealing with the same. Foo, Merrick, and Kazantzis (2006) write about how South-East Asian cultures which emphasize honor and self-esteem prevent individuals from actively seeking help. The entry of psychotherapy as a discipline in Asian countries such as India, China, Hong Kong. and Taiwan has been recent, largely due to the return of scholars trained in the West. The origins of the discipline are rooted in the colonial past, which has persisted in education, theory, and praxis. The twenty-first century increase in cultural interchange and exchange as a result of globalization has contributed to the expansion of psychotherapy and the recognition of the need to internationalize the discipline (Duan et al., 2011; Sriram, 2016).

Counseling in China In China, while the work of Freud was translated in the 1920s, psychology as a discipline was banned by Mao Zedong in the 1960s, and psychiatry followed a biomedical model. In the present times, there is a scarcity of psychiatrists; and psychology has reemerged as a profession, accompanied by the understanding that psychotherapy can play a role in alleviating mental distress. Younger, city dwelling, more educated individuals are more accepting of therapy instead of drugs as compared to older individuals. However, fundamental contradictions between Western psychotherapy and Chinese cultural traditions exist. Western therapy emphasizes the development of the individual self, which goes against the eastern belief of the need to overcome the self. Many Western philosophers emphasize the individual, while the person in context is what is emphasized in most Chinese thought (Brannigan, 2014; Duan et al., 2011).

In the early part of the twenty-first century, many therapists were certified by the Ministry of Labor through programs which had no clinical exposure at all, resulting in poorly trained professionals. The passing of the Mental Health Law in China in 2013 resulted in restrictions on those who can practice psychotherapy. The Law has resulted in psychotherapy being used by psychiatrists and practitioners in hospital settings. The Mental Health Law in China was passed because of the need to professionalize the field, to ensure that practitioners below standard levels of training could not practice. However, psychological services are concentrated in urban areas mostly situated at clinics in universities, medium-size and large general hospitals, and professional centers for psychotherapy and counseling services (Chang, Tong, Shi, & Zeng, 2005). Chinese individuals with severe mental problems visit hospitals and are treated as patients akin to those with physical problems; and the therapists are identified as psychological doctors (xinli yisheng) (Hou & Zhang, 2007). Mental health issues are thus often equated with mental diseases.

In order to comply with the Law, university-trained therapists used the term counseling for their practice. The effort is being made to professionalize the field by improving training provided both by private institutions and the university system (Clay, 2019; Huang, 2015; Zhao, 2014). The Chinese Psychological Society (CPS) sets up a registration system for professional organizations and individual practitioners in clinical and counseling psychology, aimed to regulate and improve counseling and psychotherapy in China. In 2007, the Chinese Psychological Society registration criteria for professional organizations and individual practitioners in clinical and counseling psychology and the Code of Ethics for clinical and counseling psychological practice of the Chinese Psychological Society (CPS, 2007) were decreed. Other professional bodies such as the Chinese Association for Mental Health (CAMH) were re-established in 1985 (Chen, 2005) after a long suspension since 1936. The first issue of the Journal of Chinese Mental Health was published in 1987. In 1990, the Committee of Counseling and Psychotherapy in CAMH was created; and in 1991, the Committee of Counseling College Students in CAMH was set up (Qian, 1994). The Committee of Clinical and Counseling Psychology in the Chinese Psychological Society was created in 2001, and the first national conference on counseling and psychotherapy was held in 2003 (Zeng, Zhao, & Zhu, 2003).

Counseling in India While there have been rapid strides made in the development of counseling in India, concerns have emerged alongside. While education for the training of counselors is available in many colleges and universities in the country, it is a harsh reality that the number of professionally qualified counselors and therapists in India is barely adequate to serve the needs of the population (Bhola, Kumaria, & Orlinsky, 2012; Malhotra, Chakrabarti, & Shah, 2013; Manickam, 2010). While there has been a proliferation of professional training programs and courses for counselor education in India, there is no standard curriculum followed. The need for licensing and regulation of the profession has been expressed by practitioners and academics in the field; however, there have been limited efforts to regulate the profession. There has been limited research in India related to the field of counseling psychology and the effects of counseling and therapy on issues and individuals. The existing research is scattered and rarely disseminated to academics and practitioners in the field (Bhola et al., 2012; Manickam, 2010; Sriram, 2016)

Schoonover et al. (2014) in a study on perceptions of traditional healing for mental illness in rural Gujarat found that patients sought the help of traditional healers first. Despite recognizing that doctors were more effective in treating mental illness as compared to traditional healers, there was tremendous faith reposed on the traditional healers, indicating the degree to which they were integrated into the local community. The findings indicate the necessity for collaboration between medical practitioners and faith healers for the treatment of mental illness. Until recently in India, specialized services of counseling offered by trained professionals did not exist; however, forms of counseling were available within social relationships, such as the "guru-shishya parampara" (teacher–disciple tradition) wherein the guru (teacher) had the onus of molding the lives of the students, and by general practitioners, indigenous doctors, and lay therapists (Bhola et al., 2012).

Economic reforms over the past three decades have transformed lifestyles and enhanced the pace of change. There are more individuals and families who require professional assistance to deal with changes in their lives, often due to the unavailability of supportive interventions. The role of counselors and counseling services becomes more necessary and relevant in these situations and contexts. Despite the economic progress made by India, it has been seen that about 80 percent of those who need mental healthcare are outside the purview of treatment. Community healthcare services in India are scarce, and mental health service providers are unevenly distributed (Kumar, 2011; Thara & Patel, 2010). The problem of service delivery is compounded by negative attitudes and lack of knowledge among the population, which prevents the timely seeking of help. Recent regulations in the field of psychology have come into practice with the introduction of the updated Mental Health Care Act 2017, which proposes a more patient-centric role and attempts a definition of mental health professionals (Mental Healthcare Act, 2017).

Mental health literacy is one of the aims of the National Mental Health Program (NMHP) through public awareness with information, education, and communication material. One of the added tasks of the NMHP is the reduction of stigma and discrimination meted out to persons with mental illness in both rural and urban areas. Enhancing mental health literacy of people will contribute to better access to services and provide a more conducive environment for individuals with mental illness and their families. Data from India indicate that mental health education needs are yet to be met (Gaiha, Sunil, Kumar, & Menon, 2014). Western approaches to psychology form the basis of most available counseling services and models for training in the discipline in India. These approaches are not always based on the Indian cultural context, wherein relationships are given importance over individual notions of the self. Kapur, Shamasundar, and Bhatti (1996), p. 6.) cite the importance for theoretical constructs suitable to Indian social reality, without which the entire process of learning and practice of psychotherapy would appear abstruse. At times therapists grieve that Indian patients are unsuitable for psychotherapy. The level of awareness of the social reality is in direct proportion to the depth of the understanding, training, and practice of psychotherapy. In the absence of a consolidated Indian model of psychotherapy, it is important that therapists do not blindly follow Western models. Much of the training done for counselors in India draws from Western models and therapies. There are few attempts to consider how to contextualize these Western models to Indian contemporary reality. The need to develop indigenous models of therapy has been expressed often; however, the development of such contextual models has been slow (Arulmani, 2007; Kapur et al., 1996; Sidhu, 2017; Sriram, 2016).

Counseling in Japan Iwakabe (2008) writes about how psychotherapy in Japan has developed slowly, primarily due to cultural factors associated with mental illness. Social stigma and shame still prevent individuals from seeking help for psychological distress. Mental illness has been seen as a weakness and a failure of self-discipline. This results in reluctance to seek help when needed and postponing help-seeking till it is unavoidable. The first line of assistance is usually medical personnel for psychosomatic complaints; if these do not provide ease, the individual is referred to psychiatrists who use medication instead of therapy. Psychiatrists in Japan indicate that patients are not comfortable with speaking about themselves and prefer directive advice from experts and rarely provide therapy as seen in the West. Changes in therapeutic practice in Japan were seen over the last three decades, with an increase in problems associated with children and adolescents, which brought about the development of child and adolescent psychotherapy. School counseling has developed over the last two decades in response to the problems of school refusal and bullying (Yagi, 2008).

Japanese psychologists prefer the use of the term counseling to psychotherapy, as the latter is associated more with treatment. In 2002, the President of the Japanese Association of Counseling Science formed a special committee tasked with conceptualizing counseling and officially declaring the definition to the members of the Association as well as to the public (Tagami & Ozawa, 2005). However, confusion persists in Japan regarding counseling and counselors. Professionalization of counseling in Japan has been described as a challenge due to some aspects of the Japanese Association of Counseling Sciences which has been recognized as the only professional organization since 1968. Its membership is still open to individuals and groups who are engaged in any kind of "caring" and "human service" work without any special qualifications. Japanese Clinical Psychology programs typically offer a master's degree which enables holders to apply for registration and certification as a clinical psychologist (through the Japan Society of Certified Clinical Psychologists) or as a psychotherapist (through the Japan Federation for Psychotherapy). However, the government does not license or regulate psychological practice. The Japanese government licenses medical doctors (including psychiatrists) and social workers. Psychologists are not able to seek reimbursement for services through the Japanese national health insurance system, unless theyreceive this reimbursement indirectly by working under the direction of a licensed psychiatrist, typically in a hospital setting (Watanabe-Muraoka, 2007).

Counseling in South Korea Counseling has steadily grown as a profession in South Korea with the advent of school and career counseling to practices and models that cater to the diverse mental health needs of the population (Lee, Suh, Yang, & Jang, 2012). The Korean Counseling Association was established in 2000; however, a national licensure system for professional counselors has not yet been established. Bae, Joo, and Orlinsky (2003) bring out the problems faced by therapists in Korea, in adapting the practice to the cultural context. McDonald (2011) brings to the forefront aspects arising from religious and cultural contexts of Korea, which emphasize stoicism, diligence, and modesty, where individual concerns are secondary. Koreans prefer to see fortune tellers rather than mental health professionals. Bae et al. (2003) remarked upon efforts at adapting Western models of psychotherapy to the Korean context, and they found the philosophies of Hong-Ik-In-Gan, Zen Buddhism, and Confucianism to be most well integrated into person-centered therapy. Person centered therapy emphasizes values that resonate with the Korean culture, i.e., empathy, harmony, and relationships (Joo, Lee, & Joo, 2007). Onmeum and reality dynamic counseling have emerged as popular therapeutic approaches. School counseling appears to be a widespread profession with support from the government (Lee et al., 2012).

In Summation In most Asian countries, psychotherapy has been provided by doctors in hospital and clinical settings, where the number of psychiatrists outnumbered that of psychologists. Often patients arrived at hospitals after visiting faith healers and priests and continued with alternate sources of healthcare, in conjunction with medicines and therapy. The situation is compounded by inadequate health insurance coverage especially for psychiatric medication and therapy. The stigma associated with mental illness can be seen across Asian countries, where seeking help from mental health professionals would be only after help is sought from family and friends. While the demand for therapy is on the rise, the need to culturally adapt techniques is becoming increasingly evident. That said, there is a preference for CBT with many Asian clients, which could be due to the attributes of the therapy – evidence-based, structured, problem-focused, present-focused, action-oriented, and short-term psychotherapy, which fit the requirements of clients as seen in studies from Singapore (Foo et al., 2006; Yeo, Tan, & Neihart, 2013), Japan (Iwakabe, 2008), Pakistan (Naeem, Gobbi, Ayub, & Kingdon, 2009), and India (Gupta et al., 2019; Halder & Mahato, 2019).

Therapist Characteristics and Their Influence on Therapy

The profession of psychotherapy is one where the self of the therapist plays a significant role in the effectiveness of therapy. Qualities of the therapist are one of the four factors identified as contributing to therapeutic change (Lambert, 2013; Wheeler, 2000). Therapists bring their personal experiences, attitudes, beliefs, and values into the therapy session, which implies that these will influence their inter-actions with the clients. This makes it imperative to understand what contributes to make a "good" or an effective therapist. Data indicates that effective therapists with greater degrees of engagement with their clients see faster recovery with fewer sessions of therapy (Lambert, 2013). The notion of the therapist as a *wounded healer* has been propounded by many researchers, starting from the work of Jung. The postulate is that adverse childhood experiences result in a heightened awareness of their own distress and that of others, directing them towards the profession (Farber, Manevich, Metzger, & Saypol, 2005; Gilbert, Hughes, & Dryden, 2014; Lambert, 2013; Mander, 2004).

Wheeler's (2000) analysis of what makes a good therapist listed some characteristics: "generally a good person, intelligent, creative, sincere, energetic, warm towards others, responsible and of sound judgement" (p. 66). An anxious therapist did not inspire confidence in their clients. Pope and Kline (1999) created a Counselor Characteristic Inventory from 22 personality characteristics gleaned from studies related to counseling competence. Experts were asked to rank order ten characteristics that were deemed to be both the most important and the least teachable, which were then incorporated into the inventory. The ten characteristics that emerged were acceptance, emotional stability, open-mindedness, empathy, genuineness, flexibility, interest in people, confidence, sensitivity, and fairness. He concluded that these characteristics needed to be present in all counselors selected for training.

Effective counselors have some identifiable, exceptional features, referred to as common factors which cut across therapeutic orientation, and are associated with positive client outcomes. These common factors have been further subdivided into support factors, learning factors, and action factors. Support factors include being able to have a good therapeutic relationship, being supportive, genuine, warm, trusting, empathetic, respectful, and accepting. Learning factors refer to the ability to give feedback and provide insight and advice. Action factors are related with the ability to model and encourage. According to client-centered therapy, these common factors are the necessary and sufficient conditions for change in the client: empathy, warmth, unconditional positive regard, and genuineness or congruence (Rogers, 1951).

According to Norcross and Lambert (2019), the therapist effect was directly related to the severity with which the client presented; the more the disturbance, the greater the importance of which therapist the client worked with. Common factors contribute as much as 30 percent to the improvement in clients in therapy. The other factors that impact the success of therapy are 15 percent related to the techniques used by the therapist, another 15 percent are attributed to expectancy or placebo factors, and the remaining 40 percent are ascribed to the client – the extra-therapeutic factors such as motivation and the need to change, social support, all of which play a substantial role in ensuring positive outcomes in a therapeutic setting.

Effective counselors are capable of reflection, conceptualization, and critical thinking, which allows them to use theory for diagnosis and for developing effectual interventions. The capacity for critical thinking allows therapists to make changes in the intervention plan depending on the progress made by the client. According to Wampold, Baldwin, Holtforth, and Imel (2017), professional self-doubt in therapists leads to greater effectiveness of therapeutic outcomes, by increasing reflectivity and critical examination of their practice. The ability to form therapeutic alliances with a variety of clients, irrespective of age, gender, and nature and severity of diagnosis, coupled with mature, well-defined interpersonal skills contributed to effectiveness of the therapist. The ability and the willingness to take part in deliberate practice of psychotherapy as a means to improve expertise has been mentioned as an additional weapon in the arsenal of effective therapists. Deliberate practice can take multiple forms such as participation in workshops, exercises, seeking supervision in multiple formats, and reading (Chow et al., 2015; Hill & Castonguay, 2017; Rousmaniere, 2017; Wampold et al., 2017).

The data about effective counselors indicates that identifying the right candidates for counseling and therapy training is important; not everyone can become a good counselor. The use of the self is essential for counselor development. While training can help in using the self and empathy effectively, empathy itself has to come from within.

Counselor and Therapist Competence

Before discussing counseling training, it is important to examine counselor competency, as training provides the scaffold for the development of the professional practitioner. Corey, Corey, and Callanan (2011) speak about the lifelong search for competence among mental health professionals. They assert that therapist competence is vital for the development of the profession and for safe-guarding the interests of the clients. For therapists, competence is never a single point achievement; the need for continuing professional development is a prerequisite. Competence requires levels of knowledge, skills, abilities, values, and attitudes to provide services effectively. According to Welfel (2016), professional competence is not easy to define; she includes diligence to knowledge and skill as prerequisites of competence in a therapist. Sperry (2010) talks about six basic therapist competencies: conceptual foundations, relationship, intervention planning, intervention implementation, intervention evaluation, and cultural and ethical sensitivity (p. 13).

Conceptual foundations and knowledge refer to the basic theoretical orientation and approach used by the practitioner. This orientation influences the way in which the practitioner understands normality and the deviation from it and the related frameworks for therapy and change. The conceptual foundations influence the other core competencies such as relationship building and intervention planning. Knowledge can be provided through accredited training programs which offer curated content depending on the need of the professional.

Competent counselors are skilled in knowing which interventions to use and how they need to be used. Skills of counselors include *clinical* and *technical* skills (Welfel, 2016). Clinical skills are those used in developing a therapeutic alliance, empathy, communicating effectively, and exploring client issues with sensitivity. Spruill et al. (2004) refer to *additional clinical skills*, which are foundational for competence in therapists. These include *critical thinking, awareness about legal and ethical guidelines, and cultural competence*. Technical skills refer to the ability to use specific therapeutic interventions, or use an individual assessment measure if needed. Skillfulness implies that the professional is knowledgeable enough to make a judgment about the appropriate interventions, keeping in mind the nature of the therapeutic alliance with the client, the current evidence available from literature, and the preferences and ideals of the client.

Welfel (2016) speaks of *diligence* as a vital counselor competence. Diligence consists of the need for "consistent attentiveness to the client's needs that takes priority over other concerns" (p. 89). Diligence requires attention to be paid to assessment, intervention, and follow-up. The diligent professional ensures that the best services are provided for the client and will provide referral if they feel the issue at hand is beyond their competence. They will follow-up with the client to determine outcomes, which benefits practitioners and the clients. The other aspect of diligence refers to what Pope and Vasquez (2011) refer to as *emotional competence*, which requires self-awareness and recognition as being fallible human beings. Emotional competence requires an assessment of individual abilities, rather than over-stating success. Spruill et al. (2004) and Welfel (2016) emphasize that diligent practice can only happen in consultation with other practitioners about the quality and effectiveness of their work.

While speaking of therapist competence, it is necessary to mention the ability of a professional to deal with clients in a *culturally and ethically sensitive manner*. This need has grown over the years. Therapists need to develop the competence to recognize ethical issues and dilemmas and to respond in culturally appropriate ways. Cultural sensitivity and competence are vital in the globalizing world, with migration of people and the issues arising thereof being a reality for mental health practitioners. Cultural sensitivity implies the ability to respond appropriately to attitudes, values, beliefs, and practices of people belonging to different cultural, ethnic, religious, and racial traditions. Cultural sensitivity needs to translate into cultural competence through the therapeutic alliance. Counselors are required to be aware of and to practice within the ethical code of their choosing, in the absence of uniform and culturally sanctioned code of ethics in their country.

The nature of the field of counseling and therapy complicates the issues of competence. No professional therapist can be skilled in all interventions. The diversity of populations and issues is such that therapists need to identify age groups, settings, and issues they are comfortable working with, which defines the scope of practice. While some professionals choose to develop competence, in particular, issues such as depression, or school refusal, others may specialize in working with particular groups of individuals such as couples, older adults, or adolescents. Another way of developing competence is through choice of a particular therapeutic modality; e.g., working with individuals recovering from trauma. As Welfel (2016) puts it: "Beware the professional who claims to do everything well: Either some of those skills are underdeveloped, or that person is a fraud" (p. 89).

Spruill et al. (2004) have developed a competence continuum from incompetent to exceptionally competent. They identify five levels of competence from novice to expert, comparable to Rønnestad and Skovholt (2001, 2003) stages of professional development from lay helper to the senior professional.

A competent professional is always seeking to enhance current skills and knowledge but the aim is not perfection. Instead, competence implies, at a minimum, adequate care and is partially measured in a comparative fashion. One is competent when one's knowledge and skills are as well developed as those of other professionals previously demonstrated to be competent in the specified area. In other words, one is deemed competent if, after education and supervised practice, one can carry out an intervention at least as well as supervisors or colleagues. (Welfel, 2016, p. 91)

Competence assessment can be done through monitoring one's effectiveness in helping clients, in developing plans for counseling, in implementing those plans, and in evaluating the outcomes of services (Spruill et al., 2004). Competence is achieved through care that aids the client and avoids unnecessary risk. Additionally, competence can be evaluated through the guidelines and standards of practice laid down by various professional associations; e.g., the American Psychological Association has produced specialty guidelines for providing services in clinical, counseling, school, and organizational psychology (APA, 2003) that identify skills essential for competence with multicultural clients.

While discussing competence, it is important to recognize factors that could impede performance. It is not possible to be equally competent with all clients; fatigue, distraction, and stress can affect the service offered to the client. There could be unforeseen circumstances such as health conditions, a sudden illness, burnout, or extraneous events that affect the mental health of the therapist. Environmental circumstances such as bad working conditions, unsupportive colleagues, poorly defined job roles, and limited opportunity for supervision and growth are not conducive to competence. Most Asian countries have poorly remunerated counselors and therapists as compared to their compatriots in the West, which affects the entry into the profession, sustainability, and seeking continuing professional development.

Thériault and Gazzola (Thériault & Gazzola, 2005, 2008 and 2010) have researched and written extensively about feelings of incompetence among therapists at various stages of professional development. "Feelings of incompetence (FOI) are the emotions and thoughts that arise when therapists' beliefs in their abilities, judgements, and/or effectiveness in their role as therapists are reduced or challenged internally" (Thériault, Gazzola, & Richardson, 2009, p. 106). FOI can contribute to stress and burnout among therapists, along with premature exit from the field itself. While FOI may be crippling for novice therapists, it can affect experienced therapists as well. Generally, FOI has been found to decrease with experience, though it can emerge due to various factors, both external and internal to the therapist.

In the profession of psychotherapy, many therapists continue way past the official retirement age; they have a continued commitment to grow professionally, to serve as mentors for novice professionals, to develop reflective and ethical practice, and to bring about changes in policies related to the field.

Technology and Its Influence on Mental Health Services

Traditionally, counseling and psychotherapy have been delivered in the face-to-face mode. Changes in technology have resulted in variations in the ways in which mental health services are being provided to clients. While the telephone was the first means of providing telemental health, the Internet has given rise to myriad ways of providing and accessing support through computer-mediated communication – through email, chat rooms, and other such methods (Carter, 2019; Fukkink & Hermanns, 2009; Overholser, 2019).

Telephone Services for Mental Health Provisioning mental health through telephone services arose in the middle of the twentieth century through the services provided by the Samaritans in the United Kingdom. The Samaritans helpline and other similar helplines that have opened in countries all over the world are focused on providing emotional support by trained volunteers, for those in need, more specifically to help deal with crisis situations such as suicide.

In many countries, telephone counseling helplines run by professionals have been set up to supplement the delivery of mental health services. In countries like Australia, telephone helplines offer mental health services to people located in remote parts of the country, where resources are scarce. Helpline counseling in these cases acts as an adjunct service to individual and group therapy. The popularity of helpline counseling is attributed to low cost, ease of access for remote locations, and immediacy of assistance. Telephone counseling presents itself as an ideal modality for elderly healthcare as seen in centers in Japan (Sarai, Karnasuta, & Ohara, 2019).

A review of 14 studies by Leach and Christensen (2006) indicated that telephone-administered therapy was effective in reducing symptoms of mental illness. Telephone interventions have been effective in reducing depression, anxiety, eating disorders, alcohol use, and rehospitalization for schizophrenia (King, Bambling, Reid, & Thomas, 2006; Leach & Christensen, 2006; Reese, Conoley, & Brossart, 2002). Telephone helplines have been found to be particularly efficacious in dealing with issues pertaining to children and adolescence (Christogiorgos et al., 2010; Fukkink & Hermanns, 2009). The telephone is recognized today as a medium for multiple therapeutic endeavors, from suicide to hypnosis (Henden, 2008). Data indicate that even professionals who primarily use a face-to-face mode for therapy have begun to use technology to provide services. A survey carried out in 2008 on psychology health services providers by the American Psychological Association (APA) indicated that the telephone was the technology most widely used to provide health services, with 85 percent of the respondents stating their preference for the telephone. Of the 85 percent, about 35 percent used the telephone at least once a week or more (Jacobsen & Kohout, 2010).

Telephone counseling offers valuable alternatives in countries where the delivery of mental health services is strapped by the shortage of professionals and other resources.

Computer-Assisted Therapy Computer-assisted therapies (CAT) are offered to the client through devices such as personal computers, laptops, personal digital assistants, interactive telephone messaging, and text messaging. Alternately, they can be offered directly through video interface, which increases the degree of interaction with the client. The complexity of content can vary from reading material such as a brochure to interactive virtual reality formats, which have become more effective with high-speed Internet connections (Carroll & Rounsaville, 2010). The degree of interaction with therapists and others can vary in CAT, from no interaction with others at all to moderated chat rooms to a great deal of therapist interaction and involvement. In cases where there is substantial email correspondence between the therapist and the client, it can be referred to as e-therapy. There has been an increase in the number of practitioners using email in their clinical practice, with 45 percent of respondents reporting the use of email for health provision (Jacobsen & Kohout, 2010).

Most CAT therapies and programs are intended to be stand-alone platforms, to allow users to access them alone, without any other contact or interchange with a therapist. Often CAT are developed to deal with a particular problem such as anxiety, depression, or substance use. Most forms of psychotherapy are now offered through digital modalities including psychoanalysis with sessions offered face to face usually on a weekly basis echoing the rhythm of in-person therapies (Fairburn & Patel, 2017). Some interventions for depression have been crafted in the form of a game (Merry et al., 2012) which might especially appeal to younger users. Stand-alone diploma and certificate courses are being offered to help practitioners master the art of practicing digitally, such as at the Ofer Zur Institute. It has been found that virtual reality and artificial intelligence programs help treat mental illness without face-to-face interactions and often result in reducing inhibition, where clients may admit to symptoms which they may not admit in face-to-face interactions (Carter, 2019).

CAT can be used to broaden the access to support services and to allow clients access to quality mental healthcare in geographical regions with a paucity of professionals. Developing countries see a clustering of mental health professionals in urban areas with semi-urban and rural areas depending upon general physicians and para-professionals to meet their mental health needs (Garg, Kumar, & Chandra, 2019). A fast growing smart phone market and widespread network coverage now enable a larger than ever population access to mental health services. Tele-supervision is another developing field within mental health, and psychologists can now access quality supervision across geographical lines of city and country (Inman, Soheilian, & Luu, 2019; Martin, Kumar, & Lizarondo, 2017). This paper was written before the Covid-19 pandemic, which has resulted in CAT being used by therapists all over the world, in order to allow for the access of services by clients. This paper does not have the scope of examining CAT in detail.

Education and Training for Counseling and Therapy

Since its inception, the field of counseling and psychotherapy have seen many theories and approaches regarding the training and development of practitioners. In the 1960s, both Carkhuff and Bergin proposed models for teaching helping skills to facilitate the process of counseling. These early models focused on skills that the practitioner could utilize to facilitate insight and change in the client. Both models were trans-theoretical in their approach and emphasized skill building as the focus of counselor training and education. Most education for counselors takes place within the university system, which provides the basic training. Advanced skill development and training in specific therapies and client populations is provided most often through independent training bodies and organizations who offer diploma and certificate programs.

Models of Therapist Training As the field developed over time, several training models and theories of therapist development emerged (Blocher, 1983; Fleming, 1953; Grater, 1985; Hess, 1987; Hogan, 1964; Littrell, Lee-Borden, & Lorenz, 1976; Loganbill, Hardy, & Delworth, 1982; Stoltenberg, 1981; Stoltenberg & Delworth, 1987). Egan (1998) and Hackney and Cormier (2001) provide models for counselor training that are grounded in client-centered practice and in cognitive behavior therapy, respectively. Rønnestad and Skovholt's (2001, 2003) model of stages of counselor development has been one of the most popular and comprehensive models along with Orlinsky's work on the Generic Model of Psychotherapy (Orlinsky & Howard, 1984). The integrated development model (Stoltenberg, McNeill, & Delworth, 1998) is an alternative supervision model that focuses primarily on the growth of graduate counseling students in training.

Entry Point for Therapist Training Most counseling courses in the world aim at perspective building with some introductory programs on theories and models of counseling, which are offered at the graduate level. Actual training for therapy and counseling begins at the tertiary education level of postgraduate education at a Master's level and can range from 1 to 3 years, depending on the population and the issues that the therapist would like to work with. Therapists working with clinical populations usually require more intensive training as compared to those working on issues such as school or career counseling (McQuaid, 2014).

The Master's level education can be followed by MPhil, PsyD, and PhD courses which require more intensive field experience accompanied by research (McQuaid, 2014). Many counselors augment the skills acquired during basic academic training by attending further skill-based programs, often offered by practicing therapists. The need to continually update oneself and one's therapeutic skills has been emphasized for developing competence. Often the basic training in therapy is theoretical and does not provide enough hands-on skills for working with clients. This increases the feeling of incompetence and inadequacy of the student; it has to be recognized that inadequate training is detrimental for novice counselors and for the field as a whole (Ridley & Mollen, 2011; Thériault et al., 2009).

Graduate programs in the developed world usually accept students with a background in psychology; however, in countries like India, student intake spans a larger educational milieu. Counselors from developing countries like India are drawn from varied backgrounds and disciplines, ranging from human resource professionals, teachers and educationists, and social workers to clinical and counseling psychologists, nurses, and psychiatrists. Each discipline emphasizes different aspects of counseling in the training offered. While process skills are uniformly acquired in the basic academic training, the emphasis on therapeutic skills varies. Licensing exams follow basic training of therapists, depending on the requirements for license for practice, which vary across countries.

Furthermore, higher education in the field of counseling and psychotherapy has been splintered in its availability and quality. Duan et al. (2011) surveyed counseling psychologists in Australia, Canada, New Zealand, South Africa, South Korea, Taiwan, the United Kingdom (UK), and the United States (US). A clear demarcation between the developed and the developing world was witness, with respondents who held a doctorate ranging from 100 percent in the United States to 10.9 percent in South Korea. Similarly, the proportion of counseling psychologists employed as faculty members in universities or professional schools of psychology ranged from none in Taiwan to 55.7 percent in the United States. This may result in a dilution of quality education, with inadequately equipped educators, with limited knowledge and experience.

In India, a PhD in Clinical Psychology located in hospital settings such as NIMHANS (NIMHANS – The National Institute of Mental Health and Neurosciences in Bangalore, India. A premier institution that provides training in mental health and neurosciences) and offering a strongly bio-neurological focus is the highest qualification available. The penultimate qualification of an MPhil degree in Clinical Psychology from an institute certified by the Rehabilitation Council of India (RCI) makes the recipient eligible to hold a license to practice as an independent professional. Licensing has been mandated as a requirement for psychological assessment and providing treatment with a focus on continued professional development; however, there is no formal organization to monitor professional practice. Therefore, clients are left with no forum of redressal should clinical error or malpractice happen. The Mental Health Care Act (2017) in India does not provide or lay down clear frameworks for quality and ethical conduct.

Content of Therapist Education The curriculum for therapist education can be divided into a taught component, supervised clinical practice, and personal development. The taught component of counseling training programs around the world shares certain key elements, i.e., a focus on different therapeutic approaches, theories of psychopathology, ethics, psychological assessment, and training in microskills of counseling as well as elements of research and practicum and internship. Counseling is a profession wherein the self of the counselor is an important therapeutic aid in determining the process and the outcomes. This necessitates the counselor to do intense self-reflection and introspection on individual motivations, values, beliefs, assumptions, and prejudices about clients and client groups. The person of the therapist model (Aponte & Kissil, 2016) has been influential in incorporating the use of the self in the training curriculum through experiential and reflective exercises in course work, gaining practical experience, and supervision. Counselor training helps trainees acquire knowledge, along with technical and clinical skills necessary for working with clients, to develop a therapeutic relationship and plan interventions specific to the needs to the client.

Keeping the social justice perspective of psychotherapy in mind, therapy training and education has to include the rights of the client. All trainee therapists have to be informed about what information a client or patient should receive about the assessment, diagnosis, and the interventions planned and implemented. This information may be influenced by the cultural context the client comes from; e.g., older clients from rural parts of India are content to take the word of the "expert" mental health practitioner, without questioning what is being done. This may be very different from the position taken by a client from a metropolitan city who wants to be informed about every step of the process, has access to information from the Internet, and is aware about their rights. Coming to a mental health practitioners does not mean that the client will not access other informal sources, such as faith healers. Counseling training has to prepare trainees to deal with a variety of clients, with differing needs, values, beliefs, and expectations. Psycho-educating clients about mental health, therapeutic interventions, and outcomes will go a long way in remedying the lack of awareness, misinformation, and stigma associated with mental illness and its treatment.

The use of technology for counselor training is limited. In countries like India and China, most of the resources available are Western textbooks on therapy, augmented by journal articles many of which are also from Western sources. While the importance of experiential, skill-based training is considered vital for the development of effective counselors, in practice much of the training is theoretical and does not incorporate adequate supervised fieldwork. The textual material that describes contextual cultural experiences is sparse and not readily available. It is left to individual trainers to try and develop a contextual understanding which is relevant. While all trainers and counselors recognize the importance of supervision for trainee counselors, supervision is not always available or adequate and may at times be harmful. The multilingual nature of clients, trainees, and trainers in diverse cultural contexts makes the process of supervision cumbersome and not entirely effective (Grover, 2014; Hoch, 1990; Sriram, 1990).

Thorne and Dryden (1991) expressed the importance of trainers being practicing counselors,

> Core members should themselves be practicing counselors and this goes without saying for there can be few occupations where the continuing interaction between practice and theory is of such primary value in the training process. The trainer who is no longer practicing as a counselor will quickly lose the immediacy of experience which provides the major stimulus for creativity and is the principal source of his or her credibility in the eyes of trainees. (Thorne & Dryden, 1991, p. 13)

It is necessary for trainers to keep track of developments in the counseling field. The "self" of the trainer and supervisor can be bolstered through continuing professional enhancement, accompanied by accessing supervision, good quality of life, relationships, and leisure. This can help in preventing burnout and the growing counseling field will be supported.

Research has shown that most of the training available for counselors in India is carried out in English; and English language textbooks are referenced and used exclusively in education. If we consider the country's linguistic diversity, this monolingual training of counselors does not prepare them adequately to work with clients in other languages. Often the lexicon of emotional terms that counseling students and novice counselors have access to is inadequate to allow for effective counseling practice. Supervision can resolve issues emerging from working with clients from varied linguistic and cultural backgrounds; however, training material and literature in languages other than English is scarce. There has been a hegemony of English speaking counselors, without adequately recognizing the needs of populations other than urban, middle-class English speaking groups. There is a pressing need for counselors in the vernacular medium, and dearth of skilled trainers and the absence of indigenous models of psychotherapy compound the challenge.

Supervision Supervision is a crucial requirement of postgraduate counseling training programs and is a part of developing and evaluating counseling students' competency (Borders, 1992) and overall development into effective counselors (Bernard & Goodyear, 2014). The ACA Code of Ethics (2014) states that supervision involves a process of monitoring "client welfare and supervisee performance and professional development" (Standard F.1.a). Furthermore, supervision can be used as a tool to provide supervisees with necessary knowledge, skills, and ethical guidelines to provide safe and effective counseling services that benefit the trainee therapist and the clients (Bernard & Goodyear, 2014; Hill, Spiegel, Hoffman, Kivlighan, & Gelso, 2017). Guidelines for supervision have been developed by organizations such as APA (2014, 2015) and the Association of State and Professional Psychology Boards (ASPPB, 2015). Approval of the guidelines for practice (APA, 2014, 2015), and for regulatory purposes (ASPPB, 2015), is a giant step forward in the United States. American Counseling Association (ACA, 2014), the Council for Accreditation of Counseling and Related Educational Programs (CACREP, 2009), and the Association for Counselor Education and Supervision (ACES, 2011) have articulated standards for best practices in supervision. For example, ACES' (2011) Standards for Best Practices Guidelines highlight 12 categories as integral components of the supervision process. The categories include responsibilities of supervisors and suggestions for actions to be taken in order to ensure best practices in supervision.

In the United States of America, the United Kingdom, and some countries in Europe, programs have been specifically developed to train supervisors. Developing the skills and practice for supervision is integral to the development of the profession of counseling. According to Holloway and Carroll (1999), specific training for supervision has come to the forefront only since the 1980s. Prior to this, the belief was that the training to become a good counselor would suffice to develop effective supervisors. The awareness of the need for separate training for supervision has emerged from the developmental and the social role systems models of supervision (Holloway & Carroll, 1999). In India, there is no formal training available for becoming a supervisor. While the importance of supervision has been reiterated, one of the issues besetting counselors is the lack of adequate supervision, especially in the early stage of the career. Training for supervision may better equip practitioners to provide supervision to counselors at various stages of the career.

Personal Therapy In many parts of Asia, it is not necessary for trainee counselors to go through counseling or therapy themselves, before they begin to work as counselors. This is accompanied by inadequate supervision, during training and during the early phase of career development, which can lead to intense distress, feelings of inadequacy and incompetence, and an inability to apply what is learnt in theory to practice. In the United Kingdom, mandatory personal therapy of 40 hours is a requirement for accreditation by the British Association for Counseling and Psychotherapy (BACP) (Murphy, 2005; Oteiza, 2010). While certain schools of therapy such as the psychoanalytic and psychodynamic orientations have mandated personal therapy for all potential therapists, other formats do not have such a requirement (Grimmer, 2005).

Personal therapy is a crucial factor of counseling training. It is recommended that counselors or psychotherapeutic practitioners undergo therapy to resolve personal issues and to experience being a client. Resolving one's own issues becomes important before commencing practice. There are more chances of enactment and unaddressed transference and countertransference if the practitioner's self-healing has not happened. In order to build self-confidence and the ability to think clearly, one of the aids is personal therapy.

Personal therapy has been found to profoundly impact the personal and profes-sional development of the trainee therapist (Hill et al., 2017; Murphy, 2005; Murphy, Irfan, Barnett, Castledine, & Enescu, 2018). According to Oteiza (2010), personal therapy was "a difficult but helpful and enriching experience" (p. 225). Personal therapy helped therapists identify their personal issues and accept their humanity, to be guided and accompanied and to be challenged. Personal therapy played a role in allowing practitioners to experience the role of the client, from the view of social justice and equity. However, most studies on personal therapy during training hesitate to equivocally mandate its requirement. This has been due to the expenses of personal therapy, if they are to be borne by the trainee. Alongside the benefits of personal therapy during training, there are cautionary tales about unprofessional and unethical practice. Poor quality mandated therapy can do more harm to the trainee. Additionally, evidence-based research supporting the rationale for mandated per-sonal therapy is not readily available. Murphy et al. (2018) state that training institutions that mandate personal therapy should provide lists of available thera-pists, which are updated periodically, to ensure that no harm comes to trainees.

Licensing and Regulation India and China require licensure for the practice of psychotherapy. The RCI provides a license to practice for individuals with an MPhil degree in Clinical Psychology. China has traditionally offered licenses to psychia-trists who wish to practice psychotherapy, rendering other trained professionals without formal recognition. Recent developments allow the Chinese Ministry of Labor and Social Security Affairs (CMLSS) to license professional psychological counselors with criteria that allow for easy qualification. A more rigorous registration is offered by the Clinical and Counseling Psychology Registration System (CCPRS) with an aim at voluntary registration and quality control. However, both India and China do not have legal infrastructure to enforce the standards of practice mandated by the RCI and CMLSS, respectively. Clients do not have any legal recourse for malpractice as is available for other healthcare services.

Japan notably does not require any licensure for the practicing of counseling. A lack of professional authority and regulation further compounds the problem of fragmentation of counseling services. This makes it challenging to establish a professional identity and encourage psychologists to engage in continued professional development. A lack of agreed upon and legally enforceable ethics and standards of practice leaves individuals vulnerable to malpractice and exploitation.

Conclusion: Meeting the Challenges of Counselor Training and Education

Providing mental health services in culturally diverse countries requires culturally competent counselors, who can work with people from different caste, ethnic, sociocultural, economic, regional, and linguistic backgrounds. The counseling trainer's job is a herculean task. Trainers navigate responsibilities of teaching, along with mentoring students for the "real" practice, while offering an emotionally safe and reflective space. This can be an emotionally taxing experience. Therapy training goes beyond mere didactic teaching, in that there is the need to integrate theory with practice. The fact that many trainers are themselves practitioners increases the pressures on them. While being practitioners allows the ready integration of therapeutic narratives as illustrations, there is the responsibility of training, and translating the lessons learned through practice, thereby building theory.

We believe that access to quality mental healthcare is a growing need, and raising the quality of training and education in the developing world requires a multipronged approach. We reiterate that while training and education of counselors can help develop competence, creating comprehensive criteria and methods for identifying suitable candidates a requirement that institutions need to formalize.

The following recommendations can be instrumental in preparing competent mental health professionals to deal with the challenges of the twenty-first century:

Redesigning Curricula and Pedagogy There is considerable diversity among institutes and regions in curriculum design and pedagogy of counseling and psychotherapy courses. Countries like India, China, and Japan follow universities in Europe and the United States as models upon which to base their teaching. Faculty training and knowledge determine the theoretical course content on offer. Limited access to professionals trained in emerging approaches often leads to a fall back on traditional and at times outdated course content such as classical behavior therapy, classical client-centered therapy, etc. It is recommended that current existing curricula be supplemented with course material that addresses local and global sociopolitical changes and diversity in a culturally sensitive manner, especially topics like LGBTQ psychology, disability, migration, terrorism, marginalization, etc. To meet the increasing needs of client diversity, counseling curricula need to be revised to include units dedicated to client advocacy and social justice and multicultural practice tailor made for local population groups. Keeping in mind the collectivistic nature of societies in Asia (Laungani, 2004), counseling curricula often do not devote sufficient time to systemic approaches, such as working with families, groups, and the community. Inclusion of community mental health practice in training would help graduates to be better equipped to address the disparate ratio between service providers and seekers and to provide resources that may prove more accessible to a majority.

Professionals in the twenty-first century have to be equipped to practice in the digital age through exposure to telemental health and computer-assisted therapy via didactic, experiential, and supervised practice. Training to develop competent supervisors is urgently needed to develop skilled professionals. Varied pedagogy and methods of evaluation with an inclusion of experiential activities and a person of the therapist approach would serve to equip professionals with the skills to reflexively cater to a clinical population, teach and supervise students, and research and publish.

Additional Skills   Considering the demands of the profession beyond the therapeutic space, counselors in today's age need to be equipped with knowledge and skills that extend beyond the subject. Most counseling courses follow a biopsychosocial approach and train students in mainstream therapeutic approaches like cognitive behavior therapy, psychodynamic therapy, and client-centered therapy. These approaches often leave students to graduate suitably trained with skills required to work in a hospital setting or a psychiatric clinic. Entrepreneurship skills which may enable graduates to build an independent practice are notably missing from the curriculum. Twenty-first century skills such as social media management, marketing, administrative skills, etc. are lacking. Students should be encouraged to participate in and shape public discourse as an effort to increase awareness and to tackle the mystery and stigma that often enfolds mental illness.

Deliberate Practice   Just as rehearsal helps hone perfection in the fields of sports and music, deliberate practice outside the therapy room has to be consciously inculcated by the therapist. The advantageous use of deliberate practice has to be reinforced by trainers, and space and opportunity for the same have to be encouraged. The individual methods for deliberate practice can be refined to allow for the development of competent, self-aware, reflective professionals.

Self-Care and Burnout Prevention   Therapists have to acquire the self-care skills to prevent burnout and compassion fatigue. Burnout of novice counselors can be high when there is a heavy workload coupled with inadequate supervision. Systemic factors of organizational support, even distribution of workload, and availability of supervision in a collaborative work environment can help in preventing burnout. Alongside, personal factors such as awareness about one's emotions and value congruity of the individual and the workplace can help in protecting against burnout. Encouraging personal therapy during training can be an additional protective factor.

Training Centers and Universities Skill building for existing faculty and educators can develop through international exchange programs to teach and supervise more skillfully. Each center for learning/university/institute has to take an active role in building a professional body that liaises with the government to shape mental health policies. Encouraging students working towards postgraduate and PhD degrees to examine issues that are unique to the sociocultural context will help in building locally sourced educational materials over time. Conducting research on best practices in psychotherapy pedagogy at the global and local levels will further the reach of therapy. Programs for counseling education have to be developed with an emphasis on delivering counseling in the region's vernacular, so that the benefits of therapy can accrue for all individuals.

Theorizing Practice One of the lacunae that arises in therapy and counseling is a reluctance for practitioners to theorize their practice. Opportunities for collaboration between academic institutions and practitioners can provide valuable information about the state of the field and about how practitioners are modifying techniques and practices depending on the needs of the clients. This is a possible way to develop contemporary and locally relevant psychotherapy, suitably informed by theory. Trainees can benefit from the live experiences of practitioners. Healthy debate between academia and practitioners can ensure the promotion of synergic development of the field. Facilitating research and publication by practitioners showcasing methods such as case studies, phenomenological research, ethnography, psychobiography, discourse, and narrative analysis can contribute subjective and process-oriented work.

International Dialogue Driven by the needs and challenges arising from globalization, the ambition of creating an International Counselors' Association may be realized. National bodies can work to create an international body that serves professionals across the world in a manner comparable to the functioning of the ACA, BACP, etc., with global representation. This body can help to truly internationalize the training and practice of counseling and psychotherapy, facilitating curricular development, research, and multicultural practice. Encouraging collaboration among various international training institutions can facilitate a common curriculum for counselor training and supervision across geographies.

Ethical Codes Most countries adapt ethical guidelines from either the APA or the ACA or the BACP. Leach and Harbin (1997) took on the ambitious task of analyzing the ethical codes of 24 countries in comparison to the APA code of ethics, and they found many similarities with Canadian and European countries. However, differences were noted among countries like China that hold a relativist rather than absolutist perspective. There was a high percentage of agreement with ten standards found in 75 percent of the codes surveyed. These standards were Privacy, Confidentiality, Competence, Avoiding Harm, Exploitive Relationships, Supervision, Fees and Financial Arrangements, Avoidance of False or Deceptive Statements, Informed Consent to Therapy, and Informed Consent to Research. However, some differences were noted including emphasis on school testing, forensic and legal issues, the use of torture, respect for diversity, and sexual misconduct. We propose that national bodies adapt existing ethical codes to better reflect their current sociocultural context and, in the tradition of APA, periodically revise the codes to keep up with the changing landscape.

DiFilippo et al. (2003, p. 270), caution "Approximately half of what is learned in graduate school is outdated ten years later"; necessitating continuous examination, review and updating of course content and pedagogy. A lack of exposure and supervision during formal training renders even professionally trained counselors ill prepared to meet the challenges of a dynamic sociopolitical context. In present times, both developed and developing nations are going through flux such as economic downturn, political upheavals, changing government regimes and policies, sexual and gender diversity, migration, terrorism, increased intolerance and violence against minorities, etc. Emerging needs such as using telephonic and digital modalities of therapy, working with LGBTQ, polyamorous, BDSM and kinky clients, clients facing systemic violence and refugees, etc. are not covered in formal curricula. Graduates are left to their own devices to adapt their newly minted repertoire of skills, explore literature from other cultural contexts, and seek short-term courses or supervision to help equip them to meet the needs of these groups. More often than not, novice counselors face problems in building a professional identity and integrating into the extant mental health infrastructure; further learning and skill building is often deferred or ignored. The more nuanced the training and education, the greater the unfurling of the potential of the therapist.

Asia's connections with colonialism are so strong, that even in present times, psychotherapy remains shackled by the hegemony of Eurocentric ideas. Since counseling is a reflexive discipline, its application in multiple cultural settings requires priority be given to the local cultural heritage and the social circumstances in which interventions are developed and carried out.

References

American Counseling Association. (2014). *ACA code of ethics*. Alexandria, VA: American Counseling Association.

American Psychological Association. (2003). Guidelines for multicultural education, training, research, practice, and organizational change for psychologists. *American Psychologist, 58*, 377–402.

American Psychological Association. (2006). *APA task force on the assessment of competence in professional psychology: Final report.* Retrieved from http://www.apa.org/ed/resources/competency-revised.pdf

American Psychological Association. (2014). *Guidelines for Clinical Supervision in Health Service Psychology.* Retrieved from http://apa.org/about/policy/guidelines-supervision.pdf

American Psychological Association. 2017. *Multicultural Guidelines: An Ecological Approach to Context, Identity, and Intersectionality.* Retrieved from: http://www.apa.org/about/policy/multicultural-guidelines.pdf

American Psychological Association, Commission on Accreditation. (2015). *Standards of Accreditation for Health Service Psychology.* Retrieved from http://www.Apa.org/ed/accreditation/about/policies/standards-of-accreditation.pdf

Aponte, H., & Kissil, K. (Eds.). (2016). *Person of the therapist training model: Mastering the use of self.* New York: Routledge.

Arulmani, G. (2007). Counseling psychology in India: At the confluence of two traditions. *Applied Psychology: An International Issue, 56*(1), 69–82.

Association for Counselor Education and Supervision Taskforce on Best Practices in Clinical Supervision. (2011, April). *Best practices in clinical supervision.* Retrieved from www.acesonline.net/wp-content/uploads/2011/10/ACES-Best-Practices-in-clinicalsupervision-document-FINAL.pdf.

Association of State and Provincial Psychology Boards. (2015). *Supervision guidelines for education and training leading to licensure as a health service provider.* Retrieved from https://www.asppb.net/

Bae, S. H., Joo, E., & Orlinsky, D. E. (2003). Psychotherapists in South Korea: Professional and practice characteristics. *Psychotherapy: Theory, research, practice, training, 40*(4), 302.

Bernard, J. M., & Goodyear, R. K. (2014). *Fundamentals of clinical supervision* (5th ed.). Upper Saddle River, NJ: Pearson Education.

Bhola, P., Kumaria, S., & Orlinsky, D. E. (2012, July 5). Looking within: Self-perceived professional strengths and weaknesses among psychotherapists in India. *Asia Pacific Journal of Counseling and Psychotherapy, 1–14.*

Blocher, D. H. (1983). Toward a cognitive developmental approach to counseling supervision. *The Counseling Psychologist, 11*(1), 27–34.

Borders, L. D. (1992). Learning to think like a supervisor. *The Clinical Supervision, 10*(2), 135–148.

Brannigan, T. (2014, September 3). It's good to talk: China opens up to psychotherapy. *The Guardian.*

Carroll, K. M., & Rounsaville, B. J. (2010). Computer-assisted Therapy in psychiatry: Be brave— It's a new world. *Current Psychiatry Reports, 12*(5), 426–432. https://doi.org/10.1007/s11920-010-0146-2

Carter, K. (2019). *How computer-assisted therapy helps patients and practitioners (Pt. 1) VR and AI therapy programs offer practitioners new tools to help treat patients.* https://www.apa.org/members/content/computer-assisted-therapy

Chang, D. F., Tong, H., Shi, Q., & Zeng, Q. (2005). Letting a hundred flowers bloom: Counseling and psychotherapy in the people's Republic of China. *Journal of Mental Health Counseling, 27*(2), 104–116.

Chen, X. S. (2005). The evolution and task of mental health in China. *Journal of Chinese Mental Health, 19,* 649–650.

Chinese Psychological Society. (2004). *Psychology in China.* Beijing, China: Chinese Psychological Society.

Chinese Psychological Society. (2007). *Code of ethics for counseling and clinical practice.* Beijing, China: Chinese Psychological Society.

Chow, D. L., Miller, S. D., Seidel, J. A., Kane, R. T., Thornton, J. A., & Andrews, W. P. (2015). The role of deliberate practice in the development of highly effective psychotherapists. *Psychotherapy, 52*(3), 337–345.

Christogiorgos, S., Vassilopoulou, V., Florou, A., Xydou, V., Douvou, M., & Tsiantis, J. (2010). Telephone counseling with adolescents and counter-transference phenomena: Particularities and challenges. *British Journal of Guidance & Counseling, 38*(3), 313–325. https://doi.org/10.1080/03069885.2010.482394

Clay, R. (2019). *Psychotherapy in China.* [online] https://www.apa.org. Available at: https://www.apa.org/monitor/2019/10/psychotherapy-china (Accessed 13 Nov. 2019).

Cook, A. L., Lei, A., & Chiang, D. (2010). Counseling in China: Implications for counselor education preparation and distance learning instruction. *Journal for International Counseling Education, 2*, 60–73.

Corey, G., Corey, M. S., & Callanan, P. (2005). An approach to teaching ethics courses in human services and counseling. *Counseling and Values, 49*(3), 193–207.

Corey, G., Corey, M. S., & Callanan, P. (2007). *Issues and ethics in the helping professions* (7th ed.). Pacific Grove, CA: Brooks/Cole.

Corey, G., Corey, M. S., Callanan, P., & Learning, T. (2011). *Issues and Ethics in the helping professions.* Cengage Learning.

Council for Accreditation of Counseling and Related Educational Programs. (2009). 2009 standards. Alexandria, VACouncil for Accreditation of Counseling and Related Educational Programs.

DiFilippo, J. M., Sloan, D. M., Butler, R. W., & Stefan, E. (2003). The future of psychotherapy. *Journal of Contemporary Psychotherapy, 33*(4), 261–272.

Dryden, W., & Thorne, B. (Eds.). (1991). *Training and supervision for counseling in action* (Vol. 14). Sage.

Duan, C., Nilsson, J., Wang, C. C. D., Debernardi, N., Klevens, C., & Tallent, C. (2011). Internationalizing counseling: A Southeast Asian perspective. *Counseling Psychology Quarterly, 24*(1), 29–41.

Edwards, J. (2018). Counseling and Psychology Student Experiences of Personal Therapy: A Critical Interpretive Synthesis. *Frontiers in Psychology, 9*, 17–32.

Egan, G. (1998). *The skilled helper: A problem-management approach to helping.* Pacific Grove, Calif: Brooks/Cole.

Ellenberger, H. F. (1970). *The discovery of the unconscious: The history and evolution of dynamic psychiatry.* London: Allen Lane.

Fairburn, C. G., & Patel, V. (2017). The impact of digital technology on psychological treatments and their dissemination. *Behaviour research and therapy, 88*, 19–25.

Farber, B. A., Manevich, I., Metzger, J., & Saypol, E. (2005). Choosing psychotherapy as a career: Why did we cross that road? *Journal of Clinical Psychology, 61*(8), 1009–1031.

Fernandez, M. (2013). *A Model of Pedagogy for Beginning Counselor Educators.* [online] Counseling.org. Available at: https://www.counseling.org/knowledge-center/vistas/by-subject2/vistas-education-and-supervision/docs/default-source/vistas/a-model-of-pedagogy-for-beginning-counselor-educators (Accessed 4 Nov 2019).

Fleming, J. (1953). The role of supervision in psychiatric training. *Bulletin of the Menninger Clinic, 17*(5), 157.

Fleuridas, C., & Krafcik, D. (2019, January-March). Beyond four forces: The evolution of psychotherapy. *SAGE Open*, 1–21.

Foo, K. H., Merrick, P. L., & Kazantzis, N. (2006). Counseling/psychotherapy with Chinese Singaporean clients. *Asian Journal of Counseling, 13*(2), 271–293.

Fukkink, R., & Hermanns, J. (2009). Counseling children at a helpline: Chatting or calling. *Journal of Community Psychology, 37*(8), 939–948.

Gaiha, S. M., Sunil, G. A., Kumar, R., & Menon, S. (2014). Enhancing mental health literacy in India to reduce stigma: The fountainhead to improve health-seeking behaviour. *Journal of Public Mental Health, 13*(3), 146–158.

Gao, Y. (2001). Directive approach to telephone counseling in the People's Republic of China: Underlying cultural traditions and transitions. *The Counseling Psychologist, 29*, 435–453.

Garg, K., Kumar, C. N., & Chandra, P. S. (2019). Number of psychiatrists in India: Baby steps forward, but a long way to go. *Indian Journal of Psychiatry, 61*, 104–105.

Gilbert, P., Hughes, W., & Dryden, W. (2014). The therapist as a crucial variable in psychotherapy. In W. Dryden & L. Spurling (Eds.), Classic Edition *On becoming a psychotherapist*. New York: Routledge.

Gonsiorek, J. C., Richards, P. S., Pargament, K. I., & McMinn, M. R. (2009). Ethical challenges and opportunities at the edge: Incorporating spirituality and religion into psychotherapy. *Professional Psychology: Research and Practice, 40*(4), 385–395.

Grater, H. A. (1985). Stages in psychotherapy supervision: From therapy skills to skilled therapist. *Professional Psychology: Research and Practice, 16*(5), 605.

Grimmer, A. (2005). Mandatory personal therapy for therapists: Professional and ethical issues. In *Handbook of professional and ethical practice for psychologists, counselors and psychotherapists*, 277-289.

Grover, N. (2014). An experiential account of the journey of psychotherapy training in India. *Psychological Studies, 60*(1), 114–118.

Gupta, T. (2019). *Journal of Indian Association for Child and Adolescent Mental Health, 15*(3), 90–98.

Gupta, A. K., Sharma, E., Kar, S. K., Tripathi, A., Reeves, T., Arjundas, R., & Dalal, P. K. (2019). Training and clinical impact of cognitive behaviour therapy workshops in a teaching hospital in North India. *Indian Journal of Psychological Medicine, 41*(4), 343.

Hackney, H., & Cormier, L. S. (2001). *The professional counselor: A process guide to helping*. Boston: Allyn and Bacon.

Halder, S., & Mahato, A. K. (2019). Cognitive behavior therapy for children and adolescents: Challenges and gaps in practice. *Indian Journal of Psychological Medicine, 41*(3), 279.

Henden, J. (2008). *Preventing suicide: The solution focused approach*. Chichester, UK: Wiley.

Heppner, P. P., & Roehlke, H. J. (1984). Differences among supervisees at different levels of training: Implications for a developmental model of supervision. *Journal of Counseling Psychology, 30*, 252–262.

Hess, A. K. (1987). Advances in psychotherapy supervision: Introduction. *Professional Psychology: Research and Practice, 18*(3), 187.

Higgins, L. T., & Sun, C. H. (2002). The development of psychological testing in China. *International Journal of Psychology, 77*(4), 246–254.

Hill, C. E. & Castonguay, L. G. (2017). Therapist effects: Integration and conclusions. In *How and why are some therapists better than others? Understanding therapist effects*, L. G. Castonguay and C. E. Hill (Eds.). pg. 325-341. Washington DC: American Psychological Association.

Hill, C. E., Spiegel, S. B., Hoffman, M. A., Kivlighan, D. M., & Gelso, C. J. (2017). Therapist expertise in psychotherapy revisited. *The Counseling Psychologist*, 1–47.

Hoch, E. M. (1990). Experiences with psychotherapy training in India. *Psychotherapy Psychosomatic, 53*, 14–20.

Hogan, R. A. (1964). Issues and approaches in supervision. *Psychotherapy: Theory, Research & Practice, 1*(3), 139.

Holloway, E. L. (1987). Developmental models of supervision: Is it development? *Professional Psychology: Research and Practice, 18*, 209–216.

Holloway, E., & Carroll, M. (1999). Introduction. In E. Holloway & M. Carroll (Eds.), *Training counseling supervisors* (pp. 1–7). London: Sage Publications.

Hook, J.N., Captari, L.E., Hoyt, W., Davis, D.E., McElroy, S.E., & Worthington, E.L. (2019). Religion and spirituality. In J.C. Norcross and B.E. Wampold (eds.) *Psychotherapy relationships that work. Volume 2: Evidence-based therapist responsiveness.* (3rd Ed.) pg. 212–263. New York: Oxford University Press.

Hou, Z. J., & Zhang, N. J. (2007). Counseling psychology in China. *Applied Psychology: An International Review, 56*, 33–50.

Huang, H. Y. (2015). From psychotherapy to psycho-boom: A historical overview of psychotherapy in China. *Psychoanalysis and Psychotherapy in China, 1*(1), 1–30.

Inman, A. G., Soheilian, S. S., & Luu, L. P. (2019). Telesupervision: Building bridges in a digital era. *Journal of Clinical Psychology, 75*(2), 292–301.

Iwakabe, S. (2008). Psychotherapy integration in Japan. *Journal of Psychotherapy Integration, 18*(1), 103.

Jacobsen, T., & Kohout, J. (2010). *2008 APA survey of psychology health service providers: Telepsychology, medication and collaboration.* APA Center for Workforce Studies. Washington D.C.: American Psychological Association. Retrieved October 14, 2015, from http://www.apa.org/workforce/publications/08-hsp/telepsychology/report.pdf.

Joo, E., Lee, H., & Joo, E. (2007). An investigation of Korean Humanistic counseling model based on the self-report of experienced humanistic counselors in Korea. *Korean Journal of Counseling and Psychotherapy, 19*, 569–586.

Kapur, M., Shamasundar, C., & Bhatti, R. (1996). *Psychotherapy training in India.* Bangalore: NIMHANS.

King, R., Bambling, M., Reid, W., & Thomas, I. (2006). Telephone and online counseling for young people: A naturalistic comparison of session outcome, session impact and therapeutic alliance. *Counseling and Psychotherapy Research, 6*(3), 1405–1746.

Kumar, A. (2011). Mental health services in rural India: Challenges and prospects. *Health, 3*(12), 757–761.

Kumaraswamy, N. (2007). Psychotherapy in Brunei Darussalam. *Journal of Clinical Psychology, 63*(8), 735–744.

Lambert, M. J. (2013). The efficacy and effectiveness of psychotherapy. In M. J. Lambert (Ed.), *Bergin and Garfield's handbook of psychotherapy and behavior change* (6th ed.). Hoboken NJ: John Wiley & Sons.

Laungani, P. (2004). *Asian perspectives in counseling and psychotherapy.* London: Routledge.

Leach, L., & Christensen, H. (2006). A systematic review of telephone-based interventions for mental disorders. *Journal of Telemedicine and Telecare, 12*(3), 122–129.

Leach, M. M., & Harbin, J. J. (1997). Psychological ethics codes: A comparison of twenty-four countries. *International Journal of Psychology, 32*(3), 181–192.

Lee, S. M., Suh, S., Yang, E., & Jang, Y. J. (2012). History, current status, and future prospects of counseling in South Korea. *Journal of Counseling & Development, 90*(4), 494–499.

Li, Z., Guo, Z., Wang, N., Xu, Z., Qu, Y., Wang, X., & Kingdon, D. (2015). Cognitive–behavioural therapy for patients with schizophrenia: A multicentre randomized controlled trial in Beijing, China. *Psychological Medicine, 45*(9), 1893–1905.

Lim, S., Lim, B., Michael, R., Cai, R., & Schock, C. K. (2010). The trajectory of counseling in China: Past, present, and future trends. *Journal of Counseling & Development, 88*, 4–8.

Littrell, J. M., Lee-Borden, N., & Lorenz, J. (1976). A developmental framework for counseling supervision. *Counselor Education and Supervision, 19*(2), 129–136.

Loganbill, C., Hardy, E., & Delworth, U. (1982). Supervision: A conceptual model. *The Counseling Psychologist, 10*(1), 3–42.

Malhotra, S., Chakrabarti, S., & Shah, R. (2013). Telepsychiatry: Promise, potential, and challenges. *Indian Journal of Psychiatry, 55*(1), 3.

Mander, G. (2004). The selection of candidates for training in psychotherapy and counseling. *Psychodynamic Practice, 10*(2), 161–172.

Manickam, L. S. S. (2010). Psychotherapy in India. *Indian Journal of Psychiatry, 52*(Suppl1), S366.

Martin, P., Kumar, S., & Lizarondo, L. (2017). Effective use of technology in clinical supervision. *Internet Interventions, 8*, 35–39.

McDonald, M. (2011). Stressed and depressed, Koreans avoid therapy**.** *The New York Times, 6.* https://www.nytimes.com/2011/07/07/world/asia/07iht-psych07.html

McQuaid, C. (2014). *What you really need to know about counseling and psychotherapy training.* Hove, UK: Routledge.

Merry, S. N., Stasiak, K., Shepherd, M., Frampton, C., Fleming, T., & Lucassen, M. F. (2012). The effectiveness of SPARX, a computerised self help intervention for adolescents seeking help for depression: Randomised controlled non-inferiority trial. *Bmj, 344*, e2598.

Miars, R. D., Tracey, T. J., Ray, P. B., Cornfeld, J. L., O'Farrell, M., & Gelso, C. J. (1983). Variation in supervision process across trainee experience levels. *Journal of Counseling Psychology, 30*, 403–412.

Murphy, D. (2005). A qualitative study into the experiences of mandatory personal therapy during training. *Counseling and Psychotherapy Research, 5*, 27–32.

Murphy, D., Irfan, N., Barnett, H., Castledine, E., & Enescu, L. (2018). A systematic review and meta-synthesis of qualitative research into mandatory personal psychotherapy during training. *Counseling and Psychotherapy Research., 18*(2), 199–214.

Naeem, F., Gobbi, M., Ayub, M., & Kingdon, D. (2009). University students' views about compatibility of cognitive behaviour therapy (CBT) with their personal, social and religious values (a study from Pakistan). *Mental Health, Religion & Culture, 12*(8), 847–855.

Norcross, J. C., & Lambert, M. J. (2019). Evidence- based psychotherapy relationships: The third task force. In J. C. Norcross & M. J. Lambert (Eds.), *Psychotherapy relationships that Work Volume 1: Evidence based therapist contributions* (3rd ed.). New York, NY: Oxford University Press.

Orlinsky, D. E., & Howard, K. I. (1984). A generic model of psychotherapy. Paper presented at the 1st annual meeting of the Society for the Exploration of Psychotherapy Integration (SEPI), Annapolis, MD.

Orlinsky, D. E., & Howard, K. I. (1986). Process and outcome in psychotherapy. In S. L. Garfield & A. E. Bergin (Eds.), *Handbook of psychotherapy and behavior change* (pp. 311–384). New York: Wiley.

Oteiza, V. (2010). Therapists' experiences of personal therapy: A descriptive phenomenological study. *Counseling and Psychotherapy Research: Linking Research with Practice, 10*(3), 222–228.

Overholser, J. C. (2019). 50 Years of psychotherapy: Erudition, evolution, and evaluation. *Journal of Contemporary Psychotherapy.*

Patel, V., & Thara, R. (Eds.). (2003). *Meeting the mental health needs of developing countries: NGO innovations in India*. Sage Publications India.

Pope, V. T., & Kline, W. B. (1999). The personal characteristics of effective counselors: What 10 experts think. *Psychological Reports, 84*(3), 1339–1334.

Pope, K. S., & Vasquez, M. J. T. (2011). *Ethics in psychotherapy and counseling* (4th ed.). San Francisco, CA: Jossey-Bass.

Post, B. C., & Wade, N. G. (2009). Religion and spirituality in psychotherapy: A practice friendly review of research. *Journal of Clinical Psychology, 65*(2), 131–146.

Qian, M. Y. (1994). Counseling and psychotherapy. Peking University Press.

Qian, M., Gao, J., Yao, P., & Rodriguez, M. A. (2009). Professional ethical issues and the development of professional ethical standards in counseling and clinical psychology in China. *Ethics & Behavior, 19*(4), 290–309.

Reese, R. J., Conoley, C. W., & Brossart, D. F. (2002). Effectiveness of telephone counseling: A Field-based investigation. *Journal of Counseling Psychology, 49*(2), 233–242.

Reising, G. N., & Daniels, M. H. (1983). A study of Hogan's model of counselor development and supervision. *Journal of Counseling Psychology, 30*, 235–244.

Ridley, C. R., & Mollen, D. (2011). Training in counseling psychology: An introduction to the major contribution. *The Counseling Psychologist, 39*(6), 793–799.

Rogers, C. R. (1951). *Client-centered therapy*. Boston: Houghton Mifflin.

Rønnestad, M. H., & Skovholt, T. M. (2001). Learning arenas for professional development: Retrospective accounts of senior psychotherapists. *Professional Psychology: Research and Practice, 32*(2), 181.

Rønnestad, M. H., & Skovholt, T. M. (2003). The journey of the counselor and therapist: Research findings and perspectives on professional development. *Journal of Career Development, 30*(1), 5–44.

Rousmaniere, T. (2017). *Deliberate practice for psychotherapists: A guide to improving clinical effectiveness*. New York: Routledge.

Russell, R. K., & Petrie, T. (1994). Issues in training effective supervisors. *Applied and Preventive Psychology, 3*, 27–42.

Sarai, K., Karnasuta, K., & Ohara, M. (2019). Long-term care (LTC) system for the elderly in Japan. *Journal of Thai Interdisciplinary Research, 14*(4), 1–8.

Schoonover, J., Lipkin, S., Javid, M., Rosen, A., Solanki, M., Shah, S., & Katz, C. L. (2014). Perceptions of traditional healing for mental illness in rural Gujarat. *Annals of Global Health, 80*, 96–102.

Segal, Z. V., Williams, J. M. G., & Teasdale, J. D. (2001). *Mindfulness-based cognitive therapy for depression: A new approach to preventing relapse.* New York: Guilford Press.

Sidhu, G. (2017). The Application of Western Models of Psychotherapy by Indian Psychotherapists in India: A Grounded Theory. *Dissertations & Theses, 377*.

Sipps, G. J., Sugden, G. J., & Favier, C. M. (1988). Counselor training level and verbal response type: Their relationship to efficacy and outcome expectations. *Journal of Counseling Psychology, 35*, 397–401.

Skovholt, T. M., & Ronnestad, M. H. (1992). *The evolving professional self.* New York: Wiley.

Sperry, L. (2010). *Highly effective therapy: Developing essential clinical competencies in counseling and psychotherapy.* Routledge.

Spruill, J., Rozensky, R. H., Stigall, T. T., Vasquez, M. J. T., Bingham, R. P., & Olvey, C. D. (2004). Becoming a competent clinician: Basic competencies in intervention. *Journal of Clinical Psychology, 60*, 741–754.

Sriram, T. G. (1990). Psychotherapy in developing countries: A public health perspective. *Indian Journal of Psychiatry, 32*(2), 138.

Sriram, S. (2016). Counseling in India: An introduction to the volume. In S. Sriram (Ed.), *Counseling in India: Reflections on the process* (pp. 1–11). Singapore: Springer.

Stoltenberg, C. (1981). Approaching supervision from a developmental perspective: The counselor complexity model. *Journal of Counseling Psychology, 28*(1), 59.

Stoltenberg, C. D., & Delworth, U. (1987). *Supervising counselors and therapists: A developmental approach.* Jossey-Bass.

Stoltenberg, C. D., & Delworth, U. (1988). Developmental models of supervision: It is development—Response to Holloway. *Professional Psychology: Research and Practice, 19*, 134–137.

Stoltenberg, C. D., McNeill, B., & Delworth, U. (1998). *IDM supervision: An integrated developmental model for supervising counselors and therapists.* San Francisco: Jossey-Bass.

Tagami, F., & Ozawa, Y. (2005). Kaunseringu towa nanika [What is counseling?]. In S. Geshi et al. (Eds.), *Kanunseringu no tenbou [Perspectives on counseling]* (pp. 3–14). Tokyo: Brain.

Thara, R., & Patel, V. (2010). Role of non-governmental organizations in mental health in India. *Indian Journal of Psychiatry, 52*(Suppl1), S389.

The Mental HealthCare Act; 2017. Available from: https://www.indiacode.nic.in/bitstream/123456789/2249/1/A2017-10.pdf. (Last accessed on 2019 Nov 19).

Thériault, A., & Gazzola, N. (2005). Feelings of inadequacy, insecurity, and incompetence among experienced therapists. *Counseling and Psychotherapy Research, 5*(1), 11–18.

Thériault, A., & Gazzola, N. (2008). Feelings of incompetence among experienced therapists: A substantive theory. *European Journal of Qualitative Research in Psychotherapy, 3*, 19–29.

Thériault, A., & Gazzola, N. (2010). Therapist feelings of incompetence and suboptimal processes in psychotherapy. *Journal of Contemporary Psychotherapy, 40*, 233–243.

Thériault, A., Gazzola, N., & Richardson, B. (2009). Feelings of incompetence in novice therapists: Consequences, coping, and correctives. *Canadian Journal of Counseling and Psychotherapy/Revue canadienne de counseling et de psychothérapie, 43*(2).

Thorne, B., & Dryden, W. (1991). Approaches to the training of counselors. In W. Dryden (Ed.), *Training and supervision for counseling in action* (pp. 15–32). London: SAGE Publications.

Tracey, T. J., Hays, K. A., Malone, J., & Herman, B. (1988). Changes in counselor response as a function of experience. *Journal of Counseling Psychology, 35*, 119–126.

Wampold, B. E., Baldwin, S. A., Holtforth, M. G., & Imel, Z. E. (2017). What characterizes effective therapists? In L. G. Castonguay & C. E. Hill (Eds.), *How and why are some therapists better than others? Understanding therapist effects* (pp. 37–54). Washington DC: American Psychological Association.

Watanabe-Muraoka, A. M. (2007). A perspective on counseling psychology in Japan: Toward a lifespan approach. *Applied Psychology, 56*(1), 97–106.

Welfel, E. R. (2016). *Ethics in counseling and psychotherapy standards, research, and emerging issues* (6th ed.). Boston, MA: Cengage Learning.

Wheeler, S. (2000). What makes a good counselor? An analysis of ways in which counselor trainers construe good and bad counseling trainees. *Counseling Psychology Quarterly, 13*(1), 65–83.

Wiley, M., & Ray, P. B. (1986). Counseling supervision by developmental level. *Journal of Counseling Psychology, 33*, 439–445.

Worthington, E. L. (1984). An empirical investigation of supervision of counselors as they gain experience. *Journal of Counseling Psychology, 31*, 63–75.

Yagi, D. T. (2008). Current developments in school counseling in Japan. *Asian Journal of Counseling, 15*(2), 141–155.

Yeo, L. S., Tan, S. Y., & Neihart, M. (2013). Counseling in Singapore. In T. H. Hohenshil, N. E. Amundson, & S. G. Niles (Eds.), *Counseling around the world: An international handbook* (pp. 127–136). Alexandria, VA: American Counseling Association.

Zeng, Q. F., Zhao, X. D., & Zhu, Z. H. (2003). The summary of the first conference of clinical and counseling committee in the Chinese Psychological Society. *Journal of Chinese Mental Health, 17*, 795.

Zhao, X. (2014). Opportunities and challenges for promoting psychotherapy in contemporary China. *Shanghai Archives of Psychiatry, 26*(3), 157–159.

Gender Studies

Teaching Gender in Psychology

27

Tissy Mariam Thomas and U. Arathi Sarma

Contents

T. M. Thomas (✉) · U. A. Sarma
Department of Psychology, University of Kerala, Thiruvananthapuram, Kerala, India

© Springer Nature Switzerland AG 2023
J. Zumbach et al. (eds.), *International Handbook of Psychology Learning and Teaching*,
Springer International Handbooks of Education,
https://doi.org/10.1007/978-3-030-28745-0_31

Abstract

Studying gender, a dynamic process embedded within the patriarchal frame-work, traverses academic, societal, economic, legislative, and administrative platforms. Intersectionality of gender reveals fluidity of other multiple identities wherein gender discourses undergo a revolutionary transition. The discipline of psychology, with its expertise in understanding the subtleties of human inter-actions, has the potential to contribute immense knowledge on the origin, maintenance, and modification of the social construction of gender. However, a review of gender discussions in the theory and practice of psychology gives tremendous insights on the depth and power of gendered representations, which have even penetrated into psychological theories, assessment, research, diag-nosis, and therapy. Gender-informed approaches in psychology are now of growing priority, due to the global sensitization towards the empowerment of marginalized gender. Despite formal commitments to gender equality as a universal agenda, voices of lived realities of marginalized gender have boosted the development of broader multicultural frameworks of gender mainstreaming across various domains of health, relationships, education, media, occupation, and policy-making. Thus, it remains the skill and expertise of informed acade-micians and professionals to elucidate appropriate practices towards gender fluidity and pluralism. The present chapter offers a comprehensive, inquisitive space for acquainting with gender discourses in psychology, new lines of research in gender studies, systematic efforts at gender integration, and best practices that facilitate gender-informed approaches.

Keywords

Feminist movement · Gender gap · Gender-based violence · Gender-informed approaches in psychology · Gender empowerment and policy-making · Gender sensitivity in media and educational resources

Introduction

Opening up of gender discussions in a psychology classroom often ends up with animated arguments between male and female students in an urge to prove that they live up to the gender stereotypes assigned in a patriarchal society. An informed instructor, then, might need to initiate discussions from basic conceptual clarifications, patterns of gender socialization, and development of gender-based criticisms in academic and practicing psychology. Consequences of the construction of a gendered self which results into distorted communication, power equations, and mental health guarantee psychological imbalances embedded in societal structure itself.

Recently, a pedagogical change has been observed in the teaching space while carrying out these deliberations, by placing gender concerns through the perspective of gender sensitive governance and policy-making. Rather than the promises of concluding the gender discourses focusing on the need for an inclusive approach in each class, strong forms of gender empowerment instances and events have been brought out from the social, economic, and political gender models globally. The present chapter includes a) brief analysis of the gender-sensitive approaches in academic psychology in terms of theoretical models, assessment and research methods, and mental health practice; b) implementation of various gender empowerment approaches in relationship, health, media, and educational resources in the government and nongovernment settings; and c) discussions on the empowerment of marginalized gender initiatives through the evaluation of global gender gap and human development reports.

Gender-based violence across the world has been criticized for the poor preventive mechanisms as the authorities of the world nations, tended to act after the violence had occurred, and reported by WHO in 2002. The absence of poor preventive mechanisms would have devastating effects among the youth in understanding of women rights and issues such as violence, justice, equality, etc. With a motive to understand and establish a baseline of democratic citizenship values and attitudes of youth in urban India, Children's Movement for Civic Awareness (CMCA) survey tested the awareness of young Indians on topics like democracy, rights, and responsibilities, adherence to civic rules, gender equality, social justice, and environmental conservation among 6600 school students and 4400 college students (Children's Movement for Civic Awareness, 2014). Refer to Fig. 1.

The score shows wide prevalence of gender-biased attitudes and negative stereotypes amongst the young population in urban India. Young students justify society's protectiveness in violence which tremendously alarm the nations to take necessary steps to promote prevention of violence from occurring. Having gender-based violence as still the main focus in approaching gender studies, the history of feminist movement and the changes it brought to academic psychology would worth an exercise.

The "World report on violence and health: Summary," published by WHO in 2002, analyzed the violence across the world and criticized the poor preventive mechanisms of the authorities of the world nations, who tended to act after the violence had occurred. Advocating preventive actions targeting vulnerable groups, particularly those in lower socioeconomic status, the report put forward complacency, usually reinforced by self-interests, as a barrier to tackle violence and political commitment as a resource to tackle violence. Relying on the ecological model for understanding the multiple faces of violence, the report organizes existing efforts at

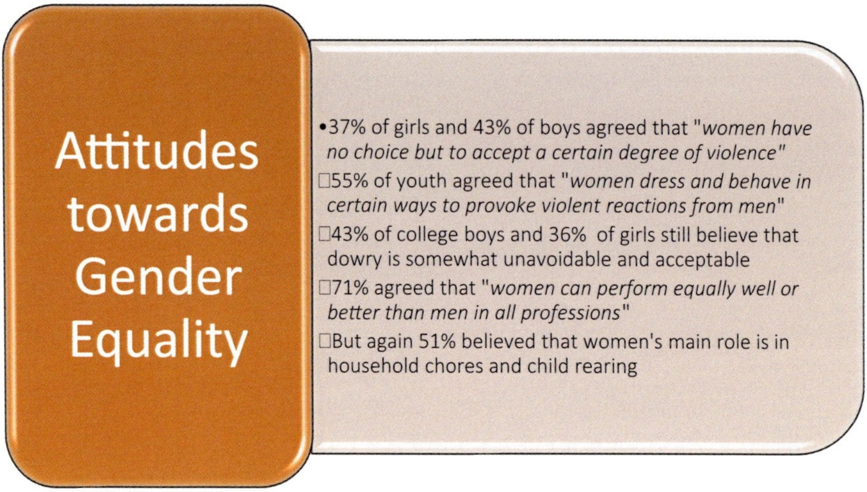

Fig. 1 Yuva Nagarik Meter Report on attitude toward gender equality. (Source: Children's Movement for Civic Awareness, 2014)

curbing violence under individual,[1] relationship,[2] community based,[3] and societal[4] approaches (WHO, 2002).

Even though these approaches are in place at different levels of execution, it's effectiveness in reaching out various communities of gender is far from implementation. One needs to go through the brief history of feminist movement in order to understand the current status of gender discourses.

Feminist Movement

Debates over the roles of women and men dated back in history. Gender differences had been subjected to theories, perspectives, research, measurement, and therapies in psychology. The *essentialist* view proposes of an underlying biological component

---

[1] Target the attitudes and behaviour of young adults, children, women and men as well as those who have committed violence

[2] Focus on the relationships between victims and predators of violence.

[3] Aims at creating public awareness, making debates on these issues to mobilise actions and facilitating social support for the victims

[4] Focus on the cultural, social and economic factors like legislative and judicial remedies, international treaties to prevent violence, polices that can make families free from poverty and inequality, efforts to change social and cultural norms that discriminates people on race, creed and gender etc., and implementing disarmament and demobilizations

which makes gender differences and *minimalist*[5] and *maximalist*[6] views bring out the nature of gender differences (Epstein, 1988).

When the structuralist school of psychology established analytical ways of studying the structure of "generalized adult mind" through experimentation, individual differences were assumed to be based on the data drawn from and by men (Brannon, 2017), and women were prohibited from this tradition expressly in the United States. Functionalist psychologists drew a wider variety of participants such as children, women, and animals to research and theorize. Consequently, behaviorism and psychoanalysis came into existence, both emphasizing minimal role gender in human behavior.

Eighteenth century is marked with the political, social, and intellectual developments of women's studies which have affected the way psychology understands gender differences. The first and second waves of feminism propagated changes in women's roles and legal status followed by development of women's studies. Even though many disputes the notion of third wave feminism (post feminism), it remains as a common belief that feminism is no longer necessary as women have achieved equal treatment and opportunities.

The terminology of sex which emphasizes the biological differences is replaced by an alternative term, gender, proposed by (1999) which describes the traits and behaviors that are regarded by the culture as appropriate to women and men.

Sooner, feminist orientation has influenced academic development in the field of psychology like other sciences and social sciences. National Council of Women Psychologists is formed in 1941, and only in 1973, American Psychological Association (APA) professionally accepted women's movement as a Division 35, Society for the Psychology of Women, after repeated rejections. Feminist-oriented research has increased in great volume which integrated study of women with current psychological thinking. Questioning the roles and stereotypes of women has incorporated intersections of race, caste, religion, language, and ethnicity with gender. Gendered reflections of these intersections are better explained as seen below. Social meanings attached to the perception of genderlessness are powerful in reflecting the inner selves of individuals.

Facts and beyond

Gendered Reflection of Race

"When you wake up in the morning and look in the mirror, what do you see?" a Black woman asked a White woman (Kimmel & Messner, 1992, p. 2). "I see a woman," said the White woman.

---

[5] Gender differences are small with few large enough to be important caused through stereotyping and differential treatment for males and females

[6] Gender differences are large and important caused through evolutionary history and sex hormones.

"That's precisely the issue," the Black woman replied. "I see a Black woman. For me, race is visible every day, because it is how I am not privileged in this culture. Race is invisible to you, which is why our alliance will always seem somewhat false to me" (p. 2).

This exchange surprised Michael Kimmel, who examined his own thoughts and realized that when he looked into the mirror, he "saw a human being: universally generalizable. The generic person" (p. 2).

Just as the White woman did not see her ethnicity, gender does not matter for men. And those who are privileged with gender, caste, religion and language do not identify themselves with these social identities. Kimmel and Messner (1992) analyzed these experiences "Certainly, we can see the biological sex of individuals, but we rarely understand the ways in which gender - that complex social meanings that is attached to biological sex – is enacted in our daily lives."

See Exercise No. 1 for reflection.

Gender studies worldwide have gone through changes in various forms in countries on every continent initiated by women's movements. Women's movements have buffered movements for peace, ecological conservation, and sustainable scientific inventions. Education free of gender bias has an influential power to change their own lives and also the social order (Howe, 1997). Despite national and regional differences, remarkable increase has been observed in the number of researches in gender studies and worldwide experiences. Gender studies in Asia, Africa, and Eastern Europe have raised gendered consciousness as a cause and consequence of activism. New trends in research methods are emerged that address the experience of women and transgender who are least privileged (participatory research) which would change public policies and education. Emergence of researches in subjective experiences (phenomenology) based on feminist paradigms marks a new era of bringing out the retrospective history of marginalized gender.

A revitalized research perspective, free of gender, unmasked the biases in psychological theories, assessment, and traditional research findings.

Section A: Analysis of Gender-Sensitive Approaches in Academic Psychology and Mental Health Practice

Gender in Psychological Theories

In the late nineteenth century, when psychology emerged as an independent systematic and scientific field, the then-commonly-held gender norms and stereotypes rooted in evolutionary theory and reinforced by social and cultural constraints made their way into psychological theorizing. Rutherford (2018), in an attempt to trace the intellectual history of gender in psychology, points out the beliefs consistent with the "doctrine of separate spheres" that differentiates men as more agentic and suitable for public worlds and women as passive and excellent for private engagements as well as the "variability hypothesis" that upheld the inferiority of female intellect. Mary Whiton Calkins (1863–1930), Helen Thompson Woolley (1874–1947), and Leta Hollingworth

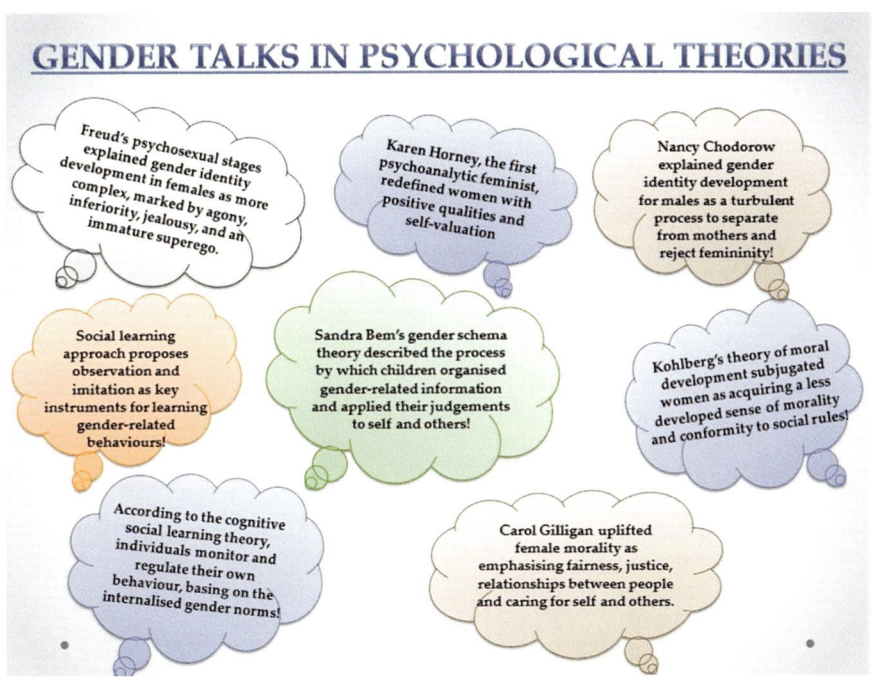

Fig. 2 Psychological theories that discuss gender and gender differences. (Source: Brannon, 2017)

(1886–1939) were the pioneers who ventured out to challenge these and many other sexist beliefs in psychology (Rutherford, 2018).

Sociobiological explanations for the differential standards and women's entitlement to child care, geared by the evolutionary theory, feature the concepts of fitness, parental investment in the offspring, and the uncertainty of paternity, despite the feminist criticisms of androcentric bias and overuse of biology in explaining behavior. Among the traditional psychological theories, psychoanalysis is often credited with explicit discourses of sexuality and gender identity development, with an inherent "phallocentric" view. Feminist psychologists who challenged mainstream psychology for incorporating the Victorian notions of patriarchal control of women converged on controversial debate on the psychoanalytic view of women. The era that followed saw several women psychoanalysts and feminists proposing modifications on the psychoanalytic theory. In addition, contemporary theories also attempt to explain gender identity development and gender differences, as seen in Fig. 2.

Gender in Psychological Measurement

With the advent of new statistical techniques and the resultant proliferation of psychological tests, gender also fell under the "psychometric scale." As one of the earliest attempts at measuring masculinity-femininity, Termanand Miles

(1936) at Stanford University postulated it as a central feature of temperament, but their conceptual frame reflected gender conservative beliefs about sex differences and nurtured the problematic and homophobic representations of gender non-conformity (Rutherford, 2018). Conventionally, the clinical usage of gender-measuring inventories purported to diagnose homosexuality as a pathological condition, which the masculinity-femininity scale of Minnesota Multiphasic Personality Inventory (MMPI-Mf) explicitly serves, but with the psychology's typical error of referring to male characteristics as the norm (Kosterina, 2009). Obviously, MMPI and similar inventories that followed its model conceive gender as a unidimensional bipolar construct, despite vagueness in the definitions of gender identity and masculinity-femininity, as reviewed by Kosterina (2009).

A feminist revamping of the construct came with Bem Sex Role Inventory (BSRI) which measured masculine and feminine traits as bidimensional. The hallmark of BSRI is androgyny, instead of masculinity, as the psychological ideal (Rutherford, 2018). Despite wide acclaims as a gender-inclusive measure that overthrew gender polarization, BSRI faced criticisms, primarily on the concept of androgyny and on the reiteration of gender stereotypes (Kosterina, 2009).

Luyt (2015) conducted a systematic review on how gender theories in psychology informed specific approaches to measuring gender, in line with the criticisms raised by several researchers like Constantinople (1973). He segregates existing measures based on whether they define gender as an innate individual trait (the "gender orientation" approach) like MMPI-Mf scale and BSRI or as socioculturally defined and individually internalized and endorsed social norms (the "gender ideology" approach), examples being the Male Role Norms Inventory and Adolescent Femininity Ideology Scale.

Further, informed by social constructionism, Luyt (2015) adds a gender (re) presentation approach to measurement, wherein gender is viewed as a situated social practice, influenced by social interactions that are mediated by language and other symbols. Assessment of gender representations requires appropriate theoretical content and research context that elicit dominant gender norms and power structures and the individual's way of "doing gender." This can be looked up through the lens of Judith Butler's notion of performativity, wherein gender is constructed through the repetition of conventional gendered acts (Butler, 2010). The gender (re)presentation approach offers a promising inclusive space for studying gender non-conformity as well, since it assesses gender as an individual's subjective position in the social realm of gender.

Outlines of Gender in Psychological Research

When gender transformed from a nonsense secondary variable to an important study variable, common-held notions about gender differences that penetrated into psychological research got replaced by empirical evidence and logical conclusions about gender. Brannon (2017) contrasts between the quantitative research methods that study biological sex, gender, and sexual orientation, either as inherent subject variable studied by ex post facto designs or as a social variable employing experimental designs. Among qualitative research methods, though more popular in interdisciplinary studies, the interview method accounted for more than 50% of articles in leading journals on psychology and gender (Brannon, 2017).

One of the major findings of Kosterina (2009) revolved around the nature of gender-measuring inventories as regulatory mechanisms in the society, imposing stereotypical gender roles portrayed within their content on the test takers' perception of gendered self, as indicated by her analysis of the interviews with test takers. The result points towards an immediate need for making psychological research gender-neutral and devoid of gender stereotypes. Gender bias in research takes multiple forms – the inbuilt masculine bias in the very framework of science in general, overemphasis on biological sex differences to explain psychological constructs like personality; procedures involved in research formulation, planning, data analysis, and evaluation; and overreliance on statistical rather than practical significance (Brannon, 2017).

Sexism and stereotyping have long been subject to psychological research. BSRI and its successor, Personal Attributes Questionnaire, are widely employed as explicit measures of gender stereotyping, which can be contrasted with measures assessing implicit attitudes, like Gender Implicit Association Test that offers better possibilities (Brannon, 2017). A shift in methodology' is also underway. In a remarkable work, Melchiori and Mallet (2018) advocate the practicability of high-impact laboratory experiments with high psychological realism in examining responses to sexism. They elaborate on the experimental techniques, needed resources, logistical challenges, and benefits associated with creating a study that mimics the pressures faced by women when responding to sexism in the real world.

Intersectionality of gender studies is an emerging area that opens up pathways of marginalization which is not limited only as "the woman problem" (Gill & Pires, 2019). This perspective has changed the direction of gender studies and is interpreted as a methodological challenge and promoting positive social change (Shields, 2008). An individual's social identity such as religion, ethnicity, class, language, etc. influences how one perceives and conducts gender. The power relations embedded in gender and other social identities are mutually constitutive which takes its meaning as a category in relation to another category. Feminist researchers after the second wave of feminism addressed the question of "Which women's experience?", thus unfolded a model of layered oppression of multiple identities. Therefore, "the whiteness of women, the maleness of people of color and the heterosexuality of everyone" (Risman, 2004 cited in Shields, 2008) has been challenged, and "woman" as a stable category is critiqued.

Gender research in psychology nurtured the naturalization of gender categories in order to identity differences, through simplistic questions as "In what way do men and women differ?" which do not explain whether gender operates as a system of oppression or as an aspect of identity (Shields, 2008). Gender as the most pervasive, visible, and codified category intersects subordinate identities and calls for a renewed theoretical and methodological approach in psychology. Studies on intersectionality offer explanations to these differences considering the structural and political oppression of gender. Intersectionality approach demands that psychology should move out of its disciplinary boundaries in exploring individual experiences, and these experiences should be learnt through social stratification. Shields (2008) calls for "mainstreaming" psychology with intersectionality approach and focus on gender as a central issue "to see things from the worldview of other" (Walker, 2003 Shields, 2008).

Intersectionality perspective is inclusive enough to accommodate transgender identities which problematized the overemphasis of heterosexuality as the normal category. Concerns toward intersectionality also posed a challenge to "theories of feminist identity that elaborates predicates of color, sexuality, ethnicity, class and ablebodiedness" (Butler, 1990 cited in Shields, 2008). Thus, queer theories began to challenge the binary approach to oppressor/oppressed relations (masculine/feminine, white/non-white, heterosexual/homosexual). The binary lens gave way to pluralistic perspective which decentralizes and decolonizes power relations and, thus, policies. Queer theories oppose the binary approaches to gender and demand critical alternatives in mainstream psychology theories and researches.

The heterosexual identity and its issues have always been in the research focus of psychology as a discipline, but multicultural studies now point out the need to understand sexual minorities as well. Research, development of theories, community support, and alliance building are necessary to facilitate the protection of the human rights of these minorities. Looking at the transgender community as a culture that serves like the biological home for the minorities, Thomas (2014) explored the clan culture (Gharana) of transgenders/Hijras in Bangalore, India. Through in-depth interviews, observations, and focus group discussions, the study unveiled the issues faced by Hijras in search for identity (gender) within and outside the Gharana as an individual in society, as well as the structural and cultural specificities of these Gharanas. At present, their clan culture exists as a supportive mechanism that opens up a social, cultural, and political space for those struggling under shame, isolation, discrimination, and violence. The development of feminine identity of Hijras during childhood and adolescence is marked by lack of opportunities for self-expression and intolerance for their effeminate ways, but their initial encounters with other transgenders served as the catalyst for identity formation. Gharana, being a self-contained community with an organized structure, well-defined roles, and traditions, is also emerging as a socializing platform that makes political and legal negotiations with the mainstream community (Thomas, 2014).

Feminist readings on Michael Foucault's concept of "biopower" rethink binaries of animacy and inanimacy and life versus death. In the History of Sexuality: Volume I, Foucault (1990) explains the link between biological existence and political existence to be reflected in knowledge's field of control and power's sphere of intervention. McWhorter (2016) suggested to develop a theory of life and historical and cultural representations of bodies as mutually constitutive. In a response to an ingrained "anti-biologism" existing in the late twentieth century feminists, tenth International Somatechnics Conference in 2016 stressed on "the political and conceptual status of 'real' bodies or materiality to recognize the cultural and political contexts in which they are located and to consider the way biopower, bioethics and biopolitics are currently reconfiguring the boundaries of life" (Stephen &Sellberg, 2019). Critical models of alternatives in binary approaches of life (and death) are sought by Hinton (2017) who proposes "a concept of life as a generative force that emerges within the friction between opposing concepts,. . . . . . stepping out of the shifting boundaries linking life and death." Foucault argues that "biopolitics" not only refers to the political structures but also offers the possibility of escaping and resisting these power formations. Somatechnics of life and death extends to transgender histories and future with its methodological and conceptual challenges. The meaning of being alive is reconstructed through the new boundaries, stories, and emotions of life and death.

Gender-Sensitive Trends in Diagnosis and Therapy

Psychology's trend of using male-based norms in defining healthy versus problem behavior was reflected in the early versions of international classificatory systems of mental illness, particularly DSM, which have been criticized for perpetuating stereotypical behaviors, medicalizing normal female functions, and making women more susceptible to diagnosis and the gender bias surrounding the description of personality disorders (Brannon, 2017). Enns (2000) summarizes early writings on feminist therapies as arguing that such diagnostic labels "reflect the inappropriate application of social power, minimize the impact of environmental factors on symptoms, and reduce therapists' respect for clients."

However, recent revisions in the classificatory systems create a gender inclusive platform for addressing mental health concerns. A remarkable revision brought about in DSM 5, on its release in 2013, was the change of name of Gender Identity Disorder to Gender Dysphoria and the decoupling of Gender Identity Disorder from the Sexual Dysfunctions and Paraphilias section with the intention of depathologizing gender identity and presenting "dysphoria" or distress as the clinical problem (Zucker et al., 2013). Similarly, the stigma arising from the intersection of transgender status and mental health and the resultant violations of human rights, healthcare needs, and legal security served as a strong impetus for WHO to rename gender identity disorders as gender incongruence in ICD 11, and it is no longer classified as a mental and behavioral disorder (Reed et al., 2016).

Eradicating gender biases and working towards the development of appropriate gender identities remain the central goal of gender-sensitive interventions that are widely represented in the mental health and therapeutic settings in diverse forms. Figure 3 represents the different forms of gender-sensitive therapies, therapeutic procedures, as well as those factors that impede effective therapy. It is to be noted that in the therapeutic process, though varied by the theoretical orientation,

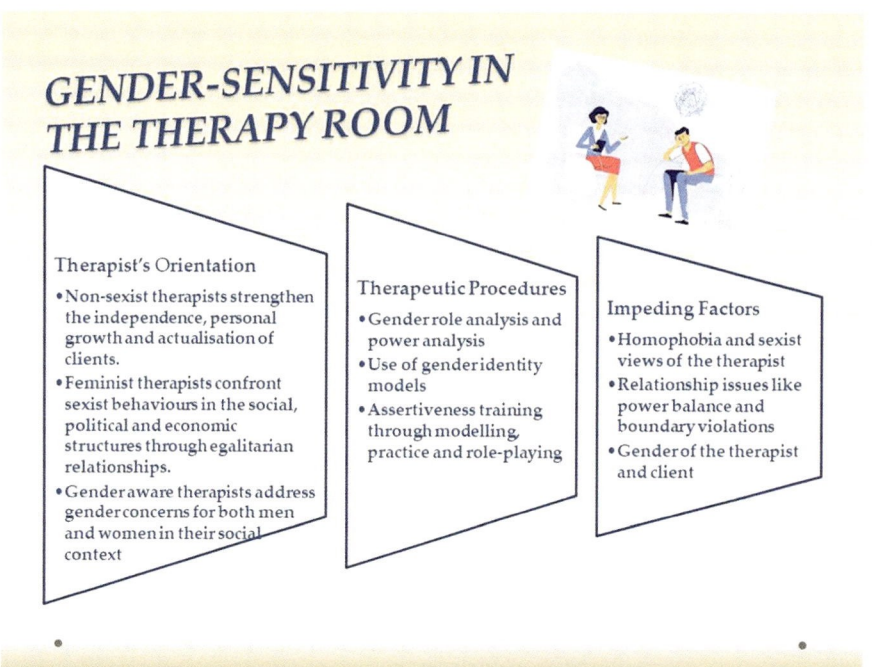

GENDER-SENSITIVITY IN THE THERAPY ROOM

Therapist's Orientation
- Non-sexist therapists strengthen the independence, personal growth and actualisation of clients.
- Feminist therapists confront sexist behaviours in the social, political and economic structures through egalitarian relationships.
- Gender aware therapists address gender concerns for both men and women in their social context

Therapeutic Procedures
- Gender role analysis and power analysis
- Use of gender identity models
- Assertiveness training through modelling, practice and role-playing

Impeding Factors
- Homophobia and sexist views of the therapist
- Relationship issues like power balance and boundary violations
- Gender of the therapist and client

Fig. 3 Gender-sensitive trends and practices in therapy. (Source: Enns, 2000)

nuances of confirming gendered messages and reinforcing power differentials and stereotypical behaviors are widely observed. Contemporary forms of sexism, including neosexism, ambivalent sexism, and modern sexism, do not openly endorse gender discrimination, but make it unrecognized within cultural norms (Enns, 2000). The release of "APA Guidelines for Psychological Practice with Girls and Women," "Guidelines for Psychological Practice with Boys and Men," and "Guidelines for Psychological Practice with Transgender and Gender Non-conforming People" is seen as instrumental in empowering clients, systematizing therapeutic care, removing stigma, and guiding towards a future of fluidity and pluralism.

In a world constructed by heterosexuals, where lesbian, gay, or bisexual individuals are subjugated to silence, shame, prejudice, homophobia, pathology, and stigma, affirming their sexuality becomes the vital point of their existence and dignity. Ramada and Chakravarthy (2013) describe Gay Affirmative Counselling Practice (GACP) to address their unique issues and stressors difficulties with self-acceptance, coming out of the notions of compulsory heterosexuality, invisibility or hiding self, discrimination, and harassment and relationship issues. In the resource and training manual for GACP, the authors give exercises for counsellors to get nuances of the experiences of homo avoidance and methods to develop gay affirmative language and promote self-acceptance of their gay clients.

Facts and Beyond

Female Counsellors to Male Clients: Gender Matters!

In the thesis submitted to York University, Toronto, for the Graduate Program in Social Work, Robbins (1999) investigated female counsellors' experiences of working with male clients. She reported that the attitudes, assumptions, and stereotypes held about men resulted in many conflicts and dilemmas for female counsellors including guilt for their inability to empathize with men and maintain a professional stance. Even though their professional role has sanctioned their authority over the clients, the counsellors struggled to assume power due to the internalized power structures.

See Exercise No. 2 for a better understanding.

Informed by the underrepresentation of marginalized gender in the patriarchal social structure, empowerment is considered as a universal agenda in the illustration of gender equality.

Section B: Empowerment of Marginalized Gender

Evaluating four decades of the evolution of development policy for women, Moser (1993) brings out five approaches in terms of its ability to meet needs of women which must be met to change their status in the society. *Welfare approach* emphasizes on women's reproductive roles and its links to poverty. *Equity approach* focuses on gender equality which enhanced women's civil and political rights and impacted on the social legislation in many countries. *Anti-poverty approach* enhanced women's productive role through wage work and income generation. *Efficiency approach* stresses women's reaction to the debt crises through their participation in the newly restructured economies. Women in development (WID) approaches consider the fifth approach, *empowerment* has the key focus of development programs which transforms oppressive laws and structures and represents grass root organizing of women's strategic needs.

As per the Global Gender Gap Report 2018 released by the World Economic Forum, there exists a 32% of global gender gap to be closed in the 149 countries covered. Even though the progress is in a slow phase, most countries are moving towards greater gender equality, following Iceland, which has 85% of its overall gender gap closed. The sub-indexes – educational attainment and health and survival – have almost achieved global gender equivalence with gaps 5% and 4% to be filled, respectively. Gender gap remains the broadest – 23% in Political Empowerment, which is untouched since 2017. The Economic Participation and Opportunity sub-index has 58% of gap to be closed, with 19 countries showing 50% of gender gap. In workplaces, only 34% of global managers are women, and the economic power is still in the hands of men. Implicating current trends to future, 108 years are estimated as necessary to close the average global gender gap. The most challenging gaps are in the economic (202 years) and political empowerment (107 years) indexes, while education-specific gender gap gets closed within 14 years (The Global Gender Gap Report, 2018).

The gender inequality index of the Human Development Report 2019 that measures women's empowerment in health, education, and economic status implicates that the overall progress towards gender parity is decreasing in the recent years and the gender gaps are deeper than originally thought. This trend is interpreted as a reflection of the glass ceiling effect, wherein women's progress is faster and greater when individual empowerment or social power is lower. But when it comes to enhanced capabilities that assume greater responsibilities, leaderships, and social payoffs, women fall behind. The Report also links gender inequality with the multidimensional gender social norms indices, which measure biases, prejudices, and social beliefs that impede gender equality. It is quite surprising that only 14% of women and 10% of men reported to have no gender social norm bias.

The need for proactive, strategic, and deep-rooted efforts at empowerment is strongly recommended, as changing gender roles in families, workplaces, and politics seem to have created a backlash and resistance to changing power relations. One major form of backlash and the cruellest form of women's disempowerment is violence against women, which is very well encouraged by traditional social norms. As per worldwide report, nearly a quarter of girls of age group 15–19 reported of having been victim of violence after age 15. The forms of violence vary – psychological, emotional, physical, sexual, or economic – and the digital age has opened up new space for cyber violence as well. The #MeToo and #NiUnaMenos movements are remarkable in breaking the silence and revealing the oppressive experiences of women across the globe (The Human Development Report, 2019).

Section C: Models of Empowerment

Gender equality, Goal 5 of the Sustainable Development Goals in the 2030 Agenda for Sustainable Development, has always been a global priority, and with consistent efforts of international agencies like the United Nations and other organizations for marginalized gender, extensive research, campaigning, and corrective measures are currently underway. Growing gender sensitization has initiated gender-sensitive interventions across the globe that incorporate systematic efforts at alleviating gender biases and promoting development of appropriate gender identities. Diverse areas like economics, policy-making, budgeting and resource allocation, governance, law, developmental initiatives, and healthcare have developed interventions that target gender mainstreaming through institutions or processes with heightened gender responsiveness. The upcoming discussions on prominent models of empowerment are intended to review notable initiatives in the domain of health and relationships, informed by increasing reports of gender-based and domestic violence. In addition, the emerging preventive models of empowerment in the various agents of socialization that stand critical in the social construction of gender are also compiled under various domains.

Domain A: Health and Relationships

Healthcare has witnessed an ever-growing number of grass root level gender-based interventions, and a review of 58 such interventions across the world has found out that when boys and men are actively engaged in discussion, questioning, and transformation of traditional gender scripts, changes in their attitudes and behavior related to sexual and reproductive behavior, maternal, new born and child health, fatherhood, and gender-based violence are observed, thereby reducing gender inequities (Barker et al., 2007). It is widely observed that breaking the patriarchal and stereotypical representations of gender is essential towards the promotion of mental health as well.

Successful gender-responsive interventions relevant to mental health are the Girls Circle Model practiced in the mid-1990s to build healthy relationships, skills, and resilience among girls and Stop Now and Plan (SNAP) Girls crime prevention program developed in Canada to reduce problematic behaviors. Another remarkable one is PACE's gender-responsive model for prevention and early intervention that brings gender-responsive principles into practice and targets academic progress, interpersonal skills, self-efficacy, confidence, goal-setting, and risky behaviors (Treskon & Bright, 2017). A detailed understanding of the model (see Case Study 1) renders proper insights on planning interventions with adequate attention to the multifaceted experiences of girls in their day-to-day lives.

Case Study 1

Bridging Gender-Responsive Principles and Practice: The PACE Model
PACE Center for Girls in Florida, founded in 1985, offers an important opportunity both to describe how gender-responsive principles translate to a real-world setting and to investigate whether the program accomplishes its service. The realization that girls represent about one-quarter of juvenile arrests nationwide and girls in the juvenile justice system are different from boys – in their histories, their offenses, and their experiences in the system – led PACE Center to a thorough investigation of risk factors and tailoring of intervention strategic programs. The PACE Model adopts a multiperspective approach that is trauma-based, relational, and strengths-based and imparts life skill training and health education ensuring physical and emotional safety.

PACE's gender-responsive model is specified through a set of broad principles that articulate the organization's overall mission and approach and a manual that provides particulars about how services should be provided. PACE provides its staff – managers, counselors, teachers, and support staff – with comprehensive training on its model and conducts ongoing quality assurance. PACE Center for Girls currently operates 19 nonresidential, year-round program sites across Florida for girls between the ages of 11 and

(continued)

17, who are typically struggling academically and may exhibit behavioral problems, along with other risk factors for delinquency. PACE is unusual among gender-responsive programs in that it is a prevention and early intervention model, serving those at risk as well as those already involved with the justice system. Girls live primarily at home and attend PACE daily during normal school hours and receive academic and social services. Parents and guardians participate in intake activities, including visiting the center before a girl's enrollment.

Impact studies show that girls loved the safe place as the staff treated and cared them lot and counselors were able to recognize their potentials and gain self-esteem and also the girls had a personal time with them. PACE provides one example of how gender-responsive principles can be put into action. Research found that PACE was successful in implementing its model as planned, owing to an approach that specified the intended program components and focused on training staff.

Reflective Questions:

1. Have you noticed any violations of law by girl children of your town?
2. What do you think are the unique factors that lead girl children in your town to such violations and ultimately to judicial custody?
3. What are the major obstacles that you face when attempting to intervene with such children?
4. Have you come across any activities or organizations who target the behavioral and emotional needs of such children?
5. If yes, how far they have been successful? Why or why not?

The social existence of human beings is nurtured by appropriate interpersonal exchanges in culturally driven ways, and violations of the appropriateness mark traumatic impacts on their psychological functioning. Internalized gender norms play their part in interpersonal exchanges, as established by the study of Zimmerman and West (1975) where they observed gender differences in the interruptions and turn-taking behaviors in conversations, that is, men interrupted more often than women in cross-sex conversations. With the rationale that interpersonal abuse and mental health are interrelated in a negatively correlated manner so that efforts to prevent interpersonal abuse will contribute to enhance mental health and efforts to actively promote mental health will pave way to prevent interpersonal abuse, Muktha Foundation from Bangalore, India, commits to prevent all forms of interpersonal abuse and promote mental health. Founded in 2017, the Foundation constitutes mental health professionals, social workers, lawyers, affiliates, and volunteers from diverse domains as its team members.

(continued)

The foundation developed "I-CARE" model which enables community members to identify those in distress, connect with them, and offer preliminary psychological support and guidance to survivors of abuse and trauma. I-CARE is an acronym which stands for Identify, Connect, Acknowledge, Refer, and Engage. Different therapists associated with Muktha Foundation employ the 4Cs (Calm, Contain, Care, Cope) proposed by Kimberg and Wheeler (2019) in the trauma-informed care approach and response-based therapeutic practice, alongside expressive therapy-based interventions and positive psychological interventions in their individual and group work with survivors of abuse and trauma. Read Case Study 2 for a detailed understanding on how expressive artistic therapies empower women undergoing critical life experiences.

Case Study 2

Women, Mothers, and Stories
Siewert (2019) provides an outcome of how the artistic experience can enhance the learning of self-knowledge, respect, and listening to the other through playback theater, i.e., a relational form of theater while explaining the status of violence against women in Brazil that one in three women suffered some type of violence in 2017 in Brazil (Santos, 2017 cited in Siewert, 2019). Siewert (2019) brings up the need to guide actions of institutions and research. Siewert, being an actor and a conductor in playback theater, in her 8 months pregnancy realized the power over her body through narrative about motherhood in a solo show in a Dionisos Teatro Project, a theater group. The woman as the protagonist of these processes, she met with different view of pregnancy and childbirth which resulted in the birth of DeMaes playback theater, to share stories among mothers which rely on feminine empowerment as the central concept.

DeMaes, a woman's consciousness raising group, heard the stories of childbirth, post-partum depression, somatization, sexual harassment, maternal guilt, sexuality, separation, obstetric violence and stories of solidarity among women, pride of children, and over coming. Differing from the traditional pattern of playback theater, DeMaes included and expected mother with their children in learning the short forms (fluid sculpture, transition and pairs), the improvisation of stories, and the work of music. "Later during the performances, the situation was repeated; babies on the scene, children in music, actresses having to leave the stage sometimes" …. the leave learned a new way of generating empathy that mothers with their children need to have their space.

It is a complex artistic practice to discuss feelings, beliefs, romantics, and judgements.

(continued)

Voices of Members

"During the months of the workshop I heard stories of abuse, violence and abandonment with truths that remain latent in my memory. Just as I also heard stories of achievement, joys and lots of love! To see the other, too hear the other, really, as equals, teaches us to be more human and to better understand and respect our feminine and maternal essence, without so many guilts and judgments. (. . .) Throughout the classes we formed a beautiful and diverse group of women and children. And yes, the fact that our children could be there, with us, being a part of it, was fundamental to finding that bond and also the balance needed to deal with such deep and complex issues".

"Being able to share the difficulties of motherhood and being a woman with other women, from different realities and contexts, brought us closer together because we had the opportunity to know ourselves better in the pains and joys of being a mother/woman. Especially, the difficulties, because positive things are easier to share with other people. In this space, it was possible to hear and be heard".

On the personal level, Siewert (2019) comments that the empowerment of women refers here to the process of achieving autonomy and self-determination, while at the political level, it concerns the development of women's political and social strength as a group or minority. But one depends on the other, both working towards the liberation of women from the bonds of patriarchal gender oppression (Sardenberg, 2018 cited in Siewert, 2019). Sardenberg (2018) stresses the fundamental role of feminine empowerment in women's consciousness-raising groups which emphasizes collective action and personal growth.

Reflective Questions:

1. What do you think are the advantages of artistic and narrative models of empowering women?
2. Does your culture offer a space for women to express themselves?
3. How can you, as a gender-informed professional, intervene in your culture to create a welcoming space for the self-expression of women?
4. Are there any consciousness-raising groups who work in your town to encourage women's voices to be heard?
5. What do you think about the practicability of applying such artistic and self-expressive models to empowering gender non-conforming people?

The therapeutic platform is always open for innovations, which are created by the empathetic therapist's concern, commitment, perseverance, and skill to tackle challenges. Getting to know about innovative practices is inspiring for budding professionals to explore their possibilities, address issues through multiple perspectives, examine available resources for their utility, and deliver effective

(continued)

mental health support. One of its kind, the Man Therapy Campaign becomes a perfect example on how the invincible problem of therapy with men was tackled through a change of perspective – manly stereotypes really help in getting men talk it out! (Read Case Study 3).

Case Study 3

The Man Therapy Campaign: Taming the "Tough Guy" Script

Therapy with men is widely acknowledged as far more challenging, primarily due to the incongruence of help-seeking behaviors with traditional masculine gender scripts. The Man Therapy Campaign (Spencer-Thomas et al., 2012) presents an innovative and humorous approach to tackle social norms surrounding men's unwillingness to access therapy and disclose themselves, even in desperation. Launched by the combined efforts of multiple agencies including Colorado Office of Suicide Prevention and Cactus, Man Therapy addresses the booming rates of suicides among working men in the USA. In its interactive web portal, men in distress meet a witty and humorous fictional therapist named Dr. Rich Mahogany, who lets men know that talking out is the initial step to solving problems, encourages them in honest talk and self-assessment, and provides "manly mental health tips" and referrals to professionals, if needed.

Systematic research behind the campaign advocates few approaches that are pivotal in getting men talk about their problems and fix themselves. Avoiding the mental health language, using role models of hope and recovery, connecting physical symptoms with emotional issues, situating communication at the point clients stand, and offering opportunities to make meaning in life through volunteering or spiritual growth are part of the wide array of actions that support men and their loved ones along the process of recovery. The campaign was widely welcomed by men for being humorous, reassuring, and manly (Spencer-Thomas et al., 2014). Following the trend, Australia and Wisconsin developed their own versions of Man Therapy.

Reflective Questions

1. What are the traditional masculine gender norms that restrict men from seeking help?
2. What are the differences in the way gender stereotyping has influenced men and other genders?
3. How do men in your culture cope with the stress related to gender stereotyping?

(continued)

4. 'Manly stereotypes really help in getting men talk it out!' - do you think that the therapist's adherence to stereotypes can build a gender-informed community of men?
5. Are the people in your culture receptive to innovative technology-driven interventions?

Recent discourses on gender inclusiveness, powered by activist movements across the world, unanimously blame the field of psychology for constructing and maintaining the oppressive structures against gender non-conforming people. However, mental health practitioners in India have now developed great interests in extending services to those non-heterosexual individuals, obviously due to the decriminalization of homosexuality declared by the revoking of Section 377 of Indian Penal Code.

In this context, the Mariwala Health Initiative (MHI), a Mumbai-based funding agency for promoting innovative mental health initiatives in the marginalized communities, questioned dominant approaches to sexuality in the mental health practice sector for their ethical work with queer clients (Chakravarty, 2018). Noticing the lack of an authentic curriculum for experiential training, MHI developed a 6-day certificate course on Queer Affirmative Counselling Practice (QACP) that provided mental health practitioners with an opportunity for perspective building – to recognize marginalization of LGBTQIA+ individuals, reorient towards anti-oppressive therapeutic practice, and reflect on the need for politicizing mental health promotions. In the first 6 months, over 50 mental health professionals were provided with the perspectives and tools to make their practice queer-affirmative. The authenticity of queer-affirmative knowledge being delivered through the course is assured by the fact that it was generated from the realities, struggles, and politics of queer people in India, as against the dominant narratives of queer and sexuality (Chakravarty, 2018). MHI's approach to training and practice serves as an educative model for pursuing authentic and valid mental health practice, in general as well as in marginalized communities.

Domain B: Agents of Socialization: Educational Resources

Interlinking the two prominent Sustainable Development Goals in the 2030 Agenda for Sustainable Development, Education Progress, and Gender Equality, the 2016 Global Education Monitoring Report published by UNESCO introduced an evidence-based monitoring framework to focus on gender parity in education participation and attainment and education system characteristics, in the broader socioeconomic context. The 2019 Gender Report summarizes the existing scenario of gender parity in education worldwide, identifies the priority areas to work on, and provides substantial recommendations to identify aids in education that create sustainable results (UNESCO, 2019). According to the Report, despite progress, especially in Central and Southern Asia, a major proportion of countries still lack gender parity in education enrolment across primary and secondary levels, while in the education completion rates, poverty worsens the disadvantage of girls.

The Report identifies discriminatory social institutions, practices, and norms as "harmful," referring to popular beliefs like "a university education is more important for a boy." With the alarming finding that 117 countries and territories still have not abolished child marriage, the need for strong political action and policy reforms is raised as the inevitable ingredients for achieving gender parity. Lack of gender-inclusiveness in structural education system, as evident in reports on school-related gender-based violence, lack of sanitation facilities for menstrual hygiene, inadequate deployment of female teachers, and lack of gender-sensitive teaching are noted as major constraints. Further, the report advances the need for comprehensive sexuality education that expands education opportunities and questions gender norms and stereotypes in the classroom. An analysis of the donor aid to gender equality in education in 20 countries for their key priorities revealed that cash and in-kind transfers are the most popular policy, while reforms in curriculum and textbook content, girls' participation in STEM courses, and safe access to schools are the least popular priorities (UNESCO, 2019).

Facts and Beyond

Gender Bias in Fairytales, Media, and Schools: A Personal Perspective

Biwei Huang who worked at the Centre for Mental Health in Schools at the University of California, Los Angeles (UCLA), had a particular interest in gender bias and narrates her personal perspective about gender bias in traditional fairy tales, media, and also school settings. Fairytales are one of the most important parts of childhood life, especially for girls. The story will be usually of a beautiful princess portrayed as fair, young, and slim, who is trapped by a dark, ugly, fat, evil woman and is waiting for a brave handsome prince who will fight with the evil, rescue her, and finally marry her. Similarly, in popular children's movies, stereotypical portrayal of female characters underscore *"the idea that women are valued by men mainly for their bodies"* (Huang, n.d.). Such biased representations, not often glorified as in fairytales, penetrate into education as well. Pictures in textbooks portraying a female nurse and male doctor; classroom discussions that require girls to be passive, non-assertive, and quiet; and socialization activities that require gender-based grouping are examples of how gender stereotypes are perpetuated in education.
Go to Exercise No. 3 for reflection.

Emerging trends informed by social learning theory and gender schema theory and supportive research on the harm effects of gender stereotyping have created gender-inclusive practices in education across the world. The Vietnamese Education Sector as part of eliminating gender disparities has considered recommendations of the Gender Equality and Girls' Education Initiative in Viet Nam project (2015–2017) under the UNESCO Malala Fund for Girls' Right to Education to mainstream gender equity into educational planning, management, and policy-making (UNESCO, 2018), The curriculum developers trained in the project worked with the Ministry of Education and Training and revised textbooks for primary and secondary education to eliminate content that perpetuate gender discrimination and bias. Another remarkable step by the School Education Department of Tamil Nadu, India, to sensitize youth about gender non-conforming community, a chapter on the success story of the renowned transgender Bharatanatyam dancer, Ms. Narthaki Natarajhas has been included in the Tamil language textbook at the higher secondary level (Kolappan, 2018) (Fig. 4).

As stated by the definition about "gender competence" by the Gender Competence Centre Berlin (2006), the incorporation of a gender perspective in teaching and learning requires "will," "knowledge," and "ability" – the will to execute gender-fair

Fig. 4 Proposed suggestions for revision in the textbooks of Vietnamese Education Sector. (Source: UNESCO, 2018)

curricula, the familiarity with new gender-sensitive content, and the ability for structural change. The Bologna process model introduces concrete organizational forms of how to incorporate these subject matters into both teaching and studying (see Case Study 4).

Case Study 4

The Bologna Process: A Challenge for Gender and Academic Policy
The Bologna process model namely "Women's and Gender Studies into the Curriculum" by the Women's and Gender Research Network NRW is incorporated within the framework of the "Gender in Bachelor's and Master's programs" (Kortendiek, 2011). The model, constructed from the analysis of 54 academic curricula, singles out categories for a gender-sensitive restructuring of particular disciplines, as well as three issues of interdisciplinary scope, and describes four concrete approaches to the integration of gender studies in higher education curricula, namely (1) general course objectives related to gender issues, (2) subject-specific gender studies content, (3) concrete forms of integrating gender studies content into the curriculum, and (4) the degree stage at which the particular content should be taught.

The Bologna model highlighted the importance of reflection on the gendered learning one school delivers: legitimate, marginal, or missing, particularly in the context of convincing gender gaps in work, well-being, education, and politics. Diverse statistics, in numerous nations, discusses the pervasiveness of gender gap, which should be comprehended and examined so as to adapt better. The Bologna process establishes gender balance as a criterion for studying, teaching, and strategic concepts implemented by institutions of higher education and recommendations for facilities of higher education, politicians, the accreditation council, and accreditation agencies.

Reflective Questions

1. How do you rate the educational institutions you have attended, on the importance given to gendered learning?
2. Have you attended any course in or related to gender studies as part of your higher education curriculum? If not, do you feel it as a major drawback of your educational system?
3. How did the course in gender studies influence (or is expected to influence) your academic and professional life?
4. What do your peers in other subjects think of including gender in their studies?
5. What are the ways in which you, as a gender-informed professional, can educate your peers as well as institutional authorities on incorporating gender in the pedagogy?

(continued)

Undoubtedly, gender has become fundamental determinants of life and society. This has affected the field of research also. Research and higher education institutions reproduce social values leading to gender bias. According to the "She Figures 2012" that provides different indicators on gender equality in research and innovation at pan-European level, only 33% of European researchers were women, and the percentage of female PhD graduates was also less than 50% (European Union, 2013). The prevalent male dominance is attributed to the gender-science stereotype that associates science with masculinity and the implicit gender bias that affects the judgements during selection and recruitment process (EIGE, 2016a, b).

However, the She Figures 2018 presents a relatively higher annual growth rate of doctoral graduates among women (2.3%) than men (1.4%) even though graduate women are less likely to pursue their education to doctoral level when compared to graduate men. Segregation of subject preference is also evident in doctoral research, with women underrepresenting research in information and communication technologies (21%) and engineering, manufacturing, and construction (29%). Extending to the employment of researchers, the report adds that, over the period of 2013 to 2017, underrepresentation of women in science and technology professions and reduced pay for women employed in scientific R&D activities prevail, despite marginal increases in the number of women heading higher education institutions.

Facts and Beyond

The GEAR Tool of the European Institute of Gender Equality

In the history of European Union (EU), from the treaty of Rome in 1957 to the 2009 Lisbon treaty, equality between men and women is enforced as a fundamental principle, and gender-based violence is regarded as a threat to the integrity and dignity of women and men. The European Institute of Gender Equality (EIGE) coordinates the gender mainstreaming efforts across EU and supports institutions and government bodies to adopt gender perspective with the help of several online tools. The Gender Equality in Academia and Research (GEAR) tool, one of its kind, stands relevant in the context of Horizon 2020, which is the ever-largest Research and Innovation Program of EU that serves as the financial instrument to transform EU's global competitiveness.

According to the GEAR tool, the three major objectives of gender equality in research are stated as "*fostering equality in scientific careers, ensuring gender balance in decision making processes and bodies, integrating the gender dimension in research and innovation content*" (European Institute of Gender Equality, 2016b). For achieving these objectives, an institutional change is brought about by the European Commission's Gender Equality Plan that consists of a set of actions through different phases. All stakeholders of a higher education institution are mobilized for implementing the Gender Equality Plan. Apart from overcoming the gender-biased and gender blind practices in the field of research, it helps to enhance women's representation and retention in scientific careers; prevent verbal, psychological, and physical gender-based offenses; ensure an unbiased, safe work environment; and retain the talented and potential ones irrespective of gender, hence ensuring the excellence and quality in research work (EIGE, 2016b).

See Exercise No. 4 for more insights.

The gender segregation in subject choice and underrepresentation of women in technical and professional fields continue to be an intriguing problem for educationalists striving to achieve gender equality in education. Wrote a pioneering work on breaking the stereotypical gender barriers associated with the professional areas of physical sciences, mathematics, and engineering. The suggestions revolve around rethinking the way science is taught – curricula, problem sets, laboratory exercises, and teaching techniques – to make it more appealing to women. In an Egyptian School for Girls, Mahdi and Roehrig (2019) found that support from teachers, challenging STEM curriculum, formative assessment, student-centered pedagogies, female friendly teaching, and a positive school environment were critical in enriching the potential of Egyptian female students to pursue STEM fields in higher education.

One of the preliminary initiatives, UNICEF, in partnership with the Uweso Trust and the Government of South Africa has set up the TechnoGirl mentorship program in 2005, which is an innovative job shadowing program that identified academically well-performing high school girls from disadvantaged communities. With the objective of encouraging girls' entry and learning in Science, Technology, Engineering, and Mathematics (STEM) – the technical fields critical for the economy. The program helps girls to link their academic learning with professional skills through corporate mentorship and skill development programs and make informed career choices through life skills programs that target prevention of HIV, teenage pregnancies, and gender-based violence. Currently, with its public-private partnership, TechnoGirl offers first-hand training for girls in more than 200 companies in STEM fields where women are underrepresented, along with academic scholarships (UNICEF, 2017).

Domain C: Agents of Socialization: Media

Gender and media have always caught research attention acknowledging the tremendous contribution of media towards the creation, maintenance, and eradication of gender stereotypes. Informed by developmental theories and large-scale comparative studies, media are now emerging as watchdogs of gender equality and diversity in the social, political, and economic realms. The pioneering yet long-running efforts at underscoring the representation of women in media were taken up by the Global Media Monitoring Project (GMMP) in 1995 conducted by the World Association for Christian Communication. Being the largest and longest research and advocacy initiative of gender mainstreaming in news media, the latest GMMC Report in 2015 highlights unchanging percentages of women stories in news content though marginal increases in reporting of gender inequality issues, gender-based violence, and gender stereotyping are observed. Even in digital newsrooms, women's invisibility is prominent, though stark differences in selecting news sources of same gender are seen between male and female reporters (WACC, 2015).

The 6th GMMP is currently underway and is expected to release in 2020 with promising insights on the advocacy of gender equality, particularly in the context of changing scenarios geared by massive campaigns like the #MeToo movement. The "Global Report on the Status of Women in the News Media" by the International Women's Media Foundation (2011) and the study on decision-making in media organizations by the European Institute for Gender Equality (2013) are some other prominent publications that portrayed the status of women in news media and presented important statistics as well as recommendations for advancing gender equality in the media profession.

The #MeToo movement, possibly the largest of its kind, serves as the best example of how media energized survivors of sexual harassment to open up their silenced voices against oppression and violence. This innovative and creative movement in social media traversed beyond cultural and political boundaries and questioned the patriarchal and misogynistic notions upheld by cultures. The waves touched academic discourses too, with inquiries into the factors that silenced women (Bhattacharya, 2018) and framing of the movement as a global learning moment (Regulska, 2018).

Distinctly, a deliberate attempt at mass mobilization on gender-based violence through social media was made by United Nations Development Programme (UNDP) in Costa Rica. Surrounding the 2018 presidential elections that generated heated discussions on the patriarchal norms, gender stereotyping, gender gaps in economic participation and opportunities, and gender-based violence, UNDP initiated an online social media campaign to combat discrimination against women and gender non-conforming people and promote gender equality. With the help of simple, constructive, and high-impact messaging in a series of digital video clips and an online banner campaign, the advocacy for human rights and the issues of gender-based violence reached out to more than 30,000 people in the social media under the hashtag "#NoDejarNadieAtras." Alliances with NGOs, digital news outlets, LGBTI and feminist organizations, faith-based organizations, and traditional media platforms heightened the impact of the campaign and augmented the continuing efforts of UNDP in the country to prevent gender-based discrimination and violence and promote gender equity (UNDP, 2019).

UNESCO in 2012 has released "Framework of Indicators to Gauge Gender Sensitivity in Media Operations and Content" which underlined the best practices for incorporating gender perspective in the operations of media of all forms and the media content. These non-prescriptive indicators serve as general guidelines for all media institutions to make necessary adaptations so that gender equality becomes more transparent and comprehensible to the public as well as to reflect and enhance gender-sensitive responsiveness in their internal policies and practices. The publication describes the indicators and the means of verification under several strategic objectives that include gender balance among decision makers of media managements, gender equality in work conditions, equal pay, safe environments, gender equality in the unions, clubs and associations of media personnel and other media self-regulatory bodies, editorial policies or initiatives for promoting gender-conscious journalists, and gender equality awareness training for teachers/trainers and students pursuing studies in communication and media.

Pertaining to the content of media, specifically news and advertising, fair, representative, balanced, and non-stereotypical portrayal of gender and coverage of gender equity issues and gender-based violence with accurate and holistic understanding are also addressed. Case studies about the gender mainstreaming efforts of media organizations from across the world, including Asia-Pacific region, the Caribbean region, Europe, Arab states, and Latin America, have also been included (UNESCO, 2012).

Facts and Beyond

The Super Prepared Asian Mother

The theme of gender neutrality strikes cultures worldwide where parenting itself marks a transition with non-traditional family models on the rise. Mothering Excellence (Roy & Sharma, 2019) is a two-part research study (in 2015 and 2018) across eleven markets in Asia to identify key trends and changes in manifestations of mothers' brand preferences and thereby delve deeper into the core motivations of Asian mothers. In 2018, the study was updated with key emerging trends in mothering behavior, the new tensions, and unique coping strategies. The "super prepared Asian mother" is depicted as the one who "*f*inds her inner child," "*e*xpresses her identity," and "*i*s paddling furiously." Her independent and experimental mothering strategies are parting with traditions, as she chases fun and interests of her own. She wisely manages her mothering duties by delegating tasks to the father, grandparents, babysitters, and helpers. For marketers, the shift holds plenty of possibilities, including legitimizing the fun aspect of traditionally hectic family moments such as the morning breakfast and acting as enablers of experiences that showcase her self-expression. The study directs marketers to take heed to emphasize boldness and spontaneity in their communications – and do away with the mum shaming rhetoric and guilt tonality. It counts on the four ways to win over Asian mothers – "Be her inspiration, be her voice for change, be her anchor, be her productivity ally."

Go to Exercise No. 5 for a critical review.

Domain D: Agents of Socialization: Occupation

The gendered nature of segregations and discriminations at work has its roots in the stereotypes about masculine and feminine emotions, those that attribute men with agentic traits and women with communal traits. The differential emotional competencies in turn lead to distinct resources and mechanisms for dealing with psychosocial risks and workplace stressors. Consistent with this idea, Gartzia et al. (2019) critically examine literature on psychosocial risks at work from a gender perspective to find that emotional competencies are critical in dealing with such risks and propose emotional androgyny as a potential resource for dealing with the dynamics and complexities of work environments.

There is yet another way of relating gender to work. A person's subjective sense of well-being is largely a matter of gendered socialization, and work-life balance is a consistent contributor that sustains and distorts one's well-being. Bernard (2019) looked up at subjective well-being, though a popular research variable with numerous quantitative assessment measures, from a gender perspective and conducted a socio-analytic inquiry into work-life experiences of women in their midlife. From the data gathered through social dream drawings and interpreted through phenomenological hermeneutic analysis, the author developed metaphors that reflect women's subjective well-being, which is continually being challenged by their projective identifications with internalized gender role norms on work-life balance. Proposing well-being as a dynamic phenomenon, the author concludes with a note to organizations about the significance of creating self-reflective spaces within them to enhance women's well-being.

The International Trade Union Confederation (ITUC) World Congress in Copenhagen has propounded an ambitious mandate based on four pillars of action, "equality" being the fourth, to frame strategic plans for 2022. The fourth pillar stood for bringing up a feminist agenda to facilitate economic integration of women through equal economic participation in the labor market, women's leadership, organizing against discrimination and exclusion, and eradication of violence and harassment in the world of work. One of its three frontline campaigns is a New Social Contract between governments, workers, and business to ensure protection from harassment, equal pay, and economic participation of women, in the light of diminishing trust on the global economic model (ITUC, 2019).

The Violence and Harassment Convention 2019 of the International Labor Organization (ILO) was the product of massive campaigning by ITUC. It adopts an "inclusive, integrated and gender-responsive approach" and calls for all ILO member states to "address violence and harrassment in the world of work in labor and employment, occupational safety and health, equality and non-discrimination law, and in criminal law, where appropriate" (ILO, 2019). ITUC plans for 2020 are ratification and implementation of the 2019 Convention and inclusion of its contents in collective bargaining, social dialogue, and policy, primarily through regional campaigns for social protection and minimum wages, leadership training for women, and exposing the injustices in working women's lives (ITUC, 2019). Johnson and Otto's Integrative model serves a good example of locating, analyzing, and alleviating gender-based discrimination and harassment at workplace (see Case Study 5).

Instances of exclusion, discrimination, and harassment against LGBTI+ individuals are widely prevalent throughout the stages of the employment cycle – education, access to work, work environments, and job security. However, the last 20 years have witnessed many countries bringing up policies for protecting them for non-discrimination, thanks to the rigorous efforts of several NGOs and LGBTI+ groups and the recognition of such discrimination as a violation of human rights by the international human rights law framework and UN Conventions. The "Information Paper on Protection against Sexual Orientation, Gender Identity and Expression and Sexual Characteristics (SOGIESC) Discrimination" (Thomas & Weber, 2019) reports that 18 countries in North America, Latin America, and the Caribbean; 17 countries in Asia, Pacific, and Arab States; 7 countries in Africa; and 42 countries in Europe are waiving off discriminatory laws and practices against LGBTI+ persons prevalent in the employment sector. The paper extensively analyzes the policies and practices of the member states of ILO based on SOGIESC dimensions, with prime focus on discrimination in employment and occupation, with key remarks on issues like law enforcement and access to justice.

Case Study 5

An Integrative Model for Gender Equality in the Workplace
The term gender-based discrimination and harassment (GBDH) represents multiple manifestations of sexism and heterosexism and takes up different forms in the workplace from sexual harassment to gender microaggressions and other disguised forms. Johnson and Otto (2019) venture out to analyze the antecedents and consequences of GBDH towards women and LGBTQ community in the workplace and developed an integrative model (Fig. 5).

With this model, Johnson and Otto (2019) have thrown some important insights on employing organizational resources to neutralize existing mechanisms that perpetuate gender oppression and framing gender and sexuality in inclusive ways. Further, an integration of queer and feministic perspectives with the intersectional approach will help individuals with multiple marginalized identities to have inclusive and respectful working environments. Johnson and Otto (2019) comment on the synergy of the intersectional, queer, and feminist approaches as follows:

Applying these complementary approaches helps to analyse how women and people from the LGBTQ community are defined (e.g., deconstructivist approach), essentialized (e.g., deconstructivist and intracategorical approaches), and oppressed by social actors (e.g., intercategorical approach) and institutionalized sexism. It also allows the analysis of the oppression reinforced by members of the dominant group (intercategorical approach), as well as by minority members that enjoy other forms of privilege (e.g., white privilege), and endorse hegemonic values (deconstructivist and intracategorical approaches). In addition, the analyses within the inter- and intra-categorical framework allow approaching the problems faced by

(continued)

individuals in the intersections between sexism, heterosexism, cissexism, and monosexism (e.g., transgender women, lesbians, bisexuals), as well as considering the way classism, racism, ableism, and ethnocentrism shape their experiences (e.g., disabled women, transgender men of color).

Imagine yourself as a psychology professional, sent for an assignment of supporting HR managers to combat GBDH in a corporate company.

1. What are the specific elements that you will look up in the databases of the employees to plan your assignment?
2. What are the ways in which you can sensitize employees and company heads about GBDH in its micro and disguised forms?
3. How will you convince the company heads to change the organizational climate and policies so as to create an inclusive space?
4. Prepare a flowchart that shows the action plan of your assignment.
5. How will you evaluate the effectiveness of your intervention, with respect to the outcomes of health and occupational well-being?

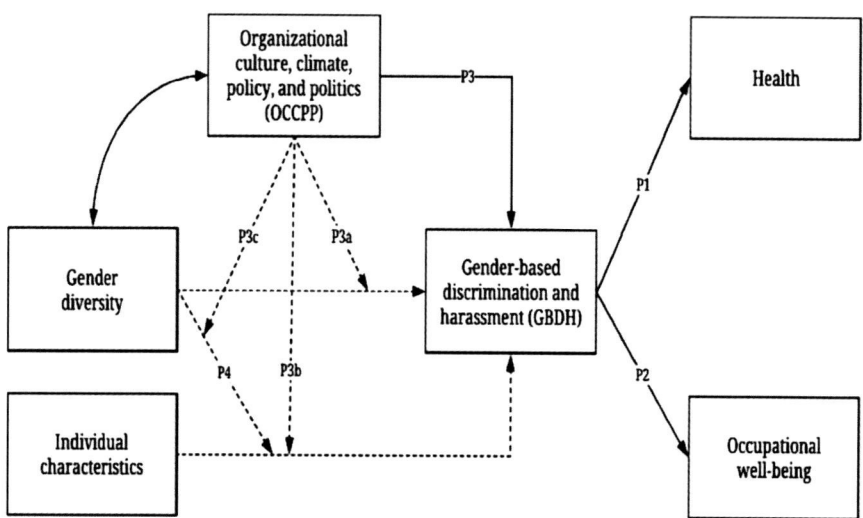

An integrated model of GBDH in the workplace. Continuous paths represent direct relationships. Dashed paths represent fully moderated relationships. The double-ended arrow signals the relationship between gender diversity and OCCPP, which follows a circular causation logic.

Fig. 5 An integrative model of gender equality in the workplace for HRM academics and practitioners

Domain E: Agents of Socialization: Government/Policy-Making Models

The latest ever report that analyses the laws and regulations in 190 economies that influence the economic opportunities of women is the "Women, Business and the Law 2020." The pace of policy reforms along the eight indicators that align with the economic decisions of women throughout their lives – mobility, workplace, pay, marriage, parenthood, entrepreneurship, assets and pension – is traced over the last 50 years. The trend is definitely progressive, and women now hold around three quarter of the rights of men in the measured indicators. Parenthood and Pay are the indicators in which economies have reformed the most; still they have the largest gaps to be closed. The report thus provides the benchmark of the regulatory environments that restrict women from work and business and projects on to the changes that can potentially enact smart economic policies that equally achieve gender equity and economic development.

In many international conferences such as Beijing Platform for Action, the Beijing +5 Declaration and Resolution, the Cairo Program of Action, the Millennium Declaration, and the Convention on the Elimination of All Forms of Discrimination against Women have made policy statements on the international development agenda (Warsi & Chaudhury, 2014). Warsi and Chaudhury (2014) support democratic decentralization as good governance to increase participation of women in political decision-making structures from the grass root levels of governance. They bring up the challenge of involving women in politics especially when the provision of co-option of two women in Panchayati Raj Institution System (PRI) is existing in India since October 2, 1959. It has been observed that women are bound to confirm in their patriarchal male-dominated family with the primary identities of wife and/or mother. This has been projected as their lack of knowledge or interest to participate in the political scenario. Therefore, political decisions taken by the male representatives in India have overlooked and underestimated the oppression-related issues faced by women in general. Rudimentary attitudinal change in family system, the smallest unit in society, and other structural socializing agencies could be brought through imparting psychosocial education in local governance itself.

Participation of people irrespective of gender in the process of development of a country and to improve per capita income has led to the "empowerment approach" of women to narrow the gender gaps in social achievement. The process of Participatory Planning, which began in Kerala about two decades ago, opened up the opportunity to the people in designing the destiny of the state, in terms of local level plan. While discussing the policy approach to women in planning in Kerala, argue that with the Ninth Plan formulation and the introduction of Women's Component Plan (WCP) of Government of Kerala named People's Planning Campaign, Kerala makes a decisive break in the history of Indian planning in the approach to women in development. However, decentralization need not necessarily lead to greater gender injustice, according to the study by, but it does open up new opportunities for intervention, particularly, given the one-third reservation for women in LSGIs (Local Self Governments) (cited from Deepthi, 2014).

Gender socialization in Indian families has multiple levels of consequences which even lead to reproductive role of women and unequal sharing of household responsibilities between men and women and the impact of decision-making and control over resources which continue to perpetuate women's social and economic vulnerability (Eapen, 2004). As a response to the gender gap obvious in social development areas in Kerala. She points out that due to the rising visibility of gender-based violence, in particular, domestic violence, Kerala's uneven social development is very often linked to dowry demands, mental ill-health manifested increasingly as suicide, downtrends in women's property rights, and rapid growth and spread of dowry, even as levels of education could not break down patriarchal structures which needs to move beyond gender parity in literacy rates to the gender differentiated patterns of education and skill acquisition and its impact on employment and earnings.

There are instances existing in a patriarchal family context wherein the state mechanisms need to intervene the family issues to sort them out. Two such mechanisms (see Case Study 6) are brought here to explain its effectiveness.

Case Study 6

The Kudumbashree Model of Gender and Social Change
The State Poverty Eradication Mission of the Government of Kerala, India, implemented a poverty eradication and women empowerment program in 1997 named Kudumbashree, with an extensive women community network. With the integration of gender analysis in its approach, Kudumbashree initiated several interventions to promote gender equality, centering on the three interlocking dimensions – prevention of gender-based violence and discriminations, support for reclaiming rights, and transformation of mind-sets towards gender equality. The Kudumbashree model of gender and social change evolved to be a cyclical and dynamic process along the stages of analysis and planning, community initiatives like gender self-learning program and vulnerability mapping, demand for legislations and institutions, and enabling community-based responses.

Kudumbashree' s foundational work, the Gender Self Learning Program (GSLP), sensitizes lakhs of women in local groups about their rights and supports them to reconstruct their own worlds in terms of employment, health, mobility, and gender qquity. Gender resource centers are established at Panchayat/village level to integrate gender problems into governance. Another initiative is the Snehitha Gender Help Desk, a 24x7 service that offers temporary shelter, counselling services, and legal support for women experiencing violence. Moreover, the Rangashree Community Theater, a network of

(continued)

women's theatre groups, provides liberating opportunities to render performances on social issues.

With its 70,000+ vigilant group members, 2200 gender resource persons, and 350 community counsellors, Kudumbashree has been successful in Kerala to reduce violence against women and increase women's income, their access and control over income, and their participation in non-traditional jobs/roles. Another major accomplishment is an increase in the number of men who are sensitive to women's needs.

Jaagratha Samithi: Vigilance Against Violence.

Case 1: A woman who belong to a lower caste got married to a man in the upper caste, at both of their consent but without the consent of their parents. Later, her husband and mother-in-law tortured her at home, but she was tolerating the torments silently. Jaagratha Samithi took suo moto cognizance of the issues. The Samithi called all the parties for hearing, and separate counselling sessions were given to them. The husband and the mother-in-law finally accepted their mistake and promoted not to harass her again. Several follow-ups were conducted so as to make sure that the family conducted so as to make sure that the family has sorted out the issues and us lining happily.

Jaagratha Samithi means vigilance committee constituted by Kerala State Women's Commission (KWC) to address to the atrocities against girls and women. As per the State Crime Record Bureau, crime against women has increased from a total no. of 9381 in 2007 to 13,002 in2012. Studies done by INCLEN and ICRW domestic violence in Kerala found that as high as 62.3% and 61.61% of the women in Kerala are subjected to physical torture and mental harassment to as compared to 37% and 35.5% at the national level. Jaagratha Samithis are headed by the District Collectors and have representatives from police department, social welfare, and other judicial aids. Built on the principles of gender equity and justice, the Samithi lifts up the local support by strengthening the networks available at the local level and coordinates the different networking systems to arrive at a proper solution (Anon, 2007). Jaagratha Samithi has marked their effectiveness in settling civil, criminal, and family issues through confidentiality, accessibility, immediacy, and integrity and encourages no political interference.

Reflective Questions

1. What are the methods adopted by local bodies and community workers in your country in addressing gender-based and domestic violence?
2. How far community level gender sensitive interventions are initiated and coordinated successfully in your country?
3. Are such mechanisms vigilant and capable enough to identify those silenced voices of domestic violence and bring them to the Judiciary?

(continued)

4. What do you think is the role of men in combating gender discrimination and gender-based violence at the grass root level?
5. Can you critically examine the possibility of applying similar mechanisms to address the discrimination and violence faced by gender non-conforming people?

International Lesbian, Gay, Bisexual, Trans, and Intersex Association (ILGA World) publishes annually an update of the Global Legislation Overview of the State-Sponsored Homophobia report, which tracks the laws surrounding sexual orientation across the world. Its 2019 update covers provisions and laws categorized into criminalization (of consensual same-sex sexual acts), restriction (to freedom of expression on SOGIESC issues and formation of association like sexual orientation related civil society organizations), protection (from discrimination at different levels), and recognition (of same-sex marriages, joint adoptions, and second parent adoptions). Extensive accounts of global legislations are listed with summarized findings that project a progressive trend towards gender equality. However, the report communicates an uncanny feeling, of a new wave of resistance by conspiring conservative actors, as observed in certain countries, particularly those with a declining trend (ILGA World, 2019). The edited monograph "Anti-Gender Campaigns in Europe: Mobilizing against Equality" adopts a "transnational and comparative approach" to understanding gender mobilizations, set along the lines of religious politics, in contemporary Europe (Kuhar & Paternotte, 2017).

Facts and Beyond

Gender Impact Assessment: A Reflective Practice

Gender impact assessment (GIA) is another EIGE tool, which serves as a timely function for all institutional structures to enable reflection on their own practices through the lens of gender mainstreaming – their current gender-related position (EIGE, 2016a). With an ex ante evaluation, in a preventive way, of the likelihood of a given decision having negative consequences for the state of equality between women and men, GIA stands relevant in the early stages of policy-making to support policy design as well as its planning. There are different ways to carry out a GIA, depending on the institutional settings and different people involved. Irrespective of the approach, GIA proceeds through five main steps – definition of the policy in connection with gender equality, checking gender relevance, gender-sensitive analysis of the potential impact, weighing the gender impact, and findings and proposals for improvement.

Undoubtedly, GIA serves as the explicit model for policy-makers and public servants to analyze and improve their gender capacity and make gender-informed decisions especially during budget allocation and policy implementations. When gender equality has emerged as a universal agenda and gender mainstreaming occupies a prominent space in institutional declarations worldwide, evaluative mechanisms like GIA stand highly relevant, lighting up the way towards practical action, rather than formal commitment and structures. Such mechanisms are so insightful, though not always preferred, as they unravel the invisible effects of long-held gender stereotypes and discriminatory practices embedded within the tradition of any institution or culture.

See Exercise No. 6 for a critical analysis.

Conclusion

Psychology as a discipline can contribute towards the subtleties of gender construction of self and can provide better insights and directions to gender studies by reworking on the existing gender biases in the discipline. Gender discourses in multidisciplinary arena promise new avenues to the intersectional approaches of gender studies in psychology.

Despite the diversity in the range of actions, the WHO underlines the major shortcomings of lack of evaluative measures that study the effectiveness of diverse programs; lack of attempts at primary prevention, when compared to secondary and tertiary prevention, under emphasis of community and societal programs; and the need for developing or adapting programs for developing countries. Scientific and comprehensive violence prevention is proposed as the single solution for violence (WHO, 2002). Best practices for professionals helping with gender-based violence are suggested including personal therapy and extensive self-work as a strong tool for enhanced awareness of one's own sexist attitudes and beliefs as well as to deal with emotional exhaustion, fatigue, and other psychological issues. It is worth commenting that mindfulness enables counsellors to become aware of self, meet the diverse demands of counselling, and reduce burnout. Friedman (2017) reports that practicing mindfulness techniques has supported counsellors to improve their self-awareness, cognitive empathy and flexibility, resilience, self-efficacy, tolerance for difficult emotions, resistance to burnout, and overall well-being. Professionals should also get equipped with the necessary experience, awareness, and accessibility to resources that aid transformations of gendered attitudes and behaviors. Especially when working with gender non-conforming clients, the APA guidelines guide psychologists to acquaint themselves with different mental health, educational, and community resources and to pursue education course work for increased awareness of their unique needs and extending training, supervision, consultation, and guidance (American Psychological Association, 2015).

Exercises

1. Reflect upon the multiple social identities you carry and how they intersect with your gender in shaping the specific experiences of daily living.
2. Imagine yourself as a trained counsellor capable of handling complex issues in families and marriages. As the first case on a fine morning, you met a client of your same gender, and later, you saw a client of different gender from you. Compare and contrast the distinct attitudes, expectations, judgements, and behaviors you held and performed for clients of the same and different gender.
3. List down the favorite stories you read and cartoons and movies watched in your childhood days. Recollect how they portrayed characters of different gender – their physique, social status, attitudes and values, responsibilities, privileges, and the like. Reflect upon how dominant representations have influenced your attitudes and behaviors towards people of different gender.
4. Think about the gender-biased and gender-blind practices you have carried out during the course of your undergraduate research work – right from the formulation of problem to data interpretation and thesis writing. Write down the possible alternatives you could have tried to make your research gender-neutral and gender-informed.
5. Identify those advertisements that portray modern mothers as independent, self-expressed, and inspiring and those that picturize traditional mothers. Form pairs with your classmates, and find out the differences in the presentations of the advertisements of the two types.
6. With the help of your teachers, conduct a group discussion to critically review the current gender-related position of your educational institution. The institution's declarations, governing bodies, decision-making process, traditions followed, educational resources, facilities offered, developmental activities, and redressal mechanisms can be subjected to scrutiny following the model of gender impact assessment.

References

Achieve gender equality and empower all women and girls. (2019) *Sustainable development goals.* Retrieved from https://sustainabledevelopment.un.org/sdg5

American Psychological Association. (2015). Guidelines for psychological practice with transgender and gender nonconforming people. *American Psychologist, 70*(9). https://doi.org/10.1037/a0039906

Anon. (2007). *Jaagratha Samithi: The panchayat vigilance committee for women's rights.* Thiruvananthapuram: SDC Cap-Deck.

Barker, G., Ricardo, C. &Nascimento, M. (2007). *Engaging men and boys in changing gender-based inequity in health: Evidence from programme interventions.* World Health Organization. Retrieved from https://www.who.int/gender/documents/Engaging_men_boys.pdf

Barnard, A. (2019). Well-being, more than a dream: Women constructing metaphors of strength. In E. Cifre & M. Vera (Eds.), *Psychosocial risks and health at work from a gender perspective: A current overview.* Lausanne: Frontiers Media. https://doi.org/10.3389/978-2-88963-014-1

Bhattacharyya, R. (2018). # metoo movement: An awareness campaign. *International Journal of Innovation, Creativity and Change, 3*(4).

Boring, A. (2015). *Gender biases in student evaluations of teachers*. France: Pfce-Presage-Science po.

Brannon, L. (2017). *Gender: Psychological perspectives* (7th ed.). New York: Routledge.

Butler, J. (2010). Performative agency. *Journal of Cultural Economy, 3*(2), 147–161. https://doi.org/10.1080/17530350.2010.494117

Byerly, C. M. (2011). *Global Report on the status of women in the news media*. Washington, USA: International Women's Media Foundation.

Centra, J. A & Gaubatz N. B (2007) *Is there gender bias in student evaluation of teaching*. Educational Testing services.

Chakravarthy, S. (2018). *Queering mental health practice*. Mariwala health initiative: Investing in collective mental health. Retrieved from https://mhi.org.in/voice/details/queering-mental-health-practice/ on 15 December 2019.

Children's Movement for Civic Awareness (2014). *Yuva Nagarik Meter Report.* Retrieved from https://issuu.com/cmcaindia/docs/yuva_nagarik_meter_report

Conel, W. (1996). *Teaching the boys, new research on masculinity and gender strategy for schools.* Teachers college record: APA.

Constantinople, A. (1973). Masculinity-femininity: An exception to a famous dictum? *Psychological Bulletin, 80*(5), 389–407. https://doi.org/10.1037/h0035334

Deepthi, M. U. (2014). Redressal mechanisms for women: The case of Jaagratha Samithi on Kerala. In P. P. Balan, S. George, & T. P. Kunhikannan (Eds.), *Deeping democracy: Issues on gender and basic needs*. Thrissur: Kerala Institute of Local Administration (KILA).

Eapen, M. (2004). *Report on gender analysis of select gram (village) panchayat plan-budgets in Thiruvananthapuram District*. New Delhi: Human Development Resource Centre.

Enns, C. Z. (2000). Gender issues in counselling. In S. D. Brown & R. W. Lent (Eds.), *Handbook of counseling psychology* (3rd ed., pp. 601–638). New York: Wiley.

Epstein, C. F. (1988). *Deceptive distinction: Sex, gender and the social order*. New Haven: Yale University Press.

European Institute for Gender Equality (2013). *Review of the implementation of the Beijing platform for action in the EU member states: Women and the media —Advancing gender equality in decision-making in media organisations*. Vilnius, Lithuania

European Institute for Gender Equality. (2016a). *Gender impact assessment: Gender mainstreaming toolkit*. Luxembourg: European Institute for Gender Equality.

European Institute for Gender Equality. (2016b). *Gender equality in academia and research: GEAR tool*. Luxembourg: European Institute for Gender Equality.

European Union. (2013). *She figures 2012 gender in research and innovation: Statistics and indicators*. Luxembourg: European Union.

European Union. (2019). *She figures 2018*. Luxembourg: European Union.

Formations of Gender and Higher Education Pedagogies. (2013). *The higher education academy*. London: University of Roehampton.

Foucault, M. ([1976] 1990). *The history of sexuality: Volume 1*. London: Penguin.

Four ways to teach gender equity in your class room. (2018). Retrieved from https://www.participatelearning.com/blog/4-ways-to-teach-about-gender-equity-in-your-classroom/

Friedman, K. (2017). Counselor self-care and mindfulness. *Contemporary Buddhism, 18*(2), 321–330. https://doi.org/10.1080/14639947.2017.1373437

Gartzia, L., Pizarro, J., & Baniandres, J. (2019). Emotional androgyny: A preventive factor of psychosocial risks at work? In E. Cifre & M. Vera (Eds.), *Psychosocial risks and health at work from a gender perspective: A current overview*. Lausanne: Frontiers Media. https://doi.org/10.3389/978-2-88963-014-1

Gender Competence Centre Berlin (2006). *Gender competence*. Retrieved from http://www.genderkompetenz.info/eng/gender-competence-2003-2010/Gender%20Competence.html

Gender Sensitive Indications for Media (2012). *United Nations educational, scientific and cultural organisation, France*.

Gill, A., & Pires, T. (2019). From binary to intersectional to imbricated approaches: Gender in a decolonial and diasporic perspective. *Contexto Internacional, 41*(2). https://doi.org/10.1590/s0102-8529.2019410200003

Gordon, L. (2016). 'Intersectionality', socialist feminism and contemporary activism: Musings by a second-wave socialist feminist. *Gender & History, 28*(2).

Hill, A. S. (2002). Teaching and doing gender in African families. *Sex Roles, 47*(11), 12.

Hinton, P. (2017). A sociality of death: Towards a new materialist politics and ethics of life itself. In K. Vicki (Ed.), *What if culture was nature all along?* (pp. 223–247). Edinburgh: University of Edinburgh Press.

Howe, E. (1997). "Promises to keep": Trends in women's studies worldwide. *Women's studies quarterly.* 25, (1/2). Looking back, moving forward: 25 years of women's studies history (Spring- Summer, 1997) (pp. 404–421).

Huang, B. (n.d.). *Gender bias faced by girls and what we can do: One Student's perspective and appended information from the center.* UCLA Center. Retrieved from http://smhp.psych.ucla.edu/pdfdocs/genderbias.pdf

Human Development Report. (2019). *United Nations Development Programme*, New York

Hyde, J. S., & Else-Quest, N. (2013). *Half the human experience: The psychology of women* (8th ed.). Belmont: Wadsworth.

ILGA World. (2019). *State-sponsored homophobia 2019: Global legislation overview update* Geneva

International Labor Organisation. (2019). Eliminating violence and harassment in the world of work: Convention No. *190, Recommendation No. 206, and the accompanying resolution.* Geneva, Switzerland.

International Trade Union Confederation. (2019). *ITUC frontline campaigns and four pillars for action 2020.* Retrieved from https://www.ituc-csi.org/ituc-frontline-campaigns-and-pillars

Johnson, C. P. G., & Otto, K. (2019). Better together: A model for women and LGBTQ equality in the workplace. In E. Cifre & M. Vera (Eds.), *Psychosocial risks and health at work from a gender perspective: A current overview.* Lausanne: Frontiers Media. https://doi.org/10.3389/978-2-88963-014-1

Kimberg, L. S., & Wheeler, M. (2019). Trauma and trauma-informed care. *Trauma-Informed Healthcare Approaches*, 25–56. https://doi.org/10.1007/978-3-030-04342-1_2

Kimmel, M. S., & Messner, M. A. (1992). *Men's lives* (2nd ed., pp. 1–11). New York: Macmillan.

Kolappan, B. (2018) *The lesson on Bharathanatyam dancer Narthaki Nataraj highlights her success story.* Retrieved from https://www.thehindu.com/news/national/tamil-nadu/transgenders-find-a-place-in-tamil-textbook-for-plus-one/article24125352.ece/amp/

Kortendiek, B. (2011). Supporting the Bologna process by gender mainstreaming: A model for the integration of gender studies in higher education curricula. In L. Grunberg (Ed.), *From gender studies to gender IN studies: Case studies on gender- inclusive curriculum in higher education.* UNESCO-CEPES: Bucharest.

Kosternia, E. (2009). Psychological gender inventories: Constructing the concept of gender through measuring. In *Thesis submitted to the degree of master of arts in gender studies.* Budapest: Central European University.

Kuhar, R., & Paternotte, D. (Eds.). (2017). *Anti-gender campaigns in Europe: Mobilizing against equality.* Lanham: Rowman and Littlefield International.

Kumar, A. Gender gap in as in commercial (2019). Retrieved from https://youtu.be/lcy3owbTqp8

Luyt, R. (2015). Beyond traditional understanding of gender measurement: The gender (re)presentation approach. *Journal of Gender Studies, 24*(2). https://doi.org/10.1080/09589236.2013.824378

McWhorter, L. (2016). Foreword. In H. Sharp & C. Taylor (Eds.), *Feminist philosophies of life* (pp. xi–xxiii). Kingston: Magill-Queens University Press.

Melchiori, K. J., & Mallett, R. K. (2018). Examining responses to sexism using a high-impact, high-psychological realism lab study. *SAGE Research Methods Cases in Psychology.* https://doi.org/10.4135/9781526439031

Moser, C. O. N. (1993). *Gender planning and development: Theory, practice and training.* London: Routledge.

Nabbuye, H. (2018). *Gender sensitive pedagogy.* Brookings: Centre for universal education.

Nelson- Jones, R. (2015). *Nelson-Jones' theory and practice of counselling and psychotherapy* (6th ed.). Sage Publications.

Nicols, E., et al. (1995). Gender inclusive science teaching: A feministic constructivist approach. *Journal of Research in Science Teaching., 32*(9), 897–924.

Ranade, K., & Chakravarty, S. (2013). *Gay-affirmative counselling practice: Resource and training manual.* Mumbai: Saksham.

Reddy, G., & Nanda, S. (2016). Hijras: An 'alternative' sex/gender in India. In C. B. Brettell & C. F. Sargent (Eds.), *Gender in cross-cultural perspective.* London: Routledge.

Reed, G. M., et al. (2016). Disorders related to sexuality and gender identity in the ICD-11: Revising the ICD-10 classification based on current scientific evidence, best clinical practices, and human rights considerations. *World Psychiatry, 15*(3), 205–221. https://doi.org/10.1002/wps.20354

Regulska, J. (2018). The #MeToo movement as a global learning moment. *International Higher Education, 94,* 5–6. https://doi.org/10.6017/ihe.2018.94.10514

Robbins, M. (1999). *Gender matters: Women counsellors' experience of working with male clients.* Thesis submitted to the Graduate Program of Social Work, York University, Toronto, Ontario.

Rosher, V. (1995). *Teaching the majority: Breaking the gender barrier in science, math and engineering.* New York: Teachers College Press. Columbia University.

Roy, R. & Sharma, A. (2019). How the Asian mother is changing: Human insights for marketers. IPSOS Views

Rutherford, A. (2018). Psychological perspectives on gender: An intellectual history [under review]. In R. Sternberg & W. E. Pickren (Eds.), *Handbook of the intellectual history of psychology: How psychological ideas have evolved from past to present.* Cambridge University Press.

Shields, S. A. (2008). Gender: An intersectionality perspective. *Sex Roles, 59,* 301–311. https://doi.org/10.1007/s11199-008-9501-8

Siewert, C. S. (2019). Women, mothers and their stories: Empowerment through playback theatre. In B. Tasker & B. Gopal (Eds.), *Playback theatre around the world: Diversity of application.* Bangalore: CHRIST (Deemed to be University).

Spencer-Thomas, S., Hindman, J. & Conrad, J. (2012).*Man therapy: An innovative approach to suicide prevention for working aged men.* Retrieved from www.ManTherapy.org

Spencer-Thomas, S., Hindman, J. & Conrad, J. (2014). *Man therapy: Outreach and impact on Men's mental health program 18 months after launch.* Retrieved from www.ManTherapy.org

Sreekumar, S. S. (2014). *Educate decentralization and empowerment of women: A study on Andaman & Nicobar Islands.* Thrissur: Kerala Institute of Local Administration (KILA).

Stephens, E., & Sellberg, K. (2019). The somatechnics of life and death: Recent trends in gender studies. *Australian Feminist Studies, 34*(99).

Stress and Gender (2019). APA retrieved from https://www.apa.org/news/press/releases/stress/2011/gender

Studies on Higher Education (2011). UNESCO, Bucharest

Tech Mahindra Introduced same sex adoption leave, other measurers to create a more inclusive work place. (2019) D Q India Retrieved from https://mhi.org.in/voice/details/need-rights-based-lens-educatio/

Terman, L. W., & Miles, C. C. (1936). *Sex and personality.* London: McGraw-Hill.

The Global Gender Gap Report (2018). *World Economic Forum.* Retrieved from http://www3.weforum.org/docs/WEF_GGGR_2018.pdf

Thomas, T. M. (2014). *Gender identity and status among hijras: Clan culture of gharanas inBangalore.* Bangalore: Christ University Publications.

Thomas, C., & Weber, C. (2019). *Information paper on protection against sexual orientation, gender identity and expression and sexual characteristics (SOGIESC) discrimination.* Geneva: International Labor Organisation.

Treskon, L., & Bright, C. L. (2017). *Bringing gender-responsive principles into practice: Evidence from the evaluation of the PACE Center for Girls*. New York: MDRC. Retrieved from https://www.mdrc.org/publication/bringing-gender-responsive-principles-practice/file-full

UNDP. (2019). *UNDP's engagement with the Media for Governance*. Oslo: Sustainable Development and Peace.

UNESCO. (2012). *Gender-sensitive indicators for media: Framework of indicators to gauge gender sensitivity in media operations and content*. Paris: France.

UNESCO. (2018). *Gender equality and girls' education initiative in Viet Nam: Empowering girls and women for a more equal society; final evaluation Report*. Hanoi: UNESCO Office.

UNESCO. (2019). *Global education monitoring Report – Gender Report: Building bridges for gender equality*. Paris: UNESCO.

UNICEF (2017).*Techno Girl: Empowering girls to be next generation leaders*. Retrieved from https://www.unicef.org/southafrica/SAF_brief_technogirl.pdf

Warsi, S., & Chaudhary, E. (2014). *Women empowerment through democratic decentralization*. Thrissur: Kerala Institute of Local Administration (KILA).

World Association for Christian Communication. (2015). *Global media monitoring project 2015*. London, UK.

World Bank. (2020). *Women, business and the law 2020*. Washington, DC: World Bank. https://doi.org/10.1596/978-1-4648-1532-4

World Health Organisation. (2002). *World report on violence and health: Summary*. Geneva: World Health Organisation.

Zeisler, A. (2017). *Media's gender gap*. Media Impact Project, The Norman Lear Centre.

Zimmerman, D., & West, C. (1975). Sex roles, interruptions and sciences in conversations. In B. Thomas & N. Henly (Eds.), *Language and sex*. Newbury House: Rowley, Mass.

Zucker, K. J., Cohen-Kettenis, P. T., Drescher, J., Meyer-Bahlburg, H. F., Pfäfflin, F., & Womack, W. M. (2013). Memo outlining evidence for change for gender identity disorder in the DSM-5. *Archives of Sexual Behaviour, 42*(5), 901–914. https://doi.org/10.1007/s10508-013-0139-4

Teaching School Psychology to Psychologists

28

M. Beatrice Ligorio, Stefano Cacciamani, and Emanuela Confalonieri

Contents

Abstract

In this chapter, we offer some insights for teaching psychology and training school psychologists. Five points are made. The first one is about the historical perspective that will help to understand the current development in school psychology. The second point deals with the professional profile of school psychologists, and it indicates the different domains of their interventions. The third point explores the knowledge and competencies school psychologists should master to effectively carry out their work. The fourth point addresses the question of how to train professional school psychologists.

M. B. Ligorio (✉)
University of Bari, Bari, Italy
e-mail: mariabeatrice.ligorio@uniba.it

S. Cacciamani
University of Valle D'Aosta, Aosta, Italy
e-mail: s.cacciamani@univda.it

E. Confalonieri
Catholic University of the Sacred Heart of Milan, Milan, Italy
e-mail: emanuela.confalonier@unicatt.it

© Springer Nature Switzerland AG 2023
J. Zumbach et al. (eds.), *International Handbook of Psychology Learning and Teaching*,
Springer International Handbooks of Education,
https://doi.org/10.1007/978-3-030-28745-0_32

The fifth and final point shows how strongly school psychology is rooted into the social and cultural context schools are part of. To this aim, we propose Active Theory as a theoretical framework able to describe and interconnect all the different levels and actors involved when looking at school as a system.

Keywords

History of school psychology · School psychologist profile · School psychologist training · Activity Theory

Introduction

Teaching means making concepts clear, coherent, understandable, and useful to students. The aim is for students to understand the knowledge presented in class and to use it to build their professional future.

The aim of the present chapter is to offer some insights to those who are teaching psychology and training school psychologists. To achieve this, we appreciate that both the content conveyed when teaching school psychology and the method used to teach and to organize the content should be clear. Therefore, the present chapter attempts to articulate both content and method as clearly as possible. The chapter comprises five main points, each discussed in a dedicated paragraph. Considered together, such five points cover what school psychology is in terms of content and teaching method. While illustrating these points, we will also refer and briefly review contents and frameworks developed by the main international associations that have addressed this topic.

The first point we make is that understanding school psychology from an historical perspective is crucial. Therefore, we dedicate a paragraph to an historical overview of school psychology and psychologists working in schools. The said paragraph outlines the main steps that led to the current definition of school psychology and its disciplinary field.

In the second point, we emphasize the contribution of some important associations that deals with the professional profile of school psychologists, and it indicates the different domains of their interventions.

The third point explores the knowledge and competencies school psychologists should master to effectively carry out their work. In other words, it illustrates the ideal knowledge this practitioner is expected to acquire to carry out school-based activities. To achieve this, we discuss the content of the teaching programs that should be proposed at a university level, to psychologists intending to focus on schools.

The fourth point addresses the question of how to train professional school psychologists. We aim at providing guidelines on teaching methods and strategies to effectively teach school psychology, focusing on the necessary theoretical framework as well as on operational and practical implications. Relatedly to this, we take into consideration the level of specialization and the importance of using case studies and technologies to enrich teaching.

The fifth and final point addresses how strongly school psychology is rooted into the social and cultural context schools are part of. Based on this assumption, school ought to be considered as a complex system with its own characteristics. Therefore, an adequate theoretical perspective is needed to avoid simplification and to encompass the complexity of school psychology. We propose Active Theory as a theoretical framework to describe and interconnect all the different levels and actors involved when looking at school as a system.

Historical Notes on School Psychology

On an international level, the specialization of the school psychologist was introduced more than a century ago and has since become increasingly established. Nevertheless, depending on the period and the country in which it was implemented, this specific professional profile has undergone contrasting developments. The present paragraph sketches the history of school psychology, recalling its most relevant steps.

According to Tharinger, Pryzwansky, and Miller (2008), school psychology emerged first in the United States in 1892, with the founding of American Psychological Association (APA). A few years later, in 1896, school psychology recorded a major step forward: The University of Pennsylvania opened the first school-based psychological clinic to assess children's learning and behavioral differences. This important event reflects the recognition that pupils in schools need purposely trained specialists to understand their needs and potentialities. Three years later, in 1899, the city of Chicago established for the first time such a clinic inside public schools (Fagan & Wise, 2007). The relevance of this achievement is amplified by the contemporary advent of compulsory schooling, but, for decades, the focus remains on students' special needs. Children's mental health issues are still now recognized as a public health crisis, since about 10% of the students experiences serious problems and another 10% moderately serious problems (U.S. Department of Health and Human Services, 1999; New Freedom Commission on Mental Health, 2003). Drawing on this acknowledgment, it may be said that the origins of school psychology are closely related with the clinical-functionalistic field of psychology (Fagan, 1992). Unlike clinical psychology, however, school psychology was not interested in assessing the mental state of individual children in general but solely in relation to specific behaviors and learning tasks (Phillips, 1990).

In 1945, APA's internal organization founded the School Psychology Division 16, marking an especially relevant achievement for the field (D'Amato, Zafiris, McConnell, & Dean, 2011). Nowadays, this Division is still a landmark for anyone who wishes to work in this field or is interested in understanding what school psychology is. The website of Division 16 reads: "School Psychology is composed of scientific-practitioner psychologists whose major professional interests lie with children, families and the schooling process. The division represents the interests of psychologists engaged in the delivery of comprehensive psychological services to children, adolescents and families in schools and other applied settings. The division is dedicated to facilitating the professional practice of school psychology and actively advocates in domains, such as education and health care reform, which have significant implications for the practice of psychology with children" (https://www.apa.org/about/division/div16).

Another crucial step for the development of school psychology is the so-called Thayer Conference, organized by APA in August 1954 in the State of New York, more precisely in the Thayer Hotel, after which it is conventionally named. This summit was organized to shed light on the role of the school psychologist, not yet sufficiently appreciated at the time. A pilot survey reported that in the 1950s, there was a school psychologist for every 1000–3000 students, covering just a few basic functions (Ysseldyke & Schakel, 1983).

The Thayer Conference sets the goal of individuating the skills school psychologists should have and how they should be trained (Cutts, 1955). The main goal of the 48 participants was to provide a definition of school psychologist as the psychologist specializing in education who uses specific knowledge of assessment, learning, and interpersonal relationships to help enrich the experience and growth of children, including cases such as deficits or surplus endowments (Ysseldyke & Schakel, 1983). The standard functions attributed to the school psychologist were also identified. Among the latter, the most relevant were the evaluation of the individuals, planning interventions, outline research, and offered coaching to teaching staff to obtain the best for as many pupils as possible (Cutts, 1955).

The Thayer Conference is still regarded as one of the most significant events in the history of school psychology. One reason is that at the time of the conference, psychologists who worked in the school field had different professional labels – estimates suggest there were at least 75 (Fagan, 2005a). By establishing standard requirements, the Thayer Conference ensured that school psychologists were nationally recognized as such, with adequate training common to all (Shick Tryon, 1986).

The historical evolution of American school psychology following the Thayer Conference merged into the experience of the Spring Hill symposium in 1980 (Ysseldyke, 1982). The 69 attendees were selected among the leading experts of school psychology from different countries and among the trainers of the field (Bray & Kehle, 2011). They examined the practical experiences of the last 30 years and tried to update the profile of school psychologist considering the cultural and economic events that affected the American society at that time (Shick Tryon, 1986). At the end of the symposium, the reflections that emerged were reorganized to form proposals and operational guidelines for future professionals (Ysseldyke & Schakel, 1983).

Europe contributed enormously to the dissemination and consolidation of school psychology. To begin with, the expression "school psychology" was first coined by German colleague Hugo Münsterberg, who introduced this label as early as 1898 and defined this professional profile at the intersection between a developmental psychologist and a teacher (Fagan, 2005b). German psychologist William Stern is credited with plundering the expression "school psychologist" by strictly associating it to specific needs of individual students, especially those who experience hardships related to school (Fagan & Delugach, 1984). Starting from this, school psychology in Europe has developed according to national policies, with each country regulating and recognizing the profile of the school psychologist through different paths. Despite this, many organizations strived to overcome the national specificities and to ultimately develop a common perspective. To this aim, numerous meetings were hosted. The first one was organized by UNESCO, and it was held in 1948 with representatives from 43 countries, with the aim of comparing their respective governments' indications and promoting common guidelines for services of school psychology. A second meeting, held in 1956, focused on an even more thorough effort to identify which services could be improved. Both written by William Douglas Wall (1956), the final reports of these conferences stressed the need to increase the number of professionals specialized in school psychology. The most active nations in putting into practice this recommendation were the United Kingdom, Denmark, Sweden, and France, which were the first European countries to regulate the professional activity of school psychologists.

The objectives of these two UNESCO conferences were further pursued with the foundation of the International School Psychology Association (ISPA). In synergy with the psychological associations of 20 European countries, this association offers advice to those wishing to inquire about the practice of school psychology (Lee, 2005).

In this very short description of the evolution of school psychology, it is possible to recognize a trajectory that started with considering school psychology as a discipline focused on students' special needs and soon shifted focus towards the complex relationships that children have with parents, family, and peers (D'Amato et al., 2011). This has generated what may be perceived as somewhat of a paradox for school psychology: to facilitate change in a child, it is necessary to work with adults (Reynolds & Gutkin, 1999).

In the next paragraph, we detail the professional profile of school psychologists.

School Psychologists' Professional Profile

This paragraph presents the perspectives of two important international associations and one Italian association of psychologists to better define areas and competencies of the school psychologist. Putting their perspectives together will help sketching a possible professional profile.

The first association under consideration is the National Association of School Psychologists (NASP), which suggests a specific working model (NASP Practice Model). This model supports the development and implementation of effective practices at the individual level as well as at the systemic level. To achieve this, the model outlines the skills and possible activities that school psychologists can carry out in 10 domains of intervention. It describes the general framework and the organizational principles within which the services should be provided. The model also clarifies the connection between school psychologists' training, the professional standards, and the activities implemented. It also emphasizes the importance of a comprehensive approach that includes all the school components and the contextual

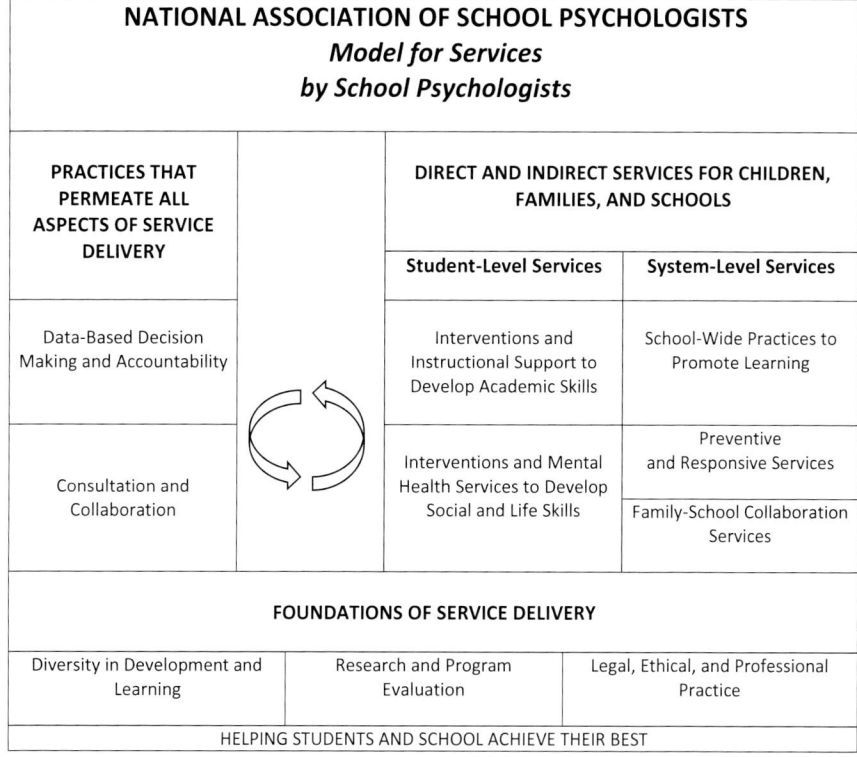

Fig. 1 The 10 domains of school psychology according to NASP. (Source, Skalski et al., 2015)

elements, to encourage interventions aimed at promoting wellbeing and treating discomfort in the educational setting. The need to create collaboration between all the actors inside and outside the school is also strongly emphasized, supporting the general functioning of the school and the ability of all to improve students' performance and wellbeing.

This model underlines how professional approaches vary depending on the context and on the school features, such as the school local traditions, the characteristics of the territory (e.g., rural, urban, suburban), the expectations of the school towards the school psychologist, the relationships between students and teachers, the quality of students' needs, and, finally, the available funding.

Overall, the 10 domains identified by this model describe the practice of school psychology (Fig. 1).

The competencies of these 10 domains describe the knowledge and skills that school psychologists should have. They are collapsed into three large domains.

Firstly, the model identifies "practices that permeate all aspects of service delivery" and that are articulated into two domains:

- Domain 1: Data-Based Decision-Making and Accountability, articulated into knowledge of assessment methods and data collection; confidently developing effective services and programs; deploying assessment tools to measure progress and results.
- Domain 2: Consultation and Collaboration, referring to knowledge of consultation models and strategies, collaboration, and communication useful for individuals, groups, and families.

Subsequently, the model identifies another possible articulation related to "direct and indirect services for children, families, and schools," articulated into two domains concerning students' services and three domains about systems-level services.

The two domains about students' services are as follows:

- Domain 3: Interventions and Instructional Support to Develop Academic Skills including knowledge of cultural and social influences on academic skills, of cognitive and development processes, and of teaching strategies.
- Domain 4: Interventions and Mental Health Services to Develop Social and Life Skills. This domain includes knowledge of cultural, developmental, and social influences on mental health and of behavioral and emotional influences on learning, promoting psychological wellbeing.

The three domains about systems-level services are as follows:

- Domain 5: School-Wide Practices to Promote Learning which focuses on the organization of the school as a system, education for young people with additional support needs, technology resources, and promoting learning.
- Domain 6: Preventive and Responsive Services that include the knowledge of protective and risk factors in learning and mental health, in implementing and supporting multi-level prevention and evidence-based strategies in emergency and critical situation.
- Domain 7: Family–School Collaboration Services that refer to knowledge of family as a system and of its characteristics, supporting families in children's relationship with school and promoting collaboration between families and schools.

Lastly, the model addresses the "Foundations of School Psychological Service Delivery" articulated in the following three domains:

- Domain 8: Diversity in Development and Learning which includes knowledge of individual differences, abilities, disabilities and of diversity factors related to culture, context, role differences referred to children, families, and schools, improving services related to diversity and inclusive process.

- Domain 9: Research and Program Evaluation based on knowledge of research design, statistics, and program analysis to collect and understand data in applied settings.
- Domain 10: Legal, Ethical, and Professional Practice that considers knowledge of the history of school psychology, of principle models and methods of service; knowledge of ethical, legal, and professional standards; and of all factors linked to professional identity and work practice as school psychologists.

As mentioned, a further international association, the European Federation of Psychologists' Associations (EFPA), has been promoting the profile of the school psychologist at the European level for years, emphasizing characteristics and skills. According to EFPA, school psychology is one of the most important branches of applied psychology since it includes in-depth and wide, complex knowledge on human development, psychopathology, organizational psychology, neuroscience, learning theory, and parental and family functioning. School psychologists are required to put in practice into schools such complex knowledge by following a holistic approach and a broad and all-encompassing perspective. Furthermore, EFPA underlines how the professional activities of school psychologists vary over time, circumstances, and contexts, with interventions that differ in terms of objectives and are aimed at both individual and group users. This recommendation is outlined through a matrix (Table 1), built starting from three functions (prevention, evaluation, and intervention) which are divided into four possible levels (individual, group, system, and social). Such a matrix highlights the wide range of professional activities falling into the school psychologists' competencies.

According to EFPA, psychologists working within the education system play a crucial role in many ways: (i) by contributing and implementing lifelong learning policies; (ii) by providing counselling and forming positive attitudes towards learning by working with children and adolescents with learning difficulties; (iii) by promoting programs to train skills needed to cope with societies that undergo increasingly rapid technological, social, and economic changes; (iv) by helping students that require specific learning activities and programs to sustain those that have dropped out; (v) by offering advice on pedagogical issues; and (vi) by providing teacher training and systemic school counselling.

Recently, an Italian association, the Italian Association of Psychology (AIP), has also proposed a possible profile for school psychologists in continuity with what is proposed by the two associations mentioned above. This profile is articulated according to the role and possible objects of intervention of school psychologists, always considering school complexity, that includes individuals (students, teachers, operators) and groups (classes, families, teaching, and non-teaching staff), operating in a wider territorial context. The figure of school psychologists emerges as a professional committed to promote health and wellbeing, to counteract risk phenomena, and to spread good psychological practices by using different tools, such as interviews, standardized instruments, role-playing, and observations. Furthermore, the capability to understand and manage the relationships between the different social actors involved is a transversal skill school psychologist should have.

Table 1 Synopsis of EFPA recommendations about school psychologist competencies. (Source: EFPA Police Paper, 2010)

Function/ level	Society	System	Group	Individual
Prevention	Provide information on living conditions, psychological development, risk/protective factors; initiate research programs in relevant areas; influence necessary reforms and legal regulations in all areas concerning optimal learning environments	Provide counselling for administrators, school leaders, teachers, parents, students, and their representatives; initiate and coordinate projects in relevant areas; encourage useful structural changes; promote changes in pedagogical thinking and tradition when needed; initiate formulation of action plans and evaluate their implementation	Provide counselling; offer supervision; stimulate teamwork; observe group behavior and interaction; provide information/ knowledge. Support the implementation and evaluation of relevant projects (e.g., learning, bullying, drugs prevention, mental health, crisis management)	Offer consultation, guidance, and supervision; observe and evaluate individual symptoms and interaction skills
Evaluation	Analyze data samples for documentation on a group, local, regional, or national level. Define the necessary psychological knowledge, skills, and methods in the evaluation	Follow up on projects and methods used; monitor action plans; apply new knowledge into practice	Interviews, questionnaires, videotaping, etc. all of which can be used to identify and examine groups to distinguish cultural aspects, social norms and interaction, intellectual levels and needs, motivation for change, etc.	Evaluate by interviews, questionnaires, or tests to distinguish: intellectual functioning; learning capacities; behavioral, emotional, or personality, social, or family problems; need for further examination (e.g., referral to neurology, psychiatry). Evaluation should be oriented towards treatment and inclusion

(continued)

Table 1 (continued)

Function/level	Society	System	Group	Individual
Intervention	Influence necessary reforms and legal regulations concerning optimal learning environments; facilitate access to psychological services and school support structures; outline qualifications, competencies needed for psychological practice; improve quality of SP at all levels (school, local, communal, regional)	Promote co-coordinated routines, provide methods for teamwork (also cross-professional teams); execute relevant parts of action plans. Provide training and information as part of special programs for school heads/ teachers/ parents/ students	Initiate projects for groups of school heads/ teachers/ students/parents; guide or supervise training groups; guide or supervise therapeutic groups, e.g., family therapy; develop new methods and materials for psychological-pedagogical use	Offer or provide: special education; specific training; therapy; change of school, change of class, develop new materials (tests and training), coordinate relevant external assistance to examination; seek and participate in relevant supplementary (post-graduate) training

Therefore, school psychologists' areas of intervention can be classified as follows: (i) teacher training; (ii) support for educational evaluation and experimentation; (iii) management of professional and organizational problems; (iv) support for school-family relationship; (v) help in intervening in cases of learning difficulties; (vi) promote health and wellbeing; (vii) direct help to children, teenagers, and families, through psychological counselling; and viii) direct help to teachers, for classroom management and group dynamics.

Even if the professional profiles emerging from these three associations lead to different matrices, it is possible to identify some common elements. Firstly, they all suggest that school psychologists should address all stakeholders within the school as well as the school's immediate surroundings. Secondly, their interventions can target individuals, groups, or the wider social context. Furthermore, through their interventions, school psychologists promote collaboration among professionals from fields other than their own, with whom they share an educational mission. Finally, school psychologists' activities should be aimed both at promoting psychological wellbeing in all the participants to the school world and at intervening on possible difficulties that may arise at school and in the immediate contexts surrounding school.

Training Programs for School Psychologists

After examining some proposals outlined by some professional associations about the profile of the school psychologist, we now report the elements relevant to training the skills of this professional figure. As Farrell (2010) points out, again professional associations play an important role defining criteria for the accreditation of the professional training and for monitoring whether the training courses comply with these criteria.

For instance, NASP requires a school psychology training program at a specialist or doctoral level to ensure that all candidates demonstrate basic professional skills, including knowledge and skills in the 10 domains identified in the NASP Practice Model (2015).

The American Psychological Association (APA) accredits only doctoral training programs and stresses that basic knowledge of the school psychologist should be rooted in psychology and education and includes, as necessary components of training, an area relating to modalities of intervention and another that could be described as concerning the object of the intervention. The first area refers to knowledge on psychoeducational assessment and diagnosis, intervention, prevention, and health promotion and recommends programs focused on the development of children and young people in the context of schools, families, and other educational systems. The second area concerns the knowledge of theories relating to cultural contexts, to address culturally or linguistically different individuals and to enrich learning and teaching, also addressing family and parenting educational processes.

The International School Psychology Association (ISPA) carries out a more articulated analysis, based on several internationally surveys related to school psychology conducted in more than 40 countries (Jimerson et al., 2004; Jimerson, Oakland, & Farrell, P. T. (Eds.)., 2007) from which they drew the elements to define the guidelines for the accreditation of professional training in School Psychology (ISPA, 2020). In these guidelines, ISPA identifies six main objectives for training in school psychology, each of which is linked to certain standards and articulated into indicators of knowledge and professional performance (Table 2).

Below we examine in detail the six goals proposed by ISPA (ISPA, 2020), also considering some of the implications.

Goal 1 – Core Knowledge in Psychology and Education

ISPA recommends that school psychology programs should focus on the core knowledge about developmental psychology, learning and cognition, personality, social psychology, experimental psychology, and neuropsychology. Programs should also promote the understanding of the educational curriculum and the related educational contexts. Psychologists should demonstrate the acquisition of this fundamental knowledge with its applications.

This goal is based on three standards, related to cognition and learning (Standard 1.1), social and emotional development (Standard 1.2), and individual differences (Standard 1.3). The first standard focuses on issues related to cognitive development and learning (also with reference to motivational aspects). It is worth noting the reference to the theories of education and to theories on the use of technological tools as mediators of teaching and learning. The second standard focuses on issues related

Table 2 Goal and standard provided by ISPA

Goals	Standards
1 – Core Knowledge in Psychology and Education	1.1 – Cognition and Learning 1.2 – Social and Emotional Development 1.3 – Individual Differences
2 – Professional Knowledge and Skills in Assessment and Intervention	2.1 – Evidence-Based Decision Making and Accountability 2.2 – Prevention, Mental Health Promotion and Crisis Intervention 2.3 – School and Systems Organization, Policy Development, and Implementation 2.4 – Home-School-Community Collaboration
3 – Transnational/Multicultural School Psychology	3.1 Role and functions of school psychologists nationally and internationally 3.2 Working with children and families from culturally diverse communities
4 – Professional Practice of School Psychologists	4.1 – Legislation that impacts on education policy and practice 4.2 – Ethical issues in professional practice 4.3 – Report writing
5 – Interpersonal Skills	5.1 Self-awareness and reflexivity 5.2 Interviewing 5.3 Consultation
6 – Research Methods	6.1 Research design and implementation 6.2 Analysis and interpretation of research findings

to social and emotional development, with a strong focus on promoting personal wellbeing and adapting the school context to students' needs. The third standard concerns the knowledge of theories on individual characteristics, assessment, and intervention strategies for students with special educational needs, including those who are intellectually gifted, to promote their inclusion in school contexts. The first two standards focus on the conditions of development and learning that can be defined as typical, while the third draws attention to the management of atypical conditions, from an inclusive perspective. The performance indicators of this objective describe the characterization of the intervention of the school psychologist as aimed at a plurality of recipients, as already highlighted in the professional profiles: students, teachers, and families.

Goal 2 – Professional Knowledge and Skills in Assessment and Intervention

ISPA highlights the need for school psychology programs to promote the development of diagnostic and decision-making skills related to the accurate description of the behavior and personal characteristics of the subjects who are being taken cared of. This includes fostering skills in the use of assessment techniques and analytical and problem-solving skills. School psychology programs should also promote the development of skills associated with the implementation of interventions at an individual, group, and system level. This goal includes four standards, concerning Evidence-Based Decision-Making and Accountability (Standard 2.1); Prevention, Mental Health Promotion, and Crisis Intervention (Standard 2.2); School and Systems Organization, Policy Development, and Implementation (Standard 2.3); and Home-School-Community Collaboration (Standard 2.4). The first standard focuses on evaluation theories, methods, and techniques for data collection that can then lead to evidence-based intervention decisions. The second standard concerns knowledge and skills related to interventions aimed at preventing and helping to overcome situations of child and adolescent psychopathology, or crises at school level and to promote students' wellbeing. The third standard emphases knowledge about the school context from an organizational point of view and on the promotion of skills while working with individuals and groups. The fourth standard promotes knowledge and skills necessary to work effectively with families, educators of other services, and promoting collaboration across schools.

Among the performance indicators, it is interesting to note the systemic reference to interventions on school organization and the construction of collaborative networks between subjects from different contexts.

Goal 3 – Transnational/Multicultural School Psychology

According to ISPA, school psychologists should be familiar with the state of the art and the development of the profession in school psychology at national and international level and be aware of the existence of different working models adopted in different countries. They are also expected to know theory and research on the potential influences of racial and/or ethnic, cultural, sociopolitical, religious, socioeconomic, gender, and linguistic factors on the development of individuals. School psychologists are, therefore, called upon to develop multicultural skills to be used in their work on assessment, intervention, and prevention, including the ability to work effectively with people of different backgrounds and to engage in successful cross-professional collaboration. This goal comprises two standards: knowing national and international roles and functions of school psychologists (Standard 3.1) and working with children and families from culturally diverse communities (Standard 3.2). The first standard emphasizes elements concerning the knowledge about the role of school psychologist and its professional growth, based on the plurality of work models to which they contribute. The focus of the second standard is twofold. On the one hand, it focuses on the attention that school psychologists should pay to the influence of the differences mentioned above on development and education. On the other hand, it focuses on the influence that such differences can have on their work. As an upshot of this, school psychologists should adopt an explicitly anti-discriminatory stance.

The attention to raising awareness about the professional role and on the need for professional updating is certainly relevant since preservice training. To this aim, it could be suggested to put this theme more in the foreground by creating a specific goal, distinct from the one related to the influence of cultural diversity, central in the second standard which, instead, concerns the object of the interventions.

Goal 4 – Professional Practice of School Psychologists

ISPA argues that school psychology programs should prepare students to work in schools and in community settings by acquiring different methods of assessment and intervention. The effectiveness of their work partly depends also on their knowledge of the legislative framework in education, their understanding and implementation of the fundamental ethical principles underlying their professional practice, and their written communication skills about their business. This goal comprises three standards: legislation that impacts education policy and practice (Standard 4.1), ethical issues in professional practice (Standard 4.2), and report writing (Standard 4.3). The first standard emphasizes that school psychologists should be familiar with key regulatory aspects at the local, regional, and national levels that directly impact the education of all children, especially those who may have learning and/or behavior issues. The second standard concerns the need to promote knowledge about the national and international ethical standards that regulate the profession, as well as attitudes and behaviors that comply with them. The third standard argues that educational programs should prepare future school psychologists to be able to formulate accurate written reports for stakeholders, including parents, teachers, and other professionals.

This goal acts on those founding elements of the profession represented by ethical and regulatory aspects and places emphasis on accountability related to professional activities of which the construction of reports constitutes a relevant formal element.

Goal 5. Interpersonal Skills

School psychology programs promote the interpersonal skills needed to work effectively at school with families and in other educational settings. There are three standards envisaged in this objective, respectively, addressing self-awareness and reflexivity (Standard 5.1) and interviewing (Standard 5.2) and consultation (Standard 5.3). The first standard emphasizes the promotion of school psychologists' awareness of the limits of their professional competence and the impact of their professional style on others, as well as a reflective approach to learning from experience. The second standard promotes competence in conducting interviews with different recipients. The third standard highlights the need to master different consulting models and to know how to use them to flexibly adapt to various situations.

Controlling the area of interpersonal skills at a training level is a significant strategic junction considering the plurality of recipients the school psychologist's activity is addressed to and the complexity of the school context.

Goal 6 – Research Methods

School psychology programs promote the understanding and use of quantitative and qualitative research and assessment methods by future school psychologists. This should enable attendees to engage in research and evaluation studies that address issues relevant to school psychology and education. This goal comprises two standards: research design and implementation (Standard 6.1) and analysis and interpretation of research findings (Standard 6.2). While the former provides training on research paradigms and their influence on research methodology in school psychology and related areas, to promote research design skills, the latter aims to enable school psychologists to conduct appropriate analyses and interpretations of qualitative and quantitative data and to disseminate the results both orally and in a written format.

The skills provided in this area strengthen the concept of school psychologists as professionals who, in addition to mastering research data, are also uniquely positioned to conduct research in their own professional context.

Guidelines for Teaching

Defining guidelines concerning "how to teach" psychological disciplines means to identify relevant criteria to design a learning environment to promote effective students' learning in this area. Upton and Taylor (2010) highlighted those guidelines to create such conditions need to be grounded in psychological concepts. The authors identify the following key principles for an effective teaching of psychology in higher education:

- *Encourage student-staff contact:* This kind of contact is useful for establishing and maintaining students' motivation and involvement in learning activities.
- *Encourage cooperation among students:* As suggested by the socio-constructivist perspective and research on collaborative learning, when students may collaborate, at least for part of the time, instead of working alone, their learning is more effective.
- *Encourage active learning:* Course material is better understood and retained when the students are actively engaged by talking, writing, questioning, debating, applying, and relating to what they already know, rather than passively receive information from lectures, videos, or other prepackaged formats.
- *Give prompt feedback:* When students receive feedback about what they know and what they do not know, they can profit from mistakes and draw satisfaction from progress, being able to focus their efforts to learn.
- *Emphasize "time on task":* Paying attention and dedicating time to the task of learning is an important condition for an effective learning to be highlighted to the students.
- *Communicate high expectations*: Teachers' high expectations, when communicated to the students, can maximize the performance of all students. Students will better learn and perform if teachers communicate them their high expectations.
- *Be organized and prepared:* The organization and planning of curriculum clarify what students will learn and how easily they will learn it.
- *Communicate enthusiasm:* Effective teachers tend to communicate to the students their enthusiasm for psychology and for teaching.

– *Be fair and ethical:* Teachers should be fair and ethical in presenting material, dealing with students, and evaluating to propose an effective, high-quality teaching.

In addition, guidelines to teach psychological disciplines in school psychology programs should consider the specific training needs. In this way, a strong focus is on the applicative dimension within the school context, as highlighted by many professional associations. For instance, NASP (2021) highlights that to become a school psychologist a specialization program that awards a degree (specialist level and/or doctorate) specifically in school psychology should be completed. Most of the school psychology degrees already include academic courses, supervised fieldwork, and an internship to gain the necessary professional knowledge and skills. NASP recommends a minimum of three years of postgraduate studies, including one-year internship consisting of at least 1.200 hours of supervised practice, of which 600 to be spent at school. Furthermore, ISPA (2020) emphasizes how school psychologists training needs to account for an organized sequence of the courses, emphasizing psychology applied to educational contexts. AIP (2019) argues that postgraduate university education (Laurea Magistrale), followed by a year of professional training, may meet the demands for training required to work as a psychologist in school and educational contexts. Additionally, AIP emphasizes that such training courses necessitate specific training goals, envisaging school and educational contexts as primary employment opportunities.

Considering all this, now we deal with the question of how to design a program training really situated into school contexts. To develop guidelines for this purpose, we elaborate upon the distinction proposed by Paavola and Hakkarainen (2005), based on a previous work by Sfard (1998), between three different metaphors that express three main visions of learning, found in several theories and theoretical models. According to the first metaphor, learning is a process aimed at acquiring knowledge, and it is a property of the mind. This metaphor reflects the emphasis placed by the cognitivist approach on the role of mental models or schemes in the learning process, which, however, are liable to the risk of strengthening a narrow notion of the mind as a container of knowledge. Learning is a process of storing knowledge within that container. Furthermore, the authors consider this vision as emphasizing the role of cognitive structures built by the subject, at an individual level. The focus of individual cognitive activity leads the authors to define this metaphor as "monological." The second metaphor is that of participation, which views learning as a process aimed at acquiring the skills to become a competent member of a community, to communicate and act according to that community's social norms. Through participation in various cultural practices and in shared activities, cognition is shaped, and it develops according to sociocultural dimensions. The centrality of interaction with others and with culture warrants that the authors define this second metaphor as "dialogic." The third metaphor is that of "knowledge creation," which defines learning as a process aimed at creating new conceptual and material artefacts. Within this metaphor can be included theoretical models that underline the central role of communities that create knowledge, such as the Knowledge Building model (Scardamalia & Bereiter, 2010), the Expansive Learning model (Engeström, 1987), and the model of Knowledge Creating Companies (Nonaka & Takeuchi, 1995). Lately, it has been proposed to rename this metaphor as "trialogic," because it emphasizes how people collaboratively develop objects that support cross-boundary trajectories (Paavola, Lakkala, Muukkonen, Kosonen, & Karlgren, 2011). These are objects able to accompany learners from one context (the educational one they are embedded into) to other contexts (workplaces, other educational agencies, etc.) (Sansone, Cesareni, & Ligorio, 2016).

School psychologists training can be operationalized and situated by referring to theoretical models that can be placed within the metaphor of the creation of "trialogical" knowledge. Therefore, it is necessary to create a collaborative community that operates starting from authentic problems related to the school context, linked to the educational objectives of the school psychology training program. Theoretical knowledge, methods, and techniques of investigation and evaluation become conceptual and procedural "tools" through which to carry out progressive problem-solving activities about the content to be learnt. To this aim, methods focused on case studies and project-based learning should be included into the training courses.

As indicated by Sudzina (1997), a case study is the description of a realistic dilemma that can be examined from a plurality of perspectives; it is a situation that poses a problem to be addressed in a "situated" way (Merseth, 1991). A good case study refers to big ideas that are meaningful for a particular subject area (Wassermann, 1993). Sudzina (1997) also stresses the need to oversee three main aspects to integrate the case study approach into a teaching program, which will be synthesised here from the perspective of knowledge creating communities:

(a) Course organization and content. Teachers must consider the time necessary to identify appropriate cases for the educational objectives of their course, plan an appropriate time within the course to examine the proposed cases, announce the case in advance to give students the opportunity to adequately examine the case, and, finally, structure the moments of discussion during the lessons.

(b) Case selection and implementation. Case selection and its implementation are strongly interconnected. Selection implies deciding which sources to use, the content of the cases, the context into which place them, as well as how many are appropriate and what assignment to give to students. It also requires defining the structure of the activity related to case study. For instance, a case could be assigned to a certain group to be analyzed and discussed; later another group of students could hypothesize solutions and present them to the rest of the class, triggering in this way further discussion.

(c) Case analysis and evaluation. Case analysis can be conducted by the students based on guidelines provided by the teacher or based on case analysis models (e.g., identify the problem, identify the point of view of the actors involved in the case, etc.). The evaluation can take various forms: for instance, by proposing a case at the outset of course to activate students' prior knowledge and by re-proposing the same case at the end of the course to detect the course impact.

It is also possible to introduce cases halfway through the course to monitor the progress. Regardless of when the cases are proposed, peer feedback can be used as evaluation.

Case analysis is conceived as a versatile training method, capable of assigning to students an active role in the process of building the professional competence of a school psychologist. The project-based learning (PBL) approach aims at creating a meaningful learning experience by presenting a contextual situation requiring the development of a project, whether individually or in working groups (Ching & Hsu, 2013). In developing projects, students take responsibility, and they engage in a wide variety of tasks, including processing information, collaborative interactions and, when possible, peer feedback. They also deliver outputs by applying what they had previously learned or by using the information they had sought and acquired. The artefacts created represent external representations of the solutions adopted that can be shared and critically evaluated by both the teacher and the peers, fostering a collective progressive improvement. Koh, Herring, and Hew (2010) proposed four guidelines for online PBL implementation: (i) assigning a design problem to students, (ii) structuring the stages of the project to facilitate the construction of knowledge, (iii) asking students to finalize their learning activity to the development of the output, and (iv) facilitating learning using several tools and formats. In this scenario, digital technologies can greatly help users in gathering information in different formats (e.g., written texts, charts and images, audio, and videos). This is a positive opportunity for both case study and project development because it improves the possibility for the trainees to receive multiple-source information and, therefore, to know the contexts to which this information belongs from different angles. In addition, technology can support synchronous collaborative activity (e.g., through group videoconferencing) as well as asynchronous (e.g., through web-forum discussion). Lastly, digital technologies can play a relevant role for students to prepare, present, share, and discuss their outcomes.

The perspective here reported allows students' agency to play a central role (Jones & Healing, 2010). In other words, students can assume collective responsibility within their community by dealing with significant problems for school psychologists'. Furthermore, they can engage in processes of knowledge creation, crucial to be the best school psychologist possible.

A Proposal

The present section summarizes some of the most compelling points mentioned in the chapter, and it proposes a more comprehensive framework to include the multiple aspects examined above.

The American Psychological Association (APA) defines school psychology as "a field of psychology concerned with the psychoeducational problems and other issues arising in primary and secondary schools. We learnt that the responsibilities of the school psychologist include involvement in overall curriculum planning,

individualized curriculum assessment and planning, administration of psychoeducational tests, interviews with parents concerning their child's progress and problems, pupils' behavioural problems, counselling of teachers and students, and
research on systematic educational questions and issues." (https://dictionary.apa.
org/school-psychology)

In other words, school is clearly the specific focus of school psychologists.
Although the previous statement may seem trivial at a first glance, it soon becomes
clear that school encompasses many different items, dimensions, and actors. To
begin with, it is possible to look at schools from four different perspectives:

i) With a focus on a single person, whether a student, a teacher, or anyone involved
   in the institution
ii) With a focus on the classroom
iii) With a focus on the internal functioning of the institution, considering teaching
   staff, administrative department, the principal, and any other professional entering the school organization
iv) With a larger focus, including all the interconnections schools may have with
   other agencies

This means that school psychologists should support students' ability to learn and
teachers' ability to teach. They should know learning and teaching dynamics, and
they should understand cognitive and social processes and emotional and cultural
dimensions at work within educational contexts. Furthermore, school psychologists
should know how to promote and value students' and teachers' mental health and
how to help children and youth succeed academically, socially, behaviorally, and
emotionally. Furthermore, the competencies of school psychologists should include
issues connected to social inclusion, special needs, and cultural diversity.

School psychologists should also tend to support internal relationships between
all the professionals involved: teachers, administrative staff, school collaborators,
and principals. Supporting a healthy community is one of the tasks school psychologists should take up. This means monitoring any possible internal conflicts, preventing or eventually solving burnout or disengagement, and offering good solutions
to organizational crises that may concern the school as institutions.

Within a broader scope, school psychologists should help maintain positive and
fruitful relationships with any agency that interfaces with school, first families, but
also nearby schools, workplaces, and local organizations offering service to students
and families such as sport, clubs and recreation clubs, social services, and parishes.
Such broader perspective is paramount in preventing schools from becoming self-
referential bubbles and to ensure the best environment possible, considering the
various contexts students engage with, whether presently or in the future. Schools
should understand what is happening outside their walls and build solid bridges to
contribute to students' development in their entirety and prepare them to contribute
to society. Therefore, concepts such as lifelong learning, innovation, sustainability,
and active citizenship should be included within school psychologists'
competencies.

The result is a depiction of an expert with cross-borders competencies, both among different specializations of psychology – cognitive, educational and developmental, social and dynamic, general and organizational, health, and sport – and as well between psychology and contiguous sciences, such as sociology, pedagogy, pediatrics, medicine, and computer sciences, and any other discipline may be instrumental to the proper functioning of schools.

A theory that encompasses such a far-reaching vision is necessary for a good overview of school psychologists' profile. Our proposal is to refer to the Activity Theory (hereafter, AT) (Engeström, 1999), which is a theoretical framework that represents the most important legacy of Soviet philosophy and psychology. Strongly connected to Vygotsky's vision (Vygotsky, 1978), AT is increasingly viewed as a potentially fertile paradigm in understanding human behavior. Although we acknowledge that this theoretical choice may present some challenges – for instance, there are still debates surrounding what an activity *is* and whether all human activities are worthy of attention (Bakhurst, 2009) – we see this approach as able to include the many levels through which school psychologists can perform their activity.

AT has a historical-cultural perspective, as it studies the cultural "residues" that can be traced in the various transformation processes of which humans are at the same time the product and the producer. Based on this assumption, some authors (Chaiklin, 2001; Cole & Engeström, 1993) prefer to use the label of Cultural Historical Activity Theory (CHAT). In any case, the assumption is that humans are unable to have a direct relationship with nature as such relationship is always mediated by material and symbolic tools. AT assigns a crucial role to mediation objects, referred to as artefacts. Humans have always been able to use, create, and improve tools capable of enhancing their action in the world, and they pass them on to next generations. In its original elaboration, AT aims to develop a meta-theory capable of providing interpretative frameworks for human action (Kaptelinin & Nardi, 1997). Its overall goal is not only to understand human action but also to offer indications on how to improve the human condition by understanding those complex actions of which only humans are capable of. In this sense, we consider AT as appropriate to outline the school psychologist's profile.

In its latest evolution, AT looks at individuals within groups or communities made up of people who share objectives and rules, functional to the implementation of common actions, performed by using artefacts, finalized to the creation of objects. This ensemble – individuals, groups, communities, roles, artefacts, and shared objects – makes clear that no action can be performed individually but always within an activity system composed of the six elements just mentioned. For instance, an activity system could include a psychologist working with a computer science expert to introduce digital educational tools at school, involving teachers, students, and their parents. This activity system, nevertheless, does not exist in a vacuum. On the contrary, it is strictly interconnected to the culture students are embedded into, including all the every-day contexts lived by the students that contribute to making sense of using digital tools. Therefore, also other activity systems may play a role in implementing the innovation, for instance, after-school communities where students may already use videogames or other digital resources. This highlights how an activity system is never isolated, but it is always in connection with other systems, feeding them and fed by them. The latest generation of AT focuses exactly on understanding the multiplicity of perspectives that take place within and between systems, as well as the nature and dynamics of the networks that are created between the various systems of activities that interact with each other (Engeström & Glăveanu, 2012).

AT allows to holistically analyze the dimensions and the fundamental contextual areas that characterize the role of the school psychologists in its complexity, thus producing a "matrix" through which to orient the intervention. To build this matrix, we need first to distinguish between two different ways of conceiving school psychologists' intervention: (i) as intervention when critical situations occur and (ii) as promotion of wellbeing, conceived not only as prevention but also as care and attention. On the side of problem-solving, there are many topics of intervention, including some that recently gained attention such as specific learning disorders, dropping out of or missing compulsory schooling, anxiety and depression, bullying and cyberbullying, and difficulties of inclusion of disabled pupils or problems in carrying out an educational action that allows academic success also to foreign students, just to mention only the most frequent. However, there is also a side of commitment that concerns the promotion of wellbeing in school, for instance, improving teacher training, attention to the socio-affective aspects of learning, sexual and emotional education, introducing innovations, and promoting classroom management techniques.

"Complexity" is, therefore, the keyword guiding school psychologists who must know how to intervene on problems and how to prevent discomfort, avoiding improper simplifications. Hence, school should be considered as a set of contextual areas marked by tasks that different actors are committed to tackle through some specific procedures. For this reason, we propose to distinguish two dimensions: (a) school as a professional organization and (b) school as an educational community.

Therefore, we already have two different types of intervention – problem-solving and wellbeing promotion – and both can be applied by considering school as a professional organization or as an educational community.

AT proposes to consider, for each activity, the following six elements: (i) the objects of the activity, the end results of the task; (ii) mediating tools – including the practices – used to achieve the objects; (iii) the individuals involved; (iv) the professional and social community involved; (v) the rules functional to the achievement of the activity; and (vi) the division of labor according to consolidated practices or to new orientations. Once these elements are identified, school psychologists can co-construct a working model able to give feedback not only about the current situation but also to indicate possible solutions. At this point, action can take place and school psychologists are also required to reflect on the change they induced, to evaluate the results, and finally consolidate the new practices introduced. In other words, school psychologists can work on three types of activities: consultancy, training, and research, and for each of them, it is required to plan the

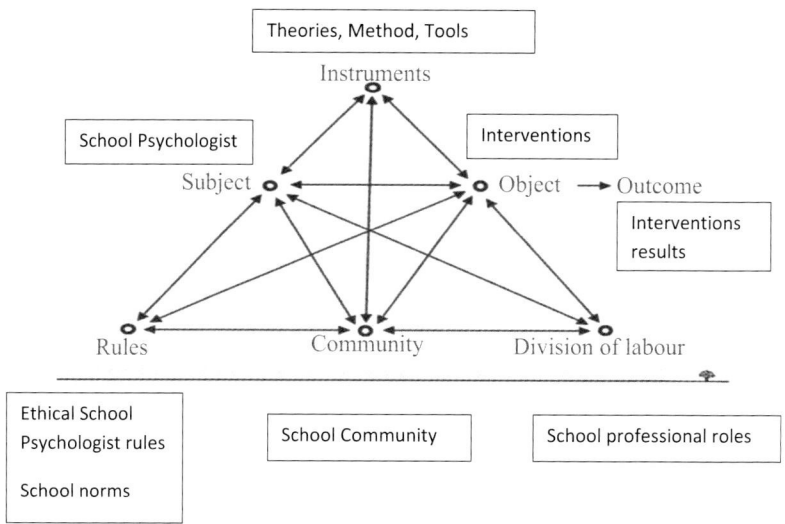

Fig. 2 The AT triangle instantiated with the school psychology elements

interventions or the activities, to manage the activities proposed, and, finally, to assess and consolidate the intervention.

To visually present our proposal, we borrow the famous triangle used to represent the AT with the instantiation of the elements defining school psychology (Fig. 2).

This figure synthesizes the types of intervention a school psychologist can propose, together with the perspectives from which school can be considered and the elements highlighted by AT. As anticipated, the AT elements would acquire a specific instantiation according to the specific type of activity – consultancy, training, and research. For example, when offering consultancy concerning school as a professional organization, the object could be the development of a new organization chart, created by using the documents already available (mediating tool), involving the whole school community, attending the roles set by the government on this matter, clarifying that the principal is the one that has to implement the proposal and that the final assessment should be in charge of the school psychologist (division of labor).

Our proposal is not intended as an addition to the existing conceptualizations. Rather, it should be considered as an attempt to systematize the various ideas already circulating about school psychology. As evidence, we can show how AT can help in organizing the components of the training program defined by ISPA. To this purpose, we display in Fig. 3 again the AT triangle this time to illustrate the activity system, and the training goals outlined by ISPA.

A first set of goals focuses on the provision of tools, understood as theories, methods, and techniques relating to the object as well as to the methods of interventions. Among such tools, we can consider Goal 1, explicitly devoted to core knowledge and skills about the content (can it be – for instance – cognition and learning, social and emotional development, individual differences) to which it can

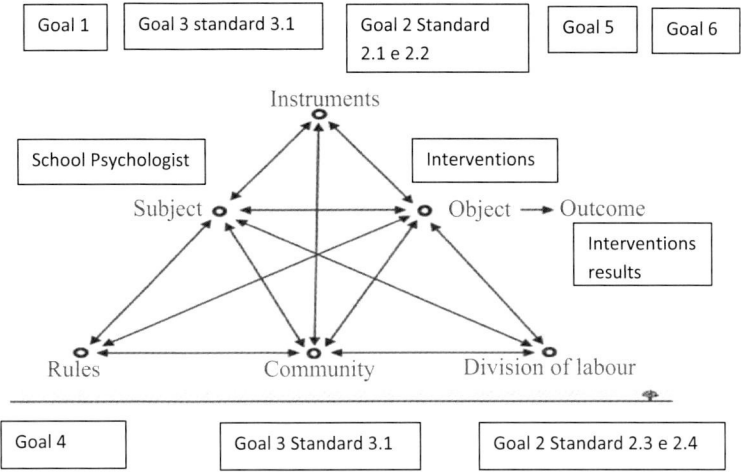

Fig. 3 The activity system in the training programs

be added the standard 3.1 of Goal 3 dedicated to working with children and families from culturally diverse communities. Subsequently, there is a set of goals focusing on the methods of intervention, such as the first two standards relating to Goal 2: Evidence-Based Decision-Making and Accountability (Standard 2.1) and Prevention, Mental Health Promotion, and Crisis Intervention (Standard 2.2). Goal 5, related to interpersonal skills, and Goal 6, related to knowledge and use of research methods, can be further added. Goal 4, instead, focused on the mediating rules of interventions and deals with ethical issues and with the skills for a formal written restitution of the interventions. As far as the community is concerned, Goal 3 (Standard 3.1) underlines the importance of membership in the community of psychologists at a national and international level. Finally, regarding the division of labor, Goal 2 with the 2.3 and 2.4 standards enables training aimed at understanding the organizational functioning of the school context, the roles envisaged therein, and the possibilities for internal and external collaboration.

Therefore, the re-reading of the ISPA guidelines in the framework of the AT outlines the vision of a proposal articulated in all the fundamental aspects of the professional activity of school psychology. Indeed, it is necessary to situate this proposal within the sociocultural context, and it needs to be constantly updated to reflect changes in social and specific cultural conditions (e.g., themes for intervention arising from the emergency created by the Covid-19 pandemic and in the aftermath of the emergency).

Conclusions

In conclusion, we hope to have given a good overview of how school psychology developed and its potentialities in supporting the educational mission of school and the wellbeing of all the actors involved. School psychologists can help schools promote positive educational practices and teach everyone in an inclusive and effective way. As we already stated, a large variety of knowledge and skills are necessary to work at school and to propose interventions for different actors (students, teachers, families, school staff) and with multiple objectives, by using different approaches and tools. The challenge is to continue to promote this figure and its services in schools to support the educational institution, both in terms of health promotion and intervention on critical events.

International associations and universities provide theoretical and professionalizing coordinates. Although today it seems possible to have clear ideas on what knowledge, what skills school psychologists should have and through what training methods they should be prepared, we should keep in mind that school psychologists should remain strictly connected to the territory and sensitive to cultural changes. Therefore, school psychology should be flexible and able to take in consideration new and unexpected instances and demands. School psychologists are called to implement interventions aimed at supporting learning, solving behavioral problems, dealing with mental health, and improving school organization. They should be equipped to prevent critical situations and to intervene when needed. Their mission is to facilitate school paths of students, training teachers, and collaboration between schools and between school, family, and other extra-school agencies and to improve the organizational climate in school.

The more universities and associations work together to train and promote school psychology and psychologists specialized in it, the more school will benefit from the interventions that will be proposed and implemented. The benefits generated by school psychologists will impact the present *and* the future and will reverberate on the whole society.

References

AIP. (2019). *Istituzione della figura professionale dello psicologo scolastico.* Approfondimenti. Last retrieved on June 15th, 2021 from: https://aipass.org/sites/default/files/documento%20finale_Psicologo%20Scolastico.pdf

APA. (2020). *School Psychology.* Last retrieved on June 15th, 2021 from: https://www.apa.org/ed/graduate/specialize/school

Bakhurst, D. (2009). Reflections on activity theory. *Educational Review, 61*(2), 197–210.

Bray, M. A., & Kehle, T. J. (2011). *The Oxford handbook of school psychology.* Oxford: Oxford University Press.

Chaiklin, S. (2001). *The theory and practice of cultural-historical psychology.* Aarhus: Aarhus University Press.

Ching, Y. H., & Hsu, Y. C. (2013). Peer feedback to facilitate project-based learning in an online environment. *International Review of Research in Open and Distributed Learning, 14*(5), 258–276.

Cole, M., & Engeström, Y. (1993). A cultural-historical approach to distributed cognition. In G. Salomon (Ed.), *Distributed cognitions: Psychological and educational considerations* (pp. 1–46). Cambridge University Press: New York.

Cutts, N. E. (1955). *School psychologists at midcentury: A report of the Thayer conference on the function, qualifications, and training of school psychologists.* Washington D.C.: American Psychological Association.

D'Amato, R. C., Zafiris, C., McConnell, E., & Dean, R. S. (2011). *The history of school psychology: Understanding the past to not repeat it.* In M. Bray & T. Kehle (Eds.), *Oxford handbook of school psychology* (pp. 9–60). New York, NY: Oxford.

Engeström, Y. (1987). *Learning by expanding.* Helsinki: Orienta-Konsultit Oy.

Engeström, Y. (1999). Activity theory and individual and social transformation. *Perspectives on Activity Theory, 19*(38), 19–30.

Engeström, Y. (2000). Activity theory as a framework for analyzing and redesigning work. *Ergonomics, 43*(7), 960–974.

Engeström, Y., & Glăveanu, V. (2012). On third generation activity theory: Interview with Yrjö Engeström. *Europe's Journal of Psychology, 8*(4), 515–518

Fagan, T. K. (1992). Compulsory schooling, child study, clinical psychology, and special education: Origins of school psychology. *American Psychologist, 47*(2), 236–243.

Fagan, T. K. (2005a). The 50th anniversary of the Thayer conference: Historical perspectives and accomplishments. *School Psychology Quarterly, 20*(3), 225.

Fagan, T. K. (2005b). Literary origins of the term "school psychologist" revisited. *School Psychology Review, 34*(3), 432–434.

Fagan, T. K., & Delugach, F. J. (1984). Literary origins of the term "school psychologist". *School Psychology Review, 13*(2), 216–220.

Fagan, T. K., & Wise, P. S. (2007). *School psychology: Past, present, and future* (3rd ed.). Bethesda, MD: National Association of School Psychologists.

Farrell, P. (2010). School psychology: Learning lessons from history and moving forward. *School Psychology International, 31*(6), 581–598.

ISPA. (2020). The Accreditation of Professional Training Programs in School Psychology. Last retrieve on June 15th, 2021 from: https://www.ispaweb.org/wp-content/uploads/2020/05/Microsoft-Word-STANDARDS-January-2020-cx.-1.pdf

Jimerson, S. R., Graydon, K., Farrell, P., Kikas, E., Hatzichristou, C., Boce, E., . . . ISPA Research Committee. (2004). The international school psychology survey: Development and data from Albania, Cyprus, Estonia, Greece and Northern England. *School Psychology International, 25*(3), 259–286.

Jimerson, S. R., Oakland, T. D., & Farrell, P. T. (Eds.). (2007). *The handbook of international school psychology.* Thousand Oaks: Sage.

Jones, C., & Healing, G. (2010). Net generation students: Agency and choice and the new technologies. *Journal of Computer Assisted Learning, 26*(5), 344–356.

Koh, J. H. L., Herring, S. C., & Hew, K. F. (2010). Project-based learning and student knowledge construction during asynchronous online discussion. *Internet and Higher Education, 13*, 284–291.

Kaptelinin, V., & Nardi, B. A. (1997). Activity Theory: Basic Concepts and Applications. CHI 97 Tutorial.

Lee, S. W. (2005). International school psychology association. In S. W. Lee (Ed.), *Encyclopedia of school psychology* (pp. 272–273). London: Sage.

Merseth, K. (1991). *The Case for Cases in Teacher Education.* Washington, D.C.: American Association for Higher Education and the American Association of Colleges for Teacher Education.

NASP. (2021). *Selecting a graduate program.* Last retrieved June 15th, 2021 from:https://www.nasponline.org/about-school-psychology/selecting-a-graduate-program

New Freedom Commission on Mental Health. (2003). *Achieving the promise: Transforming mental health care in America, Final Report* (DHHS Publication No. SMA-03–3832). Rockville, MD: Substance Abuse and Mental Health Services Administration, Center for Mental Health Service

Nonaka, I., & Takeuchi, H. (1995). *The knowledge-creating company: How Japanese companies create the dynamics of innovation.* New York: Oxford University Press.

Paavola, S., & Hakkarainen, K. (2005). The knowledge creation metaphor–An emergent epistemological approach to learning. *Science & Education, 14*(6), 535–557.

Paavola, S., Lakkala, M., Muukkonen, H., Kosonen, K., & Karlgren, K. (2011). The roles and uses of design principles in a project on trialogical learning. *Research in Learning Technology, 19*(3), 233–246.

Phillips, B. N. (1990). *School psychology at a turning point: Ensuring a bright future for the profession*. San Francisco: Jossey-Bass.

Reynolds, C. R., & Gutkin, T. B. (Eds.). (1999). *The handbook of school psychology* (3rd ed.). New York: Wiley.

Sansone, N., Cesareni, D., & Ligorio, M. (2016). The trialogical learning approach to innovate teaching. *Italian Journal of Educational Technology, 24*(2), 82–82.

Scardamalia, M., & Bereiter, C. (2010). A brief history of knowledge building. *Canadian Journal of Learning and Technology/La revue canadienne de l'apprentissage et de la technologie, 36*(1).

Sfard, A. (1998). On two metaphors for learning and the dangers of choosing just one. *Educational researcher, 27*(2), 4–13.

Shick Tryon, G. (1986). *The professional practice of psychology*. Westport, CT: Greenwood.

Skalski, A. K., Minke, K., Rossen, E., Cowan, K. C., Kelly, J., Armistead, R., & Smith, A. (2015). *NASP practice model implementation guide*. Bethesda, MD: National Association of School Psychologists.

Sudzina, M. R. (1997). Case study as a constructivist pedagogy for teaching educational psychology. *Educational Psychology Review, 9*(2), 199–260.

Tharinger, D. J., Pryzwansky, W. B., & Miller, J. A. (2008). School psychology: A specialty of professional psychology with distinct competencies and complexities. *Professional Psychology: Research and Practice, 39*(5), 529.

U.S. Department of Health and Human Services. (1999). *Mental health: A report of the Surgeon General*. Rockville, MD: U.S. Department of Health and Human Services, Substance Abuse and Mental Health Services Administration.

Upton, D., & Taylor, C. (2010). *Teaching psychology in higher education*. John Wiley & Sons.

Vygotsky, L. S. (1978). *Mind in society. The development of the higher psychological processes*. In M. Cole, V. John-Steiner, S. Scribner, & E. Souberman (Eds.). Cambridge, MA: Harvard University Press.

Wall, W. D. (1956). *Psychological services for schools*. New York: New York University Press.

Wassermann, S. (1993). *Getting down to cases: Learning to teach with case studies*. New York: Teachers College Press.

Ysseldyke, J. E. (1982). The spring hill symposium on the future of psychology in the schools. *American Psychologist, 37*(5), 547–552.

Ysseldyke, J. E., & Schakel, J. A. (1983). The school psychologist: An introduction. In G. W. Hynd (Ed.), *Directions in school psychology* (pp. 3–26). Syracuse N.Y.: Syracuse University Press.

Community Psychology and Psychological Distress

29

Principles, Practices and Pedagogy

Paul Rhodes

Contents

Abstract

Dominant approaches to support people in psychological distress are individualistic, emphasizing intervention conducted in the privacy of the therapy room, focused on exploring and resolving intrapsychic problems. This approach, originating with Freud, now has a wide variety of permutations, including self-psychology, cognitive models, and those inspired by Buddhism, dialectics, somatics, and more. This personal approach to mental distress, however, is limited, given that it fails to recognize the wider social, political, and cultural determinants of such distress and cuts the person off from their community, where solidarity, solace, and healing might also take place. The aim of this chapter is to introduce the reader to community psychology, as employed for the amelioration of psychological concerns. In particular, it serves as a primer for the content that might be included in teaching this subject to future activist-practitioners, with particular attention to the

P. Rhodes (✉)
Clinical Psychology Unit, University of Sydney, Sydney, Australia
e-mail: p.rhodes@sydney.edu.au

© Springer Nature Switzerland AG 2023   725
J. Zumbach et al. (eds.), *International Handbook of Psychology Learning and Teaching*,
Springer International Handbooks of Education,
https://doi.org/10.1007/978-3-030-28745-0_33

critical pedagogy involved. A case study will also be provided, outlining how a clinical psychology program was modified to include a community psychology curriculum. The development of activist-scholars focused on community psychology will also be discussed, with reference to a series of studies currently in progress.

Keywords

Community · Mental health · Pedagogy · Lived experience

The Dominance of Individualism

In 1907, Witmer, follower of Wundt, defined clinical psychology as "the study of individuals, by observation or experimentation, with the intention of promoting change" (Compas & Gotlib, 2002, p42). Since then, the most dominant models of practice centered on psychological distress have focused on the sole agent and the workings of the mind. This emphasis has meant that fields which conceptualize distress beyond this narrow focus have been marginalized. The field of family therapy places the etiology of distress interpersonally rather than intrapsychically (Rhodes & Wallis, 2011), with origins on cybernetics, anthropology, and sociology (Hoffman, 2002). This field has been applied to a wide variety of psychic problems, including eating disorders (Rhodes, 2003), mood disturbance (Diamond, Siqueland, and Diamond (2003), drug use (Slesnick, Gizem, & Brigham, 2013), and child abuse (MacKinnon, 1999). Family therapists look beyond the individual to the structures, patterns, strengths, and stories of families, deviating from a paradigm that would pathologize and diagnose children caught in forces beyond their control (Carr, 2000). Community psychology, however, extends this process beyond the family, taking the systemic lens to consider wider social, political, and cultural contexts for the psyche (Bronfenbrenner, 1979). Mental pathology can be reconfigured, beyond both the phenomenological and familial, and reconstructed, as a symptom of wider marginalization, or poverty, racism, collective trauma, and the like (Prilleltensky, 1997).

Introducing Community Psychology

Any curriculum in community psychology must include the basic components of history, principles, and practice. I include these here, with specific examples of practice from my own setting in Australia. Clearly, this must be adapted for local conditions and needs.

Origins

Community psychology is seen as having started in the 1960s in the USA, as part of the social movements of civil rights and feminism (Swift, Bond, & Serrano-Garcia, 2000). Psychologists aimed to create a form of practice that was informed by social justice and emphasize the empowerment of local communities to respond to their own needs (Levine & Perkins, 1997; Nelson & Prilleltensky, 2005). The recognized birthplace of the field is the Swampscott conference held in 1965, where community psychologists developed the key principles including an ecological orientation, social justice, and a focus on the participation and empowerment of communities (Orford, 1992). Rappaport's (1977) Community Psychology: Values, Research, and Action became the seminal text, establishing him as one of the key figures in the field.

Despite these claims, the origins of community psychology can be actually found in Austria in the 1930s (Fryer, 2008). The Marienthal project is conducted by left-wing social scientists who were concerned to ease the distress of unemployed communities. They described how their "psychic life has contracted; a narrowing of the sphere of wants occurred…we defined this psychic attitude as resignation" (Lazarsfeld, 1932, p. 154). These symptoms would be seen by psychotherapists as a depressive disorder; "a diminution of expectation and activity, a disrupted sense of time, and a steady decline into apathy through a variety of stages and attitudes" (Jahoda-Lazarsfeld & Zeisel, 1933, p. 128.). These early community psychologists, however, conducted qualitative and quantitative research to demonstrate the direct relationship between these intrapsychic phenomenon and the loss of employment.

South America also looms large when considering the history of community psychology. While the field formally began in the 1960s and early 1970s, its principles can be seen in the grassroots liberation theology of the Catholic Church which tied spiritual matters to sociopolitical oppression (Reich et al., 2017). In practice, therapeutic communities and other social psychiatry projects were happening during the 1960s in Chile, Argentina, and Brazil, with the movement propelled by the transformative philosophies of Paulo Friere. The first formal degree program was developed in 1975 in Puerto Rico, with others soon following in Mexico and the Dominican Republic (Reich et al., 2017).

In my own country of Australia, community psychology followed their US counterparts, given similar sociopolitical conditions in the 1960s and 1970s under the government of Whitlam. Psychologists focused especially on issues such as the needs of migrants, the problem of domestic violence, and the needs of indigenous Australians (Gridley, Fisher, Thomas, & Bishop, 2007). In 1974, the Australian Psychological Society started a Committee on Social Issues that would later become the College of Community Psychology. The first university courses emerged in Queensland and Western Australia in the mid-1970s.

Key Principles

Clinical psychology and traditional approaches to psychotherapy focus on intrapsychic processes, failing to situate distress in a wider context. Community psychology follows an ecological model which resists reductionism in favor of recognizing the interdependence of contextual factors. Psychological intervention need not simply focus on first-order change within one person or one family, but instead look to second-order change, within local communities, institutions, structures, and cultures

(Watzlawick, 1977). Second-order change is arguably more challenging than the first, involving changes to the relationships and rules that govern a system, but in turn has wider impacts concerning the number of those that can benefit and the enhanced sustainability of that change.

Bronfenbrenner's (1979) ecological model is the most influential in the field, differentiating between the microsystem, mesosystem, exosystem, and macro-system. The first consists of the relationships between the individual and their personal network of interactions across the domains of home, local community, and employment. The second consists of the relations between major settings in a person's life, such as between the household and school environments, or between one's place of employment and home. The exosystem looks to wider socio-structural issues, such as the role of the media, the culture of work, and problems in public institutions, serving to have an indirect impact on the person. The macrosystem relates to both formal and unwritten laws, and values contextualize all the other systems. Analyzing the composition of these systems as well as interactions between them is seen as crucial in community psychology assessment.

For the community psychologist, however, direct intervention is primarily focused on the micro and meso-systems, while being cognizant of an analysis of how wider discourses and structures impinge on these settings. Of course a psychologist can serve as a social activist, speaking out about social justice issues and advocating for changes in public policy. More local practice, however, focusses on the development of communities that can prevent psychological distress from occurring, or ameliorate distress when it does. Key to this practice, of course, is a requirement for any involvement in communities to be both participatory and empowering. While tradi-tional psychology can be expert-driven, relying on the therapist to provide answers, community psychology relies on the democratic involvement of community members, who might position themselves as instigators, leaders, and organizers in community psychology initiatives. Empowerment is actually the primary focus of community psychology (Rappaport, 1977), with the psychologists supporting the consciousness-raising, solidarity, and efficacy of communities.

Given the local focus of community psychology initiatives will differ widely between communities, nations, and cultures. While clinical psychology bases its therapeutic models on claims of generalizability, community psychology initiatives, as participatory, emerge from the ground up and as such are each a unique co-construction. For the purpose of this paper, I will describe three specific initiatives that are relevant to my own country of Australia. These examples have been chosen to demonstrate the potential for community psychology to address critical national problems, albeit at local grass roots levels.

Practice Exemplars

1. Aboriginal Social and Emotional Well-Being

Over 2000 Australians commit suicide annually in Australia, but the rate of Aborig-inal suicide is twice that of non-Aboriginal, particularly among the adolescent population (Ridani, Shand, & Christiansen, 2014). Our leading psychologist, Pat Dudgeon (2017), argues for local, participatory responses, whereby Aboriginal Indigenous are supported to find their own solutions. Her approach differs widely from that of mainstream clinical psychology, which if applied to these communities would serve as a form of cognitive-behavioral colonialism. She argues for a practice that is both community lead and radically decolonized, based on Aboriginal constructs rather than Western views of pathology. The construct of "mental health" itself is rejected in favor of Social and Emotional Well-Being (Dudgeon & Calma, 2013), one which mirrors the ecological model of community psychology. Here distress experienced by the self, and well-being, is understood as a function of multiple interrelated connections, to kinship, community, country, and culture, all understood in the context of wider social and historical determinants.

Ridani et al. (2014) demonstrate the potential for Aboriginal-led initiatives directed at youth suicide, reviewing nearly 70 community-based programs. Many focused on the development of community connectedness, cultural practices, and identities, held on country, in workshops and camps, not within the four walls of the solitary therapy room.

Any collaboration between Aboriginal communities and non-Aboriginal psychological services must emphasize local empowerment, rather than expert-driven intervention. The Australian Psychological Society (2010) has recognized that this type of collaboration might best be done between Aboriginal healing practices and the school of narrative therapy that was originated by white mental health practitioners (Ralph & Ryan, 2017). Narrative therapy focusses on social justice and empowerment through story which as cultural relevance for Aboriginal communities (Wingard & Lester, 2001). Community-based narrative practices, such as the definitional ceremony (White, 1995), have been modified in consultation with Aboriginal leaders, (Denborough et al., 2006), to focus on the task of preventing and responding to suicide. These practices support communities to remember those who has been lost and via story cycles. Stories are recorded and re-told between communities to build solidarity and resilience.

The approaches of Social and Emotional Well-Being and narrative community practice demonstrate the potential for community psychology to respond to one of our nation's most critical problems. An ecological approach, community-led and focused on empowerment, provides a culturally valid alternative to mainstream psychological methods.

2. Refugees

The plight of refugees is a particularly National concern in Australia, particularly due to our Government's policy of turning back asylum seekers boats and imprisoning those who arrive as a deterrent. Those who do receive visas enter a country that would be seen as hostile or at least ambivalent towards refugees, one which has perpetrated further traumas despite our reputation as free and fair. Psychological work with recent migrants is conducive to community psychology, given many form of local communities in this country. Our own research in Western Sydney with Relationships Australia (Karageorge, Rhodes, Gray, & Papadopoulos,

2018) describes a community-based approach to relational repair with families from a variety of countries, including South Sudan, Iran, and Syria. Partnerships were established between local bicultural health workers who were members of these communities and professional family therapists trained in post-Milan systemic family therapy. Deep cultural expertise combined with family therapy skills allowed for innovative culturally valid approaches to the improvement of fractured family relationships. The bicultural workers were supervised by the family therapists in responding to family dynamics, while the family therapy teams were advised on cultural responsiveness and adaptation of methods. Local community-based cultural events and multi-family meetings were held in order to engage and then work with families. Groups included culturally relevant activities, including sports and arts, providing a soft engagement prior to facilitated conversations about more challenging family issues.

This project demonstrates how innovative community-based approaches to psychological issues can be and the means by which mainstream therapeutic practices can be transformed to meet the participatory local needs of communities.

3. Psychosis

Community-based approaches, though, not only are relevant to work conducted with specified culture groups but can be applied, in communities, to a wide range of clinical problems experienced by members of all cultures. Open dialogue is a method, developed in Finland two decades ago, which provides a community-based approach to early psychosis that is a radical alternative to the dominant medical model (Seikkula et al., 2003). This approach aims to lessen a reliance on hospital admission, fostering the establishment of personalized networks, democratic decision-making communities consisting of the person hearing voices, friends, family members, and mental health professionals. This approach has suited young people experiencing their first crisis due to psychosis. Family therapists meet in the persons' own residence, returning daily with the network until things stabilize. Medications are not the first decision to be made, but instead emphasis is placed on developing a safe space with a dialogue, where all voices can be heard equally, including the voices heard by the young person due to psychosis. The general atmosphere is one of slow respectful listening, including across the professional and non-professional divides, tolerating uncertainty so that impulsive decisions are avoided. Traditionally, a crisis leads to quick decisions to medicate and hospitalize which can set the course of a young person's mental health career (Seikkula et al., 2003). Buus et al. (2017) reviewed 33 studies of Open Dialogue, showing promise for this emergent approach. This method provides an example of how community work is an activist practice, directly challenging the hierarchical and pathologizing culture of the medical system.

These practice exemplars of community work, with Indigenous peoples, refugee populations and those who hear voices, demonstrate the key principles of community psychology. All three involve an ecological model, which utilizes the strengths of local resources for the amelioration of psychological distress. Practices involve the participation and empowerment of family, cultural, and social network groups and the enhancement of democratic rather than hierarchical relations between these subsystems and these within therapeutic and mental health services.

A Pedagogy for Community Psychology

Traditional teaching in clinical psychology follows a competence model, emphasizing technical skills and positioning practice as the development of proficiency in specific models of intervention, including cognitive-behavior therapy, schema-therapy, integrative psychotherapy, and others. Given the dominance of the scientist-practitioner model in this field, the person of the therapist receives little attention, in the form of psychotherapy or self-development (Salter & Rhodes, 2018; Turnbull & Rhodes, 2019) and nothing regarding the politics of mental health. Community psychology curricula also involve a variety of competencies including ecological assessment, cybernetics and systems, group processes, empowerment practices, mental health prevention and promotion, crisis management, program evaluation methods, and participatory action research. Unique to community psychology education, however, is the need to also prepare students personally and politically for their future roles, developing activists capable of performing as agents of change in settings where marginalization and oppression is likely. Educating students for this kind of role is a unique and challenging task that requires different forms of pedagogy to competence-based learning. Pedagogy must be critical and include a variety of specific components, a liberatory classroom (hooks, 1994) where a personal reckoning with privilege is possible, where cultural humility can be developed, where students have direct access to the lived experience and insider knowledge of communities, and where dialogue and witnessing are learned.

These components will be explored here, with vignette examples from my own classroom at The University of Sydney. This class is a community psychology component of a Masters of Clinical Psychology Degree, where three half-day immersive workshops are held with a variety of educative, creative, and dialogical exercises and experiences. The workshops follow the three areas discussed earlier in this paper: Aboriginal social and emotional well-being, refugee community work, and Open Dialogue for severe mental health problems in young people.

A Critical Pedagogy

The starting point for any community psychology student must be to turn the lens inward towards the field of mainstream psychology, rather than out into community practice. A large majority of community psychology programs will be post-graduate, with students having been trained in mainstream settings in post-positivist psychology. Psychology, as a discipline, insists on individualism as a form of "habitus" (Bourdieu, 1977) and has become our collective identity. As a field we have neglected, however, to implicate neo-liberalism in the development of psychological distress (Sugarman, 2015) and instead have colluded in the development of an industry that pathologizes the sole agent (client). This implies that psychologists can perpetuate the isolation of this person, rather than focusing on issues related to attachment, belonging, and community (Verhaeghe, 2014). The confidentiality of the consultation room may support personal responsibility, but also promotes blame in the face of marginalization, oppression, or and socioeconomic disadvantage. Moreira (2015) requires a critical psychopathology, following Merleau-Ponty's (1960) argument that clients embody historico-cultural traumas. Beyond the walls of the therapy room, community work is a moral as well as a clinical imperative (Prilleltensky, 1997).

The education of psychologists who can question the practices of mainstream psychology and the development of morality in the classroom centered around social justice requires a critical pedagogy, one founded by Paulo Freire (1970) and developed by bell hooks (1994) and others. Freire criticized what he labeled the banking model of education.

Instead of communicating, the teacher issues communiqués and makes deposits which the students patiently receive, memorize, and repeat. This is the 'banking' concept of education, in which the scope of action allowed to students extends only as far as receiving, filing, and storing the deposits. [3]:58 Freire, Paulo (Freire, 1970).

Instead, he embraces a model of education where knowledge is both unlearned and then co-created between educator and student, an active process based on dialogue. The first step is an authentic liberation or humanizing of the student, which can only be done through unlearning and consciousness raising.

A Pedagogy of the Privileged

Freire originally wrote Pedagogy of the Oppressed (1970) in relation to the empowerment of oppressed Latin American students, but as Allen and Rossatto (2008) point out, the majority of students taking psychology classes are likely to instead be benefactors of social privilege. The aim of critical pedagogy in this respect is not to empower the oppressed student but rather to challenge the oppressor student to come to terms with their place on the hegemony and how they have benefited from structural inequality. Allen and Rossatto (2008) rightly point out that critical pedagogy for privileged students is undertheorized, but follow bell's (1992) admission that, despite the significant challenges, it must be attempted. Cresswell, Karimova, and Brock (2013) correctly name this Pedagogy of the Privileged. In order for students to come to terms with their own privilege, it must be a significant emotional experience, rather than just an intellectual one. Mezirow's (2000) transformational learning theory speaks to this experience, highlighting the disorientation of learning about injustice, the shame and guilt, and eventually critical reflection on personal assumptions and moral complicity. Typical confessional dialogues and exercises about "the knapsack of privilege" are likely to be ineffectual in promoting this kind of change (Margolin & Martiniello, 2015). Classes need to be designed as immersive encounters (Addleman, Brazo, and Cevallos (2011) with the paid participation of community leaders alongside academics, with creative or narrative material presented alongside intellectual, and with direct encounters with communities. Barnum and Illari (2016) call this bringing "the town to the gown." Further are some of the components used for this purpose at The University of Sydney, presented as part of three half-day immersive workshops.

1. Community Educators in the Classroom

Academics are often unlikely to be members of the communities in which many of their students will conduct their future work in or at least will be privileged members of those communities due to education and employment. It is critical that the academic serves not as an ally, given this term implies an identity, open to false performativity, but rather as an accomplice which implies pedagogy as collective action to challenge injustice. These terms also imply that risks are being taken in the classroom, rather than more tokenistic involvement of marginalized groups (Clemens, 2017). Critical too is that all members of communities are paid for their work in the classroom.

In our own workshops, we have enabled direct education from community members in a variety of ways. In the case of the workshop on Aboriginal Social and Emotional Well-Being, the entire process was run by two aboriginal academics from other Universities. Our workshop on Refugee Mental Health was conducted in a highly innovative manner, with Syrian psychologists working in refugee services teaching students directly through zoom from their home country. In addition, asylum seekers working as mental health scholars at another University where employed to visit and tell their story, both their personal narrative of fleeing their home country, incarceration in Australian detention, and their roles as researchers. Our workshop on Open Dialogue and youth mental health employed a large team of educators, including professional Peer Workers, parents of young people who have attempted suicide, a Peer Academic, a Peer Poet and Educator, and others.

2. Open Dialogue

While a small component of each workshop involves formal didactic lectures, the majority of time is dedicated to the practice of Open Dialogue. The classroom is organized in a circle of chairs, rather than the traditional arrangement with educators up front and students behind desks. This practice allows for the democratization of learning, a polyphonic space, where no one voice is privileged (Olson, Seikkula, & Ziedonis, 2014). The process typically involves a dialogue between the teaching team, where the topics and issues are discussed in a conversational exchange, tentative, embodied, and informal. This is then followed by an opportunity for the student group to reflect on that conversation, while the teaching group turn their chairs slightly away from the student group, serving as witnesses to the conversation. The teaching group in turn then reflects back and so on. This process, common to dialogical inquiry (Wells et al., 2020), is conducted as a form of slow scholarship (Harland, 2016), promoting an encounter rather than just knowledge translation.

Below is a short excerpt of recollections by a student and another of a young person who has experienced suicidality. They both look back on a particular emotional experience in the Open Dialogue circle.

Student: *Looking around me I saw my peers – friends – sitting in a larger circle, eagerly anticipating what might happen. Six of us sat in the smaller inner circle. To my left was a woman I'd never met before, who had selflessly offered to share her story with us about her child's struggle with mental illness. The outer circle slowly faded out of my awareness. It is hard to recall exactly what was said. I remember feeling somewhat anxious, humbled, out of my comfort zone, curious, I listened closely.*

Mother: *I spoke about one particular experience as the mother of my then 17-year-old daughter, Anna. At the time of the episode that I described, Anna had been managed under several psychiatrists, for about 3 years, and had been under her current team for about 18 months.*

Student: *The story felt delicate.*

Mother: *Her diagnosis was still emerging, however, medication was part of her management. I began describing the telephone call from Anna's school counsellor, telling me that Anna was not doing well. I then went on to talk about my panicked exit from home, and my thoughts as I raced to her school. I had then began to verbalise the dialogue in my head, reciting what might be Anna's eulogy,*

Student: *The words felt so precious.*

Mother: *whilst simultaneously telephoning the mental health team to tell them we were coming and needed urgent help, and then telephoning the social worker on the team to ask if she could find a bed in the youth psychiatric ward, and then calling my husband. I remember becoming quite emotional as I described this episode.*

Student: *She spoke of a certainty that her child would not live to be 21 years old, fearing that they'd have taken their own life or died in a horrific accident before this time. I saw the joy on her face when she told us her family had in fact recently celebrated this milestone birthday. They spoke of the pain that is navigating the public and private health systems, and that people rarely took the time to truly listen to them.*

Student: *The utter sadness and fear that she had carried for so many years.*

Mother: *It was the first time I have never told anyone what it feels like for me.*

Mother: *It was at this time that I noticed one of the students in the session had tears running down her face. She kept apologising and insisted that I continue, however she also continued to silently cry.*

Student: *To articulate my thoughts was difficult. What I can say is that this experience was a privilege, an overwhelming privilege to listen with all parts of myself.*

Mother: *At first, I thought she may have been through something similar. The student later explained that she had never really understood what happened during a psychiatric crisis and had never considered what a carer/parent experienced. I think the realisation that she and the others in the room were able to comprehend what it feels like to experience this, made me feel 'heard.'*

Student: *I thought about how different this setting felt to the clinical therapy room.*

Mother: *My hope is that all of the students will 'hear,' when they are seeing clients and include the clients' carer/parent/significant person."*

Student: *I thought about why I cared so much about mental health in the first place, what mattered to me, and the people that matter most. How that related to each person's story. When it was my turn to speak, I started crying, overwhelmed by the kindness, sacrifice, and genuine humanity in the room.*

Here one can read reflections on a democratic pedagogical encounter, deeply moving, and offering the possibility for the student to learn through emotional rather than simply intellectual means. This is what Michael Oakeshott (1991) calls a "dramatic friendship"; in the context of education, an "affective pedagogy" (Patience, 2008) is a field defined by technique.

3. Creative Arts

The creative arts also offer an important vehicle through which this kind of learning might take place, serving as a natural fit for social justice learning and allowing for an appreciation and even confrontation of alterity that might not be possible through text (Kraehe & Brown, 2011). In our case, we have used a variety of modalities, including holding an exhibition of Syrian civil war photography in the classroom and employing a Peer Educator in the consumer/ex-patient/survivor movement to perform her award-winning poetry in class. The poem is presented below and provides a visceral acknowledgement of empowerment and survivorship in the mental health system.

Grief for Hire by Alise Blayney
I AM grief for hire, a Poetess — not PTSDs marauded Duchess, nor the Black Dog's mistress. I used to be the clinical Countess of Distress!

I HAVE a broken aorta, when under hypnosis ticks with postmodern tacky-cardia.

I HEAR absinthe's green fairy whirlpool crash like car smash glass into community houso's observation hole.

I SEE invisible cloaked entities dressed as spiritual emergencies, infecting those whose senses are not anaesthetised. They incubi and succubi my white hospital gown like a djinn and tonic lullaby.

I WOULD drop vowels for Rhett Butler, do post traumatic time behind the fishbowl for Scarlett O'Hara.

I WANT soft asylum, 33 inch vinyl and spinning Roy Orbison.

I AM Rimbaud's THIEF of FIRE, a Poetess. Not PTSDs marauded Duchess, nor the Black
Dog's mistress. I used to be the clinical Countess of Distress.

I PRETEND that 9 years ago, I wasn't a sensory deprived TANKED mess.

I FEEL ambidextrous with the crookedness, and RAGE over the cuckoo clock's rooftops.

I TELL Blake his RINTRAH has gone too far — knockout pills and acute amnesia wrack with wrath, a reprobate wrecking ball.

I TOUCH marriage of perception through chemical incarceration and sink into delirium — the quack tells me I look like the spokesperson for vandalism!

I WORRY that the rough of the dialogue does your head in and that the curse of the coarse is coercion of sin.

I CRY because Mr Disney never told me the looking glass felt so like sheer fucking fear.

I SMILE when you spit delirious 'the road of HER excess leads you to the palace of resilience.'

I AM the serrated jaw of Dante's grand larceny circle. I lurk between the 5th of anger, the 7th of murder.

I UNDERSTAND when God gives you a gift, the angel of shibboleth gives you a whip.

I SAY drink the sweet elixir and watch your syntax sizzle off my rapid cycling tongue, to a beat that just belts on and on and on.

I DREAM of astral travel and meeting you in the ether, lucid and tender, where

I TRY to exalt this zyprexa stupor into the stars / release my pressure points into the ooh la la stars.

I HOPE to enter your white wonderland chamber, but your syntactical activist tongue

SHIPWRECKS my lips, until I'm trembling and sick.

I LOVE that you said poetry is both confession and exorcism — so we should Houdini out of the syntax straight jacket by sticking it to big pharma!

I am GRIEF FOR HIRE. Tell seclusion and restraint I want ceasefire.

Permission granted for reproduction from poet.

4. Grassroots Publications

Teaching in community psychology is also augmented by alternative forms of knowledge, generated in community, rather than simply academic peer review. Funding was granted by our National Center for Cultural Competence to allow us to produce a quarterly magazine The Activist Practitioner, with issues published on the topics presented in lecturers. Pieces were written by people with lived experience, community leaders, and local practitioners, to allow students further access to diverse voices and knowledge systems. This magazine, available for free online, also serves as a community resource. One novel aspect of the magazine is the process of cultural review, whereby each piece submitted must be approved by local aboriginal community representatives. Art works related directly to the topic of each issue were also commissioned from a local aboriginal community. Honoring first nations peoples in this way provides an important source of modeling for future community psychologists.

Developing Activist Scholars

Part of the education of community psychologists will also involve supporting them as higher degree research scholars, not simply teaching them in the classroom. Quantitative methods may be appropriate at times, but may not always align with the discipline's epistemological stance, given that research must be valid and participatory culture (Lyons et al., 2013). Participatory action research is a likely method of choice, seeking local solutions for locally identified issues (Barnes, 2003), rather than guided by academic careers and concerns. This form of "sovereignty on the ground" (Kral & Idlout, 2009) requires collaboration over a significant amount of time, preferably from students who already have links to community. Here lies, of course, one of the significant problems, especially for elite Universities that do not assertively seek out students from marginalized communities. The solution here lies with assertive equity-based admission processes and research scholarships which are the topic for another paper.

As a supervisor of Masters of Philosophy and Ph.D. Students at the University of Sydney, my students have a wide variety of projects underway in relation to community psychology. Three examples are provided as follows:

a. Decolonizing Attachment and Developing Guidelines for the Children's Court to Prevent Child Removals (Wright, Dudegon, & Rhodes)

This series of studies involves the development of a participatory indigenous methodology to decolonize the idea of maternal attachment as being primary when considering aboriginal ways of being. In particular, immersive yarning circles are being held with aboriginal elders and children, allowing for an arts-augmented exploration of the community-based nature of aboriginal attachment. Findings from this study will be used to develop specific guidelines for clinicians assessing child protection cases in the Children's Court.

b. Lived Experience and Alcoholics Anonymous (Glassman, Buus, & Rhodes)

This series of studies explored the lived experience of members of alcoholics anonymous, including those who leave the organization and those who commit for multiple decades. Our aim is to explore the ways in which this iconic community organization mediates meaning-making and belonging and how this might facilitate long-term membership beyond sobriety and why some leave disillusioned.

c. Decolonizing Clinical Psychology

Two studies are underway in this area, one which looks at international perspectives, based on in-depth interviews with leading academics who have engaged in a substantial process of decolonizing clinical psychology programs, in the USA, South Africa, Italy, and Australia, including the incorporation of community psychology ideals and practice (Cullen, Brockmann, & Rhodes). Another study explores the personal narratives of psychologists who have developed careers and lives based on the principles of cultural humility, community activist, and decolonization (Bogle, Hunt, & Rhodes).

Supporting student studying in these areas can be a challenging endeavor, especially if this work is occurring in a wider faculty setting unaccustomed to knowledge systems, research methods, and critical perspectives at odds with mainstream scientist practice. There are many lessons being learned about how best to provide this support, including the development of auxiliary supervision teams from non-dominant cultures, the recruitment of safe allies within the University to advocate for and support students through formal processes, and the development of solidarity and support among students with critical perspectives.

Conclusion

Community psychology is a field which focusses on the sociopolitical nature of human distress as differentiated from the intrapsychic pathologization common to clinical approaches. This field has a long history, dating back to the 1930s, and provides a framework for a social justice practice built for the participatory empowerment of local communities from diverse cultures. Preparing students for this type of practice has many specific challenges, least of which is developing activist-practitioners who have developed an acute awareness of their own privilege, are culturally humble, and confident to represent non-mainstream forms of knowledge and practice in the academy. Teaching must not simply be technical in nature, but also incorporate aspects of critical and affective pedagogy, inclusive of lived experience and creative content.

References

Addleman, R., Brazo, C., & Cevallos, T. (2011). Transformative learning through cultural immersion. *Northwest Passage: Journal of Educational Practices., 9*, 55–67.

Allen, R. L., & Rossatto, C. A. (2008). Does critical pedagogy work with privileged students? *Teacher Education Quarterly, 36*, 163–180.

Australian Psychological Society (2010). Evidence-based psychological interventions in the treatment of mental disorders: A literature review (3rd ed.). Retrieved from https://www.health.gov.au/internet/main/publishing.nsf/content/2A8C027E06EBA6DACA257BF0001FA175/$File/review.pdf

Barnes, C. (2003). What a difference a decade makes: Reflections on doing 'emancipatory' disability research. *Disability & Society, 18(1)*, 3–17.

Barnum, A., & Illari, J. (2016). Teaching issues of inequality through a critical pedagogy of place. *Journal of Sustainability Education, 25*, 11.

Bourdieu, P. (1977). *Outline of a theory of practice*. Cambridge: Cambridge University Press.

Bronfenbrenner, U. (1979). *The ecology of human development: Experiments by nature and design*. Cambridge, MA, USA: Harvard University Press.

Buus, B., Aida, B., Jacobsen, E., Muller-Nielson, K., Jorgen, A., & Rossen, C. (2017). Adapting and implementing open dialogue in the Scandinavian countries: A scoping review. *Issues in Mental Health Nursing, 38(5)*, 391–401.

Carr, A. (2000). *Family therapy: Concepts, process and practice*. Chichester, Eng: Wiley.

Clemens, C. (2017). *Ally or accomplice? The language of activism*. Retrieved from https://www.tolerance.org/magazine/ally-or-accomplice-the-language-of-activism

Compas, B., & Gotlib, I. (2002). *Introduction to clinical psychology*. New York, NY: McGraw-Hill Higher Education.

Cresswell, M., Karimova, Z., & Brock, T. (2013). Pedagogy of the privileged: Elite universities and dialectical contradictions in the UK. *Journal of Critical Education Policy Studies, 1740-2743(11)*, 25–48.

Denborough, D., Koolmatrie, C., Mununggirritj, D., Marika, D., Dhurrkay, W., & Yunupingu, M. (2006). Linking stories and Initiatives: A narrative approach to working with the skills and knowledge of communities. *International Journal of Narrative Therapy and Community Work, 2,* 19–51.

Diamond, G. S., Siqueland, L., & Diamond, G. M. (2003). Attachment-based family therapy for depressed adolescents: Programmatic treatment development. *Clinical Child and Family Psychology Review, 6,* 107–127.

Dudgeon, P. (2017). Australian indigenous psychology. *Australian Psychologist, 52*(4), 251–252.

Dudgeon, P., & Calma, T. (2013). The social and emotional wellbeing of Aboriginal & Torres Strait Islander Peoples. *Perspectives – Mental Health & Wellbeing in Australia, 1,* 36–39.

Freire, P. (1970). *Pedagogy of the oppressed.* New York: Herder and Herder.

Fryer, S. (2008). Some questions about the history of community psychology. *Journal of Community Psychology, 36*(5), 572–586.

Gridley, H., Fisher, A., Thomas, D., & Bishop, B. (2007). Development of community psychology in Australia and Aotearoa/New Zealand. *Australian Psychologist, 42,* 15–22.

Harland, T. (2016). Deliberate subversion of time: Slow scholarship and learning through research. In F. Trede & C. MCewen (Eds.), *Educating the deliberate professional. Professional and practice-based learning* (Vol. 17). Cham: Springer.

Hoffman, L. (2002). *Family therapy: An intimate history.* New York, NY: W.W. Norton & Co.

Hooks, B. (1994). *Teaching to transgress: Education as the practice of freedom.* New York: Routledge.

Jahoda-Lazarsfeld, M., & Zeisel, H. (1933). *Die Arbeitslosen von Marienthal: Ein soziographischer versuch uber die wirkungen langdauernder Arbeitslosigkeit mit einem Anhangzur Geschichte der Soziographie.* [The unemployed of Marienthal: A sociographic investigation into the consequences of long term unemployment with an appendix on the history of sociography]. Leipzig: Hirzel.

Karageorge, A., Rhodes, P., Gray, R., & Papadopoulos, R. K. (2018). Family therapy for refugees: A single-site investigation of client and staff experiences. *Australian and New Zealand Journal of Family Therapy, 39,* 303–319.

Kraehe, A., & Brown, K. (2011). Awakening teachers' capacities for social justice with/in arts-based inquiries. *Equity & Excellence in Education., 44,* 488–511.

Kral, M. J., & Idlout, L. (2009). Community wellness and social action in the Canadian Arctic: Collective agency as sunjective well-being. In L. J. Kirmayer & G. G. Valaskakis (Eds.), *Healing traditions: The mental health of Aboriginal peoples in Canada. Vancouver* (pp. 231–324). BC, Canada: University of British Columbia Press.

Lazarsfeld, P. F. L. (1932). An unemployed village. *Character and Personality, 1,* 147–151.

Levine, M., & Perkins, D. (1997). *Principles of community psychology: Perspectives and applications* (2nd ed.). New York, NY: Oxford University Press.

Lyons, H., Bike, D., Ojeda, L., Johnson, A., Rosales, R., & Flores, L. (2013). Qualitative research as social justice practice with culturally diverse populations. *Journal for Social Action in Counseling and Psychology, 5*(2), 10–25.

MacKinnon, L. (1999). *Trust and betrayal in the treatment of child abuse.* New York, NY: Guilford.

Margolin, L., & Martiniello, M. (2015). Unpacking the invisible knapsack: The invention of white privilege pedagogy. *Cogent Social Sciences., 1*(1).

Merleau-Ponty, M. (1960). *Signes.* Paris, France: Gallimard.

Mezirow, J. (2000). Learning to think like an adult. In J. Mezirow & Associates (Eds.), *Learning as transformation* (pp. 3–33). San Francisco, CA: Jossey-Bass.

Moreira, V. (2015). Critical psychopathology. *Radical Psychology.* Spring, *4*(1).

Nelson, G., & Prilleltensky, I. (Eds.). (2005). *Community psychology in pursuit of liberation and well-being.* Hampshire, MA: Palgrave Macmillan.

Oakeshott, M. (1991). *Rationalism in politics and other essays. New and Expanded Edition.* Indianapolis: Liberty Press.

Olson, M., Seikkula, J., & Ziedonis, D. (2014). *The key elements of dialogic practice in open dialogue.* Worcester, MA, USA: The University of Massachusetts Medical School.

Orford, J. (1992). *Community psychology: Theory and practice.* Chichester, UK: Wiley and Sons Ltd.

Patience, A. (2008). The art of loving in the classroom: A defence of affective pedagogy. *Australian Journal of Teacher Education, 33*(2), 55–67.

Prilleltensky, I. (1997). Values, assumptions, and practices: Assessing the moral implications of psychological discourse and action. *American Psychologist, 52*(5), 517–535.

Ralph, S., & Ryan, K. (2017). Addressing the mental health gap in working with Indigenous *youth: Some considerations for non-Indigenous psychologists working with Indigenous youth. Australian Psychologist, 52*(4), 288–298.

Rappaport, J. (1977). *Community psychology: Values, research, & action.* New York, NY: Holt, Rinehart & Winston.

Reich, S., Bishop, B., Carolissen, R., Dzidic, P., Portillo, N., Sasao, T., & Stark, W. (2017). Catalysts and connections: The (brief) history of community psychology throughout the world. In M. A. Bond, I. Serrano-García, & C. B. Keys (Eds.), *APA handbook of community psychology: Theoretical foundations, core concepts, and emerging challenges.* American Psychological Association (APA).

Rhodes, P. (2003). The Maudsley model of family-based treatment for anorexia nervosa: Theory, practice and empirical support. *Australian and New Zealand Journal of Family Therapy, 24*(4), 191–198.

Rhodes, P., & Wallis, A. (Eds.). (2011). *Working with families: A practical guide.* Melbourne, VA, Australia: IP Communications.

Ridani, R., Shand, F., & Christiansen, H. (2014). Suicide prevention in Australian Aboriginal communities: A review of past and present programs. *Suicide & Life-Threatening Behaviour, 45*(1), 111–123.

Salter, M., & Rhodes, P. (2018). On becoming a therapist: A narrative inquiry of personal-professional development. *Australian Psychologist., 53*(6), 486–502.

Seikkula, J., Alakare, B., Aaltonen, J., Holma, J., Rasinkangas, A., & Lehtinen, V. (2003). Open dialogue approach: Treatment principles and preliminary results of a two-year follow-up on first episode schizophrenia. *Ethical Human Sciences and Services, 5*(3), 163–182.

Slesnick, N., Gizem, E., Bartle-Haring, S., & Brigham, G. (2013). Intervention with substance-abusing runaway adolescents and their families: Results from a randomized clinical trial. *Journal of Consulting and Clinical Psychology, 81*(4), 600–614.

Sugarman, J. (2015). Neoliberalism and psychological ethics. *Journal of Theoretical and Philosophical Psychology, 35*(2), 103–116.

Swift, C. F., Bond, M. A., & Serrano-Garcia, I. (2000). Women's empowerment: A review of community psychology's first 25 years. In J. Rappaport & E. Seidman (Eds.), *Handbook of community psychology* (pp. 857–895). Dordrecht, Netherlands: Kluwer Academic Publishers.

Turnbull, M., & Rhodes, P. (2019). Burnout and growth: Narratives of Australian psychologists. *Qualitative Psychology.* https://doi.org/10.1037/qup0000146

Verhaeghe, P. (2014). *What About Me? The Struggle for Identity in a Market-Based Society.* Melbourne: Scribe.

Watzlawick, P. (1977). *The language of change.* New York, NY: Basic Books.

Wells, R., Barker, S., Boydell, K., Buus, N., Rhodes, P., & River, J. (2020). Dialogical inquiry: Multivocality and the interpretation of text. *Qualitative Research.* https://doi.org/10.1177/1468794120934409

White, M. (1995). Reflecting teamwork as definitional ceremony. In M. White (Ed.), *ReAuthoring lives: Interviews and essays* (pp. 172–198). Adelaide: Dulwich Centre Publications.

Wingard, B., & Lester, J. (2001). *Telling our stories in ways that make us stronger.* Adelaide: Dulwich Centre Publications.

Indigenous Psychology

30

Danilo Silva Guimarães

Contents

Abstract

Indigenous psychology is an intellectual worldwide movement against the hegemony of Eurocentric psychologies, in their reflected or unreflected missionary path of promoting Eurocentric tradition under a scientific appearance. The core teaching and learning objectives in indigenous psychology includes the understanding that colonialism produced threatening impacts to indigenous peoples around the world. The core contents and topics of indigenous psychology involves three main set of contents: (1) to understand, from the history and philosophy of psychology, the predicate of psychological theories and systems in its articulation with specific sociocultural contexts, through ontological reflection; (2) to understand possibilities and limits of dialogues between distinct traditions of knowledge construction, approaching socio-historical distances between psychological communities and indigenous communities, through indigenous and ethnographic approaches focusing concrete communities; (3) to understand that the theoretical

D. Silva Guimarães (✉)
Universidade de São Paulo, São Paulo, Brasil
e-mail: danilosg@usp.br

© Springer Nature Switzerland AG 2023
J. Zumbach et al. (eds.), *International Handbook of Psychology Learning and Teaching*,
Springer International Handbooks of Education,
https://doi.org/10.1007/978-3-030-28745-0_34

and document-based works about indigenous issues are distinct from the concrete work with indigenous peoples – demanding the development of expertise in social dialogue, availability to participate in indigenous communities' life and support their struggles. The approaches and strategies for teaching, learning, and assessment in indigenous psychology involve two main dimensions, (1) reading and discussion of pertinent bibliography concerning the core contents and topics and (2) engaging the students in co-authored works with concrete indigenous peoples and communities. The integration of both dimensions depends on supervised dialogues at the indigenous communities and at the university. We argue that distinct social and personal realities are constructed, grounded in the rites and myths people learn and transform from their relation with the sociocultural environment. The learned and transformed rites and myths guide perceptions, imaginations, and human actions within each tradition. Besides, there is a border of unknown between the predication of the distinct traditions, demanding the assessment of limits and the creation of conditions for equitable dialogues, bringing ontological reflections to the process of psychological knowledge construction.

Keywords

Epistemology · Ontology · Ethics · Tradition · Predication · Dialogicality

Introduction

The term "indigenous" is of Latin origin. It refers to that which is native to the land, generated in its own land. Despite its widespread use to refer to non-European populations in remote regions, who were there before colonization, the term formerly encompassed any autochthonous group native to a land or country that was later colonized. Therefore, any group of people are indigenous in relation to their original territory and cease to be when they assume a colonialist relation with their surroundings.

Indigenous psychology is an intellectual worldwide movement against the mainstream psychology, in its reflected or unreflected missionary path of promoting European tradition under a scientific appearance (see APA [Retrieved from https://www.apadivisions.org/division-32/leadership/task-forces/indigenous, January 2, 2021.]). Indigenous psychology claims that local problems need to be solved through indigenous practices and applications, including respectful dialogues between different traditions. For indigenous psychology, the generality of psychological systems depends on the openness to ontological issues grounding diverse theoretical systems and practices. It is a field of knowledge that emerges in the border between the science of psychology, historically exported to the colonized portions of the world, and the knowledge produced in indigenous contexts. It relates with historically threatened and silenced sociocultural perspectives, arising at the resilient border of differentiation from colonized perspectives, where the colonization of peoples, territories, and knowledge still advance. Indigenous psychologies are counterparts of the colonial process, a resistance movement assuming that indigenous knowledge and ontology contribute to psychological descriptions, theories, and methods. It converges with an ethical horizon, committed to the attention and care to the peoples and communities and understanding that science is a sociocultural production. Scientific knowledge depends on the relational processes involving multiple perspectives and meanings about human experiences.

The study of the role of culture in the constitution of the Self is part of psychology in its multiple theories and systems. Historically, the border between psychology and anthropology is tenuous and the demarcation between these disciplines is not precise from the very beginning of their differentiation (cf. Jahoda, 1982). The efforts of disciplinary differentiation and their limits were grounded in predication, such as (1) the psychological processes are natural, therefore, their explanatory models are the same, to be verified in all human beings and social communities, or (2) the psychological processes are social, therefore, need to be comprehended in the particularity of historical and community-based settings. Both claims are based on the naturalistic ontology that grounds most, if not all, modern sciences. From naturalistic predication, psychological studies seek the confirmation of theories proposed as universals, disputing the validation of these theories to encompass a larger number of phenomena located in cultural contexts increasingly diverse. And idiographic psychology is reduced to a contextual descriptive method without any explanatory power. Both conceptions constitute European and North American psychological tradition spread across the globe, finding resistance from the peoples they met.

Contemporary cultural and dialogical psychologies criticize the Eurocentrism of psychological theories and methodologies (cf. Boesch, 2007; Hermans, Kempen, & van Loon, 1992; Oliveira e Guimarães, 2016; Valsiner, 2007). Cross-cultural concerns based on the qualitative homogeneity and temporal stability of culture and people (cf. Valsiner, 2007) approach culture as an independent variable, consider plausible to collect representative samples to compare different cultures, and consider the equivalence of meanings of measurement instruments in different cultures. The personal idiosyncrasies of researchers and the fact that the specificities of the research problems meet the demands of the researcher's culture are not included as part of the investigation. It assumes that the participants' information fits comfortably with the information required by the researcher. However, for cultural and indigenous psychologists, the psychological study of other people should not happen as if they were just a source of data for a supposedly well-intentioned investigation (Boesch, 2007). Cross-cultural psychologies work with concepts and methodologies that come from and are more adequate to the reality of WEIRD (Western, Educated, Industrialized, Rich and Democratic) societies (cf. Groot, Hodgetts, Nikora, & Leggat-Cook, 2011; Hwang, 2015; Teo, 2011). A study from Henrich, Heine, and Norenzayan (2010) showed that 96% of psychological samples of the top journals in six sub-disciplines of psychology come from countries with only 12% of the world's population. Of the remaining 4%, the samples used in these countries are not representative of the population as a whole (cf. Brock, 2016). In this context, cross-cultural psychologies tend to construct psychological processes as part of the human nature but categories constructed according to the view of particular traditions (cf. Valsiner, 2017a; Guimarães, 2018).

Cultural psychology proposes a relevant theoretical and methodological turn in order to understand the diversity of senses and meanings constructed in multiple cultural fields of actions (Boesch, 1991). Collective and personal cultures are constructed through human actions of semiotic elaboration from experiences in the dynamic stream of embodied lived temporality (cf. Simão, Guimarães, & Valsiner, 2015). The theoretical and methodological turn of cultural psychology (cf. Valsiner, 2017a, 2017b, 2019, 2020) addresses the construction of psychological theories as semiotic elaborations about investigated processes. Knowledge advances through case studies that problematize sample studies point-like schemes about human mind, in their static form as a time-freed epistemological stance.

Alongside cultural and dialogical psychologies, ethnopsychiatry, and ethnopsychoanalysis emerged from troubled dialogues between psychoanalysis and anthropology throughout the twentieth century (cf. Barros e Bairrão, 2010). Ethnopsychoanalysts attempted to articulate theories from psychoanalysts and anthropology combined with their clinical practice (Martins-Borges, Lodetti, Jibrin, & Pocreau, 2019). However, they avoided a fusion between the different areas of knowledge, preserving interdisciplinarity. Assuming the dimension of alterity between fields of knowledge, ethnopsychiatry and ethnopsychoanalysis articulate differences in the ways of understanding health and disease, between Eurocentric naturalistic predication and the predication from the ontologies of different ethnicities, which have health concepts and care practices sophisticated and distinct from each other. Some basic assumptions of the field (cf. Borges e Pocreau, 2009) can be articulated with contemporary issues of indigenous psychology: (1) the difference of the other exceeds the explanatory models of psychological theories and systems, demanding approaches to the philosophical notion of alterity, to anthropological theories and to indigenous reflection; (2) suffering is a universal human condition that expresses itself in culturally diverse ways; and (3) the need of open-ended theories and methodologies for the development of technical devices of intervention and psychological attention.

The training of indigenous people in psychology, in the universities that spread the psychological knowledge worldwide, strengthened indigenous psychology movements, highlighting the limits of hegemonic psychologies for the understanding of local events and processes of psychological interest. This movement has gained strength in Asia Pacific part of the world (Groot, Grice, Le, & Nikora, 2019; Hwang, 2014, 2015, 2017; Kim, 2000; Li, Hodgetts, & Foo, 2019; Shiah, 2016; Liu, 2014; Hwang, Shiah, & Yit, 2017; Sundararajan, 2014; Yin, 2018). Simultaneously, in Africa and the Americas, a criticism to persistent impact of colonialist parasitism in countries that have gained their independence but which support local elites international relations that, directly or indirectly, inherited the forms of social parasitism founded in the colonial period (cf. Bomfim, 2012; Mignolo, 2017; Quijano, 1993, 2005) face hegemonic psychologies from Europe and the United States.

Among the aims of indigenous psychologies, in general, are the claims to broaden empirical data of studies including more diverse sociocultural contexts, and the revision of methods of construction, analysis, and interpretation of the data, addressing the elimination of epistemic violence (cf. Held, 2020; Gonzalez & Guimarães, 2020; Teo, 2011) in the processes of knowledge construction.

Indigenous psychology emphasizes the need for an ontological turn, since theoretical and methodological reviews are not enough to establish an equitable dialogue including basic indigenous prediction that guide reflections and practices for indigenous knowledge construction (cf. Guimarães, 2011, 2015, 2016, 2018, 2019, 2020b; Kawaguchi & Guimarães, 2019; Guimarães & Simão, 2017). For example, the ontological naturalism, prevalent in European societies after the renaissance, have a foundational role in modern sciences, but the knowledge produced by indigenous peoples around the world are based on distinct presuppositions. Descola (2005), comparing ethnographic data from different societies around the world, concluded that all can be framed into at least one of four possible ontologies, according to how they classify existing beings and their forms of relationship (cf. Kawaguchi & Guimarães, 2019, p. 377). Each ontology brings different distinct predicate concerning the dualities (1) interiority (in psychological terms, soul, spirit or mind) versus exteriority (body, appearance or physical attributes) and (2) similarity (the assumption of a contiguity between beings, as per in evolutionary theory) versus difference (a clear separation and distinction between the different types of beings).

Indigenous psychology, then, propose an ontological turn to general psychology (cf. Guimarães, 2020b), since psychological reflections of researchers are situated and formed in concrete socially situated chronotopos, that is, it is attuned to a rhythm of exchanges that is characteristic of each society. Temporality here is not chronology or history; it is not a regular calendar system or a series of events that can be situated in chronological time. Temporality is the sense of the passing of time, of experiences lived in reciprocal activity, in which "the person, performing their tasks, also answers to other's demands" (Ingold, 2000, p. 196). Temporality emerges from reciprocal actions, in which those involved, human and non-human. Therefore, the chronotopos of psychology is configured by the tension in the melting pot of different traditions that meet each other through human and environmental exchanges. Psychological theories and practices reflect the ontological ground of knowledge construction, through which the psychologists speak and act in the world with others. Some conscious or unconscious predicate underlie as a foundation for all possible rational knowledge.

The ontological turn is being proposed in anthropology in dialogue with phenomenological philosophy (cf. Pedersen, 2020), involving issues that connect the anthropological discussion with psychological ones. For instance, an anthropological-philosophical reflection carried out in the context of Americanist anthropology proposes multinaturalism as a predicate that unfolds from the academic reflection on the Amerindian ethos (cf. Viveiros de Castro, 1998, 2004). Attentive to Amerindian reflections, unfolding them, the anthropologist proposed, as one of the contrasting features of Amerindian thought, that the indigenous do not apprehend or reflect about the environment that surrounds them presupposing the unity of nature given by the objective universality of body and substance. Besides, they do not understand the relation between human beings and societies as based on the plurality of cultures, subjective particularity of psyche, and meaning. Rather, the Amerindian multinaturalism (in contrast with other Eurocentric conceptions of cultural pluralism and natural monism) proposes a relational ontology:

> Kinship terms are relational pointers; they belong to the class of nouns that define something in terms of its relations to something else (linguists have special names for such nouns—"two-place predicates" and such like). Concepts like fish or tree, on the other hand, are proper, self-contained substantives: they are applied to an object by virtue of its intrinsic properties. Now, what seems to be happening in Amerindian perspectivism is that substances named by substantives like fish, snake, hammock, or beer are somehow used as if they were relational pointers, something halfway between a noun and a pronoun, a substantive and a deictic. (There is supposedly a difference between "natural kind" terms such as fish and "artifact" terms such as hammock: a subject worth more discussion later.) You are a father only because there is another person whose father you are. Fatherhood is a relation, while fishiness is an intrinsic property of fish. In Amerindian perspectivism, however, something is a fish only by virtue of someone else whose fish it is. (Viveiros de Castro, 2004, pp. 472–473)

The issue of the social construction of objective and subjective realities is not a novelty to the European phenomenological philosophy and sociology in the twentieth century (see, for instance, Berger & Luckmann, 1991). Ontological issues become more crucial in dialogue with Amerindian knowledge because it conflicts with the monologue of naturalist ontology in science, addressing an effective inclusion of multiple traditions and their predication. For indigenous psychology, the diversity of psychological systems and theories is reflected taking into account their ontological conceptions. It addresses the creation of an ethical ground for open dialogues with the multiplicity of ontological routes traveled by distinct human traditions. Nevertheless, differences between scientific and indigenous worldviews continue to create barriers to meaningful collaboration, as does the widespread assumption that science (based on the naturalistic ontology) is superior to other knowledge systems (cf. United Nations Educational, Scientific and Cultural Organization about Indigenous Knowledge and Biodiversity (retrieved in January, 2021 at https://en.unesco.org/).) Indigenous knowledge is frequently associated to devaluated irrational myths and rites at a delayed stage in relation to the superiority of the scientific knowledge, making dialogue between the indigenous and the psychologists unfeasible in the dialogical sense of the term. For an understanding of the opposition between higher and lower thinking and the dialogical ways of overcoming this dichotomy, see Marková (2016), focusing on the ontological and ethical predication of dialogism.

Purposes and Rationale of the Curriculum in Indigenous Psychology

The core teaching and learning objectives in indigenous psychology include the understanding that colonialism produced threatening impacts to indigenous peoples around the world. These impacts are persistent and create limitations for human life in the globe. Colonialism is foundational for modernity: configures nationalities, institutions, arts, and sciences. It hierarchizes inferior and superior thinking, desensitizing the perception of the suffering of those considered inferior. This hierarchy is correlated to other modern dichotomies, such as logos versus myth; rationality versus irrationality, and science versus shamanism. It is relevant to understand that significant studies in indigenous psychology need to approach the consequences of the lack, or poverty, of ethically oriented reflections and actions from the macrosocial to the microsocial levels of human interaction. Indigenous psychology does not advocate irrational relativism as a solution to the threatening impacts of colonialism, but the rational epistemology together with the naturalistic ontology, grounding modern sciences, is insufficient to face relevant issues that impact human life in the planet.

Psychology emerged as a field of knowledge in the border between great dichotomies of modern societies, i.e., mind versus body; spiritualism versus materialism, nomothetic versus idiographic, conscience versus unconscious, etc. It collaborates with the creation of semiotic devices for communicating differences. Therefore, indigenous psychology does not exclude Western psychology but argues the benefits of including all indigenous perspectives in the dialogue, recognizing the traditions that originated psychology and reflecting on how other traditions contribute to it, sustaining the heterogeneity in our field of knowledge and work.

Indigenous psychology has diversified worldwide and gained visibility in the field of dispersion characteristic of the contemporary scenario of psychology as science and profession. The demands for psychological work with indigenous populations also increase, as the circulation of goods, information, and people become more intense and dynamic worldwide. Along with this movement, we see expanded indigenous demands: for public health policies, education, and for fundamental human rights, in which psychology can articulate knowledge that contribute to a scenario of complex attempts at dialogue. Understanding the specificity of this scenario of increasing visibility of diversity is relevant for the students addressing the production of collaborative ways of knowledge construction and professional work with the indigenous peoples and communities.

Therefore, teaching and learning indigenous psychology involves a twofold aim: on the one hand, to criticize the unreflected coloniality in psychological theories, focusing on history and philosophy that ground psychological systems, theories, and methodologies; on the other hand, it involves an engagement with indigenous communities, participation in the communities' life, sharing their struggles, predicate, and openness to dialogue.

According to the IWGIA, 5 thousand indigenous peoples resist around the world. (International Work Group for Indigenous Affairs (https://iwgia.org/).) Diversity and complexity are associated to obstacles for the dialogue of psychology and indigenous peoples, for instance, (1) linguistic, the need to include the spoken language of the indigenous people; (2) time-space, to reach the communities, usually far from the cities and universities; (3) extra-verbal, to adapt to new environmental conditions, social routines, rites, and rituals; (4) suspicion, the indigenous do not necessarily trust science as contributing to crucial issues that concerns the contemporary world;

and (5) implication, the indigenous usually need to check the level of implication of the teachers and students with coloniality, its threatening impacts to their communities and environment.

A barrier is an area that is difficult to overcome and may need particular interposed actions for the passage; once the barrier crossed, however, the action can proceed more or less as before (cf. Boesch, 1991). Overcoming some barriers without consequences for the psychological knowledge is not sufficient for learning indigenous psychology. Possible dogmatic attitude of some learning and teaching practices prevent the development of their criticism to rigid theoretical-methodological boxes, avoiding the dialogue with other conceptions and procedures about topics of knowledge approached in indigenous psychology (i.e., indigenous, shamanic understandings), disqualifying them as inferior or unnecessary to science. The eclectic attitude could also prevent some students from the contact with the different, by disqualifying the difference itself, as if the understanding of the other could be easily translated into preshaped scientific knowledge, values, and beliefs. For a discussion about the eclectic and dogmatic attitudes in psychology, see Vygotski (1991) and Figueiredo (2007). Rather, indigenous psychology is a frontier, in Boesch's (1991) sense, that is, it marks the separation between two areas of behavior, which requires an area-specific adaptation in the form, and direction of action taken by the individual. It demands theoretical and methodological innovations emerging from specific dialogues with concrete indigenous communities, traditions, and predicate.

Core Contents and Topics of Indigenous Psychology

The core contents and topics of indigenous psychology involves three main set of contents: (1) to understand, from the history and philosophy of psychology, the predicate of psychological theories and systems in its articulation with specific sociocultural contexts, through ontological reflection; (2) to understand possibilities and limits of dialogues between distinct traditions of knowledge construction, approaching socio-historical distances between psychological communities and indigenous communities, through indigenous and ethnographic approaches focusing concrete communities; and (3) to understand that the theoretical and document-based work about indigenous issues is distinct from the concrete work with indigenous peoples, demanding the development of expertise in social dialogue, availability to participate in indigenous communities' life, and support their struggles.

Concerning the first set of contents, the student of indigenous psychology needs to understand that science, arts, and other spheres of human symbolic action (cf. Boesch, 1991) are specific modes of meaning construction, emerged from personal activity in a socially shared reality (cf. Simão, 2004, 2005, 2010, 2015, Guimarães, 2020a). Modern thinking is based on belief in the progress of reason and the criticism of the limits of methodical experience of the world. Its roots go back to long-term history of secularization of Christianity, after the silencing of the pagan gods (cf. Gadamer, 2010a). Nevertheless, the myth, referring to what is said (fable), the testimony accepted, but not questioned, remains at the base of human experiences, for which the reflective experience is episodic and circumscribed to social interests and needs:

> The idea of an absolute reason is an illusion. The reason is only as a real historical reason. It is difficult for our thinking to recognize this. So great is the dominance exercised by ancient metaphysics over the self-understanding of human existence that it is known to be historical and finite. (Gadamer, 2010a, p. 62)

Reasoning is, therefore, a possibility to answer the needs emerged from an experience or interpretation of a belief, the elaboration of a demonstrative speech, able to gather and enumerate the objects referred in the speech (cf. Gadamer, 1981/2010b). Lived experiences reported and reflected are social constructions, as the objects produced in the socio-environment we live in. Foucault (1980/2017) presents a genealogy of the medical clinics showing how the discourse that makes the human beings objects of scientific studies is similar to the discourse that allowed the emergence of psychology. While medicine is born as a science of the individual from the reflection about the death in the medical thinking, psychology is born from deranging experiences of the unreason.

Nevertheless, life and death, reason and madness, are reflected through distinct predicate in different traditions, guiding other procedures for knowledge construction. While science constructs a language able to gather and enumerate the bodies according to simple and objective regularities, for the Amerindians, for instance, to know something is to configure it as a subject (cf. Viveiros de Castro, 2006).

The aim of gathering and enumerating psychological processes led psychologists to create concepts and categories that ranked and downgraded indigenous peoples around the world. These peoples were viewed as belonging to a less developed mental stage, because of their supposed more primitive living condition, which deprived them of the necessary transitions in order to overcome the "series of intermediate steps to the more developed and higher civilizations" (Wundt, 1916, p. 4). Representations of native inhabitants from diverse parts of the world pervaded the European intellectual circles and gave support to the racist scientific theories on the nineteenth century. Philosophers, artists, and scientists built their knowledge and took it as true, convinced that their hierarchy of human societies and cultures was justified (Jahoda, 1999). This knowledge was founded on ancient preconceptions and prejudices, which taint to this day the European tradition's approach to foreigners. Their vestiges are as stones embedded in the towers of academic and common sense knowledge. Valsiner (2000) discussed the issue of the European ethnocentrism in different theories in psychology throughout the twentieth century, especially until World War II. The European ethnocentrism of the nineteenth century was marked by the fascination that took over the Europeans in relation to the ways of life of "natural people" (e.g., indigenous people), in contrast to their own ways of life, which they affirmed to be the ways of "the person who has culture" (Valsiner, 2000, p. 284). The former were seen as less developed than the later. Valsiner (2000) points out that the nineteenth-century European psychologies clearly projected this distinction in their views of the considered as primitive man. Wundt and other psychologists in the twentieth century incorporated the consensual view that the distinction between nature and culture applied to the European distinction "us – them" (Valsiner, 2000; p. 284).

Quijano (1993, 2005), Mignolo (2017), and other Latin American sociologists discuss on how the intended universality of the scientific thinking of modern societies ends up as an irrational superimposition of the ontological perspective from a specific ethnic tradition over other traditions. The violence of this superimposition distorts and blocks the multiplicity of perceptions and imaginations grounding indigenous frameworks of knowledge construction, leading the indigenous to vanish their own memories and predication, when assuming the European predication as the only valid and true.

The study of Todorov (2011) about the European invasion of the continent now called the Americas argues that to know the history of colonization is relevant because it offers us an instructive example. It allows us to reflect on ourselves, the similarities as the differences between our present attitudes and those of the invaders, since "we resemble and we differ from them; [. . .] we will never be sure that, by not behaving like them, we are precisely not imitating them, adapting to new circumstances" (pp. 214–215). Todorov (2011) acknowledges the invasion of the Americas and the knowledge of the Amerindians as "the most astonishing encounter in our history" (p. 8), due to the feeling of radical strangeness it produced. The invasion of the Americas founded the identity of modern societies, transformed the existential, political, and epistemological bases of the contemporary society where psychology is included as a science and profession.

All these philosophical and historical reflections are, then, instances of relevant content preparing the students in indigenous psychology to the second set of contents, where possibilities and limits for the dialogue between psychology and indigenous peoples will be assessed. Here is relevant to get in contact with the diversity of indigenous peoples, through the main ethnographic studies about them, in parallel with the indigenous documented discourses and the published work of indigenous psychologists. From the multiplicity of indigenous psychologies, the student can deepen the understanding of specific local realities and the impact of colonization and coloniality on selected peoples in focus. Contributions to these studies come from a broad approach on diverse anthropological and interdisciplinary studies discussing the notion ontological turn. They are relevant to prepare the students to recognize approximations and distances between indigenous traditions and psychological traditions as part of the challenges for dialogues proposed in the field of indigenous psychology.

Another content in the formation of an indigenous psychologist involves the awareness that working with indigenous issues is different from working with indigenous persons (cf. Lima, Martim, & Guimarães, 2019). Here, the main readings are about methodological issues concerning the construction of dialogical grounds for co-authoring teaching and learning projects between the academic community of the psychologist and the indigenous communities. Peu, Mulaudzi, Rikhotso,

Ngunyulu, and Rasweswe (2020), for instance, discuss how academic health practitioners have to adapt their protocols to the needs of indigenous settings in Africa. Groot, King, Nikora, Beckford, and Hodgetts (2020) discuss that "people take shape through their interactions with others that are in turn molded by the histories and traditions of the groups with whom they belong" (p. 151), reflecting on a ritual of encounter indigenous to *Aotearoa* New Zealand. Guimarães (2020b) reflects on a series of meetings with people from the indigenous communities in *Pindorama* Brazil, in order to identify psycho-social vulnerabilities faced by them, aiming at collaboratively elaborating possible strategies to overcome some persistent threatening impacts of the colonial processes. From these works, the participation in the rites and rituals of the communities is relevant to researching, teaching, and learning indigenous psychology, addressing misconceptions that can emerge when the translation between psychological terms and practices dos not involve the necessary semantic rectifications in the daily life sharing. Semantic rectifications are about the transformation of meanings, from a tradition to another, due to the encounter between people with distinct predication about the topics approached in the dialogue (cf. Achatz & Guimarães, 2018). Important to this topic are methodological reflections on observant participation (cf. Bastien, 2007), controlled equivocation (Viveiros de Castro, 2004), and dialogism (Guimarães, 2020a).

Teaching, Learning, and Assessment in Indigenous Psychology

Approaches and Strategies

The approaches and strategies for teaching, learning, and assessment in indigenous psychology involve two main dimensions, (1) reading and discussion of pertinent bibliography concerning the core contents and topics and (2) engaging the students in co-authored works with concrete indigenous peoples and communities. The integration of both dimensions depends on supervised dialogues at the indigenous communities and at the university.

Based on these approaches and strategies, we developed a culture and extension program called Indigenous Support Network at the Institute of Psychology (*Universidade de São Paulo*, Brazil) (cf. Gonzalez & Guimarães, 2020; Lima et al., 2019; Guimarães, Lima Neto, Soares, Santos, & Carvalho, 2019; Bertholdo & Guimarães, 2018; Achatz & Guimarães, 2018; Achatz, Souza, Benedito, & Guimarães, 2016), working with distinct indigenous communities near the university, located in the forest and urban areas. The approaches and strategies adopted in this network converge with other experiences of indigenous psychology around the world (cf. Peu & cols. 2021; Groot & cols. 2020).

Indigenous Support Network is organized in distinct workgroups the students are invited to engage. For instance, one of these workgroups approaches the elaboration and implementation of psychological assistance, in different modalities, to indigenous people. Social and community particularities of indigenous peoples require transformations of theoretical-methodological and technical conceptions of psychological interventions. To an adequate training, we maintain a regular group of studies and regular supervision of the practical work, such as psychotherapy.

Another workgroup concerns the promotion of inter-ethnic encounters. It emerged from psycho-social demands of the communities for increasing the visibility of the indigenous presence in São Paulo, addressing the reversal of prejudices from the dominant society. Our meetings are, usually, promoted at the University, interacting people from all ages about topics of indigenous interest. Aligned with the inter-ethnic meetings workgroup, we address educational, ecological and community-based tourism. We support the communities' projects focusing to welcome students and educators as well as tourists interested in knowing indigenous lifestyle and challenges they face. This workgroup is in line with the need for local development and social inclusion, with the socioeconomic insertion of the local population in activities related to the expression of indigenous culture and values through tourism. It points to indigenous identity strengthening when some communities demand it to our network.

Teaching and learning of indigenous languages and lifestyle are the focus of another workgroup. We develop, in co-authorship with indigenous teachers from the communities, educational materials and the infrastructure for the open courses they offer at the university.

All workgroups from the Indigenous Support Network are concerned with the three set of core contents of indigenous psychology discussed in the previous topic of this chapter, approaching them through collaborative works with indigenous people in the construction of concrete projects, addressing distinct objects of interest, i.e., psychotherapy, meetings, tourism, indigenous languages, etc. The collaborative work is improved with studies about the indigenous tradition of the peoples and communities engaged and with regular visits to communities to better approaching and understanding their struggles and proposals to the network. The exposure of the body of the student to ritualized contexts from different cultural patterns, in contrast to their original culture, gives rise to unease and disquieting feelings that characterize the relationship with alterity (cf. Guimarães et al., 2019). As tools for the elaboration of this mode of relation, the indigenous communities propose dialogues in which the priority is to establish an adequate attunement to the attunement of the other (cf. Rommetveit, 1992). Such attunement is a preliminary condition to discuss and forward projects that deals with challenging issues related to situations of psycho-social vulnerabilities the focused communities face (cf. Peu & cols. 2021; Groot & cols. 2020).

The diversity of themes and communities articulated in the network is reflected at regular meetings, where spokespersons from all working groups participate, communicating their challenges in the preparation and execution of ongoing projects. These are moments of assessment, when the network listens and comments, supporting affective-cognitive processes of each student learning indigenous psychology. This strategy of Indigenous Support Network resonates with traditional Indigenous restorative justice systems (cf. Hand, Hankes, & House, 2012), especially those involving the experience of one person talking at once with everyone respectfully listening. The *Japyxaka* (Guarani term for the mutual listening process involving all members of the community, from all ages and genders) that happens every evening in the communities was, then, introduced as a regular practice at the university, for teaching, learning, and assessment in indigenous psychology. It happens at an adequate space we built at the campus, the House of Indigenous Cultures.

The House of Indigenous Cultures is a traditional *Mbya Guarani opy*, built by a group of Mbya persons in the Institute of Psychology (Universidade de São Paulo, Brazil), as the result of a collaboration between our academic service and the Jaraguá community. The *Opy'i* is a typical house for community meetings, where activities range from informal talks to ceremonies. In the later, they dance, sing, and have the *Japyxaka*, preparing the community for relevant and shared decisions. The house, at the Institute of Psychology, received the Guarani name *Xondaro kuery xondaria kuery onhembo'ea ty apy*, that is, a place for teaching, learning, and protecting indigenous knowledge, for caring persons and communities, protecting them against possible menaces (cf. Lima et al., 2019). The implantation of the house at the university changed the academic environment through distinct architectural features, inclusive of indigenous ways of communication.

Durie (2002), reflecting about the Maori academic context in *Aotearoa* New Zealand, argues that the encounters commonly witnessed on a *Marae* in modern times "point toward Maori world views as well as providing a basis for understanding distinctive ways of knowing and behaving" (p. 19). The Maori *Marae*, as the Guarani *Opy'i*, configures specific indigenous *ethos*, that is, ways of "[. . .] propitiating, configuring shaping and constituting human beings and their worlds—their dwellingplace, both subjects and their objects, social, private and "subjective" experiences of each individual" (Figueiredo, 2013, p. 48). The inclusion of traditional indigenous architecture at the universities is a sign of openness for an equitable dialogue on knowledge construction, addressing to overcome the historical barriers of indigenous access and permanence at the universities and producing a frontier (cf. Boesch, 1991) where indigenous and psychological predication exchanges.

The etymology of the word ethics goes back to the Greek notion of ethos, used to designate human ways of being and relating. Figueiredo (2013) discusses it as a mode of propitiate, configure, shape, and construct people and their worlds, including socially shared and secretive experiences. Ethos and ethics have an etymological root that link them to the notion of ethnicity (from Greek ethnikos) (cf. Partridge, 2006). Originally used to refer to the foreigners, heathen peoples, expressing an opposition between "us" and "the others," today ethnicity is a category to address people that share, among other aspects, an ethos. In this sense, ethics as a branch of philosophy concerned with the duties and effects of human actions in the world with others, addressing varied understandings of well-being that differ among peoples and communities.

Considering that indigenous psychology is in the border between persistent coloniality, strengthening indigenous paths of resistance, is relevant to understand that methodologically, it learns from the observation through participation, collaborating with indigenous resistance in concrete communities. Theoretically, it reflects the dialogue with shamanic meanings and practices. Indigenous psychology validity is based on the ethical effectiveness of its propositions, addressing duties and effects of human actions in the world with others, a commitment with sheltering varied understandings of well-being that differ among peoples and communities.

Therefore, next to the epistemological and ontological philosophical reflections, the assessment in indigenous psychology teaching and learning involves ethical concerns. Figueiredo (2013) distinguishes two ways the term ethics can be used, as a noun or as an adjective. As a noun, ethics refers to implicit patterns or explicit codes of conduct that prescribes or forbid human actions or behavior as much as the modes of implication and obedience of someone to the socially convened rules. Some cultural fields are stricter or more rigid or flexible, accepting one or multiple interpretations of the rule. As an adjective, ethics refers to an existential dimension concerning the relations between humans, between humans and other beings, and the environment. It implies value-oriented attitudes to the others and the world, next to the necessary or efficient goals of human actions.

Nowadays, intense migratory movement of people with different ethnicity amplifies the need for understanding the conditions for dialogue and for implementing desirable modes of mutual coexistence with the other, between distinct ethos. For Coelho Junior (2008), Emmanuel Lévinas' philosophy of ethics reflects that the intersubjective relations imply dislocation, splitting or modification of subjective experience. Ethics is, then, a permanent reflection that acknowledges the precedence of other guiding and making the Self possible:

> Undoubtedly, Lévinas' great statement is that the relationship with the other is not an act of knowledge, it is not situated, therefore, at the epistemological level, but it is, above all, an ethical relationship that institutes subjectivity itself. The subjective experience is conceived as a permanent and inevitable opening to the other, in its alterity. (Coelho Junior, 2008, p. 220)

Ethical, ontological, and epistemological issues are, then, relevant dimensions for cultural psychology studies, and all sciences, since the instrumental rationality defines modern sciences, in contrast to a contemplative knowledge, supposedly neutral and unimplicated of the problems that afflict our social life. These considerations touch the interests and the thoughtless of other aspects that exceeds the reason methodically employed in the formulation of scientific knowledge (cf. Gadamer, 2010a, 2010b), demanding the reflection on the mythopoetic roots and their extra scientific truths grounding all semiotic elaborations of human experiences.

From the reflections presented above, teaching, learning, and assessment in indigenous psychology involves stages promoting dialogical process between psychology and indigenous peoples. Their progress can be assessed as the following (cf. Guimarães, 2020a, 2020b): The first stage implies the follow-up of the activities that are ongoing in the community, attentively listening and actively collaborating with it. This way of participation allows the construction of the pair expectancy-confidence. The second stage implies the construction of collaborative projects when the topics of dialogue are selected and start to be further detailed and sophisticated.

Finally, the development of the agreed projects, in which each interlocutor contributes from their own asymmetric position. The interethnic relationship is converted into co-authorship, which implies dedifferentiation and differentiation actions addressing indigenous and psychological types of knowledge.

Challenges and Lessons Learned

From our experience in learning and teaching indigenous psychology, in the context of the Amerindian Support Network, we implemented a culture and extension service hitherto nonexistent at the Institute of Psychology (Universidade de São Paulo, Brazil). This service feeds our theoretical and methodological reflections, listening to the other and transforming preconceptions about the other. We learned how distinct social and personal realities are constructed, grounded in the rites and myths, guiding perceptions, imaginations, and human actions within each tradition. Nevertheless, deal with a border of unknown, a territory of ignorance, between the paths followed by the distinct traditions in dialogue, constraining human actions. Psychologists are largely unaware about meaningful dimensions of the sociocultural multiplicity of constructed realities.

Through the regularity of meetings in which the listening and the participation in the community activities are fundamental, the construction of trust, through the expectancy of the presence and collaboration of the participant in the inter-ethnic dialogue can be achieved. Within each socially constructed reality, there are objects referred in the language from a specific culture or from a specific cultural field that are nonexistent in the other sociocultural field. For instance, the House of Indigenous Cultures we have built at USP is referred in Guarani language as a *Opy'i*, a sort of house that we found equivalence in the university's culture of Maori indigenous people in *Aotearoa* New Zealand. Nevertheless, there is not a translation to *Marae* or *Opy'i* in English terms and a literal translation is not possible. They are terms and objects that exists in a cultural field but that are nonexistent in the other cultural field.

Similarly, other terms are untranslatable. For instance, from Guarani to English, there is no literal translation notion of *Teko Porã*, important for studies on indigenous psychology in Brazil: *Teko Porã* is being translated to English as well-live. On one hand, it could be confused with things the capitalist propaganda understands as a good life (cf. Guimarães, 2020b; Sousa, Gonzalez, & Guimarães, 2020). On the other hand, indigenous myths and rites, in their variation, guide indigenous reflection addressing the *Teko Porã*. It implies the construction of people attentive to the interdependent network involving our social life, including human beings, animals, vegetables, mineral beings, and aquatic, terrestrial, aerial, visible and invisible beings, under some circumstances. Besides, the word psychology is a term that exists in English, from the cultural tradition of modern Eurocentric societies; however, it has no referent or equivalent, in Guarani language. Therefore, translation issues are basic to indigenous psychology approaches, considering the diversity of indigenous languages used to describe rites, to narrate myths, to construct, and to understand the environment.

Indigenous psychology understands communication as creative approximations. When the translations are sought, many times, similar words are used to address distinct objects, for instance, the notion of *land*. Although it is usually conceived by the market logic from part of Brazilian society that makes the property speculation, interested in seizing the indigenous lands or interested, somehow, treat the land as commodity, for the indigenous peoples, the use of the word land has distinct meanings. It refers to the experience we have in relation to something that cannot be bought or sold; it is a common space for all beings, where all beings would inhabit, and does not have an owner. This is the case when the use of the same word ends up referring very distinct objects, considering indigenous and non-indigenous backgrounds.

There are words without translation between sociocultural traditions; on the other hand, the same words used by people from different cultural fields, although they use the same word, are referring to very distinct objects. Therefore, we observe that translation produce mistakes (cf. Viveiros de Castro, 2004; Achatz & Guimarães, 2018), because the terms of the other address distinct objects and subjects to each other socially constructed reality. Although communication produce mistakes, some senses and meanings about the experiences can be shared. Some shares are produced or constructed through the participation with the other in regular activities. It has a consequence for methodological propositions, when we are interested in knowledge construction, because to know depends on a participation in the social environment.

From the participation in indigenous life and struggles, however, some topics of personal interest to explore in more detail emerge, addressing the construction of joint projects. At this stage, the self and the other achieve a common task in the interethnic dialogical process, with the definition of a shared horizon for the future of the interethnic relation. The participation allows embodied awareness, guiding perceptions and imaginations in the engagement with the other (cf. Guimarães, 2020b; Guimarães et al., 2019). Such engagement is essential for knowledge construction. Then, indigenous psychology learning and teaching propitiate a series of meetings with the other, encounters with the diversity different from the colonialist violence in persistent coloniality that threatens peoples and communities. We promote them as encounters that, in fact, propitiate engagement, exchanges, knowledge construction; and not domination or elimination of the difference.

The process of domination and elimination of the difference, transforming the other in object for the control of a specific social group, is recurrently happening in the history of our societies. The meetings with alterity have been disastrous encounters, from the colonization, with the invasion of the indigenous lands, the transformation of the lands in commodity, and the transformation of the people in commodity makers. Modern sciences contributed with objectivation of the world and the objectivation of the people. However, the indigenous paths address another direction, the valuation of the other as subject, and the possibility of reciprocity in the exchanges.

The continuity of the interethnic dialogue demands the recognition of the asymmetric and nonhierarchical positions in the dialogue, including the dynamic process of dedifferentiation-differentiation. Then, the psychologist needs to be able to sustain the availability to the community's active elaboration of their cultural reflexivity and ethnic self-affirmation through the continuous increment of pertinent changes in the path of interaction. The verbal content of the interaction is not the only aspect to be observed in the construction of the interethnic trust; the rhythmical attunement is a relevant dimension to grasp the quality of the dialogical exchange. When the psychologists occupy a protagonist role in the relation, seeking for coherence from the people in relation to the psychologist's expectancies uttered solely in verbally agreed contracts they usually enter in a process of silencing the other. The same happens when the psychologists are not able to persist in offering his/her availability, uncritically giving up the previously paths agreed in the dialogical process or passively waiting for his/her inclusion in the otherness' protagonist path.

Indigenous psychologies suppose that the encounter with the other will be always harmonic. More research is needed to understand the process for the construction of reciprocity, diplomacy, and exchanges between the diversity of indigenous and the psychological generality, which could be valuable for both sides, although, considering all the challenges the encounter with the different could bring. The presentation of alterity, dimensions of oneself, of others, and of things that cannot be assimilated, produces disquieting feelings (cf. Simão, 2015, 2016) that demand a semiotic mediation in order not to threaten the fragile affective self-organization of the psychologist. It would be great if people became used to facing diversity from early childhood, then they might not be so frightened in adult life and/or feel the need to better protect themselves subjectively when facing disruptive experiences. Feeling protected is, then, a condition to cast oneself in the flow of the experience with others, to house their performances/utterances and better elaborate the experience during and after living it.

Teaching, Learning, and Assessment Resources

Complimentary information can be found in:

- Portal of Indigenous Support Network hosted by the Institute of Psychology, Universidade de São Paulo, Brazil: https://redeindigena.ip.usp.br/
- Portal of the Ngā Pae o te Māramatanga (NPM) is New Zealand's Māori Centre of Research Excellence (CoRE) funded by the Tertiary Education Commission (TEC) and hosted by The University of Auckland. http://www.maramatanga.co.nz/
- Page of Indigenous Psychology Task Force From Division 52, Society for Humanistic Psychology, American Psychological Association: https://www.apadivisions.org/division32/leadership/task-forces/indigenous
- Page of UNESCO policy on engaging with indigenous peoples: https://en.unesco.org/indigenous-peoples/policy
- Portal of the International Work Group for Indigenous Affairs: https://iwgia.org/
- Portal of the Brazilian Articulation of Indigenous Peoples: https://apiboficial.org/

Cross-References

▶ Community Psychology and Psychological Distress
▶ Developmental Psychology
▶ Epistemology of Psychology
▶ Qualitative Methodology
▶ The Methodology Cycle as the Basis for Knowledge

Acknowledgements

The author is funded by the CNPq Productivity scholarship (National Council for Scientific and Technological Development of Brazil, grant number 306227/ 2020-7).

References

Achatz, R. W., & Guimarães, D. S. (2018). An invitation to travel in an interethnic arena: Listening carefully to Amerindian Leaders' speeches. *Integrative Psychological and Behavioral Science, 52*(4), 595–613.

Achatz, R. W., Sousa, F. R., Benedito, M. A., & Guimarães, D. S. (2016). Considerações sobre o trabalho com comunidades indígenas a partir do serviço "Rede de Atenção à Pessoa Indígena". In: CRPSP (Org.), *Povos indígenas e psicologia: a procura do bem viver* (pp. 189–198). São Paulo, Brasil: CRPSP.

Barros, M. L., & Bairrão, J. F. M. H. (2010). Etnopsicanálise: embasamento crítico sobre teoria e prática terapêutica. *Revista da SPAGESP – Sociedade de Psicoterapias Analíticas Grupais do Estado de São Paulo, 11*(1), 45–54.

Bastien, S. (2007). Observation participante ou participation observante? Usages et justifications de la notion de participation observante en sciences sociales. *Recherches Qualitatives, 27*(1), 127140.

Berger, P. B., & Luckmann, T. (1991). *The social construction of reality: A treatise in the sociology of knowledge*. London, England: Penguin books. (Original text published in 1966).

Bertholdo, M., & Guimarães, D. S. (2018). Amerindian support network. In: S. Schliew, N. Chaudhary, & G. Marsico (Orgs.), *Cultural psychology of intervention in the globalized world* (pp. 119–134). Charlotte, NC: Information Age Publishing.

Boesch, E. E. (1991). *Symbolic action theory and cultural psychology*. Berlin, Germany: Springer.

Boesch, E. E. (2007). The Seven Flaws of cross-cultural psychology: The story of a conversion. In W. J. Lonner & S. A. Hayes (Eds.), *Discovering cultural psychology: A profile and selected readings of Ernest E. Boesch* (pp. 247–258). Charlotte, NC: Information Age Publishing. (Texto original publicado em 1996).

Borges, L. M., & Pocreau, J.-B. (2009). Reconhecer a diferença: o desafio da etnopsiquiatria. *Psicologia em Revista, 15*(1), 232–245.

Brock, A. C. (2016). The universal and the particular in psychology and the role of history in explaining both. In S. H. Klempe & R. Smith (Eds.), *Centrality of history for theory construction in psychology* (pp. 75–90). Cham, Switzerland: Springer.

Coelho Junior, N. (2008). Da fenomenologia à ética como filosofia primeira: notas sobre a noção de alteridade no pensamento de E. Lévinas. *Estudos e Pesquisas em Psicologia, 8*(2):213–223.

Descola, P. (2005). *Par-delà nature et culture*. Paris, França: Gallimard.

Durie, M. (2002). Keynote address: Is there a distinctive Māori psychology? In: *The Proceedings of the National Māori Graduates of Psychology Symposium*, University of Waikato.

Figueiredo, L. C. M. (2007). *A invenção do psicológico: quatro séculos de subjetivação 1500–1900*. São Paulo, Brasil: Escuta (Trabalho original publicado em 1992).

Figueiredo, L. C. M. (2013). *Revisitando as psicologias: da epistemologia à ética das práticas e discursos psicológicos*. Petrópolis, RJ: Vozes. (Trabalho original publicado em 1996).

Foucault, M. (2017). *O nascimento da clínica* (trad. Roberto Machado). Rio de Janeiro, Brasil: Forense universitária. (Original publicado em 1980)

Gadamer, H.-G. (2010a). Mito e Razão. In H.-G. Gadamer (Ed.), *Hermenêutica da Obra de Arte*. São Paulo, Brasil: Martins Fontes. (Texto original publicado em 1954).

Gadamer, H-G. (2010b). Mito e Logos. In H.-G. Gadamer (Ed.), *Hermenêutica da Obra de Arte* (pp. 6568). São Paulo, Brasil: Martins Fontes. (Texto original publicado em 1981).

Gonzalez, R., & Guimarães, D. S. (2020). For a knowledge with the other in psychological science. *Theory & Psychology, 30*(3), 419–424.

Groot, S., Hodgetts, D., Nikora, L. W., & Leggat-Cook, C. (2011). A Maori homeless woman. *Ethnography, 12*(3), 375–397.

Groot, S., Le Grice, J., & Nikora, L. W. (2019). Indigenous psychology in New Zealand. In W. W. Li, D. Hodgetts, & K. H. Foo (Eds.), *Asia-Pacific perspectives on intercultural psychology*. Abingdon, UK: Routledge.

Groot, S., King, P., Nikora, L. W., Beckford, K. A., & Hodgetts, D. (2020). Commentary 2: Pōwhiri: Rituals of encounter, recognition and engagement: A commentary on 'dialogical multiplication: Principles for an indigenous psychology'. In D. S. Guimarães (Ed.), *Dialogical multiplication: Principles for an indigenous psychology* (pp. 151–159). Cham, Switzerland: Springer. (2020b).

Guimarães, D. S. (2011). Amerindian anthropology and cultural psychology: Crossing boundaries and meeting otherness' worlds. *Culture & Psychology, 12*(2), 139–157.

Guimarães, D. S. (2015). Temporality as reciprocity of activities: Articulating the cyclical and the irreversible in personal symbolic transformations. In L. M. Simão, D. S. Guimarães, & J. Valsiner (Eds.), *Temporality: Culture in the flow of human experience* (pp. 331–358). Charlotte, NC: Information Age Publishing.

Guimarães, D. S. (2016). *Amerindian paths: Guiding dialogues with psychology*. Charlotte, NC: Information Age Publishing.

Guimarães, D. S. (2018). Affectivation: A cut across the semiotic hierarchy of feelings. In: C. Cornejo, G. Marsico, & J. Valsiner (Eds.), *I activate you to affect me* (Annals of cultural psychology, Vol. 3, pp. 203–223). Charlotte, NC: Information Age Publishing.

Guimarães, D. S. (2019). Towards a cultural revision of psychological concepts. *Culture & Psychology, 25*(2), 135–145.

Guimarães, D. S. (2020a). Co-authorship in interethnic dialogues: Reflections on the Amerindian support network. In M. Lopes-de-Oliveira, A. Branco, & S. Freire (Eds.), *Psychology as a dialogical science* (pp. 169–184). Cham, Switzerland: Springer.

Guimarães, D. S. (2020b). *Dialogical multiplication: Principles for an indigenous psychology*. Cham, Switzerland: Springer.

Guimarães, D. S., Lima Neto, D. M., Soares, L. M., Santos, P. D., & Carvalho, T. S. (2019). Temporalidade e corpo numa proposta de formação do psicólogo para o trabalho com povos indígenas. *Psicologia: Ciência e Profissão, 39*(special issue), 147–158.

Guimarães, D. S., & Simão, L. M. (2017). Mythological constrains to the construction of subjectified bodies. In M. Han (Org.), *The subjectified and subjectifying mind* (pp. 3–21). Charlotte, NC: Information Age Publication.

Hand, C. A., Hankes, J., & House, T. (2012). Restorative justice: The indigenous justice system. *Contemporary Justice Review, 15*(4), 449–467.

Held, B. S. (2020). Epistemic violence in psychological science: Can knowledge of, from, and for the (othered) people solve the problem? *Theory & Psychology, 30*(3), 349–370.

Henrich, J., Heine, S. J., & Norenzayan, A. (2010). The weirdest people in the world? *Behavioral and Brain Sciences, 33*(2/3), 61–135.

Hermans, H. J. M., Kempen, H. J. G., & van Loon, R. J. P. (1992). The dialogical self: Beyond individualism and rationalism. *American Psychologist, 47*(1), 23–33.

Hwang, K.-K. (2014). Cultural system vs. Pancultural dimensions: Philosophical reflection on approaches for indigenous psychology. *Journal for the Theory of Social Behaviour, 45*(1), 2–25.

Hwang, K.-K. (2015). Cultural system vs. pan-cultural dimensions: Philosophical reflection on approaches for indigenous psychology. *Journal for the Theory of Social Behaviour, 45*(1), 2–25.

Hwang, K.-K. (2017). The rise of indigenous psychologies: In response to Jahoda's criticism. *Culture & Psychology, 23*(4), 551–565.

Hwang, K.-K., Shiah, Y.-J., & Yit, K. (2017). Editorial: Eastern philosophies and psychology: Towards psychology of self-cultivation. *Frontiers in Psychology, 8*, 1083.

Ingold, T. (2000). *The perception of the environment: Essays on livelihood, dwelling and skill*. Abingdon, Oxon/New York, NY: Routledge.

Jahoda, G. (1982). *Psychology and anthropology: A psychological perspective*. New York, NY: Academic Press Inc. (270p).

Jahoda, G. (1999). *The images of savages: Ancient roots of modern prejudice in western culture*. New York, NY: Routledge. (320p).

Kawaguchi, D., & Guimarães, D. S. (2019). Is everybody human? The relationship between humanity and animality in Western and Amerindian myth narratives. *Culture & Psychology, 25*(3), 375–396.

Kim, U. (2000). Indigenous, cultural, and cross-cultural psychology: A theoretical, conceptual, and epistemological analysis. *Asian Journal of Social Psychology, 3*(3), 265–287.

Li, W. W., Hodgetts, D., & Foo, K. H. (Eds.). (2019). *Asia-Pacific perspectives on intercultural psychology*. Abingdon, UK: Routledge.

Lima R. V., Martim J. A., Guimarães D. S. (2019). Nhembo'ea Reko Regua: Trajectories of the Mbya Guarani Struggle for a differentiated education. In P. Hviid & M. Märtsin (Eds.), *Culture in education and education in culture* (Cultural psychology of education, vol. 10). Cham, Switzerland: Springer.

Liu, J. (2014). Globalizing indigenous psychology: An East Asian form of hierarchical relationalism with worldwide implications. *Journal for the Theory of Social Behavior, 45*(1), 8294.

Marková, J. (2016). *The dialogical mind: Common sense and ethics*. Cambridge, UK: Cambridge University Press.

Martins-Borges, L., Lodetti, M. B., Jibrin, M., & Pocreau, J.-B. (2019). Inflexões epistemológicas: a Etnopsiquiatria. *Fractal: Revista de Psicologia, 31*(spe), 249–255.

Mignolo, W. D. (2017). Colonialidade: O lado mais escuro da modernidade. *Revista Brasileira de Ciências Sociais, 32*(94), e329402.

Oliveira, M. C. L., & Guimarães, D. S. (2016). [Apresentação] Dossiê: Psicologia dialógica. *Psicologia USP, 27*(2), 165–167.

Partridge, E. (2006). *Origins: A short ethymological dictionary of modern English*. London, England/New York, NY: Routledge. 4218p. (Original published in 1958).

Pedersen, M. A. (2020). Anthropological Epochés: Phenomenology and the ontological turn. *Philosophy of the Social Sciences, 50*(6), 610–646.

Peu, M., Mulaudzi, F., Rikhotso, S., Ngunyulu, R., & Rasweswe, M. (2020). Reflections on accessing indigenous research settings: Encounters with traditional health practitioners and leaders in Vhembe district, South Africa. *Culture & Psychology, 27*(2), 227–242. https://doi.org/10.1177/1354067X20971249

Quijano, A. (1993). Colonialidad del Poder, Eurocentrismo y América Latina. In E. Lander (org.), *La Colonialidad del Saber: Eurocentrismo y Ciencias Sociales* (Perspectivas Latinoamericanas, pp. 201–246). Buenos Aires, Argentina: CLACSO.

Quijano, A. (2005). Don Quixote e os moinhos de vento na América Latina. Dom Quixote e os moinhos de vento na América Latina. *Estudos Avançados, 19*(55), 9–31.

Rommetveit, R. (1992). Outlines of a dialogically based socio-cognitive approach to human cognition and communication. In A. H. Wold (Ed.), *The dialogical alternative: Towards a theory of language and mind* (pp. 19–44). Oslo, Norway: Scandinavian University Press.

Shiah, Y.-J. (2016). From self to nonself: The nonself theory. *Frontiers in Psychology, 7*, 124.

Simão, L. M. (2004). Alteridade no diálogo e construção do conhecimento. In: A. M. Martínez & L. M. Simão (Orgs.), *O outro no desenvolvimento humano: diálogos para a pesquisa e a prática profissional em psicologia* (pp. 29–39). São Paulo, Brasil: Pioneira Thomson Learning.

Simão, L. M. (2005). Bildung, culture and self; A possible dialogue with Gadamer, Boesch and Valsiner? *Theory & Psychology, 15*(4), 549–574.

Simão, L. M. (2010). *Ensaios Dialógicos: compartilhamento e diferença nas relações eu outro*. São Paulo, Brasil: HUCITEC.

Simão, L. M. (2015). The contemporary perspective of semiotic cultural constructivism: For an hermeneutical reflexivity in psychology. In R. Marsico & S. Salvatore (Eds.), *Reflexivity and psychology* (pp. 65–85). Charlotte, NC: Information Age Publishing.

Simão, L. M. (2016). Culture as a moving symbolic border. *Integrative Psychological and Behavioral Science, 50*, 14–28.

Simão, L. M., Guimarães, D. S., & Valsiner, J. (Eds.). (2015). *Temporality: Culture in the flow of human experience* (pp. 331–358). Charlotte, NC: Information Age Publishing.

Sousa, F. R., Gonzalez, R., & Guimarães, D. S. (2020). Luta e resistência: dimensões para a promoção de saúde Mbya Guarani. *Psicologia USP, 31*, e180070.

Sundararajan, L. (2014). Indigenous psychology: Grounding science in culture, why and how? *Journal for the Theory of Social Behavior, 45*(1), 64–81.

Teo, T. (2011). Empirical race psychology and the hermeneutics of epistemological violence. *Human Studies, 34*(3), 237–255.

Todorov, T. (2011). *A conquista da América: A questão do outro*. São Paulo, Brasil: Martins Fontes. (Texto original publicado em 1982).

Valsiner, J. (2000). *The social mind: Construction of the idea*. Cambridge, UK: Cambridge University press. (504p).

Valsiner, J. (2007). Human development as migration: Striving toward the unknown. In L. M. Simão & J. Valsiner (Eds.), *Otherness in question: Labyrinths of the self* (pp. 349–378). Charlotte, NC: Information Age Publishing.

Valsiner, J. (2017a). *Between self and societies: Creating psychology in a new key*. Tallin, Estonia: ACTA. 420p.

Valsiner, J. (2017b). *From methodology to methods in human psychology*. Cham, Switzerland: Springer. 115p.

Valsiner, J. (2019). Cultural psychology as a theoretical project / La psicología cultural como proyecto teórico. *Estudios de Psicología, 40*(1), 10–47.

Valsiner, J. (2020). Where occidental science went wrong: Failing to see systemic unity in diversity. *Psychology and Developing Societies, 32*(1), 7–14.

Viveiros de Castro, E. B. (1998). Cosmological deixis and the Amerindian perspectivism. *The Journal of the Royal Anthropological Institute, 4*(3), 469–488.

Viveiros de Castro, E. B. (2004). Perspectival anthropology and the method of controlled equivocation. *Tipití: Journal of the Society for the Anthropology of Lowland South America, 2*(1), 1–22.

Viveiros de Castro, E. B. (2006). A floresta de cristal: Notas sobre a ontologia dos espíritos amazônicos. *Cadernos de Campos, 14*(15), 319–338.

Vygotski, L. S. (1991). El Significado Histórico de la crisis em Psicología [The historical meaning of the crisis in psychology: A methodological investigation (van der Veer, R. Translator)]. Em Vygotsky (1991) *Obras escogidas I: problemas teóricos y metodológicos de la Psicología* (pp. 257–407). Madrid, Spain: A. Machado Libros, S. A. (Original work published in 1927).

Wundt, W. (1916). *Elements of folk psychology*. London, England: George Allen and Unwin Ltd. 533p.

Yin, J. (2018). Beyond postmodernism: A non-western perspective on identity. *Journal of Multicultural Discourses, 13*(3), 193–219.

Teaching Psychopharmacology for Undergraduates

31

Jennifer M. J. McGee

Contents

Abstract

Psychopharmacology is the study of the effects of drugs on behavior, cognition, and the mind. It is the field dedicated to understanding the way human and nonhuman animals respond to both recreational drugs and drugs to treat mental illness. Undergraduate students are statistically very likely to have exposure to or experience with many psychoactive substances, but few have had a comprehensive and accurate education on the effects these drugs have on behavior and on the central nervous system. This chapter is meant to offer ideas for the development of learning objectives and best practices for teaching a psychopharmacology course to undergraduate students. The proposed learning objectives were derived, in part, from national organizations in North America dedicated to educating professionals in the field and the suggestions for assessments and

J. M. J. McGee (✉)
Department of Psychology, Oxford College of Emory University, Atlanta, GA, USA
e-mail: jmjuerg@emory.edu

© Springer Nature Switzerland AG 2023
J. Zumbach et al. (eds.), *International Handbook of Psychology Learning and Teaching*,
Springer International Handbooks of Education,
https://doi.org/10.1007/978-3-030-28745-0_35

deep learning activities are based on empirical research. Though the target students for such a class are likely to be junior or seniors majoring in a related discipline (psychology, neuroscience, or other pre-health fields), these recommendations can be tailored for any level of education, regardless of student background.

Keywords

Psychopharmacology · Teaching · Undergraduate · Drug · High-impact teaching strategies · Assessment

This chapter will attempt to provide a framework for an undergraduate course in psychopharmacology, including learning outcomes derived in part from an advanced graduate curriculum and course activities and assessments derived from peer reviewed sources. I will also offer suggestions for how to organize your course. I hope you will consider these recommendations merely as a starting point and that they might lead you to engage in on-going conversations about best practices in teaching and learning psychopharmacology.

Introduction

Often referred to as "traditional medicine," humans have used plants and herbs to relieve suffering for thousands of years. Prehistoric humans may have foraged and used plants such as chamomile and yarrow for medicinal purposes (Hardy 2019), and early written accounts from China (Houghton 2007), India (Shakya 2016), Europe (Rackham et al. 1938), and Africa (Dawson 1934) outline hundreds of plants and herbs that were used to treat a variety of ailments. As early humans sought out the best ways to use the plants that grew naturally around them, they came across some that not only treated ailments of the body but also emotional or mental problems with no known bodily origin. Many ancient writers from Europe, including Greek historian Diodorus Siculus, recorded that the sap of the poppy flower's seed pod could alleviate anger and grief (Hayter 1968). In China, *Ginkgo biloba* was used to prevent memory decline (Nakanishi 2005). And in the Americas, American skullcap was used to treat anxiety and depression (Uritu et al. 2018).

These early civilizations discovered plants whose active compounds could pass through the blood-brain barrier to interfere with neural signaling. While their mechanisms of action may not have been discovered until centuries later, oral and written traditions passed down recipes, dose recommendations, warnings, and other fruitful information. In short, psychopharmacology is an ancient field of study that reflects contributions from all over the world.

Technological advances in the last 150 years have exponentially increased the speed of scientific discovery, and this acceleration eventually decreased reliance on and trust in the medicinal power of plants in favor of synthetic pharmaceuticals.

However, there is now a resurgence of interest by consumers, researchers, and physicians into plant-based medicines, and modern psychopharmacology now has the tools available to ensure safety and consistency of these compounds.

While the modern field of pharmacology developed slowly from these ancient traditions, the modern field of *psycho*pharmacology burst onto the scene in the mid-twentieth century with the synthesis of chlorpromazine (Thorazine). This drug marked a new scientific approach to mental illness not only because it showed remarkable success in the symptomatic treatment of agitation and psychosis but because of a complex confluence of factors including the United States interest in deinstitutionalization and the impact of the changing nature of psychology as a discipline. As psychology was turning from its philosophical roots, early experimental scientists developed tests of behavior based on operant and classical conditioning principles that are still widely used today by psychopharmacologists. As most drugs of abuse were unregulated during the turn of the twentieth century, many notable scientists, among them Emil Kraepelin, B.F Skinner, and John B. Watson, used opiates, cocaine, and alcohol in their experimentation on animal behavior. When the pharmaceutical revolution began in earnest in the 1950s, the field was already saturated with behavioral methodology including using animal behavior as a proxy for human behaviors and operant conditioning chambers with variable schedules of reinforcement. Due to increasingly stringent governmental controls on certain plant-based drugs, the next 70 years of drug investigation focused on psychopharmacotherapy that used synthetic pharmaceuticals, which helped to usher in the biological psychology and neuroscience revolution. So, although psychopharmacology may have stemmed from an ancient tradition of using plants for medicine and recreation, it is now marked by influences from the earliest days of experimental psychology as well as by cutting-edge techniques in neuroscience. It is commonly defined as the study of the effects of drugs on behavior, cognition, and the mind and is the field dedicated to understanding the way human and nonhuman animals respond to both recreational drugs and drugs to treat mental illness.

Today, many mental health conditions are treated with psychopharmaceuticals and the psychopharmaceutical business accounts for billions in sales. As the stigma surrounding mental illness and treatment continues to fade, this business will likely continue to grow. Currently, one in six adults in the United States is using a drug to treat a mental health condition (Moore and Mattison 2017). It is therefore imperative that we educate our students about the many topics associated with the clinical use of drugs, including the mechanism of action, effectiveness, and potential adverse events.

Though often omitted from psychopharmacology courses, we should also be telling our students about the science behind drugs that we humans have long used for relaxation, entertainment, and for communion with others and with our gods. Worldwide, peak levels of drug use are seen among those aged 18–25 (United Nations Office on Drugs and Crime, World Drug Report 2017), and in the United States, nearly 64% of adults aged 19 to 28 have tried at least one illicit drug in their lifetime and 85% have used alcohol (U.S. Department of Health and Human Services 2018). For one thing, the study of recreational and illicit drugs has, like the study of their medicinal counterparts, provided insights into the ways in which our brain works. A foremost example appeared when Candace Pert's discovery of opiate receptors led to the identification of endorphins. So students should know about these drugs – how they work, their impact, how to use them responsibly, and what we can learn by studying them.

The central psychopharmacology research paradigm has always consisted of the observation of behavior before and after drug administration, but modern techniques have allowed more and more refined methods of analysis. We now regularly employ methods that not only allow us to observe behavior in living and conscious human and nonhuman animals, but also to conduct real-time imaging of the brain, brain tissue manipulations including site-specific intracerebral injections and deep brain stimulation of targeted neurons, and numerous genetic manipulations including optogenetics and gene targeting (including CRISPR). Like many other subfields related to neuroscience, psychopharmacology is trending toward a more molecular perspective. Increasingly, scientists are trying to parse the effects of various receptors, receptor complexes, and small-scale neural circuits in drug experiences.

As we learn more about how the brain interacts with the body and how the introduction of drugs can shape the effects of the brain-body connection, we begin to see specialized psychopharmacological subfields, such as those defined by age (childhood, adolescence, geriatric) and by reason for drug use (medicinal, recreational). We are only just beginning to explore important variables such as the role of polydrug use in recreational drugs and prescribed medication, how sex hormones interfere with drug experiences, and how the user's expectation of the drug experience may alter a drug's effects. Other emerging avenues of exploration focus on pharmacogenomics, historically under-researched drugs such as ayahuasca, and new drugs such as synthetic marijuana.

In short, psychopharmacology has come a long way from its roots as a plant-centric way to alleviate acute suffering of the body and mind, but we still have a long way to go to fully understand the way in which drugs interact with the brain and nervous system. Progress has been impeded, though, by laws and regulations applying both to the pharmaceutical industry and to the black market for drugs deemed illicit in various countries. The impact of these laws and regulations on the cost of developing and producing new therapeutic drugs has stifled some innovation for the rarer disorders, and the drug scheduling system of the United States and World Health Organization has substantially decreased research on the effects (including the pharmacokinetics/pharmacodynamics) of even well-known and commonly used drugs like marijuana.

Purposes and Rationale of the Curriculum in Psychopharmacology

Progress has been made in clearly articulating and stating learning objectives for psychopharmacology courses in graduate programs, particularly in nursing, but there remains a distinct need to modify them for undergraduate education. Indeed, at the undergraduate level, there are currently no widely accepted core teaching and learning objectives specific to the psychopharmacology curriculum. Here is a suggested core set of learning objectives (LO) that is derived in part from standards at other levels of education in North America, including the Faculty for Undergraduate Neuroscience Blueprints for Undergraduate Education (LO #1); the National Institute on Drug Abuse (NIDA) Strategic Plan (LO # 2); the American Psychiatric Nurses Association Specific Core Nursing Content as well as the Association of American Medical Colleges (AAMC) and the Howard Hughes Medical Institute (HHMI) Scientific Foundations for Future Physicians (LO #3); and the American Psychological Association (APA) Guidelines for the Undergraduate Psychology Major (LO # 4).

Learning Objectives in an Undergraduate Psychopharmacology Course

Students completing an undergraduate course in psychopharmacology should:

1. *Know* the facts, theories, principles, processes, and general concepts within the field of psychopharmacology. These should include:
   (a) Basic knowledge of neural anatomy, electrophysiology, and neurotransmission and how these inform the underlying assumptions of neuroscience.
   (b) An understanding of the historical and contemporary research methods in psychopharmacology.
   (c) The ability to explain the processes of pharmacokinetics and pharmacodynamics for each major drug class.
   (d) The ability to understand, compare, and evaluate current theories of addiction.
   (e) Be able to articulate knowledge of the neurobiological mechanism for various psychotropic medications.
2. *Understand* some of the biological, environmental, behavioral, and social causes and consequences of drug use and addiction across the lifespan.
3. *Apply* the principles of pharmacology to *evaluate* options for safe, rational, and optimally beneficial psychotropic drug therapy and medication-assisted treatment for drug dependency.
4. *Recognize* the systemic influences of sociocultural, theoretical, and personal biases on the research enterprise and *evaluate* the effectiveness with which researchers address those influences in psychological research.

Core Contents and Topics of Psychopharmacology

The field of psychopharmacology combines methods of psychology, pharmacology, and, increasingly, neuroscience. Students therefore should be exposed to the various ways of knowing that arise from each discipline and be encouraged to ask meaningful questions that combine these perspectives. But the impact of psycho-pharmacology transcends those disciplinary frameworks and influences our social and political lives in many ways. As a result, it is a challenge to cover all necessary information in a single introductory course. Recognizing that most universities and colleges offer only a single, elective, course on psychopharmacology, what follows is an attempt to cover the most important content while also allowing room for students to explore the various ways in which drugs have affected and continue to affect the culture in which they live.

Considerations in Developing a Three-Unit Psychopharmacology Curriculum

By way of introduction, the first unit should center around the history, nomenclature, and research paradigms central to psychopharmacology. The second unit should take a more in-depth look at the various drugs and drug classes. The third unit should be reserved for learning broadly about drug use, misuse, addiction, and drug-related public policy.

Unit 1: History, nomenclature, and research paradigms. The goals for this unit come from the above Learning Objectives 1a, 1b, 1c, and 4. Exactly what is covered in this unit will depend on the level of your students' preparation. Ideally, they will have already taken an Introduction to Psychobiology course and therefore have a working knowledge of basic brain anatomy, neural structure and communication, and the biological basis of learning and memory. Alternatively, there is a strong argument in favor of designing the course so that any student can enroll, regardless of disciplinary preparation. This would allow students from diverse disciplines to offer their perspectives to a topic that is likely to have importance in their nonacademic lives. Either way, it is advisable to begin the semester with a review of the structure and function of the nervous system, as described here:

1. History of the Field of Psychopharmacology
   (a) Briefly describe the state of the field prior to the nineteenth century. Specific drug histories will be included in Unit 2, but a discussion of traditional medicines and serendipity in medical development should be included in this unit.
   (b) Describe the impact that the development of chlorpromazine had on the field.
   (c) Particular attention should be paid to the role of behaviorism in the early days of psychopharmacology. Not only was behaviorism the most popular per-spective in psychology when chlorpromazine was invented, but its techniques are still widely used today.
   (d) Describe common experimental paradigms. US Department of Health and Human Services.
   (e) Preferably leave time to consider the future of psychopharmacology. As noted already, psychopharmacology is becoming much more genetically and

molecularly focused and our students need to be prepared to enter the field as it is now and as it is evolving while still being equipped with the lessons of the past to guide them.

2. Structure and Function of the Central Nervous System
   (a) Neurons: Types, structure, electrical transmission, and chemical signaling
       (i) Five steps of neurotransmission (neurotransmitter synthesis, storage, release, activation, termination of the signal)
   (b) Glia: Types, structure, role in neural function
       (i) Blood-brain barrier
   (c) Brain: Gross anatomy and microanatomy of relevant structures (i.e., nucleus accumbens, ventral pallidum, ventral tegmental area, and limbic regions of prefrontal cortex)
   (d) Related theories of CNS functioning
       (i) Hebbian learning
       (ii) Dale's Principle
3. Principles of Psychopharmacology
   (a) Pharmacokinetics, pharmacodynamics, and pharmacogenetics. While this course is not intended to be a pure pharmacology course, the ability to converse in the field is dependent on understanding these concepts.
       (i) Particular attention should be paid to routes of administration, as this concept is important for discussions about drug addiction as well as drug efficacy in medicine.
       (ii) Tolerance and sensitization
   (b) Receptor theory

Unit 2: In-depth look at various drugs and drug classes. The goals for this unit come from Learning Objectives 1c, 1e, 3, and 4. There is no single "right" way to organize this unit. If you use a textbook, they often make a distinction between familiar drugs (e.g., caffeine) and restricted drugs (e.g., psychedelics). Others distinguish between drugs of abuse (e.g., opioids) and psychotherapeutic drugs (e.g., antidepressants). Still others make no distinction and simply address each drug sequentially. As you make your own organizing decisions, you might find it useful to consider the following list of drugs that are both commonly used and commonly found in introductory psychopharmacology textbooks and other readings:

1. Opioids
2. Cocaine, amphetamines, and other psychostimulants
3. Cannabis
4. Nicotine
5. Alcohol
6. Caffeine
7. Psychedelics
8. Benzodiazepines and other anxiolytics
9. Antidepressants
10. Antipsychotics

Other drugs, or drug classes, that may be considered if there is time or interest are:

1. Inhalants
2. Performance enhancers
3. Alzheimer's treatments
4. Herbal supplements or over-the-counter drugs
5. Designer or new drugs

For each drug or drug class, it is advisable that students are exposed to the following information:

1. History: Contextualizing the role of drug use in societies across time and cultures is essential to learning objectives 3 and 4. For example, although psychopharmacology was named and proliferated as a science in the mid-twentieth century, descriptions of how psychoactive plants changed behavior have been around for centuries. Knowing the history of where these plants grew, how they were used, and by whom, as well as what was known of their action, can help inform students' understanding of modern perceptions of drug use and the laws that regulate or criminalize them.
   (a) For plant-based drugs:
       (i) In what area of the world the plant was first cultivated
       (ii) How civilizations in those regions used the plant (for medical, religious, ritualistic, or textile use, or pleasure)
       (iii) How use proliferated across borders
       (iv) How, where, when, and why these drugs became more potent
           1. Examples: coca leaves → powered cocaine → crack; marijuana → "shatter"; Opium → morphine → heroin → fentanyl
   (b) Non-plant-based drugs:
       (i) How, where, when, and why these drugs were invented
       (ii) How usage patterns changed over time
2. ADME: Absorption, distribution, metabolism, and excretion.
3. Mechanisms of action (neural disruption)
4. Behavior profile:
   (a) With evidence from human and nonhuman animals
5. Highlights (for illicit drugs):
   (a) Tips for responsible use, when possible
   (b) A timeline of drug regulation, with important dates
   (c) Discussion of evidence (or lack thereof) for using nonprescription ADHD medication as a study drug
6. Highlights (for prescription drugs):
   (a) Prescription guidelines
   (b) Discussions of specific populations (e.g., children, the elderly)
   (c) Side effects

Unit 3: Drug use, abuse, and dependence. The goals for this unit come from Learning Objectives 1d, 2, and 4. This unit is the capstone of the course. If you are using a textbook you will find that many of them begin with this material, but I suggest it is better held until after students have learned about the history, effects, and neural mechanisms of action of each drug class. Many students enter this class with an incomplete understanding of who uses drugs, what addiction is, and why their country's drug policies have been put into place. By ending with this material, students will already have established some understanding of the history of drugs and will have had some practice with the complex vocabulary of neuroscience. Here is a suggested content outline for this unit:

1. Definitions
   (a) Deviant drug use, misuse, abuse, addiction, dependence
2. Epidemiology
   (a) Trends across time
   (b) Use among subgroups (age, race, sex, education)
   (c) Risk and protective factors
3. Nosology of substance abuse
   (a) DSM-V and ICD-10
   (b) Historical notions of substance abuse
4. Current theories of addiction (with an emphasis on how these theories complement rather than compete with each other)
   (a) Incentive-sensitization
   (b) Developmental
   (c) Genetic
   (d) Biopsychosocial Model
5. Substance abuse treatment (with an emphasis on how these treatments complement rather than compete with each other)
   (a) Pharmacotherapy
       (i) Future directions, including vaccines and deep brain stimulation
   (b) Psychotherapy
   (c) Alcoholics Anonymous and Narcotics Anonymous
6. Public Policy
   (a) Current conceptions of drug sales, use, and abuse in the penal system in your country
   (b) International comparisons
   (c) Impact of the criminal justice system
       (i) If you are teaching in the United States, particular attention should be focused on the available statistics regarding the effects of the War on Drugs on minority populations.

Teaching, Learning, and Assessment in Psychopharmacology: Approaches and Strategies

In the United States, and in many other countries, the use of psychotropic medications is exceedingly common from childhood through adulthood. For example, approximately 25% of college students in the United States are using these medications and traditional-aged college students are also at heightened risk for drug and alcohol use, misuse, and dependence. So you might expect that curriculum planners in higher education would include a comprehensive introductory course on psycho-pharmacology. Yet, in the United States, at least, the course is rarely required for any academic major, though it is often available as an upper-class elective housed in a psychology or neuroscience program (Norcross et al. 2016; Wiertelak et al. 2018). Even in medical schools and graduate programs in nursing, where courses on psychopharmacologic principles are often required, it is rare that substantial time is dedicated to the review of illicit drugs or other drugs of abuse, such as alcohol and nicotine.

So most undergraduate psychopharmacology courses are likely to be populated by third or fourth year students in psychology or neuroscience. Given that many students from those majors are interested in working in a health-related field (APA 2018; Ramos et al. 2016), we should not only provide the knowledge they will need in their jobs, but also promote the skills they will need to be successful in those jobs. Students entering health-care fields should be experienced in reading (and under-standing) primary literature, creative and critical thinkers, and good writers and speakers who have developed a high level of empathy. Class activities and assess-ments should recognize, evoke, develop, and practice those skills.

Course Assessments and Activities

Several high-impact teaching practices work particularly well to increase student engagement and learning in this field and simultaneously prepare them for future careers. While a lab-based course provides an especially useful venue for these practices, but many colleges and universities either cannot provide the necessary lab space or choose to offer the course online. So although a few examples in this section are particularly valuable lab exercises, most of them can be accomplished outside a laboratory.

Whether you are teaching with or without a laboratory component, I recommend that you consider using backwards course design, an idea often attributed to Wiggins and McTighe's 2005 book, *Understanding by Design*. In this approach, you start by establishing the desired learning outcomes (LOs), determine what evidence will demonstrate that students have achieved those outcomes, and then plan learning experiences, instruction, and resources that will help students to show that they have met the learning outcomes.

The specific types of activities and assessments you choose should be based on the characteristics of your course and the context in which you will be teaching it. You need to consider class size, your access to a laboratory, any particular student-outcomes required by your college, budget constraints, instructional delivery methods (e.g., online vs. face to face), and your other academic and nonacademic obligations and workload. But regardless, try to choose assessment techniques that are varied, perceived by students as fair and attainable, and that provide opportuni-ties to evaluate student learning both objectively and subjectively.

To help you think through course preparation for your particular situation, the following section presents ideas for assessment of the LOs described earlier, along with activities designed to prepare students for those assessments, and for developing some of the skills they will need for success in a job or in post-baccalaureate education.

Learning Objective #1: Know the facts, theories, principles, processes, and general concepts within the field of psychopharmacology. This learning objective provides the fundamental information necessary for future coursework in neuroscience, biological psychology, and pharmacology. As such, precision and accuracy of information are paramount. Assessment techniques aimed at this learning objective should value declarative learning, with the classic exemplar being multiple-choice questions (MCQ). Because this type of knowledge lays the groundwork for the other learning objectives, nearly all activities will contribute to successful mastery of this learning objective.

Forced-choice items (e.g., MCQ and true/false) are often considered to reflect only surface-level thinking, but there is value in declarative learning as it can be an important step towards a deeper understanding of the material. For example, asking students to identify "Which neurotransmitter is released by cells located in the ventral tegmental area?" may represent the base level of Blooms taxonomy, but familiarity with the midbrain dopamine system is an essential prerequisite for later teasing out the nuances of the role of dopamine in addiction. Of course, forced-choice questions do not have to be surface-level. Careful item design can tap into higher order thinking and critical thinking skills (Tractenberg et al. 2013). These are the types of questions commonly found on graduate school entrance exams and in medical. For example, to answer correctly the item from the popular online study resource KahnAcadamy.org quoted below, students must have a clear understanding of the basic facts regarding the mechanism of action for caffeine, but must also be able to engage critical thinking in applying that knowledge

"Caffeine belongs to a class of general stimulants, which all increase the metabolic activity in cells. What is the process that causes jitters from excess amounts of coffee or other highly caffeinated beverages?

(A) Caffeine inhibits an enzyme that breaks down dopamine. The increase in dopamine increases GABA production. This increase in cellular activity results in action potentials that are briefer and released in bursts.

(B) Caffeine inhibits an enzyme that breaks down cyclic adenosine monophosphate (cAMP). The increase in cAMP increases glutamate production. This increase in cellular activity results in action potentials that are briefer and released in bursts.

(C) Caffeine inhibits an enzyme that breaks down serotonin. The increase in serotonin increases glutamate production. This increase in cellular activity results in action potentials that are briefer and released in bursts

(D) Caffeine inhibits an enzyme that breaks down norepinephrine. The increase in norepinephrine increases GABA production. This increase in cellular activity results in action potentials that are briefer and released in bursts."

Frequent low-stakes quizzes with well-crafted forced-choice items like this one can be important feedback tools for students (Karpicke and Roediger 2007). They can identify areas of weakness in students' understanding of the material, signal which definitions are most important to learn, and help students to tease out nuanced differences between concepts (e.g., agonist vs. antagonist). To make these quizzes even more effective for promoting learning and retention, I suggest that you offer feedback explaining what makes the answers correct or incorrect. This type of assessment can also be completed using learning management software (LMS) such as WebCT, Blackboard, or ClassFronter, thus reducing your workload while still providing a good student learning opportunity. Some evidence suggests that timed, multiple-choice quizzes presented online may not be as effective as in-class quizzes because of students' tendency to draw on outside sources rather than on their memories.

When designing each of your quizzes, you might want to prepare a pool of items that is large enough to allow students to take more than one quiz on the same topic areas. (The items do not have to be completely different; you can just rephrase them or change certain details.) If you do this, quizzes can serve as both a learning activity designed to reinforce understanding and as an assessment strategy for LO #1. You might also consider allowing students to drop or replace their lowest quiz grade. While the evidence for this policy is limited and mixed (see MacDermott 2013), this practice recognizes the fact that assessment of student learning often includes assessing skills that are not in our learning objectives – such as ability to work under time pressure – and that our students do not always perform to their potential. Finally, do not be afraid to let students challenge the fairness of the items. Let's face it, sometimes forced-choice questions are confusing, or can be interpreted in multiple ways depending on the students' background and experiences. Allowing students to submit a challenge to a question can help them demonstrate the depth of their knowledge (suggestions for item-challenge forms are presented in a number of sources (e.g., Bernstein et al. 2020)).

Here are some suggestions for **LO#1 activities** that will help prepare your students for doing well on forced-choice questions.

The first is to ask students to write their own multiple-choice questions. There is some evidence that these *student-derived questions* provide an active learning strategy that helps students to learn (Bobby et al. 2012; Craft et al. 2017). Having these questions to edit later can also increase your pool of available quiz or test items.

Second, you can present frequent, anonymous, *un-graded forced choice items* as you deliver your lecture. Some teachers use them at the beginning and end of class (Mandla et al. 2016), but you can also use them to slow down the pace of your lecturing and allow your students to indicate their level of understanding for each topic covered. Clickers, Plickers.com, colored response cards, scratch off cards, and hand raising are all equally effective response systems that can increasing student learning (see Zayac et al. 2016).

Third, consider using some *team-based learning (TBL)* activities. TBL is a cooperative strategy in which students complete a short forced-choice quiz alone and then in a team, and then getting instant feedback about their team answers (see

Michaelsen and Sweet 2008). This strategy effectively prepares students for assessment (Swanson et al. 2019) and may increase their emotional intelligence (Clarke 2010), a trait important for future health professionals.

Finally, you might want to employ *tactile models. In one example students use* modeling clay (Herur et al. 2011), trash/found objects (McGee 2018), food (Carter and Smith 2013), or other material to reproduce biological systems, such as a brain or a part of a brain. Such activities have been shown to increase student engagement with and retention of course content (Hardiman et al. 2019). Two of examples are designed to help students learn and remember the steps of the action potential. One of them comes from the Society for Neuroscience (Conley and Shepley 1996) and another can be found at wardsci.com (MacMullan n.d.). Both activities have been associated with better student performance on activity-related multiple-choice assessments when compared to assessment scores following a standard lecture (Keen-Rhinehart et al. 2009).

LO #2: Understand some of the biological, environmental, behavioral, and social causes and consequences of drug use and addiction across the lifespan. As you move up a level in cognitive taxonomies, your assessments should begin to vary in complexity and depth. While forced choice-test questions can still be used to assess this domain, other assessment techniques and activities can enhance students' communication skills.

Consider, for example, *short answer and/or short essay exams and quizzes.* Like forced choice quizzes, these assessments are commonly used for summative assessment, but when used as frequent quizzes, can also help students to practice retrieval and enhance learning and retention (e.g., McDaniel et al. 2007; Butler and Roediger 2007; Smith and Karpicke 2014). To increase the effectiveness of this type of assessment:

1. Set clear expectations for student answers. For example, ask students to "Compare and contrast the neurobiological approach to addiction with the socio-developmental theory of addiction" instead of to "Discuss two theories of addiction."
2. Ask more questions requiring shorter answers rather than asking just a few questions that demand longer answers. This will allow you to gauge students' knowledge of the course material more broadly.
3. Consider providing students with a list of questions in advance, then select a subset of that list for the actual exam. This helps ensure that students will prepare answers to questions spanning the content you want them to learn, but reduces the amount of time you will have to spend on grading;
4. Develop a grading rubric and stick to it. Rubrics are an assessment tool for clearly communicating teacher expectations for student answers. Short answer questions are not as objective as forced choice questions, so rubrics help increase grading reliability (Jonsson and Svingby 2007).

Students' performance on your short-answer and essay assessments can be enhanced through activities that require some of the same speaking, writing, and reading skills that employers and graduate programs typically value. For example, writing does not have to be assessed in a formal way to be valuable; including writing opportunities as low-stakes activities can enhance a student's confidence when it comes time to complete open-ended exam questions, research papers, or case studies (Spix and Brasier 2018). Here are some ideas for bringing writing into your classroom:

(a) *Informal writing.* Blogs (Spix and Brasier 2018), discussion boards (Sheen et al. 2017), and journaling can help students to learn the discipline's technical vocabulary (LO #1), deal with the complexities of drug addiction (LO #2), and assess systemic issues in the field (LO #4). More formal writing such as letters to the editor or to elected officials (Kennedy 2016; McGee, 2018) or writing an opinion piece on related topics for the student newspaper (Kennedy 2016) increases engagement with the material, helps develop scientific literacy in students and their readers, and raises the students' (and the topic's) public profile.

(b) *Grant proposals.* Many of your students will go on to graduate school (APA 2018), where grant writing will be an important part of their education. What better way to enhance writing about a course topic then to assign students to write a mock grant proposal? This strategy builds upon the "inquiry as pedagogy" framework favored by many STEM disciplines. Students often find the process of writing grants to meaningful contribute to their learning of factual information (LO #1; Köver et al. 2014). Consider using peer review or oral questioning procedures to help evaluate the grant proposals.

As with writing, *speaking* is a communication skill that takes practice to master, is transferable, and does not need to be formally assessed to be valuable. Your current formal assessment techniques or rubrics may not include a speaking component, but consider allowing students the opportunity to speak about certain topics, because doing so may enhance their ability to synthesize information more effectively. Here are some ideas for creating such opportunities:

(a) *Debates* can be used to assess LO #4 but can also be used as preparation for a longer research paper or for short answer questions on a more traditional exam. Students have reported a better understanding of course material following a debate, even if they were at first nervous about the debate format (Kennedy 2009). Debates can even be used with success in an online environment (Jugdev et al. 2004). Debate topics may include drug legislation or other controversial topics such as medication-assisted treatment. For a review, with tips for implementation and assessment, see Kennedy 2007.

(b) *In-class discussions* can be used as an assessment strategy (particularly for LOs #2-#4), but if your class size is larger than 25, it may be difficult for all students to contribute. Therefore, these are better used as an ungraded "developmental playground" in which students can talk about ideas they will use in papers, short answer exams, or other assessment techniques.

(c) *Presentations* (live or recorded) require students to have a strong understanding of the material so they can apply it to related phenomena, making this an appropriate way to assess LO #2 and #4 while giving the students the opportunity to practice public speaking. Recorded presentations (or other video formats) work particularly well in online classrooms, and in large classes, presentations can be based on peer evaluations. l

(d) *Jigsaw* is a cooperative learning strategy that gives students the chance to study a particular reading or topic in small groups, thereby allowing them to master the content together before teaching it to others in the class. Each group is given a reading on one of several related concepts. For example, one group might read an article on the biological approach to addiction while the other groups read articles on the developmental, cognitive, or social approaches to addiction. After determining the main points and identifying other important information, the groups are rearranged so that each new group is comprised of one member from each of the original groups. The new groups now discuss the various topics or approaches they have mastered in order to compare and contrast them, create policy recommendations, write a grant proposal, or the like. In these small group settings, it is often easier to promote conversation among students, particularly for those who are introverted or anxious, and thus jigsaw may be a particularly inclusive teaching strategy for reinforcing oral communication.

Reading activities, too, can also be important parts of your course. Learning how to read and critique primary literature, how to distinguish fact from opinion, and how to critically examine popular press articles are all skills that are highly sought after in graduate programs and employment settings. Undergraduate engagement with primary literature has been associated with improved critical thinking (Segura-Totten and Dalman 2013) and increased application to graduate and medical schools (Kozeracki et al. 2006). As such, it is not surprising that enhancing these skills can lead to improved performance on many of the assessment techniques for each of the four learning outcomes of the psychopharmacology course. However, if you decide to use readings as the basis for classroom discussions, consider administering pre-discussion quizzes about those readings in order to ensure that students actually do the reading and also to enhance their learning of the material (Heiner et al. 2014; Hodges et al. 2015; Connor-Greene 2016). These quizzes might include questions that can only be answered correctly by those who have done the assigned reading, but you can also ask questions that are sufficiently open ended that students can answer them using material from any classroom source (textbooks, lectures, activities, or readings). Here are three ideas for incorporating reading into your psychopharmacology classroom:

Journal clubs: Designate certain days as "primary source days" and have a class discussion about 3–4 related journal articles (see Miller and Mercer 2017). In online classes, you can utilize your LMS discussion board (or breakout rooms if there is a synchronous component). In large classes, you can have students discuss the material in small groups with a peer leader.

Nonfiction reading: There are many nonfiction books on addiction that can enhance student learning about the topic. Pollack (2015) and Lynd-Balta (2006) chose the memoir genre and identified strong gains in critical thinking and student engagement.

Primary source-only pedagogy: This approach uses primary source literature as the main source of knowledge about the topic. Many instructors have successfully employed this style in their classroom (e.g., Willard and Brasier 2014).

LO #3: Apply the principles of pharmacology to evaluate options for safe, rational, and optimally beneficial psychotropic drug therapy and medication-assisted treatment for drug dependency. Learning objective #3 represents another step up in cognitive taxonomies and as teachers our assessments should again increase in complexity and depth. While the previous assessment strategies such as forced-choice and short essay questions also work well for this learning objective, evaluating medical options can best be practiced using case studies or grant proposals. Because successful completion of a case study is best prepared through related practice, for this learning objective assessments and activities can be one and the same. Although grant proposals, short essay questions, and well-crafted forced-choice questions may suffice for this learning objective, assessments in the form of case studies are optimal. They are recommended because of their utility for the target students, their ubiquitous use in further health professional training, and their tremendous value in promoting critical thinking (Tsui 2002; Popil 2011).

Case studies can be used as an assessment technique by assigning each student to prepare a formal response to the case and then providing feedback and a grade. Case studies can also be used in the classroom as a deep-learning activity to prepare students for a different type of assessment (such as a short-answer or essay exam). If you choose to use case studies as a learning activity, consider allowing students to work on the case in small groups, because there is some evidence that small-group work improves students' critical thinking skills (Jones and Carter 1998; Springer et al. 1999; Quitadamo et al. 2007; Greenwald and Quitadamo 2014). Consider also the possibility of asking your students to generate their own case studies. Doing so could provide an opportunity for a student-led publication. Here are four resources for locating and structuring case studies relevant to psychopharmacology.

(a) In one of two fictional scenarios, students answer questions related to a newly discovered neurotransmitter. In the other, they are acting as a consultant to a police department that is trying to understand the mechanisms of a novel illicit drug (Cammack 2017).

(b) Two teachers (Greenwald and Quitadamo 2014) successfully used Blumenfeld's clinical case studies (Blumenfeld 2002) to enhance student's critical thinking skills and their understanding of neuroanatomy.

(c) Two other teachers (Nagel and Nicholas 2017a) developed for class use seven mini case-studies representing each major drug class that later mapped onto increases in student understanding of the material (Nagel and Nicholas 2017b).

(d) For more case studies, see Stahl (2011) and visit http://sciencecases.lib.buffalo. edu/cs/collection/.

LO #4: Recognize the systemic influences of sociocultural, theoretical, and personal biases on the research enterprise and evaluate the effectiveness with which researchers address those influences in psychological research. This LO is at the highest level of Blooms taxonomy and requires students to express their own ideas and critiques of the status quo. One way for students to assess systemic influences that affect the research enterprise is to engage in experiential learning opportunities beyond the classroom. If it is not possible for students to engage in off-campus experiences in the service of this LO, other assessments such as open-ended exam questions, debates, in-class discussions, journaling, presentations, research papers, or even forced choice questions will have to suffice. Nevertheless, here are some examples of how teachers of psychopharmacology have combined in-class activities with experiential ones. As you can see, these activities encourage students to engage thoughtfully with the challenges and controversies of the field, while allowing you to gain information about what they are learning.

(a) Clinical Neuroscience in Practice is an upper-level course at Virginia Tech University in Virginia, USA. Professors in neuroscience there have teamed up with clinicians in neurosurgery at a local hospital to give students observational access to the surgeries and students accompany doctors on pre- and postsurgical rounds. In class, psychopharamcology students are taught basic course material through multiple active learning techniques, including case studies, in-class discussions, and partner presentations. See Simonds et al. 2018 for a full description.

(b) Mead and Kennedy (2012) describe how they sent psychopharmacology students out to share their knowledge about the brain with audiences ranging from elementary school students to residents of senior living facilities. This activity gave the students teaching experience while spreading scientific literacy and volunteering in the community.

(c) Susan Kennedy (2016, 2018) outlines the final project requirements for two courses, Health Psychology and Psychopharmacology, in which her students developed materials related to stimulant and alcohol misuse for distribution across the campus. Not only did these projects reinforce the students' knowledge of course content and contribute to their scientific literacy, their distribution efforts had a direct and beneficial impact on their fellow students.

(d) Colpitts, Seymour, and Harris Bozer (2019) described a project in which they developed and implemented a low-cost neuroscience summer academy for local high school students. The academy was taught by volunteer undergraduates in the neuroscience major. The authors provide an outline of the four-day academy experience as well as suggestions for teachers who might like to implement a similar course. Even if a summer academy may be outside the scope of your teaching, the features described in this article could be well suited to a semester-long project with local high school or advanced elementary school partners (see Brown et al. 2019; Vollbrecht et al. 2019).

(e) Finally, there are several laboratory-based experiences that have been empirically shown to enhance student learning. If you do not have, and cannot create, a neuroscience lab, consider partnering with a local institution (McCoy et al. 2018) that does. Here are some laboratory experiments that are recommended for use in a psychopharmacology course:

Howerter, D. D., Larson, J. G., & Hill, E. M. (2018). The Behavioral Effects of Oral Psychostimulant Ingestion on a Laboratory Rat Sample: An Undergraduate Research Experience. *Journal of Undergraduate Neuroscience Education*, *17*(1), A72.

Pagán, O. R., Coudron, T., & Kaneria, T. (2009). The Flatworm Planaria as a Toxicology and Behavioral Pharmacology Animal Model in Undergraduate Research Experiences. *Journal of Undergraduate Neuroscience Education*, *7*(2), A48.

Bergstrom, B. P. (2012). Using In Vivo Voltammetry to Demonstrate Drug Action: A Student Laboratory Experience in Neurochemistry. *Journal of Undergraduate Neuroscience Education*, *10*(2), A113.

Pritchard, L. M., Van Kempen, T. A., Williams, H., & Zimmerberg, B. (2008). A Laboratory Exercise for a College-Level, Introductory Neuroscience Course Demonstrating Effects of Housing Environment on Anxiety and Psychostimulant Sensitivity. *Journal of Undergraduate Neuroscience Education*, *7*(1), A26.

Peterson, H. P., Troconis, E. L., Ordoobadi, A. J., Thibodeau-Beganny, S., & Trapani, J. G. (2018). Teaching Dose-Response Relationships Through Aminoglycoside Block of Mechanotransduction Channels in Lateral Line Hair Cells of Larval Zebrafish. *Journal of Undergraduate Neuroscience Education*, *17*(1), A40.

Vilinsky, I., Hibbard, K. L., Johnson, B. R., & Deitcher, D. L. (2018). Probing Synaptic Transmission and Behavior in Drosophila with Optogenetics: A Laboratory Exercise. *Journal of Undergraduate Neuroscience Education*, *16*(3), A289.

Mirrione, M. M., Ruth, N., Alexoff, D., Logan, J., Fowler, J., & Kernan, M. (2014). Positron Emission Tomography (PET) and Graphical Kinetic Data Analysis of the Dopamine Neurotransmitter System: An Exercise for an Undergraduate Laboratory Course. *Journal of Undergraduate Neuroscience Education*, *12*(2), A114.

A Summary of Activity and Assessment Options

There are obviously many activities that can be organized both in and out of the classroom to help deepen students' understanding of the material in psychopharmacology courses, but it essential to select those that support your learning objectives and assessment strategies. Best practices for assessing student learning in psychopharmacology can include a mix of frequent multiple choice quizzes, short open-ended responses (orally, as in a discussion, or written), case studies, and more time-intensive student-driven work, such as research papers, presentations or posters, or experiential learning opportunities. As suggested by the backwards course design approach, it is ideal to prepare your assessments before selecting the activities and other teaching methods you will employ. This means a lot of advance planning, including writing questions for all your quizzes and exams and developing rubrics for the case studies, research papers, or other forms of assessments you will be using. For excellent rubrics related to many of these assessments, be sure to read the AAC&U Value Rubrics, found online at www.aacu.org/value/rubrics. For sample course syllabi, visit Project Syllabus at the website of the Society for the Teaching of Psychology (teachpsych.org).

Teaching, Learning, and Assessment Resources

Tips for Teaching Psychopharmacology

1. **You cannot cover everything**: Given all the thousands of substances people take for recreation and for treating diseases and conditions, it will be up to you to decide which of them to include in your course, and what is most essential for your students to learn. Some teachers focus on substances that are most likely to be used or abused by the local population. Others select the ones that allow them to explore fundamental concepts of neuroscience. But no one can cover them all, so you will be doing your students a service if you dive deeply into select content instead of offering a shallow overview of every drug that could possibly be of interest.

2. **Choose activities wisely**: There is no right way to teach. Do discussions fill you with dread? Does the thought of reading student writing samples keep you up at night? Then do not assign them! Select activities if they match your assessment plans and learning objectives but also consider your strengths as a teacher and the characteristics of your students. If most of your students are working full time, caring for family, or driving long distances to class, then service-learning activities might not work to enhance their learning (and could detract from it). If many of your students will be continuing into nursing, perhaps adding an activity on correct dosing would be advisable.

3. **Do not change too much too fast**: Have you been inspired by the literature cited in this chapter and in the rest of this book? Are you excited to redesign your course? Do not start from scratch. Incremental changes with opportunities for self-reflection, evaluation, and student input will be more manageable to handle and are more likely to lead to results that work for you and your students.

4. **Link content meaningfully**: There are many ways to organize your material, so do not feel obliged to follow a particular sequence, such as a textbook's table of contents. For example, I like to teach about cocaine and amphetamines early in the semester because it is a classically addictive drug that affects very discrete

areas of the brain in very predictable ways. I then discuss biological theories of addiction. This sequence gives students something concrete to hold on to when thinking theoretically about how addiction may be driven by biological mechanisms. Later, after discussing marijuana, I cover behavioral theories of addiction. Similarly, I introduce long-term potentiation in the marijuana unit due to marijuana's impact on glutamate receptors its common side effect of memory impairment. But you should feel free to create a sequence that makes sense to you.

5. **Establish a communication network with other teachers of psychopharmacology**: Too often the teachers of psychopharmacology are the only biological psychologists in a department, making it difficult to share successes and discuss challenges with others teaching the same course. So make contact with those others at conferences (e.g., Society of Teaching Psychology Annual Conference on Teaching; Faculty for Undergraduate Neuroscience) or online (e.g., Facebook group: Teaching Resources for Biological Psychology and Neuroscience).

Annotated List of Recommended Websites

1. World Health Organization: https://www.who.int/substance_abuse/en/
   The World Health Organization (WHO) is an agency of the United Nations that is concerned with international public health concerns, including substance use and abuse. They collect and summarize data from over 155 participating counties regarding trends in substance use, education, and treatment. This site is rich with facts, figures, policy suggestions, and publications about substance use as a global issue.

2. Learn.Genetics: https://learn.genetics.utah.edu/ & https://teach.genetics.utah.edu
   These websites at the University of Utah offer sources for teaching and learning about genetics and how genes influence behaviors. They offer modules on topics such as basic genetics, precision medicine, and addiction. Learn.genetics.utah. edu is student-centered and rich with images, videos, and other interactive tools such as virtual labs and other hands-on activities. Teach.genetics.utah.edu is teacher-focused and offers lesson plans, full lab protocols, discussion guides, worksheets with answer keys, and classroom demonstrations. The very popular Mouse Party (https://learn.genetics.utah.edu/content/addiction/mouse/) is also hosted here, but currently uses a Flash plug-in which will be obsolete in 2020. The team at the Genetic Learning Science Center at the University of Utah is working on converting it and will hopefully relaunch it soon.

3. Dana Foundation & Brain Awareness: http://www.dana.org/ & https://brain aware ness.org/
   The Dana Foundation is a private philanthropic organization dedicated to advancing understanding about the brain in health and disease through research grants and public outreach. Their website contains several educational resources on

neuroscience, including lesson plans for student activities, links to webcasts and podcasts on neuroscience, and resources for science communication. The Dana Foundation also supports Brain Awareness Week, a global campaign to foster public enthusiasm and support for brain science, by providing planning tools, resources, and ideas for implementation.

4. National Institute of Drug Abuse (NIDA): http://nida.nih.gov
   NIDA is a component of the National Institutes of Health, US Department of Health and Human Services. NIDA supports much of the world's research on the health aspects of drug use and addiction. Their web page includes resources about drugs and their effects on the brain, written in accessible language. Infographics, videos, and factsheets will help students learn the basics of drug science and addiction, but they also highlight and summarize recent research in the field which can extend student learning beyond the classroom.

5. Neuroscientifically Challenged: https://www.neuroscientificallychallenged.com
   This website is run by Marc A. Dingman, Director of the Online Bachelor of Science Degree and Associate Teaching Professor of Biobehavioral Health at the Pennsylvania State University College of Health and Sciences, USA. It features blog posts on topics ranging from the role of dopamine in reward to the origins of psychotherapeutic drugs. There are also links to the very popular 2-minute neuroscience videos hosted on YouTube, that Dr. Dingman also creates and that can be very valuable to college students. Dr. Dingman just published a book, *Your Brain, Explained*, which was written to be a "friendly, engaging introduction to the human brain and its quirks using real-life examples and Dingman's own, hand-drawn illustrations."

6. Neuroscience for Kids: http://faculty.washington.edu/chudler/neurok.html
   A comprehensive website from the University of Washington features child-friendly activities and resources for neuroscience education. While these resources were not designed for higher education students, many of the activities can be adapted or used as-is for your college or university level course. Each drug class is represented and many college students will appreciate the accessible language in the educational modules. This would also be a great resource for any community outreach your students are interested in performing.

7. Backyard Brains: https://backyardbrains.com/experiments/
   Backyard Brains is an online store that sells kits that help students learn about the workings of the nervous system. While there is a charge for their products, they offer lesson plans, step-by-step instructions, and video tutorials free of charge.

8. Art of Neuroscience: https://aon.nin.knaw.nl/
   The Art of Neuroscience is an annual competition for inspiring and provocative imagery from neuroscience labs hosted by the Netherlands Institute for Neuroscience (NIN), an institute of the Royal Netherlands Academy of Arts and Sciences (KNAW). While not directly related to psychopharmacology, showing students the beauty and art of neuroscience can encourage them to take a different perspective. You could pair this with your lesson on types of neurons and the role of Santiago Ramón y Cajal.

Cross-References

▶ Neuroscience in the Psychology Curriculum

References

American Psychological Association. (2018). Degree pathways in psychology [Interactive data tool]. Retrieved from https://www.apa.org/workforce/data-tools/degrees-pathways

Bernstein, D. A., Frantz, S., & Chew, S. L. (2020). *Teaching psychology: A step by step guide* (3rd ed.). New York: Routledge.

Blumenfeld, H. (2002). *Neuroanatomy through clinical cases*. Sunderland: Sinauer Associates.

Bobby, Z., Radhika, M. R., Nandeesha, H., Balasubramanian, A., Prerna, S., Archana, N., & Thippeswamy, D. N. (2012). Formulation of multiple choice questions as a revision exercise at the end of a teaching module in biochemistry. *Biochemistry and Molecular Biology Education, 40*(3), 169–173.

Brown, A. R., Egan, M., Lynch, S., & Buffalari, D. (2019). Neuroscience and education colleagues collaborate to design and assess effective brain outreach for preschoolers. *Journal of Undergraduate Neuroscience Education: JUNE: a publication of FUN, Faculty for Undergraduate Neuroscience, 17*(2), A159–A167.

Butler, A. C., & Roediger, H. L. (2007). Testing improves long-term retention in a simulated classroom setting. *European Journal of Cognitive Psychology, 19*, 514–527. https://doi.org/10.1080/09541440701326097.

Cammack, K. M. (2017). A critical thinking activity on drug tolerance for undergraduate neuroscience courses. Journal of undergraduate neuroscience education: JUNE: a publication of FUN. *Faculty for Undergraduate Neuroscience, 15*(2), A157–A161.

Carter, K. E., & Smith, C. (2013). Synaptic snacks: Using food to teach neuroscience. Poster presented at the American Psychological Association Convention, Honolulu.

Clarke, N. (2010). Developing emotional intelligence abilities through team-based learning. *Human Resource Development Quarterly, 21*(2), 119–138.

Colpitts, K. N., Seymour, K. P., & Bozer, A. H. (2019). Development of an introductory neuroscience teaching experience for undergraduates with a low-cost neuroscience summer academy. *Journal of Undergraduate Neuroscience Education, 17*(2), A125.

Connor-Greene, P. A. (2016). Assessing and promoting student learning: Blurring the line between teaching and testing. *Teaching of Psychology, 27*(2), 84–88.

Conley, T., & Shepley, B. (1996). Action potential – Epilepsy. In M. L. Bellamy & K. Frame (Eds.), *Neuroscience laboratory and classroom activities* (pp. 191–214). Washington, DC: Society for Neuroscience.

Craft, J. A., Christensen, M., Shaw, N., & Bakon, S. (2017). Nursing students collaborating to develop multiple-choice exam revision questions: A student engagement study. *Nurse Education Today, 59*, 6–11.

Dawson, W. R. (1934). Studies in the Egyptian medical texts – III. *The Journal of Egyptian Archaeology, 20*(1), 41–46. https://doi.org/10.1177/030751333402000108.

Greenwald, R. R., & Quitadamo, I. J. (2014). A mind of their own: Using inquiry-based teaching to build critical thinking skills and intellectual engagement in an undergraduate neuroanatomy course. *Journal of Undergraduate Neuroscience Education: JUNE: A Publication of FUN, Faculty for Undergraduate Neuroscience, 12*(2), A100–A106.

Hardiman, M. M., JohnBull, R. M., Carran, D. T., & Shelton, A. (2019). The effects of arts-integrated instruction on memory for science content. *Trends in Neuroscience and Education, 14*, 25–32.

Hardy, K. (2019). Paleomedicine and the use of plant secondary compounds in the Paleolithic and Early Neolithic. *Evolutionary Anthropology, 28*, 60–71. https://doi-org.proxy.library.emory.edu/10.1002/evan.21763.

Hayter, A. (1968). *Opium and the romantic imagination*. Berkeley: Univeristy of California Press.

Herur, A., Kolagi, S., Chinagudi, S., Manjula, R., & Patil, S. (2011). Active learning by play dough modeling in the medical profession. *Advances in Physiology Education, 35*(2), 241–243.

Heiner, C. E., Banet, A. I., & Wieman, C. (2014). Preparing students for class: How to get 80% of students reading the textbook before class. *American Journal of Physics, 82*(10), 989–996.

Hodges, L., Anderson, E., Carpenter, T., Cui, L., Gierasch, T. M., Wagner, C., Leupen, S., & Nanes, K. (2015). Using reading quizzes in STEM classes–the what, why, and how. *Journal of College Science Teaching, 045*(01).

Houghton, P. (2007). Ethnopharmacology of medicinal plants: Asia and the Pacific. *British Journal of Clinical Pharmacology, 64*(2), 248. https://doi.org/10.1111/j.1365-2125.2007.02888.x.

Jones G. M., & Carter, G. (1998). Small groups and shared constructions. In J. J. Mintzes, J. H. Wandersee & J. D. Novak (Eds.), *Teaching science for understanding: A human constructivist view* (pp. 261–279). San Diego, CA: Academic Press.

Jonsson, A., & Svingby, G. (2007). The use of scoring rubrics: Reliability, validity and educational consequences. *Educational Research Review, 2*(2), 130–144.

Jugdev, K., Markowski, C., & Mengel, T. (2004). Using the debate as a teaching tool in the online classroom. *Online Cl@ssroom, 1*(10), 4–6.

Karpicke, J. D., & Roediger, H. L., III. (2007). Expanding retrieval practice promotes short-term retention, but equally spaced retrieval enhances long-term retention. *Journal of Experimental Psychology: Learning, Memory, and Cognition, 33*(4), 704.

Keen-Rhinehart, E., Eisen, A., Eaton, D., & McCormack, K. (2009). Interactive methods for teaching action potentials, an example of teaching innovation from neuroscience postdoctoral fellows in the fellowships in research and science teaching (FIRST) program. *Journal of Undergraduate Neuroscience Education, 7*(2), A74.

Kennedy, R. (2007). In-class debates: Fertile ground for active learning and the cultivation of critical thinking and oral communication skills. *International Journal of Teaching & Learning in Higher Education, 19*(2), 183.

Kennedy, R. R. (2009). The power of in-class debates. *Active Learning in Higher Education, 10*(3), 225–236.

Kennedy, S. (2016). Lights! Camera! Action projects! Engaging psychopharmacology students in service-based action projects focusing on student alcohol abuse. *Journal of Undergraduate Neuroscience Education, 14*(2), A138.

Kennedy, S. (2018). Raising awareness about prescription and stimulant abuse in college students through on-campus community involvement projects. *Journal of Undergraduate Neuroscience Education, 17*(1), A50.

Köver, H., Wirt, S. E., Owens, M. T., & Dosmann, A. J. (2014). "Thinking like a neuroscientist": Using scaffolded grant proposals to foster scientific thinking in a freshman neuroscience course. *Journal of Undergraduate Neuroscience Education: JUNE: a publication of FUN, Faculty for Undergraduate Neuroscience, 13*(1), A29–A40.

Kozeracki, C. A., Carey, M. F., Colicelli, J., Levis-Fitzgerald, M., & Grossel, M. (2006). An intensive primary-literature–based teaching program directly benefits undergraduate science majors and facilitates their transition to doctoral programs. *CBE—Life Sciences Education, 5*(4), 340–347.

Lynd-Balta, E. (2006). Using literature and innovative assessments to ignite interest and cultivate critical thinking skills in an undergraduate neuroscience course. *CBE Life Sciences Education, 5*(2), 167–174. https://doi.org/10.1187/cbe.05-08-0108.

McGee, M. J. (2018). Using found object art to learn neuroanatomy [Unpublished Manuscript]. Department of Psychology, Emory University.

MacDermott, R. J. (2013). The impact of assessment policy on learning: Replacement exams or grade dropping. *Journal of Economic Education, 44*(4), 364–371.

MacMullan, C. (n.d.). Ward's® manipulate your own action potential neuron. Retrieved 25 Oct 2019, from https://www.wardsci.com/store/product/8865622/ward-s-manipulate-your-own-action-potential-neuron

Mandla, J., Shaik, H., Pidigundla, D., & Katepogu, V. (2016). Evaluation of lectures by pre & post-test MCQS. *Journal of Education Technology in Health Sciences, 3*(2), 65–67.

McCoy, J. G., Heather, J. Y., Niznikiewicz, M., McKenna, J. T., & Strecker, R. E. (2018). Partnerships in neuroscience research between small colleges and large institutions: A case study. *Journal of Undergraduate Neuroscience Education, 16*(2), A159.

McDaniel, M. A., Anderson, J. L., Derbish, M. H., & Morrisette, N. (2007). Testing the testing effect in the classroom. *European Journal of Cognitive Psychology, 19*, 494–513. https://doi.org/10.1080/09541440701326154.

Mead, K. S., & Kennedy, S. (2012). Service learning in neuroscience courses. *Journal of Undergraduate Neuroscience Education, 11*(1), A90.

Michaelsen, L. K., & Sweet, M. (2008). The essential elements of team-based learning. *New Directions for Teaching and Learning, 2008*(116), 7–27.

Miller, L. N., & Mercer, S. L. (2017). Drugs of abuse and addiction: An integrated approach to teaching. *Currents in Pharmacy Teaching & Learning, 9*(3), 405–414.

Moore, T. J., & Mattison, D. R. (2017). Adult utilization of psychiatric drugs and differences by sex, age, and race. *JAMA Internal Medicine, 177*(2), 274–275. https://doi.org/10.1001/jamainternmed.2016.7507.

Nagel, A., & Nicholas, A. (2017a). Drugs & the brain: Case-based instruction for an undergraduate neuropharmacology course. *Journal of Undergraduate Neuroscience Education, 15*(2), C11.

Nagel, A., & Nicholas, A. (2017b). Don't believe the gripe! Increasing course structure in a large non-majors neuroscience course. *Journal of Undergraduate Neuroscience Education, 15*(2), A128.

Nakanishi, K. (2005). Terpene trilactones from Gingko biloba: From ancient times to the 21st century. *Bioorganic & Medicinal Chemistry, 13*(17), 4987–5000. https://doi.org/10.1016/j.bmc.2005.06.014.

Norcross, J. C., Hailstorks, R., Aiken, L. S., Pfund, R. A., Stamm, K. E., & Christidis, P. (2016). Undergraduate study in psychology: Curriculum and assessment. *American Psychologist, 71*(2), 89–101. https://doi.org/10.1037/a0040095.

Pollack, A. E. (2015). Non-fiction memoirs in the neuroscience classroom: A window into the minds of those affected by addiction. *Journal of Undergraduate Neuroscience Education: JUNE: A Publication of FUN, Faculty for Undergraduate Neuroscience, 14*(1), A39–A45.

Popil, I. (2011). Promotion of critical thinking by using case studies as teaching method. *Nurse Education Today, 31*(2), 204–207.

Quitadamo, I. J., Kurtz, M. J., & Kincaid, W. B. (2007). Learning to improve: Using writing to increase critical thinking performance in general education biology. *CBE—Life Sciences Education, 6*(2), 140–154.

Rackham, H., Andrews, A., Eichholz, D., Jones, W., & Pliny. (1938). *Natural history* (Loeb classical library; 330, 352–353, 370–371, 392–394, 418–419). Cambridge, MA: Harvard University Press.

Ramos, R. L., Guercio, E., Levitan, T., O'Malley, S., & Smith, P. T. (2016). A quantitative examination of undergraduate neuroscience majors applying and matriculating to osteopathic medical school. *Journal of Undergraduate Neuroscience Education: JUNE: a publication of FUN, Faculty for Undergraduate Neuroscience, 14*(2), A87–A90.

Segura-Totten, M., & Dalman, N. E. (2013). The CREATE method does not result in greater gains in critical thinking than a more traditional method of analyzing the primary literature. *Journal of Microbiology & Biology Education, 14*(2), 166–175. https://doi.org/10.1128/jmbe.v14i2.506.

Shakya, A. K. (2016). Medicinal plants: Future source of new drugs. *International Journal of Herbal Medicine, 4*(4), 59–64.

Sheen, M., AlJassmi, M. A., & Jordan, T. R. (2017). Teaching about psychological disorders: A case for using discussion boards in the classroom. *Teaching of Psychology, 44*(1), 74–77. https://doi.org/10.1177/0098628316679971.

Simonds, G. R., Marvin, E. A., Apfel, L. S., Elias, Z., Howes, G. A., Witcher, M. R., . . . Rogers, C. M. (2018). Clinical neuroscience in practice: An experiential learning course for undergraduates offered by neurosurgeons and neuroscientists. *Journal of Undergraduate Neuroscience Education, 16*(2), A112.

Smith, M. A., & Karpicke, J. D. (2014). Retrieval practice with short-answer, multiple-choice, and hybrid tests. *Memory, 22*(7), 784–802.

Spix, T. A., & Brasier, D. J. (2018). Using blogs as practice writing about original neuroscience papers enhances students' confidence in their critical analysis of research. *Journal of Undergraduate Neuroscience Education: JUNE: a publication of FUN, Faculty for Undergraduate Neuroscience, 16*(2), A120–A125.

Springer, L., Stanne, M. E., & Donovan, S. S. (1999). Effects of small-group learning on undergraduates in science, mathematics, engineering, and technology: A meta-analysis. *Review of Educational Research, 69*(1), 21–51.

Stahl, S. M. (2011). *Case studies: Stahl's essential psychopharmacology*. New York: Cambridge University Press.

Swanson, E., McCulley, L. V., Osman, D. J., Scammacca Lewis, N., & Solis, M. (2019). The effect of team-based learning on content knowledge: A meta-analysis. *Active Learning in Higher Education, 20*(1), 39–50.

Tractenberg, R. E., Gushta, M. M., Mulroney, S. E., & Weissinger, P. A. (2013). Multiple choice questions can be designed or revised to challenge learners' critical thinking. *Advances in Health Sciences Education, 18*(5), 945–961.

Tsui, L. (2002). Fostering critical thinking through effective pedagogy: Evidence from four institutional case studies. *The Journal of Higher Education, 73*(6), 740–763.

U.S. Department of Health and Human Services, Substance Abuse and Mental Health Services Administration, Center for Behavioral Health Statistics and Quality. (2018). *National Survey on Drug Use and Health 2018* (NSDUH-2018-DS0001). Retrieved from https://datafiles.samhsa.gov/

United Nations Office on Drugs and Crime, World Drug Report (2017). (ISBN: 978-92-1-148291-1, eISBN: 978-92-1-060623-3, United Nations publication, Sales No. E.17.XI.6).

Uritu, C. M., Mihai, C. T., Stanciu, G. D., Dodi, G., Alexa-Stratulat, T., Luca, A., . . . Tamba, B. I. 2018). Medicinal plants of the family Lamiaceae in pain therapy: A review. *Pain Research & Management, 2018*, 7801543. https://doi.org/10.1155/2018/7801543.

Vollbrecht, P. J., Frenette, R. S., & Gall, A. J. (2019). An effective model for engaging faculty and undergraduate students in neuroscience outreach with middle schoolers. *Journal of Undergraduate Neuroscience Education: JUNE: a publication of FUN, Faculty for Undergraduate Neuroscience, 17*(2), A130–A144.

Wiertelak, E. P., Hardwick, J., Kerchner, M., Parfitt, K., & Ramirez, J. J. (2018). The new blueprints: Undergraduate neuroscience education in the twenty-first century. *Journal of Undergraduate Neuroscience Education: JUNE: a publication of FUN, Faculty for Undergraduate Neuroscience, 16*(3), A244–A251.

Willard, A. M., & Brasier, D. J. (2014). Controversies in neuroscience: A literature-based course for first year undergraduates that improves scientific confidence while teaching concepts. *Journal of Undergraduate Neuroscience Education, 12*(2), A159.

Zayac, R. M., Ratkos, T., Frieder, J. E., & Paulk, A. (2016). A comparison of active student responding modalities in a general psychology course. *Teaching of Psychology, 43*(1), 43–47.